THE FOOTBALLERS' WHO'S WHO

2004/2005

Editor and Statistician
Barry J Hugman

Assistant Editor
Ian Nannestad

Photographs by
Getty Images

QUEEN ANNE PRESS

First published in Great Britain in 2004 by
Queen Anne Press
a division of Lennard Associates Limited
Mackerye End, Harpenden
Hertfordshire AL5 5DR

A CIP catalogue record for this book
is available from the British Library

ISBN 1 85291 660 5

Typeset and designed by
Typecast (Artwork & Design)
Labrador Way, Northfield Lane
Watergore, South Petherton
Somerset TA13 5LH

Printed and bound in Great Britain by
The Bath Press

Foreword

Once again, I am extremely pleased to give the PFA's full endorsement and recommendation to the Footballers' Who's Who, now in its 10th year. In this modern age of such tremendous interest in the professional football game it is good to have at hand the definitive book on statistics and profiles for every one of our members playing in first-team football throughout the Premier League and Football League in England and Wales.

This book gives the background to what the game is all about – the players. Having to deal with 4,000 PFA members, the book gives me a valuable source of information in an easily accessible, attractive and enjoyable format. It is a must for anybody involved in the game as an administrator, player, manager, spectator and commentator, and is especially invaluable for any football 'Brain of Britain' or football quiz aspirant!

The publication is compiled by Barry Hugman, whose record in this field is unsurpassed, and he is aided by a team of close on 100 people who provide him with the invaluable aspects of local information, which gives this book such credibility.

Gordon Taylor
Chief Executive, The Professional Footballers' Association

TEN DECADES' SERVICE TO FOOTBALL

FOUNDED AT THE IMPERIAL HOTEL, MANCHESTER IN 1907, THE PROFESSIONAL FOOTBALLERS' ASSOCIATION TODAY COMMANDS AN ENVIABLE REPUTATION AS THE WORLD'S LONGEST-ESTABLISHED PROFESSIONAL SPORTSMEN'S UNION.

This status stands as testament to the unswerving determination, dedication and commitment of all its contributors, from its earliest forefathers such as Billy Meredith right through to its current Management Committee.

The result is that the PFA is now involved in every aspect of a player's career, from financial management and pensions, to education and training, coaching, commercial, accident insurance and medical & benevolent assistance.

The PFA is also a key factor in both the Youth Training/Football Scholarship Scheme and Football In The Community Programme, ensuring that the players of tomorrow receive the best possible start to their careers.

THE PFA – PROTECTING THE PLAYERS, PROTECTING THE GAME.

20 Oxford Court, Bishopsgate, Manchester M2 3WQ

THE PFA SAYS LET'S KICK RACISM OUT OF FOOTBALL

it's only
the colour
of the shirt
that counts

Acknowledgements

Formerly known as the *Factfile* and now in its tenth edition, the *Who's Who* has, hopefully, become an invaluable part-work which, in due course, will cover the season-by-season career record of all professional footballers operating at that time in the Premier and Football Leagues. To this end, I would once again like to express my thanks to **Gordon Taylor**, the chief executive, and all those at the PFA who are genuinely supporting and helping to establish the *Footballers' Who's Who*. Their help is invaluable and much appreciated.

The massive task of editing the text this year was again carried out by the assistant editor, **Ian Nannestad**, who has also been a long-standing contributor to the publication on matters regarding Lincoln City.

For the past couple of years it has been my pleasure to work on the statistical side of the book with **Michael Joyce**, the author of *Football League Players' Records, 1888 to 1939*. This title, which is still available from SoccerData, 4 Adrian Close, Beeston, Nottingham NG9 6FL, slots in perfectly with my *Post-War Premier and Football League Players' Records*. Michael, who despite now living in Norfolk has supported Arsenal for as long he can remember, has accumulated data for a complete Football League database over many years and used it to produce the player indexes for the Definitive series of club histories and several other publications.

The editorial team were also lucky to be able to call upon **David Barber** (English FA), **Sandy Bryson** (Scottish FA), **Rebecca Burnett** (FA Premier League), **Ceri Stennett** (FA of Wales), and **Marshall Gillespie** (editor of the Northern Ireland Football Yearbook). Others who gave their time were **Alan Platt** (Where Did They Go?) and **Jenny Hugman** (proof reading), and many Premier and Football League members up and down the country.

For details provided on players, I have listed below, in alphabetical order, the names of the team, without whose help this book would not have been possible to produce. Once again, I thank every one of them for all the hard work they put in.

Audrey Adams (Watford): Producer and statistician for BBC Radio Sport and a Watford supporter since the days of Cliff Holton, Audrey was the club statistician for *The Ultimate Football Guide*. Regardless of how the club performed last season her devotion to the Hornets remains undimmed.

Geoff Allman (Walsall): A retired university lecturer, having worked for 49 years without taking a day off, he saw his first ever game in February 1944, Walsall versus Wolves. Has written for Walsall's programme for over 30 seasons and, at one time or another, has provided articles for more than half of the clubs currently in the Premiership and Football League. A keen cricketer, he says that although making few runs he prided himself on being able to hold his end up. Geoff is also a Methodist local preacher and press officer.

Stuart Basson (Chesterfield): Stuart is the club's official historian and has written for the Factfile/Who's Who since its inception. The author of three successful books about the club, he produces previews and reports for the club's official website and is also the regular summariser for home match commentaries on the club's Spireites World site.

David Batters (York City): A supporter since 1948, David is the club historian and a contributor to the matchday programme. He is also the author of *York City: A Complete Record, 1922-1990*, the compiler of *Images of Sport: York City FC* and commentates on matches for York Hospital Radio.

Harry Berry (Blackburn Rovers): As a season ticket holder ever since starting work, Harry has followed Blackburn Rovers for over 50 years, having been born only three miles from Ewood Park and living within 15 miles all his life. Has been a road runner for many years and has completed a few marathons. By profession a financial director, prior to retirement he worked for the largest manufacturer in Blackburn.

Tony Bluff (Doncaster Rovers): First watched the Rovers in 1953. The club historian and statistician for the past 20 years, Tony has contributed to the programme for many of those years but now contributes to the web site and club newspaper with historical data and match reports for the first team and reserves. Is co-author of the official history of the club.

Eddie Brennan (Sunderland): A season ticket holder at the Stadium of Light, and a former contributor to *The Ultimate Football Guide*, Eddie has been a regular supporter since 1976 and like any other Wearsider cannot wait for the team to get back to the Premiership.

Jim Brown (Coventry City): The club's official statistician and historian and contributor to the programme, he also pens a weekly column in the *Coventry Evening Telegraph* answering readers queries. He is also the author of *Coventry City: The Elite Era* (1998 and 2001) and *The Illustrated History* (2000), in addition to being the co-author of the *Breedon Complete Record* (1991). Has been a Coventry fan since 1962 and has an almost complete collection of Coventry programmes since the war, as well as having a large library of football writings and carrying out research for a number of commercial bodies. Jim has also written critically acclaimed books on *Huddersfield Town's glory years (1923-26)* and the *Busby Era at Old Trafford (1946-71)*.

Mark Brown (Plymouth Argyle): Helped by his wife, Nicola, in putting together the profiles for this publication, Mark has been supporting the club for over 25 years, having been introduced to them at the tender age of five by his Argyle-mad family. Follows most of their games, whether home or away, and is a member of the travel club. Recently became the proud father of Libby Margaret, who, with brother Ben, are almost certain to become Pilgrims!

Gavin Buckland (Everton): A life-long Everton supporter of over 30 years and co-author of *Everton: The Ultimate Book of Stats and Facts* and two other football quiz books, Gavin has also worked as a researcher and question setter on several TV quiz programmes. As the club statistician, he has a trivia and facts column in every Everton home programme and provides factual data for Radio Merseyside.

Trevor Bugg (Hull City): A supporter of the Tigers for over 30 years, Trevor contributes to Hull City's official web site as well as the matchday programme and also continues to pursue a career in football statistics.

Bob Cain (Fulham): Bob has supported Fulham for 33 years, during which time he has not missed a single home match in any first team competition. In all he has clocked up almost 1,600 first team games. A strong advocate of all seater stadiums, he is looking forward to returning to Craven Cottage and has been a contributor to the club programme for over a decade.

Tim Carder (Brighton & Hove Albion): Tim is chairman of both the Supporters' Club and the Albion's Collectors' and Historians' Society. Along with Roger Harris, he co-authored *Seagulls: The Story of Brighton and Hove Albion FC* and *Albion A to Z: A Who's Who of Brighton and Hove Albion FC*. He is also a respected local historian on matters ranging far beyond the Albion.

Wallace Chadwick (Burnley): A Clarets' supporter for over 40 years, and programme contributor for the last 17, Wallace has assisted on several publications about the club. A member of the AFS from 1980 until its untimely demise, he is an accountant by profession, a statistician by nature, and a supporter by unbreakable habit.

Gary Chalk and **Dave Juson** (Southampton): are both official historians of Southampton FC and members of Hagiology, a collective dedicated to publishing accurate and informative works on the Saints. Gary is co-author, with Duncan Holley, of *Saints: a complete History, 1885-1987*, *The Alphabet of Saints* (1992) and last year's lectern-crushing, *In That Number: A post war history of Southampton FC*. Dave is a regular contributor to the Saints' programme and was co-author, with David Bull, of *Full-Time at The Dell* (2001), a narrative history of the Saints, now in its third edition, and, along with Gary, a major contributor to *Match of the Millennium* (2000). Dave's next publication will be *Saints v Pompey*, in collaboration with Clay Aldworth, David Bull and Barry Bendel.

Paul Clayton (Charlton Athletic): Author of the book, *The Essential History of Charlton Athletic*, Paul wrote a regular feature in the club programme between 1993 and 1998, having previously written other articles for the now defunct Charlton Athletic magazine and *Valiant's Viewpoint* (Supporters Club newsletter/fanzine). He has also provided the Charlton statistics for a number of publications, including the *Ultimate Football Guide* from 1987 to its final publication in 1999, along with the Charlton player information for the *Factfile/Who's Who* since its inception in 1995. A long-standing season ticket holder at The Valley, Paul rarely misses a game, home or away, despite living in Wiltshire.

David Copping (Barnsley): David is a life-long Barnsley fan who has been a regular columnist in the Club matchday programme for many seasons. He also is one of the club statisticians and is currently involved in setting up a museum at Oakwell. For many seasons he commentated on both hospital radio and the club videos.

Frank Coumbe (Brentford): Hasn't missed a competitive Brentford home game since December 1977, a club record. He has also been Brentford's statistician for this book since it began and acted in a similar capacity for *The Ultimate Football Guide* until its demise. Frank continued to write the *Frankly Speaking* column for the Brentford programme, TW8, throughout 2003-04, while on the field, following Martin Allen's appointment as manager with just nine games to go and relegation looking a certainty, 18 points were gained and survival was ensured.

Peter Cullen (Bury): A Bury fan for more than 30 years, Peter has watched the Shakers play on all but five league grounds. A former secretary of the Supporters Assocation and the official club historian, he has written three books on the club, edited/contributed to the matchday programme for 20 years and also worked full time at the club as ticket office manager/ programme editor for three and a half years.

Mick Cunningham (Bournemouth): 44-year-old Mick has been the AFC Bournemouth programme editor and club photographer since 1995, not missing a home or away game in that time, providing coverage of the Cherries for local and national media. Mick has been a supporter since 1966.

John Curtis (Scunthorpe United): A life-long Scunthorpe fan, John is a former editor of the award-winning club matchday programme. He also covered the club's affairs for the *Scunthorpe Telegraph*, where he now works as the chief sub editor.

Carol Dalziel (Tranmere Rovers): Having watched Tranmere for over 30 years, Carol is a regular contributor to the matchday programme and operates the club's electronic scoreboard.

Denise Dann (Aston Villa): In her own words, Denise is a mad, crazy Villa supporter, who follows them up and down the country without fail. With the PFA Footballers' *Factfile/ Who's Who* since its inception, her only previous football work was to help with the club's profiles required for the *Premier League: The Players* publication.

Gareth Davies (Wrexham): Gareth is the co-author of the *Who's Who on Welsh International Footballers* (1991) with Ian Garland; editor/compiler of *Coast of Soccer Memories*, the centenary publication of the North Wales Coast FA (1994); co-author of *The Racecourse Robins* with Peter Jones; *Who's Who of Wrexham FC, 1921-99* (1999); co-author of Tempus' *Images of Sport: Wrexham FC, 1872-1950* (2000) with Peter Jones and *Wrexham FC, 1950-2001* (2001) with Peter Jones. He is also a contributor to the Wrexham official programme, *The Holyhead Hotspur* (Cymru Alliance), as the club's press officer, the Welsh Football magazine and various articles and info for other magazines and books.

David Downs (Reading): David has the honorary title of club historian as well as being employed by Reading FC as its welfare and child protection officer. Has worked for the club in a part-time capacity for over 20 years and also contributes to each issue of the Royals' matchday programme. David has other interests outside football, however, as he is a member of The Betjeman Society, The Tony Hancock Appreciation Society and The Sherlock Holmes Society of London.

Ray Driscoll (Chelsea): A life-long Blues' fan, born and bred two miles away from Stamford Bridge, whose 45 years' spectating encompasses the era from Jimmy Greaves to Jimmy Floyd Hasselbaink. He still can't believe the changes to the club over the past 12 months! An all-round sports 'nut', he has contributed to many football books as well as other sports such as cricket, golf, rugby and tennis. Has also contributed to more 'cerebral' literature such as reference books.

Brian Ellis (Luton Town): One of the co-authors of *The Definitive Luton Town*, Brian has been a Hatter since he was first taken to a game at Kenilworth Road in April 1967, but he first got interested in statistics and details of Town's history following the 2-0 win at West Ham in the opening game of the 1980-81 season. Having wondered whether such an unlikely event had occurred before he visited the libraries and was hooked. Brian is currently compiling a long-awaited *Who's Who on Luton Town*, which he hopes will be published around Christmas.

Dean Enderby and **Eddie Collins** (Nottingham Forest): A season ticket holder at Forest, this is the first book Dean has contributed to but would like to assist in others in the future. He is currently waiting for his wife to give birth to their first child in August and has already bought a small Nottingham Forest miniature kit much to her disgust. Eddie has been watching Forest since 1956 and derives much pleasure from being involved in this publication. He is also a member of the AFS.

Mark Evans (Leeds United): Has supported United for over 30 years and describes his association with the club as one of the loves of his life. The Leeds' statistician for *The Ultimate Football Guide* for nearly nine years, he was also involved in the two editions of *The FA Carling Premiership: The Players*.

Colin Faiers (Cambridge United): A Cambridge United fan for over 30 years, Colin has witnessed their rise from non-league football. A chartered accountant in the day, he is the club statistician and occasional contributor to the club programme and web site.

Harold Finch (Crewe Alexandra): March 2004 saw club historian, Harold, celebrate his 70th year as a Crewe Alexandra supporter. Still actively involved with articles for the programme and providing statistics on the club and players, following the success of his publication, *Crewe Alexandra FC – A Pictorial History of the Club*, he has now added another title, *Crewe Alexandra FC – 100 Greats* to his list. Is a keen collector of programmes involving Crewe and all types of memorabilia of the club and photographs.

Mick Ford and **Richard Lindsay** (Millwall): A life-long Millwall fan, Mick has followed the club for more than 50 years and looks forward to the day when the Lions reach the Premiership. Despite living in Worcester, he only misses a handful of games a season and without the understanding of his wife, Sue, would find it difficult to continue his passion. Has an extensive memorabilia collection, which he adds to when the right items come up. Meanwhile, his *Who's Who* partner, Richard, the author of *Millwall: A Complete Record*, continues to help establish the Millwall FC Museum at the New Den. Both Mick and Richard delighted in their big day at the Millenium Stadium, the result almost being irrelevant as Millwall finally, against all odds, arrived in an FA Cup final.

Andrew Frazier (Kidderminster Harriers): Has been following the Harriers since 1978, and hasn't missed a game, home or away, for over ten years. Is a contributor to the club programme, is the club statistician, and a member of the Association of Football Statisticians.

Jon Gibbes (Torquay United): Saw his first game on Boxing Day 1970 aged seven, the beginning of an unhealthy obsession with Torquay United, which at times leads to the woeful neglect of wife, Julie, and children, Rosie and Tommy. After having disproved the long-held belief that the club was formed in 1898, Jon co-wrote *Torquay United FC: The Official Centenary History, 1899-1999* with Leigh Edwards and John Lovis.

Harry Glasper (Middlesbrough): Now in his 38th year of supporting Middlesbrough, Harry has experienced the painful and peculiarly personal abysses of relegation on five separate occasions. These abject lows have been redressed by the relative joy of promotion on six occasions, but because the Boro had never won a major trophy he had only tasted the pangs of emptiness and misery always associated with returning empty-handed from a miscellany of Wembley finals, accompanied by a silent coach full of fellow sufferers. All this, of course, changed on February 29th, 2004 at the Millennium Stadium in Cardiff when the Carling Cup – yes, a major trophy! – was held aloft by captain, Gareth Southgate, and although Harry was in a crowd numbering over 76,000 he was alone with his personal thoughts and memories and freely admits that tears flowed. He also admits that, if accompanied by his wife, Leap Year day 2004 was the second best day of his life!

Paul Godfrey (Cheltenham Town): Paul watched his first Cheltenham Town game at the age of ten – the Robins losing 2-1 to Yeovil Town in an FA Cup Fourth Qualifying Round match. He followed similar near misses and disappointments religiously before events took a dramatic turn in the late 1990s. Having become the club's programme editor in 1990, he was able to witness at first hand the transformation at Whaddon Road brought about by Steve Cotterill and the Board, headed by the chairman, Paul Baker. He joined the club on a full-time basis in 2001 and now combines managing the club's website with his role as the secretary. He is still struggling manfully with the task of compiling the club history.

Frank Grande (Northampton Town): Author of *The Cobblers: A History of Northampton Town FC* and *The Northampton Town Who's Who*, Frank also compiled *The Definitive Northampton Town FC, A Centenary History* and a biography of Tommy Fowler, the club's longest serving player. Currently working on a book related to the 1940s of national interest, he has been a contributor to the club programme for well over 20 years.

Roy Grant (Oxford United): A life-long Oxford United fan, Roy previously produced the Oxford United matchday programme and had a spell as club statistician. A contributor in this publication since its first issue, Roy has also written for several football club programmes as well as contributing to football websites and productions such as *The Official Football League Yearbook* and *The Ultimate Football Guide*.

Michael Green (Bolton Wanderers): Despite being a fanatical Newcastle United supporter, Michael covers Bolton for this publication and his excellent efforts are much appreciated. Has a yearning to get involved in the area of freelance journalism, preferably concerning football or popular entertainment (music, films etc).

Alan Harding (Swindon Town): Alan has been supporting Swindon Town since 1968, is a season ticket holder, travels home and away, and has been researching match stats and line-up details, plus details of players, since 1981. Is also a member of the AFS.

Roger Harrison (Blackpool): A life-long supporter who has seen the Pool play every other league side, both home and away, and joint programme editor and club statistician, Roger has contributed to other publications, including *Rothmans Football Yearbook* and *The Ultimate Football Guide*.

Richard Hayhoe (Tottenham Hotspur): Involved since the start of this publication, Richard is happy to write about the men who play for his favourite team and hopes that Spurs can get among the elite in the forthcoming season. He is still delighted to be with the *Who's Who*, despite giving up his season ticket after 15 years. Whilst football and Spurs remain a great love, spending all his free time with his daughter, Holly, now six years old, is his most enjoyable pastime'.

Des Hinks (Stockport County): Des has now been following his beloved Hatters for 40 years and along with updating the club's website on a daily basis he also plays a key role in the production of their official matchday magazine. He's also a member of the independent team that produces County's award-winning reserve team programme.

Adrian Hopper (Yeovil Town): Joined Yeovil Town as media manager in 2002 after a long association through a local newspaper he owned. Also known as 'Fat Harry', Adrian is now a devoted Yeovil Town supporter attending every game, but has been known to have a slight leaning towards a certain team that plays in red at a Theatre!

Mike Jay (Bristol Rovers): Mike, the club's official historian and programme contributor, has had four books published on Rovers, namely *Bristol Rovers: A Complete Record, 1883-1987*, *Pirates in Profile: A Who's Who of Players, 1920-94* and *Bristol Rovers FC: Images of England Photographic History* (1999). His latest book, in conjunction with Stephen Byrne, is *The Definitive Bristol Rovers, 1883-2003*. Mike is currently working with Stephen Byrne on a project called *Bristol Rovers: The Men Who Made It*, which is due to be published in 2004-05.

Colin Jones (Swansea City): A fan since the early 1960s, and a contributor to the club programme for seven years, four of which were spent as editor, Colin played non-league football before being involved in training and coaching. Prior to the start of the 2000-01 season, he also made a significant contribution in setting out all the stats in grid form for David Farmer's book, *The Swans, Town & City*.

Andrew Kirkham (Sheffield United): A Blades' supporter since 1953, and a regular contributor to the club programme and handbook since 1984, Andrew is a member of the AFS and 92 Club. He was also a contributor to *Sheffield United: The First 100 Years*, and co-author of *A Complete Record of Sheffield United Football Club, 1889-1999*.

Geoff Knights (Macclesfield) Geoff is a retired bank manager who has supported Macclesfield Town since the late 1980s. Describing himself as an ordinary supporter from the terraces, and one who enjoys the friendly atmosphere of a small club, he keeps detailed statistics and records on the club, which are used in response to media and other enquiries.

Geoffrey Lea (Wigan Athletic): A life-long supporter for over 30 seasons who first started watching the club during the non-league days, Geoff has been the editor of the matchday programme for the last nine seasons. He is also the official matchday clubcall reporter and, as the club's statistician, he performs a number of jobs for Wigan as a labour of love. Has missed only a handful of games over the last 12 seasons and has also worked for a number of local radio stations and newspapers following the club's progress.

Mark Lea (Rushden & Diamonds): Mark has been covering Diamonds full-time for the *Northamptonshire Evening Telegraph* over the last five seasons, charting two championships, one runners-up spot in the Conference, a trip to the Millenium Stadium for the Division Three Play-Off final and then relegation for the first time in the club's 12-year history. Born in Boston, he also follows the fortunes of his hometown club, along with those of West Ham.

Gordon Macey (Queens Park Rangers): Has supported Queens Park Rangers since the early 1960s and has been collecting and compiling statistics on the club, at all levels, for many seasons. Recognised by many areas of the media as the 'expert' on QPR, in 1993 Gordon was invited to be the club's official historian following the publication of his successful *Queens Park Rangers: The Complete Record* and to mark the Millennium he published an update in August 1999. His three children are all regular attendees at the Rangers' games and help with some of the research at newspaper and local archives. Gordon's work, as an implementer of Financial and Logistic Business Systems, involves travel throughout Europe and other parts of the world. This gives him the opportunity of watching football (and his other interest of ice hockey) in a number of different countries.

John Maguire (Manchester United): A one-club man since this publication began, John has continued to work on several sports-related projects during 2004, particularly in the new book market. He is currently enjoying other aspects of writing, involving short stories, radio and scriptwriting.

Carl Marsden (Oldham Athletic): A life-long supporter, Carl has been involved with his beloved Athletic on several levels. Once the chairman of SAFE (Secure Athletic's Future Existence), a website editor and regular fanzine contributor, he now fronts the sports coverage of the *Oldham Advertiser* newspaper as the paper's Sports Editor and does live radio commentary on the club's matches for the Latics Live service. He can be reached by email on OldhamSport@gmwn.co.uk.

Carl Marston (Colchester United): Has been reporting on the fortunes of Colchester United since they regained their Football League status in 1992, both for the *East Anglian Daily Times* and the *Green 'Un* newspapers. Carl has only missed a handful of games during the last 12 years, usually when away, running for Suffolk in cross country races.

Tony Matthews (West Bromwich Albion): The official statistician and curator at The Hawthorns, his 60 plus publications include complete records/histories of Aston Villa, Birmingham City, Stoke City, Walsall, West Bromwich Albion and Wolverhampton Wanderers; The Essential Histories of Leicester City and Wolverhampton Wanderers, also assisting with same on Aston Villa and West Bromwich Albion; A-Z Encyclopaedias of Aston Villa, Birmingham City, Bolton Wanderers, Manchester United, Sheffield United, Stoke City, Tottenham Hotspur, West Bromwich Albion, Wolverhampton Wanderers and *Devon Football* (featuring Exeter City, Plymouth Argyle & Torquay United and published in 2002); Who's Whos of Villa, Blues, Manchester United (1945-85), Nottingham Forest, Stoke City, Albion and Wolves; *A Who's Who of England World Cup Players/Managers, The World Cup History: 1930-2002*; wartime and photographic books; *Smokin' Joe: The Cyrille Regis Story* (2002); he also contributes to programmes of Premiership/Nationwide League clubs. His most recent works are a *Who's Who of Aston Villa* (up-dated to 2004) and *Everton (1878-2004), 125 years of West Midland's Soccer 1879-2004* and following on will be books on Soccer Firsts and Football Oddities.

Peter Miles and **David Goody** (Southend U): Peter has supported United since 1976 and remains a regular watcher of matches, both home and away, while David has also supported the club from his youth. Peter has had eight books on football published, four of them about the Shrimpers and all co-authored with David. The Southend related titles are *Potted Shrimps: An Encyclopedia, Southend United: Images of Sport, 100 Greats* and, more recently, *Southend United: 50 Classic Matches*.

Ian Mills (Arsenal): An Arsenal fan for 28 years, Ian first visited 'The Home of Football' in 1982 and has been a regular contributor to the premier Arsenal fanzine, The Gooner, since 1997. As the chairman and secretary, he also writes and publishes a fanzine for his local Sunday football team, Rushden United, entitled *Sunday Bloody Sunday*. Always to be found in the North Bank Upper Tier at Highbury on matchdays, he also gets to away games when he can and is a keen historian on Arsenal.

Paul Morant (Leyton Orient): Working for an insurance company in London, Paul is an out-and-out Orient fan who rarely misses a game, home or away, and takes great pride in being this publication's Orient contributor.

Gerald Mortimer (Derby County). Gerald first visited the Baseball Ground in 1946 and for 32 years, until his retirement from full-time journalism in 2002, covered the club for the *Derby Evening Telegraph*. The main author of *Derby County: A Complete Record*, which became an important club series by Breedon Books in 1984, he went on to produce a second version in 1988. His revised and updated *Who's Who of Derby County* is due out this autumn.

Donald Nannestad (Boston United): Reporting on the fortunes of the Pilgrims for Raymonds Press Agency since the club's entry to Division Three, Donald, who is a journalist by profession, has a second role in life as a local councillor in Lincoln and he served as the city's 797th Mayor in 2003-04.

Ian Nannestad (Lincoln City): Ian has followed the Imps for more than 35 years and is co-author with his brother, Donald, of *A Who's Who of Lincoln City, 1892-1994* and *Lincoln City: The Official History*. A freelance writer and book editor, in April 2002 he established a new quarterly magazine devoted to the history of the game, titled *Soccer History*. Readers wishing to know more about the magazine can contact Ian by writing to 52 Studland Road, Hall Green, Birmingham, B28 8NW. He was previously editor of the AFS Report.

John Northcutt (West Ham United): Has supported the Hammers since 1959 and is the co-author of *West Ham: A Complete Record* and *The Illustrated History*. A regular contributor to the club programme, John was the club adviser to *The Ultimate Football Guide*. He also answers all the questions put to the Vintage Claret section on the club's web site and has recently produced *The West Ham Definitive*, which is currently on sale through SoccerData Publications.

Richard Owen (Portsmouth): A life-long supporter and official club historian for Portsmouth, Richard performs several jobs for the club as labour of love and has been a regular contributor to the club programme for the past 26 years, missing only a handful of away games in the past 28 years, having watched Pompey on 111 league grounds. An avid programme collector, with an almost complete set of post-war Portsmouth home and away issues, in 1998 he co-published *The Centenary Pictorial History of Portsmouth FC* and *A Team Collection*, which featured every team picture of Pompey since 1898. His third book, *Pompey's Rise to the Premiership* was published in July 2003 and he is currently working on two further titles. Richard has now built up a full library of club histories on all British Football League clubs.

Simon Parker (Bradford City): Following City closely due to his work at the *Bradford Telegraph & Argus*, Simon stepped in late in the day to help the *Who's Who* out of a crisis and developed material to a high standard.

Steve Peart and **Dave Finch** (Wycombe Wanderers): A former programme editor of the club and a supporter for over 30 years, Steve put together the player profiles, while the club statistics were supplied by Dave, the official Wycombe statistician. Both were authors of *Wycombe Wanderers, 1887-1996: The Official History*, published in 1996. Dave has supported Wycombe regularly since 1964 and has been a member of the club's programme editorial team since 1990.

Steve Phillipps (Rochdale): A Rochdale supporter for nearly 40 years, and the club's official historian, Steve is the author of *The Survivors: The Story of Rochdale AFC* (1990), *The Definitive Rochdale* (1995) and, more recently, *The Official History of Rochdale AFC*. A founder member of the AFS, away from football he is a university lecturer.

Terry Phillips (Cardiff City): Terry is the chief sports writer for the *South Wales Echo*, mainly covering City home and away, and a sports journalist for over 30 years – *Kent Evening Post* (1970-1977), *Derby Evening Telegraph* (1977-1986), *Gloucester Citizen* (1986-1994) – he has previously covered clubs at all levels, including Brian Clough's Nottingham Forest, Derby County, Gillingham, and Gloucester City. His specialist subjects are Cardiff City FC and Cardiff Devils (Ice Hockey).

Alan Platt (Liverpool): Is a dedicated football statistician and a follower of Liverpool FC since 1960, and whilst resident in London, a member and official of the London branch of the LFC Supporters Club. He has assisted Barry Hugman in an editorial capacity on all his football publications since 1980, namely the four updates of *Football League Players Records*, the two editions of *Premier League: The Players* and, for the last seven years, the *PFA Footballers' Who's Who* (formerly *The Factfile*) when not working overseas in his profession of transport planner. Now resident in Manchester, his main interest today is in non-league football and he keeps detailed records on all the senior semi-professional leagues, having compiled a database of over 6,000 players participating in that level of football.

Kevan Platt (Norwich City): As City's former programme editor and now club secretary, Kevan has always had an interest in football statistics and he combines his role with that of in-house club historian and statistician. Now in his 25th year of employment with the club, having first watched the Canaries in 1968, he has enjoyed and endured the many ups and downs City have had in those 36 years. Co-authored, with Mike Davage, the club's centenary book, *Canary Citizens*.

Mike Purkiss (Crystal Palace): Having supported Palace since 1950 and producing stats on them since 1960, Mike is the author of *Crystal Palace: A Complete History, 1905-1989*.

Was the club statistician for *The Ultimate Football Guide* and also contributed to *Premier League: The Players*.

Mick Renshaw (Sheffield Wednesday): Has followed Wednesday for over 40 years, despite all the ups and downs of a club that won the First Division title four times in past years, and will continue to do so regardless. Mick, who is a great supporter of European soccer, also produced the club section for *The Ultimate Football Guide*.

Mick Robinson (Peterborough United): Another life-long fan, for a number of years Mick has contributed to the club programme and was the joint editor of *The Posh*, the official Peterborough history. Was also club statistician for *The Ultimate Football Guide*.

Phil Sherwin (Port Vale): Phil is the Port Vale club statistician and has been a fan since 1968, when they had to seek re-election to the old Fourth Division. Travelling to away games since 1973, he has only missed a handful of matches since then and has contributed to the club programme, various books on the club, the now defunct *Football Club Directory*, and the local newspaper, as well as radio and television.

Mike Slater (Wolverhampton Wanderers): The Wolves' contributor to this publication since its inception, Mike wrote a book on the club's history called *Molineux Memories*, which he published in 1988. Well-known as the compiler of *The Brain of Wolves' Quiz*, he also produced a booklet in 1996 containing all of Wolves' competitive results and records against every other club. As a follow-up to *Molineux Memories*, Mike has recently produced a booklet, *Took 14 Years, It Only Took 14 Years*, on Wolves' efforts to get back to the top flight from 1989 (when it was Division 1) to 2003.

Gordon Small (Hartlepool United): Has supported the Pool since October 1965 and for the past 30 odd years has collected and compiled statistics on his adopted club. Has contributed to all ten editions of the *PFA Footballers' Who's Who* and, in 1998, was the author of *The Definitive Hartlepool United*. Has a wide range of football interests and, in particular, has ambitions to produce books on the history of soccer in Lancashire.

Dave Smith (Leicester City): Dave has been the official Leicester City statistician and historian for many years and is a regular contributor to both the club programme and the club's extensive media guide. He is also the co-author of both *Of Fossils and Foxes* and *The Foxes Alphabet* and was editor of both *Farewell to Filbert Street* and *Keeping the Faith*, which together charted the final season at Filbert Street and the first campaign at the Walkers Stadium

Phil Smith (Wimbledon): A supporter of Wimbledon FC for over 20 years, Phil continued to follow the club throughout its troubled first season at its new home and is looking forward to continuing his involvement with the renamed Milton Keynes Dons for the 2004-05 season. Is a regular contributor to the club's official programme.

Gerry Somerton (Rotherham United): The club's media and communications officer, Gerry has contributed to the *Who's Who* since its inception. Has written four books on the club, his latest being the *Definitive Rotherham United*, which is a complete Who's Who of every player since 1893. Widely accepted as the club's official historian, he broadcasts a full match commentary on every Miller's game for the club website.

Paul Stead (Huddersfield Town): Now in his seventh year with the *Who's Who*, Paul is a life-long supporter of his hometown football club, and a regular spectator both home and away. Over the last four years, Huddersfield Town have been involved in two relegations and now two play offs, after missing out on direct promotion on the last day of the 2004 season. He has, however, been fortunate in seeing Huddersfield promoted from both Wembley and The Millennium Stadium.

David Steele (Carlisle United): David has been involved with the *PFA Footballers' Who's Who* since its inception in 1995. Has also been a regular contributor to the Carlisle matchday programme since 1989, as well as giving assistance to a wide variety of publications on matters connected with the club's history.

Bill Swann (Newcastle United): A supporter since the Jackie Milburn days of the early 1950s, and a long-term shareholder in the club, along with his wife and three children (all season ticket holders), he is a keen collector of memorabilia connected with the club. Having consolidated his information on club matches, teams, scorers, and players into a database for easy access and analysis, Bill assisted in the production of the club's volume in the Complete Record series, is a co-author of the recent *Essential History of Newcastle United* and is in his ninth year as a contributor to this publication. His 18 year-old son, Richard, also a Newcastle fanatic, and an England Independent Schools goalkeeper, kept him right on some of the detailed information in the player biographies.

Colin Tattum (Birmingham City): Colin is the chief sports writer on the *Birmingham Evening Mail* newspaper,with more than 15 years experience in his field and has special responsibility to cover the day-to-day fortunes of Birmingham City.

Paul Taylor (Mansfield Town): A Mansfield Town supporter of over 30 years standing, Paul has contributed to many publications over the last few years, including the club's centenary history published in 1997. He is the club's official historian, the official Mansfield Town statistician for the AFS and is also president of the Stags Supporters' Association (formed this season from the old Stags Supporters' Club and Support Our Stags members club).

Richard and **Sarah Taylor** and **Ian Mills** (Notts County): Richard is a life-long Notts County fan from a Notts County family, travelling the length and breadth of the land in following the Magpies, and has seen them on all but a few current league grounds and many non-current grounds too. In the summer, he umpires cricket matches to while away the close season. Sarah, like her father and two brothers, became a dedicated fan at an early age and has made regular excursions home from university to support the Magpies. Having seen his first game at Gay Meadow in 1959-60, Ian, who once ran the matchday programme sales, has been hooked ever since and has now completed 1000 consecutive games for County, being presented with a momento by Chris Hull of Nationwide on the pitch last season. This coming season he will be sitting in the press box at County doing the press officer's job, after 22 seasons of programme involvement and wanting a change.

Les Triggs (Grimsby Town): A retired librarian, Les first saw the Mariners in a wartime league match whilst the club was in exile at Scunthorpe's Old Show Ground and has been a regular supporter since their days as a then First Division side. Became involved in the historical side of the club when asked to assist in the staging of the Centenary Exhibition in 1978. The co-author of *Grimsby Town: A Complete Record* and the Grimsby statistician for the *Ultimate Football Guide*, he is also an occasional contributor to the club fanzine.

Roger Triggs (Gillingham): Roger has been a Gillingham supporter for over 40 years and has been collecting statistics and records on the club since he was a schoolboy. Co-author of the highly acclaimed centenary book, *Home of the Shouting Men*, produced in 1993, Roger has since produced his images collection in conjunction with Tempus Publishing Company

and, in August 2001, brought out *The Complete Who's Who of Gillingham's Football League Players, 1920-1938 & 1950-2001*.

Frank Tweddle (Darlington): The club's official historian and statistician, Frank has regularly contributed articles to the Darlington programme for the last 29 seasons and has avidly supported the Quakers home and away for nigh on 50 years. A member of the 92 Club and the AFS, he is the author of *'Darlington's Centenary History'* published in 1983 and *'The Definitive Darlington 1883 - 2000'* and has produced work for various other football publications. Now early-retired, Frank can devote even more time to delving into Darlington's fascinating, if undistinguished past 121 years!

Paul Voller (Ipswich Town): Has been a life-long Town fan and started attending matches at Portman Road in 1963. A member of the Ipswich Town Supporters' Media Committee, he edits the supporters' page in the matchday magazine and the supporters' weekly page in the local *Evening Star*. Was the Ipswich statistician for the *Rothmans Football Yearbook* and the *Football Club Directory* during the 1990s and was joint author of *The Essential History of Ipswich Town*.

Andrew Waldon (Manchester City): Andrew has been a regular supporter of City for the past quarter of a century and has seen his favourite club play on over 160 different grounds. His creative writing talents have seen him make regular literary contributions to several publications, including the club's official handbook, monthly magazine and website. He also contributes to the matchday magazine in his role as the official reserve team reporter and has produced several books on his beloved team. Was responsible for a large proportion of the Tempus publication, *Images of Manchester City*, as well as co-writing *Manchester City Classics*. He then flew solo with two other publications, *Maine Road Voices* and *Waiting for the Whistle*.

Tony Woodburn and **Martin Atherton** (Preston North End): Both North End fans for well over 30 years, Tony and Martin provide statistical and historical information on the club for various outlets and maintain the National Football Museum's permanent Preston North End collection, as well as writing for the club programme and, of course, the *Who's Who*.

David Woods (Bristol City): An Ashton Gate regular since March 1958, and a shareholder since 1972, David has been involved with seven books on Bristol City, the most recent being *Bristol City: The Early Years, 1894-1915*, published by Desert Island. Was also involved in a history on the Bristol Bulldogs Speedway side. A life-member of the AFS, he belongs to the 92 Club on visiting all the Football League grounds following a match at Lincoln on 18 April 1970. David is also the club's official historian. A graduate of the Open University, his other interests include geology, history, cricket (Gloucestershire), rugby (Bristol), speedway (Somerset Rebels) and tennis.

Peter Wyatt (Stoke City): Having seen the return of Stan Matthews from Blackpool in October 1961, the first match he can remember, Peter has been researching the club for over 25 years and assisted Tony Matthews on the *Encyclopedia of Stoke City* and the *Stoke City A to Z*. Has had articles published in the old AFS magazines and in the Stoke City fanzine, *The Oatcake*. He also admits to once thinking that Alan Hudson was a Supreme Being !!

Finally, on the production side of the book, my thanks go to **Jean Bastin**, of Typecast (Artwork & Design) for her patience and diligent work on the typesetting and design, which again went far beyond the call of normal duty and was much appreciated.

Thierry Henry, the PFA Player of the Year

Editorial Introduction

Following on from last year's edition, the Who's Who portrays the statistical career record of every FA Barclaycard Premiership and Nationwide League player who made an appearance in 2003-04, whether it be in league football, the Football League Cup (Carling Cup), FA Cup (Sponsored by AXA), Community Shield (formerly the Charity Shield), UEFA Champions League, UEFA Cup, Inter-Toto Cup, LDV Vans Trophy, or in the Play Offs. Not included are Welsh Cup matches. It goes beyond mere statistics, however, with a write up on all of the 2,300 plus players involved, and also records faithfully last season's playing records separately by club.

The work falls into three sections, all inter-relating. Firstly, the main core, PFA Footballers' Who's Who: A-Z (pages 13 to 452); secondly, FA Barclaycard Premiership and Nationwide League Clubs: Summary of Appearances and Goals for 2003-2004 (pages 453 to 474); and thirdly, Where Did They Go? (pages 475 to 479); lists all players shown in the previous edition who either moved on or did not play in 2003-04. Below is an explanation on how to follow the PFA Footballers' Who's Who.

As the title suggests, all players are listed in alphabetical order and are shown by Surnames first, followed by full Christian names, with the one the player is commonly known by shown in bold. Any abbreviation or pseudonym is bracketed.

Birthplace/date: You will note that several players who would be predominately classified as British, were born in places like Germany and India, for example. My book, Premier and Football League Players' Records, which covers every man who has played league football since the war, has, in the past, used the family domicile as a more realistic 'birthplace'. But, for our purposes here, I have reverted to that which has been officially recorded.

Height and Weight: Listed in feet and inches, and stones and pounds, respectively. It must be remembered that a player's weight can frequently change and, on that basis, the recorded data should be used as a guide only, especially as players are weighed several times during the season.

Club Honours: Those shown, cover careers from the Conference and FA Trophy upwards. For abbreviations, read:- European Honours: EC (European Cup, now UEFA Champions League), ESC (European Super Cup), ECWC (European Cup Winners' Cup) and UEFAC (UEFA Cup). English Honours: FAC (FA Cup), FLC (Football League Cup), CS (Community Shield), FMC (Full Members Cup, which took in the Simod and Zenith Data sponsorships), AMC (Associated Members Cup – Freight Rover, Sherpa Van, Leyland DAF, Autoglass, Auto Windscreens and LDV Vans), AIC (Anglo-Italian Cup), GMVC (GM Vauxhall Conference), FC (Football Conference), NC (Nationwide Conference), FAT (FA Trophy), FAYC (FA Youth Cup). Scottish Honours: SPD (Scottish Premier Division), S Div 1/2 (Scottish Leagues), SC (Scottish Cup), SLC (Scottish League Cup). Please note that medals awarded to P/FL, FLC, and AMC winners relate to players who have appeared in 25%, or over, of matches, while FAC, EC, ESC, ECWC and UEFAC winners' medals are for all-named finalists, including unused subs. For our purposes, however, Community Shield winners' medals refer to

men who either played or came on as a sub. Honours applicable to players coming in from abroad are not shown at present, but the position continues to be reviewed.

International Honours: For abbreviations, read:- E (England), NI (Northern Ireland), S (Scotland), W (Wales) and RoI (Republic of Ireland). Under 21 through to full internationals give total appearances (inclusive of subs), while schoolboy (U16s and U18s) and youth representatives are just listed. The cut-off date used for appearances was up to and including 4 July 2004.

Player Descriptions: Gives position and playing strengths and, in keeping the work topical, a few words on how their season went in 2003-04. This takes into account, in a positive fashion, key performances, along with value to the team, injuries, honours, and other points of interest, etc.

Career Records: Full appearances, plus substitutes and goals, are given for all FA Barclaycard Premiership and Nationwide League games and, if a player who is in the book has played in any of the senior Scottish Leagues, his appearances with the club in question will also be recorded at the point of signing. Other information given, includes the players' source (clubs in the non-leagues, junior football, or from abroad), registered signing dates (if a player signs permanently following a loan spell, for our purposes, we have shown the initial date as being the point of transfer. Also, loan transfers are only recorded if an appearance is made) and transfer fees (these are the figures that have been reported in newspapers and magazines and should only be used as a guide to a player's valuation). Appearances, substitutions and goals are recorded by P/FL (Premiership and Football League), PL (Premier League), FL (Football League), FLC (Football League Cup), FAC (FA Cup), and Others. Other matches take in the Play Offs, LDV Vans Trophy, Community Shield, and European competitions, such as the European Champions League, UEFA Cup, European Super Cup and Inter-Toto Cup. All of these matches are lumped together for reasons of saving space. Scottish appearances for players on loan to P/FL clubs in 20032-04 are shown at the point of transfer and do not include games following their return to Scotland. That also applies to players transferred from England to Scotland. FA Cup appearances, subs and goals are only recorded when they are made playing for a P/FL club and do not cover appearances made by Conference sides prior to joining or after relegation from the Football League.

Career statistics are depicted as
Appearances + Substitutes/Goals

Whether you wish to analyse someone for your fantasy football team selection or would like to know more about a little-known player appearing in the lower reaches of the game, the PFA Footballers' Who's Who should provide you with the answer.

Barry J. Hugman, Editor, PFA Footballers' Who's Who

A

ABBEY George Peterson
Born: Port Harcourt, Nigeria, 20 October 1978
Height: 5'10" **Weight:** 11.13
International Honours: Nigeria: 10
George made four appearances at right back for Nigeria during the 2003 close season returning to Macclesfield a more confident and accomplished player. He appeared regularly until the middle of December when suspension and international duties took over, then his appearances were restricted by a hamstring problem. George uses his pace well especially when moving up the right flank and often delivers telling crosses into the penalty box. He was an ever-present for Nigeria in the African Nations' Cup finals, finishing up with a medal when his team finished in third place.
Macclesfield T (Signed from Sharks FC, Port Harcourt, Nigeria on 20/8/1999) FL 79+21/1 FLC 5+1 FAC 5+4 Others 2

ABBEY Zema
Born: Luton, 17 April 1977
Height: 6'1" **Weight:** 12.11
Zema was desperately unlucky to suffer his second cruciate ligament injury in three seasons playing for Norwich City at Sheffield United last August, thus restricting his first-team appearances in 2003-04 to just three. A strong, quick and athletic striker, he was out of contract in the summer and his future was uncertain at the time of writing.
Cambridge U (Signed from Hitchin T on 11/2/2000) FL 16+6/5 FLC 1+1 FAC 1 Others 1
Norwich C (£350,000 on 15/12/2000) FL 30+29/7 FLC 1 FAC 1+2/1

ABBOTT Pawel Tadeusz Howard
Born: York, 2 December 1981
Height: 6'1" **Weight:** 11.12
International Honours: Poland: U21
Pawel struggled to gain a regular place at Preston last season, despite featuring for Poland U21s and scoring the only goal of the game on his first start at Nottingham Forest. The tall front man had to be content with an irregular place on the bench before joining Huddersfield on loan. He made a dream debut as a substitute in the away draw at Bristol Rovers by scoring the equaliser, then netting the winners against both Lincoln and Yeovil Town. One of his best goals

came from a wonderful overhead kick against Southend.
Preston NE (£125,000 + from LKS Lodz, Poland on 16/2/2001) FL 8+17/6 FLC 0+1 FAC 1+3
Bury (Loaned on 9/8/2002) FL 13/5 FLC 2 Others 1
Bury (Loaned on 18/3/2003) FL 4/1
Huddersfield T (Signed on 16/2/2004) FL 12+1/5 Others 1+1

ABIDALLAH Nabil
Born: Amsterdam, Holland, 5 August 1982
Height: 5'7" **Weight:** 9.6
International Honours: Morocco: Yth
This skilful attacking midfield player began the 2003-04 season with Ipswich Town's reserve team before joining Northampton on loan early in the new year. However, he made just two appearances from the substitutes' bench for the Cobblers, suffering an injury in his second outing in the LDV Vans Trophy tie against Colchester. Soon after returning to Portman Road Nabil was made available on a free transfer and he spent the remainder of the campaign on trial with clubs in Holland.
Ipswich T (Free from Ajax, Holland on 19/7/2000) PL 0+2 FAC 0+1
Northampton T (Loaned on 16/1/2004) FL 0+1 Others 0+1

ACHTERBERG John
Born: Utrecht, Holland, 8 July 1971
Height: 6'1" **Weight:** 13.8
John enjoyed another outstanding season as Tranmere's undisputed number one goalkeeper in 2003-04, deservedly winning both the supporters' and his team mates' 'Player of the Year' Awards. A near ever-present, he kept 19 clean sheets with the highlight of his campaign was undoubtedly a penalty save at Millwall that kept Rovers in the quarter-final of the FA Cup. John's calmness, reliability and determination play a large part in inspiring confidence in his defenders, and indeed there are few weaknesses in his all-round game.
Tranmere Rov (Free from Eindhoven FC, Holland, ex NAC Breda, on 22/9/1998) FL 180+3 FLC 14+1 FAC 21 Others 4

ADAMS Daniel (Danny) Benjamin
Born: Manchester, 3 January 1976
Height: 5'8" **Weight:** 13.9
Danny was a near ever-present for Macclesfield for most of last term, featuring at left back in a back-four

formation. Always a consistent performer, he is not afraid to make firm tackles and is confident when moving forward on the overlap. In March he moved on to near-neighbours Stockport County, where he made an immediate impact, his arrival signalling the start of an impressive 11-match unbeaten run which ultimately helped County avoid relegation.
Macclesfield T (£25,000 from Altrincham on 31/8/2000) FL 146+2/1 FLC 5+1 FAC 12 Others 3/1
Stockport Co (Signed on 5/3/2004) FL 12

ADAMS Stephen (Steve) Marc
Born: Plymouth, 25 September 1980
Height: 6'0" **Weight:** 11.10
Club Honours: Div 3 '02; Div 2 '04
Steve once again proved to be a valuable member of Plymouth Argyle's squad last term. Early on he struggled to earn a starting role but soon regained his central-midfield position. Steve's main attribute is his tactical awareness of the game. He often breaks things up in midfield thanks to his useful knack of reading opposition passes.
Plymouth Arg (From trainee on 6/7/1999) FL 114+23/6 FLC 3 FAC 7+3 Others 4+2

ADEBOLA Bamberdele (Dele)
Born: Lagos, Nigeria, 23 June 1975
Height: 6'3" **Weight:** 12.8
This tall centre forward started the season as first-choice striker for Coventry and scored on his debut against Peterborough in the Carling Cup. Despite never giving less than 100 per cent Dele struggled for form and found goals hard to come by. With opportunities looking bleak in the new year he joined Burnley on loan. The type of big target man the Clarets had lacked since the departure of Gareth Taylor, Dele unfortunately made little impact due to injury and was restricted to three substitute appearances, although he did score a consolation goal in the Easter Monday home defeat by Watford.
Crewe Alex (From trainee on 21/6/1993) FL 98+26/39 FLC 4+3/2 FAC 8+2/3 Others 10+1/2
Birmingham C (£1,000,000 on 6/2/1998) FL 86+43/31 FLC 13+4/8 FAC 2+1/2 Others 1+2/1
Oldham Ath (Loaned on 20/3/2002) FL 5
Crystal Palace (Free on 15/8/2002) FL 32+7/5 FLC 5/2 FAC 4
Coventry C (Free on 2/7/2003) FL 15+13/2 FLC 2/1 FAC 2+1
Burnley (Loaned on 25/3/2004) FL 0+3/1

John Achterberg (centre)

AGOGO Manuel (Junior)
Born: Accra, Ghana, 1 August 1979
Height: 5'10" **Weight:** 11.7
International Honours: E: SP-3
After joining Bristol Rovers in the summer of 2003 Junior picked up a knee injury before the start of the campaign. This affected his movement and eventually required surgery, so it was not until the final third of the season that he flourished under the new management team at the club. Junior scored some vital goals, none better than the winner against Swansea which ultimately saved the club from relegation.
Sheffield Wed (Free from Willesden Constantine on 8/10/1996) PL 0+2 FAC 0+1 (Free to Colorado Rapids, USA on 2/2/2000)
Oldham Ath (Loaned on 18/7/1999) FL 2
Chester C (Loaned on 3/9/1999) FL 10/6
Chesterfield (Loaned on 11/11/1999) FL 3+1
Lincoln C (Loaned on 17/12/1999) FL 3/1
Queens Park R (Free from San Jose Earthquakes, USA on 28/3/2002) FL 0+2 (Free to Barnet on 4/7/2002
Bristol Rov (£110,000 + on 1/7/2003) FL 28+10/6 FLC 1

AGYEMANG Patrick
Born: Walthamstow, 29 September 1980
Height: 6'1" **Weight:** 12.0
After three years of being in and out of the Wimbledon starting line-up, Patrick began the 2003-04 season as the club's main striker and duly scored in the opening day win over Crewe. From then on he coped manfully leading the attack, displaying his usual tricks and blistering pace, but too often he lacked support. A winning goal at Gillingham in November prompted interest from that club and two months later the Dons administrators were unable to resist. Patrick not only featured as leading scorer for both clubs, he scored the winner for the Dons at Gillingham and the winner for the Gills at Wimbledon!
Wimbledon (From trainee on 11/5/1999) FL 68+53/20 FLC 3+2/1 FAC 8+3/1
Brentford (Loaned on 18/10/1999) FL 3+9 FAC 1
Gillingham (£200,000 on 13/1/2004) FL 20/6

AHMED Adnan
Born: Burnley, 7 June 1984
Height: 5'10" **Weight:** 11.12
This promising Huddersfield reserve midfielder made his Football League debut from the bench in the away draw at Rochdale last September. This was followed by two appearances as a non-playing substitute, before a double hernia

operation cut short his season. Strong and powerful on the ball, the eager youngster will be looking to establish himself next season.
Huddersfield T (From trainee on 22/8/2003) FL 0+1

AINSWORTH Gareth
Born: Blackburn, 10 May 1973
Height: 5'9" **Weight:** 12.5
This wide-right midfielder joined Queens Park Rangers in the summer of 2003 and made an immediate impact by scoring within five minutes of his debut. Gareth was a regular starter for the first team until he suffered an injury in December and was sidelined for three months. A popular player with the fans, his most memorable performance came at Rushden when he scored two spectacular goals in the 3-3 draw.
Preston NE (Signed from Northwich Vic, ex Blackburn Rov YTS, on 21/1/1992) FL 2+3 Others 1/1
Cambridge U (Free on 17/8/1992) FL 1+3/1 FLC 0+1
Preston NE (Free on 23/12/1992) FL 76+6/12 FLC 3+2 FAC 3+1 Others 8+1/1
Lincoln C (£25,000 on 31/10/1995) FL 83/37 FLC 8/3 FAC 2 Others 4/1
Port Vale (£500,000 on 12/9/1997) FL 53+2/10 FLC 2/1 FAC 2
Wimbledon (£2,000,000 on 3/11/1998) P/FL 21+15/6 FLC 1+1 FAC 5+2/1
Preston NE (Loaned on 28/3/2002) FL 3+2/1
Walsall (Loaned on 5/12/2002) FL 2+3/1
Cardiff C (£50,000 on 17/3/2003) FL 9
Queens Park R (Free on 17/7/2003) FL 21+8/6 FLC 2+1/1 FAC 1 Others 2

AKINBIYI Adeola (Ade) Peter
Born: Hackney, 10 October 1974
Height: 6'1" **Weight:** 12.9
International Honours: Nigeria: 1
Ade returned to Stoke on a permanent basis last September and took a little time to regain full fitness, but he then showed the form that had eluded him since the early days of his career. An injury saw him out of the side towards the end of the season but with a full summer's training schedule behind him he should be a threat to opposing defences again. Ade finished the campaign as the club's joint-top scorer and was voted 'Player of the Season' by the fans.
Norwich C (From trainee on 5/2/1993) P/FL 22+27/3 FLC 2+4/2 FAC 0+2 Others 0+1
Hereford U (Loaned on 21/1/1994) FL 3+1/2
Brighton & Hove A (Loaned on 24/11/1994) FL 7/4
Gillingham (£250,000 on 13/1/1997) FL 63/28 FLC 2 FAC 2/1 Others 0+1

Bristol C (£1,200,000 on 28/5/1998) FL 47/21 FLC 5/4 FAC 1
Wolverhampton W (£3,500,000 on 7/9/1999) FL 36+1/16 FAC 3
Leicester C (£5,000,000 on 28/7/2000) PL 49+9/11 FLC 1/1 FAC 5+1/1 Others 2
Crystal Palace (£2,200,000 + on 6/2/2002) FL 11+13/3 FAC 0+4
Stoke C (Loaned on 27/3/2003) FL 4/2
Stoke C (Free on 15/9/2003) FL 23+7/10 FLC 0+1 FAC 1

AKINFENWA Saheed **Adebayo**
Born: London, 10 May 1982
Height: 5'11" **Weight:** 13.0
This powerfully built striker started last term with Welsh Premier League club Barry Town, featuring in their European Champions' League qualifier against Vardar Skopje. In October he had a brief spell with Boston United, scoring on his debut against Swindon Town in the LDV Vans Trophy and setting up two goals in the home win over Torquay. He proved popular, but chose to move on after four weeks at York Street. Next stop was Leyton Orient, where he made a couple of appearances, and then Rushden, where he failed to make the first team. In March he signed for Doncaster and became an instant hit with the fans for his hard work and ability, his deft footwork and aerial ability complementing Gregg Blundell's pace as they formed a useful partnership.
Boston U (Free from Barry T, ex FK Atlantas, on 15/10/2003) FL 2+1 Others 1/1
Leyton Orient (Free on 31/10/2003) FL 0+1 FAC 0+1
Rushden & Diamonds (Free on 11/12/2003)
Doncaster Rov (Free on 18/2/2004) FL 4+5/4

ALBRIGHTON Mark
Born: Nuneaton, 6 March 1976
Height: 6'1" **Weight:** 12.7
Club Honours: Div 3 '04
Mark found himself on the sidelines at Doncaster at the start of last season due to the excellent form of regular central backs Dave Morley and Steve Foster. However, when given his chance at Cambridge he seized the opportunity and, he then featured regularly during the remainder of the campaign. Mark's strong tackling and ability in the air marked him out as the rock on which opposing forwards foundered, although his combative style was not always appreciated by referees.
Doncaster Rov (Signed from Telford U, ex Nuneaton Borough, Atherstone U, on 5/7/2002) FL 27+1/3 FAC 1 Others 1

ALCOCK Daniel (Danny) James
Born: Stafford, 15 February 1984
Height: 5'11" **Weight:** 11.3
Danny joined Barnsley after a successful trial spell, but he was second-choice 'keeper for the entire 2003-04 season. His only first-team appearance came when he came off the bench to replace the injured Marlon Beresford in the home game against Queens Park Rangers in April. He was one of a number of players released at the end of the season.
Barnsley (From trainee at Stoke C on 31/10/2003) FL 0+1

ALEXANDER Gary George
Born: Lambeth, 15 August 1979
Height: 5'11" **Weight:** 13.0

Gary was again the first-choice centre forward for Leyton Orient last term and finished the campaign as the club's leading goal-scorer with 15 strikes. He impressed the fans with his tremendous work rate and was regularly to be found helping out the defence when required. Gary was made club captain in the new year and he was rewarded with a new long-term contract in March.
West Ham U (From trainee on 6/7/1998)
Exeter C (Loaned on 19/8/1999) FL 37/16 FLC 1 FAC 3/1 Others 4/2
Swindon T (£300,000 on 11/8/2000) FL 30+7/7 FLC 3 FAC 2+1 Others 2+1/2
Hull C (£160,000 on 21/6/2001) FL 64+4/23 FLC 3/2 FAC 3/2 Others 4/3
Leyton Orient (Signed on 27/1/2003) FL 56+5/17 FLC 1 FAC 2/1 Others 0+1

ALEXANDER Graham
Born: Coventry, 10 October 1971
Height: 5'10" **Weight:** 12.7
Club Honours: Div 2 '00
International Honours: S: 14; B-1
Graham was again a permanent feature in the Preston side in 2003-04, and he also regained his international place with Scotland. Playing in a right-wing-back role, he can deliver dangerous crosses from out wide although he often prefers to drift inside rather than go down the line. Highlights of his season included making his 600th senior appearance against his hometown club, Coventry City, and scoring with a penalty in his 200th League game for North End. His consistency from the spot was again remarkable and he also hit a screamer

Neil Alexander

from 30 yards on the last day of the season.
Scunthorpe U (From trainee on 20/3/1990) FL 149+10/18 FLC 11+1/2 FAC 12/1 Others 13+4/3
Luton T (£100,000 on 8/7/1995) FL 146+4/15 FLC 17/2 FAC 7+1 Others 6+2
Preston NE (£50,000 on 25/3/1999) FL 225/36 FLC 16/4 FAC 13/4 Others 6

ALEXANDER John David
Born: Middlesbrough, 24 September 1985
Height: 5'11" **Weight:** 12.0
This young second-year scholar made three appearances as a substitute for Darlington last term as he continued to develop at a steady pace. A tall, rangy striker, he will be pushing for a place in the starting line-up in 2004-05 following some impressive performances in the reserves.
Darlington (Trainee) FL 0+4

ALEXANDER Neil
Born: Edinburgh, 10 March 1978
Height: 6'1" **Weight:** 11.0
Club Honours: S Div 2 '99; S Div 1 '01
International Honours: S: B-1; U21-10
Neil started the 2003-04 season as first-choice goalkeeper for Cardiff City, but lost his place following the 2-1 defeat at Watford at the end of December. He spent the remainder of the campaign as deputy to Martyn Margetson and added just one further appearance from the substitutes' bench.
Stenhousemuir (Free from Edina Hibs on 8/8/1996) SL 48 SLC 1 SC 1 Others 1
Livingston (Signed on 22/8/1998) SL 60 SLC 2 SC 8 Others 5
Cardiff C (£200,000 on 6/8/2001) FL 110+1 FLC 2 FAC 8 Others 5

ALEXANDERSSON Niclas
Born: Halmstad, Sweden, 29 December 1971
Height: 6'2" **Weight:** 11.8
International Honours: Sweden: 68
This skilful winger found himself completely out of favour at Everton last term and was restricted to reserve-team football. In September he joined West Ham on loan, but he sometimes struggled to find his form. His best display was in his final appearance against Burnley, when he delivered many telling crosses and was unlucky not to score with a superb flick that was turned round the post by the 'keeper. Niclas returned to Sweden to sign for IFK Goteborg in the new year.

Sheffield Wed (£750,000 from Gothenburg, Sweden, ex Halmstad, on 9/12/1997) PL 73+2/8 FLC 4+1/2 FAC 8/2
Everton (£2,500,000 on 20/7/2000) PL 49+9/4 FLC 2 FAC 4+2/1
West Ham U (Loaned on 11/9/2003) FL 5+3

ALIADIERE Jeremie
Born: Rambouillet, France, 30 March 1983
Height: 6'0" **Weight:** 11.8
Club Honours: FAYC '01; PL '04
International Honours: France: U21; Yth
This young Arsenal prospect excelled in the Carling Cup as he hit four goals in three games during the club's run to the semi-finals. He also featured ten times in the Premiership including three starts, however an injury sustained in the home win over Middlesborough ruled him out until April before earning a surprise recall for the FA Cup semi-final against Manchester United. Jeremie continues his exciting development as a striker with good pace, close control and a fine finisher.
Arsenal (From trainee on 4/4/2000) PL 3+11/1 FLC 3+2/4 FAC 1 Others 0+1

ALJOFREE Hasney
Born: Manchester, 11 July 1978
Height: 6'0" **Weight:** 12.1
Club Honours: Div 2 '04
International Honours: E: Yth
Hasney became more of a first-team regular for Plymouth Argyle last season. He began the campaign on the bench, but managed to break into the starting line-up in his preferred position of centre back in November. Strong in the air and with lots of ability he reads the game extremely well and is a very solid defender. Hasney has a great left foot and enjoys taking the odd strike at goal at set-piece situations.
Bolton W (From trainee on 2/7/1996) F/PL 6+8 FLC 4+2 FAC 0+2
Dundee U (Signed on 9/6/2000) SL 52+2/4 SLC 5+1 SC 5+1/3
Plymouth Arg (Signed on 30/8/2002) FL 39+4/1 FLC 2 FAC 1 Others 2

ALLBACK Marcus
Born: Gothenburg, Sweden, 5 July 1973
Height: 6'0" **Weight:** 12.4
International Honours: Sweden: 42
Marcus was picked for Aston Villa's opening Premiership match at Portsmouth but he then injured his hamstring playing for Sweden. After returning to the side, he scored his only goal of the season

against Spurs in November. However, a succession of injuries then hampered him and it seemed that just as he recovered fitness he was struck down again. Illness, a groin problem and then further hamstring trouble all kept him on the sidelines at various times, but he returned to the Villa side to make an appearance from the substitutes' bench against Newcastle. Marcus was a regular for Sweden when fit.
Aston Villa (£2,000,000 from Heerenveen, Holland, ex Orgryte, on 30/5/2002) PL 16+19/6 FLC 1+5 Others 3/1

ALLEN Graham
Born: Bolton, 8 April 1977
Height: 6'1" **Weight:** 12.8
International Honours: E: Yth
A versatile, uncompromising and composed defender, Graham can be employed equally effectively in either the right-back or centre-back berth, although he prefers the latter role. He relishes the opportunity to go forward to support the attack whenever he can, although he managed just a single goal last season. A tough, no-nonsense tackler, his disciplinary record improved but nevertheless he was released in the summer.
Everton (From trainee on 10/12/1994) PL 2+4
Tranmere Rov (Free on 28/8/1998) FL 193+7/10 FLC 14+2/1 FAC 19 Others 3

ALLEN-PAGE Daniel (Danny) Liam
Born: London, 30 October 1983
Height: 5'8" **Weight:** 10.13
This young Brentford right back made his debut when coming on as substitute for the closing stages of the LDV Vans Trophy tie at Peterborough last November. However, this proved to be his only senior appearance for the Bees for he was released in the new year and signed for Farnborough soon afterwards.
Brentford (From trainee on 9/7/2002) Others 0+1

ALLISON Wayne Anthony
Born: Huddersfield, 16 October 1968
Height: 6'1" **Weight:** 12.6
Club Honours: Div 2 '96
Although he had a spell in the starting line up when other strikers were injured, Wayne's appearances for Sheffield United were mainly as a substitute last term. He was used as a target man, being powerful in the air and able to hold the ball until the speedier front men arrived. Whatever

the circumstances he always worked hard for the team and was given an extension to his contract.

Halifax T (From trainee on 6/7/1987) FL 74+10/23 FLC 3/2 FAC 4+1/2 Others 8+1/3
Watford (£250,000 on 26/7/1989) FL 6+1
Bristol C (£300,000 on 9/8/1990) FL 149+46/48 FLC 4+5/2 FAC 12+1/5 Others 6+2/3
Swindon T (£475,000 on 22/7/1995) FL 98+3/31 FLC 9/3 FAC 7/2 Others 3
Huddersfield T (£800,000 on 11/11/1997) FL 71+3/15 FLC 3+1/2 FAC 6/2
Tranmere Rov (£300,000 on 3/9/1999) FL 85+18/26 FLC 4+3/1 FAC 6+1/5 Others 1
Sheffield U (Free on 30/7/2002) FL 29+44/7 FLC 7+1/1 FAC 4+4/2 Others 0+2

ALLOTT Mark Stephen

Born: Manchester, 3 October 1977
Height: 5'11" **Weight:** 12.6
Mark was one of Chesterfield's most improved players in 2003-04, when he fully embraced his move into midfield. He can operate on either wing but looks most effective in a central role. Although always attack-minded he can tackle with tenacity when called upon. A hamstring injury robbed the club of his services at a vital time, emphasising his growing importance to the side.

Oldham Ath (From trainee on 14/10/1995) FL 105+49/31 FLC 7+3/2 FAC 8+7 Others 2+3
Chesterfield (Free on 19/12/2001) FL 78+16/6 FLC 2+1/1 FAC 2 Others 2+2/1

ALLSOPP Daniel (Danny)

Born: Australia, 10 August 1978
Height: 6'1" **Weight:** 12.0
International Honours: Australia: U23-7; Yth
The pairing of Danny with Ben Burgess proved to be the key to Hull's promotion from Division Three last term, as the goal-hungry duo notched a combined tally of 33. Danny's contribution would have been even greater had he not succumbed to a series of injuries in mid-season. However, he finished the campaign back in the line-up and his calm ruthlessness in front of goal will be a source of great hope for the Tigers in the 2004-05 season.

Manchester C (£10,000 from Carlton, Australia, ex South Melbourne Lakers, on 7/8/1998) P/FL 3+26/4 FLC 0+7/1 Others 1+1/1
Notts Co (Loaned on 5/11/1999) FL 3/1
Wrexham (Loaned on 25/2/2000) FL 3/4
Bristol Rov (Loaned on 12/10/2000) FL 4+2
Notts Co (£300,000 on 22/11/2000) FL 97+8/42 FLC 3/4 FAC 8/4 Others 2+2/3
Hull C (Free on 7/5/2003) FL 31+5/15 FLC 1

[ALPAY] OZALAN Fehmi

Born: Izmir, Turkey, 29 May 1973
Height: 6'2" **Weight:** 13.7
International Honours: Turkey: 84
Following an extremely disappointing campaign in 2002-03, the arrival of a new manager, gave Alpay the opportunity to show that he was worthy of a regular place in the Aston Villa team. He gained a recall for the opening game of the season against Portsmouth, made a couple of appearances from the substitutes' bench and played a further three games, standing in for the injured Olof Mellberg. He even managed to score with a superb volley during the home match against Charlton – his first goal for the club. However, it was no secret that Alpay hadn't enjoyed the best of relationships with Villa supporters and his contract was cancelled by mutual consent at the end of October.

Aston Villa (£5,600,000 from Fenerbahce, Turkey, ex Altay, Besiktas, on 31/7/2000) PL 56+2/1 FLC 3 FAC 2 Others 8

ALSOP Julian Mark

Born: Nuneaton, 28 May 1973
Height: 6'4" **Weight:** 14.0
Club Honours: Div 3 '00
Last term proved somewhat frustrating for Julian as he struggled to find the goal-scoring form of the previous two seasons, however, he formed a useful partnership up front with Steve Basham. Julian missed a number of games through suspension, but was recalled for a successful outing on the final day of the campaign. A high spot was undoubtedly the excellent team goal at Rochdale, which he both started and applied the finishing touch to.

Bristol Rov (£15,000 from Halesowen on 14/2/1997) FL 20+13/4 FLC 2/1 FAC 1/1 Others 2
Swansea C (Loaned on 20/1/1998) FL 5/2
Swansea C (£30,000 on 12/3/1998) FL 73+12/14 FLC 4+2 FAC 6+1/1 Others 5
Cheltenham T (Free on 3/7/2000) FL 99+18/35 FLC 4+1 FAC 8+2/6 Others 6+1/3
Oxford U (Free on 8/7/2003) FL 26+3/5 FLC 1 FAC 1

AMANKWAAH Kevin Osei-Kuffour

Born: Harrow, 19 May 1982
Height: 6'1" **Weight:** 12.0
International Honours: E: Yth
This tall, rangy right back or central defender joined Cheltenham on loan early on last term and was a regular in the line-up, producing some useful displays. He returned to action with Bristol City in October and scored twice in the FA Cup

victory over Bradford Park Avenue, only to have his season curtailed shortly afterwards by a serious knee injury.

Bristol C (From trainee on 16/6/2000) FL 34+15/1 FLC 2+1/1 FAC 1+1/2 Others 4+2/1
Torquay U (Loaned on 25/1/2003) FL 6
Cheltenham T (Loaned on 16/8/2003) FL 11+1

AMBROSE Darren Paul

Born: Harlow, 29 February 1984
Height: 5'11" **Weight:** 10.5
International Honours: E: U21-3; Yth
This attacking midfielder had pre-season shin problems so his first appearance for Newcastle in the 2003-04 campaign came in late September, when he scored his first-ever goal for the club after coming on as a substitute in the UEFA Cup tie at home to NAC Breda. Darren became a regular on the bench, and scored his first Premiership goal at Leicester on Boxing Day. Nobby Solano's departure in January created an opportunity for him and he made his first-ever Premiership start at Birmingham at the end of January, following which he made the starting line-up on a regular basis, playing wide on the right of midfield and performing with increasing assurance, leading to a 'Man of the Match' display against Chelsea in April. A busy, skilful player, Darren continued to be selected for the England U21 side.

Ipswich T (From trainee on 3/7/2001) F/PL 20+10/8 FLC 2/1 FAC 1+1/1 Others 3+1/1
Newcastle U (£1,000,000 on 25/3/2003) PL 10+15/2 FLC 0+1 FAC 0+1 Others 6+5/1

AMBROSIO Marco

Born: Brescia, Italy, 30 May 1973
Height: 6'1" **Weight:** 13.4
This experienced goalkeeper joined Chelsea alongside Jurgen Macho as Ed de Goey and Rhys Evans left in the uncertain pre-Abramovich climate. Marco had spent the majority of his career as a 'bench-warmer' in Serie A and the lower Italian divisions but was unexpectedly thrust into the number two slot when Macho damaged cruciate ligaments in a pre-season training accident. He made his first-team debut in October in a Carling Cup tie against Notts County and looked decidedly unsettled as County put him under severe pressure and put two late goals past him. Marco got an unexpected second chance five months later at the Reebok Stadium following Carlo Cudicini's broken finger and Neil Sullivan's thigh strain, when he produced an inspired performance to deny a Bolton

Shola Ameobi

onslaught to keep a creditable clean sheet. He went on to keep goal in the next ten matches – including a Champions' League semi-final against Monaco – during which he kept three clean sheets.

Chelsea (Free from Chievo, Italy on 9/7/2003) PL 8 FLC 1 Others 3

AMEOBI Foluwashola (Shola)

Born: Zaria, Nigeria, 12 October 1981
Height: 6'2" **Weight:** 12.0
International Honours: E: U21-21
This highly striker became Newcastle's most capped England U21 player last term. Tall with a deceptively casual air he has excellent ball skills and a growing confidence to use them to good effect. Used primarily as a substitute at the beginning of the season, Craig Bellamy's knee injury thrust him into the starting line-up where he remained until late December when he broke a cheekbone at Charlton. On his return to fitness a month later he reverted to the bench until another injury to Bellamy enabled him to end the season in the starting line-up. His finest moment came in the UEFA Cup tie at home to Valerenga when he came off the bench to score twice.

Newcastle U (From trainee on 19/10/1998) PL 42+47/14 FLC 3+1/2 FAC 2+3 Others 18+11/9

AMOO Ryan Lee

Born: Leicester, 11 October 1983
Height: 5'10" **Weight:** 9.12
Club Honours: FAYC '02
Ryan began the 2003-04 season as a regular in defence for Aston Villa's reserve team, but on transfer-deadline day he was allowed to move to Northampton Town. He went on to make his senior debut when coming off the substitutes' bench in the home fixture with Oxford at the beginning of April.

Aston Villa (From trainee on 26/7/2001)
Northampton T (Free on 23/3/2004) FL 0+1

AMORUSO Lorenzo

Born: Bari, Italy, 28 June 1971
Height: 6'2" **Weight:** 13.10
Club Honours: SPD '99, '00, '03; SC '98, '99, '02, '03; SLC '99, '02, '03
Signed to take over from Henning Berg in the centre of the Blackburn defence, Lorenzo struggled to fit in at Ewood Park last term. A knee injury required surgery, keeping him out of action for five months but he reappeared for the final last-ditch battle against relegation when his fire and

commitment helped compensate for his lack of pace. A threat at set pieces, he headed two goals and struck a free kick for a third.

Glasgow R (£5,000,000 from Fiorentina, Italy, ex Bari, on 29/5/1997) SL 149/13 SLC 13/2 SC 21+2/5 Others 41/4
Blackburn Rov (£1,400,000 on 15/7/2003) PL 11+1/3 Others 2

ANDERSON Iain

Born: Glasgow, 23 July 1977
Height: 5'8" **Weight:** 9.10
Club Honours: Div 2 '00
International Honours: S: U21-15
Iain began his Grimsby Town career in fine style, scoring three times in the early-season fixtures last term. However, a knee injury then sidelined him for several months and when he did recover fitness he found it difficult to establish himself in the side. He is a talented winger who can play on either flank.

Dundee (From juniors on 10/8/1994) SL 90+37/16 SLC 3+5 SC 6+3/2 Others 6+1/2 (Signed by Toulouse, France on 28/7/1999)
Preston NE (£500,000 from Toulouse, France on 18/2/2000) FL 46+36/13 FLC 5 FAC 3+1/1 Others 1+2
Tranmere Rov (Loaned on 27/3/2003) FL 7/2
Grimsby T (Free on 7/7/2003) FL 24+5/5 FLC 1/1 FAC 2 Others 1

ANDERSON Ijah Massai

Born: Hackney, 30 December 1975
Height: 5'8" **Weight:** 10.6
Club Honours: Div 3 '99
Ijah finally overcame his injury problems of recent seasons and became a regular in the Bristol Rovers line-up last term. The attacking left back also showed his versatility by playing a handful of matches on the left-hand side of midfield in the final months of the campaign. Ijah was made available on a free transfer in the summer.

Southend U (From trainee at Tottenham H on 2/8/1994)
Brentford (Free on 31/7/1995) FL 196+6/4 FLC 19/1 FAC 5+3 Others 12+1
Wycombe W (Loaned on 27/11/2002) FL 5
Bristol Rov (Free on 7/2/2003) FL 51+2 FLC 1 Others 1

ANDERSON John

Born: Greenock, 2 October 1972
Height: 6'2" **Weight:** 12.2
Club Honours: S Div 2 '95; S Div 1 '01
This experienced central defender suffered a broken foot during the pre-season and when he recovered fitness he found it impossible to break into the Hull City line-

up last term. In the new year he moved on to Bristol Rovers where he helped give the defence a more solid look and played a key role in the final run which saw the club retain their Football League status.

Morton (Signed from Gourock YAC on 25/11/1994) SL 97+3/18 SLC 5/1 SC 9/2 Others 5+1/1
Livingston (Signed on 5/6/2000) SL 42+1/3 SLC 3 SC 7/2 Others 4/2
Hull C (Free on 17/6/2002) FL 42+1/1 FLC 1 FAC 1
Bristol Rov (Free on 25/3/2004) FL 8

ANDERTON Darren Robert

Born: Southampton, 3 March 1972
Height: 6'1" **Weight:** 12.5
Club Honours: FLC '99
International Honours: E: 30; B-1; U21-12; Yth
This talented midfielder's career has been blighted by much-reported injury. Last season was no exception and Darren struggled to get a decent run of injury-free performances to find any sort of consistency. At his best he is an attacking midfielder who adds pace and creativity in the centre of the park. Darren scored three goals, including one at Highbury in November. However, he was released by Spurs in the summer.

Portsmouth (From trainee on 5/2/1990) FL 53+9/7 FLC 3+2/1 FAC 7+1/5 Others 2
Tottenham H (£1,750,000 on 3/6/1992) PL 273+26/34 FLC 30+1/8 FAC 26+2/6

ANDRESEN Martin

Born: Norway, 2 February 1977
Height: 5'11" **Weight:** 11.12
International Honours: Norway: 12; U21; Yth
A loan signing in the January transfer window, Martin firstly had to recover match fitness before he broke into the Blackburn side. A solid, central midfielder he concentrated on the basics and when played in this role he brought some stability in the centre of the park, although he seemed to struggle to cope with the pace and hustle of the Premiership. When the club introduced a diamond midfield he acted as back man and although his performances passed unremarked, his quiet efficiency and organisation contributed much to the club's survival.

Wimbledon (£2,000,000 from Stabaek, Norway on 8/10/1999) PL 4+10/1 FLC 0+1 FAC 1 (Returned to Stabaek, via loan spell at Molde, Norway on 21/12/2000)
Blackburn Rov (Loaned from Stabaek, Norway on 31/1/2004) PL 11

Juan Pablo Angel

ANDREWS Keith Joseph
Born: Dublin, 13 September 1980
Height: 5'11" **Weight:** 11.5
The combative Wolves midfielder needed a run of games last term after his previous season had been disrupted by injuries. He began a loan spell at Stoke, where he impressed with his passing ability and all-action style. On his return he made only three appearances for Wolves, and was not in the squad for any other match. His solitary Premiership game was against Newcastle, when he acquitted himself well. He was loaned to Walsall for the later stages of the campaign where his firm tackling and surging runs raised the morale of colleagues and fans alike. Keith scored with a spectacular free-kick against Ipswich and then snapped up another chance against Millwall soon afterwards.
Wolverhampton W (From trainee on 26/9/1997) FL 27+18 FLC 1 FAC 4
Oxford U (Loaned on 10/11/2000) FL 4/1 Others 1
Stoke C (Loaned on 9/8/2003) FL 16
Walsall (Loaned on 13/3/2004) FL 10/2

ANDREWS Lee David
Born: Carlisle, 23 April 1983
Height: 6'0" **Weight:** 10.12
Lee enjoyed a more consistent spell in the heart of the United defence last term. Blessed with speed and strength in the tackle, he gave a number of outstanding performances, notably in the home games against Yeovil and Hull City. Lee benefited from a more settled regime at Brunton Park and despite the club's relegation to the Conference he agreed terms for the 2004-05 season.
Carlisle U (From trainee on 27/6/2001) FL 81+10 FLC 1+1 FAC 4+1 Others 3
Rochdale (Loaned on 25/2/2003) FL 8

ANDREWS Wayne Michael Hill
Born: Paddington, 25 November 1977
Height: 5'10" **Weight:** 11.12
This experienced front-runner did not disappoint for Colchester last term. Wayne's target was to beat his goal tally from the previous season and he achieved that in early March, finishing with a total of 14 in all competitions. His swift turn of speed caused opposing defenders no end of problems, resulting in a flurry of goals and free kicks. Wayne's early-season form helped the U's into the play-off zone, but both the striker and the team faded a little after the turn of the year.
Watford (From trainee on 5/7/1996) FL 16+12/4 FLC 3+2/1 FAC 0+2 Others 2/1 (Free to St Albans C during 1999 close season)

Cambridge U (Loaned on 2/10/1998) FL 1+1
Peterborough U (Loaned on 5/2/1999) FL 8+2/5
Oldham Ath (Free from Chesham U on 30/5/2002) FL 28+9/11 FLC 1+2 FAC 2+1 Others 3/1
Colchester U (Free on 9/8/2003) FL 32+9/12 FAC 4+1 Others 3+1/2

ANELKA Nicolas
Born: Versailles, France, 14 March 1979
Height: 6'0" **Weight:** 12.3
Club Honours: PL '98; FAC '98; CS '98
International Honours: France: 28
In his second season at Manchester City Nicolas continued to find the net with impressive consistency. He started the campaign in impressive style with a wonder goal against Blackburn Rovers and the scoring feast continued with a hat-trick against Aston Villa. The goals continued to flow and he finished the season as the club's leading scorer with a tally of 25 in all competitions.
Arsenal (£500,000+ from Paris St Germain on 6/3/1997) PL 50+15/23 FLC 3 FAC 13+1/3 Others 7+1/2 (£22,900,000 to Real Madrid, Spain on 20/8/1999)
Liverpool (Loaned from Paris St Germain on 24/12/2001) PL 13+7/4 FAC 2/1
Manchester C (£13,000,000 from Paris St Germain, France on 16/7/2002) PL 69+1/30 FLC 4 FAC 5/4 Others 5/4

ANGEL Juan Pablo
Born: Medellin, Colombia, 24 October 1975
Height: 6'0" **Weight:** 11.6
International Honours: Colombia: 24; Yth
Although out of favour at Aston Villa during 2002-03, Juan Pablo revived his career following a change in management at the club. The talented striker made an impressive start to the season, scoring seven goals in nine games, and was a regular in the line-up throughout the campaign. He certainly found his shooting boots, scoring a total of 23 goals in all competitions including a hat-trick in the Carling Cup tie against Wycombe. His stunning, swerving 20-yarder against Chelsea in the Carling Cup was voted as Villa's 'Goal of 2003' and he was also voted as the supporters' 'Player of the Season'. Juan Pablo continued to add to his tally of caps for Colombia during the campaign.
Aston Villa (£9,500,000 + from River Plate, Argentina, ex Atletico Nacional, on 19/1/2001) PL 74+12/30 FLC 6+3/8 FAC 4/1 Others 2+2/4

ANGEL Mark
Born: Newcastle, 23 August 1975
Height: 5'10" **Weight:** 12.4
Club Honours: NC '02
International Honours: E: SP-3
Mark found it difficult to win a regular place in the Boston United team during the season. When selected he did a valuable job on the left flank with his ability to beat a man and get the ball into the box to set up chances for his colleagues. The arrival of Danny Thomas saw him pushed out of the starting line-up and he was released at the end of the campaign.
Sunderland (Free from Walker Central on 31/12/1993)
Oxford U (Free on 9/8/1995) FL 40+33/4 FLC 4+4 FAC 4+2 Others 2+1/1
West Bromwich A (Free on 2/7/1998) FL 4+21/1 FLC 0+1 FAC 1+1
Darlington (Free on 8/8/2000) FL 1+4 FLC 2+1/1
Queen of the South (Free on 22/1/2001) SL 4+1/1
Boston U (Free on 13/6/2001) FL 36+18/6 FLC 2 FAC 1 Others 3/1

ANGUS Stevland (Stev) Dennis
Born: Westminster, 16 September 1980
Height: 6'0" **Weight:** 12.0
Club Honours: FAYC '99
This pacy centre back was a near ever-present for Cambridge United last term when he formed an excellent early-season partnership with Mark Venus. Stevland scored his first-ever Football League goal back-heeling home a late winner at Boston in September. He was also used at right back during the campaign.
West Ham U (From trainee on 2/7/1999)
Bournemouth (Loaned on 11/8/2000) FL 7+2
Cambridge U (Free on 19/7/2001) FL 120+1/1 FLC 4 FAC 10 Others 9+1

ANTOINE-CURIER Mickael
Born: Orsay, France, 5 March 1983
Height: 6'0" **Weight:** 12.4
This tall, pacy striker created a new record last term when he became the first player in the history of the Football League to play for six different clubs in a peacetime season. Several of his brief spells appear to have been linked; thus he scored a brilliant goal for Oldham against Sheffield Wednesday, and later in the campaign had a brief spell with the Owls; he played for Kidderminster against Lincoln one week and the following week for Rochdale against the same opposition, when he scored in a 1-1 draw. Mickael's other ports of call comprised Burnley (where he was on non-contract forms and

did not feature in the first team) Notts County and Grimsby. His overall tally of five goals from 18 starts amounted to a quite useful haul.

Preston NE (Signed from Nancy, France on 29/11/2000)

Nottingham F (Free on 22/6/2001)

Brentford (Loaned on 10/3/2003) FL 11/3

Oldham Ath (Free on 8/8/2003) FL 5+3/2 FLC 1/1

Kidderminster Hrs (Free on 19/9/2003) FL 0+1

Rochdale (Free on 23/9/2003) FL 5+3/1 FAC 0+1 Others 0+1

Sheffield Wed (Free on 21/11/2003) FL 0+1

Notts Co (Free on 19/2/2004) FL 4/1

Grimsby T (Free on 19/3/2004) FL 3+2

ARANALDE Zigor
Born: Guipuzcoa, Spain, 28 February 1973
Height: 6'1" **Weight:** 13.5
This attacking left-sided defender missed more games than in his three previous seasons with Walsall, but still looked exciting when going forward. At times he struggled with the defensive side of his game, and he failed to add to his tally of goals for the Saddlers.
Walsall (Free from CD Logrones, Spain, ex Albacete, Marbella, Seville, on 11/8/2000) FL 155+10/5 FLC 11/1 FAC 11 Others 3

ARASON Arni Gautur
Born: Reykjavik, Iceland, 7 May 1975
Height: 6'2" **Weight:** 13.5
International Honours: Iceland: 33; U21-12; Yth
Brought in as cover for David James during the January transfer window, this experienced goalkeeper made his debut for Manchester City in the FA Cup replay at Tottenham. He was left dazed and confused as the defence in front of him crumbled and allowed Spurs to race into a three-goal lead, but he remained unruffled and pulled off a stunning double save in the second half to help his side launch a remarkable comeback. Arni is a very good shot-stopper who is agile and an excellent communicator. However, his contract with the Blues was not renewed and he left the club following the final game of the season.
Manchester C (Free from Rosenborg, Norway, ex IA Akranes, Stjarnan, on 16/1/2004) FAC 2

ARBER Mark Andrew
Born: Johannesburg, South Africa, 9 October 1977
Height: 6'1" **Weight:** 12.11
This talented left-sided central defender

was a near ever-present for Peterborough United last term. He again showed what an effective player he is, proving to be good in the air and a confident ball player on the ground. Mark was out of contract in the summer and his future was unclear at the time of writing.
Tottenham H (From trainee on 27/3/1996)
Barnet (£75,000 on 18/9/1998) FL 123+2/15 FLC 4 FAC 3 Others 8/1
Peterborough U (Free on 9/12/2002) FL 67+2/5 FLC 1 FAC 3 Others 2

ARCA Julio Andres
Born: Quilmes Bernal, Argentine, 31 January 1981
Height: 5'10" **Weight:** 11.6
International Honours: Argentina: Yth (World Yth '01)
Julio was one of the real stars for Sunderland in 2003-04. Whereas he had been previously used exclusively as a left-sided midfielder, he initially operated at left back, before moving upfield to form a potent left-wing partnership with George McCartney. Julio is comfortable running with the ball, whilst his ability to beat a man often creates scoring chances for team mates. His presence was sorely missed for the last month of the season when a cartilage injury ended his campaign prematurely. He was Sunderland's sole representative in the PFA First Division team of the season.
Sunderland (£3,500,000 from Argentinos Juniors, Argentine on 31/8/2000) P/FL 84+9/7 FLC 4/2 FAC 12/3

ARDLEY Neal Christopher
Born: Epsom, 1 September 1972
Height: 5'11" **Weight:** 11.9
International Honours: E: U21-10
Neal, an experienced professional with more than 300 League appearances under his belt, played for most of the 2003-04 season in his favoured position of central midfield, just in front of the defence. However, he also appeared to good effect in right midfield and at right back and was an inspiring stand-in captain. A fine passer of the ball and an expert at set pieces, Neal was one of Watford's most consistent players.
Wimbledon (From trainee on 29/7/1991) F/PL 212+33/18 FLC 22+3/5 FAC 27+4/3
Watford (Free on 9/8/2002) FL 77+4/3 FLC 2 FAC 7

ARMSTRONG Alun
Born: Gateshead, 22 February 1975
Height: 6'1" **Weight:** 11.13
Club Honours: Div 1 '98
Alun was a surprise selection for Ipswich

when he led the line against West Ham at the end of August considering that he hadn't even been on the bench for the club's first five fixtures. The striker retained his place in the side during September during which he notched a couple of goals, but after a spell on the bench he was sidelined by injury. Once he regained his fitness he had a loan spell at Bradford, during which he netted the goal that enabled Bradford to pull off a surprise win at Norwich. Unfortunately a thigh strain curtailed the loan and Alun was not able to force his way back into the Ipswich first team until the very last game of the season – the second leg of the play-off semi-final at West Ham – when he came on as a second-half substitute.
Newcastle U (From trainee on 1/10/1993)
Stockport Co (£50,000 on 23/6/1994) FL 151+8/48 FLC 22/8 FAC 10+1/5 Others 7
Middlesbrough (£1,500,000 on 16/2/1998) P/FL 10+19/9 FLC 4
Huddersfield T (Loaned on 23/3/2000) FL 4+2
Ipswich T (£500,000 + on 8/12/2000) P/FL 50+29/14 FLC 2+2/1 FAC 2+1/1 Others 5+3/3
Bradford C (Loaned on 27/12/2003) FL 6/1 FAC 1

ARMSTRONG Christopher (Chris)
Born: Newcastle, 5 August 1982
Height: 5'10" **Weight:** 10.8
International Honours: E: Yth
Chris signed for Sheffield United during the 2003 close season. He began the campaign as a regular in the squad but making most of his appearances from the bench. Playing on the left side of midfield or as a left wing back he showed determination, being quick to defend and making positive use of the ball. Just as it seemed he might have made the breakthrough into the starting line-up he was sidelined with a cartilage problem in December which ended his season.
Bury (From trainee on 2/3/2001) FL 33/1 FLC 1 Others 3
Oldham Ath (£200,000 on 22/10/2001) FL 64+1/1 FLC 2 FAC 6 Others 6
Sheffield U (£100,000 on 1/8/2003) FL 4+8/1 FLC 1

ARMSTRONG Christopher (Chris) Peter
Born: Newcastle, 19 June 1971
Height: 6'0" **Weight:** 13.3
Club Honours: Div 1 '94; FLC '99
International Honours: E: B-1
Much was expected of Chris on returning to Wrexham last term, but he seemed to

struggle to gain match fitness early on and was then sidelined by a troublesome achilles problem. He was much more involved in the second half of the campaign, scoring the only goal of the game at Brentford, and two in as many minutes at home to Grimsby in March. Chris will be hoping for an injury-free time in the 2004-05 campaign.

Wrexham *(Free from Llay Welfare on 3/3/1989) FL 40+20/13 FLC 2+1 FAC 0+1 Others 5+1/3*
Millwall *(£50,000 on 16/8/1991) FL 11+17/5 FLC 3+1/2 FAC 0+1 Others 0+1*
Crystal Palace *(£1,000,000 on 1/9/1992) F/PL 118/45 FLC 8/6 FAC 8/5 Others 2/1*
Tottenham H *(£4,500,000 on 30/6/1995) PL 117+24/48 FLC 15/10 FAC 9+5/4 Others 3*
Bolton W *(Free on 28/8/2002) FLC 1*
Wrexham *(Free on 22/7/2003) FL 19+7/5 FAC 0+1/1 Others 1/1*

ARMSTRONG Steven Craig
Born: South Shields, 23 May 1975
Height: 5'11" **Weight:** 12.10
This hard-working left-sided midfield player failed to impress in his few opportunities for Sheffield Wednesday last season. He always gave 100 per cent effort, but it was not enough to force him into the manager's plans and he ended up on loan at Grimsby, where he gained a regular first-team place before being sidelined by injury.

Nottingham F *(From trainee on 2/6/1992) P/FL 24+16 FLC 6+2/2 FAC 1*
Burnley *(Loaned on 29/12/1994) FL 4*
Bristol Rov *(Loaned on 8/1/1996) FL 4*
Bristol Rov *(Loaned on 28/3/1996) FL 9+1*
Gillingham *(Loaned on 18/10/1996) FL 10 FLC 2 Others 1*
Watford *(Loaned on 24/1/1997) FL 3*
Watford *(Loaned on 14/3/1997) FL 12*
Huddersfield T *(£750,000 on 26/2/1999) FL 101+6/5 FLC 7+1 FAC 2 Others 1+1*
Sheffield Wed *(£100,000 on 15/2/2002) FL 29+6/1 FLC 3 Others 2*
Grimsby T *(Loaned on 24/2/2004) FL 9/1*

ARMSTRONG Ian
Born: Kirkby, 16 November 1981
Height: 5'7" **Weight:** 10.2
International Honours: E: Yth; Sch
This tricky Port Vale winger spent the majority of the 2003-04 season on the substitutes' bench. He began the campaign in the line-up, but a succession of niggling injuries meant that he only started a handful of games. Very dangerous when in full flow he scored just the one goal against Colchester United, helping Vale to a 4-3 victory after they had twice been behind.

Liverpool *(From trainee on 16/12/1998)*
Port Vale *(Free on 2/7/2001) FL 44+36/11 FLC 0+1 FAC 1+2 Others 5+1/3*

ARNDALE Neil Darren
Born: Bristol, 26 April 1984
Height: 5'9" **Weight:** 10.0
International Honours: E: Yth
Neil was a regular in Bristol Rovers reserves last term, and managed to net a hat-trick (albeit with two penalties) against Oxford reserves. However, his first-team appearances were limited to just three outings. The stocky left back also gained further experience with a loan spell at Dr Martens League club Clevedon Town. Neil was released at the end of the season.

Bristol Rov *(From trainee on 1/7/2003) FL 2+3 Others 1*

ARNISON Paul Simon
Born: Hartlepool, 18 September 1977
Height: 5'10" **Weight:** 10.12
This right-sided utility player began the 2003-04 season in the Hartlepool United first team, but lost his place after the opening game and thereafter his opportunities were limited. Paul moved on to Carlisle and produced some spirited performances for the Brunton Park club. However, he will best be remembered for his stunning 30-yard strike against Torquay in December. Voted the club's 'Goal of the Season' it also clinched Carlisle's first win after 12 successive League defeats.

Newcastle U *(From trainee on 1/3/1996)*
Hartlepool U *(Free on 10/3/2000) FL 53+24/3 FLC 2 FAC 2+1 Others 8/2*
Carlisle U *(Free on 31/10/2003) FL 20+6/1 Others 1*

ARPHEXAD Pegguy Michel
Born: Abymes, Guadeloupe, 18 May 1973
Height: 6'2" **Weight:** 13.5
Club Honours: FLC '00, '01; FAC '01; UEFAC '01; ESC '01
Pegguy joined Coventry shortly after the start of the 2003-04 season, but for most of the season he was the second-choice goalkeeper to Scott Shearer. His short-term contract was extended after Christmas, but he was allowed to join Notts County on loan when the Magpies required cover for injuries. He produced the occasional moments of brilliance, but soon after his return to Highfield Road he was released.

Leicester C *(Free from Lens, France on 20/8/1997) PL 17+4 FLC 4 FAC 3+1*

Liverpool *(Free on 13/7/2000) PL 1+1 FLC 2 Others 2*
Stockport Co *(Loaned on 29/9/2001) FL 3*
Coventry C *(Free on 26/8/2003) FL 5*
Notts Co *(Loaned on 11/3/2004) FL 3*

ARTELL David (Dave) John
Born: Rotherham, 22 November 1980
Height: 6'2" **Weight:** 13.9
This no-nonsense centre back joined Mansfield on a short-term contract in the summer of 2003. Dave showed good form, netting some useful goals from set pieces and his initial contract was extended until the end of the season. He formed a fine partnership with Rhys Day and shared the second central defensive position with Luke Dimech until the emergence of Alex John-Baptiste.

Rotherham U *(From trainee on 1/7/1999) FL 35+2/4 FAC 3 Others 1*
Shrewsbury T *(Loaned on 26/9/2002) FL 27+1/1 FAC 3 Others 5*
Mansfield T *(Free on 7/8/2003) FL 24+2/3 FLC 1 FAC 3+1 Others 0+1*

ARTHUR Adam Joseph
Born: Nottingham, 27 October 1985
Height: 5'9" **Weight:** 11.0
A product of York City's youth scheme, Adam was called up to first-team action for the Minstermen for the last three games of the 2003-04 season. A right-sided midfielder or forward, he was a regular scorer for the youth and reserve sides during the campaign and showed some neat touches and control on his step up to senior level.

York C *(Trainee) FL 2+1*

ASABA Carl Edward
Born: Westminster, 28 January 1973
Height: 6'2" **Weight:** 13.4
This pacy Stoke striker is comfortable with the ball at his feet and also has a good eye for goal. Carl began last term playing off either Gifton Noel-Williams or Ade Akinbiyi in a front two, or wide right when the manager preferred to play a front three. However, he failed to win a regular place in the side and became unsettled, before knuckling down to play his part as the club settled into a mid-table position. He was planning to spend part of the summer break doing extra training to raise his fitness levels for the 2004-05 campaign.

Brentford *(Free from Dulwich Hamlet on 9/8/1994) FL 49+5/25 FLC 5 FAC 4 Others 7/2*
Colchester U *(Loaned on 16/2/1995) FL 9+3/2*
Reading *(£800,000 on 7/8/1997) FL 31+2/8 FLC 7+2/3 FAC 3/1*

*Gillingham (£600,000 on 28/8/1998) FL
65+12/36 FLC 3/2 FAC 1+1 Others 9/2
Sheffield U (£92,500 + on 8/3/2001) FL
52+15/23 FLC 6+1/1 FAC 2+1 Others 3
Stoke C (Free on 6/8/2003) FL 26+11/8 FLC 1
FAC 2*

ASAMOAH Derek
Born: Ghana, 1 May 1981
Height: 5'6" **Weight:** 10.12
Derek enjoyed an excellent season with
Northampton last term, although nearly
all of his appearances came from the
substitutes' bench. Playing as a wide
striker he has pace, ability and the skills
on the ball to change the course of a
game. Derek will be remembered for his
winning goal against Plymouth in the FA
Cup second round tie and then hitting
the post in the fourth round match
against Manchester United. He has
become a great favourite with the
Sixfields faithful.
*Northampton T (Free from Slough T, ex
Barking, Hampton & Richmond Borough, on
26/7/2001) FL 27+86/10 FLC 0+3 FAC 6+3/2
Others 5+3/1*

ASHBEE Ian
Born: Birmingham, 6 September 1976
Height: 6'1" **Weight:** 13.7
International Honours: E: Yth
With his goal-scoring contributions relying
much more on quality rather than
quantity, it was appropriate that Ian's 25-
yard curler into the top corner should
confirm Hull City's first promotion success
in 19 years. He produced some
wholehearted displays throughout a
memorable campaign and his wonder
strike at Yeovil was a real highlight.
Operating as a midfield enforcer he
constantly cajoled his colleagues to
greater efforts and was voted into third
place in the club's 'Player of the Year'
awards.
*Derby Co (From trainee on 9/11/1994) FL 1
Cambridge U (Free on 13/12/1996) FL
192+11/11 FLC 7 FAC 15 Others 9+1
Hull C (Free on 3/7/2002) FL 70/3 FLC 2/1
FAC 2*

ASHBY Barry John
Born: Park Royal, 2 November 1970
Height: 6'2" **Weight:** 13.8
Club Honours: FAYC '89
Persistent injury problems restricted Barry's
appearances last season, but when
Gillingham were down to the bare bones,
he came through as a shining example to
the many youngsters around him. Who
could forget his contender for 'Tackle of
the Season' at Crystal Palace when he got

Ian Ashbee

Jon Ashton

back to whip the ball off the boot of Andy Johnson? Despite his advancing years, the reliable defender returned for the crucial final game at Stoke and played a blinder.

Watford *(From trainee on 1/12/1988) FL 101+13/3 FLC 6 FAC 4 Others 2+1*
Brentford *(Signed on 22/3/1994) FL 119+2/4 FLC 11 FAC 9/1 Others 11+1*
Gillingham *(£140,000 on 8/8/1997) FL 248+3/7 FLC 17 FAC 18/1 Others 10/1*

ASHCROFT Kane John
Born: Leeds, 19 March 1986
Height: 5'9" **Weight:** 11.11
A product of York City's School of Excellence, Kane almost scored with his first touch at senior level when coming off the bench in the final home game of the season against Leyton Orient, but his effort was well saved by the visitors' 'keeper. A strong-tackling and pacy midfielder, he made his full debut for City in the following match at Swansea.
York C *(Trainee) FL 1+1*

ASHDOWN Jamie Lawrence
Born: Wokingham, 30 November 1980
Height: 6'3" **Weight:** 14.10
An extended loan spell on first-team duty at Rushden sharpened and improved Jamie's game to the extent that he was recalled to Reading in March as a replacement for the injured Marcus Hahnemann. Jamie played in the last ten League games of the season, and his powerful physique, which enables him to dominate his area, allied to quick reflexes, made him a target for Premiership clubs. He was reported to have signed for Portsmouth in the summer.
Reading *(From trainee on 26/11/1999) FL 12+1 FAC 1 Others 2*
Bournemouth *(Loaned on 22/8/2002) FL 2*
Rushden & Diamonds *(Loaned on 14/11/2003) FL 19*

ASHTON Dean
Born: Crewe, 24 November 1983
Height: 6'1" **Weight:** 13.11
International Honours: E: U21-2; Yth
The 2003-04 season saw Dean top the scoring list for Crewe Alexandra with a total of 20 goals in all competitions. One of the highlights in his campaign came in the fixture at Wigan in March when he netted his first-ever Football League hat-trick. After previously appearing for England at U19 level, he stepped up to the U21s last term, scoring against Holland and Sweden. Dean also passed the half-century mark of goals for the club.

Crewe Alex *(From trainee on 6/2/2001) FL 108+27/43 FLC 3+1/1 FAC 6+3/5 Others 3/5*

ASHTON Jonathan (Jon) James
Born: Nuneaton, 4 October 1982
Height: 6'2" **Weight:** 13.7
Jon joined Oxford in the summer of 2003, initially on loan, but impressed greatly in the opening two months and a permanent contract was agreed. A quick, young, centre back, he was signed initially as cover for the injured Paul McCarthy but retained his place on the strength of some fine performances. Jon also f e a t u red at right back during the campaign and captained the side on one occasion.
Leicester C *(From trainee on 29/1/2001) P/FL 3+6 FLC 0+1*
Notts Co *(Loaned on 8/11/2002) FL 4*
Oxford U *(Free on 8/8/2003) FL 30+4 FLC 2 FAC 1 Others 1*

ASHTON Neil John
Born: Liverpool, 15 January 1985
Height: 5'10" **Weight:** 11.12
A product of the successful youth scheme at Tranmere, Neil signed his first professional contract with the club in the 2003 close season. He started last term as a regular in the youth team, before stepping up to a place in the reserves in the second half of the campaign. A versatile player who is comfortable in several midfield or defensive roles, Neil made his Football League debut for Rovers when coming on as substitute at Brentford in January.
Tranmere Rov *(From trainee on 10/4/2003) FL 0+1*

ATHERTON Peter
Born: Orrell, 6 April 1970
Height: 5'11" **Weight:** 13.12
International Honours: E: U21-1; Sch
The experienced defender managed to steer clear of the injury problems that have dogged his career since joining Bradford in 2000. Naturally a hard-tackling central defender, his versatility has proved crucial with Peter looking equally effective in the 'holding' role in front of the back four. He also scored two goals, against West Ham and Derby, making it his most prolific scoring campaign since leaving Hillsborough. Before Bryan Robson was appointed manager, Peter assisted Wayne Jacobs in a caretaker capacity in charge for Bradford's match at Stoke.
Wigan Ath *(From trainee on 12/2/1988) FL 145+4/1 FLC 8 FAC 7 Others 12+1*
Coventry C *(£300,000 on 23/8/1991) F/PL 113+1 FLC 4 FAC 2*

Sheffield Wed *(£800,000 on 1/6/1994) PL 214/9 FLC 16 FAC 18 Others 3*
Bradford C *(Free on 6/7/2000) P/FL 78/3 FLC 3 FAC 2 Others 4*
Birmingham C *(Loaned on 15/2/2001) FL 10 Others 2*

ATKINSON Robert (Rob) Guy
Born: Beverley, 29 April 1987
Height: 6'1" **Weight:** 12.0
Rob made his debut for Barnsley as a second-half substitute in the home game with Luton Town in March, Paul Hart's first match in charge. He is a promising young defender who made a big impression at Academy and reserve-team level.
Barnsley *(Trainee) FL 0+1*

AUSTIN Kevin Levi
Born: Hackney, 12 February 1973
Height: 6'0" **Weight:** 14.0
International Honours: Trinidad & Tobago: 1
This experienced central defender had to be patient early on last season, but after establishing himself in the Bristol Rovers first team in January he responded with some very consistent performances. Although Kevin occasionally ran into disciplinary problems he was a real asset to the side as they fought their way to safety from relegation.
Leyton Orient *(Free from Saffron Walden on 19/8/1993) FL 101+8/3 FLC 4/1 FAC 6 Others 7*
Lincoln C *(£30,000 on 31/7/1996) FL 128+1/2 FLC 9 FAC 6 Others 4*
Barnsley *(Free on 5/7/1999) FL 3 FLC 2+1*
Brentford *(Loaned on 27/10/2000) FL 3*
Cambridge U *(Free on 21/11/2001) FL 4+2 Others 1*
Bristol Rov *(Free on 12/7/2002) FL 52+4 FAC 4+1*

AUSTIN Neil Jeffrey
Born: Barnsley, 26 April 1983
Height: 5'10" **Weight:** 11.11
International Honours: E: Yth
Neil signed a short-term deal for Barnsley at the start of the 2003-04 season as the club were in administration, however, in January his contract was extended until the end of the season. He was a regular in the line-up during the campaign and although he played a number of games at left back and in midfield he was always more comfortable at right back. A tough, uncompromising tackler who never gave less than 100 per cent, Neil was offered a new contract by manager Paul Hart in the summer.
Barnsley *(From trainee on 27/4/2000) FL 64+7 FLC 0+1 FAC 5+1 Others 0+1*

Kevin Austin

B

BA Ibrahim
Born: Dakar, Senegal, 12 November 1973
Height: 5'10" **Weight:** 11.9
International Honours: France: 8
Initially signed on a short term contract in September as a free agent, this vastly experienced midfielder was offered a deal in January until the end of the season. The former international had a disappointing spell with AC Milan and was keen to re-establish himself with Bolton. This, however, proved to be quite some challenge and Ibrahim didn't make a single start in the Premiership, his appearances limited to fleeting cameos from the bench. As with the rest of the Bolton 'squad' players, Ibrahim did start four of the club's Carling Cup games, but he didn't make enough of an impression to force his way into the regular starting line-up and was released by the club at the end of the season.
Bolton W (Free from AC Milan, Italy, ex Le Havre, Bordeaux, on 12/9/2003) PL 0+9 FLC 5+1 FAC 1

BABAYARO Celestine
Born: Kaduna, Nigeria, 29 August 1978
Height: 5'8" **Weight:** 11.0
Club Honours: FLC '98; ESC '98; FAC '00; CS '00
International Honours: Nigeria: Full; U23 (OLYM '96); Yth (World-U17 '93)
The longest serving player at Chelsea – the last survivor of the Ruud Gullit regime – Celestine Babayaro made only sporadic appearances during the 2003-04 season owing to a combination of niggling injuries, African Nations' Cup duty in Tunisia and the exceptional form shown by new signing Wayne Bridge. This notwithstanding, Chelsea fans were treated to one of his trademark goal celebrations at Leicester following a thunderous left-foot drive – double somersault with tuck! This may be the last time he performs the eccentric routine in a Chelsea shirt as the club scour Europe for elite talent, and with his contract running down, new fields may beckon for the Nigerian international. He certainly has the talent and athleticism to play regular Premiership football as he is far too good a player to spend his time warming the bench.
Chelsea (£2,250,000 from Anderlecht, Belgium on 20/6/1997) PL 115+13/5 FLC 13+2 FAC 16+1 Others 29+3/3

BABB Philip (Phil) Andrew
Born: Lambeth, 30 November 1970
Height: 6'0" **Weight:** 12.3
Club Honours: FLC '95
International Honours: RoI: 35; B-1
This veteran centre back had been told he could leave Sunderland following the club's relegation in 2002-03, but he played in the first two games of the new season due to injuries. Following another spell in the wilderness, Phil returned to the side in December where he stayed for the remainder of the campaign, also playing at left back for a spell. He showed he still had plenty to offer, dominating in the air, and turning in some outstanding defensive displays in the Black Cats run to the promotion play-offs and the FA Cup semi-final. Phil was released by the club in the summer.
Millwall (From trainee on 25/4/1989)
Bradford C (Free on 10/8/1990) FL 73+7/14 FLC 5+1 FAC 3 Others 3+1
Coventry C (£500,000 on 21/7/1992) PL 70+7/3 FLC 5/1 FAC 2
Liverpool (£3,600,000 on 1/9/1994) PL 124+4/1 FLC 16 FAC 12 Others 12+2 (Free to Sporting Lisbon, Portugal during 2000 close season)
Tranmere Rov (Loaned on 21/1/2000) FL 4 FLC 1 FAC 2
Sunderland (Free on 11/6/2002) PL 48 FLC 2 FAC 8 Others 2

BABBEL Markus
Born: Munich, Germany, 8 September 1972
Height: 6'3" **Weight:** 12.10
Club Honours: UEFAC '01; FLC '01, '03; FAC '01; ESC '01; CS '01
International Honours: Germany: 51
This experienced defender joined Blackburn on loan from Liverpool and was expected to fit in alongside Lorenzo Amoruso and provide experience. However, he seemed to struggle to settle in, whether used in a central role or at right back. A danger from set pieces he contributed three headed goals, two of them in the game against Middlesbrough.
Liverpool (Free from Bayern Munich, Germany, ex SV Hamburg, on 10/7/2000) PL 42/3 FLC 7/1 FAC 5/1 Others 17+2/1
Blackburn Rov (Loaned on 27/8/2003) PL 23+2/3 FLC 1 FAC 1 Others 1

BAGGIO Dino
Born: Camposampiero, Italy, 24 July 1971
Height: 6'2" **Weight:** 13.5
International Honours: Italy: 60
Dino struggled to make an impact for Blackburn last term, and his only appearance in the starting line-up came in the first leg of the UEFA Cup tie against Genclerbirligi. Although frequently used as a substitute, the experienced midfielder soon departed for a spell back in Italy with Ancona.
Blackburn Rov (Free from Lazio, Italy, ex Torino, Inter Milan, Juventus, Parma, on 1/9/2003) PL 0+9/1 FAC 0+1 Others 1+1

BAILEY Mark
Born: Stoke, 12 August 1976
Height: 5'8" **Weight:** 10.12
This right wing back had another steady season for Lincoln despite injury problems. Mark's defensive abilities fitted in well with the Imps' back five and he gave the team another attacking option with his runs down the flank. Mark missed the start of the campaign with a hamstring injury and soon after recovering fitness he underwent a hernia operation. His only League goal was a spectacular 70-yard effort in his team's victory at Carlisle. Mark was reported to have signed for Macclesfield during the summer.
Stoke C (From trainee on 12/7/1994)
Rochdale (Free on 10/10/1996) FL 49+18/1 FLC 5 FAC 1 Others 4 (Free to Winsford U during 1999 close season)
Lincoln C (Free from Northwich Vic, ex Lancaster C on 8/10/2001) FL 97+1/1 FLC 1 FAC 3+1 Others 8/3

BAINES Leighton John
Born: Liverpool, 11 December 1984
Height: 5'8" **Weight:** 11.10
This promising teenager became the first choice left back for Wigan last term and was one of the most consistent performers in the second half of the season. Composed and confident on the ball, he displayed the maturity of a seasoned professional. A left-footed player, Leighton showed tremendous consistency based on solid defensive techniques such as well-timed tackling and excellent covering. He deservedly collected the club's 'Young Player of the Season' award for the second successive season.
Wigan Ath (From trainee on 4/1/2003) FL 29+3 FLC 2+1 FAC 3 Others 1+1

BAIRD Christopher (Chris) Patrick
Born: Ballymoney, 25 February 1982
Height: 5'10" **Weight:** 11.11
International Honours: NI: 11; U21-6; Yth
A quick, tenacious right back Chris had to wait until December before Gordon Strachan selected him for bench-warming

Markus Babbel

duty, and his single start was in the depleted defence that faced Arsenal at St Mary's later the same month; that aside his first-team appearances were confined to loan periods at Walsall and Watford. He was impressive during a spell at Bescot in the autumn, and also did well with the Hornets once he had the measure of First Division football. Recalled by Paul Sturrock early in May, with the Saints suffering an injury crisis, Chris made a single appearance from the substitutes' bench. He also featured at international level for Northern Ireland.
Southampton (From trainee on 15/1/2001) PL 2+5 FAC 1
Walsall (Loaned on 26/9/2003) FL 10
Watford (Loaned on 16/3/2004) FL 8

BAKER Thomas (Tom)
Born: Salford, 28 March 1985
Height: 5'5" **Weight:** 9.0
Tom was one of several promising Barnsley youngsters introduced to first-team football last term. He made his debut as a second-half substitute of the final home game of the season against Bristol City. A scholar attached to the club's Academy, he can play either in midfield or up front.
Barnsley (Trainee) FL 0+1

BAKKE Eirik
Born: Sogndal, Norway, 13 September 1977
Height: 6'2" **Weight:** 12.9
International Honours: Norway: 25; U21-34; Yth
Eirik missed the first half of last season due to an injury suffered on international duty with Norway and he did not return to first-team action with Leeds until the Boxing Day fixture with Aston Villa. The forceful midfielder was sorely missed in a struggling season, and after scoring in the home draw with Liverpool, injury again kept him out of the side until April.
Leeds U (£1,000,000 + from Sogndal, Norway on 13/7/1999) PL 107+22/8 FLC 6/1 FAC 9+1/6 Others 31+3/5

BALDACCHINO Ryan Lee
Born: Leicester, 13 January 1981
Height: 5'9" **Weight:** 12.3
This pacy winger appeared in two early-season matches for Carlisle before moving across the border to sign for Gretna. Ryan then featured regularly for the Scottish Third Division team during the remainder of the campaign, scoring a total of five goals.
Blackburn Rov (From trainee on 25/2/1999)
Bolton W (Free on 16/3/2001)

Carlisle U (Free on 9/8/2002) FL 11+12 FLC 1 FAC 1+2 Others 1+3

BALDRY Simon Jonathan
Born: Huddersfield, 12 February 1976
Height: 5'10" **Weight:** 11.6
Simon was a regular for Notts County for much of the 2003-04 season. A traditional right winger, who on his day can produce exciting and match-winning displays, he is capable of delivering a fine cross into the box. He scored twice, netting in the Carling Cup tie against Ipswich Town and also struck home the winner against Hartlepool in November. Simon was released in the summer.
Huddersfield T (From trainee on 14/7/1994) FL 87+59/8 FLC 5+5/1 FAC 2+2 Others 3+3/1
Bury (Loaned on 8/9/1998) FL 0+5
Notts Co (Free on 7/8/2003) FL 32+3/1 FLC 2/1 FAC 3 Others 1

BALDWIN Patrick (Pat) Michael
Born: City of London, 12 November 1982
Height: 6'2" **Weight:** 10.12
This young central defender failed to establish himself in the Colchester United line-up over the course of the 2003-04 season, starting just one League match, the 2-1 win over Bristol City in August. The following month, he started one more game at Rotherham in the Carling Cup, but otherwise he was either on the bench or found himself well down the pecking order of defenders at Layer Road. Pat had a spell on loan at St Albans City in the new year.
Colchester U (Free from trainee at Chelsea on 16/8/2002) FL 14+9 FLC 2 FAC 1 Others 0+2

BALMER Stuart Murray
Born: Falkirk, 20 September 1969
Height: 6'0" **Weight:** 12.11
Club Honours: AMC '99
International Honours: S: Yth; Sch
This solidly built central defender gave Boston United experience in the middle of their back four. He was involved in coaching during the season which he combined with playing until a change of management. He was released in the summer.
Glasgow Celtic (From juniors on 1/8/1987)
Charlton Ath (£120,000 on 24/8/1990) FL 201+26/8 FLC 15 FAC 9+1 Others 11/1
Wigan Ath (£200,000 on 18/9/1998) FL 99+2/4 FLC 7 FAC 8 Others 12/1
Oldham Ath (Free on 20/7/2001) FL 35+1/6 FLC 2 FAC 4 Others 2
Scunthorpe U (Loaned on 10/10/2002) FL 6 Others 1

Boston U (Free on 13/12/2002) FL 46+1/ FAC 1

BANKS Steven (Steve)
Born: Hillingdon, 9 February 1972
Height: 6'0" **Weight:** 13.2
Steve joined Wimbledon just prior to the start of the season on the recommendation of former Bolton team mate Dean Holdsworth and, apart from missing a few starts through an arm injury, was the club's first-choice 'keeper until deciding to accept the security of a two-year contract he was offered at Gillingham. He was immediately installed in the line-up at Priestfield and kept a clean sheet on his debut at Preston, retaining his place in the line-up until the season's end.
West Ham U (From trainee on 24/3/1990) Others 1
Gillingham (Free on 25/3/1993) FL 67 FAC 7 Others 2
Blackpool (£60,000 on 18/8/1995) FL 150 FLC 13 FAC 8 Others 11
Bolton W (£50,000 on 25/3/1999) P/FL 20+1 FLC 7 FAC 5 Others 3
Rochdale (Loaned on 14/12/2001) FL 15
Bradford C (Loaned on 30/8/2002) FL 8+1
Stoke C (Free on 6/12/2002) FL 14 FAC 2
Wimbledon (Free on 1/8/2003) FL 24 FLC 1 FAC 3
Gillingham (Signed on 12/3/2004) FL 13

BARACLOUGH Ian Robert
Born: Leicester, 4 December 1970
Height: 6'1" **Weight:** 12.2
Club Honours: Div 3 '98
International Honours: E: Yth
This committed player showed tremendous versatility for Notts County last term, featuring in a variety of positions in defence and midfield, however, he proved unable to save the Magpies from relegation. Ian was one of several players released in the summer and was subsequently reported to have signed for Scunthorpe United.
Leicester C (From trainee on 15/12/1988) FAC 1 Others 0+1
Wigan Ath (Loaned on 22/3/1990) FL 8+1/2
Grimsby T (Loaned on 21/12/1990) FL 1+3
Grimsby T (Free on 13/8/1991) FL 1
Lincoln C (Free on 21/8/1992) FL 68+5/10 FLC 7/1 FAC 4 Others 7
Mansfield T (Free on 6/6/1994) FL 47/5 FLC 7 FAC 4 Others 4
Notts Co (Signed on 13/10/1995) FL 107+4/10 FLC 5+1/1 FAC 8 Others 5
Queens Park R (£50,000 on 19/3/1998) FL 120+5/1 FLC 7 FAC 6
Notts Co (Free on 5/7/2001) FL 93+8/5 FLC 6 FAC 6+1 Others 3+1

Y Philip (Phil)

ord, 28 June 1985
5'11" **Weight:** 11.8
...onours: FAYC '03
...e again, Sir Alex Ferguson turned to
...e Carling Cup to gauge the progress of
one of his up-and-coming young players.
Slotting in at full back for the trip to the
Hawthorns against West Bromwich Albion
in December, Phillip's debut might have
ended in defeat but he showed some nice
touches, which suggested his chance will
come again.
*Manchester U (From trainee on 2/7/2003)
FLC 1 FAC 0+1*

BARKER Christopher (Chris)
Andrew
Born: Sheffield, 2 March 1980
Height: 6'0" **Weight:** 11.8

This solid left-sided defender was a
regular in the Cardiff City line-up for most
of last season, but towards the end of the
campaign he found himself battling for a
starting place. Strong and versatile, he is
able to play either at full back or in the
centre of the defence. Chris again failed
to register a goal for the Bluebirds last
term.
*Barnsley (Signed from Alfreton on
24/8/1998) FL 110+3/3 FLC 11+1 FAC 4
Others 0+1*
*Cardiff C (£600,000 on 12/7/2002) FL 65+14
FLC 3 FAC 5 Others 4*

BARKER Richard (Richie) Ian
Born: Sheffield, 30 May 1975
Height: 6'0" **Weight:** 13.5
International Honours: E: Yth; Sch
There can surely be no more willing
worker in the Rotherham United squad

than Richie who mainly had to settle for a
role on the substitutes' bench last term.
However, whenever called upon he could
always be relied on to give his best both
in his normal striker's role and also when
needed to help out in his own penalty
area, where his aerial ability was more
than useful. One of his goals earned an
FA Cup replay at Northampton and he
also netted a fine effort at West Ham
United.
*Sheffield Wed (From trainee on 27/7/1993)
Others 1+1 (Free to Linfield on 22/8/1996)*
*Doncaster Rov (Loaned on 29/9/1995) FL
5+1 Others 0+1*
*Brighton & Hove A (Free on 19/12/1997) FL
48+12/12 FLC 1+1/1 FAC 1/1 Others 1*
*Macclesfield T (Free on 5/7/1999) FL 58/23
FLC 6/2 FAC 3 Others 1/1*
*Rotherham U (£60,000 on 3/1/2001) FL
53+70/12 FLC 6+2/2 FAC 5/2*

Ian Baraclough

BARKER Shaun
Born: Nottingham, 19 September 1982
Height: 6'2" **Weight:** 12.8
This versatile player really came into his own for Rotherham last term as he established a regular place for himself in the first team. He featured for much of the season at right back but he was also employed at centre back, a position many regard as his best. In the last few games of the season Shaun was switched to become a ball-winning midfield player and he settled into that role with ease as well. He is a long-throw specialist and picked up a number of the end-of-season 'Player of the Year' awards.
Rotherham U (From trainee on 10/7/2002) FL 47/2 FLC 3 FAC 2

BARLOW Matthew (Matty)
John
Born: Oldham, 25 June 1987
Height: 5'11" **Weight:** 10.2
This young striker came to prominence last term as a member of the successful Oldham Athletic youth team. Matty was a consistent performer and industrious worker for the side and got his reward in the shape of a call up for the final first-team game of the season at Notts County. He came on as a second-half substitute for Scott Vernon and did nothing wrong.
Oldham Ath (Trainee) FL 0+1

BARLOW Stuart
Born: Liverpool, 16 July 1968
Height: 5'10" **Weight:** 11.0
Club Honours: AMC '99
This veteran striker enjoyed an impressive first season at Stockport last term, scoring 12 goals. After the serious injury to Luke Beckett, the club found a striker they could rely on as Stuart struck ten times in the first half of the campaign. His energetic and committed displays made him a firm favourite with the supporters and he also rescued the side on a couple of occasions coming off the bench to score a late winner against Bournemouth, and finding the net late on to salvage a point against Brentford.
Everton (Free from Sherwood Park on 6/6/1990) F/PL 24+47/10 FLC 3+5/1 FAC 4+3/2 Others 0+2
Rotherham U (Loaned on 10/1/1992) Others 0+1
Oldham Ath (£450,000 on 20/11/1995) FL 78+15/31 FLC 5+1 FAC 6+1/1 Others 1
Wigan Ath (£45,000 on 26/3/1998) FL 72+11/40 FLC 6/3 FAC 5/3 Others 9+3/6
Tranmere Rov (Free on 5/7/2000) FL 62+32/19 FLC 6+3/3 FAC 5+5/3 Others 1+1/2

Stockport Co (Free on 8/8/2003) FL 15+15/8 FLC 1+1/1 FAC 1 Others 2+1/3

BARMBY Nicholas (Nick)
Jonathan
Born: Hull, 11 February 1974
Height: 5'7" **Weight:** 11.3
Club Honours: FLC '01; UEFAC '01; CS '01
International Honours: E: 23; B-2; U21-4; Yth; Sch
Nick struggled to rediscover the form that once made him an exciting talent and spent the whole of the 2003-04 season out of the first-team picture at Leeds, firstly under Peter Reid and then under Eddie Gray. His only start came in the home game with Tottenham in January and soon afterwards he swapped one relegation battle for another when he moved on loan to Nottingham Forest. Nick struck up a promising partnership up front with Gareth Taylor, but following the return of David Johnson to fitness he returned to Elland Road.
Tottenham H (From trainee on 9/4/1991) PL 81+6/20 FLC 7+1/2 FAC 12+1/5
Middlesbrough (£5,250,000 on 8/8/1995) PL 42/8 FLC 4/1 FAC 3/1
Everton (£5,750,000 on 2/11/1996) PL 105+11/18 FLC 2+3/3 FAC 12/3
Liverpool (£6,000,000 on 19/7/2000) PL 23+9/2 FLC 3+4/1 FAC 2+3/1 Others 10+4/4
Leeds U (£2,750,000 on 8/8/2002) PL 17+8/4 FLC 1 FAC 0+2 Others 3/1
Nottingham F (Loaned on 27/2/2004) FL 6/1

BARNARD Darren Sean
Born: Rintein, Germany, 30 November 1971
Height: 5'9" **Weight:** 12.3
International Honours: W: 22; E: Yth; Sch
Darren was finally able to establish himself as first choice at left back for Grimsby Town last term. One of only a handful of players to appear regularly for the Mariners throughout the season, he also featured on the left-hand side of midfield when required. Darren produced a series of consistent performances and continued to represent Wales at international level during the campaign.
Chelsea (£50,000 from Wokingham T on 25/7/1990) F/PL 18+11/2 FLC 1+1 FAC 1+1
Reading (Loaned on 18/11/1994) FL 3+1
Bristol C (£175,000 on 6/10/1995) FL 77+1/15 FLC 4/1 FAC 6 Others 6/1
Barnsley (£750,000 on 8/8/1997) P/FL 151+19/28 FLC 16+3/5 FAC 9/3 Others 3
Grimsby T (Free on 2/8/2002) FL 55+8/4 FLC 1 FAC 3 Others 1

BARNARD Donny Gary
Born: Forest Gate, 1 July 1984
Height: 6'0" **Weight:** 11.3
Donny-missed the start of the 2003-04 campaign for Leyton Orient due to an injury sustained in pre-season training. However, once he returned to full fitness he made the right-back spot his own. Donny has the knack of timing a tackle to win the ball and is quick to support an attack down the flanks. He can also play in central midfield.
Leyton Orient (From trainee on 4/3/2003) FL 45+17 FLC 0+2 FAC 1+1 Others 2/1

BARNES Paul Lance
Born: Leicester, 16 November 1967
Height: 5'11" **Weight:** 13.6
As the leading goal-scorer in the Conference in 2002-03, Paul looked forward to appearing again in League football last term. However, the increased competition for places in the Doncaster line-up meant the veteran striker was restricted to just a couple of starts and in December he moved on to join Tamworth.
Notts Co (From apprentice on 16/11/1985) FL 36+17/14 FAC 0+1 Others 7+6/5
Stoke C (£30,000 on 23/3/1990) FL 10+14/3 FLC 0+2 Others 3+1/2
Chesterfield (Loaned on 8/11/1990) FL 1 FAC 1/1
York C (£50,000 on 15/7/1992) FL 147+1/76 FLC 10/5 FAC 5 Others 16/4
Birmingham C (£350,000 on 4/3/1996) FL 15/7
Burnley (£350,000 + on 6/9/1996) FL 63+2/30 FLC 5 FAC 5/1
Huddersfield T (Signed on 16/1/1998) FL 13+17/2 FLC 0+3 FAC 1+1
Bury (£40,000 on 15/3/1999) FL 31+23/8 FLC 0+1 FAC 4 Others 2
Doncaster Rov (Free on 4/7/2001) FL 2+5 FLC 0+2/1 FAC 0+1 Others 2

BARNES Philip (Phil) Kenneth
Born: Sheffield, 2 March 1979
Height: 6'1'' **Weight:** 11.1
Club Honours: AMC '02
Although Phil began the 2003-04 season as Blackpool's first-choice 'keeper, he lost his place after the opening game against Queens Park Rangers and thereafter he was in and out of the side. A sound shot-stopper, he was released in the summer.
Rotherham U (From trainee on 25/6/1997) FL 2
Blackpool (£100,000 on 22/7/1997) FL 141 FLC 7 FAC 7 Others 14

..IESS Anthony

c: Lewisham, 25 March 1973
Height: 5'10" Weight: 13.1
Club Honours: Div 1 '00
Anthony was on his way to West Ham in a loan deal in January before being called back to the Reebok due to a defensive crisis. The majority of his Premiership appearances followed this recall, when he displayed his versatility by covering both the right- and left-back positions with equal aplomb. A regular starter in the cup games, and perhaps the most reliable squad member at Sam Allardyce's disposal, Anthony continued to give assured performances whenever called to first-team action last season.
Charlton Ath (From trainee on 6/3/1991) FL 21+6/1 FLC 2 FAC 3 Others 1+1/1
Chelsea (£350,000 on 8/9/1992) PL 12+2 FLC 2 Others 2+1
Middlesbrough (Loaned on 12/8/1993) Others 1
Southend U (Loaned on 2/2/1996) FL 5
Charlton Ath (£165,000 on 8/8/1996) P/FL 83+13/3 FLC 5 FAC 3+1 Others 1+1
Bolton W (Free on 6/7/2000) P/FL 68+17 FLC 8+2 FAC 7 Others 3

BARNETT Leon Peter

Born: Stevenage, 30 November 1985
Height: 6'1" Weight: 11.3
Leon received his first start for Luton in the LDV Vans Trophy tie against Stevenage last October when he produced a confident performance. He also featured in the LDV tie against Rushden and in the FA Cup first round win over Thurrock. A promising young central defender who can also play at full back, he will be looking for more senior experience in 2004-05.
Luton T (Trainee) FAC 1 Others 2+1

BAROS Milan

Born: Czechoslovakia, 28 October 1981
Height: 6'0" Weight: 11.12
Club Honours: FLC '03
International Honours: Czech Republic: 30; U21-19; Yth
Last season should have been the season that this young striker established himself as a Premiership striker and Michael Owen's partner in the Liverpool line-up, however, he suffered a broken ankle and was out of action for several weeks. Milan returned to action in late February but despite scoring two fine goals, one in the 2-2 draw at Leeds and another in the home leg of the UEFA Cup quarter-final with Olympique Marseille, he lost his place in mid-March and thereafter only appeared as a substitute. Milan was in

excellent form for the Czech Republic during Euro 2004 where he finished as the tournament's leading scorer with five goals.
Liverpool ((£3,400,000 from Banik Ostrava, Czechoslovakia, on 24/12/2001) PL 23+17/10 FLC 2+2/2 FAC 0+2 Others 5+10/2

BARRAS Anthony (Tony)

Born: Billingham, 29 March 1971
Height: 6'0" Weight: 13.0
This vastly experienced central defender was a regular in the Notts County line-up last term, impressing with his no-nonsense approach to the game. A highlight of his campaign was scoring an equaliser for the Magpies in the Carling Cup tie at Chelsea, although the London club eventually won through by a 4-2 margin. Tony's form showed a steady improvement under new manager Gary Mills and he will be looking to guide the club to promotion in the 2004-05 campaign.
Hartlepool U (From trainee on 6/7/1989) FL 9+3 FLC 2 FAC 1
Stockport Co (Free on 23/7/1990) FL 94+5/5 FLC 2 FAC 7 Others 19+1
Rotherham U (Loaned on 25/2/1994) FL 5/1
York C (£25,000 on 18/7/1994) FL 167+4/11 FLC 16/2 FAC 10/1 Others 8+1/1
Reading (£20,000 on 19/3/1999) FL 4+2/1
Walsall (£20,000 on 7/6/1999) FL 91+14/9 FLC 9+2/2 FAC 5/1 Others 4
Plymouth Arg (Loaned on 22/11/2002) FL 4
Notts Co (Free on 7/8/2003) FL 38+2/2 FLC 3/1 FAC 2/1 Others 0+1

BARRASS Matthew (Matt) Robert

Born: Bury, 28 February 1980
Height: 5'11" Weight: 12.0
It was a big blow to Bury when Matt damaged his knee in training last September – an injury which kept him out for two months. His season got much better, though, as he gained an extended run at right back in the Shakers side throughout the second half of the campaign, signed an extended contract and captained the side in the closing three games. He even scored his first goal for four years in the 1-1 home draw against Darlington.
Bury (From trainee on 19/5/1999) FL 69+6/2 FLC 3+1 FAC 1 Others 3

BARRETT Adam Nicholas

Born: Dagenham, 29 November 1979
Height: 5'10" Weight: 12.0
This inspirational central defender was a near ever-present for Bristol Rovers last term when he missed just one Third

Division match. Adam captained the side and also contributed four goals – none better than his volley that helped clinch a 2-1 win at Cheltenham in April.
Plymouth Arg (Free from USA football scholarship on 13/1/1999) FL 47+5/3 FLC 4 FAC 6+1 Others 1
Mansfield T (£10,000 on 1/12/2000) FL 34+3/1 FAC 3 Others 2
Bristol Rov (Free on 2/7/2002) FL 90/5 FLC 2 FAC 5/1 Others 2

BARRETT Graham

Born: Dublin, 6 October 1981
Height: 5'10" Weight: 11.7
Club Honours: FAYC '00
International Honours: RoI: 5; U21-24; Yth (UEFA-U16 '98); Sch
This youngster had a mixed season at Coventry last term. Graham scored on his debut in the Carling Cup win over Peterborough and was first choice on the right side of midfield until November. His strong running and good crosses allied to his tackling back won him many admirers and he showed his shooting power by scoring a 30-yard goal in the 4-2 win over Stoke. His form tailed off in November and he suffered an ankle ligament injury playing for the reserves. Graham returned to the squad for the last few games of the season and was rewarded with a full cap for the Republic of Ireland against Poland in April.
Arsenal (From trainee on 14/10/1998) PL 0+2 FLC 1
Bristol Rov (Loaned on 15/12/2000) FL 0+1
Crewe Alex (Loaned on 11/9/2001) FL 2+1 FLC 0+1
Colchester U (Loaned on 14/12/2001) FL 19+1/4
Brighton & Hove A (Loaned on 29/8/2002) FL 20+10/1 FAC 1
Coventry C (Free on 3/7/2003) FL 20+11/2 FLC 1+1/1

BARRETT Paul David

Born: Newcastle, 13 April 1978
Height: 5'11" Weight: 11.5
International Honours: E: Yth
Paul was in and out of the Wrexham line-up last term without ever really becoming a regular. He does not get on the score sheet too often, but since the winner late on in the match at Stockport County on Boxing Day, and added a fine volley at home to Hartlepool in mid-March. An industrious midfielder, he is a good passer of the ball and strong in possession. Paul was released by the club in May.
Newcastle U (From trainee on 20/6/1996)
Wrexham (Free on 24/3/1999) FL 98+22/5 FLC 2+1 FAC 2+1 Others 5+1

BARRON Michael (Micky) James

Born: Chester le Street, 22 December 1974
Height: 5'11" **Weight:** 11.9
A great competitor and a captain who leads by example, Micky was once again the first choice at right back for Hartlepool last term. Overall he had a good campaign in 2003-04, but he had a few injury set backs in the closing stages. He returned in time for the play-off semi-final, but received a bad head injury in the latter stages of the second leg tie.
Middlesbrough (From trainee on 2/2/1993) P/FL 2+1 FLC 1 Others 3+3
Hartlepool U (Loaned on 6/9/1996) FL 16
Hartlepool U (Free on 8/7/1997) FL 250+2/3 FLC 8+1 FAC 11/1 Others 21

BARROWMAN Andrew

Born: Wishaw, 27 November 1984
Height: 5'11" **Weight:** 11.6
International Honours: S: Yth
This rangy, aggressive striker joined Crewe Alexandra on loan last October and made three starts for the First Division outfit, scoring in the 3-0 win over Derby. He returned to St Andrews and was a regular in the Blues squad towards the end of the season. He made a brief Premiership debut as an 87th minute substitute in the home defeat by Leicester City in March.
Birmingham C (From trainee on 11/12/2001) PL 0+1
Crewe Alex (Loaned on 13/10/2003) FL 3+1/1

BARRY Gareth

Born: Hastings, 23 February 1981
Height: 6'0" **Weight:** 12.6
International Honours: E: 8; U21-27; Yth
In the absence of Olof Mellberg, Gareth was appointed captain for Aston Villa's opening fixture of the season against Portsmouth. During the same game, he calmly converted a penalty six minutes from time to give Villa a fleeting glimmer of hope. With the exception of a short suspension he was in the starting line-up for every game and captained the side whenever Mellberg was absent. Although primarily a left-sided midfielder, Gareth was switched to a more central role alongside Gavin McCann for several games in mid-season, but he always looked more comfortable playing on the left. He added a couple more appearances for England U21s during the campaign.
Aston Villa (From trainee on 27/2/1998) PL 174+11/9 FLC 19/1 FAC 12+2/1 Others 17+1/1

BARRY-MURPHY Brian

Born: Cork, Ireland, 27 July 1978
Height: 6'0" **Weight:** 12.4
International Honours: Rol: U21-6; Yth
A near ever-present for Sheffield Wednesday last term, this left-sided defender filled in as a wing back and an orthodox left back without ever hitting the heights. A good team man, he brought some stability to a shaky looking defence and distributed the ball effectively. Brian was one of 13 players released by Wednesday in the summer.
Preston NE (Free from Cork C on 3/8/1999) FL 6+15 FLC 1+3 FAC 1+1 Others 1
Southend U (Loaned on 11/2/2002) FL 8/1
Hartlepool U (Loaned on 30/10/2002) FL 7 FAC 2
Sheffield Wed (Free on 31/1/2003) FL 55+3 FLC 1 FAC 2 Others 6

BART-WILLIAMS Christopher (Chris) Gerald

Born: Freetown, Sierra Leone, 16 June 1974
Height: 5'11" **Weight:** 11.6
Club Honours: Div 1 '98
International Honours: E: B-1; U21-16; Yth
Chris joined Ipswich last September, initially on a three-month loan, but eventually signing up for the whole season. When he arrived Ipswich were struggling in the table and his steadying influence in midfield was a contributory factor in the club's climb towards a play-off place. Ironically most of his best displays came during his loan period because a back injury picked up in mid-January effectively ended his season, although he did make a substitute appearance in the first leg of the play-off semi-final against West Ham.
Leyton Orient (From trainee on 18/7/1991) FL 34+2/2 FLC 4 Others 2
Sheffield Wed (£275,000 on 21/11/1991) F/PL 95+29/16 FLC 10+6/4 FAC 9+3/2 Others 1+3/2
Nottingham F (£2,500,000 on 1/7/1995) F/PL 200+7/30 FLC 16/3 FAC 14/2 Others 7+1
Charlton Ath (free on 3/12/2001) PL 17+12/1 FAC 3+1
Ipswich T (Free on 12/9/2003) FL 23+3/2 FAC 1 Others 0+1

BARTLETT Thurston Shaun

Born: Cape Town, South Africa, 31 October 1972
Height: 6'1" **Weight:** 12.4
International Honours: South Africa: 66
Shaun started the season as Charlton's first choice striker, scoring twice in the Addicks' 4-0 win at Wolves in August and grabbing a late winner at Portsmouth in October. However he suffered an ankle injury in this game, which was to sideline him for four months and it was not until February that he returned to the side. One of the highlights of his season came when he scored a dramatic headed goal at Anfield to give Charlton their first win at Liverpool for 50 years. His workmanlike performances made him first choice for the remainder of the season. The South African international has good close control and is quick and strong with a powerful shot. He is also excellent in the air, and uses this strength when defending corners and set pieces, as well as when going for goal. He covers a lot of ground during a game and his work rate is second to none.
Charlton Ath (Signed from FC Zurich, Switzerland, ex Cape Town Spurs, Colorado Rapids, NY/NJ Metro Stars, Cape Town Spurs, on 1/12/2000) PL 64+18/17 FLC 3 FAC 4+1

BARTON Joseph (Joey) Anthony

Born: Huyton, 2 September 1982
Height: 5'9" **Weight:** 11.2
International Honours: E: U21-2
An England U21 international, Joey is earmarked for a bright and prosperous future at the City of Manchester Stadium. He was one of the few bright spots for Manchester City last season playing with a maturity that belied his inexperience. A hard-working and talented midfielder who started in 24 of the team's Premiership matches, he was voted 'Young Player of the Year' by the supporters.
Manchester C (From trainee on 5/7/2001) PL 31+4/2 FLC 2 FAC 3+1 Others 2+3

BARTON Warren Dean

Born: Stoke Newington, 19 March 1969
Height: 6'0" **Weight:** 12.0
International Honours: E: 3; B-3
Warren left Derby County by mutual consent in September and soon afterwards he joined Queens Park Rangers on a non-contract basis. He made two appearances, but was injured on the second occasion and was later appointed as player-coach of Wimbledon. However, despite showing plenty of experience in a central-midfield role he was unable to prevent the club from losing the first five games he started. He then wisely decided to hang up his boots and subsequently helped out with the coaching duties until the season's end.
Maidstone U (£10,000 from Leytonstone on 28/7/1989) FL 41+1 FLC 0+2 FAC 3/1 Others 7

*...oledon (£300,000 on 7/6/1990) F/PL
...8+2/10 FLC 16/1 FAC 11 Others 2*
Newcastle U *(£4,500,000 on 5/6/1995) PL
142+22/4 FLC 12/1 FAC 19+3 Others 20+2*
Derby Co *(Signed on 1/2/2002) P/FL 53 FLC
2 FAC 1*
Queens Park R *(Free on 7/10/2003) FL 2+1
Others 2*
Wimbledon *(Free on 27/2/2004) FL 5*

BARTRAM Vincent (Vince)
Lee

Born: Birmingham, 7 August 1968
Height: 6'2" **Weight:** 13.4
How Gillingham could have done with a
fit and available Vince Bartram as back-up
to Jason Brown last term. Unfortunately,
his season ended after one match
following his recall for the home game
with Millwall, when he suffered a broken
arm following a collision with an
opponent. Vince was released by the Gills
in January.
Wolverhampton W *(From juniors on
17/8/1985) FL 5 FLC 2 FAC 3*
Blackpool *(Loaned on 27/10/1989) FL 9
Others 2*
Bournemouth *(£65,000 on 24/7/1991) FL
132 FLC 10 FAC 14 Others 6*
Arsenal *(£400,000 on 10/8/1994) PL 11 FLC
0+1*
Huddersfield T *(Loaned on 17/10/1997) FL
12*
Gillingham *(Free on 20/3/1998) FL 186+1
FLC 12 FAC 13 Others 10*

BARWICK Terence (Terry)
Patrick

Born: Doncaster, 11 January 1983
Height: 5'11" **Weight:** 11.2
This combative central midfielder finally
established himself in the Scunthorpe
United first team during the 2003-04
campaign. After starting out on the
substitutes' bench, Terry broke into the
line-up in October and kept his place for
most of the season, working hard and
improving his passing game. He netted his
first senior goal against Huddersfield in
November.
Scunthorpe U *(From trainee on 2/7/2002) FL
35+11/1 FLC 2+1 FAC 6 Others 3+2*

BASHAM Steven (Steve)
Brian

Born: Southampton, 2 December 1977
Height: 5'11'' **Weight:** 12.0
Club Honours: Div 2 '00
Steve showed himself to be one of the
best strikers in the Third Division last term
and he topped the Oxford scoring list
with 16 goals, most of them coming in

the first half of the season. One of his
most memorable strikes was when he
netted the winner at Millwall in the first
round of the Carling Cup. Steve is not
only a prolific goal-scorer, but works hard
for the team, and by the start of 2004-05
he will hope to have fully recovered from
the niggling hamstring, which caused him
to miss a number of games in the new
year.
Southampton *(From trainee on 24/5/1996)
PL 1+18/1 FLC 0+1*
Wrexham *(Loaned on 6/2/1998) FL 4+1*
Preston NE *(£200,000 on 5/2/1999) FL
37+31/15 FLC 5+2/1 FAC 1+2*
Oxford U *(Free on 8/8/2002) FL 63+6/22 FLC
2/1 FAC 4 Others 1*

BASTOCK Paul Anthony
Born: Leamington, 19 May 1970
Height: 5'10" **Weight:** 13.12
Club Honours: NC '02
This experienced 'keeper continued to
improve in a season which saw him see
off the competition from Steve Croudson.
Paul showed excellent stop stopping skills
and was an ever present for Boston
United for the second consecutive season.
He agreed a new contract in the summer.
Cambridge U *(Free from trainee at Coventry
C on 22/3/1988) FL 12 FLC 1 (Free to Sabah,
Malaysia during 1989 close season)*
Boston U *(Free from Kettering T, via Fisher
Ath, on 3/8/1992) FL 92 FLC 3 FAC 2
Others 4*

BATTY David
Born: Leeds, 2 December 1968
Height: 5'8" **Weight:** 12.0
Club Honours: Div 2 '90, Div 1 '92; CS
'92
International Honours: E: 42; B-5;
U21-7
This veteran midfielder had become Leeds
United's forgotten man prior to Peter
Reid's arrival at the club. David's
combative no-nonsense style seemed
ideal to help the club in their quest for
Premiership survival and he received a
standing ovation when returning as a
substitute in the opening game against
Newcastle. He went on to play a more
permanent role in the side, before falling
out of favour once more under Eddie
Gray.
Leeds U *(From trainee on 3/8/1987) F/PL
201+10/4 FLC 17 FAC 12 Others 17*
Blackburn Rov *(£2,750,000 on 26/10/1993)
PL 53+1/1 FLC 6 FAC 5 Others 6*
Newcastle U *(£3,750,000 on 2/3/1996) PL
81+2/3 FLC 6 FAC 9/1 Others 16*
Leeds U *(£4,400,000 on 9/12/1998) PL
79+11 FLC 4 FAC 4 Others 16+2*

BAUDET Julien
Born: Grenoble, France, 13 January 1979
Height: 6'3" **Weight:** 14.2
A player who is comfortable at the heart
of the defence or in midfield, Julien's first-
team opportunities were limited at
Rotherham last term and his longest run
of successive games came in the early
part of the season when the side was
struggling. A big, strong player, Julien is
blessed with a powerful kick in either
foot. He was released in the summer.
Oldham Ath *(Free from Toulouse, France on
9/10/2001) FL 34+10/3 FLC 2 FAC 2+2
Others 2*
Rotherham U *(Free on 6/8/2003) FL 8+3 FLC
0+1*

BAXTER Lee Stuart
Born: Helsingborg, Sweden, 17 July 1976
Height: 6'1" **Weight:** 13.6
This experienced 'keeper joined Sheffield
United on loan during the Swedish close
season. Faced with a goalkeeping crisis,
the Blades signed both Lee and Alan
Fettis two days before the game at
Burnley. Lee started the game, but after a
couple of errors he was substituted at the
interval and was released later the same
month. He subsequently returned to
Sweden and signed on loan for IFK
Goteborg until June.
Sheffield U *(Loaned from Malmo, Sweden,
ex Vissel Kobe, AIK, on 5/12/2003) FL 1*

BAYLISS David Anthony
Born: Liverpool, 8 June 1976
Height: 5'11" **Weight:** 12.4
After recovering from injury David was
recalled for Luton at Brighton last
September. The experienced defender
proved a valuable addition to the squad,
showing himself to be a good reader of
the game and a leader on the field. He
scored his only goal of the season in the
Carling Cup tie against Charlton, but
soon afterwards his campaign was
effectively ended when he picked up an
achilles tendon injury.
Rochdale *(From trainee on 10/6/1995) FL
169+17/9 FLC 11 FAC 5+3 Others 11+1*
Luton T *(Free on 7/12/2001) FL 28+9 FLC 2/1*

BAZELEY Darren Shaun
Born: Northampton, 5 October 1972
Height: 5'10" **Weight:** 11.7
Club Honours: Div 2 '98
International Honours: E: U21-1
One of Walsall's most consistent players
during the 2003-04 season, Darren
regained his first-team place in December
after losing out during Chris Baird's loan

spell and missed only one game from then on. Although he occasionally struggled defensively against fast left flank attackers, Darren worked tirelessly to set up attacks when going forward.

Watford (From trainee on 6/5/1991) FL 187+53/21 FLC 13+5/2 FAC 12+1/3 Others 9+1/1
Wolverhampton W (Free on 13/7/1999) FL 69+1/4 FLC 7 FAC 3
Walsall (Free on 16/7/2002) FL 76+6 FLC 5 FAC 5

BEADLE Peter Clifford William James
Born: Lambeth, 13 May 1972
Height: 6'1" **Weight:** 13.10
Club Honours: AMC '03
This tall, experienced centre forward joined Brentford on a one-month contract at the start of last season. Peter made his debut in the opening game at Tranmere, but was unfortunately sent off after just 12 minutes. Injury and suspension then kept him out of contention before he left Griffin Park for Barnet. At the end of the year Peter joined Team Bath as player-coach.

Gillingham (From trainee on 5/5/1990) FL 42+25/14 FLC 2+4/2 FAC 1+1 Others 1
Tottenham H (£300,000 on 4/6/1992)
Bournemouth (Loaned on 25/3/1993) FL 9/2
Southend U (Loaned on 4/3/1994) FL 8/1
Watford (Signed on 12/9/1994) FL 12+11/1 FLC 1
Bristol Rov (£50,000 on 17/11/1995) FL 98+11/39 FLC 2+1 FAC 5/2 Others 7+1/1
Port Vale (£300,000 on 6/8/1998) FL 18+5/6 FLC 2 FAC 1
Notts Co (£250,000 on 18/2/1999) FL 14+8/3 FLC 1+3
Bristol C (£200,000 on 19/10/1999) FL 51+31/14 FLC 1+1 FAC 6+4/1 Others 6+6/4
Brentford (Free on 7/8/2003) FL 1

BEAGRIE Peter Sydney
Born: Middlesbrough, 28 November 1965
Height: 5'8" **Weight:** 12.0
International Honours: E: B-2; U21-2
This veteran left winger started the 2003-04 season with a flourish for Scunthorpe United, scoring in the first three League games. A mesmerising player with superb ball skills, Peter was at his brilliant best before Christmas, hitting a double-figure goal tally and booking his place in the PFA Division Three team of the year. However, niggling injuries kicked in after the festive period, with hamstring and calf problems restricting him to just ten League starts in the final five months.

Middlesbrough (From juniors on 10/9/1983) FL 24+9/2 FLC 1 Others 1+1

Sheffield U (£35,000 on 16/8/1986) FL 81+3/11 FLC 5 FAC 5 Others 4
Stoke C (£210,000 on 29/6/1988) FL 54/7 FLC 4 FAC 3/1
Everton (£750,000 on 2/11/1989) F/PL 88+26/11 FLC 7+2/3 FAC 7+2 Others 5+1/1
Sunderland (Loaned on 26/9/1991) FL 5/1
Manchester C (£1,100,000 on 24/3/1994) F/PL 46+6/3 FLC 8/1 FAC 4+1/1
Bradford C (£50,000 on 2/7/1997) P/FL 113+18/20 FLC 9/3 FAC 5+1 Others 0+1
Everton (Loaned on 26/3/1998) PL 4+2
Wigan Ath (Free on 16/2/2001) FL 7+3/1 Others 2
Scunthorpe U (Free on 12/7/2001) FL 96+10/27 FLC 2+1/1 FAC 8 Others 7/2

BEAN Marcus Tristam
Born: Hammersmith, 2 November 1984
Height: 5'11" **Weight:** 11.6
A midfield player who can take either of the central positions, Marcus started last season as a regular on the substitutes' bench for Queens Park Rangers. After coming on in five successive games he earned a place in the starting line-up, retaining his place until he was sidelined by injury. He was out from January to March before returning to the side once more. Marcus scored his first and only goal for the club in the away win at Wrexham in September.

Queens Park R (Trainee) FL 27+11/1 FLC 1 FAC 1 Others 3+1

BEARDSLEY Christopher (Chris) Kelan
Born: Derby, 28 February 1984
Height: 6'0" **Weight:** 12.4
Chris was a regular on the bench for Mansfield in the early-season matches last term and scored his first senior goal in the 2-0 win over York in October, which was also his first time in the starting line-up. Chris was loaned out to Worksop Town in January, a result of the club's policy of giving the younger players experience of first-team football. He was released at the end of the season.

Mansfield T (From trainee on 4/7/2003) FL 3+17/1 FAC 0+1 Others 1

BEATTIE James Scott
Born: Lancaster, 27 February 1978
Height: 6'1" **Weight:** 12.0
International Honours: E: 5; U21-5
James had something of a frustrating season for Southampton, what with his international aspirations on hold and goals proving harder to come by than he, and his many admirers, have come to expect. The problem was certainly not down to lack of effort, as he continued to

run hard and get involved in all quarters of the field, but the supply of balls from an erratic midfield was less than satisfactory. Further: the Saints' midfielders repeatedly failed to get forward fast enough to exploit the chances he so frequently carved out for them; usually from unpromising situations. Still, when presented with the opportunities he was not found wanting: whether in the air, on the ground or on the volley, he remains a formidable striker.

Blackburn Rov (From trainee on 7/3/1995) PL 1+3 FLC 2 FAC 0+1
Southampton (£1,000,000 on 17/7/1998) PL 150+43/65 FLC 11+3/6 FAC 14+1/2 Others 2

BECK Daniel (Dan) Gordon
Born: Worthing, 14 November 1983
Height: 5'10" **Weight:** 10.11
This young Brighton winger broadened his football experience in 2003-04 with a spell on loan at Bognor Regis Town and then enjoyed a brief appearance as a substitute in the 4-0 defeat at Brentford for his Football League debut. Dan has been given a three-month contract at Withdean for 2004-05 to prove he has a future at the club.

Brighton & Hove A (From trainee on 7/7/2003) FL 0+1

BECKETT Luke John
Born: Sheffield, 25 November 1976
Height: 5'11" **Weight:** 11.6
It looked as though it would be another fantastic season for Stockport's star striker when he scored four goals early on last term. However, the talented striker damaged his cruciate knee ligament in the 2-2 draw with Port Vale at the beginning of September, and this kept him out of action for most of the remainder of the campaign. When he returned to the side as a substitute against Grimsby in late April he received a huge ovation from the County faithful who have already cast him as an Edgeley Park legend.

Barnsley (From trainee on 20/6/1995)
Chester C (Free on 11/6/1998) FL 70+4/25 FLC 5/5 FAC 4/2 Others 1
Chesterfield (£75,000 on 19/7/2000) FL 58+4/22 FLC 4/2 FAC 3/2 Others 5
Stockport Co (£100,000 on 14/12/2001) FL 64+5/38 FLC 3/1 FAC 2/1 Others 1

BECKWITH Robert
Born: London, 12 September 1984
Height: 6'2" **Weight:** 13.5
Robert started the 2003-04 season as first-choice goalkeeper for Luton Town. His handling and positioning enabled him

James Beattie

to keep two clean sheets early on, but his lack of experience showed and he was rested following the victory over Tranmere in October. A training ground accident in which he damaged a cruciate knee ligament then kept him out of action for the remainder of the campaign. Robert signed his first professional contract for the Hatters in the summer.

Luton T (Trainee) FL 17 FLC 2

BEDEAU Anthony (Tony)
Charles Osmond
Born: Hammersmith, 24 March 1979
Height: 5'10" **Weight:** 11.0
International Honours: Grenada
This experienced striker was hampered by injuries early on last term, and later saw Jason Fowler and then Liam Rosenior preferred in his favourite position, wide on the right. Tony continued to show excellent speed and stamina, and gave his all when called upon – often from the bench. His season was spiced up when called up by Grenada for their World Cup qualifying campaign and he made his international debut from the substitutes' bench against Guyana in March.

Torquay U (From trainee on 28/7/1997) FL 176+63/47 FLC 7+1/3 FAC 11+3/1 Others 2+8
Barnsley (Loaned on 1/2/2002) FL 0+3

BEECH Christopher (Chris)
Born: Congleton, 5 November 1975
Height: 5'10" **Weight:** 11.12
International Honours: E: Yth; Sch
After helping Doncaster Rovers to return to the Football League in 2002-03, Chris started last season at left back but soon lost his place and was unable to reclaim it. Captain of the reserve team, he always gave 100 per cent and was particularly effective at going down the left flank before putting over a good cross. Chris was placed on the transfer list in the summer.

Manchester C (From trainee on 12/11/1992)
Cardiff C (Free on 7/8/1997) FL 46/1 FLC 2 FAC 6
Rotherham U (Free on 30/6/1998) FL 40+15/1 FLC 7 FAC 0+1
Doncaster Rov (Free on 10/12/2002) FL 11 FLC 1 Others 1

BEECH Christopher (Chris)
Stephen
Born: Blackpool, 16 September 1974
Height: 5'11" **Weight:** 11.12
The 2003-04 season followed much the same pattern as the previous one for Chris, who started the campaign in a midfield slot for Rochdale but almost

immediately lost his place through injury. A brief mid-season run of games was also halted by injury and Chris was not seen again after limping out of the game at Yeovil last January. He was released by Dale in May.

Blackpool (From trainee on 9/7/1993) FL 53+29/4 FLC 4+4 FAC 1 Others 3+3/2
Hartlepool U (Free on 18/7/1996) FL 92+2/23 FLC 5/1 FAC 3/1 Others 3/1
Huddersfield T (£65,000 on 27/11/1998) FL 63+8/12 FLC 6/1 FAC 2/2
Rochdale (Free on 22/7/2002) FL 25+7/1 FLC 1 FAC 2/1

BEEVERS Lee Jonathan
Born: Doncaster, 4 December 1983
Height: 6'1" **Weight:** 12.10
International Honours: W: Yth
Lee had an excellent season for Boston United last term, earning himself a regular first-team place. He was mostly used on the right side of a four-man defence but also appeared at centre back. He was rewarded with a new two-year contract in the summer. Lee was recognised by his colleagues who chose him as the club's 'Players' Player of the Year'. He also won the Manager's 'Young Player of the Year' award.

Ipswich T (From trainee on 19/3/2001)
Boston U (Free on 27/3/2003) FL 40+1/2 FAC 1 Others 2/1

BEHARALL David (Dave)
Alexander
Born: Jarrow, 8 March 1979
Height: 6'0" **Weight:** 11.12
David is a strong centre half who was expected to benefit last term from the close-season departure of several Oldham stars. However, the cultured player's season was dogged with injury problems and he made just seven League starts before being sidelined for two months. He scored both Latics' goals in a battling 2-2 draw at Plymouth in November but then things rapidly turned sour. He finally returned to action in February but struggled to find favour following a change in management and will have to work hard to establish himself back in the side in 2004-05.

Newcastle U (From trainee on 4/7/1997) PL 4+2
Grimsby T (Loaned on 10/8/2001) FL 13+1 FLC 1
Oldham Ath (£150,000 on 19/11/2001) FL 55+2/3 FLC 4 FAC 7 Others 4

BELL Andrew (Andy)
Born: Blackburn, 12 February 1984
Height: 5'10" **Weight:** 12.6

Signed on a non-contract basis in the 2003 close season, Andy immediately impressed in Wycombe's reserves as a striker with a nose for goal. He scored two goals on his first-team debut, in the 5-2 home defeat against Oldham in September, and then signed a three-month deal. He played well in his brief appearances and scored again at Tranmere, but left the club in February. Soon afterwards he signed a short-term contract for York City where he looked lively and contributed another goal but was released in the summer.

Blackburn Rov (From trainee on 16/2/2001)
Wycombe W (Free on 18/9/2003) FL 3+8/3 FLC 1 Others 1
York C (Free on 27/2/2004) FL 3+7/1

BELL David Anthony
Born: Kettering, 21 April 1984
Height: 5'10" **Weight:** 11.6
Club Honours: Div 3 '03
International Honours: RoI: Yth
This skilful midfielder established himself as a key member of Rushden's first-team squad last term. He operated in both a central and wide role as Diamonds slipped agonisingly to relegation, scoring his only goal with a brilliant long-range strike in the 2-1 victory at Tranmere Rovers in August. David represented the Republic of Ireland at the World Youth Championships in the UAE during the season.

Rushden & Diamonds (From juniors on 24/7/2001) FL 57+11/4 FLC 2 FAC 2+2 Others 2+1

BELL Lee
Born: Crewe, 26 January 1983
Height: 5'10" **Weight:** 11.10
Lee featured three times for Crewe as a substitute in the early part of the 2003-04 season before joining Conference club Shrewsbury Town in a long-term loan arrangement. The hard-working midfielder eventually returned to Gresty Road, but added no further senior appearances.

Crewe Alex (From trainee on 6/2/2001) FL 3+17/1 FAC 0+2 Others 1+3

BELL Michael (Mickey)
Born: Newcastle, 15 November 1971
Height: 5'9" **Weight:** 11.4
Club Honours: AMC '03
Whilst he wasn't a regular throughout 2003-04, this popular wing back was at the top of his form for Bristol City at the end of the campaign. Unfortunately Mickey picked up an injury in the last game of the regular season, and this

...d to keep him out of action in the
...ay-offs.
Northampton T *(From trainee on 1/7/1990)*
FL 133+20/10 FLC 7+2 FAC 5/1 Others 9+2/1
Wycombe W *(£45,000 on 21/10/1994) FL
117+1/5 FLC 5 FAC 9/2 Others 3+1*
Bristol C *(£150,000 on 2/7/1997) FL
250+11/33 FLC 14/1 FAC 16+1 Others 14/3*

BELLAMY Craig Douglas
Born: Cardiff, 13 July 1979
Height: 5'9" **Weight:** 10.12
International Honours: W: 25; U21-8;
Yth; Sch
Fiery Craig is a key component of
Newcastle's attack, his searing pace and
all-action style making him a constant
threat to any opposition and an ideal foil
to the more measured approach of fellow
striker Alan Shearer. His early season was
disrupted by injuries, and in October he
went to the USA for surgery for tendonitis
in his knee. Craig returned to the side at
the end of January and immediately made
an impact, scoring seven times in ten
games. However, he tore a hamstring at
Villa Park in April bringing his season to a
premature close, although he did make a
substitute appearance in the final game at
Anfield. When fit he continued to be a
first choice for Wales.
Norwich C *(From trainee on 20/1/1997) FL
71+1/13 FLC 6/2 FAC 1*
Coventry C *(£6,500,000 on 17/8/2000) PL
33+1/6 FLC 3/1 FAC 2/1*
Newcastle U *(£6,000,000 on 11/7/2001) PL
66+6/20 FLC 2+1/4 FAC 4 Others 19+1/8*

BELLION David
Born: Sevres, France, 27 November 1982
Height: 5'11" **Weight:** 11.5
International Honours: France: U21
Signed on a free transfer from Sunderland
in the close season, David made only
sporadic appearances for Manchester
United from August to December. Having
been used as a playing substitute in the
early stages of the Champions' League,
he enjoyed two outings in the Carling
Cup games, celebrating with a goal in the
3-2 success at Leeds. At the turn of the
year, United's involvement in three major
competitions meant there was little
chance for David to establish himself in
the team.
Sunderland *(Free from AS Cannes, France
on 17/8/2001) PL 5+15/1 FLC 3 FAC 0+1*
Manchester U *(Signed on 1/7/2003) PL
4+10/2 FLC 2/1 FAC 1+1 Others 0+4*

BENEFIELD James (Jimmy)
Patrick
Born: Torbay, 6 May 1983
Height: 5'10" **Weight:** 11.2

This promising youngster was regularly
involved for Torquay in the first half of the
2003-04 season, making a handful of
starts mainly as a striker rather than in
midfield. Jimmy's best performances came
in cup football, his two goals coming in
the LDV Vans Trophy tie against
Peterborough and the FA Cup first round
game against Burton. The return of a
number of players from injury then limited
his opportunities and he was released at
the end of the season.
Torquay U *(From trainee on 12/7/2001) FL
6+26 FLC 0+2 FAC 1+2/1 Others 1+1/1*

BENJAMIN Trevor Junior
Born: Kettering, 8 February 1979
Height: 6'2" **Weight:** 13.2
International Honours: Jamaica: 2; E:
U21-1
This powerfully built striker underwent
knee surgery in the summer of 2003,
then spent much of the season building
up his experience through a series of loan
deals. Trevor did well in spells at
Gillingham and Rushden and made a
notable impact on the South Coast with
Brighton, where he impressed with five
goals from ten appearances and some
effective forward play. He was recalled to
the Walkers Stadium following the club's
well-publicised off-the-field crisis and
made a belated first start in the surprise
victory at St Andrews. Back in September
he added to his international caps with a
recall to the Jamaican squad, facing
Australia at the Madejski Stadium.
Cambridge U *(From trainee on 21/2/1997)
FL 96+27/35 FLC 7+3/4 FAC 9+1/5 Others 3/2*
Leicester C *(£1,000,000 + on 14/7/2000)
P/FL 31+40/9 FLC 2+3/1 FAC 2+3*
Crystal Palace *(Loaned on 20/12/2001) FL
5+1/1*
Norwich C *(Loaned on 8/2/2002) FL 3+3*
West Bromwich A *(Loaned on 27/3/2002)
FL 0+3/1*
Gillingham *(Loaned on 20/9/2003) FL 1+3/1*
Rushden & Diamonds *(Loaned on
14/11/2003) FL 5+1/1*
Brighton & Hove A *(Loaned on 16/1/2004)
FL 10/5*

BENNETT Dean Alan
Born: Wolverhampton, 13 December
1977
Height: 5'10" **Weight:** 11.0
Club Honours: NC '00
International Honours: E: SP-1
Dean finished the 2003-04 season as
Kidderminster's leading scorer, although
he only managed to find the net seven
times in all competitions. Four of his goals
came in the FA Cup as he single-handedly

tried to drag Harriers into the third round.
Normally playing wide on the right he
showed he still has the power to terrify
opposition defenders when running at
them with the ball.
West Bromwich A *(Free from Aston Villa
juniors on 19/12/1996) FL 0+1 (Free to
Bromsgrove Rov on 14/9/98)*
Kidderminster Hrs *(£30,000 on 29/1/1999)
FL 136+18/16 FLC 3 FAC 7+3/4 Others 3+3/1*

BENNETT Ian Michael
Born: Worksop, 10 October 1971
Height: 6'0" **Weight:** 12.10
Club Honours: Div 2 '95; AMC '95
Birmingham City's longest-serving player,
Ian was understudy to Maik Taylor last
term and came on as substitute when
Taylor was sent-off at Manchester United
in October and against Portsmouth in
April. He also kept a clean sheet at
Arsenal in May. Always alert and a good
kicker of the ball, Ian was reliable
whenever called upon.
Newcastle U *(From trainee at Queens Park R
on 20/3/1989)*
Peterborough U *(Free on 22/3/1991) FL 72
FLC 10 FAC 4 Others 4*
Birmingham C *(£325,000 on 17/12/1993)
P/FL 285+2 FLC 38 FAC 16 Others 13*

BENNETT Julian
Born: Nottingham, 17 December 1984
Height: 6'0" **Weight:** 12.7
Julian was a regular in the Walsall reserve
team that just missed out in the Pontins
League Premier Division championship
race last season. A promising young
central defender he showed great
confidence during his one first-team
substitute appearance at Wigan in
February.
Walsall *(Trainee) FL 0+1*

BENNETT Thomas (Tom)
McNeill
Born: Falkirk, 12 December 1969
Height: 5'11" **Weight:** 11.8
This skilful midfield man showed his
versatility by turning out in a number of
different positions for Boston United last
term. He played in both the wide-left and
wide-right midfield positions as well as in
the centre of the park. Tom's passing
ability and his commitment proved assets
for the Pilgrims in their second season of
Division Three football. He agreed a new
contract in the summer.
Aston Villa *(From apprentice on 16/12/1987)*
Wolverhampton W *(Free on 5/7/1988) FL
103+12/2 FLC 7 FAC 5+2 Others 3+1*
Stockport Co *(£75,000 on 23/6/1995) FL
105+5/5 FLC 20/2 FAC 10 Others 6+1*

Walsall *(Loaned on 30/12/1999) FL 4/1*
Walsall *(Free on 23/3/2000) FL 75+10/7 FLC 1+1 FAC 5/1 Others 3*
Boston U *(Free on 9/8/2002) FL 64+4/1 FLC 3 FAC 2 Others 3*

BENT Darren Ashley
Born: Wandsworth, 6 February 1984
Height: 5'11" **Weight:** 11.7
International Honours: E: U21-5; Yth
Despite only playing for two thirds of the 2003-04 season because of injury, Darren was still able to notch enough goals to finish up as leading scorer for Ipswich. He played mainly up front and used his pace to get behind defences and latch on to balls played over the top. The highlight of his season was his first senior hat-trick which he scored at Walsall in March. The first was a scrambled effort after a shot rebounded into his path, the second a low right-foot shot and for the third he turned in a cross at the far post. Darren also scored the goal that gave Ipswich a slender play-off semi-final first leg advantage.
Ipswich T *(From trainee on 2/7/2001) P/FL 58+19/29 FLC 4+1/3 FAC 1+2/3 Others 3+4/2*

BENT Jason
Born: Toronto, Canada, 8 March 1977
Height: 5'9" **Weight:** 11.7
Club Honours: Div 3 '02; Div 2 '04
International Honours: Canada: 32; U23-7; Yth
Jason delivered some vibrant displays in the centre of midfield during the first couple of months of 2003-04 for Plymouth Argyle, netting his only goal of the season against Stockport at Home Park in August. However, his campaign was again interrupted by injuries and he missed a lengthy spell in the middle of the season. Jason added further caps for Canada during the campaign, but was released by Argyle in the summer.
Plymouth Arg *(Free from Colorado Rapids, USA on 21/9/2001) FL 52+12/5 FLC 1 FAC 4+2/1 Others 3*

BENT Marcus Nathan
Born: Hammersmith, 19 May 1978
Height: 6'2" **Weight:** 12.4
International Honours: E: U21-2
Marcus played in the first four games of 2003-04 for Ipswich, scoring in the home game against Coventry before joining Leicester on loan for the remainder of the season, just 20 minutes before the transfer window closed. He made an early impact in the home win over Leeds and soon demonstrated his firepower with a

well-taken strike at Anfield. He also demonstrated his versatility throughout the campaign, sometimes being used on the right side of midfield to supply the ammunition for fellow strikers, Paul Dickov and Les Ferdinand. A steady supply of goals flowed, including a dramatic last-gasp header to salvage a point against Everton and a beautifully judged chip at the Valley, and Marcus could look back on the campaign with a degree of personal satisfaction despite relegation.
Brentford *(From trainee on 21/7/1995) FL 56+14/8 FLC 7/1 FAC 8/3 Others 5+1/1*
Crystal Palace *(£150,000 + on 8/1/1998) P/FL 13+15/5 FLC 0+2 FAC 0+1*
Port Vale *(£375,000 on 15/1/1999) FL 17+6/1 FLC 1*
Sheffield U *(£300,000 on 28/10/1999) FL 48/20 FLC 5/3 FAC 3/1*
Blackburn Rov *(£1,300,000 + on 24/11/2000) P/FL 22+15/8 FLC 0+1 FAC 5+1/3*
Ipswich T *(£3,000,000 on 23/11/2001) PL 51+10/21 FLC 0+2 FAC 4/1 Others 2+1/1*
Leicester C *(Loaned on 1/9/2003) PL 28+5/9 FAC 2/1*

BENTLEY David Michael
Born: Peterborough, 27 August 1984
Height: 5'10" **Weight:** 11.0
International Honours: E: U21-2; Yth
David is one of the real hopes for Arsenal's future, and of course he is a home grown product. A player of great potential, he signed a long-term contract with the club during the season. David scored one of the goals of the campaign with an audacious chip in the FA Cup fourth round tie against Middlesborough and later made his Premiership bow in May. He was a regular in the England U21 side and scored a wonderful goal on his debut in the 3-2 victory over Holland.
Arsenal *(From trainee on 8/9/2001) PL 1 FLC 4 FAC 0+3/1 Others 0+1*

BENTLEY Mark James
Born: Hertford, 7 January 1978
Height: 6'2" **Weight:** 13.0
Mark began last term with Conference outfit Dagenham & Redbridge and he took a while to get accustomed to the pace of Third Division football following his arrival at Roots Hall. However, once he had adjusted, he became an invaluable piece in Southend's midfield jigsaw. A real box-to-box player, Mark's battling qualities allied to his support of the forward line endeared him to the Blues faithful, who voted him their 'Player of the Month' for April.

Southend U *(Signed from Dagenham & Redbridge on 15/1/2004) FL 15+6/2*

BERESFORD David
Born: Middleton, 11 November 1976
Height: 5'5" **Weight:** 11.4
International Honours: E: Yth; Sch
David struggled to break into Plymouth Argyle's first team last season and in fact made only one substitute appearance before joining Macclesfield on loan in October. The tricky winger produced some sterling performances, but then became Brian Little's first signing for Tranmere Rovers. He immediately added a new dimension to the side with his ability to play out wide on either flank and became a provider of some useful crosses into the box. David grabbed his first goal for Rovers in the away win at Bournemouth and signed a new, longer-term contract as the season ended.
Oldham Ath *(From trainee on 22/7/1994) P/FL 32+32/2 FLC 3+3 FAC 0+1 Others 3*
Swansea C *(Loaned on 11/8/1995) FL 4+2*
Huddersfield T *(£350,000 on 27/3/1997) FL 24+11/3 FLC 2+3 FAC 1+1*
Preston NE *(Loaned on 17/12/1999) FL 1+3 FAC 0+1 Others 1*
Port Vale *(Loaned on 15/9/2000) FL 4*
Hull C *(Free on 4/7/2001) FL 33+8/1 FLC 2 FAC 1 Others 3*
Plymouth Arg *(Free on 23/7/2002) FL 6+11 Others 2*
Macclesfield T *(Loaned on 2/10/2003) FL 5 Others 0+1*
Tranmere Rov *(Free on 5/11/2003) FL 13+12/1 FAC 6*

BERESFORD Marlon
Born: Lincoln, 2 September 1969
Height: 6'1" **Weight:** 13.6
Marlon did an excellent short-term job early in the season for Bradford after injuries robbed them of both senior goalkeepers. He recorded a clean sheet on his debut to help the Yorkshire club to their first-ever win over Crystal Palace at Selhurst Park. A commanding figure between the posts, he moved on to Luton where he quickly organised his defence and kept three consecutive clean sheets. By far the most impressive of the four goalkeepers who played for the Hatters last term, he returned north to sign for Barnsley at the end of the year. Marlon quickly showed his worth with a string of outstanding performances, but missed the last few games of the campaign due to a back injury.
Sheffield Wed *(From trainee on 23/9/1987)*
Bury *(Loaned on 25/8/1989) FL 1*

David Beresford

*Northampton T (Loaned on 27/9/1990) FL
13 Others 2*
Crewe Alex (Loaned on 28/2/1991) FL 3
*Northampton T (Loaned on 15/8/1991)
FL 15*
*Burnley (£95,000 on 28/8/1992) FL 240 FLC
18 FAC 20 Others 16*
*Middlesbrough (£500,000 on 10/3/1998)
P/FL 8+2 FLC 3*
Sheffield Wed (Loaned on 12/1/2000) FL 4
Burnley (Loaned on 31/1/2002) FL 13
Burnley (Free on 19/7/2002)
York C (Free on 5/8/2002) FL 6
*Burnley (Free on 10/10/2002) FL 33+1 FLC 4
FAC 5*
Bradford C (Free on 15/9/2003) FL 5
*Luton T (Free on 24/10/2003) FL 11 FAC 5
Others 1*
Barnsley (Free on 26/1/2004) FL 14

BERGER Patrik
Born: Prague, Czechoslovakia, 10
November 1973
Height: 6'1" **Weight:** 12.6
Club Honours: FAC '01; UEFAC '01;
CS '01
International Honours: Czech Republic:
44; Czechoslovakia: 2; Yth (UEFA-U16
'90)
This vastly experienced and hugely
talented midfielder assisted Pompey last
season with five goals in 23 games. Cool
and confident, often the catalyst behind
the team's attacking moves, he scored a
double against Spurs on Boxing Day to
prove he is still a major threat, but missed
the second half of the campaign with a
knee injury. Patrik underwent knee
surgery in Colorado and has made good
progress throughout the summer.
*Liverpool (£3,250,000 from Borussia
Dortmund, Germany, ex Slavia Prague, on
15/8/1996) PL 106+42/28 FLC 9+2/3 FAC 4+4
Others 17+12/4*
*Portsmouth (Free on 12/7/2003) PL 20/5 FLC
1+1 FAC 1*

BERGKAMP Dennis Nicolaas
Born: Amsterdam, Holland, 18 May 1969
Height: 6'0" **Weight:** 12.5
Club Honours: PL '98, '02, '04; FAC '02,
'03; CS '98, '02
International Honours: Holland: 79;
U21
The magnificent Dutchman remains a
huge influence at Arsenal despite his
advancing years. Whilst he may not score
the volume of goals he did earlier in his
career, his advancing years have adjusted
his role at the club to creator rather than
scorer. He still registered five goals during
the club's record-breaking campaign

including the winner at home to Blackburn in December. The quality of his passing, general vision and awareness of his team mates' runs remain unsurpassed in the Premiership. There was no finer example of this than his contribution to Arsenal's last game of the season against Leicester. Two exemplary passes created the opportunity to turn what could have been defeat into a historic achievement. His fine season earned him a new deal in May.

Arsenal (£7,500,000 from Inter Milan, Italy, ex Ajax, on 3/7/1995) PL 225+37/77 FLC 15/8 FAC 29+5/14 Others 35+8/10

BERKOVIC Eyal

Born: Haifa, Israel, 2 April 1972
Height: 5'7'' **Weight:** 10.6
Club Honours: SLC '00; Div 1 '02
International Honours: Israel: 77; U21
This influential midfield playmaker started just three games for Manchester City last season. A series of niggling injuries kept him out of the side and when he returned he was unable to force his way into manager Kevin Keegan's plans. He joined Pompey during the transfer window. The little magician showed the ability to light up games, producing magnificent passes to set up goals for his colleagues after making his debut against his former team.

Southampton (Loaned from Maccabi Tel Aviv, Israel on 11/10/1996) PL 26+2/4 FLC 5+1/2 FAC 1
West Ham U (£1,700,000 on 30/7/1997) PL 62+3/10 FLC 6 FAC 7+1/2
Glasgow Celtic (£5,500,000 on 20/7/1999) SL 29+3/9 SLC 0+2 SC 1 Others 3+3
Blackburn Rov (Loaned on 9/2/2001) FL 4+7/2 FAC 3
Manchester C (£1,500,000 on 2/8/2001) P/FL 48+8/7 FLC 3+2/1 FAC 3+1/1 Others 2
Portsmouth (Free on 9/1/2004) PL 10+1/1 FAC 4

BERNARD Narada Michael

Born: Bristol, 30 January 1981
Height: 5'2" **Weight:** 10.5
International Honours: Jamaica: 1
Narada began the 2003-04 campaign with Woking before being offered a trial at Torquay. However, although he had looked a useful attacking left back for the Gulls in friendly matches, his only competitive appearance was cut short by injury after he came on as a substitute in the home game with York. He made a surprise debut in international football when he featured as a late substitute for Jamaica in their Unity Cup game against the Republic of Ireland in June.

Arsenal (From trainee at Tottenham H on 9/7/1999)
Bournemouth (Free on 31/7/2000) FL 13+16 FAC 2+1 Others 6+1 (Freed during 2003 close season)
Torquay U (Free from Woking on 17/11/2003) FL 0+1

BERNARD Olivier

Born: Paris, France, 14 October 1979
Height: 5'9" **Weight:** 12.6
Olivier has now established himself as first-choice left back for Newcastle, and the experience of playing regularly has enabled him to continue to improve his defensive qualities without compromising his attacking flair. A strong, quick tackler with a good turn of pace, his positional awareness grew during the 2003-04 campaign making him a difficult defender to overcome, while his left flank understanding with fellow countryman Laurent Robert facilitated his enjoyment of raiding down the wing and delivering dangerous crosses into the opposition's penalty box. His goals tend to be both rare and dramatic, as demonstrated by his counter at Highbury in September when he outflanked the Gunners' defence to run on to a Kieron Dyer pass and crash the ball into the roof of the net.

Newcastle U (Signed from Lyon, France, on 26/10/2000) PL 63+18/6 FLC 4 FAC 5 Others 21+5
Darlington (Loaned on 13/3/2001) FL 9+1/2

BERTHE Sekou

Born: Bamako, Mali, 7 October 1977
Height: 6'4" **Weight:** 13.0
International Honours: Mali
A tall, solid, wide-back defender, Sekou made his first appearance for West Bromwich Albion as a trialist during a tour to Denmark in July 2003. He impressed, was subsequently signed by manager Gary Megson and made his senior debut in the 2-1 Carling Cup win at Hartlepool two months later. He failed to establish himself in the side, however, and languished in the reserves for long periods.

West Bromwich A (Signed from Troyes, France, ex Monaco, on 3/9/2003) FL 2+1 FLC 1

BERTHELIN Cedric

Born: Courreres, France, 25 December 1976
Height: 6'4" **Weight:** 14.12
Cedric began last season as second choice to Matt Clarke for Crystal Palace, but when Clarke was injured he was given an extended run in the side. However, the big goalkeeper found himself sharing the

jersey with loanees Thomas Myhre and Nico Vaesen in the second half of the campaign.

Luton T (Free from ASOR Valence, France, ex RC Lens, on 1/10/2002) FL 9
Crystal Palace (Free on 31/12/2002) FL 26 FLC 3 FAC 3+1

BERTOS Leonida (Leo) Christos

Born: Wellington, New Zealand, 20 December 1981
Height: 6'0" **Weight:** 12.6
International Honours: New Zealand: Full; U23; Yth; Sch
Leo quickly became a permanent fixture in the Rochdale line-up last term, where he was employed in a right-wing role. In addition to his skills on the flank, he also showed considerable expertise with free kicks and became a regular contributor to the team's goals-for column. Leo remained one of the bright lights of the team during the second half of the campaign when Dale struggled at the wrong end of the table and he hit his tenth goal of the season in the crucial victory at Kidderminster. He made his full international debut for New Zealand against Iran in October and later spent a month away with the All Whites Olympic qualifying team, which narrowly failed to qualify for the Athens tournament.

Barnsley (Signed from Wellington Olympic, New Zealand on 1/9/2000) FL 4+8/1 FAC 0+1
Rochdale (Free on 25/7/2003) FL 40/9 FLC 1 FAC 1/1 Others 1

BESWETHERICK Jonathan (Jon) Barry

Born: Liverpool, 15 January 1978
Height: 5'11" **Weight:** 11.4
Club Honours: Div 3 '02
Jon had a somewhat disappointing time at Sheffield Wednesday last term when he again failed to win a regular place in the line-up. He spent a month on loan at Macclesfield to cover for suspensions and featured at left back and in a wide-left midfield role, but this failed to ignite his season at Hillsborough. Jon was one of several out-of-contract players released by the club in the summer.

Plymouth Arg (From trainee on 27/7/1996) FL 133+13 FLC 3 FAC 14+2 Others 4
Sheffield Wed (Free on 6/6/2002) FL 9+2 FAC 2+1 Others 1+1
Swindon T (Loaned on 21/2/2003) FL 3
Macclesfield T (Loaned on 16/1/2004) FL 3+1

BETSY Kevin Eddie Lewis

Born: Seychelles, 20 March 1978
Height: 6'1" **Weight:** 11.12
International Honours: E: SP-1

Kevin was Barnsley's leading appearance maker during the 2003-04 season, featuring in a variety of positions during the campaign. He was always at his best when he was able to run at defenders, and he scored a fine goal in the home match with Stockport. Kevin was the Reds' leading scorer with 11 goals in all competitions, but despite this he was made available for transfer in the summer.
Fulham (£80,000 + from Woking on 16/9/1998) P/FL 3+12/1 FLC 2+1 FAC 0+1 Others 1
Bournemouth (Loaned on 3/9/1999) FL 1+4
Hull C (Loaned on 26/11/1999) FL 1+1 Others 1
Barnsley (£200,000 on 28/2/2002) FL 84+10/15 FLC 2 FAC 6/1 Others 3

BETTS Robert
Born: Doncaster, 21 December 1981
Height: 5'10" **Weight:** 11.0
Robert began last term at Rochdale, where he played a handful of games and even managed to score twice at Torquay. However, he was unable to agree terms with the club and moved on to Kidderminster, where he had a brief run in the side but then rarely featured following a change in management. The defensive midfielder was released in March when he signed for Conference club Hereford United.
Doncaster Rov (Trainee) FL 2+1
Coventry C (From trainee on 23/12/1998) P/FL 5+8 FLC 1/1 FAC 2+1
Plymouth Arg (Loaned on 16/2/2001) FL 3+1
Lincoln C (Loaned on 11/10/2001) FL 1+2 Others 0+1
Rochdale (Free on 5/8/2003) FL 4+1/2 FLC 0+1
Kidderminster Hrs (Free on 12/9/2003) FL 8+1 FAC 0+1

BEVAN Scott Anthony
Born: Southampton, 16 September 1979
Height: 6'6" **Weight:** 15.10
Scott was well down the pecking order of goalkeepers at Southampton last term and he went out on loan to Woking and then Wycombe Wanderers, where he showed a commanding presence and impressed with his shot-stopping abilities. In March he made a permanent move to Wimbledon where he soon established himself in the side and quickly became a firm favourite with the club's supporters.
Southampton (From trainee on 16/1/1998)
Huddersfield T (Loaned on 27/7/2002) FL 30 FLC 2 FAC 1 Others 1
Wycombe W (Loaned on 16/1/2004) FL 5
Wimbledon (Free on 12/3/2004) FL 10

BEWERS Jonathan
Born: Wellingborough, 10 September 1982
Height: 5'9" **Weight:** 10.2
International Honours: E: Yth; Sch
Jonathan featured for Aston Villa's reserves last term, but was unable to force his way into the senior squad. After trials with Macclesfield and Bournemouth he was allowed to join Notts County on transfer-deadline day. A versatile player who can feature in midfield or in the centre of defence, he failed to impress in a handful of appearances from the substitutes' bench and was released in the summer.
Aston Villa (From trainee on 16/9/1999) PL 0+1
Notts Co (Free on 25/3/2004) FL 0+3

BIGGINS James William
Born: Nottingham, 6 June 1985
Height: 5'9" **Weight:** 11.8
International Honours: E: Yth
This young right back is another product of the Nottingham Forest Academy and made his senior debut against Port Vale in the Carling Cup last September. James also captained the reserves during a season which saw him collect the club's 'Academy Player of the Year' award. He will be hoping to get more chances in the first team in 2004-05.
Nottingham F (From trainee on 25/6/2002) FLC 1

BIGNOT Marcus
Born: Birmingham, 22 August 1974
Height: 5'10" **Weight:** 11.2
Club Honours: Div 3 '03
International Honours: E: SP-1
This talented right back was an ever-present for Rushden until mid-January, but on transfer-deadline day he re-joined Queens Park Rangers. He had a brief run in the side, helping the Loftus Road club win automatic promotion, but missed out on the last couple of games. Earlier in the season Marcus had scored his first goal for the Diamonds at Oldham.
Crewe Alex (£150,000 + from Kidderminster Hrs on 1/9/1997) FL 93+2 FLC 8 FAC 3
Bristol Rov (Free on 7/8/2000) FL 26/1 FLC 5/2 FAC 1 Others 3
Queens Park R (Signed on 16/3/2001) FL 49+5/1 FLC 1 FAC 1 Others 1
Rushden & Diamonds (Free on 8/8/2002) FL 68/2 FLC 1+1 FAC 4 Others 3
Queens Park R (Free on 25/3/2004) FL 6

BILLY Christopher (Chris) Anthony
Born: Huddersfield, 2 January 1973
Height: 5'11" **Weight:** 11.8

A hard-working and committed figure in Carlisle's midfield engine room, Chris got off to a slow start last term before producing some impressive performances. He was particularly effective in the away games at Bury and Huddersfield, but his presence and experience were missed in the crucial final weeks of the season, ironically just after he had opened his account with the winning goal in the 3-2 victory at Scunthorpe.
Huddersfield T (From trainee on 1/7/1991) FL 76+18/4 FLC 8+2 FAC 5 Others 15+2/2
Plymouth Arg (Signed on 10/8/1995) FL 107+11/9 FLC 5 FAC 8/1 Others 5+1
Notts Co (Signed on 10/8/1995) FL 3+3 FLC 2
Bury (Free on 17/9/1998) FL 165+13/11 FLC 6+1 FAC 7/1 Others 5+1
Carlisle U (Free on 7/8/2003) FL 39/1 FLC 0+1 Others 3

BIMSON Stuart James
Born: Liverpool, 29 September 1969
Height: 5'11" **Weight:** 11.12
This experienced left-footed defender joined Cambridge in the 2003 close season and was appointed as team captain. He was a regular in the side for the first half of the campaign, occasionally featuring in left or central midfield, before injury problems struck. Stuart also passed his UEFA coaching licence in preparation for when his playing days are over.
Bury (£12,500 from Macclesfield T on 6/2/1995) FL 36 FLC 5 Others 3
Lincoln C (Free on 29/11/1996) FL 157+18/4 FLC 2 FAC 7+2 Others 14+1/1
Cambridge U (Free on 31/7/2003) FL 21+3 FLC 1 FAC 1

BIRCH Gary Stephen
Born: Birmingham, 8 October 1981
Height: 5'10" **Weight:** 11.6
After getting the match winner in a pre-season game against Aston Villa, Gary enjoyed an extended run in the Walsall first team from October to February and scored in successive games against Norwich and Nottingham Forest in the space of four days early in November. He held the ball up well and at times used his weight to shake off opponents. He was loaned to Barnsley in the latter part of the campaign where he impressed with his work rate and ability to lead the line. Gary was an instant hit with the Reds' fans after scoring a late winner against Plymouth.
Walsall (From trainee on 31/10/1998) FL 31+24/5 FLC 0+2 FAC 1 Others 2/1
Exeter C (Loaned on 22/3/2001) FL 6+3/2

Exeter C (Loaned on 10/8/2001) FL 5+10 Others 1
Barnsley (Loaned on 25/3/2004) FL 8/2

BIRCH Mark

Born: Stoke, 5 January 1977
Height: 5'10" **Weight:** 12.5
Mark made only two early-season appearances for Carlisle last term before making the ten-mile journey across the border to sign for Gretna along with several of his former colleagues at Brunton Park. He scored a rare goal on his debut for the Scottish Third Division side against Stranraer and was a regular in the line-up for most of the campaign.
Stoke C (From trainee on 8/7/1995. Free to Northwich Vic on 22/7/98)
Carlisle U (£10,000 on 10/8/2000) FL 109+3/1 FLC 4 FAC 8 Others 4+1

BIRCHALL Christopher (Chris)

Born: Stafford, 5 May 1984
Height: 5'9" **Weight:** 12.12
This promising Port Vale right winger made a number of appearances from the substitutes' bench last term, the longest and most productive being a 45-minute stint at Notts County when he caused the home defence plenty of problems. His only full start was in the home defeat by Plymouth but he didn't let the experience affect him and retained his confidence.
Port Vale (From trainee on 1/5/2004) FL 1+12 FLC 0+1 FAC 1+2

BIRCHAM Marc Stephen John

Born: Wembley, 11 May 1978
Height: 5'10'' **Weight:** 12.4
Club Honours: Div 2 '01
International Honours: Canada: 17; U23-1
This competitive central-midfield player was a regular in the Queens Park Rangers line-up last term apart from injury and suspension, and contributed a couple of goals against Port Vale and Grimsby. Marc continued to represent Canada at international level during the campaign.
Millwall (From trainee on 22/5/1996) FL 86+18/3 FLC 3+1 FAC 6+1/1 Others 5+1
Queens Park R (Free on 10/7/2002) FL 70+4/4 FLC 3 FAC 2 Others 5

BIRD David Alan

Born: Gloucester, 26 December 1984
Height: 5'8" **Weight:** 12.2
David missed the opening stages of the 2003-04 campaign for Cheltenham through injury. However, once he had recovered fitness he settled down to enjoy a run of matches in the right-back

position leading up to Christmas. David later reverted to his preferred position, operating in the centre of either a four- or five-man midfield and finished the season in good form.
Cheltenham T (Signed from Cinderford T on 1/2/2001) FL 30+8 FLC 1 FAC 2 Others 1

BISCAN Igor

Born: Yugoslavia, 4 May 1978
Height: 6'3" **Weight:** 12.8
Club Honours: FLC '01, '03; ESC '01; CS '01
International Honours: Croatia: 15
After spending two seasons making little impact at Anfield, this midfielder enjoyed an unexpectedly long run in the Liverpool team as Sami Hyypia's partner in central defence from the start of the 2003-04 campaign. He was mostly deputising for Stephane Henchoz, but there came a point when it seemed that he had replaced the Swiss international in the team. However, he rarely looked comfortable in a central-defensive role.
Liverpool (£3,500,000 from Dynamo Zagreb, Croatia, ex Samobar, on 7/12/2000) PL 42+11 FLC 8+1/1 FAC 4+2 Others 6+9

BISCHOFF Mikkel

Born: Denmark, 3 February 1982
Height: 6'4" **Weight:** 13.5
International Honours: Denmark: U21-4; Yth
This promising Manchester City youngster is primarily a right-sided central defender but he is just as comfortable using his left foot. He made one senior appearance last season in the UEFA Cup qualifier second leg against TNS before being sidelined through injury. Mikkel had a frustrating time during the remainder of the campaign, when he was restricted to just nine appearances in the reserves as a string of injuries hampered his progress.
Manchester C (£750,000 from FC Copenhagen, Denmark on 2/7/2002) PL 1 Others 1

BISHOP Andrew (Andy) Jamie

Born: Stone, 19 October 1982
Height: 6'0" **Weight:** 11.2
This promising young Walsall striker spent much of the 2003-04 campaign out on loan, starting off with a spell at Kidderminster. He scored one of Harriers' goals with a long-range effort in the victory at Darlington in August. Later in the year Andy was off to Rochdale and he also spent time at Yeovil for whom he netted a vital winning goal on his debut against Oxford United. Andy

was out of contract with the Saddlers at the end of the season and at the time of writing his future was uncertain.
Walsall (From trainee on 9/8/2002)
Kidderminster Hrs (Loaned on 18/11/2002) FL 30+10/7 Others 0+1
Rochdale (Loaned on 20/11/2003) FL 8+2/1 FAC 1
Yeovil T (Loaned on 5/2/2004) FL 4+1/2

BJORKLUND Joachim

Born: Vaxjo, Sweden, 15 March 1971
Height: 6'1" **Weight:** 12.10
Club Honours: SPD '97; SLC '96
International Honours: Sweden: 75
Joachim had been told he could leave the Stadium of Light following Sunderland's relegation from the Premiership, but following a succession of injuries he began the 2003-04 campaign in the first team. Although he sustained a hamstring injury at Notts Forest on the opening day, Joachim returned in November and stayed in the side until February when he lost his place due to suspension. The experienced centre back is extremely quick, effective in the air, and an excellent man-marker and he played a crucial role in the Black Cats' run to the promotion play-offs. It has since been announced that Joachim will not be offered a new contract for 2004-05.
Glasgow R (Signed from Vicenza, Italy, ex Osters, Brann Bergen, Goteborg, on 15/7/1996) SL 59 SLC 5 SC 8 Others 13 (Transferred to Valencia, Spain during 1998 close season)
Sunderland ((£1,500,000 on 1/2/2002) P/FL 49+8 FLC 1 FAC 4+1 Others 1+1

BLACK Christopher (Chris) David

Born: Ashington, 7 September 1982
Height: 6'0" **Weight:** 12.0
This versatile young midfielder made just a single appearance for Sunderland last term, coming off the bench in the 3-0 defeat at Crewe in November. Later in the campaign he moved on to join Doncaster Rovers and made his debut in the game at Oxford shortly afterwards. Chris will be looking to establish himself in the line-up at Belle Vue during the 2004-05 campaign.
Sunderland (From trainee on 25/8/2000) P/FL 2+1
Doncaster Rov (Free on 25/3/2004) FL 1

BLACK Thomas (Tommy) Robert

Born: Chigwell, 26 November 1979
Height: 5'7" **Weight:** 11.4
This small busy striker signed a long-term

contract for Crystal Palace during the 2003 close season, but he was unable to produce his best form last term. A regular in the starting line-up in the first half of the campaign, thereafter his appearances came from the substitutes' bench.
Arsenal *(From trainee on 3/7/1998) PL 0+1 FLC 1*
Carlisle U *(Loaned on 25/8/1999) FL 5/1*
Bristol C *(Loaned on 17/12/1999) FL 4*
Crystal Palace *(£250,000 + on 21/7/2000) FL 67+59/10 FLC 13+3/5 FAC 3+1/2*

BLACKMAN Lloyd Jason
Born: Ashford, Middlesex, 24 September 1983
Height: 5'10" **Weight:** 12.3
This Brentford reserve-team striker had a disappointing time last season and made just four first-team appearances, all from the substitutes' bench. Lloyd spent time out on loan at Scarborough, Chelmsford and Cambridge City, but was released in the summer.
Brentford *(From trainee on 9/7/2002) FL 1+3 FLC 0+1*

BLAKE Nathan Alexander
Born: Cardiff, 27 January 1972
Height: 5'11" **Weight:** 13.2
Club Honours: WC '92, '93; Div 3 '93, Div 1 '97
International Honours: W: 29; B-1; U21-5; Yth
This powerful striker had a frustrating season as Wolves often played with just one man up front, Nathan or Steffen Iversen, and it was a demanding role. His only Premiership goal came at home to Newcastle in November, and was coolly taken. He had a calf injury at Spurs soon after and did not play again for a month. Nathan made his tenth Premiership start at Charlton in January, but then suffered a neck injury, which ultimately ended his season.
Cardiff C *(From trainee at Chelsea on 20/8/1990) FL 113+18/35 FLC 6+2 FAC 10/4 Others 13+2/1*
Sheffield U *(£300,000 on 17/2/1994) P/FL 55+14/34 FLC 3+1/1 FAC 1 Others 1*
Bolton W *(£1,500,000 on 23/12/1995) F/PL 102+5/38 FLC 10+1/8 FAC 6/2*
Blackburn Rov *(£4,250,000 on 30/10/1998) P/FL 37+17/13 FLC 3/1 FAC 5+3/2*
Wolverhampton W *(£1,400,000 on 13/9/2001) F/PL 70+5/24 FLC 3/1 FAC 2 Others 5/1*

BLAKE Robert (Robbie) James
Born: Middlesbrough, 4 March 1976
Height: 5'9" **Weight:** 12.6

Burnley's First Division survival in 2003-04 owed much to the form of Robbie Blake. His total of 22 goals for the season was comfortably his career best, but his contribution to the Clarets' cause was much more than as a pure finisher. Usually employed up front but sometimes behind a lone striker, he was a constant bag of tricks. Small, but strong, and difficult to shake off the ball, he was instrumental in most of the side's best moves and as often the maker as well as the taker of goals.
Darlington *(From trainee on 1/7/1994) FL 54+14/21 FLC 4+2/1 FAC 3+1 Others 3+1/1*
Bradford C *(£300,000 on 27/3/1997) P/FL 109+44/40 FLC 8+3/4 FAC 7/1 Others 3+1/2*
Nottingham F *(Loaned on 22/8/2000) FL 9+2/1 FLC 1*
Burnley *(£1,000,000 + on 25/1/2002) FL 79+17/32 FLC 7/2 FAC 6+1/4*

BLATHERWICK Steven (Steve) Scott
Born: Hucknall, 20 September 1973
Height: 6'1" **Weight:** 14.6
Steve continued to dominate at the centre of Chesterfield's defence last term. Almost unbeatable in the air, he thrived on responsibility, organising and cajoling his team mates. Steve often carried the attack at set pieces, flicking on long throws and remaining up to unsettle defences. At the time of writing the Spireites were hoping he would accept the offer of a new deal.
Nottingham F *(From trainee at Notts Co on 2/8/1992) FL 10 FLC 2 FAC 1 Others 2*
Wycombe W *(Loaned on 18/2/1994) FL 2 Others 1*
Hereford U *(Loaned on 11/9/1995) FL 10/1 Others 2*
Reading *(Loaned on 27/3/1997) FL 6+1*
Burnley *(£150,000 on 18/7/1997) FL 16+8 FLC 5 FAC 1+1 Others 3*
Chesterfield *(Loaned on 18/9/1998) FL 2*
Chesterfield *(£50,000 on 1/12/1998) FL 151+7/4 FLC 8 FAC 2+1 Others 9/1*

BLAYNEY Alan
Born: Belfast, 9 October 1981
Height: 6'2" **Weight:** 13.12
International Honours: NI: U23-1; U21-4
A perennial reserve, in a very useful second string, Alan was catapulted into first-team duty when a mystery virus saw Antti Niemi withdraw from the Southampton squad ten minutes before the warm-up of the penultimate game of the season, against Newcastle United. Alan acquitted himself well in a 'Man of the Match' performance in an exhilarating 3–3 draw, pulling off a brilliant close-

range stop from an Alan Shearer header. Noted as possessing an incredible throwing arm and comfortable in all his duties, Alan has had a lengthy wait for his Saints' debut.
Southampton *(From trainee on 13/7/2001) PL 2*
Stockport Co *(Loaned on 29/10/2002) FL 2 Others 1*
Bournemouth *(Loaned on 24/12/2002) FL 2*

BLINKHORN Matthew David
Born: Blackpool, 2 March 1985
Height: 5'11" **Weight:** 10.10
Club Honours: AMC '04
This young striker stepped up to the professional ranks with Blackpool last term, but was hampered by injury early on. Matthew came back strongly, scoring the winner in the LDV Vans Trophy game at Stockport County in December and was subsequently a regular member of the squad. A highlight of his campaign was coming off the bench in the final of the LDV Vans Trophy against Southend.
Blackpool *(From trainee on 28/6/2003) FL 7+15/3 Others 1+5/1*

BLIZZARD Dominic John
Born: High Wycombe, 2 September 1983
Height: 6'2" **Weight:** 13.5
Dominic, a product of the Watford Academy, made his first-team debut as a substitute against Norwich last April and marked the occasion with a goal. Normally a midfield player, he also caught the eye playing as a central defender for the reserves, combining his height with good technique and application. He was offered a new contract before the end of the season.
Watford *(From trainee on 19/4/2002) FL 1+1/1*

BLONDEL Jonathan
Born: Belgium, 3 April 1984
Height: 5'8" **Weight:** 10.12
International Honours: Belgium: 3; U21-7; Yth
This highly rated midfielder found chances few and far between at Tottenham last term, and made just two first-team appearances. A player who favours the attacking midfield role, he also has the ability to hold the midfield line when required. Concerned over a lack of first-team opportunities impacting upon his international career he returned to Belgium during the January transfer window, signing for Bruges.
Tottenham H *(£900,000 from Royal Excelsior Mouscron, Belgium on 16/7/2002) PL 0+2 FLC 1+1*

George Boateng (above)

BLOOMER Matthew (Matt) Brian
Born: Grimsby, 3 November 1978
Height: 6'0" **Weight:** 13.0
Matt proved a versatile player in the Lincoln back five. He fitted in well at both right wing back and centre back when needed. He was also used regularly from the substitutes' bench mainly to bolster the defence in the later stages of games or as a target man to hold the ball up front. At the end of the campaign he was offered a new 12-month contract with the Imps.
Grimsby T (From juniors on 3/7/1997) FL 3+9 FLC 0+2 Others 0+1
Hull C (Free on 5/7/2001) FL 0+3 FLC 1
Lincoln C (Loaned on 22/3/2002) FL 4+1
Lincoln C (Free on 31/12/2002) FL 17+23/1 FLC 1 FAC 2/1 Others 4+2

BLOOMFIELD Matthew (Matt) James
Born: Ipswich, 8 February 1984
Height: 5'9" **Weight:** 11.3
International Honours: E: Yth
Matt made his debut for Ipswich as a substitute in the Carling Cup game at Notts County but was given no further opportunities to experience first-team football before being allowed to join Wycombe. The busy midfielder stood out in his debut at home to Rushden, but then became a squad player, making the odd substitute appearance before a run of starts near the end of the season. His well-taken goal in the 2-2 home draw with Queens Park Rangers was a highlight of his campaign.
Ipswich T (From trainee on 3/7/2001) FLC 0+1
Wycombe W (Free on 24/12/2003) FL 10+2/1

BLUNDELL Gregg Steven
Born: Liverpool, 3 October 1977
Height: 5'10" **Weight:** 12.2
Club Honours: Div 3 '04
This talented striker started his first season in the Football League by scoring Doncaster's first goal in the competition for five years and was then a regular in the starting line-up throughout the campaign. A prolific goal-scorer in non-league circles, he coped well with the step-up to senior football and finished as Rovers' leading scorer with 20 goals in all competitions.
Tranmere Rov (From trainee on 9/7/1996. Free to Knowsley U on 30/11/1996)
Doncaster Rov (Free from Northwich Vic on 27/3/2003) FL 41+3/18 FLC 2/2 FAC 1

BOA MORTE Luis
Born: Lisbon, Portugal, 4 August 1977
Height: 5'10" **Weight:** 11.5
Club Honours: PL '98; Div 1 '01; CS '98, '99
International Honours: Portugal: 13; U21-28; Yth
Luis enjoyed an impressive season in which he was Fulham's second-highest goal-scorer with ten goals in all competition. He was at his best when used in a wide role on the left-hand side, where his pace and trickery unsettled opposing defences. Following the departure of Louis Saha he was occasionally played up front as a lone striker. Luis was again selected for Portugal on a number of occasions including an appearance against England, although he was omitted from the squad for Euro 2004.
Arsenal (£1,750,000 + from Sporting Lisbon, Portugal on 25/6/1997) PL 6+19 FLC 3/2 FAC 2+3/1 Others 2+4/1
Southampton (£500,000 + on 27/8/1999) PL 6+8/1 FLC 0+2 FAC 1
Fulham (£1,700,000 on 31/7/2000) P/FL 93+31/30 FLC 7+4/5 FAC 10+1/1 Others 10+2/2

BOATENG George
Born: Nkawkaw, Ghana, 5 September 1975
Height: 5'9" **Weight:** 11.7
Club Honours: FLC '04
International Honours: Holland: 2; U21-18
This likeable midfielder enjoyed another memorable season for Middlesbrough, missing only three Premiership games and his tremendous contribution to the club's historic season saw him voted as the supporters' 'Player of the Year'. Of course, George was a vital member of the Carling Cup winning squad and he reached his 250th senior appearance in England in the 2-1 victory over Bolton Wanderers.
Coventry C (£250,000 from Feyenoord, Holland, ex Excelsior, on 19/12/1997) PL 43+4/5 FLC 3/1 FAC 8/1
Aston Villa (£4,500,000 on 22/7/1999) PL 96+7/4 FLC 9+1/1 FAC 9 Others 13
Middlesbrough (£5,000,000 on 8/8/2002) PL 63 FLC 6 FAC 2

BOCANEGRA Carlos
Born: Alta Loma, California, USA, 25 May 1979
Height: 6'0" **Weight:** 12.4
International Honours: USA: 25
This defender joined Fulham during the mid-season transfer window and after an impressive debut at Newcastle established

himself immediately at left back replacing the injured Jerome Bonnissel. Solid in the tackle he proved a big asset to the Fulham back four and linked well with Luis Boa Morte on the left-hand side. Ever-present for the rest of season when available, Carlos continued to feature in the USA side after joining Fulham.
Fulham (Free from Chicago Fire, USA on 14/1/2004) PL 15 FAC 4

BOERTIEN Paul
Born: Haltwhistle, 21 January 1979
Height: 5'10" **Weight:** 11.2
When Paul went on loan to Notts County, it seemed as if his Derby days were numbered. He gave way earlier in the season to Luciano Zavagno and loan-signing Peter Kennedy, then Jamie Vincent joined the Rams. Paul slotted in well at left back during his stay at Meadow Lane, but was recalled to Pride Park to cover for injuries. He then produced his usual wholehearted commitment, making supporters wonder why he had not featured more regularly, but his season ended after the home match against Walsall at the beginning of April, when he injured cruciate knee ligaments and an ankle tendon.
Carlisle U (From trainee on 13/5/1997) FL 16+1/1 FLC 0+2 FAC 1 Others 1
Derby Co (£250,000 on 25/3/1999) P/FL 82+21/2 FLC 4+1 FAC 3+2
Crewe Alex (Loaned on 11/2/2000) FL 2
Notts Co (Loaned on 23/1/2004) FL 5

BOLAND William (Willie) John
Born: Ennis, Ireland, 6 August 1975
Height: 5'9" **Weight:** 11.2
International Honours: RoI: B-1; U21-11; Yth; Sch
This tenacious defensive midfield player was again in outstanding form for Cardiff City last term. He produced a series of consistent displays while his passing game improved as the season developed. However, despite his efforts he failed to win a call up for the Republic of Ireland international team in the summer.
Coventry C (From juniors on 4/11/1992) PL 43+20 FLC 6+1 FAC 0+1
Cardiff C (Free on 24/6/1999) FL 158+15/3 FLC 8+1 FAC 11+4/1 Others 6

BOLDER Adam Peter
Born: Hull, 25 October 1980
Height: 5'8" **Weight:** 11.0
After being absent only once in 2002-03, Adam found he had to fight for his place in the Derby midfield last season. He was prepared to battle hard in the reserves

Carlos Bocanegra

and whenever called on for the senior side he added a necessary urgency. Adam is not a complicated player but there is never any doubt about his courage and commitment. His eye for a goal was less evident, although he scored in the decisive victory over Millwall.
Hull C (From trainee on 9/7/1999) FL 18+2 Others 2+1
Derby Co (Signed on 3/4/2000) P/FL 51+31/7 FLC 2 FAC 3

BOLDER Christopher (Chris) James
Born: Hull, 19 August 1982
Height: 5'11" **Weight:** 12.4
This hard-tackling midfielder found it difficult to make an impression at Grimsby last term and managed just a handful of appearances in the starting line-up. Chris had a brief spell in the team early on, but then failed to make the squad until the arrival of Nicky Law as manager. He was released in the summer.
Grimsby T (From trainee at Hull C on 9/7/2001) FL 13+6 FAC 0+1

BOLLAND Paul Graham
Born: Bradford, 23 December 1979
Height: 5'11" **Weight:** 11.0
Paul was a regular member of the Notts County first-team squad in 2003-04. A hard-running, industrious midfielder who has also performed well as a full back, he netted just once, producing the winner at Chesterfield in September. Following last term's relegation, he will be looking forward to the challenge of gaining promotion for the Magpies in the 2004-05 campaign.
Bradford C (From trainee on 20/3/1998) FL 4+8 FLC 2
Notts Co (£75,000 on 14/1/1999) FL 115+17/5 FLC 1+6 FAC 4+1 Others 2+3/1

BOND Kain
Born: Torquay, 19 June 1985
Height: 5'8" **Weight:** 10.10
After graduating from the junior ranks, this young striker managed just one brief substitute appearance in his first campaign as a professional for Torquay United last term. However, he impressed sufficiently to earn an offer to stay at Plainmoor for the 2004-05 season.
Torquay U (From trainee on 2/7/2003) FL 0+2 FAC 0+1

BONNER Mark
Born: Ormskirk, 7 June 1974
Height: 5'10" **Weight:** 11.0
This gutsy, tenacious midfield player had a rather frustrating time at Cardiff last

season and after a good spell in the team in the first half of the campaign he dropped out of favour. In March he jumped at the chance of first-team football at Boundary Park and signed up for Oldham. Mark quickly became a regular in the line-up and produced a series of eye-catching displays for the Latics.
Blackpool (From trainee on 18/6/1992) FL 156+22/14 FLC 15+3 FAC 11 Others 10+3/1
Cardiff C (Free on 17/7/1998) FL 113+30/2 FLC 8 FAC 7+1 Others 8+3/1
Hull C (Loaned on 8/1/1999) FL 1/1
Oldham Ath (Free on 25/3/2004) FL 6+1

BONNISSEL Jerome
Born: Montpelier, France, 16 April 1973
Height: 5'8" **Weight:** 11.11
International Honours: France: B-5
Jerome joined Fulham in the summer of 2003 following successful trials during pre-season tours of Austria and Scotland. He immediately set about establishing himself as the first-choice left back and was ever-present in the opening 15 Premiership games before sustaining an ankle injury, despite a brief attempt at a comeback the injury eventually required an operation and ended his season. An attacking left-sided defender, Jerome linked up well with Luis Boa Morte.
Glasgow R (Loaned from Marseilles, France, ex Deportivo Coruna, Montpelier, on 27/1/2003) SL 2+1 SLC 1
Fulham (Free on 1/8/2003) PL 16

BOOK Steven (Steve) Kim
Born: Bournemouth, 7 July 1969
Height: 5'11" **Weight:** 11.1
Club Honours: FAT '98; NC '99
International Honours: E: SP-3
Steve found his opportunities at Cheltenham limited during 2003-04 due to the form of Shane Higgs. Steve began the season as the regular first-team 'keeper, but lost his place after just a handful of matches and spent much of the remainder of the campaign in the reserves. An agile goalkeeper, great shot stopper and irrepressible character, Steve was released in the summer.
Cheltenham T (Signed from Forest Green Rov on 23/7/1997) FL 171+1 FLC 7 FAC 12 Others 8

BOOTH Andrew (Andy) David
Born: Huddersfield, 6 December 1973
Height: 6'0" **Weight:** 13.0
International Honours: E: U21-3
Huddersfield's favourite son started last season alongside the young Jon Stead, and the big target man soon hit the goal-scoring trail with some important strikes.

Andy leads the line well and always causes plenty of trouble for opposition defenders, especially in the air. He finished the campaign as leading scorer for the Terriers and netted his 100th goal for the club in the final fixture of the regular season against Cheltenham Town.
Huddersfield T (From trainee on 1/7/1992) FL 109+14/54 FLC 10+1/3 FAC 8/3 Others 12+1/4
Sheffield Wed (£2,700,000 on 8/7/1996) P/FL 124+9/28 FLC 10+1/1 FAC 9+1/5
Tottenham H (Loaned on 30/1/2001) PL 3+1
Huddersfield T (£200,000 on 22/3/2001) FL 106+8/33 FLC 3/1 FAC 3 Others 11/3

BOOTY Martyn James
Born: Kirby Muxloe, 30 May 1971
Height: 5'8" **Weight:** 11.2
This experienced defender assumed the right-back berth for Huddersfield at the start of last season. A tough tackler with good distribution skills, Martyn also proved to be a good crosser of the ball. A change in team formation saw him sidelined on the bench and later in the campaign he was appointed as a member of the club's coaching staff.
Coventry C (From trainee on 30/5/1989) FL 4+1 FLC 2 FAC 2
Crewe Alex (Free on 7/10/1993) FL 95+1/5 FLC 6 FAC 8/1 Others 13
Reading (£75,000 on 18/1/1996) FL 62+2/1 FLC 10+1 FAC 7/1
Southend U (Free on 7/1/1999) FL 78+2 FLC 4 FAC 5 Others 2
Chesterfield (Free on 9/8/2001) FL 75+3/2 FLC 3 FAC 4 Others 3
Huddersfield T (Free on 7/8/2003) FL 3+1

BOPP Eugene
Born: Kiev, Ukraine, 5 September 1983
Height: 5'10" **Weight:** 12.4
Last season was a disappointing time for this young Nottingham Forest midfielder who found it difficult to string together a run of consistent performances. He made his first start against Portsmouth in the Carling Cup in October when he scored two goals, but he soon found himself out of the team again and after a change in management he found himself out of favour. Eugen returned to Germany to have a trial with Bundesliga side Hamburg in April before finishing the season in Forest's reserves.
Nottingham F (From trainee on 11/9/2000) FL 31+16/4 FLC 3+3/2 FAC 1

BORROWDALE Gary Ian
Born: Sutton, 16 July 1985
Height: 6'0" **Weight:** 12.1
International Honours: E: Yth

This promising youngster was a regular in the Crystal Palace squad until January of last season when he dropped out of contention. Gary is a versatile left-sided player who can feature in midfield or at full back. He was a member of the England U19 squad during the campaign.
Crystal Palace (From trainee on 6/12/2002) FL 22+14 FLC 2+3 FAC 1+1

BOSHELL Daniel (Danny) Kevin
Born: Bradford, 30 May 1981
Height: 5'11" **Weight:** 11.10
This cultured midfield player was enjoying his best season to date with Oldham until injury struck last March. In only the third game under new manager Brian Talbot, Danny damaged a knee ligament and this effectively ended his. He signed a new contract for the Latics in the summer.
Oldham Ath (From trainee on 10/7/1998) FL 35+19/1 FLC 4/1 FAC 3+1 Others 3/1

BOSSU Bertrand (Bert)
Born: Calais, France, 14 October 1980
Height: 6'7" **Weight:** 14.0
Bertrand joined Gillingham soon after the start of last season and made his debut for the club at Walsall soon afterwards. He was recalled for the FA Cup third round tie against Charlton on 3 January and won national headlines with his heroics. His joy was short-lived, however, as he was dropped for the next home game against Sheffield United and replaced by on-loan 'keeper Nico Vaessen from Birmingham. Bertrand added a handful more appearances towards the end of the campaign.
Barnet (Signed from RC Lens, France on 21/10/1999) Others 0+1 (Transferred to Hayes on 3/8/2001)
Gillingham (Free on 9/9/2003) FL 3+1 FAC 2

BOSSY Fabien
Born: Marseilles, France, 1 October 1977
Height: 6'2" **Weight:** 12.6
This hard-tackling but creative midfielder made his debut for Darlington in the penalty-shoot-out win at Bradford City in the Carling Cup last August. However after a handful of appearances in early-season games Fabien failed to figure in the first team after Christmas and was released before the end of the campaign.
Clydebank (Signed from Visieux, France, ex Montpelier, Academica, on 16/2/2001) SL 41+2 SLC 1 SC 2 Others 2
Ayr U (Signed on 1/8/2002) SL 1 SLC 1
Clyde (Signed on 12/8/2002) SL 11+4
Darlington (Free on 8/8/2003) FL 4+2 FLC 1 Others 1

BOSVELT Paul
Born: Doetinchem, Holland, 26 March 1970
Height: 6'0" **Weight:** 13.3
International Honours: Holland: 24
Paul jumped at the opportunity to come and chance his arm in the Premiership, joining Manchester City during the 2003 close season. He is a powerful, athletic and astute user of the ball but had a tough start to life at the City of Manchester Stadium and took time to adjust to the English game. However once settled he kept his place in the side with a series of polished displays in the middle of the park.
Manchester C (Signed from Feyenoord, Holland, ex GAE Deventer, Twente Enschede, on 29/7/2003) PL 22+3 FLC 1 FAC 4/1 Others 4+1

BOUAZZA Hameur
Born: Evry, France, 22 February 1985
Height: 5'10" **Weight:** 12.0
Hameur, a left-sided striker developed by the Watford Academy, made his Football League debut as a substitute against Sunderland last February. Speedy and strong, he did well enough to start the next match, against Preston, and claimed his first senior goal. Unfortunately, he suffered an ankle injury in the same game, which ruled him out until just before the end of the season. Hameur was offered a professional contract before the end of the season.
Watford (Trainee) FL 6+3/1

BOUCAUD Andre
Born: Enfield, 9 October 1984
Height: 5'10" **Weight:** 11.4
International Honours: Trinidad & Tobago: 3
Andre started the 2003-04 season on loan with Peterborough again and showed once more what a talented youngster he is. The skilful midfielder was not afraid to take on opponents with his speed and close ball control, and opened his goal-scoring account with an exquisite chip at Brentford. However, on his return to the Madejski Stadium he failed to make a breakthrough and was released in the summer. He was reported to have signed permanently for Posh soon afterwards. Andre also featured at international level for Trinidad during the summer.
Reading (From trainee on 25/3/2002)
Peterborough U (Loaned on 27/3/2003) FL 12+2/1 FLC 1

BOULDING Michael (Mick) Thomas
Born: Sheffield, 8 February 1976
Height: 5'10" **Weight:** 11.4
This pacy striker began the 2003-04 season in fine form for Grimsby Town, finding the net regularly. However, despite being the club's leading scorer Michael seemed to lose his appetite for goals and following a change in management at Blundell Park he was sold to Barnsley. After a while settling in at Oakwell he began to show a new lease of life before injury brought his campaign to a premature close.
Mansfield T (Signed from Hallam FC on 2/8/1999) FL 28+38/12 FLC 2+2 FAC 2+1 Others 1+1
Grimsby T (Free on 24/8/2001) FL 24+11/11 FLC 0+2 FAC 0+2
Aston Villa (Free on 9/7/2002) Others 2/1
Sheffield U (Loaned on 29/9/2002) FL 3+3 FLC 1/1
Grimsby T (Free on 10/1/2003) FL 37+2/16 FLC 1 FAC 1/1 Others 0+1
Barnsley (£50,000 on 12/2/2004) FL 5+1

BOUND Matthew (Matt) Terence
Born: Melksham, 9 November 1972
Height: 6'2" **Weight:** 14.6
Club Honours: Div 3 '00
Matt was the one of the best of the centre backs employed by Oxford last term and the big man had a very impressive season. Strong in the air and very committed, he let very few players pass him easily. He scored a late goal in the defeat at Hull but missed out on a few games towards the end of the season when a new defensive formation was employed. Matt's contract was not renewed in the summer but he will surely find a club in need of a rugged defender.
Southampton (From trainee on 3/5/1991) F/PL 2+3
Hull C (Loaned on 27/8/1993) FL 7/1
Stockport Co (£100,000 on 27/10/1994) FL 44/5 FLC 1 FAC 3/1 Others 3/1
Lincoln C (Loaned on 11/9/1995) FL 3+1 Others 1
Swansea C (£55,000 on 21/11/1997) FL 173+1/9 FLC 8/2 FAC 10 Others 8+1/2
Oxford U (Free on 21/12/2001) FL 96+4/2 FLC 5 FAC 4 Others 2

BOUSSATTA Dries
Born: Amsterdam, Holland, 23 December 1972
Height: 5'8" **Weight:** 10.6
International Honours: Holland: 3
Dries signed for Sheffield United in

November until the end of the season. His opportunities were limited, with just four starts playing an attacking role on the right side of midfield. He showed good control and produced some useful crosses. After being subbed, for tactical reasons, only 14 minutes after coming on as a substitute he amicably agreed to terminate his contract early.

Sheffield U (Free from SC Excelsior, Holland, ex Telstar, Ajax, Haarlem, FC Utrecht, AZ Alkmaar, on 5/11/2003) FL 3+3 FAC 1

BOWDITCH Dean Peter

Born: Bishops Stortford, 15 June 1986
Height: 5'11" **Weight:** 11.7
International Honours: E: Yth
Dean scored his first goal for Ipswich in extra-time of the Carling Cup match against Kidderminster and made his first start in the next round of the same competition, at Notts County. Joe Royle was very protective of his talent and only used him sparingly from the substitutes' bench but when he did appear he excited the crowd with his ability to beat players. He had a run in the team in March and created club history when he became the youngest player to score a hat-trick, achieving the feat against Watford at Portman Road.

Ipswich T (From trainee on 28/7/2003) FL 7+14/4 FLC 1+1/1 FAC 0+1 Others 0+1

BOWEN Jason Peter

Born: Merthyr Tydfil, 24 August 1972
Height: 5'7" **Weight:** 11.0
Club Honours: AMC '94
International Honours: W: 2; B-1; U21-5; Yth; Sch
One of the most skilful players on the books at Cardiff City, Jason could not find the consistency to earn a first-team place and made only two First Division appearances, both from the substitutes' bench. His best role has always been sitting just behind the front two strikers, but he is also effective in a wide-right position and as an out-and-out striker. His balance and skill can pull defences apart, but he was eventually released in April.

Swansea C (From trainee on 1/7/1990) FL 93+31/26 FLC 6+1/2 FAC 9+2/1 Others 10+2/4
Birmingham C (£350,000 on 24/7/1995) FL 35+13/7 FLC 4+6/2 FAC 1+4 Others 2/2
Southampton (Loaned on 2/9/1997) PL 1+2
Reading (£200,000 on 24/12/1997) FL 12+3/1 FLC 1+1 FAC 5
Cardiff C (Free on 12/11/1999) FL 105+29/34 FLC 6/2 FAC 15+2 Others 2+2/1

BOWER Mark James

Born: Bradford, 23 January 1980
Height: 5'10" **Weight:** 11.0
Mark had earned a regular slot on the left side of central defence for Bradford City in the 2002-2003 campaign, but found himself behind Jason Gavin in the pecking order last season. He did not play his first game until Wimbledon away in November, when he partnered Gavin because David Wetherall was injured. A hard-working performer who does the job with the minimum of fuss, Mark never let anyone down when he was called into the side. After being left out following a 3-1 loss at Ipswich, Mark did particularly well on his recall a month later against Wigan.

Bradford C (From trainee on 28/3/1998) P/FL 57+7/2 FLC 3 FAC 2+1 Others 1
York C (Loaned on 16/2/2000) FL 15/1
York C (Loaned on 30/11/2000) FL 21/1 FAC 3 Others 0+1

BOWRY Robert (Bobby) John

Born: Hampstead, 19 May 1971
Height: 5'9" **Weight:** 10.8
Club Honours: Div 1 '94
International Honours: St Kitts & Nevis
Bobby spent much of the 2003-04 season on the substitutes' bench, until he finally dislodged Thomas Pinault from the centre of midfield for Colchester. A defensive midfielder, at his best when shadowing opponents, he nevertheless rarely wasted a pass. Bobby's recall to the team coincided with the 2-0 home win over Grimsby in February, after which he missed only one more game.

Crystal Palace (Free from Carshalton on 4/4/1992) F/PL 36+14/1 FLC 10 FAC 1
Millwall (£220,000 on 5/7/1995) FL 125+15/5 FLC 9+1 FAC 6 Others 4
Colchester U (Free on 25/7/2001) FL 78+17/2 FLC 2+2 FAC 3+1 Others 5+1

BOWYER Lee David

Born: London, 3 January 1977
Height: 5'9" **Weight:** 10.6
International Honours: E: 1; U21-13; Yth
Lee's 2003-04 season at Newcastle was blighted by injuries. A foot operation impaired his pre-season preparation, although he played regularly until late November when a hip problem sidelined him for three months, and after he returned he continued to suffer from a niggling hamstring. A versatile midfielder full of energy and with a biting tackle, his trademark runs behind the opposing defence have yet to be properly exploited by the Magpies. Used primarily on the

right flank of midfield, he prefers the central role. He turned in a 'Man of the Match' performance when ten-man United held Villa to a draw in April, and again in the home draw with Wolves in May, when he netted his first goal for the club, following up with a second three days later.

Charlton Ath (From trainee on 13/4/1994) FL 46/8 FLC 6+1/5 FAC 3/1 Others 2
Leeds U (£2,600,000 on 5/7/1996) PL 196+7/38 FLC 7+1/1 FAC 16/3 Others 38/13
West Ham U (£100,000 on 8/1/2003) PL 10 FAC 1
Newcastle U (Free on 7/7/2003) PL 17+7/2 Others 0+1

BOXALL Daniel (Danny) James

Born: Croydon, 24 August 1977
Height: 5'8" **Weight:** 11.10
Club Honours: Div 3 '99
International Honours: RoI: U21-8
Danny was a regular at right back for Bristol Rovers during the first three months of last season before falling out of favour and asking to be transfer listed. He returned to the starting line-up in January but unfortunately then picked up a knee injury, which necessitated surgery and ruled him out for the remainder of the campaign. Danny was released in the summer.

Crystal Palace (From trainee on 19/4/1995) F/PL 5+3 FLC 1+1
Oldham Ath (Loaned on 21/11/1997) FL 6 Others 1
Oldham Ath (Loaned on 27/2/1998) FL 12
Brentford (Free on 9/7/1998) FL 62+6/1 FLC 6 FAC 4 Others 5+1
Bristol Rov (Free on 2/7/2002) FL 58+5 FLC 2 FAC 4 Others 2

BOYCE Emmerson Orlando

Born: Aylesbury, 24 September 1979
Height: 5'11" **Weight:** 11.10
Emmerson's overall game continued to improve last season and this was recognised when he swept the board at Luton's annual awards evening in May. A central defender who is equally at home playing as a full back, his positional sense and reading of the game were valuable assets for the team. He was out of contract in the summer and his future was unclear at the time of writing.

Luton T (From trainee on 2/4/1998) FL 171+15/8 FLC 11 FAC 9+3/1 Others 3

BOYD Adam Mark

Born: Hartlepool, 25 May 1982
Height: 5'9" **Weight:** 10.12
Adam found himself out of the first-team

picture at Hartlepool last term following a change in management. He was loaned out to Boston United, where he was a revelation playing on the right side of a two-man attack. However, when a proposed transfer fell through he was added to the Hartlepool first-team squad, and almost immediately everything fell into place. Adam finished the season a scoring sensation, with his 12 goals in the last ten games being a major factor in the club's success in winning a place in the Division Two play-offs.

Hartlepool U (From trainee on 20/9/1999) FL 34+44/27 FLC 1 FAC 0+2 Others 5+3
Boston U (Loaned on 14/11/2003) FL 14/4

BOYD Marc Edward
Born: Carlisle, 22 October 1981
Height: 5'10" **Weight:** 12.4
This skilful midfield player began the 2003-04 season with Port Vale, but found himself in and out of the line-up. In March he decided to return to his hometown club, Carlisle where he featured regularly in the closing stages of the campaign. He scored with a long-range strike at Scunthorpe but was released following the Cumbrian club's relegation to the Conference.

Newcastle U (From trainee on 22/10/1998)
Port Vale (Free on 1/7/2002) FL 39+3/3 FLC 1 FAC 4 Others 2+1/1
Carlisle U (Free on 18/3/2004) FL 9/1

BRACKENRIDGE Stephen (Steve) James
Born: Rochdale, 31 July 1984
Height: 5'8" **Weight:** 11.3
After progressing through the Macclesfield youth ranks, Steve was awarded his first professional contract in the summer of 2003. His opportunities in the senior squad came when others were either injured or suspended, with most of his appearances coming from the substitutes' bench. Steve netted on two consecutive occasions in December including the winning goal at Darlington. A regular in the reserve side playing in a wide-right midfield position, he is an excellent passer of the ball and always displays pace and confidence.

Macclesfield T (From trainee on 4/7/2003) FL 2+7/2 FAC 1+1

BRACKSTONE John
Born: Hartlepool, 9 February 1985
Height: 5'11" **Weight:** 10.8
A third-year scholar with Hartlepool, this promising young left back has excelled with the youth team. Proud to be playing for his hometown club, he was gradually

introduced to first-team football last term, and in mid-season was rewarded with a short run with the seniors. He received good reports for his defensive displays, but was unable to win a regular place and his progress was later beset with a bout of pleurisy. John was rewarded with a professional contract shortly before the end of the campaign.

Hartlepool U (From trainee on 16/3/2004) FL 5+1 FAC 1/1

BRACKSTONE Stephen (Steve)
Born: Hartlepool, 19 September 1982
Height: 5'11" **Weight:** 11.2
International Honours: E: Yth
This young midfielder never fully established himself in the York City side last term. The high points of his season came when he netted a fine goal in the home win over Cambridge United and then when he scored the equaliser in the 2-2 draw at Leyton Orient. Steve did not figure in the first team for the Minstermen in the final three months of the campaign and was released by the club in the summer.

Middlesbrough (From trainee on 7/7/2000)
York C (Signed on 27/2/2002) FL 32+12/4 FLC 1 FAC 2+1 Others 1

BRADBURY Lee Michael
Born: Isle of Wight, 3 July 1975
Height: 6'2" **Weight:** 13.10
International Honours: E: U21-3
This bustling striker was out of the reckoning for a first-team place at Portsmouth last season and began the new campaign on loan at Derby. He actually had two spells at Pride Park, returning to Pompey in between to recuperate from a broken bone in his foot. However, he never really showed his sharpest form and he was unable to find the goals that Derby needed so desperately. Later in the campaign he signed a short-term contract for Walsall, but although he battled hard he was unable to save the club from relegation and was released in the summer.

Portsmouth (Free from Cowes on 14/8/1995) FL 41+13/15 FLC 1+2 FAC 4/2
Exeter C (Loaned on 1/12/1995) FL 14/5
Manchester C (£3,000,000 + on 1/8/1997) FL 34+6/10 FLC 6/1
Crystal Palace (£1,500,000 on 29/10/1998) FL 28+4/6 FLC 3+1/1 FAC 1/1
Birmingham C (Loaned on 25/3/1999) FL 6+1 Others 1+1
Portsmouth (£380,000 on 14/10/1999) FL 90+9/28 FLC 3+2 FAC 2/1
Sheffield Wed (Loaned on 24/12/2002) FL 2+1

Sheffield Wed (Loaned on 1/3/2003) FL 8/3
Derby Co (Loaned on 14/8/2003) FL 1
Derby Co (Loaned on 20/11/2003) FL 6
Walsall (Free on 25/3/2004) FL 7+1/1

BRAIN Jonathan (Jonny) Robert
Born: Carlisle, 11 February 1983
Height: 6'2" **Weight:** 12.4
This tall, commanding goalkeeper joined Port Vale last August as cover for the injured Mark Goodlad. Jonny made his debut in the LDV Vans Trophy defeat of Scarborough, did well in the following week's 2-0 victory over Queens Park Rangers and retained his place for the rest of the season. Despite being a relative novice his confidence grew and he turned in some excellent performances.

Port Vale (Free from trainee at Newcastle U, via trials at Carlisle U, on 21/8/2003) FL 32 FAC 3 Others 1

BRAMBLE Tesfaye (Tes) Walda Simeon
Born: Ipswich, 20 July 1980
Height: 6'1" **Weight:** 13.10
Last term proved to be a disappointing time for this young Southend striker, for he made almost as many appearances from the substitutes' bench as in the starting line-up. Unable to regularly displace Drewe Broughton, Leon Constantine and Lawrie Dudfield in the Southend attack, Tes had little chance to show the skills that he undoubtedly possesses, and at times he was on the fringes of the first-team squad. He will be looking to regain his place in the line-up in the 2004-05 season.

Southend U (Signed from Cambridge C on 19/1/2001) FL 91+28/28 FLC 1+2 FAC 13/7 Others 9+2/3

BRAMBLE Titus Malachi
Born: Ipswich, 21 July 1981
Height: 6'1" **Weight:** 13.10
International Honours: E: U21-10
Titus is a big strong defender who plays at the centre of Newcastle's back four. Although he started the 2003-04 season on the bench he was quickly called up into the starting line-up and became a regular for most of the campaign, scoring his first goal for the club in the UEFA Cup tie at home to NAC Breda in September, and following up with further strikes against Basel and Mallorca. Comfortable on the ball, he distributes it well over long and short distances and visibly grew in confidence as the season progressed, helped undoubtedly by the composed presence of Jonathan Woodgate.

Ipswich T (From trainee on 24/8/1998) P/FL 41+7/1 FLC 4+1/2 FAC 4+1 Others 4/1
Colchester U (Loaned on 29/12/1999) FL 2
Newcastle U (£5,000,000 on 19/7/2002) PL 40+5 FLC 1 FAC 1 Others 19/3

BRAMMER David (Dave)
Born: Bromborough, 28 February 1975
Height: 5'10" **Weight:** 12.0
Club Honours: AMC '01
This hard-working midfielder was again captain of Crewe Alexandra last term. He missed a large part of the campaign through injury, but came back for the last six games when his skills were well in evidence in the centre of the park. Dave only scored once in the season, that being in the opening game at Wimbledon.
Wrexham (From trainee on 2/7/1993) FL 118+19/12 FLC 6+2 FAC 8+2/1 Others 12+1/1
Port Vale (£350,000 + on 24/3/1999) FL 71+2/3 FLC 2 FAC 2/1 Others 7
Crewe Alex (£500,000 on 10/8/2001) FL 86+1/4 FLC 6/1 FAC 8/1 Others 2

BRANCH Graham
Born: Liverpool, 12 February 1972
Height: 6'2" **Weight:** 12.2
Installed as Burnley's captain before the start of the season, Graham began last term in central defence. Sadly, his form at the back rarely lived up to the promise of the previous campaign and his season developed into something of a stop-start affair, with his versatility again becoming both his best asset and the main drawback to an automatic starting place. He was also plagued by injury, a calf muscle tear keeping him sidelined for a month, but he ended the season on a high, playing in a more attacking role and sometimes as an out-and-out striker. Graham's goal in the home game against West Ham was his first for three years and he added two more before the end of the season.
Tranmere Rov (Free from Heswall on 2/7/1991) FL 55+47/10 FLC 4+8/1 FAC 1+2 Others 2+1
Bury (Loaned on 20/11/1992) FL 3+1/1 Others 1
Wigan Ath (Loaned on 24/12/1997) FL 2+1
Stockport Co (Free on 31/7/1998) FL 10+4/3 FLC 1
Burnley (Free on 31/12/1998) FL 140+39/12 FLC 8+3 FAC 8+5 Others 1

BRANCH Paul Michael
Born: Liverpool, 18 October 1978
Height: 5'10" **Weight:** 11.7
International Honours: E: U21-1; Yth; Sch

A nimble and speedy striker, Michael made an immediate impact for Bradford City by coming off the bench to score a stoppage-time equaliser against Norwich on his home debut. That was the first of six goals for the former Wolves player, who also netted against Crystal Palace to help the Bantams earn their first-ever win at Selhurst Park. However, the best moment of his season came in Bryan Robson's first game in charge against Millwall in November. Bradford were 2-0 down at half-time but roared back in the second half to win with Michael showing a cool head to burst clear one-on-one with goalkeeper Tony Warner and slot home the decisive goal.
Everton (From trainee on 24/10/1995) PL 16+25/3 FLC 0+1 FAC 1+2
Manchester C (Loaned on 29/10/1998) FL 4
Wolverhampton W (£500,000 + on 25/11/1999) FL 61+11/10 FLC 2+1 FAC 4
Reading (Loaned on 21/3/2002) FL 0+2
Hull C (Loaned on 4/10/2002) FL 6+1/3
Bradford C (Free on 17/7/2003) FL 29+4/6 FLC 1 FAC 0+1

BRANDON Christopher (Chris) William
Born: Bradford, 7 April 1976
Height: 5'7" **Weight:** 10.3
Always a potential match-winner, Chris's individuality made him a bit of a luxury player at Chesterfield last term until he developed the defensive side of his game. Chris put the dangerous Martin Rowlands in his pocket when Queens Park Rangers visited, and eventually matured into a significant member of the side. He bravely played through several months of intermittent cramp attacks, which doctors and dieticians are working on to further improve his effectiveness.
Torquay U (Free from Bradford PA on 5/8/1999) FL 64+7/8 FLC 4/1 FAC 5/1 Others 3
Chesterfield (Free on 9/7/2002) FL 74+5/11 FLC 2+1/1 FAC 2 Others 4/4

BRANIFF Kevin Robert
Born: Belfast, 4 March 1983
Height: 5'11" **Weight:** 12.0
International Honours: NI: U23-1; U21-8; Yth; Sch
This tricky Millwall forward has good pace and a stinging shot. However, owing to the quality of other strikers at the club, Kevin was in and out of the team last term, but whenever he was called upon, he acquitted himself well, putting many a defender under pressure. He was reported to have signed for Rushden during the summer.

Millwall (From trainee on 12/4/2000) FL 13+19/1 FLC 3+2/1 FAC 2+6/1

BRANNAN Gerard (Ged) Daniel
Born: Prescot, 15 January 1972
Height: 6'0" **Weight:** 12.3
Unable to break into the Wigan Athletic first-team squad, Ged joined Rochdale on loan last autumn. He filled the need for an experienced midfielder, and he played regularly throughout a two-month spell at Spotland. However, soon after returning to Wigan he made a permanent move to Conference outfit Accrington Stanley.
Tranmere Rov (From trainee on 3/7/1990) FL 227+11/20 FLC 26+1/4 FAC 10+1 Others 26+1/1
Manchester C (£750,000 on 12/3/1997) FL 38+5/4 FLC 2 FAC 1
Norwich C (Loaned on 21/8/1998) FL 10+1/1 FLC 1
Motherwell (£378,000 on 28/10/1998) SL 81/16 SLC 3+1 SC 7/2
Wigan Ath (£175,000 on 16/2/2001) FL 49+3 FLC 1/1 Others 2
Dunfermline Ath (Loaned on 31/1/2003) SL 8 SC 4
Rochdale (Loaned on 11/9/2003) FL 11/1 FAC 1 Others 1

BRANSTON Guy Peter Bromley
Born: Leicester, 9 January 1979
Height: 6'0" **Weight:** 13.12
First-team opportunities were few and far between for Guy at Rotherham last term, and although he took his tally of starting League appearances for the Millers to the century mark he spent much of the season out on loan. In September he arrived at Wycombe to help shore up a leaky defence and impressed as a robust left-sided central defender. He also performed a similar role for Peterborough in the final three months of the season, where he was again in fine form. Guy was released by Rotherham in the summer and was reported to have signed for neighbours Sheffield Wednesday.
Leicester C (From trainee on 3/7/1997)
Colchester U (Loaned on 9/2/1998) FL 12/1 Others 1
Colchester U (Loaned on 7/8/1998) FL 0+1
Plymouth Arg (Loaned on 20/11/1998) FL 7/1 Others 1
Lincoln C (Loaned on 10/8/1999) FL 4 FLC 2
Rotherham U (£50,000 on 15/10/1999) FL 101+3/13 FLC 5+1 FAC 4 Others 2
Wycombe W (Loaned on 19/9/2003) FL 9 Others 2/1
Peterborough U (Loaned on 25/2/2004) FL 14

BRASS Christopher (Chris) Paul
Born: Easington, 24 July 1975
Height: 5'10" **Weight:** 12.6
Last season proved to be a rather traumatic one for York City's young player-manager as the club finished bottom of the Third Division table and slipped into the Conference. Chris was, as usual, an energetic and inspirational leader both on and off the field and he approached management with total commitment. A near ever-present in defence, he managed to score once, netting in the home win over Carlisle in January.
Burnley (From trainee on 8/7/1993) FL 120+14/1 FLC 8+1 FAC 6+1 Others 8+2
Torquay U (Loaned on 14/10/1994) FL 7 FAC 2 Others 1
Halifax T (Loaned on 22/9/2000) FL 6
York C (Free on 15/3/2001) FL 128+2/5 FLC 3/1 FAC 8/1 Others 1+1

BRAYSON Paul
Born: Newcastle, 16 September 1977
Height: 5'7" **Weight:** 10.10
International Honours: E: Yth
Paul was again in and out of the first team at Cheltenham last term. Quick, with clever movement and a good finisher, he excelled at finding pockets of space in and around the opposition penalty area with darting runs and a delicate touch. Paul scored eight goals in all competitions, but was often used as an impact player, changing the nature of the attack when coming off the substitutes' bench. However, an inability to hold down a regular place resulted in his being released at the end of the season.
Newcastle U (From trainee on 1/8/1995) FLC 1+1
Swansea C (Loaned on 30/1/1997) FL 11/5
Reading (£100,000 on 26/3/1998) FL 15+26/1 FLC 0+2 FAC 1+1 Others 2
Cardiff C (Free on 16/3/2000) FL 48+36/19 FLC 2 FAC 3+4/1 Others 1
Cheltenham T (Free on 7/8/2002) FL 34+17/8 FLC 0+1 FAC 3+1/2 Others 2/2

BRAZIER Matthew Ronald
Born: Leytonstone, 2 July 1976
Height: 5'8" **Weight:** 11.6
Matthew started last season as a first choice in midfield for Leyton Orient and scored a cracking 25-yard effort in the home game against Yeovil. However, he then fell out of favour and was transfer listed at his own request. Matthew subsequently spent time on trial with Oxford and Queens Park Rangers

before being released on a free transfer during the summer.
Queens Park R (From trainee on 1/7/1994) P/FL 36+13/2 FLC 3+2/1 FAC 3
Fulham (£65,000 on 20/3/1998) FL 4+5/1 FAC 2+1 Others 1
Cardiff C (Loaned on 28/8/1998) FL 11/2
Cardiff C (£100,000 on 9/7/1999) FL 43+13/3 FLC 2+3/1 FAC 5+1/1 Others 2
Leyton Orient (Free on 31/1/2002) FL 46/2 FLC 3 FAC 0+1 Others 0+1

BRECKIN Ian
Born: Rotherham, 24 February 1975
Height: 6'0" **Weight:** 12.9
Club Honours: AMC '96
After waiting patiently for his chance, this Wigan Athletic centre back was an automatic choice last season, putting in some excellent performances. A classy and composed central defender, he formed an effective partnership firstly with Matt Jackson and then Jason De Vos in the heart of the defence. An honest, committed and dedicated player, Ian is strong in the tackle and effective in the air. The final game of the season against West Ham United was his 50th League start for the club.
Rotherham U (From trainee on 1/11/1993) FL 130+2/6 FLC 6 FAC 5 Others 11
Chesterfield (£100,000 on 25/7/1997) FL 208+4/8 FLC 16/1 FAC 9/1 Others 12/1
Wigan Ath (£150,000 on 25/6/2002) FL 50+4 FLC 3 FAC 3 Others 1

BREEN Gary Patrick
Born: Hendon, 12 December 1973
Height: 6'2" **Weight:** 12.0
International Honours: RoI: 60; U21-9
An excellent bit of business by Sunderland boss Mick McCarthy saw this Republic of Ireland centre back join Sunderland on a free transfer last August. A commanding stopper, Gary is an excellent defensive organiser and distributor, and his presence was missed when a medial ligament injury kept him out for three months from December. He continued to represent his countryand contributed three goals to Sunderland's promotion campaign.
Maidstone U (From Charlton Ath juniors on 6/3/1991) FL 19
Gillingham (Free on 2/7/1992) FL 45+6 FLC 4 FAC 5 Others 1
Peterborough U (£70,000 on 5/8/1994) FL 68+1/1 FLC 6 FAC 6 Others 6/1
Birmingham C (£400,000 on 9/2/1996) FL 37+3/2 FLC 4 FAC 1
Coventry C (£2,400,000 on 1/2/1997) P/FL 138+8/2 FLC 10+3 FAC 12
West Ham U (Free on 30/7/2002) PL 9+5 FLC 2 FAC 2

Sunderland (Free on 7/8/2003) FL 32/4 FAC 4 Others 2

BRENNAN James (Jim) Gerald
Born: Toronto, Canada, 8 May 1977
Height: 5'9" **Weight:** 12.5
Club Honours: Div 1 '04
International Honours: Canada: 33 (Gold Cup 2000); U23-1
Jim took advantage of the Bosman Ruling to join Norwich on a free transfer in the summer of 2003, but an aggravating thigh injury sustained in the pre-season period prevented him from making any impact with the Canaries until late November. A cultured player who can perform at left back or on the left side of midfield, he has deceptive pace and an economic style, which appears to make the game look easy. Jim scored his first Norwich goal at Goodison Park in the FA Cup third round tie and will be hoping for an injury-free campaign in 2004-05.
Bristol C (Free from Sora Lazio, Canada on 25/10/1994) FL 51+4/3 FLC 6 FAC 1
Nottingham F (£1,500,000 on 29/10/1999) FL 117+6/1 FLC 6 FAC 6 Others 2
Huddersfield T (Loaned on 21/3/2001) 0+2
Norwich C (Free on 7/7/2003) FL 7+8/1 FAC 1/1

BREVETT Rupis (Rufus) Emanuel
Born: Derby, 24 September 1969
Height: 5'8" **Weight:** 11.6
Club Honours: Div 2 '99; Div 1 '01
Last term was a frustrating season for the West Ham left back. In the third game of the campaign he broke his ankle playing against Sheffield United. It was a bad injury and he needed to have a pin inserted in the bone. An experienced, tough-tackling full back, he was sorely missed as the Hammers made their bid for promotion. After months of rehabilitation he came back to play in two reserve games in May and was named as a substitute in the play-off final.
Doncaster Rov (From trainee on 8/7/1988) FL 106+3/3 FLC 5 FAC 4 Others 10+1
Queens Park R (£250,000 on 15/2/1991) F/PL 141+1/11 FLC 9+1 FAC 8
Fulham (£375,000 on 28/1/1998) P/FL 171+2/1 FLC 14+2/1 FAC 14 Others 12
West Ham U (Signed on 31/1/2003) P/FL 14+1 FLC 1

BRIDGE Wayne Michael
Born: Southampton, 5 August 1980
Height: 5'10" **Weight:** 11.11
International Honours: E: 17; U21-8; Yth

England international Wayne Bridge had the unenviable task of following Stamford Bridge legend Graeme Le Saux into the Chelsea left-back slot, but it speaks volumes for Wayne's class that he fitted seamlessly into the new-look Blues' line-up. Wayne was an automatic choice at Southampton but the Chelsea team-sheet is a mysterious thing and Wayne missed around a dozen games in favour of Celestine Babayaro! He formed a superb left-sided partnership with Damien Duff – signed on the same day – with the pair developing an almost telepathic understanding in an incredibly short time. Wayne has developed a reputation as one of the quickest, most attack-minded left backs in the modern game and delivers splendid crosses on the run – one of the best of the season was nodded home by Hernán Crespo to clinch the points at Fulham. Wayne had scored two goals in his pre-Chelsea career and had equalled this by the turn of the year with smartly-taken shots against Besiktas in the Champions' League – one that gave him particular pleasure – Portsmouth in the Premiership. But it was his third goal which will be fondly remembered by Chelsea fans – the brilliant winner at Highbury which put the Blues into the Champions' League semi-final at the expense of Arsenal.
Southampton (From trainee on 16/1/1998) PL 140+12/2 FLC 10+1 FAC 11
Chelsea (£7,000,000 + on 21/7/2003) PL 33/1 FAC 2 Others 11+2/2

BRIDGE-WILKINSON Marc
Born: Nuneaton, 16 March 1979
Height: 5'6 **Weight:** 11.8
Club Honours: AMC '01
This talented Port Vale midfield player was in the starting line-up at the beginning of last season before being sidelined by an injury. Although he returned to the team for a short spell in October his season never really got going until the new year. Marc can play either out wide or in the centre of midfield and has the knack of scoring spectacular goals. He netted two fine efforts against Grimsby and another against Blackpool, and also acted as the club's penalty taker.
Derby Co (From trainee on 26/3/1997) PL 0+1
Carlisle U (Loaned on 5/3/1999) FL 4+3
Port Vale (Free on 4/7/2000) FL 111+13/31 FLC 3/1 FAC 2+2/1 Others 9/3

BRIDGES David Stephen
Born: Huntingdon, 22 September 1982
Height: 6'0" **Weight:** 12.0

This Cambridge United youngster endured another injury-hit season in 2003-04. A summer ankle operation meant he was always playing catch-up with his fitness levels and then after a few substitute appearances, another injury problem meant a further spell on the sidelines. David returned to the side and scored in consecutive home matches against Carlisle and Bristol Rovers in February, but was restricted to outings from the bench in the final run-in. Out of contract at the end of the season, he had a trial with MLS outfit New England Revolution in the summer.
Cambridge U (From trainee on 20/3/2002) FL 18+27/5 FLC 2 FAC 1+3 Others 3+1

BRIDGES Michael
Born: North Shields, 5 August 1978
Height: 6'1" **Weight:** 10.11
Club Honours: Div 1 '96, '99
International Honours: E: U21-3; Yth; Sch
This talented striker was still recovering from injury at the start of last season, but eventually made his long-awaited Premiership return as a substitute for Leeds at Everton in September. However, in the new year he joined Newcastle United on loan until the end of the season, hoping to resurrect his career. Unfortunately his time at St James's Park was disrupted by further niggling injuries, and he made only occasional substitute appearances plus a single start on the right wing in the UEFA Cup tie at home to Valerenga. Tall with a good turn of pace and skilful on the ball he was out of contract in the summer and his future was unclear at the time of writing.
Sunderland (From trainee on 9/11/1995) P/FL 31+48/16 FLC 8+3/5 FAC 2
Leeds U (£4,500,000 on 29/7/1999) PL 40+16/19 FLC 3+2 FAC 1+1 Others 17+2/2
Newcastle U (Loaned on 2/2/2004) PL 0+6 Others 1+2

BRIGGS Keith
Born: Glossop, 11 December 1981
Height: 5'10" **Weight:** 11.6
This young Norwich right back suffered a frustrating season being kept out of the Canaries' side by the consistency of Marc Edworthy. Keith made just one senior start, on the opening day of the campaign at Bradford City, and just two appearances as a substitute. An attacking full back with the capability of playing in midfield if required, he will be hoping for more of a chance to impress at senior level in 2004-05.

Stockport Co (From trainee on 27/8/1999) FL 47+11/2 FLC 4/1 FAC 3+1 Others 2/1
Northampton T (£65,000 on 16/1/2003) FL 2+3

BRIGHTWELL Ian Robert
Born: Lutterworth, 9 April 1968
Height: 5'10" **Weight:** 12.5
International Honours: E: U21-4; Yth
Ian had 'retired' in May 2003, but after becoming the first-team coach at Port Vale he was registered as a player in case of emergency. He was called upon to play in the back four in the LDV Vans Trophy defeat at Scarborough and then in a couple of Second Division fixtures. In the summer he announced his departure from football to pursue his business interests outside the game.
Manchester C (From juniors on 7/5/1986) F/PL 285+36/18 FLC 29+2 FAC 19+4/1 Others 4+3
Coventry C (Free on 2/7/1998) FLC 1
Walsall (Free on 11/2/2000) FL 77+4 FLC 6 FAC 5 Others 3
Stoke C (Free on 28/3/2002) FL 3+1 Others 0+1
Port Vale (Free on 8/8/2002) FL 36+1 FLC 1 FAC 1 Others 2

BRILL Dean Michael
Born: Luton, 2 December 1985
Height: 6'2" **Weight:** 12.5
This promising young Luton goalkeeper made his senior debut when he came off the bench at Oldham last September after Robert Beckwith had been red carded. Dean then had a brief run in the starting line-up before losing his place, eventually returning for the last two games of the season.
Luton T (Trainee) FL 4+1 Others 2

BRISCO Neil Anthony
Born: Wigan, 26 January 1978
Height: 6'0" **Weight:** 11.5
Club Honours: AMC '01
This defensive midfield player missed the start of Port Vale's 2003-04 campaign through suspension and it was not until October that he made the starting line-up. Thereafter he made a further 21 appearances without being termed as regular but did his bit to help the club come close to a place in the play-offs. A no-nonsense tackler, he certainly helped stiffen up the centre of the park but a leg injury against Wrexham in April meant that he missed most of the run-in.
Manchester C (From trainee on 4/3/1997)
Port Vale (Free on 7/8/1998) FL 105+13/2 FLC 2 FAC 4+1 Others 8+1

BRISCOE Lee Stephen
Born: Pontefract, 30 September 1975
Height: 5'11" **Weight:** 11.12
International Honours: E: U21-5
Signed on a one-year deal, it was not until March that Lee was available for first-team action with Preston after a persistent hamstring injury necessitated an operation. Firm in the tackle and keen to get forward on the left, he looked ideally suited to North End's wing-back formation but a back injury in only his second start brought a premature end to a frustrating season. Lee will be hoping that a short-term contract allows him to show fans his true worth and earns him a more permanent place in the squad.
Sheffield Wed (From trainee on 22/5/1994) PL 48+30/1 FLC 5+2 FAC 0+2 Others 2+1
Manchester C (Loaned on 20/2/1998) FL 5/1
Burnley (Free on 14/7/2000) FL 100+6/7 FLC 7 FAC 6
Preston NE (Free on 29/7/2003) FL 2

BRITTAIN Martin
Born: Newcastle, 29 December 1984
Height: 5'8" **Weight:** 10.7
A product of Newcastle's Academy, midfielder Martin's performances for the reserves won him an occasional place on the first-team bench and led to substitute appearances in the home UEFA Cup tie against Valerenga in March and in the Premiership game at Manchester City. An attacking right winger with pace, energy, and a good attitude he delivers tempting crosses from both open play and set pieces, having made free kicks something of a speciality. He collected the 'Jackie Milburn Award for Young Talent' at the Sports Council in March.
Newcastle U (From trainee on 20/9/2003) PL 0+1 Others 0+1

BRITTON Leon James
Born: London, 16 September 1982
Height: 5'5" **Weight:** 9.10
International Honours: E: Yth
Leon made a dazzling start to the 2003-04 season with Swansea, producing some fine midfield performances and showing he had the ability to beat his opponent with skill and pace. He scored his first senior goal in the 3-0 win over Macclesfield Town at the Vetch Field in early September. A back injury in November forced him to miss the next match against Southend United, his first absence since establishing himself in the Swans' line-up following his arrival from West Ham.
West Ham U (From juniors on 21/9/1999)

Swansea C (Free on 13/12/2002) FL 67/3 FLC 1 FAC 5

BRKOVIC Ahmet
Born: Dubrovnik, Croatia, 23 September 1974
Height: 5'7" **Weight:** 10.8
Ahmet was used in a much deeper role by Luton last season, becoming more of a provider than a goal-scorer. The versatile midfielder was a regular in the side for much of the campaign, but managed just a single goal, netting in the 2-1 win at Peterborough in February.
Leyton Orient (Free from HNK Dubrovnik, Croatia on 14/10/1999) FL 59+10/8 FLC 3/2 FAC 4+2 Others 2+2
Luton T (Free on 4/10/2001) FL 70+19/5 FLC 2 FAC 8/3 Others 5/3

BROAD Joseph (Joe) Reginald
Born: Bristol, 24 August 1982
Height: 5'11" **Weight:** 12.7
After being released by Plymouth Joe initially joined Torquay as a trialist and then remained on monthly terms. He managed a handful of starts and a number of appearances from the bench, mostly in his favoured central midfield position, but did not figure at all in the promotion run-in and was not retained at the end of the season.
Plymouth Arg (From trainee on 15/2/2002) FL 2+10 FLC 0+1 Others 2
Torquay U (Free on 25/9/2003) FL 4+10 Others 1

BROADHURST Karl Matthew
Born: Portsmouth, 18 March 1980
Height: 6'1" **Weight:** 11.7
The 2003-04 season was without doubt the best in Karl's Bournemouth career so far. A central defender who can also play in a right-back role, he avoided the injury problems that had beset him in the past and flourished during an extended run in the side. Karl is an excellent tackler who is also dominant in the air.
Bournemouth (From trainee on 3/7/1998) FL 119+10/2 FLC 5+1 FAC 11/1 Others 6+1

BROCK Stuart Alan
Born: West Bromwich, 26 September 1976
Height: 6'1" **Weight:** 13.8
Club Honours: NC '00
Stuart began the 2003-04 season in some of the best form of his career for Kidderminster. In the Carling Cup tie at Ipswich he held the home team at bay for over 90 minutes almost single-handedly, producing a string of stunning saves. Later on Stuart lost his place to young

John Danby and he was one of several players released by Harriers at the end of the season.
Aston Villa (From trainee on 10/5/1995)
Northampton T (Free on 27/3/1997). Free to Solihull Borough during 1997 close season)
Kidderminster Hrs (Free on 17/9/1997) FL 135 FLC 4 FAC 10 Others 5

BROMBY Leigh
Born: Dewsbury, 2 June 1980
Height: 6'0" **Weight:** 11.8
International Honours: E: Sch
Once Leigh managed to get into the Sheffield Wednesday line-up last term he went from strength to strength. A sound central defender who can also operate as a right back or in a back three, he has learned to impose himself on opponents and is beginning to look a real talent. Leigh was one of 13 players released by the Owls in an end-of-season clear-out.
Sheffield Wed (Free from Liversedge on 9/7/1998) FL 98+2/2 FLC 8 FAC 6+1 Others 5
Mansfield T (Loaned on 10/12/1999) FL 10/1 Others 1
Norwich C (Loaned on 24/2/2003) FL 5

BROOKER Paul
Born: Hammersmith, 25 November 1976
Height: 5'8" **Weight:** 10.0
Club Honours: Div 3 '01; Div 2 '02
A pacy wide midfielder, Paul had relatively few opportunities to break through at Leicester during the 2003-04 season, as manager Micky Adams preferred to persevere with players who had Premiership experience. However, his effort could not be faulted whenever he did play, usually appearing from the bench, and he also contributed to Reading's push for a play-off berth during the latter stages of the campaign when at the Madejski Stadium on loan. Paul returned to Leicester for a final outing at Highbury on Arsenal's big end-of-season day.
Fulham (From trainee on 1/7/1995) FL 13+43/4 FLC 1+2/1 FAC 1+3/1 Others 3+3
Brighton & Hove A (£25,000 on 18/2/2000) FL 102+32/15 FLC 5+3 FAC 3+3 Others 3/1
Leicester C (Free on 5/7/2003) PL 0+3 FLC 2 FAC 0+1
Reading (Loaned on 27/2/2004) FL 5+6

BROOKER Stephen (Steve) Michael Lord
Born: Newport Pagnell, 21 May 1981
Height: 5'10" **Weight:** 12.4
Club Honours: AMC '01
This strong, burly striker had something of the proverbial 'season of two halves' with Port Vale last term. Before Christmas he

was affected by a succession of niggling injuries and could not find the net, but after scoring the winner at Sheffield Wednesday on Boxing Day he returned to form, leading the line superbly. Steve is very difficult to shake off the ball when in possession and altogether he notched eight goals, including a real cracker against Bristol City.
Watford (From trainee on 9/7/1999) PL 0+1 FAC 0+1
Port Vale (£15,000 on 5/1/2001) FL 111+11/30 FLC 4 FAC 4/1 Others 8+2/3

BROOMES Marlon Charles
Born: Birmingham, 28 November 1977
Height: 6'0" **Weight:** 12.12
International Honours: E: U21-2; Yth; Sch
Despite a more consistent level of performance than in his first season at Preston, a series of niggling injuries and suspensions did not help this experienced defender maintain a settled place in the side. His longest run was of only 12 games, indicating the in-and-out nature of his campaign. When he did play, Marlon operated mostly on the left side of a three-man central defence, showing himself to be quick on the deck, confident in his distribution with either foot and the possessor of a powerful spring and header.
Blackburn Rov (From trainee on 28/11/1994) P/FL 24+7/1 FLC 3 FAC 4
Swindon T (Loaned on 22/1/1997) FL 12/1
Queens Park R (Loaned on 25/10/2000) FL 5
Grimsby T (Loaned on 7/9/2001) FL 13+2 FLC 3/2
Sheffield Wed (Free on 13/12/2001) FL 18+1 FAC 1
Preston NE (Free, via trial at Burnley, on 9/8/2002) FL 51+7 FLC 3 FAC 2

BROUGH John Robert
Born: Ilkeston, 8 January 1973
Height: 6'0" **Weight:** 13.0
Club Honours: NC '99
John began last season playing alongside Michael Duff in the centre of the Cheltenham defence, but a calf injury then ruled him out for two months. Upon his return he produced some gritty and forceful performances as the team battled its way up the table and he was rewarded for his all-round contribution to the squad with the offer of a new contract. A wholehearted player with great determination and competitive spirit, John is a firm favourite among the supporters at Whaddon Road.
Notts Co (From trainee on 9/7/1991)
Shrewsbury T (Free on 6/7/1992) FL 7+9/1

FLC 1+1 FAC 1 Others 2 (Free to Telford during 1994 close season)
Hereford U (Free on 4/11/1994) FL 70+9/3 FLC 5 FAC 4/1 Others 4+2
Cheltenham T (Signed on 16/7/1998) FL 72+51/6 FLC 2+1 FAC 8+2/1 Others 1+1

BROUGH Michael
Born: Nottingham, 1 August 1981
Height: 6'0" **Weight:** 11.7
International Honours: W: U21-3; Yth
This hard-working, tough-tackling central midfield player struggled to make an impact at Notts County last term and was in and out of the squad in the first half of the season. He was released early in the new year and after a very brief spell with Stafford Rangers signed for Conference club Stevenage. Michael continued to appear for Wales at U21 level during the campaign.
Notts Co (From trainee on 1/7/1999) FL 67+22/2 FLC 1 FAC 4+5 Others 4

BROUGH Scott
Born: Scunthorpe, 10 February 1983
Height: 5'6" **Weight:** 9.10
This young left winger had a trial with Boston United during the pre-season but failed to earn a contract and went to play for Barrow in the Unibond League. Scott was given a second chance by Boston in October signing a short-term deal to cover during an injury crisis. His only first-team game was as a substitute in the LDV Vans Trophy clash with Swindon Town when he produced a number of promising crosses. Scott later played for Frickley Athletic before finishing the campaign back at Barrow.
Scunthorpe U (From juniors on 9/11/2000) FL 15+31/3 FLC 1+1 FAC 3+2 Others 2+3
Boston U (Free on 14/10/2003) Others 0+1

BROUGHTON Drewe Oliver
Born: Hitchin, 25 October 1978
Height: 6'3'' **Weight:** 12.10
A good, old-fashioned centre forward, Drewe was the goal-scoring hero of Southend United's run to the LDV Vans Trophy final at the Millennium Stadium. Five goals in seven games helped the Blues to their first major final, and although Drewe couldn't manage a similar return in the League, his 100 per cent commitment and determination brought him great respect from the club's fans. Two red cards were indicative of his combative nature, but there is no doubt that he would be only half the player if he did not possess that ruthless streak.
Norwich C (From trainee on 6/5/1997) FL 3+6/1

Wigan Ath (Loaned on 15/8/1997) FL 1+3
Brentford (£100,000 on 30/10/1998) FL 1
Peterborough U (£100,000 on 17/11/1998) FL 19+16/8 FLC 2 Others 1+1/1
Kidderminster Hrs (£50,000 on 22/1/2001) FL 70+24/19 FLC 2 FAC 2/2 Others 5/2
Southend U (Free on 13/6/2003) FL 27+8/2 FLC 1/1 FAC 0+2 Others 4+3/5

BROWN Aaron Wesley
Born: Bristol, 14 March 1980
Height: 5'10" **Weight:** 11.12
Club Honours: AMC '03
International Honours: E: Sch
What was proving to be the best-ever season for this pacy and skilful winger was cruelly cut short by a serious ankle injury received during Bristol City's home game with Rushden & Diamonds in early March. His pace and skill were badly missed in the concluding months of the campaign.
Bristol C (From trainee on 7/11/1997) FL 135+25/12 FLC 3+2 FAC 10+1 Others 12+4
Exeter C (Loaned on 6/1/2000) FL 4+1/1

BROWN Christopher (Chris)
Born: Doncaster, 11 December 1984
Height: 6'1" **Weight:** 13.4
Club Honours: Div 3 '04
International Honours: E: Yth
After missing most of the previous campaign due to a serious knee injury, this promising Sunderland striker was loaned to Doncaster Rovers in October to gain experience of senior football. He got off to a great start, netting on his debut against Bristol Rovers, but then suffered a broken toe. After recovering he remained at Belle Vue until the end of the season taking his goals tally to double figures. Chris is the son of the former Sunderland, Shrewsbury and Doncaster striker Alan Brown.
Sunderland (From trainee on 9/8/2002)
Doncaster Rov (Loaned on 3/10/2003) FL 17+5/10

BROWN Daniel (Danny)
Born: Bethnal Green, 12 September 1980
Height: 6'0" **Weight:** 12.0
Danny joined Oxford in the summer of 2003 and started the early-season games as a regular on the left-hand side of midfield. However, he then lost his place and it was a struggle to get back into what was then a table-topping side. The likeable youngster benefited from the appointment of Graham Rix as manager and an injury to Matt Robinson, and he ended the season on a high with a run of games and a 'Man of the Match' performance in the final fixture. Danny is

a good crosser of the ball and one of the few left-footed players in the U's squad.
Leyton Orient *(From trainee on 5/5/1998)*
Others 1
Barnet *(Free on 25/5/1999) FL 42+11/3 FLC 0+1 FAC 1+1 Others 5*
Oxford U *(Free on 29/7/2003) FL 12 FLC 1 Others 1*

BROWN Jason Roy
Born: Southwark, 18 May 1982
Height: 5'11" **Weight:** 13.3
International Honours: W: U21-7; Yth
Jason had a frustrating time at Gillingham last term when he was hampered by a string of injuries. The promising young 'keeper was a near ever-present until the beginning of December, but thereafter spent much of the time on the sidelines. His position as the Gills' first-choice goalkeeper came under threat following the arrival of Steve Banks, but he will be hoping to regain his place in the 2004-05 campaign.
Gillingham *(Free from trainee at Charlton Ath on 19/3/2001) FL 71 FLC 5 FAC 3*

BROWN Jermaine Anthony Alexander
Born: Lambeth, 12 January 1983
Height: 5'11" **Weight:** 11.4
Club Honours: FAYC '01
This lively striker joined Colchester on a short-term contract in the autumn and made just one appearance for the U's. Coming on as an injury-time substitute at arch- rivals Wycombe, he popped up with a dramatic winner to secure a 3-2 win in the LDV Vans Trophy third round tie. He was later brought in by Boston to provide competition for places among the front men. Jermaine made his debut for the Pilgrims at Torquay but lacked experience and found it difficult to win a regular place.
Arsenal *(From trainee on 3/7/2001)*
Colchester U *(Free on 22/10/2003) Others 0+1/1*
Boston U *(Free on 26/2/2004) FL 3+2*

BROWN Marvin Robert
Born: Bristol, 6 July 1983
Height: 5'9" **Weight:** 11.1
International Honours: E: Yth
This skilful striker again struggled to make his mark at Bristol City last term and managed just a couple of first-team appearances early in the new year. He was eventually deemed surplus to requirements and was released in the summer. Marvin is the younger brother of City's Aaron Brown.

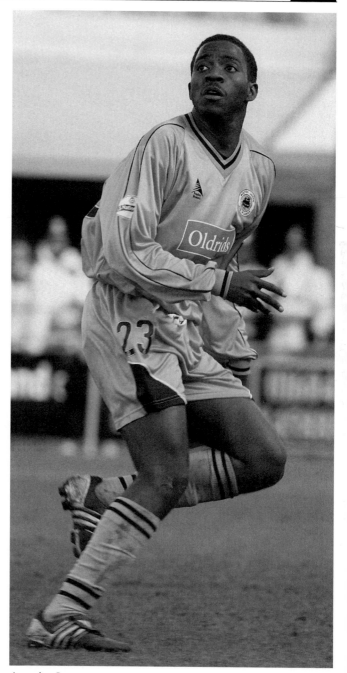

Jermaine Brown

59

Michael Brown

Bristol C (From trainee on 18/7/2000) FL 2+17 FLC 0+1 FAC 0+2 Others 2+3
Torquay U (Loaned on 26/9/2002) FL 2+2
Cheltenham T (Loaned on 30/1/2003) FL 11+4/2

BROWN Michael Robert
Born: Hartlepool, 25 January 1977
Height: 5'9" **Weight:** 11.8
International Honours: E: U21-4
Michael started the season with a foot injury and this limited his appearances for Sheffield United. As a result he did not reach his excellent high standards of the previous campaign. Nevertheless he worked hard on the left of midfield, being an effective ball-winner, and his passing and control going forward created opportunities for others. Out of contract at the end of the season, the Blades opted to sell him to Tottenham during the January transfer window. Spurs fans were delighted at the news and he fitted into the team immediately, providing some initiative and depth in the centre of the park. His defensive qualities were also evident and Michael showed he was willing to track back to gain possession when required.
Manchester C (From trainee on 13/9/1994) F/PL 67+22/2 FLC 2+4 FAC 10+1/2 Others 4
Hartlepool U (Loaned on 27/3/1997) FL 6/1
Portsmouth (Loaned on 19/11/1999) FL 4
Sheffield U (Signed on 17/12/1999) FL 146+5/27 FLC 13+1/3 FAC 6/3 Others 3/2
Tottenham H (£500,000 on 31/12/2003) PL 17/1 FAC 2

BROWN Nathaniel (Nat) Levi
Born: Sheffield, 15 June 1981
Height: 6'2" **Weight:** 12.6
Nat was often used from the substitutes' bench for Huddersfield at the start of last season, coming on to add some pace to the defence before he established himself in the line-up in November. A wing back and emergency striker, the tall youngster uses his control of the ball effectively and has the awareness to bring others into the game. His only disappointment last term was that he failed to find the net after some accomplished displays on the side.
Huddersfield T (From trainee on 8/7/1999) FL 49+10 FLC 1+2 FAC 1+1 Others 1+1

BROWN Ryan Anthony
Born: Stoke, 15 March 1985
Height: 5'9" **Weight:** 10.12
This teenaged left back started out last term in the Port Vale first team and retained his place in the line-up until October when he was left out. Following

a change in management he returned to the side in the new year, but then suffered a head injury in the game at Queens Park Rangers leaving him with a fractured eye socket and he took no further part in the campaign.
Port Vale (From trainee on 22/8/2003) FL 17+1 FLC 1

BROWN Simon Alexander
Born: West Bromwich, 18 September 1983
Height: 5'10" **Weight:** 11.0
This promising young West Bromwich Albion midfielder joined Kidderminster on loan in March to gain some experience of first-team football. Simon became an instant hero of the fans at Aggborough after scoring on his debut against Lincoln City and very easily slotted into the side. A tricky attacking midfielder or striker, he was always a threat when taking on opposition defences and will be looking to build on his experience in 2004-05.
West Bromwich A (From trainee on 9/7/2003)
Kidderminster Hrs (Loaned on 25/3/2004) FL 8/2

BROWN Simon James
Born: Chelmsford, 3 December 1976
Height: 6'2" **Weight:** 15.0
Apart from a brief spell, Simon was again first-choice 'keeper for Colchester for the whole of the 2003-04 season. He was particularly impressive away from home, highlighted by a terrific display at Yeovil in the LDV Vans Trophy tie, which resulted in the U's winning a penalty shoot-out. Simon also saved a spot kick in normal time in his team's biggest win of the season, a 4-1 triumph over Notts County. His good form on the U's travels led to him being named the away supporters' 'Player of the Year'.
Tottenham H (From trainee on 1/7/1995)
Lincoln C (Loaned on 19/12/1997) FL 1 Others 0+1
Colchester U (Free on 20/7/1999) FL 141+1 FLC 7 FAC 9 Others 8+1

BROWN Steven (Steve) Byron
Born: Brighton, 13 May 1972
Height: 6'1" **Weight:** 13.10
Club Honours: Div 1 '00
An incredibly brave player whose season was marred by injury, Steve played in fewer than half of Reading's first-team games in 2003-04. He was at his best in the opening months of the campaign, when his dogged determination at the heart of the defence saved his side on many occasions. However, his best

performance came in the 3-2 win at Cardiff, when he answered an emergency call to dash down the M4 to play, despite not being fully fit. Steve played in just one more game before being sidelined with a serious knee injury for the rest of the season.
Charlton Ath (From trainee on 3/7/1990) P/FL 194+48/9 FLC 12+4/1 FAC 19+1/1 Others 3+2
Reading (Free on 19/12/2002) FL 40/1 FLC 2 FAC 3 Others 2

BROWN Steven (Steve) Ferold
Born: Northampton, 6 July 1966
Height: 6'0" **Weight:** 11.8
After ten years at Wycombe Wanderers and in his testimonial season, Steve retired from full-time professional football in May 2004. He was given a tremendous send off by the fans in the last home game against Wrexham, and again in the final game of the season at Peterborough. He is remarkably fit despite his advancing years, a ferocious tackler with a cultured left foot, and the ability to take the game by the scruff of the neck with his driving runs.
Northampton T (From juniors on 11/8/1983) FL 14+1/3 (Free to Irthlingborough T in December 1985)
Northampton T (Free on 21/7/1989) FL 145+13/19 FLC 10/1 FAC 10+1/1
Wycombe W (£60,000 on 9/2/1994) FL 332+39/35 FLC 22+4/3 FAC 24+8/4 Others 11+4/1

BROWN Wayne Lawrence
Born: Barking, 20 August 1977
Height: 6'0" **Weight:** 12.6
Wayne, a left-sided central defender or full back who is particularly strong in the air, had a chequered season so far as Watford was concerned. He suffered a calf injury pre-season and went on loan to Gillingham in September in search of form and fitness. On his return, he enjoyed a run of first-team matches in November and December at left back, but seemed uncomfortable with his attacking responsibilities and went on loan again, this time to Colchester, where he remained until the end of the campaign. Operating alongside Alan White in the centre of the defence he produced some impressive performances and helped the U's regain their form and so finish in the top half of Division Two.
Ipswich T (From trainee on 16/5/1996) P/FL 28+12 FLC 3 FAC 2 Others 4+1/1
Colchester U (Loaned on 16/10/1997) FL 0+2

Queens Park R (Loaned on 22/3/2001) FL 2
Wimbledon (Loaned on 14/9/2001) FL 17/1
Watford (Loaned on 30/1/2002) FL 10+1/3
Watford (Free on 18/12/2002) FL 24+1/1
FAC 1
Gillingham (Loaned on 19/9/2003) FL 4/1
Colchester U (Loaned on 17/2/2004) FL 16
Others 0+1

BROWN Wesley (Wes) Michael
Born: Manchester, 13 October 1979
Height: 6'1" **Weight:** 12.4
Club Honours: EC '99; PL '99, '01, '03;
FAC '04
International Honours: E: 7; U21-8;
Yth; Sch
A solid central defender, who is
commanding in the air, with pace and
confidence to match, Wes was laid low
with a cruciate ligament injury until
December, and only returned to first-team
action as Rio Ferdinand was preparing for
his eight-month ban from English football
in January. Understandably, he took a while
to settle back into the thick of things, but
once he'd played in a steady run of games
he cemented his reputation as one of
Manchester United's most valued defenders.
Manchester U (From trainee on 13/11/1996)
PL 89+11 FLC 6+1 FAC 9+2 Others 25+5/1

BROWNE Gary
Born: Belfast, 17 January 1983
Height: 5'10" **Weight:** 10.10
International Honours: NI: U21-5
Gary began last season on trial with York
City and after a spell in the Unibond
League with Whitby Town he signed a
short-term contract with the Minstermen.
A promising striker, he showed some nice
touches in his senior appearances but was
subsequently released in the new year.
Manchester C (From trainee on 5/7/2000.
Freed during 2003 close season)
York C (Free from Whitby T on 14/11/2003)
FL 2+4

BROWNING Marcus Trevor
Born: Bristol, 22 April 1971
Height: 6'0" **Weight:** 12.10
International Honours: W: 5
The oldest player in the Bournemouth
squad last term, Marcus more than made
up for this with his enthusiasm for the
game and enjoyed another good season.
An influential player in the middle of the
park with good vision and passing ability,
Marcus missed very few games.
Bristol Rov (From trainee on 1/7/1989) FL
152+22/13 FLC 7+3 FAC 8/1 Others 13+5/3
Hereford U (Loaned on 18/9/1992) FL 7/5
Huddersfield T (£500,000 on 17/2/1997) FL
25+8 FLC 2+2

Gillingham (Loaned on 20/11/1998) FL 1
Gillingham (£150,000 on 25/3/1999) FL
60+17/3 FLC 6+1 FAC 3+3 Others 0+1
Bournemouth (Free on 9/8/2002) FL 81+4/1
FLC 2/1 FAC 6+1/2 Others 6

BRUNT Christopher (Chris)
Born: Belfast, 14 December 1984
Height: 6'1" **Weight:** 11.8
International Honours: NI: U23-1
This exciting young prospect arrived at
Sheffield Wednesday for a trial period
from Middlesbrough and was soon
signed up on a permanent contract. He
scored a cracking goal on his first start
against Brighton, and generally added
drive and skill to the left-hand side of
the Owls' midfield. Chris was called up
for Northern Ireland U23s and made an
appearance as a substitute against Serbia
& Montenegro.
Middlesbrough (From trainee on 6/7/2002)
Sheffield Wed (Free on 2/3/2004) FL 8+1/2

BRYANT Simon Christopher
Born: Bristol, 22 November 1982
Height: 5'9" **Weight:** 10.7
Simon had a rather frustrating season at
Bristol Rovers last term. Confined to the
reserves for much of the campaign, he
spent a month out on loan at Tiverton
Town. A change of manager saw the
central midfielder restored to first-team
action and in February he enjoyed six
consecutive appearances but he failed to
impress and lost his place once more.
Simon's contract was cancelled by mutual
consent in the summer.
Bristol Rov (From trainee on 17/1/2000) FL
65+22/2 FLC 5+4 FAC 3+1 Others 4+1

BUARI Malik
Born: Accra, Ghana, 21 January 1984
Height: 5'11" **Weight:** 11.11
A product of the Fulham youth system,
Malik produced some impressive
performances in a number of pre-season
games earning himself a first-team debut
as a substitute at Everton. His only
Premiership start came against Newcastle
in October, and this proved to be his final
first-team appearance of the season.
Malik usually operates in a wide-right-
sided role where he is able to
demonstrate his speed on the ball and
shooting ability.
Fulham (From trainee on 10/7/2003) PL 1+2
FLC 1

BULL Ronald (Ronnie) Rodney
Born: Hackney, 26 December 1980
Height: 5'8" **Weight:** 10.12
This combative Millwall left back joined

Yeovil on loan early on last term and
featured on the left-hand side of the
defence until injury curtailed his stay.
Ronnie then joined Brentford in another
loan deal and was a near ever-present for
the Bees in the second half of the
campaign, eventually signing permanent
terms in April. He is a strong tackler,
effective on the overlap and able to
deliver an accurate cross.
Millwall (From trainee on 12/5/1999) FL
37+13 FLC 0+2 Others 3
Yeovil T (Loaned on 3/9/2003) FL 7
Brentford (Signed on 7/1/2004) FL 20

BULLARD James (Jimmy) Richard
Born: Newham, 23 October 1978
Height: 5'10" **Weight:** 11.10
Club Honours: Div 2 '03
This inventive and classy midfield was an
ever-present for Wigan last term and has
yet to miss a League game since his move
to the JJB Stadium. Hard working and
alert, always willing to develop attacking
moves, he coupled his strong running
with an eye for goal and netted a
spectacular effort from outside the box in
the away win at Crewe Alexandra. Very
much the playmaker in the side, pulling
the strings in midfield and directing the
pattern of the game, he played a major
part in the club's first season in Division
One.
West Ham U (£30,000 from Gravesend &
Northfleet on 10/2/1998)
Peterborough U (Free on 6/7/2001) FL
62+4/11 FLC 2 FAC 6/1 Others 3/2
Wigan Ath (£275,000 on 31/1/2003) FL 63/3
FLC 3/1 FAC 1

BULLOCK Lee
Born: Stockton, 22 May 1981
Height: 5'9" **Weight:** 11.7
York City's highly rated midfielder enjoyed
another good season at Bootham
Crescent last term and with goals at a
premium for the club he played a number
of games up front for the Minstermen. He
netted seven times including an excellent
effort which earned an early-season win
at Huddersfield Town. In March he joined
Cardiff City on loan and stayed until the
end of the season. Lee produced some
good performances at Ninian Park and
scored three goals from four starts, but at
the time of writing it was unclear whether
he would make a permanent move to the
South Wales club.
York C (From trainee on 29/6/1999) FL
156+15/24 FLC 5+1/1 FAC 10+2/2
Cardiff C (Loaned on 11/3/2004) FL 4+7/3

BULLOCK Martin John
Born: Derby, 5 March 1975
Height: 5'5" **Weight:** 10.7
Club Honours: AMC '02, '04
International Honours: E: U21-1
This dangerous winger was a regular for Blackpool throughout the 2003-04 campaign. A skilful player with plenty of speed and the ability to deliver an accurate cross, Martin scored his only goal of the season in the final home game against Peterborough United. A highlight of his campaign was appearing in the final of the LDV Vans Trophy against Southend at the Millennium Stadium.
Barnsley (£15,000 from Eastwood T on 4/9/1993) F/PL 108+77/4 FLC 14+4 FAC 4+11/3 Others 1
Port Vale (Loaned on 14/1/2000) FL 6/1
Blackpool (Free on 10/8/2001) FL 104+21/4 FLC 3+3 FAC 9+1 Others 13+1/3

BULMAN Dannie
Born: Ashford, Surrey, 24 January 1979
Height: 5'10" **Weight:** 12.3
By his own high standards Dannie did not have quite his usual influential role in central midfield at Wycombe Wanderers last term, and was dropped more than once early on. He was much stronger in the second half of the season, displaying his customary commitment and non-stop running. Rather surprisingly he was released in the summer.
Wycombe W (£5,000 + from Ashford T on 17/6/1998) FL 160+42/14 FLC 8+2 FAC 14+6/1 Others 11/1

BUNJEVCEVIC Goran Petar
Born: Karlovac, Croatia, 17 February 1973
Height: 6'3" **Weight:** 12.6
International Honours: Serbia: 17
A versatile defender who has also been deployed in central midfield, Goran favours a central-defensive role where he has impressed at international level. With Tottenham manager Glenn Hoddle favouring the development of Ledley King and Anthony Gardner, Goran found it hard to displace the two promising youngsters. He spent time in the reserves but otherwise he received only rare first-team opportunities last term.
Tottenham H (£1,400,000 from Red Star Belgrade, Yugoslavia, ex FK Crvena, Zuezda, on 25/7/2001) PL 39+9 FLC 4+1

BURCHILL Mark James
Born: Broxburn, 18 August 1980
Height: 5'8" **Weight:** 10.2
Club Honours: SLC '00; Div 1 '03

International Honours: S: 6; U21-15; Sch
Mark was again completely out of the first-team picture at Portsmouth last season and was restricted to appearances for the reserves and when out on loan elsewhere. The pacy striker had a spell at Wigan early on in the campaign. Signed as cover for injuries, he impressed with an excellent first touch and an eye for goal. Towards the end of the year he was out on loan again, this time with Sheffield Wednesday. Mark tried hard during his brief stay at Hillsborough but failed to ignite the team and returned to the South Coast.
Glasgow Celtic (From Celtic BC on 3/6/1997) SL 17+34/21 SLC 3+2 SC 1+2/1 Others 4+1/3
Birmingham C (Loaned on 22/9/2000) FL 4+9/4 FLC 3+1/1
Ipswich T (Loaned on 22/1/2001) PL 2+5/1
Portsmouth (£600,000 on 24/8/2001) FL 9+15/8 FLC 1+1
Dundee (Loaned on 31/1/2003) SL 7+4/2 SC 1+3/1
Wigan Ath (Loaned on 21/8/2003) FL 1+3
Sheffield Wed (Loaned on 24/12/2003) FL 4+1

BURGESS Andrew (Andy) John
Born: Bozeat, 10 August 1981
Height: 6'2" **Weight:** 11.6
Club Honours: NC '01; Div 3 '03
Andy was a regular in the Rushden line-up last term, switching from the left wing into a central playmaker role where his superb skills were put to good use. He scored five goals including two close-range headers in the 4-0 home win over Colchester in November. Later in the campaign he featured at left back as a replacement for the departed Paul Underwood and coped well in an unfamiliar position.
Rushden & Diamonds (From juniors on 3/7/1999) FL 79+17/9 FLC 2+1 FAC 2+1 Others 3+2

BURGESS Benjamin (Ben) Kieron
Born: Buxton, 9 November 1981
Height: 6'3" **Weight:** 14.4
International Honours: RoI: U21-2; Yth
Ben began to fulfil the promise he had previously shown at the KC Stadium in 2003-04 as he led the forward line superbly in notching 18 goals to finish top scorer for Hull City. Although he uses his physical presence to provide a considerable threat in the air, Ben's awareness and dexterity on the ground also brings his fellow attackers into play.

After being an ever-present, he missed the last two games of the season following a cruciate ligament injury against Huddersfield and seems likely to be sidelined up until Christmas of 2004.
Blackburn Rov (From trainee on 25/11/1998) FL 1+1 FLC 1
Brentford (Loaned on 16/8/2001) FL 43/17 FLC 2 FAC 2/1 Others 4
Stockport Co (£450,000 on 5/8/2002) FL 17+2/4 FLC 0+1 FAC 1+1/2 Others 2
Oldham Ath (Loaned on 10/1/2003) FL 6+1 FLC 1 FAC 1
Hull C (£100,000 on 27/3/2003) FL 51/22

BURGESS Daryl
Born: Birmingham, 24 January 1971
Height: 5'11" **Weight:** 12.4
This stalwart central defender linked up with his former boss Alan Buckley at Rochdale during the 2003 close season and proved a key figure in the back line for Dale last term. Despite the team slipping down the table after a bright start, Daryl performed consistently strongly in the heart of the defence and was a near-automatic choice until injuries and competition for places limited his appearances over the last couple of months of the campaign.
West Bromwich A (From trainee on 1/7/1989) FL 317+15/10 FLC 20+2/3 FAC 9 Others 14
Northampton T (Free on 5/7/2001) FL 60+1/2 FLC 1 FAC 4 Others 3
Rochdale (Free on 6/8/2003) FL 33+2 FLC 1 FAC 2

BURGESS Oliver David
Born: Bracknell, 12 October 1981
Height: 5'10" **Weight:** 11.7
Ollie started the 2003-04 season playing in a midfield role for Northampton and produced some creditable performances, showing he was not afraid to have a shot from outside the box. However, he then picked up an injury that kept him out of the side and in October he moved on to join Basingstoke Town.
Queens Park R (From trainee on 1/7/2001) FL 6+4/1 FAC 2+1 Others 1
Northampton T (Free on 7/7/2003) FL 3+6 FLC 1+1

BURLEY Craig William
Born: Irvine, 24 September 1971
Height: 6'1" **Weight:** 13.0
Club Honours: SLC '97; SPD '98
International Honours: S: 46; U21-7; Yth; Sch
Craig began the 2003-04 season on a short-term contract at Dundee, signing on a similar basis for Preston in January. He

made four appearances in all for North End (three as a substitute) without ever having the opportunity to fully demonstrate his undoubted pedigree. He declined the offer of an extension due to the problems of commuting from Nottingham and left the club in early March. Coincidentally, Craig made his Walsall debut at Deepdale two weeks after leaving North End. However, the cultured midfield player made only a limited impact during his stay at Bescot.
Chelsea (From trainee on 1/9/1989) P/FL 85+28/7 FLC 5 FAC 12+4/4 Others 3
Glasgow Celtic (£2,500,000 on 24/7/1997) SL 61+3/20 SLC 7 SC 6/1 Others 12/1
Derby Co (£3,000,000 on 2/12/1999) P/FL 73/10 FLC 5/3 FAC 2
Dundee (Free on 1/7/2003) SL 1+1 SLC 1
Preston NE (Free on 29/11/2004) FL 1+3
Walsall (Free on 15/3/2004) FL 5

BURNELL Joseph (Joe)
Michael
Born: Bristol, 10 October 1980
Height: 5'10" **Weight:** 11.1
Club Honours: AMC '03
Joe was a regular in the Bristol City side during the opening stages of the 2003-04 season when results were not as good as expected. The hard-working midfielder always gave 100 per cent, but featured only rarely in the side after November.
Bristol C (From trainee on 24/7/1999) FL 117+14/1 FLC 3+2 FAC 4+3 Others 17+1/2

BURNS Jacob Geoffrey
Born: Sydney, Australia, 21 January 1978
Height: 5'9" **Weight:** 11.12
International Honours: Australia: 2; U23-19
After being released by Leeds United at the end of the previous season, Jacob joined Barnsley on a short-term contract last October and stayed at Oakwell until the end of the season. An impressive passer of the ball, he was a vital cog in the Reds' midfield until his campaign was ended early through injury. He was offered a new contract by manager Paul Hart at the end of the season.
Leeds U (£250,000 from Parramatta Power, Australia, ex Sydney U, on 31/8/2000) PL 5+1 FLC 1 Others 3+1
Barnsley (Free, via trial at Feyenoord, Holland, on 17/10/2003) FL 16+6/1 FAC 4 Others 1

BURNS Jamie Daniel
Born: Blackpool, 6 March 1984
Height: 5'9" **Weight:** 10.11
Club Honours: AMC '04
This promising left-sided midfielder was in

his first year as a professional at Blackpool last term. Jamie continued to make steady progress and registered his first goal in senior football in the FA Cup tie against Boreham Wood. He was a regular in the squad in the final run-in and will be looking to gain further senior experience in 2004-05.
Blackpool (From trainee on 1/7/2003) FL 7+11 FAC 1+1/1 Others 2+2

BURNS Liam
Born: Belfast, 30 October 1978
Height: 6'0" **Weight:** 12.12
International Honours: NI: U21-13; Yth
Port Vale's longest serving player, Liam was mainly used as a squad player last season. A tall central defender he gave his all when called upon and in the early part of the campaign the team kept more clean sheets when Liam played than when he didn't. He suffered a bad injury at Luton when he crashed over the goal line and ended up in the seats. Thankfully he soon recovered and scored the first goal of his senior career against Ford United in the FA Cup with a low shot. A no-nonsense defender who clears the ball first and asks questions later, Liam can always be relied upon. He was released on a free transfer in May.
Port Vale (From trainee on 2/7/1997) FL 94+24 FLC 1 FAC 7+1/1 Others 4+1

BURT Jamie Paul
Born: Blyth, 29 September 1979
Height: 5'10" **Weight:** 12.0
Jamie makes this year's Who's Who on the basis of one minute of Second Division action for Chesterfield at home to Bristol City last August. Soon afterwards he had a brief spell at Scarborough before moving on to Whitby and then Blyth Spartans. On his day Jamie is a powerful, exciting forward, difficult to dispossess and with a powerful shot.
Chesterfield (Free from Whitby T, ex Bridlington T, Scarborough, on 14/12/2001) FL 29+12/8 FLC 1+1 FAC 1 Others 2
Carlisle U (Loaned on 31/12/2002) FL 4/1

BURTON Deon John
Born: Ashford, 25 October 1976
Height: 5'9" **Weight:** 11.9
Club Honours: Div 1 '03
International Honours: Jamaica: 48
Deon spent much of the first half of last season out on loan, firstly at Walsall, where he showed plenty of energy, and then at Swindon, where he scored a fine goal against Wycombe but otherwise made little impact. He spent most of his time at Fratton Park in the reserves,

featuring on just two occasions in the first team. A capable striker or midfield player, he was released in the summer.
Portsmouth (From trainee on 15/2/1994) FL 42+20/10 FLC 3+2/2 FAC 0+2/1 Others 1
Cardiff C (Loaned on 24/12/1996) FL 5/2 Others 1
Derby Co (£1,000,000 + on 9/8/1997) P/FL 78+47/25 FLC 6+2/3 FAC 9+1/3
Barnsley (Loaned on 14/12/1998) FL 3
Stoke C (Loaned on 21/2/2002) FL 11+1/2 Others 2+1/2
Portsmouth (Loaned on 9/8/2002) FL 6/3
Portsmouth (£75,000 + on 12/12/2002) FL 5+5/1 FAC 1+1
Walsall (Loaned on 12/9/2003) FL 2+1 FLC 1
Swindon T (Loaned on 17/10/2003) FL 4/1

BURTON Steven (Steve) Paul
Born: Doncaster, 9 October 1983
Height: 6'1" **Weight:** 13.5
A well-built, strong-running forceful striker, Steve made his debut for Doncaster as a substitute against Cambridge at the end of September and the following Saturday he made his only start of the season. He added a handful more appearances from the bench, but was released in the summer.
Ipswich T (From trainee on 14/8/2002)
Boston U (Loaned on 15/8/2002) FL 6+2 FLC 1+1/1
Doncaster Rov (Free on 10/3/2003) FL 1+5 Others 0+1

BURTON Steven (Steve) Peter
Graham
Born: Hull, 10 October 1982
Height: 6'1" **Weight:** 11.5
After an encouraging 2002-03 campaign, Steve was unable to break into the promotion-chasing Hull squad in the new season save for an outing in the LDV Vans Trophy win at Darlington. He eventually rejoined his former Tigers boss Jan Molby in a loan move to Kidderminster, which then became permanent and he quickly made the left-back spot his own at Aggborough.
Hull C (From trainee on 11/7/2002) FL 2+9 FAC 1 Others 2
Kidderminster Hrs (Loaned on 24/10/2003) FL 6+1 FAC 1/1
Kidderminster Hrs (Free on 25/3/2004) FL 4+1

BURTON-GODWIN Osagyefo
(Sagi) Lenin Ernesto
Born: Birmingham, 25 November 1977
Height: 6'2" **Weight:** 13.6
Club Honours: AMC '01
International Honours: St Kitts
A fine, ball-playing, powerful central

defender, Sagi was a regular for Peterborough United for most of last season, although he occasionally ran into disciplinary problems. He was one of three Posh players called up by St Kitts for their World Cup qualifying campaign in the summer.

Crystal Palace *(From trainee on 26/1/1996)*
P/FL 19+6/1 FLC 1 FAC 0+1 Others 0+1
Colchester U *(Free on 26/5/1999) FL 9 FLC 2*
Sheffield U *(Free on 19/11/1999)*
Port Vale *(Free on 14/1/2000) FL 76+10/2*
FLC 3/1 FAC 3 Others 6+1/1
Crewe Alex *(Free on 8/8/2002) FL 1*
Peterborough U *(Free on 29/8/2002) FL*
55+6/1 FLC 2 FAC 2 Others 2/1

BUTCHER Richard Tony
Born: Peterborough, 22 January 1981
Height: 6'0" **Weight:** 12.12
This central midfield man was a key player for Lincoln with his driving runs from deep positions causing problems for opposition defences. He also contributed some spectacular long-range goals, including a stunning 30-yard shot which helped the Imps to a win at Mansfield. He was badly missed when a left knee ligament injury sustained in training kept him out from early February until the final few games of the campaign.

Rushden & Diamonds *(From trainee at Northampton T on 26/11/1999. Freed on 1/10/2001)*
Lincoln C *(Free from Kettering T on 19/11/2002) FL 49+9/9 FLC 1 FAC 2 Others 8/1*

BUTLER Andrew (Andy) Peter
Born: Doncaster, 4 November 1983
Height: 6'0" **Weight:** 13.6
An injury crisis at Scunthorpe led to Andy making his first-team debut at Leyton Orient last September, and he never looked back, becoming one of the first names on the United team sheet throughout the rest of the season. A left-sided central defender, who is superb in the air, he produced some excellent performances and was rewarded with a four-and-a-half year professional deal, the longest contract in the club's history. A regular scorer for the juniors from set pieces, he had netted two goals by the end of the season.

Scunthorpe U *(From trainee on 2/7/2003) FL 34+1/2 FLC 1 FAC 4 Others 3*

BUTLER Philip Anthony (Tony)
Born: Stockport, 28 September 1972
Height: 6'2" **Weight:** 12.0
Club Honours: AMC '03

Tony formed a sound central-defensive partnership with Danny Coles last term, helping make Bristol City's defence the most parsimonious in the Second Division. He was outstanding at Hartlepool in the play-offs as City battled to a hard-earned draw. A sound header of the ball, he is a determined and hard-working defender.

Gillingham *(From trainee on 13/5/1991) FL 142+6/5 FLC 12 FAC 12+1 Others 5+1/1*
Blackpool *(£225,000 on 30/7/1996) FL 98+1 FLC 7 FAC 4 Others 4/1*
Port Vale *(£115,000 on 25/3/1999) FL 19*
West Bromwich A *(£140,000 on 23/3/2000) FL 65+5/1 FLC 7 FAC 1+1 Others 2*
Bristol C *(Free on 30/8/2002) FL 75+1/2 FLC 4 FAC 4 Others 13*

BUTLER Martin Neil
Born: Wordsley, 15 September 1974
Height: 5'11" **Weight:** 11.9
Three substitute appearances in August was the total of Martin's first-team contribution to Reading's season, before he left for Rotherham United. However, the nippy striker left his mark with a sparkling display in a reserve game against Northampton, when he scored five times in a 7-0 victory. He proved to be a more-than-capable replacement for Alan Lee at Millmoor, topping the scoring charts and he finishing the season with a flourish, finding the net in four successive games. The highlight of his campaign was a superb hat-trick against Norwich City. Martin established a fine understanding with Michael Proctor and the pair played a major role in steering the club clear of the relegation zone.

Walsall *(From trainee on 24/5/1993) FL 43+31/8 FLC 2+1 FAC 2+5/2 Others 2+2/2*
Cambridge U *(£22,500 on 8/8/1997) FL 100+3/41 FLC 9/6 FAC 9+2/5 Others 3+1/1*
Reading *(£750,000 on 1/2/2000) FL 85+18/32 FLC 4 FAC 5/2 Others 4+1/2*
Rotherham U *(£150,000 on 2/9/2003) FL 36+1/15 FLC 1 FAC 0+1*

BUTLER Paul John
Born: Manchester, 2 November 1972
Height: 6'2" **Weight:** 13.0
Club Honours: Div 2 '97; Div 1 '99
International Honours: RoI: 1; B-1
An enthusiastic central defender, Paul was not expected to feature much in the Premiership, yet ended up being one of the Wolves' most consistent players. His game was all about hard work and determination, but those qualities are not enough to keep great strikers quiet, which Paul often did. He is surprisingly acrobatic for a big man, and having hit the woodwork against Chelsea, he scored

with a neat header against Blackburn. He missed only one Premiership game and showed his spirit in April, playing on with injuries in games against Southampton and Bolton, having broken his nose in the latter.

Rochdale *(From trainee on 5/7/1991) FL 151+7/10 FLC 8+1 FAC 6+2 Others 12+1*
Bury *(£100,000 on 22/7/1996) FL 83+1/4 FLC 8 FAC 2 Others 3/1*
Sunderland *(£600,000 + on 15/7/1998) P/FL 78+1/3 FLC 11+1/1 FAC 4*
Wolverhampton W *(Loaned on 17/11/2000) FL 5*
Wolverhampton W *(£1,000,000 on 31/1/2001) P/FL 118+1/3 FLC 5 FAC 7 Others 5*

BUTLER Thomas Anthony
Born: Dublin, Ireland, 25 April 1981
Height: 5'8" **Weight:** 10.8
International Honours: RoI: 2; U21-15; Yth
Last term was something of a disappointment for this diminutive Sunderland midfield player as he failed to establish himself as a regular in the first team. Operating mainly on the left wing, the tricky youngster suffered an ankle injury in October and subsequently found his path blocked firstly by a succession of loan signings and then the partnership of Julio Arca and George McCartney.

Sunderland *(From trainee on 25/6/1998) P/FL 16+15 FLC 1+3 FAC 0+1*
Darlington *(Loaned on 13/10/2000) FL FAC 2*

BUTT Nicholas (Nicky)
Born: Manchester, 21 January 1975
Height: 5'10" **Weight:** 11.3
Club Honours: FAYC '92; CS '96, '97, '03; PL '96, '97, '99, '00, 01, '03; FAC '96, '04; EC '99
International Honours: E: 35; U21-7; Yth; Sch
A gritty midfielder with neat skills and a hardened edge, Nicky's plans for regular first-team football at Old Trafford were severely restricted by Phil Neville's continuing progress in his customary midfield slot. By December he was subject to much tabloid speculation when both Middlesbrough and Spurs expressed an interest. Nicky opted to stay at Old Trafford, where he enjoyed his most fruitful run in the side, playing in both Champions' League games against Porto, and also in the later stages of United's successful FA Cup run. Still very much a part of Sven Göran Eriksson's England set-up, the only question mark remains his long-term United future, although Sir Alex Ferguson clearly knows his value.

Paul Butler (right)

Manchester U (From trainee on 29/1/1993)
PL 210+60/21 FLC 7+1 FAC 23+6/1 Others
67+13/4

BUTTERFIELD Daniel (Danny) Paul

Born: Boston, 21 November 1979
Height: 5'10" **Weight:** 11.10
Club Honours: AMC '98
International Honours: E: Yth
This hard-working right back was once
again a near ever-present for Crystal
Palace last season. His consecutive run of
first-team appearances was broken in
October but he provided the Eagles with
excellent service all season. Danny also
has a powerful shot and contributed a
couple of spectacular long-range goals
during the campaign.
Grimsby T (From trainee on 7/8/1997) FL
100+24/3 FLC 13+1 FAC 5+2 Others 1+1/1
Crystal Palace (Free on 7/8/2002) FL 91/5
FLC 8+1 FAC 5 Others 3/1

BUTTERS Guy

Born: Hillingdon, 30 October 1969
Height: 6'3" **Weight:** 14.2
International Honours: E: U21-3
With his career at Brighton seemingly
going nowhere, Guy knuckled down,
worked greatly on his fitness, took his
opportunity when it arose through injuries
to others early in the campaign, and
never missed another game. The
turnaround was so remarkable, and Guy's
performances so consistent, that he was
rewarded with the supporters' 'Player of
the Season' award. The veteran defender
did the simple things well: solid
headwork, laying the ball off neatly to
colleagues, clearing his lines when
required, and reading the game to make
up for his lack of pace.
Tottenham H (From trainee on 5/8/1988) FL
34+1/1 FLC 2+1 FAC 1
Southend U (Loaned on 13/1/1990) FL 16/3
Others 2
Portsmouth (£375,000 on 28/9/1990) FL
148+6/6 FLC 16+1/1 FAC 7 Others 7+2
Oxford U (Loaned on 4/11/1994) FL 3/1
Others 1
Gillingham (£225,000 on 18/10/1996) FL
155+4/16 FLC 9 FAC 14/1 Others 11
Brighton & Hove A (Free on 29/8/2002) FL
49/3 FLC 2 FAC 1 Others 6

BUXTON Jake Fred

Born: Sutton in Ashfield, 4 March 1985
Height: 5'11" **Weight:** 13.0
Jake was used as a squad player by
Mansfield Town last term, making his first
appearance at left back in the LDV Vans
Trophy tie with Stockport County. He

replaced Jamie Clarke in that position in
the Burnley match after Clarke had been
sent off and made a good impression,
and then deservedly kept his place in the
side, his confidence growing all the time.
Earlier in the campaign Jake had spent a
month on loan at Alfreton Town.
Mansfield T (From juniors on 21/10/2002) FL
12/1 FAC 0+1 Others 1+1

BUXTON Lewis Edward

Born: Newport, IoW, 10 December 1983
Height: 6'1" **Weight:** 13.10
A central defender who can also be used
as a left back, Lewis rejoined
Bournemouth last November on loan
from Portsmouth. The deal was extended
for the rest of the season and he grew in
stature with each game, showing great
maturity.
Portsmouth (From trainee on 9/4/2001) FL
27+3
Exeter C (Loaned on 21/10/2002) FL 4
Others 2
Bournemouth (Loaned on 10/3/2003) FL
15+2 FAC 1
Bournemouth (Loaned on 30/10/2003) FL
24+2 FAC 1+1

BYFIELD Darren

Born: Sutton Coldfield, 29 September
1976
Height: 5'11" **Weight:** 11.11
International Honours: Jamaica: 7
Darren started the season as Rotherham
United's first-choice striker and he was
soon topping the scoring charts helped by
his tremendous pace and tricky ball play.
He also proved to be an expert from the
penalty spot and his form soon attracted
the attention of other clubs. In February
he joined Sunderland in an exchange deal
that involved Michael Proctor moving in
the opposite direction. Initially given a
contact until the end of the season, he
produced a string of impressive
performances, starting off with a goal on
his debut as a substitute at Watford.
Darren continued to represent Jamaica at
international level during the season.
Aston Villa (From trainee on 14/2/1994) PL
1+6 FLC 1 FAC 0+1 Others 1
Preston NE (Loaned on 6/11/1998) FL 3+2/1
Others 1
Northampton T (Loaned on 13/8/1999) FL
6/1 FLC 1/1
Cambridge U (Loaned on 17/9/1999) FL 3+1
Blackpool (Loaned on 6/3/2000) FL 3
Walsall (Free on 21/6/2000) FL 45+32/13 FLC
2+3/2 FAC 4+2/1 Others 2+2/1
Rotherham U (£50,000 on 27/3/2001) FL
53+15/22 FLC 3+1/1 FAC 2
Sunderland (Signed on 6/2/2004) FL 8+9/5

BYRNE Clifford (Cliff)

Born: Dublin, 27 April 1982
Height: 6'0" **Weight:** 12.12
International Honours: RoI: U21-10;
Yth
After starring on loan the previous
season, Scunthorpe United fans were
delighted to secure Cliff's services in the
summer of 2003. A strong, determined
centre back, who can also fill in at right
back, he was a regular in the starting line-
up throughout the campaign. He marked
his first match as captain with his only
senior goal, a remarkable effort at
Kidderminster in September when he ran
from his own half to find the back of the
net. Cliff added two more appearances
for the Republic of Ireland at U21 level
during the season.
Sunderland (From trainee on 27/5/1999)
Scunthorpe U (Loaned on 21/11/2002) FL 13
FAC 3
Scunthorpe U (Free on 2/7/2003) FL 39/1
FLC 2 FAC 6 Others 4

BYRNE Daniel (Danny) Thomas

Born: Frimley, 30 November 1984
Height: 5'9" **Weight:** 10.6
International Honours: RoI: Yth
This talented young winger had previously
represented the Republic of Ireland at
U19 level, but was deemed surplus to
requirements at Manchester United last
term. Danny had a spell on loan at
Hartlepool in the autumn but failed to
make much of an impact and soon after
returning to Old Trafford he was released.
He later had a trial with Reading.
Manchester U (From trainee on 18/9/2003)
Hartlepool U (Loaned on 25/11/2003) FL 2
FAC 1

BYRNE Desmond (Des)

Born: Dublin, 10 April 1981
Height: 6'1" **Weight:** 12.8
International Honours: RoI: Yth
Although his contract with Carlisle had
been terminated during the previous
campaign, Des was given another chance
by the Brunton Park management in the
2003 close season. He enjoyed a run in
the side in his favoured left-back role but
did not feature after early November, and
his contract was later ended after a
further breach of club discipline. In April
he signed for one of his former clubs, St
Patrick's Athletic, on a weekly contract.
Stockport Co (Trainee) FL 2 (Free to St
Patricks Ath on 1/2/1999)
Wimbledon (£20,000 on 2/8/2000) FL 0+1
Cambridge U (Loaned on 8/8/2001) FL 3+1
FLC 1

Des Byrne

Carlisle U (Free on 25/10/2002) FL 18+3 FAC 0+1 Others 2

BYRNE Michael Thomas
Born: Huddersfield, 14 May 1985
Height: 5'10" **Weight:** 11.6
The young striker was thrown straight into the deep end when Stockport manager Sammy McIlroy surprisingly handed him a debut against Notts County at Meadow Lane last February. The Hatters found themselves 2-0 down when Michael got them back into the game with a coolly taken strike in front of the County fans, providing a special moment for the rookie forward.
***Stockport Co** (From trainee at Bolton W, via trial at Cardiff C, on 23/10/2003) FL 1/1*

BYRNE Shaun Ryan
Born: Chesham, 21 January 1981
Height: 5'9" **Weight:** 11.12
International Honours: RoI: U21-10; Yth (UEFA-U16 '98)
Shaun came on as a substitute for West Ham in the Carling Cup tie against Rushden but that was his only appearance for the Hammers last term. The young West Ham left back was loaned out to Swansea in February and impressed during his spell at the Vetch Field. However he was released by West Ham during the summer.
***West Ham U** (From trainee on 2/7/1999) PL 0+2 FLC 0+1*
***Bristol Rov** (Loaned on 7/1/2000) FL 1+1 Others 2*
***Swansea C** (Loaned on 30/1/2004) FL 9 FAC 1*

BYWATER Stephen (Steve) Michael
Born: Manchester, 7 June 1981
Height: 6'3" **Weight:** 13.2
Club Honours: FAYC '99
International Honours: E: U21-2; Yth
This young goalkeeper came into the West Ham side in January after David James was transferred to Manchester City. In his first match he saved a penalty against Sheffield United at Bramall Lane and soon showed what a fine prospect he is by turning on some excellent displays as the Hammers made a bid for promotion. His contributions included a breathtaking stop at Bradford, another penalty save at Millwall and a brilliant dive to thwart Bruce Dyer against Watford.
***Rochdale** (Trainee) Others 1*
***West Ham U** (£300,000 + on 7/8/1998) P/FL 21+1 FAC 3 Others 3*
***Wycombe W** (Loaned on 23/9/1999) FL 2*
***Hull C** (Loaned on 23/11/1999) FL 4*

CADAMARTERI Daniel (Danny) Leon

Born: Cleckheaton, 12 October 1979
Height: 5'7'' **Weight:** 11.12
Club Honours: FAYC '98
International Honours: E: U21-3; Yth
This former England U21 international played only a quarter of Bradford City's First Division programme because of knee and hamstring injuries. However, when he did feature, Danny was a major threat operating on either the left or right of a three-man attack. His pace and strength unsettled opponents and had he been available for larger chunks of their survival fight, City would have stood a much stronger chance of beating the drop. His three-goal tally for the season was his best since joining his hometown club.
Everton (From trainee on 15/10/1996) PL 38+55/13 FLC 6+3/2 FAC 6+3
Fulham (Loaned on 4/11/1999) FL 3+2/1
Bradford C (Free on 22/2/2002) FL 42+10/5 FLC 1/1

CADE Jamie William

Born: Durham, 15 January 1984
Height: 5'8'' **Weight:** 10.12
International Honours: E: Yth
Jamie joined Chesterfield on loan to cover for injury to Glynn Hurst and proved a useful addition to the forward line, with plenty of pace and good close control. Released by Middlesbrough, he was offered a deal by the Spireites, but sensibly opted for a longer-term one at Colchester. However, he struggled to find his best form at Layer Road and often found himself used in a position out on the right flank. Jamie managed just six starts for the U's and will be looking to make more of an impact in the 2004-05 season.
Middlesbrough (From trainee on 12/7/2001) FLC 0+1
Chesterfield (Loaned on 25/9/2003) FL 9+1/2 FAC 1 Others 1+1/1
Colchester U (Free on 27/11/2003) FL 6+9

CAHILL Timothy (Tim)

Born: Sydney, Australia, 6 December 1979
Height: 5'10'' **Weight:** 10.11
Club Honours: Div 2 '01
International Honours: Australia: 4; W Samoa: Yth
A forceful, strong-running midfielder Tim is remarkably good in the air for a player of only average height. He continued to improve last term and scored some

cracking goals. His main threat is when receiving the ball from deep when he times his runs superbly. Still only young, he has already made nearly 300 appearances for Millwall. Tim finally made his debut at international level for Australia following after FIFA altered their regulations concerning eligibility. He was selected for the PFA Division One team of the season.
Millwall (Signed from Sydney U, Australia on 31/7/1997) FL 212+5/52 FLC 9+1/1 FAC 10+2/3 Others 10+1/1

CAIG Antony (Tony)

Born: Whitehaven, 11 April 1974
Height: 6'1'' **Weight:** 13.4
Club Honours: Div 3 '95; AMC '97
Newcastle's reserve 'keeper was out of the first-team picture at St James' Park last term and his only senior action came during a loan spell at Barnsley in the new year. Tony enjoyed his three-match stay at Oakwell, showing himself to be a capable and effective shot stopper before returning to the North-East.
Carlisle U (From trainee on 10/7/1992) FL 223 FLC 16 FAC 13 Others 29
Blackpool (£40,000 on 25/3/1999) FL 49 FLC 2 FAC 3 Others 2
Charlton Ath (Free on 3/11/2000) PL 0+1
Hibernian (Free on 13/7/2001) SL 13+1 SLC 2
Newcastle U (Free on 31/1/2003)
Barnsley (Loaned on 16/1/2004) FL 3

CALDWELL Gary

Born: Stirling, 12 April 1982
Height: 5'11'' **Weight:** 12.0
International Honours: S: 8; B-4; U21-19; Yth; Sch
This Scotland international defender joined Derby on loan for two months from the start of the 2003-04 season but suffered from the team's uncertain start. He was used in the centre of defence but also played at right back against West Ham. Gary was never totally sure of a starting place, but his form improved before he returned to Newcastle. He joined Hibernian in the January transfer window and featured regularly at the Easter Road club in the second half of the season.
Newcastle U (From trainee on 19/4/1999)
Darlington (Loaned on 20/11/2001) FL 4
Hibernian (Loaned on 31/1/2002) SL 10+1 SLC 1
Coventry C (Loaned on 3/7/2002) FL 36 FLC 3 FAC 2
Derby Co (Loaned on 8/8/2003) FL 6+3 FLC 1

CALDWELL Stephen

Born: Stirling, 12 September 1980
Height: 6'0'' **Weight:** 11.5

International Honours: S: 4; B-3; U21-4; Yth
This strong, composed centre back found it difficult to break into Newcastle's first team in 2003-04 and he made only a couple of starts and two substitute appearances early in the season before joining Leeds on loan in January. He went straight into the first team and formed a useful central defensive partnership with Dominic Matteo. However, once Leeds' relegation was confirmed he was recalled to Tyneside because injuries and suspensions had left the Magpies short of centre backs, and he played in the final three games of the season, turning in sound performances, the last as an effective substitute right back. Stephen continued to represent his country at international level.
Newcastle U (From trainee on 30/10/1997) PL 20+8/1 FLC 3/1 Others 1+5
Blackpool (Loaned on 12/10/2001) FL 6 Others 1/1
Bradford C (Loaned on 7/12/2001) FL 9
Leeds U (Loaned on 2/2/2004) PL 13/1

CALVO-GARCIA Alexander (Alex)

Born: Ordizia, Spain, 1 January 1972
Height: 5'10'' **Weight:** 11.12
Alex made a dramatic start to the 2003-04 campaign when coming off the bench to score a spectacular long-range injury-time winner against Torquay. A skilful, hard-working central midfield player, his season was ruined by a damaged ankle tendon in October which ruled him out for six months. However, he appeared in the last three games of the season, being made captain for the final match as he bowed out of English football after eight years' fabulous service to Scunthorpe and retired to start work in business back in Spain.
Scunthorpe U (Free from Eibar, Spain on 4/10/1996) FL 205+28/32 FLC 10+1/4 FAC 19+2/4 Others 13/4

CAMARA Henri

Born: Dakar, Senegal, 10 May 1977
Height: 5'9'' **Weight:** 10.8
International Honours: Senegal
Henri arrived at Molineux as an exciting right winger or forward, who showed great speed and skill. His winning goal against Leicester did not prove a breakthrough, for despite an exciting approach his play didn't always produce an end product. Henri was absent from seven games as he appeared for Senegal in the African Nations' Cup, not scoring for them either. His second goal for

Wolves came on 27 March, to begin a sequence of scoring in five consecutive matches. The latter two were quite spectacular, and another powerful shot found the Everton net to make it six goals in seven games. He was playing a more central role, linking up well with Carl Cort, and was Wolves' top Premiership scorer. Henri was also voted the club's 'Player of the Season'.

Wolverhampton W (Free from Sedan, France, ex Neuchatel Xamax, Strasbourg, Grasshoper Zurich, on 6/8/2003) PL 29+1/7 FLC 2

CAMARA Mohamed (Mo)

Born: Conakry, Guinea, 25 June 1975
Height: 5'11" **Weight:** 11.9
After arriving on a free transfer shortly before the start of the season, Mo was a virtual ever-present as Burnley's left back last term. He looked good on the overlap with his considerable pace, and was generally reliable at the back although positional failings and slow reactions proved costly on a few occasions. He

often looked happier going forward, was instrumental in the build-up to several goals and was unlucky not to register on the score sheet himself.

Wolverhampton W (Loaned from Le Havre, France, ex AS Beauvais, on 11/8/2000) FL 27+18 FLC 2+1 FAC 1+1 Others 2

Burnley (Free on 18/7/2003) FL 45 FLC 3 FAC 2+1

CAMARA Zoumana

Born: Paris, France, 3 April 1979
Height: 5'10" **Weight:** 12.11
International Honours: France: 1; B-2
One of several players to join Leeds United on loan for the whole of the 2003-04 season, this experienced defender featured regularly at right back under Peter Reid. He scored in the 3-2 win at Middlesbrough, but was out of favour when Eddie Gray assumed the managerial reigns and made just one appearance in the second half of the campaign.

Leeds U (Loaned from Lens, France, ex St Etienne, Inter Milan, Empoli, Bastia, Marseilles, on 1/8/2003) PL 13/1 FLC 2

CAMERON Colin

Born: Kirkcaldy, 23 October 1972
Height: 5'6" **Weight:** 10.6
Club Honours: S: 11; S Div 1 '93, '95; SLC '94; SC '98
International Honours: S: 27
The hard-working midfielder secured Wolves' first ever Premiership win with a rare header against Manchester City. He followed it up with a brace against Leicester in the next home match, but then suffered an injury and was no more than substitute in the next six games. Colin re-established himself in the team before another brief absence in February. His return to the starting line-up at Manchester City was somewhat marred by a penalty miss, but he made amends with a quality goal at Birmingham, exchanging passes with Henri Camara before curling the ball into the net. Colin continued to be a regular for Scotland.

Raith Rov (Signed from Lochore Welfare on 13/7/1990) SL 106+16/23 SLC 8+1/5 SC 6/3 Others 9/2

Henri Camara (left)

Heart of Midlothian (£400,000 on 31/3/1996) SL 152+3/47 SLC 13/6 SC 17+1/6 Others 6+3/1
Wolverhampton W (£1,750,000 on 24/8/2001) P/FL 92+12/15 FLC 1 FAC 7 Others 5

CAMP Lee Michael John

Born: Derby, 22 August 1984
Height: 5'11" **Weight:** 11.11
International Honours: E: Yth
This promising young goalkeeper was well down the pecking order at Derby last term and in March he joined Queens Park Rangers on loan. Lee made his debut in the 4-1 away win at Hartlepool and kept his place in the side for the rest of the season, despite Chris Day's return to fitness. He quickly became a favourite with the fans with some brave performances and fine saves, and will be looking to break into the first-team squad at Pride Park in 2004-05.
Derby Co (From trainee on 16/7/2002) FL 0+1
Queens Park R (Loaned on 12/3/2004) FL 12

CAMPBELL Andrew (Andy) Paul

Born: Stockton, 18 April 1979
Height: 5'11" **Weight:** 11.7
International Honours: E: U21-4; Yth
Last season was a turning point for Andy, who shrugged off the frustration of his supporting role behind Robert Earnshaw and began to produce his best form. A key to his transformation was a switch to a role as an out-and-out striker, whereas in the past he had often featured out wide on the left. The man who scored Cardiff's winning goal in the Division Two play-off final at the Millennium Stadium can look to 2004-05 with renewed confidence.
Middlesbrough (From trainee on 4/7/1996) F/PL 28+28/4 FLC 5+5/1 FAC 2+3/2
Sheffield U (Loaned on 10/12/1998) FL 5/1
Sheffield U (Loaned on 25/3/1999) FL 6/2
Bolton W (Loaned on 9/3/2001) FL 3+3
Cardiff C (£950,000 on 25/2/2002) FL 24+37/12 FLC 2+2/1 FAC 2+4/2 Others 2+5/2

CAMPBELL Kevin Joseph

Born: Lambeth, 4 February 1970
Height: 6'1" **Weight:** 13.8
Club Honours: FAYC '88; FLC '93; FAC '93; ECWC '94; Div 1 '98
International Honours: E: B-1; U21-4
Kevin had a frustrating season for Everton, the tone being set when he pulled up with a hamstring injury in the final warm-up game of pre-season that kept him on the sidelines for six weeks.

He featured only intermittently as a consequence, the personal highlight of his campaign arriving with his 500th career game in English football which came, ironically enough, against his former club, Arsenal. He had to wait until the final game of the season, against Manchester City, to score his only goal of the campaign. At his best Kevin lends a powerful presence to the attack and is an excellent finisher both on the ground and in the air.
Arsenal (From trainee on 11/2/1988) F/PL 124+42/46 FLC 14+10/6 FAC 13+6/2 Others 15+4/5
Leyton Orient (Loaned on 16/1/1989) FL 16/9
Leicester C (Loaned on 8/11/1989) FL 11/5 Others 1/1
Nottingham F (£3,000,000 on 1/7/1995) F/PL 79+1/32 FLC 2 FAC 11/3 Others 3 (£2,500,000 to Trabzonspor, Turkey on 7/8/1998)
Everton (£3,000,000 on 25/3/1999) PL 121+18/45 FLC 5+3/3 FAC 9+1/3

CAMPBELL Stuart Pearson

Born: Corby, 9 December 1977
Height: 5'10" **Weight:** 10.8
Club Honours: FLC '97, '00
International Honours: S: U21-14
Stuart was one of Grimsby Town's most consistent players last season and was one of only a handful to appear in the line-up throughout the campaign. A tireless worker in midfield, he scored two goals including one in the 4-0 win over Chesterfield, one of the high points of an otherwise dismal season for the Mariners.
Leicester C (From trainee on 4/7/1996) PL 12+25 FLC 2+5 FAC 3+3
Birmingham C (Loaned on 23/3/2000) FL 0+2
Grimsby T (£200,000 on 15/9/2000) FL 154+1/12 FLC 6/1 FAC 7 Others 0+1

CAMPBELL Sulzeer (Sol) Jeremiah

Born: Newham, 18 September 1974
Height: 6'2" **Weight:** 14.1
Club Honours: FLC '99; PL '02, '04; FAC '02; CS '02
International Honours: E: 62; B-1; U21-11; Yth (UEFA-U18 '93)
Now widely acknowledged as the key figure in the Gunners' back four, Sol had a difficult start to the 2003-04 campaign, but his class won through. He recorded his only goal of the season against a resolute Aston Villa team and was very effective in the crucial win at Anfield. Sol was, as usual, a magnificent last line of defence, strong in the air and a fine

exponent of the defender's art, forming an impressive partnership with Kolo Toure. He was named in both the PFA Premiership team of the season and England's squad for Euro 2004.
Tottenham H (From trainee on 23/9/1992) PL 246+9/10 FLC 28/4 FAC 28+2/1 Others 2
Arsenal (Free on 10/7/2001) PL 97+2/5 FAC 17/2 Others 31

CAMPBELL-RYCE Jamal Julian

Born: Lambeth, 6 April 1983
Height: 5'7" **Weight:** 11.10
International Honours: Jamaica: 1
A skilful winger with electric pace, Jamal can be very difficult to play against. He made his first appearance of the season coming on as a substitute in the Carling Cup game against Luton Town at the Valley in September, and almost immediately raced down the left flank and put in a superb cross to set up Paolo Di Canio for a last minute equaliser, which put the tie into extra time. The same month he won a full cap for Jamaica, coming on as a substitute against Australia at Reading. He made three more appearances from the bench for Charlton without really impressing, and he was loaned to Wimbledon in February to enable him to gain more experience. He showed some neat touches for the Dons, but found it hard going in a team that was struggling badly in the table.
Charlton Ath (From trainee on 9/7/2002) PL 0+3 FLC 0+2
Leyton Orient (Loaned on 10/8/2002) FL 16+1/2 FLC 2/1
Wimbledon (Loaned on 6/2/2004) FL 3+1

CAMPO Ramos Ivan

Born: San Sebastian, Spain, 21 February 1974
Height: 6'1" **Weight:** 12.11
International Honours: Spain: 4
This well-known midfielder proved himself to be one of the most pivotal players in a fine season for Bolton Wanderers. Playing as the 'holding' midfielder, and as such allowing the likes of Youri Djorkaeff, Jay Jay Okocha and Kevin Nolan to weave their magic further up the field, Ivan controlled games with a combination of skill and passion which secured his place amongst the hearts of the Bolton fans. Fully committed, and a sublime distributor of the ball, he proved to be the vital link between defence and attack on many occasions, whilst also weighing in with four important Premiership goals over the course of the campaign.

Ivan Campo (right)

Bolton W (Loaned from Real Madrid, Spain, ex CD Logrones, Alaves, Vallencia, Valladolid, Real Mallorca, on 31/8/2002) PL 65+4/6 FLC 7 FAC 2

CANERO Peter

Born: Glasgow, 18 January 1981
Height: 5'9" **Weight:** 11.4
International Honours: S: 1; B-3; U21-17

This highly rated young full back or wide midfielder was out of contract at Kilmarnock in the summer and the club wisely chose to sell him on to Leicester during the January transfer window. Peter picked up a shoulder injury in his first outing for the Foxes' reserves, but when he did finally see some first-team action he impressed with his pace and persistence. Often appearing from the bench and being asked to operate on the right side of midfield, he came close to providing an unlikely winner at Elland Road, whilst he particularly impressed on his first start, at home to Manchester City. He was rewarded with a first call up to the senior Scotland squad in April, when he was called into action from the bench after just 15 minutes. A hip injury then brought his season to a premature close in early May, so denying him the opportunity to add to his international caps at the end of that month.
Kilmarnock (From juniors on 16/10/1997) SL 96+21/9 SLC 3+1/1 SC 5+1/1 Others 2+1
Leicester C (£250,000 on 20/1/2004) PL 2+5

CANOVILLE Lee

Born: Ealing, 14 March 1981
Height: 6'1" **Weight:** 11.3
International Honours: E: Yth; Sch
Although occasionally pushed up to right midfield, Lee established himself as a regular at right back for Torquay last term. He used his skill and pace to cover efficiently at the back and always carried a real threat on the overlap. Lee had two extended spells out injured, and was ruled out of the final promotion run-in.
Arsenal (From trainee on 3/7/1998, having earlier been transferred from Millwall juniors for an undisclosed fee on 9/7/1997) FLC 0+1
Northampton T (Loaned on 26/1/2001) FL 2
Torquay U (Free on 14/9/2001) FL 78+3/2 FLC 2 FAC 2 Others 2

CAPALDI Anthony (Tony) Charles

Born: Porsgrunn, Norway, 12 August 1981
Height: 6'0" **Weight:** 11.8
Club Honours: Div 2 '04
International Honours: NI: 5; U21-14

Tony enjoyed an excellent campaign last term, when he gained a Second Division championship medal with Plymouth and also made his full international debut for Northern Ireland. A left-sided midfield player with plenty of ability on the ball, he built up an excellent understanding with his former Birmingham City colleague Peter Gilbert. Tony also showed he has an eye for goal, netting seven times during the season.
Birmingham C (From trainee on 9/7/1999)
Plymouth Arg (Free on 3/5/2003) FL 30+4/7 FLC 1 Others 0+2

CARBON Matthew (Matt) Phillip

Born: Nottingham, 8 June 1975
Height: 6'2" **Weight:** 13.6
International Honours: E: U21-4
Matt created a surprise at the start of the season by announcing his retirement from the game but he was soon back. He linked up with his former boss Keith Alexander when he joined Lincoln on a month's loan in October to help his return to match fitness. Matt fitted into a three-man centre-back system but lasted just 45 minutes of his debut at Hull City before being forced off with a shoulder injury. Matt spent the remainder of his time at Sincil Bank on the injury list before returning to Walsall.He returned for the Saddlers in the new year and acquitted himself well whenever called upon. He was particularly impressive in the game against the strong Wigan side in February with commanding headers and strong tackles. Matt was reported to have signed for Barnsley in the summer.
Lincoln C (From trainee on 13/4/1993) FL 66+3/10 FLC 4/1 FAC 3 Others 4+3
Derby Co (£385,000 on 8/3/1996) P/FL 11+9 FLC 1 FAC 0+1
West Bromwich A (£800,000 on 26/1/1998) FL 106+7/5 FLC 7+2 FAC 4
Walsall (Free on 23/7/2001) FL 49+6/2 FLC 1 FAC 5
Lincoln C (Loaned on 24/10/2003) FL 1

CAREY Brian Patrick

Born: Cork, 31 May 1968
Height: 6'3" **Weight:** 14.4
International Honours: RoI: 3; U21-1
Brian was once again involved for Wrexham last term, combined playing duties with coaching the Racecourse youngsters. Although perhaps losing some of his pace, he still held the defence together and the back line always looked tighter for his inclusion. Although he missed time towards the end of the season with a foot injury, he headed the

opening goal in the FAW Premier Cup final against Rhyl.
Manchester U (£100,000 from Cork C on 2/9/1989)
Wrexham (Loaned on 17/1/1991) FL 3
Wrexham (Loaned on 24/12/1991) FL 13/1 FAC 3 Others 3
Leicester C (£250,000 on 16/7/1993) F/PL 51+7/1 FLC 3 FAC 0+1 Others 4
Wrexham (£100,000 on 19/7/1996) FL 272+6/15 FLC 12 FAC 22 Others 8+2

CAREY Louis Anthony

Born: Bristol, 20 January 1977
Height: 5'10" **Weight:** 11.10
Club Honours: AMC '03
International Honours: S: U21-1
This cool and cultured defender impressed in his defensive role at right back last term and it was no surprise that he was one of three Bristol City players selected for the PFA Division Two team of the season. Unfortunately the dashing runs down the right flank were less frequent than hitherto as manager Danny Wilson decided to adopt a more defensive approach for what turned out to be an unsuccessful promotion attempt.
Bristol C (From trainee on 3/7/1995) FL 301+11/5 FLC 15+1 FAC 18+1 Others 21+2/1

CARLISLE Clarke James

Born: Preston, 14 October 1979
Height: 6'1" **Weight:** 12.10
International Honours: E: U21-3
This central defender was an automatic choice for Queens Park Rangers last season when fit. He missed two months early on following an injury at Rushden in August and then suffered an ankle injury in the Easter game against Grimsby. Despite several opportunities he only added one to his goal tally for the club during the campaign. One of the reasons for the club's success was the solid central defensive partnerships that Clarke established firstly with Danny Shittu and then with Arthur Gnohere.
Blackpool (From trainee on 13/8/1997) FL 85+8/7 FLC 4+1 FAC 3/1 Others 5
Queens Park R (£250,000 on 25/5/2000) FL 93+3/6 FLC 5 FAC 6 Others 5

CARLISLE Wayne Thomas

Born: Lisburn, 9 September 1979
Height: 6'0" **Weight:** 11.6
International Honours: NI: U21-9; Yth; Sch
This quick-raiding right winger scored some important match-winning goals for Bristol Rovers last term including two in the early-season victory at Carlisle. Although Wayne's season was curtailed

prematurely following a knee operation in February, he still finished the campaign as Rovers' second-top scorer with seven goals.

Crystal Palace (From trainee on 18/9/1996) FL 29+17/3 FLC 4+3 FAC 1
Swindon T (Loaned on 12/10/2001) FL 10+1/2 FAC 2
Bristol Rov (Free on 28/3/2002) FL 62+9/14 FLC 2 FAC 3+2/1 Others 1

CARNEY David (Dave)

Born: Sydney, Australia, 30 November 1983
Height: 5'10" **Weight:** 12.5
International Honours: Australia: Yth
This young midfielder joined Oldham Athletic on a non-contract basis last August after being released by Everton. Despite showing promise in the Carling Cup defeat at Scunthorpe, Dave was released as manager Iain Dowie felt the Latics had enough midfield options. After trials with a number of clubs he signed for Halifax Town towards the end of the season.

Everton (From trainee on 15/1/2000)
Oldham Ath (Free on 8/8/2003) FLC 0+1

CAROLE Sebastien

Born: Pontoise, France, 8 September 1982
Height: 5'6" **Weight:** 11.4
Sebastien joined West Ham on loan from Monaco in March and came on as substitute against Crewe with only three minutes remaining. He has impressive technical ability and can play on either side of the midfield. He played well for the club's reserves for whom he scored some spectacular goals.

West Ham U (Loaned from Monaco, France on 31/1/2004) FL 0+1

CARPENTER Richard

Born: Sheerness, 30 September 1972
Height: 6'0" **Weight:** 13.0
Club Honours: Div 3 '01; Div 2 '02
Richard enjoyed another solid season for Brighton last term when he was once again a consistent driving-force in the midfield. Solid in the tackle, a good passer of the ball and a 90-minute player, he excited the Withdean crowd with his long-range shooting, firing the winner against Swindon to give his side a vital lead after the first leg of the play-off semi-final. A great talisman wherever he has played, Richard went on to earn the sixth promotion of his career, and his third with the Seagulls, in the narrow play-off victory over Bristol City at the Millennium Stadium.

Gillingham (From trainee on 13/5/1991) FL 107+15/4 FLC 2+1 FAC 9+1 Others 7/1
Fulham (£15,000 on 26/9/1996) FL 49+9/7 FLC 4/1 FAC 2/1 Others 2
Cardiff C (£35,000 on 29/7/1998) FL 69+6/2 FLC 3+1 FAC 8+1 Others 1
Brighton & Hove A (Free on 4/7/2000) FL 169+4/15 FLC 7+1 FAC 7/1 Others 7/2

CARR Christopher (Chris)

Paul
Born: Newcastle, 14 December 1984
Height: 5'11" **Weight:** 12.6
This young central defender began last term in Newcastle's reserve team, but in March he signed for Sheffield Wednesday after a successful trial period. Chris was immediately appointed captain of the Owls' reserve side and after some assured displays he was given his first-team debut, albeit as a last-minute substitute at Luton. He will be looking to gain further senior experience in 2004-05.

Sheffield Wed (Free from trainee at Newcastle U on 25/3/2004) FL 0+2

CARR Michael Andrew

Born: Crewe, 6 December 1983
Height: 5'9" **Weight:** 11.4
Michael progressed through the youth ranks at Macclesfield Town and was awarded his first professional contract during the summer of 2003. Captain of the reserve side, for whom he usually played as a central defender in a back-four formation, Michael deputised for George Abbey at right back, making some useful appearances and demonstrating his ability to make timely tackles. Michael was voted as Macc's 'Reserve Team Player of the Year'.

Macclesfield T (From trainee on 4/7/2003) FL 11 FAC 1

CARR Stephen

Born: Dublin, 29 August 1976
Height: 5'9" **Weight:** 12.2
Club Honours: FLC '99
International Honours: RoI: 30; U21-12; Yth; Sch
Probably the most influential player in the current Spurs line-up, when Stephen is fit and on form and commanding his wing-back position on the right the team seem to show much greater confidence, especially when moving forward. Stephen continued to grow in stature at both club and international level and looked to have recovered well from his long lay-off. He is a rock solid tackler and has matured into a great leader on the pitch. He will be eager to see what opportunities and ambitions the new

management bring to White Hart Lane in 2004-05.

Tottenham H (From trainee on 1/9/1993) PL 222+4/7 FLC 23/1 FAC 16+1 Others 6

CARRAGHER James (Jamie) Lee Duncan

Born: Bootle, 28 January 1978
Height: 6'1" **Weight:** 13.0
Club Honours: FAYC '96; FLC '01, '03; FAC '01; UEFAC '01; ESC '01; CS '01
International Honours: E: 12; B-2; U21-27; Yth
Jamie's season seemed over as early as September when he suffered a broken leg playing for Liverpool at Blackburn. To his credit, however, he returned to first-team duty in January and held his place until the end of the campaign, initially at left back before replacing Steve Finnan at right back. To cap it all he won a surprise call-up for the England squad for the Euro 2004 finals in Portugal. Jamie's versatility in any defensive position or as midfield anchor was undoubtedly a factor in his selection. In the closing weeks of the season Liverpool fans were treated to a new dimension in Jamie's play as he frequently entered the opposition half to put in some quality crosses and some fierce shots on target for goal, and if he continues in this vein his third goal for the Reds, after a six-year wait, may not be far away.

Liverpool (From trainee on 9/10/1996) PL 204+12/2 FLC 16+3 FAC 18 Others 50+1

CARRAGHER Matthew (Matt)

Born: Liverpool, 14 January 1976
Height: 5'9" **Weight:** 12.4
Club Honours: Div 3 '97; AMC '01
Matt began the 2003-04 campaign with Dr Martens League club Stafford Rangers before signing for Macclesfield in November. Although his appearances were curtailed due to two month-long absences because of injury, when fully fit he used his considerable experience and versatility filling in at right back, as a wide-right midfielder and, in the latter part of the season, as an effective sweeper. Matt is an excellent defensive player who always puts in a solid and reliable performance.

Wigan Ath (From trainee on 25/11/1993) FL 102+17 FLC 6+1/1 FAC 10+1/2 Others 7+1
Port Vale (Free on 3/7/1997) FL 190+4/1 FLC 9 FAC 5 Others 12/1 (Free to Stafford R during 2003 close season)
Macclesfield T (Free on 25/11/2003) FL 18

CARRICK Michael
Born: Wallsend, 28 July 1981
Height: 6'0" **Weight:** 11.10
Club Honours: FAYC '99
International Honours: E: 2; U21-14; Yth

At the start of the 2003-04 season Michael was troubled by a groin injury but returned to the midfield at West Ham in October. He soon rediscovered his form to show that he is one of the top midfielders in the country and proved to be the driving force behind many of the Hammers attacks. At Stoke in April he was the 'Man of the Match' showing some classy play and impressive passing skills. Michael was the runner-up in the 'Hammer of the Year' award and was selected for the PFA Division One team of the season.

West Ham U (From trainee on 25/8/1998) P/FL 128+8/6 FLC 8 FAC 11 Others 3+1
Swindon T (Loaned on 12/11/1999) FL 6/2
B i rmingham C (Loaned on 23/2/2000) FL 1+1

CARROLL Roy Eric
Born: Enniskillen, 30 September 1977
Height: 6'2" **Weight:** 12.9
Club Honours: AMC '99; PL '03; FAC '04
International Honours: NI: 14; U21-11; Yth

A highly accomplished goalkeeper, who possesses great presence, and a safe pair of hands, Roy might have found his way to regular first-team football blocked by the summer signing of Tim Howard, but he remained a trusted and patient deputy when called upon by Sir Alex Ferguson. His appearances from August to early March where limited to a solitary Champions' League outing against Stuttgart in November, two Carling Cup games against Leeds United and West Bromwich Albion, and two Premiership outings against Fulham in February and Spurs in March. However, when Sir Alex decided to rest Tim Howard following the Reds exit from the Champions' League, Roy took his chance with relish, inspiring United to their 15th FA Cup final.

Hull C (From trainee on 7/9/1995) FL 46 FLC 2 FAC 1 Others 1
Wigan Ath (£350,000 on 16/4/1997) FL 135 FLC 11 FAC 8 Others 15
Manchester U (£2,500,000 on 27/7/2001) PL 20+3 FLC 5 FAC 4+1 Others 5

CARRUTHERS Christopher (Chris) Paul
Born: Kettering, 19 August 1983
Height: 5'10" **Weight:** 12.3
International Honours: E: Yth

This promising young Northampton left back had a somewhat up-and-down season last term. He featured in over half the Cobblers first-team games, but also had his fair share of injuries, and in the FA Cup fourth round tie against Manchester United he was carried off in a neck brace. However, Chris continued to represent England at U20 level during the campaign and was a member of the squad that took part in the World Youth Championships in Dubai at the end of the year.

Northampton T (From trainee on 9/4/2002) FL 52+21/1 FLC 2 FAC 7 Others 3+1

CARRUTHERS Martin George
Born: Nottingham, 7 August 1972
Height: 5'11" **Weight:** 12.0

Martin appeared in the role of striker in the majority of matches for Macclesfield last term, but was unable to reach his goal tally of recent seasons, possibly because the level of service to him could have been better at times. Nevertheless he made a useful contribution, scoring ten goals in all competitions and complementing his main strike partner, Matthew Tipton.

Aston Villa (From trainee on 4/7/1990) F/PL 2+2 FAC 0+1 Others 0+1
Hull C (Loaned on 31/10/1992) FL 13/6 Others 3
Stoke C (£100,000 on 5/7/1993) FL 60+31/13 FLC 7+3/1 FAC 3+1 Others 10+4/6
Peterborough U (Signed on 18/11/1996) FL 63+4/21 FLC 5+1/2 FAC 6/4 Others 6
York C (Loaned on 29/1/1999) FL 3+3
Darlington (Signed on 25/3/1999) FL 11+6/2 FLC 0+2
Southend U (£50,000 on 17/9/1999) FL 69+1/26 FLC 2 FAC 5 Others 5+1/3
Scunthorpe U (£20,000 on 22/3/2001) FL 80+6/34 FLC 2 FAC 6/4 Others 5+1/1
Macclesfield T (Free on 4/7/2003) FL 30+9/8 FLC 1 FAC 3+1/2 Others 1

CARSLEY Lee Kevin
Born: Birmingham, 28 February 1974
Height: 5'10" **Weight:** 11.11
International Honours: RoI: 29; U21-1

Lee's season was very much a stop-start affair at Everton, mainly as a result of a niggling knee injury that delayed the start to his campaign and flared up again in October. He then played consistently for the first team in an extended run of games over the Christmas and New Year period, being employed either in central midfield or wide on the right, scoring in the crucial wins against Portsmouth and Leicester. A dip in fortunes followed which resulted in the combative midfielder putting his international

ambitions on hold in order to re-establish himself in the first team.

Derby Co (From trainee on 6/7/1992) P/FL 122+16/5 FLC 10+3 FAC 12 Others 3
Blackburn Rov (£3,375,000 on 23/3/1999) P/FL 40+6/10 FLC 4/1 FAC 4/1
Coventry C (£2,500,000 on 1/12/2000) P/FL 46+1/4 FLC 2/1 FAC 3
Everton (£1,950,000 on 8/2/2002) PL 44+9/6 FLC 4 FAC 3

CARSON Scott Paul
Born: Whitehaven, 3 September 1985
Height: 6'3" **Weight:** 13.7
International Honours: U21-2; Yth

Following Nigel Martyn's departure to Everton, Scott emerged as second choice to Paul Robinson in goal for Leeds. Scott made his full debut in February against Manchester United in the 1-1 draw at Old Trafford, producing a creditable performance. He added another Premiership appearance and also forced himself into the England U21 squad.

Leeds U (From trainee on 5/9/2002) PL 2+1

CARSON Stephen
Born: Ballymoney, NI, 6 October 1980
Height: 5'10" **Weight:** 12.0
International Honours: NI: U21-2

This hard-working left-sided midfielder was attached to Barnsley from the 2003 close season, but the club's financial restraints meant that he did not sign until the end of September. Stephen made an immediate impact at Oakwell, impressing with his crossing and eye for a shot, but in January it was announced that his short-term contract would not be renewed and he moved on to Hartlepool. However, he managed just a handful of appearances during his stay at the Victoria Ground and was released in the summer.

Glasgow R (Signed from Linfield on 1/7/1999) SL 1+1 SLC 0+1 SC 0+1
Dundee (£150,000 on 9/8/2001) SL 8+12 SLC 0+1 SC 1+3
Barnsley (Free on 26/9/2003) FL 9+2/1 FAC 3+1 Others 1+1
Hartlepool U (Free on 19/2/2004) FL 1+2

CARSS Anthony (Tony) John
Born: Alnwick, 31 March 1976
Height: 5'10" **Weight:** 12.0

Tony proved to be a shrewd signing for Huddersfield Town last term, adding both silk and steel to the midfield. Some all-out attacking displays were rewarded with a goal in the Carling Cup win over Sunderland and a sensational volley against Torquay, which was arguably the Terriers' 'Goal of the Season'. The left-sided player became an important cog in

Tony Carss

the club's end-of-season success and was one of the scorers in the play-off penalty shoot-out against Mansfield.
Blackburn Rov *(From trainee at Bradford C on 29/8/1994)*
Darlington *(Free on 11/8/1995) FL 33+24/2 FLC 5/1 FAC 2+1 Others 4*
Cardiff C *(Free on 28/7/1997) FL 36+6/1 FLC 2 FAC 5+1 Others 1*
Chesterfield *(Free on 7/9/1998) FL 26+9/1 FLC 2 FAC 1 Others 1+1*
Carlisle U *(Free on 11/8/2000) FL 6+1 FLC 2*
Oldham Ath *(Free on 13/10/2000) FL 58+17/5 FLC 3/1 FAC 3 Others 1+2*
Huddersfield T *(Free on 7/8/2003) FL 35+1/2 FLC 3/1 Others 1*

CARTER Darren Anthony
Born: Solihull, 18 December 1983
Height: 6'2" **Weight:** 12.5
International Honours: E: Yth
An England U20 regular, Darren was squeezed out of the Birmingham City midfield last term and was the subject of several loan inquiries. He matured physically and got stronger as the season went on. Left-footed, he gets from box to box, is quick and not afraid to tackle. His only Premiership start came at left back at Spurs when the Blues had an injury crisis.
Birmingham C *(From trainee on 13/11/2001) P/FL 16+14/1 FLC 1 FAC 0+3 Others 1+1*

CARTLEDGE Jonathan (Jon)
Born: Carshalton, 27 November 1984
Height: 6'2" **Weight:** 13.0
This young central defender spent much of last season in the Bury youth team. However, a suspension to Colin Woodthorpe gave John an unexpected chance in the first team and he made his debut at Carlisle in February. Powerful in the air, he retained his place for the next game but a dose of mumps then ended his run. Although not the finished article, John adapted well to Division Three football and he started the closing six games of the season – scoring his first-ever senior goal in the away game at Northampton.
Bury *(Trainee) FL 7+4/1*

CARTWRIGHT Lee
Born: Rawtenstall, 19 September 1972
Height: 5'8" **Weight:** 11.0
Club Honours: Div 3 '96; Div 2 '00
Lee's last Preston appearance saw him become only the fourth player ever to make 100 substitute appearances for a single club, when he came on from the bench at Gillingham. He also made a couple of starts for North End before

moving on to Stockport in the new year. Lee quickly settled in at Edgeley Park, becoming a regular on the right-hand side of midfield and playing a key role in the club's successful fight to avoid relegation.
Preston NE *(From trainee on 30/7/1991) FL 312+85/22 FLC 19+4/2 FAC 18+6/1 Others 20+5/1*
Stockport Co *(Free on 29/1/2004) FL 14+1*

CAS Marcel
Born: Breda, Holland, 30 April 1972
Height: 6'1" **Weight:** 12.8
This widely travelled right winger joined Grimsby Town during the 2003 close season and made an immediate impact with his pace and eye for a goal. However, after a short spell out of the team in October he was unable to regain a regular place in the starting line-up and thereafter was mainly used from the substitutes' bench. Marcel was released from his contract in the new year and returned to Holland to sign for RBC Roosendaal.
Notts Co *(Free from RBC Roosendaal, Holland on 4/7/2001) FL 49+9/8 FLC 3 FAC 3 Others 3*
Sheffield U *(Free on 4/2/2003) FL 3+3*
Grimsby T *(Free on 7/7/2003) FL 13+7/2 FLC 1 FAC 0+2/1 Others 1*

CASH Brian Dominick
Born: Dublin, 24 November 1982
Height: 5'9" **Weight:** 12.0
International Honours: RoI: U21-4; Yth
This young Nottingham Forest right-sided midfielder found opportunities hard to come by last term and only made one brief appearance as a last-minute substitute against Coventry in Paul Hart's final game in charge. Brian was a regular in the reserves and will be looking to gain more senior action in 2004-05.
Nottingham F *(From trainee on 15/12/1999) FL 0+7 FLC 0+1*
Swansea C *(Loaned on 19/10/2002) FL 5 Others 1*

CASKEY Darren Mark
Born: Basildon, 21 August 1974
Height: 5'8" **Weight:** 11.9
International Honours: E: Yth (UEFA-U18 '93); Sch
This hugely talented midfield player proved unable to inspire his Notts County colleagues to greater things last season and with relegation looming he joined promotion candidates Bristol City on transfer deadline day. However, he failed to break into the first team at Ashton Gate and was released in the summer. At his best Danny is a brilliant passer of the

ball and a formidable dead-ball specialist.
Tottenham H *(From trainee on 6/3/1992) PL 20+12/4 FLC 3+1/1 FAC 6+1*
Watford *(Loaned on 27/10/1995) FL 6/1*
Reading *(£700,000 on 28/2/1996) FL 180+22/35 FLC 10+2/4 FAC 9+1/5 Others 8+1/1*
Notts Co *(Free on 4/7/2001) FL 101+13/10 FLC 5 FAC 7 Others 2+2/1*

CHADWICK Luke Harry
Born: Cambridge, 18 November 1980
Height: 5'11" **Weight:** 11.0
Club Honours: PL '01
International Honours: E: U21-13; Yth
The season-long loan of Luke Chadwick from Manchester United looked like an inspired move by Burnley manager Stan Ternent in the early stages of the campaign. Often playing on the opposite flank to Glen Little, but occasionally up front, Luke lived up to the expectations, five goals in the month of September confirming him as a valuable addition to the Clarets' side. Unfortunately, he failed to maintain the good start, often seemed to tire during games and was frequently substituted. He was only an occasional starter after Christmas, injury as well as loss of form largely keeping him out of the picture.
Manchester U *(From trainee on 8/2/1999) PL 11+14/2 FLC 5 FAC 1+2 Others 1+5*
Reading *(Loaned on 7/2/2003) FL 15/1 Others 1+1*
Burnley *(Loaned on 15/7/2003) FL 23+13/5 FLC 2/1 FAC 1+1*

CHADWICK Nicholas (Nicky) Gerald
Born: Market Drayton, 26 October 1982
Height: 6'0" **Weight:** 12.8
Nick had a good pre-season during which he put in a series of excellent performances for Everton, which was followed by a campaign during which his two impressive loan spells at Millwall compensated for an unlucky time at Everton, injuries restricting his first-team opportunities to just two games. The tall, pacy striker scored on his debut for the Lions and added three more during his stay, impressing with his willingness for hard work. Nick has consistently found the net at all levels of the game and will be looking to make a breakthrough at Goodison in 2004-05.
Everton *(From trainee on 29/10/1999) PL 3+10/3 FLC 1+1/1 FAC 0+1*
Derby Co *(Loaned on 28/2/2003) FL 4+2*
Millwall *(Loaned on 26/11/2003) FL 6/2*
Millwall *(Loaned on 18/3/2004) FL 5+4/2*

Luke Chadwick

CHALLINOR David (Dave) Paul
Born: Chester, 2 October 1975
Height: 6'1" **Weight:** 12.6
International Honours: E: Yth; Sch
Stockport's captain was dropped at the start of the 2003-04 campaign, beginning the new season on the bench, but even when he got his place back he did not keep it for long. In January he joined Bury on loan, adding experience and steel to a young back line and helping to bring the best out of fellow centre half Danny Swailes. The Shakers enjoyed a good sequence of results during his spell at Gigg Lane and he was made captain for the day on his last appearance against Torquay.
Tranmere Rov (Signed from Brombrough Pool on 18/7/1994) FL 124+16/6 FLC 17+1 FAC 9+2 Others 1
Stockport Co (£120,000 on 11/1/2002) FL 78+3/1 FLC 3 FAC 2 Others 4+1
Bury (Loaned on 9/1/2004) FL 15

CHAMBERLAIN Alec Francis Roy
Born: March, 20 June 1964
Height: 6'2" **Weight:** 13.9
Club Honours: Div 1 '96; Div 2 '98
Alec started his 23rd season in senior football as Watford's first-choice goalkeeper, but lost his place after being sent off controversially at Crewe for handling outside his penalty area. Alec regained his first-team place in April, and his experience was crucial to Watford's successful battle against relegation. His excellent end-of-season form led to the offer of a new contract just before his 40th birthday.
Ipswich T (Free from Ramsey T on 27/7/1981)
Colchester U (Free on 3/8/1982) FL 188 FLC 11 FAC 10 Others 12
Everton (£80,000 on 28/7/1987)
Tranmere Rov (Loaned on 1/11/1987) FL 15
Luton T (£150,000 on 27/7/1988) FL 138 FLC 7 FAC 7 Others 7
Sunderland (Free on 8/7/1993) FL 89+1 FLC 9 FAC 8 Others 1
Watford (£40,000 on 10/7/1996) P/FL 236+3 FLC 16+1 FAC 14 Others 3

CHAMBERS Adam Craig
Born: West Bromwich, 20 November 1980
Height: 5'10" **Weight:** 11.8
International Honours: E: Yth
Unlike his twin brother James, Adam's season was split between the Hawthorns and Hillsborough. As in 2002-03 he was given only one substitute outing in West

Bromwich Albion's first team, coming on in the second-half of a 2-0 home Carling Cup victory over Manchester United in early December. A strong tackler with good technique his Premiership experience proved invaluable to Sheffield Wednesday in a loan spell towards the end of the season. However, Adam lost his place in the final run-in and later returned to the Midlands.
West Bromwich A (From trainee on 8/1/1999) P/FL 38+18/1 FLC 4+2 FAC 5+1 Others 0+1
Sheffield Wed (Loaned on 19/2/2004) FL 8+3 Others 1

CHAMBERS James Ashley
Born: West Bromwich, 20 November 1980
Height: 5'10" **Weight:** 11.8
International Honours: E: Yth
James – strong and competitive – had to battle hard to get first-team football for West Bromwich Albion last term due to the initial form shown by Swiss international right wing back Bernt Haas and the two main central defenders. Eventually he claimed Haas' position and did well during the latter stages of the season, occasionally acting as a man-marker. He did a superb job on Norwich City's Darren Huckerby in a tight promotion encounter at Carrow Road in early March. He then had a transfer request granted by the club after being left out of the side following that 0-0 at Norwich.
West Bromwich A (From trainee on 8/1/1999) F/PL 54+19 FLC 5+1 FAC 1

CHAMBERS Luke
Born: Kettering, 29 August 1985
Height: 5'11" **Weight:** 11.0
This young Northampton Town defender came on in leaps and bounds last term. He scored his first goal in a friendly match against Dundee and when selected held his own against Third Division attacks. He featured in both full-back positions as well as at centre back during the campaign and will be looking to become a regular in the starting line-up in 2004-05.
Northampton T (From trainee on 3/11/2003) FL 19+6 FLC 2 FAC 0+2 Others 1

CHAPLOW Richard David
Born: Accrington, 2 February 1985
Height: 5'9" **Weight:** 9.3
International Honours: E: U21-1; Yth
The promise shown by Richard towards the end of 2002-03 was realised with interest last season, as he soon staked a

claim to a regular place in the Burnley midfield and progressed rapidly enough to be rewarded with England honours at U19 and U21 levels. A non-stop competitor with fine passing skills who loves to join in the attack, he proved the best graduate of the Burnley youth system for many years and became a firm crowd favourite. Richard was often a fine example to the older heads around him with his constant harrying of the opposition. His first goal came in the home win against Crewe, and his best was a 25-yard left-foot screamer in the 3-0 victory against Reading.
Burnley (From trainee on 13/9/2003) FL 32+12/5 FLC 1+1 FAC 3

CHAPMAN Benjamin (Ben)
Born: Scunthorpe, 2 March 1979
Height: 5'7" **Weight:** 11.0
Ben began the 2003-2004 season as Boston United's skipper and regular left back. His incisive tackling and eagerness to get forward were important for the Pilgrim's. Although he lost his role as captain to Paul Ellender he was able to retain his place in the back four.
Grimsby T (From trainee on 11/7/1997) FL 13+8 FLC 3 FAC 3 Others 0+1
Boston U (Free on 9/8/2002) FL 70+4 FLC 1 FAC 1 Others 2+1

CHAPUIS Cyril Sylvain Thierry
Born: Lyon, France, 21 March 1979
Height: 6'0" **Weight:** 12.4
International Honours: France: U21
This experienced striker was one of three players signed from Marseille by Leeds manager Peter Reid in 12-month loan deals last term. However, the move was not a success and his only Premiership appearance came in the home defeat by Bolton. He was released from his contract in January and soon afterwards signed for Strasbourg.
Leeds U (Loaned from Marseilles, France, ex Ales, Niort, Stade Rennais, on 3/9/2003) PL 0+1 FLC 1+1

CHARLTON Simon Thomas
Born: Huddersfield, 25 October 1971
Height: 5'8" **Weight:** 11.10
International Honours: E: Yth
One of the unsung heroes at the Reebok Stadium, Simon enjoyed another solid and successful season last year. Equally as comfortable at centre back as in his favoured left-back position, Simon came into the side early in the season in place of the injured Florent Laville. He remained in the starting line-up for much of the campaign initially at left back until injury

problems prompted a move to centre back in December. Here Simon forged a fine partnership with Bruno N'Gotty, putting in his best performances of the season. A wholly committed player, Simon also featured in every game during Bolton's charge to the Carling Cup final.
Huddersfield T *(From trainee on 1/7/1989)*
FL 121+3/1 FLC 9/1 FAC 10 Others 14
Southampton *(£250,000 on 8/6/1993) PL*
104+10/2 FLC 9+4/1 FAC 8+1
Birmingham C *(£250,000 on 5/12/1997) FL*
69+3 FLC 3 FAC 3
Bolton W *(Free on 12/7/2000) P/FL 108+12*
FLC 6+2 FAC 3+1 Others 3

CHARNOCK Philip (Phil)
Anthony
Born: Southport, 14 February 1975
Height: 5'11" **Weight:** 11.2
Phil trained with Bury during the pre-season and was signed on non-contract forms last August after the Shakers' small squad was depleted by injuries to both Terry Dunfield and George Clegg. Phil made his debut at Kidderminster and ran himself into the ground, even setting up Chris Porter's goal in a 2-0 Bury win. However, the midfield battler was released in September and soon afterwards signed for Irish League club Linfield.
Liverpool *(From trainee on 16/3/1993) FLC 1*
Others 0+1
Blackpool *(Loaned on 9/2/1996) FL 0+4*
Crewe Alex *(Signed on 30/9/1996) FL*
136+21/8 FLC 13+2 FAC 5 Others 6
Port Vale *(Free on 8/8/2002) FL 14+4/1 FAC*
1 Others 3
Bury *(Free on 22/8/2003) FL 3*

CHEYROU Bruno
Born: Suresnes, France, 10 May 1978
Height: 6'1" **Weight:** 12.8
Club Honours: FLC '03
International Honours: France: 2
Bruno belatedly showed some of the form that persuaded Liverpool to fork out a substantial fee for his services two years ago. A succession of niggling injuries rendered him unavailable for the first half of the 2003-04 campaign, but when he finally returned to the fray in January he did so with a bang, scoring a glorious winning goal at Chelsea in a rare 1-0 triumph, the Reds' first victory at Stamford Bridge for 15 years. Bruno followed this up with a goal in the 1-1 draw away to Wolves and two fine goals in the FA Cup victory over Newcastle. However, he failed to establish himself in

the side and as the season progressed his appearances became fleeting. His best position is surely in the 'hole', just behind the central strikers as a playmaker, however Liverpool rarely used this tactical formation.
Liverpool *(£4,000,000 from Lille, France, ex RC Lens, Racing Club Paris, on 12/7/2002) PL 17+14/2 FLC 1+1 FAC 5+1/2 Others 4+5/1*

CHILLINGWORTH Daniel (Dan) Thomas
Born: Cambridge, 13 September 1981
Height: 6'0" **Weight:** 12.6
After a good pre-season, Dan started last term on fire for Cambridge United and scored three goals in the first three games. However, just as hopes were raised of a bumper haul he suffered an ankle injury, which restricted further appearances. Dan returned to action in the closing stages, raising his goal tally to seven, and will be hoping to steer clear of the treatment room in 2004-05.
Cambridge U *(From trainee on 14/2/2000) FL 31+28/9 FLC 1+1 FAC 1+4 Others 5+5/1*
Darlington *(Loaned on 19/11/2001) FL 2+2/1 FAC 1/1*

CHILVERS Liam Christopher
Born: Chelmsford, 6 November 1981
Height: 6'1" **Weight:** 13.5
Club Honours: FAYC '00
This young Arsenal defender spent the whole of the 2003-04 season on loan at Colchester United, beginning as a centre half before switching to left back. He was a regular alongside club skipper Scott Fitzgerald in the centre of the defence until the middle of March, showing terrific composure on the ball. However, his form then dipped and he had to be content with a place on the bench during the run-in. Liam was reported to have signed a permanent deal for the U's in the summer.
Arsenal *(From trainee on 18/7/2000)*
Northampton T *(Loaned on 22/12/2000) FL 7*
Notts Co *(Loaned on 1/11/2001) FL 9/1 FAC 2*
Colchester U *(Loaned on 24/1/2003) FL 6*
Colchester U *(Loaned on 26/8/2003) FL 29+3 FLC 1 FAC 7 Others 5*

CHOPRA Rocky Michael
Born: Newcastle, 23 December 1983
Height: 5'8" **Weight:** 9.6
International Honours: E: U21-1; Yth
Local boy Michael is a product of Newcastle's Academy and is a highly rated striker who has scored regularly at all levels for club and country, including a

strike for England U21 against Sweden in March, but who is still waiting to make an impact on the Premiership. He started the 2003-04 season on the bench and made two substitute appearances during August, but later on made his first start at home to Blackburn, plus a handful more substitute appearances. In February Michael joined Nottingham Forest on loan, but after starting brightly he soon lost his place and returned to St James's Park. Quick with good control and an eye for making runs behind defenders, he will be hoping for more opportunities to establish himself in the first team in 2004-05.
Newcastle U *(From trainee on 4/1/2001) PL 1+6 FLC 0+1 Others 0+2*
Watford *(Loaned on 25/3/2003) FL 4+1/5 FAC 1*
Nottingham F *(Loaned on 6/2/2004) FL 3+2*

CHORLEY Benjamin (Ben) Francis
Born: Sidcup, 30 September 1982
Height: 6'3" **Weight:** 13.2
Club Honours: FAYC '01
Such was Wimbledon's season that Ben started it as a first-choice central defender, was then benched after a few shaky performances, and ended up captaining the team from a newly-found central midfield position, where his tackling and determination proved to be his biggest strengths. Always encouraging his team mates even when things were clearly not going well, he emerged from a poor season with a great amount of credit, and took particular delight from the fact that his first League goal brought about a morale-boosting late-season win at Wigan.
Arsenal *(From trainee on 2/7/2001)*
Brentford *(Loaned on 14/8/2002) FL 2 FLC 1*
Wimbledon *(Free on 3/3/2003) FL 41+4/2 FLC 1 FAC 1+1*

CHRISTIANSEN Jesper
Born: Denmark, 18 June 1980
Height: 6'3" **Weight:** 13.6
This big target man joined Kidderminster during the January transfer window and made his debut for Harriers in the FA Cup third round tie against Wolves. However, Jesper found it difficult to settle in the Third Division football and was mostly restricted to outings from the substitutes' bench as the season wore on. He will be hoping for an improvement in fortunes during the 2004-05 campaign.
Kidderminster Hrs *(Free from Odense BK, Denmark on 2/1/2004) FL 11+10/1 FAC 2*

CHRISTIE Iyseden

Born: Coventry, 14 November 1976
Height: 6'0" **Weight:** 12.6
Iyseden opened his goal-scoring account for Mansfield last term with a fine hat-trick at Southend, but his season was then disrupted by suspensions and he fell out of favour. However, he worked hard to regain his place only to see his campaign end prematurely when he broke a bone in his foot at Bury in March. Iyseden is an experienced striker who causes problems for defenders with his strong running and is not afraid to have a go at goal. He was one of several players released by the Stags in the summer.
Coventry C (From trainee on 22/5/1995) PL 0+1 FLC 0+1
Bournemouth (Loaned on 18/11/1996) FL 3+1
Mansfield T (Loaned on 7/2/1997) FL 8
Mansfield T (Free on 16/6/1997) FL 44+37/18 FLC 4/5 FAC 0+4 Others 2+1
Leyton Orient (£40,000 on 7/1/1999) FL 32+26/12 FLC 4+1/1 FAC 1+2/1 Others 1
Mansfield T (Free on 9/8/2002) FL 53+11/26 FLC 2 FAC 4+1/2 Others 1

CHRISTIE Malcolm Neil

Born: Stamford, 11 April 1979
Height: 5'6" **Weight:** 11.4
International Honours: E: U21-11
Malcolm's season started brightly enough at Middlesbrough and he featured in all of the club's pre-season friendlies and also the initial Premiership games, but the luckless striker's season ended abruptly in early November when he fractured his right tibia in a training session at Rockcliffe Park. It was thought, initially, that it was not a serious injury but hopes of a quick recovery were dashed when further details of the injury were revealed. Looking back on an all-too brief season Malcolm had, at least, the satisfaction of knowing that he had scored the first goal, against Brighton at the Riverside, which launched the club on its way in Boro's historic Carling Cup winning run.
Derby Co (£50,000 + from Nuneaton Borough on 2/11/1998) P/FL 90+26/30 FLC 6+2/3 FAC 5/2
Middlesbrough (£1,500,000 + on 31/1/2003) PL 18+4/5 FLC 0+1/1

CISSE Aliou

Born: Zinguinchor, Senegal, 24 March 1976
Height: 5'11" **Weight:** 12.8
International Honours: Senegal
This hard-tackling midfielder was put on the transfer list by Birmingham manager Steve Bruce at the start of last season and

struggled to play regularly. He was outstanding in the 0-0 draw at home to Chelsea in October when he chased and closed down opponents relentlessly. Aliou also featured for Senegal in the African Nations' Cup in the new year.
Birmingham C (£1,500,000 from Montpelier, France, ex Lille, Sedan, Paris St Germain, on 26/7/2002) PL 26+10 FLC 1 FAC 0+1

CLANCY Sean

Born: Liverpool, 16 September 1987
Height: 5'8" **Weight:** 9.12
This talented schoolboy made his debut for Blackpool as a substitute against Sheffield Wednesday in April when aged just 16 years and 213 days old. Sean subsequently went on to feature in the starting line-up at left back in the following home game against Peterborough when he settled in well.
Blackpool (Associated Schoolboy) FL 1+1

CLAPHAM James (Jamie) Richard

Born: Lincoln, 7 December 1975
Height: 5'9" **Weight:** 10.11
A very reliable performer, Jamie slotted in well with Birmingham City's renowned back four last season. Clever at reading the game and able to deliver an accurate pass, Jamie went about his job steadily, working well with Stan Lazaridis down the left flank. However, he missed several games through injury, pulling a hamstring in December then being struck down by shingles.
Tottenham H (From trainee on 1/7/1994) PL 0+1 Others 4
Leyton Orient (Loaned on 29/1/1997) FL 6
Bristol Rov (Loaned on 27/3/1997) FL 4+1
Ipswich T (£300,000 on 9/1/1998) P/FL 187+20/10 FLC 19+1/4 FAC 4+3/1 Others 16+2/1
Birmingham C (£1,000,000 + on 10/1/2003) PL 38+3 FLC 1 FAC 0+1

CLARE Robert (Rob)

Born: Belper, 28 February 1983
Height: 6'1" **Weight:** 11.7
International Honours: E: Yth
The 2003-04 campaign proved to be another impressive season for Stockport's young England U20 skipper. A talented centre half, Rob also excelled when playing at right back last term. He scored his first League goal in the 1-1 draw at Grimsby Town in November before adding a couple of crucial goals in the club's nervous run-in. He netted in the 1-1 home draw with Oldham before rescuing a point for County five days later at

promotion-chasing Queens Park Rangers to send the travelling supporters ecstatic.
Stockport Co (From trainee on 10/3/2000) FL 107+10/3 FLC 4/1 FAC 4 Others 3

CLARK Benjamin (Ben)

Born: Consett, 24 January 1983
Height: 6'2" **Weight:** 13.0
International Honours: E: Yth; Sch
This highly rated Sunderland centre back began the 2003-04 season in the first team and looked to have finally established himself at the Stadium of Light. However, a badly broken nose sustained at Preston in August meant the powerfully built stopper had to watch from the sidelines as a succession of more experienced central-defensive partnerships were employed by Mick McCarthy. Ben also played in a midfield role in the Carling Cup game against Huddersfield and in the FA Cup tie versus Hartlepool.
Sunderland (From trainee on 5/7/2000) P/FL 2+4 FLC 3 FAC 2

CLARK Ian David

Born: Stockton, 23 October 1974
Height: 5'11" **Weight:** 11.7
Ian was mostly used as a left-sided defender by Darlington last term, when he was often restricted to outings from the substitutes' bench. He continued to show enthusiasm and was particularly effective with his tricky footwork and direct running when attacking down the left flank. Ian contributed four goals including a penalty at Huddersfield.
Doncaster Rov (Free from Stockton on 11/8/1995) FL 23+22/3 FLC 1+2 FAC 1+1 Others 4/1
Hartlepool U (Free on 24/10/1997) FL 109+29/17 FLC 4 FAC 4+2 Others 11+2/1
Darlington (£10,000 on 14/11/2001) FL 71+24/24 FLC 2+1 FAC 5+2/1 Others 1

CLARK Lee Robert

Born: Wallsend, 27 October 1972
Height: 5'8" **Weight:** 11.7
Club Honours: Div 1 '93, '99, '01
International Honours: E: U21-11; Yth; Sch
After recovering from the injury which saw him miss much of the previous season Lee was a fixture in the Fulham midfield for much of the 2003-04 campaign before again sustaining an injury, this time to his right calf, which needed an operation causing him to miss the final two months. Back to his best influencing the Fulham midfield, he is a ball winner capable of piercing opposition defences with some strategic passes. Although not a consistent goal-scorer he

did hit two notable efforts in successive games in October, the second of which provided the springboard for the 3-1 win at Old Trafford.
Newcastle U *(From trainee on 9/12/1989)* F/PL 153+42/23 FLC 17 FAC 14+2/3 Others 7+5/1
Sunderland *(£2,750,000 on 25/6/1997)* FL 72+1/16 FLC 4+1 FAC 4 Others 3
Fulham *(£3,000,000 on 13/7/1999)* P/FL 126+6/19 FLC 15/2 FAC 7 Others 1+1

CLARK Peter James
Born: Romford, 10 December 1979
Height: 6'1" **Weight:** 12.7
Peter started last term as the regular left back for Northampton and fitted in well, producing some exciting runs down the flank. However, he suffered an injury at Cheltenham at the beginning of September and spent the remainder of the campaign out of action.
Carlisle U *(From trainee at Arsenal on 6/8/1998)* FL 77+2/1 FLC 2 FAC 2 Others 3
Stockport Co *(£75,000 on 7/7/2000)* FL 66+6/3 FLC 2 FAC 3
Mansfield T *(Loaned on 6/9/2002)* FL 2+1 FLC 1
Northampton T *(£100,000 on 1/7/2003)* FL 6 FLC 1

CLARK Steven (Steve) Terence
Born: Stepney, 10 February 1982
Height: 6'1" **Weight:** 12.4
Steve found himself out of favour at Southend at the beginning of last term and spent a month on loan at Macclesfield where he featured as a striker and on the left-hand side of midfield. On his return to Roots Hall he proved unable to reproduce the form he had shown previously and two League starts in January was his sole return for the Blues. He was released by the club in the summer.
West Ham U *(From trainee on 21/7/2001)*
Southend U *(£12,000 + on 19/11/2001)* FL 31+20/1 FLC 0+1 FAC 1+4 Others 2+2/1
Macclesfield T *(Loaned on 26/9/2003)* FL 1+3

CLARKE Andrew (Andy) Weston
Born: Islington, 22 July 1967
Height: 5'10" **Weight:** 11.7
Club Honours: GMVC '91
International Honours: E: SP-2
This veteran striker was often used as a substitute last season, but still finished the campaign as Peterborough United's leading scorer with a total of 12 goals in all competitions. Despite his age he showed a tremendous enthusiasm for the

game and was rewarded with another contract for Posh.
Wimbledon *(£250,000 from Barnet on 21/2/1991)* F/PL 74+96/17 FLC 13+12/4 FAC 9+8/2
Port Vale *(Loaned on 28/8/1998)* FL 2+4
Northampton T *(Loaned on 15/1/1999)* FL 2+2
Peterborough U *(Free on 4/5/1999)* FL 157+40/54 FLC 3+2/2 FAC 13+2/7 Others 9/5

CLARKE Christopher (Chris) Edward
Born: Leeds, 18 December 1980
Height: 6'3" **Weight:** 12.10
Club Honours: AMC '04
This powerful defender was again a regular for Blackpool in the early part of the 2003-04 campaign. However, injury restricted his appearances after November and he eventually signed for Cambridge United on transfer-deadline day. Chris featured for the U's in central midfield after coming off the bench against Cheltenham, but did not play again and was released in the summer.
Halifax T *(From trainee at Wolverhampton W on 5/7/1999)* FL 50+1/1 FLC 2 FAC 3 Others 1
Blackpool *(£120,000 on 18/2/2002)* FL 33+13/2 FLC 2+1 FAC 4+2 Others 4/1
Cambridge U *(Free on 25/3/2004)* FL 0+1

CLARKE Clive Richard
Born: Dublin, 14 January 1980
Height: 6'1" **Weight:** 12.3
Club Honours: AMC '00
International Honours: RoI: 2; U21-11; Yth
Clive was named as club captain by Stoke for the first time last season. Although playing mostly at left back he found a new lease of life operating in the centre of midfield after an injury ruled out John Eustace. Clive showed an eye for goal and scored with several spectacular long-range efforts, notably at Sheffield United and Gillingham.
Stoke C *(From trainee on 25/1/1997)* FL 163+18/8 FLC 11+3 FAC 7+1 Others 17/1

CLARKE Darrell James
Born: Mansfield, 16 December 1977
Height: 5'10" **Weight:** 11.6
A predominantly right-sided midfielder who likes going forward and is a regular goal-scorer, Darrell is a player with great attitude, but he had a mixed time at Hartlepool in 2003-04. He held a regular place in the side during the first half of the season, but then he was mainly restricted to appearances as a substitute.

Mansfield T *(From trainee on 3/7/1996)* FL 137+24/24 FLC 7/2 FAC 4+1/1 Others 2+2
Hartlepool U *(Signed on 17/7/2001)* FL 92+19/19 FLC 3+1 FAC 2+2/1 Others 3+2/2

CLARKE James (Jamie) William
Born: Sunderland, 18 September 1982
Height: 6'2" **Weight:** 12.9
Jamie was mostly used in a supporting role by Mansfield Town last term, appearing mainly when others were unavailable. An effective full back, he can play on either flank, although he is right-footed. Jamie is the son of Jeff Clarke the former Sunderland and Newcastle central defender. He was one of several players released by the Stags in the summer.
Mansfield T *(From trainee on 5/7/2002)* FL 29+5/1 FLC 2 FAC 3+1 Others 2

CLARKE Leon Marvin
Born: Birmingham, 10 February 1985
Height: 6'2" **Weight:** 14.2
The young Wolves striker looked promising in appearances as a substitute in the Carling Cup ties against Darlington and Burnley. His third outing from the bench came in the FA Cup tie against West Ham, when he had a chance to score before he had settled into his first big match. He was then loaned out to Kidderminster on transfer-deadline day. An attacking player, he was used most often on the left wing in a position that didn't seem to suit him and he found himself in and out of the side without settling.
Wolverhampton W *(From trainee on 5/3/2004)* FLC 0+2 FAC 0+1
Kidderminster Hrs *(Loaned on 25/3/2004)* FL 3+1

CLARKE Matthew (Matt) John
Born: Sheffield, 3 November 1973
Height: 6'4" **Weight:** 13.10
This experienced 'keeper was again unfortunate with injuries for Crystal Palace last term. Matt made the starting line-up for the first four League games of the season before succumbing to a back injury. He was out of action for the remainder of the campaign and announced his retirement in April. When fully fit he is a big, strong goalkeeper who commands his area well.
Rotherham U *(From trainee on 28/7/1992)* FL 123+1 FLC 4 FAC 3 Others 10
Sheffield Wed *(£325,000 + on 10/7/1996)* PL 2+2
Bradford C *(Free on 5/7/1999)* PL 38 FLC 2 FAC 2 Others 3

Bolton W (Loaned on 20/3/2001) FL 8 Others 3
Crystal Palace (£1,350,000 on 7/9/2001) FL 38 FLC 2

CLARKE Matthew Paul
Born: Leeds, 18 December 1980
Height: 6'3" **Weight:** 12.7
This giant central defender enjoyed a fine season with Darlington last term, producing some excellent displays on the left-hand side of the defence and striking up a good understanding with Joey Hutchinson and Craig Liddle at the back. Matthew is very strong in the air and exhibits tricky footwork for a big man, overlapping effectively down the left wing and putting in telling crosses. He enjoys getting forward for set pieces and contributed four goals during the campaign.
Halifax T (From trainee at Wolverhampton W on 5/7/1999) FL 42+27/2 FAC 5+1 Others 2+2
Darlington (Free on 9/7/2002) FL 79+4/7 FLC 3 FAC 3 Others 2

CLARKE Nathan
Born: Halifax, 30 July 1983
Height: 6'2" **Weight:** 11.5
This classy youngster returned to central defence for Huddersfield Town last term after an absence of 16 months and looked like he had never been away. Showing maturity beyond his years, he is a strong tackler and reads the game extremely well. Nathan was selected on a number of occasions for the Nationwide 'Team of the Week', but his season was ended prematurely after he suffered an ankle injury in the home game with Rochdale.
Huddersfield T (From trainee on 6/9/2001) FL 63+2/2 FLC 1 FAC 2 Others 4

CLARKE Peter Michael
Born: Southport, 3 January 1982
Height: 6'0" **Weight:** 12.0
International Honours: E: U21-8; Yth; Sch
Peter continues to have a frustrating professional career, which has failed to reflect his impressive international record, during which he has captained England at every level up to U21 and made over 50 appearances for his country. His opportunities at Everton were limited to just one first-team start during the season and he had a loan spell at Coventry. Peter impressed when selected as a central defender for the Sky Blues, but sometimes struggled when switched to

right back. A speedy and tough-tackling defender with obvious leadership qualities, he was offered a new deal by Everton at the end of the season.
Everton (From juniors on 19/1/1999) PL 6+3 FLC 0+1 FAC 4
Blackpool (Loaned on 8/8/2002) FL 16/3
Port Vale (Loaned on 20/2/2003) FL 13/1
Coventry C (Loaned on 13/2/2004) FL 5

CLARKE Ryan Anthony
Born: Sutton Coldfield, 22 January 1984
Height: 5'11" **Weight:** 12.4
This youngster signed for Boston United after being released by Notts County. His only League start was in the defeat at Yeovil Town at the end of September but he gained valuable experience in the reserves. Ryan showed plenty of ability in midfield and agreed a new contract at the end of the campaign.
Boston U (From trainee at Notts Co on 11/7/2003) FL 1+3 Others 2

CLARKE Ryan James
Born: Bristol, 30 April 1982
Height: 6'1" **Weight:** 12.0
This young Bristol Rovers goalkeeper spent most of last season patiently developing in the reserves. Ryan made just two first-team appearances, at home to Huddersfield and at Bury when he managed to keep a clean sheet. He will be hoping to see more first-team action for Rovers in 2004-05 after signing a new contract during the summer.
Bristol Rov (From trainee on 4/7/2001) FL 4+1 Others 1

CLEGG George Gerald
Born: Manchester, 16 November 1980
Height: 5'10" **Weight:** 11.12
George had a disappointing season at Bury last term. He suff e red medial ligament damage to his left knee early on and it was not until November that he regained match fitness. However, this midfield man was only able to claim a place on the substitutes' bench t h e reafter and his contract was cancelled by mutual agreement at the end of the campaign.
Manchester U (From trainee on 5/7/1999)
Wycombe W (Loaned on 2/3/2001) FL 2+8 FAC 1
Bury (Free on 10/8/2001) FL 57+11/9 FLC 3 FAC 0+1 Others 4+1/1

CLEGG Michael Jaime
Born: Ashton under Lyne, 3 July 1977
Height: 5'8" **Weight:** 11.8
Club Honours: FAYC '95
International Honours: E: U21-2

Michael forced his way back into the first-team at Oldham last term following the departure of several star players during the summer of 2003. A competent defender, he was rewarded with a recall in September and the following month he was the penalty shoot-out hero as Latics beat Hartlepool in a marathon LDV Vans Trophy tie. However, Michael lost his place again under new boss Brian Talbot and has another selection battle on his hands in the 2004-05 campaign.
Manchester U (From trainee on 1/7/1995) PL 4+5 FLC 7+1 FAC 3+1 Others 1+2
Ipswich T (Loaned on 16/2/2000) FL 3
Wigan Ath (Loaned on 23/3/2000) FL 6
Oldham Ath (Free on 19/2/2002) FL 40+6 FLC 1 FAC 2 Others 2+1

CLEMENCE Stephen Neal
Born: Liverpool, 31 March 1978
Height: 5'11" **Weight:** 11.7
Club Honours: FLC '99
International Honours: E: U21-1; Yth; Sch
Stephen maintained his fine partnership with Robbie Savage in the centre of the Birmingham City midfield last season. He was always efficient and passed the ball simply, helping to keep things ticking over. An underrated threat at set pieces, he often threaded good passes for the team's attackers, but his main priority was to help protect the back four.
Tottenham H (From trainee on 3/4/1995) PL 68+22/2 FLC 7+1 FAC 7+1/1 Others 2+1
Birmingham C (£250,000 + on 10/1/2003) PL 47+3/4 FLC 1 FAC 1+1/1

CLEMENT Neil
Born: Reading, 3 October 1978
Height: 6'0" **Weight:** 12.3
International Honours: E: Yth; Sch
Neil had a mixed season for West B romwich Albion last seaso n. When left back Paul Robinson was signed from Watford he knew he had to play a lot better to keep his place in the side. A player with a terrific left foot, he was moved into midfield by his manager and did a solid job there alongside Jason Koumas, Andy Johnson and later on Mark Kinsella.
Chelsea (From trainee on 8/10/1995) PL 1 FLC 0+2 FAC 0+1
Reading (Loaned on 19/11/1998) FL 11/1 Others 1
Preston NE (Loaned on 25/3/1999) FL 4
Brentford (Loaned on 23/11/1999) FL 7+1
West Bromwich A (£100,000 + on 23/3/2000) P/FL 156+13/16 FLC 11+2/3 FAC 8/2 Others 2

Neil Clement

CLEVERLEY Benjamin (Ben) Raymond
Born: Bristol, 12 September 1981
Height: 5'7" **Weight:** 10.5
Ben found his opportunities limited in a Cheltenham squad overloaded with midfielders last term, although he continued to perform well in the reserves. Given a chance to start in the FA Cup first round tie against Hull he was named 'Man of the Match', however, this proved to be one of only four starts during the season. A left-footed midfielder with good touch and passing ability, Ben was unable to convince incoming manager John Ward to offer him an extended deal.
Bristol C (From trainee on 3/7/2001)
Cheltenham T (Free on 7/8/2003) FL 2+6 FAC 1 Others 1

CLICHY Gael
Born: Paris, France, 26 February 1985
Height: 5'9" **Weight:** 10.0
Club Honours: PL '04
International Honours: France: U21
This youngster enjoyed a marvellous first season at Arsenal last term, making his Premiership debut at Birmingham City in November and ending the campaign as the youngest-ever recipient of a Premiership winners' medal. Suspension and injury to Arsenal's regular left back Ashley Cole allowed Gael seven Premiership starts and in total he made 22 appearances in all competitions, including a start in the FA Cup semi-final. Gael is similar in both stature and style to Cole, a strong tackler with a real desire to get forward. A testament of his season was the improvement in his rival's defensive form as a result of the genuine challenge presented by Gael.
Arsenal (£250,000 from Cannes, France on 6/8/2003) PL 7+5 FLC 5 FAC 1+3 Others 1

CLIST Simon James
Born: Shaftesbury, 13 June 1981
Height: 5'9" **Weight:** 11.0
This talented Bristol City midfielder has terrific ability, but was unable to gain a regular place in the line-up last term. In January he moved into the Conference with Barnet and appeared for them in the play-offs, when they just missed out on a return to the Football League.
Bristol C (From trainee at Tottenham H on 24/7/1999) FL 54+17/6 FLC 2+1/1 FAC 8+2/2 Others 4+3
Torquay U (Loaned on 22/2/2003) FL 11/2

CLOSE Brian Aidan
Born: Belfast, 27 January 1982
Height: 5'10" **Weight:** 12.6

International Honours: NI: U23-1; U21-10; Yth
Brian was released by Middlesbrough last March and was immediately snapped up for Darlington. A versatile youngster who can play either in defence or midfield, he caught the eye with some hard tackling and crisp, accurate passing. Brian featured regularly for the Quakers following his arrival and finished the season with a place in the starting line-up.
Middlesbrough (Free from St Oliver Plunkett BC on 11/10/1999) FLC 0+1
Chesterfield (Loaned on 7/3/2003) FL 8/1
Darlington (Signed on 5/3/2004) FL 8+4

CLYDE Mark Graham
Born: Limavady, 27 December 1982
Height: 6'1" **Weight:** 12.0
International Honours: NI: U21-5
This promising Wolves central defender was restricted to one outing as a substitute in the first half of the 2003-04 season. He gradually got more involved and featured in five successive games in the spring, when he was used at right back. Mark made a good impression at Liverpool, but a calf strain at Chelsea spoiled his chance of a full debut for Northern Ireland in March. He seemed to have trouble shaking off the injury, although he did provide a perfect cross for Carl Cort to score against Middlesbrough in April.
Wolverhampton W (From trainee on 6/8/2001) P/FL 21+5 FAC 3+1
Kidderminster Hrs (Loaned on 13/9/2002) FL 4

COAD Matthew Paul
Born: Darlington, 25 September 1984
Height: 5'8" **Weight:** 11.0
One of several promising youngsters to come through at York City last term, Matthew made his debut in senior football when he came off the bench at Darlington in December and added two more appearances as a substitute before the end of the campaign. The midfielder impressed in his brief outings with his hard tackling and bustling style.
York C (Trainee) FL 0+3

COATES Jonathan Simon
Born: Swansea, 27 June 1975
Height: 5'8" **Weight:** 10.4
Club Honours: Div 3 '00
International Honours: W: B-1; U21-5; Yth
Jonathan made only occasional appearances from the substitutes' bench for Swansea in the early part of last term,

but after overcoming an ankle injury in October he became a regular member of the first-team line-up. By the end of the season he found himself at left back following injuries to Michael Howard and Leon Hylton. Jonathan is primarily a left-sided attacking midfielder, who, if he can develop the defensive side of his game, could become a permanent fixture in that position.
Swansea C (From trainee on 8/7/1993) FL 218+32/23 FLC 11+2/1 FAC 10 Others 11+3/1
Cheltenham T (Free on 18/10/2002) Others 1 (Free to Woking on 15/11/2002)
Swansea C (Free on 27/3/2003) FL 16+14 FLC 0+1 FAC 1+3 Others 1

COCHRANE Justin Vincent
Born: Hackney, 26 January 1982
Height: 6'0" **Weight:** 11.8
Justin signed for Crewe during the 2003 close season and took his place in the line-up in the opening game at Wimbledon. He retained his place in the side in a midfield role through to the closing stages of the campaign when he stepped out of the action for a while. Justin has proved to be a real asset for the club since his arrival.
Queens Park R (From trainee on 16/7/1999) FL 0+1 (Free to Hayes on 12/8/2002)
Crewe Alex (£50,000 on 19/7/2003) FL 37+2 FLC 2

COGAN Barry
Born: Sligo, Rol, 4 November 1984
Height: 5'9" **Weight:** 9.0
International Honours: Rol: U21-1
A product of Millwall's Academy, Barry enjoyed an excellent season for the club's reserves last term. This tricky and pacy winger got his first-team chance against Watford in April when he came on as a substitute and found his feet straight away, putting in a good performance. Barry stepped up to the Republic of Ireland U21 squad last term, featuring in the Madeira Tournament in February.
Millwall (From trainee on 28/11/2001) FL 0+3 FAC 0+1

COGHLAN Michael James
Born: Sunderland, 15 January 1985
Height: 5'10" **Weight:** 11.0
A product of Darlington's youth policy, this busy, sure-passing midfielder was given his chance after a series of excellent displays for the reserves. Michael made four substitute appearances early on last season, but has still to receive his first start for the Quakers.
Darlington (Trainee) FL 0+3 Others 0+1

COHEN Christopher (Chris) David
Born: Norwich, 5 March 1987
Height: 5'11" **Weight:** 10.11
International Honours: E: Yth
The youngest player to appear for West Ham for over 80 years, this promising left back was not overawed when he made his debut against Sunderland. He tackles well and is not afraid to take a shot when the occasion arises. It was an amazing season for the teenager. As members of the youth team are required to act as ball boys for first-team games, Chris was a ball boy then played for the U17s, U19s, reserves and first team all in one season. He was also called up by England for the U17 squad.
West Ham U (From trainee on 1/4/2004) FL 1+6

COID Daniel (Danny) John
Born: Liverpool, 3 October 1981
Height: 5'11" **Weight:** 11.7
Club Honours: AMC '02, '04
This left-sided player was a regular in defence or midfield for Blackpool last term. He contributed a total of six goals in all competitions, most notably the all-important second goal in the LDV Vans Trophy final against Southend at Cardiff's Millennium Stadium.
Blackpool (From trainee on 24/7/2000) FL 143+23/9 FLC 7+1 FAC 13/1 Others 16+1/2

COLDICOTT Stacy
Born: Redditch, 29 April 1974
Height: 5'8" **Weight:** 11.8
This combative midfielder returned to action following a broken leg and after just half a game with the reserves he was thrust straight into Grimsby's relegation struggle last February. Although used sparingly at first, Stacy showed he had lost none of his competitive edge. Returning to full match fitness, his battling contribution was unable to avert a second successive relegation for the Mariners.
West Bromwich A (From trainee on 4/3/1992) FL 64+40/3 FLC 6+1 FAC 2+2/1 Others 7+3
Cardiff C (Loaned on 30/8/1996) FL 6
Grimsby T (£125,000 on 6/8/1998) FL 169+20/3 FLC 12/2 FAC 6+1

COLE Andrew (Andy) Alexander
Born: Nottingham, 15 October 1971
Height: 5'11" **Weight:** 11.12
Club Honours: Div 1 '93; PL '96, '97, '99, '00, '01; FAC '96, '99; CS '97; EC '99; FLC '02

International Honours: E: 15; B-1; U21-8; Yth, Sch
Andy remained an enigmatic figure for Blackburn last term and despite the variability of his finishing he was comfortably the top goal-scorer, finding the net 11 times in total. He was particularly effective early on, scoring five times including two in the opening-day thrashing of Wolves, while he contributed a classical goal at Fulham that evoked memories of his best form.
Arsenal (From trainee on 18/10/1989) FL 0+1 Others 0+1
Fulham (Loaned on 5/9/1991) FL 13/3 Others 2/1
Bristol C (£500,000 on 12/3/1992) FL 41/20 FLC 3/4 FAC 1 Others 4/1
Newcastle U (£1,750,000 on 12/3/1993) F/PL 69+1/55 FLC 7/8 FAC 4/1 Others 3/4
Manchester U (£6,000,000 on 12/1/1995) PL 161+34/94 FLC 2 FAC 19+2/9 Others 49+8/19
Blackburn Rov (£7,500,000 on 29/12/2001) PL 74+9/27 FLC 8/7 FAC 5/3 Others 2+2

COLE Ashley
Born: Stepney, 20 December 1980
Height: 5'8" **Weight:** 10.8
Club Honours: FAC '02, '03; PL '02, '04; CS '02
International Honours: E: 30; U21-4; Yth
The one home grown player in the Arsene Wenger era to fully integrate himself in the side as an automatic first choice, Ashley once again suffered occasional absences from the team due to injury and suspension last term. Yet he enjoyed another fine season with his improving defensive ability coming to the fore, and scored one of the most important goals of Arsenal's season to keep their Champions' League hopes alive against Dinamo Kiev. Named in the PFA Premiership team of the season, he was also the regular left back for England and a member of the squad for Euro 2004.
Arsenal (From trainee on 23/11/1998) PL 107+3/6 FLC 2+1 FAC 16+1 Others 34+2/1
Crystal Palace (Loaned on 25/2/2000) FL 14/1

COLE Carlton Michael
Born: Croydon, 12 November 1983
Height: 6'3" **Weight:** 13.4
International Honours: E: U21-6; Yth
A tall, powerfully built centre forward, Carlton joined Charlton on loan from Chelsea at the start of the season. He made a couple of substitute appearances before suffering a hip injury which kept him sidelined for a couple of months. Carlton continued to be used mainly as a substitute, and scored his first goal for the

Addicks at Tottenham Hotspur in December. He made his first start in the following game, an FA Cup tie at Gillingham, and scored again. He was in and out of the side from then on, but managed a creditable five goals in total, the best of which was a close-range effort against Blackburn Rovers at the Valley. Carlton is very quick for a big man, is good in the air and has a powerful shot.
Chelsea (From trainee on 23/10/2000) PL 4+12/4 FLC 1/2 FAC 0+2/1
Wolverhampton W (Loaned on 28/11/2002) FL 5+2/1
Charlton Ath (Loaned on 20/8/2003) PL 8+13/4 FAC 1/1

COLE Joseph (Joe) John
Born: Islington, 8 November 1981
Height: 5'9" **Weight:** 11.0
Club Honours: FAYC '99
International Honours: E: 17; U21-8; Yth; Sch
After a long and somewhat expensive route Joe Cole eventually wore the blue of Chelsea, which would have delighted his family of life-long Blues' fans. Joe signed on the same day as Juan Sebastian Veron and, perhaps, that summed up his predicament in a nutshell – the intense competition for a regular midfield place. He settled quickly at the Bridge – helped in no small measure by the presence of ex-Hammers colleagues Frank Lampard and Glen Johnson, but he faces an uphill struggle to claim the starting berth his ambition and talent warrant. The first two-thirds of the season saw Joe very much as a peripheral figure in the Blues' assault on four trophies but in the latter third he figured more prominently – helped by injuries to Veron and Damien Duff – and played superbly to clinch a place in England's Euro 2004 squad. Joe has been hailed as the finest midfield talent of his generation and his eye-catching dribbling and trickery on the ball make him a firm crowd favourite.
West Ham U (From trainee on 11/12/1998) PL 108+18/10 FLC 7+1/1 FAC 10+1/2 Others 2+3
Chelsea (£6,600,000 on 6/8/2003) PL 18+17/1 FLC 2+1/2 FAC 2+1 Others 3+6

COLEMAN Kenneth (Kenny) James
Born: Cork, 20 September 1982
Height: 6'0" **Weight:** 12.3
International Honours: Rol: Yth
Injury blighted Kenny's career at Kidderminster last term, and he was eventually diagnosed as suffering from Gilmore's groin, a problem which

restricted his appearances throughout the campaign. The promising young right back was one of several players released by Harriers at the end of the season.
Wolverhampton W (From trainee on 17/7/2000)
Kidderminster Hrs (Loaned on 11/10/2002) FL 13+2 FAC 2 Others 3
Kidderminster Hrs (Free on 8/8/2003) FL 10 FLC 1 FAC 0+1 Others 1

COLES Daniel (Danny) Richard
Born: Bristol, 31 October 1981
Height: 6'1" **Weight:** 11.5
Club Honours: AMC '03
This youngster enjoyed another great season for Bristol City in 2003-04. He was outstanding at the centre of one of the meanest Football League defences throughout the whole campaign. Danny's form was such that he attracted many admirers and it remains to be seen whether the failure to win promotion will result in this prize asset moving to pastures new.
Bristol C (From trainee on 7/6/2000) FL 104+6/4 FLC 3/1 FAC 7 Others 17/1

COLGAN Nicholas (Nicky) Vincent
Born: Drogheda, 19 September 1973
Height: 6'1" **Weight:** 13.6
International Honours: RoI: 8; B-1; U21-9; Yth; Sch
Nick joined Stockport County on loan from SPL outfit Hibernian on the eve of the 2003-04 season and made his debut at Wycombe on the opening day. A competent 'keeper, he featured regularly in the early stages of the campaign before returning to Easter Road in December. However, although he featured at international level for the Republic of Ireland he was unable to replace Daniel Andersson in the Hibs goal and did not manage a single appearance. Out of contract in the summer, his future was uncertain at the time of writing.
Chelsea (From trainee on 1/10/1992) PL 1
Brentford (Loaned on 16/10/1997) FL 5
Reading (Loaned on 27/2/1998) FL 5
Bournemouth (Free on 9/7/1998)
Hibernian (Free on 29/7/1999) SL 121 SLC 8 SC 16 Others 2
Stockport Co (Loaned on 8/8/2003) FL 14+1 FLC 2

COLLETT Andrew (Andy) Alfred
Born: Stockton, 28 October 1973
Height: 6'0" **Weight:** 12.10
Andy started last term as Darlington's first-choice 'keeper but a recurrence of

the rib injury that had so blighted the previous season for him saw him on the sidelines by the end of September. Unfortunately he never fully recovered from this and in February he was forced to retire from the game on medical advice.
Middlesbrough (From trainee on 6/3/1992) PL 2 Others 3
Bristol Rov (Loaned on 18/10/1994) FL 4
Bristol Rov (£10,000 on 23/3/1995) FL 103 FLC 4 FAC 7 Others 8
Darlington (Free on 6/8/1999) FL 125 FLC 7 FAC 9 Others 4

COLLINS James Michael
Born: Newport, 23 August 1983
Height: 6'2" **Weight:** 13.0
International Honours: W: 2; U21-7; Yth
James was in and out of the Cardiff line-up in the first half of the 2003-04 campaign, but finished the season in style with a good run in the side. A powerful central defender, he began to forge an effective partnership at the back with Danny Gabbidon, the two complementing each other's styles perfectly. James won his first full cap for Wales against Norway in May, thus becoming the first player to hold caps at every level for his country.
Cardiff C (From trainee on 5/4/2001) FL 17+15/2 FLC 1 FAC 2+5/2 Others 4+2

COLLINS Samuel (Sam) Jason
Born: Pontefract, 5 June 1977
Height: 6'3" **Weight:** 14.0
Sam was again a first choice in the centre of defence for Port Vale last term and had another excellent season with the Second Division club. He scored four goals, including a last-minute 25-yard free kick that earned a 2-2 draw at Stockport County; his other strikes all coming at Vale Park: against Colchester, Peterborough and Grimsby Town. Sam is also a long-throw expert.
Huddersfield T (From trainee on 6/7/1994) FL 34+3 FLC 6+1 FAC 3
Bury (£75,000 on 2/7/1999) FL 78+4/2 FLC 5 FAC 0+2 Others 1
Port Vale (Free on 15/7/2002) FL 87/9 FLC 2 FAC 4 Others 3

COLLINS Wayne Anthony
Born: Manchester, 4 March 1969
Height: 6'0" **Weight:** 12.0
Club Honours: Div 2 '97
Wayne joined Stockport County on a short-term contract last term, but only managed to make two substitute appearances during his time at Edgeley Park. Both of his run-outs in the first team came in August when he replaced Fraser

McLachlan during the 2-1 home defeat by Luton Town and the 3-1 defeat at Plymouth a week later. He remained on the books until the new year when he was released.
Crewe Alex (£10,000 from Winsford U on 29/7/1993) FL 102+15/14 FLC 6/1 FAC 8+1 Others 14+1/3
Sheffield Wed (£600,000 on 1/8/1996) PL 16+15/6 FLC 2 FAC 1
Fulham (£400,000 + on 23/1/1998) FL 37+21/4 FLC 10+1/2 FAC 6+2/2 Others 4
Crewe Alex (Free on 9/8/2001) FL 13+7 FLC 2 FAC 1 Others 0+1
Stockport Co (Free on 15/8/2003) FL 0+2

COLLIS Stephen (Steve) Philip
Born: Harrow, 18 March 1981
Height: 6'2" **Weight:** 13.0
Steve waited patiently for his chance in the Yeovil first team last season and it came when Chris Weale was sidelined with a broken bone in his hand in March. The young 'keeper produced some outstanding displays and kept three clean sheets as he retained his place in the side until the end of the campaign.
Barnet (From juniors on 27/8/1999)
Nottingham F (Free on 11/7/2000)
Yeovil T (Free on 6/8/2001) FL 11 Others 1

COMBE Alan
Born: Edinburgh, 3 April 1974
Height: 6'1" **Weight:** 12.6
This goalkeeper had a frustrating season with Bradford City after joining them in the summer from Dundee United. Alan, who had enjoyed a successful loan spell at Valley Parade two years previously, found himself in a battle for the starting jersey with New Zealander Mark Paston. He was held up by niggling injuries as well as a period of suspension. A good shot-stopper, he will be looking to establish a regular position as the Bantams attempt to bounce straight back from relegation.
Cowdenbeath (Signed from Kelty Hearts on 13/7/1992) SL 20 SLC 1
St Mirren (Signed on 7/8/1993) SL 123+1 SLC 6 SC 4 Others 4
Dundee U (Signed on 17/6/1998) SL 73 SLC 8 SC 4
Bradford C (Loaned on 1/2/2002) FL 16
Bradford C (Free on 4/7/2003) FL 21 FAC 1

COMMONS Kristian (Kris) Arran
Born: Mansfield, 30 August 1983
Height: 5'6" **Weight:** 9.8
Now happily fully recovered from a cruciate knee ligament injury, Kris soon settled into his best form for Stoke last

term. Originally playing at left back with the reserves he developed into a left-sided midfielder, and even played up front to devastating effect against West Bromwich Albion, when he netted twice and made a third. Kris possesses a bullet-like shot, terrific pace and the ability to take on and beat opponents.

Stoke C *(From trainee on 25/1/2001) FL 20+21/5 FLC 1+2 FAC 0+1 Others 1*

Alan Combe

COMYN-PLATT Charlie

Born: Manchester, 2 October 1985
Height: 6'2" **Weight:** 12.0
Another product of the Bolton Academy to be given his chance in cup games last season, Charlie made two starts in the FA Cup and one appearance as a substitute in the Carling Cup. A versatile defender, he actually played at centre back and left back during these games, performing admirably in both roles. As one of a promising group of young players starting to make a name for themselves with Bolton's youth and reserve team set-ups, Charlie will be looking to make the step up to the first team more often during the 2004-05 season.

Bolton W *(Trainee) FLC 0+1 FAC 2*

CONLON Barry John

Born: Drogheda, 1 October 1978
Height: 6'3" **Weight:** 13.7
International Honours: RoI: U21-7
Barry had another useful campaign for Darlington last term when he finished up with a total of 14 goals, thus making him the club's leading scorer for the second year in succession. He is an excellent target man who has a strong aerial presence, while his control of the ball on his chest enables him to hold play up for his colleagues to enter the action.

Manchester C *(From trainee at Queens Park R on 14/8/1997) FL 1+6 FLC 0+1*
Plymouth Arg *(Loaned on 26/2/1998) FL 13/2*
Southend U *(£95,000 on 4/9/1998) FL 28+6/7 FAC 1 Others 1*
York C *(£100,000 on 20/7/1999) FL 33+15/11 FLC 2+2 FAC 1 Others 0+1*
Colchester U *(Loaned on 9/11/2000) FL 23+3/8 FAC 1 Others 1*
Darlington *(£60,000 on 6/7/2001) FL 114+1/39 FLC 4 FAC 4/3 Others 2*

CONNELL Alan John

Born: Enfield, 15 February 1983
Height: 5'11" **Weight:** 10.8
This young Bournemouth striker endured a frustrating time yet again in 2003-04. After missing the majority of the previous campaign, Alan recovered from a pre-season injury to earn a place on the bench. However, he made just one start and then had a further operation on his knee which kept him out of action until the summer break.

Bournemouth *(From Ipswich T juniors on 9/7/2002) FL 11+9/6 FLC 1/1*

CONNELL Lee Anthony

Born: Bury, 24 June 1981
Height: 6'0" **Weight:** 12.0

Barry Conlon

Bury's midfield general suffered a season of rather mixed fortunes in 2003-04. A goal on the opening day of the season at Swansea was the first of six that he would score by October. Lee looked confident and eager playing in a central midfield role and he netted some exquisite goals including a chip with his left foot from the edge of the area at Darlington and a wonderful strike at Cambridge which won the Shakers' 'Goal of the Season' poll – a flick over an opponent followed by a 30-yard volley. However, he was largely overlooked following a change in management and at the end of the season he was handed a free transfer.

Bury *(From trainee on 9/7/1999) FL 46+12/9 FLC 1 FAC 1+1 Others 5*

CONNELLY Sean Patrick
Born: Sheffield, 26 June 1970
Height: 5'10" **Weight:** 11.10
Sean is a calm and steady defender who featured at right back, centre half and right wing back for Tranmere last term. His experience and maturity proved to be of great help to some of his younger colleagues, and although a regular first-team choice for most of the campaign he lost his place in March, and therefore missed most of Rovers' impressive closing spell. Away from football, Sean holds a chartered physiotherapy qualification. He was released just before the final game of the season.

Stockport Co *(Free from Hallam on 12/8/1991) FL 292+10/6 FLC 29/1 FAC 15+2 Others 15+1*
Wolverhampton W *(Free on 21/3/2001) FL 11+3 FLC 1*
Tranmere Rov *(Free on 11/10/2002) FL 66+4 FLC 2 FAC 6 Others 4*

CONNOLLY David James
Born: Willesden, 6 June 1977
Height: 5'8" **Weight:** 11.4
International Honours: RoI: 40; U21
This experienced striker was a bargain summer signing for West Ham and set Upton Park alight with seven goals in his first 11 games. After scoring at Preston on the opening day of the season he went on to hit doubles in the Carling Cup tie against Rushden and in the game at Crewe. When Jermain Defoe departed in January he was switched to midfield with further success. David worked hard for his team mates with some excellent link-up play between midfield and attack and was superb in the FA Cup ties against Premiership opposition. Very confident in his own ability, he contributed a great

deal to West Ham reaching the play-off final.

Watford *(From trainee on 15/11/1994) FL 19+7/10 FLC 1 FAC 3+3/4 Others 1/1 (Free to Feyenoord during 1997 close season)*
Wolverhampton W *(Loaned on 21/8/1998) FL 18+14/6 FLC 2 FAC 0+1*
Wimbledon *(Free from Feyenoord, Holland on 27/7/2001) FL 63/42 FLC 1 FAC 4*
West Ham U *(£285,000 on 8/8/2003) FL 37+2/10 FLC 2/2 FAC 4/2 Others 3*

CONNOLLY Karl Andrew
Born: Prescot, 9 February 1970
Height: 5'10" **Weight:** 11.2
Club Honours: WC '95
After proving his fitness during pre-season training, Karl signed a 12-month contract with Swansea and went on to score his first goal for his new club in the Carling Cup tie at Bristol City. However, he struggled with a calf injury from then on, and this was further aggravated in a reserve game. Karl then suffered a fractured ankle, which sidelined him until the new year, then after a few comeback attempts, he sustained a further ankle injury in March, which set him back once more.

Wrexham *(Free from Napoli, in local Sunday League, on 8/5/1991) FL 337+21/88 FLC 22/4 FAC 37+1/16 Others 24+1/4*
Queens Park R *(Free on 31/5/2000) FL 53+19/12 FLC 2 FAC 4+2 Others 2*
Swansea C *(Free on 7/8/2003) FL 4+6/1 FLC 1/1 FAC 1*

CONNOLLY Paul
Born: Liverpool, 29 September 1983
Height: 6'0" **Weight:** 11.9
Club Honours: Div 2' 04
Paul managed to break into the Plymouth Argyle first team last November, replacing David Worrell at right back, and kept his place in the side for the remainder of the season. A confident youngster, he is brave, strong in the air and very fit. He likes to get forward on the overlap and when he does he often provides an excellent cross.

Plymouth Arg *(From trainee on 23/7/2002) FL 30+2 Others 1*

CONNOR Paul
Born: Bishop Auckland, 12 January 1979
Height: 6'1" **Weight:** 11.5
Club Honours: AMC '00
Paul spearheaded Rochdale's early-season run of good form with five goals in the first eight games. However, injuries and suspension then restricted his appearances and he found it difficult to rediscover his goal touch. He became

Swansea's first cash signing since September 1999 when he arrived at the Vetch Field last March. An experienced front runner, he scored two goals on his home debut against Scunthorpe United, also found the net in the next home game against Carlisle United. Paul impressed with an all-round willingness for hard work in the Swans' frontline.

Middlesbrough *(From trainee on 4/7/1996)*
Hartlepool U *(Loaned on 6/2/1998) FL 4+1*
Stoke C *(Free on 25/3/1999) FL 18+18/7 FLC 3+3/3 FAC 0+1 Others 2+3*
Cambridge U *(Loaned on 9/11/2000) FL 12+1/5 FAC 1*
Rochdale *(£100,000 on 9/3/2001) FL 76+18/28 FLC 3 FAC 8+1/3 Others 0+2*
Swansea C *(Signed on 12/3/2004) FL 12/5*

CONSTANTINE Leon
Born: Hackney, 24 February 1978
Height: 6'2" **Weight:** 11.10
Leon impressed during a pre-season trial earning a one-year contract, which was arguably the best business Southend United did throughout the 2003-04 campaign. A tall, gangly forward with excellent ball control, Leon scored all types of goals: close-range, headers, long-range, and he ended the season with 25 in all, the best return by a Southend player since Brett Angell in 1990-91. With the best part of his career ahead of him, Leon will be looking to build on his reputation in 2004-05.

Millwall *(Signed from Edgware T on 31/8/2000) FL 0+1 Others 1*
Leyton Orient *(Loaned on 27/8/2001) FL 9+1/3 Others 0+1*
Partick Thistle *(Loaned on 11/1/2002) SL 2 SC 1*
Brentford *(Free on 8/8/2002) FL 2+15 FLC 1+1*
Southend U *(Free on 21/8/2003) FL 40+3/21 FAC 2+1 Others 6+1/4*

CONVERY Mark Peter
Born: Newcastle, 29 May 1981
Height: 5'6" **Weight:** 10.5
Mark spent the early part of last term out of the first-team picture at Darlington, but he returned to the starting line-up in January and held his place until the end of the season with a series of dashing displays of pace down the right flank. A hard-working wide player with an accurate cross, he also possesses a fine shot and rifled in two goals from outside the box in successive games in March.

Sunderland *(From trainee on 24/3/1999)*
Darlington *(Free on 30/1/2001) FL 28+25/3 FLC 1 FAC 0+2 Others 1+2*

COOK Lee
Born: Hammersmith, 3 August 1982
Height: 5'9" **Weight:** 11.7
Lee was one of Watford's best players in a forgettable season, and played in most of their matches, albeit frequently as substitute. A skilful and direct left winger, Lee clearly benefited from a regular involvement with the first team: he appeared more accomplished as a player and his team play, particularly his awareness of defensive responsibilities, was much improved. He scored his first League goal at Nottingham Forest in November and ended up with seven in all, including outstanding long-distance strikes at Burnley and Millwall.

Watford *(Signed from Aylesbury U on 19/11/1999) FL 31+28/7 FLC 0+2 FAC 2+1*
York C *(Loaned on 2/10/2002) FL 7/1 Others 1/1*
Queens Park R *(Loaned on 20/12/2002) FL 13/1*

COOK Lewis Leon
Born: High Wycombe, 28 December 1983
Height: 5'7" **Weight:** 11.1
This speedy left winger had to be content with just one start for Wycombe last season, at Tranmere in September, plus a handful of outings from the bench. Lewis found himself loaned out, firstly to Weymouth in January and then to Cambridge City in March.

Wycombe W *(From trainee on 28/1/2003) FL 5+17 FLC 0+1 FAC 0+1 Others 3+1/1*

COOKE Stephen Lee
Born: Walsall, 15 February 1983
Height: 5'8" **Weight:** 9.8
International Honours: E: Yth
This promising young Aston Villa midfield player did well with the club's reserve team in the first half of last season and in January he rejoined Bournemouth in another loan deal. Stephen enjoyed an excellent debut against Port Vale, but then received an injury to his ankle in the game at Barnsley. He returned to start the next match, but the injury was such that this was his last appearance and he returned to Villa Park for treatment.

Aston Villa *(From trainee on 22/2/2000) PL 0+3 Others 0+1*
Bournemouth *(Loaned on 8/3/2002) FL 6+1*
Bournemouth *(Loaned on 6/1/2004) FL 3*

COOKE Terence (Terry) John
Born: Birmingham, 5 August 1976
Height: 5'7" **Weight:** 11.4
Club Honours: FAYC '95
International Honours: E: U21-4; Yth

Terry was a regular in Sheffield Wednesday's line-up early on last term, but was sidelined by a knee ligament injury and further injury problems then hampered him, so it was not until towards the end of the season that he returned to full match fitness. A right winger or wide-midfield player, he is adept as a provider of goals and added balance to the side. Terry was one of 13 players released by the Owls in the summer.

Manchester U *(From trainee on 1/7/1994) PL 1+3 FLC 1+2/1 Others 0+1*
Sunderland *(Loaned on 29/1/1996) FL 6*
Birmingham C *(Loaned on 29/11/1996) FL 1+3*
Wrexham *(Loaned on 30/10/1998) FL 10 Others 1*
Manchester C *(£1,000,000 on 13/1/1999) FL 27+7/7 FLC 3+1/1 Others 3*
Wigan Ath *(Loaned on 7/3/2000) FL 10/1*
Sheffield Wed *(Loaned on 21/9/2000) FL 12+1/1*
Sheffield Wed *(Loaned on 15/12/2000) FL 4*
Grimsby T *(Free on 28/3/2002) FL 18+10/1 FLC 1 FAC 2/1*
Sheffield Wed *(Free on 8/8/2003) FL 19+4/2 FLC 0+1 FAC 0+1 Others 0+1*

COOKSEY Ernest (Ernie) George
Born: Bishops Stortford, 11 June 1980
Height: 5'9" **Weight:** 11.4
Ernie joined Oldham in the 2003 close season and quickly made an impact at Boundary Park with his feisty displays, tireless running and aerial prowess in central midfield. He scored his first senior goal at Peterborough in October and went on to net an impressive tally of six goals, including a memorable left-footed screamer at Grimsby Town on Boxing Day. Ernie was switched to the left of midfield for the remainder of the season and was awarded a new contract in May.

Oldham Ath *(Signed from Crawley T, ex Colchester U trainee, Heybridge Swifts, Bishops Stortford, Bromley, Chesham U, on 8/8/2003) FL 22+14/4 FAC 2/2 Others 1+1*

COOPER Colin Terence
Born: Sedgefield, 28 February 1967
Height: 5'10" **Weight:** 11.9
Club Honours: Div 1 '98; FLC '04
International Honours: E: 2; U21-8
Colin surprised all when he joined Sunderland on loan last March until the end of the season. Colin, who grew up as a Black Cats' fan, had not featured in any of Middlesbrough's FA Cup games and could have played for the Wearsiders at the semi-final stage of the competition at

the start of his loan, but he was not called upon. When Boro's defensive injury crisis became severe he was recalled to the Riverside to ease the player shortage problem. He ended the season requiring an operation to flush out debris from his knee. His dedication and personal commitment to his role at the Riverside earned Colin a year's extension on his contract and he requires just one more appearance to register 400 senior games for the club.

Middlesbrough *(From juniors on 17/7/1984) FL 183+5/6 FLC 18 FAC 13 Others 19+1/3*
Millwall *(£300,000 on 25/7/1991) FL 77/6 FLC 6 FAC 2 Others 2*
Nottingham F *(£1,700,000 on 21/6/1993) F/PL 179+1/20 FLC 14/2 FAC 12/1 Others 7*
Middlesbrough *(£2,500,000 on 22/8/1998) PL 128+14/5 FLC 12+1 FAC 4+1*
Sunderland *(Loaned on 12/3/2004) FL 0+3*

COOPER Kevin Lee
Born: Derby, 8 February 1975
Height: 5'7" **Weight:** 10.7
This left-sided midfield player came on as a substitute for Wolves in the opening home game when he looked lively until he got injured. In January he was loaned to Sunderland, but ended up playing only 13 minutes in a red-and-white shirt in the 2-1 defeat at Millwall. Kevin returned to Molineux early, and in March was loaned out again, this time to Norwich. Signed to bolster the Canaries' squad for the final run-in, he made his debut at Crystal Palace. Composed on the ball, his clever passing and movement off the ball helped create many chances for his colleagues.

Derby Co *(From trainee on 2/7/1993) FL 0+2 FLC 0+2 Others 0+1*
Stockport Co *(£150,000 on 24/3/1997) FL 146+22/21 FLC 7+5/2 FAC 6 Others 1*
Wimbledon *(£800,000 + on 15/3/2001) FL 50+1/13 FLC 1 FAC 2*
Wolverhampton W *(£1,000,000 on 26/3/2002) FL 17+15/3 FAC 0+1 Others 2+1/1*
Sunderland *(Loaned on 6/1/2004) FL 0+1*
Norwich C *(Loaned on 19/3/2004) FL 6+4*

COOPER Richard Anthony
Born: Nottingham, 27 September 1979
Height: 5'9" **Weight:** 10.12
International Honours: E: Yth; Sch
Richard was a regular in York City's side last term featuring mostly in a central-midfield role. Playing with his usual tenacity and enthusiasm, he scored in the defeat at Kidderminster and added an excellent effort in the home win over Carlisle United in January, which proved to be City's last victory of the season.

Richard was released by the Minstermen in the summer.

Nottingham F *(From trainee on 2/10/1996) FL 0+3*
York C *(Free on 2/3/2001) FL 84+16/4 FLC 1 FAC 6+1 Others 2*

COOPER Shaun David
Born: Isle of Wight, 5 October 1983
Height: 5'10" **Weight:** 10.10
This young Pompey right back only featured as an unused substitute last season, but experienced first-team football after joining Leyton Orient on loan in October. Signed as cover for injuries to Matthew Joseph and Donny Barnard, Shaun proved to be a reliable defender who was always willing to join in the attack.

Portsmouth *(From trainee on 7/4/2001) FL 3+4*
Leyton Orient *(Loaned on 17/10/2003) FL 9*

COOTE Adrian
Born: Great Yarmouth, 30 September 1978
Height: 6'2" **Weight:** 12.0
International Honours: NI: 6; B-1; U21-14
This experienced target man was always well down the pecking order of strikers at Colchester United last term, and he made just one appearance as a late substitute in the Carling Cup tie at Rotherham before being released. Adrian later joined Wivenhoe Town.

Norwich C *(From trainee on 3/7/1997) FL 20+34/3 FLC 1+5 FAC 0+1*
Colchester U *(£50,000 on 21/12/2001) FL 12+23/4 FLC 0+1*
Bristol Rov *(Loaned on 21/10/2002) FL 4+1/1 Others 1*

CORBETT James (Jim) John
Born: Hackney, 6 July 1980
Height: 5'10" **Weight:** 12.0
Jim was one of several Southend players whose 2003-04 season was cruelly curtailed by injury. He made a very promising start, featuring in both midfield and up front, before he was sidelined for the majority of the second half of the campaign. His powerful physique belies a good first touch, which he uses to great effect. Jim returned to action in the final game of the season and will be hoping to stay clear of the treatment room in 2004-05.

Gillingham *(From trainee on 13/1/1998) FL 8+8/2 FLC 0+1 Others 0+1*
Blackburn Rov *(£525,000 + on 22/5/1998)*
Darlington *(Loaned on 28/2/2003) FL 9+1/2*
Southend U *(Free on 15/7/2003) FL 13+4/1 FLC 1 FAC 3+1/1 Others 1/1*

CORBETT Luke John

Born: Worcester, 10 August 1984
Height: 6'0" **Weight:** 11.2
This young striker emerged from the Cheltenham Town youth scheme to make his Football League debut when coming off the substitutes' bench against York in November. Luke finished the season as top scorer for the club's reserves and also impressed in front of goal during loan spells with Chelmsford City and Weston-super-Mare.
Cheltenham T (From juniors on 24/1/2003) FL 0+1

CORBISIERO Antonio

Born: Reading, 17 November 1984
Height: 5'8" **Weight:** 11.4
This third-year scholar made his senior debut for Swansea as a substitute against Mansfield Town at the Vetch Field early on last season, and was included as a non-playing substitute on several more occasions. The horrendous injury list at the Vetch Field saw Antonio given further first-team opportunities as the campaign progressed, and in April he made his first start against Hull City. He showed tremendous stamina in midfield, and also featured at right back for the reserve side on occasions.
Swansea C (Trainee) FL 1+4

CORDEN Simon **Wayne**

Born: Leek, 1 November 1975
Height: 5'9" **Weight:** 11.3
This skilful left winger was again a huge favourite with the Mansfield Town faithful last term and scored a few useful goals with his trademark free kicks. Wayne's tricky wing play and crosses made him a thorn in the side of many opponents and he provided a major contribution to the Stags efforts in reaching the play-off final.
Port Vale (From trainee on 20/9/1994) FL 30+36/1 FLC 4 FAC 2+1/1
Mansfield T (Free on 3/7/2000) FL 154+14/32 FLC 7/2 FAC 8+1/1 Others 7

CORICA Stephen (Steve) Christopher

Born: Queensland, Australia, 24 March 1973
Height: 5'8" **Weight:** 11.0
International Honours: Australia: 31; U23; Yth
Steve scored a splendid goal for Walsall in the opening-day win against West Bromwich Albion and converted a penalty at Millwall a few weeks later. However, the experienced midfielder then faded out of the first-team scene and rarely featured in the second half of the season.

Leicester C (£325,000 from Marconi, Australia on 11/8/1995) FL 16/2 FAC 2
Wolverhampton W (£700,000 on 16/2/1996) FL 80+20/5 FLC 5+1 FAC 3+1
(Free to Sanfrecce Hiroshima, Japan on 20/3/2000)
Walsall (Free on 8/2/2002) FL 63+10/9 FLC 5 FAC 2+2

CORNWALL Lucas (Luke) Clarence

Born: Lambeth, 23 July 1980
Height: 5'11" **Weight:** 11.6
Luke signed for Bradford City during the 2003 close season but was given few opportunities to shine last term. The pacy striker started against Reading and Ipswich and came off the bench twice. He scored two goals. Luke did not feature at all under Bryan Robson and joined Conference side Woking in March after trial spells with Sheffield Wednesday and Wimbledon.
Fulham (From trainee on 6/7/1998) FL 1+3/1 FLC 2+1
Grimsby T (Loaned on 13/3/2001) FL 9+1/4
Lincoln C (Loaned on 17/1/2003) FL 1+2
Bradford C (Free on 3/7/2003) FL 2+1 FLC 0+1

CORT Carl Edward Richard

Born: Southwark, 1 November 1977
Height: 6'4" **Weight:** 12.7
International Honours: E: U21-12
This tall striker joined Wolves after an injury-affected spell at St James's Park. He made a slow start to his Molineux career, scoring once in six outings, then came on as substitute for the next three games before regaining his place. This worked, as suddenly he was leading the line in style, holding the ball up well and retaining possession, which Wolves needed. Carl scored four goals in a five-game spell, two of them flashing headers against Middlesbrough and Everton.
Wimbledon (From trainee on 7/6/1996) PL 54+19/16 FLC 8+2/7 FAC 6+4/2
Lincoln C (Loaned on 3/2/1997) FL 5+1/1
Newcastle U (£7,000,000 on 6/7/2000) PL 19+3/7 FLC 3/1 FAC 2 Others 0+1
Wolverhampton W (£2,000,000 on 28/1/2004) PL 13+3/5

CORT Leon Terence Anthony

Born: Bermondsey, 11 September 1979
Height: 6'2" **Weight:** 13.4
Leon enjoyed another excellent season at Southend last term, enhancing his reputation as a rock in the centre of defence. He made the starting line-up for every Third Division match and was only

booked once throughout the whole season, an impressive record for a centre half. Although only troubling the scorers once, Leon's consistency was paramount in securing a comfortable place in the table for Southend.
Millwall (Free from Dulwich Hamlet on 23/1/1998)
Southend U (Free on 11/7/2001) FL 135+2/11 FLC 3 FAC 13/1 Others 8

COSTA Candido Alves

Born: Sao Joao da Madeira, Portugal, 30 April 1981
Height: 5'7" **Weight:** 11.6
International Honours: Portugal: U21
George Burley took Candido on a season-long loan from Porto and showed great faith in him as a wide midfield player. Candido, who added to his Portuguese Under 21 caps, is always eager for the ball and shows good control. He found it hard to get away from defenders, with the result that too many of his crosses were hit diagonally from deep positions. He had to adjust to the tempo of the English game and needed more time than First Division defenders were prepared to give him.
Derby Co (Loaned from FC Porto, Portugal on 5/8/2003) FL 23+11/1 FLC 1

COUGHLAN Graham

Born: Dublin, 18 November 1974
Height: 6'2" **Weight:** 13.6
Club Honours: S Div 1 '01; Div 3 '02; Div 2 '04
Graham was the only ever-present for Plymouth Argyle in their Second Division championship season in 2003-04. He is a very strong central defender, extremely good in the air and often chips in with some vital goals from set pieces, which he works extremely hard at during training. His outstanding performances were recognised when he was selected for the PFA Division Two team of the season by his fellow professionals.
Blackburn Rov (£100,000 from Bray W on 14/10/1995)
Swindon T (Loaned on 25/3/1997) FL 3
Livingston (Free on 29/3/1999) SL 53+3/2 SLC 4 SC 2 Others 5
Plymouth Arg (Free on 21/6/2001) FL 134/23 FLC 3 FAC 9 Others 2/1

COUNAGO Pablo

Born: Pontevedra, Spain, 9 August 1979
Height: 5'11" **Weight:** 11.12
Pablo had an up-and-down time with Ipswich last term. The first half of the season saw him notch ten goals by the turn of the year, including a Boxing Day

double at West Ham after coming on as substitute. However, he then picked up a groin injury in February and this effectively ended his campaign. A talented striker with the ability to wriggle past opponents, he is very unselfish and always looking to play colleagues into goal-scoring positions.

Ipswich T (Free from Celta Vigo, Spain on 19/7/2001) P/FL 47+34/28 FLC 5/2 FAC 4+1 Others 7+2/3

COWAN Thomas (Tom)
Born: Bellshill, 28 August 1969
Height: 5'9" **Weight:** 11.10
This experienced defender began last term with SPL club Dundee and made a handful of first-team appearances before the club went into administration. Tom was subsequently allowed to move on to Carlisle, for whom he soon became an automatic choice at left back. A solid tackler who reads the game well, his never-say-die attitude was a significant factor in the club's much improved form in the second half of the season.

Clyde (Free from Netherdale BC on 11/7/1988) SL 16/2 SC 2
Glasgow R (Signed on 9/2/1989) SL 8+4 SC 0+1 Others 2
Sheffield U (£350,000 on 1/8/1991) F/PL 45 FLC 5 FAC 2 Others 1
Stoke C (Loaned on 1/10/1993) FL 14 FLC 1 Others 3
Huddersfield T (£150,000 on 24/3/1994) FL 137/8 FLC 13/1 FAC 9/1 Others 6
Burnley (£20,000 on 12/3/1999) FL 17+3/1 FLC 2 Others 0+1
Cambridge U (Loaned on 22/2/2000) FL 4
Cambridge U (Free on 20/7/2000) FL 44+2/3 FLC 1 FAC 1
Peterborough U (Loaned on 18/1/2002) FL 4+1/1
York C (Free on 5/7/2002) FL 31+2/1 FLC 1
Dundee (Free on 6/8/2003) SL 4+1/1 Other 0+1
Carlisle U (Free on 28/11/2003) FL 20/1

COX Ian Gary
Born: Croydon, 25 March 1971
Height: 6'0" **Weight:** 12.2
International Honours: Trinidad & Tobago: 5
Ian joined Gillingham during the 2003 close season and made an impressive start to life at Priestfield. However, problems in both ankles forced him to undergo surgery and led to an extended absence. He returned against West Bromwich Albion in April and kept his place for the remainder of the campaign.

Crystal Palace (£35,000 from Carshalton on 8/3/1994) F/PL 2+13 FAC 1+2/1

Bournemouth (Free on 28/3/1996) FL 172/16 FLC 14 FAC 10 Others 11/1
Burnley (£500,000 on 4/2/2000) FL 107+8/5 FLC 7 FAC 8+1
Gillingham (Free on 6/8/2003) FL 32+1 FLC 3 FAC 1

COX Neil James
Born: Scunthorpe, 8 October 1971
Height: 6'0" **Weight:** 13.7
Club Honours: FLC '94; Div 1 '95
International Honours: E: U21-6
Neil, an experienced central defender or right back with more than 400 League appearances under his belt, was again one of Watford's most consistent players. As captain, he led by example and also took responsibility for penalties, scoring four times from the spot. His only absences at the start of the season were for disciplinary reasons, but a hamstring injury in March ruled him out until the last two games of the season.

Scunthorpe U (From trainee on 20/3/1990) FL 17/1 FAC 4 Others 4+1
Aston Villa (£400,000 on 12/2/1991) F/PL 26+16/3 FLC 5+2 FAC 4+2/1 Others 2
Middlesbrough (£1,000,000 on 19/7/1994) P/FL 103+3/3 FLC 14+1 FAC 5/1 Others 1+1
Bolton W (£1,200,000 on 27/5/1997) P/FL 77+3/7 FLC 9/1 FAC 1+1 Others 3
Watford (£500,000 on 5/11/1999) P/FL 177+3/20 FLC 12 FAC 9

COX Simon Peter
Born: Clapham, 24 March 1984
Height: 5'11" **Weight:** 11.0
International Honours: RoI: Yth
After patiently awaiting the chance of a first-team game due to the consistency of Andy Woodman, Simon eventually made his senior debut for Oxford against Doncaster Rovers last term, and kept a clean sheet against the eventual champions. Although small in stature for a goalkeeper, Simon commands his area well and is a good shot stopper.

Oxford U (From trainee on 8/7/2003) FL 5

COYNE Christopher (Chris) John
Born: Brisbane, Australia, 20 December 1978
Height: 6'1" **Weight:** 13.10
International Honours: Australia: U23
A model of consistency in the centre of defence for Luton Town last term, Chris's f o rm seemed to improve in every game he played. He was rarely absent all season and when Kevin Nicholls was sidelined by injury he took over the captain's armband. Chris netted three goals, including one in the home match

against champions-elect Plymouth.

West Ham U (£150,000 from Perth SC, Australia on 13/1/1996) PL 0+1
Brentford (Loaned on 21/8/1998) FL 7 FLC 1
Southend U (Loaned on 25/3/1999) FL 0+1
Dundee (Free on 31/3/2000) SL 16+4 SLC 0+2 SC 4 Others 2
Luton T (£50,000 on 18/9/2001) FL 111+4/6 FLC 3/1 FAC 7 Others 3

COYNE Daniel (Danny)
Born: Prestatyn, 27 August 1973
Height: 5'11" **Weight:** 13.0
International Honours: W: 5; B-1; U21-9; Yth; Sch
Danny spent the 2003-04 season as understudy to Ian Walker in goal for Leicester. On the rare occasions that he was called up for first-team duties he did not let anyone down and duly found himself back in international action for Wales in April. He completed the campaign with a cameo appearance at Arsenal and kept a clean sheet for the final few minutes.

Tranmere Rov (From trainee on 8/5/1992) FL 110+1 FLC 13 FAC 2 Others 2
Grimsby T (Free on 12/7/1999) FL 181 FLC 13 FAC 7
Leicester C (Free on 4/7/2003) PL 1+3 FLC 1

COZIC Bertrand Edern
Born: Quimper, France, 18 May 1978
Height: 5'10" **Weight:** 12.6
This midfield player joined Cheltenham Town on a short-term contract last August after previously being a member of the successful Team Bath side. A strong central midfielder with an eye for a pass, Bertrand made a positive impression during the pre-season and started several early-season games. He scored his first Football League goal in the 4-3 defeat against Swansea City but then suffered a hamstring injury at the end of September and was released after the change of management at the club, joining Hereford United until the end of the season.

Cheltenham T (Free from Team Bath on 8/8/2003) FL 7/1 FLC 0+1

CRADDOCK Darren
Born: Bishop Auckland, 23 February 1985
Height: 6'0" **Weight:** 12.2
A third-year scholar with Hartlepool, Darren made his debut when coming on as a substitute in the FA Cup tie against Whitby Town. The young defender acquitted himself well, and for the next two games was given a first-team place at centre back when he was preferred to captain Micky Barron. Later in the season he was tried out as a right back and

proved a great success making several appearances as the club fought their way into the play-offs.
Hartlepool U (Trainee) FL 9+1 FAC 0+1

CRADDOCK Jody Darryl
Born: Redditch, 25 July 1975
Height: 6'1" **Weight:** 12.4
This central defender faced yet another relegation battle last term, having gone down with Sunderland the previous season. After the first couple of games he settled in well at Molineux and looked a good signing, being particularly hard to beat in the air. Whilst not so convincing in mid-season, he was still an ever-present until January. A highlight was scoring at Chelsea, to give Wolves a brief lead. After a 4-1 home defeat to Southampton in April, he was dropped to give Isaac Okoronkwo a chance.
Cambridge U (Free from Christchurch on 13/8/1993) FL 142+3/4 FLC 3/1 FAC 6 Others 5
Sunderland (£300,000 + on 4/8/1997) P/FL 140+6/2 FLC 8+2 FAC 7+2 Others 3
Sheffield U (Loaned on 27/8/1999) FL 10
Wolverhampton W (£1,750,000 on 15/8/2003) PL 31+1/1 FLC 3/1 FAC 2+1

CRAIG Tony Andrew
Born: Greenwich, 20 April 1985
Height: 6'0" **Weight:** 10.13
Tony started the 2003-04 season as a member of the Millwall first-team squad. Still only a teenager he gave some fine performances early on, but then suffered an injury which kept him out for the rest of the campaign. Tony is a tough, hard-tackling, full back and has an 'old head' confirmed by his attitude when getting forward and motivating his fellow experienced professionals.
Millwall (From trainee on 13/3/2003) FL 10+1/1 FLC 1

CRAINEY Stephen Daniel
Born: Glasgow, 22 June 1981
Height: 5'9" **Weight:** 9.11
Club Honours: SPD '02
International Honours: S: 6; B-1; U21-7
Out of favour at Celtic for tactical reasons, Stephen was Gordon Strachan's last signing, arriving during the January transfer window. He made an encouraging debut at Arsenal just ten days later, on the left of a makeshift back four that conceded two goals. His opportunities to impress were then limited by a combination of Danny Higginbotham's outstanding form at left back, a brief return from Graeme Le Saux and the shifts in the Saints' management,

but towards the end of the season he looked particularly effective playing behind Anders Svensson down the left flank.
Glasgow Celtic (From juniors on 3/7/1997) SL 18+21 SLC 6+1/1 SC 2+3 Others 3+2
Southampton (£500,000 + on 31/1/2004) PL 5

CRAINIE Martin James
Born: Yeovil, 23 September 1986
Height: 6'0" **Weight:** 12.4
International Honours: E: Yth
Martin's debut for Southampton, at Chelsea in May, was not the stuff of dreams: he opened the scoring against his own side! There were mitigating circumstances for the teenager, he is accustomed to playing in central defence, and was plunged into an injury ravaged first team out of position. The goal aside, he coped manfully. Quick and comfortable with the ball, and more than useful in the air, he earned glowing reports in the last year, playing with the Saints' U19s, and featuring in the England U18 squad.
Southampton (Trainee) PL 1

CRANE Anthony (Tony) Steven
Born: Liverpool, 8 September 1982
Height: 6'1" **Weight:** 12.6
International Honours: E: Yth
This tall, powerfully-built central defender joined Grimsby Town during the 2003 close season and immediately established himself as an automatic choice for the senior squad. His combative style did not always meet with the approval of referees and his season was interrupted by a couple of suspensions.
Sheffield Wed (From trainee on 15/9/1999) FL 24+25/4 FLC 3+5/1 FAC 1+3
Grimsby T (Free on 7/7/2003) FL 37/3 FLC 1 FAC 2

CRESPO Hernan Jorge
Born: Florida, Argentina, 6 July 1975
Height: 6'0" **Weight:** 12.13
International Honours: Argentina: 46
To boost their striking power for the Champions' League campaign Chelsea invested heavily in a world-class striker with a proven pedigree. Hernan Crespo had featured in the competition for his three previous Italian clubs and had starred in Inter's progress to the 2003 semi-finals by scoring nine goals in seven matches. His most satisfactory goal was probably the opener against Lazio in the Stadio Olimpico which set Chelsea on course for a four-goal romp and diffused

the hostile reception given to him by Lazio fans. Earlier he had announced his arrival in English football with two stunning goals at Moulineux and a wonderful curling shot at Highbury. Another memorable goal was the superb header at Fulham in December, which put Chelsea back on track after two consecutive defeats. The second half of Hernán's season was disrupted by groin and calf strains and a bout of illness but he returned to finish the season in style with two brilliant goals at Villa Park and an opportunist effort in Monaco which gave the Blues a glimmer of hope in the Champions' League semi-final. Hernan is a perfect example of the contemporary front player: able to play up front alone; dangerous in and around the box and from long distance; a threat with both feet and in the air; mobile and intelligent.
Chelsea (£16,800,000 from Inter Milan, Italy, ex River Plate, Parma, Lazio, on 29/8/2003) PL 13+6/10 FLC 1+1 Others 7+3/2

CRESSWELL Richard Paul Wesley
Born: Bridlington, 20 September 1977
Height: 6'0" **Weight:** 11.8
International Honours: E: U21-4
Preston's leading scorer in each of the previous two seasons, Richard had to wait until September to get off the mark, scoring his first goal on his 150th appearance for the club. A goal in the next game seemed to see him back on top form, but that was more or less it for the rest of the campaign. His only other strike came in the FA Cup replay at Reading. A lack of fortune in front of goal never undermined Richard's work ethic and he continued to try hard for both himself and the team, which was much appreciated by the fans with whom he maintains an excellent relationship.
York C (From trainee on 15/11/1995) FL 72+23/21 FLC 3+3 FAC 4+2/3 Others 4
Mansfield T (Loaned on 27/3/1997) FL 5/1
Sheffield Wed (£950,000 + on 25/3/1999) PL 7+24/2 FLC 1+1/1 FAC 0+3
Leicester C (£750,000 on 13/3/2001) FLC 1 FAC 0+2/1 Others 0+2
Preston NE (£500,000 on 12/3/2001) FL 115+23/33 FLC 5+2/1 FAC 2+1/3 Others 1+2

CRITTENDEN Nicholas (Nick) John
Born: Bracknell, 11 November 1978
Height: 5'10" **Weight:** 11.8
International Honours: E: SP-1
This Yeovil Town midfielder had a somewhat disappointing season in 2003-04, starting in less than half the League

fixtures, although a run of injuries did not help his cause. Nick's strengths have always been his pace down the flanks and the ability to cut in and score past opposition defences. He netted three goals during the campaign including the winner at Bristol Rovers in December. Nevertheless he was released by the club in the summer.

Chelsea *(From trainee on 9/7/1997) PL 0+2 FLC 1*
Plymouth Arg *(Loaned on 19/10/1998) FL 1+1*
Yeovil T *(Free on 14/8/2000) FL 20+9/2 FLC 1 FAC 3/1 Others 1*

CROFT Gary

Born: Burton on Trent, 17 February 1974
Height: 5'9" **Weight:** 11.8
International Honours: E: U21-4
Gary missed the start of the 2003-04

campaign after being struck down by appendicitis on his return from Cardiff City's pre-season trip to Scandinavia. He did not return to first-team duties until the end of September, and subsequently enjoyed a couple of decent runs in the line-up. A consistent player who can feature in either full-back position and also in midfield, Gary was out of contract in the summer, but was offered a new deal by the club.

Grimsby T *(From trainee on 7/7/1992) FL 139+10/3 FLC 7 FAC 8+2/1 Others 3*
Blackburn Rov *(£1,700,000 on 29/3/1996) PL 33+7/1 FLC 6 FAC 4+2*
Ipswich T *(£800,000 on 21/9/1999) P/FL 20+9/1 FLC 3+1 FAC 1 Others 2+1*
Wigan Ath *(Loaned on 17/1/2002) FL 7*
Cardiff C *(Free on 28/3/2002) FL 65+11/3 FLC 2 FAC 3+2 Others 2+2*

CROFTS Andrew Lawrence

Born: Chatham, 29 May 1984
Height: 5'9" **Weight:** 10.8
International Honours: W: Yth
Andrew was used mainly as a substitute by Gillingham last season, but gave a good account of himself in his first start – a narrow 1-0 defeat at West Bromwich Albion. The promising young midfielder will be hoping to experience more senior action in 2004-05.

Gillingham *(From trainee on 6/8/2003) FL 1+8 FLC 0+2*

CROOKS Lee Robert

Born: Wakefield, 14 January 1978
Height: 6'0" **Weight:** 12.1
International Honours: E: Yth
Lee was enjoying a useful spell for Barnsley last term when an ankle injury

Hernan Crespo (left)

put him out of action. He returned to fitness in mid-January, but a series of further injuries disrupted the remainder of his campaign. His best performances came when playing just in front of the back four where he was very effective at breaking up opposition movements and starting counter attacks.

Manchester C *(From trainee on 14/1/1995) P/FL 52+24/2 FLC 5+2 FAC 5 Others 3*
Northampton T *(Loaned on 26/12/2000) FL 3*
Barnsley *(£190,000 on 2/3/2001) FL 50+17 FLC 2 FAC 2 Others 2*

CROPPER Dene James
Born: Chesterfield, 5 January 1983
Height: 6'1" **Weight:** 13.0
This solidly built target man found it difficult to force his way into the Lincoln starting line-up because of the competition for places. Dene was loaned to Gainsborough Trinity in November but returned after a month and was regularly used from the substitutes' bench until departing for neighbours Boston United in March. Signed by the Pilgrims on a short-term contract with the aim of earning himself a deal for 2004-2005, he was an instant hit at York Street scoring in the opening ten minutes of his debut at Bury. Dene then found chances hard to come by and was relegated to the bench before being released at the end of the season.
Lincoln C *(Free from trainee at Sheffield Wed on 7/8/2002) FL 29+21/3 FLC 1 FAC 1 Others 4+1*
Boston U *(Signed on 26/3/2004) FL 4+1/1*

CROSBY Andrew (Andy) Keith
Born: Rotherham, 3 March 1973
Height: 6'2" **Weight:** 13.7
Club Honours: Div 3 '01
Oxford United club captain Andy had another reliable season last term, rarely missing a match. A solid, dependable defender, he held the back line together and was again the club penalty taker, keeping up his 100 per cent record for five more. An honest, committed player, he was reported to have signed for Scunthorpe United during the summer break. Andy was selected for the PFA Division Three team of the season.
Doncaster Rov *(From trainee at Leeds U on 4/7/1991) FL 41+10 FLC 1+1 FAC 2 Others 4+1/1*
Darlington *(Free on 10/12/1993) FL 179+2/3 FLC 10 FAC 11/1 Others 9*
Chester C *(Free on 8/7/1998) FL 41/4 FLC 3 FAC 1 Others 1*

Brighton & Hove A *(£10,000 on 28/7/1999) FL 64+8/5 FLC 3 FAC 1+1 Others 7*
Oxford U *(Free on 13/12/2001) FL 109+2/12 FLC 5 FAC 4 Others 2/1*

CROSSLEY Mark Geoffrey
Born: Barnsley, 16 June 1969
Height: 6'0" **Weight:** 16.0
International Honours: W: 7; B-1; E: U21-3
Signed in the summer of 2003 as cover for Edwin van der Sar, Mark managed just two first-team appearances and a handful of reserve outings for Fulham last term. When he did appear in the Carling Cup tie at Wigan he almost stole the show in the final minute at the other end of the field, forcing a good save from his opposite number. His only Premiership outing came in the 2-1 home defeat against Liverpool. Despite his lack of club action he was regularly selected for Wales and featured in the 4-0 win over Scotland.
Nottingham F *(From trainee on 2/7/1987) F/PL 301+2 FLC 39+1 FAC 32 Others 18*
Millwall *(Loaned on 20/2/1998) FL 13*
Middlesbrough *(Free on 25/7/2000) PL 21+2 FLC 5 FAC 3*
Stoke C *(Loaned on 29/11/2002) FL 1*
Stoke C *(Loaned on 6/3/2003) FL 11*
Fulham *(£500,000 on 14/8/2003) PL 1 FLC 1*

CROUCH Peter James
Born: Macclesfield, 30 January 1981
Height: 6'7" **Weight:** 11.12
Club Honours: Div 1 '04
International Honours: E: U21-6; Yth
This tall striker is very effective in the air, but also has a deceptively neat touch, and his control and ability to hold the ball up while colleagues find good positions is one of his major strengths. After just one substitute appearance for Aston Villa in the opening game of the season Peter moved to Norwich on loan in September. He impressed during his spell at Carrow Road, helping lift the Canaries from a mid-table position to promotion contenders. On his return to Villa Park he seemed to rediscover his predatory instincts and became a more confident player. Peter made his first start of the season in the home leg of the Carling Cup semi-final match against Bolton, and then went on to score twice in the 5-0 win against Leicester – his first seeing him dive in at the far post to meet Thomas Hitzlsperger's inswinging corner with a brave header which earned him a cut from a defender's boot.
Tottenham H *(From trainee on 2/7/1998)*

Queens Park R *(£60,000 on 28/7/2000) FL 38+4/10 FLC 1+1 FAC 3/2*
Portsmouth *(£1,250,000 on 11/7/2001) FL 37/18 FLC 1/1 FAC 1*
Aston Villa *(£4,000,000 + on 28/3/2002) PL 20+17/6 FLC 1+1 Others 4*
Norwich C *(Loaned on 8/9/2003) FL 14+1/4*

CROWE Dean Anthony
Born: Stockport, 6 June 1979
Height: 5'5" **Weight:** 11.3
Dean made a handful of appearances from the substitutes' bench for Luton at the start of last season before joining York City on loan in September. The young striker featured regularly during his time at Bootham Crescent, but failed to find the net and returned to Kenilworth Road. He continued to feature on the bench with a couple of starts in the LDV Vans Trophy games until moving on to Oldham on transfer-deadline day as new Latics boss Brian Talbot looked to add more firepower to his squad. The young striker then proceeded to score his first goal for 18 months, ironically against his former club, but he was released at the end of the season.
Stoke C *(From trainee on 5/9/1996) FL 29+31/12 FLC 2+3 Others 2/1*
Northampton T *(Loaned on 11/2/2000) FL 3+2*
Bury *(Loaned on 23/3/2000) FL 4/1*
Bury *(Loaned on 11/8/2000) FL 1+6/1*
Plymouth Arg *(Loaned on 11/8/2001) 0+1*
Luton T *(Free on 29/9/2001) FL 49+20/6 FLC 1+2 FAC 1+3 Others 3*
York C *(Loaned on 26/9/2003) FL 2+3*
Oldham Ath *(Free on 25/3/2004) FL 2+3/1*

CROWE Jason William
Born: Sidcup, 30 September 1978
Height: 5'9" **Weight:** 10.9
Club Honours: Div 1 '03
International Honours: E: Yth
Jason was perhaps the most successful of the players recruited by Grimsby during the 2003 close season. He appeared at both right back and in the centre of the defence, proving to be an effective man-to-man marker and comfortable when bringing the ball forward. Jason received several 'Man of the Match' awards during the campaign.
Arsenal *(From trainee on 13/5/1996) FLC 0+2 FAC 0+1*
Crystal Palace *(Loaned on 10/11/1998) FL 8*
Portsmouth *(£750,000 + on 7/7/1999) FL 67+19/5 FLC 4 FAC 1+2*
Brentford *(Loaned on 12/9/2000) FL 9 FLC 2*
Grimsby T *(Free on 7/8/2003) FL 27+5 FLC 1 FAC 2 Others 1*

CROWELL Matthew (Matty) Thomas

Born: Bridgend, 3 July 1984
Height: 5'9" **Weight:** 10.12
International Honours: W: U21-1
This promising youngster may not as yet be the finished article, but he showed plenty of promise when given the opportunity by Wrexham last term. An enthusiastic midfielder, he was never shy of having a crack at goal and netted with a real screamer at home to Grimsby in March.
Southampton (From trainee on 13/7/2001)
Wrexham (Free on 15/7/2003) FL 9+6/1 FLC 0+1 Others 1+1

CRYAN Colin

Born: Dublin, 23 March 1981
Height: 5'10" **Weight:** 13.4
International Honours: Rol: U21-5
The form of the first-choice central defenders meant Colin made just two first-team substitute appearances for Sheffield United last term, producing solid performances, being effective in the air and showing good anticipation. Whilst at Bramall Lane he was a regular member and captain of the successful reserve side, but he spent three months on loan at Conference side Scarborough where he was involved in their impressive FA Cup run.
Sheffield U (From trainee on 6/8/1999) FL 0+5 FLC 0+3

CUDICINI Carlo

Born: Milan, Italy, 6 September 1973
Height: 6'1" **Weight:** 12.3
Club Honours: FAC '00; CS '00
International Honours: Italy: U21; Yth
The 2003-04 campaign proved to be another magnificent season for this superb goalkeeper who confirmed his status as one of the finest of contemporary custodians with a string of outstanding performances. Carlo was inspirational in the Premiership as the Blues boasted the second-meanest defensive record in the country – between October and December he conceded just one goal in 14 hours and 24 minutes of football. Incredibly, he performed even better in Chelsea's away Champions' League ties – not conceding a goal in five volatile matches. Perhaps his best display came at one of his former clubs Lazio when he broke the hearts of the Roman club's forwards with a succession of breathtaking saves before the Blues ran riot with four goals. Sadly, Carlo missed the climax of Chelsea's season through two nasty injuries – limping off with a

groin strain during the FA Cup fifth round tie with Arsenal and later breaking a finger in training, which forced him to miss 11 matches. He returned for the last four games, keeping two clean sheets, and brilliantly saved Ruud van Nistelrooy's penalty at Old Trafford which secured the one point which Chelsea needed to confirm second place in the Premiership and direct entry into the 2004-05 Champions' League.
Chelsea (£160,000 from Castel di Sangro, Italy, ex AC Milan, Prato, Lazio, on 6/8/1999) PL 113+2 FLC 9 FAC 19 Others 15+1

CULKIN Nicholas (Nick) James

Born: York, 6 July 1978
Height: 6'2" **Weight:** 13.7
This tall and commanding goalkeeper spent most of last season as second choice to Chris Day for Queens Park Rangers and was a regular on the substitutes' bench. When Day was injured in February, Nick became first choice but was then injured himself after just a handful of appearances.
Manchester U (£250,000 from trainee at York C on 27/9/1995) PL 0+1
Hull C (Loaned on 24/12/1999) FL 4
Bristol Rov (Loaned on 14/7/2000) FL 45 FLC 5 FAC 1 Others 3
Livingston (Loaned on 5/10/2001) SL 21 SLC 2 SC 2
Queens Park R (Free on 22/7/2002) FL 22 Others 3

CULLIP Daniel (Danny)

Born: Bracknell, 17 September 1976
Height: 6'1" **Weight:** 12.7
Club Honours: Div 3 '01; Div 2 '02
Brighton's inspirational captain enjoyed another fine season last term, culminating in his lifting of the Second Division play-off trophy at Cardiff to earn his third promotion with the Seagulls. Blessed with pace and good reading of the game, Danny was named in the PFA's Second Division team for the second time in his career and was runner-up to Guy Butters in the club's annual 'Player of the Season' award. Forming a great central defensive partnership with Butters, he led by example and his never-say-die attitude made him hugely popular with the Withdean supporters.
Oxford U (From trainee on 6/7/1995)
Fulham (Free on 5/7/1996) FL 41+9/2 FLC 8 FAC 2 Others 1
Brentford (£75,000 on 17/2/1998) FL 15 FLC 2
Brighton & Hove A (£50,000 on 17/9/1999) FL 198+1/7 FLC 7/1 FAC 11/2 Others 6/1

CUMMINGS Warren

Born: Aberdeen, 15 October 1980
Height: 5'9" **Weight:** 11.8
International Honours: S: U21-9
In his first full season at Bournemouth this young left back excelled to become one of the most consistent performers in the team. Warren contributed two excellent goals as his all-round game improved. He also performed in a left-midfield role when the Cherries reverted to three at the back.
Chelsea (From trainee on 5/7/1999)
Bournemouth (Loaned on 20/10/2000) FL 10/1 Others 1
West Bromwich A (Loaned on 21/3/2001) FL 1+2
West Bromwich A (Loaned on 25/7/2001) FL 6+8 FLC 0+2
Bournemouth (Free on 3/2/2003) FL 62/2 FLC 1 FAC 3 Others 3
Dundee U (Loaned on 23/8/2002) SL 7+1 SLC 1
Dundee U (Loaned on 16/11/2002) SL 0+3

CUMMINS Michael (Micky) Thomas

Born: Dublin, 1 June 1978
Height: 6'0" **Weight:** 11.11
Club Honours: AMC '01
International Honours: Rol: U21-2; Yth
This dependable Port Vale midfield player spent much of the first half of the 2003-04 campaign at right back and even featured at centre half for a couple of games as the problems created by having a small squad hit hard. This of course limited his attacking options, but then as the new year dawned he was moved back to central midfield and responded with four goals, one of which was the late winner against Luton Town. Micky is probably the best header of a ball at the club and is always dangerous at set pieces.
Middlesbrough (From trainee on 1/7/1995) PL 1+1
Port Vale (Free on 17/3/2000) FL 172+3/19 FLC 6 FAC 7/1 Others 14/1

CUNNINGHAM Kenneth (Kenny) Edward

Born: Dublin, 28 June 1971
Height: 6'0" **Weight:** 11.8
International Honours: Rol: 57; B-2; U21-4; Yth
Birmingham City's captain was inspirational in the first-half of the 2003-04 season, sweeping up attacks and reading play superbly to halt danger. He helped Matthew Upson blossom as his defensive partner and continued to perform at an excellent level in the new

year despite constant niggling injuries which often left him unable to train properly during the week.
Millwall (Signed from Tolka Rov on 18/9/1989) FL 132+4/1 FLC 10 FAC 1 Others 5+1/1
Wimbledon (£650,000 on 9/11/1994) P/FL 249+1 FLC 22+1 FAC 32+1
Birmingham C (£600,000 on 18/7/2002) PL 67 FLC 2 FAC 4

CURETON Jamie
Born: Bristol, 28 August 1975
Height: 5'8" **Weight:** 10.7
International Honours: E: Yth
This midfield player joined Queens Park Rangers in February after a spell in South Korea, the deal being funded by a group of supporters. Jamie began his Loftus Road career on the bench, with his first start coming against Grimsby in April. He made an impact in the home game against Port Vale scoring twice, including the injury-time winner.
Norwich C (From trainee on 5/2/1993) P/FL 13+16/6 FLC 0+1 FAC 0+2
Bournemouth (Loaned on 8/9/1995) FL 0+5 Others 0+1
Bristol Rov (£250,000 on 20/9/1996) FL 165+9/72 FLC 7+1/2 FAC 10/2 Others 6/3
Reading (£250,000 on 21/8/2000) FL 74+34/50 FLC 4+1/1 FAC 5+2/2 Others 6+1/2
(Free to Busan Icons, South Korea during 2003 close season)
Queens Park R (£95,000 on 2/2/2004) FL 2+11/2

CURLE Thomas (Tom) Keith
Born: Bristol, 3 March 1986
Height: 5'10" **Weight:** 10.0
This Mansfield Town youngster was given his baptism in League football when he came off the bench to replace Tony Vaughan during injury time of the game against Yeovil last September. A promising left-sided player, he then spent the remainder of the campaign developing with the club's youth team. Tom is the son of Stags' manager Keith Curle.
Mansfield T (Trainee) FL 0+1

CURRIE Darren Paul
Born: Hampstead, 29 November 1974
Height: 5'11" **Weight:** 12.7
Darren was a near ever-present for Wycombe Wanderers last term. As a truly two-footed playmaker, he was used to good effect on both wings from where he likes to deliver those accurate crosses which have become his trademark. He was the FA Cup 'Player of the Third Round' for his impressive two-goal performance against Swindon.

In spite of the team's struggles he had recorded seven goals by the end of November. In the wake of relegation, he was released by the club in the summer.
West Ham U (From trainee on 2/7/1993)
Shrewsbury T (Loaned on 5/9/1994) FL 10+2/2
Shrewsbury T (Loaned on 3/2/1995) FL 5
Leyton Orient (Loaned on 16/11/1995) FL 9+1
Shrewsbury T (£70,000 on 7/2/1996) FL 46+20/8 FLC 2+1/1 FAC 3
Plymouth Arg (Free on 26/3/1998) FL 5+2
Barnet (Free on 13/7/1998) FL 120+7/19 FLC 5/1 FAC 3/2 Others 6
Wycombe W (£200,000 on 11/7/2001) FL 109+17/14 FLC 5 FAC 6+1/5 Others 5

CURTIS John Charles Keyworth
Born: Nuneaton, 3 September 1978
Height: 5'10" **Weight:** 11.9
Club Honours: FAYC '95; FLC '02
International Honours: E: B-1; U21-16; Yth; Sch
This stylish right back made a promising start to the campaign for Leicester, but lost a little confidence as the team struggled to find a winning formula. His unfortunate last-gasp own goal at Middlesbrough was almost his final act for the Foxes before joining fellow strugglers Pompey during the January transfer window. Signed to help shore up a leaking defence, he featured on a handful of occasions but was in the squad for the final three games.
Manchester U (From trainee on 3/10/1995) PL 4+9 FLC 5 Others 0+1
Barnsley (Loaned on 19/11/1999) FL 28/2 Others 1+1
Blackburn Rov (£2,250,000 on 1/6/2000) P/FL 61 FLC 10 FAC 6 Others 4
Sheffield U (Loaned on 3/3/2003) FL 9+3 FAC 1 Others 3
Leicester C (Free on 15/8/2003) PL 14+1 FLC 1 FAC 1
Portsmouth (Free on 2/2/2004) PL 5+1

CURTIS Thomas (Tom) David
Born: Exeter, 1 March 1973
Height: 5'8" **Weight:** 11.7
This defensive midfielder began the 2003-04 season as a first choice for Mansfield Town, but following an injury he lost his place to Neil MacKenzie and it was not until Lee Williamson was suspended that he came back into the side. Tom was in tremendous form by Christmas, and although a cartilage problem saw him miss out in February he came back once more to help the

Stags in their struggle for promotion. Despite not being noted for his scoring feats, Tom netted the vital goal which levelled the aggregate score with Northampton in the play-off semi-final and took the tie to a penalty shoot-out.
Derby Co (From juniors on 1/7/1991)
Chesterfield (Free on 12/8/1993) FL 235+5/12 FLC 20/1 FAC 14/1 Others 11+1
Portsmouth (£150,000 on 4/8/2000) FL 7+6 FLC 1+1
Walsall (Loaned on 20/9/2001) FL 3+1
Tranmere Rov (Loaned on 30/8/2002) FL 8 FLC 2 Others 1
Mansfield T (Free on 20/12/2002) FL 57+4 FLC 1 FAC 3/1 Others 3/1

CUTLER Neil Anthony
Born: Cannock, 3 September 1976
Height: 6'1" **Weight:** 12.0
International Honours: E: Yth; Sch
This competent goalkeeper spent the majority of the 2003-04 season as understudy to Ed De Goey at Stoke. On his day Neil is a brilliant shot-stopper, but first-team opportunities were few and far between last term until De Goey suffered concussion against Coventry in April and he then had a brief run in the side.
West Bromwich A (From trainee on 7/9/1993)
Chester C (Loaned on 27/3/1996) FL 1
Crewe Alex (Signed on 30/7/1996)
Chester C (Loaned on 30/8/1996) FL 5
Chester C (Free on 8/7/1998) FL 23 FLC 1 FAC 1 Others 1
Aston Villa (Signed on 30/11/1999) PL 0+1
Oxford U (Loaned on 15/12/2000) FL 11
Stoke C (Free on 24/7/2001) FL 65+4 FLC 3 FAC 6+1 Others 3
Swansea C (Loaned on 28/2/2003) FL 13

CYGAN Pascal
Born: Lens, France, 19 April 1974
Height: 6'3" **Weight:** 13.10
Club Honours: PL '04
Suspensions to Martin Keown and Lauren allowed Pascal to stake his claim in the Arsenal back four last term. He featured in ten consecutive Premiership games starting with the match at Birmingham City and helped the Gunners to six wins and four draws. After a patchy first season Pascal performed much better during the club's historic campaign. Strong in the air and a good passer of the ball he remained as back up to the defence upon Lauren's return to the side.
Arsenal (£2,100,000 from Lille, France, ex Valenciennes, Wasquehal, on 8/8/2002) PL 26+10/1 FLC 3 FAC 2 Others 11+3

D

DABIZAS Nikolaos (Nikos)
Born: Amyndaeo, Greece, 3 August 1973
Height: 6'1" **Weight:** 12.7
International Honours: Greece: 67; U21; Yth
This experienced central defender signed for Leicester in January on a short-term contract. Nikos was clearly short of match practice when joining the Foxes, but soon established a promising central-defensive pairing with local prospect, Matt Heath, offering guidance and direction as needed. He was unlucky to contribute a decisive own goal at Blackburn and continued to add to his international reputation with Greece, being a member of their Euro 2004 winning squad, although he only featured on the bench.
Newcastle U (£1,300,000 from Olympiakos, Greece on 13/3/1998) PL 119+11/10 FLC 6 FAC 17+1/2 Others 21+1/1
Leicester C (Free on 2/1/2004) PL 18

DADI Eugene
Born: Abidjan, Ivory Coast, 20 August 1973
Height: 6'2" **Weight:** 12.11
A large, bustling, but surprisingly skilful striker, Eugene proved a great success at Tranmere last term and finished the season as the club's leading scorer with 19 goals in all competitions. He always looked likely to unsettle opposing defenders with his busy and determined style of play and was quick to spot and snap up the half-chance. Off the field, Eugene has proved to be a popular and worthy ambassador for the club, in addition to running his own fashion design business and being a successful part-time model.
Aberdeen (Signed from Toulouse, France, ex Laval, Sete, ASK Linz, on 24/8/2001) SL 20+8/4 SLC 1+1/1 SC 3
Livingston (Signed on 23/7/2002) SL 16+7/3 SLC 2/1 Others 1+1
Tranmere Rov (Free on 8/8/1003) FL 29+9/16 FLC 1+1/1 FAC 6+2/2 Others 1

DAGNALL Christopher (Chris)
Born: Liverpool, 15 April 1986
Height: 5'8" **Weight:** 11.9
This young striker made his first-team debut for Tranmere Rovers when he came on as a substitute in the home game against Peterborough last September. He went on to feature on several more occasions and bagged his first senior goal

at Luton the following month. A product of the club's successful youth scheme, Chris possesses a devastatingly powerful shot and is capable of scoring spectacular goals, often conjuring chances from seemingly nothing.
Tranmere Rov (From trainee on 11/7/2003) FL 5+5/1 FLC 0+1

DAILLY Christian Eduard
Born: Dundee, 23 October 1973
Height: 6'0" **Weight:** 12.10
Club Honours: SC '94
International Honours: S: 53; B-1; U21-34; Yth; Sch
The West Ham skipper had another consistent season playing as a central defender last term. He scored his first-ever goal for the club against Reading in September and later followed up with a headed goal against Rotherham. His final goal was vital when he scored against Ipswich to take the Hammers to the play-off final in Cardiff. Although not vociferous as a captain he leads by example and each of the club's three managers during the season announced they were pleased with his efforts. Christian added to his total of caps for Scotland and made his 50th appearance for his country against Holland.
Dundee U (From juniors on 2/8/1990) SL 110+33/18 SLC 9/1 SC 10+2 Others 8+1/1
Derby Co (£1,000,000 on 12/8/1996) PL 62+5/4 FLC 6 FAC 4+1
Blackburn Rov (£5,300,000 on 22/8/1998) P/FL 60+10/4 FLC 5+1 FAC 4 Others 2
West Ham U (£1,750,000 on 18/1/2001) P/FL 115+4/2 FLC 5 FAC 10+2 Others 3/1

DALEY Omar
Born: Jamaica, 25 April 1981
Height: 5'10" **Weight:** 11.0
International Honours: Jamaica
Omar joined Reading on a 12-month contract, hoping to make a name for himself with the First Division club. However, he found difficulty in adjusting to the physical demands of the English game, and made only seven first-team appearances, all as a late second-half substitute in a wide right position. For the rest of the time he was confined to reserve team appearances, and was allowed to leave the Royals to return home before his contract was due to finish.
Reading (Signed from Portmore U, Jamaica on 19/8/2003) FL 0+6 FLC 0+1

DALMAT Stephane
Born: Tours, France, 16 February 1979
Height: 6'1" **Weight:** 12.8

International Honours: France: U21
This extremely talented attacking midfielder joined Spurs in the summer of 2003 and immediately impressed with some mazy runs and a willingness to shoot from outside the box. After the departure of Glenn Hoddle, Stephane retained the support of new boss David Pleat and was given more opportunity to play a creative role. Stephane repaid that faith and his contribution triggered a turn around in early-season results for the White Hart Lane club. However, he fell out of favour in the second half of the campaign and it was announced that he would return to Italy once his loan period had ended.
Tottenham H (Loaned from Inter Milan, Italy, ex Chateauroux, RC Lens, Marseilles, Paris St Germain, on 1/9/2003) PL 12+10/3 FLC 1+2 FAC 2+1

DALY Jonathan (Jon) Marvin
Born: Dublin, Ireland, 8 January 1983
Height: 6'1" **Weight:** 12.4
International Honours: RoI: U21-9; Yth
Stockport's talented young striker found goals hard to come by early on last season and then lost his place following a period of suspension. He was loaned out to Bury at the start of the new year and made a big impression during his spell at Gigg Lane, providing the strong physical presence that manager Graham Barow was seeking. On his return to Edgeley Park Jon broke back into County's line-up and played a key role in the club's 11-game unbeaten run that ultimately ensured they avoided relegation.
Stockport Co (From trainee on 18/1/2000) FL 55+22/11 FLC 2+1/1 FAC 2/1 Others 0+1
Bury (Loaned on 2/1/2004) FL 7/1

DALY Wesley (Wes) James Patrick
Born: Hammersmith, 7 March 1984
Height: 5'9" **Weight:** 11.2
This right-sided midfield player failed to establish himself in the Queens Park Rangers line-up last term and apart from two starts he was mostly used as a substitute. In order to gain some first team experience he was loaned out to Gravesend and then to Grays Athletic, eventually signing for Grays on a permanent basis.
Queens Park R (Trainee) FL 4+5 FAC 0+1 Others 1

DANBY John Robert
Born: Stoke, 20 September 1983
Height: 6'2" **Weight:** 14.7
A product of Kidderminster's youth policy,

this young goalkeeper finally received a first-team start at Scunthorpe last March. John marked the occasion with a clean sheet and went on to produce a series of fine performances in the closing matches. One of the highlights of his career to date came when he made a crucial last-minute save to earn the Harriers a point at Cambridge.
Kidderminster Hrs *(From juniors on 14/12/2001) FL 9+2*

[DANI] FERREIRA RODRIGUES Daniel
Born: Madeira, Portugal, 3 March 1980
Height: 6'0" **Weight:** 11.8
International Honours: Portugal: U21
After a spell in Greece with Ionikos, Dani joined Yeovil on a short-term contract towards the end of last season. After regaining full match-fitness he made his debut against Bury in explosive style, netting with a classic bicycle kick. A quality striker with an eye for goal, Dani featured regularly for the Glovers in the closing fixtures, adding three more goals.
Bournemouth *(Loaned from CS Farense, Portugal on 1/10/1998) FL 0+5 Others 0+2*
Southampton *(£170,000 on 3/3/1999) PL 0+2*
Bristol C *(Loaned on 3/10/2000) FL 3+1*
Bristol C *(Loaned on 31/12/2001) FL 0+4 Others 0+1*
Walsall *(Free on 6/8/2002) FL 0+1 (Freed on 13/1/2003)*
Yeovil T *(Free from Ionikos, Greece on 25/3/2004) FL 3+1/4*

DANIELS David (Dave) WIlliam
Born: Bedford, 14 September 1985
Height: 5'8" **Weight:** 10.10
An intelligent and strong-running midfield player who was a key member of the Cambridge United youth team last term, Dave was allocated a squad number in December. He made his debut in senior football when coming off the bench in the last minute of the home game against Scunthorpe in April.
Cambridge U *(Trainee) FL 0+1*

DANNS Neil Alexander
Born: Liverpool, 23 November 1982
Height: 5'9" **Weight:** 12.1
This hard-working midfielder received few chances for Blackburn last term and his only first-team appearance came in the Premiership game at home to Bolton in January when he came on from the bench. He was loaned out to Blackpool early on in the season, where he impressed with his work rate, and later

spent the closing weeks of the campaign out on loan again at Hartlepool.
Blackburn Rov *(From trainee on 3/7/2000) PL 1+2 FLC 2 FAC 1 Others 1*
Blackpool *(Loaned on 7/8/2003) FL 12/2 FLC 2 Others 1*
Hartlepool U *(Loaned on 12/3/2004) FL 8+1/1 Others 0+2*

DARBY Duane Anthony
Born: Birmingham, 17 October 1973
Height: 5'11" **Weight:** 12.6
Club Honours: NC '01; Div 3 '03
This experienced striker recorded his 50th strike for Rushden in the six-goal thriller at home to Queens Park Rangers last August and then netted on an emotional return to his former club Notts County. However he fell out of favour with the management and was allowed to move on to join Conference club Shrewsbury Town. He went on to assist the Shrews to a quick return to Football League status following their play-off victory against Aldershot Town.
Torquay U *(From trainee on 3/7/1992) FL 60+48/26 FLC 4+3/1 FAC 1+4 Others 5+3/2*
Doncaster Rov *(£60,000 on 19/7/1995) FL 8+9/4 FLC 2 FAC 0+1 Others 1+1*
Hull C *(Signed on 27/3/1996) FL 75+3/27 FLC 5/1 FAC 4/6 Others 4/2*
Notts Co *(Free on 2/7/1998) FL 22+6/5 FLC 3+1/1*
Hull C *(Loaned on 25/3/1999) FL 4+4*
Rushden & Diamonds *(Free on 21/6/2000) FL 61+18/23 FLC 1+2/1 FAC 4+1 Others 0+1*

DARLINGTON Jermaine Christopher
Born: Hackney, 11 April 1974
Height: 5'7" **Weight:** 10.10
Jermaine again alternated between midfield and defensive duties for Wimbledon last term, playing the first half of the season at full back before ending the campaign in one of the wider attacking positions. Much more happier going forward than tackling back, he contributed well in the improved form towards the end of the season, but despite this was not offered a new deal following the club's relegation.
Charlton Ath *(From trainee on 30/6/1992) FL 1+1 (Free to Dover Ath on 23/9/1993)*
Queens Park R *(£25,000 from Aylesbury U on 25/3/1999) FL 70+1/2 FLC 2 FAC 6*
Wimbledon *(£200,000 on 16/7/2001) FL 97+8/3 FLC 3+1 FAC 4*

DAVENPORT Calum Raymond Paul
Born: Bedford, 1 January 1983
Height: 6'4" **Weight:** 14.4

International Honours: E: Yth
A product of Coventry's youth scheme, this young centre half failed to win a first-team place in the early part of last season, but once in the side he proved immovable, winning plaudits for his cool and assured performances. Calum has an immense aerial presence and looks comfort on the ball. He was again dangerous at set pieces and whilst failing to find the net he made a number of goals. He was voted as the club's 'Players' Player of the Season' and was also selected for the Nationwide Division One team of the season.
Coventry C *(From trainee on 6/1/2000) P/FL 58+11/3 FLC 2 FAC 5+1*

DAVIDSON Callum Iain
Born: Stirling, 25 June 1976
Height: 5'10" **Weight:** 11.8
Club Honours: S Div '97
International Honours: S: 17; U21-2
Callum's progress at Leicester was severely hampered by injuries during the 2003-04 season and his drive and enthusiasm were severely missed for long periods. Indeed, he started the campaign with a groin problem that kept him out of action until November. Although primarily a left-sided defender, he was often employed as a makeshift midfielder when called into action, where both his drive and enthusiasm were a distinct asset. However, with relatively few fit weeks to look back on over the past two seasons, Callum was released by Micky Adams in the summer.
St Johnstone *(From juniors on 8/6/1994) SL 39+5/4 SLC 1 Others 3*
Blackburn Rov *(£1,750,000 on 12/2/1998) P/FL 63+2/1 FLC 3+1 FAC 6 Others 1+1*
Leicester C *(£1,700,000 on 12/7/2000) P/FL 90+11/2 FLC 5+1 FAC 5+1 Others 0+1*

DAVIES Andrew
Born: Stockton, 17 December 1984
Height: 6'3" **Weight:** 14.8
International Honours: E: U21-1; Yth
This talented and promising teenaged defender started Middlesbrough's Premiership campaign as defensive cover for the likes of Gareth Southgate, Ugo Ehiogu and Chris Riggott. Andrew made a total of ten Premiership appearances and broke through into David Platt's England U21 side. However, he suffered a double break of his right leg in the away reserve match against Blackburn Rovers at Morecambe in March. He fractured his tibia and fibia in a 15th-minute challenge and as a result he was side-lined beyond the end of the season.

Middlesbrough (From trainee on 6/7/2002)
PL 9+2 FLC 1

DAVIES Arron Rhys
Born: Cardiff, 22 June 1984
Height: 5'9" **Weight:** 10.0
This promising young Southampton winger scored regularly for the club's reserve team last term and was rewarded with an extension to his contract in December. Soon afterwards he joined Barnsley on loan to gain more experience of senior football, but he had few opportunities to establish himself in the side due to a change in management at Oakwell and subsequently returned to the South Coast.
Southampton (From trainee on 11/7/2002)
Barnsley (Loaned on 13/2/2004) FL 1+3

DAVIES Clint Aaron
Born: Perth, Australia, 24 April 1983
Height: 6'2" **Weight:** 12.2
Clint began the 2003-04 season on loan at Halifax and was expected to further his education with a year of Conference football. However, thanks to Bradford City's injury problems with goalkeepers he found himself recalled to Valley Parade and made his senior debut as a substitute at Gillingham in January after Alan Combe was sent off. Clint was given his first start against Sheffield United and acquitted himself well in very windy conditions.
Birmingham C (From trainee on 1/7/2002)
Bradford C (Free on 28/7/2003) FL 1+1

DAVIES Curtis Eugene
Born: London, 15 March 1985
Height: 6'1" **Weight:** 11.13
This young Luton central defender was given his senior debut in the LDV Vans Trophy tie at Rushden last November when he showed a level of maturity beyond his years. Curtis went on to feature in a handful more games, mostly coming on in the closing stages of the campaign, impressing with his anticipation and ability in the air.
Luton T (Trainee) FL 4+2 Others 0+1

DAVIES Gareth
Born: Chesterfield, 4 February 1983
Height: 6'1" **Weight:** 12.13
Gareth was unfortunate to play as infrequently as he did for Chesterfield in 2003-04. Others were preferred to him despite a number of reliable displays in defence and midfield, and it wasn't until Gus Uhlenbeek left that Gareth was able to claim the right-back berth as his own. His response to this was to work hard

and improve, and he can surely look forward to a more regular spot in 2004-05.
Chesterfield (Free from Buxton on 20/8/2001) FL 45+17/1 FLC 2+1 FAC 2/2 Others 3

DAVIES Kevin Cyril
Born: Sheffield, 26 March 1977
Height: 6'0" **Weight:** 13.6
International Honours: E: U21-3; Yth
Kevin proved once again why Sam Allardyce is considered to be one of the best wheelers and dealers around. Left seemingly on the soccer scrap heap after a desperately disappointing season at Southampton, Kevin moved to Bolton as a free agent and proved to be one of the players of the season, a fact confirmed by the number of 'Player of the Year' awards he garnered. A big, bustling centre forward, he caused opposing defences numerous problems with his tenacious and unerring style of play. Although Kevin ended the season with a healthy total of nine Premiership goals, this figure does not tell half the story. Always willing to drop deep to influence play, his strength and ability to hold the ball up for others enabled several of his colleagues to notch healthy goal tallies. It came as no surprise when Kevin signed an extension to his original one-year deal at the end of the campaign.
Chesterfield (From trainee on 18/4/1994) FL 113+16/22 FLC 7+2/1 FAC 10/6 Others 9+2/1
Southampton (£750,000 on 14/5/1997) PL 20+5/9 FLC 3+1/3 FAC 1
Blackburn Rov (£7,250,000 on 2/6/1998) P/FL 11+12/1 FLC 3 FAC 2/1 Others 1
Southampton (Signed on 18/8/1999) PL 59+23/10 FLC 3+2/1 FAC 3+5/2
Millwall (Loaned on 13/9/2002) FL 6+3/3
Bolton W (Free on 25/7/2003) PL 38/9 FLC 4+1/1

DAVIES Sean Graham
Born: Middlesbrough, 1 June 1985
Height: 6'1" **Weight:** 12.8
This young left-sided defender progressed through the ranks at York City to make his senior debut against Hull on Boxing Day. Sean was a member of the first-team squad throughout the second half of the season and impressed with his competence and confidence in defence.
York C (Trainee) FL 6+2

DAVIES Simon
Born: Haverfordwest, 23 October 1979
Height: 5'10" **Weight:** 11.4
International Honours: W: 19; B-1; U21-10; Yth

Last term proved to be another progressive season for this talented Tottenham midfielder who has grown in stature and has grabbed opportunities at both club and international level to impress. He is a player who loves to have the ball at his feet and is happy to hold and challenge in midfield. However, his greatest strength is in getting forward and piercing opponents' defence with his pace and mazy runs. Simon's finish is accurate and he is happy to strike from outside the box. He was particularly influential in Wales' progress in the qualification stages of Euro 2004 only to have his ambitions scuppered at the final hurdle.
Peterborough U (From trainee on 21/7/1997) FL 63+2/6 FLC 4 FAC 3 Others 3
Tottenham H (£700,000 on 10/1/2000) PL 82+18/13 FLC 8+2/3 FAC 6+2/2

DAVIS Claude
Born: Jamaica, 6 March 1979
Height: 6'3" **Weight:** 14.4
International Honours: Jamaica
Signed on a season-long loan, this big central defender made an instant impression with a powerful display for Preston on his debut at the Hawthorns. A series of niggling injuries stopped him claiming a regular place in the side, but North End fans were pleased when he signed a permanent contract in March. Claude uses his strength effectively both on the ground and in the air, easing opponents off the ball without having to resort to foul play, and his ability to make apparently telescopic tackles never failed to impress the fans at Deepdale. Claude remained a regular at international level for Jamaica.
Preston NE (Signed from Portmore U, Jamaica on 15/8/2003) FL 16+6/1 FAC 2

DAVIS Kelvin Geoffrey
Born: Bedford, 29 September 1976
Height: 6'1" **Weight:** 14.0
International Honours: E: U21-3; Yth
Kelvin joined Ipswich during the summer of 2003 and made an immediate improvement to the club's last line of defence. He is a good all-round 'keeper, being particularly effective as a shot-stopper. This was aptly demonstrated during the last game of the season, the second leg of the play-off at West Ham, when he produced a fantastic one-handed save to keep out a point-blank header from Bobby Zamora and then stretched to turn a long-range effort over the bar.

101

*Luton T (From trainee on 1/7/1994) FL 92
FLC 7 FAC 2 Others 6*
*Torquay U (Loaned on 16/9/1994) FL 2 FLC 1
Others 1*
*Hartlepool U (Loaned on 8/8/1997) FL 2
FLC 1*
*Wimbledon (£600,000 + on 14/7/1999) FL
131 FLC 7 FAC 8*
*Ipswich T (Free on 6/8/2003) FL 45 FLC 2
FAC 2 Others 2*

DAVIS Sean

Born: Clapham, 20 September 1979
Height: 5'10" **Weight:** 12.0
Club Honours: Div 1 '01
International Honours: E: U21-11
Sean suffered a pre-season injury which
kept him out of first-team contention for
Fulham until November when he made a
goal-scoring return to the side at
Charlton. He then settled back into his
central-midfield role and showed the form
that brought him to the verge of
international recognition during the
previous campaign. An excellent tackler
and a tireless runner, he is to be found all
over the field at the heart of the action.
Although not a prolific goal-scorer he
produced a stunning effort in the home
win over Charlton.
*Fulham (From trainee on 2/7/1998) P/FL
128+27/14 FLC 9+5/3 FAC 15+2/2 Others
12/1*

DAVIS Solomon (Sol)

Sebastian
Born: Cheltenham, 4 September 1979
Height: 5'8" **Weight:** 11.0
This tenacious left back was a regular in
the Luton Town line-up for much of last
season. A brave tackler who reads the
game well, his forward runs proved useful
in helping start up attacking moves down
the left flank. Although he has made
almost 200 senior appearances, Sol has
yet to score in senior football, but his
willingness to shoot from long range
suggests his first goal may not be far
away.
*Swindon T (From trainee on 29/5/1998) FL
100+17 FLC 7 FAC 5+1 Others 1*
*Luton T (£600,000 + on 16/8/2002) FL 68+2
FLC 3+1 FAC 5 Others 4*

DAVIS Stephen (Steve) Mark

Born: Hexham, 30 October 1968
Height: 6'2" **Weight:** 14.7
Club Honours: Div 4 '92; AMC '04
This experienced defender joined
Blackpool in the 2003 close season and
was a regular in the line-up until the
middle of January. However, he was then
sidelined by injury and only managed a

handful more appearances during the
campaign. Steve netted his first goal for
the Seasiders in the 3-0 win at Wycombe
shortly before he was injured. He was
reported to have signed for York City
during the summer break.
*Southampton (From trainee on 6/7/1987) FL
5+1*
*Burnley (Loaned on 21/11/1989) FL 7+2
Others 2*
*Notts Co (Loaned on 28/3/1991) FL 0+2
Burnley (£60,000 on 17/8/1991) FL 162/22
FLC 10/2 FAC 18/1 Others 13*
*Luton T (£750,000 on 13/7/1995) FL
137+1/21 FLC 19/3 FAC 6/2 Others 10/1*
*Burnley (£800,000 on 21/12/1998) FL
152+4/20 FLC 9/2 FAC 6+1 Others 1*
*Blackpool (Free on 15/7/2003) FL 22+7/1
FLC 3 FAC 3 Others 1+1*

DAVISON Aidan John

Born: Sedgefield, 11 May 1968
Height: 6'1" **Weight:** 13.12
Club Honours: AMC '98
International Honours: NI: 3; B-1
After being released by Bradford City at
the close of the 2003-04 season Aidan
had considered retirement, but was
persuaded to return to Grimsby to replace
the departed Danny Coyne. Still providing
a commanding presence in the box he
was unfortunate in the fact that the
Mariners were unable to field a consistent
back four and thus clean sheets were at a
premium. However, he remained an ever-
present until sidelined by a combination
of suspension and injury in the closing
stages of the campaign.
*Notts Co (Signed from Billingham Synthonia
on 25/3/1988) FL 1*
Bury (£6,000 on 7/10/1989)
*Millwall (Free on 14/8/1991) FL 34 FLC 3
FAC 2 Others 2*
*Bolton W (£25,000 on 26/7/1993) P/FL 35+2
FAC 8 Others 4*
Hull C (Loaned on 29/11/1996) FL 9 Others 1
Bradford C (Free on 14/3/1997) FL 10
*Grimsby T (Free on 16/7/1997) FL 77 FLC 10
FAC 7 Others 10*
Sheffield U (Free on 6/8/1999) FL 1+1
*Bradford C (Free on 4/1/2000) P/FL 49+2 FLC
6 FAC 1 Others 2+1*
*Grimsby T (Free on 8/8/2003) FL 32 FLC 1
FAC 2 Others 1*

DAWS Nicholas (Nicky) John

Born: Manchester, 15 March 1970
Height: 5'11" **Weight:** 13.2
Club Honours: Div 2 '97
This experienced midfield player was
restricted to just a handful of appearances
for Rotherham United last term, but he
never let the team down when called

upon. The lack of opportunity at Millmoor
saw him spend two spells on loan at
Grimsby as the Mariners looked for a
replacement for long-term injuries to
Stacy Coldicott and Alan Pouton. A
tenacious ball winner and excellent
distributor he made a good impression at
Blundell Park, but was unable to save the
team from relegation.
*Bury (£10,000 from Altrincham on
13/8/1992) FL 356+13/16 FLC 24+2/3 FAC
19/1 Others 15+4/3*
*Rotherham U (Free on 16/7/2001) FL
54+18/2 FLC 5+1 FAC 2+1*
*Grimsby T (Loaned on 19/9/2003) FL 7
Others 1*
Grimsby T (Loaned on 17/1/2004) FL 10

DAWSON Andrew (Andy)

Born: Northallerton, 20 October 1978
Height: 5'9" **Weight:** 10.2
Andy missed the opening games of last
term after damaging knee ligaments in a
pre-season friendly for Hull City against
Canvey Island. He quickly made up for
lost time, impressing the Tigers' fans with
stunning long-distance goals against
Southend and Kidderminster in his first
two home appearances. Andy's reliable
performances at left back were a major
element of the club's promotion-winning
team, and he was deservedly selected for
the PFA Division Three team of the year.
*Nottingham F (From trainee on 31/10/1995)
FLC 1*
*Scunthorpe U (£70,000 on 18/12/1998) FL
192+3/8 FLC 6 FAC 12/1 Others 12/2*
Hull C (Free on 1/7/2003) FL 32+1/3 FAC 1

DAWSON Kevin Edward

Born: Northallerton, 18 June 1981
Height: 6'0" **Weight:** 10.10
When fit Kevin was a real asset to
Chesterfield last term, producing a
number of gritty performances in central
defence and at right back, particularly at
the business end of the season. He was
injured throughout October, but Kevin's
most obvious quality is determination,
and he battled back to remain in the
squad for the rest of the campaign.
*Nottingham F (From trainee on 25/6/1998)
FL 8+3 FAC 1*
Barnet (Loaned on 9/3/2001) FL 5
*Chesterfield (Free on 8/8/2002) FL 48+2/1
FLC 3 FAC 2 Others 2*

DAWSON Michael Richard

Born: Northallerton, 18 November 1983
Height: 6'2" **Weight:** 12.12
International Honours: E: U21-6; Yth
Last term was a frustrating time for this
talented Nottingham Forest central

defender and after missing the start of the season due to glandular fever he then suffered with hamstring problems. However, when he returned to full fitness Michael showed his leadership qualities by captaining the Forest side and he also skippered England U21s against Sweden.

Nottingham F (From trainee on 23/11/2000) FL 69/6 FLC 3 FAC 1 Others 1

DAY Christopher (Chris)
Nicholas
Born: Walthamstow, 28 July 1975
Height: 6'3" **Weight:** 13.6
International Honours: E: U21-6; Yth (UEFA-U18 '93)
This experienced goalkeeper was first choice for Queens Park Rangers last season. A near ever-present until injured in the new year, he missed out on the closing stages of the campaign as he was unable to dislodge the on-loan Lee Camp and had to settle for a place on the bench.

Tottenham H (From trainee on 16/4/1993) Others 4
Crystal Palace (£225,000 + on 9/8/1996) FL 24 FLC 2 FAC 2
Watford (£225,000 on 18/7/1997) PL 11 FLC 1 Others 1
Lincoln C (Loaned on 4/12/2000) FL 14 Others 4
Queens Park R (Free on 24/7/2001) FL 57 FLC 4 FAC 1 Others 5

DAY Rhys
Born: Bridgend, 31 August 1982
Height: 6'2" **Weight:** 13.6
Club Honours: AMC '02
International Honours: W: U21-11; Yth
This highly-rated Mansfield centre half performed excellently last term alongside a string of partners including Dave Artell, Luke Dimech and youngster Alex John-Baptiste. Magnificent in the air, he caused opponents problems when going forward for set pieces and netted some useful goals. All-in-all Rhys had a wonderful season and was rewarded with the supporters' 'Player of the Year' trophy. He continued to represent Wales at U21 level during the campaign.

Manchester C (From trainee on 21/9/1999)
Blackpool (Loaned on 31/12/2001) FL 4+5 FAC 0+1 Others 3
Mansfield T (Free on 29/11/2002) FL 63+1/7 FLC 0+1 FAC 5 Others 4/2

DEANE Brian Christopher
Born: Leeds, 7 February 1968
Height: 6'3" **Weight:** 12.7
International Honours: E: 3; B-3
This big target man found his role was reduced to understudy to Les Ferdinand

for Leicester during the early weeks of the campaign, and he eventually moved on to assist West Ham in their promotion quest. Vastly experienced and very good in the air, his physical presence caused problems for many First Division defenders. Brian was regularly used as a substitute to come on and change the game. The Hammers were losing 2-0 to Sunderland in December when he was introduced to the fray. He headed down a free kick for Jermain Defoe to score and later he flicked on the ball for the same player to equalise. Brian became a popular figure with the fans, more so when his headed goal in the last minute gave West Ham a draw at Wigan on the last day of the season.

Doncaster Rov (From juniors on 14/12/1985) FL 59+7/12 FLC 3 FAC 2+1/1 Others 2+2
Sheffield U (£30,000 on 19/7/1988) F/PL 197/82 FLC 16/11 FAC 23+1/11 Others 2/2
Leeds U (£2,900,000 on 14/7/1993) PL 131+7/32 FLC 8+3/2 FAC 13+3/4 Others 3
Sheffield U (£1,500,000 on 29/7/1997) FL 24/11 FLC 4/2 FAC 1 (£1,000,000 to Benfica, Portugal on 15/1/1998)
Middlesbrough (£3,000,000 on 16/10/1998) PL 72+15/18 FLC 4+1 FAC 3/1
Leicester C (£150,000 on 30/11/2001) P/FL 44+8/19 FLC 2 FAC 2
West Ham U (Free on 31/10/2003) FL 9+17/6 FAC 3/1 Others 0+3

DEARDEN Kevin Charles
Born: Luton, 8 March 1970
Height: 5'11" **Weight:** 13.4
Kevin was involved in coaching at Torquay last term in addition to being the club's second-choice goalkeeper. However, injuries to Arjan Van Heusden gave him two runs as first choice, and he was so impressive in his second spell that he retained his place until injury ruled him out of the run-in. An excellent shot-stopper, Kevin also communicates well and marshals his back four effectively.

Tottenham H (From trainee on 5/8/1988) PL 0+1 FLC 1
Cambridge U (Loaned on 9/3/1989) FL 15
Hartlepool U (Loaned on 31/8/1989) FL 10
Swindon T (Loaned on 23/3/1990) FL 1
Peterborough U (Loaned on 24/8/1990) FL 7
Hull C (Loaned on 10/1/1991) FL 3
Rochdale (Loaned on 16/8/1991) FL 2
Birmingham C (Loaned on 19/3/1992) FL 12
Brentford (Free on 30/9/1993) FL 205 FLC 17 FAC 13 Others 19
Barnet (Loaned on 5/2/1999) FL 1
Wrexham (Free on 4/6/1999) FL 81 FLC 3 FAC 6
Torquay U (Free on 9/8/2001) FL 93+2 FLC 3 FAC 1 Others 2

DE BOLLA Mark
Born: Camberwell, 1 January 1983
Height: 5'7" **Weight:** 11.9
Roy McFarland worked long and hard to bring this forward to Chesterfield: three times he came and, on the first two occasions, he went home injured! Mark works the ball well to his colleagues, he is difficult to dispossess,and is just as effective in an attacking-midfield role as he is up front. Released by the Addicks in March, he signed for the Spireites just before the transfer deadline.

Aston Villa (From trainee on 17/4/2000)
Charlton Ath (Signed on 25/1/2001)
Chesterfield (Loaned on 11/9/2003) FL 2+1 Others 1
Chesterfield (Free on 5/3/2004) FL 1+4/1

DEENEY David Richard
Born: Bulawayo, Zimbabwe, 12 January 1987
Height: 5'9" **Weight:** 10.6
A regular member of Luton's successful U19 team, David made his senior debut as a substitute in the LDV Vans Trophy game against Stevenage Borough last October. He also played against Southend in the same competition, when he made the starting line-up at centre half. David received no further senior opportunities, but will be hoping to gain further experience next term. He is the brother of Joe who featured for the Hatters in the 2002-03 season.

Luton T (Trainee) Others 1+1

DEENEY Saul
Born: Londonderry, 12 March 1983
Height: 6'1" **Weight:** 12.10
International Honours: RoI: Yth
This talented young goalkeeper spent most of last season in the wings at Notts County, only stepping forward to the first team for the final three matches of the campaign. A 'keeper of great potential, he produced some impressive performances in a team that was already effectively doomed to relegation. Saul was also called up to the Republic of Ireland U21 squad during the season.

Notts Co (From trainee on 8/9/2000) FL 10

DEFOE Jermain Colin
Born: Beckton, 7 October 1982
Height: 5'7" **Weight:** 10.4
International Honours: E: 2; U21-23; Yth; Sch
Jermain was the scourge of First Division defences last term and he scored a number of spectacular goals for West Ham early in the season. His tally included a hat-trick in the Carling Cup tie against

Cardiff, but in the January transfer window he moved back to the Premiership with Tottenham, Bobby Zamora moving in the opposite direction. The arrival of Jermain brought a much-needed lift to White Hart Lane and he quickly impressed with six goals in five games. He went on to win his first full cap for England and will be hoping to help revive the North London club in the 2004-05 campaign.

West Ham U (£400,000 + from trainee at Charlton Ath on 15/10/1999) P/FL 62+31/29 FLC 6+1/6 FAC 4+1/6

Bournemouth (Loaned on 26/10/2000) FL 27+2/18 FAC 1/1 Others 1

Tottenham H (£7,000,000 + on 2/2/2004) PL 14+1/7

DE GOEY Eduard (Ed)
Franciscus
Born: Gouda, Holland, 20 December 1966
Height: 6'6" **Weight:** 15.0
Club Honours: FLC '98; ECWC '98; ESC '98; FAC '00; CS '00
International Honours: Holland: 31; U21-17
This experienced 'keeper joined Stoke City during the summer of 2003 and remained as first choice for most of the campaign. He was extremely consistent and kept the challenge of Neil Cutler in the background. Ed's penalty save from Darren Huckerby almost secured a point at Norwich and, but for suffering concussion against Coventry in April, he would have kept his place in the side until the end of the season.

Chelsea (£2,250,000 from Feyenoord, Holland, ex Sparta Rotterdam, on 10/7/1997) PL 123 FLC 5 FAC 13+1 Others 37

Stoke C (Free on 1/8/2003) FL 37 FLC 1

DE LA CRUZ Bernardo Ulises
Born: Piqulucho, Ecuador, 8 February 1974
Height: 5'11" **Weight:** 11.12
International Honours: Ecuador: 67
Ulises is a right-sided midfielder who can also play at the back if required, being strong defensively as well as creative. Last season he deputised for the injured Mark Delaney in the right-back position, which resulted in him appearing in every game from February to the end of the season. He performed admirably in the role, producing some steady, reliable performances. As the season wore on he looked better in every game, earning appreciative applause for his fine anticipation and sharp tackling. Ulises continued to win caps for Ecuador during the campaign.

Hibernian (£700,000 from Liga Deportiva Universitaria, Ecuador on 18/6/2001) SL 25+7/2 SLC 2 SC 2+2/1 Others 2

Aston Villa (£1,500,000 on 2/8/2002) PL 32+16/1 FLC 5+1/1 FAC 2

DELANEY Damien
Born: Cork, 20 July 1981
Height: 6'3" **Weight:** 13.10
International Honours: RoI: U21-1; Yth
Damien produced some remarkably consistent form throughout the whole of Hull's promotion campaign last term, when he settled in on the left-hand side of the centre-back pairing. He was the Tigers' only ever-present, missing only the second-half of the visit to Mansfield following a clash of heads. Highlights included excellent goals against Rochdale and Bristol Rovers (the former voted City's 'Goal of the Season') and winning the club's, players' and supporters' 'Player of the Year' awards.

Leicester C (£50,000 from Cork C on 9/11/2000) PL 5+3 FLC 1 FAC 1+1

Stockport Co (Loaned on 15/11/2001) FL 10+2/1

Huddersfield T (Loaned on 28/3/2002) FL 1+1

Mansfield T (Loaned on 6/9/2002) FL 7

Hull C (£50,000 on 18/10/2002) FL 76/3 FLC 1 FAC 2

DELANEY Mark Anthony
Born: Fishguard, 13 May 1976
Height: 6'1" **Weight:** 11.7
International Honours: W: 26
This tough-tackling right back position is reliable, defensively composed and strong when it comes to going forward. Mark's trademarks are without doubt his sliding tackles and steady defending. He adds a different dimension to the right flank with his darting forward bursts and accurate inswinging crosses. Unfortunately, he again experienced more than his fair share of injuries last term. He was forced out of the game against Tottenham with a twisted knee and was then carried off on a stretcher with a nasty leg injury at Fulham and subsequently underwent surgery on his ankle, missing ten games. Mark continued to represent Wales during the season.

Cardiff C (Free from Carmarthen on 3/7/1998) FL 28 FLC 2 FAC 5/1

Aston Villa (£250,000 + on 10/3/1999) PL 102+14/1 FLC 8+3 FAC 4+1 Others 13

DELANY Dean
Born: Dublin, 15 September 1980
Height: 6'1" **Weight:** 13.2

Club Honours: FAYC '98
International Honours: RoI: U21-6
Dean began the 2003-04 campaign as first-choice 'keeper at Port Vale, but lost his place following the heavy home defeat by Plymouth and never regained it. A fine shot stopper, Dean was loaned out to Macclesfield Town in December, but he only featured as a non-playing substitute until being recalled six weeks later. Dean was released on a free transfer in May.

Everton (From trainee on 23/9/1997)

Port Vale (Free on 16/6/2000) FL 34+2 FLC 1 Others 1

DELAP Rory John
Born: Sutton Coldfield, 6 July 1976
Height: 6'0" **Weight:** 12.10
Club Honours: AMC '97
International Honours: RoI: 11; B-1; U21-4
Although in terms of anticipation, neat tackling and smart distribution Rory's abilities are above the average he struggled to impose himself in the Southampton midfield last season. The highlight of his campaign: his one goal, scored with a stunning overhead kick against Spurs in March. He tweaked a knee ligament against Bolton at St Mary's in April, an injury that saw him miss the last four matches of the season.

Carlisle U (From trainee on 18/7/1994) FL 40+25/7 FLC 4+1 FAC 0+3 Others 12+2

Derby Co (£500,000 + on 6/2/1998) PL 97+6/11 FLC 7/2 FAC 2+1

Southampton (£3,000,000 + on 21/7/2001) PL 72+7/3 FLC 5+1 FAC 3+1 Others 1+1

DELGADO Chala Agustin
Born: Ibarra, Ecuador, 23 December 1974
Height: 6'3" **Weight:** 14.2
International Honours: Ecuador: 54
The 'Tin Man' has made five first-team starts, ten appearances as a substitute and scored a grand total of two goals since signing for the Saints in November 2001. Between absences, caused by a succession of back and knee injuries, he has shown glimpses of the skill and power that make him a national hero in his native Ecuador but, on the eve of Paul Sturrock's arrival as manager at St Mary's, in March, Agustin was allowed home to play for Aucus and fulfil international duties.

Southampton (£3,500,000 from Necaxa, Mexico on 13/11/2001) PL 2+9 FLC 2+1/1 FAC 1

Dean Delany

Eric Deloumeaux (left)

DELL Steven (Steve) Bradley
Born: London, 6 February 1980
Height: 5'11" **Weight:** 12.8
After impressing as a trialist at the end of the 2002-03 season, and again in the club's pre-season friendlies, Steve was rewarded with a three-month contract last August. He is a gritty right back, comfortable coming forward and with plenty of stamina and a huge throw. He had a short run in the opening weeks, but did not really figure in the plans of Lawrie Sanchez or Tony Adams. After a two-month loan spell at Eastbourne Borough, Steve joined the Ryman League club on a permanent basis, moving on to Hornchurch soon afterwards.
Wycombe W (Free from Beaconsfield SYCOB on 7/8/2003) FL 3+1

DELOUMEAUX Eric Jean
Born: Montbeliard, France, 12 May 1973
Height: 5'10" **Weight:** 11.13
Eric got off to a good start at Aberdeen last term, netting early on against Rangers, but he never won a regular place in the Dons' line-up and in the new year he rejoined his former Motherwell boss Eric Black at Coventry. He made an immediate impact in the midfield anchor role when City won 6-1 at Walsall, but later switched to right back. Eric has good ball control, tackles strongly and rarely wastes the ball. He notched his first goal against Millwall with a strong header from a corner and remained an ever-present until the end of the season.
Motherwell (£100,000 from Le Havre, France, ex Geugnon, on 9/11/2001) SL 22+1 SC 1
Aberdeen (£50,000 on 10/7/2002) SL 40+3/4 SLC 4+1/1 SC 2 Others 4
CoventryC (Free on 16/1/2004) FL 19/1 FAC 2

DEMPSTER John
Born: Kettering, 1 April 1983
Height: 6'0" **Weight:** 11.10
Club Honours: Div 3 '03
International Honours: S: U21-1; Yth
John struggled to hold down a regular place in the Rushden line-up last term apart from a brief spell at the turn of the year. However, the promising young centre half was involved with the first-team squad throughout the campaign, providing useful cover for more experienced players. John also earned a call-up to the Scotland U21 squad during the season.
Rushden & Diamonds (From juniors on 24/7/2001) FL 22+15/1 FLC 1+2 FAC 1+1 Others 2

DERRY Shaun Peter
Born: Nottingham, 6 December 1977
Height: 5'10" **Weight:** 10.13
Club Honours: Div 3 '98
A hard-working no-nonsense midfield player, Shaun was a regular in the starting line-up for Crystal Palace in the first half of last season. Thereafter he was mostly a squad player, generally featuring from the substitutes' bench. He scored twice during the campaign, including a goal at champions-to-be Norwich City in September.
Notts Co (From trainee on 13/4/1996) FL 76+3/4 FLC 4+1 FAC 6+1/1 Others 3
Sheffield U (£700,000 on 26/1/1998) FL 62+10 FLC 4 FAC 7/1
Portsmouth (£300,000 + on 16/3/2000) FL 48+1/1 FLC 4 FAC 1+1
Crystal Palace (£400,000 on 6/8/2002) FL 61+15/3 FLC 6 FAC 4 Others 1+2

DESAILLY Marcel
Born: Accra, Ghana, 7 September 1968
Height: 6'1" **Weight:** 13.5
Club Honours: ESC '98; FAC '00; CS '00
International Honours: France: 116 (WC '98, UEFA '00); B-1; U21
A string of niggling injuries including hip, groin and back strains restricted Marcel 'The Rock' Desailly to just 24 starts during the 2003–04 season, but the great man still looked one of the world's best defenders whenever called upon. One of the most successful players of all time and the most-capped Frenchman, he continued his phenomenal international career into the Euro 2004 finals where he played alongside club colleague William Gallas to whom he has given invaluable advice. Marcel is an inspirational captain and he has spoken of his pride in leading the 'new' Chelsea to a brighter future. The pairing of Gallas and John Terry is undoubtedly the Blues' long-term option and both players could not have had a better master to teach them their trade.
Chelsea (£4,600,000 from AC Milan, Italy, ex Nantes, Marseilles, on 14/7/1998) PL 156+2/6 FLC 5 FAC 22 Others 36+1/1

DEVANEY Martin Thomas
Born: Cheltenham, 1 June 1980
Height: 5'10" **Weight:** 11.12
Martin was one of the more consistent performers in a general season of under-achievement by Cheltenham Town in 2003-04. He was not a regular selection at the start of the campaign, however, he broke back into the first team towards the end of September and held down a regular place in the side from then on. Martin was mostly used on the right-hand

side of midfield, where he impressed with some strong running and accurate crossing, not to mention some increasingly necessary defensive work. He contributed six goals in all competitions including a last-minute winner in an extraordinary 4-3 victory over Northampton Town.
Coventry C (From trainee on 4/6/1997)
Cheltenham T (Free on 5/8/1999) FL 117+48/28 FLC 4+1 FAC 5+3/2 Others 6+2/2

DEVLIN Paul John
Born: Birmingham, 14 April 1972
Height: 5'9" **Weight:** 11.5
Club Honours: AIC '95
International Honours: S: 10; B-1
Paul managed just two outings from the substitutes' bench for Birmingham before moving on to Watford in September. A pacy and tenacious right winger, who proved very effective at Division One level, and his wide experience gained in more than 500 senior appearances for four different clubs was invaluable. He made more starts and played more matches than anyone else at Vicarage Road and his only absence was due to a short period of suspension. Paul was again called up by Scotland during the season.
Notts Co (£40,000 from Stafford R on 22/2/1992) FL 132+9/25 FLC 11+1/1 FAC 8/1 Others 17+2/6
Birmingham C (Signed on 29/2/1996) FL 61+15/28 FLC 8+1/4 FAC 3+1/2
Sheffield U (£200,000 + on 13/3/1998) FL 122+25/24 FLC 4 FAC 8/1 Others 2
Notts Co (Loaned on 23/10/1998) FL 5
Birmingham C (£200,000 on 8/2/2002) P/FL 31+16/4 FAC 1 Others 2
Watford (£150,000 on 12/9/2003) FL 39/3 FLC 1 FAC 2

DE VOS Jason Richard
Born: Ontario, Canada, 2 January 1974
Height: 6'4" **Weight:** 13.7
Club Honours: Div 2 '03
International Honours: Canada: 46 (Gold Cup 2000); U23-14; Yth
A colossus at the heart of the Wigan Athletic defence, Jason was again an outstanding performer establishing an effective partnership with Ian Breckin. An inspirational captain, he missed the first three months of the season because of a broken foot. A positive performer, strong in every aspect of defensive play, Jason never shirks a tackle, wins most of the 50-50 balls in the air and is a great leader, always urging his colleagues on from the back. He continued to represent Canada during the season and was captain of his country. Jason was out of contract in the

Arjan De Zeeuw

summer and was reported to have signed for Ipswich Town.
Darlington (*Free from Montreal Impact, Canada on 29/11/1996*) *FL 43+1/5 FLC 3/1 FAC 4 Others 1*
Dundee (*£400,000 on 12/10/1998*) *SL 91+2/2 SLC 5+1 SC 12*
Wigan Ath (*£500,000 on 8/8/2001*) *FL 87+3/15 FLC 6 FAC 2*

DE ZEEUW Adrianus (Arjan)
Johannes
Born: Castricum, Holland, 16 April 1970
Height: 6'1" **Weight:** 13.11
Club Honours: Div 1 '03
Arjan showed he was a wholehearted player for Pompey last term, and despite his maturing years he was always involved in the action. A consistent figure in the heart of the defence he is a firm tackler, composed and with a great positional sense. A popular and well-liked professional, he was the club's 'Player of the Season' for 2003-04.
Barnsley (*£250,000 from Telstar, Holland, ex Vitesse 22, on 3/11/1995*) *F/PL 138/7 FLC 12 FAC 14*
Wigan Ath (*Free on 2/7/1999*) *FL 126/6 FLC 8 FAC 6 Others 6*
Portsmouth (*Free on 3/7/2002*) *P/FL 71+3/2 FLC 3 FAC 4*

DIALLO Drissa
Born: Nouadhibou, Mauritania, 4 January 1973
Height: 6'1" **Weight:** 12.0
International Honours: Guinea
Drissa was a regular for Ipswich in the early weeks of the 2003-04 season, but then suffered an injury in the home game with Wimbledon and thereafter his appearances were spasmodic. A strong centre back who is a particularly good tackler, he was also used at full back in some games.
Burnley (*Free from KV Mechelen, Belgium, ex RC Tilleur, Sedan, AS Brevannes, on 9/1/2003*) *FL 14/1 FAC 4/1*
Ipswich T (*Free on 6/6/2003*) *FL 16+3 FLC 1*

DIAO Salif Alassane
Born: Kedougou, Senegal, 10 February 1977
Height: 6'0" **Weight:** 11.7
Club Honours: FLC '03
International Honours: Senegal
After a disappointing first season at Anfield, this midfielder almost disappeared from view last term. Salif started only five games for Liverpool, three times at right back and twice in midfield. His first Premiership appearance came in the important home match with

Arsenal in October when he replaced Emile Heskey, not as a striker, but in a defensive midfield role. His final game of the season came in the Carling Cup defeat at home to Bolton in December. Despite being troubled by ankle and calf injuries throughout the campaign, he was selected by his country for the African Nations' Cup finals held in Tunisia in late January.
Liverpool (*£5,000,000 from Sedan, France, ex Monaco, on 9/8/2002*) *PL 15+14/1 FLC 4+1 FAC 1+1 Others 7+4/1*

DIBBLE Andrew (Andy)
Gerald
Born: Cwmbran, 8 May 1965
Height: 6'3" **Weight:** 16.8
International Honours: W: 3; U21-3; Yth; Sch
Andy continued as good as ever in the Wrexham goal last term, producing a number of outstanding performances to belie his years in the game. However, mid-March saw him sustain a broken arm in the away fixture at Peterborough, which curtailed his season. Andy presents a formidable barrier to opponents and made many important saves, among them an amazing reaction stop to prevent Stockport County getting back in the game after Wrexham had taken a late lead on Boxing Day.
Cardiff C (*From apprentice on 27/8/1982*) *FL 62 FLC 4 FAC 4*
Luton T (*£125,000 on 16/7/1984*) *FL 30 FLC 4 FAC 1 Others 1*
Sunderland (*Loaned on 21/2/1986*) *FL 12*
Huddersfield T (*Loaned on 26/3/1987*) *FL 5*
Manchester C (*£240,000 on 1/7/1988*) *P/FL 113+3 FLC 14 FAC 8+1 Others 2*
Aberdeen (*Loaned on 20/10/1990*) *SL 5*
Middlesbrough (*Loaned on 20/2/1991*) *FL 19 Others 2*
Bolton W (*Loaned on 6/9/1991*) *FL 13 Others 1*
West Bromwich A (*Loaned on 27/2/1992*) *FL 9*
Glasgow R (*Signed on 11/3/1997*) *SL 7*
Luton T (*Free on 15/9/1997*) *FL 1 FLC 2*
Middlesbrough (*Free on 30/1/1998*) *FL 2*
(*Free to Altrincham during 1998 close season*)
Hartlepool U (*Free on 25/3/1999*) *FL 6 FLC 2 Others 2+1*
Carlisle U (*Loaned on 8/10/1999*) *FL 2*
Stockport Co (*Free on 10/8/2000*) *FL 22+1 FLC 0+1 FAC 1*
Wrexham (*Free on 9/8/2002*) *FL 68 FLC 2 FAC 1 Others 1*

DI CANIO Paolo
Born: Rome, Italy, 9 July 1968
Height: 5'9" **Weight:** 11.9

This immensely skilful and vastly experienced player joined Charlton just before the start of the season, but was not fully match fit. For this reason he was used mainly as a substitute in the first few games until he built up his fitness. Paolo is marvellous to watch and does things with the ball that range from the brilliant to the amazing. Altogether he made some great contributions to the team over the season, and still remained as enthusiastic and committed as ever, but sometimes showed signs of his age. He was instrumental in setting up numerous opportunities for his colleagues during the campaign, some of which resulted in goals. Paolo himself found the net on five occasions with three coming from the penalty spot. It was not known at the time of writing whether Paolo would be offered another contact for 2004-05.
Glasgow Celtic (*Signed from AC Milan, Italy, ex AC Milan, Lazio, Ternana, Juventus, Napoli, on 3/7/1996*) *SL 25+1/12 SLC 2 SC 6/3 Others 2+1*
Sheffield Wed (*£3,000,000 on 8/8/1997*) *PL 39+2/15 FLC 4/2 FAC 3*
West Ham U (*£1,700,000 on 28/1/1999*) *PL 114+4/47 FLC 8/2 FAC 5/1 Others 10/1*
Charlton Ath (*Free on 12/8/2003*) *PL 23+8/4 FLC 1/1 FAC 0+1*

DICHIO Daniele (Danny)
Salvatore Ernest
Born: Hammersmith, 19 October 1974
Height: 6'3" **Weight:** 12.3
Club Honours: Div 1 '99
International Honours: E: U21-1; Sch
Danny Dichio started the season as West Bromwich Albion's first-choice twin striker alongside new signing Rob Hulse. Unfortunately he failed to repeat his performances from the previous campaign and with Scott Dobie and Lee Hughes both pressing hard for a place in the starting line-up, he quickly found himself out of favour and was allowed to join Derby on loan. He scored an excellent goal against Ipswich Town at Pride Park, and the Rams were keen to keep him but he was recalled to the Hawthorns. Later in the season Danny joined Millwall on loan and got off to a great start, scoring twice on his debut against Sunderland, and then repeating the feat a week later as Millwall beat Crewe at Gresty Road. He eventually agreed a permanent transfer to the South London club.
Queens Park R (*From trainee on 17/5/1993*) *P/FL 56+19/20 FLC 6/2 FAC 3+3* (*Free to Sampdoria, Italy during 1997 close season*)
Barnet (*Loaned on 24/3/1994*) *FL 9/2*
Sunderland (*£750,000, via loan spell at*

Lecce, Italy on 28/1/1998) P/FL 20+56/11 FLC 11+1/6 FAC 3+3/1 Others 1+2
West Bromwich A (Loaned on 23/8/2001) FL 3/2
West Bromwich A (£1,250,000 on 30/11/2001) P/FL 47+16/12 FLC 3+1 FAC 6/4
Derby Co (Loaned on 17/10/2003) FL 6/1
Millwall (£200,000 + on 13/1/2004) FL 15/7 FAC 5/1

DICKMAN Jonjo
Born: Hexham, 22 September 1981
Height: 5'8" **Weight:** 10.8
This young midfielder began last season in Sunderland's reserve team, before joining York City on loan in the new year. However, Jonjo's stay at Bootham Crescent was cut short when he suffered an injury in his second match for City at Kidderminster and he returned to the Stadium of Light to recuperate.
Sunderland (From juniors on 2/11/1998) PL 0+1
York C (Loaned on 25/2/2004) FL 2

DICKOV Paul
Born: Livingston, 1 November 1972
Height: 5'6" **Weight:** 11.9
Club Honours: ECWC '94
International Honours: S: 8; U21-4; Yth; Sch
This busy forward continued to find the net for Leicester City in the Premiership last term, usually partnering Les Ferdinand up front. Most notable was his goal in the demolition of Leeds at the Walkers Stadium. He was also recalled to the Scotland squad during the season, netting his first international goal, then suffering with his colleagues at the hands of Holland in the Euro 2004 play-offs. However, well-publicised off-the-field events severely disrupted the second half of his campaign, and his form was understandably affected during the final run-in.
Arsenal (From trainee on 28/12/1990) PL 6+15/3 FLC 2+2/3
Luton T (Loaned on 8/10/1993) FL 8+7/1
Brighton & Hove A (Loaned on 23/3/1994) FL 8/5
Manchester C (£1,000,000 on 23/8/1996) P/FL 105+51/33 FLC 9+4/5 FAC 5+4/1 Others 3/2
Leicester C (Signed on 22/2/2002) P/FL 81+8/32 FLC 4/2 FAC 4/3

DIMECH Luke Anthony
Born: Malta, 11 January 1977
Height: 5'11" **Weight:** 13.4
International Honours: Malta: 28
This talented centre back or midfield player joined Mansfield Town on a short-

term contract which was later extended to the whole season. A former trainee with Lincoln City, Luke had returned to Malta where his career blossomed and he is now captain of his national team. Although injured whilst on international duty in August, he came back as good as ever and enjoyed several useful runs in the side. Luke added two more caps for his country during the season.
Mansfield T (Free from Shamrock Rov, ex Lincoln C trainee, Sliema, Birkirkara, on 7/8/2003) FL 17+3/1 FLC 1 FAC 1+1

DINNING Tony
Born: Wallsend, 12 April 1975
Height: 6'0" **Weight:** 12.11
Club Honours: Div 2 '03; AMC '04
A hard-tackling defensive midfielder, Tony started the season as a regular for Wigan Athletic. A tireless ball winner playing at his best in a 'holding' role while others got forward, Tony disappeared almost entirely from the first-team scene at the JJB Stadium. Surprisingly loaned to First Division rivals Walsall, he failed to make much of an impact during his stay at Bescot Stadium. Later in the season he went out on loan at Blackpool where he scored in successive games against Port Vale and Luton and also appeared in the LDV Vans Trophy final before returning to Wigan once more.
Newcastle U (From trainee on 1/10/1993)
Stockport Co (Free on 23/6/1994) FL 159+32/25 FLC 12+5/3 FAC 4+7 Others 6+1/2
Wolverhampton W (£600,000 + on 22/9/2000) FL 35/6 FLC 1/1 FAC 1
Wigan Ath (£750,000 on 7/9/2001) FL 79+5/12 FLC 5 FAC 3
Stoke C (Loaned on 27/3/2002) FL 5 Others 3
Walsall (Loaned on 20/11/2003) FL 2+3
Blackpool (Loaned on 23/1/2004) FL 10/3 Others 3

DIOUF El Hadji Ousseynou
Born: Dakar, Senegal, 15 January 1981
Height: 5'11" **Weight:** 11.11
Club Honours: FLC '03
International Honours: Senegal
The decision to convert El Hadji from a will-o'-the wisp striker or playmaker into a right-sided midfielder may have made him more of a team player but has sometimes been to the detriment of his individual talents. Although an automatic selection for Liverpool until January, when he departed to represent Senegal in the African Nations' Cup in Tunisia, he only made four more starts for the Reds. Disappointingly he failed to add to his

tally of goals for the club during the season.
Liverpool (£10,000,000 from RC Lens, France, ex Sochaux, Rennes, on 17/7/2002) PL 41+14/3 FLC 7/3 FAC 4 Others 9+5

DISLEY Craig Edward
Born: Worksop, 24 August 1981
Height: 5'10" **Weight:** 11.0
Craig was a regular member of the Mansfield Town squad last term, although he was often used from the substitutes' bench. A solid attacking midfield player he never let the side down and popped up with some useful goals throughout the season. He was employed in a variety of positions across the centre of the park and his lively style of play always caused problems for the opposition.
Mansfield T (From trainee on 23/6/1999) FL 106+35/16 FLC 2 FAC 9+1 Others 5

DISTIN Sylvain
Born: Paris, France, 16 December 1977
Height: 6'4" **Weight:** 13.10
This elegant defender wore the captain's armband for Manchester City throughout the 2003-04 season, boss Kevin Keegan having no hesitation in making Sylvain his new leader. A player who offers 100 per cent commitment to everything he does in a match, he demonstrated that he was learning more and more with each game.
Newcastle U (Loaned from Paris St Germain, France, ex Tours, Guegnon, on 14/9/2001) PL 20+8 FLC 2 FAC 5
Manchester C (£4,000,000 from Paris St Germain, France on 4/7/2002) PL 72/2 FLC 3 FAC 6/1 Others 5

DIXON Jonathan (Jonny) James
Born: Muria, Spain, 16 January 1984
Height: 5'9" **Weight:** 11.2
A skilful, two-footed striker, Jonny continued to be a fringe player at Wycombe last season with just three starts, two of those in the final weeks of the season. He spent a month on loan at Dr Martens League pacesetters Crawley Town, but generally struggled to find his best form.
Wycombe W (From trainee on 14/2/2003) FL 16+14/5 FAC 1 Others 0+2

D'JAFFO Laurent
Born: Aquitaine, France, 5 November 1970
Height: 6'0" **Weight:** 13.5
International Honours: Benin
Laurent found himself completely out of the first-team picture at Aberdeen last term and in January his contract was

Jonny Dixon

cancelled by mutual consent. He played for Benin in the African Nations' Cup finals before joining Mansfield Town until the end of the season. Used as a target man, he made his debut for the Stags in the vital promotion clash with Hull City at Field Mill and scored the only goal of the game with a powerful header from a corner. He lost his place in the side through injury but returned during the run-in when a place in the play-offs was ensured.

Ayr U *(Signed from Red Star Paris, France on 13/10/1997) SL 21+3/10 SC 2+1*
Bury *(Free on 28/7/1998) FL 35+2/8 FLC 4+1/1 FAC 1*
Stockport Co *(£100,000 on 13/8/1999) FL 20+1/7 FLC 2/1*
Sheffield U *(£100,000 + on 4/2/2000) FL 45+24/11 FLC 0+2/1 FAC 1+2*
Aberdeen *(Free on 13/2/2002) SL 16+2/3 SC 3/2 Others 4 (Freed during 2003 close season)*
Mansfield T *(Free from Benin on 1/3/2004) FL 4+4/1 Others 0+3*

DJEMBA DJEMBA Eric Daniel
Born: Douala, Cameroon, 4 May 1981
Height: 5'9" **Weight:** 11.13
Club Honours: CS '03; FAC '04
International Honours: Cameroon
This tough-tackling midfielder signed for Manchester United in the summer of 2003 and was pitched straight into first-team action in the Community Shield opener against Arsenal, but only made sporadic appearances for the Reds in all competitions from August to December. In that time he managed two goals, the first coming in United's opening Champions' League game against Panathinaikos, and the second in the Carling Cup encounter against Leeds. Despite playing in no Premiership or F.A. Cup games from January to March, he deputised quite ably for Roy Keane in the second leg of United's ill-fated European tie against Porto, before returning to the fringes of first-team action.

Manchester U *(£3,500,000 + from Nantes, France on 29/7/2003) PL 10+5 FLC 1/1 FAC 0+1 Others 1+4/1*

DJETOU Martin Okelo
Born: Brogohlo, Ivory Coast, 15 December 1974
Height: 6'2" **Weight:** 12.8
International Honours: France: 6; B-2; U21
A quiet but effective member of the Fulham side, Martin enjoyed an excellent season, his second on loan from Parma. Comfortable in the back four or as a defensive midfielder, he was often played immediately in front of the back line.

Injured at the start of season, he did not win an immediate first-team place on his return, but enjoyed his most consistent run towards the end of the season when he showed some excellent form. Martin was outstanding in the 0-0 draw at Liverpool.

Fulham *(Loaned from Parma, Italy, ex Creteil, Strasbourg, Monaco, on 24/7/2002) PL 41+10/1 FLC 2+1 FAC 8 Others 3+1*

DJORKAEFF Youri
Born: Lyon, France, 9 March 1968
Height: 5'11" **Weight:** 11.6
International Honours: France: 82
The evergreen Frenchman had another wonderful season last year, belying his advancing years. Operating very much as an attacking midfielder (and forming a devastating partnership with Jay Jay Okocha in the process) Youri's experience and quality were vital in Bolton's success. He suffered a couple of minor injuries, although he always returned to cement his place in the starting line-up. A late flourish saw Youri notch four goals in two games (against Leeds and Everton) and as the end of the season drew near Youri hinted that he would like to add another year to his soon-to-expire contract.

Bolton W *(Free from Kaiserslautern, Germany, ex Grenoble, Strasbourg, AS Monaco, Paris St Germain, on 15/2/2002) PL 72+3/19 FLC 4+1/1 FAC 1*

DOBIE Robert Scott
Born: Workington, 10 October 1978
Height: 6'1" **Weight:** 12.8
International Honours: S: 5
Like he had done in the Premiership campaign of 2002-03, striker Scott Dobie made more substitute appearances (21) than any other West Bromwich Albion player last term, although in fairness niggling injuries (mainly to his right knee) interrupted his game quite a lot. Quick and direct with an eye for goal, he scored decisive League goals against Stoke City, Millwall and Bradford City, and also netted the clincher against Manchester United in the 2-0 Carling Cup win.

Carlisle U *(From trainee on 10/5/1997) FL 101+35/24 FLC 2+6 FAC 4+1/2 Others 6+1*
Clydebank *(Loaned on 3/11/1998) SL 6*
West Bromwich A *(£125,000 + on 11/7/2001) P/FL 56+49/20 FLC 5+4/4 FAC 1+6*

DOBSON Craig Gregory
Born: Chingford, 23 January 1984
Height: 5'7" **Weight:** 10.6
International Honours: Jamaica: 1
This pacy right-sided midfielder made three substitute appearances for Cheltenham last term, but two successive

coaching regimes at the club found it a challenge to integrate his talent into the team ethos. He spent a period on trial at Brentford mid-way through the season and returned home to London at the end of the campaign. Craig had previously achieved fame with his ball-juggling skills, winning the 2002 Nike Freestyle award and making a number of television appearances. Craig made a surprise international debut for Jamaica in their Unity Cup match with the Republic of Ireland in June.

Cheltenham T *(From trainee at Crystal Palace on 2/7/2003) FL 0+2 Others 0+1*

DOBSON Michael William
Born: Isleworth, 9 April 1981
Height: 5'11" **Weight:** 12.4
Brentford's steady right back and captain had another consistent season in 2003-04, impressing more and more as the campaign wore on. Michael led by example and was rarely absent from the line-up, contributing goals in the LDV Vans Trophy tie against Peterborough and the Second Division fixture with Hartlepool. A real 'local boy made good' he is the son of former Brentford winger George Dobson.

Brentford *(From trainee on 30/6/1999) FL 148+5/2 FLC 5+1 FAC 7/1 Others 14/4*

DODD Jason Robert
Born: Bath, 2 November 1970
Height: 5'10" **Weight:** 12.3
International Honours: E: U21-8
After a couple of seasons disrupted by injury Jason resumed his regular berth at right back and responsibilities as the Saints' skipper at the start of 2003-04, and it may truly be said that, after 15 years, 11 managers and two home grounds at Southampton, age cannot wither him, nor custom stale his infinite variety … at least until he suffered medial ligament damage to his left leg at Wolves in April resulting in a premature end to his season. A talented defender with shrewd distribution skills his influence was missed, not least in dead-ball situations – his single strike last term was converted directly from a flag kick against Portsmouth in December – unfortunately it was harshly re-designated an own-goal!

Southampton *(£50,000 from Bath C on 15/3/1989) F/PL 367+26/9 FLC 43+2/1 FAC 32+1/3 Others 7*

DOHERTY Gary Michael Thomas
Born: Carndonagh, 31 January 1980
Height: 6'2" **Weight:** 13.1
International Honours: RoI: 26; U21-7; Yth

Youri Djorkaeff

Gary is a versatile player who can feature at the back, in midfield or up front, but he is most at home in the defence. Gary continued to battle hard for Tottenham last term, although injury prevented a long run in the first team. He has the ability to turn a game, particularly when deployed in an attacking role where his height and aerial strength always pose a threat to opponents. Gary has become a regular in the Republic of Ireland team but needs more first-team opportunity at club level to fully develop his potential.
Luton T *(From trainee on 2/7/1997) FL 46+24/12 FLC 0+3/1 FAC 6+2/2 Others 1+1*
Tottenham H *(£1,000,000 on 22/4/2000) PL 45+18/4 FLC 3+3 FAC 7+1/4*

DOHERTY Sean Anthony
Born: Basingstoke, 10 May 1985
Height: 5'8" **Weight:** 10.6
International Honours: E: Yth
This talented Fulham left winger was a member of the England U20 squad that took part in the Toulon Tournament during the 2003 close season and early on last term he had a spell on loan at Blackpool. However, he managed just one appearance from the substitutes' bench for the Seasiders before returning to the West London club, where he went on to establish himself as a regular in the reserve side.
Fulham *(From trainee on 12/2/2002)*
Blackpool *(Loaned on 24/9/2003) FL 0+1*

DOHERTY Thomas (Tommy) Edward
Born: Bristol, 17 March 1979
Height: 5'8'' **Weight:** 9.13
Club Honours: AMC '03
International Honours: NI: 5
For the second consecutive season this dynamic midfielder was the undoubted star of Bristol City's side, and it was no surprise that he picked up the supporters' 'Player of the Year' award. It is difficult to visualise the Ashton Gate outfit without his combative skills. Tommy always appears to have time on the ball and his continuing international career with Northern Ireland is testimony to his great ability.
Bristol C *(From trainee on 8/7/1997) FL 130+29/6 FLC 7+1/1 FAC 5+1 Others 16+1/1*

DOIG Christopher (Chris) Ross
Born: Dumfries, 13 February 1981
Height: 6'2" **Weight:** 12.6
International Honours: S: U21-13; Yth; Sch
After starting the season in Nottingham Forest's reserves Chris was loaned out to

Northampton Town to cover for the injured Paul Reid. He impressed many at Sixfields playing in his favoured position of centre half before returning to the City Ground early due to an injury crisis. Chris was forced to play in an unfamiliar role at left back, but despite this he performed well and many felt he was unlucky to lose his place to Alan Rogers. Chris is the now the longest-serving player on Forest's books, despite still being in his early twenties.
Queen of the South *(Associated Schoolboy) SL 2+2*
Nottingham F *(From trainee on 7/3/1998) P/FL 42+14/1 FLC 6+2 FAC 3*
Northampton T *(Loaned on 15/9/2003) FL 9*

DOLAN Joseph (Joe) Thomas
Born: Harrow, 27 May 1980
Height: 6'3" **Weight:** 13.5
Club Honours: Div 2 '01
International Honours: NI: U21-6; Yth
Following nearly two years out with injury Joe made a full recovery last term. After such a long lay-off the road back was somewhat difficult, but he produced some good performances in the reserves, and received a first team-chance against Bradford City in the final game of the season. A tall, hard-tackling central defender, he has been sorely missed but will be hoping to feature regularly in 2004-05.
Millwall *(Free from Chelsea juniors on 15/4/1998) FL 47+2/3 FLC 5 FAC 3/1 Others 5*

DOMI Didier
Born: Paris, France, 2 May 1978
Height: 5'10" **Weight:** 11.4
International Honours: France: U21; Yth
A season-long loan signing who arrived at Leeds with some pedigree, Didier was used sparsely by manager Peter Reid, but at the turn of the year he was promoted to the starting line-up and made the left-back position his own. Very quick and always willing to go on the attack he was ever-present in the relegation run-in.
Newcastle U *(£3,250,000 + from Paris St Germain, France on 5/1/1999) PL 44+1/3 FLC 2+1 FAC 5+3/1 Others 4 (Transferred to Paris St Germain, France on 25/11/2001)*
Leeds U *(Loaned from Paris St Germain, France on 12/8/2003) PL 9+3 FLC 0+2*

DONALDSON Clayton Andrew
Born: Bradford, 7 February 1984
Height: 6'1" **Weight:** 11.7
With his more senior striking colleagues being in such fine form for Hull throughout the 2003-04 campaign, this

tall centre forward only managed a couple of substitute appearances in the LDV Vans Trophy. Highly rated by City boss Peter Taylor, Clayton was allowed to go out on loan to Conference clubs Scarborough in August and Halifax in February to gain further experience.
Hull C *(From trainee on 10/2/2003) FL 0+2 Others 0+3/1*

DONNELLY Ciaran
Born: Blackpool, 2 April 1984
Height: 5'10" **Weight:** 11.8
International Honours: E: Yth
Capped by England youths at several different age groups, this talented midfielder joined Blackpool on loan last March to gain some experience of senior football. Ciaran featured regularly during his stay at Bloomfield Road and made a good impression with his drive and enthusiasm.
Blackburn Rov *(From trainee on 5/7/2001)*
Blackpool *(Loaned on 24/3/2004) FL 8+1*

DONOVAN Kevin
Born: Halifax, 17 December 1971
Height: 5'8" **Weight:** 11.2
Club Honours: AMC '98
Kevin found himself completely out of favour at Barnsley last term and in mid-November his contract was cancelled by mutual consent. The following month he linked up with his former boss Alan Buckley at Rochdale, arriving on a non-contract basis. Kevin was signed to cover the right flank position while Leo Bertos was away on international duties, but the experienced midfielder was unable to make much impact, and was released when Bertos returned. Kevin subsequently had a non-contract spell at York without making a first-team appearance.
Huddersfield T *(From trainee on 11/10/1989) FL 11+9/1 FLC 1+1 FAC 1/2 Others 4*
Halifax T *(Loaned on 13/2/1992) FL 6*
West Bromwich A *(£70,000 on 1/10/1992) FL 139+29/19 FLC 9+2/6 FAC 7+1/3 Others 15+1/4*
Grimsby T *(£300,000 on 29/7/1997) FL 150+6/24 FLC 13+1/2 FAC 11/1 Others 9/3*
Barnsley *(Free on 2/7/2001) FL 48+6/1 FLC 2+1 FAC 2*
Rochdale *(Free on 23/12/2003) FL 4+3*

DOOLAN John
Born: Liverpool, 7 May 1974
Height: 6'1" **Weight:** 13.0
Club Honours: Div 3 '04
This experienced midfield player was the man who pulled the strings for Doncaster Rovers in the centre of the park last term.

John was a regular in the line-up, impressing with his distribution skills, but has yet to register a goal for Rovers in a competitive match.
Everton *(From trainee on 1/6/1992)*
Mansfield T *(Free on 2/9/1994) FL 128+3/10 FLC 8/1 FAC 7/2 Others 4+1/1*
Barnet *(£60,000 on 13/1/1998) FL 132+2/7 FLC 5+1/1 FAC 4 Others 5*
Doncaster Rov *(Signed on 20/3/2003) FL 36+3 FLC 2 FAC 1 Others 1*

[DORIVA] GHIDONI Dorival
Born: Landeara, Brazil, 28 May 1972
Height: 5'9" **Weight:** 11.7
Club Honours: FLC '04
International Honours: Brazil: 12
Midfielder Doriva became Middlesbrough's first summer capture when he signed a one-year contract having joined on loan from Celta Viga the previous January. The vastly experienced Brazilian went on to become one of Steve McClaren's best transfers and he was subsequently voted as the Middlesbrough players' 'Player of the Year'. Once described as "a no frills player who just gets on with the job but is most effective in everything he does," he was one of Boro's unsung heroes of the season in the historic Carling Cup run. He missed the closing games of the season requiring surgery to fix a troublesome groin injury.
Middlesbrough *(Free from Celta Vigo, Spain, ex Sao Paulo, Piracicaba, Atletico Mineiro, Oporto, Sampdoria, on 3/2/2003) PL 22+4 FLC 4+1*

DOUGHTY Matthew (Matt) Liam
Born: Warrington, 2 November 1981
Height: 5'8" **Weight:** 10.8
Although new manager Alan Buckley initially only offered him monthly terms to stay at Rochdale, Matt soon earned a regular slot on the left-hand side of midfield and was rewarded with a contract for the rest of the 2003-04 season. When former boss Steve Parkin returned, Matt briefly switched to his former position of left back but subsequently struggled to keep his place in the squad in the face of an influx of new players and was released in May.
Chester C *(Trainee) FL 19+14/1 FLC 2 FAC 4*
Rochdale *(Free on 20/7/2001) FL 96+12/1 FLC 2+1 FAC 8+1/1 Others 6*

DOUGLAS Jonathan
Born: Monaghan, 22 November 1981
Height: 5'10" **Weight:** 12.12
International Honours: RoI: 2; U21-1; Yth

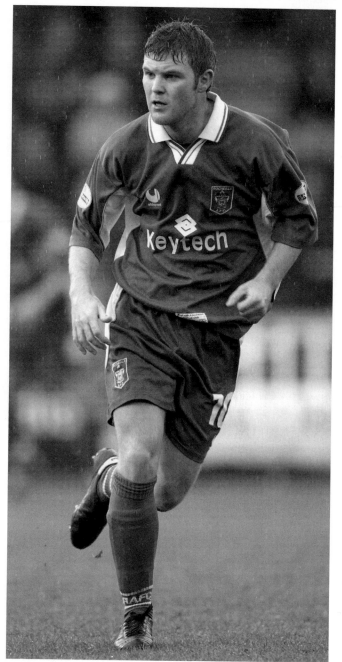

Matt Doughty

At the start of the season Jonathan was told that he was surplus to requirements at Blackburn and could join Blackpool on a season-long loan, starting with a three-month spell. He did well in his spell at Bloomfield Road, scoring three goals, and after making a surprise return to Ewood Park, he was offered the chance of playing in the wide-left role. Protecting the newly arrived Michael Gray, Jonathan found a regular role in the side, his willingness to work, tackle hard and cover in defence making him the best option the club could find for their problem position. His equaliser at Fulham was a vital goal as well as his first for the club.
Blackburn Rov (From trainee on 10/2/2000) PL 14+1/1 FLC 0+2 FAC 1+4
Chesterfield (Loaned on 26/3/2003) FL 7/1
Blackpool (Loaned on 7/8/2003) FL 15+1/3 FLC 3 Others 1

DOUGLAS Stuart Anthony
Born: Enfield, 9 April 1978
Height: 5'9" **Weight:** 11.5
This bustling, livewire striker had a couple of runs in the Boston United starting line-up last term, but was more effective when introduced from the substitutes' bench. His enthusiasm and non-stop running pepped up United's two-man attack but Stuart was allowed to leave at the end of the campaign.
Luton T (From trainee on 2/5/1996) FL 104+42/18 FLC 11+3/3 FAC 8+2/2 Others 1+1
Oxford U (Loaned on 23/10/2001) FL 1+3
Rushden & Diamonds (Loaned on 18/1/2002) FL 4+5
Boston U (Free on 20/8/2002) FL 28+30/8 FLC 2 FAC 0+2 Others 0+1

DOVE Craig
Born: Hartlepool, 16 August 1983
Height: 5'8" **Weight:** 11.6
International Honours: E: Yth
This young midfield player spent much of last season in Middlesbrough's reserve team. In October he went out on loan to York City to gain further experience of senior football, but he featured only twice for the Minstermen before returning to the Riverside Stadium. Craig was released by Boro' in the summer.
Middlesbrough (From trainee on 7/7/2000) FLC 0+2
York C (Loaned on 10/10/2003) FL 1 Others 1

DOWNER Simon
Born: Romford, 19 October 1981
Height: 5'11" **Weight:** 12.0
Simon endured another injury-ravaged

Stewart Downing

season for Leyton Orient last term, making only three senior appearances, although he managed to win the 'Man of the Match' award in the away win at Carlisle. He was eventually allowed to join Conference club Aldershot on loan, for whom he played several games at both right back and centre half.

Leyton Orient (From trainee on 4/10/1999) FL 64+15 FLC 3+2 FAC 3+1 Others 5

DOWNES Stephen

Born: Leeds, 22 November 1981
Height: 5'6" **Weight:** 9.12

This lively and enthusiastic player operated in a wide role down either flank for York City, featuring in several of the early-season matches last term. However, he never really established himself in the side and he was one of several players released by the club in the summer.

Grimsby T (Free from Osset Albion on 10/9/2001)
York C (Free on 31/7/2003) FL 4+2 Others 1

DOWNING Stewart

Born: Middlesbrough, 22 July 1984
Height: 5'11" **Weight:** 10.6
Club Honours: FLC '04
International Honours: E: U21-2; Yth

England U21 player Stewart Downing, an attacking traditional left winger, was disappointed to be only on the substitutes' bench for Middlesbrough's Carling Cup final success. However, at 19 years of age Stewart, with bags of exciting potential, has the footballing world at his feet and there will be happier days ahead of him. Stewart had a loan spell at Sunderland at the end of the year, creating quite an impression in his three months at the Stadium of Light when he scored three goals. Stewart would have been out of contract in the summer but talks between the player and club eventually led to a new long-term deal.

Middlesbrough (From trainee on 6/9/2001) PL 9+16 FLC 1+2/1 FAC 2
Sunderland (Loaned on 29/10/2003) FL 7/3

DOYLE Michael Paul

Born: Dublin, 8 July 1981
Height: 5'8" **Weight:** 11.0
International Honours: RoI: 1; U21-8

This tenacious left-footed midfielder joined Coventry in the 2003 close season, having previously played under Eric Black when he was in charge of Celtic's youth team. A strong and ambitious youngster, Michael featured in all four midfield positions, looking most comfortable on the left. His performances were

sometimes inconsistent but shooting was a strong side of his game and he netted several goals including a stunning free kick at Gillingham. His form earned him a contract extension and a place on the bench for the Republic of Ireland squad against Poland in April. Michael was voted as the Sky Blues' 'Young Player of the Season'.

Glasgow Celtic (From juniors on 1/8/1998)
Coventry C (Free on 4/7/2003) FL 38+2/5 FLC 2 FAC 3

DOYLE Nathan Luke Robert

Born: Derby, 12 January 1987
Height: 5'11" **Weight:** 11.11
International Honours: E: Yth

One of a talented trio of teenagers who first appeared in Derby's squad along with Lee Holmes and Tom Huddlestone under John Gregory, Nathan was still 16 when he made his senior debut against Preston last November but George Burley decided to let him develop in the reserves. Nathan signed a professional contract in January and graduated to the England U17 team.

Derby Co (From trainee on 21/1/2004) FL 1+1

DOYLEY Lloyd Collin

Born: Whitechapel, 1 December 1982
Height: 6'0" **Weight:** 11.10

Lloyd played the first four matches of the season at right back for Watford, but thereafter made only sporadic appearances, though he filled in creditably at centre half at the end of the season. A sound defender, he needs to develop greater confidence in his distribution and attacking play.

Watford (From trainee on 8/3/2001) P/FL 39+12 FLC 4 FAC 0+2

DRURY Adam James

Born: Cambridge, 29 August 1978
Height: 5'10" **Weight:** 11.8
Club Honours: Div 1 '04

Adam produced another exceptionally consistent set of performances at left back for Norwich City last term. He is a natural defender who times his tackles well and prevents too many crosses going into the box from the right flank. Adam took over as team captain last August, leading the side by example and developing an excellent understanding with Paul McVeigh on the left side of the Canaries' line-up, often linking well in attack to provide crosses. He had the honour of lifting the First Division championship trophy

at the club's civic celebrations in May.

Peterborough U (From trainee on 3/7/1996) FL 138+10/2 FLC 8 FAC 9 Others 10+1
Norwich C (£275,000 on 21/3/2001) FL 128/2 FLC 3 FAC 5 Others 3

DUBERRY Michael Wayne

Born: Enfield, 14 October 1975
Height: 6'1" **Weight:** 13.6
Club Honours: F LC '98; ECWC '98; ESC '98
International Honours: E: U21-5

After a consistent role in the pre-season games, Michael suffered a fractured cheekbone in Ireland, a setback which kept him out of the Leeds United side until November. He then had a good run of games, in which he scored two goals, before picking up yet another injury at Southampton. Michael has suffered more injury problems than anyone in his stop-start career at Elland Road, yet he refuses to be downcast and despite speculation about his future, will always battle for a place in the side.

Chelsea (From trainee on 7/6/1993) PL 77+9/1 FLC 8 FAC 12/2 Others 9
Bournemouth (Loaned on 29/9/1995) FL 7 Others 1
Leeds U (£4,000,000 + on 29/7/1999) PL 50+4/4 FLC 0+4 FAC 3+2 Others 9+1

DUBLIN Dion

Born: Leicester, 22 April 1969
Height: 6'1" **Weight:** 12.4
Club Honours: Div 3 '91
International Honours: E: 4

Dion is a powerful target man who is good in the air and effective at holding the ball up. He is a great motivator, a tower of strength and a sheer presence in any line-up. Last season he played in the centre of defence for Aston Villa for the majority of the time. He put in several outstanding performances and even found time to get upfield in the away game at Southampton and score the winner with an overhead kick. Following the announcement that he was to be released during the summer, Dion made his final appearance for the club from the substitutes' bench in the last game of the season against Manchester United and left the pitch to a standing ovation.

Norwich C (Free from Oakham U on 24/3/1988)
Cambridge U (Free on 2/8/1988) FL 133+23/52 FLC 8+2/5 FAC 21/10 Others 14+1/5
Manchester U (£1,000,000 on 7/8/1992) PL 4+8/2 FLC 1+1/1 FAC 1+1 Others 0+1

Adam Drury

Coventry C *(£2,000,000 on 9/9/1994) PL
144+1/61 FLC 11+2/4 FAC 13/7*
Aston Villa *(£5,750,000 on 6/11/1998) PL
120+35/48 FLC 14+2/8 FAC 5+2/1 Others
10+2/2*
Millwall *(Loaned on 28/3/2002) FL 5/2
Others 2/1*

DUDEK Jerzy
Born: Rybnik, Poland, 23 March 1973
Height: 6'2" **Weight:** 12.10
Club Honours: FLC '03
International Honours: Poland: 41
With two top class keepers to choose
from there was speculation at Anfield as
to who would be Liverpool manager
Gerald Houllier's first choice in 2003-04.
In the event it was the Polish international
who started the season. Once again,
however, the home match with
Manchester United in November proved
his downfall and from this point Chris
Kirkland became first choice. In a bizarre
reprise of the previous campaign,
however, Jerzy twice returned to first-
team duty, in December and again in
March due to injuries to Kirkland and he
ended the season with 38 games. At his
best, which he frequently is, Jerzy is a
superbly athletic shot-stopper and a
confident handler of crosses.
Liverpool *(£4,850,000 from Feyenoord,
Holland, ex GKS Tychy, Sokol Tychy, on
31/8/2001) PL 95 FLC 3 FAC 6+1 Others 28*

DUDFIELD Lawrence
(Lawrie) George
Born: Southwark, 7 May 1980
Height: 6'1" **Weight:** 13.9
Lawrie vied with Marc Richards for the
centre-forward slot at Northampton in the
early part of last season, but was then
sidelined by an injury. On his return to
fitness he was loaned to Southend where
he scored the winner on his debut. Soon
afterwards he signed permanent forms
for the Blues and netted four more times
for them during the campaign. Lawrie is a
useful striker with a great eye for goal, a
cannonball shot and the ability to hold
the ball up to bring his colleagues into
the play.
Leicester C *(Signed from Kettering T on
6/6/1997) PL 0+2*
Lincoln C *(Loaned on 15/9/2000) FL 2+1*
Chesterfield *(Loaned on 14/12/2000) FL
4+10/3 Others 3+1/1*
Hull C *(£210,000 on 2/7/2001) FL 39+20/13
FLC 2 FAC 2/2 Others 3*
Northampton T *(Signed on 14/3/2003) FL
20+9/4 FLC 1+1/1 FAC 0+1 Others 0+2/2*
Southend U *(Signed on 5/2/2004) FL 13/5*

DUFF Damien Anthony
Born: Dublin, Ireland, 2 March 1979
Height: 5'10" **Weight:** 12.0
Club Honours: FLC '02
International Honours: RoI: 43; B-1; Yth; Sch
If there was a down side to the summer of 2003 for Chelsea fans it was the loss of the iconic Gianfranco Zola, but the Blues came as close as possible to replacing the great man by signing Damien Duff for a club record fee. Fittingly, Damien signed for Chelsea on the same day as Wayne Bridge and the pair developed a formidable partnership on the Blues' left flank – interchanging and overlapping as if they had played together for years. Damien's sinuous dribbling skills were particularly effective in the Champions' League and in one memorable performance ran the Lazio defence ragged in Rome and netted a thoroughly deserved goal, just one of six in an excellent first season at Stamford Bridge, Sadly, his campaign was marred by injury – a dislocated shoulder at Fulham in December required a lengthy lay-off and on his return groin and calf strains hampered him further, but the worst blow of all fell in April when a recurrence of the shoulder injury in training put a premature end to his season.
Blackburn Rov (Signed from Lourdes Celtic on 5/3/1996) P/FL 157+27/27 FLC 16+1/5 FAC 13+5/2 Others 4/1
Chelsea (£17,000,000 on 26/7/2003) PL 17+6/5 FLC 2 FAC 0+1 Others 7+4/1

DUFF Michael James
Born: Belfast, 11 January 1978
Height: 6'1" **Weight:** 11.8
Club Honours: FAT '98; NC '99
International Honours: NI: 3
Michael enjoyed another highly consistent season for Cheltenham Town last season. A first choice in the centre of the defence, he was a near ever-present during the campaign. Tall, effective in the air and an excellent reader of the game, Michael again won a number of 'Man of the Match' awards. His performances also earned a recall to the Northern Ireland squad and he made a substitute appearance against Estonia in March.
Cheltenham T (From trainee on 17/8/1996) FL 201/12 FLC 6 FAC 15 Others 9

DUFF Shane Joseph
Born: Wroughton, 2 April 1982
Height: 6'1" **Weight:** 12.10
International Honours: NI: U21-1
Shane was hampered by an ankle injury in

the first half of last season, but returned to the Cheltenham Town line-up in the new year and operated in the centre of either a four- or five-man defence, putting in a particularly gutsy performance in the narrow defeat at Oxford United. He scored his first senior goal late in the final game of the season to deny Huddersfield Town promotion. Shane is the younger brother of Michael Duff, and the two partnered each other in central defence on a number of occasions last term.
Cheltenham T (From juniors on 20/10/2000) FL 28+5/1 FAC 0+1 Others 1

DUFFIELD Peter
Born: Middlesbrough, 4 February 1969
Height: 5'6" **Weight:** 10.4
This veteran striker was given few first-team starts by Boston United to the disappointment of many of the fans who saw him as the answer to the Pilgrims' scoring problems. He netted five goals in a time when the team was struggling with his experience being a big asset. Peter was eventually allowed to move on to Carlisle United where he made an immediate impact, bagging the only goal of the game on his debut against Huddersfield. A goal-scorer throughout his career, he netted twice more for Carlisle including the winner at Swansea when he scored with a stunning volley.
Middlesbrough (From apprentice on 4/11/1986)
Sheffield U (Free on 20/8/1987) FL 34+24/14 FLC 2+5/2 FAC 6+2/1 Others 3+2/3
Halifax T (Loaned on 7/3/1988) FL 12/6 Others 1
Rotherham U (Loaned on 7/3/1991) FL 17/4
Blackpool (Loaned on 23/7/1992) FL 3+2/1 FLC 0+1
Crewe Alex (Loaned on 15/1/1993) FL 0+2 FAC 0+1
Stockport Co (Loaned on 19/3/1993) FL 6+1/4 Others 2+1
Hamilton Ac (Signed on 24/9/1993) SL 69+3/39 SLC 2/1 SC 2 Others 3/3
Airdrie (Signed on 21/7/1995) SL 19+5/6 SLC 2+2/2 SC 3/3 Others 1
Raith Rov (Signed on 2/3/1996) SL 37+14/11 SLC 2+1/3 SC 2 Others 1+1
Morton (Signed on 8/11/1997) SL 25/9 SLC 1 SC 1
Falkirk (Signed on 27/8/1998) SL 10+7/3
Darlington (Signed on 15/1/1999) FL 31+16/14 FLC 0+2 FAC 2/1 Others 3
York C (Free on 3/7/2000) FL 41+4/19 FLC 2 FAC 2+1/2
Boston U (Free on 30/1/2003) FL 24+21/9 FLC 1 FAC 1 Others 1+1/1
Carlisle U (Free on 9/3/2004) FL 10/3

DUFFY Richard Michael
Born: Swansea , 30 August 1985
Height: 5'10" **Weight:** 10.4
International Honours: W: Yth
Richard made his first start for Swansea at Scunthorpe in September, and earned rave reviews for his cool defensive play. He scored his first League goal for the Swans in the 3-0 victory over Macclesfield Town at the Vetch Field, before moving up to the Premiership when he joined Pompey. The young defender coped well when brought on from the bench in the 1-1 draw against Fulham in May.
Swansea C (From trainee on 3/9/2002) FL 16+2/1 FAC 3+1 Others 1
Portsmouth (£300,000 on 26/1/2004) PL 0+1

DUFFY Robert James
Born: Swansea, 2 December 1982
Height: 6'1" **Weight:** 12.6
Club Honours: Div 3 '03
This young Rushden striker had a somewhat difficult season in 2003-04. He got off to a bad start after fracturing a kneecap in a freak training-ground accident shortly before the start of the campaign and it was not until January that he returned to action. He managed just four starts, all in April, as the Diamonds dropped towards the relegation zone.
Rushden & Diamonds (From juniors on 7/7/2000) FL 8+20/1 FLC 0+1 FAC 3+1/3 Others 1

DUGARRY Christophe
Born: Bordeaux, France, 24 March 1972
Height: 6'2" **Weight:** 12.4
International Honours: France: 55
Christophe underwent surgery on his knee last August and never felt right with it. He subsequently struggled to recapture his brilliance of the previous season for Birmingham and a mutual parting of the ways was announced in March. Christophe scored one goal, a towering header, against Charlton Athletic in November when he controlled the game for a 20-minute spell at the end. Sadly, that was as good as it got for the Blues.
Birmingham C (Free from Bordeaux, France, ex Bordeaux, AC Milan, Barcelona, Marseilles, on 3/1/2003) PL 28+2/6 FAC 0+1

DUGUID Karl Anthony
Born: Letchworth, 21 March 1978
Height: 5'11" **Weight:** 11.7
Colchester United's longest-serving player again gave terrific service to the club last term until he was sidelined by

Damien Duff

medial knee ligament damage in March. He was unable to recover in time to play again during the season, but by then he had already proved to be a key player either on the right wing or at left back, such is his great versatility. Karl has made more appearances for Colchester than any other player on the books, and he signed a new contract for the U's in April.

Colchester U (From trainee on 16/7/1996) FL 212+58/37 FLC 8+3 FAC 13+3/2 Others 7+5

DUKE David

Born: Inverness, 7 November 1978
Height: 5'10" **Weight:** 11.3
This versatile performer continued to give good service to Swindon during the 2003-04 campaign. A change of formation initially cost David his position in the team, but he soon returned on the left-hand side of midfield and retained his place until the end of the season. Although predominantly right-footed, he can play on either flank.
Sunderland (Free from Redby CA on 3/7/1997)
Swindon T (Free on 10/8/2000) FL 139+21/6 FLC 8+1 FAC 7+2 Others 6+2

DUNCAN Andrew (Andy)

Born: Hexham, 20 October 1977
Height: 5'11" **Weight:** 13.0
International Honours: E: Sch
A solid consistent defender and one of the more experienced players in the Cambridge United squad, Andy found himself on the bench at the start of the 2003-04 campaign, but soon battled his way back into the team. Virtually ever-present from then on, he made his 200th Football League appearance at York in October and also managed to get forward and score his first League goal for several seasons.
Manchester U (From trainee on 10/7/1996)
Cambridge U (£20,000 on 9/1/1998) FL 193+7/5 FLC 10+1/1 FAC 15 Others 16

DUNCAN Derek Henry Junior

Born: Newham, 23 April 1987
Height: 5'9" **Weight:** 10.12
Derek is a direct left winger who was given a brief taste of first-team football with a late substitute appearance for Leyton Orient n the last game of the season at home to Cambridge, as reward for a good season in both the youth and reserve team. He will be looking to gain more first-team experience in 2004-05.
Leyton Orient (Trainee) FL 0+1

DUNFIELD Terence (Terry)

Born: Canada, 20 February 1982
Height: 5'10" **Weight:** 11.6
International Honours: Canada: U23-1; Yth; E: Yth
A dislocated shoulder meant a pre-season operation for this Bury midfielder. It also meant that he missed the opening two months of the 2003-04 campaign. Terry finally started a game for the Shakers at the end of September, turning in a 'Man of the Match' performance against York. He was away playing for the Canadian U23 team during much of November but immediately established himself back in the Shakers midfield upon his return, controlling and dictating games. Terry remained a regular choice throughout the second half of the season, and although his form dipped slightly in the closing games he remains an important member of the squad.
Manchester C (From trainee on 5/5/1999) PL 0+1
Bury (Loaned on 16/8/2002) FL 15/2 FLC 3
Bury (Free on 13/12/2002) FL 41+3/2 Others 3/1

DUNN David John Ian

Born: Blackburn, 27 December 1979
Height: 5'10" **Weight:** 12.3
Club Honours: FLC '02
International Honours: E: 1; U21-20; Yth
David started the season off as Birmingham City's main creative talent in midfield, scoring the winner at Newcastle United in August. He mesmerised opponents with his clever footwork and bursts of elusive movement. He was used primarily wide on the left cutting in, but he was also very effective in the role of withdrawn striker. David tore his hamstring twice, the second time just eight minutes into the crucial FA Cup fifth round replay against Sunderland. Manager Steve Bruce felt had he stayed fit all season, the Blues push for Europe would have continued for longer.
Blackburn Rov (From trainee on 30/9/1997) P/FL 120+16/30 FLC 14+3/5 FAC 11+2/3 Others 3+1
Birmingham C (£5,500,000 on 9/7/2003) PL 20+1/2 FLC 1 FAC 3

DUNNE Alan James

Born: Dublin, 23 August 1982
Height: 5'10" **Weight:** 12.0
Alan became a full member of the Millwall first-team squad last term, but he only managed a handful of appearances

due to the consistent performances of other defenders at the club. Very assured and strong in the challenge, he is still young and will be looking to make a breakthrough in 2004-05.
Millwall (From trainee on 17/3/2000) FL 7+6 FLC 0+1

DUNNE Richard Patrick

Born: Dublin, 21 September 1979
Height: 6'1'' **Weight:** 14.0
Club Honours: FAYC '98; Div 1 '02
International Honours: RoI: 20; B-1; U21-4; Yth (UEFA-U18 '98); Sch
Richard had a solid season for Manchester City last term and put his well-documented personal problems behind him with a string of 'Man of the Match' performances. He is a powerfully built centre half, a tough-tackling defender who is always a threat in the air from set pieces. Richard was a regular in the Republic of Ireland squad and he is seen as a key member of the Blues' defence.
Everton (From trainee on 8/10/1996) PL 53+7 FLC 4 FAC 8
Manchester C (£3,000,000 on 20/10/2000) P/FL 117+5/1 FLC 6 FAC 11 Others 3+1

DUNNING Darren

Born: Scarborough, 8 January 1981
Height: 5'6" **Weight:** 11.12
This hard-working and skilful midfield player battled hard for York City last term but was unable to prevent the club from dropping out of the Football League. Voted 'Clubman of the Year' by the supporters, Darren played consistently well and showed plenty of commitment and effort. He netted four times: twice from the penalty spot and twice direct from free kicks.
Blackburn Rov (From trainee on 25/2/1999) FL 1 FLC 2/1 FAC 1
Bristol C (Loaned on 12/8/2000) FL 9
Rochdale (Loaned on 29/11/2001) FL 4+1
Blackpool (Loaned on 28/3/2002) FL 5
Torquay U (Loaned on 7/11/2002) FL 4+3/1 FAC 1
Macclesfield T (Loaned on 16/1/2003) FL 17
York C (Free on 29/7/2003) FL 42/3 FLC 1 FAC 1 Others 1/1

DURKAN Keiron John

Born: Runcorn, 1 December 1973
Height: 5'11" **Weight:** 12.10
Club Honours: WC '95
International Honours: RoI: U21-3
Keiron signed a new one-year contract for Swansea after proving his fitness and netted his first goal for the Swans in the home win over Mansfield Town at the end of August. He was included in the

squad regularly and proved himself to be very much under-rated as a wide midfielder. Despite lacking genuine pace, he produced accurate crosses from the flanks and scored a great goal in the FA Cup tie against Rushden, sprinting from the halfway line, and lobbing the goalkeeper from just outside the penalty area. Keiron departed in late February and returned to the North West, later signing for Welsh Premier League club Caernarfon Town.

Wrexham (From trainee on 16/7/1992) FL 43+7/3 FLC 3+1 FAC 4+2/2 Others 8
Stockport Co (£95,000 on 16/2/1996) FL 52+12/4 FLC 10+1 FAC 4/3 Others 4+2
Macclesfield T (£15,000 on 25/3/1998) FL 92+11/13 FLC 4+3 FAC 2+3 Others 1+1
York C (Loaned on 5/10/2000) FL 7
Rochdale (Free on 4/7/2001) FL 16+14/1 FLC 2 FAC 3 Others 1
Swansea C (Free on 10/1/2003) FL 15+6/1 FLC 1 FAC 2/1 Others 1

DUTTON Brian

Born: Malton, 12 April 1985
Height: 5'11" **Weight:** 12.0
This young striker was a college student in Yorkshire and playing for Pickering Town when snapped up by Cambridge United last term. Brian made his debut as a second-half substitute against Leyton Orient in November and added a couple more appearances from the bench, but struggled to adapt to Third Division football and was allowed to leave the club in the summer.

Cambridge U (Free from Pickering T on 28/11/2003) FL 0+3 FAC 0+2

DUXBURY Lee Edward

Born: Keighley, 7 October 1969
Height: 5'10" **Weight:** 11.13
Lee was installed as captain of Bury at the start of last term and held down a regular place in midfield for the majority of the season. He was at his best when used in a deep-lying role just in front of the defence, which allowed the other two midfield men to be more attack minded. Lee was also occasionally employed in the back three. However, he sometimes found it difficult to exert his influence on games and was relegated to a place on the substitutes' bench for the closing fixtures.

Bradford C (From trainee on 4/7/1988) FL 204+5/25 FLC 18+1/3 FAC 11 Others 13
Rochdale (Loaned on 18/1/1990) FL 9+1 FAC 1
Huddersfield T (£250,000 on 23/12/1994) FL 29/2 FLC 1 Others 3
Bradford C (£135,000 on 15/11/1995) FL 63/7 FLC 2 FAC 5 Others 3

Oldham Ath (£350,000 on 7/3/1997) FL 222+26/32 FLC 12/1 FAC 16+2/5 Others 5+1/1
Bury (Free on 7/8/2003) FL 36+1 FLC 1 FAC 1

DYCHE Sean Mark

Born: Kettering, 28 June 1971
Height: 6'0" **Weight:** 13.10
Club Honours: Div 2 '01
Sean, a gutsy and effective central defender, was one of Watford's most committed players, last term, despite being told in January that he would be released at the end of the season. After spending most of the early months on the substitutes' bench, he was drafted into the team to play Chelsea in the FA Cup, and did well. He won a regular place in the first team in February, his excellent attitude and vocal leadership doing him great credit and leading to the unexpected offer of a new contract.

Nottingham F (From trainee on 20/5/1989)
Chesterfield (Free on 1/2/1990) FL 219+12/8 FLC 9 FAC 13/1 Others 16
Bristol C (£350,000 on 11/7/1997) FL 14+3 FLC 2+1
Luton T (Loaned on 4/1/1999) FL 14/1 Others 1
Millwall (£150,000 on 5/7/1999) FL 69/3 FLC 2+1 FAC 4
Watford (Free on 12/7/2002) FL 45+4 FLC 2 FAC 1

DYER Bruce Antonio

Born: Ilford, 13 April 1975
Height: 6'0" **Weight:** 11.3
International Honours: E: U21-11
Bruce returned to Watford on a free transfer from Barnsley in the summer of 2003, having started his career at Vicarage Road more than ten years earlier. A strong, hard-working centre forward with an impressive scoring pedigree, Bruce seemed an ideal signing, but somehow the goals would not come and he failed to gel with the other forwards, leading to a loss of confidence. Manager Ray Lewington was supportive and kept him in the squad and his patience was rewarded in the last month of the season when Bruce suddenly found his form and with it his goal touch. He followed up five goals in two games for the reserves with crucial strikes in consecutive first-team matches at Rotherham and Millwall, and suddenly looked a completely rejuvenated player.

Watford (From trainee on 19/4/1993) FL 29+2/6 FLC 4/2 FAC 1 Others 2/1

Crystal Palace (£1,100,000 on 10/3/1994) F/PL 95+40/37 FLC 9+5/1 FAC 7+3/6 Others 3+2
Barnsley (£700,000 on 23/10/1998) FL 149+33/59 FLC 11+1/4 FAC 5+2/3 Others 2+1/3
Watford (Free on 10/7/2003) FL 18+14/3 FLC 2 FAC 1

DYER Kieron Courtney

Born: Ipswich, 29 December 1978
Height: 5'7" **Weight:** 9.7
International Honours: E: 23; B-2; U21-11; Yth
Injuries disrupted Kieron's 2003-4 season as torn hamstring problems sidelined him in October and again in April. When fit he demonstrated his importance to the Newcastle side based on his high energy levels and impressive change of pace, which he used to good effect to supplement his strikers with penetrating runs into the opposition box. His flexibility enabled him to perform in any of the midfield positions, and even as an emergency right back, where he had an excellent game against Aston Villa in April. After missing two matches he returned as a striker for the FA Cup tie at Southampton in January and scored twice in an outstanding performance, although he reverted to midfield on Craig Bellamy's return a few games later. When fit Kieron continued to figure in the England squads and was selected for Euro 2004.

Ipswich T (From trainee on 3/1/1997) FL 79+12/9 FLC 11/1 FAC 5 Others 5+1/2
Newcastle U (£6,000,000 on 16/7/1999) PL 125+9/14 FLC 5+1/3 FAC 10+1/3 Others 20+2/2

DYER Lloyd Richard

Born: Birmingham, 13 September 1982
Height: 5'10" **Weight:** 11.4
A fast raiding left-sided midfielder who hugs the touchline and loves to run at defenders, Lloyd went on loan to Kidderminster at the start of last season, featuring at left back or left wing back. On his return to West Bromwich Albion he was used regularly as a substitute in the second half of the campaign and he duly did the business by turning what looked like six drawn games into wins with some great wing play. He scored two goals for the Baggies, including a beauty in the 3-2 victory at Portman Road as promotion beckoned.

West Bromwich A (Signed from Aston Villa juniors on 9/7/2001) FL 2+15/2 FLC 1 FAC 0+1
Kidderminster Hrs (Loaned on 5/9/2003) FL 5+2/1

EADEN Nicholas (Nicky)
Jeremy
Born: Sheffield, 12 December 1972
Height: 5'9" **Weight:** 12.8
Club Honours: Div 2 '03
Last term was another sound season for
this Wigan Athletic defender who was
an ever-present in First Division matches.
Steady and undemonstrative, his
positional sense at right back was
excellent as he worked the flanks
unselfishly, producing solid displays. Yet
to miss a League match since signing for
the club, Nicky's experience was
invaluable as he continued to provide a
calm and confident presence in the
defence. He received the 'Man of the
Match' award in the home game against
Sunderland.
*Barnsley (From juniors on 4/6/1991) F/PL
281+12/10 FLC 18+3/3 FAC 20 Others 4+1*
*Birmingham C (Free on 6/7/2000) FL 68+6/3
FLC 13/1 FAC 1 Others 1+1/1*
*Wigan Ath (Signed on 20/9/2002) FL 83 FLC
7 FAC 4 Others 1*

EAGLES Christopher (Chris)
Mark
Born: Hemel Hempstead, 19 November
1985
Height: 6'0" **Weight:** 10.8
Club Honours: FAYC '03
International Honours: E: Yth
A talented right-sided midfielder who is
highly regarded for his dribbling and close
control, Chris made his first-team debut
for Manchester United in the Carling Cup
victory over Leeds United at Elland Road
in October, coming on as a second-half
substitute for Kieran Richardson.
Following on with an adequate
performance in the Carling Cup game
against West Bromwich Albion, Chris
showed he had all the qualities of a
bright future.
*Manchester U (From trainee on 25/7/2003)
FLC 0+2*

EARNSHAW Robert
Born: Zambia, 6 April 1981
Height: 5'8" **Weight:** 10.10
International Honours: W: 13; U21-10;
Yth
Robert is a goals ace with a mission - to
play in the Premiership. The question for
most of last season was whether it would
be for Cardiff or another club. He started
the campaign in fine form, netting a hat-
trick in the Carling Cup game against

Leyton Orient, then hitting four against
Gillingham in September. Although his
overall tally was slightly down on the
previous season, he still topped the 20-
goal mark and finished as the team's
leading scorer. Robert was also a regular
for Wales at international level, netting a
hat-trick in the 4-0 win over Scotland in
February.
*Cardiff C (From trainee on 4/8/1998) FL
137+37/84 FLC 5+2/9 FAC 11+2/9 Others
5+1/1*
*Greenock Morton (Loaned on 20/1/2000) SL
3/2 SC 1*

EASTER Jermaine Maurice
Born: Cardiff, 15 January 1982
Height: 5'8" **Weight:** 12.4
International Honours: W: Yth
This pacy young striker had a rather
disappointing time at Hartlepool last
term, for although he scored regularly
for the reserves, he failed to make any
significant breakthrough at first-team
level. After a loan spell at Spennymoor,
he joined Cambridge, also on loan, but
had a difficult start at the Abbey
Stadium, being laid low by a virus and
also suffering a clash of heads that saw
him stretchered off the pitch
unconscious. However his return to
action saw him net two goals in the 4-3
win at Darlington and he later signed
permanently for the U's.
*Wolverhampton W (From trainee on
6/7/2000)*
*Hartlepool U (Free on 17/3/2001) FL 0+27/2
Others 0+3*
*Cambridge U (Loaned on 6/2/2004) FL
10+5/2*

EASTON Clint Jude
Born: Barking, 1 October 1977
Height: 5'11' **Weight:** 10.8
Club Honours: Div 2 '98
International Honours: E: Yth
This former Watford midfielder started
nine of Norwich City's first ten matches of
the 2003-04 campaign before fading out
of the first-team picture for the remainder
of the season. An assured and creative
left-sided player, he has the vision to
make telling passes through the tightest
of defences. Strong in the air, he also gets
into good goal-scoring positions and
netted twice for the Canaries early on. His
contract at Carrow Road was cancelled in
May 2004.
*Watford (From trainee on 5/7/1996) P/FL
50+14/1 FLC 4+4/1 FAC 3+1 Others 3*
*Norwich C (£200,000 on 19/6/2001) FL
41+9/5 FLC 2 FAC 0+2 Others 3*

EATON Adam Paul
Born: Wigan, 2 May 1980
Height: 5'11" **Weight:** 11.2
Club Honours: FAYC '98
Adam missed the opening months of the
2003-04 season with a groin injury and it
was not until December that he returned
to first-team action for Mansfield. He
then suffered a set back early in the new
year with a recurrence of the injury and
went to Lilleshall for a period of
rehabilitation. Adam recovered to take his
place in the side at left back for the
penultimate match of the season against
Huddersfield and also featured in the
play-offs.
Everton (From trainee on 2/6/1997)
*Preston NE (Free on 29/6/1999) FL 7+7 FLC
2 FAC 1 Others 0+1*
Mansfield T (Loaned on 10/12/2002) FL 6
*Mansfield T (Signed on 4/2/2003) FL 17
Others 3*

EBDON Marcus
Born: Pontypool, 17 October 1970
Height: 5'10" **Weight:** 12.4
International Honours: W: U21-2; Yth
Marcus joined Leyton Orient on a monthly
contract at the start of last term after
impressing during the pre-season period.
An experienced midfielder who is capable
of breaking up attacks as well as starting
them, he featured regularly early on, but
after losing his place he was released in
October and moved on to Conference
outfit Tamworth.
Everton (From trainee on 16/8/1989)
*Peterborough U (Free on 15/7/1991) FL
136+11/15 FLC 14+2 FAC 12+3/1 Others 11+1*
*Chesterfield (£100,000 on 21/3/1997) FL
180+12/13 FLC 12+1/1 FAC 7 Others 7+1/3*
*Leyton Orient (Free on 4/8/2003) FL 10+4
FLC 1 Others 1*

EDDS Gareth James
Born: Sydney, Australia, 3 February 1981
Height: 5'11" **Weight:** 10.12
International Honours: Australia: U23-
2; Yth
The right back was one of a clutch of pre-
season signings for Bradford. Gareth
found himself straight into the side under
Nicky Law and missed only two matches
until the change of manager at the club
in November. An enthusiastic defender,
Gareth was always willing to add to
attacks and overlap on the right wing. He
found himself out of favour when Bryan
Robson took over, but Gareth still gave
some wholehearted displays when called
upon.
*Nottingham F (From trainee on 19/2/1998)
FL 11+5/1 FAC 1*

Jermaine Easter

Swindon T (Free on 9/8/2002) FL 8+6 FLC 0+1 FAC 1 Others 2
Bradford C (Free on 14/7/2003) FL 19+4 FLC 1

EDGE Lewis John Spencer
Born: Lancaster, 12 January 1987
Height: 6'2" **Weight:** 12.10
A first-year scholar with Blackpool, this young 'keeper made his senior debut in the final game of the 2003-04 season at Bristol City when he acquitted himself well, making several fine saves. Lewis is also a talented cricketer and has played at first-team level for Morecambe in the Northern League.
Blackpool (Trainee) FL 1

EDGHILL Richard Arlon
Born: Oldham, 23 September 1974
Height: 5'9" **Weight:** 11.5
International Honours: E: B-1; U21-3
Richard initially joined Queens Park Rangers on a short-term contract as cover, but following some solid performances he stayed at Loftus Road until the end of the season. In November he became a regular at right back, but then suffered a serious injury that kept him out until March. On regaining fitness he switched to left back to cover for the injured Gino Padula.
Manchester C (From trainee on 15/7/1992) P/FL 178+3/1 FLC 17 FAC 8+1 Others 3
Birmingham C (Loaned on 14/11/2000) FL 3
Wigan Ath (Free on 21/10/2002) Others 1
Sheffield U (Free on 17/11/2003) FL 0+1
Queens Park R (Free on 22/8/2003) FL 15+5 FLC 2 Others 1+1

EDMONDSON Darren Stephen
Born: Coniston, 4 November 1971
Height: 6'0" **Weight:** 12.11
Club Honours: Div 3 '95; AMC '97
This experienced defender was York City's captain last term, but was troubled by injuries throughout the season. Darren led the Minstermen to the top of the Third Division table with a 100 per cent record after four games but injury in the following match at Lincoln caused him to miss several fixtures and he never fully recovered his form on his return to first-team action. He scored just once, netting in the 2-2 draw at Leyton Orient in November, and was released by the club at the end of the campaign.
Carlisle U (From trainee on 17/7/1990) FL 205+9/9 FLC 15/1 FAC 15/3 Others 22/3
Huddersfield T (£200,000 + on 3/3/1997) FL 28+9 FLC 2 FAC 2+2
Plymouth Arg (Loaned on 11/9/1998) FL 4
York C (Free on 23/3/2000) FL 126+5/6 FLC 5 FAC 10 Others 1

[EDU] GASPAR Eduardo Cesar Daud
Born: Sao Paulo, Brazil, 15 May 1978
Height: 6'1" **Weight:** 11.4
Club Honours: FAC '02; PL '02, '04; CS '02
International Honours: Brazil: 4
Last term proved to be a defining season for Edu at Arsenal as he came to prominence in spectacular fashion. He battled with both Gilberto Silva and Ray Parlour to command a place alongside Patrick Vieira in centre midfield and as the vast majority of Gunners' fans called for him to be given a starting place he finally broke into the team as a first choice. He scored seven goals including the winner at Stamford Bridge in February and two

more away to Celta Vigo in the Champions' League, the second of which was a mesmerising solo effort. An intelligent passer of the ball and in possession of a fine shot, a fine club season was rewarded with his first cap for Brazil against Hungary.
Arsenal (£6,000,000 from Corinthians, Brazil on 18/11/2001) PL 35+32/5 FLC 7/2 FAC 13+3/3 Others 11+8/3

EDWARDS Andrew (Andy) David
Born: Epping, 17 September 1971
Height: 6'3" **Weight:** 12.10
Club Honours: Div 3 '03
Andy was a near ever-present in the Rushden defence last term until mid-

Christian Edwards

November, but then a back problem kept him out of action for three months. He returned for the run-in and even scored twice in the home win against Notts County, but unfortunately it was not enough to save the Diamonds from relegation. Andy was released in the summer and was reported to have signed for Southend United.

Southend U *(From trainee on 14/12/1989)*
FL 141+6/5 FLC 5 FAC 4 Others 9/2
Birmingham C *(£400,000 on 6/7/1995) FL*
37+3/1 FLC 12/1 FAC 2 Others 5/1
Peterborough U *(Signed on 29/11/1996) FL*
266/10 FLC 12 FAC 21/1 Others 17/2
Rushden & Diamonds *(Free on 5/3/2003) FL*
40+1/4 FLC 1 FAC 1 Others 2

EDWARDS Akenhaton **Carlos**
Born: Port of Spain, Trinidad, 24 October 1978
Height: 5'11" **Weight:** 11.9
International Honours: Trinidad & Tobago: 31
Carlos was a near ever-present for Wrexham last term when he impressed with his tricky probing runs down the right. Now a confirmed wing back since the defensive side of his game has improved considerably, he is also capable of scoring spectacular goals. Carlos was named in the PFA Second Division team for the second year running and continued to add to his total of caps for Trinidad during the campaign.

Wrexham *(£125,000 from Defence Force, Trinidad on 8/8/2000) FL 126+22/22 FLC 4+2/1 FAC 3 Others 3/1*

EDWARDS Christian Nicholas Howells
Born: Caerphilly, 23 November 1975
Height: 6'2" **Weight:** 12.8
International Honours: W: 1; B-2; U21-7
After some time out of favour at the City Ground, Christian moved on to join Bristol Rovers during the 2003 close season. The experienced central defender established himself in the team and was a near ever-present throughout the campaign. Christian produced a series of fine performances, displaying good aerial ability and some well-timed tackles.
Swansea C *(From trainee on 20/7/1994) FL 113+2/4 FLC 5 FAC 4 Others 8*
Nottingham F *(£175,000 + on 26/3/1998) P/FL 44+10/3 FLC 1 FAC 1*
Bristol C *(Loaned on 11/12/1998) FL 3*
Oxford U *(Loaned on 24/2/2000) FL 5/1*
Crystal Palace *(Loaned on 16/11/2001) FL 9*
Tranmere Rov *(Loaned on 17/9/2002) FL 12 FLC 1 FAC 2 Others 2*
Oxford U *(Loaned on 17/1/2003) FL 5+1*
Bristol Rov *(Free on 4/7/2003) FL 40+2 FLC 1 FAC 1 Others 1*

EDWARDS Jake
Born: Prestwich, 11 May 1976
Height: 6'2" **Weight:** 13.0
Strong and clinical, this experienced striker joined Yeovil shortly after the start of last season. Jake's tally of ten goals in all competitions reflected his ability in front of goal, but injuries and suspensions restricted his first-team appearances. He was released by the Glovers in the summer.
Wrexham *(Free from James Maddison University, USA on 13/8/1998) FL 4+7/2 Others 1+4/2 (Free to Telford U on 5/11/1999)*
Yeovil T *(Free on 14/8/2003) FL 17+10/6 FAC 1+1/2 Others 2/2*

EDWARDS Michael (Mike)
Born: Hessle, 25 April 1980
Height: 6'1" **Weight:** 12.0
Mike performed consistently well for Grimsby Town last term, but found himself in and out of the line-up as a series of managers juggled the side to try to stem a leaky defence. A versatile and dependable defender he has the ability to play anywhere in the back four. His only goal of the campaign came in the 4-0 win over Chesterfield in September.
Hull C *(From trainee on 16/7/1998) FL 165+13/6 FLC 8+1 FAC 11/2 Others 9+1*

Jake Edwards

Colchester U (Free on 27/3/2003) FL 3+2
Grimsby T (Free on 7/8/2003) FL 32+1/1 FAC 2 Others 1

EDWARDS Neil Ryan
Born: Aberdare, 5 December 1970
Height: 5'9" **Weight:** 11.10
International Honours: W: U21-1; Yth; Sch
Rochdale's experienced 'keeper was still recovering from surgery when the 2003-04 season started, but he returned in October and was a permanent fixture thereafter. Despite Dale's struggles he maintained an outstanding level of performance, winning several 'Man of the Match' accolades with his tremendous shot stopping. Neil passed 200 Football League appearances for the club during the campaign and has now played more games for the Dale than any other goalkeeper.
Leeds U(From trainee on 10/3/1989) Others 1
Stockport Co (£5,000 on 3/9/1991) FL 163+1 FLC 11 FAC 11 Others 31
Rochdale (£25,000 on 3/11/1997) FL 223 FLC 8 FAC 16+1 Others 12

EDWARDS Paul
Born: Manchester, 1 January 1980
Height: 5'11" **Weight:** 10.12
Paul's defensive game showed distinct improvements last term and he was in the running for the Wrexham supporters' 'Player of the Year' award. A strong-running pacy flanker who can cause defences problems when he 'goes at them' he added a much higher work rate to his attributes. His swift runs along the left touchline remind fans of the good old days when wingers were the norm.
Doncaster Rov (Free from Ashton U on 2/2/1998) FL 5+4
Swindon T (Free from Altrincham, ex Knutsford T, on 17/8/2001) FL 14+6 FLC 0+1 FAC 1/1 Others 1
Wrexham (Free on 12/7/2002) FL 73+6/4 FLC 3 FAC 0+1 Others 3

EDWARDS Paul
Born: Derby, 10 November 1982
Height: 6'0" **Weight:** 11.0
Following his introduction to senior football in 2002-03, Paul had hoped to make a breakthrough into the first-team squad at Crewe last term. However, the young striker found it hard to make an impact in the side and mostly featured from the substitutes' bench. He managed three first-team starts, the first of these being in the Carling Cup tie at Leicester.
Crewe Alex (From trainee on 6/2/2001) FL 2+10 FLC 1

EDWARDS Robert (Robbie)
Born: Manchester, 23 February 1970
Height: 5'9" **Weight:** 12.4
Rob rejoined Huddersfield Town during the summer of 2003, and was soon made club captain as he established himself in the side at left back. A confident defender with great awareness, he was keen to link with his forwards and scored with a classic low volley against Bristol Rovers at the McAlpine Stadium. A hamstring injury blighted his season, before he returned in a central-midfield role for the all-important closing fixtures. Rob scored the decisive equalising goal in the second leg of the play-off semi-final against Lincoln and also netted in the penalty shoot-out that clinched promotion for the Terriers.
Crewe Alex (From trainee on 11/7/1988) FL 110+45/44 FLC 8/5 FAC 13+5/5 Others 9+7/5
Huddersfield T (£150,000 on 8/3/1996) FL 109+29/14 FLC 12+1/1 FAC 7+1/1
Chesterfield (£20,000 on 8/9/2000) FL 89+5/7 FLC 2+1 FAC 5 Others 8
Huddersfield T (Free on 7/8/2003) FL 11+6/1 FLC 1 Others 2+1/1

EDWARDS Robert (Rob) Owen
Born: Telford, 25 December 1982
Height: 6'1" **Weight:** 12.0
International Honours: W: 6; Yth
Rob was recovering from ankle surgery at the start of last season, then found it impossible to force his way into the Aston Villa first-team squad and his only senior football came whilst out on loan. At Crystal Palace the young defender was looking good and scored with a fine header against Coventry before returning to the Midlands with an injury. He then spent three months with Derby and would have played more League games but for an attack of bronchitis. Rob's goal in his first home game for Derby, an important victory over Gillingham, owed much to Marcus Tudgay's deflection but he left a good impression, alert in defence and positive when he pressed forward. He added further caps for Wales during the season.
Aston Villa (From trainee on 4/1/2000) PL 7+1 FAC 1
Crystal Palace (Loaned on 21/11/2003) FL 6+1/1
Derby Co (Loaned on 9/1/2004) FL 10+1/1

EDWARDS Robert (Rob) William
Born: Kendal, 1 July 1973
Height: 6'0" **Weight:** 12.2
Club Honours: Div 2 '00

International Honours: W: 4; B-2; U21-17; Yth
Rob was not a regular starter for Preston last term until he came into the side during an injury crisis in March. Previously seen as a left back, he looked solid, slotting into the three-man central defensive formation favoured by Craig Brown, where his lack of pace was less of a factor. Instead, he used his experience well to cover for team mates and he showed himself particularly adept at taking responsibility for organising his less experienced colleagues. A great servant at Deepdale, Rob was out of contract at the end of the season and his future was unclear at the time of writing.
Carlisle U (From trainee on 10/4/1990) FL 48/5 FLC 4 FAC 1 Others 2+1
Bristol C (£135,000 on 27/3/1991) FL 188+28/5 FLC 16+3/1 FAC 13+2 Others 12+1/2
Preston NE (Free on 5/8/1999) FL 156+13/4 FLC 13 FAC 10 Others 5/1

EDWORTHY Marc
Born: Barnstaple, 24 December 1972
Height: 5'8" **Weight:** 11.10
Club Honours: Div 1 '04
Marc arrived at Norwich shortly before the start of the 2003-04 season and was introduced as a half-time substitute at Bradford in the opening game. Apart from one three-match spell when he was sidelined through injury, he retained the right-back berth for the remainder of the campaign. An experienced and energetic defender who covers his team mates well, he is always willing to burst forward on overlapping runs.
Plymouth Arg (From trainee on 30/3/1991) FL 52+17/1 FLC 5+2 FAC 5+2 Others 2+2
Crystal Palace (£350,000 on 9/6/1995) F/PL 120+6 FLC 8+1/1 FAC 8 Others 8
Coventry C (£850,000 + on 28/8/1998) P/FL 62+14/1 FLC 5 FAC 4
Wolverhampton W (Free on 23/8/2002) FL 18+4 FLC 1
Norwich C (Free on 8/8/2003) FL 42+1 FLC 1 FAC 1

EHIOGU Ugochuku (Ugo)
Born: Hackney, 3 November 1972
Height: 6'2" **Weight:** 14.10
Club Honours: FLC '96, '04
International Honours: E: 4; B-1; U21-15
Ugo missed almost all the first half of the season as he was recovering from a torn posterior cruciate ligament injury, an injury he picked up at the end of the previous campaign. Indeed, his return to

first-team action for Middlesbrough did not come until the end of December. Boro's imposing centre half formed a superb, almost telepathic, partnership with his former Aston Villa colleague Gareth Southgate at the heart of the defence. Ugo is solid in the tackle, deceptively fast and commanding in the air and his return to the side coincided with some positive results. When Southgate was forced out of the team through injury in March, Ugo was the natural successor to wear the captain's armband and just to show how vital he was to the team he signed an extension to his playing contract.

West Bromwich A (From trainee on 13/7/1989) FL 0+2
Aston Villa (£40,000 on 12/7/1991) F/PL 223+14/12 FLC 23+1/1 FAC 22+2/1 Others 18/1
Middlesbrough (£8,000,000 on 20/10/2000) PL 97+1/7 FLC 4 FAC 6/1

EL-ABD Adam

Born: Brighton, 11 September 1984
Height: 5'11" **Weight:** 13.9

This young Brighton defender was introduced to the first team last November and enjoyed a useful run in the side before his form dipped slightly and he was omitted from the squad for the final run-in. Nevertheless, Adam impressed with his no-nonsense style and was rewarded with a long-term contract, indicating the promise of this burly youngster. Although employed principally at right back, he can also play as a central defender, a role he occupied on a most accomplished senior debut against Boston United in the LDV Vans Trophy.

Brighton & Hove A (From trainee on 22/12/2003) FL 6+5 Others 2

ELAM Lee Patrick George

Born: Bradford, 24 September 1976
Height: 5'8" **Weight:** 10.12
International Honours: E: SP-4

This exciting midfielder began the 2003-04 season at Halifax, but in October he joined Yeovil Town on loan, a move that became permanent the following month. However, he was unable to win a regular place in the Glovers line-up and in March he went out on loan to Conference club Chester City. Lee was reported to have signed for Hornchurch during the summer break.

Yeovil T (Free from Halifax T, ex Guiseley, Southport, Morecambe, on 31/10/2003) FL 6+6/1

EL KHOLTI Abdelhalim (Abdou)

Born: Annemasse, France, 17 October 1980
Height: 5'10" **Weight:** 11.2

This versatile player featured in a number of games in a midfield role for Yeovil at the start of the 2003-04 campaign, but then dropped out of contention for a while. However, he forced his way back into the team with a string of 'Man of the Match' performances at left back in the new year. Abdou missed the closing stages of the campaign after undergoing a groin operation.

Yeovil T (Free from Raja Casablanca, Morocco on 9/10/2002) FL 19+4/1 FLC 0+1 FAC 0+1 Others 1

ELLEGAARD Kevin Stuhr

Born: Copenhagen, Denmark, 23 May 1983
Height: 6'5" **Weight:** 15.0
International Honours: Denmark: Yth

Due to injuries to those ahead of him in the queue for first-team action at Manchester City, this young goalkeeper made a dramatic Premiership debut in the defeat by Leicester in November and featured in a number of games as a deputy for the injured David Seaman, including the Carling Cup tie against Tottenham. However with the signing of England 'keeper David James during the January transfer window, it was back to the bench and time to reflect on the fact he had done enough to show he is a future number one.

Manchester C (£750,000 from Farum, Denmark on 16/11/2001) PL 2+2 FLC 1 FAC 2

ELLENDER Paul

Born: Scunthorpe, 21 October 1974
Height: 6'1" **Weight:** 12.7
Club Honours: NC '02
International Honours: E: SP-1

This big central defender held the Boston United back four together for much of the season. He worked hard and was rewarded by being handed the captain's armband in the second half of the campaign. Paul swept the board in the supporters' 'Player of the Year' awards and was given a new contract in the summer. He showed ability in the air and on the ground as well as providing the odd goal. These included a spectacular 25-yard effort to help the Pilgrims earn a point at home to Huddersfield.

Scunthorpe U (From trainee on 8/4/1993. Freed during 1994 close season)
Boston U (Signed from Scarborough, ex Gainsborough Trin, Altrincham, on 17/8/2001) FL 67+1/4 FLC 3/1 FAC 1 Others 2

ELLINGTON Nathan Levi Fontaine

Born: Bradford, 2 July 1981
Height: 5'10" **Weight:** 12.10
Club Honours: Div 2 '03

An exceptionally quick striker who has an unerring eye for goal, Nathan again topped Wigan Athletic's scoring chart, his tally of 19 goals showing that he coped adequately with the step up to Division One football. Following the arrival of Jason Roberts the two rekindled a partnership developed at Bristol Rovers and they quickly gelled together once more. Nathan was voted February's Umbro /Isotonic 'Player of the Month' following four goals in as many matches, while another highlight was his brace of goals in the home win over Crystal Palace. He always gives 100 per cent and his haul of goals was a justification of the trickery, skill, and total commitment that he showed.

Bristol Rov (£150,000 from Walton & Hersham on 18/2/1999) FL 76+40/35 FLC 7/2 FAC 6+1/4 Others 6+1/3
Wigan Ath (£750,000 + on 28/3/2002) FL 87+2/35 FLC 6+1/6 FAC 3+1/2 Others 0+1

ELLIOTT Marvin Conrad

Born: Wandsworth, 15 September 1984
Height: 5'11" **Weight:** 12.2

Another product of the Millwall Academy, Marvin joined the first-team squad last season. This tall, elegant, midfield player is a tough tackling and forward running player who is capable of causing plenty problems for the opposition. Despite his tender years he regularly stamped his authority on games and gaining a couple of 'Man of the Match' awards.

Millwall (From trainee on 6/2/2002) FL 14+8 FAC 1+3

ELLIOTT Matthew (Matt) Stephen

Born: Wandsworth, 1 November 1968
Height: 6'3" **Weight:** 14.10
Club Honours: FLC '00
International Honours: S: 18

A training ground broken toe during the second week of the season kept this experienced central defender out of action for a while, before a red card for a misjudged leap at home to Birmingham further hampered his chances of regaining his position at the heart of the Leicester defence. Matt later linked up with Ipswich Town on loan, to add experience to their back line as they made a push for promotion via the play-offs. He had a steadying effect on Town's defence using his experience to keep one step ahead of

his opponents and forged an effective partnership with John McGreal at the heart of the defence.
Charlton Ath *(£5,000 from Epsom & Ewell on 9/5/1988) FLC 1*
Torquay U *(£10,000 on 23/3/1989) FL 123+1/15 FLC 9/2 FAC 9/2 Others 16/1*
Scunthorpe U *(£50,000 on 26/3/1992) FL 61/8 FLC 6 FAC 2 Others 8*
Oxford U *(£150,000 on 5/11/1993) FL 148/21 FLC 16/1 FAC 11/2 Others 6*
Leicester C *(£1,600,000 on 18/1/1997) P/FL 238+5/27 FLC 20+1/3 FAC 18+1/3 Others 4*
Ipswich T *(Loaned on 16/3/2004) FL 10 Others 2*

ELLIOTT Stephen William
Born: Dublin, 6 January 1984
Height: 5'8" **Weight:** 11.8
International Honours: RoI; U21-7; Yth
A prolific scorer for Manchester City at reserve-team level, Stephen was on the bench for the first time against Liverpool before being given his first-team spurs in fleeting cameo roles against Bolton Wanderers and Middlesbrough. He has good movement along the front line and can hold the ball up well. A Republic of Ireland U21 international, he produced some outstanding performances for his country at the World Youth Championships in December.
Manchester C *(From trainee on 17/1/2001) PL 0+2*

ELLIOTT Steven (Steve) William
Born: Swadlincote, 29 October 1978
Height: 6'1" **Weight:** 14.0
Club Honours: AMC '04
International Honours: E: U21-2
Steve Elliott began the season in Derby's side but found it hard to win a place after Michael Johnson was signed. The central defender went on loan to Blackpool and eventually earned a contract until the end of the season. He formed a good partnership with Mike Flynn in the heart of defence and was a member of the team that was victorious in the LDV Vans Trophy final at Cardiff.
Derby Co *(From trainee on 26/3/1997) P/FL 58+15/1 FLC 8+1 FAC 3+2*
Blackpool *(Free on 14/11/2003) FL 28 Others 5*

ELLIOTT Stuart
Born: Belfast, 23 July 1978
Height: 5'10" **Weight:** 11.9
International Honours: NI: 20; U21-3
Stuart again reached a double-figure goals tally for Hull City last term, despite being hampered by a mystery virus

throughout the first three months of the season. He provided a potent attacking threat down the left flank, proving to be most effective when running at defenders and pulling back quality crosses from the wing. Despite not being the tallest of players, he has tremendous jumping ability and a superb heading technique.
Motherwell *(£100,000 from Glentoran on 20/7/2000) SL 50+20/22 SLC 2+1 SC 1+1/1*
Hull C *(£230,000 on 12/7/2002) FL 72+6/26 FLC 1 FAC 0+2*

ELLIOTT Wade Patrick
Born: Eastleigh, 14 December 1978
Height: 5'9" **Weight:** 11.1
International Honours: E: Sch
This popular Bournemouth winger enjoyed an excellent start to the 2003-04 season and was a regular in the side. After scoring an injury-time winner against Sheffield Wednesday, Wade netted three more soon afterwards, but the second half of the campaign saw him relegated to the bench as he struggled to find the form that has made him such an influential player.
Bournemouth *(£5,000 from Bashley on 4/2/2000) FL 135+42/27 FLC 3+1 FAC 14/4 Others 8+2/1*

ELLISON Kevin
Born: Liverpool, 23 February 1979
Height: 6'1" **Weight:** 12.8
Kevin only managed to make ten starts for Stockport County last season, all in the opening stages. A couple of substitute appearances followed but the powerful left winger couldn't force his way back into the side and he spent the final weeks of the season on loan at Third Division outfit Lincoln City where he was required following the departure of Paul Mayo to Watford. Kevin was used in the unfamiliar position of left wing back with some success in Lincoln's run-in to the play-offs. He showed good defensive qualities and the ability to push forward. Kevin's loan was extended to the end of May when he was offered a permanent deal by the Imps.
Leicester C *(£50,000 + from Altrincham on 13/2/2001) PL 0+1*
Stockport Co *(£55,000 on 30/11/2001) FL 33+15/2 FLC 1 FAC 1 Others 2*
Lincoln C *(Loaned on 12/3/2004) FL 11 Others 2*

EMANUEL Lewis James
Born: Bradford, 14 October 1983
Height: 5'8" **Weight:** 11.12
International Honours: E: Yth

Lewis began the 2003-04 season as a left back for Bradford City and finished it as a left-sided striker. The teenager started to fulfil his undoubted promise although he needs to develop a bit more confidence in the opposition penalty area. He scored his first senior goal in some style with a thundering 30-yarder as the Bantams won unexpectedly at Cardiff in August. Lewis, who signed a new contract in February, was also on target with a close-range header in another victory against Reading.
Bradford C *(From trainee on 5/7/2001) FL 51+15/2 FLC 3 FAC 1+1*

EMBERSON Carl Wayne
Born: Epsom, 13 July 1973
Height: 6'2" **Weight:** 14.7
Club Honours: FAYC '91
Carl arrived at Southend during the 2003 close season, but made only a handful of first-team appearances before injury forced him out of the starting line-up. Although a giant of a goalkeeper, he sometimes experienced problems dealing with high balls and after Blues signed Darryl Flahavan as cover Carl was unable to regain his place. He warmed the bench until April, when he was released.
Millwall *(From trainee on 4/5/1991) Others 1*
Colchester U *(Loaned on 17/12/1992) FL 13*
Colchester U *(£25,000 on 6/7/1994) FL 178+1 FLC 9 FAC 8 Others 16*
Walsall *(Free on 28/6/1999) FL 6+2 FLC 1 Others 2*
Luton T *(Free on 13/7/2001) FL 51+2 FLC 3 FAC 3 Others 1*
Southend U *(Free on 3/7/2003) FL 6 FLC 1*

EMBLEN Neil Robert
Born: Bromley, 19 June 1971
Height: 6'1" **Weight:** 13.11
Neil featured regularly for Walsall throughout the 2003-04 campaign, featuring in a variety of roles at different times: up front, in midfield and in defence. He opened his goal-scoring account for the Saddlers in the win over Preston in September and later on he scored match winners at Cardiff and against Wimbledon. Neil was a tower of strength in defence in the latter part of the season, battling to the last kick in the vain battle to avoid relegation.
Millwall *(£175,000 from Sittingbourne on 8/11/1993) FL 12 Others 1*
Wolverhampton W *(£600,000 on 14/7/1994) FL 80+8/9 FLC 2+2/1 FAC 7+2 Others 2+1*
Crystal Palace *(£2,000,000 on 21/8/1997) PL 8+5 FAC 1+1/2*
Wolverhampton W *(£900,000 on 26/3/1998) FL 102+12/7 FLC 8+1/1 FAC 6+1*

Peter Enckelman

Norwich C (£500,000 + on 12/7/2001) FL 6+8 FLC 0+1
Walsall (Free on 10/1/2003) FL 30+14/5 FLC 2 FAC 1

EMERTON Brett
Born: Sydney, Australia, 22 February 1979
Height: 6'1" **Weight:** 13.5
International Honours: Australia: 31; U23; Yth
A highly regarded acquisition, Brett started brightly for Blackburn, netting with a rocket goal in the opening game against Wolves. As the season floundered on he began to get sucked into the middle in a desperate attempt to even the balance and was less able to use the flank constructively. However he remained as the club's most reliable outlet for playing from defence and seldom left the field without having contributed. His goal-scoring prowess was disappointing given the style with which he strode through to score at Old Trafford. Brett lost his place in the team for the last six games when the club introduced the diamond formation in midfield.
Blackburn Rov (£2,200,000 from Feyenoord, Holland, ex Sydney Olympic, on 21/7/2003) PL 31+6/2 FLC 0+1 Others 2/1

ENCKELMAN Peter
Born: Turku, Finland, 10 March 1977
Height: 6'2" **Weight:** 12.5
International Honours: Finland: 5; U21-15
Out of favour at Villa Park following the arrival of Thomas Sorensen, Peter joined Blackburn on loan in November when the club had no reserve goalkeeper. He signed in the January transfer window, but had to wait until the final two games to make his first-team debut. He had the misfortune to come up against his old adversaries Birmingham City on the second occasion and kept his calm. Ironically the feature of the match was his kicking ability. He fielded back passes all day and kicked them huge distances.
Aston Villa (£200,000 from TPS Turku, Finland on 1/2/1999) PL 51+1 FLC 6 FAC 1 Others 7+1
Blackburn Rov (£150,000 on 7/11/2003) PL 2

ETHERINGTON Matthew
Born: Truro, 14 August 1981
Height: 5'10" **Weight:** 11.2
International Honours: E: U21-3; Yth
Matthew joined West Ham in the summer of 2003 and went on to become the most influential player in the side.

Jason Euell (left)

Featuring on the left-hand side he has pace and an array of dribbling skills. From his debut at Preston, when he set up both goals, he earned the reputation as being one of the most dangerous wingers in the First Division. He can also score goals, as a brilliant hat-trick against Wimbledon in March would testify. Matthew deservedly won the 'Hammer of the Year' award.

Peterborough U (From trainee on 15/8/1998) FL 43+8/6 FLC 1+1 FAC 2+1 Others 2
Tottenham H (£500,000 on 10/1/2000) PL 20+25/1 FLC 3+1 FAC 1+1/1
Bradford C (Loaned on 23/10/2001) FL 12+1/1
West Ham U (£1,000,000 on 8/8/2003) FL 34+1/5 FLC 3 FAC 4 Others 3/1

ETUHU Dickson Paul
Born: Kano, Nigeria, 8 June 1982
Height: 6'2" **Weight:** 13.4
Club Honours: Div 1 '02
A great favourite with the Preston fans, Dickson nevertheless had something of an inconsistent season in 2003-04. The tall young midfielder spent the first half of the campaign mostly making appearances from the bench, adding his strength in the air to the defence and making surging runs to support the strikers, which surprisingly brought him only four goals. After establishing himself in November, he was unfortunate to be injured early on against West Bromwich Albion and was out of action for nine games. Still very much a developing talent, hopefully a summer hernia operation will see him back to his best in 2004-05.
Manchester C (From trainee on 23/12/1999) FL 11+1 FLC 1
Preston NE (£300,000 on 24/1/2002) FL 72+14/12 FLC 5 FAC 3/1

EUELL Jason Joseph
Born: Lambeth, 6 February 1977
Height: 6'0" **Weight:** 12.7
International Honours: E: U21-6
Once again Jason finished the season as Charlton's top scorer with ten goals, despite playing the majority of games in midfield. He is strong, good in the air, and holds the ball up well. His unselfish play brings others into the game, and although he prefers to play up front, playing in midfield just behind the front two seems to give him more goal-scoring opportunities. Jason scored twice in the 2-2 draw with Everton at the Valley in August, both goals coming from the penalty spot, and he registered further doubles against Wolves at the Valley and in the 3-3 draw at Leeds United in May.

His best was probably the first goal against Wolves, when he ran onto a wonderful reverse pass from Paolo Di Canio and blasted the ball past the oncoming 'keeper and into the net.
Wimbledon (From trainee on 1/6/1995) P/FL 118+23/41 FLC 15+2/4 FAC 14+5/2 Others 2+2
Charlton Ath (£4,750,000 on 16/7/2001) PL 90+13/31 FLC 4+1/1 FAC 4+1/2

EUSTACE John Mark
Born: Solihull, 3 November 1979
Height: 5'11" **Weight:** 11.12

This tough-tackling midfield playmaker made his mark with some strong displays for Stoke City early on last season. A replacement for the departed James O'Connor, he seemed to attract more attention than he deserved from referees and as a result served a couple of periods of suspension. A niggling groin injury after Christmas saw him drop out of the side, but he should be back to full fitness in time for the start of the 2004-05 campaign.
Coventry C (From trainee on 5/11/1996) P/FL 62+24/7 FLC 6+2/2 FAC 3+2/1

John Eustace

Dundee U (Loaned on 17/2/1999) SL 8+3/1 SC 2
Middlesbrough (Loaned on 17/1/2003) PL 0+1
Stoke C (Free on 4/8/2003) FL 26/5 FLC 2 FAC 2/1

EVANS Gareth Joseph
Born: Leeds, 15 February 1981
Height: 6'0" **Weight:** 11.12
Club Honours: AMC '04
International Honours: E: Yth
After spending much of the previous campaign out injured Gareth was released by Huddersfield Town and linked up with Blackpool during the summer of 2003. A series of useful displays earned him a contract for the season and he made the left-back position his own. Unfortunately he was sidelined by injury shortly before the LDV Vans Trophy final and this brought his campaign to a premature close.
Leeds U (From trainee on 26/3/1998) PL 0+1 Others 0+1
Huddersfield T (Free on 9/8/2001) FL 35 FLC 1 Others 5
Blackpool (Free on 19/8/2003) FL 21+2 FLC 2 FAC 2 Others 4+1

EVANS Michael (Micky) James
Born: Plymouth, 1 January 1973
Height: 6'1" **Weight:** 13.4
Club Honours: Div 3 '02; Div 2 '04
International Honours: Rol: 1
Micky had another fantastic season for Plymouth Argyle in 2003-04. He is an extremely strong centre forward, who is very effective in the air and holds the ball up well. He became a focal point of Argyle's play on numerous occasions and contributed a useful return of 14 goals. His towering header in the crucial victory at home to Queens Park Rangers in April will live long in the memory of the Argyle fans. Micky was voted as the club's 'Player of the Year' for the season.
Plymouth Arg (From trainee on 30/3/1991) FL 130+33/38 FLC 8+1 FAC 10+2/3 Others 10/2
Southampton (£500,000 on 4/3/1997) PL 14+8/4 FLC 2+1/1
West Bromwich A (£750,000 on 27/10/1997) FL 35+28/6 FLC 3+3/2 FAC 2+2/1
Bristol Rov (£250,000 on 18/8/2000) FL 19+2/4 FLC 2 Others 3/2
Plymouth Arg (£30,000 on 22/3/2001) FL 110+24/26 FLC 2+1/1 FAC 8/1 Others 1+2/2

EVANS Paul Anthony
Born: Newcastle, South Africa, 28 December 1973
Height: 6'4" **Weight:** 15.6
International Honours: South Africa: U23-8
After being released by Sheffield Wednesday at the end of the previous campaign, this experienced goalkeeper had a trial period at Crewe before joining Rushden & Diamonds in a short-term deal last October. He soon got his chance when number one choice Billy Turley suffered a knee ligament problem, however, Paul struggled with a shoulder injury himself and was released shortly before the end of the year. He later signed for Dr Martens League outfit Bath City.
Leeds U (£50,000 from Wits University on 29/12/1995. Freed during 1997 close season)
Sheffield Wed (Free from Jomo Cosmos, South Africa, ex Wits University, Supersport U, Mamelodi Sundowns, on 9/8/2002) FL 7
Rushden & Diamonds (Free on 30/10/2003) FL 2 FAC 1 Others 2

EVANS Paul Simon
Born: Oswestry, 1 September 1974
Height: 5'8" **Weight:** 11.6
Club Honours: Div 3 '94, '99
International Honours: W: 2; U21-4; Yth
A tough-tackling midfielder with a ferocious shot, Paul was a regular member of the Bradford City side for the first three months of last season under manager Nicky Law. He scored twice in that time, firstly with a clever 25-yard lob at Reading and then a spectacular overhead kick to inspire City to battle back from two down to earn a point at Crewe. He then struggled to get back in the side and moved out to Nottingham Forest, initially on loan. Paul impressed many at the City Ground with his displays in the centre of midfield and the team was undefeated in the games that he played.
Shrewsbury T (From trainee on 2/7/1993) FL 178+20/26 FLC 12+2/4 FAC 12+1/2 Others 12/4
Brentford (£110,000 on 3/3/1999) FL 130/31 FLC 8 FAC 3 Others 13/3
Bradford C (Free on 9/8/2002) FL 36+6/5 FLC 2 FAC 1
Blackpool (Loaned on 17/1/2003) FL 10/1
Nottingham F (Signed on 25/3/2004) FL 8

EVANS Rhys Karl
Born: Swindon, 27 January 1982
Height: 6'1" **Weight:** 12.2
International Honours: E: U21-2; Yth; Sch
Rhys enjoyed a promising debut season

with his hometown club and was rewarded with a third place finish in a local 'Player of the Season' competition. He established himself as Swindon's regular goalkeeper early on in the campaign, producing a string of competent, composed performances and showing plenty of confidence in his own ability.
Chelsea (From trainee on 8/2/1999)
Bristol Rov (Loaned on 25/2/2000) FL 4
Queens Park R (Loaned on 6/11/2001) FL 11
Leyton Orient (Loaned on 10/8/2002) FL 7
Swindon T (Free on 28/7/2003) FL 41 FLC 1+1 FAC 1 Others 2

EVANS Richard Glyn
Born: Cardiff, 19 June 1983
Height: 5'9" **Weight:** 11.8
This pacy, skilful winger started off well last term and was a regular in the Sheffield Wednesday line-up. Unfortunately he suffered a serious cruciate ligament injury in September and this kept him out of action for the remainder of the campaign. The youngster will be looking to make a return to senior action when fully fit in the 2004-05 campaign.
Birmingham C (From trainee on 1/7/2002)
Sheffield Wed (Signed on 27/3/2003) FL 8+2/1 FLC 1

EVANS Stephen (Steve) James
Born: Caerphilly, 25 September 1980
Height: 6'1" **Weight:** 11.6
International Honours: W: U21-2; Yth
This tough-tackling Brentford midfielder never really established himself in the side during 2003-04. He deputised on the left wing for the injured Stephen Hunt on a couple of occasions and had a brief run out in midfield at the turn of the year, but the rest of the campaign saw him a regular on the bench. Steve came on in April to score a dramatic injury-time goal against Chesterfield, only for the Spireites to equalise.
Crystal Palace (From trainee on 31/10/1998) FL 0+6 FLC 0+1
Swansea C (Loaned on 9/11/2001) FL 4 FAC 2
Brentford (Free on 27/3/2002) FL 34+14/5 FLC 1+1 FAC 3+2 Others 4

EVANS Thomas (Tommy) Raymond
Born: Doncaster, 31 December 1976
Height: 6'0" **Weight:** 13.2
International Honours: NI: Yth
Scunthorpe's first-choice goalkeeper, Tommy suffered a shock last September when he was dropped for the first time in four seasons after a hesitant start to the

campaign. He returned in November with some fantastic displays, particularly in the FA Cup, saving three out of four penalties in a shoot-out to eliminate Sheffield Wednesday in round two. A good shot-stopper and reliable last line of defence, he kept his place for the rest of the season.
Sheffield U (From trainee on 3/7/1995)
Crystal Palace (Free on 14/6/1996)
Scunthorpe U (Free on 22/8/1997) FL 226+1 FLC 7 FAC 20 Others 12

EVANS Duncan **Wayne**
Born: Abermule, 25 August 1971
Height: 5'10" **Weight:** 12.5
After spending part of the previous term in central defence, Wayne returned to his normal right-back slot for Rochdale in 2003-04. As solid in the tackle as ever, few wingers really got the better of him during the season and he missed just one game. Wayne passed the 200 Football

League appearances mark for the club in January and played his 250th game overall at Kidderminster in April.
Walsall (Free from Welshpool on 13/8/1993) FL 173+10/1 FLC 14+1/1 FAC 15+1 Others 12+3
Rochdale (Free on 2/7/1999) FL 219/3 FLC 8/1 FAC 15 Others 10

EVATT **Ian** Ross
Born: Coventry, 19 November 1981
Height: 6'3" **Weight:** 13.11
Ian began last season in midfield for Chesterfield, but looked off the pace: a move to central defence galvanized his season, though, and he deservedly won the supporters' 'Player of the Year' awards. Ian combines power with keen anticipation and is rarely caught out in the air or on the ground. One of the keystones of the Spireites' back-line, he also got forward to score important goals from set pieces.

Derby Co (From trainee on 3/12/1998) P/FL 19+15 FLC 0+2/1 FAC 1
Northampton T (Loaned on 10/8/2001) FL 10+1 FLC 2
Chesterfield (Free on 4/8/2003) FL 43/5 FLC 1 FAC 1/1 Others 1+1

EYRE John Robert
Born: Hull, 9 October 1974
Height: 6'0" **Weight:** 12.7
Now in his second spell with Oldham, John showed his versatility by playing up front, in the middle, out wide and even in the back four last season. As a senior professional he set a fine example for the club's youngsters with his tireless work rate, even assuming the role of skipper for a time. John finished the campaign on a high, scoring twice as he spearheaded the attack when Latics beat Chesterfield to ensure they avoided relegation.
Oldham Ath (From trainee on 16/7/1993) P/FL 4+6/1 FLC 0+1
Scunthorpe U (Loaned on 15/12/1994) FL 9/8
Scunthorpe U (£40,000 on 4/7/1995) FL 151+13/43 FLC 9/2 FAC 12/3 Others 8+1/3
Hull C (Free on 5/7/1999) FL 43+9/13 FLC 5/3 FAC 4+1/2 Others 3+2/1
Oldham Ath (Free on 25/7/2001) FL 80+14/13 FLC 5 FAC 6+1/1 Others 5+2/1

EYRES David
Born: Liverpool, 26 February 1964
Height: 5'11" **Weight:** 11.8
Club Honours: Div 2 '00
David was the oldest outfield player in the Football League last term, but showed little sign of slowing down. The wily left winger was hit by a pre-season ankle injury and struggled to regain fitness early on. Following the departure of manager Iain Dowie in December he became assistant to caretaker boss John Sheridan – a move that restricted his first-team involvement even further until the arrival of Brian Talbot. After being recalled for Easter Monday's trip to Stockport, David then rolled back the years with some outstanding late-season displays, scoring a memorable 40-yard free-kick against Plymouth. In recognition of his longevity and popularity, he was voted 'Veteran Player of the Year' by listeners of BBC Radio Five Live.
Blackpool (£10,000 from Rhyl on 15/8/1989) FL 147+11/38 FLC 11+1/1 FAC 11/2 Others 13+2/4
Burnley (£90,000 on 29/7/1993) FL 171+4/37 FLC 17/7 FAC 14/8 Others 9/3
Preston NE (£80,000 on 29/10/1997) FL 85+23/19 FLC 3+4 FAC 10/3 Others 5/3
Oldham Ath (Free on 13/10/2000) FL 132+12/28 FLC 6/1 FAC 10+1/4 Others 4/2

Tommy Evans

F

FABREGAS Francesc (Cesc)
Born: Barcelona, Spain, 4 May 1987
Height: 5'9" **Weight:** 10.8
International Honours: Spain: Yth
This teenaged Spaniard arrived at Arsenal with a great reputation and made three appearances in the Carling Cup, becoming the youngest-ever player to represent the club when he lined up for the tie against Rotherham United tie in October. He made more history when he scored a goal against Wolves in the third round and in so doing became the youngest-ever Arsenal goal-scorer. Francesc competed for Spain U17s in the UEFA championships in France.
Arsenal (Trainee) FLC 2+1/1

FACEY Delroy Michael
Born: Huddersfield, 22 April 1980
Height: 5'11" **Weight:** 13.10
A promising striker, with bags of pace and power, Delroy found his chances severely limited at Bolton last term. His only appearances were as a substitute in the Premiership opener against Manchester United and two starts in the FA Cup against Tranmere in January. He spent three months on loan at Burnley in the first half of the season and proved a valuable extra link in the Clarets' attack, his bulk complementing the more delicate skills of Robbie Blake and Ian Moore. Unlucky not to score in several games, his duck was finally broken in style with a hat-trick against Walsall followed in quick succession by goals at Ipswich and West Ham. Frustrated by his lack of opportunities, Delroy moved to West Bromwich Albion in the new year. Signed by manager Gary Megson to boost the team's strike-power early in 2004, he received only occasional outings and was released in the summer.
Huddersfield T (From trainee on 13/5/1997) FL 40+35/15 FLC 1+1 FAC 1+2 Others 2
Bolton W (Signed on 4/7/2002) PL 1+9/1 FAC 4
Bradford C (Loaned on 8/11/2002) FL 6/1
Burnley (Loaned on 1/9/2003) FL 12+2/5 FLC 2
West Bromwich A (£100,000 on 30/1/2004) FL 2+7

FAGAN Craig Anthony
Born: Birmingham, 11 December 1982
Height: 5'11" **Weight:** 11.12
Last term proved to be a season of contrasts for this young front runner, but it ended on a happy note when he duly signed a permanent contract for Colchester in April. Craig arrived on a season's loan from Birmingham City, dazzling opponents and fans alike with his neat skills. Unfortunately he then accumulated several yellow cards and ran into disciplinary problems. However, the livewire striker then came good, culminating in a fine hat-trick to inflict a 4-1 defeat over Notts County. Craig scored his tenth and final goal of the campaign in the following match at Brentford.
Birmingham C (From trainee on 20/12/2001) PL 0+1 FLC 0+2 FAC 0+1
Bristol C (Loaned on 16/1/2003) FL 5+1/1 Others 1
Colchester U (Free on 5/8/2003) FL 30+7/9 FLC 2/1 FAC 5 Others 4

FALLON Rory Michael
Born: Gisbourne, New Zealand, 20 March 1982
Height: 6'2" **Weight:** 11.10
International Honours: E: Yth
Rory was a regular for Barnsley early on last season, leading the attack effectively, however, the club's financial situation meant that he was only retained on short-term contracts. He was eventually sold to Second Division rivals Swindon where he soon settled in. Generally used as a substitute, he went on to play a full part as Town successfully challenged for a play-off spot. Rory scored seven goals, including a spectacular overhead kick to earn a home draw against Bristol City, and showed good skills in the air and a useful touch despite his size.
Barnsley (From trainee on 23/3/1999) FL 33+19/11 FLC 2+1 FAC 1 Others 2
Shrewsbury T (Loaned on 14/12/2001) FL 8+3
Swindon T (£60,000 on 14/11/2003) FL 6+13/6 Others 0+2/1

FARRELL Craig Wayne
Born: Middlesbrough, 5 December 1982
Height: 6'0" **Weight:** 13.2
Craig was in and out of the Carlisle line-up in the first half of the 2003-04 campaign, but returned to his best form towards the end of the season when he was a regular in the team and netted five goals in a run of seven matches. He scored seven times in all, making him the club's joint-top scorer, the best of these coming against Yeovil when he scored from a difficult angle after rounding the 'keeper.

Leeds U (From trainee on 7/12/1999)
Carlisle U (Free on 4/10/2002) FL 52+11/18 FAC 2/1 Others 7+2/2

FARRELL David William
Born: Birmingham, 11 November 1971
Height: 5'10" **Weight:** 11.9
David was a regular for Peterborough United last term, although many of his appearances came from the substitutes' bench, from where he used his pace to create plenty of chances for his team mates. A very talented player, who on his day is one of the best wingers in the Second Division. He featured mostly on the left flank last term, but he can play on either side.
Aston Villa (£45,000 from Redditch U on 6/1/1992) F/PL 5+1 FLC 2
Scunthorpe U (Loaned on 25/1/1993) FL 4+1/1 Others 2
Wycombe W (£100,000 on 14/9/1995) FL 44+16/8 FLC 6 FAC 3+2 Others 2
Peterborough U (Free on 21/7/1997) FL 226+51/34 FLC 9+3/2 FAC 17+1/3 Others 13/5

FARRELLY Gareth
Born: Dublin, 28 August 1975
Height: 6'0" **Weight:** 13.0
International Honours: RoI: 6; B-1; U21-11; Yth; Sch
Out of the first-team picture at Bolton last term, Gareth joined Burnley on loan with team mate Delroy Facey in September. However, he made little impression at Turf Moor and later had a three-month loan spell with Bradford City, becoming manager Bryan Robson's first signing for the club. The left-sided midfielder breathed fresh impetus into City's relegation fight with his attacking runs even though he did not score. In March he signed a short-term contract for Wigan until the end of the season. However, although he showed some touches of class he was not offered a new deal in the summer.
Aston Villa (From trainee on 21/1/1992) PL 2+6 FLC 0+1
Rotherham U (Loaned on 21/3/1995) FL 9+1/2
Everton (£700,000 + on 9/7/1997) PL 18+9/1 FLC 2/1 FAC 1
Bolton W (Free on 12/11/1999) P/FL 61+17/5 FLC 4 FAC 6+2 Others 3/1
Rotherham U (Loaned on 14/3/2003) FL 6
Burnley (Loaned on 1/9/2003) FL 9+3 FLC 1+1
Bradford C (Loaned on 28/11/2003) FL 14 FAC 1
Wigan Ath (Signed on 8/3/2004) FL 3+4

FAULCONBRIDGE Craig Michael
Born: Nuneaton, 20 April 1978
Height: 6'1" **Weight:** 13.0
Injured since the previous March, Craig returned to first-team action as a target man for Wycombe Wanderers last November but found it hard to keep his place. After being transfer listed by new manager Tony Adams in January he knuckled down to some hard work and found himself back in favour in the first team. He scored in two games in a row in March but struggled to recapture his scoring touch.
Coventry C (From trainee on 5/7/1996)
Dunfermline Ath (Loaned on 27/3/1998) SL 1+12/1 SLC 0+1
Hull C (Loaned on 18/12/1998) FL 4+6 FAC 1 Others 1+1
Wrexham (Free on 6/8/1999) FL 92+19/31 FLC 4+1/1 FAC 4+2/1 Others 4/1
Wycombe W (Free on 24/7/2002) FL 40+10/8 FLC 2 FAC 3 Others 3+1

FAYE Amdy Mustapha
Born: Dakar, Senegal, 12 March 1977
Height: 6'1" **Weight:** 12.4
This tenacious and hard-tackling midfielder showed consistent quality in his appearances for Pompey last term. Although over enthusiastic at times he showed good ball skills and played his part in ensuring the club avoided relegation in their first season of Premiership football, producing several inspired performances.
Portsmouth (£1,500,000 from Auxerre, France on 14/8/2003) PL 27 FLC 1 FAC 2+1

FEATHERSTONE Lee Paul
Born: Chesterfield, 20 July 1983
Height: 6'0" **Weight:** 12.8
Lee's second season at Scunthorpe United saw him struggle to force his way into the first-team picture due to a number of minor injuries and the continued good form of veteran winger Peter Beagrie. A hard-working left winger, who is a good crosser of the ball, he turned in arguably his best display for the club when having to fill in at left back for the FA Cup third round replay win over Barnsley.
Sheffield U (From trainee on 4/7/2001)
Scunthorpe U (Free on 11/10/2002) FL 17+14 FLC 1 FAC 3+3 Others 0+3

FEENEY Warren James
Born: Belfast, 17 January 1981
Height: 5'10" **Weight:** 11.6
International Honours: NI: 3; U21-8; Yth; Sch
This Bournemouth striker started last

season on the bench, but when he came on in September to score twice against Rushden & Diamonds it signalled the start of a lengthy spell in the team and an excellent scoring run. Warren improved his all-round play and his efforts earned him a call up to the Northern Ireland U23 squad, but unfortunately he sustained an injury prior to the game and missed the end of the campaign. Out of contract in the summer, his future was undecided at the time of writing.
Leeds U (Signed from St Andrew's BC on 26/1/1998)
Bournemouth (Free on 22/3/2001) FL 83+25/36 FLC 1+1 FAC 6+4 Others 3+2/1

FENTON Nicholas (Nicky) Leonard
Born: Preston, 23 November 1979
Height: 5'10" **Weight:** 10.4
International Honours: E: Yth
Although the 2003-04 campaign did not see Nicky at his best for a struggling Notts County team, he was still a regular in the starting line-up throughout the season. A tall, strong central defender who has also played at right back, he always provides a threat when coming up to join the attack for set pieces. Nicky was one of several players released by the Magpies in the summer.
Manchester C (From trainee on 26/11/1996) FL 15 FLC 3+1 Others 1
Notts Co (Loaned on 7/10/1999) FL 13/1 Others 1
Bournemouth (Loaned on 23/3/2000) FL 8
Bournemouth (Loaned on 11/8/2000) FL 4+1
Notts Co (£150,000 on 18/9/2000) FL 153+2/9 FLC 7 FAC 12/1 Others 4

FERDINAND Anton Julian
Born: Peckham, 18 February 1985
Height: 6'0" **Weight:** 11.0
International Honours: E: Yth
This teenager made his West Ham debut at Preston on the opening day of the 2003-04 season. He acquitted himself well and continued to develop as a full back throughout the season. Useful in the air and calm under pressure, he deservedly won the award for being the 'Young Player of the Season' at Upton Park.
West Ham U (From trainee on 15/8/2002) FL 9+11 FLC 2+1 FAC 3

FERDINAND Leslie (Les)
Born: Acton, 8 December 1966
Height: 5'11" **Weight:** 13.5
Club Honours: FLC '99
International Honours: E: 17; B-1

'Sir Les' joined Leicester in the summer of 2003 and made an immediate impact with a brave headed goal on his debut at home to Southampton, although the knee injury he suffered in the process would prove a hindrance throughout the remainder of the campaign. Leicester's oldest-ever debutant provided a regular supply of goals to keep the Foxes' hopes of avoiding relegation alive for most of the season. It was not only his ability in the air that earned plaudits, as his powerful free kicks also continued to bring rewards. During the season, Les became the third-oldest player ever to score for the club. His knee injury continued to trouble him, and he rarely trained as the season wore on. A thumping free kick at the Valley on the afternoon that City were relegated was a typical response from the immensely popular striker, who bade farewell with a cameo appearance in the final home victory over Portsmouth.
Queens Park R (£15,000 from Hayes on 12/3/1987) F/PL 152+11/80 FLC 11+2/7 FAC 6+1/3 Others 1
Brentford (Loaned on 24/3/1988) FL 3
Newcastle U (£6,000,000 on 7/6/1995) PL 67+1/41 FLC 6/3 FAC 4+1/2 Others 5/4
Tottenham H (£6,000,000 on 5/8/1997) PL 97+21/33 FLC 11+4/5 FAC 15+1/1
West Ham U (£200,000 on 21/11/2003) PL 12+2/2
Leicester C (Free on 15/7/2003) PL 20+9/12 FAC 1+1/1

FERDINAND Rio Gavin
Born: Peckham, 7 November 1978
Height: 6'2" **Weight:** 12.1
Club Honours: PL '03; CS '03
International Honours: E: 33; U21-5; Yth
A consummate central defender, who possesses great strength in the air with neat skills on the ground, Rio's season collapsed in disarray in December when he was banned from football for eight months following a much publicised drugs test. Up to that stage he had only missed three Premiership matches, and played in all six of United's Champions' League qualifying games. His absence was clearly felt by the Reds defence during the crucial months of February and March.
West Ham U (From trainee on 27/11/1995) PL 122+5/2 FLC 12+1 FAC 9 Others 9
Bournemouth (Loaned on 8/11/1996) FL 10 Others 1
Leeds U (£18,000,000 on 27/11/2000) PL 54/2 FLC 2 FAC 3 Others 14/1
Manchester U (£29,100,000 + on 22/7/2002) PL 47+1 FLC 4 FAC 3 Others 18

FERGUSON Barry
Born: Glasgow, 2 February 1978
Height: 5'11" **Weight:** 11.1
Club Honours: SPD '99, '00, '03; SLC '98, '00, '03; SC '00, '02, '03
After beginning the season at Ibrox, Barry found the move to the Premiership somewhat difficult, but he had settled in to become the club's play maker and main influence when a broken knee cap at Newcastle ruled him out for half of the season. A complete box-to -box midfield man with fire and passing skills he also showed that he could finish as well as create with a superb Carling Cup goal against Liverpool.
Glasgow R (From juniors on 6/7/1994) SL 148+2/24 SLC 15/3 SC 23+2/6 Others 46+1/2
Blackburn Rov (£7,500,000 on 30/8/2003) PL 14+1/1 FLC 1/1

FERGUSON Darren
Born: Glasgow, 9 February 1972
Height: 5'10" **Weight:** 11.10
Club Honours: PL '93
International Honours: S: U21-5; Yth
Darren continued to be an influential figure in the Wrexham midfield engine room last term, setting up pointed opportunities for his front men with some fine intricate passes. A player who always seems to have time on the ball, the hallmark of a class player, he signed a new long-term deal for the club during the season.
Manchester U (From trainee on 11/7/1990) F/PL 20+7 FLC 2+1
Wolverhampton W (£250,000 on 13/1/1994) FL 94+23/4 FLC 13+2/3 FAC 9+2/3 Others 6
Wrexham (Free on 17/9/1999) FL 197+1/19 FLC 6/1 FAC 9/1 Others 7

FERGUSON Duncan
Born: Stirling, 27 December 1971
Height: 6'4" **Weight:** 14.6
Club Honours: SL '94; SLC '94; FAC '95
International Honours: S: 7; B; U21-7; Yth; Sch
The towering Scot had a greater than expected impact on Everton's fortunes during the season, appearing in almost half of his team's games, although he continued to be dogged by injury problems. A run of four goals in as many matches in September saw the striker back to his dominant best, when at times his skilful play on the floor and unmatched power in the air can make him unplayable. A series of health and off-the-field mishaps followed, which restricted his first-team opportunities, until he began a lengthy run in the first

team in December during which he regained the captaincy and showed renewed commitment and vigour. Typically his season was effectively ended by a groin injury.
Dundee U (Signed from Carse Thistle on 1/2/1990) SL 75+2/28 SLC 2+1/2 SC 8/6
Glasgow R (£4,000,000 on 20/7/1993) SL 8+6/2 SLC 2+2/3 SC 0+3 Others 1
Everton (£4,400,000 on 4/10/1994) PL 110+6/37 FLC 8/1 FAC 8+1/4
Newcastle U (£7,000,000 + on 25/11/1998) PL 24+6/8 FAC 6+2/3 Others 2+1/1
Everton (£3,750,000 on 19/8/2000) PL 39+22/17 FLC 3+1/3 FAC 5/3

FERNANDES Fabrice
Born: Paris, France, 29 October 1979
Height: 5'9" **Weight:** 11.7
Club Honours: Div 1 '01
International Honours: France: U21
A left-footed winger with a preference for playing on the right, so he can cut inside to execute a subtle through ball or unleash a stunning shot, Fabrice can delight and infuriate by turn. In what proved a mediocre Saints' midfield in 2003–04, he certainly provided most of the crowd-pleasing moments – such as his single goal: a stunning run and scorching 20-yard curler to convert the last-minute equaliser against Everton in February – but not enough to please Saints' latest manager, Paul Sturrock, and he spent the latter third of the season playing musical chairs between the midfield and the substitutes' bench.
Fulham (Loaned from Rennes, France on 3/8/2000) FL 23+6/2 FLC 4+2/1 FAC 1/1
Southampton (£1,100,000 from Rennes, France on 27/12/2001) PL 62+13/5 FLC 3/1 FAC 6+2 Others 2

FETTIS Alan William
Born: Belfast, 1 February 1971
Height: 6'1" **Weight:** 12.10
International Honours: NI: 25; B-3; Yth; Sch
This popular 'keeper's fortunes soon turned sour in his first full term back at Hull. Alan was substituted due to a knee injury at half time in the Tigers' first away game of the season at Oxford and didn't regain his place until November. Soon afterwards he went out on loan to Sheffield United as cover for the injured Paddy Kenny. Alan also had a loan spell with Grimsby where he produced some outstanding displays to ensure the Mariners' goals-against column stayed relatively respectable.
Hull C (£50,000 from Ards on 14/8/1991) FL 131+4/2 FLC 7+1 FAC 5 Others 7

West Bromwich A (Loaned on 20/11/1995) FL 3
Nottingham F (£250,000 on 13/1/1996) PL 4 FLC 1 FAC 0+1
Blackburn Rov (£300,000 on 12/9/1997) P/FL 9+2 FAC 1
York C (Free on 1/3/2000) FL 125 FLC 3 FAC 12
Hull C (Free on 23/11/2003) FL 20 FLC 1 Others 2
Sheffield U (Loaned on 5/12/2003) FL 2+1
Grimsby T (Loaned on 11/3/2004) FL 11

FIELDWICK Lee Peter
Born: Croydon, 6 September 1982
Height: 5'11" **Weight:** 12.2
Lee was a regular in the Brentford squad in the opening games of the 2003-04 season featuring at left back and from the substitutes' bench. Thereafter he was unable to win his place back and when Ronnie Bull arrived his days at Griffin Park looked numbered. On transfer deadline day he joined Swansea on loan to cover for injuries and his confidence grew game by game. However, at the end of his loan spell he returned to Griffin Park.
Brentford (From trainee on 4/7/2001) FL 10+2
Swansea C (Loaned on 25/3/2004) FL 4+1

FIGUEROA Luciano (Lucho) Gabriel
Born: Rosario, Argentina, 19 May 1981
Height: 6'0" **Weight:** 12.2
International Honours: Argentina: 1; U23
Signed from Rosario Central, Lucho struggled to adapt to the physical nature of the English game at first but became a regular later in the reserves. Slight and tall, he had a knack of ghosting in to score but at first-team level his path was blocked by more experienced players and the superb Mikael Forssell. He left for Mexican team Cruz Azul by mutual consent at the end of the year. After starring at U23 level for his country, Lucho won a surprise call up to the squad for the Copa America in the summer.
Birmingham C (£2,500,000 from Rosario Central, Argentina on 1/8/2003) PL 0+1 FLC 0+1

FILAN John Richard
Born: Sydney, Australia, 8 February 1970
Height: 5'11" **Weight:** 13.2
Club Honours: Div 2 '03
International Honours: Australia: 2; U23
Another exceptional season for the Wigan Athletic goalkeeper saw him once again form a terrific last line of defence. Utterly dependable, the experienced 'keeper played a big part in the Latics miserly defensive record, producing 17 clean sheets in the season. John has

tremendous physical presence, is decisive in one-on-one situations and is also a top-class shot-stopper. His positional sense and handling ability were impressive throughout the season and he was rewarded with the supporters' 'Player of the Year' award.
Cambridge U (£40,000 from Budapest St George, Australia on 12/3/1993) FL 68 FLC 6 FAC 3 Others 5
Coventry C (£300,000 on 2/3/1995) PL 15+1 FLC 2
Blackburn Rov (£700,000 on 10/7/1997) P/FL 61+1 FLC 6 FAC 5
Wigan Ath (£450,000 on 14/12/2001) FL 116 FLC 6 FAC 4 Others 1

FINNAN Stephen (Steve) John
Born: Limerick, 20 April 1976
Height: 5'10" **Weight:** 11.6
Club Honours: Div 3 '98; Div 2 '99; Div 1 '01
International Honours: RoI: 28; B-1; U21-8
This defender seemed an excellent signing for Liverpool in the 2003 close season, but at times he struggled to settle in to his new surroundings. An immaculate overlapping right back his campaign was disrupted by two injuries: a calf problem which sidelined him from November to January and a shoulder injury in March and April. At best Steve is a quality player and will be looking to show what he can achieve under a new manager in his second season at Anfield.
Birmingham C (£100,000 from Welling U on 12/6/1995) FL 9+6/1 FLC 2+2 Others 2+1
Notts Co (Loaned on 5/3/1996) FL 14+3/2 Others 3/1
Notts Co (£300,000 on 31/10/1996) FL 71+9/5 FLC 4 FAC 7/1 Others 1
Fulham (£600,000 on 13/11/1998) P/FL 171+1/6 FLC 10+1 FAC 18/1 Others 6
Liverpool (£3,500,000 on 30/6/2003) PL 19+3 FAC 3 Others 5+1

FINNIGAN John Francis
Born: Wakefield, 29 March 1976
Height: 5'8" **Weight:** 10.11
This hard-working midfielder produced a number of fine performances to help Cheltenham Town pull away from the Third Division relegation zone last term. After missing the opening months of the campaign with an ankle injury sustained in the first game, John returned in October and began to drive the team forward with his hard-running, energetic performances. He took over the club captaincy following the departure of Mark Yates and continued to lead by example from the heart of midfield, remaining ever

present until the penultimate game of the season.
Nottingham F (From trainee on 10/5/1993)
Lincoln C (£50,000 on 26/3/1998) FL 139+4/3 FLC 7 FAC 8+1/1 Others 7
Cheltenham T (Free on 7/3/2002) FL 78+4/4 FLC 2 FAC 6 Others 4/1

FISH Mark Anthony
Born: Cape Town, South Africa, 14 March 1974
Height: 6'3" **Weight:** 13.2
International Honours: South Africa: 62 (ANC '96)
Mark capped a fine season by being recalled to the South Africa international squad after a self-imposed three-year exile. Although equally comfortable at right back, Mark was used as a central defender by Charlton last term. He was a regular in the side for most of the season, until suffering a freak accident at home in March, when he suffered severe injuries to the left side of his chest. Fortunately he has since made a full recovery and even made the substitutes' bench for the last two games. Mark is very calm when under pressure and is also very consistent. He is strong, very good in the air and is extremely comfortable on the ball, building up strong partnerships with both Jon Fortune and Chris Perry in the middle of the Charlton defence.
Bolton W (£2,500,000 from Lazio, Italy, ex Orlando Pirates, on 16/9/1997) P/FL 102+1/3 FLC 12+1/1 FAC 6 Others 5
Charlton Ath (£700,000 on 10/11/2000) PL 95/2 FLC 4 FAC 4

FISKEN Gary Stewart
Born: Watford, 27 October 1981
Height: 6'0" **Weight:** 12.7
Gary endured a disappointing season blighted by a series of niggling injuries that prevented him from making a sustained challenge for a first-team place at Watford. A creative midfield player, he started only one match, in the Carling Cup, and made one League appearance as a substitute.
Watford (From trainee on 8/2/2000) FL 15+7/1 FLC 3+2 FAC 1

FITZGERALD Scott Brian
Born: Westminster, 13 August 1969
Height: 6'0" **Weight:** 12.12
International Honours: RoI: B-1; U21-4
Scott began the 2003-04 season as the club skipper at Colchester United, but he ended it on loan at Brentford, admitting that he had almost certainly played his last game for the Essex club. He was in supreme form at the heart of defence

alongside Liam Chilvers early on, but then lost his place in January before moving out to Griffin Park shortly before the transfer deadline. A tall, solid and reliable centre half, his organisational skills and ability to read the game stiffened up the Bees' defence and his contribution to the club's survival in Division Two cannot be understated.
Wimbledon (From trainee on 13/7/1989) F/PL 95+11/1 FLC 13 FAC 5 Others 1
Sheffield U (Loaned on 23/11/1995) FL 6
Millwall (Loaned on 11/10/1996) FL 7
Millwall (£50,000 + on 28/7/1997) FL 79+3/1 FLC 4 FAC 2 Others 5
Colchester U (Free on 17/10/2000) FL 114+2 FLC 3 FAC 5 Others 4
Brentford (Loaned on 16/3/2004) FL 9

FITZGERALD Scott Peter
Born: Hillingdon, 18 November 1979
Height: 5'11" **Weight:** 11.6
Scott was one of Watford's few unqualified successes of a forgettable campaign. In his first full season he was expected to be no more than a bit-part player, but he proved a quick learner and ended up as leading scorer with 11 goals, having started more than half of Watford's games. His long-distance effort at West Bromwich Albion was voted as the club's 'Goal of the Season'. A mobile and hard-working striker with an instinct for finding the back of the net, Scott was deservedly rewarded with a new contract before the end of the season.
Watford (Free from Northwood on 5/3/2003) FL 29+19/11 FLC 0+1/1 FAC 0+1

FLAHAVAN Darryl James
Born: Southampton, 28 November 1978
Height: 5'10" **Weight:** 12.1
After being released by Southend at the end of the 2002-03 season, Darryl found himself back between the sticks for the Blues last September following Carl Emberson's injury. He jumped at the chance of rejoining the club where he made his name, and he didn't disappoint, producing many excellent performances. A superb shot-stopper, Darryl's small stature means he sometimes struggles to deal with crosses.
Southampton (From trainee on 14/5/1996) Free to Woking on 13/8/1998)
Southend U (Free on 16/10/2000) FL 148 FLC 2 FAC 17 Others 16

FLEETWOOD Stuart
Born: Gloucester, 23 April 1986
Height: 5'10" **Weight:** 11.8
International Honours: W: Yth
This young Cardiff City striker went on

Darryl Flahavan

the team's pre-season tour to Scandinavia and was often included in the first-team squad last term. Stuart made his senior debut as a substitute in the Carling Cup tie against Leyton Orient and added two more appearances from the bench before the season's end.

Cardiff C *(From trainee on 2/2/2004) FL 0+2 FLC 0+1*

FLEMING Craig
Born: Halifax, 6 October 1971
Height: 6'0" **Weight:** 12.10
Club Honours: Div 1 '04
An ever-present in Norwich City's defensive line last term, Craig's no-nonsense approach to defending has become par for the course for the Canaries' fans. His experience ensures that he is seldom caught out of position, while he is very competitive in the air and brave in the challenge, often making important blocks as the opposition prepares to shoot for goal. He made his 250th League appearance for the club during the season and also popped up with his first goal in three years in the 4-1 home success over Cardiff in December, to be followed by another at Derby just three games later. Craig was an immensely proud winner of City's 'Player of the Season' award in 2003-04.

Halifax T *(From trainee on 21/3/1990) FL 56+1 FLC 4 FAC 3 Others 3+2*
Oldham Ath *(£80,000 on 15/8/1991) F/PL 158+6/1 FLC 12+1 FAC 11 Others 4*
Norwich C *(£600,000 on 30/6/1997) FL 252+7/10 FLC 17 FAC 9+1 Others 3*

FLEMING Craig Matthew
Born: Stockport, 1 December 1984
Height: 5'10" **Weight:** 11.2
A young bustling striker, Craig was handed his only first-team appearance for Oldham by caretaker boss John Sheridan last January when he came on as a late second-half substitute in the 1-1 draw at Blackpool. He struggled to find favour and was one of several players released by new manager Brian Talbot in the summer.

Oldham Ath *(Trainee) FL 0+1*

FLEMING Curtis
Born: Manchester, 8 October 1968
Height: 5'11" **Weight:** 12.8
Club Honours: Div 1 '95
International Honours: Rol: 10; U23-2; U21-5; Yth
This veteran right back broke into the Crystal Palace line-up in September and enjoyed a good run in the side in the first half of the season, when he was also the

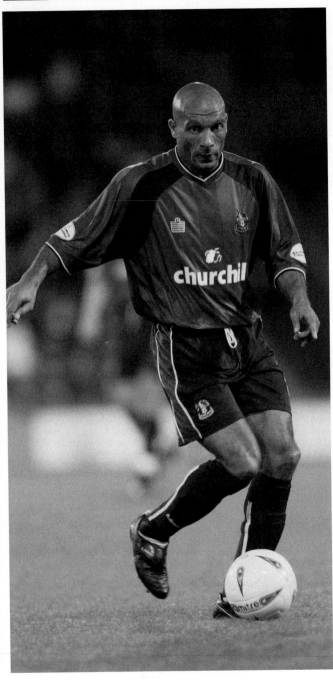

Curtis Fleming

club captain. He was in fine form but had the misfortune to suffer a fractured fibula in the game at Burnley in January and he was out of action for some time. Curtis was released by Palace in April.
Middlesbrough *(£50,000 from St Patricks on 16/8/1991) F/PL 248+18/3 FLC 24+2/1 FAC 16+1 Others 7+1*
Birmingham C *(Loaned on 16/11/2001) FL 6*
Crystal Palace *(£100,000 on 31/12/2001) FL 41+4 FLC 2+1 FAC 1*

FLEMING Terence (Terry) Maurice
Born: Marston Green, 5 January 1973
Height: 5'9" **Weight:** 10.9
A utility player who is comfortable in midfield, full back or at wing back and can even play as a striker, Terry was a first-team regular for Cambridge United until November. However, he was then dropped from the squad and it was not until a new management team was installed that he was recalled to the side.
Coventry C *(From trainee on 2/7/1991) F/PL 8+5 FLC 0+1*
Northampton T *(Free on 3/8/1993) FL 26+5/1 FLC 2 FAC 0+1 Others 0+1*
Preston NE *(Free on 18/7/1994) FL 25+7/2 FLC 4 FAC 0+1 Others 3+2*
Lincoln C *(Signed on 7/12/1995) FL 175+8/8 FLC 11+1/2 FAC 11/2 Others 4*
Plymouth Arg *(Free on 4/7/2000) FL 15+2 FLC 2 FAC 2 Others 0+2*
Cambridge U *(Free on 8/3/2001) FL 96+9/4 FLC 3 FAC 7 Others 8+2/1*

FLETCHER Carl Neil
Born: Camberley, 7 April 1980
Height: 5'10" **Weight:** 11.7
International Honours: W: 4
Carl enjoyed another season of great progress for Bournemouth last term. He came through the ranks as a central midfielder, but it has been as a centre half where he has flourished. He was outstanding for his club, and his displays earned him a call up to the full Wales international squad, making appearances against Scotland and Bulgaria.
Bournemouth *(From trainee on 3/7/1998) FL 180+7/17 FLC 5 FAC 15+1/1 Others 9+1/3*

FLETCHER Darren Barr
Born: Edinburgh, 1 February 1984
Height: 6'0" **Weight:** 13.5
Club Honours: FAC '04
International Honours: S: 8; B-1; U21-2
An elegant midfielder, who possesses good touch and passing skills, Darren continued to shine with a clutch of first-team appearances in all competitions for United last term. On the international

front too he helped Scotland to the European Championship play-offs before falling to Holland. With expectations still high, and comparisons being made with former Red David Beckham somewhat inevitable, Darren's progress was best highlighted in the FA Cup semi-final against Arsenal, where he played an inspired role.
Manchester U (From trainee on 3/2/2001) PL 17+5 FLC 2 FAC 4+1 Others 5+3

FLETCHER Gary
Born: Widnes, 4 June 1981
Height: 5'10" **Weight:** 11.7
Gary's move to Lincoln City a few weeks into the season revived his career. The busy striker quickly found his form and as well as scoring regularly he also set up many chances. Gary showed the ability to beat defenders in the tightest situations in addition to his opportunist's eye for goal. He was Lincoln's leading scorer with 18 goals including a superb solo effort at his old club Leyton Orient. Gary was voted as 'Player of the Season' by Lincoln's fans.
Hull C (Loaned from Northwich Vic on 16/3/2001) FL 1+4
Leyton Orient (£150,000 from Northwich Vic on 9/7/2001) FL 10+11/1 FLC 1/1 FAC 2 Others 4/3
Lincoln C (Free on 14/8/2003) FL 42/16 FAC 2 Others 4/3

FLETCHER Steven (Steve) Mark
Born: Hartlepool, 26 June 1972
Height: 6'2" **Weight:** 14.9
Steve enjoyed one of the best seasons of his career for Bournemouth in 2003-04. A talented striker, he deserved his reputation as one of the best target men in the Second Division. A recurrence of his old knee injury ruled him out of the final run-in and the team's results suffered, but he was given a clean bill of health and should be fit for the 2004-05 campaign.
Hartlepool U (From trainee on 23/8/1990) FL 19+13/4 FLC 0+2/1 FAC 1+2 Others 2+2/1
Bournemouth (£30,000 on 28/7/1992) FL 363+26/74 FLC 27/3 FAC 26+1/6 Others 18+3/4

FLITCROFT David (Dave) John
Born: Bolton, 14 January 1974
Height: 5'11" **Weight:** 13.5
David was appointed team captain of Macclesfield at the start of the 2003-04 campaign, but found it difficult to settle into a role in the centre of midfield. In January his contract was cancelled by mutual consent and shortly afterwards he signed for Bury as a direct replacement for Glenn Whelan who returned to

Manchester City. David struggled to find his form in his early games for the Shakers, but gradually won the fans over with a string of determined performances and by the end of the season he was a regular in the line-up.
Preston NE (From trainee on 2/5/1992) FL 4+4/2 FLC 0+1 Others 0+1
Lincoln C (Loaned on 17/9/1993) FL 2 FLC 0+1
Chester C (Free on 9/12/1993) FL 146+21/18 FLC 10+1 FAC 7 Others 8/1
Rochdale (Free on 5/7/1999) FL 141+19/4 FLC 5+2 FAC 7+4 Others 9+1
Macclesfield T (Free on 11/7/2003) FL 14+1 Others 1
Bury (Free on 30/1/2004) FL 17

FLITCROFT Garry William
Born: Bolton, 6 November 1972
Height: 6'0" **Weight:** 12.2
Club Honours: FLC '02
International Honours: E: U21-10; Yth; Sch
After signing a new contract in the close season the Blackburn Rovers captain continued to be the least noticed but most influential member of the team. Always one to lead by commitment, he provided his usual amount of tough tackling, although his creative influence was never great. He contributed vital goals against Manchester City and Aston Villa and was singled out by manager Graeme Souness for his demonstration of resilience in the first five minutes at Fulham when the club was in rapid decline.
Manchester C (From trainee on 2/7/1991) PL 109+6/13 FLC 11+1 FAC 14/2
Bury (Loaned on 5/3/1992) FL 12
Blackburn Rov (£3,200,000 on 26/3/1996) P/FL 213+12/14 FLC 10+3/1 FAC 12+1/4 Others 4/1

FLITNEY Ross Daniel
Born: Hitchin, 1 June 1984
Height: 6'1" **Weight:** 11.11
A third-year scholar at Fulham, Ross enjoyed two spells on loan in Brighton last season as cover for injuries to the club's regular goalkeepers. He made his senior debut against Chesterfield at Withdean in September and performed well in a 1-0 victory. A tall, wiry custodian, he returned to the south coast in December and made two more appearances between the posts, again playing brightly, especially in the defeat at Swindon when he came under considerable pressure. Ross subsequently returned to Fulham to continue his development.

Fulham (From trainee on 10/7/2003)
Brighton & Hove A (Loaned on 29/8/2003) FL 3

FLO Tore Andre
Born: Stryn, Norway, 15 June 1973
Height: 6'4" **Weight:** 13.8
Club Honours: FLC '98; ECWC '98; ESC '98; FAC '00; CS '00; SLC '02; SC '02
International Honours: Norway: 75; U21
Sunderland's record transfer signing made only one appearance last season, playing in an uncustomary midfield role at Mansfield in the Carling Cup, before joining Serie A side Siena for a nominal fee. At his best, Norwegian international Tore is a gifted striker with exceptional close control.
Chelsea (£300,000 from Brann Bergen, Norway, ex Sogndal, Tromso, on 4/8/1997) PL 59+53/34 FLC 7+2/3 FAC 5+5/1 Others 23+9/12
Glasgow R (£12,000,000 on 23/11/2000) SL 44+9/29 SLC 2+1/1 SC 5/4 Others 10+1/4
Sunderland (£6,750,000 on 30/8/2002) PL 23+6/4 FLC 2/2 FAC 1+1

FLOOD William (Willo) Robert
Born: Dublin, 10 April 1985
Height: 5'6" **Weight:** 9.11
International Honours: RoI: U21-4; Yth
This promising young midfielder made his debut for Manchester City in the UEFA Cup win at TNS when he acquitted himself well playing as a wing back. In March he temporarily joined Rochdale's bid to avoid Conference football and was thrust straight into the team. Willo displayed a fine touch in midfield as Dale matched several of the best sides in the Third Division before returning to City. He was voted as the Republic of Ireland's U19 'Player of the Year'.
Manchester C (From trainee on 13/4/2002) Others 1
Rochdale (Loaned on 15/3/2004) FL 6

FLYNN Michael (Mike) Anthony
Born: Oldham, 23 February 1969
Height: 6'0" **Weight:** 11.0
Club Honours: AMC '04
This powerful and determined defender won most things in the air for Blackpool in the 2003-04 season. He established an excellent partnership with Steve Elliott in the second half of the campaign and the pair helped the Seasiders to a 2-0 victory over Southend in the LDV Vans Trophy final at Cardiff's Millennium Stadium.
Oldham Ath (From apprentice on 7/2/1987) FL 37+3/1 FLC 1+1 FAC 1 Others 2
Norwich C (£100,000 on 22/12/1988)

Dave Flitcroft

Preston NE *(£125,000 on 4/12/1989) FL
134+2/7 FLC 6 FAC 6+1/1 Others 13*
Stockport Co *(£125,000 on 25/3/1993) FL
386+1/16 FLC 34/2 FAC 20/1 Others 19*
Stoke C *(Loaned on 12/1/2002) FL 11+2*
Barnsley *(Free on 15/3/2002) FL 20+1*
Blackpool *(Free on 10/1/2003) FL 50+1/1
FLC 1 FAC 2+1 Others 6+1*

FLYNN Michael John
Born: Newport, 17 October 1980
Height: 5'10" **Weight:** 12.10
Club Honours: Div 2 '03
International Honours: W: SP
This versatile performer mostly featured
from the substitutes' bench last term due
to the competition for first-team places
from several experienced players. A
youngster only in his second season with
Wigan Athletic, he was particularly
effective at supporting the forwards when
employed in the middle of the park. His
only League start was in the match
against Rotherham United, but when
called upon he never let the side down
with his willingness to work. Michael was
a regular member of the club's reserve
side that won promotion.
Wigan Ath *(£50,000 from Barry T, ex
Newport Co, on 25/6/2002) FL 4+21/1 FLC
0+4 FAC 0+2/1 Others 2*

FLYNN Sean Michael
Born: Birmingham, 13 March 1968
Height: 5'8" **Weight:** 11.8
Sean began the 2003-04 campaign as
club captain at Kidderminster, using his
years of experience to encourage and
cajole the younger players around him on
the pitch to greater things. However, a
loss of form cost him his place in the
team and he was released early in
September. Sean then signed for Evesham
United before ending the season with
Redditch.
Coventry C *(£20,000 from Halesowen T on
3/12/1991) F/PL 90+7/9 FLC 5/1 FAC 3*
Derby Co *(£250,000 on 11/8/1995) F/PL
39+20/3 FLC 3 FAC 3*
Stoke C *(Loaned on 27/3/1997) FL 5*
West Bromwich A *(£260,000 on 8/8/1997)
FL 99+10/8 FLC 11/1 FAC 0+2*
Tranmere Rov *(Free on 18/7/2000) FL
65+1/6 FLC 8/2 FAC 8/3*
Kidderminster Hrs *(Free on 8/8/2002) FL
49+2/2 FLC 2 FAC 1 Others 3*

FOFANA Aboubaka
Born: Paris, France, 4 October 1982
Height: 6'0" **Weight:** 12.4
A left-sided winger with great pace and
trickery, Aboubaka joined Millwall on a
12-month loan deal from Juventus. He

started the 2003-04 season in great form,
but after an injury at Christmas he had a
couple of months out and found it
difficult to get back in the side due to the
strength of the squad. He continued
playing in the reserves for whom he had
some excellent games.
Millwall *(Signed from Juventus, Italy on
22/8/2003) FL 9+7 FAC 0+1*

FOLAN Caleb Colman
Born: Leeds, 26 October 1982
Height: 6'1" **Weight:** 12.12
Caleb missed much of the 2003-04
season for Chesterfield with a broken leg,
a huge blow for the youngster. He had
just begun to realise his undoubted
promise, was learning from the more
experienced forwards around him and
had put in a fine performance at Queens
Park Rangers on the opening day. He
returned to the squad at the season's end:
with growing strength to add to his pace
he will emerge from the shadows in
2004-05.
Leeds U *(From trainee on 2/11/1999)*
Rushden & Diamonds *(Loaned on
5/10/2001) FL 1+5 Others 1*
Hull C *(Loaned on 30/11/2001) FL 0+1*
Chesterfield *(Free on 14/2/2003) FL 13+7/1*

FOLEY David John
Born: South Shields, 12 May 1987
Height: 5'4" **Weight:** 8.9
This first-year scholar produced some fine
early-season displays to earn an extremely
quick promotion to the Hartlepool first-
team squad last term. He was named as
one of the substitutes in the home game
against Port Vale in August, and on taking
to the field in the 82nd minute he
became the youngest-ever player to turn
out for the club, at 16 years and 105
days. This proved to be his only taste of
senior football, and he returned to the
U19s where he played the season.
Hartlepool U *(Trainee) FL 0+1*

FOLEY Kevin Patrick
Born: Luton, 1 November 1984
Height: 5'9" **Weight:** 11.2
International Honours: RoI: U21-1
This versatile Luton Town youngster can
play either at full back or in midfield. He
enjoyed a successful campaign during
2003-04, establishing himself as a regular
in the line-up and scoring his first-ever
senior goal against Port Vale in
September. Kevin was rewarded for his
efforts when he became the club's 'Young
Player of the Year' for the third
consecutive season and he won wider
recognition when called up for his debut

for the Republic of Ireland at U21 level.
Luton T *(From trainee on 8/3/2004) FL
32+3/1 FLC 2/2 FAC 3 Others 1+1*

FOLLY Yoann
Born: Togo, 6 June 1985
Height: 5'11" **Weight:** 11.0
International Honours: France: Yth
When Paul Sturrock arrived to manage at
St Mary's in March his first priority was to
invigorate a distinctly mediocre midfield.
His surprising solution was to promote
Yoann Folly from the reserves. It was
asking a lot of the teenager, but he
responded to the challenge with élan,
sitting in front of his defence, snuffing
out passes and knocking off short balls
that invariably found colleagues – in
short: keeping it simple. Yoann, whose
anticipation is remarkable in such a young
player, grew in confidence, and his
distribution, tackling and running
improved with every game. At the end of
the season he was called-up by France to
play in the prestigious U21 tournament in
Toulon.
Southampton *(£250,000 from St Etienne,
France on 31/7/2003) PL 9*

FORAN Richard (Richie)
Born: Dublin, 16 June 1980
Height: 6'1" **Weight:** 12.9
International Honours: RoI: U21-2
Last term proved to be very much the
proverbial season of two halves for Richie
at Carlisle at Brunton Park. He was a fairly
regular performer in the pre-Christmas
period and though he lacked support in
his striking role on occasions, his
commitment was never in doubt. A loan
spell at Oxford gave him the chance to
rejuvenate a career that was being
hindered by some off-the-pitch incidents.
He impressed the U's fans with some lively
performances and was unlucky not to
find the net. Richie made a surprise return
to the Carlisle side near the end of the
season, but was out of contract in the
summer and at the time of writing his
future was undecided.
Carlisle U *(£20,000 from Shelbourne on
31/8/2001) FL 84+7/25 FLC 1 FAC 6/2 Others
7+2/2*
Oxford U *(Loaned on 9/1/2004) FL 3+1*

FORBES Adrian Emmanuel
Born: Ealing, 23 January 1979
Height: 5'8" **Weight:** 11.10
International Honours: E: Yth
Adrian began the 2003-04 campaign out
of favour at Luton and it was not until
October that he really established himself
in the line-up again. Injuries let him in,

however, and he seized the opportunity, finding the net regularly. A highlight was his hat-trick in the FA Cup replay against Thurrock, and he registered doubles against Bradford City (also in the FA Cup) and Brentford. However, the talented winger was out of contract in the summer and was reported to have signed for Swansea City.

Norwich C (From trainee on 21/1/1997) FL 66+46/8 FLC 1+4 FAC 2+2

Luton T (£60,000 on 16/7/2001) FL 39+33/14 FLC 1 FAC 5/6 Others 0+1

FORBES Boniek Manuel Gomes
Born: Guinea Bissau, 30 September 1983
Height: 5'10" **Weight:** 11.0
This promising youngster made a few appearances as a late substitute for Leyton Orient last term and started just one game, in the LDV Vans Trophy defeat at Dagenham & Redbridge. An exciting left winger with pace and skill to match, Boniek was released before the end of the season and joined Ford United.

Leyton Orient (From trainee on 22/8/2003) FL 0+13 FAC 0+2 Others 1

FORBES Terrell Dishan
Born: Southwark, 17 August 1981
Height: 6'0" **Weight:** 12.8
Club Honours: FAYC '99
Terrell started the 2003-04 season as first choice at right back for Queens Park Rangers, but he suffered an ankle injury at Brighton early on and was out of action for several weeks. After recovering he was a regular choice in either of the right-sided defensive roles, however, he lost his place in March and did not return to the line-up. He was released at the end of the season.

West Ham U (From trainee on 2/7/1999)
Bournemouth (Loaned on 18/10/1999) FL 3 FAC 1
Queens Park R (Free on 24/7/2001) FL 111 FLC 5 FAC 3+1 Others 6

FORD Simon Gary
Born: Newham, 17 November 1981
Height: 6'0" **Weight:** 11.6
This young Grimsby Town central defender had high hopes of earning a permanent place in the back four and appeared to have established a promising partnership with Tony Crane at the beginning of the 2003-04 season. However, a hamstring problem proved to be the forerunner of a series of injuries and these severely limited his first-team opportunities. Simon was released by the Mariners in the summer.

Grimsby T (From trainee at Charlton Ath on 12/7/2001) FL 64+14/4 FLC 1+1 FAC 3 Others 1

FORLAN Diego
Born: Montevideo, Uruguay, 19 May 1979
Height: 5'8" **Weight:** 11.11
Club Honours: PL '03; CS '03
International Honours: Uruguay: 13
A gifted young striker with a good range of skills, Diego continued to show progress on the Old Trafford stage, despite his now limited role in the team. In the goal stakes he netted Premiership hits against Fulham, Portsmouth and Aston Villa (2) whilst in the Champions' League Panathinaikos and Glasgow Rangers felt the weight of his boot. Also scoring against Leeds in the Carling Cup, Diego's frustration when being substituted in United's Premiership match against Leicester in March suggested that his long-term future at Old Trafford might not extend into next season.

Terrell Forbes

Manchester U *(£7,500,000 from Independiente, Uruguay on 23/1/2002) PL 23+39/10 FLC 4+2/3 FAC 2+2/1 Others 8+15/3*

FORREST Daniel (Danny)
Paul Halafihi
Born: Keighley, 23 October 1984
Height: 5'10" **Weight:** 11.7
International Honours: E: Yth
Danny had a difficult second season at Bradford City last term, finding himself behind Dean Windass, Michael Branch and Danny Cadamarteri in the pecking order of strikers. Very popular with the fans, he started only two games in October but came off the bench as a substitute ten times. With Bryan Robson giving the youngsters a chance late on in the campaign, Danny found himself up front alongside Kevin Sanasy which renewed a strike partnership first formed at U10 level.
Bradford C (Trainee) FL 12+18/3 FLC 1

FORRESTER Jamie Mark
Born: Bradford, 1 November 1974
Height: 5'6" **Weight:** 11.0
Club Honours: FAYC '93
International Honours: E: Yth (UEFA-U18 '93); Sch
Despite largely being the back-up to Hull's regular strike partnership of Ben Burgess and Danny Allsopp, Jamie played a vital role in the Tigers rise from the Third Division last term. The experienced campaigner often came off the bench in the latter stages of tight games when his trickery and awareness in and around the penalty area would unlock tiring defences. After recovering from an ankle injury in October, hopes of an extended run were soon dashed when he fractured a cheekbone against Yeovil in November and he was ruled out for another month.
Leeds U (£60,000 from Auxerre, France on 20/10/1992) PL 7+2 FAC 1+1/2
Southend U (Loaned on 1/9/1994) FL 3+2
Grimsby T (Loaned on 10/3/1995) FL 7+2/1
Grimsby T (Signed on 17/10/1995) FL 27+14/6 FLC 0+1 FAC 3+1/3
Scunthorpe U (Signed on 21/3/1997) FL 99+2/37 FLC 6/1 FAC 7/4 Others 7 (Free to FC Utrecht, Holland on 1/6/1999)
Walsall (Loaned on 30/12/1999) FL 2+3
Northampton T (£150,000 on 21/3/2000) FL 109+12/45 FLC 5/1 FAC 7/2 Others 3/2
Hull C (Signed on 22/1/2003) FL 17+15/7 FAC 0+1 Others 1/1

FORSSELL Mikael Kaj
Born: Steinfurt, Germany, 15 March 1981
Height: 6'1" **Weight:** 12.8

International Honours: Finland: 29; U21-8; Yth
Birmingham City's 'Player of the Season' and 'Players' Player of the Season', Mikael's 17 Premiership goals made him the most prolific Blues striker at the highest level since Trevor Francis in 1977-78. He scored twice on his debut against Fulham in September after signing on loan from Chelsea and never looked back. Although he often didn't appear to be too involved in the build-up, he was devastating in and around the box. Not only could he finish, but he created his own chances by moving the ball from foot to foot quickly as he penetrated into the box, as shown by goals against Sunderland and Wolves. Mikael had briefly featured for Chelsea prior to his arrival at St Andrews, starting during the pre-season Asia Cup campaign and the Champions' League qualifier against MSK Zilinia.
Chelsea (Free from HJK Helsinki, Finland on 18/12/1998) PL 6+26/5 FLC 1+4/2 FAC 3+6/5 Others 2+3
Crystal Palace (Loaned on 23/2/2000) FL 44+8/16 FLC 8/2 FAC 1+1
Birmingham C (Loaned on 29/8/2003) PL 32/17 FLC 0+1 FAC 3+1/2

FORSTER Nicholas (Nicky)
Michael
Born: Caterham, 8 September 1973
Height: 5'10" **Weight:** 11.5
International Honours: E: U21-4
Nicky was back to his lively, goal-scoring best for Reading in the months leading up to Christmas, either as a lone striker in a 4-5-1 formation, or alongside new signing Shaun Goater when the team switched to 4-4-2. He had lost none of his pace, or his ability to finish clinically from the tightest of angles, and it was a huge blow to the club's hopes of a play-off place when he suffered a long-term stomach injury which kept him out of action for most of the second half of the season. His long-range volley in the 2-1 win at Sheffield United was voted Royals' 'Goal of the Season'.
Gillingham (Signed from Horley T on 22/5/1992) FL 54+13/24 FLC 3+2 FAC 6/2
Brentford (£100,000 on 17/6/1994) FL 108+1/39 FLC 11/3 FAC 8/1 Others 7+1/4
Birmingham C (£700,000 on 31/1/1997) FL 24+44/11 FLC 2+2/1 FAC 3+1
Reading (£650,000 on 23/6/1999) FL 130+27/53 FLC 10/4 FAC 4+1 Others 5+4/2

FORSYTH Richard Michael
Born: Dudley, 3 October 1970
Height: 5'11" **Weight:** 13.0
Club Honours: GMVC '94

International Honours: E: SP-3
Richard played an important role for Cheltenham Town in the opening games of the 2003-04 season. His touch, vision and passing ability gave the experienced midfielder time on the ball amidst the hustle and bustle of Division Three. He scored twice from the penalty spot in the 4-3 win over Northampton in September but was forced out of the side with a hamstring injury in mid-season. The arrival of loan signing Karl Henry pushed Richard onto the substitutes' bench and he was unable to regain a regular starting place.
Birmingham C (£50,000 from Kidderminster Hrs on 13/7/1995) FL 12+14/2 FLC 7+2 FAC 2 Others 3+1
Stoke C (£200,000 on 25/7/1996) FL 90+5/17 FLC 7/1 FAC 4 Others 1+1
Blackpool (Free on 5/7/1999) FL 10+3 FAC 0+2 Others 0+1
Peterborough U (Free on 14/7/2000) FL 61+9/2 FLC 4/1 FAC 9/1 Others 1+1
Cheltenham T (£15,000 on 11/10/2002) FL 28+11/4 FAC 4+1 Others 2/1

FORTE Jonathan Ronald James
Born: Sheffield, 25 July 1986
Height: 6'2" **Weight:** 12.2
International Honours: E: Yth
After performing well in Sheffield United's reserves, this youngster made his first-team debut as a substitute in the FA Cup tie against Nottingham Forest. Playing on the left he showed the confidence to take on defenders, his height and pace causing problems for the opposition. A regular for England U18 and voted the supporters' 'Young Player of the Year', he will be hoping to feature regularly for the Blades in 2004-05.
Sheffield U (Trainee) FL 1+6 FAC 0+1

FORTUNE Clayton Alexander
Born: Forest Gate, 10 November 1982
Height: 6'3" **Weight:** 13.10
This young Bristol City defender did well when coming on as a substitute in a couple of games last season, but his only start came at Tranmere in March. Clayton will be looking to make further progress in the 2004-05 when he will be seeking to win a regular place in the squad.
Bristol C (From trainee at Tottenham H on 22/3/2001) FL 8+9 FLC 0+1 Others 2+2

FORTUNE Jonathan (Jon) Jay
Born: Islington, 23 August 1980
Height: 6'2" **Weight:** 11.4
Jon was unlucky to be in and out of the Charlton side during the season, despite looking on a par with any of his competitors in the squad. He has become

Jon Fortune (right)

an accomplished central defender coping adequately with the Premiership's best strikers. Quick and good in the air, Jon is strong and is a formidable opponent. He started the season as first choice alongside Mark Fish, but lost his place when Chris Perry was signed from Spurs. As a former striker he likes to get into the opposing penalty area for corners, and scored in the away win at Portsmouth and the home draw with Leicester City. Jon possesses a powerful shot in addition to his aerial ability.

Charlton Ath (From trainee on 2/7/1998) PL 57+16/3 FLC 4+1/1 FAC 4+1
Mansfield T (Loaned on 18/2/2000) FL 4
Mansfield T (Loaned on 31/8/2000) FL 14

FORTUNE Quinton

Born: Cape Town, South Africa, 21 May 1977
Height: 5'11" **Weight:** 11.11
Club Honours: CS '03
International Honours: South Africa: 43; U23-18
A top-class forward or midfielder with pace and good ball skills to match, Quinton enjoyed an extended run in the Manchester United first team from August to December, and kicked off United's Champions' League campaign with a goal against Panathinaikos. Indeed, he only missed one European outing against Stuttgart in October, which coincided with United's solitary defeat in the group stages. Lauded by Sir Alex Ferguson as one of the Reds most versatile players, Quinton's season was once again blighted by injuries, particularly when he was showing real consistency. Despite his season terminating in early March, at least he was rewarded with a new contract.

Manchester U (£1,500,000 from Atletico Madrid, Spain on 27/8/1999) PL 41+18/5 FLC 4 FAC 3 Others 15+12/4

FORTUNE-WEST Leopold (Leo) Paul Osborne

Born: Stratford, 9 April 1971
Height: 6'3" **Weight:** 13.10
Club Honours: Div 3 '04
This experienced striker joined Doncaster Rovers in the summer of 2003 and went on to become a member of a promotion-winning side for the fifth time in his career as he helped Rovers to win the Third Division title. Leo started last term in fine form, netting twice on his debut for the club against Leyton Orient, and went on to finish the campaign in double figures. A highlight of his season

was netting a hat-trick in the return game against Orient at Belle Vue in January.

Gillingham (£5,000 from Stevenage Borough on 12/7/1995) FL 48+19/18 FLC 3+1/2 FAC 3+1/2
Leyton Orient (Loaned on 27/3/1997) FL 1+4
Lincoln C (Free on 6/7/1998) FL 7+2/1 FLC 2
Rotherham U (Loaned on 8/10/1998) FL 5/4
Brentford (£60,000 on 17/11/1998) FL 2+9 FAC 0+1 Others 2+1/1
Rotherham U (£35,000 on 26/2/1999) FL 59/26 FLC 4 FAC 2 Others 2
Cardiff C (£300,000 on 11/9/2000) FL 53+39/23 FLC 2+1 FAC 7+6/3 Others 5/2
Doncaster Rov (Free on 24/7/2003) FL 28+11/11 FLC 2/1 FAC 1 Others 0+1

FOSTER James Ian

Born: Liverpool, 11 November 1976
Height: 5'7" **Weight:** 11.0
Club Honours: NC '00
International Honours: E: SP-1; Sch
Ian began last term with Conference outfit Chester City, but early in the new year he returned to his former club Kidderminster Harriers on loan in an attempt to bolster the strike force. He showed he had lost none of his pace and ability to take on opposition defenders and once more became a favourite with the Aggborough faithful, scoring three times before returning to Chester.

Hereford U (Free from Liverpool juniors on 15/7/1996) FL 4+15 FLC 2+1 Others 0+1
(Free to Barrow during 1998 close season)
Kidderminster Hrs (Free on 13/8/1999) FL 37+35/11 FLC 3 FAC 3+1 Others 4+2 (Freed during 2003 close season)
Kidderminster Hrs (Loaned from Chester C on 10/2/2004) FL 10+1/3

FOSTER Stephen (Steve)

Born: Mansfield, 3 December 1974
Height: 6'1" **Weight:** 12.0
Club Honours: FAT '97; Div 3 '04
Steve was appointed as captain of Doncaster Rovers at the start of last term and went on to become a key figure in the team as they went on to win the Third Division title. An experienced centre back, he led the team superbly and was as solid as a rock in the centre of a defence that had the best record in the Football League. Tremendous in the air and effective in the tackle, very few opponents got the better of him during the season.

Mansfield T (From trainee on 15/7/1993) FL 2+3 FLC 2 (Free to Telford on 22/1/1994)

Bristol Rov (£150,000 from Woking on 23/5/1997) FL 193+4/7 FLC 14 FAC 13 Others 11
Doncaster Rov (Free on 1/8/2002) FL 44/1 FLC 2 Others 1

FOSTER Stephen (Steve) John

Born: Warrington, 10 September 1980
Height: 5'11" **Weight:** 11.8
International Honours: E: Sch
Steve is now a well-established member of the Crewe Alexandra first team and is normally to be found in the heart of the defence. The only game he missed last season was the away fixture at Sunderland. Steve is one of the players who have continued to make steady progress since promotion from the youth side and he is acknowledged to be quite a danger from set pieces.

Crewe Alex (From trainee on 19/9/1998) FL 130+15/11 FLC 6+1/1 FAC 9+1/1 Others 4

FOTIADIS Panos (Andy) Andrew

Born: Hitchin, 6 September 1977
Height: 5'11" **Weight:** 11.7
International Honours: E: Sch
Andy had a somewhat disappointing season for Peterborough last term when injury and a dip in form saw him restricted to substitute appearances. In March he was loaned out to Heybridge Swifts, but suffered a serious knee injury, which seems likely to keep him out of action until December 2004.

Luton T (From juniors on 26/7/1996) FL 50+73/18 FLC 3+6/1 FAC 5+2/1 Others 4+3
Peterborough U (Free on 7/2/2003) FL 6+13/2 Others 0+2

FOWLER Jason Kenneth George

Born: Bristol, 20 August 1974
Height: 6'3" **Weight:** 11.12
With Matt Hockley adding muscle to the centre of the park, Jason was forced to play in a wide-midfield position for Torquay last season, usually operating on the right-hand side. Although this reduced his ability to dictate the pace of games, he used the space intelligently and created chances with his skill and awareness. Continuing hip problems affected Jason's ability to play 90 minutes regularly, and led to his spending much of the promotion run-in on the bench.

Bristol C (From trainee on 8/7/1993) FL 16+9 FLC 1+1 Others 1+1
Cardiff C (Signed on 19/6/1996) FL 138+7/14 FLC 8/1 FAC 12+2/4 Others 3/1
Torquay U (Free on 30/11/2001) FL 78+7/7 FLC 2 FAC 3/1 Others 1+1

147

FOWLER Lee Anthony
Born: Cardiff, 10 June 1983
Height: 5'7" **Weight:** 10.8
International Honours: W: U21-4; Yth
Lee impressed for Huddersfield during the pre-season and initially arrived at the McAlpine Stadium in a three-month loan deal. A solid playmaker operating in the centre of midfield he never shirked a tackle, and his strong running and accurate distribution made him a key figure in the team. However, an accumulation of disciplinary points coupled with hernia and ankle problems blighted the latter part of his campaign. Lee featured as a substitute in the play-off final against Mansfield Town and scored the decisive penalty to send the Terriers up from the Third Division.
Coventry C (From trainee on 7/7/2000) FL 6+8 FAC 1+1/1
Huddersfield T (Signed on 11/8/2003) FL 27+2 FLC 3 Others 0+1

FOWLER Robert (Robbie)
Bernard
Born: Liverpool, 9 April 1975
Height: 5'11" **Weight:** 11.10
Club Honours: FLC '95, '01; FAC '01; UEFAC '01; ESC '01
International Honours: E: 26; B-1; U21-8; Yth (UEFA-U18 '93)
After a slow start to life at Manchester City, when injuries and a lack of goals stalled his career, Robbie began to hit top gear last season. Much to the delight of the Blues' supporters he began hitting the net and scored a total of ten goals in all competitions. Hard work and endeavour were spiced with creativity and this helped him win over a demanding public who understandably expected an instant return from him following his big-money transfer from Leeds United.
Liverpool (From trainee on 23/4/1992) P/FL 210+26/120 FLC 32/27 FAC 21+3/12 Others 26+12/11
Leeds U (£11,000,000 on 30/11/2001) PL 24+6/14 FAC 1+1 Others 0+1
Manchester C (£3,000,000 + on 30/1/2003) PL 35+9/9 FLC 2/1 FAC 4/1 Others 4/1

FOX Christian
Born: Stonehaven, 11 April 1981
Height: 5'10" **Weight:** 11.5
Christian had another frustrating season at York last term. He was injured in the opening game at Carlisle and only managed one other start, in the away defeat at Bury in September. The talented midfielder was subsequently released by the Minstermen at the end of the campaign.

York C (From trainee on 29/6/1999) FL 44+26/1 FLC 1 FAC 3 Others 3

FOXE Hayden
Born: Australia, 23 June 1977
Height: 6'4" **Weight:** 13.5
Club Honours: Div 1 '03
International Honours: Australia: 11; U23; Yth
Hayden started the 2003-04 season in good form for Pompey, but jittered in and out of the side in defence into the middle of the campaign, finding strong competition from Boris Zivkovic for his place in the side. A stress fracture to his foot finally took him out of the first team and he was not due to return to action until September 2004.
West Ham U (Free from Sanfrecce Hiroshima, Japan, ex Ajax, Arminia Bielefeld, on 14/3/2001) PL 7+4 FAC 0+1
Portsmouth (£400,000 on 6/6/2002) P/FL 38+4/2 FLC 2+1 FAC 1

FRAMPTON Andrew (Andy)
James Kerr
Born: Wimbledon, 3 September 1979
Height: 5'11" **Weight:** 10.10
Last term proved to be another frustrating season for this Brentford left back who was unable to displace Matt Somner and then Ronnie Bull in the side. Andy suffered a bad head injury in the Carling Cup tie at West Bromwich Albion early on and was out of action for several weeks. Most of his first-team appearances came when he deputised at centre back, although he was also a regular on the bench. Andy scored his first senior goal in the FA Cup tie against Gainsborough Trinity.
Crystal Palace (From trainee on 8/5/1998) FL 19+9 FLC 3+1 FAC 1
Brentford (Free on 28/10/2002) FL 19+12 FLC 1 FAC 4/1 Others 5

FRANCE Ryan
Born: Sheffield, 13 December 1980
Height: 5'11" **Weight:** 11.11
After starting the 2003-04 season with Unibond League club Alfreton, Ryan was snapped up by Hull City and went on to make a dream debut, scoring after only eight minutes when coming off the bench in the 6-1 demolition of Kidderminster. He had already had trials at several clubs before completing a sports science degree and signing a long-term contract with the Tigers. Ryan was mostly used as the deputy to Jason Price on the right wing last term.
Hull C (£15,000 from Alfreton T on 24/9/2003) FL 7+21/2 Others 2/1

FRANCIS Damien Jerome
Born: Wandsworth, 27 February 1979
Height: 6'1" **Weight:** 11.2
Club Honours: Div 1 '04
International Honours: Jamaica: 1
A close-season capture from Wimbledon, Damien's contribution to the Norwich City cause last season was immense. An attack-minded central midfielder who works hard to break up opposition moves, he is also effective at getting forward himself into goal-scoring positions and netted decisive goals against Sunderland and at Gillingham.
Wimbledon (From trainee on 6/3/1997) P/FL 80+17/15 FLC 7+4 FAC 9
Norwich C (Signed on 23/7/2003) FL 39+2/7 FLC 1 FAC 1

FRANCIS Simon Charles
Born: Nottingham, 16 February 1985
Height: 6'0" **Weight:** 12.6
International Honours: E: Yth
Commanding, quick and comfortable on the ball, Simon can play as a right-sided centre half, right back or in midfield. He featured regularly at right back for Bradford City last term and his powerful surges out of defence regularly lifted the Bantams' fans. His stylish performances attracted the interest of several clubs and when Bradford went into administration he opted for a move to Sheffield United. Simon made an immediate impression at Bramall Lane, playing either as a right wing back or in midfield, looking strong in the tackle and positive coming forward.
Bradford C (From trainee on 3/5/2003) FL 49+6/1 FLC 1 FAC 1
Sheffield U (Signed on 16/3/2004) FL 4+1

FRANCIS Willis David
Born: Nottingham, 26 July 1985
Height: 5'5" **Weight:** 10.10
A third-year scholar with Notts County, this speedy right-sided midfield player failed to make much of an impact at first-team level last term, managing just a handful of outings from the substitutes' bench. Early in the new year he had a spell on loan with Grantham Town and when he was released by the Magpies he signed a 12-month contract with the Lincolnshire club.
Notts Co (Trainee) FL 2+11

FRANDSEN Per
Born: Copenhagen, Denmark, 6 February 1970
Height: 6'1" **Weight:** 12.6
Club Honours: Div 1 '97

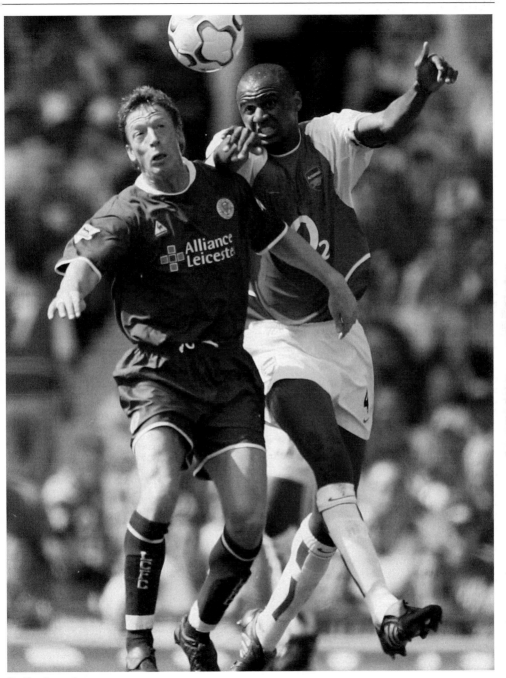

Steffen Freund

International Honours: Denmark: 23; U21; Yth
In a season when competition for midfield places was tight, Per figured frequently at the heart of the Bolton side during the 2003-04 campaign. An industrious and tenacious member of the team, as well as a phenomenal striker of the ball, Per scored just one Premiership goal last term, a header in the 2-0 home victory against Everton. In what proved to be an emotional final game of the season, Per was awarded the captain's armband against Fulham; a fitting reward for a loyal servant who will be seeking pastures new in the summer having been released by the club at the end of the season.
Bolton W (£1,250,000 from FC Copenhagen, Denmark, ex Lille, on 7/8/1996) F/PL 129+1/17 FLC 15+1/4 FAC 4+1 Others 3/1
Blackburn Rov (£1,750,000 + on 22/9/1999) FL 26+5/5 FAC 4/1
Bolton W (£1,600,000 on 24/7/2000) P/FL 116+19/13 FLC 5+1 FAC 3+3 Others 2+1/1

FRECKLINGTON Lee Craig
Born: Lincoln, 8 September 1985
Height: 5'8" **Weight:** 11.0
This promising teenager had his first taste of senior football when Lincoln included him in their starting line-up for their LDV Vans Trophy clash with Telford United. Lee gave an excellent performance in the centre of midfield. He was always keen to push foward and went close to marking his debut with a goal. His only other appearance was as a substitute in the LDV second round tie with Chesterfield.
Lincoln C (Trainee) Others 1+1

FREEDMAN Douglas (Dougie) Alan
Born: Glasgow, 21 January 1974
Height: 5'9" **Weight:** 11.2
International Honours: S: 2; B-1; U21-8; Sch
Dougie started out last term in fine form for Crystal Palace, netting a hat-trick at Burnley on the opening day. The popular striker found the net regularly throughout the campaign, and despite spending much of the period after Christmas on the substitutes' bench he finished with a respectable tally of 15 goals in all competitions. Dougie netted Palace's 'Goal of the Season' with a tremendous volley against Sunderland in April.
Queens Park R (From trainee on 15/5/1992)
Barnet (Free on 26/7/1994) FL 47/27 FLC 6/5 FAC 2 Others 2

Crystal Palace (£800,000 on 8/9/1995) F/PL 72+18/31 FLC 3+2/1 FAC 2+1 Others 3+2/2
Wolverhampton W (£800,000 on 17/10/1997) FL 25+4/10 FAC 5+1/2
Nottingham F (£950,000 on 12/8/1998) P/FL 50+20/18 FLC 8+1/4 FAC 3+1/1
Crystal Palace (£600,000 on 23/10/2000) FL 97+33/53 FLC 8/5 FAC 1+4 Others 0+1

FREESTONE Roger
Born: Newport, 19 August 1968
Height: 6'3" **Weight:** 14.6
Club Honours: Div 2 '89; Div 3 '00; AMC '94
International Honours: W: 1; U21-1; Yth; Sch
For the first time since arriving at the Vetch Field, this experienced shot-stopper failed to start the campaign as first-choice 'keeper for Swansea, following the close-season signing of Brian Murphy. By the end of August, however, 'Dodger' had reclaimed the number one jersey, soon showing his experience in goal with no sign of the back problems that he had experienced in recent seasons. Although briefly dropped once more, he was soon recalled to first-team action following a change of management at the club.
Newport Co (From trainee on 2/4/1986) FL 13 Others 1
Chelsea (£95,000 on 10/3/1987) FL 42 FLC 2 FAC 3 Others 6
Swansea C (Loaned on 29/9/1989) FL 14 Others 1
Hereford U (Loaned on 9/3/1990) FL 8
Swansea C (£45,000 on 5/9/1991) FL 549+3/3 FLC 28 FAC 35 Others 39

FREUND Steffen
Born: Brandenburg, Germany, 19 January 1970
Height: 5'11" **Weight:** 11.6
Club Honours: FLC '99
International Honours: Germany: 21; U21; Yth
Snapped up on a free transfer by Micky Adams in January 2004 after a public falling out with the staff at his Bundesliga club, Steffen soon won over the Leicester fans with his wholehearted commitment to the Foxes' cause. His long throw was often a source of danger, although his rare appearances on the goal-scoring chart were confined to friendly fixtures. Even so, Steffen was released by the club at the end of the season after relegation was confirmed.
Tottenham H (£750,000 from Borussia Dortmund, Germany, ex Motor Sud, Stahl Brandenburg, Schalke 04, on 29/12/1998) PL

92+10 FLC 14 FAC 11 Others 4 (Free to Kaiserslautern, Germany during 2003 close season)
Leicester C (Loaned on 31/1/2004) PL 13+1

FRIEDEL Bradley (Brad) Howard
Born: Lakewood, USA, 18 May 1971
Height: 6'3" **Weight:** 14.7
Club Honours: FLC '02
International Honours: USA: 82
Brad was a near ever-present for Blackburn last term, but his performances never quite matched his heroics of the previous season. His personal highlight was the last-minute goal he scored at Charlton when he struck home Paul Gallagher's cross following a corner, though the celebrations were quickly silenced as he failed to stop Charlton's winner a minute later. Hints at his value in desperate situations had come earlier when he caused such confusion going for a corner in the last minute against Middlesbrough that Markus Babbel was able to head the equaliser. Overall, however, he coped well and did his best behind a sometimes disorganised defence.
Liverpool (£1,000,000 from Columbus Crew, USA on 23/12/1997) PL 25 FLC 4 Others 1+1
Blackburn Rov (Free on 7/11/2000) P/FL 136/1 FLC 10 FAC 13 Others 6

FRIIO David
Born: Thionville, France, 17 February 1973
Height: 6'0" **Weight:** 11.7
Club Honours: Div 3 '02; Div 2 '04
David enjoyed another great season at Plymouth in 2003-04, finishing the campaign as the club's leading scorer with 15 goals from a central-midfield position. A player who is always comfortable with the ball, he is capable of spreading passes all over the pitch. His trademark runs into the opposition penalty area resulted in many of his goals. However, two that stand out were the 'Goal of the Season' at Port Vale in October, a 30-yard shot that curled into the roof of the net, and the second goal against Queens Park Rangers in April that clinched the Second Division title for the Pilgrims. David was also selected for the PFA Division Two team of the year.
Plymouth Arg (Free from ASOA Valence, France, ex Epinal, Nimes, on 30/11/2000) FL 135+4/33 FLC 1+2 FAC 8+1/4 Others 4/1

FRY Russell Harok
Born: Hull, 4 December 1985
Height: 6'2" **Weight:** 12.1

David Friio

This very promising Hull City youngster added another LDV Vans Trophy substitute appearance to his name last term. The talented midfielder came on for Ryan France after 31 minutes of the Humber 'derby' defeat by Scunthorpe at the KC Stadium in November.
Hull C *(From trainee on 16/12/2002) Others 0+2*

FRYATT Matthew (Matty) Charles
Born: Nuneaton, 5 March 1986
Height: 5'10" **Weight:** 11.0
This talented young Walsall striker made his senior debut in the Carling Cup tie at Bolton last September and was later sent out on loan to Carlisle to gain experience of senior football. Matty became one of the youngest goal-scorers in the club's history when he netted the winner against Boston in January. His combination of skill and enthusiasm made him a crowd favourite and the experience gained in his two months at Brunton Park proved time well spent. On his return to the Midlands he was introduced to the Saddlers team more often in the closing stages of the campaign and scored his first senior goal in the 2-1 win at Preston in March.
Walsall *(From trainee on 28/4/2003) FL 4+7/1 FLC 0+1*
Carlisle U *(Loaned on 18/12/2003) FL 9+1/1*

FULLARTON James (Jamie)
Born: Glasgow, 20 July 1974
Height: 5'10" **Weight:** 10.6
International Honours: S: U21-17
After joining Southend during the 2003 close season, Jamie was unable to show his tough-tackling, combative style to the Roots Hall faithful in more than fleeting bursts as first a thigh problem and then a severe groin injury meant he only started seven Third Division games. He was released in March and joined Chesterfield soon afterwards, but played only around 15 minutes in one match before missing the rest of the campaign with further injuries. In that short time he looked composed and determined, but nevertheless he was released in the summer.
St Mirren *(Free from Motherwell BC on 13/6/1991) SL 93+9/3 SLC 2 SC 4 Others 4+1 (Transferred to Bastia, France during 1996 close season)*
Crystal Palace *(Free on 7/8/1997) P/FL 40+7/1 FLC 2+1 FAC 3 Others 1*
Bolton W *(Loaned on 25/3/1999) FL 1*

Dundee U *(Free on 11/10/2000) SL 14+2 SLC 1 SC 3*
Brentford *(Free on 9/8/2002) FL 22+5/1 FLC 2 FAC 1 Others 2*
Southend U *(Free on 23/7/2003) FL 7 Others 1*
Chesterfield *(Free on 23/3/2004) FL 0+1*

FULLER Ashley John
Born: Bedford, 14 November 1986
Height: 5'9" **Weight:** 10.10
Ashley was one of several youngsters introduced to League football at Cambridge United last term. A promising midfielder who had developed through the club's youth system, he made his senior debut when coming off the bench in the last minute of the home game against York City on Good Friday.
Cambridge U *(Trainee) FL 0+1*

FULLER Ricardo Dwayne
Born: Kingston, Jamaica, 31 October 1979
Height: 6'3" **Weight:** 13.3
International Honours: Jamaica
Ricardo had very much a season of two halves for Preston in 2003-04. Returning from a serious knee injury, the striker scored nine goals in his first 16 games. The highlight of his campaign was undoubtedly his hat-trick against Burnley, in which he demonstrated all his strengths – powerful heading ability, speed and trickery on the deck and the ability to finish clinically. However, speculation over a possible transfer seemed to unsettle him and he only scored three further goals in the second half of the season.
Crystal Palace *(£1,000,000 from Tivoli Gardens, Jamaica on 19/2/2001) FL 2+6*
Heart of Midlothian *(Loaned on 19/10/2001) SL 27/8 SC 2/2*
Preston NE *(£500,000 on 1/7/2002) FL 55+1/26 FLC 2+1/2 FAC 2/2*

FURLONG Paul Anthony
Born: Wood Green, 1 October 1968
Height: 6'0" **Weight:** 13.8
Club Honours: FAT '88
International Honours: E: SP-5
This experienced striker started last season as the regular partner for Kevin Gallen in the Queens Park Rangers attack. He played around a dozen games before missing out through injury and it was not until March that he returned to the side. Paul found the net regularly throughout the campaign and finished as the club's second-top scorer with 16 goals.

Coventry C *(£130,000 from Enfield on 31/7/1991) FL 27+10/4 FLC 4/1 FAC 1+1 Others 1*
Watford *(£250,000 on 24/7/1992) FL 79/37 FLC 7/4 FAC 2 Others 3*
Chelsea *(£2,300,000 on 26/5/1994) PL 44+20/13 FLC 3+1 FAC 5+5/1 Others 7/3*
Birmingham C *(£1,500,000 on 17/7/1996) FL 104+27/50 FLC 11+2/3 FAC 5/3 Others 4*
Queens Park R *(Loaned on 18/8/2000) FL 3/1*
Sheffield U *(Loaned on 8/2/2002) FL 4/2*
Queens Park R *(Free on 8/8/2002) FL 58+11/29 FLC 2 FAC 1 Others 4+1/1*

FUTCHER Benjamin (Ben) Paul
Born: Manchester, 20 February 1981
Height: 6'4" **Weight:** 12.4
This giant Lincoln defender continued to improve last season, with his form attracting the attention of a number of higher division clubs. His tackling and blocking were important parts of his game and supported his skill in the air. Ben was pushed forward at set-piece situations with his height causing problems for opponents. He captained the team in the absence of regular skipper Paul Morgan. At the end of the season Paul's request for a transfer was granted by the Lincoln board of directors. Ben is the son of the former Luton and Barnsley player Paul Futcher.
Oldham Ath *(From trainee on 5/7/1999) FL 2+8 FAC 0+1 (Free to Stalybridge Celtic on 3/1/2000)*
Lincoln C *(Free from Doncaster Rov on 7/8/2002) FL 84+2/10 FLC 1 FAC 3/1 Others 10/2*

FYFE Graham
Born: Dundee, 7 December 1982
Height: 5'6" **Weight:** 10.6
This diminutive left-sided midfielder or defender began the 2003-04 season with some swashbuckling performances as Cheltenham Town pulled off a string of high-scoring results. Graham lost his place following a 3-1 defeat at Boston in October and took some time to win over new boss John Ward, but eventually returned to the squad for the last two months of the campaign. Some efficient performances on the left-hand side of midfield and at left wing back led to the offer of a new contract at the season's end.
Glasgow Celtic *(From juniors on 13/7/1999)*
Raith Rov *(Free on 1/1/2003) SL 8+2/1*
Cheltenham T *(Free on 7/8/2003) FL 15+5 FLC 1 Others 1*

G

GAARDSOE Thomas

Born: Randers, Denmark, 23 November 1979
Height: 6'2" **Weight:** 12.8
International Honours: Denmark: 1; U23-10

Thomas produced some sterling displays at the heart of the West Bromwich Albion defence last season and was instrumental in helping the Baggies regain their Premiership status. He didn't miss a match following his debut in the second game of the season against Brentford in the Carling Cup and he contributed four goals, two of them vital late winners against promotion-chasing rivals Sheffield United and Wigan Athletic. Skilful and confident with the ability to keep clam under pressure, he made his international debut when Denmark beat England 3-2 at Old Trafford in November 2003. Thomas was named as Albion's 'Player of the Year' for 2004.
Ipswich T (£1,300,000 from AAB Aalborg on 31/8/2001) P/FL 40+1/5 FLC 2+1/1 FAC 1/1 Others 2+2
West Bromwich A (£520,000 on 5/8/2003) FL 45/4 FLC 5 FAC 1

GABBIADINI Marco

Born: Nottingham, 20 January 1968
Height: 5'10" **Weight:** 13.4
Club Honours: Div 3 '88
International Honours: E: B-1; U21-2

Marco was a surprise close-season signing for Hartlepool but the veteran striker was a regular scorer in the early weeks of the new campaign. Most memorable was a great goal at Stockport when he took the ball past several defenders to set up a fine away win. However, he then suffered a bad knee injury, and shortly after missing out on the club's big FA Cup game at Sunderland, he was forced to announce his retirement from the game.
York C (From apprentice on 5/9/1985) FL 42+18/14 FLC 4+3/1 Others 4/3
Sunderland (£80,000 on 23/9/1987) FL 155+2/74 FLC 14/9 FAC 5 Others 9/4
Crystal Palace (£1,800,000 on 1/10/1991) FL 15/5 FLC 6/1 FAC 1 Others 3/1
Derby Co (£1,000,000 on 31/1/1992) F/PL 163+25/50 FLC 13/7 FAC 8+1/3 Others 16+1/8 (Free to Panionios, Greece during 1997 close season)
Birmingham C (Loaned on 14/10/1996) FL 0+2
Oxford U (Loaned on 31/1/1997) FL 5/1
Stoke C (Free on 24/12/1997) FL 2+6 FAC 1/1

York C (Free on 20/2/1998) FL 5+2/1
Darlington (Free on 8/7/1998) FL 81+1/47 FLC 4/1 FAC 4/1 Others 5/3
Northampton T (Free on 28/6/2000) FL 97+23/25 FLC 4/1 FAC 6+1/3 Others 4+1/1
Hartlepool U (Free on 14/7/2003) FL 9+6/5 FLC 1 FAC 1/2 Others 1

GABBIDON Daniel (Danny) Leon

Born: Cwmbran, 8 August 1979
Height: 6'1" **Weight:** 11.2
International Honours: W: 12; U21-17; Yth

Danny put his back problems of the previous season firmly behind him last term and finished the campaign at his best. He came through a dip in form following Wales' exit from the Euro 2004 championships, but remained a solid figure in the Cardiff City back line, forging an excellent central defensive partnership with young James Collins in the closing stages of the campaign. Danny is pacy, composed on the ball and has the skill to succeed at a higher level. He won several more caps for his country and was selected for the PFA First Division team of the season.
West Bromwich A (From trainee on 3/7/1998) FL 20 FLC 4+1 FAC 2
Cardiff C (£175,000 + on 10/8/2000) FL 149+3/9 FLC 6 FAC 9 Others 3

GADSBY Matthew (Matt) John

Born: Sutton Coldfield, 6 September 1979
Height: 6'1" **Weight:** 11.12

Manager Ian Britton signed Matt for Kidderminster during the 2003 close season with the intention of using him as a central defender. However, circumstances led to his being used in a variety of positions in midfield and defence but rarely in the role that had been earmarked for him. Versatile and dependable, Matt found the net twice but was one of several players released by Harriers at the end of the season.
Walsall (From trainee on 12/2/1998) FL 23+14 FLC 2 FAC 0+1 Others 2+5
Mansfield T (Free on 8/11/2002) FL 13+7 FAC 2
Kidderminster Hrs (Free on 7/7/2003) FL 23+9/2 FAC 2+1 Others 1

GAIN Peter Thomas

Born: Hammersmith, 11 November 1976
Height: 6'1" **Weight:** 11.0
International Honours: RoI: U21-1; Yth

This skilful midfield player completed his 200th senior appearance for Lincoln City in a season when the Imps again reached the play-offs. Although a naturally left-

sided player Peter was used in a slightly different role as a central-midfield man in a 3-4-3 system. He contributed seven goals during the campaign including a spell of three in four games in February.
Tottenham H (From trainee on 1/7/1995)
Lincoln C (Loaned on 31/12/1998) FL 0+1 Others 1
Lincoln C (£15,000 on 26/3/1999) FL 159+27/21 FLC 5+1 FAC 9+1/1 Others 10+2

GALL Kevin Alexander

Born: Merthyr Tydfil, 4 February 1982
Height: 5'9" **Weight:** 11.1
International Honours: W: U21-8; Yth; Sch

Kevin started last season with a flurry of goals for new boys Yeovil, including two at Rochdale in the club's first-ever Football League match. The young striker's pace proved to be a wonderful attribute together with his never-say-die attitude. A regular in the line-up throughout the campaign, the supply of goals dried up in the new year, but he still managed a double-figure tally.
Newcastle U (From trainee on 29/4/1999)
Bristol Rov (Free on 22/3/2001) FL 28+22/5 FLC 2 FAC 2+2 Others 2+2
Yeovil T (Free on 4/2/2003) FL 39+4/8 FLC 1 FAC 3/1 Others 2/1

GALLAGHER Paul

Born: Glasgow, 9 August 1984
Height: 6'1" **Weight:** 12.0
International Honours: S: 1; B-1; U21-4

This youngster proved to be the surprise package of the season for Blackburn last term, demonstrating a maturity beyond his years and an eye for an opportunity. He is perhaps the most dangerous crosser of a ball at the club, spots an opportunity early and is always willing to try the unexpected. Capped for Scotland he received fewer chances because of the gravity of the club's situation, but proved himself an opportunist, never more so than at Newcastle when his hustle produced the goal that brought the club a great win.
Blackburn Rov (From trainee on 5/2/2003) PL 12+15/3 FLC 0+1 FAC 1

GALLAS William

Born: Paris, France, 17 August 1977
Height: 6'1" **Weight:** 12.7
International Honours: France: 20; U21

Prior to the Abramovich takeover in June 2003, Premiership rivals and La Liga giants alike tracked William Gallas, anxious to lure away this excellent young centre back. The new regime nipped any transfer move in the bud and offered William a

contract extension which ties him to the club on a long-term basis. His partnership with John Terry has matured into one of the best in the game and alongside his mentor, the great Marcel Desailly, William became an automatic choice at international level for France. William is fast, powerful, good in the air and versatile – having played a few games at right back towards the end of the season. He also scores vital goals – the most recent being the winner in Prague against Sparta in a very difficult Champions' League tie. In the past 12 months every facet of the Chelsea side has undergone radical change except for the Gallas-Terry central defensive pairing, bearing out the old adage: "If it ain't broke, don't fix it!"
Chelsea *(£6,200,000 from Marseilles, France, ex SM Caen, on 4/7/2001) PL 86+11/5 FLC 8 FAC 13/1 Others 16/1*

GALLEN Kevin Andrew
Born: Chiswick, 21 September 1975
Height: 5'11" **Weight:** 12.10
International Honours: E: U21-4; Yth (UEFA-U18 '93); Sch
A striker who can also play in any midfield position, Kevin was a regular for Queens Park Rangers throughout the 2003-04 season. He forged an excellent partnership up front with Paul Furlong, finishing as the club's leading scorer with 17 goals, and was runner-up in the Supporter's Club 'Player of the Year' ballot. Kevin was also team captain whenever Steve Palmer was not in the side.
Queens Park R *(From trainee on 22/9/1992) P/FL 126+45/36 FLC 9+3/2 FAC 6+2/2*
Huddersfield T *(Free on 10/8/2000) FL 30+8/10 FAC 1*
Barnsley *(Free on 27/7/2001) FL 8+1/2 FLC 0+1*
Queens Park R *(Free on 20/11/2001) FL 110+2/37 FLC 3+1/1 FAC 1+1 Others 5+2*

GALLIMORE Anthony (Tony) Mark
Born: Crewe, 21 February 1972
Height: 5'11" **Weight:** 12.6
Club Honours: Div 3 '95; AMC '98
Tony joined Barnsley shortly before the start of the 2003-04 campaign and was a regular in the line-up until the end of the year when he was sidelined by an injury that required surgery. A hard-working, strong-tackling full back, he remained out of action until the summer when he was released by the club.
Stoke C *(From trainee on 11/7/1990) FL 6+5*
Carlisle U *(Loaned on 3/10/1991) FL 8*
Carlisle U *(Loaned on 26/2/1992) FL 8*

Carlisle U *(£15,000 on 25/3/1993) FL 124/9 FLC 8 FAC 8/1 Others 24/1*
Grimsby T *(£125,000 on 28/3/1996) FL 263+10/4 FLC 20/2 FAC 15 Others 10*
Barnsley *(Free on 8/8/2003) FL 20 FLC 1 FAC 2 Others 2*

GANEA Ioan (Ivo) Viorel
Born: Fagaras, Romania, 10 August 1973
Height: 5'10" **Weight:** 12.6
International Honours: Romania: 44
This experienced striker was loaned to Wolves in January for the rest of the season. He is a powerful man, and did not look at all overawed. After an FA Cup goal he made his Premiership debut against Arsenal, scoring with a sweet volley. A low drive at Leeds meant he scored all three of Wolves' goals in a four-match spell. After representing Romania in midweek, Ivo returned as a substitute for Wolves' next two games. He then started against Villa, but missed a penalty, and was not making such an impact. His last start was against Southampton at the beginning of April, but he came off the bench to equalise at Newcastle.
Wolverhampton W *(Loaned from Bursaspor, Turkey, ex Brasav, Rapid Bucharest, VfB Stuttgart, on 1/1/2004) PL 6+10/3 FAC 2+1/1*

GARCIA Richard
Born: Perth, Australia, 4 September 1981
Height: 6'1" **Weight:** 11.2
Club Honours: FAYC '99
International Honours: Australia: U23; Yth
This midfielder was looking to establish himself as a regular in the West Ham team last term. Richard's early-season form was impressive until he suffered a ligament injury in September. After returning to action he was selected to play for the Australian U23 team in their Olympic trials in January. Unfortunately he twisted his cartilage and the injury ruled him out for the season.
West Ham U *(From trainee on 16/9/1998) P/FL 4+11 FLC 0+5 FAC 0+1*
Leyton Orient *(Loaned on 11/8/2000) FL 18/4 FLC 3*

GARDEN Stuart Robertson
Born: Dundee, 10 February 1972
Height: 6'0" **Weight:** 12.5
Although Stuart was in Notts County's line-up for the opening game of 2003-04 against Bristol City, he did not feature again until the end of January. The reliable goalkeeper then produced some match-winning saves but was unable to prevent the Magpies from being

relegated. He was released in the summer and was reported to have signed for Ross County.
Dundee U *(Signed from Dundee NE on 1/3/1993)*
Brechin C *(Free on 1/9/1995) SL 91+2 SLC 4 SC 8 Others 3*
Forfar Ath *(Free on 4/8/1999) SL 67 SLC 1 SC 1 Others 1*
Notts Co *(Free on 5/7/2001) FL 51+1 FLC 1 FAC 1 Others 2*

GARDNER Anthony
Born: Stone, 19 September 1980
Height: 6'5" **Weight:** 13.8
International Honours: E: 1; U21-1
An impressive young defender with great aerial ability, Anthony has matured into a more rounded player and has grown in confidence on the ball. After putting his previous injuries behind him, a regular starting place brought consistency, so much so that a surprise call-up to the full England squad saw the pundits raise an eyebrow or two. Those who have watched this talent week-in, week-out would not have been so surprised. Like his central defensive colleague Ledley King, Anthony is a super prospect who will undoubtedly benefit from some stability in the coaching staff at White Hart Lane in 2004-05.
Port Vale *(From trainee on 31/7/1998) FL 40+1/4 FLC 2 FAC 1*
Tottenham H *(£1,000,000 on 28/1/2000) PL 60+8/1 FLC 8 FAC 4*

GARDNER Ricardo Wayne
Born: Jamaica, 25 September 1978
Height: 5'9" **Weight:** 11.0
International Honours: Jamaica: 54
The 2003-04 campaign was one of new challenges and mixed emotions for Ricardo. He began the season in the unaccustomed position of left back (although he has played that role for Jamaica) in the 4-0 defeat at the hands of Manchester United. Despite that initial setback, he quickly adapted to the role and became a very effective attacking wing back. Ricardo's trickery proved vital when going forward and his electrifying pace enabled him to track back when required. The season was progressing well until he suffered knee ligament damage in the return game with Manchester United in January, an injury which kept him sidelined until coming on as a substitute in the final game of the campaign against Fulham.
Bolton W *(£1,000,000 from Harbour View, Jamaica on 17/8/1998) P/FL 152+24/15 FLC 13+4/2 FAC 6+3 Others 6/2*

Glyn Garner

GARDNER Ross
Born: South Shields, 15 December 1985
Height: 5'8" **Weight:** 10.6
International Honours: E: Yth
Ross is a left-sided midfielder who joined
Nottingham Forest last August from
Newcastle. His form for the reserve-team
at the City Ground was such that he was
called up for senior action much earlier
than expected, making his senior debut as
a substitute in the 6-0 home victory over
Wimbledon shortly after signing. He only
managed one other appearance during
the season but will be looking to make a
breakthrough in 2004-05. Ross was a
member of the England U19 squad
during the campaign.
Newcastle U (From trainee on 15/5/2002)
Nottingham F (Signed on 11/8/2003) FL 1+1

GARNER Darren John
Born: Plymouth, 10 December 1971
Height: 5'9" **Weight:** 12.7
Club Honours: AMC '96
After starting the 2003-04 season in the
Rotherham United first team, Darren's
campaign was blighted by a succession of
injuries which kept him out of action for
longer than he would have hoped. His
best spell came in the early part of the
new year when he made eight successive
appearances. Darren is a good passer of
the ball from his midfield position and he
will be looking for an injury free 2004-05
campaign.
Plymouth Arg (From trainee on 15/3/1989)
FL 22+5/1 FLC 2+1 FAC 1 (Free to Dorchester
T on 19/8/1994)
Rotherham U (£20,000 on 26/6/1995) FL
231+15/23 FLC 13+2 FAC 15+2/6 Others 9/1

GARNER Glyn
Born: Pontypool, 9 December 1976
Height: 6'2" **Weight:** 13.6
Glyn enjoyed an outstanding season in
goal for Bury last term when he was the
club's only ever-present. He displayed a
high level of consistency, turning in
impressive performances week after
week. A great shot-stopper, he also
managed to save two penalties during the
campaign – against Southend and
Rochdale. Glyn's progress was recognised
when the Shakers' fans named him as
'Player of the Season'.
Bury (Free from Llanelli on 7/7/2000) FL
97+2 FLC 4 FAC 3 Others 9

GARRARD Luke Edward
Born: Barnet, 22 September 1985
Height: 5'10" **Weight:** 11.9
This young midfielder was again on the
fringes of the Swindon Town first team

last term and made a couple of
appearances from the substitutes' bench
when he showed himself to be a steady
player with a good touch. Towards the
end of the season he was included as a
non-playing substitute on a number of
occasions.
Swindon T (From Tottenham H juniors on
8/7/2002) FL 0+2 Others 0+1

GAVIN Jason Joseph
Born: Dublin, 14 March 1980
Height: 6'1" **Weight:** 12.7
International Honours: RoI: U21-6; Yth
(UEFA-U18 '98)

Jason enjoyed his second spell under
Bradford boss Bryan Robson, who first
gave him a chance with Middlesbrough. A
right-sided centre half, Jason grew more
confident as the season wore on and
forged a solid partnership with David
Wetherall in the middle, although he also
had the occasional game at right back.
Middlesbrough (From trainee on 26/3/1997)
PL 19+12 FLC 5+1 FAC 1+2
Grimsby T (Loaned on 1/11/2002) FL 8+2
Huddersfield T (Loaned on 14/3/2003) FL
10/1
Bradford C (Free on 16/7/2003) FL 37+1 FAC
0+1

Jason Gavin

GAYLE Marcus Anthony
Born: Hammersmith, 27 September 1970
Height: 6'1" **Weight:** 12.9
Club Honours: Div 3 '92
International Honours: E: Yth. Jamaica: 14
Watford's player of the season in 2002-03, Marcus failed to find his best form last term, mainly because of a series of leg injuries, notably a torn hamstring in January. At his best he is a fine central defender, commanding in the air and uncomplicated on the ground.
Brentford (From trainee on 6/7/1989) FL 118+38/22 FLC 6+3 FAC 6+2/2 Others 14+6/3
Wimbledon (£250,000 on 24/3/1994) P/FL 198+38/37 FLC 23+1/7 FAC 18+7/3
Glasgow R (£900,000 on 9/3/2001) SL 28+8/4
Watford (£900,000 on 8/8/2001) FL 90+9/5 FLC 4+1/2 FAC 8/2

GEARY Derek Peter
Born: Dublin, 19 June 1980
Height: 5'6" **Weight:** 10.8
Derek firmly established himself in the Sheffield Wednesday line-up last term when he was a near ever-present in the side. A hard-working full back who is equally effective as a conventional right back or as a right-sided wing back, he is hugely popular with the fans. Derek was one of 13 out-of-contract players released by the Owls in the summer.
Sheffield Wed (Signed from Cherry Orchard on 17/11/1997) FL 95+9 FLC 12+2 FAC 4 Others 5

GEMMILL Scot
Born: Paisley, 2 January 1971
Height: 5'11" **Weight:** 11.6
Club Honours: FMC '92; Div 1 '98
International Honours: S: 26; B-2; U21-4
Scot was injured at the start of last term and then found it impossible to break into the first-team picture at Everton. In March he followed in the footsteps of his father Archie when he joined Preston on loan. He settled in well, despite not having played all season and added some skill and guile to the midfield area. His only goal clinched all three points against Bradford City, but he was injured against Nottingham Forest and returned to Goodison. Scot was released in the summer.
Nottingham F (From trainee on 5/1/1990) F/PL 228+17/21 FLC 29+2/3 FAC 19+2/1 Others 13+1/4
Everton (£250,000 on 25/3/1999) PL 79+18/5 FLC 3+1 FAC 7+2
Preston NE (Loaned on 12/3/2004) FL 7/1

GEORGE Liam Brendan
Born: Luton, 2 February 1979
Height: 5'9" **Weight:** 11.3
International Honours: RoI: U21-4; Yth (UEFA-U18 '98)
This clever ball playing forward made a bright start for York City last term as they went top of Division Three in the early weeks of the season. Liam proved popular with the supporters after netting goals against Southend and Darlington, but he then suffered a series of injury setbacks. He returned to the attack in the closing stages of the campaign and again showed glimpses of his skill, scoring in the 1-1 draw at Bootham Crescent against Bury. Nevertheless he was released at the end of the campaign.
Luton T (From trainee on 20/1/1997) FL 81+21/20 FLC 3+6 FAC 9+1/4 Others 2+1
Clydebank (Free on 16/3/2002) SL 2 (Free to Stevenage Borough on 27/3/2002)
Bury (Free on 7/8/2002) FL 3+5/1 Others 2
Boston U (Free on 13/2/2003) FL 1+2 (Free to St Patricks in April 2003)
York C (Free on 15/8/2003) FL 14+8/3 FAC 0+1 Others 0+1

[GEREMI] N'JITAP FOTSO Geremi Sorele
Born: Cameroon, 20 December 1978
Height: 5'11" **Weight:** 12.8
International Honours: Cameroon
Perseverance certainly paid off for Chelsea when they finally landed Geremi from Real Madrid a year after showing interest in the experienced Cameroon skipper. The versatile midfielder had enjoyed an impressive loan season at Middlesbrough who could not agree a fee with the Madrid giants. Claudio Ranieri used Geremi all across his four-man midfield, even the critical 'holding' central role when ex-Real colleague Claude Makelele was unavailable. Usually a regular goalscorer, Geremi surprisingly scored just the once for Chelsea but what a goal indeed – a sensational 30-yard volley against Portsmouth. Geremi had a very satisfactory season for the Blues for whom his all-round versatility, shooting power and accurate crossing make him a valuable asset even in a squad which has such strength in depth in midfield.
Middlesbrough (Loaned from Real Madrid, Spain, ex Racing Baffoussam, Cerro Porteno, Genclerbirligi, on 31/7/2002) PL 33/7 FAC 1
Chelsea (£7,000,000 on 1/8/2003) PL 19+6/1 FLC 3 FAC 1 Others 7+3

GERKEN Dean Jeffery
Born: Southend, 22 May 1985
Height: 6'3" **Weight:** 13.0

There was a surprise call-up to the Colchester United senior team for this third-year scholar just hours before the visit to Brentford in mid-April. Dean had been on the bench for nearly half the season due to an injury to reserve goalkeeper Richard McKinney, but he was not expecting to make his debut until number one choice Simon Brown fell ill before the Griffin Park clash. Dean gave a competent display in the 3-2 defeat, but made no further senior appearances.
Colchester U (Trainee) FL 1

GERRARD Paul William
Born: Heywood, 22 January 1973
Height: 6'2" **Weight:** 14.4
International Honours: E: U21-18
Paul found himself well down the pecking order of goalkeepers at Everton last term and his only opportunities of senior action came while out on loan. He had a spell at Sheffield United early on in the season, covering for the injured Paddy Kenny, and produced some solid performances for the Blades. Towards the end of the campaign he was loaned out to Nottingham Forest where he again impressed and was a key figure in the club's revival in the closing stages of the season. Paul was released by Everton in the summer.
Oldham Ath (From trainee on 2/11/1991) P/FL 118+1 FLC 7 FAC 7 Others 2
Everton (£1,000,000 + on 1/7/1996) PL 89+1 FLC 6 FAC 3
Oxford U (Loaned on 18/12/1998) FL 16
Ipswich (Loaned on 16/11/2002) FL 5
Sheffield U (Loaned on 29/8/2003) FL 16
Nottingham F (Loaned on 25/3/2004) FL 8

GERRARD Steven George
Born: Huyton, 30 May 1980
Height: 6'2" **Weight:** 12.4
Club Honours: FLC '01, '03; FAC '01; UEFAC '01; ESC '01
International Honours: E: 28; U21-4; Yth
Steven stood head and shoulders above his Liverpool colleagues last term. His displays got better and better as the campaign progressed and at times it seemed that he single-handedly drove the Reds into fourth place in the Premiership. In retrospect manager Houllier's decision to transfer the club captaincy from Sami Hyypia to Steven was inspired as he led by example. In the first half of the season he was relatively subdued, but only because he was required to fill in the injured Didi Hamann's role as midfield anchor. However, once Hamann returned to

Steven Gerrard (left)

action Steven was free to do what he does best, driving forward with the ball, making blindside runs and supplying the angled crosses and threaded balls in the channel for Michael Owen to finish off. He scored five excellent goals from open play and one penalty and was a regular for England, featuring in the squad for the Euro 2004 finals in Portugal. Steven was also selected for the PFA Premiership team of the season.
Liverpool (From trainee on 26/2/1998) PL 151+19/20 FLC 11+1/2 FAC 11+2/1 Others 43+2/5

GIANNAKOPOULOS Stilianos (Stelios)
Born: Athens, Greece, 12 July 1974
Height: 5'8" **Weight:** 11.0
Club Honours: Div 2 '04
International Honours: Greece: 38
Voted as Greece's 'Player of the Year' in his final season in his homeland, and widely considered to be the most important member of the national team, Stelios was considered to be a shrewd acquisition when signing for Bolton. Although he only started half of the club's Premiership games, and figured quite often from the bench, Stelios quickly won the hearts of the Reebok faithful with some skilful, all-action displays. Despite not being the tallest player in the squad, he showed a tenacious side to his nature, in addition to his undoubted natural skill and pace. Stelios went on to assist his country to a surprise victory over Portugal in the final of the Euro 2004 tournament.
Bolton W (Free from Olympiakos, Greece on 15/7/2003) PL 17+14/2 FLC 4+2/2 FAC 2

GIBB Alistair (Ally) Stuart
Born: Salisbury, 17 February 1976
Height: 5'9" **Weight:** 11.7
The previous season had seen Ali become a popular figure at Edgeley Park with his mazy runs down the right flank, but he struggled to find that kind of form last term, despite being a regular in the line-up. He subsequently joined Bristol Rovers just prior to the transfer deadline, scoring on his debut against York and retaining his place in the line-up until the end of the campaign.
Norwich C (From trainee on 1/7/1994)
Northampton T (Loaned on 22/9/1995) FL 9/1
Northampton T (£30,000 on 5/2/1996) FL 51+71/3 FLC 8+4 FAC 5+3 Others 6+3
Stockport Co (£50,000 on 18/2/2000) FL 157+8/1 FLC 6 FAC 6 Others 3
Bristol Rov (Free on 25/3/2004) FL 8/1

GIBBS Paul Derek
Born: Gorleston, 26 October 1972
Height: 5'10" **Weight:** 11.10
This left-sided defender or midfield player found himself to be only a bit-part player at Barnsley last term and his contract was cancelled by mutual consent in October. Paul then had trial spells with a number of clubs and also featured for both Gravesend & Northfleet and Canvey Island.
Colchester U (Signed from Diss T on 6/3/1995) FL 39+14/3 FAC 1+1 Others 8+1
Torquay U (Free on 26/7/1997) FL 40+1/7 FLC 4/1 FAC 3/1 Others 3/1
Plymouth Arg (Free on 7/7/1998) FL 30+4/3 FLC 2
Brentford (Free on 10/7/2000) FL 49+5/3 FLC 3 FAC 3/1 Others 6+1
Barnsley (Free on 15/3/2002) FL 27+6/1 FLC 1 FAC 1 Others 1

GIDDINGS Stuart James
Born: Coventry, 27 March 1986
Height: 6'0" **Weight:** 11.8
International Honours: E: Yth
The young left back won England Youth honours last term and put in consistently good performances in the Coventry reserve team. He was a surprise choice on the bench for the final game of the season and was given seven minutes on the pitch.
Coventry C (Trainee) FL 0+1

GIER Robert (Rob) James
Born: Bracknell, 6 January 1980
Height: 5'9" **Weight:** 11.7
Rob had a difficult campaign at Wimbledon last term. A fully-committed central defender, his lack of inches again showed up when dealing with deep crosses into the box, and he was eventually left out of the side towards the end of the season. Out of contract in the summer, he was not offered a new deal.
Wimbledon (From trainee on 11/5/1999) FL 67+4 FLC 4+3 FAC 4

GIGGS Ryan Joseph
Born: Cardiff, 29 November 1973
Height: 5'11" **Weight:** 10.9
Club Honours: ESC '91; FAYC '92; FLC '92; PL '93, '94, '96, '97, '99, '00, '01, '03; CS '93, '94, '96, '97, '03; FAC '94, '96, '99, '04; EC '99
International Honours: W: 48; U21-1; Yth. E: Sch
An outstanding left winger, who can play equally well as a front line striker, Ryan put aside his indifferent form of the previous campaign, and showed why he is still so highly regarded at Old Trafford. He

continued to hit his fair quota of goals with contributions coming against Bolton (2), Birmingham, Liverpool (2) and Middlesbrough in the Premiership, and a solitary effort against Stuttgart in the Champions' League game. Elevated to team captain in the absence of Roy Keane, Ryan saved his best form for the vital run-in to the season's conclusion. That included an inspired performance against Arsenal in the FA Cup semi-final, which gave Ryan a further chance of glory in his hometown in May. Despite his longevity at the club, there were still rumours in the media that his services might come under review during the summer months. His form, however, indicated otherwise.
Manchester U (From trainee on 1/12/1990) F/PL 370+45/86 FLC 21+5/6 FAC 44+4/9 Others 96+6/20

GILBERT Peter
Born: Newcastle, 31 July 1983
Height: 5'11" **Weight:** 12.13
Peter joined Plymouth Argyle in the summer of 2003, signing a long-term contract, and quickly made the left-back position his own. Powerful in the tackle and deceptively quick, he was one of the main reasons that Argyle notched up a run of seven consecutive clean sheets during the season, a new club record.
Birmingham C (From trainee on 1/7/2002)
Plymouth Arg (Signed on 8/7/2003) FL 40/1 FLC 1 FAC 1 Others 2/1

GILCHRIST Philip (Phil) Alexander
Born: Stockton on Tees, 25 August 1973
Height: 5'11" **Weight:** 13.12
Club Honours: FLC '00
Owing to injury and the form of other quality defenders, Phil made only 21 first-team appearances for West Bromwich Albion during 2003-04. He missed the start of the campaign, regained his place in the side in late September, was sidelined for a short time after that and then, after returning for a second time, ended the campaign on loan at Rotherham. The experienced central defender proved to be a very valuable acquisition in helping the Millers to avoid relegation. He was released by Albion in the summer.
Nottingham F (From trainee on 5/12/1990)
Middlesbrough (Free on 10/1/1992)
Hartlepool U (Free on 27/11/1992) FL 77+5 FLC 4+1 FAC 4 Others 5
Oxford U (£100,000 on 17/2/1995) FL 173+4/10 FLC 16 FAC 9/1 Others 3

Leicester C (£500,000 on 10/8/1999) PL
23+16/1 FLC 6+1 FAC 4+1
West Bromwich A (£500,000 on 22/3/2001)
P/FL 89+1 FLC 6+1 FAC 5+1 Others 2
Rotherham U (Loaned on 12/3/2004) FL 10

GILES Christopher (Chris)
Born: Milborne Port, 16 April 1982
Height: 6'2" **Weight:** 13.0
Club Honours: FAT '02
A former striker who has successfully
switched to central defence, Chris only
made one substitute appearance for
Yeovil during the season and was
transferred to Aldershot on deadline day,
featuring in their play-off games.
*Yeovil T (Signed from Sherborne on
5/6/2000) FL 0+1*

GILKS Matthew (Matt)
Born: Oldham, 4 June 1982
Height: 6'1" **Weight:** 12.7
With Neil Edwards still finding fitness
after a summer operation, Matthew
started the2003-04 campaign in the
Rochdale goal and put in some first-class
performances over the opening games.
However when the team began to slide
down the table, the experienced Edwards
was recalled and Matthew had to spend
the rest of the campaign on the bench,
until being recalled for the last game of
the season.
*Rochdale (From trainee on 4/7/2001) FL
52+2 FLC 2 FAC 3+1 Others 1*

GILL Jeremy (Jerry) Morley
Born: Clevedon, 8 September 1970
Height: 5'7" **Weight:** 11.0
International Honours: E: SP-1
Jerry spent much of last season recovering
from a serious knee injury suffered
towards the end of the previous
campaign and once fit he moved on to
join Cheltenham Town on a non-contract
basis. He showed his versatility with
appearances at right back, in midfield and
as a sweeper in a five-man defence. A
bubbly character who added maturity to
an increasingly youthful dressing room,
Jerry missed the closing matches with a
hamstring problem, but had already done
enough to earn a new contract with the
Robins.
*Leyton Orient (Free from Trowbridge T on
16/12/1988. Free to Weston super Mare on
1/7/1990)*
*Birmingham C (£30,000 from Yeovil T on
14/7/1997) FL 43+17 FLC 11+1 FAC 3
Others 1*
*Northampton T (Free on 9/8/2002) FL 41
FLC 1 FAC 2 Others 2*
Cheltenham T (Free on 27/2/2004) FL 5+2

GILL Matthew James
Born: Cambridge, 8 November 1980
Height: 5'11" **Weight:** 12.10
Matthew enjoyed another good campaign
for Peterborough last term. A regular in
the first half of the season, he was mostly
used on the right flank of a five-man
defensive line, but he is also at home in
midfield. Matthew was reported to have
signed for Notts County during the
summer.
*Peterborough U (From trainee on 2/3/1998)
FL 121+30/5 FLC 3+1 FAC 6+1 Others 3+4*

GILL Robert
Born: Nottingham, 10 February 1982
Height: 6'0" **Weight:** 12.0
A product of the Doncaster Rovers youth
scheme, this young striker spent much of
last term shuttling between the reserve
team and loan spells at Chester City,
Dagenham & Redbridge and Burton
Albion. His only starts came in the LDV
Vans Trophy ties and at the end of the
season he was placed on the transfer list.
*Doncaster Rov (From trainee at Nottingham
F on 4/8/2000) FL 0+1 Others 2*

GILLESPIE Keith Robert
Born: Bangor, 18 February 1975
Height: 5'10" **Weight:** 11.3
Club Honours: FAYC '92; FLC '02
International Honours: NI: 55; U21-1;
Yth; Sch
This experienced right winger struggled to
establish a regular place in the Foxes' line
up last term and Leicester's fans did not
really see the best of the flying Irishman.
He did, however, continue to earn
selection for his country, even leading
them out on the occasion of his 50th cap,
though they too were struggling through
a record goalless spell at the time.
Ironically, on the night that the Irish did
finally break their drought, Keith
managed to contribute an own goal just
60 seconds later. A very well publicised
off-the-field event did little to enhance his
prospects in the second half of the
campaign and he had rather drifted to
the fringes of the squad by the end of the
season.
*Manchester U (From trainee on 3/2/1993) PL
3+6/1 FLC 3 FAC 1+1/1*
*Wigan Ath (Loaned on 3/9/1993) FL 8/4
Others 2*
*Newcastle U (£1,000,000 on 12/1/1995) PL
94+19/11 FLC 7+1/1 FAC 9+1/2 Others 11+5*
*Blackburn Rov (£2,250,000 on 18/12/1998)
P/FL 67+46/5 FLC 8+3 FAC 6+4/1 Others 0+3*
*Wigan Ath (Loaned on 1/12/2000) FL 4+1
FAC 2*
Leicester C (Free on 9/7/2003) PL 7+5 FLC 0+1

GILROY David Miles
Born: Yeovil, 23 December 1982
Height: 5'11" **Weight:** 11.3
This young striker made a handful of
appearances as a substitute for Bristol
Rovers last term but his only start came at
Kidderminster in December shortly before
being released. David also had loan spells
at Clevedon Town and Forest Green
Rovers before leaving to join Dr Martens
League outfit Weston-super-Mare for
whom he scored on his debut on New
Year's Day.
*Bristol Rov (From trainee on 2/7/2002) FL
6+13 FAC 0+2/1 Others 0+1*

GIVEN Seamus (Shay) John
Born: Lifford, 20 April 1976
Height: 6'0" **Weight:** 13.4
Club Honours: Div 1 '96
International Honours: RoI: 60; U21-5;
Yth
Goalkeeper Shay remained a vital member
of Newcastle's defence last term, as
demonstrated by his being an ever-
present in the Premiership for the third
season in succession, in the process
setting a new all-time record for
consecutive appearances in the
competition, his current total being 129.
Athletic but undemonstrative, he
continued to show that he is a 'keeper of
the highest quality and reliability,
delivering 17 clean sheets in the season,
form which continued to earn him
selection as first choice for the Republic of
Ireland. His highlights of the season were
probably the 1-0 win at Middlesbrough in
October, when he made three world-class
saves, and at Charlton in December when
a superb double save from Jason Euell
helped earn a point in a 0-0 draw.
*Blackburn Rov (From Glasgow Celtic juniors
on 8/8/1994) PL 2 FLC 0+1*
Swindon T (Loaned on 4/8/1995) FL 5
Sunderland (Loaned on 19/11/1996) FL 17
*Newcastle U (£1,500,000 on 14/7/1997) PL
217 FLC 4+1 FAC 20 Others 40*

GLEESON Daniel (Dan) Edward
Born: Cambridge, 17 February 1985
Height: 6'1" **Weight:** 12.8
This tall and strong Cambridge United
defender came up through the ranks and
broke into the first team after a good run
in the reserves. Dan made his senior
debut at Kidderminster in November
when he featured in midfield. Later in the
season he had a brief run in the starting
line-up when he showed some good
defensive skills.
*Cambridge U (From trainee on 25/2/2004)
FL 3+4*

Shay Given

GLENNON Matthew (Matty) William
Born: Stockport, 8 October 1978
Height: 6'2" **Weight:** 14.9
Matty was a near ever-present for Carlisle last season and was one of the most consistent performers at the club. A fine shot-stopper and a 'keeper who commands his area, his campaign was marked by a number of outstanding displays. His last-minute penalty save at Mansfield in April which preserved United's Football League status for a little longer was singled out by the Carlisle Supporters' Trust for their 'Outstanding Achievement' award and evoked memories of the heroics of Jimmy Glass five years earlier.
Bolton W (From trainee on 3/7/1997)
Bristol Rov (Loaned on 15/9/2000) FL 1
Carlisle U (Loaned on 10/11/2000) FL 29 FAC 3 Others 1
Hull C (£50,000 on 20/6/2001) FL 35 FLC 3 FAC 2 Others 2
Carlisle U (Free on 18/10/2002) FL 76 FLC 1 FAC 4 Others 10

GNOHERE David Arthur
Born: Ivory Coast, 20 November 1978
Height: 6'2" **Weight:** 12.13
Arthur started the season as first choice in the centre-back department for Burnley, but lost his place with the arrival of David May and soon afterwards was loaned to Queens Park Rangers as cover for the injured Clarke Carlisle. He returned to Turf Moor in October and had a decent run in the side, but lost out again following the team's poor defensive showing around the Christmas period. With his first-team chances clearly limited at Burnley, he returned to Loftus Road on a permanent transfer following the long-term injury to Danny Shittu and was a near ever-present during the remainder of the campaign.
Burnley (Free from SM Caen, France, ex AS Cannes, on 9/8/2001) FL 74+7/6 FLC 7 FAC 5
Queens Park R (Loaned on 4/9/2003) FL 6 Others 1/1
Queens Park R (Free on 19/2/2004) FL 11+1

GOATER Leonard Shaun
Born: Hamilton, Bermuda, 25 February 1970
Height: 6'1" **Weight:** 12.0
Club Honours: AMC '96
International Honours: Bermuda: 19; Yth
Signed from Manchester City at the start of the 2003-04 season, the big striker justified his fee by becoming Reading's leading goal-scorer with 14 goals from 38 appearances. He created chances for his colleagues too, and his control of the long ball out of defence meant that supporting players were brought into the attack quickly. Shaun also became the team's reliable penalty taker, and fans will be hoping for an even better return from him in 2004-05. He is the holder of the MBE for services to youth sport in Bermuda.
Manchester U (Free from North Village, Bermuda on 8/5/1989)
Rotherham U (Free on 25/10/1989) FL 169+40/70 FLC 13+4/4 FAC 12+3/7 Others 15+4/5
Notts Co (Loaned on 12/11/1993) FL 1

Dan Gleeson

*Bristol C (£175,000 on 17/7/1996) FL
67+8/40 FLC 7/2 FAC 5 Others 5+1/1
Manchester C (£400,000 on 26/3/1998) P/FL
164+20/84 FLC 13/9 FAC 9+3/9 Others 3/1
Reading (£500,000 on 4/8/2003) FL 30+4/12
FLC 1+1 FAC 2/2*

GOMA Alain

Born: Sault, France, 5 October 1972
Height: 6'0" **Weight:** 13.0
International Honours: France: 2; B-1;
U21; Yth
A commanding central defender who is
strong in the tackle and rarely beaten in
the air, Alain proved to be one of the
stars of the Fulham side in the opening
weeks of the 2003-04 campaign before
losing his place briefly through injury.
Once back in the side he gave some
outstanding performances, notably in the
latter part of the season and particularly
away from home at Manchester City and
Liverpool. His run of form coincided with
the fact that Fulham conceded just one
goal in their last five away games of the
season.
*Newcastle U (£4,750,000 from Paris St
Germain, France, ex Auxerre, on 9/7/1999) PL
32+1/11 FLC 4 FAC 2 Others 2
Fulham (£4,000,000 on 16/3/2001) P/FL
87+1 FLC 1 FAC 15 Others 13*

GOODFELLOW Marc David

Born: Swadlincote, 20 September 1981
Height: 5'8" **Weight:** 10.6
Marc had few first-team opportunities for
Stoke last term and his only starts came in
the Carling Cup ties against Rochdale and
Gillingham. In January he was sold to
Bristol City where he received more
regular first-team action. An exciting
winger with great pace who demonstrated
his goal-scoring ability on his debut
against Notts County, although it was his
88th minute header against Hartlepool in
the play-off semi-finals that most City
fans will remember.
*Stoke C (From juniors on 29/1/1999) FL
17+37/6 FLC 3+3/2 FAC 1+6 Others 4/1
Bristol C (£50,000 on 9/1/2004) FL 7+8/4
Others 0+2/1*

GOODHIND Warren Ernest

Born: Johannesburg, South Africa, 16
August 1977
Height: 5'11" **Weight:** 11.6
Warren missed the start of last season for
Cambridge United as he was still
recovering from a cartilage operation.
However, he fought his way back into the
side and once again he was a consistent
performer in a team that struggled
throughout the campaign. Warren is a

versatile defender who featured either at
right back or at centre half.
*Barnet (From trainee on 3/7/1996) FL
73+20/3 FLC 5+2 FAC 2 Others 4/1
Cambridge U (£80,000 on 21/9/2001) FL
70+7 FLC 1 FAC 8 Others 5+3*

GOODISON Ian

Born: Jamaica, 21 November 1972
Height: 6'3" **Weight:** 12.10
International Honours: Jamaica
Ian linked up with his former Hull City
boss Brian Little at Tranmere last term and
after a short settling-in period fitted
comfortably into the defence. He soon
became a firm favourite with the Prenton
Park faithful with his no-nonsense
tackling, team work and never-say-die
approach. Ian will undoubtedly be one of
the key players in the manager's
ambitious plans for the 2004-05 season
and will bring maturity and stability to a
young back line.
*Hull C (Free from Olympic Gardens, Jamaica
on 22/10/1999) FL 67+3/1 FLC 2 FAC 6+1
Others 5 (Free to Seba U, Jamaica during
2002 close season)
Tranmere Rov (Signed on 20/2/2004) FL 12
FAC 2*

GOODWIN James (Jim)

Born: Waterford, 20 November 1981
Height: 5'9" **Weight:** 12.2
International Honours: RoI: 1; U21-14
Jim enjoyed another good season for
Stockport County last term, producing a
number of committed performances. The
combative midfielder scored a total of six
goals, the best of which came in the 2-0
victory against Bristol City when he
smashed the ball high into the top corner
of the net for a 'Goal of the Season'
contender.
*Glasgow Celtic (Signed from Tramore on
25/11/1997) SL 1
Stockport Co (Free on 7/6/2002) FL 51+16/7
FLC 2 FAC 3/1 Others 5/1*

GORDON Dean Dwight

Born: Croydon, 10 February 1973
Height: 6'0" **Weight:** 13.4
Club Honours: Div 1 '94
International Honours: E: U21-13
This veteran full back was out in the cold
for much of last term at Coventry. He
played in only a handful of games and
with his contract coming to an end in the
summer he was allowed to join Reading
until the end of the campaign. He made
just three appearances as a composed
substitute defender, but still found time to
be involved in one of the most bizarre
goals of the season. Late in the home

game against Norwich City, with the score
at 0-0, Dean's headed clearance deflected
off referee Neale Barry to Phil Mulryne,
who volleyed the ball home for the only
goal of the match.
*Crystal Palace (From trainee on 4/7/1991)
F/PL 181+20/20 FLC 16+3/2 FAC 14+1/1
Others 5+1
Middlesbrough (£900,000 on 17/7/1998) PL
53+10/4 FLC 5 FAC 3
Cardiff C (Loaned on 23/11/2001) FL 7/2
Coventry C (Free on 1/8/2002) FL 33+2/1
FLC 2 FAC 4+1
Reading (Loaned on 23/3/2004) FL 0+3*

GORDON Kenyatta Gavin

Born: Manchester, 24 June 1979
Height: 6'1" **Weight:** 12.0
A striker with pace, agility and aerial
power, Gavin did not put these assets
together often enough to win a regular
place in the Cardiff City line-up last term.
He briefly replaced Peter Thorne in the
side in the autumn, but by the end of the
campaign he was restricted to the
occasional outing from the substitutes'
bench. Gavin was released by the club in
the summer.
*Hull C (From trainee on 3/7/1996) FL
22+16/9 FLC 1+4/1 Others 1+1
Lincoln C (£30,000 on 7/11/1997) FL
87+12/28 FLC 2/1 FAC 9/2 Others 4+1
Cardiff C (£275,000 + on 18/12/2000) FL
26+24/5 FLC 0+2 FAC 2/1 Others 1+1/6
Oxford U (Loaned on 27/9/2002) FL 3+3/1
FLC 0+1*

GORDON Michael Alexander

Born: Tooting, 11 October 1984
Height: 5'6" **Weight:** 10.4
Michael began the 2003-04 season in the
starting line-up for Wimbledon, and
contributed impressively during the
opening-day win over Crewe. Sadly, he
failed to approach that level of form for
the remainder of the campaign. A very
skilful winger with a good turn of foot,
he sometimes disappointed with his final
delivery. Mostly consigned to the reserves
after Christmas, he was released in the
summer.
*Wimbledon (Free from trainee at Arsenal on
11/3/2003) FL 8+11 FLC 1 FAC 0+1*

GORRE Dean

Born: Surinam, 10 September 1970
Height: 5'8" **Weight:** 11.7
International Honours: Holland: U21
Dean provided the main attacking threat
for Barnsley last term and was the club's
leading scorer until an injury put him out
of action at the end of November. He only
managed two brief outings from then on

and the team's performances declined as a result. Dean was one of several players released by the Reds in the summer.
Huddersfield T (£330,000 from Ajax, Holland on 16/9/1999) FL 49+13/6 FLC 4/1 FAC 1+1
Barnsley (£50,000 on 24/7/2001) FL 48+17/9 FLC 3/1 Others 2

GOSLING Jamie John
Born: Bath, 21 March 1982
Height: 6'0" **Weight:** 10.6
This young midfielder joined Yeovil after an encouraging pre-season trial, but managed only a handful of starts at the beginning of the campaign before dropping down the pecking order. He later spent time on loan at Aldershot for whom he featured in the Conference play-off final against Shrewsbury when the Shots missed out on their bid to regain Football League status. Jamie was released by the Glovers in the summer.
Yeovil T (£20,000 from Bath C on 31/7/2003) FL 4+8/1 FLC 1 FAC 0+2 Others 0+2

GOULD Jonathan Alan
Born: Paddington, 18 July 1968
Height: 6'1" **Weight:** 13.7
Club Honours: SPD '98, '01; SLC '98, '00, '01
International Honours: S:2; B-1
Jonathan was one of several Preston players to find his 2003-04 campaign disrupted by injury whilst also experiencing some personal highs. He was recalled to the Scotland squad for the Euro 2004 play-offs on the back of some quite remarkable goalkeeping performances in the early part of the season. A persistent thigh injury saw him out of action in the new year, and on his return he made several uncharacteristic lapses, which suggested he might not have fully recovered. However, his overall performances showed him to be one of the best 'keepers to have played for North End for many years and his close-quarter work in particular was often of international class.
Halifax T (Free from Clevedon T on 18/7/1990) FL 32 FLC 2 FAC 5 Others 5
West Bromwich A (Free on 30/1/1992)
Coventry C (Free on 15/7/1992) PL 25 FLC 1+1
Bradford C (Free on 29/3/1996) FL 18 FLC 2 Others 3
Gillingham (Loaned on 28/10/1996) FL 3
Glasgow Celtic (Signed on 2/8/1997) SL 109+1 SLC 14+1 SC 12 Others 21
Preston NE (Free on 9/1/2003) FL 50+1 FLC 1 FAC 3

GOWER Mark
Born: Edmonton, 5 October 1978
Height: 5'11" **Weight:** 11.12
Club Honours: FLC '99
International Honours: E: SP-4; Yth; Sch
Mark was in excellent form for Southend throughout last season and was deservedly voted as the club's 'Player of the Year' by the fans. A winger with hypnotising skills who is equally comfortable on either foot, he scored nine goals and provided many more for his colleagues. His influence on the team as a whole was never more obvious than when he was absent injured. When firing on all cylinders, Mark has enough skill to win a match on his own, and the Blues fans will be looking forward to seeing more of those skills in the 2004-05 season.
Tottenham H (From trainee on 1/4/1997) FLC 0+2
Motherwell (Loaned on 12/3/1999) SL 8+1/1
Barnet (£32,500 on 19/1/2001) FL 10+4/1 Others 1/1
Southend U (£25,000 on 25/7/2003) FL 40/6 FLC 1 FAC 5/2 Others 7/1

GRABBI Corrado (Ciccio)
Born: Turin, Italy, 29 July 1975
Height: 5'11" **Weight:** 12.12
Club Honours: FLC '02
Ciccio was again out of favour at Blackburn last term and his only start came in the home leg of the UEFA Cup tie against Genclerbirligi. His best moment came with the immaculate cross he delivered in the last minute at Bolton, which brought Dwight Yorke an equalising header. Ciccio was eventually offloaded to Ancona during the January transfer window.
Blackburn Rov (£6,750,000 from Ternana, Italy on 12/7/2001) PL 11+19/2 FLC 2+3/1 FAC 1+2/1 Others 2+1/1

GRAHAM Daniel (Danny)
Anthony William
Born: Gateshead, 12 August 1985
Height: 5'11" **Weight:** 12.5
A prolific scorer with Middlesbrough's U19 team, this highly rated young striker signed his first professional contract last March and soon afterwards he joined Darlington on loan to gain some valuable experience of senior football. Danny impressed with some strong running and an obvious eye for goal, and found the net twice during his stay with the Quakers.
Middlesbrough (From trainee on 6/3/2004)
Darlington (Loaned on 19/3/2004) FL 7+2/2

GRAHAM David
Born: Edinburgh, 6 October 1978
Height: 5'10" **Weight:** 11.5
International Honours: S: U21-8
A summer hernia operation left David short of match fitness at the start of last season. However, he scored two cracking goals after coming off the bench for Torquay in the home match with Leyton Orient in September and from then on never looked back. With fitness problems resolved, his undoubted skills were now complemented by a voracious work rate and an ever-improving team-awareness. David capped a fine campaign by being voted United's 'Player of the Season' and winning a place in the PFA's Division Three team of the season.
Glasgow R (From juniors on 1/7/1995) SL 0+3 Others 1+1
Dunfermline Ath (Signed on 15/11/1998) SL 17+23/4 SLC 1 SC 3/1 Others 0+1
Inverness Caledonian Thistle (Loaned on 5/1/2001) SL 0+2 SC 0+2
Torquay U (Free on 22/3/2001) FL 103+17/47 FLC 3+1/2 FAC 4 Others 1+1

GRAINGER Martin Robert
Born: Enfield, 23 August 1972
Height: 5'11" **Weight:** 12.0
Martin joined Coventry on loan from Birmingham in February after being out of the game for over a year with injuries. However, he soon got the pace of Division One football and made a strong impression in his short time at Highfield Road demonstrating good positional sense, simple but effective distribution and impressive dead-ball delivery. An injury crisis at St Andrews cut short his loan period and Coventry's play-off hopes suffered after his departure. The tough-tackling full back came on for the Blues against Manchester United in April and scored with a free kick. But the luckless defender then snapped knee ligaments and was ruled out of six months.
Colchester U (From trainee on 28/7/1992) FL 37+9/7 FLC 3 FAC 2 Others 3/1
Brentford (£60,000 on 21/10/1993) FL 100+1/12 FLC 6/1 FAC 9/1 Others 8/2
Birmingham C (£400,000 on 25/3/1996) P/FL 205+21/25 FLC 21+2/2 FAC 9+1/1 Others 7
Coventry C (Loaned on 13/2/2004) FL 3

GRAND Simon
Born: Chorley, 23 February 1984
Height: 6'1" **Weight:** 10.12
With skipper Gareth Griffiths out injured, Simon began the 2003-04 season as Rochdale's first-choice centre half as they briefly challenged towards the top of the

table. Later he provided cover for other defensive positions, and was on the bench, at least, for virtually every game until the last couple of months of the season when Dale brought in a string of new defensive players. He was released by the club in May.

Rochdale (From trainee on 3/7/2002) FL 33+7/2 FLC 1 FAC 7 Others 1

GRANT Anthony (Tony) James
Born: Liverpool, 14 November 1974
Height: 5'10" **Weight:** 10.2
Club Honours: CS '95
International Honours: E: U21-1
Last term was arguably Tony's best season at Turf Moor to date. He was a near automatic starter in the side before unfortunately missing the crucial run-in due to injury. A key man in central midfield, he was often an important feature of Burnley's build-up play, effective in the tackle and arguably the best passer of a ball at the club. He formed a useful partnership in the engine room with Richard Chaplow, Tony's experience and cool head providing the ideal complement to the youngster's energy and drive.

Everton (From trainee on 8/7/1993) PL 43+18/2 FLC 5+1 FAC 4+4 Others 2+2/1
Swindon T (Loaned on 18/1/1996) FL 3/1
Tranmere Rov (Loaned on 2/9/1999) FL 8+1 FLC 1/1
Manchester C (£450,000 on 24/12/1999) P/FL 11+10 FLC 1 FAC 2+1
West Bromwich A (Loaned on 1/12/2000) FL 3+2
Burnley (£250,000 on 11/10/2001) FL 84+15/1 FLC 5+1 FAC 11

GRANT Lee Anderson
Born: Watford, 27 January 1983
Height: 6'2" **Weight:** 13.4
International Honours: E: U21-4; Yth
Lee took full advantage of Andy Oakes' injury to compile a good run in Derby's goal and add to his England U21 caps last term. Tall and athletic, he made use of the chance to develop his game. There were some stunning saves at important moments in a difficult season and firm evidence of the right temperament in the way he dismissed mistakes from his mind. The future is promising as he gathers experience.

Derby Co (From trainee on 17/2/2001) FL 62+3 FLC 1 FAC 2

GRANVILLE Daniel (Danny) Patrick
Born: Islington, 19 January 1975
Height: 5'11" **Weight:** 12.5

Club Honours: FLC '98, ECWC '98; Div 1 '02
International Honours: E: U21-3
Danny missed the start of the 2003-04 season following a hernia operation, but once he had recovered fitness he found himself out of favour and on the transfer list at Crystal Palace. However, his fortunes changed in the new year when he was restored to the line-up at left back and he retained his place for the remainder of the campaign, helping Palace win a place in the Premiership via the play-offs. Danny is an experienced defender who is effective when pushing down the flank and a free-kick specialist.

Cambridge U (From trainee on 19/5/1993) FL 89+10/7 FLC 3+2 FAC 2+2 Others 4+2
Chelsea (£300,000 + on 21/3/1997) PL 12+6 FLC 3 Others 4+1/1
Leeds U (£1,600,000 on 8/7/1998) PL 7+2 FLC 1 FAC 3 Others 0+1
Manchester C (£1,000,000 on 7/8/1999) P/FL 56+14/3 FLC 1+4 FAC 5
Norwich C (Loaned on 27/10/2000) FL 6
Crystal Palace (£500,000 on 28/12/2001) FL 67+5/6 FLC 4 FAC 3+3 Others 3

GRAVES Wayne Alan
Born: Scunthorpe, 18 September 1980
Height: 5'8" **Weight:** 12.10
Utility player Wayne had a frustrating season for Scunthorpe United in 2003-04, having to settle for a bit-part role due to collecting a number of minor injuries. A very quick, committed player who loves to get forward, he found himself used equally as a central midfield player or at right wing back. Appearances, though, were limited and his longest run in the starting line-up was just three matches from the end of February.

Scunthorpe U (From trainee on 24/3/1999) FL 97+38/6 FLC 4+3 FAC 7+5 Others 4+2

GRAVESEN Thomas
Born: Vejle, Denmark, 11 March 1976
Height: 5'10" **Weight:** 12.4
International Honours: Denmark: 47; U21-6
Thomas continued to both impress and frustrate for Everton, for his crisp passing and strong running were sometimes dogged by inconsistency. A knee injury curtailed his impressive start to the campaign, but over the Christmas period he put in some eye-catching displays during the best period of his Goodison career so far. He carried this good form into the new year, the highlight of which was a brilliant goal against Aston Villa that showed his ability to beat players with ease when in the mood. A knee

injury four games from the end finished his season and the fact that the Blues lost all these games indicates his importance to the side. At international level he continued to be an inspirational figure, exemplified by his 'Man of the Match' performance for Denmark in their win against England at Old Trafford.

Everton (£2,500,000 from SV Hamburg, Germany, ex Vejle BK, on 9/8/2000) PL 111+9/7 FLC 5 FAC 6+1

GRAY Andrew (Andy) David
Born: Harrogate, 15 November 1977
Height: 6'1" **Weight:** 13.0
International Honours: S: 2; B-3; Yth
Andy was an ever-present for Bradford last term before his move to Sheffield United in February. He began the season in centre midfield and also operated on the left and right wings but he was at his most effective leading the line up front. He impressed with his strong running and positional play and was the club's joint top scorer with six goals when he left for Bramall Lane. Andy proved to be an immediate hit for the Blades, scoring in his first three games. Used as a striker, he worked hard, showing a good instinct for goal, both with his head and feet. He linked up particularly well with his former team mate, Ashley Ward and then with Jack Lester.

Leeds U (From trainee on 1/7/1995) PL 13+9 FLC 3+1 FAC 0+2
Bury (Loaned on 11/12/1997) FL 4+2/1
Nottingham F (£175,000 on 2/9/1998) P/FL 34+30/1 FLC 3+4 FAC 4+1
Preston NE (Loaned on 23/2/1999) FL 5
Oldham Ath (Loaned on 25/3/1999) FL 4
Bradford C (Free on 9/8/2002) FL 77/20 FLC 2 FAC 2/1
Sheffield U (Signed on 27/2/2004) FL 14/9

GRAY Ian James
Born: Manchester, 25 February 1975
Height: 6'2" **Weight:** 13.0
This big goalkeeper joined Huddersfield Town during the summer of 2003 and quickly established himself as the club's number one 'keeper. He controlled his area well, showing confidence on crosses and the ability to turn defence into attack in a moment. Ian is a great shot-stopper, and was responsible for many fine saves before he suffered a hand injury in the FA Cup defeat by Accrington Stanley and this ended his season in November.

Oldham Ath (From trainee on 16/7/1993)
Rochdale (Loaned on 18/11/1994) FL 12 Others 3
Rochdale (£20,000 on 17/7/1995) FL 66 FLC 4 FAC 5 Others 4

Michael Gray (right)

Stockport Co (£200,000 + on 30/7/1997) FL 14+2 FLC 3
Rotherham U (Free on 10/7/2000) FL 38+2 FLC 2 FAC 3 Others 1
Huddersfield T (Free on 7/8/2003) FL 17 FLC 3 FAC 1 Others 1

GRAY Julian Raymond
Born: Lewisham, 21 September 1979
Height: 6'1" **Weight:** 11.10
Julian was transfer-listed by Crystal Palace in the summer of 2003 and after trials with a number of Premiership clubs he was loaned out to Cardiff in October. He spent a month getting fit and then, after a second month, returned to Selhurst Park. The talented left winger went on to help transform the Eagles' fortunes as they rose from the relegation zone to the play-offs and eventually clinched the ultimate prize, a place in the Premiership for the 2004-05 season.
Arsenal (From trainee on 13/7/1998) PL 0+1
Crystal Palace (£250,000 + on 21/7/2000) FL 100+25/10 FLC 5+6/1 FAC 6/2 Others 2
Cardiff C (Loaned on 13/10/2003) FL 5+4

GRAY Kevin John
Born: Sheffield, 7 January 1972
Height: 6'0" **Weight:** 14.0
This experienced and committed full back made a handful of early-season appearances for Tranmere, but following a change in management at Prenton Park he moved on to Carlisle where he proved to be a successful signing. An excellent leader, he quickly established himself as one of the dominant figures both on the pitch and in the dressing room. Rarely beaten in the air, his committed approach rubbed off on those around him and he should be a key figure as Carlisle face their first season in the Conference.
Mansfield T (From trainee on 1/7/1990) FL 129+12/3 FLC 8/1 FAC 6+1 Others 12+2/2
Huddersfield T (Signed on 18/7/1994) FL 214+16/6 FLC 12+1 FAC 15 Others 11
Stockport Co (Loaned on 11/8/2000) FL 1
Tranmere Rov (Free on 8/7/2002) FL 11+1/1 FLC 1 FAC 1+1 Others 2+1
Carlisle U (Free on 25/11/2003) FL 25/3

GRAY Michael
Born: Sunderland, 3 August 1974
Height: 5'7" **Weight:** 10.10
Club Honours: Div 1 '96, '99
International Honours: E: 3
Sunderland's former club captain made his final appearance for his hometown club at Mansfield in the Carling Cup in August before moving to Celtic on loan and subsequently joining Blackburn Rovers on a free transfer. Arriving at

Ewood Park towards the end of the January transfer window, Michael settled down to become a huge favourite with his determined forward running and sharp tackling.
Sunderland (From trainee on 1/7/1992) P/FL 341+22/16 FLC 23+4 FAC 17+1/1 Others 3+1
Glasgow Celtic (Loaned on 31/8/2003) SL 2+5 SLC 1 Others 1+1
Blackburn Rov (Free on 28/1/2004) PL 14

GRAY Stuart Edward
Born: Harrogate, 18 December 1973
Height: 5'11" **Weight:** 11.2
Club Honours: Div 3 '03
International Honours: S: U21-7
This cultured Rushden midfielder spent some time battling against a groin injury last term, before succumbing to surgery. He returned to the side once he had recovered fitness and produced some influential displays even though Diamonds slipped to relegation as a result of a disastrous end-of-season spell. Stuart is the son of former Leeds United star Eddie Gray.
Glasgow Celtic (Signed from Giffnock North AFC on 7/7/1992) SL 19+9/1 SC 1 Others 2+1
Reading (£100,000 on 27/3/1998) FL 46+6/2 FLC 8 FAC 1+1 Others 2
Rushden & Diamonds (Free on 23/3/2001) FL 79+6/12 FLC 3+1 FAC 4 Others 4+1/1

GRAY Wayne William
Born: Camberwell, 7 November 1980
Height: 5'10" **Weight:** 12.10
It took Wayne 25 games to open his goal-scoring account for Wimbledon last term, and after finally netting his first of the campaign against Preston in early April, he promptly added an added-time equaliser in the same game before scoring in the following two matches against Sheffield United and Bradford City. A very pacy striker, but one who often struggled to impose himself in the opposing box, a final tally of four for the season was not enough to earn him a new deal. He was reported to have signed for Southend United in the summer.
Wimbledon (From trainee on 10/2/1999) P/FL 33+42/6 FLC 1+1 FAC 1+7/1
Swindon T (Loaned on 3/3/2000) FL 8+4/2
Port Vale (Loaned on 6/10/2000) FL 2+1
Leyton Orient (Loaned on 30/11/2001) FL 13+2/5 FAC 2/1
Brighton & Hove A (Loaned on 27/3/2002) FL 3+1/1

GRAYSON Simon Nicholas
Born: Ripon, 16 December 1969
Height: 6'0" **Weight:** 13.7
Club Honours: FLC '97; AMC '04

This experienced defender was again a regular in the Blackpool first-team squad in 2003-04. Equally effective either at right back or in the centre of the defence, a high point of his season came with an appearance in the LDV Vans Trophy final at Cardiff's Millennium Stadium.
Leeds U (From trainee on 13/6/1988) FL 2 Others 1+1
Leicester C (£50,000 on 13/3/1992) F/PL 175+13/4 FLC 16+2/2 FAC 9 Others 13+1
Aston Villa (£1,350,000 on 1/7/1997) PL 32+16 FLC 1+1 FAC 4+1/2 Others 6+3
Blackburn Rov (£750,000 + on 29/7/1999) FL 31+3 FLC 1+1 FAC 2+1
Sheffield Wed (Loaned on 11/8/2000) FL 5
Stockport Co (Loaned on 12/1/2001) FL 13 FAC 1
Notts Co (Loaned on 6/9/2001) FL 10/1 FLC 1 Others 2
Bradford C (Loaned on 15/2/2002) FL 7
Blackpool (Free on 1/8/2002) FL 72+6/4 FLC 3+1 FAC 5 Others 5+1

GREAVES Mark Andrew
Born: Hull, 22 January 1975
Height: 6'1" **Weight:** 13.0
Mark had another good season for Boston United. He was a first-team regular being used both as a central defender and in midfield where he provided extra power and strength. Mark was quick on the ground as well as solid in the air. He was given an extension to his contract at the end of the season.
Hull C (Free from Brigg T on 17/6/1996) FL 152+25/10 FLC 8/1 FAC 11/1 Others 6+2
Boston U (Free on 29/8/2002) FL 58+5/1 FLC 2 FAC 1 Others 3

GREEN Adam
Born: Hillingdon, 12 January 1984
Height: 5'9" **Weight:** 10.11
This impressive young left back made his senior debut for Fulham in the Carling Cup tie at Wigan. He was given his Premiership debut at Middlesbrough in January and later he enjoyed a three-match run, including two games against Manchester United in successive weeks when deputising for the suspended Carlos Bocanegra. Calm and assured on the ball he shows a maturity beyond his years and is possibly the best Fulham academy product since Sean Davis.
Fulham (From trainee on 4/7/2003) PL 4 FLC 1 FAC 2

GREEN Francis James
Born: Nottingham, 25 April 1980
Height: 5'9" **Weight:** 11.6
Francis had few opportunities for

Peterborough early on last season and finally signed for Lincoln City in September after being targeted by the Imps for several months. He was introduced gradually into the first team before winning a regular place on the right side of a three-man strike force. Francis worked hard and deserved more than the eight goals he netted during the campaign.

Peterborough U (£25,000 + from Ilkeston T on 2/3/1998) FL 51+57/14 FLC 4+3 FAC 5 Others 3+4/2
Lincoln C (£7,500 on 16/9/2003) FL 28+7/7 FAC 1 Others 2+2/1

Simon Grayson

GREEN Paul Jason
Born: Sheffield, 10 April 1983
Height: 5'10" **Weight:** 10.12
Club Honours: Div 3 '04
This young Doncaster Rovers midfielder took to Third Division football like a duck to water last season, impressing with his skill on the ball and his capacity for hard work. A box-to-box player he can be defending one minute and then be at the other end to put the ball in the net in the next minute. Paul is an exciting player and the Rovers' fans love him.
Doncaster Rov (From trainee on 16/8/2000) FL 38+5/8 FLC 1 FAC 1 Others 1

GREEN Robert Paul
Born: Chertsey, 18 January 1980
Height: 6'2" **Weight:** 12.2
Club Honours: Div 1 '04
International Honours: E: Yth
Robert forced his way into Sven-Göran Eriksson's England squad for the final international friendly of the season in Sweden but missed out on a place in the Euro 2004 squad. His outstanding reputation was enhanced by another tremendous season between the posts for Norwich City as they claimed the First Division title. A calm and authoritative figure, he makes difficult saves look easy with his tremendous positioning and quick reflexes. Robert was a member of the PFA's Division One team for the season.
Norwich C (From juniors on 3/7/1997) FL 142+1 FLC 3 FAC 6 Others 3

GREEN Stuart
Born: Whitehaven, 15 June 1981
Height: 5'10" **Weight:** 11.4
Stuart was in fine form for Hull City last term and a key figure in enabling the club to win promotion. A talented midfield player with tremendous passing skills, his increased work rate and consistency took the eye throughout the campaign and he weighed in with a total of six goals.
Newcastle U (From trainee on 8/7/1999)
Carlisle U (Loaned on 14/12/2001) FL 16/3
Hull C (£150,000 on 3/7/2002) FL 65+5/12 FLC 1 FAC 2
Carlisle U (Loaned on 19/2/2003) FL 9+1/2 Others 3

GREENACRE Christopher (Chris) Mark
Born: Halifax, 23 December 1977
Height: 5'11" **Weight:** 12.8
This quick-thinking and nippy striker was again hampered by injuries at Stoke last term. He was a regular in the starting line-up in the first few weeks of the season, but thereafter mostly featured from the substitutes' bench. A groin problem then saw him return to the treatment room in March. Chris will be hoping to establish himself in the first team during 2004-05.
Manchester C (From trainee on 1/7/1995) FL 3+5/1 FAC 0+1
Cardiff C (Loaned on 22/8/1997) FL 11/2
Blackpool (Loaned on 5/3/1998) FL 2+2
Scarborough (Loaned on 10/12/1998) FL 10+2/2 Others 1
Mansfield T (Free on 5/11/1999) FL 120+1/49 FLC 5/3 FAC 5/6 Others 2+1
Stoke C (Free on 8/7/2002) FL 26+17/6 FLC 1 FAC 4+1/2

GREENING Jonathan

Born: Scarborough, 2 January 1979
Height: 5'11" **Weight:** 11.7
Club Honours: EC '99; FLC '04
International Honours: E: U21-18; Yth
Jonathan started last term in
Middlesbrough's Premiership squad and
he was enjoying regular first-team
football until the end of the December
but, as the New Year came and went, he
then found that he was often overlooked
while injury problems did not help him.
However, Jonathan was handed a rare
start on the left wing in Boro's 5-3
demolition of Birmingham City at the
Riverside in March and he scored his only
goal of the season in this game.
York C (From trainee on 23/12/1996) FL
5+20/2 FLC 0+1 Others 1
Manchester U (£500,000 + on 25/3/1998)
PL 4+10 FLC 6 FAC 0+1 Others 3+3
Middlesbrough (£2,000,000 on 9/8/2001)
PL 91+8/4 FLC 5 FAC 4+1

GREGAN Sean Matthew

Born: Guisborough, 29 March 1974
Height: 6'2" **Weight:** 14.7
Club Honours: Div 2 '00
For the West Bromwich Albion skipper,
2003-04 was, in terms of overall
performances, perhaps his best season as
a professional footballer. He produced
some solid and determined displays in
both midfield and defence and his drive
and enthusiasm, all-out commitment and
urgency went a long way in helping the
Baggies regain their place in the
Premiership. He missed only five games
during the campaign and in November
reached the personal milestone of 400
League appearances in his club career.
Darlington (From trainee on 20/1/1991) FL
129+7/4 FLC 8 FAC 7 Others 10+1/1
Preston NE (£350,000 on 29/11/1996) FL
206+6/12 FLC 14 FAC 15/1 Others 10
West Bromwich A (£1,500,000 on
6/8/2002) P/FL 76+3/2 FLC 4 FAC 2

GRESKO Vratislav

Born: Pressburg, Bratislava, Slovakia, 24
July 1977
Height: 5'11" **Weight:** 11.5
International Honours: Slovakia: 19
Although he recovered from the broken
foot he suffered at the end of the
previous season Vratislav started the
2003-04 campaign in indifferent form for
Blackburn. Ironically he was just showing
signs of returning to his best, with a goal
and a magnificent display against Bolton,
when the club signed Michael Gray who
was immediately handed the left-back
shirt.

Blackburn Rov (£1,200,000 from Parma,
Italy, ex Dukla Banska, Inter Bratislava, Bayer
Leverkusen, Inter Milan, on 31/1/2003) PL
32+2/11 FLC 1 FAC 1 Others 2

GRIEMINK Bart

Born: Holland, 29 March 1972
Height: 6'4" **Weight:** 15.4
Bart began the 2003-04 season as
Swindon's first-choice 'keeper, but soon
found himself behind Rhys Evans in the
pecking order. Thereafter he was usually
confined to the substitutes' bench,
although he managed a rare outing at
former club Peterborough. He was out of
contract in the summer and was released
by the Robins.
Birmingham C (Free from WK Emmen,
Holland on 9/11/1995) FL 20 FLC 3 FAC 1
Others 1+1
Peterborough U (£25,000 on 11/10/1996)
FL 58 FLC 1 FAC 4 Others 4
Swindon T (Loaned on 5/2/2000) FL 4
Swindon T (Free on 27/7/2000) FL 118+2
FLC 8 FAC 7 Others 5

GRIFFIN Adam

Born: Salford, 26 August 1984
Height: 5'7" **Weight:** 10.5
After spending almost 18 months without
starting a League game for Oldham,
Adam made the line-up for the visit to
Colchester last December, Iain Dowie's
final game in charge. Despite previously
being seen as a left-sided midfielder, he
was asked to operate at left back and
thereafter became a virtual ever-present in
that position. A solid and gritty defender,
Adam also likes to venture forward and
scored a memorable first senior goal in
the 6-0 thumping of Grimsby Town in
February, his effort receiving the club's
'Goal of the Season' award.
Oldham Ath (From trainee on 9/8/2003) FL
25+2/1 FAC 0+1

GRIFFIN Andrew (Andy)

Born: Billinge, 7 March 1979
Height: 5'9" **Weight:** 10.10
International Honours: E: U21-2; Yth
This tenacious defender began the 2003-
04 season as first-choice right back in
Newcastle's back four. However, after
appearing in the squad for the first dozen
games Andy's opportunities were seriously
curtailed from October onwards by
hamstring and achilles injuries, although
he did reappear for the final game of the
season at Anfield when he turned in a
fine performance. A fierce tackler with
good stamina and a liking for joining his
attack, he was the subject of a bid from
Portsmouth in the January transfer

window, and although this was turned
down he agreed a move there at the end
of the season to secure regular first-team
football.
Stoke C (From trainee on 5/9/1996) FL
52+5/2 FLC 4+1 FAC 2
Newcastle U (£1,500,000 + on 30/1/1998)
PL 63+13/2 FLC 8 FAC 6 Others 14/1

GRIFFIN Antony Richard

Born: Bournemouth, 22 March 1979
Height: 5'11" **Weight:** 11.2
Antony was one of six players used in the
right-back position by Cheltenham Town
last term. A pacy attacking full back who
can also play on the right-hand side of
midfield, Antony started off in the first
team but soon found himself displaced.
Following a spell in the reserves he
returned to first-team duties in the new
year but finished the season on the
substitutes' bench. Antony was released
in the summer.
Bournemouth (From trainee on 7/7/1997) FL
1+5
Cheltenham T (£20,000 on 27/7/1999) FL
67+29/1 FLC 4+1 FAC 5 Others 3+2

GRIFFIN Daniel (Danny)
Joseph

Born: Belfast, 19 August 1977
Height: 5'10" **Weight:** 10.5
Club Honours: S Div 1 '97
International Honours: NI: 29; U21-10
This experienced central defender made a
number of appearances for Dundee
United in the early part of last season, but
then fell out of favour. He linked up with
his former Northern Ireland boss Sammy
McIlroy in the new year and made a huge
impact at Edgeley Park before being
stretchered off at Blackpool in March with
an achilles injury, which ruled him out of
action until the summer. Danny continued
to represent his country during the
campaign.
St Johnstone (Signed from St Andrew's BC
on 18/2/1994) SL 42+12/2 SLC 6+1/2 SC 4/2
Others 2
Dundee U (£600,000 on 17/6/2002) SL
72+5/4 SLC 4/1 SC 6
Stockport Co (Free on 9/1/2004) FL 15/1

GRIFFIT Leandre

Born: Maubeuge, France, 21 May 1984
Height: 5'11" **Weight:** 11.1
Brought to St Mary's during the summer
as a goal-scoring winger, Leandre was
converted to a wide midfielder with no
little success. Fleet and skilful of foot and
a cool customer in front of goal, he
marked his debut, in October against
Blackburn Rovers, with a deftly taken goal

less than five minutes after coming on as a substitute. Used sparingly afterwards – rather than be lost in a lacklustre midfield – he repeated the feat in May against Newcastle United; outpacing the defence, cutting in and slotting the ball home through Shay Given's legs.
Southampton *(Free from Amiens, France on 23/7/2003) PL 2+3/2*

GRIFFITHS Gareth John
Born: Winsford, 10 April 1970
Height: 6'4" **Weight:** 14.0
Rochdale's centre half and skipper missed the first month of the 2003-04 campaign through injury before re-establishing himself in the side. He provided his usual dominant presence in the air at the back, but niggling injuries and the presence of a number of other central defenders in the Dale ranks meant that he was in and out of the side in the last couple of months of the season. Still a player you would want on your side when the going gets tough, though, he was there to help Dale to crucial late victories to preserve their Football League status.
Port Vale *(£1,000 from Rhyl on 8/2/1993) FL 90+4/4 FLC 8 FAC 7/1 Others 7*
Shrewsbury T *(Loaned on 31/10/1997) FL 6*
Wigan Ath *(Free on 2/7/1998) FL 44+9/2 FLC 4/1 FAC 5 Others 5+1*
Rochdale *(Free on 18/7/2001) FL 111+5/11 FLC 3 FAC 6/1 Others 5*

GRITTON Martin
Born: Glasgow, 1 June 1978
Height: 6'1" **Weight:** 12.7
This willing centre forward's second season at Torquay never really scaled the heights of his first term with the club. After missing the start of the campaign with a badly gashed leg, he rushed back into action only to be ruled out for a further three months with a groin injury. The lack of a prolonged run of starts meant that Martin did not fully regain match sharpness to go with his work rate and strength on the ball.
Plymouth Arg *(Free from Porthleven on 7/8/1998) FL 15+29/7 FLC 2+2/1 FAC 0+4 Others 3/1*
Torquay U *(Signed on 8/8/2002) FL 56+18/17 FLC 1 FAC 2/3 Others 1*

GRONKJAER Jesper
Born: Nuuk, Denmark, 12 August 1977
Height: 6'1" **Weight:** 12.8
International Honours: Denmark: 49; U21-13
Famous for his crucial goal which put

Chelsea into the Champions' League, the flying Danish winger waited 51 weeks for his next goal! Jesper certainly ended the 2003-04 season with a flourish scoring three of the Blues' last four goals – a delightful curling left-footer against AS Monaco, a rasping right-footed drive at Old Trafford and a diving header which clinched the final Premiership match of the season against Leeds United. Jesper lost his place on the wide right at the start of the season to the newly-arrived Geremi but Claudio Ranieri is a firm believer in pace on the flanks and Jesper reclaimed his position for the latter two-thirds of the campaign – with Damien Duff on the opposite flank Chelsea fielded possibly the two most effective wide men in the Premiership.
Chelsea *(£7,800,000 from Ajax, Holland, ex Aalborg BK, on 21/12/2000) PL 56+32/7 FLC 3+2 FAC 10+4/3 Others 8+4/1*

GROVES Paul
Born: Derby, 28 February 1966
Height: 5'11" **Weight:** 11.5
Club Honours: AMC '98
Grimsby's player-manager appeared to have decided to concentrate on his managerial duties last term and after the first few weeks of the season remained mainly on the bench as a second successive relegation season threatened. However, he was relieved of his management post in February and after a brief spell on the playing staff at Blundell Park he moved on to local rivals Scunthorpe. Paul's experience proved invaluable to the Iron midfield, firstly in midfield and latterly in the centre of defence as the team successfully avoided relegation.
Leicester C *(£12,000 from Burton A on 18/4/1988) FL 7+9/1 FLC 1/1 FAC 0+1 Others 0+1*
Lincoln C *(Loaned on 20/8/1989) FL 8/1 FLC 2*
Blackpool *(£60,000 on 25/1/1990) FL 106+1/21 FLC 6/1 FAC 9/4 Others 13/3*
Grimsby T *(£150,000 on 12/8/1992) FL 183+1/38 FLC 10+1/2 FAC 12/2 Others 4/1*
West Bromwich A *(£600,000 on 8/7/1996) FL 27+2/4 FLC 2/1 FAC 1*
Grimsby T *(£250,000 on 21/7/1997) FL 262+8/33 FLC 25+1/5 FAC 13/1 Others 10/2*
Scunthorpe U *(Free on 27/2/2004) FL 13/3*

GUDJOHNSEN Eidur Smari
Born: Reykjavik, Iceland, 15 September 1978
Height: 6'1" **Weight:** 13.0
Club Honours: CS '00

International Honours: Iceland: 27; U21-11; Yth
Chelsea's pursuit of top-class front players in the aftermath of the Russian takeover appeared, at first glance, to put Eidur Gudjohnsen's position in jeopardy but the club showed their faith in the Icelandic striker by awarding him a one-year extension to his contract. Eidur started the ball rolling for the 'new' Chelsea back in early August by scoring the opening goal of the season at MSK Zilina in a Champions' League qualifier. However, newcomers Adrian Mutu and Hernan Crespo plus Jimmy-Floyd Hasselbaink mainly occupied the striking berths in the first two-thirds of the season, reducing Eidur to cameo appearances from the bench. Given more action in the last three months, Eidur played brilliantly – scoring with a thunderous left-footer against Fulham and playing a big part in the elimination of Arsenal from the Champions' League by scoring in the first leg and creating Wayne Bridge's winner with an intuitive pass. In a case of 'what might have been', he rattled the Monaco crossbar with a bullet header in the semi-final when Chelsea had the French club at their mercy.
Bolton W *(Free from KR Reykjavik, Iceland, ex Valur, PSV Eindhoven, on 6/8/1998) FL 48+7/18 FLC 8+1/3 FAC 4+1/4 Others 4/1*
Chelsea *(£4,000,000 on 12/7/2000) PL 80+43/40 FLC 6+3/5 FAC 12+7/8 Others 12+6/6*

GUDJONSSON Bjarni
Born: Iceland, 26 February 1979
Height: 5'9" **Weight:** 11.9
Club Honours: AMC '00
International Honours: Iceland: 12; U21-20; Yth
Bjarni joined Coventry on loan last January and had a major impact on the team as a run of excellent results briefly raised play-off hopes. His crosses and corners created numerous chances and a willingness to shoot brought him three goals. A clinical finish at Wimbledon, when he had an outstanding game, was followed by a brace at home to Preston: a stunning, dipping 30-yard effort and a superb header. Bjarni's form won him a recall to the Iceland team before the end of the season.
Newcastle U *(£500,000 from Akranes, Iceland on 14/7/1997. £125,000 to KRC Genk on 12/11/1998)*
Stoke C *(£250,000 on 10/3/2000) FL 119+13/11 FLC 7/2 FAC 8+1/1 Others 9+4/2*
(Freed during 2003 close season)

Coventry C *(Loaned from VfL Bochum, Germany on 16/1/2004)* FL 17+1/3 FAC 1+1

GUDJONSSON Johannes (Joey) Karl
Born: Akranes, Iceland, 25 May 1980
Height: 5'8" **Weight:** 11.5
International Honours: Iceland: 15; U21-10; Yth
Joey joined Wolves on a long-term loan basis and after a couple of appearances from the bench he made the starting line-up against Chelsea. He scored with a long-range effort in the Carling Cup tie against Darlington, and enjoyed a four-match run, but found there was plenty of competition for places in midfield. Joey had a torrid time at Arsenal, playing in an unfamiliar right-back role, but although he continued to be involved with the Iceland team, he was rarely seen in a Wolves' shirt after Christmas.
Aston Villa (Loaned from Real Betis, Spain, ex IA Akranes, KRC Genk, MVV Maastricht, RKC Waalwijk, on 27/1/2003) PL 9+2/2
Wolverhampton W (Loaned from Real Betis, Spain on 29/8/2003) PL 5+6 FLC 3/1 FAC 1+1

GUERET Willy July
Born: Guadeloupe, 3 August 1973
Height: 6'1" **Weight:** 13.5
Willy was restricted to just a handful of appearances for Millwall last term due to the exceptional form of Tony Warner. However, he continued to plug away and had a short run in the side when Warner was injured, during which time the team was undefeated. With the arrival of Andy Marshall, Willy dropped back to the bench. He is an excellent shot-stopper, good in the air and with a great presence in the area.
Millwall (Free from Le Mans, France on 31/7/2000) FL 13+1 FAC 3 Others 2

GULLIVER Philip (Phil) Stephen
Born: Bishop Auckland, 12 September 1982
Height: 6'2" **Weight:** 13.6
This promising central defender did well in a two-month loan spell with Bury last autumn and soon after his return to the Riverside Stadium he moved out on loan again, this time to Scunthorpe. He showed himself to be strong in the air but stayed just a month with the Iron. A regular in the Middlesborough reserve team, and captain on occasions, Phil was released in the summer.
Middlesbrough (From trainee on 7/7/2000)

Blackpool *(Loaned on 29/11/2002)* FL 2+1 FAC 1
Carlisle U *(Loaned on 31/12/2002)* FL 1
Bournemouth *(Loaned on 27/3/2003)* FL 4+2 Others 3
Bury (Loaned on 10/10/2003) FL 10 FAC 1
Scunthorpe U (Loaned on 16/1/2004) FL 2 Others 1

GUNBY Stephen (Steve) Robert
Born: Boston, 14 April 1984
Height: 5'11" **Weight:** 13.3
This young Bury midfielder featured as a substitute in a handful of games last term and was given his first senior start at Torquay in October. However, he suffered a shoulder injury in training in November and at the end of January his contract was terminated. Soon afterwards Steve signed for Conference outfit Leigh RMI.
Bury (From trainee on 13/11/2002) FL 1+5 Others 0+1

GUNNARSSON Brynjar Bjorn
Born: Iceland, 16 October 1975
Height: 6'1" **Weight:** 11.12
International Honours: Iceland: 39; U21-8; Yth
This defensive midfielder originally joined Nottingham Forest on trial just prior to the start of last season and after impressing the management he was rewarded with a one-year contract. Unfortunately he found it difficult to win a regular place in the side and even briefly featured at right back. In March he rejoined Stoke on loan, then on a short-term contract. However, he was used sparingly by the Potters in the closing weeks of the campaign. Brynjar was reported to have signed for Watford in the summer.
Stoke C (£600,000 from Orgryte IS, Sweden on 4/1/2000) FL 128+3/16 FLC 7/1 FAC 7/2 Others 12+1/1
Nottingham F (Free on 1/8/2003) FL 9+4 FAC 1
Stoke C (Free on 19/3/2004) FL 1+2

GUPPY Stephen (Steve) Andrew
Born: Winchester, 29 March 1969
Height: 5'11" **Weight:** 11.12
Club Honours: FAT '91, '93; GMVC '93; FLC '00; SPD '02
International Honours: E: 1; B-1; U21-1; SP-1
Steve made just one first-team appearance for Celtic last term, coming on as a substitute in the Scottish League Cup tie at Partick in December. The

following month he opted for a move back to Leicester, one of his former clubs. Steve was soon back in harness supplying a series of quality crosses from the left wing or from dead-ball situations. However, even he could not turn the Foxes' fortunes around single-handedly and injury problems later saw him have to settle for a string of substitute appearances rather than starts. Consequently, Steve was released by Micky Adams at the end of the campaign.
Wycombe W (Signed from Colden Common on 1/9/1989) FL 41/8 FLC 4 FAC 3 Others 10/2
Newcastle U (£150,000 on 2/8/1994) FLC 0+1
Port Vale (£225,000 on 25/11/1994) FL 102+3/12 FLC 7 FAC 8 Others 7+1/1
Leicester C (£950,000 on 28/2/1997) PL 133+3/19 FLC 15 FAC 9/1 Others 4
Glasgow Celtic (£350,000 on 2/8/2001) SL 22+11 SLC 2+1 SC 4 Others 4+5
Leicester C (Free on 16/1/2004) PL 9+6

GURNEY Andrew (Andy) Robert
Born: Bristol, 25 January 1974
Height: 5'10" **Weight:** 11.6
Andy enjoyed another consistent season for Swindon last term when he was once again a regular in the line-up. A combative, tenacious right back, he weighed in with his customary contribution of goals, opening his account with a spectacular effort to secure all three points against Wrexham.
Bristol Rov (From trainee on 10/7/1992) FL 100+8/9 FLC 7/1 FAC 5 Others 15
Torquay U (Free on 10/7/1997) FL 64/10 FLC 6 FAC 5/1 Others 3
Reading (£100,000 on 15/1/1999) FL 55+12/3 FLC 5 FAC 5+1 Others 5+1
Swindon T (Free on 2/7/2001) FL 126/20 FLC 4/1 FAC 4/2 Others 4+1

GUTTRIDGE Luke Horace
Born: Barnstaple, 27 March 1982
Height: 5'5" **Weight:** 9.7
This brave, two-footed young central midfielder enjoyed an excellent season for Cambridge United last term. He was the U's only ever-present and finished the campaign as leading scorer. A series of fine performances bought him to the attention of bigger clubs and he spent time training with Charlton. Luke was voted 'Player of the Season' by the U's fans.
Torquay U (Trainee) FL 0+1
Cambridge U (Free on 15/8/2000) FL 113+6/17 FLC 1+2 FAC 6+1/1 Others 9+3/2

Steve Guppy

HAAS Bernt
Born: Vienna, Austria, 8 April 1978
Height: 6'1" **Weight:** 12.8
International Honours: Switzerland: 31
A confident, hard-working and composed wingback, Bernt joined West Bromwich Albion following Igor Balis' retirement, and went on to produce some impressive displays with his blistering pace down the right flank. He didn't have the happiest of debuts, however, featuring in a 4-1 defeat at Walsall on the opening day of the season. Bernt scored a cracking volleyed goal when Albion defeated Manchester United 2-0 in the Carling Cup in December but during the second half of the season served suspension, was injured and also lost his first-team place to James Chambers. Bernt was a regular for Switzerland, featuring in their squad for the Euro 2004 finals in the summer.
Sunderland (£750,000 from Grasshopper Zurich, Switzerland on 10/8/2001) PL 27 FLC 0+1 FAC 1
West Bromwich A (£400,000 + on 8/8/2003) FL 36/1 FLC 5/2 FAC 1

HACKETT Christopher (Chris) James
Born: Oxford, 1 March 1983
Height: 6'0" **Weight:** 11.6
Chris was one of several players to benefit from the appointment of Graham Rix as manager of Oxford United towards the end of last season. The tall, speedy winger, a former county sprint champion, did well when called upon and scored his only goal of the campaign with a clever lob at York.
Oxford U (From trainee on 20/4/2000) FL 22+45/3 FLC 0+2 FAC 1+2 Others 2+2

HACKWORTH Anthony (Tony)
Born: Durham, 19 May 1980
Height: 6'1" **Weight:** 13.7
International Honours: E: Yth
Tony had a rather disappointing season at Notts County last term and never managed to establish himself in the first team. In March the young striker was loaned out to Conference club Scarborough, where he finally found his goal touch, netting three times in 11 appearances for the Conference outfit.
Leeds U (From trainee on 23/5/1997) FLC 0+1 Others 0+2
Notts Co (£150,000 on 16/7/2001) FL 17+37/1 FLC 0+3 FAC 2+1 Others 4/1

HADDRELL Matthew (Matt) Charles
Born: Stoke, 19 March 1981
Height: 6'1" **Weight:** 14.0
Most of Matt's appearances for Macclesfield last season came when other players were either injured or suspended. In his role as a central defender in a back-four formation he made good use of his heading ability, but also occasionally came on from the bench as a striker. Unfortunately, Matt had been unable to settle into League football to the degree he would have liked, resulting in his contract being cancelled by mutual consent in February 2004. Shortly afterwards he signed for Unibond League club Leek Town.
Macclesfield T (£35,000 from Vauxhall Motors, ex Kidsgrove, Newcastle T, on 21/3/2003) FL 6+8/1 FLC 1 FAC 2+1

HADJI Moustapha
Born: Ifrane, Morocco, 16 November 1971
Height: 6'0" **Weight:** 11.10
International Honours: Morocco
Moustapha made a solitary appearance as a substitute for Aston Villa against Manchester City last September before leaving to join Espanyol on a short-term contract. A creative midfielder, he can play on either flank, but prefers a role just behind the main two strikers.
Coventry C (£4,000,000 from Deportivo La Coruna, Spain, ex Nancy, Sporting Lisbon, on 3/8/1999) PL 61+1/12 FLC 4+1 FAC 3/1
Aston Villa (£4,500,000 on 6/7/2001) PL 24+11/2 FLC 3 FAC 0+1 Others 4+5/1

HADLAND Phillip (Phil) Jonathan
Born: Warrington, 20 October 1980
Height: 5'11" **Weight:** 11.8
This tricky winger joined Colchester United during the 2003 close season, but failed to make much of an impression at Layer Road in the opening stages of the campaign. He was on the bench for five games, making two brief appearances, before returning north to sign for Leek Town.
Reading (From trainee on 22/6/1999) FLC 1
Rochdale (Free on 8/8/2000) FL 12+20/2 FLC 0+1 FAC 1 Others 1
Leyton Orient (Free on 9/7/2001) FL 0+5/1 FLC 0+1
Carlisle U (Loaned on 19/11/2001) FL 4/1 FAC 1
Brighton & Hove A (Free on 19/3/2002) FL 0+2
Darlington (Free on 16/8/2002) FL 4+2 FLC 1
Colchester U (Free on 8/8/2003) FL 0+1 FLC 0+1

HAHNEMANN Marcus Stephen
Born: Seattle, USA, 15 June 1972
Height: 6'3" **Weight:** 16.2
International Honours: USA: 4
Marcus maintained his run of consecutive appearances in the Reading goal until near the end of the season, when an injury to his right knee forced him to be taken off in the home game against Stoke City. Up to that point he had been at his consistent best. He returned to fitness by May, but was only able to warm the substitutes' bench for the last two games. Popular as ever with the fans, he always throws his 'keeper's jersey into the crowd at the end of each match.
Fulham (£80,000 from Colorado Rapids, USA on 9/7/1999) FL 2 FLC 2
Rochdale (Loaned on 12/10/2001) FL 5 Others 2
Reading (Loaned on 14/12/2001) FL 6
Reading (Free on 14/8/2002) FL 77 FLC 5 FAC 4 Others 2

HAINING William (Will) Wallace
Born: Glasgow, 2 October 1982
Height: 5'11" **Weight:** 10.10
Domineering in the air and a good reader of the game, Will endured a frustrating start to the 2003-04 season when he was hampered by a hamstring injury. After returning to the centre of the defence in November, he found himself in and out of the Oldham line-up with the arrival of new manager Brian Talbot. Will then teamed up at the heart of defence with on-loan Gareth Owen and latterly Danny Hall as the side conceded just seven goals in their last eight games. He became out of contract this summer but was offered a new deal and at the time of writing looked likely to stay at Boundary Park.
Oldham Ath (From trainee on 17/10/2001) FL 56+5/4 FLC 1+1 FAC 1+1/1 Others 3

HALDANE Lewis Oliver
Born: Trowbridge, 13 March 1985
Height: 6'0" **Weight:** 11.13
This exciting young teenage striker made rapid progress last term after starting the season on loan at Dr Martens League club Clevedon Town. Lewis scored on his first start for Bristol Rovers at Darlington and added another super strike against Bury. He completed his first season as a professional with six goals and was voted by the fans as 'Young Player of the Season'.
Bristol Rov (From trainee on 13/10/2003) FL 16+11/5 FAC 1 Others 1/1

HALFORD Gregory (Greg)
Born: Chelmsford, 8 December 1984
Height: 6'4" **Weight:** 13.10
Greg really came of age for Colchester last term, when he was transformed from a hopeful youth-team player to a senior professional, bursting onto the scene in dramatic fashion at right back. Taking advantage of skipper Karl Duguid's knee injury, Greg played in every game bar one from the beginning of March. His height gave an extra dimension to the U's set plays, and he proceeded to plunder four goals inside two months, including a bullet of a free kick at Chesterfield.
Colchester U (From trainee on 8/8/2003) FL 16+3/4 FAC 2 Others 4

HALL Christopher (Chris)
Michael
Born: Manchester, 27 November 1986
Height: 6'1" **Weight:** 11.4
A burly young striker, Chris made two first-team appearances as a substitute for Oldham in the early part of the 2003-04 campaign after impressing in youth and reserve-team outings. He made his debut as a late substitute in the 2-2 draw at Peterborough United in October and had a goal disallowed in his next appearance, the FA Cup tie against Carlisle United at Boundary Park. Chris's chief attribute is his physical presence and he is a real handful in the opposition penalty box.
Oldham Ath (Trainee) FL 0+1 FAC 0+1

HALL Daniel (Danny) Andrew
Born: Ashton under Lyne, 14 November 1983
Height: 6'2" **Weight:** 12.7
A determined central defender, Danny earned regular first-team football during the 2003-04 season after impressing in Oldham Athletic's reserve and U19 sides. His big break came about after a pre-season injury to Michael Clegg and he seized his opportunity well. He scored his first senior goal in September's 5-2 win at Wycombe and despite being sidelined with injury at the turn of the year he was restored to the side when on-loan Gareth Owen returned to Stoke City in March.
Oldham Ath (From trainee on 7/8/2003) FL 28+5/1 FLC 1 FAC 1+1 Others 1

HALL Fitz
Born: Leytonstone, 20 December 1980
Height: 6'1" **Weight:** 13.4
In last year's edition of the *PFA Footballers' Who's Who* it was stated that Fitz, of Second Division Oldham, was: "A skilful defender with a silky touch and an eye for the pass [who] also poses an

attacking threat at set pieces." Nothing has changed, other than he's now looking just as good for Southampton in the Premiership. A bargain buy, he had to wait until December for the opportunity to demonstrate his undoubted promise at St Mary's, and while he may not be quite ready to displace either Claus Lundekvam or Michael Svensson in the centre of Saints' defence, he has now established himself as a contender rather than a stand-in.
Oldham Ath (£20,000 + from Chesham U,

ex Staines T, on 15/3/2002) FL 44/5 FLC 4 FAC 3/1 Others 2+1
Southampton (£250,000 + on 14/7/2003) PL 7+4 FLC 1

HALL Marcus Thomas
Born: Coventry, 24 March 1976
Height: 6'1" **Weight:** 12.2
International Honours: E: B-1; U21-8
This tall and pacy Stoke player settled in at left back last season following Clive Clarke's conversion to a midfield role. A regular in the side for most of the

Marcus Hall

campaign, Marcus is also able to operate on the left-hand side of midfield if required.
Coventry C *(From trainee on 1/7/1994) P/FL 113+19/2 FLC 14+1/2 FAC 8+2*
Nottingham F *(Free on 7/8/2002) FL 1*
Southampton *(Free on 30/8/2002)*
Stoke C *(Free on 6/12/2002) FL 57+2 FLC 2 FAC 4*

HALL Paul Anthony
Born: Manchester, 3 July 1972
Height: 5'9" **Weight:** 11.0
Club Honours: Div 3 '03
International Honours: Jamaica: 41
This experienced winger found it difficult to make an impact for Rushden last term, and although he provided plenty of assists for his colleagues, he only found the target twice at Nene Park. Paul eventually found himself fighting to hold down a regular starting role and on transfer-deadline day he moved on to Tranmere on a short-term contract. He slotted easily into the Rovers' line-up, adding further options on the right-hand side, and was given a new contract at the end of the season.
Torquay U *(From trainee on 9/7/1990) FL 77+16/1 FLC 7 FAC 4+1/2 Others 5+1/1*
Portsmouth *(£70,000 on 25/3/1993) FL 148+40/37 FLC 10+3/1 FAC 7+1/2 Others 5+2/2*
Coventry C *(£300,000 on 10/8/1998) PL 2+8 FLC 2+1/1*
Bury *(Loaned on 18/2/1999) FL 7*
Sheffield U *(Loaned on 17/12/1999) FL 1+3/1*
West Bromwich A *(Loaned on 10/2/2000) FL 4*
Walsall *(Free on 17/3/2001) FL 46+6/10 FLC 4+1 FAC 3/1 Others 3*
Rushden & Diamonds *(Free on 11/10/2001) FL 106+6/26 FLC 3 FAC 4+2 Others 4+2/3*
Tranmere Rov *(Free on 25/3/2004) FL 9/2*

HALLS John
Born: Islington, 14 February 1982
Height: 6'0" **Weight:** 11.4
Club Honours: FAYC '00
International Honours: E: Yth
John arrived at Stoke on loan from Arsenal last October and went straight into the line-up. Although he prefers to play in midfield his performances at right back were something of a revelation and the transfer was eventually made permanent. A good tackler he likes to get forward and although he has yet to find the net it is surely only a matter of time. John won several 'Man of the Match' awards and was runner-up to Ade

Akinbiyi in the fans' 'Player of the Season' poll.
Arsenal *(From trainee on 18/7/2000) FLC 0+3*
Colchester U *(Loaned on 18/1/2002) FL 6*
Stoke C *(£100,000 on 4/10/2003) FL 34 FAC 2*

HAMANN Dietmar
Born: Waldsasson, Germany, 27 August 1973
Height: 6'3" **Weight:** 12.2
Club Honours: FLC '01; FAC '01; UEFAC '01; ESC '01; CS '01
International Honours: Germany: 57; U21; Yth
This unassuming and unspectacular midfield anchor for Liverpool is often more noticed when he is missing than when he plays! When he is in the team the Reds operate with more cohesion and efficiency but when he is absent the team loses its fluency and starts to struggle. So when Didi missed the first three months of the season with a shin injury, Liverpool fans were praying for his early return to enable the team to start playing as a coherent unit. Didi returned to action in November and remained virtually ever-present to the end of the season, but the Reds continued to splutter in fits and starts. Although an infrequent scorer his goals are always memorable, for their power and timing rather than their rarity. A volley into the top corner in the Christmas game at Manchester City was surpassed by a stunning swerving and dipping volley from a lay-back by Michael Owen against Portsmouth in March, without doubt Liverpool's 'Goal of the Season'.
Newcastle U *(£4,500,000 from Bayern Munich, Germany, ex Wacker Munchen, on 5/8/1998) PL 22+1/4 FLC 1 FAC 7/1*
Liverpool *(£8,000,000 on 23/7/1999) PL 138+6/8 FLC 4+4 FAC 14/1 Others 40+2/1*

HAMILTON Derrick (Des) Vivian
Born: Bradford, 15 August 1976
Height: 5'11" **Weight:** 13.0
International Honours: E: U21-1
After a frustrating couple of seasons this combative midfielder arrived at Blundell Park to fill the gap left by the long-term absence of key Grimsby players Alan Pouton and Stacy Coldicott. He established himself firmly in the senior squad, but then a change in management saw him deemed as surplus to requirements and he was released by mutual consent shortly before the transfer deadline. Des then signed non-contract forms for Barnet but did not appear at

first-team level for the Conference club.
Bradford C *(From trainee on 1/6/1994) FL 67+21/5 FLC 6/1 FAC 6 Others 4+1/2*
Newcastle U *(£1,500,000 + on 27/3/1997) PL 7+5 FLC 1+1/1 FAC 1 Others 2+1*
Sheffield U *(Loaned on 16/10/1998) FL 6*
Huddersfield T *(Loaned on 15/2/1999) FL 10/1*
Norwich C *(Loaned on 22/3/2000) FL 7*
Tranmere Rov *(Loaned on 25/10/2000) FL 2 FLC 1*
Tranmere Rov *(Loaned on 10/1/2001) FL 3+1 FAC 3*
Cardiff C *(Free on 3/7/2001) FL 16+9 FLC 0+1 FAC 4+1/1 Others 4*
Grimsby T *(Free on 10/7/2003) FL 20+7 FLC 1 FAC 2 Others 1*

HAMMOND Dean John
Born: Hastings, 7 March 1983
Height: 6'0" **Weight:** 12.4
This promising young Brighton midfielder spent most of the first half of the 2003-04 campaign out on loan, firstly at Aldershot and then at Leyton Orient, where he impressed with his willingness to join in the attack. Dean then returned to the Withdean and a place in Albion's reserve side, captaining the team to victory over Worthing in the Sussex Senior Cup final.
Brighton & Hove A *(From trainee on 10/6/2002) FL 1+3 FLC 1/1 Others 0+1*
Leyton Orient *(Loaned on 17/10/2003) FL 6+2 FAC 1*

HAMMOND Elvis Zark
Born: Accra, Ghana, 6 October 1980
Height: 5'10" **Weight:** 10.10
This promising Fulham youngster had a spell on loan at Norwich early on last season. A quick and direct striker with a prodigious leap, he played in a handful of games as a substitute before returning to the West London club with an injury. Soon afterwards he suffered a fractured knee cap and only returned to first-team training in the closing stages of the campaign. Elvis will be hoping to make a breakthrough for Fulham in 2004-05.
Fulham *(From trainee on 1/7/1999) PL 3+7 FLC 0+1*
Bristol Rov *(Loaned on 31/8/2001) FL 3+4 FLC 0+1*
Norwich C *(Loaned on 14/8/2003) FL 0+4*

HAND Jamie
Born: Uxbridge, 7 February 1984
Height: 5'11" **Weight:** 11.10
International Honours: E: Yth
Jamie was a regular member of the first-team squad at the start of last season and has now made more than 50 League

appearances for Watford, his only club. An enthusiastic and hard-working midfield player who is always eager to be involved, Jamie never stopped trying but found it difficult to assert himself in a struggling team.

Watford (From trainee on 17/4/2002) FL 40+15 FLC 1+2 FAC 1+2

HANDYSIDE Peter David
Born: Dumfries, 31 July 1974
Height: 6'1" **Weight:** 13.8
Club Honours: AMC '98
International Honours: S: U21-7
Peter was appointed as club captain by Barnsley at the start of last season, although like several of his colleagues he was initially taken on rolling three-year contracts. The solid defender was a regular in the side until an injury in early November put him out of action. He made his return in mid-January, however, a change of manager then saw him become more of a squad player. Peter was released at the end of the season.

Grimsby T (From trainee on 21/11/1992) FL 181+9/4 FLC 18+1 FAC 12+1 Others 13+1
Stoke C (Free on 10/7/2001) FL 78 FLC 2 FAC 5/1 Others 3
Barnsley (Free on 8/8/2003) FL 28 FLC 1 FAC 2 Others 1

HANKIN Sean Anthony
Born: Camberley, 28 February 1981
Height: 5'11" **Weight:** 12.4
Sean started the 2003-04 season as first choice at left back for Torquay, despite only being on a short-term contract. However, he quickly lost his place through injury and was not subsequently offered an extended contract. Sean later had brief spells with Margate and Northwich, before joining Crawley Town, helping his new club go on to win the Dr Martens League title.

Crystal Palace (From trainee on 29/6/1999) FL 0+1
Torquay U (£20,000 on 15/10/2001) FL 45+2/1 FLC 2 FAC 2 Others 1

HANLON Richard (Richie) Kenneth
Born: Wembley, 26 May 1978
Height: 6'1" **Weight:** 13.7
After a lengthy battle against knee ligament problems Richie returned to first-team action with Rushden as a second-half substitute in their 2-0 defeat at Barnsley last October. He completed 90 minutes in the LDV Vans Trophy tie at Oxford and then scored a superb last-minute goal from 30 yards as Diamonds beat Grimsby Town 3-1. The midfielder

continued to work hard but he was in and out of the side in the closing stages. He was released at the end of the season.

Southend U (From trainee at Chelsea on 10/7/1996) FL 1+1 (Free to Welling U on 18/9/1997)
Peterborough U (Signed from Rushden & Diamonds on 9/12/1998) FL 0+4/1 Others 1 (Free to Welling U on 12/8/1999)
Peterborough U (Free on 17/12/1999) FL 30+13/2 FLC 1+1 FAC 0+1 Others 3+2
Rushden & Diamonds (£30,000 on 10/9/2001) FL 51+11/7 FLC 0+1 FAC 2+1/2 Others 3

HARDIKER John David
Born: Preston, 17 July 1982
Height: 6'0" **Weight:** 11.4
John enjoyed another good campaign for Stockport County last term when he was a regular in the line-up for almost all the season. Although he featured on the bench early on he was soon back in the starting line-up, playing mostly at right back, but also occasionally filling in as a central defender.

Stockport Co (£150,000 from Morecambe on 28/1/2002) FL 68+6/3 FLC 3+1 FAC 2 Others 5

HARDING Benjamin (Ben) Scott
Born: Carshalton, 6 September 1984
Height: 5'10" **Weight:** 11.2
In terms of notable debuts, Ben's ranks fairly highly. A tall and well-balanced midfielder, he was given his chance for Wimbledon at Rotherham in November, and after doing well enough found himself ending the match in goal as a result of an injury and a sending off to the club's designated 'keepers! The fact that he failed to concede during his 25 minutes between the posts set him up well for the remainder of the season, when he shone in a struggling team. A naturally left-footed player, his physique lends itself much more to a central than a wide position, where he often ended up featuring late on in the campaign.

Wimbledon (From trainee on 15/10/2001) FL 10+5 FAC 1

HARDING Daniel (Dan) Andrew
Born: Gloucester, 23 December 1983
Height: 6'0" **Weight:** 11.11
Used by Brighton as a substitute or as cover for left midfield during the first half of the 2003-04 season, Dan came into his own when he replaced the suspended Kerry Mayo at left back in February. He performed so well that he held onto his

place for the final run-in that culminated in the play-off final triumph at Cardiff. Tenacious in the tackle and adept at clearing his lines, Dan is still learning and can only improve with more experience.

Brighton & Hove A (From trainee on 28/7/2003) FL 17+7 FLC 0+2 Others 4+1

HARDING William (Billy)
Born: Carshalton, 20 January 1985
Height: 6'0" **Weight:** 12.7
A striker with Wycombe's youth team, Billy displayed great promise in the pre-season friendlies, scoring against Spurs. He was rewarded with his senior debut on the opening day of the campaign, coming on as a substitute at home to Stockport. He only managed one more appearance and, after a loan spell at Beaconsfield SYCOB, was released by new manager Tony Adams, linking up with Ryman League club Carshalton Athletic soon afterwards. Billy is the son of the former Notts County, Birmingham and Cardiff midfielder Paul Harding.

Wycombe W (Trainee) FL 0+2

HAREWOOD Marlon Anderson
Born: Hampstead, 25 August 1979
Height: 6'1" **Weight:** 11.0
Marlon was the most improved striker in the First Division last term. He started the season with 11 goals in 19 games for Nottingham Forest, a considerable feat bearing in mind the absence of David Johnson. However, after announcing he would not sign a new contract at the end of the campaign he was allowed to join West Ham for a bargain fee in November. He was an instant hit for the Hammers, scoring two goals against Wigan on his debut. A fast, powerful player, his energetic displays made him a favourite with the fans and he finished the campaign as the club's leading scorer with 14 goals.

Nottingham F (From trainee on 9/9/1996) P/FL 124+58/51 FLC 12+4/3 FAC 3+2/1 Others 2
Ipswich T (Loaned on 28/1/1999) FL 5+1/1
West Ham U (£500,000 on 25/11/2003) FL 28/13 FAC 4/1 Others 3

HARGREAVES Christian (Chris)
Born: Cleethorpes, 12 May 1972
Height: 5'11" **Weight:** 12.2
Chris found himself out of the starting line-up for Northampton at the start of last term, but very quickly won his place back and remained in the side for the rest of the season. A powerhouse midfielder

who has plenty of running in him, a hard tackle and an eye for the odd goal, Chris is a great favourite of the fans at the Sixfields Stadium.

Grimsby T (From trainee on 6/12/1989) FL 15+36/5 FLC 2+2/1 FAC 1+2/2 Others 2+4
Scarborough (Loaned on 4/3/1993) FL 2+1
Hull C (Signed on 26/7/1993) FL 34+15 FLC 1 FAC 2+1/1 Others 3+1
West Bromwich A (Free on 13/7/1995) FL 0+1 Others 0+1
Hereford U (Free on 19/2/1996) FL 57+4/6 FLC 3+1 FAC 1 Others 2
Plymouth Arg (Free on 20/7/1998) FL 74+2/5 FLC 4 FAC 11/2 Others 1
Northampton T (Free on 7/7/2000) FL 144+7/6 FLC 5+1/1 FAC 11/2 Others 8/2

HARKINS Gary
Born: Greenock, 2 January 1985
Height: 6'2" **Weight:** 12.10
This young midfield player was a regular in Blackburn's reserve side last term and later went on loan to Third Division club Huddersfield Town. Signed as cover for injuries and suspensions, Gary proved to be a powerful tackler and looked confident when attacking with the ball.
Blackburn Rov (From trainee on 22/1/2004)
Huddersfield T (Loaned on 24/3/2004) FL 1+2

HARLEY Jonathan (Jon)
Born: Maidstone, 26 September 1979
Height: 5'9" **Weight:** 10.3

Club Honours: FAC '00
International Honours: E: U21-3; Yth
A plethora of left-sided defenders at Fulham again restricted Jon's appearances in the side and he was loaned out to Sheffield United early in the season. A favourite with the Blades' fans, he quickly settled in at left wing back, producing some classy performances, tackling and defending well, and being prominent in attack. His loan was extended but after five games he was injured and returned to London. Jon's three Fulham starts all came in December following an injury to Jerome Bonnissel, but the signing of Carlos Bocanegra saw him move out again on loan, this time to West Ham. He

Ben Harding (right)

went straight into the Hammers' line-up, ironically at Sheffield United, and scored a brilliant 20-yarder on his debut. He then settled into the side with a string of fine performances and was a regular until he returned to Fulham in April.
Chelsea *(From trainee on 20/3/1997) PL 22+8/2 FLC 0+1 FAC 7 Others 1+3*
Wimbledon *(Loaned on 20/10/2000) FL 6/2*
Fulham *(£3,500,000 on 8/8/2001) PL 19+6/1 FLC 2 FAC 4+1 Others 4*
Sheffield U *(Loaned on 30/10/2002) FL 8+1/1 FLC 2*
Sheffield U *(Loaned on 16/9/2003) FL 5*
West Ham U *(Loaned on 16/1/2004) FL 15/1 FAC 1*

HARNWELL Jamie
Born: Perth, Australia, 21 January 1977
Height: 6'3" **Weight:** 12.0
After scoring the goal that clinched Australia's NSL title for Perth Glory, Jamie decided to try his luck in England. The experienced central defender impressed in pre-season training at Leyton Orient and was signed on a short-term contract. However, after just a handful of first-team appearances he was released and moved on to join Welling United.
Leyton Orient *(Free from Perth Glory, Australia on 8/8/2003) FL 1+2*

HARPER James (Jamie) Alan John
Born: Chelmsford, 9 November 1980
Height: 5'10" **Weight:** 11.7
Still a young and exciting prospect in the Reading midfield, Jamie is now virtually an automatic choice in the first-team line-up. He has added consistency and determination to his undoubted flair, and extended his repertoire by playing occasionally in wide positions as well as centrally. An assiduous trainer and keen student of the game, he looks set to be a vital part of the Royals' squad for many years to come. Maybe he needs to score more goals, but his creativity makes regular chances for his team mates.
Arsenal *(From trainee on 8/7/1999)*
Cardiff C *(Loaned on 29/12/2000) FL 3*
Reading *(£400,000 on 28/2/2001) FL 97+16/5 FLC 5/1 FAC 5 Others 4+2*

HARPER Kevin Patrick
Born: Oldham, 15 January 1976
Height: 5'6" **Weight:** 10.10
Club Honours: Div 1 '03
International Honours: S: B-1; U21-7; Sch
Kevin was used as a substitute by Portsmouth last term and his only starts came during a loan spell at Norwich. His

arrival helped galvanise the Canaries' promotion campaign. A hard-working right-sided player he has a tremendous awareness of his defensive responsibilities as well as enthusiastic attacking instincts. Kevin was also a regular member of Scotland's international squad.
Hibernian *(Signed from Hutchison Vale BC on 3/8/1992) SL 73+23/15 SLC 4+5 SC 9+1/3*
Derby Co *(£300,000 + on 11/9/1998) PL 6+26/1 FLC 1+5 FAC 0+3/1*
Walsall *(Loaned on 17/12/1999) FL 8+1/1*
Portsmouth *(£300,000 on 6/3/2000) F/PL 85+34/9 FLC 1+2 FAC 5*
Norwich C *(Loaned on 12/9/2003) FL 9*

HARPER Lee Charles Phillip
Born: Chelsea, 30 October 1971
Height: 6'1" **Weight:** 13.11
Lee began last term as second-choice 'keeper for Northampton, but he regained his place at the beginning of September and never looked back. He made several penalty stops during the campaign, including two in the shoot-out that decided the LDV Vans Trophy match against Hereford and a memorable save in the FA Cup tie against Manchester United. Lee is a superb shot stopper and was voted as the PFA Fans' Division Three 'Player of the Season'.
Arsenal *(£150,000 from Sittingbourne on 16/6/1994) PL 1*
Queens Park R *(£125,000 + on 11/7/1997) FL 117+1 FLC 8+1 FAC 4*
Walsall *(Free on 20/7/2001) FL 3 FLC 2*
Northampton T *(Free on 18/7/2002) FL 70 FLC 1 FAC 7 Others 5+1*

HARPER Stephen (Steve) Alan
Born: Easington, 14 March 1975
Height: 6'2" **Weight:** 13.0
Newcastle's longest-serving player, Steve is now into his second decade at the club, but continues to find his path blocked by the excellence of first-choice goalkeeper Shay Given. Steve is a good all-round 'keeper whom numerous judges believe would hold down a first-team place at many other Premiership clubs, but his opportunities on Tyneside were restricted during the 2003-04 season to an away game at NAC Breda in the UEFA Cup, when he made a number of important saves and kept a clean sheet, and the Carling Cup tie at home to West Bromwich Albion, when he was honoured by becoming one of the few 'keepers ever to captain a Newcastle first team.
Newcastle U *(Free from Seaham Red Star on 5/7/1993) PL 29+2 FLC 9 FAC 7+1 Others 8*
Bradford C *(Loaned on 18/9/1995) FL 1*

Hartlepool U *(Loaned on 29/8/1997) FL 15*
Huddersfield T *(Loaned on 18/12/1997) FL 24 FAC 2*

HARRAD Shaun Nicholas
Born: Nottingham, 11 December 1984
Height: 5'10" **Weight:** 12.4
This promising young striker continued to make progress in Notts County's reserves last term and added several more appearances from the substitutes' bench during the campaign. A versatile player who can also feature in an attacking midfield role, Shaun signed a professional contract with the Magpies shortly before the end of the season.
Notts Co *(From trainee on 22/4/2004) FL 0+13 FAC 0+1*

HARRIS Neil
Born: Orsett, 12 July 1977
Height: 5'11" **Weight:** 12.9
Club Honours: Div 2 '01
Neil continued to feature regularly for Millwall last term, although many of his appearances came from the substitutes' bench. He scored ten goals including a vital strike in the FA Cup sixth round replay over Tranmere and is now closing in on the club's all-time aggregate goal-scoring record. He was as fast and tricky as ever and signed a new contract at the New Den during the season.
Millwall *(£30,000 from Cambridge C on 26/3/1998) FL 181+40/92 FLC 5+1 FAC 13+2/2 Others 11+1/3*

HARRIS Richard Lewis Scott
Born: Croydon, 23 October 1980
Height: 5'11" **Weight:** 10.9
Richard impressed up front for Wycombe at the start of the 2003-04 season. His powerfully headed brace knocked Wimbledon out of the Carling Cup, but an injury at Blackpool saw the start of both his and the team's decline. He spent loan periods at Woking and Maidenhead United before leaving the Chairboys in April after just seven starts. Richard played as a makeshift goalkeeper for nearly an hour at Rushden in September after 'keeper Frank Talia was sent off.
Crystal Palace *(From trainee on 22/12/1997) FL 2+7 FLC 2+2*
Mansfield T *(Loaned on 28/9/2001) FL 0+6*
Wycombe W *(Free on 26/3/2002) FL 13+22/5 FLC 1+3/3 FAC 1 Others 2*

HARRISON Daniel (Danny) Robert
Born: Liverpool, 4 November 1982
Height: 5'11" **Weight:** 12.5
Danny made good progress at Tranmere

last term, recovering from an early-season ankle injury to become a regular choice under new manager Brian Little. A solid central midfielder who works hard and is effective in the tackle, he relishes the chance to go forward. Danny has benefited greatly from playing alongside Micky Mellon and he reached the landmark of 50 first-team appearances mark for Rovers by the end of the campaign.
Tranmere Rov (From trainee on 16/5/2002) FL 40+5/2 FLC 1 FAC 7+1 Others 2+1/1

HARRISON Lee David
Born: Billericay, 12 September 1971
Height: 6'2" **Weight:** 12.7
Lee started last season as first-choice goalkeeper for Leyton Orient, but lost his place to Glenn Morris towards the end of the year and thereafter rarely featured in the line-up. An excellent shot-stopper who never let the team down when called upon, he will be looking to regain his place in the team in 2004-05.
Charlton Ath (From trainee on 3/7/1990)
Fulham (Loaned on 18/11/1991) Others 1
Gillingham (Loaned on 24/3/1992) FL 2
Fulham (Free on 18/12/1992) FL 11+1 FAC 1 Others 6
Barnet (Free on 15/7/1996) FL 183 FLC 9 FAC 3 Others 12
Peterborough U (Loaned on 12/12/2002) FL 12
Leyton Orient (Signed on 14/3/2003) FL 25+1 FLC 1 FAC 1+1 Others 1

HARROLD Matthew (Matt) James
Born: Leyton, 25 July 1984
Height: 6'1" **Weight:** 11.10
This young Brentford centre forward burst onto the scene last season with a hat-trick in the FA Cup tie against Gainsborough Trinity. A pelvic injury then saw him drop out of contention before new manager Martin Allen recalled him to the side. Matt repaid his faith by scoring against both Colchester and Wycombe.
Brentford (Free from Harlow T on 12/8/2003) FL 5+8/2 FAC 1/3 Others 1

HARSLEY Paul
Born: Scunthorpe, 29 May 1978
Height: 5'9" **Weight:** 11.10
Paul failed to get much of a look-in at Northampton last term and was restricted to the odd appearance as cover for injury or suspension. Early in the new year he moved on to Macclesfield Town where he quickly won a regular place in the side, netting two goals including the winner in the home match against Swansea City.

Paul is a pacy midfield player who causes problems when running at the opposition and gives 100 per cent throughout every match.
Grimsby T (From trainee on 16/7/1996)
Scunthorpe U (Free on 7/7/1997) FL 110+18/5 FLC 6 FAC 4+2/1 Others 5+1
Halifax T (Free on 1/7/2001) FL 45/11 FLC 1 FAC 3/1 Others 1
Northampton T (Free on 8/7/2002) FL 46+13/2 FLC 2 FAC 3+2/1 Others 2+2
Macclesfield T (Free on 13/2/2004) FL 16/2

HART Gary John
Born: Harlow, 21 September 1976
Height: 5'9" **Weight:** 12.8
Club Honours: Div 3 '01; Div 2 '02
Still one of Brighton's most popular players, as much for his all-out effort, Gary may be disappointed by a return of just three goals from the 2003-04 campaign. Now used mainly as a winger, he can also play as an out-and-out forward when needed. Towards the end of the season Gary was often a substitute, but he came off the bench in the play-off semi-final matches to such good effect that he secured his place in the starting line-up for the showdown against Bristol City at Cardiff. Gary's greatest strengths are his ability to take on opposition defenders and a willingness to chase back to support his own defence.
Brighton & Hove A (£1,000 from Stansted on 18/6/1998) FL 223+26/39 FLC 8+3 FAC 8 Others 7+4/1

HARTE Ian Patrick
Born: Drogheda, 31 August 1977
Height: 5'10" **Weight:** 11.8
International Honours: RoI: 56; U21-3
This experienced left back, began the season out of the first-team picture at Leeds, but injuries meant that he was recalled to the squad at the end of August. However, it was not until Eddie Gray was installed as caretaker-manager that he featured regularly, and after a run in the side he was replaced by Didier Domi, only to return to the line-up for the final fixtures.
Leeds U (From trainee on 15/12/1995) PL 199+14/28 FLC 10+2/2 FAC 16+2/3 Others 45/6

HASLAM Steven (Steve) Robert
Born: Sheffield, 6 September 1979
Height: 5'11" **Weight:** 10.10
International Honours: E: Yth; Sch
Steve enjoyed a consistent season for Sheffield Wednesday last term, although he missed out on the last couple of

months due to a hernia injury. He was generally used in a midfield 'holding' role, but also occasionally featured at centre half (his favoured position) and full back. He was one of 13 out-of-contract players released by the Owls in the summer.
Sheffield Wed (From trainee on 12/9/1996) P/FL 115+29/2 FLC 10+1 FAC 9+1 Others 5+1

HASSELBAINK Jerrel (Jimmy Floyd)
Born: Surinam, 27 March 1972
Height: 6'2" **Weight:** 13.4
Club Honours: CS '00
International Honours: Holland: 23
Following the influx of Russian wealth into Chelsea the player who seemed most vulnerable was Jimmy-Floyd Hasselbaink as the big-spending Blues cast their net looking at world-class strikers. But the ebullient hitman vowed to stay and fight for his place and proved true to his word in the opening Premiership match at Anfield when he came off the bench to rifle home a dramatic late winner. Although Hernan Crespo and Adrian Mutu were the preferred partnership for the Champions' League matches, Jimmy still scored regularly in the Premiership whenever he got the chance – particularly when he played in tandem with his old strike partner Eidur Gudjohnsen. Jimmy had a memorable 32nd birthday against Wolves – coming off the bench to score a 13-minute hat-trick and break the 100 Premiership-goal barrier in the process. Despite featuring in just over half of Chelsea's fixtures Jimmy still retained his customary position as top-scorer with 17 goals in all competitions in what turned out to be, both personally and for the club, a very satisfactory season.
Leeds U (£2,000,000 from Boavista, Portugal, ex Campomaiorense, on 18/7/1997) PL 66+3/34 FLC 5/2 FAC 9/5 Others 4/1 (£12,000,000 to Atletico Madrid, Spain on 20/8/1999)
Chelsea (£15,000,000 on 12/7/2000) PL 119+17/69 FLC 10/7 FAC 16/7 Others 11+4/4

HASSELL Robert (Bobby) John Francis
Born: Derby, 4 June 1980
Height: 5'9" **Weight:** 12.6
Bobby was once again troubled with niggling injuries at the start of the 2003-04 season but was soon back to his best for Mansfield Town. First choice at right back throughout the campaign, he formed a tremendous partnership with Liam Lawrence down the right flank. Bobby is a solid defender who likes to get forward as much as possible.

Ian Harte

*Mansfield T (From trainee on 3/7/1998) FL
151+9/3 FLC 6+1 FAC 9 Others 4*

HATSWELL Wayne Mervin
Born: Swindon, 8 February 1975
Height: 6'0" **Weight:** 13.10
Wayne began last term with Conference
outfit Chester City before returning to
Football League action with
Kidderminster. The transfer proved to be
an astute piece of business as the no-
nonsense central defender slotted
comfortably into the back line and
immediately steadied the defence.
Handed the captaincy by Jan Molby,
Wayne soon became a firm fans' favourite
and deservedly won the club's 'Player of
the Year' award at the end of the season.
*Oxford U (£35,000 from Forest Green Rov
on 1/12/2000) FL 47+1 FLC 1 FAC 1 Others 2
(Free to Chester C on 1/6/2002)*
*Kidderminster Hrs (£15,000 on 16/10/2003)
FL 32/2 FAC 4*

HAW Robert (Robbie) Andrew
Born: York, 10 October 1986
Height: 5'8" **Weight:** 10.10
A product of York City's youth system this
promising young midfielder made his
senior debut when coming on as a
substitute in the Minstermen's final game
of the season at Swansea City, by which
time the club's relegation to the
Conference had been confirmed.
York C (Trainee) FL 0+1

HAWKINS Peter Steven
Born: Maidstone, 19 September 1978
Height: 6'0" **Weight:** 11.6
A versatile player who can occupy any of
the back-four positions, Peter missed the
middle part of the 2003-04 season
through an ankle injury and was never
able to reclaim a regular starting berth for
Wimbledon on his return to action.
Probably best suited to the full-back
positions, he always competed well and
rarely did anything too catastrophic.
Although not offered a new deal by the
club at the end of the season, he is a very
competent defender who would be a
useful addition to most lower-division
squads.
*Wimbledon (From trainee on 6/3/1997) FL
113+7 FLC 6 FAC 9+1*
York C (Loaned on 22/2/2000) FL 14

HAWLEY Karl Leon
Born: Walsall, 6 December 1981
Height: 5'7" **Weight:** 12.0
After appearing for Walsall in the pre-
season win over Aston Villa, Karl was
loaned out to Raith Rovers at the start of

Wayne Hatswell

the 2003-04 campaign. He scored twice in ten appearances for the Scottish First Division club and on his return made just one substitute appearance for Walsall, coming on for the last few seconds of the FA Cup tie at Millwall. Karl was released towards the end of the season and signed for Hednesford Town.

Walsall *(From trainee on 26/1/2001) FL 0+1 FAC 0+1 Others 0+2*

Raith Rov *(Loaned on 9/8/2002) SL 15+2/7 SLC 1 SC 1+2/1*

Raith Rov *(Loaned on 29/8/2003) SL 4+5/2 SLC 1*

HAWORTH Simon Owen
Born: Cardiff, 30 March 1977
Height: 6'2" **Weight:** 13.8
Club Honours: AMC '99
International Honours: W: 5; B-1; U21-12; Yth
This pacy Tranmere striker has the ability to score spectacular goals and found the back of the net on seven occasions last term. The club's leading scorer by some margin in the previous campaign, he showed excellent form until his season was ended prematurely when he suffered a double fracture of his right leg during the game at Brentford in January. Away from football, Simon is a keen racing fan and part owns a horse with team mate Gareth Roberts.

Cardiff C *(From trainee on 7/8/1995) FL 27+10/9 FLC 4 FAC 0+1 Others 4/1*

Coventry C *(£500,000 on 4/6/1997) PL 5+6 FLC 2/1 FAC 0+1*

Wigan Ath *(£600,000 on 2/10/1998) FL 99+18/44 FLC 8/6 FAC 4/4 Others 12+1/4*

Tranmere Rov *(£125,000 on 28/2/2002) FL 75+1/31 FLC 3/1 FAC 4/2 Others 3*

HAY Alexander (Alex) Neil
Born: Birkenhead, 14 October 1981
Height: 5'10" **Weight:** 11.5
This enthusiastic, committed striker was once again a cornerstone of Tranmere's reserve team last season. However, although he featured regularly for the first team from the substitutes' bench he rarely appeared in the starting line-up and was released shortly before the end of the campaign. Alex has since signed a contract for Rushden & Diamonds.

Tranmere Rov *(From trainee on 24/3/2000) FL 16+25/3 FLC 2 FAC 0+6 Others 1*

HAY Daniel (Danny) John
Born: Auckland, New Zealand, 15 May 1975
Height: 6'4" **Weight:** 14.11
International Honours: New Zealand
After holding down a regular defensive

place in the Walsall line-up during the first four months of the season Danny lost a little form. In December he decided to return to New Zealand and soon afterwards he was reported to have signed a long-term contract with the Auckland Kingz. At his best he proved himself to be a powerful wholehearted defender during his season-and-a-half with the Saddlers.

Leeds U *(£200,000 from Perth Glory, Australia on 25/8/1999) PL 2+2 FLC 1 Others 0+1*

Walsall *(Free on 5/8/2002) FL 40+5 FLC 3 FAC 3*

HAYES Paul Edward
Born: Dagenham, 20 September 1983
Height: 6'0" **Weight:** 12.2
After making a huge impact when he broke into Scunthorpe United's first team during the second half of 2002-03, Paul endured a disappointing season last term. He started off in the first team but soon lost his place to Steve MacLean and spent most of the campaign resigned to a substitute's role. A strong centre forward who likes running at defences, he scored seven times – five of which came in cup ties but failed to find the net after December.

Scunthorpe U *(From trainee at Norwich C on 22/3/2003) FL 27+26/10 FLC 1+1/2 FAC 3+2/2 Others 3+2/1*

HAYLES Barrington (Barry) Edward
Born: Lambeth, 17 May 1972
Height: 5'9" **Weight:** 13.0
Club Honours: GMVC '96; Div 2 '99; Div 1 '01
International Honours: Jamaica: 10; E: SP-2
Barry enjoyed his best form at the start of the season when he hit three goals in two games for Fulham, including a double at Tottenham when his performance stole the show. Sadly his season was then disrupted by an injury sustained on international duty for Jamaica against Australia. Barry did not fit easily into the single-striker formation favoured by Fulham and often found himself used as a substitute prior to the departure of Louis Saha. A combative player who uses his experience and physique to gain a yard on defenders, he continued to feature for Jamaica.

Bristol Rov *(£250,000 from Stevenage Borough on 4/6/1997) FL 62/32 FLC 4/1 FAC 5/2 Others 3+2/1*

Fulham *(£2,100,000 on 17/11/1998) P/FL 116+59/44 FLC 10+2/5 FAC 12+7/6 Others 2+5/2*

HAYTER James Edward
Born: Sandown, IoW, 9 April 1979
Height: 5'9" **Weight:** 11.2
James completed an excellent season for Bournemouth, finishing as 'Player of the Year', leading scorer, and the holder of a new record. A whirlwind few days saw him become a father for the first time, and because of this he was put on the bench against Wrexham, coming on after 85 minutes. He scored with his first touch and completed his hat-trick 140 seconds later! James is a hard-working player who tends to play just behind the front two.

Bournemouth *(From trainee on 7/7/1997) FL 181+50/45 FLC 3+3/1 FAC 12+2/3 Others 9+4/5*

HAYWARD Steven (Steve) Lee
Born: Pelsall, 8 September 1971
Height: 5'11" **Weight:** 12.5
Club Honours: AMC '97; Div 2 '99
International Honours: E: Yth
Steve played in a number of midfield positions for Barnsley last season and when Paul Hart took over as manager he found himself in a 'holding' position where his experience was put to effective use. Steve was one of several players released by the Reds in the summer.

Derby Co *(From juniors on 17/9/1988) FL 15+11/1 FLC 0+2 FAC 1 Others 3+4*

Carlisle U *(£100,000 on 13/3/1995) FL 88+2/13 FLC 6/1 FAC 15/1*

Fulham *(£175,000 on 23/6/1997) FL 108+7/7 FLC 16+3/1 FAC 9+2/3 Others 3*

Barnsley *(£25,000 on 19/1/2001) FL 40+8/2 FLC 1 FAC 4 Others 1*

HAZELL Reuben
Born: Birmingham, 24 April 1979
Height: 5'11" **Weight:** 12.0
A pre-season knee injury led to a long lay off for Reuben and on his return to fitness he had to content himself with occasional outings at full back interspersed with spells on the bench, before replaying the final five games at right back due to an injury to Lee Canoville. Reuben rarely showed his best form during the campaign due to prolonged inactivity, playing out of position and ongoing knee problems, which required further treatment at the end of the season.

Aston Villa *(From trainee on 20/3/1997)*

Tranmere Rov *(Free on 5/8/1999) FL 38+4/1 FLC 8 FAC 3 Others 1*

Torquay U *(Free on 10/1/2002) FL 77+7/2 FLC 1 FAC 2 Others 1*

HEALD Gregory (Greg) James
Born: Enfield, 26 September 1971
Height: 6'1" **Weight:** 12.8
International Honours: E: SP-1; Sch
Greg began last term as Leyton Orient's
team captain, but injury problems
restricted his appearances and in the new
year he was released from his contract.
Shortly afterwards he signed for
Rochdale, and he proved to be the
experienced campaigner the team
required. A hard-as-nails central defender,
Greg put in a string of superb
performances, despite turning out with a
cracked rib, until Dale's future was
secured.
*Peterborough U (£35,000 from Enfield on
8/7/1994) FL 101+4/6 FLC 8 FAC 8+1 Others
11/2*
*Barnet (Signed on 8/8/1997) FL 141/13 FLC
8/1 FAC 4 Others 7/1*
Leyton Orient (£9,000 on 27/3/2003) FL 9/1

HEALD Paul Andrew
Born: Wath on Dearne, 20 September
1968
Height: 6'2" **Weight:** 14.0
This experienced 'keeper began last
season on the bench, where he had spent
most of his Wimbledon career, but
reclaimed the starting berth soon after
and kept it until being forced out of
action with a knee injury that ultimately
made it necessary for him to hang up his
playing boots. A very popular figure at
the club, Paul had been doubling up as
goalkeeping coach prior to his playing
retirement, and most definitely has all the
attributes necessary for a solid future
career in that role.
Sheffield U (From trainee on 30/6/1987)
*Leyton Orient (Signed on 2/12/1988) FL 176
FLC 13 FAC 9 Others 21*
Coventry C (Loaned on 10/3/1992) PL 2
Swindon T (Loaned on 24/3/1994) PL 1+1
*Wimbledon (£125,000 on 25/7/1995) P/FL
36+3 FLC 7*
*Sheffield Wed (Loaned on 22/1/2002) FL 5
FLC 1*

HEALY Colin
Born: Cork, 14 March 1980
Height: 5'11" **Weight:** 9.12
Club Honours: SPD '01; SLC '01
International Honours: RoI: 13; U21-10
This talented young midfielder arrived at
Sunderland at the start of the 2003-04
season and made an impact as a strong-
tackling schemer who was always willing
to support his strikers. He soon
established himself in the line-up, but his
campaign ended prematurely when he
suffered a double fracture of his right leg

at Coventry in December. Colin also filled
in at right back for the Black cats on one
occasion. He added further caps for the
Republic of Ireland before his injury.
*Glasgow Celtic (Signed from Wilton U,
Ireland on 7/7/1998) SL 16+14/1 SLC 5+1/2
SC 3+1 Others 3+5*
Coventry C (Loaned on 29/1/2002) FL 17/2
Sunderland (Free on 22/8/2003) FL 16+4

HEALY David Jonathan
Born: Downpatrick, 5 August 1979
Height: 5'8" **Weight:** 11.0
International Honours: NI: 35; B-1;
U21-8; Yth; Sch
Preston's Northern Ireland striker made
national headlines when he broke his
country's goal-scoring drought against
Norway, and in the summer he
established a new career record of goals
for the national team. Having almost left
Deepdale the previous season, David
buckled down to winning back the home
crowd and his hard work brought its
rewards with a regular place from
October, which resulted in a flood of
goals, 15 in all during the season. Scoring
in four consecutive games got David back
on track, and showed that his best
position was floating behind the two
main strikers, from where he could attack
the box late, strike powerfully from
distance or deliver telling crosses for team
mates.
*Manchester U (From trainee on 28/11/1997)
PL 0+1 FLC 0+2*
Port Vale (Loaned on 25/2/2000) FL 15+1/3
*Preston NE (£1,500,000 on 29/12/2000) FL
93+35/39 FLC 6+1 FAC 7+1 Others 3/1*
Norwich C (Loaned on 30/1/2003) FL 5/1
Norwich C (Loaned on 13/3/2003) FL 5+3/1

HEARN Charles (Charley)
Richard
Born: Ashford, Kent, 5 November 1983
Height: 5'11" **Weight:** 11.9
This very talented midfield player had a
promising start to the 2003-04 season for
Millwall, appearing in four matches and
carrying on where he left off in the
previous campaign. Charlie is a tricky
player who shows some delicate touches
for one so young. Unfortunately he took
a nasty injury that kept him out of action
for most of the campaign, but he was
back in action for the reserves before the
summer break.
*Millwall (From trainee on 27/4/2001) FL 9+9
FLC 1+1 FAC 2+2*

HEATH Matthew (Matt) Philip
Born: Leicester, 1 November 1981
Height: 6'4" **Weight:** 13.13

This promising young Leicester defender
was loaned out to Stockport in the
autumn and produced a commanding
performance in the heart of the County
defence on his debut at Brighton. He
featured regularly during his stay at
Edgeley Park and once he returned to the
Foxes he was recalled to the side, forming
a useful central defensive partnership with
Nikos Dabizas during the latter stages of
the season.
*Leicester C (From trainee on 17/2/2001) P/FL
25+4/3 FLC 2 FAC 3+2*
*Stockport Co (Loaned on 24/10/2003) FL 8
Others 2*

HECKINGBOTTOM Paul
Born: Barnsley, 17 July 1977
Height: 5'11" **Weight:** 12.0
Left back Paul missed only three matches
in his first season with Bradford and he
was named the club's 'Player of the Year'
by both the fans and his team mates. He
also filled in at left midfield and at centre
half when required, but Paul made the
full-back spot his own with his consistent,
unflustered performances. He is a player
who tends to keep things simple, but he
is also willing to push forward up the
wing to support the attack.
*Sunderland (From trainee at Manchester U
on 14/7/1995)*
*Scarborough (Loaned on 17/10/1997) FL
28+1 Others 1*
Hartlepool U (Loaned on 25/9/1998) FL 5/1
*Darlington (Free on 25/3/1999) FL 111+4/5
FLC 4 FAC 8/1 Others 8*
*Norwich C (Free on 5/7/2002) FL 7+8 FLC
0+1*
*Bradford C (Free on 17/7/2003) FL 43 FLC 1
FAC 1*

HEEROO Gavin
Born: Haringey, 2 September 1984
Height: 5'11" **Weight:** 11.7
International Honours: Mauritius
This combative central midfielder featured
several times on the bench for Crystal
Palace last term, but the only time when
he was called into action was during the
closing stages of the home game against
Preston in November. Gavin later had a
trial with Leyton Orient and was released
by Palace in the summer. He is already a
full international having represented
Mauritius on a number of occasions in
friendly matches.
*Crystal Palace (From juniors on 7/9/2001) FL
0+1*

HEFFERNAN Paul
Born: Dublin, Ireland, 29 December 1981
Height: 5'10" **Weight:** 10.7

International Honours: Rol: U21-3
This talented young striker finally established himself as a regular in the Notts County line-up during the 2003-04 season and enjoyed a superb campaign. He finished leading scorer with 21 goals to his name, an achievement in a team that struggled against relegation. Personal highlights included hitting four goals against Stockport County in February and a hat-trick against Queens Park Rangers on Boxing Day.
Notts Co (Signed from Newtown, Co Wicklow on 22/10/1999) FL 74+26/36 FLC 2+3/1 FAC 2+2/1 Others 2+3

HELGUSON Heidar

Born: Iceland, 22 August 1977
Height: 6'0" **Weight:** 12.2
International Honours: Iceland: 25; U21-6; Yth
Watford's Icelandic international centre forward suffered a cruciate ligament injury in September and his dynamic and hard-working performances were sorely missed. He returned to first-team action ahead of schedule in December and was outstanding as a lone striker against Chelsea in the FA Cup, terrorising the Blues' renowned back line and scoring Watford's first goal. Heidar's excellence in the air made him a constant menace to opposing defences, although his commitment occasionally spilled over. He suffered further knee ligament problems in April, and was again badly missed at the end of the campaign. He did wait to score nine goals in a truncated season.
Watford (£1,500,000 from SK Lillestrom, Norway, ex Throttur, on 13/1/2000) P/FL 96+39/39 FLC 3+7/2 FAC 6+2/3

HENCHOZ Stephane

Born: Billens, Switzerland, 7 September 1974
Height: 6'1" **Weight:** 12.10
Club Honours: FLC '01, '03; FAC '01; UEFAC '01; ESC '01; CS '01
International Honours: Switzerland: 68; U21; Yth
The absence of this Swiss international central defender for much of the season was a major factor in Liverpool's defensive frailty in 2003-04. Although Stephane started the first two games, an ankle injury then ruled him out until October, but his return was short lived as subsequent knee and groin problems sidelined him again until January. Finally restored to full fitness he returned to first-team duty at right back for four games before replacing Igor Biscan in his more familiar central defensive position.

However, having re-established himself he was in and out of the side thereafter. Reds' fans will be hoping his superb defensive partnership with Sami Hyypia is fully restored in the 2004-05 campaign.
Blackburn Rov (£3,000,000 from Hamburg, Germany, ex FC Bulle, Neuchatel Xamax, on 14/7/1997) PL 70 FLC 3+1 FAC 6 Others 2
Liverpool (£3,750,000 on 20/7/1999) PL 132+3 FLC 13 FAC 15 Others 37+1

HENDERSON Darius Alexis

Born: Sutton, 7 September 1981
Height: 6'0" **Weight:** 12.8
Darius began the 2003-04 season on loan at Brighton, partnering Leon Knight in the attack. He produced a few useful performances before returning to Reading in November to make a brief 11-minute substitute appearance in the 1-0 home win over Millwall. He then returned to reserve-team football before being transferred to Gillingham in the new year. Darius scored in the FA Cup fourth round tie at Burnley, but was then hampered by injuries and did not feature in the line-up after February.
Reading (From trainee on 15/12/1999) FL 5+66/11 FLC 2+2/2 FAC 1+2 Others 4+1/2
Brighton & Hove A (Loaned on 8/8/2003) FL 10/2
Gillingham (£25,000 on 2/1/2004) FL 4 FAC 1+1/1

HENDERSON Ian

Born: Norwich, 24 January 1985
Height: 5'8" **Weight:** 10.10
Club Honours: Div 1 '04
International Honours: E: Yth
A regular member of the England U19 squad, Ian consolidated his place within the Norwich team, making 21 first-team appearances and scoring four goals in 2003-204. His preferred position is as an out-and-out striker, but the majority of his appearances were made as an attacking right-sided midfield player, where his appetite for hard work combined well with his natural desire to appear in the penalty area looking for goal-scoring opportunities.
Norwich C (From trainee on 3/2/2003) FL 18+21/5 FLC 1 FAC 0+3

HENDERSON Kevin Malcolm

Born: Ashington, 8 June 1974
Height: 6'3" **Weight:** 13.2
Although he is a proven goal-scorer with a reputation for being a hard worker, Kevin was unable to win a regular place in the Hartlepool line-up in the early part of the 2003-04 season. He was loaned out to Carlisle United, where he was soon

among the goals and in October he signed permanently for the Cumbrians. Injury problems restricted his contribution, particularly in the new year, although he appeared from the bench in the last match at Doncaster.
Burnley (Signed from Morpeth T on 17/12/1997) FL 0+14/1 FLC 0+2 Others 0+4/1
Hartlepool U (Free on 2/7/1999) FL 82+49/29 FLC 3+3 FAC 1+1 Others 6+3/3
Carlisle U (Free on 12/9/2003) FL 10+9/2 FAC 0+1 Others 2

HENDERSON Wayne

Born: Dublin, 16 September 1983
Height: 5'11" **Weight:** 12.2
Club Honours: FAYC '02
International Honours: Rol: U21-5; Yth
Third choice at Aston Villa, Wayne featured regularly in the reserves last season and had loan spells at Tamworth and Wycombe. He joined the Chairboys for the final three games of the season, making his senior debut at Brentford. A confident goalkeeper who commands his area well, he represented the Republic of Ireland in the World Youth Championships and also featured for the U21s. Wayne is from a family of goalkeepers, his father Paddy played for Shamrock and two of his brothers are also 'keepers.
Aston Villa (From trainee on 27/9/2000)
Wycombe W (Loaned on 23/4/2004) FL 3

HENDRIE Lee Andrew

Born: Birmingham, 18 May 1977
Height: 5'10" **Weight:** 10.3
International Honours: E: 1; B-1; U21-13; Yth
This quick-witted midfielder worked hard throughout the season and consequently had a more successful time for Aston Villa, being rarely absent. The arrival of Gavin McCann meant a switch to the right of midfield during the first half of the campaign, but Lee was restored to his more favoured central role in the new year, and relished the challenge thrown down by David O'Leary. He scored a magnificent goal at Bolton, an impudent 25-yard lob which was a contender for 'Goal of the Season'.
Aston Villa (From trainee on 18/5/1994) PL 170+35/21 FLC 13+2/3 FAC 9+8 Others 14+5/2

HENRIKSEN Bo

Born: Denmark, 7 February 1975
Height: 5'10" **Weight:** 11.10
Bo started last season in good form for Kidderminster, netting two goals in the opening-day victory over Mansfield, but a

Thierry Henry

niggling groin injury then left him struggling to reach match fitness. On transfer deadline day he was released and he joined up with Bristol Rovers for the rest of the campaign. Bo managed just one start for Rovers, against Swansea at the Memorial Stadium, when he impressed by setting up a goal in a vital win.

Kidderminster Hrs *(Free from Herfolge, Denmark, ex Odense BK, on 9/11/2001) FL 74+10/30 FLC 1 FAC 5+2 Others 1+1*
Bristol Rov *(Free on 25/3/2004) FL 1+3*

HENRY Karl Levi Daniel
Born: Wolverhampton, 26 November 1982
Height: 6'1" **Weight:** 10.13
International Honours: E: Yth
This Stoke City youngster made a number of appearances in the first half of last season prior to joining Cheltenham Town on loan in the new year. He put in some impressive performances during his time at Whaddon Road and scored in the 4-2 win over Mansfield. On his return to Stoke he showed tremendous improvement, looking much stronger and more determined. Karl is a talented midfield player who can feature in a central role or on the right-hand side.
Stoke C *(From trainee on 30/11/1999) FL 38+24/1 FLC 2+1 FAC 4+1 Others 1+1*
Cheltenham T *(Loaned on 13/1/2004) FL 8+1/1*

HENRY Thierry
Born: Paris, France, 17 August 1977
Height: 6'1" **Weight:** 12.2
Club Honours: FAC '02, '03; PL '02, '04; CS '02
International Honours: France: 63 (UEFA '00); Yth (UEFA-U18 '96)
This excellent striker enjoyed another marvellous season for Arsenal and became only the fourth player in Premiership history to score 30 goals in a season. With pace to burn allied to spellbinding skill and lightning quick feet, Thierry tied just about every Premiership defence in knots throughout an outstanding personal campaign. His hat-trick against Liverpool including a breathtaking individual effort, and in the immediate aftermath of the exits from the FA Cup and Champions' League, he registered four more against Leeds to turn the title race decisively in the Gunners' favour. Runner-up in both the World and European 'Player of the Year' awards, he became the first player to win the PFA and Football Writers' Association 'Player of the Year' Awards in successive seasons.

The awards kept on coming for Thierry as he claimed the PFA Fans' Premiership 'Player of the Season', French 'Sportsman of the Year' and the French 'Footballer of the Year' titles. He was a member of the PFA Premiership team of the season and the France squad for Euro 2004.
Arsenal *(£8,000,000 from Juventus, Italy, ex Monaco, on 6/8/1999) PL 158+15/112 FLC 2/1 FAC 14+6/6 Others 56+5/32*

HERRING Ian
Born: Swindon, 14 February 1984
Height: 6'1" **Weight:** 11.12
This promising young midfielder or defender was given a six-month contract extension in a bid to prove himself at Swindon last season. Ian made a handful of appearances, notably coming on as a substitute in the Carling Cup tie at Leeds when he confidently netted in the penalty shoot-out that decided the tie. Soon afterwards he started at right back in the game at Bristol City when he gave a typical battling performance, but he was eventually released and moved on to join Chippenham Town.
Swindon T *(From trainee on 14/7/2003) FL 3+3 FLC 0+1 Others 1*

HERZIG Nico
Born: Pobneck, Germany, 10 December 1983
Height: 5'10" **Weight:** 11.0
A strongly-built young central defender, Nico made his debut for Wimbledon in the memorable 1-0 win at West Bromwich Albion last October and kept his place for the next few matches, showing gritty determination and a keen willingness to compete for every ball. A striker when playing junior football back in Germany, he was given a couple of attacking chances in the second half of the season before reverting back to his defensive duties, and although not ending the season in the starting line-up, he showed plenty of promise for the future.
Wimbledon *(Signed from Carl Zeiss Jena, Germany on 12/10/2001) FL 18+1*

HESKEY Emile William Ivanhoe
Born: Leicester, 11 January 1978
Height: 6'2" **Weight:** 13.12
Club Honours: FLC '97, '00, '01, '03; FAC '01; UEFAC '01; ESC '01; CS '01
International Honours: E: 43; B-1; U21-16; Yth
There is no doubt of Emile's talent or his enthusiasm and commitment to the cause, and he reached a respectable, if slightly disappointing tally of 12 goals for Liverpool last term. Very much a team

player, his goal tally would undoubtedly increase if he were to develop a greater streak of selfishness. One of his finest performances for the Reds came in the penultimate fixture, away to Birmingham City, when he scored once himself and set up Michael Owen and Steven Gerrard for the others in a 3-0 victory. Ironically, he then made a move to the St Andrews club during the close season. Emile again featured regularly for England during the campaign and was a member of the squad for the Euro 2004 finals in Portugal.
Leicester C *(From trainee on 3/10/1995) PL 143+11/40 FLC 25+2/6 FAC 11 Others 5*
Liverpool *(£11,000,000 on 10/3/2000) PL 118+32/39 FLC 7+5/2 FAC 9+5/6 Others 42+5/13*

HESSENTHALER Andrew (Andy)
Born: Dartford, 17 June 1965
Height: 5'7" **Weight:** 11.5
International Honours: E: SP-1
Gillingham's player-manager has suggested he will continue to play on in the 2004-05 season and the team will surely miss him if he doesn't. Although age may have diminished his powers, he regularly put some of the club's younger players to shame with his fitness levels and determination. The Gills always looked a better side with him in the line-up, and he contributed two goals, including one in the late-season victory at Wimbledon.
Watford *(£65,000 from Redbridge Forest on 12/9/1991) FL 195/12 FLC 13/1 FAC 5/2 Others 4*
Gillingham *(£235,000 on 7/8/1996) FL 245+25/19 FLC 22+2/3 FAC 17+2/2 Others 9+1/3*

HESSEY Sean Peter
Born: Whiston, 19 September 1978
Height: 5'10" **Weight:** 12.6
Sean struggled to win a regular place in the Kilmarnock line-up last term and following a change in management he was allowed to return south and sign for Blackpool. The tall central defender struggled with injuries during his spell at Bloomfield Road and an ankle problem brought his campaign to a premature close. He was released in the summer.
Leeds U *(From Liverpool juniors on 15/9/1997)*
Wigan Ath *(Free on 24/12/1997)*
Huddersfield T *(Free on 12/3/1998) FL 7+4 FAC 1 (Freed on 30/6/1999)*

Kilmarnock *(Free on 31/8/1999) SL 38+6/1 SLC 2 SC 1*
Blackpool *(Free on 12/2/2004) FL 4+2 Others 0+1*

HEWLETT Matthew (Matt) Paul

Born: Bristol, 25 February 1976
Height: 6'2" **Weight:** 11.3
International Honours: E: Yth
Matt enjoyed a fine season for Swindon Town in 2003-04 and was one of the driving forces behind the club's successful campaign. A spell as team captain really saw his form improve and a series of competitive displays in midfield helped propel the team towards the play-offs. A hard-working midfielder who gives his all for the cause, he weighed in with three goals during the season.
Bristol C *(From trainee on 12/8/1993) FL 111+16/9 FLC 10+2 FAC 4+1/2 Others 7+2/1*
Burnley *(Loaned on 27/11/1998) FL 2 Others 1*
Swindon T *(Free on 27/7/2000) FL 145+3/5 FLC 9 FAC 3 Others 3*

HEYWOOD Matthew (Matty) Stephen

Born: Chatham, 26 August 1979
Height: 6'2" **Weight:** 14.0
A reliable and consistent performer at the heart of the Swindon defence who relishes the aerial battles, Matty has now accumulated over 150 Football League appearances for the club. He enjoyed a steady campaign last term, rarely letting his side down, although distribution was not always his strong point. He will be disappointed to have found the net only once during the season, netting in the 4-2 defeat at Peterborough in April.
Burnley *(From trainee on 6/7/1998) FL 11+2 FAC 1 Others 1*
Swindon T *(Free on 22/1/2001) FL 148+3/7 FLC 5 FAC 6/1 Others 7/1*

HIBBERT Anthony (Tony) James

Born: Liverpool, 20 February 1981
Height: 5'8" **Weight:** 11.3
Club Honours: FAYC '98
Tony got off to a slow start for Everton last term following hernia surgery. The tigerish defender featured in most of the matches without building on the promise of his excellent 2002-03 season, one reason being that he missed the presence of the injured Steve Watson, with whom he had built an excellent understanding. When playing to his best he is a speedy and mobile right back who can tackle cleanly at speed to great effect, but he

will need to improve his distribution if international honours are to be a realistic target.
Everton *(From trainee on 1/7/1998) PL 55+7 FLC 4+1 FAC 4*

HIGDON Michael

Born: Liverpool, 2 September 1983
Height: 6'1" **Weight:** 11.5
Michael is yet another promising youngster to emerge through the renowned youth system at Crewe. The tall attacking midfielder missed much of the 2002-03 campaign with injury, but came back strongly last term. He made his senior debut as a substitute at Crystal Palace in December and featured on several occasions thereafter. Michael scored his first senior goal in the 3-1 win over Coventry in April.
Crewe Alex *(From trainee on 6/2/2001) FL 7+3/1 FAC 1*

HIGGINBOTHAM Daniel (Danny) John

Born: Manchester, 29 December 1978
Height: 6'1" **Weight:** 12.6
After being brought in on loan in January 2003 from Derby County, Danny became a fully-fledged Saint during the summer for a very reasonable fee. At his best in the centre of defence he had the misfortune of being understudy to the exemplary Michael Svensson, and spent most of last season at left back, standing in for Graeme Le Saux; a position in which he looked very comfortable. An adept, versatile and intelligent footballer, it has been argued that if he could hold down a regular place at centre back for Southampton he might well be a contender for honours with England.
Manchester U *(From trainee on 10/7/1997) PL 2+2 FLC 1 Others 1+1*
Derby Co *(£2,000,000 on 12/7/2000) P/FL 82+4/3 FLC 7+1/1 FAC 3+1*
Southampton *(Signed on 31/1/2003) PL 27+9 FLC 2 FAC 2 Others 1*

HIGGS Shane Peter

Born: Oxford, 13 May 1977
Height: 6'2" **Weight:** 12.12
One of the few genuine success stories of a disappointing season for Cheltenham Town, Shane was voted 'Player of the Season' by both players and supporters in 2003-04. A tall, strong goalkeeper with excellent reflexes and the ability to kick the length of the pitch, he firmly established himself as the club's number one 'keeper. Shane's saves played a big part in staving off the threat of relegation, and he very nearly scored when his

mammoth clearance against Torquay United was touched in by the faintest of deflections from Damian Spencer.
Bristol Rov *(From trainee on 17/7/1995) FL 10 Others 2 (Free to Worcester C on 11/7/1998)*
Cheltenham T *(£10,000 on 21/6/1999) FL 52+2 FAC 3 Others 3*

HIGNETT Craig John

Born: Prescot, 12 January 1970
Height: 5'9" **Weight:** 11.10
Club Honours: Div 1 '95; FLC '02
This experienced midfielder mostly featured from the substitutes' bench for Leicester during the early weeks of the 2003-04 season, but a hamstring injury at Anfield put him out of action for a while. He grabbed his single goal with a last-gasp touch to deny Arsenal victory at the Walkers Stadium just before Christmas. However, with prospects of a place in the starting line up diminishing, he took up the offer of a return to Crewe on loan during the second half of the campaign. He featured regularly during his stay at Gresty Road, but failed to contribute any goals. Craig was released by the Foxes at the end of the season.
Crewe Alex *(From trainee at Liverpool on 11/5/1988) FL 108+13/42 FLC 9+1/4 FAC 11+1/8 Others 6+1/3*
Middlesbrough *(£500,000 on 27/11/1992) F/PL 126+30/33 FLC 19+3/12 FAC 10+2/3 Others 5+1*
Aberdeen *(Free on 1/7/1998) SL 13/2 SLC 2*
Barnsley *(£500,000 on 26/11/1998) FL 62+4/28 FLC 2 FAC 6/5 Others 3/2*
Blackburn Rov *(£2,250,000 on 14/7/2000) P/FL 20+33/8 FLC 5+1/3 FAC 4+4/3 Others 1*
Coventry C *(Loaned on 1/11/2002) FL 7+1/2 FLC 1*
Leicester C *(Free on 25/7/2003) PL 3+10/1 FLC 1 FAC 1*
Crewe Alex *(Loaned on 20/2/2004) FL 11+4*

HILL Clinton (Clint) Scott

Born: Huyton, 19 October 1978
Height: 6'0" **Weight:** 11.6
This tall, no-nonsense central defender joined Stoke during the summer of 2003 after missing most of the previous season due to a broken leg. However, his injury problems followed him to the Potteries and he failed to make an appearance until October. A leg injury and a bout of influenza further disrupted his campaign, but Clint secured a regular place on the bench towards the end of the campaign.
Tranmere Rov *(From trainee on 9/7/1997) FL 138+2/16 FLC 18/3 FAC 11+1/1*

Matt Hill

Oldham Ath (Signed on 16/7/2002) FL 17/1 FLC 4 FAC 2 Others 2
Stoke C (£120,000 on 22/7/2003) FL 9+3

HILL Kevin
Born: Exeter, 6 March 1976
Height: 5'8" **Weight:** 10.3
Kevin spent most of the 2003-04 season in his preferred position wide on the left of midfield for Torquay United, although he also featured at left back during the campaign. His wholehearted attitude makes him a favourite with fans and he possesses exceptional leaping and heading ability. Highlights of the season for Kevin included a spectacular overhead effort against Macclesfield and scoring twice in the 4-1 win over Carlisle in March.
Torquay U (Free from Torrington on 8/8/1997) FL 254+33/34 FLC 12+1/1 FAC 13+1/2 Others 8+1/1

HILL Matthew (Matt) Clayton
Born: Bristol, 26 March 1981
Height: 5'7" **Weight:** 12.6
Club Honours: AMC '03
This left-sided defender is a good header of the ball, despite his lack of inches, and displays good pace and honest commitment, qualities which endear him to the Bristol City fans. Matt was a near ever-present in the side last year when City came so close to gaining promotion via the play-offs.
Bristol C (From trainee on 22/2/1999) FL 159+16/6 FLC 6 FAC 13 Others 17+4

HILL Stephen Bryan
Born: Prescot, 12 November 1982
Height: 5'10" **Weight:** 11.2
After breaking through to the Rochdale first-team squad in 2002-03, Stephen was handed only one start last time around, when regular left back Michael Simpkins was suspended. Unfortunately Dale were beaten 3-2 by bottom club Carlisle and Stephen dropped out of contention thereafter. He was loaned to Morecambe towards the end of the season before being released in May.
Rochdale (From trainee on 3/7/2002) FL 10+1 FAC 2

HILLIER Ian Michael
Born: Neath, 26 December 1979
Height: 6'0" **Weight:** 11.10
International Honours: W: U21-5
Ian's season never really got going at Luton last term and he only featured in the squad in the first half of the campaign when he was in and out of the side. A versatile player who can fill in at

full back, in the centre of the defence or in central midfield, he will be looking for a decent run of first-team action in 2004-05.
Tottenham H (From trainee on 2/7/1998)
Luton T (Free on 18/8/2001) FL 31+25/1 FLC 0+2 FAC 3+2 Others 5

HILLS John David
Born: Blackpool, 21 April 1978
Height: 5'9" **Weight:** 11.2
Club Honours: AMC '02
The talented left back was one of Gillingham's most impressive performers in the 2003-04 season. John defended soundly throughout and caused problems for the opposition with his effective raiding down the flank and some accurate crosses. His ability in dead-ball situations was an added bonus and he would have been in the running for the club's 'Player of the Year' award if it had not been for injury.
Blackpool (From trainee on 27/10/1995)
Everton (£90,000 on 4/11/1995) PL 1+2
Swansea C (Loaned on 30/1/1997) FL 11
Swansea C (Loaned on 22/8/1997) FL 7/1
Blackpool (£75,000 on 16/1/1998) FL 146+16/16 FLC 12/2 Others 13+1/2
Gillingham (Free on 6/8/2003) FL 27+2/2 FLC 3/1 FAC 2

HILTON Kirk
Born: Flixton, 2 April 1981
Height: 5'7" **Weight:** 10.6
Club Honours: AMC '04
This promising young left back joined Blackpool in the 2003 close season and was seen as a direct replacement for the departed John Hills. However, although Kirk began the season in the starting line-up he soon lost his place and thereafter was generally restricted to the occasional outing on the left-hand side of midfield or on the substitutes' bench. He was released in the summer.
Manchester U (From trainee on 7/7/1999)
Blackpool (Free on 1/7/2003) FL 12+2/1 FLC 1 FAC 1 Others 2

HINDS Richard Paul
Born: Sheffield, 22 August 1980
Height: 6'2" **Weight:** 11.0
Richard originally signed for Hull on a short-term contract, but made such a significant impression that by October he had agreed a long-term deal. His versatility proved to be an important ingredient in the Tigers' promotion campaign, notably during Alton Thelwell's absence when he performed admirably at right back. Richard was also a reliable central defensive deputy but it

was from midfield that he scored the first goal of his senior career with a long-range effort against Macclesfield in November.
Tranmere Rov (From juniors on 20/7/1998) FL 42+13 FLC 3+5 FAC 5 Others 1
Hull C (Free on 1/7/2003) FL 34+5/1 FLC 1 FAC 1 Others 0+1

HINSHELWOOD Adam
Born: Oxford, 8 January 1984
Height: 5'10" **Weight:** 12.10
After starting last season as a central defender alongside Danny Cullip, Adam switched to right back following an injury to Paul Watson and kept his place in the Brighton line-up until November. It was then another five months before the strapping youngster appeared in the first team again as a substitute. On the bench for all three play-off games, Adam could easily have stolen the show in the semi-final second leg against Swindon, twice going close to scoring after coming on late in the game as a winger. Still learning the game, he is a solid defender but needs to work on his distribution.
Brighton & Hove A (From trainee on 28/7/2003) FL 20+4 FLC 2 FAC 1 Others 1+1

HINTON Craig
Born: Wolverhampton, 26 November 1977
Height: 6'0" **Weight:** 12.0
Club Honours: NC '00
This ever-dependable central defender passed the 250-appearance milestone for Kidderminster when he came off the bench at Swansea last October. Craig was often used at right back instead of in a more central role and his form suffered, but he did manage to get his name on the score sheet when he was the only player brave enough to take a penalty in the game at Boston.
Birmingham C (From trainee on 5/7/1996)
Kidderminster Hrs (Free on 12/8/1998) FL 172+1/3 FLC 5 FAC 10 Others 8

HIRSCHFELD Lars
Born: Edmonton, Canada, 17 October 1978
Height: 6'4" **Weight:** 13.8
International Honours: Canada: 16; U23-1
Lars was again well down the pecking order of goalkeepers at Tottenham last term and his only first-team action came during a loan spell at Gillingham. He impressed on his debut in the 1-0 defeat at Crystal Palace in February, but only made one further appearance before being recalled to White Hart Lane

189

Thomas Hitzlsperger (right)

following an injury to second-choice 'keeper Rob Burch.

Tottenham H *(Free from Calgary Storm, Canada, ex Edmonton Drillers, Energie Cottbus, via trial at Portsmouth, on 31/8/2002)*
Luton T *(Loaned on 22/2/2003) FL 5*
Gillingham *(Loaned on 27/2/2004) FL 2*

HISLOP Neil **Shaka**
Born: Hackney, 22 February 1969
Height: 6'4" **Weight:** 14.4
Club Honours: Div 2 '94; Div 1 '03
International Honours: Trinidad & Tobago: 15; E: U21-1
Shaka kept goal for Pompey in their first-ever Premiership season on 29 occasions, keeping seven clean sheets, and was often the 'Man of the Match' keeping the score down with some great finger-tip saves, excellent reactions and command of his area. His vast frame helps cover the goal area and his uninterrupted spell from January until the end of the season suggested he would be the club's number one 'keeper again in 2004-05. A solid, reliable goalkeeper he is approaching the prime years of his career.

Reading *(Signed from Howard University, USA on 9/9/1992) FL 104 FLC 10 FAC 3 Others 9*
Newcastle U *(£1,575,000 on 10/8/1995) PL 53 FLC 8 FAC 6 Others 4*
West Ham U *(Free on 8/7/1998) PL 105 FLC 11 FAC 7 Others 9*
Portsmouth *(Free on 3/7/2002) P/FL 76 FLC 2 FAC 5*

HITCHEN Steven (Steve) James
Born: Salford, 28 November 1976
Height: 5'8" **Weight:** 11.7
At the beginning of the 2003-04 season Steve was the longest-serving player in the current squad at Macclesfield, but despite being a useful and able right back he found it difficult to gain a regular place in the starting line-up due to the form of George Abbey. In January his contract was cancelled by mutual consent and shortly afterwards he signed for Welsh Premier League side Bangor City on non-contract forms, rejoining former Macclesfield manager Peter Davenport.
Blackburn Rov *(From trainee on 4/7/1995)*
Macclesfield T *(Free on 14/7/1997) FL 143+8/1 FLC 7+2 FAC 11+1 Others 3*

HITZLSPERGER Thomas
Born: Munich, Germany, 5 April 1982
Height: 6'0" **Weight:** 12.5
International Honours: Germany: U21-20; Yth
This talented Aston Villa midfielder packs

a powerful shot and has the capability to score spectacular goals from distance. Thomas struggled to maintain a regular place in the side at the beginning of the season. After a six-week spell without any first-team action, he came on as an impressive second-half substitute against Everton and followed up with a stunning long-range winner in the Carling Cup tie against Leicester. Thomas established himself in the line-up in the second half of the campaign and looked sharper and stronger as the season wore on.
Aston Villa *(Free from Bayern Munich, Germany on 8/8/2000) PL 57+14/6 FLC 4+4/4 FAC 0+1 Others 4*
Chesterfield *(Loaned on 27/10/2001) FL 5 Others 1*

HOBBS Shane Michael
Born: Bristol, 30 April 1985
Height: 5'7" **Weight:** 10.7
This young Bristol Rovers scholar made good progress in the club's reserve team last season and was given his senior debut as a substitute against Cambridge in October. Shane also gained valuable experience during a loan spell at Dr Martens League club Clevedon Town for whom he scored ten goals. However, the promising winger was released at the end of the season.
Bristol Rov *(Trainee) FL 0+2*

HOCKING Matthew (Matt) James
Born: Boston, 30 January 1978
Height: 5'11" **Weight:** 11.12
This central defender began the campaign as first choice in the Boston United back four but quickly found himself pushed out. He suffered a back injury and was then relegated to the substitutes' bench. Matt did not start after the management change-over in February and was later released.
Sheffield U *(From trainee on 16/5/1996)*
Hull C *(£25,000 on 19/9/1997) FL 55+2/2 FLC 6 FAC 4 Others 4*
York C *(£30,000 on 25/3/1999) FL 83+14/2 FLC 2+1 FAC 6+2 Others 2*
Boston U *(Free on 9/8/2002) FL 60+7/1 FLC 2+1 FAC 1+1 Others 4*

HOCKLESS Graham
Born: Hull, 20 October 1982
Height: 5'7" **Weight:** 10.6
This promising young midfielder continued to make steady progress at Grimsby last term. An intelligent player who has plenty of skill on the ball, he always performed well when given his chance and notched up a goal in the 4-0

home win over Chesterfield in September. Later in the campaign Graham scored with a spectacular effort at Stockport and produced several outstanding performances when coming on from the substitutes' bench. He was voted as the Mariners' 'Young Player of the Year'.
Grimsby T *(From Hull C juniors on 9/7/2001) FL 5+9/2*

HOCKLEY Matthew (Matt)
Born: Paignton, 5 June 1982
Height: 5'10" **Weight:** 11.7
After previously being used as a utility player by Torquay, Matt started last season in his preferred central-midfield role and quickly made the position his own. His tremendous enthusiasm and work rate accompanied by some ferocious tackling added steel for the Gulls in the centre of the park. Matt also showed he could do the simple things consistently well, thus complementing the ball-playing skills of his colleagues.
Torquay U *(From trainee on 4/7/2000) FL 85+18/8 FLC 1 FAC 5 Others 3*

HODGES Lee Leslie
Born: Plaistow, 2 March 1978
Height: 5'5" **Weight:** 10.2
International Honours: E: Sch
Lee joined Bristol Rovers permanently during the summer of 2003 and enjoyed the start of the season, coming off the bench to score against Scunthorpe United and Kidderminster. Unfortunately he sustained a knee injury, which required an operation in October, and this kept him out of action for four months. Lee then had to be content with a few substitute appearances but failed to regain his place in the starting line-up.
West Ham U *(From trainee on 2/3/1995) PL 0+3 FAC 0+3*
Exeter C *(Loaned on 13/9/1996) FL 16+1*
Leyton Orient *(Loaned on 28/2/1997) FL 3*
Plymouth Arg *(Loaned on 6/11/1997) FL 9 Others 1*
Ipswich T *(Loaned on 20/11/1998) FL 0+4*
Southend U *(Loaned on 25/3/1999) FL 10/1*
Scunthorpe U *(£50,000 on 8/7/1999) FL 97+16/20 FLC 4 FAC 9/2 Others 4/2*
Rochdale *(Free on 9/8/2002) FL 3+4 Others 1*
Bristol Rov *(Free on 21/3/2003) FL 12+9/2 FLC 0+1*

HODGES Lee Leslie
Born: Epping, 4 September 1973
Height: 6'0" **Weight:** 12.1
Club Honours: Div 3 '02; Div 2 '04
International Honours: E: Yth
Lee proved to be an invaluable member

of Plymouth Argyle's Second Division championship-winning squad in 2003-04. He played in a variety of positions throughout the campaign including left back and central midfield, his favoured position. He is a hard tackler and is good in the air, for although not the tallest of players, he has fantastic spring. Lee scored three goals including the opener in the 7-0 demolition of Chesterfield at Home Park in January.

Tottenham H (From trainee on 29/2/1992) PL 0+4
Plymouth Arg (Loaned on 26/2/1993) FL 6+1/2
Wycombe W (Loaned on 31/12/1993) FL 2+2 FAC 1 Others 1
Barnet (Free on 31/5/1994) FL 94+11/26 FLC 6+1 FAC 6+1/4 Others 4+1
Reading (£100,000 on 29/7/1997) FL 58+21/10 FLC 7+3 FAC 7+1/1 Others 0+2
Plymouth Arg (Free on 17/8/2001) FL 108+13/11 FLC 2 FAC 7+1 Others 2+1

HOEKSTRA Peter

Born: Groningen, Holland, 4 April 1973
Height: 6'3" **Weight:** 12.8
International Honours: Holland: 5
This supremely skilful left winger remained at Stoke last season and again showed good form. On his day no defence was safe when he had the ball at his feet and his scintillating displays made him a crowd favourite. Unfortunately an ankle injury kept Peter out of the side for lengthy periods. His best performance came against Reading in December when he netted a hat-trick, his second goal, a thunderbolt volley from 20 yards, was voted as the Potters' 'Goal of the Season'. Peter has since announced his retirement from the game due to his ankle problems, but it will be a long time before his like will be seen again at the Britannia Stadium.

Stoke C (Free from Ajax, Holland, ex PSV Eindhoven, on 27/7/2001) FL 66+12/11 FLC 2+1 FAC 5+2/1

HOGG Christopher

Born: Middlesbrough, 12 March 1985
Height: 6'0" **Weight:** 12.7
International Honours: E: Yth
This young defender gave some solid performances for Boston United after signing on loan from Ipswich Town. Chris took the opportunity to increase his senior experience at right back but his move eventually proved disappointing for both player and club.

Ipswich T (From trainee on 12/8/2002)
Boston U (Loaned on 10/10/2003) FL 10 FAC 1 Others 2

HOLDEN Dean Thomas John

Born: Salford, 15 September 1979
Height: 6'0" **Weight:** 11.0
International Honours: E: Yth
Dean had an excellent season for Oldham Athletic in 2003-04. He was a model of consistency whether asked to play at full back or in the centre of defence. Although still relatively young, he was often the senior player in the rearguard and shouldered the responsibility well. Dean also likes to get forward from the channels and netted four goals, ending the season on a personal high with a superb strike from just inside the area in the 1-1 draw at Notts County. His preferred position is right back and following a change in management, he made that position his own in the latter stages of the campaign.

Bolton W (From trainee on 23/12/1997) FL 7+6/1 FLC 3+1 FAC 3+1
Oldham Ath (Free on 12/10/2001) FL 59+9/8 FLC 0+1 FAC 3 Others 4+1

HOLDSWORTH Andrew (Andy)

Born: Pontefract, 29 January 1984
Height: 5'9" **Weight:** 11.2
A product of the Huddersfield Town Academy, Andy broke into the first-team ranks last September and never looked back. A right wing back or wide-midfield player, he showed maturity beyond his years and created many chances for his colleagues with some accurate crossing. Andy scored with a close-range effort in the Carling Cup win over Sunderland and was selected for the Nationwide 'Team of the Week' on a number of occasions.

Huddersfield T (From trainee on 6/12/2003) FL 31+5 FLC 2/1 FAC 1 Others 4

HOLDSWORTH Dean Christopher

Born: Walthamstow, 8 November 1968
Height: 5'11" **Weight:** 11.13
Club Honours: Div 3 '92
International Honours: E: B-1
Though clearly not the player he was during his first spell with the club, Dean performed with great credit for Wimbledon throughout the 2003-04 season and fittingly scored the club's first goal at its new Milton Keynes home. He had been willing to join a team that was clearly going to have a difficult campaign, but was a figurehead player the Dons' new supporters responded well to, and the ovation he received when appearing off the bench during the final game of the season was both generous and very well merited.

Watford (From apprentice on 12/11/1986) FL 2+14/3 Others 0+4
Carlisle U (Loaned on 11/2/1988) FL 4/1
Port Vale (Loaned on 18/3/1988) FL 6/2
Swansea C (Loaned on 25/8/1988) FL 4+1/1
Brentford (Loaned on 13/10/1988) FL 2+5/1
Brentford (£125,000 on 29/9/1989) FL 106+4/53 FLC 7+1/6 FAC 6/7 Others 12+2/9
Wimbledon (£720,000 on 20/7/1992) PL 148+21/58 FLC 16+3/11 FAC 13+7/7
Bolton W (£3,500,000 on 3/10/1997) P/FL 97+6/39 FLC 11+5/4 FAC 5+2/3 Others 5/3
Coventry C (Free on 29/11/2002) FL 13+4 FAC 3/1
Rushden & Diamonds (Free on 27/3/2003) FL 4+3/2
Wimbledon (Free on 17/7/2003) FL 14+14/3 FLC 0+1 FAC 2

HOLE Stuart Mark

Born: Oxford, 17 July 1985
Height: 6'0" **Weight:** 11.11
A third-year scholar at Wycombe, Stuart had loan spells at Berkhamsted and Beaconsfield SYCOB before being given his senior debut as a late substitute in the final game of the season at Peterborough. A former striker, he has successfully converted to a left-sided central-defensive role. He was released in the summer.

Wycombe W (Trainee) FL 0+1

HOLLAND Christopher (Chris) James

Born: Clitheroe, 11 September 1975
Height: 5'9" **Weight:** 11.5
International Honours: E: U21-10; Yth
This industrious midfielder was restricted to just two starts for Huddersfield Town last term. Always willing to graft for his team mates, the non-stop playmaker continued to be involved from the substitutes' bench. Chris was one of a number of new players brought in by Boston United following a change of management in the second half of the season. He made only a handful of appearances in the centre of midfield and will be looking to win a regular place in the starting line-up in 2004-05.

Preston NE (Trainee) FL 0+1 Others 1
Newcastle U (£100,000 on 20/1/1994) PL 2+1 FLC 0+1
Birmingham C (£600,000 on 5/9/1996) FL 39+31 FLC 7+5 FAC 4 Others 1+1
Huddersfield T (£150,000 on 3/2/2000) FL 113+7/2 FLC 4 FAC 5 Others 9+1/1
Boston U (Free on 22/3/2004) FL 3+2

HOLLAND Matthew (Matt) Rhys

Born: Bury, 11 April 1974
Height: 5'9" **Weight:** 11.12

International Honours: Rol: 43; B-1
Made club captain on his debut, Matt
was an ever-present in his first season for
Charlton. He started the season on the
right of midfield, but switched to his
preferred central-midfield role after the
sale of Scott Parker in January. Matt took
a while to settle, but then started to put
in some sterling performances for the
club and became a crowd favourite. A
strong tackler with good positional sense,
he is very comfortable on the ball and has
good passing ability. He looked a better
player when moved to the centre of
midfield and chipped in with some
valuable goals, including two headers in
the 2-1 win at Birmingham in March,
and a 25-yard screamer in the 1-0 home
win over Middlesbrough in March. His
headed goal in Charlton's 4-2 home win
against Chelsea was also a beauty. Matt
finished the season as second-top scorer
with six goals, and looks like a great
acquisition.
West Ham U (From trainee on 3/7/1992)
Bournemouth (Signed on 27/1/1995) FL
97+7/18 FLC 6 FAC 3 Others 3
Ipswich T (£800,000 on 31/7/1997) P/FL
259/38 FLC 23+1/6 FAC 12 Others 17+2/2
Charlton Ath (£750,000 on 17/6/2003) PL
38/6 FLC 2 FAC 1

HOLLIGAN Gavin Victor
Born: Lambeth, 13 June 1980
Height: 5'10" **Weight:** 12.0
Gavin missed the start of the 2003-04
campaign with a groin strain, but then
enjoyed a seven-week run in the
Wycombe line-up, netting twice against
Bristol City. Following a loan spell at
Crawley he then joined Hornchurch, also
on loan, but an injury saw him return to
Adams Park in March. He was released by
manager Tony Adams and was reported
to have secured a permanent deal with
Havant & Waterlooville. Gavin is a cool,
tricky striker, capable of scoring
spectacular goals.
West Ham U (£100,000 from Kingstonian
on 5/3/1999) P/L 0+1
Leyton Orient (Loaned on 17/9/1999) FL 1
FLC 1
Exeter C (Loaned on 17/10/2000) FL 3
Wycombe W (Free on 9/8/2001) FL 20+23/8
FLC 1 FAC 3/1 Others 3/1

HOLLOWAY Darren
Born: Crook, 3 October 1977
Height: 5'10" **Weight:** 12.2
International Honours: E: U21-1
Darren's last season with Wimbledon was
notable for the reception he received
from the Sunderland fans when being

substituted after 30 minutes during the
December match at the Stadium of Light.
A right-sided defender who can also play
the 'holding' role in midfield, he was
loaned out to Scunthorpe later in the
campaign and scored with a header on
his debut against Yeovil. He featured in
the centre of midfield for the Iron, but
returned before the season's end and was
subsequently not offered a new deal by
Wimbledon.
Sunderland (From trainee on 12/10/1995)
P/FL 46+12 FLC 3 FAC 2 Others 3
Carlisle U (Loaned on 29/8/1997) FL 5
Bolton W (Loaned on 14/12/1999) FL 3+1
Wimbledon (£1,250,000 on 2/10/2000) FL
84+8 FLC 4 FAC 6
Scunthorpe U (Loaned on 27/2/2004) FL 5/1

HOLMES Derek
Born: Lanark, 18 October 1978
Height: 6'0" **Weight:** 13.2
This tall striker had to be content with a
place in the Bournemouth reserve side for
the majority of the 2003-04 season,
although he found the net regularly.
However, an injury to Steve Fletcher gave
Derek a run in the first team at the end of
the campaign and allowed him to pass
the 100-appearance mark for the
Cherries.
Heart of Midlothian (From juniors on
5/11/1995) SL 1+6/1 SLC 0+2/2 Others 0+3/1
Ross Co (Free on 15/10/1999) SL 39+19/14
SLC 1+1/1 SC 1+1 Others 3
Bournemouth (£40,000 on 14/9/2001) FL
55+37/14 FLC 1+1 FAC 0+5/1 Others 4+2

HOLMES Lee Daniel
Born: Mansfield, 2 April 1987
Height: 5'7" **Weight:** 10.6
International Honours: E: Yth
Already the youngest player to appear for
Derby County, Lee's goal in the home
defeat by Coventry last October made
him the youngest scorer in the club's
history, at the age of 16 years and 206
days. The winger excites because he
whips in telling crosses and makes things
happen, but after being a regular in the
squad for the first half of the season, he
was then used more sparingly. While
being nursed at club level, Lee progressed
to the England U19 team and scored
spectacularly against Germany.
Derby Co (From trainee on 15/5/2004) FL
17+8/2 FAC 0+2

HOLMES Peter James
Born: Bishop Auckland, 18 November
1980
Height: 5'10" **Weight:** 10.6
International Honours: E: Yth; Sch

Peter was still recovering from an injury
suffered the previous term at the start of
the 2003-04 campaign, and it was not
until November that he returned to action
for Luton Town. He then enjoyed a useful
run in the side only to be sidelined by a
further injury in March which brought his
season to a close. A skilful midfield player
who can play on the right-hand side or in
a more central role, he is an excellent
passer of the ball.
Sheffield Wed (From trainee on 2/12/1997)
Luton T (Free on 1/8/2000) FL 35+23/6 FLC
3+2 FAC 5+2 Others 4+1/1

HOLMES Shaun Paul
Born: Derry, 27 December 1980
Height: 5'9" **Weight:** 11.3
International Honours: NI: 1; U21-13;
Yth; Sch
Shaun had limited opportunities to stake
a regular place in the Wrexham starting
line-up last term, partly due to the
systems employed by the team. However,
he was still a valued member of the
squad and could always be counted on to
do a good job. He came on as a
substitute on several occasions, and made
a great contribution at Tranmere when he
delivered a spectacular 25-yard goal to
win the game for the Racecourse club.
Shaun was released in the summer and
was reported to have signed for Irish
League club Glentoran.
Manchester C (From trainee on 10/1/1998)
Wrexham (Free on 9/8/2001) FL 55+28/2
FLC 1+2 FAC 3 Others 3+1/1

HOLT Andrew (Andy)
Born: Stockport, 21 May 1978
Height: 6'1" **Weight:** 12.7
Andy became one of the unsung heroes
of Hull City's promotion success last term.
Used by manager Peter Taylor as a
defensive midfielder rather than an
orthodox full back, he regularly came on
in the final stages of games to replace
Stuart Elliott on the left flank. A popular
figure amongst colleagues and fans alike,
Andy's only goal of the season – the
opener in an important 3-0 defeat of
Lincoln – won wide acclaim.
Oldham Ath (From trainee on 23/7/1996) FL
104+20/10 FLC 8 FAC 4 Others 3
Hull C (£150,000 on 15/3/2001) FL 45+26/3
FLC 1 FAC 1 Others 5+1
Barnsley (Loaned on 15/8/2002) FL 4+3
FLC 1
Shrewsbury T (Loaned on 27/3/2003) FL 9

HOLT Gary James
Born: Irvine, 9 March 1973
Height: 6'0" **Weight:** 12.11

Club Honours: SC '98; Div 1 '04
International Honours: S: 6
Gary won a recall to Berti Vogts' Scotland squad towards the end of the 2003-04 season following a fantastic campaign at the heart of Norwich City's midfield. He was an ever-present in Nigel Worthington's side, showing his versatility with three appearances at right back early on in the campaign. Renowned for his energetic displays, his distribution is always simple and he has become a key figure in the Canaries' line-up since signing from Kilmarnock. His performances earned him a new contract in April.
Stoke C (From Glasgow Celtic N/C on 20/10/1994)
Kilmarnock (Free on 18/8/1995) SL 138+13/9 SLC 10+1 SC 13 Others 8
Norwich C (£100,000 on 22/3/2001) FL 140+1/3 FLC 3 FAC 6 Others 3

HOLT Grant
Born: Carlisle, 12 April 1981
Height: 6'1" **Weight:** 12.7
After a promising breakthrough into the Sheffield Wednesday line-up the previous season, Grant found it difficult to impress last term. He scored twice against Brentford, but in the new year he became Rochdale manager Steve Parkin's first permanent signing. The big target man proved a real handful for opposition defences and his goals helped Dale avoid relegation to the Conference.
Halifax T (Signed from Workington on 16/9/1999) FL 0+6 FLC 1/1 Others 1 (Free to Barrow during 2001 close season)
Sheffield Wed (Free on 27/3/2003) FL 12+12/3 FLC 0+1 FAC 2/1 Others 1+2
Rochdale (Signed on 30/1/2004) FL 14/4

HOPE Christopher (Chris)
Jonathan
Born: Sheffield, 14 November 1972
Height: 6'1" **Weight:** 12.7
Chris was a regular for Gillingham for much of last term, even though by his own high standards he was not always at his best. A cool and unruffled central defender he contributed three goals during the campaign.
Nottingham F (From Darlington juniors on 23/8/1990)
Scunthorpe U (£50,000 on 5/7/1993) FL 278+9/19 FLC 13+1 FAC 18/1 Others 18/2
Gillingham (£250,000 on 12/7/2000) FL 175/10 FLC 13 FAC 10/2

HOPE Richard Paul
Born: Stockton, 22 June 1978
Height: 6'2" **Weight:** 12.6

This commanding central defender played consistently well in the heart of York City's defence as the Minstermen struggled to remain in the Football League last season. Strong in the air, he was on the mark twice with goals against Southend and Oxford United.
Blackburn Rov (From trainee on 9/8/1995)
Darlington (Free on 17/1/1997) FL 62+1/1 FLC 3 FAC 1 Others 0+1
Northampton T (Signed on 18/12/1998) FL 113+22/7 FLC 3 FAC 5+3 Others 7+1
York C (Free on 8/8/2003) FL 36/2 FLC 1 FAC 1 Others 1

HORLOCK Kevin
Born: Erith, 1 November 1972
Height: 6'0" **Weight:** 12.0
Club Honours: Div 2 '96; Div 1 '02
International Honours: NI: 32; B-2
After previously being a youth and reserve player at West Ham, Kevin returned last August to make his long-awaited first-team debut. Now an established Northern Ireland international, he added a great deal of experience to the midfield. Kevin had an outstanding game at Coventry in November with some tigerish tackling. He is always a reliable member of the squad and when needed he can also play in defensive positions.
West Ham U (From trainee on 1/7/1991)
Swindon T (Free on 27/8/1992) F/PL 151+12/22 FLC 15+2/1 FAC 12/3 Others 5+2
Manchester C (£1,250,000 on 31/1/1997) P/FL 184+20/37 FLC 15+1/3 FAC 9/1 Others 3/1
West Ham U (£300,000 on 15/8/2003) FL 23+4/1 FLC 2 FAC 4

HORSFIELD Geoffrey (Geoff)
Malcolm
Born: Barnsley, 1 November 1973
Height: 5'10" **Weight:** 11.0
Club Honours: FC '98; Div 2 '99
This all-action striker was soon on his way out of St Andrews last term, leaving Birmingham City for Wigan Athletic. He impressed as an old-fashioned centre forward at the JJB Stadium, scoring a winner against West Bromwich Albion, but after three months in the North West he returned to the Midlands, signing for the Baggies. He immediately added impetus to the front-line and scored some important goals while helping the club regain their Premiership status at the first attempt.
Scarborough (From juniors on 10/7/1992) FL 12/1 FAC 1 Others 0+2 (Free to Halifax T on 31/3/1994)
Halifax T (Free from Witton A on 8/5/1997) FL 10/7 FLC 4/1

Fulham (£325,000 on 12/10/1998) FL 54+5/22 FLC 6/6 FAC 8+1/3
Birmingham C (£2,000,000 + on 12/7/2000) P/FL 75+33/23 FLC 10+1/3 FAC 1+1 Others 5/2
Wigan Ath (Signed on 6/9/2003) FL 16/7 FLC 1
West Bromwich A (£1,000,000 on 18/12/2003) FL 20/7 FAC 1

HOSKINS William (Will)
Richard
Born: Nottingham, 6 May 1986
Height: 5'11" **Weight:** 11.2
International Honours: E: Yth
This young striker burst on to the Rotherham first-team scene on Boxing Day hitting both goals with some aplomb in an unexpected 2-1 win at Wigan Athletic. Will had been a prolific scorer for both the reserve and junior teams and would probably have had further senior opportunities towards the end of the season but for a back injury. His excellent potential was rewarded when he made his debut for England U18s in April.
Rotherham U (Trainee) FL 0+4/2 FAC 0+1

HOULT Russell
Born: Ashby de la Zouch, 22 November 1972
Height: 6'3" **Weight:** 14.9
Once again goalkeeper Russell Hoult had a fine season between the posts for West Bromwich Albion, despite playing on through the pain barrier during the second half of the campaign with a back problem. Confident on his line, strong and safe in the air, he produced some stunning saves to keep the Baggies in the game on many occasions and in his 44 League games conceded only 39 goals, helping his team reclaim their place in the Premiership.
Leicester C (From trainee on 28/3/1991) FL 10 FLC 3 Others 1
Lincoln C (Loaned on 27/8/1991) FL 2 FLC 1
Bolton W (Loaned on 3/11/1993) FL 3+1 Others 1
Lincoln C (Loaned on 12/8/1994) FL 15 Others 1
Derby Co (£300,000 on 17/2/1995) F/PL 121+2 FLC 8 FAC 7
Portsmouth (£300,000 + on 21/1/2000) FL 40 FLC 4
West Bromwich A (£500,000 on 5/1/2001) P/FL 139 FLC 8 FAC 7 Others 2

HOWARD Brian Richard William
Born: Winchester, 23 January 1983
Height: 5'8" **Weight:** 11.1
International Honours: E: Yth
Brian had a promising debut season for Swindon during 2003-04 and after

establishing himself as a regular member of the first team he was involved throughout the campaign. A left-footed midfielder who likes to get forward, he was one of the main reasons behind the much improved delivery of corners. Brian also scored some useful goals, none more impressive than a spectacular chip at Stockport in February.

Southampton *(From trainee on 27/1/2000)*
Swindon T *(Free on 6/8/2003) FL 21+14/4 FLC 1+1 FAC 1 Others 3*

HOWARD Michael Anthony
Born: Birkenhead, 2 December 1978
Height: 5'9" **Weight:** 11.13
Club Honours: Div 3 '00
Despite missing out on a place in the

line-up at the start of last season when Leon Hylton was preferred at left back, Michael again proved all the doubters wrong to regain a regular spot in the Swansea City line-up. He struggled through the second half of the campaign with injury problems, and in early April was forced to have surgery to a hernia problem, which then needed a second operation.

Tranmere Rov *(From trainee on 9/7/1997)*
Swansea C *(Free on 6/2/1998) FL 221+7/2 FLC 9 FAC 15 Others 8*

HOWARD Steven (Steve) John
Born: Durham, 10 May 1976
Height: 6'2" **Weight:** 14.6

This experienced striker was leading scorer for Luton Town for the third season in succession, despite missing a third of the campaign through injury and suspension. A traditional English-style centre forward, brave, bustling and effective in the air, he sometimes performed when not fully fit and coped adequately with a succession of striking partners.

Hartlepool U *(Free from Tow Law on 8/8/1995) FL 117+25/26 FLC 7+1/1 FAC 5/2 Others 7/3*
Northampton T *(£120,000 on 22/2/1999) FL 67+19/18 FLC 4 FAC 2+1 Others 2*
Luton T *(£50,000 on 22/3/2001) FL 129/63 FLC 5/2 FAC 4 Others 1*

Steve Howard (left)

HOWARD Timothy (Tim) Matthew

Born: North Brunswick, New Jersey, USA, 6 March 1979
Height: 6'3" **Weight:** 14.12
Club Honours: CS '03; FAC '04
International Honours: USA: 10

A solid performer, who is quick off his line, Tim signed for Manchester United in the summer of 2003. Immediately installed as Sir Alex Ferguson's first-choice goalkeeper at the start of the campaign, he fully justified the manager's faith in him with a string of consistent performances. From August to December, he conceded only 11 Premiership goals whilst only Stuttgart managed to breach his defence in the Champions' League qualifying rounds. Superseded by Roy Carroll later in the campaign, Tim came back to action against Charlton in April. He was also selected for the PFA Premiership team of the season.
Manchester U (£2,300,000 from New York/New Jersey Metrostars, USA on 22/7/2003) PL 32 FAC 4 Others 8

HOWARTH Russell Michael

Born: York, 27 March 1982
Height: 6'1" **Weight:** 13.10
International Honours: E: Yth

Russell's first-team opportunities at Tranmere were again severely restricted by the outstanding form of regular goalkeeper John Achterberg last term. He was called upon to make just one full start, and that came in the away game at Swindon Town when John was injured. Russell is a confident 'keeper and toiled away uncomplainingly in the reserves side while awaiting his chance of further senior action.
York T (From trainee on 26/8/1999) FL 6+2 FLC 3 Others 3
Tranmere Rov (Free on 5/11/2002) FL 3+1 FAC 0+1

HOWELLS Lee David

Born: Perth, Australia, 14 October 1968
Height: 5'11" **Weight:** 11.12
Club Honours: FAT '98; NC '99
International Honours: E: SP-2

Lee missed the start of last season with an achilles problem and made his first start for Cheltenham in 18 months in the 2-0 defeat at Bristol Rovers. A strong, fit central midfielder with plenty of appetite for running and the ability to get into goal-scoring positions, Lee found it hard to break into the squad. He made a total of seven starting appearances, but spent the final three months of the season on loan to Merthyr Tydfil in the Dr Martens League.

Bristol Rov (From apprentice on 17/10/1986. Freed on 1/7/1988)
Cheltenham T (Signed from Brisbane Lions, Australia on 1/12/1991) FL 119+2/6 FLC 2 FAC 10/2 Others 4

HOWEY Stephen (Steve) Norman

Born: Sunderland, 26 October 1971
Height: 6'2" **Weight:** 11.12
Club Honours: Div 1 '93, '02
International Honours: E: 4

This experienced defender signed for Leicester in the 2003 close season and established a promising central defensive partnership with Riccardo Scimeca during the Foxes' best run of the season, but injury problems dogged his time at the Walkers Stadium, culminating in his withdrawal during the warm up for the FA Cup replay with Manchester City. He was allowed to move to Bolton during the January transfer window, signing on a short-term contract. However, he did not get the chance to establish himself as a regular in the first team at the Reebok and made just two starts, in the games against Manchester City and Middlesbrough. Steve was released by Bolton at the end of the season.
Newcastle U (From trainee on 11/12/1989) F/PL 167+24/6 FLC 14+2/1 FAC 21+2 Others 10+2
Manchester C (£2,000,000 + on 14/8/2000) P/FL 94/11 FLC 6 FAC 3
Leicester C (£300,000 on 4/7/2003) PL 13/1 FLC 2
Bolton W (Free on 30/1/2004) PL 2+1

HOWSON Stuart Leigh

Born: Chorley, 30 September 1981
Height: 6'1" **Weight:** 12.12

A series of recurring injuries decimated Stuart's 2003-04 season for Chesterfield. Although previously effective as a defender, he was used as much in midfield when he did play - testament, of course, to his well-timed tackling, composure and distribution skills. In the event, though, the injuries won, and Stuart was released in May.
Blackburn Rov (From trainee on 22/7/1999)
Chesterfield (Free on 15/2/2002) FL 51+4/3 FLC 2 FAC 1 Others 3

HOYTE Justin Raymond

Born: Waltham Forest, 20 November 1984
Height: 5'11" **Weight:** 10.10
International Honours: E: U21-2; Yth

Justin was one of several Arsenal youngsters to make significant progress last term. The right back made his

Premiership debut as a substitute in the game against Birmingham City in November and also started in the Carling Cup ties against Rotherham and Wolves. He was on the bench on a number of occasions, as well as featuring regularly for the club's reserve team.
Arsenal (From trainee on 1/7/2002) PL 0+2 FLC 2

HREIDARSSON Hermann

Born: Iceland, 11 July 1974
Height: 6'1" **Weight:** 13.1
Club Honours: Div 3 '99
International Honours: Iceland: 52; U21-6

Hermann was used mainly as a left back by Charlton during the season, but played the last few games as a central defender alongside Jon Fortune when all the club's other experienced central defenders were injured. Tall and uncompromising, he is good in the air, skilful on the ground and very strong. Hermann is very quick and likes to overlap down the left wing and get in an accurate cross. He even managed to find the net himself on two occasions, in the away win at Blackburn Rovers with a diving header, and in the home win over Chelsea with another header in the opening minute. Hermann added five more international caps for Iceland during the campaign and was voted runner-up to goalkeeper Dean Kiely as the season's 'Player of the Year'.
Crystal Palace (Signed from IBV, Iceland on 9/8/1997) P/FL 32+5/2 FLC 5/1 FAC 4 Others 2
Brentford (£850,000 on 24/9/1998) FL 41/6 FLC 2 FAC 2/1 Others 3/1
Wimbledon (£2,500,000 on 14/10/1999) P/FL 25/1 FAC 2
Ipswich T (£4,000,000 + on 19/8/2000) P/FL 101+1/2 FLC 11 FAC 6 Others 9/1
Charlton Ath (£500,000 + on 27/3/2003) PL 33/2 FLC 1 FAC 1

HUCKERBY Darren Carl

Born: Nottingham, 23 April 1976
Height: 5'10" **Weight:** 11.12
Club Honours: Div 1 '02, '04
International Honours: E: B-1; U21-4

Darren scored in his only start for Manchester City in the UEFA Cup tie against TNS. However, with fierce competition for places in the Blues' attack the quicksilver striker saw his opportunities limited and he finally joined Norwich City after a successful three-month loan period. The deal was clinched on Boxing Day and the announcement that preceded the home match with Nottingham Forest that day seemed to set the tone for the remainder of the Canaries' title-winning season. An electric

Hermann Hreidarsson (foreground)

Tom Huddlestone

performer with fantastic pace and dribbling skills to frighten even the best of defences, his 14 goals made him the club's top scorer. A real hero for Norwich fans, he was voted runner-up in the club's 'Player of the Season' award and was named as the PFA Fan's Division One 'Player of the Season'.

Lincoln C *(From trainee on 14/7/1993) FL 20+8/5 FLC 2 Others 1/2*
Newcastle U *(£400,000 on 10/11/1995) PL 0+1 FAC 0+1*
Millwall *(Loaned on 6/9/1996) FL 6/3*
Coventry C *(£1,000,000 on 23/11/1996) PL 85+9/28 FLC 2+1 FAC 12/6*
Leeds U *(£4,000,000 on 12/8/1999) PL 11+29/2 FLC 1+1/2 FAC 1+2 Others 1+11/2*
Manchester C *(£2,250,000 + on 29/12/2000) P/FL 44+25/22 FLC 2+3/6 FAC 6+1/2 Others 1/1*
Nottingham F *(Loaned on 24/2/2003) FL 9/5 Others 2*
Norwich C *(Loaned on 12/9/2003) FL 16/5*
Norwich C *(£750,000 on 27/12/2003) FL 20/9 FAC 1*

HUDDLESTONE Thomas (Tom) Andrew

Born: Nottingham, 28 December 1986
Height: 6'3" **Weight:** 14.12
International Honours: E: Yth

By any standards, Tom had a remarkable first season for Derby County. He began it hoping for a few later outings but, although not 17 until the end of December, he was in from the start and made more appearances than any other player. His impressive physique caused many to query his age, but his smooth touch on the ball in midfield and passing ability were immediately obvious. His tackling and heading will gain authority with increased strength so, given luck in avoiding injuries, he should have a bright future. Tom continued his progress through the England age groups by appearing at U19 level and was an inevitable choice as Derby's 'Young Player of the Year'.

Derby Co *(From trainee on 27/2/2004) FL 42+1 FLC 1 FAC 1*

HUDSON Mark

Born: Bishop Auckland, 24 October 1980
Height: 5'10" **Weight:** 11.3

Mark ascended to the captaincy of Chesterfield last term and clearly relished the challenge. His vision and passing ability remained unaffected by any additional pressure and when joined by a ball winner in Derek Niven, Mark took his game to another level. He ran the midfield against Queens Park Rangers in

January and killed the game off with a firm shot: many similar subsequent displays were seen once Mark could concentrate on the creative side of his play.
Middlesbrough *(From trainee on 5/7/1999) PL 0+5 FAC 0+1*
Chesterfield *(Loaned on 13/8/2002) FL 15+1/1 FLC 1 FAC 0+1 Others 0+1*
Carlisle U *(Loaned on 10/12/2002) FL 14+1/1*
Chesterfield *(Free on 21/3/2003) FL 40+3/4 FLC 1 Others 2*

HUDSON Mark Alexander
Born: Guildford, 30 March 1982
Height: 6'3" **Weight:** 12.6
This commanding young central defender made excellent progress last term and finished the season on the bench for Fulham, although he has yet to make his debut in the Premiership. He started the campaign on loan at Oldham where he was effective in the middle of a three-man central defensive system. He certainly impressed manager Iain Dowie, and when Dowie moved to Crystal Palace he signed Mark on loan again. He went on to establish an excellent central-defensive partnership with Tony Popovic helping the Eagles in their rise from the relegation zone to the play-offs before returning to Loftus Road.
Fulham *(From trainee on 6/4/1999) FLC 2+1*
Oldham Ath *(Loaned on 25/8/2003) FL 15 Others 1*
Crystal Palace *(Loaned on 16/1/2004) FL 14*

HUGHES Aaron William
Born: Cookstown, NI, 8 November 1979
Height: 6'0" **Weight:** 11.2
International Honours: NI: 35; B-2; Yth
Aaron reads the game well and is comfortable on the ball, while his versatility enables him to play in any of the defensive roles, or as a marking midfielder. His clean-tackling skills were highlighted by the fact that he was booked only once during the season. He began the 2003-04 campaign competing with Andy Griffin for the right-back spot in Newcastle's back four, but by October he was established as first choice which he remained for the rest of the season, although he occasionally featured in the centre of the defence and even at left back. Aaron continued to represent Northern Ireland, and was honoured with the captaincy of his country.
Newcastle U *(From trainee on 11/3/1997) PL 175+8/3 FLC 8 FAC 14+3/1 Others 30+4/2*

HUGHES Andrew (Andy) John
Born: Manchester, 2 January 1978
Height: 5'11" **Weight:** 12.1

Club Honours: Div 3 '98
Andy put in another successful season of solid, consistent performances, and along with Steve Sidwell, made more first-team appearances than any other Reading player. He operated mostly on the right or left flank, but also contributed from the centre of midfield. However, some of his best performances came in the closing weeks of the campaign when he filled in as an emergency left back, a position which still allows him to make penetrating runs forward. Andy also chipped in with the occasional goal.

Michael Hughes

Oldham Ath *(From trainee on 20/1/1996) FL 18+15/1 FLC 1+1 FAC 3+1 Others 1+2*
Notts Co *(£150,000 on 29/1/1998) FL 85+25/17 FLC 6+1/1 FAC 10/2 Others 2*
Reading *(Free on 16/7/2001) FL 117+8/18 FLC 5 FAC 3+1 Others 3*

HUGHES Bryan
Born: Liverpool, 19 June 1976
Height: 5'10" **Weight:** 11.2
Club Honours: WC '95
Bryan was a frustrated spectator last season until injuries gave him his chance for Birmingham City in January and from

Lewis Hunt

then on he never looked back. He kept his place, either in central midfield or on either flank, and got into great attacking positions. Bryan's knack of arriving in the box just at the right time brought five goals, including two in the 4-1 win over Leeds United in March.

Wrexham (From trainee on 7/7/1994) FL 71+23/12 FLC 2 FAC 13+3/7 Others 6+1/1
Birmingham C (£750,000 + on 12/3/1997) P/FL 197+51/34 FLC 17+5/3 FAC 8+5/4 Others 6+2/1

HUGHES Christopher (Chris)

Born: Sunderland, 5 March 1984
Height: 6'0" **Weight:** 11.6
This lively young midfielder joined Darlington during the 2003 close season and after featuring as a substitute in the first four games made a dream full debut when he scored the winner against Leyton Orient at the end of August. Chris always gave 100 per cent and established himself in the starting line-up after Christmas, impressing with some hard running and strong tackling.

Darlington (From trainee on 1/7/2003) FL 24+6/2 FLC 1+1 FAC 1

HUGHES Ian

Born: Bangor, 2 August 1974
Height: 5'10" **Weight:** 12.8
Club Honours: Div 2 '97; AMC '02
International Honours: W: U21-12; Yth
This experienced defender started last term at centre half for Huddersfield Town before switching to the right-back berth. Ian tackled effectively and linked up well with the front-line players. Praised for his valuable work rate, he enjoyed an early-season goal at Boston United, but was hampered by injury later in the campaign.

Bury (From trainee on 19/11/1991) FL 137+24/1 FLC 14+3 FAC 6+2 Others 14+4/1
Blackpool (£200,000 on 12/12/1997) FL 139+21/3 FLC 11/1 FAC 8 Others 8+4/1
Huddersfield T (Free on 7/8/2003) FL 12+1/1 FLC 1 Others 1

HUGHES Lee

Born: Smethwick, 22 May 1976
Height: 5'10" **Weight:** 11.6
International Honours: E: SP-4
Striker Lee Hughes claimed the 100th League goal of his career last term, and then reached the milestone of a century of goals for West Bromwich Albion in May. A well-publicised off-the-field problem certainly affected his performances either side of Christmas, but when selected to play he gave nothing less than 100 per cent. Lee

netted some crucial goals, including the extra-time decider at Newcastle United in the Carling Cup.

West Bromwich A (£250,000 + from Kidderminster Hrs on 19/5/1997) FL 137+19/78 FLC 10+3/4 FAC 6/2 Others 2/1
Coventry C (£5,000,000 on 9/8/2001) FL 38+4/15 FLC 1+1
West Bromwich A (£2,500,000 on 30/8/2002) P/FL 35+20/11 FLC 2+3/2

HUGHES Michael Eamonn

Born: Larne, 2 August 1971
Height: 5'7" **Weight:** 10.13
International Honours: NI: 69; U23-2; U21-1; Yth; Sch
After missing out on the whole of the 2002-03 campaign due to contractual problems, Michael was back in action last term, and after a successful trial he signed for Crystal Palace. The diminutive, hard-working midfielder showed great vision and produced several fine performances for the Eagles. A high point was scoring the winning penalty in the shoot-out that decided the play-off semi-final against Sunderland. Michael also added to his total of caps for Northern Ireland during the campaign.

Manchester C (From trainee on 17/8/1988) FL 25+1/1 FLC 5 FAC 1 Others 1 (£450,000 to RS Strasbourg, France on 3/8/1992)
West Ham U (Loaned on 29/11/1994) PL 15+2/2 FAC 2
West Ham U (Loaned on 2/10/1995) PL 28 FLC 2 FAC 3/1
West Ham U (Free on 12/8/1996) PL 33+5/3 FLC 5 FAC 2
Wimbledon (£1,600,000 on 25/9/1997) P/FL 99+16/13 FLC 5+1/2 FAC 8+1/2
Birmingham C (Loaned on 28/3/2002) FL 3
Crystal Palace (Free on 14/8/2003) FL 34/3 FLC 3 FAC 1 Others 3

HUGHES John Paul

Born: Hammersmith, 19 April 1976
Height: 6'0" **Weight:** 12.10
International Honours: E: Sch
This gifted Luton Town midfielder was again affected by injuries which restricted his appearances last term. He started the season in good form, and scored a brilliant individual goal against Bournemouth, but that was the last that was seen of him until he was called upon as a substitute in February. Restored to the first team, Paul once again provided the Hatters with class and maturity in the centre of the park. He was out of contract in the summer and his future is unclear at the time of writing.

Chelsea (From trainee on 11/7/1994) PL 13+8/2 FAC 1 Others 1

Stockport Co (Loaned on 17/12/1998) FL 7
Norwich C (Loaned on 24/3/1999) FL 2+2/1
Southampton (Free on 23/3/2000)
Luton T (Free, via trial at Burnley, on 10/8/2001) FL 62+17/6 FLC 5 FAC 1 Others 2

HUGHES Richard Daniel

Born: Glasgow, 25 June 1979
Height: 5'9" **Weight:** 9.12
International Honours: S: 2; U21-9; Yth
Richard showed plenty of class in Portsmouth's reserves last term and this paid off towards the end of the season when, having overcome an ankle injury himself, injuries to first-teamers gave him the chance to show his skills in the Premiership. A hard-working midfielder who always gives 100 per cent commitment, he scored the winner in the FA Cup replay against Liverpool at Fratton Park.

Arsenal (Free from Atalanta, Italy on 11/8/1997)
Bournemouth (£20,000 on 5/8/1998) FL 123+8/14 FLC 9+1 FAC 8/2 Others 5
Portsmouth (£100,000 on 13/6/2002) F/PL 12+5 FLC 1 FAC 2+2/1
Grimsby T (Loaned on 21/2/2003) FL 12/1

HUGHES Stephen (Steve) Thomas

Born: High Wycombe, 26 January 1984
Height: 6'1" **Weight:** 12.10
Although a regular on the substitutes' bench for the first two-thirds of the 2003-04 season, this left-sided midfielder only actually started one game for Brentford. He then dropped out of contention before joining Basingstoke on loan in April. Steve was released at the end of the season.

Brentford (From trainee on 9/7/2002) FL 3+9 FLC 0+1 FAC 1+3 Others 0+2

HULBERT Robin James

Born: Plymouth, 14 March 1980
Height: 5'9" **Weight:** 10.5
International Honours: E: Yth; Sch
This young midfielder's Bristol City career was disrupted by minor injuries just when he got himself into the first team last season. Robin made only three substitute appearances, all in cup competitions, before moving on to join Conference outfit Telford United in November.

Swindon T (From trainee on 25/9/1997) FL 12+17 FLC 1+1 FAC 2
Bristol C (£25,000 on 23/3/2000) FL 21+18 FLC 1+4 Others 5+3
Shrewsbury T (Loaned on 27/3/2003) FL 4+3

HULSE Robert (Rob) William
Born: Crewe, 25 October 1979
Height: 6'1" **Weight:** 11.4
Chased by one or two big-named clubs, striker Rob Hulse was eventually snapped up by West Bromwich Albion boss Gary Megson following the transfer request by Jason Roberts. A hard-working player with an eye for goal, he made his senior debut for the Baggies on the opening day of the season at Walsall and looked the part when he claimed 12 goals before Christmas. But then he lost his form and his place in the side following Geoff Horsfield's arrival from Wigan, returning late on to help his colleagues regain their Premiership status.
Crewe Alex (From trainee on 25/6/1998) FL 97+19/46 FLC 6+1/2 FAC 5+1 Others 2/4
West Bromwich A (£750,000 + on 8/8/2003) FL 29+4/10 FLC 5/3 FAC 1

HUME Iain
Born: Brampton, Ontario, Canada, 31 October 1983
Height: 5'7" **Weight:** 11.2
International Honours: Canada: 6; Yth
This pacy, energetic striker scored some extraordinary goals for Tranmere last term, including one against Bolton in the FA Cup third round. Iain was Rovers' second-highest scorer netting 14 times in all, although it took him until October to get off the mark. A successful campaign saw him selected as Rovers' 'Young Player of the Season' and also take home the club's 'Goal of the Season' award. Iain represented Canada at the World Youth Championships and added three more caps for the full international team.
Tranmere Rov (From juniors on 6/11/2000) FL 55+47/16 FLC 2+3 FAC 7+2/3 Others 1+3/1

HUMPHREYS Richard (Richie) John
Born: Sheffield, 30 November 1977
Height: 5'11" **Weight:** 14.6
International Honours: E: U21-3; Yth
Ritchie began last season as an author, with his book *'From Tears To Cheers'* being a best seller – at least in Hartlepool. An attacking midfielder who likes to entertain, he showed his best form in the latter stages of the season as the club battled to earn a place in the Division Two play-offs. He was an ever-present and contributed four valuable goals during the campaign.
Sheffield Wed (From trainee on 8/2/1996) P/FL 34+33/4 FLC 4+2 FAC 5+4/5
Scunthorpe U (Loaned on 13/8/1999) FL 6/2
Cardiff C (Loaned on 22/11/1999) FL 8+1/2 FAC 1 Others 1

Cambridge U (Free on 2/2/2001) FL 7/3
Hartlepool U (Free on 18/7/2001) FL 134+4/19 FLC 4 FAC 6/1 Others 6

HUNT David
Born: Dulwich, 10 September 1982
Height: 5'11" **Weight:** 11.9
David started last season at right back for Leyton Orient, but moved into his favoured position in central midfield in September. A specialist with long throws and in dead-ball situations, he scored with a spectacular free kick in the home game with Hull and also hit the bar on several occasions. A player who is strong in the tackle, he will be looking to collect fewer bookings next term.
Crystal Palace (From trainee on 9/7/2002) FL 2 FLC 0+1
Leyton Orient (Signed on 11/7/2003) FL 35+3/1 FLC 1 FAC 2 Others 1

HUNT James Malcolm
Born: Derby, 17 December 1976
Height: 5'8" **Weight:** 10.3
James was a near ever-present in the Oxford midfield last term, working hard in a 'holding' role. Mostly taking up a position just in front of the defence, he seemed to cover acres of ground in each game and managed to find time to venture forward to score a couple of goals – one of which was a cracking volley at Macclesfield. James was out of contract in the summer and his future was uncertain at the time of writing.
Notts Co (From trainee on 15/7/1994) FL 15+4/1 FAC 0+1 Others 2+2/1
Northampton T (Free on 7/8/1997) FL 150+22/8 FLC 8+2 FAC 7+3/1 Others 10+1/1
Oxford U (Free on 12/7/2002) FL 75+5/3 FLC 4/1 FAC 3

HUNT Jonathan Martin
Born: Leeds, 11 September 1984
Height: 5'10" **Weight:** 12.4
A third-year scholar with Scunthorpe United, Jonathan came back from missing most of the previous season through injury to force his way into the first-team squad last term. A hard-working midfielder who likes to go from box to box, he made two brief substitute appearances, against Shrewsbury in the FA Cup in November and then at Yeovil in the League the following month. Jonathan was rewarded with a one-year professional contract.
Scunthorpe U (Trainee) FL 0+1 FAC 0+1

HUNT Lewis James
Born: Birmingham, 25 August 1982
Height: 5'11" **Weight:** 12.8

Lewis Hunt, by preference a central defender, played at right back in Derby's alarming home defeat by Stoke City on the opening day. It was his only appearance before joining Southend United on loan and this was eventually extended to cover the remainder of the season. At Roots Hall he produced some assured displays in both central defence and midfield. Quietly confident on the ball with excellent aerial ability for someone who is not the tallest of defenders, Lewis oozed quality and went about his task neatly, wherever he was asked to play.
Derby Co (From trainee on 17/2/2001) FL 8+3 FLC 0+2
Southend U (Loaned on 28/10/2003) FL 23+3 FAC 3 Others 5

HUNT Nicholas (Nicky) Brett
Born: Westhoughton, 3 September 1983
Height: 6'1" **Weight:** 10.8
International Honours: E: U21-1
Nicky proved to be one of the finds of the season with a magnificent campaign for Bolton last term. Despite only having featured in the FA Cup during the previous season, Nicky was handed his first Premiership start in last term's opening defeat at Manchester United. He was given further chances and matured as the campaign progressed he made the right-back position his own. A combative and powerful defender, he is just as adept at making surging runs forward as he is at stopping the opposition, as testified when scoring his first senior goal in the home draw with Liverpool. Nicky's fine form did not go unnoticed outside Bolton, as he made his England U21 debut in the 3-2 victory over Holland in February.
Bolton W (From trainee on 7/7/2001) P/FL 28+4/1 FLC 6 FAC 2+1

HUNT Stephen (Steve)
Born: Port Laoise, Ireland, 1 August 1980
Height: 5'7" **Weight:** 12.6
International Honours: RoI: U21-1
This exciting ball-playing left winger was usually Brentford's best option for creating a goal last term. Steve had a couple of brief spells out of action through injury, but nevertheless finished the campaign as the club's leading scorer. In the 4-0 win over Brighton last October the referee awarded the Bees three penalties, Steve took them all, scoring twice and having one saved. He deputised as captain when Michael Dobson was absent.
Crystal Palace (From trainee on 29/6/1999) FL 0+3

Brentford *(Free on 6/8/2001) FL 113+4/22 FLC 2+2 FAC 7/2 Others 8/3*

HUNT Warren David
Born: Portsmouth, 2 March 1984
Height: 5'9" **Weight:** 10.7
This Pompey youngster joined Leyton Orient on loan on transfer-deadline day. He showed he was able to play as a forward or in midfield and displayed some brief touches of class before returning to Fratton Park. Warren will be looking to make a breakthrough into the Portsmouth squad in 2004-05.
Portsmouth (From trainee on 20/11/2001)
Leyton Orient (Loaned on 25/3/2004) FL 6

HUNTER Barry Victor
Born: Coleraine, 18 November 1968
Height: 6'3" **Weight:** 13.2
Club Honours: Div 3 '03
International Honours: NI: 15; B-2; Yth
Barry was a key figure at the heart of the Rushden defence throughout the 2003-04 campaign and also contributed four goals at the other end of the pitch, including strikes in successive games against Stockport and Barnsley in early April. It was generally a very eventful time for the big defender who had a spell as caretaker-manager and picked up several 'Player of the Year' trophies at the season's end.
Newcastle U (Signed from Coleraine on 2/11/1987. Freed during 1988 close season)
Wrexham (£50,000 from Crusaders on 20/8/1993) FL 88+3/4 FLC 6 FAC 7+1/1 Others 8
Reading (£400,000 on 12/7/1996) FL 76+8/4 FLC 5/1 FAC 3+1/1 Others 6+1
Southend U (Loaned on 12/2/1999) FL 5/2
Rushden & Diamonds (Free on 14/9/2001) FL 106/6 FLC 2 FAC 5

HURST Glynn
Born: Barnsley, 17 January 1976
Height: 5'10" **Weight:** 11.10
Glynn had a lean spell for Chesterfield at the start of the 2003-04 season and spent several months out injured. He used this time to think: by his own admission he worked hard on general fitness and returned to the line-up as a far more lively and dangerous forward with pace, courage and the stamina to last for 90minutes. He finished as the side's leading scorer, netted the goal that kept them up in the 88th minute of the final match and was the first Spireite to make double figures in the League for three years.
Barnsley (From trainee at Tottenham H on 13/7/1994) FL 0+8 FLC 1 (Freed on 27/3/1997)

Swansea C *(Loaned on 15/12/1995) FL 2/1*
Mansfield T *(Loaned on 18/11/1996) FL 5+1 Others 0+1*
Ayr U *(£30,000 from Emley on 23/3/1998) SL 78/49 SLC 6/2 SC 10 Others 1+2*
Stockport Co *(£150,000 on 16/2/2001) FL 22+4/4 FLC 0+1*
Chesterfield *(Free on 14/12/2001) FL 77+7/29 FLC 1 FAC 0+1*

HURST Kevan
Born: Chesterfield, 27 August 1985
Height: 6'0" **Weight:** 11.7
A product of the Sheffield United youth system this versatile midfielder or striker was a regular member of the reserve side last term, making his senior debut as a late substitute in the Carling Cup tie against Queens Park Rangers. On transfer-deadline day he moved on loan to Boston United and gained valuable senior experience. His direct style caused problems for opposing defences and he quickly became a favourite of the fans. Kevan returned to Bramall Lane at the end of the season.
Sheffield U (From trainee on 24/3/2004) FLC 0+1
Boston U (Loaned on 25/3/2004) FL 3+4/1

HURST Paul Michael
Born: Sheffield, 25 September 1974
Height: 5'4" **Weight:** 9.4
Club Honours: AMC '96
A one-club man who was rewarded with a richly-deserved testimonial for ten years' loyal service, Paul willingly switched from his usual left-back position to do a specific man-marking job for Rotherham towards the end of last season. Although small in stature he is big in heart and he never gives anything less than 100 per cent commitment to the team's cause. Paul netted two goals with excellently delivered free kicks from just outside the penalty area.
Rotherham U (From trainee on 12/8/1993) FL 297+43/13 FLC 10+2 FAC 20+2/3 Others 14+1

HUSBANDS Michael Paul
Born: Birmingham, 13 November 1983
Height: 5'9" **Weight:** 9.13
Club Honours: FAYC '02
Last term proved to be a somewhat disappointing campaign for Michael after he had looked particularly effective in the pre-season fixtures. Incredibly quick with exceptional close control, he impressed so much against Gillingham in a friendly that the Kent side tried to sign him, only for Michael to pledge his future to the Blues. Unfortunately, a series of injuries meant

he only started three Third Division matches and he will be hoping to steer clear of the treatment room in the 2004-05 season.
Aston Villa (From trainee on 2/4/2002)
Southend U (Free on 31/7/2003) FL 3+6 FLC 1 FAC 0+2 Others 0+2

HUTCHINSON Edward (Eddie) Stephen
Born: Kingston, 23 February 1982
Height: 6'1" **Weight:** 12.7
After three years in the Brentford squad this box-to-box midfielder finally established himself in the Bees' first team last term. Eddie's willingness to put his head in where the action was saw him pick up countless cuts and bruises. He scored five goals, all with headers, and he was equally useful defending set pieces. He picked up an ankle injury in December, which saw him out of action for several weeks during which time the Bees failed to win a match.
Brentford (£75,000 from Sutton U on 21/7/2000) FL 64+11/5 FLC 3 FAC 1+1 Others 1+2

HUTCHINSON Jonathan (Joey)
Born: Middlesbrough, 2 April 1982
Height: 6'0" **Weight:** 12.0
Joey went straight into the Darlington first team following his arrival shortly before the start of last season and made his debut at Hull City in the opening game. Unfortunately he suffered an injury, which kept him out for the remainder of August, but once back in the side he showed his top-flight pedigree, impressing with some calm defensive play and his reading of the game. Joey performed consistently well all season striking up an excellent partnership with Craig Liddle in the centre of the Quakers' defence.
Birmingham C (From trainee on 1/7/2000) P/FL 1+3 FLC 2 FAC 1
Darlington (Free on 8/8/2003) FL 38+1 FLC 1 FAC 0+1 Others 1

HUTCHISON Donald (Don)
Born: Gateshead, 9 May 1971
Height: 6'1" **Weight:** 11.8
International Honours: S: 26; B-2
Although dogged by injuries throughout the campaign, Don was still able to contribute vital goals as West Ham attempted to win promotion last term. Playing on the right side of midfield he added balance and experience to the team. He scored a last-minute winner at Derby and a late equaliser against Burnley.

In the vital home match with Watford he scored twice, the first with a free kick and then he touched on Christian Dailly's header for the second. Don added to his Scotland caps by playing against Holland and Lithuania.
Hartlepool U (From trainee on 20/3/1990) FL 19+5/2 FLC 1+1 FAC 2 Others 1
Liverpool (£175,000 on 27/11/1990) F/PL 33+12/7 FLC 7+1/2 FAC 1+2 Others 3+1/1
West Ham U (£1,500,000 on 30/8/1994) PL 30+5/11 FLC 3/2 FAC 0+1
Sheffield U (£1,200,000 on 11/1/1996) FL 70+8/5 FLC 3+2 FAC 5/1 Others 2+1
Everton (£1,000,000 + on 27/2/1998) PL 68+7/10 FLC 4+1/1 FAC 9
Sunderland (£2,500,000 on 19/7/2000) PL 32+2/8 FLC 2/2 FAC 3
West Ham U (£5,000,000 on 31/8/2001) F/PL 34+24/5 FLC 2 FAC 3+1 Others 0+1

HUTH Robert
Born: Berlin, Germany, 18 August 1984
Height: 6'2" **Weight:** 12.12
International Honours: Germany: U21-2; Yth
An extremely powerful, left-footed centre back Robert Huth is gaining iconic status with the Chelsea crowd during his sporadic appearances. He tackles with bone-jarring ferocity and wins every challenge in the air. Robert played outstandingly alongside John Terry in the pre-season Asia Cup triumph and in August scored his first senior goal with an unstoppable header from a corner against MSK Zilinia – this should be the first of many as he is dominant in the air and a considerable threat at set pieces with howitzer-like shooting. Robert had an extended run in the first team at the end of the season, again paired with Terry, owing to injuries to William Gallas and Marcel Desailly. He showed maturity and composure way beyond his limited experience and looks to be a fine prospect for the future.
Chelsea (From trainee on 23/8/2001) PL 10+9 FLC 1 FAC 0+2 Others 2+2/1

HYDE Graham
Born: Doncaster, 10 November 1970
Height: 5'8" **Weight:** 11.11
This experienced midfielder continued to impress with some accurate passing and solid ball-winning skills for Bristol Rovers last term. He featured regularly in the starting line-up and contributed valuable goals against Huddersfield and in the vital home win over Swansea City. He was released in the summer.
Sheffield Wed (From trainee on 17/5/1988)

F/PL 126+46/11 FLC 17+3/1 FAC 13+5/2 Others 8/1
Birmingham C (Free on 5/2/1999) FL 35+17/1 FLC 2+2/1 FAC 2
Chesterfield (Loaned on 18/8/2001) FL 8+1/1
Peterborough U (Loaned on 20/9/2002) FL 8+1
Bristol Rov (Free on 28/11/2002) FL 54+4/3 FAC 3 Others 1

HYDE Micah Anthony
Born: Newham, 10 November 1974
Height: 5'9" **Weight:** 11.5
Club Honours: Div 2 '98
International Honours: Jamaica: 12
Micah, a combative midfield player with more than 350 League appearances under his belt, had a frustrating season for Watford marred by a recurring hamstring injury sustained in September. He struggled to regain his consistency, but came good in the last three months of the campaign, and it was no coincidence that the team's form improved at the same time. Micah remained a member of the Jamaican international squad, but was out of contract in the summer and his future was unclear at the time of writing.
Cambridge U (From trainee on 19/5/1993) FL 89+18/13 FLC 3 FAC 7+2 Others 4+1
Watford (£225,000 on 21/7/1997) P/FL 235+18/24 FLC 16+1/4 FAC 13 Others 3

HYLDGAARD Morten Lauridsen
Born: Denmark, 26 January 1978
Height: 6'6" **Weight:** 13.6
International Honours: Denmark: U21
Morten joined Hibernian during the 2003 close season, but apart from the odd pre-season game he failed to win a place in the line-up at Easter Road and in January he signed for Luton Town. He became a regular for the Hatters in the second half of the campaign, proving to be a good shot-stopper, although he sometimes seemed to lack the confidence to dominate his area. He was released in the summer.
Coventry C (£200,000 from Ikast FS, Denmark on 9/7/1999) FL 27 FLC 1 FAC 3
Scunthorpe U (Loaned on 7/1/2000) FL 5 Others 2
Hibernian (Free on 1/7/2003)
Luton T (Free on 29/1/2004) FL 18

HYLTON Leon David
Born: Birmingham, 27 January 1983
Height: 5'9" **Weight:** 11.3
International Honours: E: Yth
Shortly after representing England at U20

level in the Toulon Tournament during the 2003 close season, Leon signed permanent forms for Swansea City. He was first choice at left back at the start of the new campaign, but then suffered groin and ankle injuries in September, which affected his first-team opportunities throughout the season. He made a few attempts at a return, but after playing in an FAW Premier Cup tie at Rhyl, suffered a hamstring problem which kept him out of action until the summer break.
Aston Villa (From trainee on 23/2/2000)
Swansea C (Free on 7/2/2003) FL 17+2 FLC 1 FAC 0+1

HYNES Peter Joseph
Born: Dublin, 28 November 1983
Height: 5'9" **Weight:** 11.12
Club Honours: FAYC '02
Aston Villa's young reserve striker had spells on loan at Doncaster and Cheltenham last term in order to gain experience of senior football. Peter showed plenty of pace in his time at Whaddon Road, preferring to play with the goal in front of him. He can also operate on the left-hand side of midfield.
Aston Villa (From trainee on 29/11/2000)
Doncaster Rov (Loaned on 13/12/2003) FL 0+5/1
Cheltenham T (Loaned on 23/1/2004) FL 2+2

HYYPIA Sami
Born: Porvoo, Finland, 7 October 1973
Height: 6'4" **Weight:** 13.5
Club Honours: FLC '01, '03; FAC '01; UEFAC '01; ESC '01; CS '01
International Honours: Finland: 61; U21-27; Yth
This central defender was one of very few players in the Liverpool squad to remain injury free in 2003-04, playing in all but one game of the Reds' 52-match programme. He also scored his usual quota of goals from corners and set pieces. He had a mixed season, and although not always showing his best form, there were occasions when he was outstanding. He appeared to miss the presence of his usual defensive partner, Stephane Henchoz, and his understanding with Igor Biscan often appeared uneasy. Of his five goals, all headers, the most vital was one in the last minute of the home game with Wolves in March, the additional two points they earned edging Liverpool ahead of their rivals for fourth place in the Premiership.
Liverpool (£2,600,000 from Willem II, Holland, ex MyPa, on 7/7/1999) PL 184/16 FLC 14/1 FAC 17 Others 49/5

IBEHRE Jabo Oshevire
Born: Islington, 28 January 1983
Height: 6'2" **Weight:** 12.10
Jabo is an exciting centre forward who likes nothing better than to bring the ball down and run at defenders. He is strong and quick and has become a real favourite of the Leyton Orient fans. Jabo featured regularly in the first-team squad last term, although often used from the substitutes' bench, netting five goals in total. He was rewarded with a new contract in March and will be looking to become a first-team regular in 2004-05.
Leyton Orient (From trainee on 18/7/2001) FL 50+46/15 FLC 1+3/2 FAC 3+3/1 Others 5+1

IFIL Jerel Christopher
Born: Wembley, 27 June 1982
Height: 6'1" **Weight:** 12.11
Jerel, a central defender nurtured by the Watford Academy, spent the first half of the 2003-04 season on loan at Swindon where he impressed the fans with his ferocious tackling. On his return to Vicarage Road, he had the chance of a run in the first team and demonstrated strength, pace and good passing skills, although his concentration and positional sense sometimes betrayed his inexperience. Nevertheless, he showed enough promise to win himself a new contract and the prospect of further chances in the future.
Watford (From trainee on 8/2/2000) FL 10+1
Huddersfield T (Loaned on 28/3/2002) FL 1+1 Others 2
Swindon T (Loaned on 30/1/2003) FL 5+4
Swindon T (Loaned on 4/9/2003) FL 6
Swindon T (Loaned on 14/11/2003) FL 10

IFILL Paul
Born: Brighton, 20 October 1979
Height: 6'0" **Weight:** 12.10
Club Honours: Div 2 '01
International Honours: Barbados
A tall, clever player, Paul won over the New Den faithful with his pace, tricky ball skills and unpredictability. After beginning as an out-and-out striker, he successfully switched to a wide midfield role and is at his best running at opposition defences. Paul has also improved his defensive capabilities, as was proved on a number of occasions last season when he made many vital interceptions inside the danger zone. Paul made his debut for Barbados against St Kitts in a World Cup qualifying tie during the summer.
Millwall (From trainee on 2/6/1998) FL 179+33/36 FLC 5/1 FAC 15/2 Others 8+1

IGOE Samuel (Sammy) Gary
Born: Staines, 30 September 1975
Height: 5'6" **Weight:** 10.0
A lively performer Sammy, was a popular acquisition for Swindon Town last term, providing a creative spark from the right-hand side of midfield. His season was disrupted by a bizarre wrist injury, but generally he was a first choice throughout the campaign. Although small in stature, he can prove a real handful for defenders whether running at them with the ball or delivering a range of passes.
Portsmouth (From trainee on 15/2/1994) FL 100+60/11 FLC 7+5 FAC 2+3
Reading (£100,000 on 23/3/2000) FL 53+34/7 FLC 4+1 FAC 4+2 Others 6+1
Luton T (Loaned on 27/3/2003) FL 2
Swindon T (Free on 14/7/2003) FL 33+3/5 FLC 2 Others 2

ILIC Sasa
Born: Melbourne, Australia, 18 July 1972
Height: 6'4" **Weight:** 14.0
International Honours: Yugoslavia: 2
This experienced 'keeper made his debut for Barnsley on the opening day of the 2003-04 season and did well in the early fixtures. Although he lost a little confidence in dealing with crosses as the campaign developed it was still a surprise when it was announced that his monthly deal would not be renewed. He subsequently signed for Sheffield United on a contract to the end of the season, but did not feature at first-team level for the Blades.
Charlton Ath (Free from St Leonards Stamcroft on 5/10/1997) P/FL 51 FLC 3 FAC 2 Others 3 (Freed on 30/6/2002)
West Ham U (Loaned on 24/2/2000) PL 1
Portsmouth (Loaned on 7/9/2001) FL 7
Portsmouth (Free from Zalaegerszegi, Hungary on 20/2/2003)
Barnsley (Free on 8/8/2003) FL 25 FLC 1 FAC 5 Others 2
Sheffield U (Free on 26/2/2004)

IMPEY Andrew (Andy) Rodney
Born: Hammersmith, 30 September 1971
Height: 5'8" **Weight:** 11.2
Club Honours: FLC '00
International Honours: E: U21-1
This right-sided winger or wing back had few opportunities to impress with Leicester, during the 2003-04 campaign and was allowed to link up with neighbours Nottingham Forest on loan, where he immediately found his goal-scoring boots when he netted with his first touch for the club on his debut against Walsall. Andy continued to be a valuable member of the side showing his versatility by finishing the season as a right back. His future was uncertain at the season's close after being released by Leicester.
Queens Park R (£35,000 from Yeading on 14/6/1990) F/PL 177+10/13 FLC 15+1/3 FAC 7+3/1 Others 0+2/1
West Ham U (£1,300,000 on 26/9/1997) PL 25+2 FLC 4 FAC 3
Leicester C (£1,600,000 on 25/11/1998) P/FL 132+20/1 FLC 9+4 FAC 10+1 Others 2
Nottingham F (Loaned on 13/2/2004) FL 15+1/1

INAMOTO Junichi
Born: Kagoshima, Japan, 18 September 1979
Height: 5'11" **Weight:** 11.13
International Honours: Japan: 50
Junichi enjoyed a second season on loan at Fulham where he has a sizeable Japanese following. After starting out as a regular, scoring in the opening game against Middlesbrough, his most memorable contribution was the goal that clinched victory at Manchester United in October. An industrious player who is always in the thick of the action, he operated as a central or left-sided midfielder. Although he rarely started a game in the second half of the campaign he let no one down when called upon. Junichi continued to appear regularly for Japan and featured in the early qualifying games for the 2006 World Cup.
Arsenal (Loaned from Gamba Osaka, Japan on 24/7/2001) FLC 2 Others 0+2
Fulham (Loaned from Gamba Osaka, Japan on 23/7/2002) PL 24+17/4 FLC 3 FAC 3+1/1 Others 3+7/4

INCE Clayton
Born: Trinidad, 13 July 1972
Height: 6'3" **Weight:** 14.2
International Honours: Trinidad & Tobago
Clayton was again first-choice goalkeeper for Crewe Alexandra last term and was an ever-present in the side until suffering an injury against West Ham in March and this kept him out until the summer. A popular and very capable 'keeper, he continued to add to his tally of caps for Trinidad during the season.
Crewe Alex (£50,000 from Defence Force, Trinidad on 21/9/1999) FL 97+3 FLC 6 FAC 7

INCE Paul Emerson Carlyle
Born: Ilford, 21 October 1967
Height: 5'11" **Weight:** 12.2
Club Honours: CS '93, '94; FAC '90, '94; ECW '91; ESC '91; FLC '92; PL '93, '94
International Honours: E: 53; B-1; U21-2; Yth
This veteran Wolves midfielder showed he could still hack it in the Premiership, although he had to wait until December for his first goal, at Tottenham. He played in all but six of the Premiership games and netted with a well-taken goal to set up victory over Fulham. However, it was his insistence that nothing was a lost cause that took the eye, making long runs to get in vital tackles even if the game was lost.
West Ham U (From apprentice on 18/7/1985) FL 66+6/7 FLC 9/3 FAC 8+2/1 Others 4/1
Manchester U (£1,000,000 on 14/9/1989) F/PL 203+3/25 FLC 23+1/2 FAC 26+1/1 Others 24/1 (£8,000,000 to Inter Milan, Italy on 13/7/1995)
Liverpool (£4,200,000 on 22/7/1997) PL 65/14 FLC 6/1 FAC 3/1 Others 7/1
Middlesbrough (£1,000,000 on 3/8/1999) PL 93/7 FLC 6/1 FAC 7/1
Wolverhampton W (Free on 6/8/2002) P/FL 67+2/4 FLC 3+1 FAC 4/1 Others 3

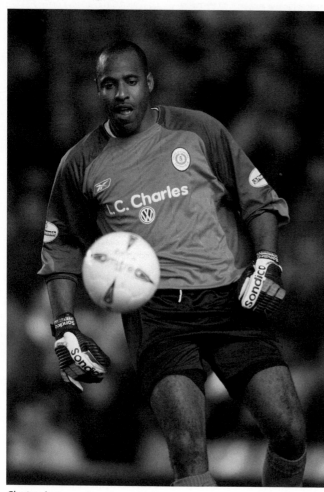

Clayton Ince

INGHAM Michael Gerard
Born: Preston, 7 September 1980
Height: 6'4" **Weight:** 13.12
International Honours: NI: U21-4; Yth
This young goalkeeper made a solitary appearance for Sunderland last term in the Carling Cup tie defeat against Huddersfield in September, finding his way to a regular first-team place barred by the more experienced Mart Poom and Thomas Myhre. Later in the season he joined Wrexham on loan as cover for the injured Andy Dibble and featured regularly for the Racecourse club in the final run-in. Michael produced many spectacular saves, none more so than a stunning flying effort against Hartlepool on Easter Monday. A member of the Northern Ireland international squad, he toured the Caribbean in the summer but missed out on his first cap after dislocating a finger during training.
Sunderland (£30,000 from Cliftonville on 28/7/1999) FLC 2
Carlisle U (Loaned on 1/10/1999) FL 7
Stockport Co (Loaned on 23/8/2002) FLC 1
Darlington (Loaned on 22/11/2002) FL 3
York C (Loaned on 24/1/2003) FL 17
Wrexham (Loaned on 16/3/2004) FL 11

INGIMARSSON Ivar
Born: Iceland, 20 August 1977
Height: 6'0" **Weight:** 12.7
International Honours: Iceland: 12; U21-14; Yth
Steve Coppell's first signing as Reading manager proved to be one of the bargains of the season. Ivar immediately brought resilience and no little class to a defence that had looked decidedly uncertain at times. Although not the tallest, he jumps well and heads powerfully, and scored his first goal for the Royals with a towering header in the 3-2 win at Cardiff. He retained his place in the Icelandic international team, and also played in the Reading reserve team that won the Pontins Combination play-off final.
Torquay U (Loaned from IBV Vestmannaeyjar, Iceland on 21/10/1999) FL 4/1
Brentford (£150,000 from IBV Vestmannaeyjar, Iceland on 18/11/1999) FL 109+4/10 FLC 6 FAC 3 Others 13/1
Wolverhampton W (Free on 2/7/2002) FL 10+3/2 FLC 2
Brighton & Hove A (Loaned on 10/2/2003) FL 15
Reading (£100,000 + on 23/10/2003) FL 24+1/1 FLC 2 FAC 1

INNES Mark
Born: Glasgow, 27 September 1978
Height: 5'10" **Weight:** 12.1

Injury prevented this determined but cultured midfielder from getting a run with Chesterfield until December of last season, but he featured in almost every game thereafter. Normally working on the left, from full back or midfield, he has the skill to break down opposition moves and the vision to start them off.
Oldham Ath (From trainee on 10/10/1995) FL 52+21/1 FLC 4+3 FAC 4+2 Others 3+1
Chesterfield (Free on 19/12/2001) FL 44+11/2 Others 0+1

IRELAND Craig
Born: Dundee, 29 November 1975
Height: 6'3" **Weight:** 13.9
Craig joined Barnsley shortly before the start of last season after spending a trial period at Oakwell and remained until the end of the campaign. A steady defender, strong in the air and with good distribution, Craig was always a threat from set pieces and took over the captaincy when Peter Handyside was injured. It was a surprise when he was

released in the summer.
Aberdeen (From juniors on 5/10/1994) SLC 1
Dunfermline Ath (Free on 12/2/1996) SL 61+6/2 SLC 0+2 SC 0+1
Dundee (Free on 27/10/1999) SL 14/1 SC 1
Airdrieonians (Loaned on 12/10/2000) SL 12/2 Others 1
Notts Co (£50,000 on 2/2/2001) FL 77+3/2 FLC 2 FAC 1
Barnsley (Free on 8/8/2003) FL 43/3 FLC 1 FAC 5 Others 2

IRIEKPEN Ezomo (Izzy)
Born: London, 14 May 1982
Height: 6'1" **Weight:** 12.4
Club Honours: FAYC '99
International Honours: E: Yth
This young central defender arrived at the Vetch Field on a two-week trial shortly after the start of last season. A good competitor who possesses the ability to win the ball in the air and on the ground, Izzy is extremely quick when covering back. He signed a long-term deal at the end of November, but missed a number

of games in the last third of the campaign through an ankle injury.
West Ham U (From trainee on 25/5/1999)
Leyton Orient (Loaned on 22/10/2002) FL 5/1 FAC 1 Others 2/1
Cambridge U (Loaned on 28/2/2003) FL 13/1
Swansea C (Free on 22/8/2003) FL 33+1/1 FAC 5

IRWIN Joseph **Denis**
Born: Cork, 31 October 1965
Height: 5'8" **Weight:** 11.0
Club Honours: CS '93, '96, '97; ECWC '91; ESC '91; FLC '92; PL '93, '94, '96, '97, '99, '00, '01; FAC '94, '96; EC '99
International Honours: RoI: 56; B-1; U23-1; U21-3; Yth; Sch
Denis thought long and hard about extending his career, but decided to give it one more season with Wolves. Far from having a supporting role, the right back played in the first 16 Premiership games. He was rarely outclassed in the top flight, and his know-how and calming influence were vital at times. He was feeling the strain a little by the new year, briefly losing his place to Mark Cyde. Denis was given a tremendous ovation on 15 May, as he retired after a long and successful career, spanning some 900-odd club appearances.
Leeds U (From apprentice on 3/11/1983) FL 72/1 FLC 5 FAC 3 Others 2
Oldham Ath (Free on 22/5/1986) FL 166+1/4 FLC 19/3 FAC 13 Others 5
Manchester U (£625,000 on 20/6/1990) F/PL 356+12/22 FLC 28+3 FAC 42+1/7 Others 85+2/4
Wolverhampton W (Free on 25/7/2002) F/PL 73+2/2 FLC 1+1 FAC 5 Others 3

ISTEAD Steven Brian
Born: South Shields, 23 April 1986
Height: 5'8" **Weight:** 11.4
An exciting prospect, this skilful winger was a member of the Hartlepool first-team squad for most of the 2003-04 season. He was usually employed as a substitute introduced late in the game, and in this role was able to add pace and enthusiasm to a tiring forward line. Still only a second-year scholar, he was chosen as the club's 'Young Player of the Year'.
Hartlepool U (Trainee) FL 1+36/1 FLC 0+2/1 FAC 0+2

IVERSEN Steffen
Born: Oslo, Norway, 10 November 1976
Height: 6'1'' **Weight:** 11.10
Club Honours: FLC '99
International Honours: Norway: 45; U21-23; Yth

Ivar Ingimarsson

This tall striker was a surprising recruit for Wolves. However, he gained the distinction of scoring the club's first-ever Premiership goal, and found the net again in the 1-1 draw with Birmingham. It seemed to be a contest between Steffen and Nathan Blake to be the target man for Wolves. Steffen was good in the air, and not afraid to shoot from a distance. A Christmas double against Leeds meant he had scored four in eight starts, and he led the line well against Manchester United and Liverpool. However, the latter occasion proved to be his last start, and he lost his place with the arrival of Carl Cort. Steffen also found the net in his appearances for Norway during the season.

Tottenham H *(£2,700,000 from Rosenborg, Norway, ex Nationalkam, on 7/12/1996) PL 112+31/36 FLC 11+4/6 FAC 10+5/4 Others 4/1*

Steffen Iversen

Wolverhampton W *(Free on 15/8/2003) PL 11+5/4 FLC 2 FAC 1+1*

IWELUMO Christopher (Chris) Robert
Born: Coatbridge, 1 August 1978
Height: 6'3" **Weight:** 13.8
This giant striker failed to win a regular place at Stoke last term following the arrival of several new players and made most of his appearances from the substitutes' bench. In March he joined Brighton and made an instant impression by scoring with a spectacular 25-yard strike in a 2-0 win at Chesterfield. He added three more goals to as he tried to forge a 'little-and-large' partnership up front with Leon Knight, but the combination met with only limited success. With Chris's ability in the air making him an obvious target, Albion's approach tended to become somewhat

one-dimensional, but he played a significant part in the play-off triumph in Cardiff, earning the penalty which his striking partner put away to secure victory over Bristol City.

St Mirren *(From juniors on 5/8/1996) SL 7+19 SLC 0+3/1 SC 1+1/1 Others 0+2 (Free to Aarhus Fremad, Denmark during 1998 close season)*
Stoke C *(£25,000 from Aarhus Fremad, Denmark on 1/3/2000) FL 40+44/16 FLC 2+4/2 FAC 6+2/4 Others 4+1/1*
York C *(Loaned on 10/11/2000) FL 11+1/2 FAC 4/1*
Cheltenham T *(Loaned on 13/2/2001) FL 2+2/1*
Brighton & Hove A *(Signed on 16/3/2004) FL 10/4 Others 3*

IZZET Kemal (Kem)
Born: Whitechapel, 29 September 1980
Height: 5'8" **Weight:** 10.5
Kem was his usual tigerish self in central midfield for Colchester United last term. Much of his best work was defensive, and indeed he didn't score his first goal until the end of January, but he then regained his scoring touch, adding three more before the end of the season. His strength is his ability to hustle and bustle in the middle of the park, closing down opponents quickly. Kem is the younger brother of Muzzy Izzet.

Charlton Ath *(From trainee on 11/1/1999)*
Colchester U *(Signed on 22/3/2001) FL 127+8/15 FLC 5/1 FAC 8 Others 7/2*

IZZET Mustafa (Muzzy) Kemal
Born: Mile End, 31 October 1974
Height: 5'10" **Weight:** 10.12
Club Honours: FLC '97, '00
International Honours: Turkey: 8
This right-footed midfielder continued to be the driving force in the centre of the park for Leicester in 2003-04, also acting as skipper for much of the campaign. He did not score as often as in previous years, although he certainly made up for that in quality, with a terrific long-range effort at Elland Road. Although his contract was due to expire at the end of the season, there was never any thought of either the club or player cashing-in during the January transfer window, as Muzzy remained fully committed to City's cause throughout. Hamstring trouble cut short his final home appearance, but not before he had come close to a couple of spectacular efforts against Pompey. Muzzy was reported to have signed for Birmingham City during the summer.

Chelsea *(From trainee on 19/5/1993)*
Leicester C *(£650,000 + on 28/3/1996) P/FL 265+4/38 FLC 24+3/4 FAC 16/4 Others 7/1*

J

JAASKELAINEN Jussi
Born: Vaasa, Finland, 19 April 1975
Height: 6'3" **Weight:** 12.10
International Honours: Finland: 17;
U21-14; Yth
For the second season in succession, Jussi
was an ever-present in the Premiership for
Bolton. He is now regarded as one of the
best 'keepers in the competition; a
reputation he has built up during his
seven fantastic years with the club. Jussi
will continue to improve and should have
many years of top-flight football left in
him. A fantastic shot-stopper, he now has
more of a commanding presence within
the team, a fact which seems to have
instilled greater confidence in his defence.
Jussi would surely have more international
caps if it were not for the form of Antti
Niemi – another outstanding Finnish
stopper.
*Bolton W (£100,000 + from VPS Vaasa,
Finland, ex MPS, on 14/11/1997) P/FL 204+1
FLC 13 FAC 5 Others 2*

JACK Darren
Born: Norwich, 9 August 1983
Height: 6'2" **Weight:** 13.3
After being released by Motherwell at the
end of the previous season, Darren joined
Barnsley on a non-contract basis at the
beginning of January following a
successful trial spell. He made his debut
as a substitute in the FA Cup tie against
Scunthorpe, but this proved to be his only
first-team appearance. A tall, strong
forward, Darren left Oakwell shortly
afterwards and signed for Eircom League
club Sligo Rovers. Darren is the son of
Ross Jack the former Norwich, Lincoln
and Dunfermline striker.
*Ross Co (From juniors on 1/9/2000) SL 0+1
Motherwell (Signed on 1/8/2002) SL 0+2
Barnsley (Free on 2/11/2004) FAC 0+1*

JACK Michael Lawrence
Born: Carlisle, 2 October 1982
Height: 5'8" **Weight:** 10.5
Although he had previously been
released by Carlisle United, Michael
returned to Brunton Park for the 2003-
04 campaign. A local-born midfielder, his
five first-team appearances included only
one in the starting line-up, but after
featuring briefly in the final match at
Doncaster he will be hoping for more
senior action in 2004-05.
*Carlisle U (From trainee on 27/6/2001) FL
19+23 FLC 0+1 FAC 3+1 Others 0+2*

JACK Rodney Alphonso
Born: Kingstown, St Vincent, 28
September 1972
Height: 5'7" **Weight:** 10.9
International Honours: St Vincent &
Grenadines
The talented striker arrived in Rushden in
the 2003 close season and had a
successful season at Nene Park in 2003-
04. Rodney formed a useful partnership
up front with Onandi Lowe and netted a
respectable total of 13 goals. He featured
both as an out-and-out striker and in a
position wide on either flank, from where
he supplied numerous chances for his
colleagues.
*Torquay U (Free from Lambada, St Vincent
on 10/10/1995) FL 82+5/24 FLC 6/1 FAC 6
Others 6/3*
*Crewe Alex (£650,000 on 14/8/1998) FL
140+23/33 FLC 12/5 FAC 8+2 Others 3/4*
*Rushden & Diamonds (Free on 21/7/2003)
FL 44+1/12 FLC 1 FAC 1 Others 2/1*

JACKMAN Daniel (Danny)
James
Born: Worcester, 3 January 1983
Height: 5'5" **Weight:** 10.2
Danny joined Stockport on loan from
Aston Villa at the end of October and
made his debut in the 2-1 home defeat
by Queens Park Rangers. A permanent
move soon followed and he quickly
became a favourite with the Edgeley Park
faithful following a series of fine
performances at left back. He found his
scoring touch towards the end of the
season as well, netting the Hatters' third
goal at Chesterfield and adding another
during the crucial 2-1 win over Grimsby
Town.
*Aston Villa (From trainee on 4/4/2001)
Cambridge U (Loaned on 14/2/2002) FL
5+2/1 Others 1+1*
*Stockport Co (£70,000 on 31/10/2003) FL
27/2 Others 2*

JACKSON John (Johnnie)
Born: Camden, 15 August 1982
Height: 6'1" **Weight:** 13.0
International Honours: E: Yth
This left-sided midfielder joined Coventry
on loan last November and made a strong
impression during his time at Highfield
Road, scoring two vital goals when
coming off the bench. On returning to
Tottenham he made a breakthrough into
the first-team squad and featured
regularly in the second half of the
campaign. He added width to the attack,
showing a willingness to get forward and
take on opponents. Johnnie has a keen

eye for goal and scored in the 4-2 win at
Charlton in February.
*Tottenham H (From trainee on 23/3/2000)
PL 9+2/1 FAC 1+2*
*Swindon T (Loaned on 13/9/2002) FL
12+1/1 FAC 2 Others 2/1*
*Colchester U (Loaned on 11/3/2003) FL 8
Coventry C (Loaned on 21/11/2003) FL
2+3/2*

JACKSON Kirk Stewart Samuel
Born: Doncaster, 16 October 1976
Height: 6'0" **Weight:** 13.0
Club Honours: NC '03
International Honours: E: SP-6
After leading the scoring charts for Yeovil
the previous campaign, Kirk began last
term in similar fashion, netting four goals
in the early-season matches. However, he
then seemed to lose his touch somewhat
and in January he spent time on loan with
Conference club Dagenham & Redbridge.
A mobile and bustling striker, Kirk was
reported to have signed for Hornchurch
during the summer break.
*Sheffield Wed (From trainee on 15/5/1995)
Scunthorpe U (Free on 23/7/1996) FL 0+4/1
Others 0+1*
*Chesterfield (Free on 6/8/1997) FL 0+3 FLC
0+1 FAC 0+1 Others 1 (Free to Grantham T
on 7/8/1998)*
*Darlington (£30,000 from Worksop T on
1/3/2001) FL 6+15/11 FLC 0+1 FAC 1+1 Others
2 (Free to Stevenage Borough on 18/1/2002)*
*Yeovil T (Signed on 28/11/2002) FL 19+11/5
FLC 1 FAC 1+2*

JACKSON Mark Graham
Born: Barnsley, 30 September 1977
Height: 6'0" **Weight:** 11.12
International Honours: E: Yth
Matt was appointed Scunthorpe United's
club captain in the summer and started
the 2003-04 season in good form in the
centre of defence, where his strength and
aerial prowess make him a key figure.
However, his season was to end
prematurely just before Christmas when
ankle and knee cartilage problems ruled
him out of the closing five months of the
campaign.
*Leeds U (From trainee on 1/7/1995) PL 11+8
FAC 4*
*Huddersfield T (Loaned on 29/10/1998) FL 5
Barnsley (Loaned on 14/1/2000) FL 1
Scunthorpe U (Free on 9/3/2000) FL
126+7/4 FLC 3 FAC 11 Others 7+1/1*

JACKSON Mark Philip
Born: Preston, 3 February 1986
Height: 5'11" **Weight:** 11.9
Called into the first-team squad during a
late-season injury crisis, Mark's second

inclusion on the Preston bench led to a debut appearance for the last few minutes of the heavy defeat at Derby. The youngster was a regular in the reserves during the campaign, where he played all across the midfield as well as upfront.
Preston NE (Trainee) FL 0+1

JACKSON Matthew (Matt) Alan
Born: Leeds, 19 October 1971
Height: 6'1" **Weight:** 12.12
Club Honours: FAC '95; Div 2 '03
International Honours: E: U21-10; Sch
A composed and impressive central defender, Matt produced a series of reliable and impressive performances at the heart of the Wigan Athletic defence, showing excellent anticipation and the ability to tackle under pressure. He was the stand-in captain when the club went to the top of the table early in the season. The polished and experienced defender netted his only goal with a dramatic injury-time equaliser in the away draw at Coventry.
Luton T (From juniors on 4/7/1990) FL 7+2 FLC 2 Others 0+1
Preston NE (Loaned on 27/3/1991) FL 3+1 Others 1
Everton (£600,000 on 18/10/1991) F/PL 132+6/4 FLC 9 FAC 14/2 Others 4
Charlton Ath (Loaned on 26/3/1996) FL 8 Others 2
Queens Park R (Loaned on 20/8/1996) FL 7
Birmingham C (Loaned on 31/10/1996) FL 10
Norwich C (£450,000 on 24/12/1996) FL 158+3/6 FLC 6 FAC 5
Wigan Ath (Free on 19/10/2001) FL 94+1/2 FLC 8 FAC 3+1 Others 2

JACKSON Michael James
Born: Runcorn, 4 December 1973
Height: 6'0" **Weight:** 13.8
Club Honours: Div 2 '97, '00
International Honours: E: Yth
Michael remained both a favourite with the Preston fans and a regular in the starting line up last season, where he featured in a trio of central defenders. The only games he missed came as a result of a suspension and on the final day when he was rested. He again showed his tenacity in the tackle and an uncomplicated method of clearing his lines, although he was less of a threat when joining the attack at set pieces.
Crewe Alex (From trainee on 29/7/1992) FL 5 FLC 1 FAC 1 Others 2
Bury (Free on 13/8/1993) FL 123+2/9 FLC 9/1 FAC 3 Others 12

Preston NE (£125,000 on 26/3/1997) FL 237+8/17 FLC 16/2 FAC 14 Others 8
Tranmere Rov (Loaned on 18/12/2002) FL 6

JACKSON Richard
Born: Whitby, 18 April 1980
Height: 5'8" **Weight:** 10.12
For the first time since he joined Derby County, Richard gained the confidence that comes with regular selection. Always a neat and unfussy defender, he also proved adaptable, playing equally effectively at right or left back. For all Derby's problems, it was a season of sound development for Richard, who

increasingly showed an ability to contribute when going forward. After making the important breakthrough, it is vital that he continues to progress into a more assertive player. The foundations are laid.
Scarborough (From trainee on 27/3/1998) FL 21+1 FLC 2
Derby Co (£30,000 + on 25/3/1999) P/FL 57+11 FLC 2

JACOBS Wayne Graham
Born: Sheffield, 3 February 1969
Height: 5'9" **Weight:** 11.2
Bradford City's longest-serving player had

Michael Jackson

David James

an eventful season even though he missed long spells through calf and hamstring injuries. Wayne, who has been awarded a testimonial for the forthcoming campaign, had a one-match stint as caretaker manager before Bryan Robson was appointed. Unfortunately Bradford lost that game 1-0 to Stoke but it has whetted his appetite for coaching in the future. The reliable defender received a rare outing at right back against Sheffield United at Bramall Lane when he put in a 'Man of the Match'display. He played in the same role equally effectively in the last game of the season at Millwall.

Sheffield Wed (From apprentice on 3/1/1987) FL 5+1 FLC 3 Others 1

Hull C (£27,000 on 25/3/1988) FL 127+2/4 FLC 7 FAC 8 Others 6

Rotherham U (Free on 5/8/1993) FL 40+2/2 FLC 4 FAC 1 Others 2

Bradford C (Free on 5/8/1994) P/FL 289+15/12 FLC 17+2 FAC 13/2 Others 7

JAGIELKA Philip (Phil)
Nikodem
Born: Manchester, 17 August 1982
Height: 5'11" **Weight:** 12.8
International Honours: E: U21-6; Yth
Phil had a very good season for Sheffield United last term. Playing mainly as a right wing back he showed speed and accuracy in the tackle, and the ability to use the ball well when coming forward. Due to injuries to others he had a spell in central defence, using his height and anticipation to good effect and being quick to cover when required. His potential as a substitute goalkeeper meant Neil Warnock rarely had a 'keeper on the bench, and when Paddy Kenny was injured at Crystal Palace Phil spent 50 minutes in goal, conceding one goal (a penalty), the Blades winning 2-1. He made three more appearances for England U21s, scoring against Macedonia, and was chosen in the PFA Division One team of the year.

Sheffield U (From trainee on 8/5/2000) FL 101+23/6 FLC 13/1 FAC 8/1 Others 3

JAMES Craig Peter
Born: Middlesbrough, 15 November 1982
Height: 6'2" **Weight:** 11.8
A left-sided midfielder or full back, Craig made his senior debut for Sunderland at Stoke in September and also featured in the Carling Cup tie against Huddersfield. Towards the end of the year he was allowed to join Darlington on loan and slotted in well on the right side of the defence. His overlapping wing play

allowed him to get forward frequently and he scored one goal during his stay, netting in the 3-0 win against York City. In March he joined Port Vale on loan. Used in a more familiar left-back role, he made a good impression at Vale Park and signed a long-term contract for the club before the end of the season.

Sunderland (From trainee on 12/7/2000) FL 1 FLC 1

Hibernian (Loaned on 29/8/2002) SL 20+2/2 SLC 1 SC 2

Darlington (Loaned on 14/11/2003) FL 10/1

Port Vale (Signed on 19/3/2004) FL 8

JAMES David Benjamin
Born: Welwyn Garden City, 1 August 1970
Height: 6'5" **Weight:** 14.5
Club Honours: FAYC '89; FLC '95
International Honours: E: 28; B-1; U21-10; Yth
Now installed as England's number one goalkeeper, David started the campaign in top form for West Ham with 'Man of the Match' performances in the difficult games against Millwall and Cardiff. In January he was allowed to move on to Manchester City where he looked one of the bargains of the season. A 'keeper who thrives on tension, he finds something extra when there is an additional edge to a game and made some crucial saves from the penalty spot in his side's fight to avoid relegation from the Premiership. David was a regular in the England set-up and represented his country in the Euro 2004 finals in Portugal in the summer.

Watford (From trainee on 1/7/1988) FL 89 FLC 6 FAC 2 Others 1

Liverpool (£1,000,000 on 6/7/1992) PL 213+1 FLC 22 FAC 19 Others 22

Aston Villa (£1,800,000 on 23/6/1999) PL 67 FLC 6 FAC 8 Others 4

West Ham U (£3,500,000 on 17/7/2001) P/FL 91 FLC 5 FAC 6

Manchester C (£1,300,000 + on 14/1/2004) PL 17

JAMES Kevin Ernest
Born: Southwark, 3 January 1980
Height: 5'9" **Weight:** 10.7
A pacy midfielder or wing back, this Gillingham youngster received limited opportunities during the 2003-04 season and managed just one goal, netting in the 2-1 win at Millwall at the end of December. Kevin filled in for a time during the Gills' injury crisis and even spent some time at right back, but with his contract due to finish in the summer and a stalemate in new negotiations, he was released by the club in April.

Charlton Ath (From trainee on 2/7/1998)

Gillingham (Free on 21/8/2000) FL 18+31/4 FLC 1+2 FAC 1+1

JANSEN Matthew (Matt)
Brooke
Born: Carlisle, 20 October 1977
Height: 5'11" **Weight:** 10.13
Club Honours: AMC '97; FLC '02
International Honours: E: U21-6; Yth
There were hopes that Matt would return to the form that he was showing for Blackburn before he suffered a head injury in a motor accident in 2002. A well-struck goal at Bolton gave him early confidence but although there were always signs of the old Matt Jansen, the club was never in a position to allow him time to play himself back into form. He suffered a severe concussion in the reserves, but fortunately came through unscathed. Matt is the best offensive header of the ball at Ewood Park and a great defender from the front, but he is still looking to re-establish himself in the side.

Carlisle U (From trainee on 18/1/1996) FL 26+16/10 FLC 4+1/3 FAC 1+3 Others 3+3

Crystal Palace (£1,000,000 + on 12/2/1998) P/FL 23+3/10 FLC 4 FAC 0+1 Others 2

Blackburn Rov (£4,100,000 on 19/11/1999) P/FL 100+42/42 FLC 8+4/8 FAC 8+4/4 Others 2+1/1

Coventry C (Loaned on 13/2/2003) FL 8+1/2

[JARDEL] RIBEIRO DE ALMEIDA Mario Jardel
Born: Fortaleza, Brazil, 18 September 1973
Height: 6'2" **Weight:** 13.3
International Honours: Brazil: 7
The former European 'Golden Boot' winner was signed in August of last year with massive expectations. A prolific marksman throughout his career, it was apparent that he was carrying some extra weight, although the belief was that the Bolton back-room team would soon help him back to full fitness. Whilst it is true that he did initially lose some of the excess weight he arrived with, he seemed to struggle with the pace of the Premiership, making only seven appearances, all from the bench. Whilst he fared a little better in the Carling Cup, making four appearances and scoring three goals, it came as little surprise when he signed on loan for the basement club in Serie A, Ancona, in January.

Bolton W (£400,000 from Sporting Lisbon, Portugal on 15/8/2003) PL 0+7 FLC 3+1/3 FAC 1

JARRETT Albert Ojumiri
Born: Sierra Leone, 23 October 1984
Height: 5'11" **Weight:** 11.2
A skilful left winger, Albert made his debut for Wimbledon as a substitute in the early-season Carling Cup defeat at Wycombe, showing enough promise to be given his first League start at Ipswich soon after. A good crosser of the ball, he was never able to impose himself and certainly playing in a team that was constantly struggling didn't help his cause. On his day he is an exciting

attacker, but he generally reserved those displays for the club's second team, when he appeared much more relaxed and confident, and it was no great surprise when he was released at the end of the season.
Wimbledon *(Signed from Dulwich Hamlet on 17/4/2003) FL 3+6 FLC 0+1*

JARRETT Jason Lee Mee
Born: Bury, 14 September 1979
Height: 6'0" **Weight:** 12.4
Club Honours: Div 2 '03

A forceful player, who is not afraid to make hard tackles, Jason is a solid and consistent performer in the Wigan Athletic midfield who has the ability to pass the ball with accuracy. One of the most improved players, this energetic, consistent box-to-box player showed a liking for hard work in the centre of midfield. Comfortable on the ball he also finds time to create danger with his runs into the opposition penalty area. The 2003-04 season saw him complete his 100th Football League start.
Blackpool *(From trainee on 3/7/1998) FL 2 FAC 0+1 Others 1*
Wrexham *(Free on 8/10/1999) FL 1*
Bury *(Free on 13/7/2000) FL 45+17/4 FLC 0+1 FAC 2+2 Others 3/1*
Wigan Ath *(£75,000 on 27/3/2002) FL 63+18/1 FLC 7/2 FAC 3 Others 1+1/1*

JARVIS Matthew (Matt) Thomas
Born: Middlesbrough, 22 May 1986
Height: 5'8" **Weight:** 11.7
The teenager was the driving force behind Gillingham's exploits in the FA Youth Cup and when called up by the senior side he showed glimpses of his undoubted talent. Matt made a wonderful cameo appearance against Walsall and came close to scoring a debut goal. Mainly used as a substitute last term, he will be looking to make a breakthrough in the 2004-05 campaign.
Gillingham *(From trainee on 13/5/2004) FL 2+8 FAC 0+1*

JARVIS Ryan Robert
Born: Fakenham, 11 July 1986
Height: 5'11" **Weight:** 11.0
Club Honours: Div 1 '04
International Honours: E: Yth
Last term proved to be a season of consolidation for Norwich City's England U19 striker. Ryan made just one start, in the Carling Cup at Northampton, but became the club's youngest-ever scorer when he netted against Watford at Carrow Road in November. A clever striker with great touch and vision, he is adept at dropping off the front line to receive the ball and then looking to set up attacks from there.
Norwich C *(From trainee on 5/8/2003) FL 2+13/1 FLC 1 FAC 0+1*

JASZCZUN Antony (Tommy) John
Born: Kettering, 16 September 1977
Height: 5'10" **Weight:** 10.10
Club Honours: AMC '02, '04
This experienced Blackpool defender

Jason Jarrett

spent much of the 2003-04 season out of action through injury. He managed just two brief spells in the line-up, but earned a winners' medal from the LDV Vans Trophy final after replacing the injured Gareth Evans. Tommy was released in the summer.

Aston Villa *(From trainee on 5/7/1996) FLC 0+1*
Blackpool *(£30,000 on 20/1/2000) FL 107+15 FLC 7 FAC 5/1 Others 12/1*

JEFFERS Francis
Born: Liverpool, 25 January 1981
Height: 5'10" **Weight:** 10.7
Club Honours: FAYC '98
International Honours: E: 1; U21-16; Yth; Sch
Francis came on as a substitute for Dennis Bergkamp in the FA Community Shield against Manchester United and soon afterwards he went out on a season-long loan to his former club Everton. Unfortunately he failed to recover the

form that had made him one of the most sought after young strikers in the country, and he returned to Highbury at the end of the season. Francis failed to find the net in the Premiership although he did so twice in the FA Cup tie against Fulham. A lack of regular first-team football clearly affected his form and he had only limited opportunities to display the darting runs and goal-poaching ability that once made him such an elusive figure in the penalty area.

Everton *(From trainee on 20/2/1998) PL 37+12/18 FLC 2+2/1 FAC 6+1/1*
Arsenal *(£8,000,000 + on 27/6/2001) PL 4+18/4 FLC 1/1 FAC 7+1/3 Others 1+7*
Everton *(Loaned on 1/9/2003) PL 5+13 FLC 1 FAC 0+3/2*

JEFFS Ian David
Born: Chester, 12 October 1982
Height: 5'7" **Weight:** 10.0
This Crewe Alexandra youngster returned to Gresty Road last term after spending

much of the previous campaign in Iceland. A promising midfielder, Ian made a single appearance from the substitutes' bench in the FA Cup defeat by Conference club Telford United. He was released by the club in the summer and soon afterwards returned to Iceland to sign for IBV.

Crewe Alex *(From trainee on 6/2/2001) FAC 0+1*

JELLEYMAN Gareth Anthony
Born: Holywell, 14 November 1980
Height: 5'10" **Weight:** 10.6
International Honours: W: U21-1; Yth
This pacy attacking full back had a rather indifferent season for Peterborough last term when he was in and out of the line-up. Unfortunately his campaign ended prematurely when he suffered a bad injury in the game at Queens Park Rangers in February.

Peterborough U *(From trainee on 5/8/1998) FL 69+18 FAC 5+2 Others 11+1*

Gareth Jelleyman (right)

JENAS Jermaine Anthony
Born: Nottingham, 18 February 1983
Height: 5'11" **Weight:** 11.2
International Honours: E: 6; U21-9; Yth
This young midfield player continued his development as a fine prospect with another solid season in which he made an important contribution to Newcastle's performances. Mature beyond his years he is tall and rangy with good control and pace on the ball, and as he grows older he is becoming stronger and better able to compete physically in the engine room, while his reading of the game has developed and he has added penetrating runs to his repertoire. Jermaine started the 2003-04 season on the bench but once he broke into the starting line-up he was there to stay until he damaged a tendon behind his knee against Villa in April bringing his campaign to an early conclusion. His talent and potential were recognised through several more appearances in the England shirt.
Nottingham F (From trainee on 19/2/2000) FL 29/4 FLC 2 FAC 2
Newcastle U (£5,000,000 on 5/2/2002) PL 55+20/8 FLC 1 FAC 3/1 Others 18+2/1

JENKINS Lee David
Born: Pontypool, 28 June 1979
Height: 5'9" **Weight:** 11.0
Club Honours: Div 3 '00
International Honours: W: U21-9; Yth; Sch
Despite making a number of appearances for Swansea during the early part of last season, Lee was re-united with his former Swans boss Jan Molby at Kidderminster Harriers towards the end of the year. However, surgery to correct a knee problem kept him out of action for some time and he only managed a handful of appearances for his new club. Signed to stiffen up the Harriers' midfield Lee is also an accomplished right back and adds versatility to a small squad in the 2004-05 season.
Swansea C (From trainee on 20/12/1996) FL 125+44/3 FLC 3+1 FAC 3+1 Others 9+1
Kidderminster Hrs (Free on 12/12/2003) FL 5+2

JENKINS Neil
Born: Carshalton, 6 January 1982
Height: 5'6" **Weight:** 10.8
International Honours: E: Yth
Neil had a mixed season at Southend last term and never managed to put together a decent run of first-team appearances. A wide-left player who is equally comfortable at the back or

rampaging forward, Neil found himself unable to replace Mark Gower in the Blues line-up. He started only seven matches, scoring just once, at Boston in March, and he was released by the club in the summer.
Wimbledon (From trainee on 17/7/2000)
Southend U (Free on 7/8/2002) FL 36+14/8 FLC 1 FAC 5+1 Others 2+2

JENKINS Stephen (Steve) Robert
Born: Merthyr Tydfil, 16 July 1972
Height: 5'11" **Weight:** 12.3
Club Honours: AMC '94
International Honours: W: 16; U21-2; Yth
Steve joined Notts County during the 2003 close season and after being appointed as captain he became a regular in the line-up at right back. However, he never really seemed settled at Meadow Lane and in the new year he moved on to join Peterborough United. Although he featured in both midfield and defence for the Posh he failed to establish himself in the side and he spent much of the campaign warming the substitutes' bench.
Swansea C (From trainee on 1/7/1990) FL 155+10/1 FLC 12+1 FAC 10+1 Others 22
Huddersfield T (£275,000 on 3/11/1995) FL 257+1/4 FLC 18 FAC 14 Others 5
Birmingham C (Loaned on 15/12/2000) FL 3 FLC 1
Cardiff C (Free on 5/2/2003) FL 4
Notts Co (Free on 8/8/2003) FL 17 FLC 3 FAC 2 Others 1
Peterborough U (Free on 15/1/2004) FL 6+2

JENNINGS Steven (Steve) John
Born: Liverpool, 28 October 1984
Height: 5'7" **Weight:** 11.7
A mainstay of Tranmere's reserve team last term, this promising youngster made his bow in senior football as a substitute against Oldham in October, starting his first full match in December. He scored some spectacular goals for the second string when operating in a role in the centre of the park, but can also play at right wing back if required.
Tranmere Rov (From trainee on 28/10/2002) FL 1+3 FAC 1

JENSEN Brian
Born: Copenhagen, Denmark, 8 June 1975
Height: 6'1" **Weight:** 12.4
Brian had a mixed campaign for Burnley last term, but he remained all but

unopposed as the Clarets' first-choice 'keeper. When on form he was a key to some of the season's best results, such as the 1-1 draw at Sunderland when he was equal to all that the home attack could throw at him, but on occasions little seemed to go right for him. An imposing figure between the posts, he is more agile than his considerable bulk might suggest and is a fine shot-stopper from all angles.
West Bromwich A (£100,000 from AZ Alkmaar, Holland, ex B93, Hvidovre, on 3/3/2000) FL 46 FLC 4
Burnley (Free on 18/7/2003) FL 46 FLC 3 FAC 3

JENSEN Claus William
Born: Nykobing, Denmark, 29 April 1977
Height: 5'11" **Weight:** 12.6
International Honours: Denmark: 33; U21-17
One of Charlton's most important players, Claus is also one of the most skilful individuals at the club and put in some outstanding displays in midfield. He is able to run with ease with the ball at his feet, and is an accurate passer, not afraid to hit a 40-yard pass. He is also extremely dangerous at corners and set pieces, with the ability to bend a free kick into the goal from the edge of the penalty area. Claus scored with two such free kicks during the season at Wolves and Arsenal. He also grabbed a dramatic injury-time winner against Blackburn Rovers at the Valley after the visitors' goalkeeper Brad Friedel had equalised in the 90th minute. Claus is now established in the Danish international side, and was named in their squad for Euro 2004.
Bolton W (£1,600,000 from Lyngby, Denmark, ex Naestved, on 14/7/1998) FL 85+1/8 FLC 12/2 FAC 6 Others 5
Charlton Ath (£4,000,000 on 21/7/2000) PL 112+10/16 FLC 7/1 FAC 4

JEPHCOTT Avun Cyd
Born: Coventry, 16 October 1983
Height: 6'2" **Weight:** 14.0
A product of Coventry City's Academy, Avun made one substitute appearance last term, coming on in the Carling Cup first round victory over Peterborough. A tall striker with a good touch, he was a regular for the reserves and scored several good goals. He also had a spell on loan at Notts County, but did not make it off the substitutes' bench during his time at Meadow Lane.
Coventry C (From trainee on 19/2/2003) FL 0+1 FLC 0+1

JESS Eoin
Born: Aberdeen, 13 December 1970
Height: 5'9" **Weight:** 11.10
Club Honours: SLC '89
International Honours: S: 18; B-2; U21-14
Eoin had a much better campaign for Nottingham Forest last term when he played the majority of his games in the centre of midfield. He scored a vital last-minute goal to earn the Reds a draw against Rotherham at a time when the team were in deep relegation trouble. Eoin finished the season in an unfamiliar role, proving his adaptability on the right wing without any fuss. He was out of contract in the summer and his future was unclear at the time of writing.
Aberdeen *(From Glasgow R juniors on 13/11/1987) SL 167+34/50 SLC 19+2/4 SC 14+2/3 Others 8+2/6*
Coventry C *(£1,750,000 on 24/2/1996) PL 28+11/1 FLC 1 FAC 4/2*

Sun Jihai

Aberdeen *(£700,000 on 3/7/1997) SL 108+3/29 SLC 8+1/1 SC 6/1*
Bradford C *(Free on 29/12/2000) P/FL 60+2/17 FLC 2 FAC 2*
Nottingham F *(Free on 9/8/2002) FL 38+28/5 FLC 0+3*

JEVONS Philip (Phil)
Born: Liverpool, 1 August 1979
Height: 5'11" **Weight:** 11.10
Club Honours: FAYC '98
Phil found himself out of the first-team picture at Grimsby Town in the opening months of the 2003-04 campaign and it was not until November that he returned to the squad. He immediately hit the goal trail and he became the first Mariner in 25 years to score four times in a match in the 6-1 defeat of Barnsley. A well-struck penalty against fellow strugglers Rushden made him the club's joint-top scorer with Michael Bolding. Phil was voted as the Mariners' 'Player of the Year'.
Everton *(From trainee on 10/11/1997) PL 2+6 FLC 1*
Grimsby T *(£150,000 + on 26/7/2001) FL 46+17/18 FLC 4/2 FAC 3/1*
Hull C *(Loaned on 5/9/2002) FL 13+11/3 FLC 1 FAC 1*

JIHAI Sun
Born: Dalian, China, 30 September 1977
Height: 5'10" **Weight:** 10.12
International Honours: China
A talented utility player who can play anywhere across the back line or as a holding midfielder, this experienced international was in his second spell in English football after previously spending a couple of seasons at Crystal Palace. Principally a fleet-footed right back, he is a regular member of his country's international squad and he is revered by his fans in China.
Crystal Palace *(£500,000 from Dalian Wanda, China on 10/9/1998) FL 22+1 FLC 1 FAC 1 (£500,000 to Dalian Wanda, China on 27/7/1999)*
Manchester C *(£2,000,000 on 26/2/2002) P/FL 56+12/3 FLC 3 FAC 4 Others 5/1*

JOACHIM Julian Kevin
Born: Boston, 20 September 1974
Height: 5'6" **Weight:** 12.2
International Honours: E: U21-9; Yth; (UEFA-U18 '93)
Julian bounced back to regain his first-team place for Coventry last November and was a virtual ever-present for the rest of the season. His fitness improved with regular football and he was soon showing the speed that had terrorised Premiership defences in the past. His form stepped up

appreciably after Christmas when he was paired with Gary McSheffrey and he was an ever-present until suffering a chest injury in the penultimate home game with Rotherham. His performance at home to Burnley was superb with his speed exposing a sluggish away defence. Out of contract in the summer he was reported to have signed for Leeds.

Leicester C *(From trainee on 15/9/1992) F/PL 77+22/25 FLC 7+2/3 FAC 4+1/1 Others 4+2/2*
Aston Villa *(£1,500,000 on 24/2/1996) PL 90+51/39 FLC 10+1/3 FAC 8+4/2 Others 6+3/1*
Coventry C *(Signed on 11/7/2001) FL 41+15/11 FLC 1 FAC 4/3*

JOB Josephe-Desire
Born: Lyon, France, 1 December 1977
Height: 5'10" **Weight:** 11.3
Club Honours: FLC '04
International Honours: Cameroon (ANC '00)

Joseph-Desire completed his fourth season at the Riverside, with last term being his most successful to date. He was a regular in the team until a knee injury kept him out for three months from September to early January. He returned for the 2-0 FA Cup win at the Riverside against Notts County and was, again, a regular in the side. The Cameroon international has not scored too many goals for the club but the most vital one was the one he tapped in at the Millennium Stadium in Cardiff to send Boro' on the way to victory in the Carling Cup final against Bolton Wanderers. With that goal he has written himself into Boro' folklore. Out of contract in the summer his future was unclear at the time of writing.

Middlesbrough *(£3,000,000 from RC Lens, France, ex Lyon, on 7/8/2000) PL 52+16/12 FLC 2+4/1 FAC 3/1*

JOHANSSON Jonatan (JJ)
Lillebror
Born: Stockholm, Sweden, 16 August 1975
Height: 6'1" **Weight:** 12.8
Club Honours: SPL '99, '00; SLC '99
International Honours: Finland: 55; U21-7

JJ featured in most of Charlton's games throughout the season, although a lot of them were from the substitutes' bench. He worked hard and used his pace to get behind the opposition defence, but only found the net on four occasions. One of these was a diving header in the home game with Bolton, and another two came in the home win against Fulham in

November when he put in a great all round performance, finishing the game on the right wing. The Finnish international striker is very quick, possesses a powerful shot and is able to set up goals for other players using his pace and ability to turn a defender. Although used mainly as a striker, JJ can also play wide on the left, a position he sometimes occupies for his international side, and is an excellent crosser of the ball.

Glasgow R *(From FC Flora Tallinn, Estonia, ex TPS Turku, on 13/8/1997) SL 22+25/14 SLC 4/1 SC 2+4/3 Others 9+8/7*
Charlton Ath *(£3,250,000 + on 1/8/2000) PL 74+44/23 FLC 6+1/3 FAC 4+1/2*

JOHANSSON Nils-Eric
Born: Stockholm, Sweden, 13 January 1980
Height: 6'1" **Weight:** 12.7
Club Honours: FLC '02
International Honours: Sweden: 3; U21-21

With so many centre backs absent at Blackburn last term, Nils-Eric ought to have been able to profit but he received only one chance, at Manchester City, when both he and Markus Babbel won praise. He made other starts at left back and on the left-hand side of midfield and in these did well but his occasional substitute appearances were not exceptional. Unexpectedly brought back for the final three games of the season, he produced a fine display against Manchester United.

Blackburn Rov *(£2,700,000 from Nuremburg, Germany, ex Brommapojkarna, AIK Solna, Bayern Munich, on 5/10/2001) PL 41+23 FLC 7+2/1 FAC 4+1/1 Others 4*

JOHN Collins
Born: Zwandru, Liberia, 17 October 1985
Height: 6'0" **Weight:** 12.11
International Honours: Holland: Yth

Signed from Twente Enschede in the January transfer window, Collins' debut was delayed by a series of niggling injuries and he finally made it into Premiership action as a second-half substitute at Chelsea, two months after his arrival. He did not score that day but it proved worth the wait as he fit four goals in two games over Easter demonstrating a predatory instinct in front of goal. A natural striker who leads the line well, he was selected for the Holland U19 squad at the end of the season.

Fulham *(£600,000 from Twente Enschede, Holland on 31/1/2004) PL 3+5/4*

JOHN Stern
Born: Trinidad, 30 October 1976
Height: 6'1" **Weight:** 12.12
International Honours: Trinidad & Tobago

Stern was continually used as back-up striker for Birmingham City last term, coming off the bench and developing the knack of scoring late goals. He rescued a point against Newcastle United at St Andrews in January and scored the dramatic equaliser in the derby at Villa Park, four minutes into added time, to help the Blues come back from 2-0 down. Highly skilful with the ball at his feet, Stern's work rate also went up a notch. He continued to add to his caps for Trinidad during the season.

Nottingham F *(£1,500,000 + from Columbus Crew, USA on 22/11/1999) FL 49+23/18 FLC 3/2 FAC 4+1*
Birmingham C *(Free on 8/2/2002) P/FL 42+32/16 FLC 2/3 FAC 1+2/1 Others 3/1*

JOHN-BAPTISTE Alexander (Alex) Aaron
Born: Sutton in Ashfield, 31 January 1986
Height: 5'11" **Weight:** 11.7

The pick of the crop from the Mansfield Town youth team, this teenager was chosen by Sky TV's *Soccer AM* as their sponsored player. However, injury and illness affected his progress in the early part of last term and he was loaned out to Tamworth for a month in December for match practice. Alex returned to first-team action when resources were stretched and did not let the side down. After a second loan period, this time with Burton Albion, he became a regular in the line-up and went on to produce a series of excellent performances in the centre of the defence.

Mansfield T *(From trainee on 5/2/2003) FL 18+3 Others 4*

JOHNROSE Leonard (Lenny)
Born: Preston, 29 November 1969
Height: 5'10" **Weight:** 12.6
Club Honours: Div 2 '97

Lenny started the 2003-04 season in an unfamiliar central defensive role for Swansea until a hamstring injury kept him out of action. Returning to his usual midfield role, he was an influential figure in the Swans' exciting FA Cup run, but returned for his third spell at Turf Moor on transfer-deadline day, and featured in most of the games in Burnley's run-in. He proved something of a surprise package to many, but remained a solid and dominating figure in the centre of

the park and sometimes an inspiration to the flagging younger players around him.
Blackburn Rov *(From trainee on 16/6/1988)* FL 20+22/11 FLC 2+1/1 FAC 0+3 Others 2
Preston NE *(Loaned on 21/1/1992)* FL 1+2/1
Hartlepool U *(£50,000 on 28/2/1992)* FL 59+7/11 FLC 5+1/4 FAC 5/1 Others 5
Bury *(Signed on 7/12/1993)* FL 181+7/19 FLC 16+2/2 FAC 9/1 Others 9/1
Burnley *(£225,000 on 12/2/1999)* FL 51+27/4 FLC 2 FAC 1+2/1 Others 1
Bury *(Free on 21/10/2002)* FL 5+1 Others 2
Swansea C *(Free on 24/1/2003)* FL 36+4/3 FLC 1 FAC 3
Burnley *(Free on 25/3/2004)* FL 4+3

JOHNSEN Jean **Ronny**
Born: Norway, 10 June 1969
Height: 6'2" **Weight:** 13.2
Club Honours: PL '97, '99, '01; CS '97; FAC '99; EC '99
International Honours: Norway: 61
This experienced central defender struck up a formidable partnership in the centre of defence with Olof Mellberg for Aston Villa last term. Ronny was as solid and consistent as ever, and displayed steady and reliable form. A string of niggling injuries restricted his appearances, but he scored his first goal for Villa in the home game against Leeds when he met Nolberto Solano's inswinging free kick from the left with a glancing header which left the 'keeper helpless. Ronny added further caps for Norway during the season.
Manchester U *(£1,200,000 from Besiktas, Turkey, ex Lyn, Lillestrom, on 26/7/1996)* PL 85+14/7 FLC 3 FAC 8+2/1 Others 35+3/1
Aston Villa *(Free on 29/8/2002)* PL 46+3/1 FLC 5+1 FAC 1

JOHNSON Andrew (Andy)
Born: Bedford, 10 February 1981
Height: 5'9" **Weight:** 9.7
International Honours: E: Yth
This pacy striker had an excellent campaign for Crystal Palace last term and finished the season as the club's leading scorer with 32 goals earning him the First Division's 'Golden Boot' award. His tally included hat-tricks against Stoke in February and at Crewe in April, plus numerous doubles. Andy finished the campaign as the club's 'Player of the Year' and was also voted into the PFA Division One team of the season.
Birmingham C *(From juniors on 11/3/1998)* FL 44+39/8 FLC 6+9/5 FAC 1 Others 1+3
Crystal Palace *(£750,000 on 5/8/2002)* FL 67+3/38 FLC 6/7 FAC 4 Others 3/1

JOHNSON Andrew (Andy) James
Born: Bristol, 2 May 1974
Height: 6'0" **Weight:** 13.0
Club Honours: Div 1 '98
International Honours: W: 14; E: Yth
An attacking midfielder, Andy once again worked his socks off in the West Bromwich Albion engine room, but perhaps on his own admission, he could and should have scored more goals than he did. He was a regular at international level for Wales and reached two career milestones during the season: 250 League appearances and 300 outings in all competitions.
Norwich C *(From trainee on 4/3/1992)* F/PL 56+10/13 FLC 6+1/2 FAC 2
Nottingham F *(£2,200,000 on 4/7/1997)* P/FL 102+17/9 FLC 6+1/1 FAC 2
West Bromwich A *(£200,000 on 19/9/2001)* P/FL 91+11/7 FLC 4+1 FAC 6/1

JOHNSON Damien Michael
Born: Lisburn, 18 November 1978
Height: 5'9" **Weight:** 11.2
Club Honours: FLC '02
International Honours: NI: 29; U21-11; Yth
Damien was one of Birmingham City's best players last season when he was singled out by manager Steve Bruce as an unsung hero. Damien worked the right flank tirelessly, always helping out the defence and carrying the ball forward with determination. Very competitive, he was never one to shirk a challenge. He maintained a reliable level of consistency, even when asked to help out at right back on several occasions.
Blackburn Rov *(From trainee on 2/2/1996)* P/FL 43+17/3 FLC 12+3/1 FAC 3+4 Others 0+1
Nottingham F *(Loaned on 29/1/1998)* FL 5+1
Birmingham C *(Signed on 8/3/2002)* P/FL 68+5/3 FLC 1+1 FAC 5 Others 1

JOHNSON David Anthony
Born: Kingston, Jamaica, 15 August 1976
Height: 5'6" **Weight:** 12.3
Club Honours: FAYC '95; Div 2 '97
International Honours: Jamaica: 4; E: B-1; Sch
This Nottingham Forest striker had an unhappy start to the 2003-04 season after suffering a broken leg against Sheffield United in September. David returned to the side as a substitute against Crystal Palace in March still short of match fitness, but he showed the Forest fans what they had been missing. He scored five goals in the last four

games of the season, including a double against his former side Ipswich Town, to help ensure that relegation was avoided. David will be hoping to be back to full fitness for the 2004-05 campaign.
Manchester U *(From trainee on 1/7/1994)* **Bury** *(Free on 5/7/1995)* FL 72+25/18 FLC 8+3/4 FAC 1+1 Others 3+2/1
Ipswich T *(£800,000 on 14/11/1997)* P/FL 121+10/55 FLC 13/5 FAC 7/2 Others 7
Nottingham F *(£3,000,000 + on 12/11/2001)* FL 86+14/37 FLC 5/2 FAC 1+1 Others 2/2
Sheffield Wed *(Loaned on 5/2/2002)* FL 7/2
Burnley *(Loaned on 12/3/2002)* FL 8/5

JOHNSON Edward (Eddie) William
Born: Chester, 20 September 1984
Height: 5'10" **Weight:** 13.7
International Honours: E: Yth
A promising young forward who joined Manchester United from Crewe Alexandra's Centre of Excellence, Eddie got his first taste of senior action in October when he came on as a second-half substitute for Darren Fletcher in the 3-2 Carling Cup win over Leeds United at Elland Road.
Manchester U *(From trainee on 4/10/2001)* FLC 0+1

JOHNSON Gavin
Born: Stowmarket, 10 October 1970
Height: 5'11" **Weight:** 12.0
Club Honours: Div 2 '92; Div 3 '97
After more than a year on the sidelines with a broken leg, Gavin made his long-awaited comeback for Colchester United at Wycombe last December. The left-sided specialist then remained on the fringe of the team until making a big impact during the last two months of the campaign. Gavin created several goals for his team mates with his deliveries from crosses, corners and free kicks, and scored himself in the final home game of the season against Rushden.
Ipswich T *(From trainee on 1/3/1989)* P/FL 114+18/11 FLC 10+1/2 FAC 12+1/2 Others 3+1/1
Luton T *(Free on 4/7/1995)* FL 4+1
Wigan Ath *(£15,000 on 15/12/1995)* FL 82+2/8 FLC 4 FAC 3 Others 1
Dunfermline Ath *(Free on 1/7/1998)* SL 18 SC 0+1
Colchester U *(Free on 12/11/1999)* FL 98+12/4 FLC 4+1 FAC 4 Others 3+1

JOHNSON Glen McLeod
Born: London, 23 August 1984
Height: 6'0" **Weight:** 12.0
International Honours: E: 1; U21-7; Yth
Chelsea certainly had an eye on the

future with the influx of the Abramovich millions, the first signing under the new regime being England U21 right back Glen Johnson from West Ham United. Although comparatively inexperienced Glen made meteoric progress in his first three months at Stamford Bridge, scoring his first two senior goals against MSK Zilinia and Newcastle United and then winning his first full cap against Denmark in November – becoming in the process one of Chelsea's 'Famous Five' who played in the match. He looked comfortable at both Premiership and Champions' League level, being sharp and confident on the ball and eager to attack and, remarkably, displaced one of the most solid right backs in the country in Mario Melchiot. His third goal was the sensational last-minute pile driver that

secured a win at Ewood Park and kept Chelsea, fleetingly at least, on Arsenal's coat-tails. Glen created the only goal of the Champions' League knockout phase at Stuttgart before a nasty ankle injury forced him to miss 11 matches until his reappearance against Southampton when he scored yet again with a nicely-taken side-footed effort.
West Ham U (From trainee on 25/8/2001) PL 14+1 FAC 0+1
Millwall (Loaned on 17/10/2002) FL 7+1
Chelsea (£6,000,000 on 22/7/2003) PL 17+2/3 FLC 3 FAC 1 Others 8+1/1

JOHNSON Jermaine
Born: Kingston, Jamaica, 25 June 1980
Height: 5'9" **Weight:** 11.5
International Honours: Jamaica
Jermaine again found it difficult to break

into the Bolton first-team squad last term and in November he joined Oldham Athletic on loan. He eventually spent three months at Boundary Park, operating up front with a variety of partners. Quick-footed and pacy, he proved to be a bright attacking asset who was only let down at times by some wayward and impulsive finishing. He returned to the Reebok in February before the two clubs agreed a deal that saw Latics take over his contract until the end of the season. Jermaine finished with a respectable tally of six goals from 19 starts and was considering the offer of a contract with the club at the time of writing.
Bolton W (£750,000 from Tivoli Gardens, Jamaica on 19/9/2001) PL 4+8 FLC 3 FAC 1+1
Oldham Ath (Free on 28/11/2004) FL 18+2/5 FAC 1/1

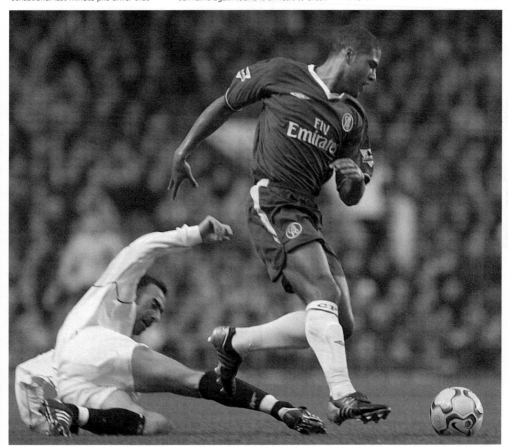

Glen Johnson

JOHNSON Lee David
Born: Newmarket, 7 June 1981
Height: 5'6" **Weight:** 10.7
Club Honours: FAT '02; NC '03
International Honours: E: SP-5
Lee produced a string of impressive performances in midfield for Yeovil Town last term when he was a leading contender for the club's 'Player of the Year' award. A busy individual who was always in the thick of the action, he set up numerous chances for his colleagues. Lee was a near ever-present in the side and scored five goals, two of which were a result of stunning strikes from free kicks.
Watford (From trainee on 3/10/1998)
Brighton & Hove A (Free on 4/9/2000) Others 1/1
Brentford (Free on 22/3/2001)
Yeovil T (Free on 12/7/2001) FL 45/5 FLC 1 FAC 3 Others 2

JOHNSON Leon Dean
Born: Shoreditch, 10 May 1981
Height: 6'0" **Weight:** 12.4
This promising Gillingham youngster was called upon in the latter part of the season and never let anyone down when selected. Leon looked assured in the centre of the defence, whether playing in a back four or as one of three defenders.
Southend U (From trainee on 17/11/1999) FL 43+5/3 FLC 1 FAC 1+3 Others 8
Gillingham (Free on 15/8/2002) FL 26+12 FLC 1 FAC 1+1

JOHNSON Michael Owen
Born: Nottingham, 4 July 1973
Height: 5'11" **Weight:** 11.12
Club Honours: AIC '95
International Honours: Jamaica: 14
George Burley soon realised Derby's defence had to be strengthened and was happy that Birmingham were prepared to release Michael, who set a fine example of commitment for the remainder of the season. Michael suffered from a variety of strains and pulls but seldom missed a match, so keen was he to play. He was most unfortunate to be sent off against Walsall, a red card that was rescinded by the FA disciplinary committee. It did not, however, cancel the penalty through which Walsall won at Pride Park. Michael added a Jamaican cap after joining Derby.
Notts Co (From trainee on 9/7/1991) FL 102+5 FLC 9 FAC 4 Others 15+1
Birmingham C (£225,000 on 1/9/1995) P/FL 227+35/13 FLC 25+6/5 FAC 6+4 Others 11
Derby Co (Signed on 15/8/2003) FL 39/1 FAC 1

JOHNSON Richard Mark
Born: Newcastle, Australia, 27 April 1974
Height: 5'11" **Weight:** 12.4
Club Honours: Div 2 '98
International Honours: Australia: 1
This experienced central midfield player played only one match for Watford last term before leaving the club by mutual consent in September. After a brief spell at Colchester, where his only appearance was as a substitute in the LDV Vans Trophy tie against Yeovil, he joined Stoke City on a three-month contract. However, he had few chances to shine with the Potteries club and finished the season at Queens Park Rangers. Richard made one of the central-midfield positions his own at Loftus Road, producing some useful performances, but was injured at Bristol City at the beginning of April and only returned for the final three games of the campaign.
Watford (From trainee on 11/5/1992) P/FL 210+32/20 FLC 14+1/1 FAC 13+2/1 Others 5+1
Northampton T (Loaned on 7/2/2003) FL 5+1/1
Colchester U (Free on 27/10/2003) Others 0+1
Stoke C (Free on 17/11/2003) FL 3+4 FAC 1+1
Queens Park R (Free on 18/2/2004) FL 10+1

JOHNSON Roger
Born: Ashford, 28 April 1983
Height: 6'3" **Weight:** 11.0
Roger started the 2003-04 season as an automatic choice as a central defender at Wycombe but lost his place to loan signing Guy Branston at the end of September. However, he was pretty much ever-present in the second half of the campaign, leading by example with his gritty, committed performances. Dominant in the air, he scored a headed goal against Tranmere on Easter Monday as a makeshift centre forward, earning him a start in the same position for the next game. This did not work out and he was soon back in his familiar defensive role. In a wretched season for the club, his never-say-die attitude deservedly won him the supporters' 'Player of the Season' award.
Wycombe W (From trainee on 10/7/2001) FL 61+9/6 FLC 3 FAC 3 Others 4+2/1

JOHNSON Seth Art Maurice
Born: Birmingham, 12 March 1979
Height: 5'10" **Weight:** 11.0
International Honours: E: 1; U21-15; Yth
Seth had a better time at Elland Road last term following his injury problems of the

previous season. He settled into a central-midfield role, showing some tenacious tackling and an array of passing ability. Seth remained committed to the cause in a season of struggle and scored two goals, both coming in the 2-1 victory over Blackburn in October.
Crewe Alex (From trainee on 12/7/1996) FL 89+4/6 FLC 5 FAC 2/1 Others 0+3
Derby Co (£3,000,000 on 21/5/1999) PL 73/2 FLC 6+1 FAC 0+1
Leeds U (£7,000,000 + on 19/10/2001) PL 39+9/3 FLC 1 FAC 3+1

JOHNSON Simon Ainsley
Born: West Bromwich, 9 March 1983
Height: 5'9" **Weight:** 12.0
International Honours: E: Yth
This young striker did well in the Leeds United reserve team last term and towards the end of the year he was loaned out to Blackpool. Simon featured on a number of occasions, scoring in the Boxing Day against Tranmere. On his return to Elland Road he made a handful of Premiership appearances in the closing stages of the season.
Leeds U (From trainee on 7/7/2000) PL 2+7 FAC 0+1
Hull C (Loaned on 12/8/2002) FL 4+8/2 FLC 0+1
Blackpool (Loaned on 13/12/2003) FL 3+1/1 FAC 0+1

JOHNSON Thomas (Tommy)
Born: Newcastle, 15 January 1971
Height: 5'11" **Weight:** 12.8
Club Honours: FLC '96; SPD '01; SLC 00; SC '01
International Honours: E: U21-7
This experienced professional has been dogged by injury problems during his time at Gillingham. It sometimes seemed that every time he returned from one injury he was sidelined by another one. A capable striker, he produced some creditable performances when fit, shining in the FA Cup win over Charlton and netting two goals in the draw at Coventry to earn the Gills a valuable point.
Notts Co (From trainee on 19/1/1989) FL 100+18/47 FLC 7+2/5 FAC 3+2/1 Others 14+3/4
Derby Co (£1,300,000 on 12/3/1992) FL 91+7/30 FLC 9+1/2 FAC 5/1 Others 16/8
Aston Villa (£1,450,000 on 6/11/1995) FL 38+19/13 FLC 5/2 FAC 5+2/1 Others 1+1/1
Glasgow Celtic (£2,400,000 on 27/3/1997) SL 23+12/18 SLC 3+1/3 SC 2+4 Others 0+3/1
Everton (Loaned on 24/9/1999) PL 0+3
Sheffield Wed (Free on 8/9/2001) FL 8/3 FLC 1
Kilmarnock (Free on 22/12/2001) SL 7+3/7 SC 1+1

Gillingham (Free on 7/8/2002) FL 18+23/5 FLC 0+4/1 FAC 2+1/1

JONES Bradley (Brad)
Born: Armadale, Australia, 19 March 1982
Height: 6'3" **Weight:** 12.3
Club Honours: AMC '04
International Honours: Australia: U23-3; Yth
With his Riverside opportunities restricted during the season Brad was loaned out to Rotherham United, where he made no first-team appearances, and Blackpool, where he impressed, to gain invaluable experience. With Middlesbrough's number two Carlo Nash injured Brad was on the substitutes' bench for most of the season, patiently awaiting his opportunity. He eventually featured in two games, the FA Cup tie against Notts County and the Premiership win over Fulham.
Middlesbrough (From trainee on 26/3/1999) PL 1 FAC 1
Stockport Co (Loaned on 13/12/2002) FL 1
Blackpool (Loaned on 4/11/2003) FL 5 Others 2

JONES Darren Lee
Born: Newport, 28 August 1983
Height: 6'0" **Weight:** 12.6
International Honours: W: Yth; Sch
This tall, strong central defender was out of the first-team picture at Bristol City last term. He spent three months on loan at Cheltenham Town in the opening part of the season where he played alongside Michael Duff in the centre of a four-man defence. Shortly after returning to Ashton Gate he went out on loan to Forest Green Rovers and eventually moved on to sign for Newport County.
Bristol C (From trainee on 22/9/2000) FL 1+1 Others 0+3
Cheltenham T (Loaned on 25/8/2003) FL 14/1

JONES Gary Roy
Born: Birkenhead, 3 June 1977
Height: 5'10" **Weight:** 12.0
This midfield stalwart was completely out of the first-team picture at Barnsley last term and jumped at the chance to rejoin Rochdale, initially on loan, mid-way through the season. Despite a lack of match practice and a nasty foot injury picked up in his first game, Gary was soon back covering every blade of grass in the team's cause. Fittingly it was Gary who netted the goal against Southend that guaranteed the club's survival in the battle at the foot of Division Three.

Swansea C (Signed from Caernarfon T on 11/7/1997) FL 3+5 FLC 0+1
Rochdale (Free on 15/1/1998) FL 123+17/22 FLC 4+1 FAC 6+3 Others 7+2/3
Barnsley (£175,000 on 30/11/2001) FL 56/2 FLC 1
Rochdale (Free on 13/11/2003) FL 26/4 FAC 1

JONES Gary Steven
Born: Chester, 10 May 1975
Height: 6'3" **Weight:** 14.0
This versatile and committed Tranmere Rovers player featured in defence, midfield and up front last term and finished the campaign with the captain's armband. Primarily used as a striker, he reached a double-figure goals tally and it was fitting that he should score the goal in the FA Cup quarter-final replay against Millwall which briefly gave Rovers hope of pulling off another famous victory. Gary again caused plenty of problems for opposition defenders with his height and physical presence.
Tranmere Rov (From trainee on 5/7/1993) FL 117+61/28 FLC 17+4/3 FAC 9+2/3 Others 1+1
Nottingham F (Free on 3/7/2000) FL 24+12/2 FLC 1+1 FAC 1
Tranmere Rov (Free on 29/8/2002) FL 76+6/15 FLC 4 FAC 9+1/2 Others 4/2

JONES Graeme Anthony
Born: Gateshead, 13 March 1970
Height: 6'0" **Weight:** 13.0
Club Honours: Div 3 '97; AMC '99
This experienced striker proved invaluable for Boston United in the second half of the season. He used his strength and ability to hold the ball up to great effect. Graeme set up scoring opportunities for his colleagues as well as netting six League goals himself. At the end of the campaign Graeme left the York Street club and was reported to have signed for Bury.
Doncaster Rov (£10,000 from Bridlington T on 2/8/1993) FL 80+12/26 FLC 4+1/1 FAC 2+1/2 Others 5/1
Wigan Ath (£150,000 on 8/7/1996) FL 76+20/44 FLC 4+3/1 FAC 4/1 Others 6+2/6
St Johnstone (£100,000 on 19/11/1999) SL 31+10/7 SLC 2 SC 1
Southend U (£35,000 on 30/7/2002) FL 18+3/2 FLC 1 FAC 2+1 Others 1/1
Boston U (Free on 21/3/2003) FL 33+3/7 FLC 0+1

JONES Lee
Born: Pontypridd, 9 August 1970
Height: 6'3" **Weight:** 14.4
Club Honours: AMC '94; '04

This experienced custodian joined Blackpool during the 2003 close season and quickly took over the 'keeper's jersey from Phil Barnes. However, although Lee remained the club's number one choice for most of the campaign he was hampered by a series of injuries that restricted his appearances.
Swansea C (£7,500 from AFC Porth on 24/3/1994) FL 6 Others 1
Bristol Rov (Signed on 7/3/1998) FL 76 FLC 6 FAC 7 Others 4
Stockport Co (£50,000 on 19/7/2000) FL 72+3 FLC 5 FAC 4
Blackpool (Free on 8/8/2003) FL 21 FLC 2 FAC 2 Others 4

JONES Philip Lee
Born: Wrexham, 29 May 1973
Height: 5'9" **Weight:** 10.8
International Honours: W: 2; B-1; U21-14; Yth
Injuries once again were a big part of Lee's season last term, hampering him in his quest for a regular spot in the Wrexham side. He notched all of his eight goals in September and October, including a double in the 2-1 win over Port Vale, and a hat-trick in the LDV Vans Trophy game against Morecambe at the Racecourse. However, he failed to feature for much of the rest of the season and was one of five senior players to be released in May.
Wrexham (From trainee on 5/7/1991) FL 24+15/10 FLC 2 FAC 1+2/1 Others 4/2
Liverpool (£300,000 on 12/3/1992) PL 0+3 FLC 0+1
Crewe Alex (Loaned on 3/9/1993) FL 4+4/1
Wrexham (Loaned on 26/1/1996) FL 20/9
Wrexham (Loaned on 31/1/1997) FL 2+4
Tranmere Rov (£100,000 on 27/3/1997) FL 58+28/16 FLC 7+3/2 FAC 0+1
Barnsley (Free on 3/7/2000) FL 17+23/5 FLC 3+4/2 FAC 0+1 (Free to Oswestry T on 27/3/2002)
Wrexham (Free on 28/3/2002) FL 25+24/14 FLC 1 FAC 1+1 Others 3+1/5

JONES Mark Alan
Born: Wrexham, 15 August 1983
Height: 5'11" **Weight:** 10.10
International Honours: W: U21-1
Although not making the starting line-up in his first season as a full-time professional Mark is a very promising player of whom much is expected at Wrexham. The young midfielder managed to get on the score sheet against Oldham in October, turning his defender and beating the opposing 'keeper with a superb shot. Mark also featured in the Wales U21 squad during the campaign.

Wrexham *(From trainee on 9/7/2003) FL 0+14/1 Others 1+1/1*

JONES Nathan Jason
Born: Rhondda, 28 May 1973
Height: 5'7" **Weight:** 10.12
Club Honours: Div 3 '01
Nathan was a regular in the starting line-up for Brighton last term, but his season was still something of a mixed bag. A talented winger and master of trickery with the ball, his 'step over' routine now seems to be handled by opposition players, but he developed a new flick,

which is spectacular when it leaves a defender for dead. One of those flair players who can light up a game, Nathan wasn't always able to find the finishing pass to match his runs and he was substituted on several occasions.
Luton T *(£10,000 from Merthyr Tydfil on 30/6/1995. Freed on 20/12/1995)*
Southend U *(Free from Numancia, Spain on 5/8/1997) FL 82+17/2 FLC 6+2 FAC 3+1/1 Others 0+3*
Scarborough *(Loaned on 25/3/1999) FL 8+1*
Brighton & Hove A *(Free on 7/7/2000) FL 106+34/7 FLC 5+2/1 FAC 6+1 Others 8+1*

Nathan Jones

JONES Paul Steven
Born: Chirk, 18 April 1967
Height: 6'3" **Weight:** 14.8
International Honours: W: 38
Paul began the Premiership campaign in goal for the Saints due to the injury Antti Niemi picked up at the previous May's FA Cup final, but as soon as the Finnish 'keeper was fit it was back to bench-warming duties, which did not suit Paul's aspirations to stay in the reckoning for Wales. He was eventually loaned to Liverpool in January to cover for injuries, but after two appearances he was transferred Wolves. Although he frustrated Portsmouth in a 0-0 draw on his debut, he sometimes had a difficult time playing in a struggling team at Molineux. Paul was at his best in one-on-one situations, and he always seemed to somehow block the shot, notably against Everton. He finished the season well, with a fine low penalty stop from Alan Shearer at Newcastle and a brilliant reflex save against Tottenham.
Wolverhampton W *(£40,000 from Kidderminster Hrs on 23/7/1991) FL 33 FLC 2 FAC 5 Others 4*
Stockport Co *(£60,000 on 25/7/1996) FL 46 FLC 11 FAC 4 Others 4*
Southampton *(£900,000 on 28/7/1997) PL 192+1 FLC 16+1 FAC 11+1 Others 1*
Liverpool *(Loaned on 9/1/2004) PL 2*
Wolverhampton W *(£250,000 on 29/1/2004) PL 16*

JONES Richard John Stanley
Born: Swansea, 6 January 1985
Height: 5'10" **Weight:** 10.1
International Honours: W: Yth
After spending two weeks at the Vetch Field on a trial basis shortly after the start of the 2003-04 campaign, Richard then signed a season-long loan transfer from Premiership side Southampton. A central midfield player who had experienced reserve-team football with the Saints, he made only one senior appearance for Swansea, appearing in the LDV Vans Trophy tie against Southend United. Richard also represented Wales at both U19 and U20 levels during the campaign.
Southampton *(From trainee on 11/1/2002)*
Swansea C *(Loaned on 4/9/2003) Others 1*

JONES Robert (Rob) William
Born: Stockton, 30 November 1979
Height: 6'7" **Weight:** 12.2
This tall, powerful centre back looked to be a sound investment for Stockport in the opening few weeks of the 2003-04

season, however a loss of form and then a change in management saw him loaned out to Macclesfield in October. He played just once during his stay at Moss Rose, being hampered by a succession of training ground injuries, and returned to Edgeley Park in February, where he added just a couple more appearances before the end of the campaign.

Stockport Co *(Signed from Gateshead on 9/4/2003) FL 14+2/2 FLC 2 Others 1*
Macclesfield T *(Loaned on 31/10/2003) FL 1*

JONES Stephen (Steve)
Graham
Born: Derry, 25 October 1976
Height: 5'4" **Weight:** 10.9
International Honours: NI: 11
Steve was firmly established in the Crewe front line last term and finished the season as the club's second-top scorer with a total of 16 goals in all competitions. A striker who causes problems for opposition defenders with his pace, he was also a regular at international level for Northern Ireland during the campaign.

Blackpool *(Free from Chadderton on 30/10/1995)*
Bury *(Free on 23/8/1996. Free to Sligo Rov during 1997 close season)*
Crewe Alex *(£75,000 + from Leigh RMI, ex Bray W, Chorley, on 4/7/2001) FL 62+20/24 FLC 1+1/1 FAC 3+1/1 Others 2+2/1*
Rochdale *(Loaned on 5/2/2002) FL 6+3/1*

JONES Stuart Clive
Born: Bristol, 24 October 1977
Height: 6'1" **Weight:** 14.0
Plucked from the relative obscurity of Weston super Mare, Stuart joined Brighton on a short-term contract as back-up for Ben Roberts after first choice 'keeper Michel Kuipers suffered a knee injury. Stuart's tenure of the substitutes' bench lasted just 45 minutes when Roberts suffered a knee injury at Wycombe, and the newcomer was thrust between the posts for the second half, producing a couple of excellent stops. He then made two more appearances before stepping down following Roberts' recovery. Although looking a little rusty at times, Stuart did enough to earn himself a deal to the end of the season.

Sheffield Wed *(£20,000 + from Weston super Mare on 26/3/1998)*
Torquay U *(£30,000 on 3/2/2000) FL 32 FLC 2 FAC 2 Others 1 (Free to Hereford U on 26/10/2001)*
Brighton & Hove A *(Free from Weston super Mare on 6/2/2004) FL 2+1*

JONES Stuart John
Born: Aberystwyth, 14 March 1984
Height: 6'0" **Weight:** 11.8
International Honours: W: Yth
After signing a professional contract in the 2003 close season, Stuart began last term as Swansea's first-choice right back. He also featured in the centre of defence, but a training ground injury saw him sidelined for almost all of September. He appeared as a substitute on a number of occasions before a hamstring injury saw him sidelined once more. Stuart was included in the Wales U21 squad in May.

Swansea C *(From trainee on 28/7/2003) FL 21+9 FLC 1 FAC 1 Others 2*

JONES William (Billy)
Born: Shrewsbury, 24 March 1987
Height: 5'11" **Weight:** 13.0
International Honours: E: Yth
Although this talented youngster was only a first-year scholar at Crewe, he proved to be one of the finds of the season for manager Dario Gradi. Billy made an impressive debut as a substitute in the home game against Derby County in October, and went on to establish himself as a regular in the first-team line-up. A versatile defender, his best role is in the centre of the defence. His only goal to date was a spectacular effort against Wigan in December. Billy represented England at U17 and U19 levels during the campaign.

Crewe Alex *(Trainee) FL 23+4/1 FAC 1*

JONES William (Billy) Kenneth
Born: Chatham, 26 March 1983
Height: 6'0" **Weight:** 11.7
Billy started the 2003-04 season playing at centre half for Leyton Orient due to injuries and only switched to his preferred position of left back when Matt Lockwood was injured. Billy has a cultured left foot and is a dead-ball specialist.

Leyton Orient *(From trainee on 10/7/2001) FL 68+4 FLC 2 FAC 3+1 Others 0+1*

JORDAN Andrew (Andy)
Joseph
Born: Manchester, 14 December 1979
Height: 6'1" **Weight:** 13.1
International Honours: S: U21-4
A left-sided central defender, Andy had suffered badly with injuries in recent seasons and had not played any first-team football during the 2002-03 season. He was one of new Hartlepool manager Neale Cooper's close-season signings, and went straight into the first team,

featuring in several early games last term. However, Andy was then rested and for the remainder of the season he was restricted to reserve football.

Bristol C *(From trainee on 5/12/1997) FL 10+1 FLC 1+1/1 Others 1*
Cardiff C *(£30,000 on 26/10/2000) FL 3+2 FAC 1*
Hartlepool U *(Free on 1/8/2003) FL 4+1 FLC 1*

JORDAN Stephen (Steve)
Robert
Born: Warrington, 6 March 1982
Height: 6'0" **Weight:** 11.13
A promising young defender who is looking to make his mark on the Premiership, Stephen is a product of the Manchester City Academy. Stephen made a fleeting appearance at Bolton before coming on as a substitute for his home debut against Everton. He will be hoping that he gets more chances to impress in the near future as he looks to establish himself in the first team.

Manchester C *(From trainee on 11/3/1999) PL 0+3*
Cambridge U *(Loaned on 4/10/2002) FL 11 Others 3*

JORGENSEN Claus Beck
Born: Denmark, 27 April 1979
Height: 5'11" **Weight:** 11.0
Although Claus impressed during the pre-season period for Coventry he struggled to make an impact at Highfield Road. His best performance was as a substitute in the Carling Cup defeat by Tottenham when he pepped up an ailing attack with some positive running and probing passes. Claus went on loan to Bournemouth after Christmas where he proved popular with the fans and enjoyed a good run in the side.

Bournemouth *(Free from AC Horsens, Denmark on 12/7/1999) FL 77+10/14 FLC 6/1 FAC 6 Others 1+1*
Bradford C *(Free on 23/7/2001) FL 41+9/12 FLC 2+1 FAC 1*
Coventry C *(Free on 5/8/2003) FL 4+4 FLC 1+1*
Bournemouth *(Loaned on 23/1/2004) FL 16+1*

JOSEPH Marc Ellis
Born: Leicester, 10 November 1976
Height: 6'0" **Weight:** 12.10
This cultured right-sided centre back fully justified Hull City manager Peter Taylor's faith in him last term when he established an outstanding partnership with Damien

Delaney. Although affected by a knee problem in the early stages of the campaign Marc recovered to become a regular in the line-up, his calmness in possession of the ball was a vital quality as opponents often employed a defensive strategy at the KC Stadium. He scored his only goal of the campaign at Macclesfield in April as the Tigers closed in on their promotion target.

Cambridge U (From trainee on 23/5/1995) FL 136+17 FLC 7 FAC 5+2 Others 7+1
Peterborough U (Free on 3/7/2001) FL 60+1/2 FLC 3 FAC 6 Others 3
Hull C (£40,000 on 22/11/2002) FL 54+1/1 FAC 1 Others 1

JOSEPH Matthew Nathaniel
Born: Bethnal Green, 30 September 1972
Height: 5'8" **Weight:** 10.7
International Honours: E: Yth. Barbados: 2
Matthew started last season as first-choice right back for Leyton Orient and only lost his place due to injury and the form of Donny Barnard. Matthew showed his versatility by also playing as a left back during the second half of the campaign. He is hard to knock off the ball and despite his size rarely loses out to bigger opponents. Matthew was released during the summer, despite being the O's longest serving player.

Arsenal (From trainee on 17/11/1990)
Gillingham (Free on 7/12/1992) Others 1
Cambridge U (Signed on 19/11/1993) FL 157+2/6 FLC 6+1 FAC 7 Others 5
Leyton Orient (£10,000 on 22/1/1998) FL 219+5/2 FLC 9+1 FAC 16+1 Others 5+1

[JUAN] MALDONDO DUARTE Juan
Born: Sao Paulo, Brazil, 6 February 1982
Height: 5'6" **Weight:** 9.7
After missing most of the 2002-03 campaign with a cruciate ligament injury, the young Arsenal left back joined Millwall on a three-month loan deal last term. He featured in most of the pre-season friendlies, but made just four first-team appearances before returning to Highbury. Juan subsequently had a trial with PSV and in the new year he returned to Brazil, signing for Fluminense.

Arsenal (Signed from Sao Paulo, Brazil on 9/7/2001) FLC 1 FAC 1
Millwall (Loaned on 1/8/2003) FL 2+1 FLC 1

JUDGE Matthew Peter
Born: Barking, 18 January 1985
Height: 6'0" **Weight:** 11.7
International Honours: RoI: Yth

This young striker spent most of last season developing with Luton's U19 team. He appeared as a substitute in the LDV Vans Trophy tie at Stevenage, when he came off the bench to score the winner, and also featured in the following game against Brentford. Matthew represented the Republic of Ireland at U19 level during the campaign, but was surprisingly released in the summer.

Luton T (Trainee) FL 0+2 FAC 0+1 Others 1+2/1

JULIAN Alan John
Born: Ashford, 11 March 1983
Height: 6'2" **Weight:** 13.5
International Honours: NI: Yth
This tall, commanding Brentford goalkeeper got an early run in the side when Paul Smith was suspended and then took over again when Smith was sold to Southampton. However, after six games Alan was replaced by new signing Stuart Nelson and only returned again when the newcomer was suspended.

Brentford (From trainee on 4/7/2001) FL 16 FLC 0+1 Others 1

[JUNINHO] JUNIOR GIROLDO Oswaldo
Born: Sao Paulo, Brazil, 22 February 1973
Height: 5'5" **Weight:** 10.4
Club Honours: FLC '04
International Honours: Brazil: 50
To many Middlesbrough fans the two most endearing memories of recent footballing times revolve around one player, Brazilian international Juninho, a much loved and spiritually adopted son of Teesside. The first etched memory is of a dejected and tearful Juninho sat on the Elland Road turf in May 1997. The second endearing memory is one of an old promise finally fulfilled last season at the Millennium Stadium in Cardiff. The little fellow, in his third spell with the club, collected a well-deserved Carling Cup winner's medal at his fourth attempt and at the club's seemingly umpteenth try. Those Boro' fans that were present on that memorable afternoon and those that watched the game on television 290 miles away on Teesside were united in common kinship as they shared the magic moments when the team finally and successfully rose to overcome the failure of 128 years. In the same moment mature and hardened Northern folk laughed and cried as Juninho jigged and beamed his way around the pitch with the Carling Cup held high above his head.

Middlesbrough (£4,750,000 from Sao Paulo, Brazil, ex Ituano, on 3/11/1995) PL 54+2/14 FLC 9/1 FAC 9/2 (£12,000,000 to Atletico Madrid, Spain on 25/8/1997)
Middlesbrough (Loaned from Atletico Madrid, Spain on 21/9/1999) PL 24+4/4 FLC 4/1 FAC 1
Middlesbrough (Signed from Atletico Madrid, Spain on 14/8/2002) PL 35+6/11 FLC 5+1/1 FAC 0+1

[JUNIOR] GUIMARAES SANIBIO Jose Luis
Born: Fortaleza, Brazil, 20 July 1976
Height: 6'0" **Weight:** 13.0
The biggest blow to Derby's season came at the end of September when Junior injured cruciate knee ligaments against Nottingham Forest at the City Ground. The Brazilian, signed after complex negotiations, soon showed his eye for goal and blended well with Mathias Svensson, who was recalled by Charlton less than a fortnight later. Junior made a good recovery and returned to the bench at the beginning of April, although still feeling his way before starting in the final match against Wimbledon.

Walsall (Free from Treze, Brazil, via loan spells at Beveren and Ajaccio, ex U.Espanola, Cordoba, Aleanza, Beveren, on 3/8/2002) FL 28+8/15 FLC 3/1 FAC 3
Derby Co (Free on 22/8/2003) FL 6+6/4

JUPP Duncan Alan
Born: Guildford, 25 January 1975
Height: 6'0" **Weight:** 12.12
International Honours: S: U21-9
Duncan joined Southend United during the summer of 2003 and enjoyed a steady season at Roots Hall. He quickly made the right-back berth his own, overcoming the injury problems that have hampered his career in recent seasons. His impressive raids on the right flank and an ability to deliver high quality crosses were instrumental in the Shrimpers showing improved form in the second half of the campaign. Duncan was rewarded for his sterling efforts with a new contract with the Blues.

Fulham (From trainee on 12/7/1993) FL 101+4/2 FLC 10+2 FAC 9+1/1 Others 9+1/2
Wimbledon (£125,000 + on 27/6/1996) P/FL 23+7 FLC 8+2 FAC 3+2
Notts Co (Free on 8/11/2002) FL 6+2 FAC 0+1
Luton T (Free on 28/2/2003) FL 2+3
Southend U (Free on 17/7/2003) FL 39+1 FLC 1 FAC 2 Others 5

K

KABBA Stephen (Steve)
Born: Lambeth, 7 March 1981
Height: 5'10" **Weight:** 11.12
The skilful and speedy striker had a good pre-season for Sheffield United, but tendonitis in his knee kept him out of competitive action until Christmas. Then 28 minutes into his return he broke his ankle following an innocuous challenge. On the brink of returning at the end of April he ruptured his achilles tendon in a reserve game and is likely to be out until around December 2004.
Crystal Palace (From trainee on 29/6/1999) FL 2+8/1 FLC 0+1
Luton T (Loaned on 28/3/2002) FL 0+3
Grimsby T (Loaned on 23/8/2002) FL 13/6 FLC 1
Sheffield U (£250,000 on 15/11/2002) FL 19+7/7 FAC 5/3 Others 1+2/1

KACHLOUL Hassan
Born: Agadir, Morocco, 19 February 1973
Height: 6'1" **Weight:** 11.12
International Honours: Morocco
Hassan had a disappointing time at Aston Villa last term, and the only hint of any first-team action came when he sat on the bench as an unused substitute in one match early on. The left-sided midfielder went out on loan to Wolves, but injuries restricted him to four outings as substitute. Yet he showed a lot of composure when helping steer Wolves to their first two wins of the season. He came on at half time as Wanderers trailed 3-0 to Leicester, and when he neatly let the ball through for Henri Camara to score, it gave Wolves a 4-3 win. In fact the games Hassan played in resulted in three wins and a draw.
Southampton (£250,000 from St Etienne, France, ex Nimes, Dunkerque, Metz, on 20/10/1998) PL 73+13/14 FLC 5 FAC 4+2/1
Aston Villa (Free on 1/7/2001) PL 17+5/2 FLC 2 Others 6+2
Wolverhampton W (Loaned on 1/9/2003) PL 0+4

KAMARA Malvin Ginah
Born: London, 17 November 1983
Height: 5'11" **Weight:** 13.7
After having been given a few tastes of first-team football last season, Malvin stepped up for regular action after the club's enforced mid-season sales and ended the campaign attracting the attention of several higher-level outfits. An enthusiastic right-sided midfielder who

can also play at full back when required, he went close to scoring on several occasions before finally breaking his duck at home to Sunderland. In a season of much disappointment for the club, his all-round energy and obvious ability were at least something positive to emerge from a generally gloom-laden campaign.
Wimbledon (From trainee on 17/7/2003) FL 15+14/2

KANOUTE Frederic (Fredi)
Born: Sainte Foy Les Lyon, France, 2 September 1977
Height: 6'4" **Weight:** 12.10
International Honours: Mali; France: B-1; U21
This towering striker made a terrific impact at Tottenham early on last term. Back at his very best, Fredi became a key figure in the team, showing the ability to score from outside the box, with his head and through penetrating deep in opponents defence. His great pace and power added urgency in attack and without him the team struggled for creativity up front. Fredi finished as second-top scorer with a total of 12 goals and represented Mali in the African Nations' Cup finals.

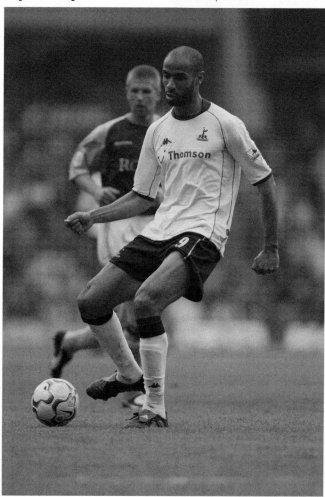

Fredi Kanoute

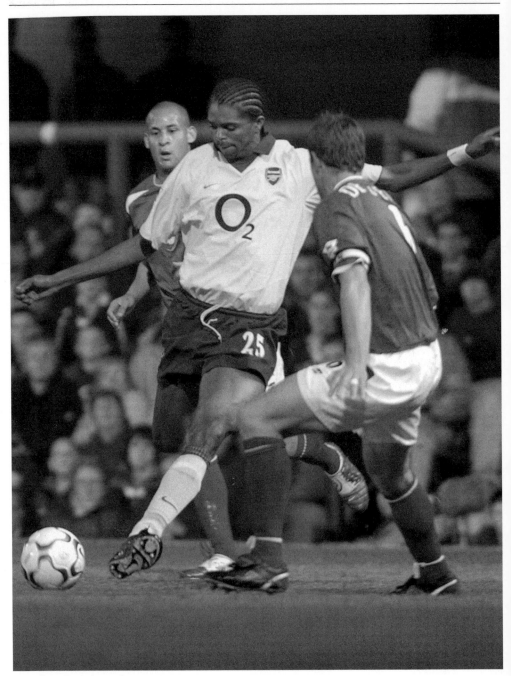

Nwankwo Kanu (centre)

West Ham U *(£4,000,000 from Lyon, France on 23/3/2000) PL 79+5/29 FLC 3 FAC 5/4* **Tottenham H** *(£3,500,000 + on 6/8/2003) PL 19+8/7 FLC 2+1/2 FAC 1/3*

KANU Christopher
Born: Owerri, Nigeria, 4 December 1979
Height: 5'8" **Weight:** 11.4
International Honours: Nigeria
Christopher joined Peterborough during the 2003 close season and featured regularly in the line-up in the first half of the campaign, either at full back or in a midfield role. However, he gradually faded from the scene and rarely featured in the squad after Christmas. Christopher is the younger brother of Arsenal's Nwankwo Kanu.
Peterborough U *(Free from TOP Oss, Holland on 12/8/2003) FL 16+5 FLC 1 FAC 2 Others 2+1*

KANU Nwankwo
Born: Owerri, Nigeria, 1 August 1976
Height: 6'4" **Weight:** 13.3
Club Honours: CS '99; FAC '02, '03; PL '02, '04
International Honours: Nigeria: Full; U23 (OLYM '96); Yth (World-U17 '93)
Nwankwo had another disappointing campaign with Arsenal last term and on his brief forays from the bench he seemed to struggle to make an impact. He provided just three goals all season and only one in the Premiership, in the 1-1 draw at Everton. He remains a player who undoubtedly possesses tremendous skill as he displayed in his first two seasons at the club, but was hotly tipped to be one of those to depart Highbury in the summer.
Arsenal *(£4,500,000 from Inter Milan, Italy, ex Fed Works, Iwuanyanwu National, Ajax, on 4/2/1999) PL 63+56/30 FLC 8/4 FAC 5+12/3 Others 28+26/7*

KAVANAGH Graham Anthony
Born: Dublin, 2 December 1973
Height: 5'10" **Weight:** 12.11
Club Honours: AMC '00
International Honours: RoI: 5; B-1; U21-9; Yth; Sch
Cardiff City's skipper was again in excellent form last term following the club's return to Division One, however, having been given his first start by the Republic of Ireland against Canada he was promptly injured. After several weeks out he recovered to take his place in the side once more, but eventually required surgery to his ankle and missed the closing stages of the campaign. Graham is a skilful midfielder who is

capable of scoring spectacular long-range goals.
Middlesbrough *(Signed from Home Farm on 16/8/1991) F/PL 22+13/3 FLC 1 FAC 2+2/1 Others 7*
Darlington *(Loaned on 25/2/1994) FL 5*
Stoke C *(£250,000 + on 13/9/1996) FL 198+8/35 FLC 16+2/7 FAC 6 Others 15/4*
Cardiff C *(£1,000,000 on 6/7/2001) FL 112+2/25 FLC 4 FAC 9/3 Others 5*

KAY Antony Roland
Born: Barnsley, 21 October 1982
Height: 5'11" **Weight:** 11.8
International Honours: E: Yth
After a number of seasons as a bit-part player Antony became a regular for Barnsley last term. His versatility saw him play in several outfield positions, although he was most comfortable in central defence or in the centre of midfield. Antony was voted 'Player of the Season' by the club's supporters and was offered a new contract by manager Paul Hart in the summer.
Barnsley *(From trainee on 25/10/1999) FL 55+12/3 FLC 1 FAC 5/1 Others 3*

KEANE Keith Francis
Born: Luton, 20 November 1986
Height: 5'9" **Weight:** 11.1
A young scholar with Luton Town, Keith was pressed into service in the LDV Vans Trophy game against Rushden last November. He continued his development in the Hatters' U19 team, before returning to enjoy a useful run in the first team in the closing stages of the campaign. A versatile youngster who can play either at full back or in midfield, he is strong and brave in the tackle. The highlight of his career to date came when he scored a last-minute spot in the 3-2 win over Bristol City in April.
Luton T *(Trainee) FL 14+1/1 FAC 0+1 Others 1*

KEANE Michael Thomas Joseph
Born: Dublin, 29 December 1982
Height: 5'7" **Weight:** 10.10
International Honours: RoI: U21-7; Yth
This young midfielder turned down a move to Grimsby over the summer to fight for his place at Preston, in which he was partially successful by starting just under half the club's games. Popular with the fans for his all-action, never-say-die attitude, he still has much to learn and faded from the first-team picture towards the end of the season. Michael was reported to have signed for Hull City during the summer.
Preston NE *(From trainee on 7/8/2000) FL 39+18/3 FLC 2+1 FAC 5*
Grimsby T *(Loaned on 27/3/2003) FL 7/2*

KEANE Robert (Robbie) David
Born: Dublin, 8 July 1980
Height: 5'9" **Weight:** 11.10
International Honours: RoI: 52; B-1; Yth; (UEFA-U18 '98)
A quick-thinking striker who loves to loiter deep in the opposition half ready to pick up play from midfield, Robbie struggled with injury initially last term, and then a slight goal drought struck before he finished the campaign in top form. He looked exciting playing alongside new arrival Jermain Defoe and also benefited from the height of Fredi Kanoute. Robbie continued to impress at international level for the Republic of Ireland and his country's chances of Euro 2004 qualification were blighted by his lack of availability due to injury.
Wolverhampton W *(From trainee on 26/7/1997) FL 66+7/24 FLC 7+2/3 FAC 3+2/2*
Coventry C *(£6,000,000 on 20/8/1999) PL 30+1/12 FAC 3 (£13,000,000 to Inter Milan, Italy on 31/7/1999)*
Leeds U *(£12,000,000 on 22/12/2000) PL 28+18/13 FLC 2/3 FAC 2 Others 6/3*
Tottenham H *(£7,000,000 on 31/8/2002) PL 60+3/27 FLC 5+1/1 FAC 4/1*

KEANE Roy Maurice
Born: Cork, 10 August 1971
Height: 5'10" **Weight:** 12.10
Club Honours: FMC '92; CS '93, '96, '97, '03; PL '94, '96, '97, '99, '00, '01, '03; FAC '94, '96, '99, '04
International Honours: RoI: 59; U21-4; Yth; Sch
An inspirational midfield general who possesses excellent skills with a hardened edge to match, Roy showed that not even the double signing of World Cup winner Kleberson, or Djemba Djemba was going to curtail his input to United's cause in 2004. Though Sir Alex Ferguson tried to rest him from certain games, Roy was quick to show his commitment was never in doubt. Still the biggest jewel in the United crown, he missed only one Premiership outing from August to December, and netted vital goals against Leicester, Leeds United and Portsmouth. Having been red carded in United's vital Champions' League game against Porto in February, he had to sit out a disappointing end to the European campaign. In April, Roy ended his enforced exile from the Republic of Ireland side, hoping for one last chance of glory on the international stage.
Nottingham F *(£10,000 from Cobh Ramblers on 12/6/1990) F/PL 114/22 FLC 17/6 FAC 18/3 Others 5/2*

Manchester U *(£3,750,000 on 22/7/1993)*
PL 277+13/32 FLC 11+2 FAC 40+2/1 Others
85+1/16

KEARNEY Thomas (Tom) James
Born: Liverpool, 7 October 1981
Height: 5'9" **Weight:** 11.0
After spending a year out of action following a cruciate ligament injury, Tom's return was greeted keenly by the Bradford faithful. However, the tenacious midfielder was a bit too eager to get back and it was not until November that he really established his place once again, beginning a run of ten starts in 11 games. The former Everton trainee is still looking to score his first senior goal.
Everton (From trainee on 15/10/1999)
Bradford C (Free on 21/3/2002) FL 22+4 FLC 1 FAC 1

KEATES Dean Scott
Born: Walsall, 30 June 1978
Height: 5'6" **Weight:** 10.10
Dean struggled to retain his place at Hull City last term and his hopes of a return to a regular starting place were thwarted by an ankle ligament injury in December. He then accepted an offer to rejoin his former boss Jan Molby at Kidderminster. However, after just a handful of games for the Harriers he picked up a knee injury in the game at Scunthorpe which required surgery and kept him out for the rest of the season. A tigerish midfield player, he opened his account for Kidderminster with a real screamer in the win over Northampton.
Walsall (From trainee on 14/8/1996) FL 125+34/9 FLC 15+1/1 FAC 10+4 Others 14+1/3
Hull C (Free on 23/8/2002) FL 45+5/4 FLC 1+1 Others 2
Kidderminster Hrs (Signed on 10/2/2004) FL 8/2

KEEGAN Paul Anthony
Born: Dublin, 5 July 1984
Height: 5'10" **Weight:** 11.7
International Honours: RoI: U21-5; Yth
This promising young Leeds United player made his bow for the Republic of Ireland at U21 level at the start of the 2003-04 campaign and in October he joined Third Division Scunthorpe United on loan to gain experience of senior football. Paul made two substitute appearances for the Iron, looking comfortable on the ball in a central-midfield role, before returning to Elland Road. He was a regular for the reserves during the rest of the season and featured as an unused substitute for the

Premiership game at Birmingham in March.
Leeds U (From trainee on 6/7/2001)
Scunthorpe U (Loaned on 21/10/2003) FL 0+2

KEEN Peter Alan
Born: Middlesbrough, 16 November 1976
Height: 6'0" **Weight:** 12.0
A good all-round goalkeeper, the form of Matty Glennon meant that Peter's first-team opportunities were limited at Carlisle last term. He managed a couple of appearances when deputising for Glennon and did all that was asked of him when the occasion required.
Newcastle U (From trainee on 25/3/1996)
Carlisle U (Free on 4/8/1999) FL 60+1/1 FAC 3+1 Others 1
Darlington (Loaned on 13/3/2001) FL 7

KEITH Joseph (Joe) Richard
Born: Plaistow, 1 October 1978
Height: 5'7" **Weight:** 10.6
Joe had a rather frustrating time at Colchester last term when he was often kept on the bench due to the presence of Rowan Vine. However, he bounced back in the new year, taking his chance by scoring both goals in the FA Cup replay win over Accrington Stanley in January. A left-footed player, Joe even reinvented himself as a right winger, and his moment of fame duly arrived when he scored the winner at Sheffield Wednesday with a deft chip from outside the box.
West Ham U (From trainee on 9/7/1997)
Colchester U (Free on 5/7/1999) FL 151+26/19 FLC 8+2 FAC 8+1/2 Others 8+2/1

KEITH Marino
Born: Peterhead, 16 December 1974
Height: 5'10" **Weight:** 12.11
Club Honours: SCC '98; Div 3 '02; Div 2 '04
This lively striker scored several important goals for Plymouth Argyle last season. Although he had some niggling injuries during the campaign, when he was fully fit and had a run of games under his belt he was a real handful for any centre half. Perhaps his most vital goal was the injury-time winner at Swindon to clinch victory after the home team had fought back from two goals down with ten minutes remaining.
Dundee U (Free from Fraserburgh on 11/10/1995) SL 0+4 SC 0+1
Falkirk (Free on 9/9/1997) SL 53+8/27 SLC 2/1 SC 7/1 Others 1+1
Livingston (Signed on 30/7/1999) SL 15+5/7 SLC 1+3 SC 2/3 Others 2

Plymouth Arg *(Free on 8/11/2001) FL 61+39/29 FLC 1 FAC 4+3 Others 3+1/2*

KELL Richard
Born: Bishop Auckland, 15 September 1979
Height: 6'1" **Weight:** 10.13
International Honours: E: Sch
Richard was released by Scunthorpe United in the summer of 2003, but the club gave him another chance to prove his fitness pre-season and he shone, forcing his way back into the centre of midfield where his passing and work rate added an extra dimension. By mid-October he had scored three goals but his chances of adding to that were ended when he had to have a groin operation in February.
Middlesbrough (From trainee on 2/7/1998)
Torquay U (Free on 8/2/2001) FL 15/3
Scunthorpe U (Free on 12/9/2001) FL 37+3/3 FLC 2 FAC 6+1 Others 5+2/1

KELLER Kasey C
Born: Olympia, Washington, USA, 27 November 1969
Height: 6'2" **Weight:** 13.12
Club Honours: FLC '97
International Honours: USA: 70
Kasey remained as Tottenham's first-choice goalkeeper throughout the 2003-04 season, comfortably seeing off the challenge of Neil Sullivan to become an ever-present in first-team fixtures during the campaign. Despite his relative seniority in years, Kasey is surprisingly agile and maintains an extraordinary level of fitness. He was busy during the campaign, a result of playing behind a rather leaky defence, and is likely to have more competition for his place next term if rumours of potential arrivals at White Hart Lane prove to be correct.
Millwall (Free from Portland University on 20/2/1992) FL 176 FLC 14 FAC 8 Others 4
Leicester C (£900,000 on 17/8/1996) PL 99 FLC 16 FAC 8 Others 2 (Signed for Rayo Vallecano, Spain during 1999 close season)
Tottenham H (Free on 16/8/2001) PL 85 FLC 8 FAC 4

KELLY Darren
Born: Derry, 30 June 1979
Height: 6'1" **Weight:** 12.10
Darrren was one of a number of Carlisle United players who were more prominent in the early part of last season. On his day a reliable and committed defender, he gave one of his best displays at Lincoln when he held together a back line weakened by injury to one central defender and the sending

off of another. Darren played little part in United's post-Christmas revival although he remains on the books for next term.
Carlisle U (£100,000 from Derry C on 21/8/2002) FL 39+3/2 FLC 1+1 FAC 2 Others 8

KELLY Garry
Born: Drogheda, 9 July 1974
Height: 5'8" **Weight:** 11.8
International Honours: RoI: 52; U21-5; Yth; Sch
When Danny Mills moved to Middlesbrough on a season-long loan, Gary started the 2003-04 campaign as first-choice right back for Leeds, and remained virtually ever present throughout. In a poor season his experience was needed more than ever, and he didn't disappoint. A full back of pace and ability he gave his all for the club, and was vital in helping the young players around him.
Leeds U (Signed from Home Farm on 24/9/1991) PL 316+11/2 FLC 23+2 FAC 28+1/1 Others 35+1

KELLY Marcus Philip
Born: Kettering, 16 March 1986
Height: 5'7" **Weight:** 10.0
One of several talented youngsters on the books at Rushden, Marcus enjoyed a successful season with the club's youth team last term and stepped up to make his senior debut against Bournemouth at the end of March. He then retained his place in the squad for the closing fixtures, producing some exciting performances down the flanks. Marcus received the Diamonds' 'Young Player of the Season' award for his efforts.
Rushden & Diamonds (From juniors on 27/11/2003) FL 4+4

KELLY Stephen Michael
Born: Dublin, 6 September 1983
Height: 5'11" **Weight:** 12.4
International Honours: RoI: U21-11; Yth
This promising Tottenham defender was loaned to Watford last September and played 13 matches before returning to White Hart Lane just before Christmas. A cultured right back and a sound defender, he seemed to gain confidence with every game and his attacking play in particular improved markedly. Stephen subsequently broke into the first-team squad and featured regularly in the starting line-up in the final run-in.
Tottenham H (From juniors on 11/9/2000) PL 7+4
Southend U (Loaned on 30/1/2003) FL 10

Queens Park R (Loaned on 27/3/2003) FL 7 Others 2
Watford (Loaned on 24/9/2003) FL 13

KELTIE Clark Stuart
Born: Newcastle, 31 August 1983
Height: 6'1" **Weight:** 12.7
Clark was a regular for Darlington during the first half of last season, but lost his place due to injury in December and struggled to regain it due to the good form of others. He showed greater

maturity in midfield, but although he possesses a fierce shot he managed just a single goal, netting in the home defeat by Cambridge in March.
Darlington (Free from Walker Central on 19/9/2001) FL 50+12/4 FLC 2 FAC 4 Others 1

KENNA Jeffrey (Jeff) Jude
Born: Dublin, 27 August 1970
Height: 5'11" **Weight:** 12.2
International Honours: RoI: 27; B-1; U21-8; Yth; Sch

Stephen Kelly

After starting the 2003-04 season for Birmingham City, Jeff was replaced at right back by Damien Johnson and then by Olivier Tebily, and he seemed to face a bleak future at St Andrews. He responded when he got another chance in December and played with great intelligence. Jeff's positional play and calmness helped the defence and he scored two vital goals, including the winner against Southampton in January. He also helped out at left back when Jamie Clapham was injured. Jeff had been a Derby target for several months before he was signed in March, immediately adding his Premiership and international experience to the side. His ability to perform in any defensive position was valuable in a team frequently disrupted by injuries and he was especially helpful to the club's younger players, assisting to calm them in an edgy relegation battle. He twisted an ankle in the Easter Monday victory over Bradford City but was back for the decisive win against Millwall.

Southampton (From trainee on 25/4/1989) F/PL 110+4/4 FLC 4 FAC 10+1 Others 3
Blackburn Rov (£1,500,000 on 15/3/1995) P/FL 153+2/1 FLC 17+2 FAC 13 Others 7
Tranmere Rov (Loaned on 20/3/2001) FL 11
Wigan Ath (Loaned on 2/11/2001) FL 6/1 FAC 1
Birmingham C (Free on 24/12/2001) P/FL 71+4/3 FLC 1 FAC 5 Others 3
Derby Co (Free on 11/3/2004) FL 9

KENNEDY Mark

Born: Dublin, 15 May 1976
Height: 5'11" **Weight:** 11.9
International Honours: RoI: 34; U21-7; Yth; Sch
This Wolves left winger started three of the first 11 Premiership games last term, but then struggled to make an impact. He scored a good goal at Villa, but did not really come into top form until the new year. Mark had an outstanding game away to his old club Manchester City, scoring with a first-time shot and having a free-kick lead to another Wolves goal. He produced a perfect centre for Carl Cort to score the winner over Everton. No wonder he was recalled to the Republic of Ireland squad at the end of the season.

Millwall (From trainee on 6/5/1992) FL 37+6/9 FLC 6+1/2 FAC 3+1/1
Liverpool (£1,500,000 on 21/3/1995) PL 5+11 FLC 0+2 FAC 0+1 Others 0+2
Queens Park R (Loaned on 27/1/1998) FL 8/2
Wimbledon (£1,750,000 on 27/3/1998) PL 11+10 FLC 4+1/1 FAC 2

Manchester C (£1,000,000 + on 15/7/1999) P/FL 56+10/8 FLC 5+4/3 FAC 2
Wolverhampton W (£1,800,000 on 6/7/2001) P/FL 93+4/10 FLC 2+1 FAC 8/1 Others 3+1/1

KENNEDY Peter Henry James

Born: Lurgan, 10 September 1973
Height: 5'9" **Weight:** 11.11
Club Honours: Div 2 '98, '03
International Honours: NI: 20; B-1
A versatile player, who can operate at both full back and in midfield, Peter had rather a difficult season with Wigan Athletic last term. Robust, solid and blessed as an excellent crosser and dangerous at free kicks, he was a regular in the left-back berth in the first couple of months but quickly faded from the scene. Out of favour at the club, he joined Derby County on loan where he was used at left back. He scored with a classic free kick against Ipswich on his first appearance at Pride Park and was skilful enough to give the Rams excellent value in his month at the club. Peter subsequently returned to Wigan before being released at the end of the season. He continued to be a regular for Northern Ireland during the campaign.

Notts Co (£100,000 from Portadown on 28/8/1996) FL 20+2 FLC 1 FAC 2+1/1 Others 0+1
Watford (£130,000 on 10/7/1997) P/FL 108+7/18 FLC 9/2 FAC 7/2 Others 3
Wigan Ath (£300,000 on 18/7/2001) FL 60+5/2 FLC 6 FAC 4 Others 3
Derby Co (Loaned on 31/10/2003) FL 5/1

KENNEDY Thomas (Tom) Gordon

Born: Bury, 24 June 1985
Height: 5'10" **Weight:** 11.1
One of the most pleasing aspects of Bury's 2003-04 season was the introduction and development of teenaged left wing back Tom Kennedy. He made his full debut in the LDV Vans Trophy tie against Oldham in November, then following a change in management he was given the chance to establish himself in the first team and he kept his place throughout the second half of the campaign. Tom is not afraid to push forward and take players on, while he is an excellent passer of the ball. He was voted 'Young Player of the Season' by the Bury supporters. He is the son of former Shakers full back Keith and nephew of former Liverpool and England defender Alan Kennedy.

Bury (From trainee on 2/11/2002) FL 22+5 Others 1

KENNY Patrick (Paddy) Joseph

Born: Halifax, 17 May 1978
Height: 6'1" **Weight:** 14.6
International Honours: RoI: 2
Paddy began the 2003-04 season in excellent form for Sheffield United, but a serious ankle injury sustained at Crystal Palace in August sidelined him until Christmas. Excellent as a shot-stopper and in one-on-one situations, he shows good command of his area and is quick and decisive in response to a through ball. He tied himself to the Blades on a long-term contract and was chosen for the Republic of Ireland squad in March, gaining his first cap as a late substitute against the Czech Republic.

Bury (£10,000 + from Bradford PA on 28/8/1998) FL 133 FLC 5 FAC 7 Others 5
Sheffield U (Signed on 26/7/2002) FL 72 FLC 8 FAC 8 Others 3

KENTON Darren Edward

Born: Wandsworth, 13 September 1978
Height: 5'10" **Weight:** 11.11
Brought over from Norwich City on a 'Bosman Free' during the close season, Darren had a long wait for an opportunity to play in the Premiership. Injury saw him sidelined at the beginning of the campaign, and by the time he had recovered he was behind Danny Higginbotham and Fitz Hall for a place in the central defenders' berths. When he was called upon it was within an injury-ravaged and distinctly inexperienced defence. Assured in the air, and combining superior acceleration with smart tackling skills he earned glowing reports – being universally designated as 'Man of the Match' in a decidedly experimental back three that conceded four goals at Chelsea in May.

Norwich C (From trainee on 3/7/1997) FL 142+16/9 FLC 9+1 FAC 2+2 Others 3
Southampton (Free on 19/5/2003) PL 3+4

KEOWN Martin Raymond

Born: Oxford, 24 July 1966
Height: 6'1" **Weight:** 12.4
Club Honours: PL '98, '02, '04; FAC '98, '02, '03; CS '98, '99, '02
International Honours: E: 43; B-1; U21-8; Yth
The elder statesman of the Arsenal side, Martin started only three Premiership games in total and ended the season making cameo appearances on the right wing in the dying moments of the club's remarkable unbeaten campaign. However, no one could begrudge Martin his seventh major club honour as he made a final appearance against Leicester. His

Harry Kewell

loyalty to the Gunners, which spans 447 games over two spells, was rewarded with a testimonial the following day against an England XI.
Arsenal *(From apprentice on 2/2/1984) FL 22 FAC 5*
Brighton & Hove A *(Loaned on 15/2/1985) FL 21+2/1 FLC 2/1 Others 2/1*
Aston Villa *(£200,000 on 9/6/1986) FL 109+3/3 FLC 12+1 FAC 6 Others 2*
Everton *(£750,000 on 7/8/1989) F/PL 92+4 FLC 11 FAC 12+1 Others 6*
Arsenal *(£2,000,000 on 4/2/1993) PL 282+28/4 FLC 21+2/1 FAC 32+3 Others 46+8/3*

KERR Brian
Born: Motherwell, 12 October 1981
Height: 5'8" **Weight:** 11.2
International Honours: S: 3; B-2; U21-14; Yth; Sch
This Newcastle reserve midfielder spent most of last term out on loan. He was a regular for SPL side Livingston in the early part of the campaign, only to suffer a broken right leg towards the end of November. Once fit again he spent the last six weeks of the season on loan at Coventry. He performed solidly in central midfield but then lost his place when Youssef Safri returned from injury. Brian continued to represent Scotland at international level but was released by Newcastle in the summer.
Newcastle U *(From trainee on 4/12/1998) PL 4+5 FAC 0+2 Others 1+1*
Coventry C *(Loaned on 24/10/2002) FL 2+1 FLC 1*
Livingston *(Loaned on 8/8/2003) SL 11+2 SLC 2*
Coventry C *(Loaned on 17/3/2004) FL 5+4*

KEWELL Harold (Harry)
Born: Sydney, Australia, 22 September 1978
Height: 6'0" **Weight:** 11.10
Club Honours: FAYC '97
International Honours: Australia: 15; Yth
The signing of this mercurial striker in the summer of 2003 was assumed by many to be the missing piece of the jigsaw as Gerald Houllier sought to assemble a Liverpool team capable of mounting a serious challenge for the Premiership. However, despite an excellent start to his Anfield career, Harry's own form dipped as the season progressed. By the end of November he had notched up eight goals, most of them excellent angled drives from the left side of the box, but he subsequently netted only three more, and none at all after February. This may have

been due in part to his constantly changing roles. Although predominantly deployed on the left side of midfield, he sometimes played as a striker or, in his preferred position just behind the front men.
Leeds U *(Signed from the Australian Academy of Sport on 23/12/1995) PL 169+12/45 FLC 8/4 FAC 16/6 Others 34+3/8*
Liverpool *(£5,000,000 on 9/7/2003) PL 36/7 FLC 0+2/1 FAC 3 Others 8/3*

KIELY Dean Laurence
Born: Salford, 10 October 1970
Height: 6'1" **Weight:** 13.5
Club Honours: Div 2 '97; Div 1 '00
International Honours: RoI: 8; B-1; E: Yth; Sch
Once again Dean had a brilliant season in the Charlton goal, keeping a total of ten clean sheets. He missed the opening game through suspension, but played in every other match. Dean is an excellent shot-stopper who is very comfortable at dealing with crosses, and commands his area well. He made some outstanding saves during the campaign, playing particularly well in the away game at Birmingham in November. His performances earned him the supporters' 'Player of the Year' award for the second time in three years.
Coventry C *(From trainee on 30/10/1987)*
York C *(Signed on 9/3/1990) FL 210 FLC 9 FAC 4 Others 17*
Bury *(£125,000 on 15/8/1996) FL 137 FLC 13 FAC 4 Others 3*
Charlton Ath *(£1,000,000 on 26/5/1999) P/FL 183 FLC 9 FAC 11*

KIGHTLY Michael John
Born: Basildon, 24 January 1986
Height: 5'9" **Weight:** 9.12
This exciting youngster burst onto the scene at Southend during the middle part of the 2003-04 campaign and netted his first senior goal in the 3-0 defeat of Luton Town in the LDV Vans Trophy. He thrilled the Roots Hall faithful with a string of dazzling performances characterised by scintillating speed and skilful dribbling. Southend boss Steve Tilson wisely limited his appearances towards the season's end to avoid burn out. Michael will be looking to see more regular first-team action during 2004-05.
Southend U *(From trainee on 12/12/2003) FL 2+10 FAC 1+2 Others 2+1/1*

KILBANE Kevin Daniel
Born: Preston, 1 February 1977
Height: 6'0" **Weight:** 12.10
International Honours: RoI: 53; U21-11

This tall, skilful left winger played in Sunderland's first six games of the season before joining Everton in September. A few eyebrows were raised with the transfer deadline deal that brought Kevin to Goodison Park. However, the Republic of Ireland international was one of the major plus points of the club's season, being a consistent and spirited performer down the left flank, where he showed fine dribbling skills and accurate crossing ability. The winger also scored four goals and his heading ability was always a threat from set pieces. He missed only one Premiership game in his first seven months in the team and it was only at the tail-end that his form began to dip, when he was handicapped by hamstring and ankle injuries, which necessitated him sitting out the last few games.
Preston NE *(From trainee on 6/7/1995) FL 39+8/3 FLC 4 FAC 1 Others 1+1*
West Bromwich A *(£1,000,000 on 13/6/1997) FL 105+1/15 FLC 12/2 FAC 4/1*
Sunderland *(£2,500,000 on 16/12/1999) P/FL 102+11/8 FLC 4 FAC 3+4/1*
Everton *(£750,000 on 2/9/2003) PL 26+4/3 FAC 3/1*

KILFORD Ian Anthony
Born: Bristol, 6 October 1973
Height: 5'10" **Weight:** 11.0
Club Honours: Div 3 '97; AMC '99
Ian started the 2003-04 season as first choice in the centre of the Scunthorpe United midfield where his composed play and passing ability helped a young team. But the season turned sour for him in September when he was laid low for five weeks by a mystery virus and then struggled to get over it in the following months. Other minor injuries followed and he didn't manage to start two consecutive league matches during the closing six months of the campaign.
Nottingham F *(From trainee on 3/4/1991) FL 0+1*
Wigan Ath *(Loaned on 23/12/1993) FL 7+1/3 FAC 0+1*
Wigan Ath *(Free on 13/7/1994) FL 170+4/29 FLC 14+3/1 FAC 14+2/2 Others 15+2/2*
Bury *(Free on 16/8/2002)*
Scunthorpe U *(Free on 8/11/2002) FL 38+8/3 FLC 1 FAC 5+2 Others 4*

KILGALLON Matthew Shaun
Born: York, 8 January 1984
Height: 6'1" **Weight:** 12.5
International Honours: E: U21-1; Yth
A tall central defender, who is quick in the tackle and assured on the ball, Matthew spent three months on loan at

West Ham at the beginning of last season. He produced some impressive performances and was in particularly good form during the Carling Cup game against Tottenham. He returned to Elland Road and made his Premiership debut against Aston Villa on Boxing Day, then had a short run in the side, scoring his first senior goal at Southampton in January.

Leeds U (From trainee on 10/1/2001) PL 7+3/2 FAC 1 Others 0+1

West Ham U (Loaned on 23/8/2003) FL 1+2 FLC 1

KILLEN Christopher (Chris) John

Born: Wellington, New Zealand, 8 October 1981
Height: 5'11" **Weight:** 11.3
International Honours: New Zealand
Chris endured another frustrating season at Oldham last term when his campaign was again affected by injuries. Firstly a hamstring problem ruled him out then a broken foot bone and further hamstring trouble kept him on the sidelines. The talented young striker continued to represent New Zealand at international level when fit.

Manchester C (Free from Miramar Rangers, New Zealand on 8/3/1999) FL 0+3

Wrexham (Loaned on 8/9/2000) FL 11+1/3

Port Vale (Loaned on 24/9/2001) FL 8+1/6 Others 1

Oldham Ath (£200,000 + on 31/7/2002) FL 18+22/5 FLC 2+1/1 FAC 1+2 Others 1

KILLOUGHERY Graham Anthony

Born: London, 22 July 1984
Height: 5'10" **Weight:** 11.7
This promising left-sided midfielder graduated to the professional ranks at Torquay last term. However, Graham managed just four appearances from the substitutes' bench and at the end of October his contract was cancelled by mutual consent.

Torquay U (From trainee on 2/7/2003) FL 1+5 Others 0+1

KING Ledley Brenton

Born: Stepney, 12 October 1980
Height: 6'2" **Weight:** 13.6
International Honours: E: 7; U21-12; Yth
This extremely talented central defender impressed at Tottenham last term, showing that he could more than adequately fill the boots of the departed Sol Campbell. Great in the air, Ledley is extremely agile for one so tall, and he enjoys getting forward where his height

and ability to create space around him provide a real threat. He made his full debut for England against Portugal in February, marking the occasion with a goal, and then made the squad for the Euro 2004 finals in the summer.

Tottenham H (From trainee on 22/7/1998) PL 105+3/2 FLC 10/1 FAC 11+1/2

KING Marlon Francis

Born: Dulwich, 26 April 1980
Height: 6'1" **Weight:** 11.12
International Honours: Jamaica: 5
This exciting striker started the 2003-04 campaign with Gillingham and impressed with his pace, skill ability with free kicks. However, in November he joined Nottingham Forest as a replacement for the departed Marlon Harewood. Unfortunately Marlon struggled at the outset along with the rest of the team, but after waiting seven games for his first goal he scored a penalty in the FA Cup tie against West Bromwich Albion. He continued to frustrate but had an upsurge in form towards the season's close as he seemed to come to grips with the Forest style of play. He was rewarded for his efforts by scoring on his debut for Jamaica against Venezula in April, then contributing a hat trick in the World Cup qualifier against Haiti in June.

Barnet (From trainee on 9/9/1998) FL 36+17/14 FLC 0+2 FAC 0+1 Others 2+2

Gillingham (£255,000 on 28/6/2000) FL 82+19/40 FLC 6+3/4 FAC 5+1/3

Nottingham F (£950,000 on 27/11/2003) FL 23+1/5 FAC 2/1

KINSELLA Mark Anthony

Born: Dublin, 12 August 1972
Height: 5'9" **Weight:** 11.8
Club Honours: GMVC '92; FAT '92; Div 1 '00
International Honours: RoI: 48; B-1; U21-8; Yth
This consistent right-sided midfielder struggled to gain a regular place in the Aston Villa side during the first half of the season and was mostly on the substitutes' bench. He moved on to neighbours West Bromwich Albion at the turn of the year, adding some steel to the Baggies' engine-room. Mark produced some solid performances as Gary Megson's side regained their Premiership status, while also adding to his total of full caps for the Republic of Ireland. Mark was released by the club in May.

Colchester U (Free from Home Farm on 18/8/1989) FL 174+6/27 FLC 11+1/3 FAC 9/2 Others 12+2/5

Charlton Ath (£150,000 on 23/9/1996) P/FL 200+8/19 FLC 4+2 FAC 8+1/3 Others 3

Aston Villa (£750,000 on 23/8/2002) PL 17+4 FLC 2+2 FAC 1

West Bromwich A (Free on 15/1/2004) FL 15+3/1

KIRKLAND Christopher (Chris)

Born: Leicester, 2 May 1981
Height: 6'6" **Weight:** 11.7
Club Honours: FLC '03
International Honours: E: U21-8; Yth
Kris was again unfortunate with injuries last term. The talented 'keeper started out playing second fiddle to Jerzy Dudek but replaced his rival in November. However, after a short run in the side he suffered a broken finger in the Boxing Day clash with Bolton. Chris returned to first-team duty in February to play five games before sustaining a wrist injury in training and this sidelined him for the remainder of the season. In February he was selected for the England squad for the first time in the friendly match with Portugal as a substitute but was not used.

Coventry C (From trainee on 6/5/1998) P/FL 24 FLC 3+1 FAC 1

Liverpool (£6,000,000 + on 31/8/2001) PL 15 FLC 6 FAC 3 Others 7

KIROVSKI Jovan

Born: Escondido, California, USA, 18 March 1976
Height: 6'1" **Weight:** 12.4
International Honours: USA: 62
This midfielder played a bit-part role for Birmingham City last season, coming off the bench for fleeting appearances. Jovan was versatile, often going up front or playing anywhere in the centre of the park. He was eventually released from his contract in March and signed for MLS club Los Angeles Galaxy.

Crystal Palace (£350,000 from Sporting Lisbon, Portugal, ex San Diego Nomads, Borussia Dortmund, on 9/8/2001) FL 25+11/5 FLC 2 FAC 1

Birmingham C (Free on 15/8/2002) PL 5+18/2 FLC 1+2 FAC 1+1

KISHISHEV Radostin Prodanov

Born: Bulgaria, 30 July 1974
Height: 5'10" **Weight:** 12.4
International Honours: Bulgaria: 50
Radostin probably had his best-ever season playing for Charlton, featuring at right back and on the right side of midfield. The skilful and versatile player is a strong tackler who is very comfortable on the ball and is not afraid to try something unexpected such as a 40-yard pass to switch the play. He also likes to get forward and has a powerful shot.

Radostin performed very well at right back when deputising for the injured Luke Young for almost half the campaign, but looked more at ease when playing in midfield as he had more room to express himself.
Charlton Ath (£300,000 + from Liteks Lovech, Bulgaria, ex Neftokhimik Burgas, Bursapor, on 14/8/2000) PL 82+15/2 FLC 3 FAC 5+1

KITAMIRIKE Joel Derick
Born: Kampala, Uganda, 5 April 1984
Height: 5'10" **Weight:** 13.1
International Honours: E: Yth
This young Chelsea central defender joined Brentford on loan last September and eventually stayed the whole season. Joel showed a great deal of composure

on the ball and passed well, but his lack of inches sometimes saw him beaten in the air. A regular in the side until the beginning of March, he was then left out of the team for the closing stages.
Chelsea (From trainee on 6/4/2001) Others 1
Brentford (Loaned on 19/9/2003) FL 21+1 FAC 1 Others 2

KITSON David (Dave) Barry
Born: Hitchin, 21 January 1980
Height: 6'3" **Weight:** 12.11
This prolific striker carried on where he had left off the previous season at Cambridge, regularly hitting the back of the net, and by mid-November he had eleven goals. However, in January he was sold to Reading where he proved to be an astute signing by incoming manager Steve

Copell. Although Dave took a while to achieve full fitness, and his first seven appearances were as a substitute, he soon became a first-choice in the line-up, partnering either Shaun Goater or Lloyd Owusu. The goals began to accumulate too, none more spectacular than the overhead strike at Bradford City, although he will be best remembered for the double he netted in the 2-0 home win over West Ham. Raw and uncomplicated he may be at present, but as a tough forward who also does his share of defending, he has considerable potential.
Cambridge U (Signed from Arlesey T on 16/3/2001) FL 97+5/40 FLC 4/1 FAC 9/2 Others 7+1/4
Reading (£150,000 on 30/12/2003) FL 10+7/5

Dave Kitson (left)

KITSON Paul

Born: Murton, 9 January 1971
Height: 5'11" **Weight:** 10.12
International Honours: E: U21-7
Paul initially arrived at Rushden on trial at the start of last season and signed on a non-contract basis until switching to monthly deals. His first goal for Diamonds was the midweek winner at Blackpool at the end of October. A few days later he struck twice against Wrexham at Nene Park and the much-travelled striker also found the target past local rivals Peterborough United and Luton Town. However, he was released in the wake of the club's relegation at the end of the campaign.
Leicester C (From trainee on 15/12/1988) FL 39+11/6 FLC 5/3 FAC 1+1/1 Others 5/1
Derby Co (£1,300,000 on 11/3/1992) FL 105/36 FLC 7/3 FAC 5/1 Others 13+1/9
Newcastle U (£2,250,000 on 24/9/1994) FL 26+10/10 FLC 3+2/1 FAC 6+1/3 Others 0+1
West Ham U (£2,300,000 on 10/2/1997) PL 46+17/18 FLC 2+3/1 FAC 4+1/1 Others 3+5/2
Charlton Ath (Loaned on 21/3/2000) FL 2+4/1
Crystal Palace (Loaned on 14/9/2000) FL 4
Brighton & Hove A (Free on 20/8/2002) FL 7+3/2
Rushden & Diamonds (Free on 26/9/2003) FL 18+10/5 Others 2

[KLEBERSON] PEREIRA KLEBERSON Jose

Born: Urai, Brazil, 19 June 1979
Height: 5'9" **Weight:** 10.5
International Honours: Brazil: 21
This Brazilian midfielder joined Manchester United from Atletico Paranense, but only made sparse appearances for the Reds, particularly as United motored along in all the major competitions with more seasoned campaigners. On the few opportunities he had to shine, he opened his goal-scoring account on his third outing with a strike against Blackburn Rovers in November, and netted against Everton in the 3-2 win at Goodison in December. With even fewer first-team opportunities coming from January to May, Kleberson became something of a fringe team player, with his long-term future being debated in the media.
Manchester U (£5,930,000 from Atletico Paranense, Brazil, ex PSTC-Lodrina, on 13/8/2003) PL 10+2/2 FLC 1 FAC 1 Others 1+1

KNIGHT Leon Leroy

Born: Hackney, 16 September 1982
Height: 5'4" **Weight:** 9.10

International Honours: E: Yth
Signed on loan from Chelsea, Leon made an instant impression at Brighton, scoring four times early on last term. His brace against Queens Park Rangers prompted the London side to make an immediate bid for him, but Albion secured his services permanently and he went on to score 27 times over the course of the season. A sharp finisher with the ability to turn any opponent, Leon scored a number of memorable goals, but his expertly-taken penalty to secure victory over Bristol City in the play-off final at the Millennium Stadium will linger long in the memory of Albion fans. Leon was also selected for the PFA's Division Two team of the season.
Chelsea (From trainee on 17/9/1999) Others 0+1
Queens Park R (Loaned on 9/3/2001) FL 10+1
Huddersfield T (Loaned on 23/10/2001) FL 31/16 FAC 2/1 Others 4
Sheffield Wed (Loaned on 8/7/2002) FL 14+10/3 FLC 2 FAC 0+1
Brighton & Hove A (£100,000 on 24/7/2003) FL 43+1/25 FLC 2 FAC 1 Others 6/2

KNIGHT Zatyiah (Zat)

Born: Solihull, 2 May 1980
Height: 6'6" **Weight:** 13.8
International Honours: E: U21-4
Zat established himself as one of the first-choice central defenders in the Fulham side last season. An excellent reader of the game, he uses his height well and is calm when in possession of the ball on the ground. Zat enjoys coming forward and likes to try his luck from distance. Although he has yet to score he produced a memorable moment in the FA Cup tie at Old Trafford when he surged forward to strike the crossbar from fully 35 yards.
Fulham (Signed from Rushall Olympic on 19/2/1999) PL 50+8 FLC 6 FAC 8+2 Others 3+2
Peterborough U (Loaned on 25/2/2000) FL 8

KONCHESKY Paul Martyn

Born: Barking, 15 May 1981
Height: 5'10" **Weight:** 10.12
International Honours: E: 1; U21-15; Yth
On Charlton's transfer list at his own request, mainly because he wanted to play regularly at left back, Paul played in Charlton's opening fixture against Manchester City at the Valley and then moved to Tottenham on loan, where he stayed until the end of the year. Ironically he was used on the left-hand side of

midfield at White Hart Lane, before returning to the Valley where he was a regular in the Addicks' line-up for the remainder of the season. Paul is quick, as well as being a strong tackler and can play at left back, in central defence or on the left side of midfield. He looks comfortable in the midfield role, despite his reluctance to play there, and some think his long-term future may lie in this position. He has a powerful shot and is a dead-ball specialist.
Charlton Ath (From trainee on 25/5/1998) P/FL 76+45/4 FLC 5+4/1 FAC 7+1
Tottenham H (Loaned on 1/9/2003) PL 10+2 FLC 2+1

KONJIC Muhamed (Mo)

Born: Bosnia, 14 May 1970
Height: 6'4" **Weight:** 13.7
International Honours: Bosnia-Herzegovina: 38
Mo continued to endear himself to the Coventry fans last term with his strong physical presence and mazy dribbles upfield. He never gave less than 100 per cent, but the form of Steve Staunton and Calum Davenport meant he had to sit out several games. His wonderful glancing header against Burnley at home was amazingly his first goal for two years and he followed it up with a thunderous header in the final game against Crystal Palace. Mo was surprisingly allowed to join Derby at the end of the season.
Coventry C (£2,000,000 from AS Monaco, France, ex Slobada Tuzla, Croatia Belisce, Croatia Zagreb, FC Zurich, on 5/2/1999) P/FL 130+8/4 FLC 9+1 FAC 7

KOUMANTARAKIS George

Born: Athens, Greece, 27 March 1974
Height: 6'4" **Weight:** 13.3
International Honours: South Africa: 12
Big George signed a one-year deal with Preston following his loan in 2002-03, but he was injured when the season started and was not seen in first-team action until January. Controversially called up by South Africa for the African Nations' Cup despite not playing for nine months, he was sent back after the coach was suspended. His first Preston appearance for ten months was as a substitute at West Ham, and he scored in his first start at Reading in the FA Cup replay. The tall striker's strengths lie, not surprisingly, in the aerial aspects of the game and he made a total of nine appearances, scoring twice.
Preston NE (Signed from Basle, Switzerland, ex Manning R, Supersport U, Lucerne, on 23/1/2003) FL 11+6/4 FAC 2/1

Mo Konjic

KOUMAS Jason
Born: Wrexham, 25 September 1979
Height: 5'10" **Weight:** 11.0
International Honours: W: 9
For most of the season West Bromwich Albion's Welsh international midfielder played superbly well, but occasionally he performed below par and this resulted in him being relegated to the substitutes' bench. Nevertheless, on his day he was a class act and produced the goods when it mattered most. Blessed with excellent close control and dribbling skills, besides creating chances aplenty for his colleagues, he scored some wonderful and vital goals himself including Albion's first in the League at Walsall, two extra-specials in the 3-0 victory at Nottingham Forest and the late clincher in the promotion clash at Sunderland. Jason was selected for the PFA Division One team of the season.
Tranmere Rov (From trainee on 27/11/1997) FL 96+31/25 FLC 9+5/2 FAC 9/5
West Bromwich A (£2,500,000 on 29/8/2002) P/FL 64+10/14 FLC 4 FAC 3

KOZLUK Robert (Rob)
Born: Mansfield, 5 August 1977
Height: 5'8" **Weight:** 11.7
International Honours: E: U21-2
After signing a new contract, Rob had a very good season for Sheffield United in 2003-04, being consistent and reliable throughout. He played either as a right or left wing back, using his pace and anticipation to good effect in defence and being effective coming forward, making improved use of the final ball. He used his long throw to good effect and although his long-range shooting could be better, he managed a goal at Stoke.
Derby Co (From trainee on 10/2/1996) PL 9+7 FLC 3 FAC 2+1
Sheffield U (Signed on 12/3/1999) FL 146+12/2 FLC 6+1 FAC 10 Others 3
Huddersfield T (Loaned on 7/9/2000) FL 14

KUIPERS Michel
Born: Amsterdam, Holland, 26 June 1974
Height: 6'2" **Weight:** 14.10
Club Honours: Div 3 '01; Div 2 '02
Although he lost his place as number one goalkeeper for Brighton last term, Michel could so easily have lost considerably more in a serious car accident that kept him out of contention for two months. A knee injury then sidelined him for another seven weeks. Ironically he had begun the season on loan at Hull after recovering from another injury suffered during the previous campaign. He impressed the

Jason Koumas

Tigers' faithful with some superb performances and then enjoyed a brief run in the Albion line-up in the autumn.
Bristol Rov *(Free from SDW Amsterdam, Holland on 20/1/1999) FL 1*
Brighton & Hove A *(Free on 4/7/2000) FL 103+1 FLC 3 FAC 6 Others 6*
Hull C *(Loaned on 29/8/2003) FL 3*

KUQI Shefki
Born: Albania, 10 November 1976
Height: 6'2" **Weight:** 13.10
International Honours: Finland: 34
This big striker began last term with Sheffield Wednesday, but in September he joined Ipswich in a three-month loan deal and this was later converted into a permanent contract. His non-stop running and commitment immediately endeared him to the Portman Road faithful. The fans didn't have to wait long for his first goal as he scored with only his second touch after coming on as a substitute at Watford. Shefki held his place in the side for much of the season but lost out in the last month when Joe Royle gave his young strikers a chance to show what they could do.
Stockport Co *(£300,000 from FC Jokerit, Finland, ex HJK Helsinki, on 31/1/2001) FL 32+3/11 FLC 2/1 FAC 1*
Sheffield Wed *(£700,000 + on 11/1/2002) FL 58+6/19 FLC 3 FAC 1*
Ipswich T *(Free on 26/9/2003) FL 29+7/11 FAC 1+1/1 Others 1+1*

KYLE Kevin Alistair
Born: Stranraer, 7 June 1981
Height: 6'3" **Weight:** 13.7
International Honours: S: 8; B-3; U21-12
This tall centre forward firmly established himself at Sunderland last term scoring 16 goals, including one in each leg of the club's unsuccessful play-off campaign. His combative style made him a difficult opponent for many First Division defences, while his deft flicks set up numerous chances for his colleagues. and he generally terrorised First Division defences with his combative style. An old-fashioned style centre forward, he will be looking to lead the Black Cats to promotion in 2004-05.
Sunderland *(Free from Ayr Boswell on 25/9/1998) P/FL 45+25/10 FLC 3+2/4 FAC 7+2/1 Others 2/2*
Huddersfield T *(Loaned on 8/9/2000) FL 0+4*
Darlington *(Loaned on 1/11/2000) FL 5/1 FAC 3/1*
Rochdale *(Loaned on 26/1/2001) FL 3+3*

Shefki Kuqi

L

LABARTHE TOME Alberto Gianfranco

Born: Lima, Peru, 20 September 1984
Height: 5'10" **Weight:** 10.7
International Honours: Peru: Yth
The young Peruvian forward was described as one for the future by Derby County manager George Burley, although he began the season in the senior squad. He has skill and good control, becoming a steady scorer in the reserves.
Huddersfield T (Free from Sport Boys, Peru, ex Cantolao, on 30/1/2003) FL 0+3
Derby Co (Free on 5/8/2003) FL 0+3 FLC 1

LAMBERT Rickie Lee

Born: Liverpool, 16 February 1982
Height: 5'10" **Weight:** 11.2
Rickie enjoyed a fantastic season with Stockport in 2003-04 and deservedly picked up the club's 'Player of the Year' award at the end of the campaign. His first goal didn't arrive until mid-September when he unleashed a superb long-range free kick straight into the top corner against Blackpool, but 12 more followed throughout the campaign. His winner in the home game over Sheffield Wednesday came close to picking up the 'Goal of the Season' award, while his late penalty against Rushden in April secured three points which effectively staved off the threat of relegation.
Blackpool (From trainee on 17/7/2000) FL 0+3
Macclesfield T (Free on 2/3/2001) FL 36+8/8 FAC 4/2 Others 1
Stockport Co (£300,000 on 30/4/2003) FL 61+8/14 FLC 3 FAC 1 Others 4/1

LAMPARD Frank James

Born: Romford, 20 June 1978
Height: 6'0" **Weight:** 12.6
International Honours: E: 23; B-1; U21-19; Yth
One of the most improved players in English football is Chelsea and England midfielder Frank Lampard who had a magnificent 2003-04 season. Even with the Abramovich millions pouring into Chelsea and the squad enlarging accordingly, Frank still figured in 58 of the 59 first-team fixtures – a sign of the high esteem in which he was held by Claudio Ranieri for whom 'rotation' is a byword! Frank made a sensational start to the season, being voted Barclaycard Player of the Month for September and passing 100 consecutive Premiership matches in

the process. The acquisition of Claude Makelele allowed Frank greater freedom to move further forward to support the front players and his total of 15 goals was remarkable for a midfield player. He bagged doubles against Blackburn and Southampton, plus crucial Champions' League goals against Arsenal and the one against Monaco which gave Chelsea the required 2-0 score line and fleetingly gave the club a glimpse of the final. Frank received the accolade of his peers of being voted second in the PFA 'Player of the Year' poll, and was also selected for the PFA Premiership team of the season.
West Ham U (From trainee on 1/7/1995) PL 132+16/23 FLC 15+1/9 FAC 13/2 Others 10/4
Swansea C (Loaned on 6/10/1995) FL 8+1/1 Others 1+1
Chelsea (£11,000,000 on 3/7/2001) PL 109+4/21 FLC 8+1 FAC 16+1/3 Others 18+2/6

LANGLEY Richard Barrington Michael

Born: Harlesden, 27 December 1979
Height: 5'10" **Weight:** 11.4
International Honours: Jamaica: 17; E: Yth
This talented central midfield player made two appearances for Queens Park Rangers at the start of the 2003-04 season, scoring on both occasions, before moving on to join Cardiff City, the team that had defeated Rangers in the previous campaign's Second Division play-off final. He took time to settle at Ninian Park, but showed flashes of real ability and the club have high hopes for him for 2004-05. Richard added a number of caps for Jamaica during the season.
Queens Park R (From trainee on 31/12/1996) FL 123+10/18 FLC 6/2 FAC 7 Others 2/1
Cardiff C (£250,000 on 15/8/2003) FL 39+5/6 FAC 1

LANGMEAD Kelvin Steven

Born: Coventry, 23 March 1985
Height: 6'1" **Weight:** 13.6
Kelvin was a regular scorer for Preston's U19 and reserve teams last term and also enjoyed spells out on loan with Tamworth and Carlisle. Although mainly used as a substitute during his time at Brunton Park, the young striker scored his first senior goal when he netted the winner in the 3-2 victory at Mansfield in April. Kelvin received North End's 'Star of the Future' award for the club's most promising youngster at the end of the season.
Preston NE (From trainee on 26/2/2004)
Carlisle U (Loaned on 27/2/2004) FL 3+8/1

LARKIN Colin

Born: Dundalk, Ireland, 27 April 1982
Height: 5'9" **Weight:** 10.4
International Honours: RoI: Yth
Colin was again troubled by injuries in the early stages of last season when he was in and out of the Mansfield Town line-up. A central striker who can also operate on the right wing, he possesses a useful turn of pace. Colin opened his scoring account with a brace against Cheltenham at Field Mill in October and began to look much sharper towards the end of the season, knocking in some useful goals during the run-in.
Wolverhampton W (From trainee on 19/5/1999) FL 1+2 FLC 0+1/1
Kidderminster Hrs (Loaned on 14/9/2001) FL 31+2/6 Others 1+1/1
Mansfield T (£135,000 on 9/8/2002) FL 32+27/14 FAC 3+1/1 Others 2+3

LARRIEU Romain

Born: Mont-de-Marsan, France, 31 August 1976
Height: 6'4" **Weight:** 13.11
Club Honours: Div 3 '02
This popular Plymouth Argyle 'keeper missed virtually the whole of the 2003-04 season after suffering a serious knee injury in the match against Brentford in September. Romain eventually returned to the first-team squad in April, but by then Luke McCormick had established himself in the side and he was restricted to a place on the substitutes' bench.
Plymouth Arg (Free from ASOA Valence, France, ex Montpellier, on 30/11/2000) FL 108+1 FLC 3 FAC 8 Others 3

[LAUREN] BISAN-ETAME MAYER Laureano

Born: Lodhji Krib, Cameroon, 19 January 1977
Height: 5'11" **Weight:** 11.4
Club Honours: FAC '02, '03; PL '02, '04; CS '02
International Honours: Cameroon (ANC '00, '02; OLYM '00)
Last term proved to be the most consistent season yet for the midfielder who was converted to a right back by Arsene Wenger. Always willing to bring the ball forward in attack he played his full part in a back four that conceded just 26 goals in the club's history-making season. Lauren started the season in less than auspicious circumstances, scoring an own goal at the City of Manchester Stadium, but he went on to display such fine form that he saw off the challenge of Moritz Volz. Lauren was one of several

Colin Larkin (left)

Arsenal players to make the PFA Premiership team of the season.
Arsenal (£7,200,000 from Real Mallorca, Spain, ex Cant Sevilla, Utrera, Seville, Levante, on 16/6/2000) PL 98+6/5 FLC 1 FAC 18/2 Others 36+6/1

LAVILLE Florent

Born: Valence, France, 7 August 1973
Height: 6'0" **Weight:** 13.0
Last season was expected to be one of greatness for Florent. After impressing so much during his loan spell in the 2002-03 campaign, Florent delighted Bolton fans by agreeing a contract in the close season. He began at the heart of the defence but disaster struck in just the fifth game, at home to Middlesbrough, when he suffered a ruptured cruciate ligament. The injury ruled Florent out for the rest of the season and was a desperate blow to Bolton's ambitions. Although he did not play again Florent showed signs of returning to fitness by the end of the campaign and the cultured centre back will be looking to return to the team during 2004-05.
Bolton W (£500,000 from Lyon, France on 1/2/2003) PL 15

LAW Graeme

Born: Kirkcaldy, 6 October 1984
Height: 5'10" **Weight:** 10.10
International Honours: S: Yth
This talented young right back made his senior debut for York City as a substitute at home to Macclesfield last April and impressed with his steadiness and control. Graeme added three more appearances for the Minstermen in the last few games of the season and was deservedly voted as the club's 'Youth Player of the Year'.
York C (Trainee) FL 2+2

LAWRENCE Denis William

Born: Trinidad, 1 August 1974
Height: 6'7" **Weight:** 12.7
International Honours: Trinidad & Tobago: 40
This tall, ungainly central defender established himself as a firm favourite with the Wrexham fans last term, so much so that he was voted as the club's 'Player of the Season'. Denis dominates the back line and is surprisingly skilful for such a big man. His height was also a big advantage when pushing forward for corners and free kicks, indeed he was the team's leading goal-scorer for the first two months of the season. He continued to add to his total of caps for Trinidad during the campaign.

Wrexham (£100,000 from Defence Force, Trinidad on 10/3/2001) FL 105+7/8 FLC 3 FAC 1+1 Others 3

LAWRENCE James (Jamie) Hubert

Born: Balham, 8 March 1970
Height: 5'11" **Weight:** 12.11
Club Honours: FLC '97
International Honours: Jamaica: 19
This hard-working midfielder only played a bit-part role at Walsall last term. Jamie jumped at the chance to rejoin his former manager Paul Jewell at Wigan Athletic in November, but only featured as a substitute during his stay with the club. He subsequently joined Grimsby Town and was awarded the rare accolade of being handed the captain's armband for his debut against Chesterfield, contributing a goal in the same match. However, he suffered a severe gashed leg in only his third game for the club and was missing until the final games of the season, too late to contribute to the Mariners doomed struggle against relegation.
Sunderland (Signed from Cowes on 15/10/1993) FL 2+2 FLC 0+1
Doncaster Rov (£20,000 on 17/3/1994) FL 16+9/3 FLC 2 FAC 1 Others 3
Leicester C (£125,000 on 6/1/1995) P/FL 21+26/1 FLC 3+4/2 FAC 1+1
Bradford C (£50,000 on 17/6/1997) P/FL 133+22/12 FLC 8+1/1 FAC 4+1/1 Others 0+2
Walsall (Free on 27/3/2003) FL 12+10/1 FLC 1 FAC 0+1
Wigan Ath (Loaned on 20/11/2003) FL 0+4
Grimsby T (Free on 23/3/2004) FL 5/1

LAWRENCE Liam

Born: Retford, 14 December 1981
Height: 5'10" **Weight:** 11.3
Liam was in fine form for Mansfield Town at the start of the 2003-04 season and played a starring role in the 5-0 defeat of Scunthorpe at Field Mill. He netted all three goals to remove Wycombe Wanderers from the FA Cup in December, and after becoming the club's penalty taker he scored 12 times from the spot to create a new club record. Liam finished the campaign with 22 goals in all competitions but was unable to lead the Stags to victory in the play-off final. A versatile midfielder, his best position appears to be wide on the right, but he can also play in a more central role. Liam was also honoured with a place in the PFA Division Three team of the season.
Mansfield T (From trainee on 3/7/2000) FL 120+16/34 FLC 3 FAC 8/5 Others 4+2

LAWRENCE Matthew (Matt) James

Born: Northampton, 19 June 1974
Height: 6'1" **Weight:** 12.12
Club Honours: Div 2 '01
International Honours: E: Sch
Matt received limited opportunities for Millwall at the start of the 2003-04 season, but when Dennis Wise took over as manager he was paired alongside Darren Ward in the centre of the defence. The two established a formidable partnership and Matt produced some excellent displays to ensure that he earned a new contract that will keep him at the New Den for the foreseeable future.
Wycombe W (£20,000 from Grays Ath on 19/1/1996) FL 13+3/1 FLC 4 FAC 1 Others 0+1
Fulham (Free on 7/2/1997) FL 57+2 FLC 4+1 FAC 2 Others 5
Wycombe W (£86,000 + on 2/10/1998) FL 63/4 FLC 4 FAC 7 Others 3
Millwall (£200,000 on 21/3/2000) FL 143+6 FLC 7+1 FAC 16 Others 6

LAZARIDIS Stanley (Stan)

Born: Perth, Australia, 16 August 1972
Height: 5'9" **Weight:** 11.12
International Honours: Australia: 53; U23; Yth
Stan had another excellent season in midfield for Birmingham City last term. He was often the team's main threat and supplier to the forwards thanks to his rangy running with the ball and searching crosses. When he wasn't in the team, the Blues' attacking potency was reduced. He also played at left back very impressively, maintaining his forward forays whilst coping easily with defensive duties.
West Ham U (£300,000 from West Adelaide, Australia on 8/9/1995) PL 53+16/3 FLC 6+1 FAC 9+1 Others 0+1
Birmingham C (£1,600,000 on 29/7/1999) P/FL 116+38/8 FLC 12+3 FAC 3+1 Others 2+5

LEACOCK Dean Graham

Born: Croydon, 10 June 1984
Height: 6'2" **Weight:** 12.4
International Honours: E: Yth
Dean made only a handful of first-team appearances for Fulham last term, his three Premiership starts coming in successive games in October. Although he operated as a right back in these games he is more comfortable playing in a central-defensive role. Dean looked set to keep his place in the side but sustained a medial ligament injury during the warm-up at Old Trafford, which kept him out of action for a lengthy period.

Stan Lazaridis

*Fulham (From trainee on 17/7/2002) PL 3+1
FLC 2*

LEADBITTER Grant
Born: Chester le Street, 7 January 1986
Height: 5'9" **Weight:** 10.3
International Honours: E: Yth
This promising young midfielder made a
solitary appearance for Sunderland last
term, featuring as a substitute in the
Carling Cup defeat by Huddersfield. Grant
is a skilful player who distributes the ball
well and represented England at U19 level
during the season.
*Sunderland (From trainee on 9/1/2003) FLC
0+1*

LEARY Michael Antonio
Born: Ealing, 17 April 1983
Height: 5'11" **Weight:** 12.3
International Honours: RoI: Yth
Michael was one of several youngsters
who featured in first-team action for
Luton Town last term. A neat, skilful
midfielder he can play either in the centre
of the park or on the right-hand side.
Michael featured in the first team on a
number of occasions and the highpoint of
his campaign came when he scored two
well-taken goals at Hartlepool in April.
*Luton T (From juniors on 3/8/2001) FL 8+6/2
FLC 0+1 FAC 1+1 Others 3+2/1*

LEE Alan Desmond
Born: Galway, 21 August 1978
Height: 6'2" **Weight:** 13.9
International Honours: RoI: 7; U21-5
Alan played just twice for Rotherham at
the start of last season before joining
Cardiff City for what was a new record
transfer fee for the Millers. Although
troubled by injury at Ninian Park, he was
a regular in the closing stages of the
campaign and scored three goals. A
powerful striker who has great speed for
a big man, Alan featured regularly for the
Republic of Ireland when fit.
*Aston Villa (From trainee on 21/8/1995)
Torquay U (Loaned on 27/11/1998) FL 6+1/2
Others 2/1
Port Vale (Loaned on 2/3/1999) FL 7+4/2
Burnley (£150,000 on 8/7/1999) FL 2+13
FLC 1+1 FAC 0+2 Others 1/1
Rotherham U (£150,000 on 21/9/2000) FL
105+6/37 FLC 5/2 FAC 4+1/1 Others 1/1
Cardiff C (£850,000 + on 15/8/2003) FL
17+6/3 FAC 0+1*

LEE David John Francis
Born: Basildon, 28 March 1980
Height: 5'11" **Weight:** 11.8
David had a spell on loan at Ryman
League club Thurrock last season and on

his return made his first appearance in the
starting line-up for Brighton in the LDV
Vans Trophy match at Queens Park
Rangers in December. He then added a
second start, filling in for Gary Hart at
Sheffield Wednesday in March. New
manager Mark McGhee had promised to
give all the playing staff a fair chance and
the young midfielder was a beneficiary of
that policy, doing enough to earn a three-
month contract to prove himself in
2004-05.
Tottenham H (From trainee on 17/7/1998)

*Southend U (Free on 2/8/2000) FL 37+5/8
FLC 2 FAC 3 Others 5/2
Hull C (Free on 1/6/2001) FL 2+9/1 FLC 0+1
FAC 0+1 Others 0+1
Brighton & Hove A (Free on 11/1/2002) FL
1+5 Others 1
Bristol Rov (Loaned on 16/10/2002) FL 5
Others 1*

LEE Graeme Barry
Born: Middlesbrough, 31 May 1978
Height: 6'2" **Weight:** 13.7
Graeme followed his former boss Chris

Alan Lee

Turner to Sheffield Wednesday last term and proved an excellent signing for the Owls. An effective central defender who can head, tackle and distribute the ball, he missed several matches as a result of a problem with shin splints.
Hartlepool U *(From trainee on 2/7/1996) FL 208+11/19 FLC 7+2/1 FAC 8+1 Others 13+2/2*
Sheffield Wed *(Free on 2/7/2003) FL 30/3 FLC 1/1 FAC 3 Others 3/1*

LEE Robert (Rob) Martin
Born: West Ham, 1 February 1966
Height: 5'11" **Weight:** 11.13
Club Honours: Div 1 '93
International Honours: E: 21; B-1; U21-2
A West Ham supporter since boyhood, the veteran midfielder was pleased to join the Hammers last August. Playing in midfield his experience was invaluable to the youngsters around him. Toiling tirelessly he was particularly impressive in early-season victories over Preston and Reading. Robert was a regular in the side until November when he suffered a knee injury which forced him to miss the remainder of the campaign.
Charlton Ath *(Free from Hornchurch on 12/7/1983) FL 274+24/59 FLC 16+3/1 FAC 14/2 Others 10+2/3*
Newcastle U *(£700,00 on 22/9/1992) F/PL 292+11/44 FLC 22+1/3 FAC 27/5 Others 28/4*
Derby Co *(£250,000 + on 7/2/2002) P/FL 47+1/2 FLC 2*
West Ham U *(Free on 8/8/2003) FL 12+4 FLC 2 FAC 0+1*

LEGG Andrew (Andy)
Born: Neath, 28 July 1966
Height: 5'8" **Weight:** 10.7
Club Honours: WC '89, '91; AIC '95
International Honours: W: 6
Peterborough United's player-coach played more games at centre back or centre midfield than in his more familiar full-back role last season. An enthusiastic player with terrific ability in his left foot, his long throw again provided a threat to opposition defences.
Swansea C *(Signed from Britton Ferry on 12/8/1988) FL 155+8/29 FLC 9+1 FAC 16/4 Others 15+3/5*
Notts Co *(£275,000 on 23/7/1993) FL 85+4/9 FLC 11 FAC 7+1/2 Others 13+2/3*
Birmingham C *(Signed on 29/2/1996) FL 31+14/5 FLC 3+1 FAC 2+1*
Ipswich T *(Loaned on 3/11/1997) FL 6/1 FLC 1*
Reading *(£75,000 on 20/2/1998) FL 12 FLC 1*
Peterborough U *(Loaned on 15/10/1998) FL 5*

Cardiff C *(Free on 16/12/1998) FL 152+23/12 FLC 8+1 FAC 17+4 Others 4*
Peterborough U *(Free on 8/7/2003) FL 38+4 FLC 1 FAC 1+1 Others 0+2*

LEGWINSKI Sylvain
Born: Clermont-Ferrand, France, 6 October 1973
Height: 6'3" **Weight:** 11.7
International Honours: France: B-3; U21
Sylvain enjoyed an excellent season for Fulham when he was almost ever-present when available. He played much of the campaign in a role just in front of the back four, as well as appearing in a more conventional central-midfield role. A combative midfielder who works tirelessly for the team, he is a great favourite with the Fulham fans. Despite often instigating attacking moves he surprisingly failed to net a Premiership goal last term.
Fulham *(£3,500,000 from Bordeaux, France, ex AS Monaco, on 22/8/2001) PL 93+7/7 FLC 2+1/1 FAC 12/1 Others 10+2/2*

LEHMANN Jens
Born: Essen, Germany, 10 November 1969
Height: 6'3" **Weight:** 13.10
Club Honours: PL '04
International Honours: Germany: 18
Jens joined Arsenal in the summer of 2003 from Borussia Dortmund and immediately established himself as the club's first-choice 'keeper. Not without its critics in his first season in England, he produced a near flawless Premiership season and was the club's only ever-present in the remarkable unbeaten championship success. He is very commanding in his area coming for every cross with real conviction, and is very assured in his handling in the area as well as being a sound shot stopper. He kept 15 clean sheets in the Premiership.
Arsenal *(£1,250,000 from Borussia Dortmund, Germany, ex SW Essen, Schalke 04, AC Milan, on 5/8/2003) PL 38 FAC 5 Others 11*

LEIGERTWOOD Mikele Benjamin
Born: Enfield, 12 November 1982
Height: 6'1" **Weight:** 13.11
A robustly built young central defender, Mikele did his best to hold together the Wimbledon back line during the first part of last season. He was the one shining defensive light early on, and with cash at the club at an absolute premium it was no great surprise that the club's administrators accepted an offer from Crystal Palace just prior to Christmas. He

broke into the Eagles' line-up for the closing stages and featured in the end-of-season play-offs.
Wimbledon *(From trainee on 29/6/2001) FL 55+1/2 FLC 4/1 FAC 5*
Leyton Orient *(Loaned on 19/11/2001) FL 8 FAC 2*
Crystal Palace *(£150,000 on 2/2/2004) FL 7+5 Others 3*

LEITAO Jorge Manuel
Born: Oporto, Portugal, 14 January 1974
Height: 5'11" **Weight:** 13.4
Although Jorge's fourth season at Walsall was not his most successful, he still ended up as leading scorer with nine goals in all competitions. He ran tirelessly throughout the campaign whatever the situation, but luck was not always with him and he was desperately unfortunate to be sent off in the FA Cup-tie at Millwall in a game in which he had earlier opened the scoring.
Walsall *(£150,000 from SC Farense, Portugal, ex Avintes, on 10/8/2000) FL 136+29/44 FLC 9/5 FAC 10+1/4 Others 3*

LENNON Aaron Justin
Born: Leeds, 16 April 1987
Height: 5'5" **Weight:** 9.12
International Honours: E: Yth
Aaron became the youngest Premiership player ever when he featured as a substitute for Leeds at Tottenham last August when he was just 16 years and 129 days old. A diminutive winger or striker, he made his full debut in the Carling Cup tie with Swindon the following month. Highly skilful, he stayed in and around the first team all season, and will be looking for more opportunities in 2004-05.
Leeds U *(Trainee) PL 0+11 FLC 1+1 FAC 0+1*

LE SAUX Graeme Pierre
Born: Jersey, 17 October 1968
Height: 5'10" **Weight:** 12.2
Club Honours: PL '95; FLC '98; ESC '98; CS '00
International Honours: E: 36; B-2; U21-4
Brought to St Mary's as part of the deal that took Wayne Bridge to Chelsea, Graeme was an instant hit with the Southampton faithful, manifesting the sort of form that had made him an automatic choice at left back for England. Unfortunately, just as the Saints' back four was beginning to look as effective on the offensive as it was on the defensive, Graeme sustained the first of a series of niggling injuries that were to restrict his appearances throughout the season. Problematical: because attacking

defenders as effective as Graeme Le Saux are difficult to find at international, never mind club, level.

Chelsea *(Free from St Paul's, Jersey on 9/12/1987) F/PL 77+13/8 FLC 7+6/1 FAC 7+1 Others 8+1*
Blackburn Rov *(£750,000 on 25/3/1993) PL 127+2/7 FLC 10 FAC 8 Others 6+1*
Chelsea *(£5,000,000 on 8/8/1997) PL 133+7/4 FLC 10/1 FAC 18+2/2 Others 20+2*
Southampton *(£500,000 on 21/7/2003) PL 19 FLC 1/1 Others 1*

LESCOTT Aaron Anthony
Born: Birmingham, 2 December 1978
Height: 5'8" **Weight:** 10.9
This hard-working midfielder struggled to find his best form at times for Stockport last season, although he enjoyed a brief run in the line-up in September. However, he then dropped out of the reckoning and spent the final month of the campaign on loan at Bristol Rovers. He featured regularly during his stay at the

Memorial Stadium and helped the Pirates steer clear of relegation to the Conference.

Aston Villa *(From trainee on 5/7/1996) FAC 0+1*
Lincoln C *(Loaned on 14/3/2000) FL 3+2*
Sheffield Wed *(£100,000 on 3/10/2000) FL 19+18 FLC 3+1 FAC 2*
Stockport Co *(£75,000 on 14/11/2001) FL 65+7/1 FLC 2+1 FAC 2+1 Others 2+1*
Bristol Rov *(Loaned on 25/3/2004) FL 8*

LESTER Jack William
Born: Sheffield, 8 October 1975
Height: 5'10" **Weight:** 11.8
Club Honours: AMC '98
International Honours: E: Sch
Jack signed for Sheffield United in the summer of 2003 and quickly became a favourite with the fans. Apart from a spell out with injury in February he was a regular member of the squad, playing mainly as a striker but sometimes behind the front two. Hard working, he was

effective in either role, causing defenders problems in the box with his ability to turn with the ball. His goal tally was boosted by eight coolly taken penalties.

Grimsby T *(From juniors on 8/7/1994) FL 93+40/17 FLC 13+4/6 FAC 8+1/2 Others 4+4*
Doncaster Rov *(Loaned on 20/9/1996) FL 5+6/1*
Nottingham F *(£300,000 on 28/1/2000) FL 73+26/21 FLC 3/3 FAC 1 Others 0+1*
Sheffield U *(Free on 1/8/2003) FL 25+7/12 FLC 2/2 FAC 2/1*

LE TALLEC Anthony
Born: Hennebont, France, 3 October 1984
Height: 6'0" **Weight:** 11.7
International Honours: France: U21; Yth
Anthony finally arrived at Anfield in the summer of 2003 after picking up some very useful experience with Le Havre in France. Due to the long injury list he was thrown into action, making his debut as a

Aaron Lescott (right)

substitute at Blackburn in September. He made his first start a week later and scored his first goal for the Reds in the UEFA Cup tie at home to Olimpija Ljubljana of Slovenia soon afterwards. After a run of appearances up to November, mostly as a substitute, his opportunities became more sporadic as the club's injury list shortened, but he did enjoy another short run on the right side of midfield early in the new year. However, his campaign came to a premature end in March following an ankle injury.

Liverpool *(Signed from Le Havre, France on 18/7/2003) PL 3+10 FLC 2 FAC 1+3 Others 2+2/1*

LEWINGTON Dean Scott
Born: Kingston, 18 May 1984
Height: 5'11" **Weight:** 11.2
Following a brief substitute appearance the previous season, Dean was given his chance for Wimbledon in the home win over Bradford City last November, and after an assured display he became a regular first-team starter from then on. A tall and fiercely determined left back, he got better and better as the season progressed, and had the honour of captaining the team late on at Burnley. The son of Watford manager Ray Lewington, he looks to be a very good prospect for the future.

Wimbledon *(From trainee on 17/7/2003) FL 28+1/1 FAC 3*

LEWIS Edward (Eddie) James
Born: Cerritos, California, USA, 17 May 1974
Height: 5'9" **Weight:** 11.12
International Honours: USA: 57
After playing for the USA in the summer's Gold Cup, Eddie could have been excused for starting the 2003-04 season slowly, but this was not the case as he scored the first goal of the new campaign after only 92 seconds in the early kick-off against West Ham. Eddie is a lively left winger who can deliver a telling cross and he is also adept at ghosting in on the blind side for some valuable goals, whilst his dead-ball strikes are rapidly becoming the stuff of legend at Deepdale. A hernia operation in March seemed to signal the end of his season and a much-needed rest, but he surprised all by returning for the final three games, scoring the opener on his return against Cardiff.

Fulham *(£1,300,000 from San Jose Clash, USA on 17/3/2000) P/FL 8+8 FLC 6/1*
Preston NE *(Signed on 5/9/2002) FL 60+11/11 FLC 3+1/1 FAC 3*

LEWIS Karl Junior
Born: Wembley, 9 October 1973
Height: 6'5" **Weight:** 12.4
Club Honours: Div 2 '02
Junior found himself completely out of the first-team picture at Leicester last term and in October he joined Swindon Town on loan. The tall and lanky midfielder acquitted himself well during his stay at the County Ground before returning to the Walkers Stadium. Junior spent the closing stages on loan at Hull, where he linked up with his former boss Peter Taylor once more and proved to be a valuable asset to the Tigers' promotion campaign. He was released by Leicester in the summer.

Fulham *(From trainee on 3/7/1992) FL 4+2 FAC 1 (Free to Dover Ath during 1993 close season)*
Gillingham *(Free from Hendon on 3/8/1999) FL 47+12/8 FLC 4+2 FAC 7+2 Others 4*
Leicester C *(£50,000 on 30/1/2001) P/FL 24+6/1 FLC 3 FAC 1*
Brighton & Hove A *(Loaned on 8/2/2002) FL 14+1/3*
Swindon T *(Loaned on 19/3/2003) FL 9*
Swindon T *(Loaned on 21/10/2003) FL 4*
Hull C *(Loaned on 25/2/2004) FL 13/1*

LEWIS Matthew (Matt) Thomas
Born: Coventry, 20 March 1984
Height: 6'1" **Weight:** 11.7
Matt managed just one first-team start for Kidderminster last term and in September he was sent out on loan to Hinckley United for whom he scored a bagful of goals. The promising young striker was eventually allowed to leave Harriers and signed permanent forms for Hinckley in December.

Kidderminster Hrs *(Free from Coventry Marconi on 23/7/2001) FL 1+7 FLC 0+1 FAC 0+1 Others 0+1*

LIBURD Richard John
Born: Nottingham, 26 September 1973
Height: 5'9" **Weight:** 11.1
This experienced player established himself in the Lincoln City starting line-up from the commencement of the 2003-04 season after signing in the summer. His mobility and work rate proved real assets to the team in midfield and also when switched to wing back. An ankle ligament injury meant he made only one start in the second half of the campaign and he was released at the end of the season.

Middlesbrough *(£20,000 from Eastwood T on 25/3/1993) FL 41/1 FLC 4 FAC 2 Others 5*
Bradford C *(£200,000 on 21/7/1994) FL 75+3/3 FLC 6+2 FAC 2+2 Others 2*

Carlisle U *(Free on 26/2/1998) FL 9*
Notts Co *(Free on 4/8/1998) FL 127+27/9 FLC 5+2 FAC 8+4/2 Others 1+1*
Lincoln C *(Free on 5/8/2003) FL 19+5 FLC 1 Others 2+1*

LIDDELL Andrew (Andy) Mark
Born: Leeds, 28 June 1973
Height: 5'7" **Weight:** 11.6
Club Honours: AMC '99; Div 2 '03
International Honours: S: U21-12
Last term saw Andy break Wigan Athletic's Football League scoring record, his first goal in the win over Crystal Palace surpassing the previous record of 66 goals set by current first-team coach David Lowe. A talented right-footed striker and tireless worker with good pace and vision, he can make or score goals. Andy finished the season as the team's second-top scorer, despite spending much of the campaign on the right side of midfield. The Latics longest-serving player, he was out of contract in the summer and his future was unclear at the time of writing.

Barnsley *(From trainee on 6/7/1991) F/PL 142+56/34 FLC 11+4/3 FAC 5+7/1 Others 2+1*
Wigan Ath *(£350,000 on 15/10/1998) FL 206+11/70 FLC 11/1 FAC 7/1 Others 14+1*

LIDDLE Craig George
Born: Chester le Street, 21 October 1971
Height: 5'11" **Weight:** 12.7
Craig was again outstanding in the centre of defence for Darlington last term, taking his total of appearances for the Quakers to 300 in all competitions by the end of the season. He led the team by example and his commitment and dedication were great motivators for his colleagues. Strong in the air, quick into the tackle and a good distributor of the ball from the heart of the defence, Craig enjoys getting forward for set pieces and was rewarded with four goals during the campaign.

Aston Villa *(From trainee on 4/7/1990. Free to Blyth Spartans in August 1991)*
Middlesbrough *(Free on 12/7/1994) P/FL 20+5 FLC 3+2 FAC 2 Others 2*
Darlington *(Free on 20/2/1998) FL 265/16 FLC 11 FAC 13/1 Others 11/3*

LINCOLN Greg Dean
Born: Enfield, 23 March 1980
Height: 5'9" **Weight:** 10.3
International Honours: E: Yth
Greg broke into the Northampton Town midfield last November and held his own in the company of more experienced

players around him. However, he then fell victim to the club's injury jinx and spent much of the second half of the campaign out of action. Greg is an aggressive and tenacious midfield player with a high work rate.

Arsenal *(From trainee on 3/7/1998. Freed during 2001 close season)*
Northampton T *(Free from Hammarby IF, Sweden on 9/7/2002) FL 9+10/1 FAC 2 Others 1*

LINDEGAARD Andrew (Andy) Rindom

Born: Taunton, 10 September 1980
Height: 5'8" **Weight:** 11.4
Club Honours: FAT '02; NC '03
Andy featured fairly regularly in the Yeovil Town squad last term, although he was often on the substitutes' bench. He had a spell on loan with Weymouth towards the end of the year, but ended the season with some excellent performances at right back as the Glovers pushed for a place in the play-offs. Andy is a pacy defender or midfielder who causes many a problem for opposition defences when going forward and is always likely to chip in with a goal.

Yeovil T *(Signed from Westlands Sports on 5/6/2000) FL 12+11/2 FLC 0+1 FAC 0+1*

LINDEROTH Tobias

Born: Marseilles, France, 21 April 1979
Height: 5'9" **Weight:** 10.12
International Honours: Sweden: 39; U21-22
This midfielder had a generally good season for Everton, and was at his best when employed in the midfield anchor role that plays to his strengths of breaking up play and delivering the simple but effective pass. Tobias was arguably Everton's star performer in the first month of the campaign and he scored his first goal for the club in the Carling Cup victory over Charlton. After a period out of the side in December and January, he returned to the side for the last third of the season, when he continued his quiet, effective presence in the team.

Everton *(£2,500,000 + from Stabaek, Norway, ex Hassleholm, Elfsborg, on 1/2/2002) PL 29+11 FLC 2+1/1 FAC 2+1*

LINWOOD Paul Anthony

Born: Birkenhead, 24 October 1983
Height: 6'2" **Weight:** 12.8
This young central defender signed his first professional contract for Tranmere in the summer of 2003 and stepped up to first-team duties following the arrival of new boss Brian Little. His unruffled

demeanour and maturity marked him out as a natural leader, but he was used sparingly in the senior side and eventually picked up a stomach injury which ruled him out of the final run-in.

Tranmere Rov *(From trainee on 3/4/2002) FL 18+2 FAC 3+1 Others 1*

LIPA Andreas

Born: Vienna, Austria, 26 April 1971
Height: 6'2" **Weight:** 12.4
International Honours: Austria: 1
This experienced midfield player signed for Port Vale during the 2003 close season. It was his first foray into English football and he impressed early on, particularly in the Carling Cup tie against Nottingham Forest. Despite being very skilful on the ball, he admitted that he was finding it difficult to adjust to the pace of the game, but nevertheless continued to draw on his experience. A leg injury curtailed his appearances following a change of manager at the Vale in February he could not regain his place in the starting line-up.

Port Vale *(Free from Xanthi, Greece, ex Austria Vienna, Casino Salzburg, SC Lustenau, Grazer AK, on 14/7/2003) FL 27+3/2 FLC 1 FAC 2*

LISBIE Kevin Anthony

Born: Hackney, 17 October 1978
Height: 5'8" **Weight:** 10.12
International Honours: Jamaica: 9; E: Yth
Kevin was playing the best football of his career before injury struck in late November. Five goals in ten games, of which he only started six, gave him sort of goal-scoring statistics he had been looking for since making his debut in 1996. His best game was undoubtedly against Liverpool at the Valley when he hit a hat-trick in a 3-2 win. His third goal in this game was a brilliant individual effort which was voted 'Goal of the Season' by the Addicks' supporters. He picked up a knee injury in the following game, which put him out for a month, and then after a couple more games, suffered a back problem, which put him out for the rest of the season. Kevin has electric pace, is very skilful on the ball and can play as a central striker or wide on the right. Kevin played for Jamaica in the end-of-season Unity Cup tournament.

Charlton Ath *(From trainee on 24/5/1996) P/FL 49+75/15 FLC 3+7/3 FAC 2+5*
Gillingham *(Loaned on 5/3/1999) FL 4+3/4*
Reading *(Loaned on 26/11/1999) FL 1+1*
Queens Park R *(Loaned on 1/12/2000) FL 1+1*

LITA Leroy Halirou

Born: DR Congo, 28 December 1984
Height: 5'9" **Weight:** 11.2
Bristol City's 'super-sub' came off the bench on nearly 30 occasions last term, but although the team often struggled for goals during the campaign he received only a couple of starts. The popular striker scored five times and will be looking to feature in the starting line-up on a regular basis in 2004-05.

Bristol C *(From trainee on 6/3/2003) FL 2+39/7 FLC 0+1 FAC 0+3/2 Others 1+3*

LITTLE Colin Campbell

Born: Wythenshawe, 4 November 1972
Height: 5'10" **Weight:** 12.2
Colin experienced a difficult season at Macclesfield last term, when he was asked to play in a wide-left midfield position rather than in his more accustomed role as a striker. Nevertheless he put in some sterling performances, often making an impact when coming on from the substitutes' bench, and even though goal-scoring opportunities were limited he netted six times. His best strike provided a last-minute equaliser against Kidderminster when the match looked lost. Towards transfer-deadline day, Colin's contract was cancelled by mutual consent and shortly afterwards he signed for Conference outfit Halifax Town.

Crewe Alex *(£50,000 from Hyde U on 7/2/1996) FL 135+58/33 FLC 16+2/8 FAC 5/1 Others 5/3*
Mansfield T *(Loaned on 24/10/2002) FL 5*
Macclesfield T *(Loaned on 13/12/2002) FL 1*
Macclesfield T *(Free on 27/3/2003) FL 21+8/6 FLC 1 FAC 4/1*

LITTLE Glen Matthew

Born: Wimbledon, 15 October 1975
Height: 6'3" **Weight:** 13.0
Glen returned to the Burnley side at the start of last season, but quite soon he was loaned out again, this time to Bolton where he had a brief first taste of Premiership football but made little impact. Returning to Turf Moor in October, his season from then on was thankfully free of the injury problems that had plagued him for some time and he enjoyed a solid if unspectacular campaign, only occasionally displaying the dazzling skills that had previously had him rated as one of the First Division's finest. Used on both wings and sometimes in central midfield, he rarely let the side down and his transfer to Reading at the end of the season brought an end to the Turf Moor career of arguably Burnley's best player of recent times.

*Crystal Palace (From trainee on 1/7/1994.
Free to Glentoran on 11/11/1994)*
*Burnley (£100,000 on 29/11/1996) FL
211+35/32 FLC 11+4 FAC 11+6/3 Others
4+1/1*
*Reading (Loaned on 27/3/2003) FL 6/1
Others 1*
Bolton W (Loaned on 1/9/2003) PL 0+4

LITTLEJOHN Adrian Sylvester
Born: Wolverhampton, 26 September
1970
Height: 5'9" **Weight:** 11.0
International Honours: E: Yth
This pacy wide player began the 2003-04
season in fine style for Port Vale, scoring a
late winner against Bournemouth on the
opening day, and always looked
dangerous in his usual role on the left-
hand side. Adrian netted seven times for
Vale, including two 20-yard rockets in the
fixtures against Sheffield Wednesday.
Nonetheless, he was released on a free
transfer in May.
*Walsall (From trainee at West Bromwich A
juniors on 24/5/1989) FL 26+18/1 FLC 2+1
FAC 1+1 Others 4+1*
*Sheffield U (Free on 6/8/1991) F/PL
44+25/12 FLC 5+1 FAC 3+2/1 Others 2/1*
*Plymouth Arg (£100,000 on 22/9/1995) FL
100+10/29 FLC 6 FAC 6+2/3 Others 6*
*Oldham Ath (Signed on 20/3/1998) FL
16+5/5 FLC 2/1*
*Bury (£75,000 on 13/11/1998) FL 69+30/14
FLC 4/1 FAC 6/1 Others 2+1*
*Sheffield U (Free on 22/10/2001) FL 1+2
(Freed in December 2001)*
*Port Vale (Free, after spells in China and the
USA, via a trial at Barnsley, on 19/2/2003) FL
36+13/10 FLC 1 FAC 3 Others 1*

LIVERMORE David
Born: Edmonton, 20 May 1980
Height: 5'11" **Weight:** 12.1
Club Honours: Div 2 '01
After having played over 200 games for
Millwall, David is now becoming
something of a legend at the club due to
his tough tackling and never-say-die
attitude. The left-footed youngster
produced some determined
perfomances in the centre of midfield
and was a key figure in the club's
successes last term.
Arsenal (From trainee on 13/7/1998)
*Millwall (£30,000 on 30/7/1999) FL 187+4/8
FLC 9/1 FAC 16 Others 5*

LIVESEY Daniel (Danny)
Richard
Born: Salford, 31 December 1984
Height: 6'2" **Weight:** 13.0
Danny spent much of last season on loan

firstly at Notts County, where he was
probably the best defender at the club
during his spell, and later on at Rochdale,
where he provided cover for Dale's other
more experienced centre backs. Between
these loan spells Danny found time to
make a couple of first-team appearances
for Bolton in the two FA Cup games
against Tranmere, acquitting himself well
at the heart of the defence.
*Bolton W (From trainee on 17/8/2002) PL
0+2 FLC 1 FAC 3*
*Notts Co (Loaned on 5/9/2003) FL 9+2
Others 1*
Rochdale (Loaned on 6/2/2004) FL 11+2

LIVINGSTONE Stephen
(Steve) Carl
Born: Middlesbrough, 8 September 1968
Height: 6'1" **Weight:** 13.6
Club Honours: AMC '98
Steve did not have the happiest of spells
at Carlisle last term. Initially chosen as a
striker, he looked more comfortable when
playing in the back four, but a
combination of injuries and disciplinary
problems restricted his overall
contribution and eventually his contract
was cancelled. Steve is the son of Joe
Livingstone, who played for Carlisle in the
early 1960s.

David Livermore

Freddie Ljungberg (left)

Coventry C *(From trainee on 16/7/1986) FL 17+14/5 FLC 8+2/10 Others 0+1*
Blackburn Rov *(£450,000 on 17/1/1991) F/PL 25+5/10 FLC 2 FAC 1/1*
Chelsea *(£350,000 on 23/3/1993) PL 0+1*
Port Vale *(Loaned on 3/9/1993) FL 4+1*
Grimsby T *(£140,000 on 29/10/1993) FL 226+63/43 FLC 15+5/4 FAC 12+5/4 Others 4+3*
Carlisle U *(Free on 7/8/2003) FL 6 FLC 0+1 Others 2*

LJUNGBERG Karl **Fredrik** **(Freddie)**
Born: Sweden, 16 April 1977
Height: 5'9" **Weight:** 11.6
Club Honours: CS '99; PL '02, '04; FAC '02, '03
International Honours: Sweden: 44; U21-12; Yth
A firm favourite with the Highbury faithful, this talented midfielder suffered numerous injuries in a frustrating season in 2003-04. He scored the winner at the City of Manchester Stadium in August and finished with ten goals in all competitions, although only four of these came in the Premiership. Freddie plays with his heart on his sleeve; always prepared to run himself into the ground, fight for every ball and with a keen eye for goal. He remains a key player in the midfield particularly when supported by Dennis Bergkamp as the two appear to share a telepathic understanding. Freddie is able to play in any position in midfield as well as a support striker. He was named in Sweden's squad for Euro 2004.
Arsenal *(£3,000,000 from BK Halmstad, Sweden on 17/9/1998) PL 127+20/35 FLC 2 FAC 20+3/8 Others 46+9/11*

LLEWELLYN **Christopher** **(Chris)** Mark
Born: Swansea, 29 August 1979
Height: 5'11" **Weight:** 11.6
International Honours: W: 3; B-1; U21-14; Yth; Sch
Chris was brought to Wrexham to partner Chris Armstrong up front, however, it was obvious from the start he seemed more of a midfield operator than an out-and-out striker. Nonetheless, he also showed he could score goals, notching a notable double against Blackpool just after Christmas, and the only goal in the win against Barnsley at the Racecourse in February. Chris was called up to the Wales squad for the end-of-season friendlies against Norway and Canada.
Norwich C *(From trainee on 21/1/1997) FL 103+39/17 FLC 7+3 FAC 3+3/1*
Bristol Rov *(Loaned on 21/2/2003) FL 14/3*

Wrexham *(Free on 6/8/2003) FL 46/8 FLC 1 FAC 1 Others 1+1*

LLOYD **Anthony** Francis
Born: Taunton, 14 March 1984
Height: 5'7" **Weight:** 11.0
A product of the Huddersfield Town Academy, this promising youngster occupied the left-wing-back role with great maturity last season, holding down a regular place in the side from September onwards. A tenacious tackler, who is strong on the ball, Anthony scored three goals during the campaign, including a sublime lob in the 3-0 win over Swansea City.
Huddersfield T *(From trainee on 22/8/2003) FL 30+1/3 FAC 1 Others 4*

LOCKETT **Ryan** David Carl William
Born: Cambridge, 11 November 1986
Height: 5'10" **Weight:** 11.8
Ryan had scored regularly at youth-team level for Cambridge United and was given his senior debut when coming on for the last 20 minutes at Hull in January. A striker with explosive pace who can provide the link from midfield to attack, he featured in the starting line-up for the Good Friday fixture at home to York City.
Cambridge U *(Trainee) FL 1+1*

LOCKWOOD **Adam** Brian
Born: Wakefield, 26 October 1981
Height: 6'0" **Weight:** 12.7
Club Honours: FAT '02; NC '03
International Honours: E: SP-2
Adam enjoyed another consistent season at Yeovil last term when he featured both at full back and in the centre of defence. He produced some committed displays and proved a valuable asset to the Glovers squad. Adam is a great crowd favourite at Huish Park and is always a threat at set pieces and corners.
Reading *(From trainee on 19/3/1999)*
Yeovil T *(Free on 17/10/2001) FL 43/4 FLC 1 FAC 3 Others 2*

LOCKWOOD **Matthew** Dominic
Born: Southend, 17 October 1976
Height: 5'9" **Weight:** 10.12
Matthew was again first-choice left back for Leyton Orient last term until he broke his toe in the game at Doncaster in January. He briefly returned at the end of the season but will be looking for an injury free time in 2004-05 after a couple of nightmare campaigns. The O's dead-ball expert, Matthew was awarded a new long-term contract in March.
Queens Park R *(From trainee at Southend U on 2/5/1995)*

Bristol Rov *(Free on 24/7/1996) FL 58+5/1 FLC 2+1 FAC 6 Others 4+2*
Leyton Orient *(Free on 7/8/1998) FL 194+8/25 FLC 13/2 FAC 15/1 Others 10/3*

LOGAN **Richard** James
Born: Bury St Edmunds, 4 January 1982
Height: 6'0" **Weight:** 12.5
International Honours: E: Yth; Sch
After a successful first season at Boston United, Richard found it harder to repeat that in 2003-2004 when he was used on the right side of midfield rather than in his role as a central striker. He was loaned out to Peterborough United with the move eventually becoming permanent. However, he spent most of the time as a substitute at London Road, as Posh's playing style didn't suit his strengths. He still managed to score nine goals from 15 starts. A powerful leader of the line with a good physical presence, what he lacks in pace he makes up for with his skill on the ball and ability in the air.
Ipswich T *(From trainee on 6/1/1999) FL 0+3 FLC 0+1 FAC 0+1*
Cambridge U *(Loaned on 25/11/2001) FL 5/1*
Torquay U *(Loaned on 13/12/2001) FL 16/4*
Boston U *(Free on 30/11/2002) FL 30+5/10 FLC 0+1*
Peterborough U *(Free on 24/9/2003) FL 12+17/7 FAC 2+1/1 Others 1+1/1*

LOMAS **Stephen (Steve)** Martin
Born: Hanover, Germany, 18 January 1974
Height: 6'0" **Weight:** 12.8
International Honours: NI: 45; B-1; Yth; Sch
Steve missed virtually all of the 2003-04 season due to an ongoing ankle injury. He returned briefly to the West Ham midfield in February for an FA Cup tie against Fulham but was not fully fit. He therefore made his first League appearance of the season in April against Derby County. Steve provided some much-needed steel and his attitude and experience proved invaluable as the Hammers qualified for the play-offs.
Manchester C *(From trainee on 22/1/1991) P/FL 102+9/8 FLC 15/2 FAC 10+1/1*
West Ham U *(£1,600,000 on 26/3/1997) P/FL 161+3/9 FLC 12/2 FAC 10+3/1 Others 13*

LOMAX Kelvin
Born: Bury, 12 November 1986
Height: 5'11" **Weight:** 12.3
Kelvin caught the eye of Oldham boss Brian Talbot as the club's youth side notched an impressive league and cup

double last term. A versatile defender who can play anywhere across the back line, Kelvin was rewarded with a first-team call up for the final game of the season at Notts County. He came on as a second-half substitute for Darren Sheridan and slotted into central midfield, showing composure and some neat touches that belied the fact that he was still only a first-year scholar.

Oldham Ath (Trainee) FL 0+1

LONERGAN Andrew (Andy)
Born: Preston, 19 October 1983
Height: 6'4" **Weight:** 13.2

International Honours: Rol: Yth; E: Yth Preston's England Youth 'keeper moved up to second choice on the back of his international appearances at U20 level. Andy finally returned to first-team action three years after his debut when he kept a clean sheet against West Bromwich Albion and he made eight consecutive appearances in all before Jonathan Gould returned from injury. He is a calm and composed young man, commanding in his area and excellent on ground shots for such a tall player. A broken hand prevented him from adding to his tally at the season's end.

Preston NE (From trainee on 21/10/2000) FL 9 FLC 1
Darlington (Loaned on 20/12/2002) FL 2

LORAN Tyrone
Born: Amsterdam, Holland, 29 June 1981
Height: 6'2" **Weight:** 13.11
International Honours: Holland: U21 Tyrone made a permanent move to Tranmere during the 2003 close season and started the new campaign brightly enough. However, the defender and occasional midfielder was ruled out of action for some time with a cruciate ligament injury and he did not return to

Matthieu Louis-Jean (right)

fitness until February. A great favourite with the Rovers' fans, Tyrone is a calm, intelligent player, who is not only a tough tackler but also possesses excellent vision. At the end of the campaign he had established himself in the right-back berth.

Manchester C *(£60,000 from Volendam, Holland on 16/7/2002)*
Tranmere Rov *(Signed on 31/12/2002) FL 42+3 FLC 1 FAC 2 Others 1*

LOUIS Jefferson Lee
Born: Harrow, 22 February 1979
Height: 6'2" **Weight:** 13.2
This big, strong, but deceptively quick Oxford forward started last season on loan at Woking, but a fine run of goal-scoring prompted a quicker than expected return to the Kassam Stadium. Jefferson quickly made his mark, scoring with a soaring header in the Carling Cup tie against Reading. He has still a lot to learn in the full-time game, but three goals in seven starts showed he has plenty to offer. Although out of favour for a while, he ended the season on a high, scoring and creating a goal against Cambridge.

Oxford U *(Free from Thame U, ex Aylesbury U, on 4/3/2002) FL 18+37/8 FLC 1+2/1 FAC 1+3/1 Others 2*

LOUIS-JEAN Matthieu
Born: Mont St Aignan, France, 22 February 1976
Height: 5'9" **Weight:** 10.12
International Honours: France: U21; Yth
Matthieu was again a regular in the Nottingham Forest line-up last season playing on the right-hand side of defence. At his best when he is attacking down the flank, Louis-Jean is also dangerous at set pieces. He returned to the side as a substitute in the final game of the campaign after being out for a short spell due to a thigh injury.

Nottingham F *(Signed from Le Havre, France on 14/9/1998) P/FL 166+7/3 FLC 12+2 FAC 5 Others 2*

LOW Joshua (Josh) David
Born: Bristol, 15 February, 1979
Height: 6'1" **Weight:** 12.0
International Honours: W: U21-4; Yth
Josh started the 2003-04 campaign in fine style for Northampton, scoring a great individual goal in the Carling Cup tie against Norwich City. However, he missed a large chunk of the season through injury before returning with a

bang, scoring another brilliant effort against Leyton Orient. Josh is a match-winning wide man with pace, ball control and a cannonball shot in either foot, and quickly became a firm favourite of the Cobblers fans.

Bristol Rov *(From trainee on 19/8/1996) FL 11+11 FLC 0+2 FAC 2+2 Others 2*
Leyton Orient *(Free on 27/5/1999) FL 2+3/1 FLC 1*
Cardiff C *(Free on 20/11/1999) FL 54+21/6 FLC 1+1 FAC 2+3 Others 3+1*
Oldham Ath *(Signed on 12/8/2002) FL 19+2/3 FLC 2 FAC 2/1 Others 2*
Northampton T *(£165,000 on 8/8/2003) FL 28+5/3 FLC 1/1 FAC 2/1 Others 4/1*

LOWE Onandi
Born: Kingston, Jamaica, 2 December 1973
Height: 6'3" **Weight:** 13.12
Club Honours: Div 3 '03
International Honours: Jamaica
The giant striker finished as top scorer for Rushden last season with 16 goals even though he was among four key players who left on transfer-deadline day. After being absent for a couple of months with a groin injury at Bournemouth, he recovered to lead the Diamonds attack once more but with the side slipping down the table he moved on to Coventry. However, although he scored for the Sky Blues on his first start at Crewe he was rested by the club following a well-publicised off-the-field problem.

Port Vale *(Loaned from Rochester Rhinos, USA, ex Harbour View, Montreal Impact, Waterhouse, Richmond Kickers, on 1/2/2001) FL 4+1/1 Others 1/1*
Rushden & Diamonds *(Free from Kansas Wizards on 30/11/2001) FL 87+3/49 FLC 1/1 FAC 2+1/1 Others 4/1*
Coventry C *(Free on 25/3/2004) FL 1+1/1*

LOWNDES Nathan Peter
Born: Salford, 2 June 1977
Height: 5'11" **Weight:** 11.6
Club Honours: Div 2 '04
Nathan enjoyed a much more productive season for Plymouth last term, although many of his appearances came from the substitutes' bench. A talented striker, his main attributes are the ability to finish with either foot, good pace and a refusal to allow opposition defenders time to settle on the ball. His total of ten goals helped the Pilgrims towards their Second Division championship success.

Leeds U *(From trainee on 1/4/1995)*
Watford *(£40,000 on 3/10/1995) FL 1+6 FLC 0+1 FAC 1+1 Others 1*

St Johnstone *(£50,000 on 21/8/1998) SL 30+34/14 SLC 2+2/2 SC 4+2 Others 2+1*
Livingston *(Free on 20/7/2001) SL 7+14/3 SLC 0+2 SC 0+2*
Rotherham U *(Loaned on 28/3/2002) FL 2*
Plymouth Arg *(Free on 23/7/2002) FL 24+25/10 FLC 1 FAC 0+1 Others 3+1/2*

LUA LUA Lomano Tresor
Born: Zaire, 28 December 1980
Height: 5'8" **Weight:** 12.2
International Honours: DR Congo
Lomano struggled to win a place in Newcastle's side last term and his only starts came in the Carling Cup tie against West Bromwich Albion and the Premiership games at Wolves and Leicester, so he welcomed the opportunity to move to Portsmouth on loan with a view to a permanent transfer at the end of the season. He enjoyed a consistent run in the Pompey team, scoring four times included a last-minute equaliser against his parent club. His fast, mazy runs down the flank caused all sorts of problems and he proved to be a very entertaining player. Lomano captained the DR Congo side in the African Nations' Cup finals in January.

Colchester U *(From Leyton College on 25/9/1998) FL 37+24/15 FLC 4/4 FAC 1/1 Others 1*
Newcastle U *(£2,250,000 on 29/9/2000) PL 14+45/5 FLC 2+3 FAC 0+7 Others 5+12/4*
Portsmouth *(Loaned on 3/2/2004) PL 10+5/4*

LUCAS David Anthony
Born: Preston, 23 November 1977
Height: 6'2" **Weight:** 13.10
International Honours: E: Yth
David made only two appearances for Preston last term as he slipped behind Andy Lonergan in the goalkeeping pecking order and he joined Sheffield Wednesday on loan in October. The move was a success and he enjoyed a second spell at Hillsborough, only to suffer medial ligament damage at Port Vale and this effectively ended his season.

Preston NE *(From trainee on 12/12/1994) FL 117+5 FLC 10 FAC 7 Others 11*
Darlington *(Loaned on 14/12/1995) FL 6*
Darlington *(Loaned on 3/10/1996) FL 7*
Scunthorpe U *(Loaned on 23/12/1996) FL 6 Others 2*
Sheffield Wed *(Loaned on 1/10/2003) FL 17 Others 1*

LUCKETTI Christopher (Chris) James
Born: Rochdale, 28 September 1971
Height: 6'0" **Weight:** 13.6

Lomano Lua Lua

Club Honours: Div 2 '97
Captain Chris was one of a number of Preston players to miss out due to injury in 2003-04, suffering a broken toe in December. Trying to play on only exacerbated the problem and on his return he suffered a further injury which kept him out for an extended period. Playing at the heart of the defence, Chris is an inspiration to those around him, leading by example in his determination to clear his lines. The fairness of his play was illustrated by a mere two bookings, whilst he scored just once during the campaign, with a stylish drive against Nottingham Forest.
Rochdale (Trainee) FL 1
Stockport Co (Free on 23/8/1990)
Halifax T (Free on 12/7/1991) FL 73+5/2 FLC 2/1 FAC 2 Others 4
Bury (£50,000 on 1/10/1993) FL 235/8 FLC 16 FAC 11/1 Others 15/1
Huddersfield T (£750,000 + on 14/6/1999) FL 68/1 FLC 7/1
Preston NE (£750,000 on 23/8/2001) FL 120/5 FLC 6 FAC 5

LUMSDON Christopher (Chris)
Born: Newcastle, 15 December 1979
Height: 5'7" **Weight:** 10.6
Chris started the 2003-04 campaign in excellent form for Barnsley. However, he lost his place in the side in October and thereafter most of his first-team appearances came from the substitutes' bench. Despite having a season left on his contract he was made available for transfer in the summer.
Sunderland (From trainee on 3/7/1997) P/FL 2 FLC 1+1
Blackpool (Loaned on 3/2/2000) FL 6/1
Crewe Alex (Loaned on 11/9/2000) FL 14+2
Barnsley (£350,000 on 8/10/2001) FL 70+15/13 FLC 2+1 FAC 3+3 Others 2+1

LUNDEKVAM Claus
Born: Norway, 22 February 1973
Height: 6'3'' **Weight:** 12.10
International Honours: Norway: 28; U21-16
Claus continued to be among the most arresting centre backs in the Premiership, and, whether he was playing in tandem with Michael Svensson or Danny Higginbotham, the Saints' central defensive partnership was arguably one of the best in the country. Physically imposing, he is predictably commanding in the air, but surprisingly dextrous on the deck, being subtle in the challenge and astute going forward. His only weakness,

to date, has been a failure to score. After eight years and 295 appearances in red and white his goal drought ended at Wolverhampton in April. The other landmark of the past season: his 300th appearance for the Saints, against Aston Villa at St Mary's in May.
Southampton (£400,000 from SK Brann, Norway on 3/9/1996) PL 250+6/1 FLC 24+3 FAC 17 Others 2

LUNT Kenneth (Kenny) Vincent
Born: Runcorn, 20 November 1979
Height: 5'10" **Weight:** 10.0
International Honours: E: Yth; Sch
This long-serving Crewe Alexandra midfielder was once again a near ever-present during the 2003-04 campaign and has now topped 300 senior appearances for the club. A talented player with good vision, he can be relied upon to score several goals during a season, especially from dead-ball situations, and netted seven times last term.
Crewe Alex (From trainee on 12/6/1997) FL 254+30/26 FLC 17+4/1 FAC 13+1 Others 4/1

LUZHNY Oleg
Born: Ukraine, 5 August 1968
Height: 6'1" **Weight:** 12.3
Club Honours: CS '99; FAC '03
International Honours: Ukraine: 52; USSR: 8
The first of Wolves summer signings, this veteran right back came on as a substitute at Blackburn in the first match, but did not seem ready for first-team duties, and did not feature again until the Carling Cup-tie with Darlington. He managed a brief run in December and showed signs of the strong tackles and composure that had given him a good career in football. After that he had the occasional outing but could not win a regular place in the side.
Arsenal (£1,800,000 from Dinamo Kiev, Ukraine on 9/7/1999) PL 58+17 FLC 4 FAC 9 Others 2
Wolverhampton W (Free on 24/7/2003) PL 4+2 FLC 2 FAC 2

LUZI-BERNARDI Patrice
Born: Ajaccio, France, 8 July 1980
Height: 6'2" **Weight:** 14.1
This young goalkeeper was third in line behind Jerzy Dudek and Chris Kirkland at Liverpool last term. He made his first-team debut for the Reds in January, replacing the injured Dudek for the last

fifteen minutes of the vital game at Chelsea. Patrice did well to protect his team's narrow 1-0 lead, but the club then signed the experienced Paul Jones as short-term cover for the next two games and Patrice made no further appearances.
Liverpool (Free from Monaco, Monte Carlo on 5/8/2002) PL 0+1

LYNCH Simon George
Born: Montreal, Canada, 19 May 1982
Height: 6'0" **Weight:** 10.0
International Honours: S: B-1; U21-13
Simon had not made a start for Preston when he was loaned to Stockport in December. He took a couple of games to settle in, but soon showed why he is highly rated as he scored three goals in successive games. On his return, the lively young striker's first start came in midfield at Sunderland and he featured regularly in the squad for the remainder of the season. His only Preston goal came with a crisp strike at Wimbledon, but he will be hoping for more first-team opportunities in 2004-05.
Glasgow Celtic (From juniors on 13/7/1999) SL 2+1/3 Others 1+1
Preston NE (£130,000 on 8/1/2003) FL 12+24/2
Stockport Co (Loaned on 12/12/2003) FL 9/3

LYTTLE Desmond (Des)
Born: Wolverhampton, 24 September 1971
Height: 5'9" **Weight:** 12.13
Club Honours: Div 1 '98
After being released by West Bromwich Albion, Des began last term training with Telford United. He then had a very brief spell with Dr Martens League club Stourport Swifts before joining Northampton on a short-term contract, which was eventually extended to cover the remainder of the season. An experienced right back who likes to push forward, he featured regularly in the starting line-up for the Cobblers.
Leicester C (From trainee on 1/9/1990)
Swansea C (£12,500 from Worcester C on 9/7/1992) FL 46/1 FLC 2 FAC 5 Others 3
Nottingham F (£375,000 on 27/7/1993) F/PL 177+8/3 FLC 19+1 FAC 16 Others 8
Port Vale (Loaned on 20/11/1998) FL 7
Watford (Free on 28/7/1999) PL 11 FLC 1
West Bromwich A (Free on 21/3/2000) P/FL 61+15/1 FLC 8 FAC 2+1 Others 2 (Freed during 2003 close season)
Northampton T (Free from Stourport Swifts on 4/11/2003) FL 23+4 FAC 5 Others 3

M

MABIZELA Oldjohn **Mbulelo**
Born: Pietermaritzburg, South Africa, 16 September 1980
Height: 5'10" **Weight:** 12.6
International Honours: South Africa: 31
Despite captaining his country while still in his early 20s, this strong defender found first-team opportunities few and far between at Tottenham last term and managed just a handful of appearances from the substitutes' bench. Mbulelo is a traditional defender, strong in the tackle, tenacious and good vision. Whilst not being the tallest defender in the line up, he makes his presence felt with his organisational skill and international experience.
Tottenham H (Signed from Orlando Pirates, South Africa on 26/8/2003) PL 0+6/1 FLC 0+1

McALISKEY John James
Born: Huddersfield, 2 September 1984
Height: 6'5" **Weight:** 12.7
This promising Huddersfield Town striker enjoyed a dream debut, coming off the bench to score in the home win over Macclesfield Town in March. He did even better when given his first start, scoring two goals in the final three minutes to snatch an unlikely victory over Scunthorpe. A fine prospect who also possesses pace and good control, John signed a new contract for the Terriers during the season.
Huddersfield T (From trainee on 1/5/2004) FL 5+3/4 Others 0+2

McALLISTER Gary
Born: Motherwell, 25 December 1964
Height: 6'1" **Weight:** 11.12
Club Honours: S Div 1 '85; Div 1 '92; CS '92, '02; FLC '01; FAC '01; UEFAC '01; ESC '01
International Honours: S: 57; B-2; U21-1
Coventry's player-manager continued to be the fulcrum of the team's early-season performances but in October and again in early December he temporarily stepped down from management duties in order to spend more time with his family and a month later the club reluctantly accepted his resignation. His midfield skill was missed after his departure but several players were forced to take more responsibility within the team and overall the performances improved. Soon after leaving Highfield Road Gary confirmed that his playing career was over.

Motherwell (Signed from Fir Park BC on 5/9/1981) SL 52+7/6 SLC 3+1 SC 7/2
Leicester C (£125,000 on 15/8/1985) FL 199+2/46 FLC 14+1/3 FAC 5/2 Others 4
Leeds U (£1,000,000 on 2/7/1990) F/PL 230+1/31 FLC 26/4 FAC 24/6 Others 14/4
Coventry C (£3,000,000 on 26/7/1996) PL 119/20 FLC 11/5 FAC 10/1
Liverpool (Free on 6/7/2000) PL 35+20/5 FLC 3+3/1 FAC 4+1 Others 10+11/3
Coventry C (Free on 5/7/2002) FL 55/10 FLC 2/1 FAC 3/1

McANUFF Joel (Jobi) Joshua Frederick
Born: Edmonton, 9 November 1981
Height: 5'11" **Weight:** 11.10
International Honours: Jamaica: 1
The only surprise about Jobi's last season with the Dons was how long it took for the club's administrators to sell him. An exciting, pacy right winger possessing a ferocious shot with both feet, he netted a glorious late winner in the backs-to-the-wall win at West Bromwich Albion, and scored another cracker at Crystal Palace in late January, which proved to be his last game before he was sold to West Ham for a bargain fee. He scored a stunning goal for the Hammers against Crewe, leaving a trail of defenders behind as he sped from the halfway line and hit a low shot into the corner. Another superb run made a goal for Marlon Harewood in the match against Watford. He is a player who excites the crowd and will surely become a big favourite with the Hammers' fans.
Wimbledon (From trainee on 11/7/2000) FL 76+20/13 FLC 2/1 FAC 4+2/1
West Ham U (£300,000 on 4/2/2004) FL 4+8/1 Others 0+1

McATEER Jason Wynn
Born: Birkenhead, 18 June 1971
Height: 5'10" **Weight:** 11.12
International Honours: RoI: 52; B-1
This experienced midfielder started the 2003-04 campaign as club captain at Sunderland but saw his campaign interrupted by a succession of injuries beginning with a back problem during the season opener at Nottingham Forest. Jason also suffered hamstring problems throughout the season but a high point for him came in February when he was recalled to the Republic of Ireland side after 18 months in the international wilderness. With the ability to operate in central midfield or wide on the right, Jason's versatility experience, and enthusiasm+were missed by the Black Cats

when he was sidelined, but he played a vital role in the Wearsiders' run to the FA Cup semi-finals. He was released by the club in the summer.
Bolton W (Signed from Marine on 22/1/1992) P/FL 109+5/8 FLC 11/2 FAC 11/3 Others 8+1/2
Liverpool (£4,500,000 on 6/9/1995) PL 84+16/3 FLC 12+1 FAC 11+1/3 Others 12+2
Blackburn Rov (£4,000,000 on 28/1/1999) P/FL 58+14/4 FLC 4 FAC 7
Sunderland (£1,000,000 on 19/10/2001) P/FL 53/5 FAC 6 Others 2

MACAULEY Stephen (Steve) Roy
Born: Lytham, 4 March 1969
Height: 6'1" **Weight:** 12.10
Club Honours: FAYC '86
Steve was recovering from a knee operation at the start of last season, which was the prelude to an injury-strewn campaign such that he was unable to sustain a regular run of appearances for Macclesfield. His experience as a central defender in a back-four formation missed, especially his ability in the air and his marshalling of the players around him. Towards the end of the season he lost his place in the side and his contract was cancelled by mutual consent at the beginning of April.
Manchester C (From trainee on 5/11/1987. Released during 1988 close season)
Crewe Alex (£25,000 from Fleetwood T on 24/3/1992) FL 247+14/26 FLC 20 FAC 16/1 Others 20/3
Macclesfield T (Loaned on 14/12/2001) FL 4 FAC 1
Macclesfield T (Loaned on 15/2/2002) FL 8 Rochdale (Free on 29/7/2002) FL 6 Others 1
Macclesfield T (Loaned on 22/11/2002) FL 4/1
Macclesfield T (Free on 16/1/2003) FL 32 FAC 2 Others 1

McBRIDE Brian Robert
Born: Arlington Heights, USA, 19 June 1972
Height: 6'1" **Weight:** 12.7
International Honours: USA: 76
Brian returned to the Premiership when Fulham signed him from Columbus Crew during the January transfer window. He made an immediate impact, scoring minutes after coming on as a substitute against Tottenham. A player who holds the ball up well, he creates chances for others. He also has a lethal shot and scored an exceptional goal to help Fulham gain a draw at Portsmouth. Possibly his best game came in the 2-0 win at Bolton when he netted both goals. As well as

appearing up front he was also used as an attacking midfielder on a number of occasions. He was selected for the USA during the summer.
Preston NE (Loaned from Columbus Crew, USA, ex St Louis University, VFL Wolfsburg, on 15/9/2000) FL 8+1/1 FLC 1 FAC 1
Everton (Loaned from Columbus Crew, USA on 5/2/2003) PL 7+1/4
Fulham (£600,000 from Columbus Crew, USA on 27/1/2004) PL 5+11/4 FAC 3/1

McCAFFERTY Neil
Born: Derry, 19 July 1984
Height: 5'7" **Weight:** 10.6
This promising young Charlton midfielder was a regular in the reserves last term and in December he joined Cambridge United on loan to gain experience of first-team football. Neil made his debut in the Boxing Day game against Southend when he featured on the right-hand side of midfield and enjoyed a short run in the U's line-up before returning to the Valley.
Charlton Ath (From trainee on 2/8/2001)
Cambridge U (Loaned on 23/12/2003) FL 5+1

McCALL Andrew **Stuart** Murray
Born: Leeds, 10 June 1964
Height: 5'7" **Weight:** 12.0
Club Honours: Div 3 '85; SPL '92, '93, '94, '95, '96; SLC '92, '93; SC '92, '93, '96
International Honours: S: 40; U21-2
Following the departure of Kevin Blackwell, Stuart took on duties as first-team coach for Sheffield United whilst continuing his involvement with the reserves. He also played more than 40 games for the Blades, featuring as a defensive midfielder, picking up and distributing the loose ball, being available when his side had possession and closing down opponents as well as more than occasionally going forward. He scored two goals, one in the defeat of his former club Bradford City and the second which made him the oldest player to score a League goal for the Blades.
Bradford C (From apprentice on 1/6/1982) FL 235+3/37 FLC 19/3 FAC 11/3 Others 16/3
Everton (£850,000 on 1/6/1988) FL 99/4/6 FLC 11/1 FAC 16+2/3 Others 9+1
Glasgow R (£1,200,000 on 15/8/1991) SL 186+8/14 SLC 15/3 SC 25+2 Others 28/2
Bradford C (Free on 4/6/1998) P/FL 154+3/8 FLC 5+3/1 FAC 5+1 Others 4
Sheffield U (Free on 2/7/2002) FL 69+2/2 FLC 7 FAC 9 Others 0+1

McCAMMON Mark Jason
Born: Barnet, 7 August 1978
Height: 6'5" **Weight:** 14.5
Mark had an unfortunate time with injuries for Millwall last term. He spent much of the campaign recovering from a knee injury suffered at the end of the 2002-03 season and did not return to first-team action until February. Then soon afterwards he suffered a head injury at Ipswich causing another setback. A tall target man, he is strong, excellent in the air, holds the ball up well and can shoot with either foot.
Cambridge U (Free from Cambridge C on 31/12/1996) FL 1+3 FAC 0+1 Others 1
Charlton Ath (Free on 17/3/1999) FL 1+3 FLC 0+1
Swindon T (Loaned on 3/1/2000) FL 4
Brentford (£100,000 + on 18/7/2000) FL 46+29/10 FLC 4/1 FAC 3+1/1 Others 3+5/3
Millwall (Free on 27/3/2003) FL 10+4/2 FAC 0+1

McCANN Gavin Peter
Born: Blackpool, 10 January 1978
Height: 5'11" **Weight:** 11.0
International Honours: E: 1
This committed midfielder joined Aston Villa during the 2003 close season. Noted for his ball-winning and distribution qualities in a deep-lying role, he is also capable of knocking in a few goals. Gavin played in the 'holding' role in midfield for Villa and despite missing out occasionally through injury he was a vital presence in the team. He produced displays of relentless running and biting tackles, also proving his ability to hit a range of passes with either foot. Gavin scored his first goal for the club when heading home against Crystal Palace in the Carling Cup.
Everton (From trainee on 1/7/1995) PL 5+6
Sunderland (£500,000 on 27/11/1998) P/FL 106+10/8 FLC 4+3/2 FAC 11+1/3
Aston Villa (£2,250,000 on 31/7/2003) PL 28 FLC 6/2 FAC 1

McCANN Grant Samuel
Born: Belfast, 14 April 1980
Height: 5'10" **Weight:** 12.0
International Honours: NI: 9; U21-11
This talented left-footed midfield player enjoyed a fine season at Cheltenham Town last term. Operating either on the left-hand side or in the centre of midfield, he proved a valuable asset to the team with his skills on the ball and range of passing. Grant also showed he had an eye for goal, finishing as the Robins' leading scorer with 12 goals in all competitions, including a spectacular 25-yard effort in the FA Cup tie against Fulham. He added

further international caps for Northern Ireland against Armenia and Estonia during the season.
West Ham U (From trainee on 6/7/1998) PL 0+4
Livingston (Loaned on 27/8/1999) SL 0+4
Notts Co (Loaned on 11/8/2000) FL 2 FLC 1
Cheltenham T (Loaned on 17/10/2000) FL 27+3/3 FAC 2 Others 1
Cheltenham T (Loaned on 4/10/2002) FL 8 Others 2/1
Cheltenham T (£50,000 on 29/1/2003) FL 62/14 FLC 1/1 FAC 3/3 Others 1

McCANN Neil Doherty
Born: Greenock, 11 August 1974
Height: 5'10" **Weight:** 10.4
Club Honours: SPD '99, '00, '03; SC '98, '99, '00, '02, '03; SLC '02
International Honours: S: 22; B-2; U21-9
The positive aspect of Neil's move from Glasgow to Southampton last August was that it brought an instant recall to the Scotland squad (for whom he scored in the 3-1 win over the Faroe Islands in September), the negative: he failed to impress the more critical St Mary's regulars. A natural left winger, happy to track back and help his defence, he showed glimpses of true class, but a series of petty injuries, from September onwards, and the unsettled managerial situation from December were not conducive to a player making a bid for regular first-team consideration.
Dundee (Signed from Port Glasgow on 14/5/1992) SL 73+6/5 SLC 5/1 SC 6 Others 4
Heart of Midlothian (Signed on 30/7/1996) SL 68+6/19 SLC 8+1/3 SC 10/2 Others 4/2
Glasgow R (£2,000,000 on 14/12/1998) SL 66+47/19 SLC 6+1 SC 18+4/3 Others 13+16/3
Southampton (£1,500,000 on 7/8/2003) PL 9+9 FLC 0+2 Others 0+1

McCANN Ryan Patrick
Born: Bellshill, 21 September 1981
Height: 5'8" **Weight:** 11.3
An attacking midfielder who has an eye for goal, Ryan was an early-season signing for Hartlepool from Glasgow giants Celtic. Initially lacking in match fitness, he was a regular in the club's successful reserve team, although he failed to make the anticipated first-team breakthrough and was restricted to a handful of substitute appearances.
Glasgow Celtic (From juniors on 10/7/1998) SL 1
St Johnstone (Loaned on 26/7/2002) SL 13+3/2 SLC 2 Others 1/1
Hartlepool U (Free on 29/8/2003) FL 0+4 FLC 0+1

MACCARONE Massimo
Born: Galliate, Italy, 9 September 1979
Height: 6'0" **Weight:** 11.12
Club Honours: FLC '04
International Honours: Italy 2; U21
Massimo suff e red an early-season
setback when he injured ankle ligaments
in a pre-season friendly at Hull City in
July and he did not feature in
Middlesbrough's first team until mid-
October. As a consequence he struggled
to find both form and confidence and
was in and out of the side for most of
the campaign. He was inconsolable
when he was left out of the Carling Cup
final team against Bolton Wanderers at
the Millennium Stadium. However,
instead of re t reating into his shell he
knuckled down and the Riverside fans
saw a revitalised player end the season in
fine style, finishing on a total of seven
goals in all competitions.
*Middlesbrough (£8,150,000 from Empoli,
Italy, ex AC Milan, Modena, on 20/7/2002) PL
39+18/15 FLC 5/1 FAC 0+2*

McCARTHY Paul Jason
Born: Cork, 4 August 1971
Height: 5'10" **Weight:** 13.12
International Honours: Rol: U21-10;
Yth; Sch
This experienced defender was a regular
when fit for Oxford United last term, but
injuries restricted his appearances
somewhat. A good organiser at the back
and comfortable when pushing the team
forward, Paul also grabbed a couple of
useful goals against Kidderminster and
Cambridge. He was released by the U's in
the summer.
*Brighton & Hove A (From trainee on
26/4/1989) FL 180+1/6 FLC 11/1 FAC 13
Others 12/1*
*Wycombe W (£100,000 on 5/7/1996) FL
199+13/9 FLC 17+1/5 FAC 21/5 Others 8*
Oxford U (Free on 27/3/2003) FL 34+1/3

McCARTNEY George
Born: Belfast, 29 April 1981
Height: 6'0" **Weight:** 12.6
International Honours: NI: 16; U21-5;
Yth; Sch
George firmly established himself at left
back for Sunderland last season, finishing
the campaign as club captain. An
excellent attacker down the flanks, he
forged a superb partnership with Julio
Arca which produced many a goal for the
team. George led Sunderland to the FA
Cup and play-off semi-finals, and
although the Wearsiders fell short on
both fronts the experience was invaluable
for the youngster. With the club missing

out on promotion, it was a relief when it
was announced that George had signed a
new contract that will keep him at the
Stadium of Light. He added several more
caps for Northern Ireland during the
campaign.
*Sunderland (From trainee on 28/5/1998)
P/FL 69+16 FLC 6+2 FAC 8+3 Others 2*

McCLARE Sean Patrick
Born: Rotherham, 12 January 1978
Height: 5'10" **Weight:** 11.12
International Honours: Rol: U21-3

One of three summer signings for
Rochdale, Sean was a mainstay in the
cent re of midfield last term. Playing with
a succession of partners he
demonstrated an excellent passing game,
although unfortunately he was unable to
get himself on the score sheet. Sean
missed a few games through suspension
and lost his place briefly as new boss
Steve Parkin juggled with the side, but
he was back, in a midfield five, for the
crucial run-in at the end of season
bef o rebeing released.

Jamie McCombe (left)

Barnsley *(From trainee on 3/7/1996)* FL 29+21/6 FLC 10+3 FAC 5+1/1
Rochdale *(Loaned on 22/3/2000)* FL 5+4
Port Vale *(Free on 20/10/2001)* FL 28+12/1 FAC 1+1 Others 2+3
Rochdale *(Free on 24/7/2003)* FL 33+5 FLC 1 FAC 1 Others 1

McCOMBE Jamie Paul
Born: Scunthorpe, 1 January 1983
Height: 6'5" **Weight:** 12.6
After starting in six of Scunthorpe United's first ten League games, Jamie fell out of favour and was sent to Nationwide Conference outfit Halifax Town on loan in October. He returned after a month, but had to settle mainly for a substitutes' role, coming off the bench in January as a makeshift centre forward to curl home a superb goal in the 2-0 FA Cup victory over Barnsley. A giant central defender, who is strong in the air, he was allowed to join local rivals Lincoln City in March. He came into the team as the right-sided player in a three-man centre-back formation and was occasionally pushed up front as an extra striker, but knee and rib injuries meant he missed the final games. He was offered a new 12-month contract in the summer. Jamie is the brother of Huddersfield Town youngster John McCombe.
Scunthorpe U *(From trainee on 28/11/2001)* FL 42+21/1 FLC 1 FAC 5+1/2 Others 4+1/1
Lincoln C *(Free on 11/3/2004)* FL 8 Others 1+1

McCORMACK Alan
Born: Dublin, 10 January 1984
Height: 5'8" **Weight:** 10.0
International Honours: RoI: Yth; Sch
Loaned to Orient in August, this young Preston midfielder impressed as a hard-working player always willing to put a foot in to win the ball. On his return to Deepdale he gradually broke into the first-team squad, making his debut from the bench at Burnley, and then starting in the next game at Sunderland. An aggressive ball-winning midfielder, Alan moves around the park well in support of both defence and attack.
Preston NE *(Signed from Stella Maris BC on 14/8/2002)* FL 2+3
Leyton Orient *(Loaned on 29/8/2003)* FL 8+2 Others 1

McCORMICK Luke Martin
Born: Coventry, 15 August 1983
Height: 6'0" **Weight:** 13.12
Club Honours: Div 2 '04
Luke was given his chance for Plymouth

following the injury to Romain Larrieu last September and made the most of his opportunity, keeping his place in the line-up until the end of the campaign. The young 'keeper was an inspiration to his team mates, his handling from crosses was excellent and he made many saves in one-on-one situations. Luke managed a run of 624 minutes without conceding a goal, a new club record, and he capped a fine season by being voted as Argyle's 'Young Player of the Year'.
Plymouth Arg *(From trainee on 9/7/2002)* FL 43+1 FAC 1 Others 4

McCOURT Patrick (Paddy) James
Born: Derry, 16 December 1983
Height: 5'10" **Weight:** 11.0
International Honours: NI: 1; U21-6
Rochdale's enigmatic young winger had another stop-start season during 2003-04. Paddy managed only a handful of Football League starts indeed, he had two spells on trial away from Spotland, at Norwich and Crewe and rarely seemed to be 100 per cent fit. On the other hand he continued to provide some wonderful cameos, such as when he dribbled virtually the length of the field to win a penalty at Orient, and when on his game can run through any defence.
Rochdale *(From trainee on 11/2/2002)* FL 28+45/8 FLC 0+2 FAC 2+4/1 Others 0+5

McCREADY Christopher (Chris) James
Born: Runcorn, 5 September 1981
Height: 6'0" **Weight:** 11.11
This tall, versatile defender had a couple of decent runs in the Crewe Alexandra line-up last term, but was hampered by injuries that restricted his appearances. Chris is yet to score his first senior goal but remains confident that it will come.
Crewe Alex *(From trainee on 30/5/2000)* FL 21+10 FLC 1+1

McCULLOCH Lee Henry
Born: Bellshill, 14 May 1978
Height: 6'5" **Weight:** 13.6
Club Honours: Div 2 '03
International Honours: S: B-1; U21-14
A tall player with good physical presence, Lee again showed his versatility last term, playing the first half of the season out wide left in midfield, before moving up front to provide striking cover for Nathan Ellington and Jason Roberts. An honest, energetic and bustling player who never gives less than 100 per cent effort, what he lacks in pace he makes up for in

determination. Lee chipped in with seven goals, including the club's first-ever goal in Division One in the home draw against Preston North End. His best performance was in the home match against Crewe Alexandra when he scored twice.
Motherwell *(Signed from Cumbernauld U on 17/8/1995)* SL 75+47/28 SLC 5+2/2 SC 11+3/4
Wigan Ath *(£700,000 on 2/3/2001)* FL 98+25/21 FLC 5/1 FAC 2+1 Others 1+1

McDERMOTT John
Born: Middlesbrough, 3 February 1969
Height: 5'7" **Weight:** 11.0
Club Honours: AMC '98
After agreeing new terms for Grimsby this veteran defender was out of the side for the early matches of the 2003-04 campaign with sciatica. However, when he regained his place John struggled to find his form and then in the new year a hernia problem was diagnosed necessitating surgery and keeping him out of the side for the rest of the season.
Grimsby T *(From trainee on 1/6/1987)* FL 535+18/8 FLC 36+2 FAC 32+1/2 Others 21

McDONAGH William (Will)
Born: Dublin, 14 March 1983
Height: 6'1" **Weight:** 11.12
One of the most versatile members of the Carlisle United squad, Will is equally at home in midfield or in central defence where his stamina and strength in the tackle can be used to advantage. Last term he was disrupted by injury, particularly in the second half of the season, but his overall performances reflected an increasing maturity in his play.
Carlisle U *(Signed from Bohemians, Ireland on 16/10/2001)* FL 40+23/4 FLC 1 FAC 4 Others 7+2/3

McDONALD Scott
Born: Melbourne, Australia, 21 August 1983
Height: 5'8" **Weight:** 12.4
International Honours: Australia: U23-2; Yth
Scott joined Wimbledon on a short-term contract after scoring whilst on trial and made his debut as a substitute in the August home defeat by Crystal Palace. A sturdily-built left-footed striker with good close control, he had a couple of decent matches at reserve level, but failed to impress for the first team and was released almost as quickly as he signed. Later in the campaign he joined Motherwell and made an immediate

Luke McCormick

impact, scoring on his debut against St Johnstone. He was a regular for 'Well in the second half of the campaign and signed a new contract in the summer.
Southampton (Signed from Eastern Pride, Australia on 23/8/2000) PL 0+2 FLC 1
Huddersfield T (Loaned on 27/7/2002) FL 7+6/1 FLC 0+1
Bournemouth (Free on 27/3/2003) FL 3+4/1 Others 0+1
Wimbledon (Free on 19/8/2003) FL 0+2

McEVELEY James (Jay)
Michael
Born: Liverpool, 11 February 1985
Height: 6'1" **Weight:** 12.11
International Honours: E: U21-1
This strapping young defender arrived at Burnley on loan from neighbours Blackburn Rovers last December, and showed promise in four substitute appearances. Jay was preferred to Mo Camara at left back for the FA Cup tie at Mansfield, but that proved to be his only start for the club as he dislocated his knee in that game, effectively ending his season.
Blackburn Rov (From trainee on 8/7/2002) PL 9 FLC 3+1 FAC 2
Burnley (Loaned on 15/12/2003) FL 0+4 FAC 1

McEVILLY Lee Richard
Born: Liverpool, 15 April 1982
Height: 6'0" **Weight:** 13.0
International Honours: NI: 1; U23-1; U21-9
Lee began the 2003-04 campaign on the bench for Rochdale, but soon reappeared to score penalties in three successive games. However, his season was disrupted by suspension and when Steve Parkin returned as manager, Lee was sent out on loan to Accrington Stanley. After the sale of Paul Connor he was recalled to take his place up front and scored with a superb header against champions Doncaster but signed permanently for Stanley in May. Lee continued to represent Northern Ireland at U21 and U23 levels during the season.
Rochdale (£20,000 from Burscough on 24/12/2001) FL 55+30/25 FAC 5+2/1 Others 3/1

McFADDEN James
Born: Glasgow, 14 April 1983
Height: 5'10" **Weight:** 10.10
International Honours: S: 14; B-1; U21-7
The arrival of one of the most sought after talents from north of the border was a major boost for Everton fans in a generally disappointing season. Initially employed as a left winger, James had an

excellent start to his Blues career with superb performances in the victories over Stockport and Leeds, although he suffered a subsequent dip in form when many thought his talents could be best used in a forward role. When showing his best form, James is a mesmerising dribbler who is difficult to dispossess and he also has fine two-footed crossing and finishing ability – the latter shown in the three goals he has scored in his embryonic Scotland career.
Motherwell (From juniors on 31/7/1999) SL 52+11/26 SLC 1/1 SC 5+1/5
Everton (£1,250,000 on 8/9/2003) PL 11+12 FLC 3 FAC 1

McFAUL Shane
Born: Dublin, 23 May 1986
Height: 6'1" **Weight:** 11.10
One of several promising youngsters on the books at Notts County, Shane is a skilful midfield playmaker with excellent vision and a wide range of passing. He made his senior debut as a substitute at Swindon at the end of August and also featured in several more first-team games in the first half of the season.
Notts Co (From trainee on 28/2/2004) FL 2+4 Others 1

McGHEE David (Dave)
Christopher
Born: Worthing, 19 June 1976
Height: 5'11" **Weight:** 12.4
Dave had another injury-hit season for Leyton Orient last term and managed only a handful of appearances as a centre half and in central midfield, although he was the club captain. He was eventually released from his contract in March and joined Canvey Island.
Brentford (From trainee on 15/7/1994) FL 95+22/8 FLC 5+2/1 FAC 9/1 Others 8+1 (Freed on 22/1/1999)
Leyton Orient (Free from Stevenage Borough on 11/11/1999) FL 108+7/7 FLC 5 FAC 9 Others 7

McGILL Brendan
Born: Dublin, 22 March 1981
Height: 5'8" **Weight:** 9.8
International Honours: RoI: Yth (UEFA-U16 '98)
Brendan was a near ever-present for Carlisle United last term and was rewarded for his consistency with the club's 'Player of the Year' award. He was also voted the 'Most Improved Performer' and his clever and determined running, particularly on the right flank, posed a constant threat to opposition defences. Brendan's seven goals made him United's

joint-top scorer, and thanks to his close-range effort at home to Cheltenham he now holds the distinction of scoring the club's last goal in the Football League.
Sunderland (Signed from River Valley Rangers on 29/7/1998) FLC 0+1
Carlisle U (Loaned on 7/9/2001) FL 27+1/2 FAC 3 Others 1
Carlisle U (Free on 15/8/2002) FL 64+14/10 FLC 1/1 FAC 3+1 Others 6+2

McGLEISH Scott
Born: Barnet, 10 February 1974
Height: 5'9" **Weight:** 11.3
Red-hot striker Scott enjoyed his best ever season for Colchester last term, finishing up as the club's leading scorer with some 17 goals, including his first-ever senior hat-trick in the LDV Vans Trophy tie against Northampton. A real handful in the air, he spent some time out of the team towards the end of the season before returning for the closing fixtures.
Charlton Ath (Free from Edgware T on 24/5/1994) FL 0+6
Leyton Orient (Loaned on 10/3/1995) FL 4+2/1 Others 1/1
Peterborough U (Free on 4/7/1995) FL 3+10 FLC 0+1 FAC 0+1 Others 3+1/2
Colchester U (Loaned on 23/2/1996) FL 10+5/6 Others 2
Cambridge U (Loaned on 2/9/1996) FL 10/7 FLC 1
Leyton Orient (£50,000 on 22/11/1996) FL 36/7 FLC 3/1 FAC 1 Others 1
Barnet (£70,000 on 1/10/1997) FL 106+28/36 FLC 5/4 FAC 3 Others 7+2/2
Colchester U (£15,000 on 11/1/2001) FL 118+26/38 FLC 4 FAC 9+1/2 Others 7+2/7

McGLINCHEY Brian Kevin
Born: Londonderry, 26 October 1977
Height: 5'7" **Weight:** 10.2
Club Honours: Div 3 '01
International Honours: NI: B-1; U21-14; Yth
Brought in on loan to fill Torquay's problem left-back slot, Brian stayed for three months before returning to Plymouth. After agreeing a settlement on his contract, he returned to Plainmoor on a permanent basis. Brian is a highly polished orthodox left back, who likes to get forward but not to the detriment of his defensive duties.
Manchester C (From trainee on 4/12/1995)
Port Vale (Free on 1/7/1998) FL 10+5/1 FLC 0+1 FAC 1
Gillingham (Free on 3/8/1999) FL 7+7/1 FLC 3+1 FAC 4/1 Others 1
Plymouth Arg (Free on 1/12/2000) FL 54+14/2 FLC 1 FAC 3+2 Others 4+1
Torquay U (Free on 12/9/2003) FL 34

McGOLDRICK David
Born: Nottingham, 29 November 1987
Height: 6'1" **Weight:** 11.10
This talented young striker made excellent progress in Notts County's youth and reserve teams and went on to make his debut in senior football whilst still a local schoolboy. He made a handful of appearances in the first team, when he impressed with his talent, but chose not to sign a contract for the Magpies at the end of the season.
Notts Co *(Associated Schoolboy) FL 2+2*

McGRATH John Matthew
Born: Limerick, 27 March 1980
Height: 5'10" **Weight:** 10.8
International Honours: RoI: U21-5
John was snapped up by Doncaster Rovers during the 2003 close season, but found it difficult to break into the first-team squad last term. The left-sided midfielder produced some terrific displays for the club's reserves, but only figured occasionally in the first team because of

the good form of Michael McIndoe.
Aston Villa *(Signed from Belvedere YC on 3/9/1999) PL 0+3*
Doncaster Rov *(Free on 10/7/2003) FL 4+7 FLC 1 FAC 1 Others 1*

McGREAL John
Born: Liverpool, 2 June 1972
Height: 5'11" **Weight:** 12.8
John was unable to make a first-team appearance for Ipswich until December last term, a legacy of the previous season's injuries, but he gave the defence more stability whenever he played. He formed a particularly effective defensive unit with Matt Elliott at the end of the season, but injuries had the last laugh when a calf strain picked up in the first leg of the play-off semi-final with West Ham prevented him from playing in the return game.
Tranmere Rov *(From trainee on 3/7/1990) FL 193+2/1 FLC 20+1 FAC 8 Others 7+2*
Ipswich T *(£650,000 on 4/8/1999) P/FL 120+3/4 FLC 12 FAC 5 Others 10/1*

McGREGOR Mark Dale Thomas
Born: Chester, 16 February 1977
Height: 5'11" **Weight:** 11.5
The 2003-04 season started late for Mark, as a knee injury kept him out of first-team contention until November. Once in the side, he proved difficult to replace and he added a solid feel to the Burnley defence that had previously been lacking, in partnership in the middle with David May or occasionally Graham Branch. Although he contributed one goal to the cause, and is not averse to trying his luck upfield, Mark is at his best as a pure no-nonsense defender, solid in the tackle and usually in the right place to clear any danger.
Wrexham *(From trainee on 4/7/1995) FL 237+7/11 FLC 9 FAC 24+1 Others 11*
Burnley *(Free on 20/7/2001) FL 46+8/2 FLC 4/1 FAC 5+2*

McGURK David Michael
Born: Middlesbrough, 30 September 1982
Height: 6'0" **Weight:** 11.10

James McFadden

This tall, young defender started the 2003-04 season on the right-hand side of the defence for Darlington but lost his place following the defeat by Hornchurch in the FA Cup and featured in only a handful more games. Strong in the tackle and effective in the air, he showed a much greater composure in his game last term.

Darlington *(From trainee on 9/8/2002) FL 35+8/4 FLC 3 FAC 1+1 Others 2*

McHALE Christopher (Chris) Mark
Born: Birmingham, 4 November 1984
Height: 6'0" **Weight:** 12.0
After working his way up through the youth ranks Chris was finally promoted to the Kidderminster first-team squad last March as emergency back-up. He is mainly a central defender, but can also play in the centre of midfield. However, when he made his debut for the final three minutes of the last game of the season against Boston United he featured at right back.

Kidderminster Hrs *(From juniors on 25/3/2004) FL 0+1*

McHUGH Frazer Joseph
Born: Nottingham, 14 July 1981
Height: 5'9" **Weight:** 12.5
A hard-working defensive midfielder, Frazer was restricted to three starting appearances in a Bradford shirt last term. He played in the final two games of Nicky Law's reign and also started for caretaker-boss Wayne Jacobs at Stoke before Bryan Robson was appointed. The high point of his time at Valley Parade was provided by two thundering long-range strikes for the reserves when he played at right back. Frazer was released from his contract and snapped up by Notts County on a short-term deal. However, he failed to impress sufficiently to earn a longer contract during his time at Meadow Lane.

Swindon T *(From trainee on 5/8/1999) FL 13+6 FLC 0+2 Others 2+1 (Freed during 2001 close season)*
Bradford C *(Free from Halesowen, ex Tamworth, Gainsborough Trin, Bromsgrove Rov, on 27/3/2003) FL 5*
Notts Co *(Free on 22/1/2004) FL 9+4*

McINDOE Michael
Born: Edinburgh, 2 December 1979
Height: 5'8" **Weight:** 11.0
Club Honours: FAT '02; NC '03; Div 3 '04
International Honours: S: B-1
Michael joined Doncaster Rovers during the 2003 close season and had a good

campaign at Belle Vue last term. Taking up a position on the left-hand side of midfield he impressed with his pace and dribbling skills, while his crosses set up many chances for his colleagues. His success brought him to the attention of the Scotland manager Bertie Vogts, who selected him for the Futures side against Turkey in December and he gained further recognition with a place in the PFA Division Three team of the year and when winning the Rovers' Supporters Club 'Player of the Year' title.

Luton T *(From trainee on 2/4/1998) FL 19+20 FLC 4+1 FAC 0+3 Others 1 (Free to Hereford U on 20/7/2000)*
Doncaster Rov *(£50,000 from Yeovil T on 5/8/2003) FL 45/10 FLC 2 FAC 1 Others 2*

McINTOSH Martin Wyllie
Born: East Kilbride, 19 March 1971
Height: 6'2" **Weight:** 12.0
International Honours: S: B-2; Sch
A commanding left-footed central defender, Martin was regarded as the backbone of the Rotherham defence last season. However, he suffered a knee injury just before Christmas and it took some time before it was revealed he had damaged a cruciate ligament. Martin was forced to undergo surgery and this brought his campaign to a premature close.

St Mirren *(From trainee at Tottenham H on 30/11/1988) SL 2+2*
Clydebank *(Signed on 17/8/1991) SL 59+6/10 SLC 2 SC 4+1/1 Others 3/1*
Hamilton Academical *(Signed on 1/2/1994) SL 99/12 SLC 5 SC 5 Others 5/1*
Stockport Co *(£80,000 on 15/8/1997) FL 96+3/5 FLC 5+1 FAC 4*
Hibernian *(£250,000 on 10/2/2000) SL 13 SLC 3 SC 2*
Rotherham U *(£125,000 on 17/8/2001) FL 99/11 FLC 6 FAC 3*

MACKAY Malcolm (Malky) George
Born: Bellshill, 19 February 1972
Height: 6'1" **Weight:** 11.7
Club Honours: Div 1 '04
International Honours: S: 3
So proud to receive his first full Scotland cap in the April friendly in Denmark, Malky enjoyed another fantastic season at the heart of the Norwich rearguard. A traditional-style centre half, he is strong, brave and commanding in the air. A big hero for City fans, his place in Canary folklore was further cemented by his two-goal display against local rivals Ipswich Town at Carrow Road in March, in what was his 200th League appearance for the

club. His contribution to the cause was further recognised when he was voted into the PFA Division One team of the season.

Queens Park *(From juniors on 8/12/1989) SL 68+2/6 SLC 3/2 SC 2 Others 2*
Glasgow Celtic *(Signed on 6/8/1993) SL 32+5/4 SLC 5+1 SC 4/1 Others 4+1*
Norwich C *(£350,000 on 18/9/1998) FL 198+14/15 FLC 8+1 FAC 8 Others 3/1*

MACKEN Jonathan (Jon) Paul
Born: Manchester, 7 September 1977
Height: 5'10" **Weight:** 12.8
Club Honours: Div 2 '00
International Honours: E: Yth
Jon has endured a troubled run through injury and last season was no different when further knee and toe injuries restricted his appearances for Manchester City. He was finally given the chance to shine when Nicolas Anelka had to step aside and became the hero of the hour when heading the Blues' winner in an epic FA Cup confrontation with Tottenham. He soon followed that up with his first-ever goal in the Premiership in the game against Manchester United. A proven goalscorer, he is particularly effective when holding the ball up.

Manchester U *(From trainee on 10/7/1996)*
Preston NE *(£250,000 on 31/7/1997) FL 155+29/63 FLC 12+2/8 FAC 10+5/2 Others 9+3/1*
Manchester C *(£4,000,000 + on 5/3/2002) P/FL 11+17/6 FLC 0+1/1 FAC 1+2/2 Others 1+1*

McKENNA Paul Stephen
Born: Chorley, 20 October 1977
Height: 5'7" **Weight:** 11.12
Club Honours: Div 2 '00
Paul is now an established starter at Preston, having made his 250th career appearance for the club last term, and he was one of the first names on the team sheet every week. A wholehearted terrier in midfield who breaks up play well, Paul is an excellent passer of the ball, both short and long range, and is always ready to surge forward in support of the attack. The possessor of a tremendous shot, he finally found the net on a regular basis towards the end of the season with four goals in the last six games.

Preston NE *(From trainee on 2/2/1996) FL 214+18/21 FLC 12 FAC 9+2/2 Others 6+2*

McKENZIE Leon Mark
Born: Croydon, 17 May 1978
Height: 5'11" **Weight:** 11.2
Club Honours: Div 1 '04

Fans' favourite Leon had an injury-free start to the season, scoring 12 times for Peterborough before being sold to Norwich in December. He made an unbelievable start to his Canary career scoring both goals for City in their 2-0 away win at local rivals Ipswich, a victory which took the team to the top of Division One. Deceptively strong when receiving the ball with his back to goal, he is sharp on the turn and likes to take his shots at goal early, often catching defenders and goalkeepers unaware.
Crystal Palace *(From trainee on 7/10/1995) F/PL 44+41/7 FLC 5+2/1 FAC 2+4*
Fulham *(Loaned on 3/10/1997) FL 1+2*
Peterborough U *(Loaned on 13/8/1998) FL 4/3*
Peterborough U *(Loaned on 30/11/1998) FL 10/5 Others 1/1*
Peterborough U *(Free on 13/10/2000) FL 83+7/45 FLC 2 FAC 7+1/1 Others 3/4*
Norwich C *(£325,000 on 15/12/2003) FL 12+6/9*

MacKENZIE Neil David
Born: Birmingham, 15 April 1976
Height: 6'2" **Weight:** 12.12
Club Honours: AMC '02
This attacking midfield player was in and out of the Mansfield Town side last season, despite scoring a hat-trick against Bishop's Stortford in the first round of the FA Cup. He broke three fingers in a freak accident at home, which ruled him out at the turn of the year, but returned to the line-up at the end of January. Neil's chief asset is his distribution, and his accurate passes and crafty through balls unlocked many a defence during the campaign.
Stoke C *(From trainee at West Bromwich A on 9/11/1995) FL 15+27/1 FLC 1+1 FAC 0+1 Others 0+1*
Cambridge U *(Loaned on 24/3/1999) FL 3+1/1*
Cambridge U *(£45,000 on 14/10/1999) FL 20+8 FLC 1+1 FAC 5 Others 0+1*
Kidderminster Hrs *(Free on 24/11/2000) FL 20+3/3 FAC 0+1 Others 2*
Blackpool *(Free on 9/7/2001) FL 6+8/1 FLC 1+1 FAC 1+3/1 Others 3/2*
Mansfield T *(Free on 6/8/2002) FL 41+15/3 FLC 1+1 FAC 4/3 Others 2+3*

MACKIE James (Jamie) Charles
Born: London, 22 September 1985
Height: 5'8" **Weight:** 11.2
Jamie made his debut for Wimbledon at Reading on Boxing Day, producing an enthusiastic attacking display to help the club to one of its best wins of the season, and from then on he was given plenty of

opportunities. A goal would have done wonders for his confidence, but as a constant snapper at defenders' heels he rivalled a Jack Russell dog for annoyance levels. Having begun the season on expenses only in the club's U19 team, his determination to succeed was a shining example to all the club's youngsters.
Wimbledon *(Signed from Leatherhead on 9/1/2004) FL 8+5 FAC 2+1*

MACKIE John
Born: London, 5 July 1976
Height: 6'0" **Weight:** 12.6
After a four-year spell with Reading, John moved on to Leyton Orient in January. He had played only a limited part in the Royals' fortunes in the early part of the season, although typically he always played to his best, and scored a brilliant headed goal in the 3-2 home win over Preston North End. The arrival of Ivar Ingimarsson meant that he was relegated to the substitutes' bench, so he moved in search of regular first-team football. The wholehearted central defender settled in quickly with the O's and when made captain on a one-off occasion seemed to relish the role.
Reading *(Free from Sutton U on 5/11/1999) FL 61+10/3 FLC 3+1 FAC 5+2 Others 1+2*
Leyton Orient *(Free on 13/1/2004) FL 20/1*

MACKIN Levi Alan
Born: Chester, 4 April 1986
Height: 6'1" **Weight:** 12.0
This young Wrexham scholar impressed immensely on his Football League debut at Wycombe on the penultimate Saturday of the 2003-04 season. Only told of his inclusion in the starting line up when team mate Paul Barrett was taken ill shortly before the kick off, Levi played alongside fellow teenagers Craig Morgan and Simon Spender and did not disappoint. He was included in the Wales U21 training squad at the end of April.
Wrexham *(Trainee) FL 1*

McKINLAY William (Billy)
Born: Glasgow, 22 April 1969
Height: 5'9" **Weight:** 11.6
International Honours: S: 29; B-1; U21-6; Yth; Sch
Billy was offered a new contract for 2003-04 and continued to make a valuable contribution in midfield to Leicester's efforts to avoid relegation whenever he was called into action. His best form of the season, just before Christmas, coincided with City's best run in the Premiership. However, age is finally beginning to catch up and Billy was duly

released with a heartfelt 'thank you' from the club in the summer.
Dundee U *(Signed from Hamilton Thistle on 24/6/1985) SL 210+10/23 SLC 21/3 SC 23+3/4 Others 17/2*
Blackburn Rov *(£1,750,000 on 14/10/1995) PL 76+14/3 FLC 4/1 FAC 7+1 Others 1*
Leicester C *(Loaned on 27/10/2000) FLC 1*
Bradford C *(Free on 24/11/2000) PL 10+1 FAC 1*
Preston NE *(Free on 25/9/2001)*
Clydebank *(Free on 24/11/2001) SL 8 SC 1*
Leicester C *(Free on 9/8/2002) P/FL 44+9/1 FLC 1+1 FAC 4*

McKINNEY Richard
Born: Ballymoney, 18 May 1979
Height: 6'3" **Weight:** 14.0
Colchester United's reserve 'keeper had a rather frustrating time with injuries last term and apart from a brief period he was unable to dislodge Simon Brown from the line-up. When he did so, Richard picked up another injury while keeping a clean sheet in the goalless draw at Oldham Athletic and never featured again.
Manchester C *(Free from Ballymena U on 25/8/1999)*
Swindon T *(Free on 18/7/2001) FL 1*
Colchester U *(Free on 9/8/2002) FL 25+1 FLC 1 FAC 1 Others 2*

McKOY Nicholas (Nick) Paul
Born: Newham, 3 September 1986
Height: 6'0" **Weight:** 12.4
A tall, gangly central midfielder, Nick made his debut for Wimbledon as a substitute in the December home defeat by Walsall. Given a couple more chances later on in the campaign, he showed distinct promise for the future, but is still very young and once he adjusts to the faster pace of senior football he should prove to be a very solid box-to-box performer.
Wimbledon *(Trainee) FL 1+2*

McLACHLAN Fraser Malcolm
Born: Manchester, 9 November 1982
Height: 5'11" **Weight:** 12.6
Last season was a mixed one for Stockport's young midfielder who was in the line-up for the opening games, but then only managed one further start until Boxing Day when he came back into the side for the home game with Wrexham. This coincided with a better run of form and Fraser found the net in the away games at Luton and Tranmere and also scored in the 1-1 home draw with promotion-chasing Brighton. Three days later, though, County's 2-1 defeat at Colchester proved to be his last start of

the campaign as he was dropped for the vital relegation battle ahead.
Stockport Co (From trainee on 11/7/2001) FL 43+10/4 FLC 1 FAC 2 Others 0+1

McLAREN Paul Andrew
Born: High Wycombe, 17 November 1976
Height: 6'0" **Weight:** 13.4
This bright, attack-minded midfielder endured an injury-ravaged season for Sheffield Wednesday last term. A driving force for the Owls in the centre of the park, he had two lengthy spells out of action but eventually returned to the line-up for the closing stages to show the fans what they had missed. Paul was one of 13 out-of-contract players released by the club in the summer.
Luton T (From trainee on 5/1/1994) FL 137+30/4 FLC 10+4/1 FAC 11/1 Others 9
Sheffield Wed (Free on 11/6/2001) FL 83+13/8 FLC 6+1/1 FAC 2 Others 1

MacLEAN Steven (Steve)
Born: Edinburgh, 23 August 1982
Height: 5'10" **Weight:** 11.1
International Honours: S: U21-4
After breaking into the first-team squad at Rangers in the 2002-03 campaign, this talented young striker joined Scunthorpe on loan for four months at the start of last term and ended up staying the full season, finishing as the Third Division's joint-leading marksman with 25 goals. A talented, skilful front runner, who is an excellent finisher, he bagged 17 goals by mid-November including three hat-tricks. He then went over three months without a goal, but after a spell out with a groin injury he returned to form in March with six goals in six games.
Glasgow R (From juniors on 17/9/1998) SL 0+3 SC 0+1
Partick Thistle (Loaned on 31/7/2002) SL 6+6/1 SLC 0+1
Scunthorpe U (Loaned on 6/8/2003) FL 37+5/23 FLC 1+1/1 FAC 5 Others 3/1

McLEOD Izale (Izzy) Michael
Born: Birmingham, 15 October 1984
Height: 6'0" **Weight:** 11.2
A cartilage operation in October interrupted Izzy's progress at Derby but the hard-running striker forced his way back into contention. He scored against Sheffield United at Pride Park by hurrying Paddy Kenny into an error and ended the season on loan at Bramall Lane. When Paul Peschisolido joined Derby, Izzy went in the opposite direction, with an agreement that neither could figure when the teams met again in March. The young

striker made a handful of lively substitute appearances for the Blades, playing wide and making good use of his pace.
Derby Co (From trainee on 7/2/2003) FL 24+15/4 FLC 1+1
Sheffield U (Loaned on 12/3/2004) FL 1+6

McLEOD Kevin Andrew
Born: Liverpool, 12 September 1980
Height: 5'11" **Weight:** 11.3
This wide left-sided midfield player joined Queens Park Rangers on a permanent basis following his successful loan period during the 2002-03 season. He continued to show good form and was a regular in the line-up until suffering an injury at Bristol City in April, eventually returning to the substitutes' bench at the end of the campaign.
Everton (From trainee on 24/9/1998) PL 0+5 FLC 1 FAC 0+1
Queens Park R (Loaned on 21/3/2003) FL 8/2 Others 3
Queens Park R (Signed on 18/8/2003) FL 26+9/3 FLC 2 FAC 1 Others 1/1

McMAHON Daryl
Born: Dublin, 10 October 1983
Height: 5'11" **Weight:** 12.2
International Honours: RoI: Yth
This promising left-sided midfielder was capped by the Republic of Ireland at U20 level last autumn and later in the campaign he had a brief loan spell with Torquay. Daryl impressed for the Gulls when coming off the bench against Yeovil, but soon afterwards returned to Upton Park. He was released by West Ham during the summer break.
West Ham U (From trainee on 16/10/2000)
Torquay U (Loaned on 24/3/2004) FL 0+1

McMAHON Lewis James
Born: Doncaster, 2 May 1985
Height: 5'9" **Weight:** 11.4
A fine young midfield prospect, Lewis made his big breakthrough for Sheffield Wednesday towards the end of last season. A calmness and maturity beyond his years, a sure touch on the ball and an eye for a good pass all mark him out as a potential talent and he will be looking to establish himself in the line-up in 2004-05.
Sheffield Wed (Trainee) PL 9+1 Others 0+1

McMAHON Stephen Joseph
Born: Southport, 31 July 1984
Height: 5'9" **Weight:** 10.5
Club Honours: AMC '04
This promising young Blackpool midfield player was in his first year as a professional at Bloomfield Road last term.

He gained further experience of senior football, including an outing from the bench in the LDV Vans Trophy final against Southend. Stephen, who is the son of former Seasiders' manager Steve McMahon, was voted as the club's 'Young Player of the Season'.
Blackpool (From trainee on 1/7/2003) FL 10+8 FAC 0+2 Others 3+3

McMANAMAN Steven (Steve)
Born: Bootle, 11 February 1972
Height: 6'0" **Weight:** 11.10
Club Honours: FAC '92; FLC '95
International Honours: E: 28; U21-7; Yth
A series of niggling injuries prevented Steve from finding his best rhythm last term and it was a frustrating season for the former Real Madrid man who returned to the Premiership with Manchester City last August. A talented winger or central midfield player, his wealth of experience at top level may prove invaluable but injuries meant he was unable to show City fans anything like his best form.
Liverpool (From trainee on 19/2/1990) F/PL 258+14/46 FLC 32+1/10 FAC 28+1/5 Others 30/5 (Free to Real Madrid, Spain on 1/7/1999)
Manchester C (Free on 30/8/2003) PL 20+2 FLC 0+1 FAC 2+1 Others 4

McMASTER Jamie
Born: Sydney, Australia, 29 November 1982
Height: 5'10" **Weight:** 11.13
International Honours: E: Yth
This talented Leeds United youngster enjoyed a successful loan spell at Chesterfield last term. Although he prefers to play up front he was used to great effect on the right of midfield by the Spireites, his ability to go past a man and think several moves ahead proving too much for many opponents. His goal at Peterborough capped a superb passing move involving six team mates and was widely regarded as the club's 'Goal of the Season'.
Leeds U (From trainee on 30/11/1999) PL 0+4
Coventry C (Loaned on 22/11/2002) FL 2+2
Chesterfield (Loaned on 7/1/2004) FL 4+2/2

McMILLAN Stephen (Steve) Thomas
Born: Edinburgh, 19 January 1976
Height: 5'10" **Weight:** 11.10
Club Honours: Div 2 '03
International Honours: S: U21-4

A versatile left-sided player, Steve was restricted to just a handful of appearances for Wigan Athletic last season. While his ability is unquestionable, his fitness often prevents him getting a consistent run in the team and that was the case again when a series of injuries restricted him to just three outings in the new year. At his best, his pace is an asset and he loves nothing better than to push forward from his full-back position to deliver a telling cross.

Motherwell (Signed from Troon Juniors on 19/8/1993) SL 144+8/6 SLC 9 SC 13+1
Wigan Ath (£550,000 on 2/3/2001) FL 76+6 FLC 5

McNAMARA Niall Anthony
Born: Limerick, 26 January 1982
Height: 5'11" **Weight:** 11.12
International Honours: RoI: Yth
This tall, hard-working player was used in a number of different positions by Lincoln City after making his debut as a striker in the Carling Cup clash with Stockport County. Niall also appeared as a wide midfield man and in centre midfield, but struggled to win a regular first-team place. Most of his appearances were from the substitutes' bench although a thigh strain caused him to miss the second half of the season. He also had a short spell on loan at Alfreton Town in September. Niall's initial six-month contract was extended but he was released at the end of the campaign.

Nottingham F (From trainee on 2/2/1999)
Notts Co (Free on 5/7/2001) FL 0+4 (Free to Belper T on 30/6/2002)
Lincoln C (Free on 5/8/2003) FL 2+8 FLC 1 FAC 1+1 Others 1

McNAMEE Anthony
Born: Kensington, 13 July 1984
Height: 5'6" **Weight:** 10.0
International Honours: E: Yth
Anthony made only two appearances for Watford last term, both as substitute. It was a disappointing season for the young winger, who possesses outstanding skills on the ball and delivers a good cross, but sometimes neglects his defensive responsibilities. Anthony went on loan to Barnet in December to widen his experience and finished the season strongly in the reserves.

Watford (From trainee on 17/4/2002) FL 3+29/1 FLC 0+1

McNIVEN Scott Andrew
Born: Leeds, 27 May 1978
Height: 5'10" **Weight:** 12.1
International Honours: S: U21-1; Yth

Scott was a regular in the right-wing-back berth for Oxford last term and was rarely absent from the line-up. A useful player when pushing forward, Scott did not manage a goal but had plenty of attempts. Honest and hard working, he showed a good level of consistency in his performances for the U's.

Oldham Ath (From trainee on 25/10/1995) FL 204+18/3 FLC 13+1 FAC 18+1/1 Others 9+2
Oxford U (Free on 11/7/2002) FL 85/1 FLC 5 FAC 4 Others 1

McNULTY James (Jimmy)
Born: Liverpool, 13 February 1985
Height: 6'1" **Weight:** 12.0
Jimmy was introduced to the Wrexham substitutes' bench for the home encounter with Bournemouth at the end of August. Although not coming on in that game he made his senior debut towards the end of the LDV Vans Trophy tie at Stockport later in the season. That was the extent of his involvement with first-team football, although he later enjoyed a loan spell with Welsh Premier League club Bangor City. Jimmy was one of several players released by the club in the summer.

Wrexham (Trainee) Others 0+1

McPHAIL Stephen John Paul
Born: Westminster, 9 December 1979
Height: 5'10" **Weight:** 12.0
Club Honours: FAYC '97
International Honours: RoI: 10; U21-7; Yth (UEFA-U18 '98)
This skilful midfielder player was allowed to join his former youth-team manager Paul Hart at Nottingham Forest on a three-month loan at the start of last season. He impressed the City Ground fans with his skill on the ball but was recalled to Elland Road, where he forced himself back into the first-team picture. Stephen featured prominently under Eddie Gray and scored his first home goal with a curling free kick in the 2-1 victory over Manchester City in March. He also represented the Republic of Ireland during the campaign.

Leeds U (From trainee on 23/12/1996) PL 52+26/3 FLC 2+4 FAC 3 Others 15+5
Millwall (Loaned on 14/3/2002) FL 3
Nottingham F (Loaned on 27/8/2003) FL 13+1 FLC 2

McPHEE Christopher (Chris) Simon
Born: Eastbourne, 20 March 1983
Height: 5'10" **Weight:** 12.4

This young centre forward came on in leaps and bounds at Brighton during 2003-04, scoring his first senior goals and enjoying his best run to date in the side. His debut goal was a spectacular overhead effort to secure victory in the Carling Cup tie at Bristol Rovers. Always willing to chase, he is still learning the game and needs to improve his effectiveness at holding the ball up before securing a permanent first-team place.

Brighton & Hove A (From trainee on 10/6/2002) FL 19+18/4 FLC 2+2/1 FAC 1/1 Others 2+2/3

McPHEE Stephen (Steve)
Born: Glasgow, 5 June 1981
Height: 5'7" **Weight:** 10.8
This talented striker had an excellent season for Port Vale last term, finishing up as top scorer with 27 goals, the second-highest tally for the club in the previous 66 years. Although small in stature, Steve was lethal when there was a chance of a goal and he rattled in five in the club's last three games before the chances of a play-off place eventually disappeared. The only Vale player to be an ever-present during the campaign, his best goal came against Swindon Town, a casual 20-yard run and then a rocket shot past the bemused 'keeper. Not surprisingly he was a runaway winner of the club's 'Player of the Year' award.

Coventry C (From juniors on 19/11/1998)
Port Vale (Free on 30/7/2001) FL 125+5/39 FLC 4/2 FAC 6/1 Others 7/2

McSHEFFREY Gary
Born: Coventry, 13 August 1982
Height: 5'8" **Weight:** 10.10
International Honours: E: Yth
After starting the season on the transfer list Gary's future at Coventry looked bleak. However, an extended loan spell at Luton re-ignited his career as he quickly found his goal-scoring touch at Kenilworth Road. His return to first-team action for the Sky Blues in the FA Cup third round win over Peterborough saw him score an excellent goal from a free kick and he was back to stay. A pacy striker with good close control, Gary began to fulfil the potential he had shown earlier in his career. He finished the campaign with a total of 22 goals, having reached double figures for both Luton and Coventry.

Coventry C (From trainee on 27/8/1999) P/FL 31+29/16 FLC 4+1/4 FAC 3+2/1
Stockport Co (Loaned on 30/11/2001) FL 3+2/1
Luton T (Loaned on 22/8/2003) FL 18/9 FLC 1/1

265

McSPORRAN Jermaine
Born: Manchester, 1 January 1977
Height: 5'8" **Weight:** 10.10
Jermaine enjoyed an impressive season for Wycombe last term, despite a four-week absence in September with an ankle injury. His 12 goals in 35 starts were, as ever, mostly spectacular, none more so than his efforts against Swindon in the FA Cup, when he ran half the length of the pitch before cutting in to coolly slot home, and against Grimsby, when he exquisitely flicked the ball into the net on the volley. His move to Walsall on transfer-deadline day came as a huge disappointment to the fans. However, the wide attacker or striker had limited opportunities to show his blistering pace at Bescot Stadium. Released at the end of the season he was reported to have signed for Doncaster Rovers.
Wycombe W *(Signed from Oxford C on 5/11/1998) FL 117+41/30 FLC 9+1/3 FAC 10+2/4 Others 5+2/4*
Walsall *(Free on 25/3/2004) FL 2+4*

McSWEENEY David (Dave)
Born: Basildon, 28 December 1981
Height: 5'11" **Weight:** 11.7
This promising youngster had a somewhat disappointing campaign at Southend last term. Dave started the season in the unfamiliar left-back slot and despite some solid performances lost his place to Jamie Stuart. He was also unable to secure a regular place his more usual centre-back berth due to the form of Leon Cort and Mark Warren. In a bid to gain regular first-team football he was loaned out to Dr Martens League side Welling United in April, but returned with a broken rib after a handful of appearances.
Southend U *(From trainee on 30/4/2001) FL 54+16/1 FLC 1+1 FAC 8+2 Others 8+1*

McVEIGH Paul
Born: Belfast, 6 December 1977
Height: 5'6" **Weight:** 10.5
Club Honours: Div 1 '04
International Honours: NI: 15; U21-11; Yth; Sch
Paul enjoyed another excellent season for Norwich last term, playing for the most part on the left-hand side of midfield, but also showing his versatility with a string of impressive displays on the right flank. A technically gifted player with a tremendous first touch, he has a great awareness of his team mates' positions when he is in possession of the ball. He poses a real threat to his defenders with his ability to go past them on the outside or to cut inside and shoot for goal. Paul missed just two matches last season as he notched up his 150th senior appearance for the Canaries in the 1-0 win at Reading in April.
Tottenham H *(From trainee on 10/7/1996) PL 2+1/1*
Norwich C *(Free on 23/3/2000) FL 117+25/28 FLC 1+2 FAC 6/1 Others 3/1*

MADDISON Lee Robert
Born: Bristol, 5 October 1972
Height: 5'11" **Weight:** 12.4
Club Honours: S Div 1 '98
Lee made just three early-season appearances for Carlisle last term, all away from home. The experienced defender then made the short journey across the border to join several former Carlisle team mates at Gretna, and he featured regularly for the Scottish Third Division side during the remainder of the campaign.
Bristol Rov *(From trainee on 18/7/1991) FL 68+5 FLC 4 FAC 2 Others 6+1*
Northampton T *(£25,000 on 22/9/1995) FL 55 FLC 3+1 FAC 3 Others 4+1*
Dundee *(Free on 23/7/1997) SL 59+6/1 SLC 3 SC 3/1*
Carlisle U *(Free on 13/10/2000) FL 59+5/1 FLC 2 FAC 5 Others 2+2*
Oxford U *(Loaned on 5/2/2002) FL 11*

Steve McPhee (left)

MADDISON Neil Stanley
Born: Darlington, 2 October 1969
Height: 5'10" **Weight:** 12.0
This experienced midfielder completed his third season with his hometown club last term, continuing to show his obvious class with quality, control and accurate passing from the centre of the park. His experience was always evident as he prompted and inspired those around him with some commanding displays in the centre of the field. Neil contributed his customary goal for the Quakers when he netted with a speculative lob at Huddersfield in February.
Southampton (From trainee on 14/4/1988) F/PL 149+20/19 FLC 9+5 FAC 8+5 Others 1
Middlesbrough (£250,000 on 31/10/1997) P/FL 32+24/4 FLC 7+1 FAC 4
Barnsley (Loaned on 4/11/2000) FL 3
Bristol C (Loaned on 16/3/2001) FL 4+3/1
Darlington (Free on 26/7/2001) FL 79+11/3 FLC 3 FAC 2+2 Others 3

MAGILTON James (Jim)
Born: Belfast, 6 May 1969
Height: 6'0" **Weight:** 14.2
International Honours: NI: 52; U23-2; U21-1; Yth; Sch
Manager Joe Royle appointed Jim as captain of Ipswich at the start of last season and Jim rewarded him by playing in every game and leading the side by example. He is the playmaker of the side, constantly demanding the ball, whether it is on the edge of his own penalty area or in the opposition half. Jim would probably be disappointed with his tally of just one goal this season as he is not afraid to have a shot from any distance, however, his only strike proved to be the match winner at Watford.
Liverpool (From apprentice on 14/5/1986)
Oxford U (£100,000 on 3/10/1990) FL 150/34 FLC 9/1 FAC 8/4 Others 7/3
Southampton (£600,000 on 11/2/1994) PL 124+6/13 FLC 12+2/2 FAC 12/3
Sheffield Wed (£1,600,000 on 10/9/1997) PL 14+13/1 FLC 2 FAC 1
Ipswich T (£682,500 on 15/1/1999) P/FL 185+15/12 FLC 12+1/1 FAC 5+2/1 Others 15+1/3

MAHER Kevin Andrew
Born: Ilford, 17 October 1976
Height: 6'0" **Weight:** 12.5
International Honours: RoI: U21-4
Southend United's longest-serving player enjoyed another fine season last term, his seventh at Roots Hall. His obvious attributes are a fearsome tackle and a wonderful repertoire of passes. He was again a vital cog in a Blues' midfield,

which was seldom as effective in his occasional absences. Kevin won the Supporters' Club 'Player of the Year' award and at the time of writing had been offered a new contract, which should take him up to a well-deserved testimonial season.
Tottenham H (From trainee on 1/7/1995)
Southend U (Free on 23/1/1998) FL 230+7/15 FLC 10/1 FAC 18 Others 14+1/1

MAHER Shaun Patrick
Born: Dublin, 20 June 1978
Height: 6'2" **Weight:** 12.6
This big central defender again had a season disrupted by injury at Bournemouth in 2003-04. Shaun marked his first appearance of the campaign with a goal against Swindon in August, but sustained an injury in the next game. On

returning to fitness he had to be content with a place on the bench. He then returned to the side for a prolonged run and was part of an impressive back line, but the campaign ended in disappointment as he was sidelined once more.
Fulham (£35,000 from Bohemians on 18/12/1997) Others 2 (Free to Bohemians on 10/9/1998)
Bournemouth (Free on 23/8/2001) FL 58+10/3 FLC 2 FAC 0+1

MAHON Alan Joseph
Born: Dublin, 4 April 1978
Height: 5'10" **Weight:** 11.5
Club Honours: FLC '02
International Honours: RoI: 1; U21-18; Yth; Sch
Alan joined Ipswich on a three-month

Neil Maddison

loan deal in September and was an instant hit with the fans because of his exciting wing play and pinpoint crosses. He opened his account at Portman Road with the only goal in the win at Bradford, but was hampered by injuries in the latter stages of his loan. He returned to Ewood Park at the turn of the year and gained an unexpected place in the left- wing spot, but after a short run in the side he was offloaded to Wigan. Alan brought a balance to the midfield showing quick feet and an excellent first touch, which seemingly gave him an extra split-second on the ball. He netted his first goal in Wigan colours in the away win at Gillingham.

Tranmere Rov (From trainee on 7/4/1995) FL 84+36/13 FLC 12+6/1 FAC 4+2 (Free to Sporting Lisbon, Portugal on 1/7/2000)
Blackburn Rov (£1,500,000 on 14/12/2000) P/FL 25+11/1 FLC 4+3 FAC 10
Cardiff C (Loaned on 24/11/2003) FL 13+2/2
Ipswich T (Loaned on 5/9/2003) FL 7+4/1 FLC 1
Wigan Ath (Free on 6/2/2004) FL 13+1/1

MAHON Gavin Andrew

Born: Birmingham, 2 January 1977
Height: 6'0" **Weight:** 13.2
Club Honours: Div 3 '99
Gavin was voted Watford's 'Player of the Year' last term after his best-ever season with the club, during which he finally won over the supporters. It was a tribute to Ray Lewington's faith in him and to his own persistence, and no coincidence that he played the majority of his matches in central midfield, where his commitment, reliability and ball-winning skills were used to best advantage. Having a regular position brought increased confidence, and Gavin at last made the Watford score sheet, heading his first goal for the club in the FA Cup tie against Chelsea. His new goal consciousness brought him a total of three by the end of the season.
Wolverhampton W (From trainee on 3/7/1995)
Hereford U (Free on 12/7/1996) FL 10+1/1 FLC 4
Brentford (£50,000 + on 17/11/1998) FL 140+1/8 FLC 8 FAC 5 Others 12
Watford (£150,000 + on 4/3/2002) FL 51+4/2 FLC 2 FAC 6+1/1

MAKELELE Claude

Born: Kinshasha, DR Congo, 18 February 1973
Height: 5'7" **Weight:** 10.12
International Honours: France: 34; B-4; U21
Chelsea pulled off a stunning transfer

coup with their last capture of 2003. Claude Makelele was described by Claudio Ranieri as the 'battery' which made the great Real Madrid side tick, occupying that crucial area in front of the back four while the 'galacticos' weaved their magic higher up the pitch. Claude swapped Madrid for London SW6 and a different set of 'galacticos', but his role was exactly the same and just as effective! He has the priceless ability to make the game look easy and snuffs out dangerous attacks by a combination of athleticism, anticipation and intelligence and, once the ball is won, its rolled with the minimum of fuss to a midfield colleague. Although not known for his goal-scoring, indeed he failed to find the net in his 46 appearances, it was Claude's fiercely struck shot which was parried by the Arsenal 'keeper for Frank Lampard to score and set Chelsea on their way to that momentous Champions' League quarter-final victory.
Chelsea (£16,600,000 from Real Madrid, Spain, ex Brest Armorique, Nantes, Marseilles, Celta Vigo, on 1/9/2003) PL 26+4 FLC 1+1 FAC 3 Others 11

MAKIN Christopher (Chris) Gregory

Born: Manchester, 8 May 1973
Height: 5'10" **Weight:** 11.2
Club Honours: Div 1 '99
International Honours: E: U21-5; Yth; Sch
This Ipswich Town defender was injured in the home game with West Ham at the end of August and he never played again during the 2003-04 season. Chris was eventually diagnosed as having damaged his hip joint and required corrective surgery. He was subsequently offered a short-term contract to enable him to prove his fitness at the start of the 2004-05 campaign.
Oldham Ath (From trainee on 2/11/1991) F/PL 93+1/4 FLC 7 FAC 11 Others 1+1 (Transferred to Marseilles, France during 1996 close season)
Wigan Ath (Loaned on 28/8/1992) FL 14+1/2
Sunderland (£500,000 on 5/8/1997) P/FL 115+5/1 FLC 13 FAC 7+1 Others 1+1
Ipswich T (£1,250,000 on 7/3/2001) P/FL 78 FLC 4 FAC 2 Others 7+1

MALBRANQUE Steed

Born: Mouscron, Belgium, 6 January 1980
Height: 5'8" **Weight:** 11.7
International Honours: France: U21
Steed was the only Fulham player to appear in every Premiership game last

season and he missed only the Carling Cup defeat at Wigan. Once again this crowd favourite was at the centre of many attacking moves, his close control outwitting opponents time and again. Steed often found himself the target of some fierce tackling but still provided some memorable efforts, not least the penalty kick coolly slotted home in the FA Cup tie at Old Trafford. After being surprisingly denied full international recognition previously, he was finally called up by France in the latter part of the season.
Fulham (£5,000,000 from Lyon, France on 14/8/2001) PL 106+6/20 FLC 1+2/1 FAC 16/7 Others 12+2/3

MALONEY Jonathan (Jon) Duncan

Born: Leeds, 3 March 1985
Height: 6'0" **Weight:** 11.12
This promising Doncaster Rovers youngster made his bow in senior football in the LDV Vans Trophy tie at Chester when he came on as a substitute at centre back just after half time. John mostly featured for the reserves in the centre of defence but he can also play in midfield and as a striker. He made his Football League debut in the final game of the season when he came off the bench against Carlisle United and helped clinch victory with a vital last-minute clearance.
Doncaster Rov (From trainee on 9/7/2003) FL 0+1 Others 0+1

MANANGU Eric Mavambu

Born: DR Congo, 9 September 1985
Height: 5'8" **Weight:** 11.7
This teenaged Rushden striker made his first-team debut as a late substitute at home to Colchester at the end of November. Just a few days later he put the club's U18 side into an early lead in their FA Youth Cup tie against Manchester United at Nene Park – only for the Red Devils to hit back with two late goals for victory. Eric is one of several highly-rated youngsters who will be looking to make an impact with the Diamonds in 2004-05.
Rushden & Diamonds (Trainee) FL 0+1

[MANEL] MARTINEZ FERNANDEZ Manuel

Born: Barcelona, Spain, 3 November 1973
Height: 6'1" **Weight:** 13.12
After being released by Espanyol, Manel joined Derby in the January transfer window. His best scoring days were with

Logrones, especially in their promotion season. Unknown in England, Manel took time to settle, hardly surprising with a lack of match fitness. Then he began to show a good touch on the ball and was unlucky to have valid goals denied by poor offside decisions. Two in the defeat of Preston helped his confidence.
Derby Co (Free from RCD Espanyol, Spain, ex Sabadell, Logrones, on 2/1/2004) FL 12+4/3 FAC 1

MANGAN Andrew Francis
Born: Liverpool, 30 August 1986
Height: 5'9" **Weight:** 10.3
A regular for Blackpool's reserve and youth teams last term, this promising youngster was drafted into the first-team squad to cover during an injury crisis. He made two brief appearances from the substitutes' bench and on both occasions looked lively and effective. He will be looking to gain more experience of first-team football in 2004-05.
Blackpool (Trainee) FL 0+2

MANSARAM Darren Timothy
Born: Doncaster, 25 June 1984
Height: 6'2" **Weight:** 11.7
Grimsby's talented but unpredictable young striker was a regular in the squad last term, but the majority of his appearances came from the substitutes' bench. When given the opportunity Darren showed that he retains the ability to cause confusion in opposition defences and with a little more consistency he will look to become a regular in the starting line-up in 2004-05.
Grimsby T (From trainee on 16/9/2002) FL 32+33/5 FLC 0+2 FAC 2+1/1 Others 1/1

MANSELL Lee Richard Samuel
Born: Gloucester, 28 October 1982
Height: 5'9" **Weight:** 10.10
Lee did well on the occasions he was called upon by Luton Town last term, but suffered somewhat due to the club's lack of a reserve side. A versatile player whose preferred position is in the centre of midfield, he has good pace and is a tenacious tackler. Lee will be looking to gain a regular place in the Hatters' line-up in 2004-05.
Luton T (From trainee on 16/5/2001) FL 35+11/8 FLC 1 FAC 6/2 Others 6

MANSOURI Yazid
Born: Revin, Algeria, 25 February 1978
Height: 5'9" **Weight:** 10.8
International Honours: Algeria
This young midfielder joined Coventry in a 12-month loan deal after impressing in

pre-season games. His lack of experience in the English game was exposed early on, but he returned to the side in December and, playing in his preferred central-midfield position, he put in several excellent appearances alongside his mentor Youssef Safri. Yazid featured for Algeria in the African Nations' Cup finals in the new year and soon afterwards his loan contract was terminated.
Coventry C (Loaned from Le Havre, France on 19/8/2003) FL 9+5 FLC 1

MAPES Charles (Charlie) Edward
Born: St Pancras, 4 July 1982
Height: 5'10" **Weight:** 11.3
This creative Wycombe midfielder scored the only goal of the game on his debut, on the opening day of the 2003-04 season against Stockport. He had recorded three by his seventh game but only made a total of 11 starts and was released at the season's end. He is always dangerous around the box, especially when arriving on late runs.
Wycombe W (Signed from Berkhamsted T, ex Tottenham H trainee, Harrow Borough, Edgware T, Wealdstone, on 1/7/2003) FL 10+5/3 FLC 1 FAC 0+1 Others 1

MARGETSON Martyn Walter
Born: Neath, 8 September 1971
Height: 6'0" **Weight:** 14.0
International Honours: W: 1; B-1; U21-7; Yth; Sch
Although Martyn began the 2003-04 campaign as second-choice 'keeper for Cardiff City, he made great strides during the season and eventually broke through to replace Neil Alexander in the line-up. Martyn kept his place through to the end of the campaign although he finished up playing with a broken finger and still maintained his excellent form! Martyn was also called up to the full Wales international squad and won his first cap after coming on as a second-half substitute in the friendly against Canada in May.
Manchester C (From trainee on 5/7/1990) F/PL 51 FLC 2+2 FAC 3 Others 1
Bristol Rov (Loaned on 8/12/1993) FL 2+1
Southend U (Free on 3/8/1998) FL 32 FLC 4 FAC 1 Others 1
Huddersfield T (Signed on 6/8/1999) FL 47+1 FLC 1 FAC 2 Others 8
Cardiff C (Free on 2/8/2002) FL 28 FLC 3 FAC 2 Others 2

MARINELLI Carlos Ariel
Born: Buenos Aires, Argentina, 14 March 1982
Height: 5'8" **Weight:** 11.6

International Honours: Argentina: Yth
Carlos spent the 2002-03 season with Italian side Torino and was linked with a move away from the Teesside, however the deal fell through and he returned to the Riverside. The Argentine striker featured in Middlesbrough's opening game at Fulham and, indeed, he scored Boro's first goal of the season in the 3-2 defeat. In November his contract was terminated by mutual consent and in February he rejoined Boca Juniors.
Middlesbrough (£1,500,000 from Boca Juniors, Argentina on 27/10/1999) PL 18+25/3 FLC 3+2/1 FAC 3+2

MARLET Steve
Born: Pithiviers, France, 10 January 1974
Height: 5'11" **Weight:** 11.5
International Honours: France: 23; B-1
Steve made just a single Premiership appearance for Fulham before starting a season-long loan at Marseilles where he was part of a side which reached the UEFA Cup final. He featured for Fulham in the opening game against Middlesbrough when he enjoyed an excellent game scoring in the 3-2 defeat of the Teeside club. Although expected to return to West London after his loan period, his future is uncertain at the time of writing.
Fulham (£13,500,000 from Lyon, France, ex Paris Red Star, Auxerre, on 3/9/2001) PL 50+5/11 FLC 1 FAC 6+2/3 Others 13+1/5

MARNEY Daniel (Danny) Gary
Born: Sidcup, 2 October 1981
Height: 5'9" **Weight:** 10.12
With just four appearances as a substitute to his name in Brighton's Second Division campaign last term, Danny will have gained more enjoyment in his role as a striker for Crawley Town, having joined on loan at the start of the season and again in February. A ball-playing, pacy forward, Danny signed permanently for the north Sussex side in March and played his part as Crawley secured the Dr Martens League championship for the first time in their history.
Brighton & Hove A (From trainee on 7/8/2001) FL 6+9 FLC 1 Others 0+1
Southend U (Loaned on 19/12/2002) FL 13+4

MARNEY Dean Edward
Born: Barking, 31 January 1984
Height: 5'9" **Weight:** 10.7
This promising right-sided midfield player was on the substitutes' bench for Tottenham in the first two Premiership games last term and he later joined Queens Park Rangers on loan. However,

he only managed a couple of starts before being injured and returning to White Hart Lane. Later in the campaign Dean featured in the starting line-up for Spurs in the 3-0 defeat at Old Trafford.
Tottenham H *(From trainee on 3/7/2002) PL 1+2*
Swindon T *(Loaned on 24/12/2002) FL 8+1*
Queens Park R *(Loaned on 16/1/2004) FL 1+1 Others 1*

MARPLES Simon James
Born: Sheffield, 30 July 1975
Height: 5'10" **Weight:** 11.11
Club Honours: Div 3 '04
International Honours: E: SP-2
Simon once again looked likely to make the right-back position his own at Doncaster Rovers last term, starting the season in terrific form. However, he was sidelined for much of the campaign by a stomach muscle problem and only returned to the first team in the closing fixtures.
Doncaster Rov *(Free from Stocksbridge Park Steels on 13/9/1999) FL 16 FLC 1 FAC 1 Others 1*

MARRIOTT Alan
Born: Bedford, 3 September 1978
Height: 6'1" **Weight:** 12.5
Alan again showed that he is one of the best 'keepers in the lower divisions last term. His confidence continued to increase and he produced some excellent performances to keep 17 clean sheets including ten away from home. Alan was an ever-present for Lincoln City and was voted 'Away Player of the Year' by the supporters. During the campaign he passed 200 senior appearances for the club.
Tottenham H *(From trainee on 3/7/1997)*
Lincoln C *(Free on 5/8/1999) FL 183 FLC 5 FAC 7 Others 11*

MARSDEN Christopher (Chris)
Born: Sheffield, 3 January 1969
Height: 5'11" **Weight:** 10.12
With Chris's successful partnership down the left with Wayne Bridge dissolved, due to the young defender's transfer to Chelsea during the summer, Southampton manager Gordon Strachan struggled to find a satisfactory combination in midfield at the beginning of the 2003-04 season. Chris's outstanding five-year career in the Saints' midfield suffered as a result. With the club hesitating with regard to renewing his contract Chris decided to accept an offer – from Ian Porterfield, his former manager at Sheffield United – to

play for Puson Icons in Korea. However, he was reported to have made a return home in the summer, signing for Sheffield Wednesday.
Sheffield U *(From apprentice on 6/1/1987) FL 13+3/1 FLC 1 Others 1*
Huddersfield T *(Signed on 15/7/1988) FL 113+8/9 FLC 15+1 FAC 6+2 Others 10*
Coventry C *(Loaned on 2/11/1993) PL 5+2*
Wolverhampton W *(£250,000 on 11/1/1994) FL 8 FAC 3*
Notts Co *(£250,000 on 15/11/1994) FL 10 FLC 1 Others 1/1*
Stockport Co *(£70,000 on 12/1/1996) FL 63+2/3 FLC 13 FAC 4 Others 4/1*

Andy Marshall

Birmingham C *(£500,000 on 9/10/1997) FL 51+1/3 FLC 5/3 FAC 2*
Southampton *(£800,000 on 2/2/1999) PL 118+11/6 FLC 8+3/1 FAC 10+1/1 Others 1*

MARSHALL Andrew (Andy) John
Born: Bury St Edmunds, 14 April 1975
Height: 6'2" **Weight:** 13.7
International Honours: E: U21-4; Yth (UEFA-U18 '93)
Andy began the 2003-04 season on loan at Wolves, where he was required as cover for Michael Oakes, but his only appearance came in the Carling Cup

defeat by Arsenal. On his return to
Portman Road he was unable to dislodge
Kelvin Davis from the line-up and with his
contract up in the summer he joined
Millwall on loan in January. Signed as a
replacement for injured 'keeper Tony
Warner, he made his Lions debut at Crewe
and thereafter was a regular in the team.
Norwich C *(From trainee on 6/7/1993) P/FL
194+1 FLC 18 FAC 5+1*
Bournemouth *(Loaned on 9/9/1996) FL 11*
Gillingham *(Loaned on 21/11/1996) FL 5 FLC
1 Others 1*
Ipswich T *(Free on 4/7/2001) P/FL 53 FLC 2
FAC 4 Others 6*
Wolverhampton W *(Loaned on 18/11/2003)
FLC 1*
Millwall *(Signed on 28/1/2004) FL 16 FAC 4*

MARSHALL Lee Keith
Born: Islington, 21 January 1979
Height: 6'0" **Weight:** 11.11
International Honours: E: U21-1
Lee found himself out of favour at West
Bromwich Albion last term and in January
he linked up with his former Leicester
boss Peter Taylor at Hull in a loan deal.
Usually employed at right back but also
used on the right-hand side of midfield,
Lee displayed calmness under pressure as
City moved close to reaching their goal of
promotion. Ill fortune was not far away,
however, as Lee's season came to a
shuddering halt when he suffered a
compound fracture to the tibia and fibula
of his right leg at Kidderminster in April.
Norwich C *(Signed from Enfield on
27/3/1997) FL 95+22/11 FLC 11+1/2 FAC 2*
Leicester C *(£600,000 on 21/3/2001) P/FL
37+8 FLC 1 FAC 2*
West Bromwich A *(£700,000 on 14/8/2002)
PL 4+5/1 FLC 1*
Hull C *(Loaned on 23/1/2004) FL 10+1*

MARSHALL Scott Roderick
Born: Edinburgh, 1 May 1973
Height: 6'1" **Weight:** 12.5
International Honours: S: U21-5; Yth
After being released by Brentford in the
summer of 2003, Scott had trials with a
number of clubs before becoming one of
Wycombe manager Tony Adams' first
signings. A very safe central defender, he
is a fine distributor of the ball but a
hamstring injury stopped his run in
February, suffering a reaction when
returning to training in March. He made
no further appearances and was released
at the end of the season. Scott is the son
of former Hearts goalkeeper Gordon
Marshall and the brother of Gordon
junior, who played in goal for Celtic and
Scotland.

Arsenal *(From trainee on 18/3/1991) PL
19+5/1 FLC 1+1*
Rotherham U *(Loaned on 3/12/1993) FL
10/1 Others 1*
Sheffield U *(Loaned on 25/8/1994) FL 17*
Southampton *(Free on 3/8/1998) PL 2*
Brentford *(£250,000 on 15/10/1999) FL
73+2/3 FLC 5 FAC 7/1 Others 7/3*
Wycombe W *(Free on 21/11/2003) FL 8
FAC 1*

MARSHALL Shaun Andrew
Born: Fakenham, 3 October 1978
Height: 6'1" **Weight:** 12.12
Sean was once again the first-choice
'keeper for Cambridge United last term,
and was an ever-present until the final
game of the season. Something of an
enigma, at times he was truly exceptional
and his reflex saves kept United in with a
chance on many occasions. A very
capable shot stopper, he just needs to
develop greater consistency in his
performances to become a first-class
goalkeeper.
Cambridge U *(From trainee on 21/2/1997)
FL 149+5 FLC 4 FAC 15 Others 8*

MARTEINSSON Petur
Born: Reykjavik, Iceland, 14 July 1973
Height: 6'1" **Weight:** 12.4
International Honours: Iceland: 27;
U21-19; Yth
This accomplished midfield player made
three early-season appearances for Stoke
last term before being allowed to leave
the Britannia Stadium. Soon afterwards
he signed for Swedish club Hammarby. A
talented player who can also feature in
defence, he never really seemed to
establish himself during his stay in the
Potteries.
Stoke C *(Free from Stabaek IF, Norway, ex
Leftur, Fram, Hammarby IF, Sweden, on
10/1/2002) FL 12+6/2 FAC 1+1*

MARTIN Benjamin (Ben)
Born: Harpenden, 15 November 1982
Height: 6'7" **Weight:** 13.8
This giant central defender was given a
one-year contract by Swindon Town after
impressing during trial games. However,
his only senior appearance came as a
substitute in the LDV Vans Trophy at
Boston. Ben went on loan to Lincoln in
October, but although he appeared on
the bench and in the reserves he did not
appear in the first team for the Imps. He
also had a loan spell at Farnborough
before being released in the summer.
Swindon T *(Signed from Aylesbury U on
7/8/2003) Others 0+1*

MARTIN David Edward
Born: Romford, 22 January 1986
Height: 6'1" **Weight:** 13.7
International Honours: E: Yth
David became the fifth goalkeeper to
appear for Wimbledon last term when
making his debut at Burnley on a late
April Tuesday evening. Despite a mix-up
for an own goal he gave a sound display,
and was also in good form in the
following game against Gillingham. A
regular in the England youth set-up, he
put in some excellent displays for the
club's reserve team throughout the
season. David is the son of former West
Ham central defender Alvin Martin.
Wimbledon *(From trainee on 19/1/2004)
FL 2*

MARTINEZ Roberto
Born: Balaguer Lerida, Spain, 13 July
1973
Height: 5'10" **Weight:** 12.2
Club Honours: Div 3 '97
After signing a new contract for Swansea
during the summer of 2003, this
influential midfielder injured knee
ligaments during the second home game
of the season against Boston United,
which kept him on the sidelines for two
months. A training ground injury then
hampered his efforts to regain fitness,
and it was only in the final month of the
campaign that Roberto was at last able to
show the fans his fitness problems were
all behind him.
Wigan Ath *(Free from CFS Vipla Balaguer,
Spain on 25/7/1995) FL 148+39/17 FLC
11+1/1 FAC 13+2/4 Others 7+5/2*
Motherwell *(Free on 3/7/2001) SL 8+9*
Walsall *(Free on 13/8/2002) FL 1+5*
Swansea C *(Free on 28/1/2003) FL 43+3/2
FLC 1 FAC 2*

MARTYN Antony Nigel
Born: St Austell, 11 August 1966
Height: 6'2" **Weight:** 14.7
Club Honours: Div 3 '90; FMC '91; Div 1
'94
International Honours: E: 23; B-6; U21-
11
There were few better signings in the
Premiership last season than the one that
brought this veteran 'keeper to Goodison,
ostensibly as back-up to Richard Wright.
Following an injury to the Blues' number-
one in September, Nigel kept the 'keeper's
jersey for the rest of the campaign, his
form in that period being nothing less
than outstanding. He was a commanding
presence throughout and showed agility
and reflexes that belied his seniority. The
highlight of his season was undoubtedly a

fantastic individual performance at Anfield, when he miraculously kept a clean sheet. He was rightly regarded as being the team's star performer during the campaign and his brilliant form saved the club from a worse fate.

Bristol Rov (Free from St Blazey on 6/8/1987) FL 101 FLC 6 FAC 6 Others 11
Crystal Palace (£1,000,000 on 21/11/1989) F/PL 272 FLC 36 FAC 22 Others 19
Leeds U (£2,250,000 on 26/7/1996) PL 207 FLC 12 FAC 18 Others 36
Everton (£500,000 on 1/9/2003) PL 33+1 FLC 3 FAC 3

MASON Christopher
Born: Newton Aycliffe, 26 June 1986
Height: 6'0" **Weight:** 12.0
A product of Darlington's youth scheme, Christopher gave a succession of excellent performances for the reserves last term and was promoted to the first-team squad towards the end of the campaign. A strong, quick-tackling right-sided defender, he finally made his debut on the last day of the season at Scunthorpe when he came off the bench for the final few minutes.
Darlington (Trainee) FL 0+1

MATIAS Pedro Manuel Miguel
Born: Madrid, Spain, 11 October 1973
Height: 6'0" **Weight:** 12.0
International Honours: Spain: U21
In what turned out to be his fifth and final season with Walsall Pedro scored with an accurate shot in the win over Gillingham in September, but was out for four months with a broken toe. On his return he showed in his occasional appearances that he still has something to offer as a wing back, in midfield or as a left flank raider. He spent the closing stages of the campaign on loan at

Roberto Martinez

Blackpool where he featured regularly and scored in the 3-1 win over Brighton on Easter Saturday.
Macclesfield T (Free from Logrones, Spain, ex Real Madrid, Almeria, on 3/12/1998) FL 21+1/2 FAC 1
Tranmere Rov (Free on 5/8/1999) FL 1+3
Walsall (Free on 7/10/1999) FL 105+36/24 FLC 4+3 FAC 6+4/1 Others 4/2
Blackpool (Loaned on 25/3/2004) FL 7/1

MATTEO Dominic (Dom)
Born: Dumfries, 28 April 1974
Height: 6'1" **Weight:** 11.12
International Honours: S: 6; E: B-1; U21-4; Yth
Dominic underwent a knee operation in the summer of 2003 to clear up a long-standing problem, but was back in action for Leeds in their opening game of the new season. An inspirational skipper and a rock in the centre of defence, he switched to a midfield role when Eddie Gray took over, but when the side returned to a 4-4-2 formation he returned to his more familiar position. Dominic contributed two Premiership goals, netting the winner in the 3-2 defeat of Fulham and another in the 4-1 victory over Wolves.
Liverpool (From trainee on 27/5/1992) PL 112+15/1 FLC 9 FAC 6+2/1 Others 10+1
Sunderland (Loaned on 24/3/1995) FL 1
Leeds U (£4,750,000 on 24/8/2000) PL 115/2 FLC 2 FAC 6 Others 23/2

MATTHEWS Lee Joseph
Born: Middlesbrough, 16 January 1979
Height: 6'3" **Weight:** 12.6
Club Honours: FAYC '97
International Honours: E: Yth
This strong, bustling striker was amongst the goals at the start of last season, scoring twice in Bristol City's 5-0 demolition of Notts County. However, he spent most of the remainder of the campaign out on loan. He had spells at Darlington, where he scored crucial goals to salvage points at Carlisle, Bristol Rovers and Yeovil before injury led to a return to Ashton Gate. Lee was released in the summer and was reported to have signed for Port Vale.
Leeds U (From trainee on 15/2/1996) PL 0+3
Notts Co (Loaned on 24/9/1998) FL 4+1
Gillingham (Loaned on 23/3/2000) FL 2+3
Bristol C (£100,000 on 16/3/2001) FL 14+29/9 FLC 0+5 FAC 0+2/1 Others 2+2/2
Darlington (Loaned on 11/12/2003) FL 6/1
Bristol Rov (Loaned on 13/1/2004) FL 9
Yeovil T (Loaned on 20/3/2004) FL 2+2

MATTIS Dwayne Antony
Born: Huddersfield, 31 July 1981
Height: 6'1" **Weight:** 10.10
International Honours: RoI: U21-2; Yth
This tough-tackling midfielder was restricted to just two starts in the midfield engine room for Huddersfield Town last term and also featured in a handful of games from the substitutes' bench. Dwayne was released by the Terriers shortly before the end of the season.
Huddersfield T (From trainee on 8/7/1999) FL 50+19/2 FLC 1+2 FAC 3+1 Others 4/1

MAWENE Youl
Born: Caen, France, 16 July 1979
Height: 6'2" **Weight:** 12.6
Youl played through Derby's pre-season programme but suffered a knee ligament injury. He was able to return in November to make his first senior appearance for 21 months, having been in danger of becoming a forgotten man at Pride Park. Youl was there for the remainder of a difficult season, showing the defensive poise and reliability that first persuaded Jim Smith to sign him. A regular place restored his confidence and Youl became a major figure as the Rams battled successfully to avoid relegation. He beat off Ian Taylor to become Derby's 'Player of the Year'.
Derby Co (£500,000 from RC Lens, France, ex Caen, on 4/8/2000) P/FL 54+1/1 FLC 2 FAC 4

MAXWELL Layton Jonathan
Born: Rhyl, 3 October 1979
Height: 5'8" **Weight:** 11.6
International Honours: W: U21-14; Yth
Layton started the 2003-04 campaign with high hopes and featured in Cardiff City's first two games, but then dropped out of the reckoning. He was eventually released and in March he joined Swansea City in a short-term deal. However, he suffered an ankle injury on his first day at the Vetch Field on trial and was later hampered by hamstring problems. He was released by the Swans in the summer.
Liverpool (From trainee on 17/7/1997) FLC 1/1
Stockport Co (Loaned on 17/7/2000) FL 8+12/2 FLC 1+1 FAC 0+1
Cardiff C (Free on 7/8/2001) FL 10+24/1 FLC 2+1 FAC 1+3 Others 3+1
Swansea C (Free on 25/3/2004) FL 1+2

MAY Benjamin (Ben) Steven
Born: Gravesend, 10 March 1984
Height: 6'1" **Weight:** 12.6
This promising young Millwall centre forward joined Brentford on loan last August and stayed the whole season. Ben

often found it difficult to make his mark in a struggling side, but nevertheless scored seven goals during the campaign. His best performance came against Tranmere in January when he netted with a crisp shot following a good turn, and then hit the crossbar with a 30-yard chip.
Millwall (From juniors on 10/5/2001) FL 4+6/1 FLC 1 FAC 0+1
Colchester U (Loaned on 27/3/2003) FL 4+2
Brentford (Loaned on 25/8/2003) FL 38+3/7 FAC 1 Others 1

MAY David
Born: Oldham, 24 June 1970
Height: 6'0" **Weight:** 13.5
Club Honours: CS '94, '96; PL '96, '97, '99; FAC '96, '99; EC '99
After several years as a squad member at Old Trafford, this experienced defender found regular first-team football on arrival at Burnley. Apart from the odd suspension or injury David was a guaranteed starter in the Clarets' team and one of the few unqualified successes of Burnley's season. On more than one occasion he was the saviour of the side as his sureness in the tackle put an end to opposition attacks. He also proved useful up front, particularly at set pieces, and weighed in with four goals.
Blackburn Rov (From trainee on 16/6/1988) F/PL 123/3 FLC 12+1/2 FAC 10/1 Others 5
Manchester U (£1,400,000 on 1/7/1994) PL 68+17/6 FLC 9/1 FAC 6 Others 15+3/1
Huddersfield T (Loaned on 24/12/1999) FL 1
Burnley (Free on 14/8/2003) FL 34+1/4 FLC 1 FAC 3

MAY Rory Joseph
Born: Birmingham, 25 November 1984
Height: 6'4" **Weight:** 12.7
An injury crisis gave this solid teenaged striker the opportunity for his senior debut in Lincoln's opening-day home clash with Oxford. Rory lacked experience but worked hard in his role as a target man. He made only one further start before being pushed out by the arrival of Gary Fletcher. Rory was loaned to Halifax Town in March before being released at the end of the season.
Lincoln C (From trainee at Coventry C on 8/8/2003) FL 1+4 FLC 1 FAC 0+2 Others 0+1

MAYLETT Bradley (Brad)
Born: Manchester, 24 December 1980
Height: 5'8" **Weight:** 10.10
Brad started the 2003-04 season in bright form for Swansea, scoring not only his first senior goal, but also netting a hat-trick in the 4-2 win over Bury at the Vetch Field. He suffered a dead leg against

Huddersfield Town, forcing him to miss several matches, then on his return from injury he was carried off with a hamstring problem. An exciting, pacy winger on his day, Brad added two more League goals to his tally by the end of the campaign, and signed a new contract with the Swans before the summer break.
Burnley *(From trainee on 19/2/1999) FL 3+42 FLC 1+2 FAC 0+1 Others 1*
Swansea C *(Free on 14/3/2003) FL 32+7/5 FLC 1 FAC 3*

MAYO Kerry
Born: Haywards Heath, 21 September 1977
Height: 5'10" **Weight:** 13.4
Club Honours: Div 3 '01; Div 2 '02
Brighton's longest-serving player missed out on the club's end-of-season play-off triumph after losing his place to Dan Harding in February, the latter coming into the side when Kerry was suspended. Although always game and eager to get

forward, the experienced defender was not enjoying his best campaign with the club before being replaced, but will certainly be trying to win back his left-back berth in the higher division as he looks forward to a testimonial.
Brighton & Hove A *(From trainee on 3/7/1996) FL 256+20/10 FLC 9+1 FAC 8+6/2 Others 7+3*

MAYO Paul
Born: Lincoln, 13 October 1981
Height: 5'11" **Weight:** 11.9
Paul established himself as first choice in the left-wing-back position for Lincoln City. His ability to push forward and his long throw-ins gave the Imps extra attacking options and he was also Lincoln's regular penalty taker. His form attracted the interest of bigger clubs but it was still a surprise when he was sold to Watford in March. It soon became evident that it was money well spent by the Hornets: Paul proved to be a reliable left-

footed defender with a dangerous long throw and a willingness to take responsibility that marked him out as a potential future captain.
Lincoln C *(From trainee on 6/4/2000) FL 92+14/6 FLC 4 FAC 5+1/1 Others 9/2*
Watford *(Signed on 8/3/2004) FL 12*

MEARS Tyrone
Born: Stockport, 18 February 1983
Height: 5'11" **Weight:** 11.10
Injured in pre-season, Tyrone made only one start before January, after which he became a fixture in the Preston side until a stress fracture in March ended his campaign early. His performance as a central defender at West Ham, when he performed a man-marking job on David Connolly, showed that the pacy defender had another string to his bow. His topsy-turvy season was encapsulated at Sunderland, when he scored an unfortunate own goal before redressing the balance at the other end of the field.

Ben May (centre)

A strong tackler and improving in the air, Tyrone is unbelievably fast and will be looking to build on a solid period as a first-team player.
Manchester C *(From juniors on 5/7/2000) FL* 0+1
Preston NE *(Signed on 10/7/2002) FL* 22+12/2 FLC 1+2 FAC 1+1

MELCHIOT Mario
Born: Amsterdam, Holland, 4 November 1976
Height: 6'1" **Weight:** 11.8
Club Honours: FAC '00; CS '00
International Honours: Holland: 11; U21-13; Yth
The story of Mario Melchiot's season is a virtual carbon copy of erstwhile full-back partner Celestine Babayaro's – club buys England international full back who takes his chance with both hands and consigns the previous incumbent to the fringes. Mario did feature in just under half the club's matches and the back four still retained that familiar solid look whenever he filled-in for Glen Johnson. Mario also did particularly well when pressed into service as an emergency central defender. The big Dutchman scored two Premiership goals during the season – against Southampton and Wolves – which were mirror images of each other; breaking through from the right flank and sliding an angled drive past the 'keeper into the opposite corner.
Chelsea *(Free from Ajax, Holland on 5/7/1999) PL 117+13/4 FLC 9 FAC 14+2 Others 9+1/1*

MELLANBY Daniel (Danny)
Born: Bishop Auckland, 17 July 1979
Height: 5'10" **Weight:** 11.9
Danny suffered another frustrating time with injuries at Darlington last term and was out of action for much of the season. He managed only five starts and a couple of substitute outings in the early part of the season before he was forced onto the sidelines. A striker with a deceptive turn in the box and an eye for goal, he was sorely missed by his colleagues. Unfortunately his problems with injuries led to his announcing his retirement from the game on medical advice in the summer.
Darlington *(Free from Bishop Auckland, ex West Auckland on 26/7/2001) FL 33+11/8 FLC 1 FAC 3+1 Others 1*

MELLBERG Erik Olof
Born: Gullspang, Sweden, 3 September 1977
Height: 6'1" **Weight:** 12.10
International Honours: Sweden: 47

An immense figure in the centre of the defence, Olof was one of Aston Villa's most consistent performers last season, turning in 'Man of the Match' displays week-in week-out. His strong tackling has made him a fan's favourite and he formed a solid defensive partnership with Ronny Johnsen. He missed a handful of games through injury, but went on to make his 100th Premiership appearance for Villa in April. Olof also represented Sweden during the campaign.
Aston Villa *(£5,000,000 from Racing Santander, Spain, ex Degerfors, AIK Solna, on 25/7/2001) PL 103/2 FLC 8 FAC 3 Others 5*

MELLIGAN John (JJ) James
Born: Dublin, 11 February 1982
Height: 5'9" **Weight:** 11.4
Club Honours: Div 3 '04
International Honours: RoI: U21-1; Yth
This promising Wolves' youngster

returned to Kidderminster for a second loan spell last October, but following a change in management at Aggborough he went back to Molineux. Shortly afterwards he joined Doncaster Rovers, also on loan, as the club sought to cover the right-midfield berth and the deal was eventually extended until the end of the campaign. He scored on his debut for Rovers against Boston United and produced some terrific displays as they went on to clinch the Third Division title.
Wolverhampton W *(From trainee on 11/7/2000) FL 0+2*
Bournemouth *(Loaned on 30/11/2001) FL 7+1 FAC 1*
Kidderminster Hrs *(Loaned on 13/9/2002) FL 28+1/10 Others 3/2*
Kidderminster Hrs *(Loaned on 3/10/2003) FL 5/1 Others 1*
Doncaster Rov *(Loaned on 17/11/2003) FL 21/2*

Micky Mellon

275

MELLON Michael (Micky) Joseph
Born: Paisley, 18 March 1972
Height: 5'10" **Weight:** 12.11
Micky was part of an impressive midfield set-up at Tranmere last term and combined well with his colleagues in whatever formation was being used. Club captain and a regular in the line-up, he likes nothing more than to instigate attacks and created many useful chances for his colleagues. A personal highlight was scoring the late winner in the FA Cup fifth round tie at Luton. Micky was out of contract in the summer and his future was unclear at the time of writing.
Bristol C (From trainee on 6/12/1989) FL 26+9/1 FLC 3 FAC 1+1 Others 5+3
West Bromwich A (£75,000 on 11/2/1993) FL 38+7/6 FLC 3+2 FAC 0+1 Others 6/1
Blackpool (£50,000 on 23/11/1994) FL 123+1/14 FLC 9/1 FAC 4 Others 7/2
Tranmere Rov (£285,000 on 31/10/1997) FL 45+12/3 FLC 4 FAC 3+1
Burnley (£350,000 on 8/1/1999) FL 72+12/5 FLC 3+1 FAC 5
Tranmere Rov (Free on 5/3/2001) FL 102+15/3 FLC 7/1 FAC 11+1/3 Others 5

MELLOR Neil Andrew
Born: Sheffield, 4 November 1982
Height: 6'0" **Weight:** 13.7
Club Honours: FLC '03
This young Liverpool striker started the 2003-04 season on loan at West Ham. Neil looked enthusiastic and eager early on and scored his first goals in November against Crystal Palace: a looping header and a tap-in. However, he then suffered an ankle injury and by the time he had recovered several new strikers had arrived at Upton Park, pushing him down the pecking order. Neil eventually returned to Anfield, where he finished off in great form for the reserves with ten goals in the last four games.
Liverpool (From trainee on 8/2/2002) PL 1+2 FLC 2/1 FAC 1
West Ham U (Loaned on 7/8/2003) FL 8+8/2 FLC 1+1 FAC 0+3

MELTON Stephen (Steve)
Born: Lincoln, 3 October 1978
Height: 5'11" **Weight:** 12.2
Club Honours: Div 3 '01
As he drifted further towards the fringes of the first-team squad, Steve's only starts for Hull in 2003-04 came in the LDV Vans Trophy games against Darlington and Scunthorpe. A skilful midfielder with an outstanding first touch, he didn't complete the latter game due to an ankle problem and later joined Boston United.

Steve gave some excellent performances on the right side of midfield for the Pilgrims. His only goal was a scrambled effort, but he provided both skill and strength in the centre of the park.
Nottingham F (From trainee on 9/10/1995) P/FL 2+1 FLC 1
Stoke C (Free on 28/2/2000) FL 0+5 Others 0+2
Brighton & Hove A (Free on 2/8/2000) FL 21+25/3 FLC 1+3 Others 4+1/2
Hull C (Free on 24/12/2002) FL 19+11 FLC 0+1 Others 2
Boston U (Signed on 19/3/2004) FL 9/1

MELVILLE Andrew (Andy) Roger
Born: Swansea, 29 November 1968
Height: 6'0" **Weight:** 13.10
Club Honours: WC '89; Div 1 '96, '01
International Honours: W: 62; B-1; U21-2
An experienced defender Andy found himself out of the Fulham side in the early part of the season, but regained his place following an injury to Alain Goma in November. A solid central defender, he uses his experience well, often making last-ditch tackles as well as exerting a calming influence on the less experienced players. In January he moved to West Ham, with Ian Pearce travelling in the opposite direction. Andy added considerable experience to the Hammers' side and helped the youngsters around him. He had a superb match at Stoke as West Ham marched on to the play-offs. Andy added further caps for Wales with appearances against Scotland and Hungary.
Swansea C (From trainee on 25/7/1986) FL 165+10/22 FLC 10 FAC 14+1/5 Others 13/2
Oxford U (£275,000 on 23/7/1990) FL 135/13 FLC 12/1 FAC 6 Others 6/1
Sunderland (£750,000 + on 9/8/1993) P/FL 204/14 FLC 18+1 FAC 11 Others 2
Bradford C (Loaned on 13/2/1998) FL 6/1
Fulham (Free on 1/7/1999) P/FL 150+3/4 FLC 12+1 FAC 13+2 Others 12
West Ham U (Signed on 16/1/2004) FL 11+3 Others 3

MENDES Albert Junior Hillyard Andrew
Born: Balham, 15 September 1976
Height: 5'8" **Weight:** 11.4
Junior began last season on the bench for Mansfield Town, but showed some scintillating form when he came into the side after Colin Larkin was injured and won several 'Man of the Match' awards. He became a valuable member of the Stags' attack, reaching a double-figure

goal tally and becoming a firm favourite of the fans. Junior is a right-sided forward, who is most effective when cutting in from a wide position.
Chelsea (From trainee on 1/7/1995)
St Mirren (Free on 29/4/1996) SL 98+22/21 SLC 6 SC 4/1 Others 0+2
Carlisle U (Loaned on 18/11/1998) FL 5+1/1
Dunfermline Ath (£20,000 on 24/7/2000) SL 7+7 SLC 2
St Mirren (Free on 22/6/2002) SL 15+2/6 SLC 1 SC 1 Others 3
Mansfield T (Free on 30/1/2003) FL 54+3/12 FLC 1 FAC 4/1 Others 3/1

MENDIETA Gaizka
Born: Bilbao, Spain, 27 March 1974
Height: 5'8" **Weight:** 10.12
Club Honours: FLC '04
International Honours: Spain: 40
This Lazio midfielder joined Middlesbrough in a 12-month loan deal, having just returned to Rome following an unsuccessful season on loan at Barcelona. The Spanish giants had spurned the chance to buy him for a cut-price fee leaving the door open for Steve McClaren to move in. A regular in the side, Gaizka's ability brought balance and guile to a Boro' side that was lacking in firepower.
Middlesbrough (Loaned from Lazio, Italy, ex Castellon, Valencia, on 26/8/2003) PL 30+1/2 FLC 6/1 FAC 1

MERRIS David Andrew
Born: Rotherham, 13 October 1980
Height: 5'7" **Weight:** 10.6
David joined York City during the 2003 close season and had an impressive first term with the Minstermen. He was a near ever-present at left wing back throughout the campaign and showed an array of talents: good pace, fine attacking skills and excellent powers of recovery.
York C (Free from Harrogate T, ex Rotherham U trainee, on 8/8/2003) FL 42+2 FLC 1/1 FAC 1 Others 0+1

MERSON Paul Charles
Born: Harlesden, 20 March 1968
Height: 6'0" **Weight:** 13.2
Club Honours: Div 1 '89, '91, '03; FLC '93; FAC '93; ECWC '94
International Honours: E: 21; B-4; U21-4; Yth
Possibly Walsall's most spectacular signing ever, Paul got off to a tremendous start with a goal in the pre-season win over his former club Aston Villa and two really brilliant goals in the 4-1 win over West Bromwich Albion in the opening First Division match. He missed a few weeks in

Gaizka Mendieta

Paul Merson

the new year, but was back in time to be appointed caretaker manager for the last four games of the season. His surging runs and probing passes were a key factor in the final day win over Rotherham that just failed to save Walsall from relegation. Soon afterwards he was appointed manager although he plans to continue to play for the Saddlers in the 2004-05 campaign.
Arsenal (From apprentice on 1/12/1985) F/PL 289+38/78 FLC 38+2/10 FAC 28+3/4 Others 27+2/6
Brentford (Loaned on 22/1/1987) FL 6+1 Others 1+1
Middlesbrough (£4,500,000 + on 15/7/1997) P/FL 48/11 FLC 7/3 FAC 3/1
Aston Villa (£6,750,000 on 10/9/1998) PL 101+16/18 FLC 6+2 FAC 11 Others 8+1/1
Portsmouth (Free on 8/8/2002) FL 44+1/12 FLC 2 FAC 1
Walsall (Free on 1/8/2003) FL 31+3/4 FLC 2/2

MIGLIORANZI Stefani
Born: Pocos de Caldas, Brazil, 20 September 1977
Height: 6'0" **Weight:** 11.12
After being rewarded with a new contract for Swindon Town last term, Stef was unfortunate with injuries. Although these tended to be from impacts and knocks and were quickly overcome they acted to disrupt his season. A classy midfielder who always looks composed and uses the ball well, he had a particularly fine game as Swindon frightened Leeds in the Carling Cup during September.
Portsmouth (Free from St John's University, NY, USA on 8/3/1999) FL 25+10/2 FLC 2+4 FAC 1
Swindon T (Free on 1/8/2002) FL 73+3/7 FLC 2+1 FAC 2 Others 3/1

MILDENHALL Stephen (Steve) James
Born: Swindon, 13 May 1978
Height: 6'4" **Weight:** 14.0
Steve was first choice in goal for Notts County for most of last season, experiencing a difficult campaign playing behind a leaky defence. He was just returning to his best form when he was sidelined by an injury which required surgery and kept him out of action until the summer.
Swindon T (From trainee on 19/7/1996) FL 29+4 FLC 2 FAC 2 Others 1
Notts Co (£150,000 on 16/7/2001) FL 74+1 FLC 5/1 FAC 6 Others 3

MILES John Francis
Born: Bootle, 28 September 1981
Height: 5'10" **Weight:** 12.9

In his first full season as a professional, John started the 2003-04 campaign playing up front alongside Martin Carruthers for Macclesfield and later on he partnered Matthew Tipton, but he found himself on the substitutes' bench when Jon Parkin was signed in February. John always played enthusiastically and scored seven goals in all competitions, using his pace to create goal-scoring opportunities for his colleagues.
Liverpool (From trainee on 27/4/1999)
Stoke C (Free on 28/3/2002) FL 0+1
Crewe Alex (Free on 16/8/2002) FL 0+5/1 FLC 1 FAC 2 Others 0+2
Macclesfield T (Signed on 27/3/2003) FL 30+7/10 FLC 1 FAC 1+1/1 Others 0+1

MILLER Justin James
Born: Johannesburg, South Africa, 16 December 1980
Height: 6'0" **Weight:** 11.10
After being mostly used in the centre of defence the previous season, Justin played more in a central-midfield role for Leyton Orient last term but still showed some excellent touches. He chipped in with a couple of goals during the campaign and will be looking to become more of a first-team regular in 2004-05. Justin is a long-throw specialist.
Ipswich T (From juniors on 26/11/1999)
Leyton Orient (Loaned on 13/9/2002) FL 13 FLC 1 FAC 2 Others 2
Leyton Orient (Free on 31/1/2003) FL 33+7/2 FLC 1 FAC 1+1

MILLER Kenneth (Kenny)
Born: Edinburgh, 23 December 1979
Height: 5'8" **Weight:** 11.3
International Honours: S: 12; B-1; U21-7
This talented Wolves striker underwent a hernia operation in the summer of 2003 and did not return to first-team action until the end of September. Often playing in a deep role or on the wing, he had only scored one goal by January, before suddenly notching four in nine days. There was an FA Cup double against Kidderminster, followed by two well-taken and important goals. He scored the winner against Manchester United, the only goal of the match, and a late equaliser at home to Liverpool. It seemed Kenny had turned the corner, but the inconsistencies crept in again and he was dropped in April.
Hibernian (Signed from Hutchison Vale BC on 22/5/1996) SL 29+16/12 SLC 1+2/1 SC 5/1
Stenhousemuir (Loaned on 25/11/1998) SL 11/8

Glasgow R (£2,000,000 on 16/7/2000) SL 12+18/8 SLC 1/1 SC 2+1/1 Others 3+2/1
Wolverhampton W (Loaned on 7/9/2001) FL 3+2/2
Wolverhampton W (£3,000,000 on 14/12/2001) P/FL 54+29/21 FLC 3+1/2 FAC 7+1/5 Others 3+2/1

MILLER Kevin
Born: Falmouth, 15 March 1969
Height: 6'1" **Weight:** 13.0
Club Honours: Div 4 '90
This experienced goalkeeper overcame a close-season knee operation to establish himself in the Bristol Rovers line-up, bringing some much-needed stability to the defence. Kevin produced many impressive performances, none more so than in the 1-1 draw at Leyton Orient in March, and was selected by the supporters as their 'Player of the Season'.
Exeter C (Free from Newquay on 9/3/1989) FL 163 FLC 7 FAC 12 Others 18
Birmingham C (£250,000 on 14/5/1993) FL 24 FLC 4 Others 2
Watford (£250,000 on 7/8/1994) FL 128 FLC 10 FAC 10 Others 3
Crystal Palace (£1,000,000 + on 21/7/1997) P/FL 66 FLC 3 FAC 5 Others 2
Barnsley (£250,000 on 27/8/1999) FL 115 FLC 11 FAC 4 Others 3
Exeter C (Free on 9/8/2002) FL 46 FLC 1 FAC 3 Others 2
Bristol Rov (Free on 11/7/2003) FL 44 FLC 1 FAC 1 Others 1

MILLER Lee Adamson
Born: Lanark, 18 May 1983
Height: 6'2" **Weight:** 11.7
Club Honours: S Div 1 '03
Great things were expected of this striker who had been Falkirk's top scorer in the 2002-03 campaign. However, despite flashes of good play, he sometimes struggled to find his best form for Bristol City last term. Nevertheless he netted a respectable total of nine goals and will be looking to increase his output in the 2004-05 campaign.
Falkirk (From juniors on 9/6/2000) SL 61/27 SLC 3/1 SC 6 Others 3/2
Bristol C (£300,000 on 30/7/2003) FL 32+10/8 FLC 2+1/1 FAC 2 Others 1

MILLER Thomas (Tommy) William
Born: Easington, 8 January 1979
Height: 6'1" **Weight:** 11.12
After a bright start – he scored Ipswich Town's first goal of the season from the penalty spot in injury time – Tommy was forced to miss a couple of months because of injury. A tenacious midfield

279

player he is most effective when filling one of the central roles, enabling him to link up with his forwards but also to provide additional defensive cover when necessary. Tommy likes nothing better than to get in shots at goal and last season he was able to reach double figures in the goals department.
Hartlepool U (From trainee on 8/7/1997) FL

130+7/35 FLC 6/3 FAC 5/1 Others 12/5
Ipswich T (£800,000 + on 16/7/2001) P/FL
56+16/17 FLC 5/1 FAC 3+1/2 Others 5+3/2

MILLS Daniel (Danny) John
Born: Norwich, 18 May 1977
Height: 5'11" **Weight:** 11.9
Club Honours: FLC '04
International Honours: E: 19; U21-14; Yth

Garry Mills

This combative and strong-running right back who can also play as a centre back joined Middlesbrough on loan from Leeds United four days after playing for England in a 3-1 win against Croatia. His first game in a Boro' shirt was against Leeds United at the Riverside: United won 3-2! He settled in well and his no-nonsense attitude to his game soon made him a favourite of the fans. He won a further England cap during his loan period in the 1-1 draw with Portugal and his first domestic honour followed soon after with Boro', a Carling Cup winner's medal, but he returned to Elland Road when his loan period expired on the final day of the Premiership season, uncertain where he would be playing his football in 2004-05.
Norwich C (From trainee on 1/11/1994) FL
46+20 FLC 3+2/1 FAC 2
Charlton Ath (£350,000 on 19/3/1998) P/FL
45/3 FLC 3 FAC 1 Others 2
Leeds U (£4,370,000 on 1/7/1999) PL
96+5/3 FLC 4/1 FAC 6+1 Others 27+2
Middlesbrough (Loaned on 22/8/2003) PL
28 FLC 7 FAC 2

MILLS Garry Leonard
Born: Faversham, 20 May 1981
Height: 5'9" **Weight:** 11.8
Club Honours: NC '01; Div 3 '03
Garry was a key figure in central midfield for Rushden last term, producing some tough-tackling displays and even managing his first senior goal when he burst forward to score with a cool finish in the 2-1 home win over Tranmere in February. However, he was left frustrated when an ankle injury ruled him out of the final run-in and the Diamonds slipped to relegation.
Rushden & Diamonds (From juniors on 3/7/1999) FL 51+18/1 FLC 4+1 FAC 3 Others 4

MILLS Pablo Simeon
Born: Birmingham, 27 May 1984
Height: 6'0" **Weight:** 11.6
International Honours: E: Yth
At one stage, Pablo was a reported target for clubs in Russia and Ukraine. He had a mixed season with Derby, a regular member of the squad before Christmas but hardly used after more experienced defenders were signed. Pablo is strong and can use the ball well but needs to work on his game. Greater concentration and discipline is needed in the centre of defence if he is to realise his undoubted talent.
Derby Co (From trainee on 16/7/2002) FL 25+10 FLC 1 FAC 2

MILNER James Philip
Born: Leeds, 4 January 1986
Height: 5'11" **Weight:** 11.0
International Honours: E: U21-1; Yth
This exciting Leeds United youngster
spent a month on loan at Swindon early
in the season, a move that was both an
enjoyable and beneficial experience for
him. James scored twice during this
period and showed himself to be an
unselfish player in possession of skill and
pace. Back at Elland Road he became an
integral member of the first team playing
on the left-hand side of midfield. For
someone so young he is a good reader of
the game, has an abundance of skill and
an eye for goal.
*Leeds U (From trainee on 12/2/2003) PL
28+20/5 FLC 1 FAC 1+4*
Swindon T (Loaned on 4/9/2003) FL 6/2

MINTO Scott Christopher
Born: Heswall, 6 August 1971
Height: 5'9" **Weight:** 12.7
Club Honours: FAC '97
International Honours: E: U21-6; Yth
Scott brought his vast experience to the
Rotherham team and this proved
invaluable during the closing weeks of the
season when the Millers were battling
against the threat of relegation. A full
back who reads the game well and isn't
afraid to play the simple ball to get out of
danger, he is always willing to join in the
attack with overlapping runs. The fact
that Scott had played at the highest level
held him in good stead, particularly
during the last few weeks of the season
when a cool head was needed.
*Charlton Ath (From trainee on 2/2/1989) FL
171+9/7 FLC 8/2 FAC 8+2 Others 7/1*
*Chelsea (£775,000 on 28/5/1994) PL 53+1/4
FLC 3/1 FAC 9 Others 5+1 (Free to Benfica,
Portugal on 30/6/1997)*
*West Ham U (£1,000,000 on 15/1/1999) PL
44+7 FLC 4 FAC 2 Others 5*
*Rotherham U (Free on 8/8/2003) FL 28+4
FLC 2 FAC 1*

MIRFIN David Matthew
Born: Sheffield, 18 April 1985
Height: 6'2" **Weight:** 14.5
This teenaged defender was involved
with the Huddersfield Town first team
throughout the 2003-04 season. The
tall centre back settled in remarkably
well into the right side of the defence,
and was also used from the substitutes'
bench to lead the attack. A powerful
tackler who reads the game well, David
scored the winning goal in the first leg

James Milner

of the play-off semi-final against Lincoln.

Huddersfield T (From trainee on 6/12/2003) FL 15+7/2 FLC 1 Others 4/1

MITCHELL Craig Richard
Born: Mansfield, 6 May 1985
Height: 6'0" **Weight:** 12.4
This young Mansfield Town striker managed just a single first-team outing from the substitutes' bench last term, featuring against Yeovil in September when the squad was decimated by injury. He subsequently spent time on loan at Harrogate and Northwich Victoria before being released in the summer.

Mansfield T (From trainee on 4/7/2003) FL 3+13/1

MITCHELL Paul Alexander
Born: Stalybridge, 26 August 1981
Height: 5'11" **Weight:** 12.3
Club Honours: Div 2 '03
Although not a Wigan Athletic first-team regular last term, Paul was again a useful squad member. With midfield being possibly the strongest area of the team, he found it hard to break into the line-up, making just one League start in the away win at Crewe. A gutsy performer who works hard and does the simple things well, his substitute appearances were as a 'holding' player in the centre of midfield. Paul also showed his versatility with an excellent performance at left back in the away draw at Crystal Palace. His contract was due to expire in the summer and his future was unclear at the time of writing.

Wigan Ath (From trainee on 3/7/2000) FL 30+33 FLC 4+3 FAC 2+2 Others 3+2
Halifax T (Loaned on 22/3/2001) FL 11

MITCHELL Scott Andrew
Born: Ely, 2 September 1985
Height: 5'11" **Weight:** 12.0
A product of the Ipswich Town Academy, Scott is a versatile youngster who can play in midfield or defence. He made his bow in senior football last term, making two appearances as a substitute.

Ipswich T (From trainee on 5/3/2004) FL 0+2

MOLLOY David
Born: Newcastle, 29 August 1986
Height: 5'11" **Weight:** 11.1
A winger who showed good close control, David gained some valuable experience of senior football for Carlisle United last term. He made his senior debut from the substitutes' bench at Southend in September and went on to make a handful more appearances, all in the first half of the campaign.

Carlisle U (Trainee) FL 3+4 FAC 0+1 Others 0+1

MONK Garry Alan
Born: Bedford, 6 March 1979
Height: 6'0" **Weight:** 13.0
This popular central defender joined Barnsley on loan last November and in February he signed a contract through to the end of the campaign. He impressed during his loan spell, but suffered an injury soon after signing terms and did not return to action until shortly before the end of the season. Garry was rather unlucky to be released by the Reds in the summer.

Torquay U (Trainee) FL 4+1
Southampton (Signed on 23/5/1997) PL 9+2 FLC 1 FAC 0+1
Torquay U (Loaned on 25/9/1998) FL 6
Stockport Co (Loaned on 9/9/1999) FL 2 FLC 2
Oxford U (Loaned on 12/1/2001) FL 5
Sheffield Wed (Loaned on 13/12/2002) FL 15
Barnsley (Free on 21/11/2003) FL 14+3 FAC 4/1

MONKHOUSE Andrew (Andy) William
Born: Leeds, 23 October 1980
Height: 6'1" **Weight:** 11.6
A tall left winger, Andy was in and out of the Rotherham United team last season, with his best spell being a run of six successive games. He possesses a powerful shot and he put that to good use with excellent goals against Sheffield United and Nottingham Forest to help his team gain two valuable draws. His defensive work also improved to a great extent.

Rotherham U (From trainee on 14/11/1998) FL 50+52/6 FLC 7/3 FAC 1+5 Others 1+1/1

MONTGOMERY Gary Stephen
Born: Leamington, 8 October 1982
Height: 6'1" **Weight:** 13.8
This fearless young goalkeeper received few chances at Rotherham last term due to the consistent form of Mike Pollitt. However, he didn't let the team down in any of his appearances when he proved to be a brave shot-stopper. Gary replaced the dismissed Pollitt in the Carling Cup tie at Arsenal when he saved two penalties in the shoot-out and scored himself.

Coventry C (From trainee on 31/1/2001) FL 8 FLC 1
Kidderminster Hrs (Loaned on 28/3/2002) FL 2
Rotherham U (Free on 14/7/2003) FL 3+1 FLC 0+1

MONTGOMERY Nicholas (Nick) Anthony
Born: Leeds, 28 October 1981
Height: 5'9" **Weight:** 11.8
International Honours: S: U21-2
After several seasons as a much-used substitute, Nick finally became a regular member of the Sheffield United side last term, working extremely hard and showing great commitment as a midfield ball-winner and occasionally as a man-to-man marker. He made regular forward runs both down the flanks and through the middle but his final pass or shot could be wayward. He was regularly selected for Scotland U21s, twice having to withdraw through injury or club commitments and he was also chosen for the Scottish Future squad.

Sheffield U (From trainee on 7/7/2000) FL 75+42/5 FLC 5+3/1 FAC 7+2

MOONEY Thomas (Tommy) John
Born: Billingham, 11 August 1971
Height: 5'10" **Weight:** 12.6
Club Honours: Div 2 '98
Tommy was a revelation for Swindon Town during the 2003-04 season. Enthusiastic, eager and full of running, the County Ground fans took to him from the start. His constant hard work up front was rewarded with a 20-goal haul and he was involved throughout, missing only one game when laid low by a virus. He was also not afraid to help out at the back when required and made some vital goal-line clearances. Tommy was voted as the Robins' 'Player of the Season' and can look back with pride on his contribution to a successful campaign.

Aston Villa (From trainee on 23/11/1989)
Scarborough (Free on 1/8/1990) FL 96+11/30 FLC 11+2/8 FAC 3 Others 6/2
Southend U (£100,000 on 12/7/1993) FL 9+5/3
Watford (Signed on 17/3/1994) P/FL 221+29/60 FLC 22/3 FAC 11+1/2 Others 4
Birmingham C (Free on 1/7/2001) P/FL 29+5/13 FLC 1/2 FAC 1 Others 3
Stoke C (Loaned on 13/9/2002) FL 11+1/3
Sheffield U (Loaned on 17/11/2003) FL 2+1 FLC 0+1 FAC 2/1
Derby Co (Loaned on 19/3/2003) FL 7+1
Swindon T (Free on 21/7/2003) FL 41+4/19 FLC 0+1/1 FAC 1 Others 2

MOORE Alan
Born: Dublin, 25 November 1974
Height: 5'10" **Weight:** 11.10
Club Honours: Div 1 '95
International Honours: RoI: 8; U21-4; Yth; Sch

Alan began last term as a first choice, but his starts for Burnley were rare both before and after an injury which kept him on the sidelines for over three months up to Christmas. Rarely living up to the promise shown in his early days at Turf Moor and clearly badly short of match fitness, Alan left the club at the end of the season.

Middlesbrough (From trainee on 5/12/1991) F/PL 98+20/14 FLC 9+6/1 FAC 3+2/2 Others 3+1
Barnsley (Loaned on 30/10/1998) FL 4+1
Burnley (Free on 20/7/2001) FL 42+27/4 FLC 3+2/1 FAC 8+3/3

MOORE Darren Mark
Born: Birmingham, 22 April 1974
Height: 6'2" **Weight:** 15.6
International Honours: Jamaica: 3
After missing the entire first half of the 2003-04 season with a knee problem, West Bromwich Albion's giant, rock-like central defender returned to produce some quite outstanding performances alongside Thomas Gaardsoe and his skipper Sean Gregan. Strong in the air, powerful and totally committed in the tackle his drive and enthusiasm once again brushed off on the rest of the team and he was as delighted as anyone when the Baggies reclaimed their place in the Premiership. Like he had done when promotion was achieved in 2001-02, he weighed in with two crucial goals – the equaliser at Sheffield United and the opener in a 2-0 home victory over play-off chasing Crystal Palace.

Torquay U (From trainee on 18/11/1992) FL 102+1/8 FLC 6 FAC 7/1 Others 8/2
Doncaster Rov (£62,500 on 19/7/1995) FL 76/7 FLC 4 FAC 1 Others 3/1
Bradford C (£310,000 + on 18/6/1997) FL 62/3 FLC 6/1 FAC 2
Portsmouth (£500,000 + on 15/11/1999) FL 58+1/3 FLC 5 FAC 2
West Bromwich A (£750,000 on 15/9/2001) P/FL 80+3/6 FAC 7

MOORE Ian Ronald
Born: Birkenhead, 26 August 1976
Height: 5'11" **Weight:** 12.0
International Honours: E: U21-7; Yth
Apart from missing the start of the season through suspension and the end of it through injury, Ian appeared in every game for Burnley last term. His role varied, sometimes out-and-out lone striker, sometimes in a deeper role and occasionally out wide, but whatever the demands he gave his all for the cause. A serial goal-scorer in the FA Cup, Ian's partnership with Robbie Blake blossomed

and together they were a pair to trouble most First Division defences. Although his work rate still sometimes exceeded the end product, Ian's contribution to the side in 2003-04 was never in doubt.

Tranmere Rov (From trainee on 6/7/1994) FL 41+17/12 FLC 3+2/1 FAC 1+1 Others 0+1
Bradford C (Loaned on 13/9/1996) FL 6
Nottingham F (£1,000,000 on 15/3/1997) F/PL 3+12/1 FLC 0+2 FAC 1
West Ham U (Loaned on 26/9/1997) PL 0+1
Stockport Co (£800,000 on 31/7/1998) FL 83+10/20 FLC 8/2 FAC 3/1
Burnley (£1,000,000 on 20/11/2000) FL 140+17/33 FLC 4+1/1 FAC 13/10

MOORE Luke Issac
Born: Birmingham, 13 February 1986
Height: 5'11" **Weight:** 11.13
Club Honours: FAYC '02
International Honours: E: Yth
This talented young striker made several appearances from the substitutes' bench for Aston Villa last term. He showed no nerves when making his debut for Villa in the big 'derby' clash at home to Birmingham and produced some promising displays. Luke joined Wycombe Wanderers on loan during December and scored four goals in six games including a hat-trick against Grimsby Town. He showed that he had plenty of pace and the knack for being in the right place in the penalty box.

Aston Villa (From trainee on 13/2/2003) PL 0+7
Wycombe W (Loaned on 11/12/2003) FL 6/4

MOORE Stefan
Born: Birmingham, 28 September 1983
Height: 5'10" **Weight:** 11.0
Club Honours: FAYC '02
International Honours: E: Yth
Like his brother Luke, Stefan has graduated through Villa's youth system. He is a young striker who made a handful of senior appearances, mainly from the substitutes' bench, during the first half of the season. He showed plenty of ability and scored once, in the 2-0 win at Blackburn in December.

Aston Villa (From trainee on 9/10/2000) PL 9+12/2 FLC 2+3 FAC 0+1 Others 0+2
Chesterfield (Loaned on 27/10/2001) FL 1+1 Others 1

MORENO Javier (Javi)
Born: Valencia, Spain, 10 September 1974
Height: 5'11" **Weight:** 12.4
International Honours: Spain: 5
Signed on loan during the January transfer window, Javi came to Lancashire with quite a reputation to uphold.

However, Javi only made one start for Bolton (in the home victory against Portsmouth), as well as a number of appearances from the bench, all without scoring. He admitted that the pace and the directness of the English game took him by surprise and it would appear that he never really came to terms with this during his time in the Premiership.

Bolton W (Loaned from Atletico Madrid, Spain, ex Barcelona, Cordoba, Numancia, Alaves, AC Milan, on 7/1/2004) PL 1+7 FLC 0+2

MORGAN Alan William
Born: Edinburgh, 27 November 1983
Height: 6'0 **Weight:** 12.6
International Honours: S: Yth
This promising Blackburn Rovers youngster was a regular for the reserves at left back or in a wide-left midfield position last term. In October he had a spell on loan at Darlington where he featured in midfield or up front. A strong running player, who possesses a powerful shot, he found the net for the Quakers in the away defeat at Cheltenham.

Blackburn Rov (From trainee on 22/12/2000)
Darlington (Loaned on 10/10/2003) FL 4+1/1 FAC 1 Others 1

MORGAN Christopher (Chris) Paul
Born: Barnsley, 9 November 1977
Height: 5'10" **Weight:** 12.9
Chris signed a long-term deal with Sheffield United in the summer of 2003, immediately becoming a first-choice central defender. He missed some games through injuries (a broken wrist and then a cartilage problem), but his no-nonsense approach made him a favourite with the fans. Always good in the air and strong in the tackle, his use of the ball improved as the season progressed. He was a threat at set pieces and scored from 15 yards with a scissors kick against Nottingham Forest in the FA Cup. Chris's wholehearted attitude helped to win him the supporters' 'Player of the Year' award.

Barnsley (From trainee on 3/7/1996) P/FL 182+3/7 FLC 14/1 FAC 9 Others 4
Sheffield U (Free on 1/8/2003) FL 32/1 FLC 1 FAC 3/1

MORGAN Craig
Born: St Asaph, 18 June 1985
Height: 6'1" **Weight:** 12.7
International Honours: W: U21-2; Yth
Craig made further progress at Wrexham last term and although still not the finished article in some aspects of his

game, he is emerging as a fine talent with his calm unhurried style of defending. A regular member of the Wales U21 squad, he will be looking to become a regular in the Wrexham starting line-up in 2004-05. Craig was voted as the 'Young Player of the Season' by the supporters.
Wrexham (From trainee on 10/7/2003) FL 15+11/1 FAC 0+1 Others 3

MORGAN Dean Lance
Born: Enfield, 3 October 1983
Height: 5'11" **Weight:** 11.2
Recommended to Reading by Colchester manager Phil Parkinson, Dean was originally given a contract until the end of the season but a series of impressive displays persuaded the club to extend that in the summer. Quick and tricky on either flank, he also enjoys scampering down the middle, and scored a well-taken late winner in the 3-2 win at Cardiff.Described by Steve Coppell as "the most skilful player at the club", Dean now needs to show that he can produce for the whole 90 minutes what he has been showing in longer and longer bursts.
Colchester U (From trainee on 8/8/2001) FL 23+48/6 FLC 1 FAC 0+3 Others 1+1
Reading (Free on 28/11/2003) FL 3+10/1 FAC 1+1

MORGAN Lionel Anthony
Born: Tottenham, 17 February 1983
Height: 5'11" **Weight:** 12.7
International Honours: E: Yth
One of the most gifted players to wear a Wimbledon shirt, Lionel unfortunately has also proved to be one of the most injury prone, and after another nightmare campaign that saw a persistent knee injury restrict him to just three games, he was released at the end of the season. A left-footed midfielder with a superb array of skills, he will be looking to resurrect his career elsewhere in 2004-05.
Wimbledon (From trainee on 10/8/2000) FL 13+17/2 FLC 1+1 FAC 0+1/1

MORGAN Mark Paul Thomas
Born: Belfast, 23 October 1978
Height: 6'0" **Weight:** 11.5
International Honours: NI: U21-1
Paul had another solid season at the heart of Lincoln's defence playing on the left side of a three-man centre-back system. His anticipation of situations and his skill on the ball held the defence together at times. Paul suffered from a persistent hamstring injury, which eventually forced him to sit out most of the run in to the end of the season and the play-offs.

Preston NE (From trainee on 9/5/1997) FLC 1
Lincoln C (Free on 17/7/2001) FL 118+2/1 FLC 3 FAC 3 Others 6

MORGAN Westley (Wes) Nathan
Born: Nottingham, 21 January 1984
Height: 6'2" **Weight:** 14.0
This big Nottingham Forest central defender proved to be the find of the season after making his debut as a left back in the Carling Cup tie against Port Vale last August. Wes continued to be a regular in the side, showing his versatility by also playing as a right back and he scored his first goal for the club in the 6-0 win over Wimbledon in October. However, his best role appeared to be in the centre of defence and he was very effective alongside Michael Dawson in the closing stages of the campaign.
Nottingham F (Signed from Central Midlands League side,Dunkirk, on 5/7/2002) FL 30+2/2 FLC 3 FAC 1
Kidderminster Hrs (Loaned on 27/2/2003) FL 5/1

MORISON Steven (Steve) William
Born: Enfield, 29 August 1983
Height: 6'2" **Weight:** 12.0
This tall striker found first-team places at a premium at Northampton last term with so many new faces coming into the club. However, he continued to score regularly for the reserve team and netted his only senior goal in the home win over Boston United in March.
Northampton T (From trainee on 7/7/2003) FL 6+13/2 Others 0+2

MORLEY David Thomas
Born: St Helens, 25 September 1977
Height: 6'2" **Weight:** 12.7
Club Honours: Div 3 '04
This commanding central defender shared centre-back duties with Mark Albrighton and Steve Foster for Doncaster Rovers last term. Although Dave was often the back-up he made a valuable contribution and netted his only goal in the 3-1 win at Cheltenham in December.
Manchester C (From trainee on 3/1/1996) FL 1+2/1
Ayr U (Loaned on 14/3/1998) SL 4
Southend U (Signed on 28/8/1998) FL 63+13 FLC 6 FAC 0+2 Others 2
Carlisle U (Free on 26/1/2001) FL 37+4/1 FLC 1 FAC 1 Others 1
Oxford U (Free on 14/12/2001) FL 16+2/3
Doncaster Rov (Free on 5/7/2002) FL 15+6/1 FLC 1 FAC 1 Others 2

MORNAR Ivica
Born: Split, Croatia, 12 January 1974
Height: 6'2" **Weight:** 13.1
International Honours: Croatia: 20
Ivica arrived at Pompey at the end of the January transfer window and scored on his debut in the 4-3 defeat at White Hart Lane. He proved to be a lively handful for opposition defenders, showing great close control and using his height to good effect.
Portsmouth (£400,000 from RSC Anderlecht, Belgium, ex Hajduk Split, Eintracht Frankfurt, Seville, CD Ourense, Standard Liege, on 30/1/2004) PL 3+5/1 FAC 2

MORRELL Andrew (Andy) Jonathan
Born: Doncaster, 28 September 1974
Height: 5'11" **Weight:** 12.0
Andy started last season in promising form for Coventry and scored in five consecutive games in September, including a memorable winner at Reading. However, the goals then dried up, Andy's form suffered and he lost his place. He played a number of games as a withdrawn striker on the right-hand side but did not look comfortable. Then after scoring twice in the 6-1 win at Walsall he suffered a knee injury which kept him out for three months.
Wrexham (Free from Newcastle Blue Star on 18/12/1998) FL 76+34/40 FLC 3/1 FAC 1+2 Others 2+3/2
Coventry C (Free on 2/7/2003) FL 19+11/9 FLC 1+1 FAC 2

MORRIS Glenn James
Born: Woolwich, 20 December 1983
Height: 6'0" **Weight:** 11.3
Glenn started last season as Leyton Orient's reserve goalkeeper but regained his position as first choice towards the end of the year. He again produced a series of mature displays and retained his place in the side throughout the second half of the campaign.
Leyton Orient (From trainee on 4/3/2003) FL 51+1 FLC 2+1 FAC 2 Others 3

MORRIS Jody Steven
Born: Hammersmith, 22 December 1978
Height: 5'5" **Weight:** 10.12
Club Honours: ECWC '98; FAC '00; CS '00
International Honours: E: U21-7; Yth; Sch
Signed from Chelsea at a time when many others were moving out, this busy midfielder made a dozen appearances for Leeds United last term before being blighted by a series of off-field problems.

Andy Morrell

He was eventually released from his contract in March before joining Rotherham United. It was something of a surprise when Jody stepped down to the First Division but it turned out to be a good move as he took the steps to resurrect his career. His clever ball work and midfield control proved to be valuable assets to his new club and he revelled in his new lease of life. Jody scored a superb goal in the Easter Monday victory at Stoke City, a win that played a major part in saving the Millers' season.
Chelsea *(From trainee on 8/1/1996)* PL 82+42/5 FLC 10+2/2 FAC 10+5/2 Others 11+11
Leeds U *(Free on 22/7/2003)* PL 11+1
Rotherham U *(Free on 17/3/2004)* FL 9+1/1

MORRIS Lee
Born: Blackpool, 30 April 1980
Height: 5'10" **Weight:** 11.2
International Honours: E: U21-1; Yth
Whether playing wide or in his preferred position as a central striker, Lee Morris had a good run for Derby in the first half of the season, scoring twice against Bradford City to earn a rare away win. As he admitted, he still lacked consistency but made progress. All the signs indicated a return to Sheffield United but, in January, Lee moved back into the Premiership with Leicester City. However he was sidelined by a thigh injury and although he managed to feature for the reserves in the closing stages of the campaign he failed to make a first-team appearance for his new club.
Sheffield U *(From trainee on 24/12/1997)* FL 14+12/6 FAC 2+5/2 Others 0+1
Derby Co *(£1,800,000 + on 7/6/1999)* P/FL 62+29/17 FLC 1+4/1 FAC 2+2
Huddersfield T *(Loaned on 8/3/2001)* FL 5/1
Leicester C *(£120,000 on 2/2/2004)*

MORRISON Clinton Hubert
Born: Wandsworth, 14 May 1979
Height: 6'1" **Weight:** 11.2
International Honours: RoI: 21; U21-2
Clinton established himself in the Birmingham City line-up last December when Christophe Dugarry was sidelined by injury and scored a vital goal in a 2-0 win at Leicester. He went on to develop an excellent partnership with Mikael Forssell and was credited by his team mate and Steve Bruce for helping the Finn to become so prolific. Clinton unselfishly ran down the channels and out wide and was often unlucky in front of goal, either hitting the woodwork or being denied by good saves.
Crystal Palace *(From trainee on 29/3/1997)* P/FL 141+16/62 FLC 16+3/9 FAC 4/1 Others 0+1

Birmingham C (£4,250,000 + on 3/8/2002)
PL 43+17/10 FLC 2 FAC 5/1

MORRISON James Clark
Born: Darlington, 25 May 1986
Height: 5'10" **Weight:** 10.5
International Honours: E: Yth
A key member of Middlesbrough's historic
FA Youth Cup winning team, James made
his senior debut appearance for the club
at the Riverside against Notts County in
the 2-0 FA Cup win. He had played in all
eight games as the club's juniors marched
on triumphantly to lift the FA Youth Cup
in April for the first time in Boro's long
history. He finished his memorable season
with a substitute appearance in the final
game of the season at Fratton Park, a
dismal 5-1 defeat but what a season for
James to remember.
Middlesbrough (From trainee on 14/7/2003)
PL 0+1 FAC 0+1

MORRISON John Owen
Born: Londonderry, 8 December 1981
Height: 5'8" **Weight:** 11.12
International Honours: NI: U21-7; Yth;
Sch
This talented winger struggled to combine
consistency with his undoubted ability for
Stockport last term. After the heavy home
defeat by Swindon in February he didn't
figure again until he replaced the injured
Lee Cartwright for the final two games of
the season, but he certainly made his
mark with 'Man of the Match'
performances at Bournemouth and
against Barnsley, when he scored a fine
individual goal.
Sheffield Wed (From trainee on 5/1/1999)
P/FL 31+25/8 FLC 8+2/3 FAC 1+2
Hull C (Loaned on 23/8/2002) FL 1+1
Sheffield U (Free on 21/2/2003) FL 3+5
Stockport Co (Free on 6/8/2003) FL 11+11/1
FLC 1 FAC 0+1 Others 0+2/1

MORROW Samuel (Sam)
Born: Derry, 3 March 1985
Height: 6'0" **Weight:** 12.10
International Honours: NI: Yth
This young striker made a substitute
appearance for Ipswich in the Carling Cup
tie at Notts County but was unable to
establish a regular place in the side. He
later joined Boston United on loan, but
found it difficult to adjust to the hustle
and bustle of Third Division football. He
showed skill on the ball in the couple of
brief appearances he made from the
substitutes' bench before he returned to
Portman Road. Sam was released in the
summer and was reported to have signed
a short-term contract for Hibernian.

Ipswich T (From trainee on 9/8/2002) FLC
0+1
Boston U (Loaned on 12/12/2003) FL 0+2

MOSES Adrian (Adie) Paul
Born: Doncaster, 4 May 1975
Height: 5'10" **Weight:** 12.8
International Honours: E: U21-2
This experienced professional joined
Crewe Alexandra in the 2003 close
season and proved an invaluable help to
the younger players around him. His
campaign was interrupted by an injury
which kept him out of the team for a
lengthy period, but he returned to the
side in April and played in the remaining
games. Adie is a central defender who is
very effective in the air.
Barnsley (From juniors on 2/7/1993) F/PL
137+14/3 FLC 15+1 FAC 15
Huddersfield T (£225,000 on 20/12/2000)
FL 63+6/1 FLC 1 FAC 2+1/1 Others 5
Crewe Alex (Free on 8/7/2003) FL 15+6
FLC 1

MOSS Neil Graham
Born: New Milton, 10 May 1975
Height: 6'2" **Weight:** 13.10
The 2003-04 campaign proved to be
another excellent season for this
Bournemouth goalkeeper as he was ever-
present in Second Division fixtures and
was voted as the Fans' PFA Division Two
'Player of the Year'. A commanding figure
between the posts and possessing great
agility, Neil has blossomed with regular
first-team football.
Bournemouth (From trainee on 29/1/1993)
FL 21+1 FLC 1 FAC 3+1 Others 2
Southampton (£250,000 on 20/12/1995) PL
22+2 FLC 2
Gillingham (Loaned on 8/8/1997) FL 10
FLC 2
Bournemouth (Free on 13/9/2002) FL 79 FLC
1 FAC 5 Others 6

MUGGLETON Carl David
Born: Leicester, 13 September 1968
Height: 6'2" **Weight:** 13.4
International Honours: E: U21-1
Forget Chesterfield's goal difference last
term! Carl enjoyed his best season to date
as the Spireites' custodian and fully
merited the offer of an extended contract
made in May. He caught the eye with a
number of memorable saves, usually late
in a game when his team mates were
most up against it. A point-blank, diving
stop to deny Guylain N'dumbu in the 3-1
win over Sheffield Wednesday was typical
of Carl's work.

Leicester C (From apprentice on 17/9/1986)
FL 46 FAC 3 Others 5
Chesterfield (Loaned on 10/9/1987) FL 17
Others 2
Blackpool (Loaned on 1/2/1988) FL 2
Hartlepool U (Loaned on 28/10/1988) FL 8
Others 2
Stockport Co (Loaned on 1/3/1990) FL 4
Stoke C (Loaned on 13/8/1993) FL 6 FLC 1
Others 2
Glasgow Celtic (£150,000 on 11/1/1994) SL
12 SC 1
Stoke C (£150,000 on 21/7/1994) FL 148+1
FLC 17 FAC 5 Others 6
Rotherham U (Loaned on 1/11/1995) FL 6
Others 1
Sheffield U (Loaned on 28/3/1996) FL 0+1
Mansfield T (Loaned on 9/9/1999) FL 9
Chesterfield (Loaned on 9/12/1999) FL 5
Cardiff C (Loaned on 15/3/2001) FL 6
Cheltenham T (Free on 1/7/2001) FL 7 FLC 1
Bradford C (Loaned on 28/12/2001) FL 4
FAC 1
Chesterfield (Free on 9/7/2002) FL 72 FLC 3
FAC 2 Others 3

MUIRHEAD Benjamin (Ben)
Robinson
Born: Doncaster, 5 January 1983
Height: 5'9" **Weight:** 10.5
International Honours: E: Yth
A very fast, elusive right winger, Ben
scored his first Bradford City goal in the
season-opener against Norwich and
helped turn the game on its head. He also
netted a late equaliser against Crewe but
will be best remembered by the Bantams'
fans for a storming 60-yard run from one
penalty area to the other at Reading
which set up a goal for Andy Gray. Ben
struggled to hold down a place when
Bryan Robson took charge and was told
he was not being retained when his
contract ran out in the summer.
Manchester U (From trainee on 7/11/2000)
Bradford C (Free on 6/3/2003) FL 17+19/2
FLC 0+1 FAC 0+1

MULLIGAN David James
Born: Bootle, 24 March 1982
Height: 5'8" **Weight:** 9.13
Club Honours: Div 3 '04
International Honours: New Zealand:
Full; Yth
This hard-working player was retained on
monthly contracts by Barnsley last term
due to the club's financial situation. He
received only a limited number of
opportunities, being used in an
unaccustomed role on the left-hand side
of midfield. Dave was released by the
Reds in the new year and shortly
afterwards joined Doncaster Rovers where

he was given a chance at right back and grasped it with both hands, featuring regularly during the closing stages of the campaign. He continued to represent New Zealand at international level.
Barnsley *(From trainee on 18/10/2000) FL 59+6/1 FLC 1 FAC 3 Others 1*
Doncaster Rov *(Free on 16/2/2004) FL 14/1*

MULLIGAN Lance Martin
Born: Sutton in Ashfield, 21 October 1985
Height: 5'7" **Weight:** 11.6

This stocky Mansfield youth-team striker was given a run out in the first team as substitute at Oxford when the squad was depleted. Although small in stature he has a powerful shot, however, despite netting a hat-trick in an FA Youth Cup tie he was released in November and signed for Unibond League outfit Eastwood Town.
Mansfield T *(Trainee) FL 0+1*

MULLIN John Michael
Born: Bury, 11 August 1975
Height: 6'0" **Weight:** 11.10

An ever willing worker in the midfield area, John is a player who loves to surge forward on powerful runs in support of the strikers. He enjoyed one of his most productive seasons to date for Rotherham last term, finishing the campaign with four goals to his credit, although he will almost certainly feel that should have been more. John is a specialist from dead-ball situations and took the majority of the corners and free kicks in the opposition half. After finding himself out of favour in October

Karl Munroe

he came back to become a near ever-present for the remainder of the season.
Burnley *(From trainee on 18/8/1992) FL 7+11/2 FAC 2*
Sunderland *(£40,000 + on 12/8/1995) P/FL 23+12/4 FLC 5+1 FAC 2+1*
Preston NE *(Loaned on 13/2/1998) FL 4+3 Others 1*
Burnley *(Loaned on 26/3/1998) FL 6*
Burnley *(Free on 20/7/1999) FL 38+39/8 FLC 2+1 FAC 5+1/1 Others 1*
Rotherham U *(£150,000 on 5/10/2001) FL 93+13/9 FLC 3+1 FAC 4/2*

MULLINS Hayden Ian
Born: Reading, 27 March 1979
Height: 6'0" **Weight:** 11.12
International Honours: E: U21-3
This popular midfield player was in good form for Crystal Palace early on last term and captained the side. In October he was sold to First Division rivals West Ham and he proved an excellent signing for the Hammers. Versatile and able to play in several defensive positions, he is quick, comfortable in possession and has a calm approach. He never seemed to put a foot wrong as West Ham made their bid for promotion, even featuring at left back in the closing stages to cover for injuries.
Crystal Palace *(From trainee on 28/2/1997) FL 219+3/18 FLC 24/2 FAC 9 Others 2*
West Ham U *(£600,000 on 22/10/2003) FL 27 FAC 4/1 Others 3*

MULRYNE Phillip (Phil) Patrick
Born: Belfast, 1 January 1978
Height: 5'8" **Weight:** 10.11
Club Honours: FAYC '95; Div 1 '04
International Honours: NI: 25; B-1; U21-3; Yth
A regular member of Lawrie Sanchez's Northern Ireland international set-up, Phil spent the 2003-04 season battling with Damien Francis and Gary Holt for the two central midfield positions at Norwich. His creativity and passing skills made him an integral part of the squad and his three goals included the vital late winner at Reading in mid-April. Phil likes to dictate the pattern of play by receiving the ball from his defence to get his side moving forward and is something of a specialist at dead-ball situations around the penalty area.
Manchester U *(From trainee on 17/3/1995) PL 1 FLC 3 FAC 0+1*
Norwich C *(£500,000 on 25/3/1999) FL 124+27/18 FLC 6+1 FAC 5+1/2 Others 3*

MUNROE Karl Augustus
Born: Manchester, 23 September 1979
Height: 6'1" **Weight:** 11.3
Karl was a regular in the Macclesfield line-up last term, forming a centre back partnership with Michael Welch. He held his place until the beginning of March, when the more experienced Steve Payne was signed and after this Karl often found himself on the substitutes' bench. Normally playing in a back-four formation Karl also adapted to a back-five line-up when required and made good use of his physical presence.
Swansea C *(From trainee on 9/7/1998) FL 0+1*
Macclesfield T *(Free on 14/10/1999) FL 94+25/1 FLC 5+2/1 FAC 7 Others 3*

MURPHY Brian
Born: Waterford, 7 May 1983
Height: 6'0" **Weight:** 13.1
International Honours: RoI: U21-1; Yth
Brian Murphy moved to the Vetch Field in the summer of 2003 in search of regular first-team football and began the 2003-04 campaign as Swansea's first-choice 'keeper. However, he lost his place at the end of the first month and had to wait patiently for a second opportunity. Then, after regaining his position, he received a red card at Southend, and in the last away game of the season he was carried off with a hip injury at Darlington. Brian was included in the Republic of Ireland U20 squad that took part in the World Youth Championships in the UAE last November.
Manchester C *(From trainee on 13/5/2000)*
Peterborough U *(Loaned on 2/5/2003) FL 1*
Swansea C *(Free on 8/8/2003) FL 11 FLC 1 Others 1*

MURPHY Daniel (Danny) Benjamin
Born: Chester, 18 March 1977
Height: 5'9" **Weight:** 10.8
Club Honours: FLC '01, '03; FAC '01; UEFAC '01; ESC '01; CS '01
International Honours: E: 9; U21-5; Yth; Sch
Danny was one of the few members of the Liverpool first-team squad to remain relatively injury-free last season, but never enjoyed a prolonged run in one position. The enforced absence of Didi Hamann in the first three months of the season offered a golden opportunity for Danny to establish a place in central midfield, rather than on the flanks, but after two games he lost his place to Vladimir Smicer and the rest of his season was stop-start, although in the latter stages he became

more settled in his previous role on the right side of midfield. The best dead-ball kicker at the club Danny took over as the club's penalty taker, confidently despatching spot kicks at Manchester United (for a vital 1-0 victory) and against Middlesbrough.
Crewe Alex *(From trainee on 21/3/1994) FL 110+24/27 FLC 7 FAC 7/4 Others 15+2/4*
Liverpool *(£1,500,000 + on 17/7/1997) PL 114+56/25 FLC 15+1/11 FAC 11+4/3 Others 38+10/5*
Crewe Alex *(Loaned on 12/2/1999) FL 16/1*

MURPHY David Paul
Born: Hartlepool, 1 March 1984
Height: 6'1" **Weight:** 12.3
International Honours: E: Yth
After missing the start of the 2003-04 season through injury this promising Middlesbrough left back recovered fitness and joined Barnsley on loan in the new year. He proved to be a real hit with the Reds' fans, looking effective in the air and showing tremendous distribution. However, he returned to the Riverside and was released by Boro' in the summer.
Middlesbrough *(From trainee on 20/7/2001) PL 4+9 FLC 2/1 FAC 0+1*
Barnsley *(Loaned on 12/3/2004) FL 10/2*

MURPHY John James
Born: Whiston, 18 October 1976
Height: 6'2" **Weight:** 14.0
Club Honours: AMC '02, '04
Injury prevented this experienced striker from starting a first-team game for Blackpool until last October, but he hit a hat-trick in the LDV Vans Trophy tie against Tranmere Rovers in only his third start of the season. John subsequently overcame further injury problems to finish the campaign with a double-figure tally including one of the vital goals that clinched the LDV Vans Trophy final against Southend at Cardiff's Millennium Stadium.
Chester C *(From trainee on 6/7/1994) FL 65+38/20 FLC 7+3/1 FAC 1+2 Others 3+1*
Blackpool *(Signed on 6/8/1999) FL 171+16/66 FLC 8+2/5 FAC 14/5 Others 14+3/10*

MURPHY Joseph (Joe)
Born: Dublin, Ireland, 21 August 1981
Height: 6'2" **Weight:** 13.6
International Honours: RoI: 1; U21-14; Yth (UEFA-U16 '98)
Joe Murphy again deputised for Russell Hoult in the West Bromwich Albion goal, starting games against Cardiff City (home) and Sheffield United (away) both of which the Baggies won 2-1 while also coming

Danny Murphy

on as a second-half substitute during the 3-2 win at Ipswich. A fine shot-stopper, he was rewarded with his first full cap for the Republic of Ireland as a late substitute against Turkey last September.
Tranmere Rov (From trainee on 5/7/1999) FL 61+2 FLC 8 FAC 3 Others 1
West Bromwich A (Signed on 17/7/2002) P/FL 3+2 FLC 1

MURPHY Peter
Born: Dublin, 27 October 1980
Height: 5'11" **Weight:** 12.10
International Honours: RoI: Yth
Peter found the going a little harder at Carlisle in the 2003-04 season, partly due to injuries which kept him out of the side for a period in the late autumn. Able to play either in midfield or in defence, he generally looked more comfortable as a central defender. He likes to go forward when occasion permits and created Carlisle's second goal against Oxford following a surging run that took him almost the entire length of the pitch.
Blackburn Rov (From trainee on 15/7/1998)
Halifax T (Loaned on 26/10/2000) FL 18+3/1 FAC 1 Others 2
Carlisle U (Free on 10/8/2001) FL 110+5/3 FLC 3 FAC 6 Others 8

MURRAY Adam David
Born: Birmingham, 30 September 1981
Height: 5'8" **Weight:** 10.10
International Honours: E: Yth
Adam initially came to Kidderminster on loan from Derby County last September, but didn't last the month before well-publicised off-the-field problems led to his departure. After his release by the Rams he appeared for Solihull Borough and Burton Albion before joining Notts County, where he showed tremendous potential. However, he eventually opted for a longer contract with Kidderminster where he soon began to display signs of his great vision and passing skills in midfield.
Derby Co (From trainee on 7/10/1998) P/FL 25+31 FLC 3+1 FAC 4 (Free to Solihull Borough on 11/12/2003)
Mansfield T (Loaned on 26/2/2002) FL 13/7
Kidderminster Hrs (Loaned on 29/8/2003) FL 3
Notts Co (Free from Burton A on 27/11/2003) FL 1+2 FAC 0+1
Kidderminster Hrs (Free on 9/1/2004) FL 16+3/3

MURRAY Frederick (Fred)
Anthony
Born: Clonmel, Ireland, 22 May 1982
Height: 5'10" **Weight:** 11.12

International Honours: RoI: Yth
This left-footed player was primarily used on the left-hand side of defence by Cambridge United last term, but he showed his versatility by also fitting in well in a midfield role. Although still relatively young, Fred is seen as one of the more experienced players at the Abbey Stadium.
Blackburn Rov (From trainee on 25/5/1999)
Cambridge U (Free on 14/12/2001) FL 80+8 FLC 2 FAC 3+2 Others 7

MURRAY Matthew (Matt)
William
Born: Solihull, 2 May 1981
Height: 6'4" **Weight:** 13.10
International Honours: E: U21-5; Yth
This tall Wolves goalkeeper underwent a hernia operation after the play-offs that had secured their promotion to the Premiership, but this was only a prelude to more injury problems. Matt played in the opening-day defeat at Blackburn, and made some fine saves despite the score line, but then bruised his back in an England U21 match. A stress fracture in his foot in December was expected to keep him out for a further six weeks, but in March it was announced that he needed a bone graft to repair it and would be out for the rest of the season.
Wolverhampton W (From trainee on 6/5/1998) F/PL 41 FLC 2 FAC 4 Others 3

MURRAY Paul
Born: Carlisle, 31 August 1976
Height: 5'9" **Weight:** 10.5
International Honours: E: B-1; U21-4; Yth
Paul had an exceptional campaign with Oldham Athletic in 2003-04, sweeping the club's 'Player of the Season' awards in May. One of the Latics' most consistent performers, he provides an energetic and forceful presence in central midfield and also has an eye for goal, finishing as the club's second-top scorer with a career-best tally of nine goals. Hugely popular with the Boundary Park fans, his late-season displays proved instrumental in helping the club beat the threat of relegation. However, Paul was out of contract in the summer and opted to team up again with former mentor Mick Wadsworth at Portuguese club Beira Mar.
Carlisle U (From trainee on 14/6/1994) FL 27+14/1 FLC 2 FAC 1 Others 6+1
Queens Park R (£300,000 on 8/3/1996) P/FL 115+25/7 FLC 8/1 FAC 9
Southampton (Free on 2/8/2001) PL 0+1

Oldham Ath (Free on 12/12/2001) FL 93+2/15 FLC 2 FAC 3 Others 4+1

MURRAY Scott George
Born: Aberdeen, 26 May 1974
Height: 5'10" **Weight:** 11.0
Club Honours: AMC '03
International Honours: S: B-2
Scott signed for Reading in the summer of 2003 and the fans hoped that he would continue his excellent strike rate, but this proved not to be the case, and the goals dried up after a promising early start. He netted twice in the 3-2 win at Derby County and was predicted to reach double figures for the season, but his performances as well as his scoring ratio dipped around the Christmas period and he was no longer considered an automatic choice for the wide-right position in midfield. Scott did gain selection for the Scotland Future team in their game against Turkey, but rejoined Bristol City on transfer-deadline day. City had badly missed his pace down the flanks, but injury and possible loss of confidence left the Ashton Gate faithful hoping that Scott will be back to his best in 2004-05.
Aston Villa (£35,000 from Fraserburgh on 16/3/1994) PL 4
Bristol C (£150,000 on 12/12/1997) FL 193+31/46 FLC 10+3 FAC 13+1/7 Others 18+2/8
Reading (£650,000 on 9/7/2003) FL 25+9/5 FLC 3+1 FAC 2
Bristol C (£500,000 on 25/3/2004) FL 4+2 Others 0+3

MURTY Graeme Stuart
Born: Saltburn, 13 November 1974
Height: 5'10" **Weight:** 11.10
International Honours: S: 1; B-1
An excellent 2003-04 season confirmed Graham's reputation as one of the best defenders outside the Premiership. He contributed another campaign of consistently high-class performances for Reading which were rewarded with election as the supporters' 'Player of the Year', captaincy of the team during the period of Adrian Williams absence through injury, and above all, international recognition. Selected by Berti Vogts for the Scotland Future team against Turkey, he made his full international debut as a substitute against Wales later in the campaign.
York C (From trainee on 23/3/1993) FL 106+11/7 FLC 10/2 FAC 5+1 Others 6+2
Reading (£700,000 on 10/7/1998) FL 163+11/1 FLC 4 FAC 10+1 Others 6+2

MUSCAT Kevin Vincent
Born: Crawley, 7 August 1973
Height: 5'11" **Weight:** 12.2
Club Honours: SPD '03; SL '03
International Honours: Australia: 40;
U23; Yth
This experienced tough-tackling defender
was a revelation for Millwall after signing
at the end of August. On being given the
club captaincy he led the team by
example, producing some excellent
performances. Kevin is a player who likes
to get forward to deliver crosses and with
a good football brain, he knows how to
lift his team and the supporters.
*Crystal Palace (£35,000 from South
Melbourne, Australia on 16/8/1996) FL
51+2/2 FLC 4/1 FAC 2 Others 2*
*Wolverhampton W (£200,000 on
22/10/1997) FL 178+2/14 FLC 10/1 FAC 11*
*Glasgow R (Free on 1/7/2002) SL 22+1 SLC
0+1 SC 3+1 Others 1+1*
Millwall (Free on 29/8/2003) FL 27 FAC 6

MUSSELWHITE Paul Stephen
Born: Portsmouth, 22 December 1968
Height: 6'2" **Weight:** 14.2
Club Honours: AMC '93
Although Paul began last term as Hull
City's second-choice 'keeper he was soon
called back into action when Alan Fettis
was injured early on. Paul remained
between the posts for the Tigers for
most of the first half of the season,
displaying his usual calm assurance,
before losing his place following the
arrival of Boaz Myhill.
Portsmouth (From apprentice on 1/12/1986)
*Scunthorpe U (Free on 21/3/1988) FL 132
FLC 11 FAC 7 Others 13*
*Port Vale (£20,000 on 30/7/1992) FL 312
FLC 15 FAC 21 Others 19*
*Sheffield Wed (Free, via trials at Scunthorpe
U, Darlington, on 25/8/2000)*
*Hull C (Free on 19/9/2000) FL 94+1 FAC 4
Others 5*

MUSTOE Robin (Robbie)
Born: Witney, 28 August 1968
Height: 5'11" **Weight:** 11.12
Club Honours: Div 1 '95
This hard-working, skilful player made a
major contribution to the Sheffield
Wednesday midfield last term. Robbie
covered an awful lot of ground for a so-
called 'veteran' helping to protect the
defence and break up opposition
attacks. He captained the side on several
occasions and was sorely missed when
injury kept him out towards the end of
the season. He was one of several out-
of-contract players released in the
summer.

Oxford U *(From juniors on 2/7/1986) FL
78+13/10 FLC 2 FAC 2 Others 3*
*Middlesbrough (£375,000 on 5/7/1990)
F/PL 327+38/25 FLC 44+3/7 FAC 29+1/2
Others 12+1*
Charlton Ath (Free on 30/8/2002) PL 6 FLC 1
*Sheffield Wed (Free on 11/8/2003) FL
22+3/1 FAC 3 Others 1*

MUTU Adrian
Born: Calinesti, Romania, 8 January 1979
Height: 5'11" **Weight:** 11.12
International Honours: Romania: 32;
U21; Yth
A reworking of the old cliché 'Season of
Two Halves' best sums up Adrian Mutu's
first campaign in English football. Adrian
is very much in the mould of Chelsea
legend Franco Zola and when the great
man returned to Cagliari he was seen as
the ideal replacement. Adrian scored a
stunning winning goal on his debut
against Leicester City in August. He
delighted the Chelsea crowd with his
quicksilver touches, enthusiasm and
opportunism which brought a string of
excellent goals including efforts against
Blackburn, Tottenham and Lazio before
encountering a goal drought from
November onwards. The second half of
the season brought a few highlights such
as FA Cup goals against Arsenal and
Watford before Adrian faded from the
spotlight, being superseded in the Blues'
front line. Chelsea bought Adrian Mutu to
play alongside Hernan Crespo in the
Champions' League but the partnership
never really blossomed and the Romanian
looked a forlorn figure as his form
deserted him in the final third of the
season.
*Chelsea (£15,800,000 + from Parma, Italy, ex
Arges Pitesti, Dinamo Bucharest, Inter Milan,
Verona, on 19/8/2003) PL 21+4/6 FLC 0+1
FAC 3/3 Others 6+1/1*

MYERS Andrew (Andy) John
Born: Hounslow, 3 November 1973
Height: 5'10" **Weight:** 13.11
Club Honours: FAC '97; ECWC '98
International Honours: E: U21-4; Yth
This experienced defender became a very
effective performer at left back for
Colchester last term before being
sidelined by a back injury following the
game at Queens Park Rangers at the end
of December. Andy was out of action for
the next four months, only returning as
an unused substitute at Plymouth on the
final day of the campaign.
*Chelsea (From trainee on 25/7/1991) F/PL
74+10/2 FLC 2+1 FAC 9+3 Others 4+3*
Bradford C (£800,000 on 16/7/1999) P/FL

74+15/3 FLC 5 FAC 1 Others 3+1
Portsmouth (Loaned on 23/3/2000) FL 4+4
*Colchester U (Free on 15/7/2003) FL 21 FLC
1 FAC 2 Others 2*

MYHILL Glyn (Boaz) Oliver
Born: California, USA, 9 November 1982
Height: 6'3" **Weight:** 14.6
International Honours: E: Yth
Aston Villa's young reserve goalkeeper
began last season with a three-month
loan spell at Macclesfield where he
quickly established himself in the side,
producing a number of breathtaking
saves. However, an injury forced his early
return to Villa Park, but once fit he was
out on loan again, this time to Stockport
where he was required as cover for the
injured James Spencer. He was offered a
permanent contract by the Hatters, but
opted for a move to Third Division Hull
City. He proved to be a wise investment
for the Tigers showing good command of
his area and great confidence in his own
decision-making.
Aston Villa (From trainee on 28/11/2000)
Bradford C (Loaned on 22/11/2002) FL 2
*Macclesfield T (Loaned on 8/8/2003) FL 15
FLC 1*
*Stockport Co (Loaned on 22/11/2003) FL 2
Others 1*
Hull C (£50,000 on 12/12/2003) FL 23

MYHRE Thomas
Born: Sarpsborg, Norway, 16 October
1973
Height: 6'4" **Weight:** 13.12
International Honours: Norway: 33;
U21-27; Yth
This experienced goalkeeper was second
choice to Mart Poom for Sunderland last
term and found opportunities few and far
between. In October he joined Crystal
Palace for an extended loan period and
featured regularly during his stay at
Selhurst Park. Thomas was recalled to the
Stadium of Light in April as cover for an
injury to Poom and played his part in the
excellent 3-0 win over promotion rivals
Sheffield United.
*Everton (£800,000 from Viking Stavanger,
Norway on 28/11/1997) PL 70 FLC 3 FAC 9
(£375,000 to Besiktas, Turkey on 1/11/2001)*
*Glasgow R (Loaned on 24/11/1999) SL 3 SLC
1 Others 2*
*Birmingham C (Loaned on 31/3/2000) FL 7
Others 2*
*Tranmere Rov (Loaned on 28/11/2000) FL 3
FLC 1*
*Sunderland (Free on 8/7/2002) P/FL 4+2
FLC 1*
*Crystal Palace (Loaned on 24/10/2003) FL
15 FLC 1*

Boaz Myhill

N

NACCA Francesco (Franco)

Born: Venezuela, 9 November 1982
Height: 5'7" **Weight:** 10.6
Franco was sidelined by an ankle injury until last November before making his first appearance of the season for Cambridge United in the FA Cup match at Lancaster when he was involved in the build-up to the U's first goal. A hard-working and skilful player who can play in defence or midfield, injuries continued to hamper him and he managed to start just a handful of matches during the campaign.
*Cambridge U (From trainee on 21/4/2001)
FL 11+15 FLC 0+2 FAC 4+3 Others 2+4*

NALIS Lilian Bernard Pierre

Born: Paris, France, 29 September 1971
Height: 6'1" **Weight:** 13.3
This energetic midfielder made an early dramatic impact for Leicester with a spectacular goal in a Monday night game against Leeds United, but generally it took a while for him to adjust to the pace of the game in England. Lilian showed a commendable willingness to battle his way back into first-team contention and he featured again on a number of occasions in the closing stages of the campaign. His vision and style could make him a key player in the Foxes' promotion challenge in 2004-05.
Leicester C (Free from Chievo, Italy, ex SM Caen, Laval, Guingamp, Le Havre, Bastia, on 16/7/2003) PL 11+9/1 FLC 2

NARDIELLO Daniel (Danny) Antony

Born: Coventry, 22 October 1982
Height: 5'11" **Weight:** 11.4
International Honours: E: Yth; Sch
An excellent young forward with a good range of skills, Danny made only one appearance for Manchester United last term, in the Carling Cup defeat to West Bromwich Albion at the Hawthorns. He spent time on loan at Swansea and Barnsley, and was a great hit during his spell at Oakwell, scoring two goals and impressing throughout his spell at the club. Danny is the son of former Coventry City winger Donato Nardiello.
*Manchester U (From trainee on 1/11/1999)
FLC 1+2 Others 0+1*
*Swansea C (Loaned on 24/10/2003) FL 3+1
Others 1/1*

Barnsley (Loaned on 27/1/2004) FL 14+2/7

NASH Carlo James

Born: Bolton, 13 September 1973
Height: 6'5" **Weight:** 14.1
Club Honours: Div 1 '02
Carlo arrived at the Riverside from Manchester City in August 2003 as experienced cover for Middlesbrough's number one 'keeper Mark Schwarzer. With Schwarzer in scintillating form he patiently waited for his debut chance and this eventually came in the 2-0 win at Villa Park, but this was to be his only senior appearance of the season. He was out for seven long months with a ruptured tendon in a finger and only returned to reserve-team football in early May.
Crystal Palace (£35,000 from Clitheroe on 16/7/1996) FL 21 FLC 1 Others 3
Stockport Co (Free on 7/6/1998) FL 89 FLC 5 FAC 4
Manchester C (£100,000 on 12/1/2001) P/FL 37+1 FLC 2 FAC 1
Middlesbrough (£150,000 on 14/8/2003) PL 1

NASH Gerard Thomas

Born: Dublin, 11 July 1986
Height: 6'1" **Weight:** 11.8
International Honours: RoI: Yth
This promising Ipswich Town youngster has captained age-group teams for the Republic of Ireland from U14s to U17s. Gerard made his senior debut as a substitute at Burnley last October, but was later sidelined by a cruciate injury. A central defender or midfield player he represented his country at U19 level last term.
Ipswich T (From trainee on 16/7/2003) FL 0+1

NAVARRO Alan Edward

Born: Liverpool, 31 May 1981
Height: 5'11" **Weight:** 11.7
This tough-tackling but creative midfielder recovered from a career-threatening cruciate ligament injury to make a return to the Tranmere Rovers first-team squad last term. However, Alan's first-team appearances were sporadic due to competition from the likes of Gary Jones and Tyrone Loran, but he never gave less than 100 per cent when called upon to deputise.
Liverpool (From trainee on 27/4/1999)
Crewe Alex (Loaned on 22/3/2001) FL 5+3/1
Crewe Alex (Loaned on 9/8/2001) FL 7 FLC 2
Tranmere Rov (£225.000 on 9/11/2001) FL 35+10/1 FAC 4+2/1 Others 0+1

NAYLOR Lee Martyn

Born: Walsall, 19 March 1980
Height: 5'9" **Weight:** 11.8
International Honours: E: U21-3; Yth
This young left back showed plenty of effort and enthusiasm but found it difficult to adapt to the needs of Premiership football. However, Wolves were short of full backs and Lee was involved in all 38 Premiership matches, although he might have benefited from a break. He has made more career appearances for Wolves than anyone else on the club's books, yet he was often their youngest player on the field last term.
Wolverhampton W (From trainee on 10/10/1997) P/FL 193+19/5 FLC 17 FAC 15/1 Others 3/1

NAYLOR Richard Alan

Born: Leeds, 28 February 1977
Height: 6'1" **Weight:** 13.7
Richard had one of his best seasons to date for Ipswich last term and was one of the key figures in the defence for much of the time. He had several defensive partners during the season but his pairing with Georges Santos coincided with the club's best spell. He was still able to get forward for set pieces and contributed some vital goals including a double in the 4-3 win at Crystal Palace. A very courageous player who is not afraid to go in where it hurts, he played at Walsall with a broken toe because there were no other central defenders available.
Ipswich T (From trainee on 10/7/1995) P/FL 97+84/28 FLC 7+10/1 FAC 4+5/1 Others 5+6/1
Millwall (Loaned on 29/1/2002) FL 2+1
Barnsley (Loaned on 4/3/2002) FL 7+1

NAYSMITH Gary Andrew

Born: Edinburgh, 16 November 1978
Height: 5'7" **Weight:** 11.8
Club Honours: SC '98
International Honours: S: 22; B-1; U21-22; Sch
Gary was one of the more consistent Everton performers last term in what was a difficult campaign. Employed in his favoured position at full back he added a pacy and committed presence to the Blues' left flank with the highlight of his season being a splendidly executed free-kick in the victory over Tottenham at Goodison Park on Good Friday. His season ended early due to an ankle injury and then a hernia operation. At international level he continued to be one of his country's better performing players.

Heart of Midlothian (Signed from Whitehill Welfare on 17/6/1996) SL 92+5/3 SLC 5/1 SC 10 Others 7/1
Everton (£1,750,000 on 20/10/2000) PL 91+10/5 FLC 4+1/1 FAC 8+1

NDIWA-LORD Kangana
Born: Maquela do Zombo, Angola, 28 February 1984
Height: 6'3" **Weight:** 13.3
International Honours: DR Congo; Sweden: Yth
After signing for Bolton Wanderers during the 2003 close season, this powerful young defender was sent out on loan to Oldham to gain first-team experience. He made several appearances in the centre of a three-man defensive system before returning to the Reebok the following month. Later in the season he was a

member of the DR Congo squad for the African Nations' Cup finals and he also had a spell on loan at Rochdale. However, his first-team career at Spotland was one of the shortest on record, amounting to just three minutes as a substitute. He was released by Wanderers in the summer.
Bolton W (Signed from Djurgaarden, Sweden on 15/7/2003)
Oldham Ath (Loaned on 8/8/2003) FL 3+1
Rochdale (Loaned on 6/2/2004) FL 0+1

NDLOVU Peter
Born: Bulawayo, Zimbabwe, 25 February 1973
Height: 5'8" **Weight:** 10.2
International Honours: Zimbabwe
After signing a new contract for Sheffield United in the summer, Peter made an excellent start to the Blades' campaign as

an attacking right midfielder. He scored eight goals in his first nine outings, including a hat-trick against Cardiff City. The goals then dried up but he still worked tirelessly in midfield, making vital contributions in defence as well as being dangerous in attack, but as the season ended he was in and out of the side. Peter added to his Zimbabwe caps, captaining his country in the finals of the African Nations' Cup. He was voted Zimbabwe's 'Player of the Year, 'Sportsman of the Year' and 'Sports Personality of the Year'.
Coventry C (£10,000 from Highlanders, Zimbabwe on 16/8/1991) F/PL 141+36/37 FLC 10/2 FAC 5+4/2 Others 0+1
Birmingham C (£1,600,000 on 15/7/1997) FL 78+29/22 FLC 17+2/4 FAC 3+1/1 Others 2+2

Richard Naylor

Huddersfield T (Loaned on 8/12/2000) FL 6/4
Sheffield U (Free on 2/2/2001) FL 114+21/25 FLC 6+3/2 FAC 7/2 Others 3

N'DOUR Alassane
Born: Dakar, Senegal, 12 December 1981
Height: 6'1" **Weight:** 12.5
International Honours: Senegal
One of Senegal's stars in the 2002 World Cup finals, Alassane joined West Bromwich Albion as cover and also to put pressure on left wing back Neil Clement. A positive footballer, hard but fair, he made over 40 appearances in two seasons playing in France and helped his country reach the final of the African Nations' Cup. He had an excellent debut for the Baggies in the 2-2 away draw with Crystal Palace in September, but found it difficult to get first-team football after that.
West Bromwich A (Loaned from St Etienne, France on 2/9/2003) FL 2 FLC 1

NDUMBU-NSUNGU Guylain
Born: Kinshasha, DR Congo, 26 December 1982
Height: 6'1" **Weight:** 12.8
This pacy, exciting striker initially arrived at Sheffield Wednesday on loan, but was quickly signed up on a permanent contract. He went on to finish the season as the club's leading scorer, registering ten goals in all competitions including three from the penalty spot. The Owls will be looking for him to continue in similar vein in the 2004-05 campaign.
Sheffield Wed (Signed from Amiens, France on 9/9/2003) FL 20+4/9 FAC 1+1/1 Others 5+1

NEAL Lewis Ryan
Born: Leicester, 14 July 1981
Height: 6'0" **Weight:** 11.2
Lewis featured quite regularly in the Stoke City squad last term, although he was hampered by an ankle injury at the turn of the year. A promising left-sided or central midfielder, he will be looking to make a major breakthrough at the Britannia Stadium in 2004-05.
Stoke C (From juniors on 17/7/1998) FL 19+28/1 FLC 1+1 FAC 3+3 Others 1+2/1

NEGOUAI Christian
Born: Fort de France, Martinique, 20 January 1975
Height: 6'4" **Weight:** 13.11
Christian adds a different dimension to the Manchester City midfield with his towering presence. However, his only appearance for the side came in the UEFA Cup tie against TNS at the beginning of the campaign, Plagued by fitness problems he headed for Austrian side Sturm Graz, to get games under his belt, but he soon returned to the City of Manchester Stadium, where a series of niggling injuries continued to hamper his progress.
Manchester C (£1,500,000 from RSC Charleroi, Belgium, ex Vaux en Velin, Lyon, Namur, on 16/11/2001) FL 2+3/1 FLC 1 FAC 0+1 Others 1/1

NEIL Alexander (Alex)
Born: Bellshill, 9 June 1981
Height: 5'8" **Weight:** 12.10
Alex was disrupted by injuries in the first half of the 2003-04 season and these restricted his appearances. However, a change of manager saw him become a regular in the team and he produced a number of hard-working performances in midfield for Barnsley. Nevertheless, he was released at the end of the season.
Airdrieonians (From Dunfermline Ath

Lucas Neill

295

juniors on 8/7/1999) SL 15+1/5 SC 0+1
Barnsley *(£25,000 on 11/7/2000) FL*
83+38/4 FLC 2+2 FAC 4+2 Others 1

NEILL Lucas Edward

Born: Sydney, Australia, 9 March 1978
Height: 6'1" **Weight:** 12.0
Club Honours: Div 2 '01
International Honours: Australia: 3;
U23-12; Yth
An exceptional athlete with fierce tackling
skills and great physical qualities, Lucas
was a regular in the Blackburn line-up for
most of last season. Still potentially an
outstanding prospect he was less secure
in his marking and this limited his ability
to join the attack as frequently as the club
would have liked. A highlight of his
campaign came when he scored a vital
goal in the 2-1 win at Portsmouth early
on in the season.
Millwall (Free from Australian Academy of
Sport on 13/11/1995) FL 124+28/13 FLC 6+1
FAC 4 Others 11+1
Blackburn Rov (£1,000,000 on 7/9/2001) PL
95+2/3 FLC 5 FAC 8 Others 5

NEILSON Alan Bruce

Born: Wegburg, Germany, 26 September
1972
Height: 5'11" **Weight:** 12.10
International Honours: W: 5; B-2; U21-
7
Alan started the 2003-04 season as a
first-team regular for Luton before an
injury put him on the sidelines. Thereafter
he managed only sporadic appearances,
mostly as cover for injuries and
suspensions. An excellent reader of the
game, he is a versatile player who
featured at left back, in the centre of the
defence or in midfield. Alan was recalled
for the last two games of the campaign
and looked as good as ever.
Newcastle U (From trainee on 11/2/1991)
F/PL 35+7/1 FLC 4 Others 4
Southampton (£500,000 on 1/6/1995) PL
42+13 FLC 7 FAC 1
Fulham (£250,000 on 28/11/1997) FL
24+5/2 FLC 4+2 FAC 4 Others 2
Grimsby T (Free on 19/10/2001) FL 8+2 FLC
1 FAC 1
Luton T (Free on 22/2/2002) FL 40+8/1 FLC
1+2 FAC 1+1

NELSON Michael John

Born: Gateshead, 28 March 1980
Height: 6'2" **Weight:** 13.12
A strong central defender, Michael was
signed by Hartlepool in the 2003 close
season to fill the gap left by Graeme Lee.
He fitted in immediately, and soon
justified his transfer fee, establishing a

solid centre-back partnership with Chris
Westwood. Michael received a foot injury
late in the campaign, which kept him out
for a lengthy spell, but he was back to his
best in the play-offs against Bristol City.
His consistency was recognised when he
was chosen as the Supporters' Club
'Player of the Year'.
Bury (Free from Bishop Auckland on
22/3/2001) FL 68+4/8 FLC 4 FAC 3 Others 5
Hartlepool U (£70,000 on 10/7/2003) FL
38+2/3 FLC 2 FAC 3 Others 3

NELSON Stuart James

Born: Stroud, 17 September 1981
Height: 6'1" **Weight:** 12.12
After impressing in goal for Hucknall in
the Unibond League, Stuart joined
Brentford as a replacement for
Southampton-bound Paul Smith.
Although he received a red card on his
debut at Brighton in March things
improved and he kept two clean sheets
before the end of the season. His best
performance was probably at Grimsby
when he made numerous impressive
saves.
Millwall (Signed from Cirencester T on
6/10/2000. Free to Des Moines University,
USA during 2001 close season)
Brentford (£10,000 from Hucknall T, ex
Oxford C, Doncaster Rov, on 2/2/2004) FL 9

NEMETH Szilard

Born: Kamarna, Slovakia, 8 August 1977
Height: 5'10" **Weight:** 10.10
Club Honours: FLC '04
International Honours: Slovakia: 44
Szilard had another mixed and frustrating
season at the Riverside. He played in 32
Premiership games, but he was personally
disappointed that 15 of those games
were as a substitute. His pace and a
striker's eye for goal saw him finish the
season as joint-top scorer with Juninho on
nine goals although he missed out on a
Carling Cup final appearance.
Middlesbrough (Signed from Inter
Bratislava, Slovakia, ex Slovan Bratislava,
Kosice, on 30/7/2001) PL 43+38/19 FLC
5+2/2 FAC 4+3/1

NETHERCOTT Stuart David

Born: Ilford, 21 March 1973
Height: 6'1" **Weight:** 13.8
Club Honours: Div 2 '01
International Honours: E: U21-8
This wholehearted performer started the
2003-04 season at the centre of defence
for Millwall before he was sidelined by
injury and once he had recovered he
failed to win his place back. Stuart joined
Wycombe on loan in the new year and

became one of manager Tony Adams'
best signings for the club. He was an
ever-present until the end of the
campaign, providing some much-needed
leadership in a defence clearly lacking in
confidence.
Tottenham H (From trainee on 17/8/1991)
PL 31+23 FAC 5+3/1
Maidstone U (Loaned on 5/9/1991) FL 13/1
Others 1
Barnet (Loaned on 13/2/1992) FL 3
Millwall (Signed on 22/1/1998) FL 206+9/10
FLC 8 FAC 6 Others 13
Wycombe W (Free on 2/1/2004) FL 22/1

NEVILLE Gary Alexander

Born: Bury, 18 February 1975
Height: 5'11" **Weight:** 12.8
Club Honours: FAYC '92; PL '96, '97,
'99, '00, '01, '03; FAC '96, '99, '04; CS
'96; EC '99
International Honours: E: 66; Yth
(UEFA-U18 '93)
The hub of Manchester United's
rearguard, a hard-tackling full back, who
is equally as effective in a central
defensive role, Gary missed the opening
two Premiership games of the campaign,
but returned to give the Reds sterling
service throughout a mixed campaign. His
versatility in defence was invaluable
during the troubled months between
January and February when Rio Ferdinand
was suspended, and his performance
against Porto in the Champions' League
in Ferdinand's familiar berth might give
Sven Göran Eriksson some food for
thought for Euro 2004. With more plusses
than minuses against his form, his errs are
more noticeable than most. An
uncharacteristic red card offence in the FA
Cup tie against Manchester City at Old
Trafford earned its fair share of headlines.
However, Gary redeemed himself by
netting the winner in the Premiership
meeting against Leicester in April, and
scored again two games later against
Charlton. It was a remarkable tally if only
for the fact that Gary had scored two in a
week as opposed to just four in 427
appearances previously.
Manchester U (From trainee on 29/1/1993)
PL 279+14/5 FLC 10+1 FAC 32+2 Others
91+6/1

NEVILLE Philip (Phil) John

Born: Bury, 21 January 1977
Height: 5'11" **Weight:** 12.0
Club Honours: FAYC '95; PL '96, '97,
'99, '00, '01, '03; FAC '96, '99, '04: CS
'96, '97, '03; EC '99
International Honours: E: 51; U21-7;
Yth; Sch

A versatile player who is equally comfortable at full back or as a central defender, Phil might have seen the previous season as something of a crossroads, but he really came to the fore in 2003-04. His highly impressive performances in the Reds midfield kept the likes of Kleberson, Eric Djemba Djemba and Nicky Butt waiting anxiously in the wings. His now customary goal of the season came against Glasgow Rangers in the Champions' League, which kept up that impressive record of United never having lost a match when he's scored. His only long-term absence from the team came during late March, but he was soon back in contention.
Manchester U (From trainee on 1/6/1994) PL 198+46/5 FLC 13+1 FAC 21+5/1 Others 49+19/2

NEWBY Jonathan (Jon) Philip Robert
Born: Warrington, 28 November 1978
Height: 6'0" **Weight:** 12.4
Club Honours: FAYC '96
This quick and skilful striker had a somewhat unfortunate time at Huddersfield last term, and after failing to find the net he was switched to playing in a wide role, before injuries put him on the sidelines. Later in the season he had a spell on loan with York City, where he impressed with his pace and work rate but still failed to register a goal.
Liverpool (From juniors on 23/5/1997) PL 0+1 FLC 0+1 FAC 0+2
Crewe Alex (Loaned on 3/3/2000) FL 5+1
Sheffield U (Loaned on 4/8/2000) FL 3+10
Bury (£100,000 on 2/2/2001) FL 109/21 FLC 4/1 FAC 3 Others 6/2
Huddersfield T (Free on 7/8/2003) FL 10+4 FLC 1
York C (Loaned on 25/3/2004) FL 6+1

NEWEY Thomas (Tom) William
Born: Huddersfield, 31 October 1982
Height: 5'10" **Weight:** 10.6
Tom joined Leyton Orient during the 2003 close season and went straight in the first team, retaining his place in the side until the closing stages of the campaign. Although he can play anywhere down the left-hand side, he was mostly used as a left winger in which role he showed good skills and the ability to cross the ball whilst in full flight down the flank.
Leeds U (From trainee on 4/8/2000)
Cambridge U (Loaned on 14/2/2003) FL 6 Others 1
Darlington (Loaned on 27/3/2003) FL 7/1
Leyton Orient (Free on 8/8/2003) FL 31+3/2 FLC 1 FAC 2

NEWMAN Richard (Ricky) Adrian
Born: Guildford, 5 August 1970
Height: 5'10" **Weight:** 12.6
Although he is well into the veteran stage of his career, Ricky proved a steady and abrasive performer for the Royals throughout the 2003-04 season, despite playing in a variety of positions. Equally capable in the centre of midfield, at full back or centre back, his tenacity helps him to win and retain the ball for his team, and also inspires those around him. He is now regarded as a utility player rather than a first-choice, but his commitment was rewarded with the offer in the summer of a new contract.
Crystal Palace (From juniors on 22/1/1988) F/PL 43+5/3 FLC 5 FAC 5+2 Others 2
Maidstone U (Loaned on 28/2/1992) FL 9+1/1
Millwall (£500,000 on 19/7/1995) FL 144+6/5 FLC 11 FAC 5 Others 7
Reading (Free on 17/3/2000) FL 87+17/1 FLC 5 FAC 7/1 Others 1+1

Szilard Nemeth

NEWTON Adam Lee
Born: Grays, 4 December 1980
Height: 5'10" **Weight:** 11.6
Club Honours: FAYC '99
International Honours: St Kitts; E: U21-1
Adam had a fine season with Peterborough United last term, coming to terms with the requirements of Second Division football. A regular in the line-up throughout the campaign, he was used in a more defensive role last term, although he is most impressive when attacking down the flanks. Adam was one of three Posh players called up by St Kitts for their World Cup qualifying campaign in the summer.
West Ham U (From trainee on 1/7/1999) PL 0+2 Others 0+1
Portsmouth (Loaned on 2/7/1999) FL 1+2 FLC 2
Notts Co (Loaned on 22/11/2000) FL 13+7/1 FAC 2
Leyton Orient (Loaned on 8/3/2002) FL 10/1
Peterborough U (Free on 8/7/2002) FL 59+14/4 FLC 1+1 FAC 2+2/1 Others 3+1

NEWTON Shaun O'Neill
Born: Camberwell, 20 August 1975
Height: 5'8" **Weight:** 11.7
Club Honours: Div 1 '00
International Honours: E: U21-3
This right-sided midfielder was not expected to feature much for Wolves last term, but he made the starting line-up for the first six matches and created the club's first Premiership goal. After that he seemed to fade from the picture, although he had a sequence of seven games after Christmas and was in good form, only to get injured. Shaun did not always catch the eye, but his work rate meant the team often seemed to perform better when he was playing, as he never let the opposition settle. He was a regular again by April, even helping out at right back briefly.
Charlton Ath (From trainee on 1/7/1993) P/FL 189+51/20 FLC 19+1/3 FAC 11+6/2 Others 7+1/2
Wolverhampton W (£850,000 + on 8/8/2001) F/PL 94+12/11 FLC 3+2/1 FAC 7 Others 4+1

N'GOTTY Bruno
Born: Lyon, France, 10 June 1971
Height: 6'1" **Weight:** 13.8
International Honours: France: 6; B-10
The rock at the heart of the Bolton defence, Bruno had yet another fine campaign last year. Cool, calm and collected, he is the epitome of

consistency. Despite playing with several centre-back partners throughout the season, he still turned in a number of assured displays whilst striking up effective partnerships with all who played alongside him. Also a threat at the other end of the pitch, Bruno notched four goals, including one in the famous 2-1 victory at Chelsea in December. In a move that surely pleased all Bolton fans, Bruno ended the season by signing a new deal with the club.
Bolton W (Loaned from Marseilles, France, ex Lyon, Paris St Germain, AC Milan, Venezia, on 11/9/2001) PL 79+3/4 FLC 8+1/1 FAC 1

NICHOLAS Andrew Peter
Born: Liverpool, 10 October 1983
Height: 6'2" **Weight:** 12.8
A close-season signing from Liverpool, Andrew seized his opportunity to become a regular member of the Swindon team during the 2003-04 campaign. A tall left back with good pace and a long throw, he scored his first senior goal in the 4-2 win at Stockport in February. Andrew was rewarded with an extension to his contract before the close of the season and was recognised as 'Young Player of the Year' by one of the Robins' supporters' groups.
Swindon T (From trainee at Liverpool on 21/7/2003) FL 28+3/1 FAC 1 Others 2+1

NICHOLLS Ashley Joseph
Born: Ipswich, 30 October 1981
Height: 5'11" **Weight:** 12.2
International Honours: E: Sch
This hard-working midfielder featured regularly for Darlington last term, but failed to add to his goal tally. He lost his place in the line-up at the end of January and soon afterwards went out on loan to Cambridge United. Ashley quickly settled into the side and endeared himself to the U's faithful with some tireless running in the centre of the park.
Ipswich T (Free from Ipswich W on 5/7/2000)
Darlington (Free on 7/8/2002) FL 65+2/6 FLC 2+1 FAC 4/1 Others 2
Cambridge U (Loaned on 11/2/2004) FL 15+1/1

NICHOLLS Kevin John Richard
Born: Newham, 2 January 1979
Height: 6'0" **Weight:** 11.0
International Honours: E: Yth
Kevin started the 2003-04 season in a central-midfield role for Luton, but suffered an early injury to his back that kept him out of action for several months. He returned to the line-up in January and

apart from a period of suspension kept his place for the remainder of the campaign. An enthusiastic presence in the centre of the park, Kevin contributed two goals for the Hatters.
Charlton Ath (From trainee on 29/1/1996) FL 4+8/1 FLC 2+2
Brighton & Hove A (Loaned on 26/2/1999) FL 4/1
Wigan Ath (£250,000 + on 22/6/1999) FL 19+9 FLC 2 Others 4/1
Luton T (£25,000 + on 3/8/2001) FL 98+1/14 FLC 3 FAC 2 Others 1

NICHOLSON Kevin John
Born: Derby, 2 October 1980
Height: 5'8" **Weight:** 11.5
International Honours: E: Yth; Sch
This attacking left back was in and out of the Notts County line-up in the first half of 2003-04, but never managed to hold down a regular first-team place. However, following a change in management he fell out of favour and spent the closing stages of the campaign on loan with Conference club Scarborough.
Sheffield Wed (From trainee on 22/10/1997) FL 0+1
Northampton T (Free on 26/1/2001) FL 6+1
Notts Co (Free on 8/3/2001) FL 74+21/3 FLC 4+1 FAC 2+2/1 Others 4

NICHOLSON Shane Michael
Born: Newark, 3 June 1970
Height: 5'10" **Weight:** 12.2
Club Honours: GMVC '88
Last term proved to be a rather frustrating time for this experienced Tranmere player. The defender or midfielder began well with a double in the opening day win over Brentford, but just as new boss Brian Little arrived, Shane had to undergo surgery to correct a persistently troublesome toe condition. He was then unable to force his way back into the side until February. A steady player who is an intelligent passer of the ball, Shane was released in the summer.
Lincoln C (From trainee on 19/7/1988) FL 122+11/7 FLC 8+3 FAC 4/1 Others 7+1
Derby Co (£100,000 on 22/4/1992) FL 73+1/1 FLC 4 FAC 4/1 Others 5
West Bromwich A (£150,000 on 9/2/1996) FL 50+2 FLC 4 FAC 2 Others 2
Chesterfield (Free on 21/8/1998) FL 23+1 Others 1
Stockport Co (Free on 4/6/1999) FL 73+4/3 FLC 3 FAC 3
Sheffield U (Free on 18/7/2001) FL 21+4/3 FLC 1
Tranmere Rov (Free on 17/7/2002) FL 45+9/6 FLC 1 FAC 2+3 Others 3+1/1

NICOLAS Alexis Peter
Born: Westminster, 13 February 1983
Height: 5'8" **Weight:** 10.6
This slightly-built midfield player got an unexpected chance during Chelsea's successful pre-season tour to Malaysia which culminated in the capture of the Asia Cup. Six months – and a few midfield players – later he made his first-team debut in the tricky Fourth Round FA Cup-tie at Scarborough and a fortnight later he made his Premiership bow against Charlton Athletic. He acquitted himself well in both matches and looked at ease in the Blues' slick passing game, working hard and keeping moves alive with intuitive short passes. Since the Abramovich takeover the Chelsea midfield department has become a particularly overcrowded department with even established

international players unsure of a regular place and, to be honest, Alexis faces an uphill struggle to carve out a niche at Stamford Bridge.
Aston Villa *(From trainee on 4/4/2001)*
Chelsea *(Free on 20/12/2001) PL 1+1 FAC 1*

NICOLAU Nicky George
Born: St Pancras, 12 October 1983
Height: 5'8" **Weight:** 10.8
Club Honours: FAYC '01
This promising youngster was a regular in Arsenal's reserve team last term and in March he joined Southend United on loan to gain experience of senior football. Nicky slotted in well at left back and produced a 'Man of the Match' performance on his debut for the Blues, which helped secure a vital away win at Carlisle United. He was also used on the

left-hand side of midfield where his attacking skills were seen to best effect. Nicky was reported to have signed a permanent deal for the Blues during the summer break.
Arsenal *(From trainee on 1/7/2002)*
Southend U *(Loaned on 25/3/2004) FL 9*

NIELSEN David
Born: Denmark, 1 December 1976
Height: 6'0" **Weight:** 11.13
David made just two League appearances for Norwich early on in the 2003-04 campaign before opting to return to Denmark and he signed for AaB Aalborg. An explosive striker with the ability to do the unexpected he was a great favourite with the Carrow Road fans.
Grimsby T *(Loaned from FC Copenhagen, Denmark on 12/10/2000) FL 16+1/5 FAC 1+1/1*

Kevin Nicholls (right)

Wimbledon (Signed from FC Copenhagen, Denmark on 27/3/2001) FL 15+8/4 FLC 1
Norwich C (£200,000 on 14/12/2001) FL 35+23/14 FLC 1+1 FAC 3 Others 3

NIEMI Antti
Born: Oulu, Finland, 31 May 1972
Height: 6'1" **Weight:** 13.9
Club Honours: SLC '99
International Honours: Finland: 61; U21-17; Yth
Everybody's favourite Antti, accruing 83 per cent of the votes in the Saints' supporters 'Player of the Season' poll, his performances 'Player of the Season' poll, his performances were phenomenal last season. As to his attributes: they are legion and, accepting he is not super-human, it's difficult to see, on the form of the last two years, any way in which his game can be substantially improved. Inevitably, press speculation regarding moves to 'bigger' and/or 'better' clubs, has steadily increased with every save, but, gratifyingly, he has made no indication of wanting to move. It would be a devastating blow if he were to go; whatever fee was received, because it's improbable that an adequate replacement could be found at any price.
Glasgow R (Signed from FC Copenhagen, Denmark, ex HJK Helsinki, on 22/7/1997) SL 13 SLC 1 Others 7+1
Heart of Midlothian (£400,000 on 17/12/1999) SL 89 SLC 4 SC 9 Others 4
Southampton (£2,000,000 on 28/8/2002) PL 53 FLC 5 FAC 7 Others 1

NIGHTINGALE Luke Raymond
Born: Portsmouth, 22 December 1980
Height: 5'10" **Weight:** 12.5
This young striker joined Southend on a short-term contract after an injury-affected spell at Fratton Park. However, he struggled to cope with Third Division football and was restricted to just four appearances from the substitutes' bench. Unable to make an impression at Roots Hall he moved on to Dr Martens League outfit Weymouth in September.
Portsmouth (From trainee on 23/11/1998) FL 14+31/4 FLC 2+1/3 FAC 2+1/1
Swindon T (Loaned on 24/12/2002) FL 2+1
Southend U (Free on 8/8/2003) FL 0+4

NIMMO Liam
Born: Boston, 28 December 1984
Height: 6'0" **Weight:** 11.5
A third-year scholar for Grimsby Town, this tall, powerful striker was in impressive goal-scoring form for the U19s last term. A fringe first-team player he made a couple of appearances from the bench early on. Liam was due to finish his scholarship in the summer and his future was uncertain at the time of writing. He is the son of the former Sheffield Wednesday and Doncaster striker Ian Nimmo.
Grimsby T (Trainee) FL 0+2

NIVEN Derek
Born: Falkirk, 12 December 1983
Height: 6'1" **Weight:** 11.2
Derek spent the first half of the 2003-04 season developing in Bolton's reserve team before joining Chesterfield on loan towards the end of the year. The Spireites had previously lacked a reliable ball-winner in the centre of the park, but Derek helped turn the club's season around, with fellow midfield man Mark Hudson being transformed. Although he returned briefly to the Reebok, he was released in March and the Spireites moved to pick him up on a long-term deal.
Raith Rov (From Stenhousemuir juniors on 10/7/2000) SL 0+1
Bolton W (Signed on 29/11/2001)
Chesterfield (Signed on 12/12/2003) FL 22/1

NIXON Eric Walter
Born: Manchester, 4 October 1962
Height: 6'4" **Weight:** 14.12
Club Honours: AMC '90
Sheffield Wednesday's goalkeeping coach was forced out of retirement to take his place on the substitutes' bench last term. He made a single appearance, replacing the injured Kevin Pressman at Grimsby in September, and thus became the oldest player to appear in the Football League during the season.
Manchester C (£1,000 from Curzon Ashton on 10/12/1983) FL 58 FLC 8 FAC 10 Others 8
Wolverhampton W (Loaned on 29/8/1986) FL 16
Bradford C (Loaned on 28/11/1986) FL 3
Southampton (Loaned on 23/12/1986) FL 4
Carlisle U (Loaned on 23/1/1987) FL 16
Tranmere Rov (£60,000 on 24/3/1988) FL 341 FLC 34 FAC 19 Others 45+1
Reading (Loaned on 9/1/1996) FLC 1
Blackpool (Loaned on 5/2/1996) FL 20 Others 2
Bradford C (Loaned on 13/9/1996) FL 12
Stockport Co (£100,000 on 28/8/1997) FL 43 FLC 2 FAC 2
Wigan Ath (Loaned on 28/8/1998) FL 1
Wigan Ath (Free on 24/3/1999) FL 2
Tranmere Rov (Free on 20/7/1999) FL 1+4 FLC 0+1
Kidderminster Hrs (Loaned on 12/10/2001) FL 2 Others 1
Sheffield Wed (Free on 12/9/2003) FL 0+1

NOBLE David James
Born: Hitchin, 2 February 1982
Height: 6'0" **Weight:** 12.4
Club Honours: FAYC '00
International Honours: S: B-1; U21-2; E: Yth
This classy midfielder impressed when playing for West Ham in their Carling Cup tie with Rushden. He played in a further three First Division games as a substitute but was not able to break into the side. In March he joined Boston United on loan, fitting in well on the right side of midfield, with his passing ability and vision on the ball proving big assets. The move became permanent and he agreed a contract in the summer.
Arsenal (From trainee on 13/3/2001)
Watford (Loaned on 10/7/2001) FL 5+10/1 FLC 3
West Ham U (Free on 31/1/2003) FL 0+3 FLC 1
Boston U (Free on 27/2/2004) FL 14/2

NOEL-WILLIAMS Gifton Ruben Elisha
Born: Islington, 21 January 1980
Height: 6'1'' **Weight:** 14.6
Club Honours: Div 2 '98
International Honours: E: Yth
A powerful centre forward who is good at holding the ball up and running at opposing defences, Noel joined Stoke during the summer of 2003. He got off to a good start, scoring on his debut at Derby on the opening day of the season, but as the campaign wore on his old injuries began to slow him down and the goals dried up. Noel returned to scoring form with two at Bradford City at the beginning of May and finished the campaign as the Potters' joint-top scorer with ten goals.
Watford (From trainee on 13/2/1997) P/FL 107+62/33 FLC 10+2/3 FAC 10+2/5
Stoke C (Free on 29/5/2003) FL 40+2/10 FLC 1 FAC 1

NOGAN Lee Martin
Born: Cardiff, 21 May 1969
Height: 5'9" **Weight:** 11.0
Club Honours: AMC '98
International Honours: W: 2; B-1; U21-1
York City's assistant manager, Lee was again a tireless worker for the Minstermen last term, contributing some unselfish running and general all-round experience to the cause. Although sometimes playing a deeper midfield role than previously, he still finished the campaign as the club's top marksman with nine goals to his credit. Lee netted in

early-season wins over Carlisle and Northampton and bagged a double in the 2-1 victory at Rochdale.
Oxford U *(From trainee on 25/3/1987) FL 57+7/10 FLC 4+1 FAC 2+1/1 Others 4+1/1*
Brentford *(Loaned on 25/3/1987) FL 10+1/2*
Southend U *(Loaned on 17/9/1987) FL 6/1 FLC 2 Others 1/1*
Watford *(£350,000 on 12/12/1991) FL 97+8/26 FLC 5+2/3 FAC 2/1 Others 1+2*
Southend U *(Loaned on 17/3/1994) FL 4+1*
Reading *(£250,000 on 12/1/1995) FL 71+20/26 FLC 5+1/1 FAC 2 Others 3/2*
Notts Co *(Loaned on 14/2/1997) FL 6*
Grimsby T *(£170,000 on 24/7/1997) FL 63+11/10 FLC 9+1/2 FAC 4/2 Others 8/2*
Darlington *(Free on 21/7/1999) FL 37+12/6 FLC 3/2 FAC 3 Others 1+2/1*
Luton T *(Free on 23/11/2000) FL 7/1 FAC 3/1 Others 0+1*
York C *(Free on 12/2/2001) FL 133+10/32 FLC 3 FAC 8/1 Others 2+1/1*

NOLAN Kevin Anthony Jance
Born: Liverpool, 24 June 1982
Height: 6'1" **Weight:** 13.5
International Honours: E: U21-1; Yth
This energetic midfielder really came of age last term, replicating his form of a couple of seasons ago and finishing as Bolton's top scorer. After a disappointing campaign the previous season, Kevin cemented his place at the heart of the midfield early on and remained there until the last game, giving a series of passionate and committed displays. His goals contributed to a number of vital victories, not least his double salvo in the epic 4-3 win at Blackburn. It is testimony to Kevin's growing status that he more than held is own in a midfield which also contained Jay Jay Okocha and Youri Djorkaeff.
Bolton W *(From trainee on 22/1/2000) P/FL 111+29/19 FLC 5+3/2 FAC 5+5/3 Others 2*

NOLAN Matthew (Matt) Lee
Born: Hitchin, 25 February 1982
Height: 6'0" **Weight:** 12.0
This highly-rated young striker was a regular scorer with Hitchin Town before being sold to Peterborough United last September. He made his debut for Posh as a substitute against Port Vale soon afterwards, but was then sidelined by injury. Matt later had a spell on loan with Cambridge City.
Peterborough U *(Signed from Hitchin T on 23/9/2003) FL 0+1*

NORRIS David Martin
Born: Stamford, 22 February 1981
Height: 5'7" **Weight:** 11.6

Club Honours: Div 2 '04
David had an excellent season for Plymouth Argyle in 2003-04. A right-sided midfield player with a terrific work rate, he can deliver crosses with either foot and created many goal-scoring opportunities for his colleagues. Extremely popular with the Home Park faithful, he scored five times including the final goal of the campaign against Colchester United at Home Park in May.
Bolton W *(£50,000 from Boston U on 2/2/2000) FLC 3+1 FAC 1/1*
Hull C *(Loaned on 4/3/2002) FL 3+3/1*
Plymouth Arg *(Free on 8/10/2002) FL 71+7/11 FLC 1 FAC 4 Others 0+1*

NOSWORTHY Nyron Paul Henry
Born: Brixton, 11 October 1980
Height: 6'0" **Weight:** 12.0
Nyron was a near ever-present for Gillingham at right back last term until being sidelined by a groin injury which ended his season in January. His insatiable appetite for work and dynamic forays down the right flank were both sorely missed by the Gills.
Gillingham *(From trainee on 30/12/1998) FL 115+22/5 FLC 6+2/1 FAC 7+7 Others 1+2*

NOTMAN Alexander (Alex) McKeachie
Born: Edinburgh, 10 December 1979
Height: 5'7" **Weight:** 10.11
International Honours: S: U21-11; Yth; Sch
Despite a brave attempt Alex was forced to call an end to his career following the ankle injury sustained at Ipswich in September 2002. This likeable Scot made just one brief substitute appearance for Norwich last term, in the September home win against Burnley. A clever striker who was more a maker than taker of chances, he often played on the right-hand side of midfield.
Manchester U *(From trainee on 17/12/1996) FLC 0+1*
Aberdeen *(Loaned on 11/2/1999) SL 0+2*
Sheffield U *(Loaned on 20/1/2000) FL 7+3/3*
Norwich C *(£250,000 on 28/11/2000) FL 18+36/1 FLC 1 FAC 2+1 Others 0+3*

NOWLAND Adam Christopher
Born: Preston, 6 July 1981
Height: 5'11" **Weight:** 11.6
Adam's season was transformed when he was switched from being a skilful, if somewhat lightweight, front-runner to a determined, ball-winning central midfielder. He immediately showed that he was a much better player starting from

a deeper position, being able to use his passing skills and long-range shooting ability to full effect. Not surprisingly, word soon started to spread regarding his transformation in fortune, and it didn't take the Wimbledon administrators too long to ship him off to West Ham for a bargain fee. After making his debut for the Hammers against Rotherham he was used mainly as a substitute for the rest of the campaign.
Blackpool *(From trainee on 15/1/1999) FL 18+51/5 FLC 1+5/1 FAC 2+2/1 Others 0+2*
Wimbledon *(Signed on 29/6/2001) FL 35+21/5 FLC 2+1 FAC 2/2*
West Ham U *(£75,000 on 28/1/2004) FL 2+9*

NTIMBAN-ZEH Harry Dave
Born: France, 26 September 1973
Height: 6'1" **Weight:** 12.7
One of a number of out-of-contract players looked at by Wimbledon during the 2003-04 season, Harry did enough in a couple of reserve games to earn a short-term deal, and after making his debut in late March as a substitute against Ipswich, he kept his place for the remainder of the season. A speedy central defender particularly adept at making last-ditch clearances, he managed to shore up the defensive side of things in the final weeks of the season.
Wimbledon *(Signed from Sporting Club Espinho, Portugal, ex Racing Club Paris, on 8/3/2004) FL 9+1*

N'TOYA-ZOA Tcham
Born: Kinshasha, DR Congo, 3 November 1983
Height: 5'10" **Weight:** 12.8
Tcham made a handful of appearances for French Second Division side Troyes last term before joining Chesterfield on transfer-deadline day. His signing may have been speculative but he produced a number of promising displays up front and on the right-hand side of midfield. Tcham is strong, pacy and powerful, and will be an asset if the Spireites can keep him for the 2004-05 campaign.
Chesterfield *(Free from Troyes, France on 25/3/2004) FL 3+3*

NUGENT David James
Born: Liverpool, 2 May 1985
Height: 5'11" **Weight:** 12.13
This young striker started the 2003-04 season in the Bury line-up, despite being one of five strikers at the club vying for just two places. A change of management in December seemed to reduce David's first-team opportunities

but the return of loan man Jon Daly to Stockport brought him another opportunity in March and he responded by establishing himself in the side in the closing fixtures. His work rate and pace continually unsettled opposition defenders, although he still needs to improve his finishing.

Bury *(From trainee on 8/3/2003) FL 32+30/7 FLC 1+1 FAC 1+1 Others 3+4/1*

NUGENT Kevin Patrick
Born: Edmonton, 10 April 1969
Height: 6'1" **Weight:** 13.3
International Honours: RoI: Yth
This experienced striker forged a useful partnership up front with Lee Trundle for Swansea City last term, and on occasions he captained the side. Kevin always

showed 100 per cent endeavour throughout the 90 minutes, despite carrying a hamstring injury on a number of occasions. A good battler up front, he showed he was still dangerous in aerial challenges and netted ten goals during the campaign.

Leyton Orient *(From trainee on 8/7/1987) FL 86+8/20 FLC 9+3/6 FAC 9/3 Others 9+1/1*
Plymouth Arg *(£200,000 on 23/3/1992) FL 124+7/32 FLC 11/2 FAC 10/3 Others 5+3*
Bristol C *(Signed on 29/9/1995) FL 48+22/14 FLC 2+2 FAC 3+2/1 Others 2+1*
Cardiff C *(£65,000 on 4/8/1997) FL 94+5/29 FLC 8+1/1 FAC 9/6 Others 1+1/1*
Leyton Orient *(Free on 31/1/2002) FL 17+11/4 FLC 1/1 FAC 2 Others 1*
Swansea C *(Free on 17/1/2003) FL 46+8/13 FLC 0+1 FAC 2+2/2*

NYARKO Alex
Born: Accra, Ghana, 15 October 1973
Height: 6'1" **Weight:** 12.0
International Honours: Ghana
The return of Alex to Everton after a two-year exile was a surprise to many but he did as well as can be expected in the circumstances. The midfielder made 11 appearances in the Premiership, impressing with his attitude and determination and was obviously keen to reclaim his place in the first team. A technically sound player, he displayed effective distribution skills as well as shooting with venom.

Everton *(£4,500,000 from RC Lens, France, ex Asante Kotoko, Dawu Youngsters, Sportul Studentese, FC Basle, Karlruhe SC, on 9/8/2000) PL 26+7/1 FLC 3 FAC 2*

Nyron Nosworthy

O

OAKES Andrew (Andy) Mark

Born: Northwich, 11 January 1977
Height: 6'4" **Weight:** 12.4
Unfortunate to be left out after the
opening-day disaster against Stoke, Andy
was back as Derby's number one
goalkeeper until injury halted his progress
in October. He damaged a wrist cartilage
in training and was put in plaster after an
exploratory operation. A second operation
was required in December and it was five
months before he returned to duty on the
bench. His qualities of courage and
determination will see him through, but
he would welcome a change of fortune.
*Hull C (Signed from Winsford U, ex Burnley
trainee, trial with Bury, Macclesfield T, on
8/12/1998) FL 19 Others 1*
*Derby Co (£460,000 on 7/6/1999) P/FL 43
FLC 2 FAC 1*

OAKES Michael Christian

Born: Northwich, 30 October 1973
Height: 6'2" **Weight:** 14.6
Club Honours: FLC '96
International Honours: E: U21-6
Michael started last season as second-
choice 'keeper to Matt Murray at Wolves,
but the youngster succumbed to injury
problems after one match. Michael had a
torrid return to the team, as they trailed
4-0 to Charlton after 33 minutes, yet he
was not really at fault. When Wolves
recorded their first win, against
Manchester City, it was Michael who
made a brilliant save to clinch the points.
He could not be blamed for many of the
goals Wolves conceded, and was involved
in every match until January before
making way for new signing Paul Jones.
*Aston Villa (From juniors on 16/7/1991) PL
49+2 FLC 3 FAC 2 Others 5*
*Scarborough (Loaned on 26/11/1993) FL 1
Others 1*
*Wolverhampton W (£400,000 + on
29/10/1999) P/FL 147 FLC 7+1 FAC 8
Others 2*

OAKES Stefan (Stef) Trevor

Born: Leicester, 6 September 1978
Height: 5'11" **Weight:** 12.4
Club Honours: FLC '00
After joining Walsall in the summer of
2003, Stefan was a regular in the reserves
in the first half of the season. First-team
opportunities were few and far between
and when he stepped out for his first full
game against Coventry in January he was
rather harshly sent off after just 35

minutes. In February he moved on to
Notts County where he experienced much
more regular first-team football. A central
midfield playmaker with the ability to
produce defence-splitting passes, he was
brought in by new manager Gary Mills to
become a major component in the engine
room of the side.
*Leicester C (From trainee on 3/7/1997) P/FL
39+25/2 FLC 7+1/2 FAC 5+2*
Crewe Alex (Loaned on 17/3/2003) FL 3+4
Walsall (Free on 18/7/2003) FL 1+4
Notts Co (Free on 17/2/2004) FL 14

OAKLEY Matthew (Matt)

Born: Peterborough, 17 August 1977
Height: 5'10" **Weight:** 12.1
International Honours: E: U21-4
Southampton began the season with a
six-game undefeated run which ended
with a home defeat to Middlesbrough at
the end of September, and Matt limping
from the field with what transpired to be
a cruciate ligament injury which kept him
out for the rest of the season. An
undemonstrative, skilful and tidy player,
his contribution to the Saints' midfield
over the past ten seasons (eight as a
regular) has not always been obvious, but
in his absence the team has struggled to
find any sort of rhythm, and service to the
forwards has been fitful – prompting the
notion among many supporters that
finding a better central midfielder might
prove far more expensive than had
hitherto been supposed.
*Southampton (From trainee on 1/7/1995) PL
203+22/11 FLC 21+2/2 FAC 16+2/3 Others 1*

OATWAY Anthony Philip David Terry Frank Donald Stanley Gerry Gordon Stephen James (Charlie)

Born: Hammersmith, 28 November 1973
Height: 5'7" **Weight:** 10.10
Club Honours: Div 3 '99, '01; Div 2 '02
Although Charlie's 2003-04 season was
disrupted by a severe back injury in
September, the terrier-like midfielder
came back into the Brighton line-up in
January and kept his place to the end of
the season, helping to secure promotion
for the Seagulls in the play-off final at
Cardiff. Chasing, harrying and tackling are
the key elements to his game, and he is
just the man to have in a side scrapping
to get out of the Second Division via the
play-offs.
*Cardiff C (Free from Yeading on 4/8/1994) FL
29+3 FLC 2/1 FAC 1+1 Others 2*
*Torquay U (Free on 28/12/1995) FL 65+2/1
FLC 3 FAC 1*
*Brentford (£10,000 on 21/8/1997) FL 37+20
FLC 1+2/1 FAC 4 Others 0+1*

Lincoln C (Loaned on 21/10/1998) FL 3
*Brighton & Hove A (£10,000 on 9/7/1999)
FL 152+20/7 FLC 8 FAC 10/1 Others 5*

O'BRIEN Andrew (Andy) James

Born: Harrogate, 29 June 1979
Height: 6'3" **Weight:** 12.4
International Honours: RoI: 13; U21-8;
E: U21-1; Yth
Although competition for places in
Newcastle's back four was stiff, Andy was
a regular there for most of the 2003-04
season. A determined central defender, he
clearly benefited from playing alongside
Jonathan Woodgate, improving his
positional awareness and his composure
on the ball, and when turning out
together the pair helped deliver nine
clean sheets during the campaign. His
only goal of the season came in the home
win over Fulham in January. Andy
continued to be selected for the Republic
of Ireland during the campaign.
*Bradford C (From trainee on 28/10/1996)
P/FL 113+20/3 FLC 5 FAC 8 Others 4*
*Newcastle U (£2,000,000 on 28/3/2001) PL
93+4/4 FLC 3+1 FAC 6+1/1 Others 23+3*

O'BRIEN Robert (Rob) Louis

Born: Leeds, 28 November 1983
Height: 5'10" **Weight:** 11.0
This promising Doncaster Rovers
youngster was loaned out to
Gainsborough Trinity last September and
on his return to Belle Vue he was plunged
into the first team for his Football League
debut at Kidderminster when he showed
his pace to good effect. Essentially a
right-sided midfield player, he is more like
a traditional winger, being fast and tricky
and always willing to track back and help
out in defence. Rob was released in the
summer.
*Doncaster Rov (From Leeds U juniors on
11/1/2003) FL 1*

O'BRIEN Roy Joseph

Born: Cork, 27 November 1974
Height: 6'1" **Weight:** 12.4
Club Honours: NC '03
International Honours: RoI: Yth; Sch
This cultured Yeovil Town defender was a
regular in the line-up in the opening
stages of the 2003-04 campaign before
suffering an injury in the fixture at Oxford
in October. Thereafter he was beset by
injuries which required two separate
operations and kept him out of the side
for the remainder of the season. Roy, who
can also adapt his game to a midfield
role, will be hoping to steer clear of the
treatment room in 2004-05.

Arsenal (From trainee on 6/7/1993)
Bournemouth (Free on 23/8/1996) FL 1
(Freed on 18/12/1996)
Yeovil T (Free from Dorchester T on
8/8/2000) FL 13 FLC 1

O'CALLAGHAN Brian Patrick
Born: Limerick, 24 February 1981
Height: 6'1" **Weight:** 12.1
International Honours: RoI: U21-4; Yth
Brian was a regular in the Barnsley line-up

Andy O'Brien

at the start of last term, featuring in a
variety of positions: right back, centre
back and central midfield, but wherever
he played he always looked comfortable
on the ball. Unfortunately injury brought
his season to a premature close in the
new year and he was one of several
players released by the club in the summer.
Barnsley (Signed from Pike Rov on
16/7/1998) FL 58+17/1 FLC 5+2 FAC 5+1
Others 2

O'CONNOR Garreth
Born: Dublin, 10 November 1978
Height: 5'7" **Weight:** 11.0
A very skilful midfielder, Garreth proved to
be a hard-working member of the
Bournemouth side last season. Although
he lost his place towards the end of the
campaign he showed his worth to the
squad by putting in some impressive
performances in the reserve side to regain
his first-team spot.
Bournemouth (Free from Bohemians on
5/6/2000) FL 70+58/11 FLC 2+1 FAC 9+4/1
Others 10+1/2

O'CONNOR James Kevin
Born: Dublin, 1 September 1979
Height: 5'8" **Weight:** 11.6
Club Honours: AMC '00
International Honours: RoI: U21-9; Yth
A totally committed midfielder who
prefers the left-hand side of the field,
James' has an aggressive approach to
almost every game. A strong, tenacious
tackler, he made his debut for West
Bromwich Albion against Walsall on the
opening day of the 2003-04 season and
was a regular in the side up until the new
year when he lost his place to Mark
Kinsella.
Stoke C (From trainee on 5/9/1996) FL
176/16 FLC 9/3 FAC 8+1 Others 16+1/3
West Bromwich A (Signed on 8/8/2003) FL
27+3 FLC 5 FAC 1

O'CONNOR Kevin Patrick
Born: Blackburn, 24 February 1982
Height: 5'11" **Weight:** 12.0
International Honours: RoI: U21-6
This attacking midfielder had rather a
mixed time at Brentford last term. He
started the campaign at outside right
switching to central midfield and then
played up front or as a substitute. The
fact that he took part in all bar three of
the Bees' 51 matches confirms his
contribution to the team. Kevin scored
just twice, netting in the FA Cup tie
against Gainsborough Trinity and against
Queens Park Rangers. He continued to
represent the Republic of Ireland at U21
level during the season.
Brentford (From trainee on 4/3/2000) FL
104+26/7 FLC 4+1/3 FAC 7+1/2 Others 4+5/1

ODEJAYI Olukayode (Kay)
Born: Nigeria, 21 February 1982
Height: 6'2" **Weight:** 12.2
Kayode began and finished last term in
excellent form for Cheltenham, however
he was mostly used as a substitute
during the middle part of the season. A
tall, quick striker he benefited from the

arrival of new manager John Ward and netted a total of five goals during the campaign.
Bristol C *(From trainee on 17/7/2000) FL 0+6 Others 1 (Free to Forest Green Rov on 28/9/2002)*
Cheltenham T *(£25,000 on 5/6/2003) FL 14+16/5 FLC 1 FAC 0+2 Others 0+1*

ODUNSI Saheed **Adeleke (Leke)**
Born: Lambeth, 5 December 1980
Height: 5'9" **Weight:** 11.8
After leaving full-time football in November 2002, Leke returned to the senior ranks with Southend United in the summer of 2003 and immediately won a place in the line-up as a defensive midfielder. Unfortunately, after opening his goal-scoring account for the Blues in the home game against Huddersfield

Town, he was then sidelined for the remainder of the season with a broken ankle and severe ligament damage suffered in the same match. Sadly, this resulted in Leke having to retire from the professional game at the age of 23 on medical advice.
Millwall *(From trainee on 24/2/1999) FL 5+12 FLC 1+2 Others 2+1*
Colchester U *(Loaned on 16/8/2002) FL 3+3 FLC 0+1 Others 0+1 (Freed on 2/12/2002)*
Southend U *(Free, via Kingstonian, Bromley, Carshalton, on 30/7/2003) FL 12/1 FLC 1*

OFFIONG Richard
Born: South Shields, 17 December 1983
Height: 5'11" **Weight:** 12.0
International Honours: E: Yth
The pacy Newcastle United striker spent most of last season in the reserves, but towards the end of the campaign he

joined York City on loan to gain further experience of senior football. Richard made four appearances for the Minstermen, but was unable to revive the fortunes of the struggling Third Division club.
Newcastle U *(From trainee on 26/9/2001)*
Darlington *(Loaned on 29/11/2002) FL 7/2 FAC 2/2*
Motherwell *(Loaned on 31/1/2003) SL 0+9 SC 0+1*
York C *(Loaned on 12/3/2004) FL 2+2*

O'HALLORAN Matthew (Matt) Vincent
Born: Nottingham, 18 November 1982
Height: 5'10" **Weight:** 11.6
After being released by Derby County, Matt joined Oldham on trial and he featured in a several early-season games in a variety of positions, including wing back, in central midfield and up front. However, he was allowed to leave Boundary Park and in December he signed for Chesterfield on non-contract terms, but was sidelined with injury almost from the off. Returning in April his hard work and competitive edge in midfield helped the Spireites to earn a creditable draw at Bournemouth, but he was unable to show enough to earn a contract in the summer.
Derby Co *(From trainee on 16/7/2002)*
Oldham Ath *(Free on 16/8/2003) FL 2+11/1 FLC 0+1 FAC 0+1 Others 1+1*
Chesterfield *(Free on 11/12/2003) FL 1+2*

O'HANLON Sean Philip
Born: Southport, 2 January 1983
Height: 6'1" **Weight:** 12.5
International Honours: E: Yth
A regular with Everton's reserves, Sean joined Swindon on loan to gain experience of senior football, impressed with a series of fine performances at right back and eventually signed permanently for the County Ground club. Tall, strong and powerful, he can also play at centre back and put in some useful performances as a man-marker towards the close of the season as Town just failed to make the play-off final.
Everton *(From trainee on 26/2/2000)*
Swindon T *(£150,000 on 23/1/2004) FL 17+2/2 Others 2*

O'HARE Alan Patrick James
Born: Drogheda, Ireland, 31 July 1982
Height: 6'2" **Weight:** 12.2
Alan came on in leaps and bounds for Chesterfield last season and gained great confidence from a string of consistent displays in defence. He picked up some

Garreth O'Connor

scary-looking injuries mainly through his bravery and 'team first' ethos, but he was rarely out of the side for long. Alan clearly enjoys life at Saltergate and fully merits the warm appreciation of the club's supporters.
Bolton W *(From trainee on 24/11/2001)*
Chesterfield *(Loaned on 25/11/2002) FL 19*
Chesterfield *(Free on 9/10/2002) FL 58+4/1 FLC 1 FAC 1 Others 4*

OKAI Richard **Parys**
Born: London, 23 November 1984
Height: 5'9" **Weight:** 11.5
A fast and tricky left winger, Luton spent most of the 2003-04 season developing with the club's U19 team. He was called up twice by the first team, making his

senior debut in the LDV Vans Trophy tie against Stevenage Borough and also featuring in the FA Cup replay against Thurrock. Parys was surprisingly released by the Hatters in the summer.
Luton T *(Trainee) FLC 0+1 FAC 0+1 Others 1+1*

OKOCHA Augustine Azuka (Jay Jay)
Born: Enugu, Nigeria, 14 August 1973
Height: 5'7" **Weight:** 11.2
International Honours: Nigeria
Unfortunately Jay Jay will now be known as the player with the most shots in a Premiership season without scoring a single goal, but his campaign was about so much more than that unfortunate statistic. He was in typically inspired form,

supplementing his endless box of tricks with a work ethic that was second to none. Jay Jay left for the African Nations' Cup at the end of January, signing off with a magnificent performance in the first leg of the Carling Cup semi-final against Aston Villa. His two goals, including one of the finest free kicks of the season, inspired Bolton to a famous 5-2 victory. During his time in Tunisia he was named as the 'Player of the Tournament' after a series of dazzling displays which helped Nigeria to third place.
Bolton W *(Free from Paris St Germain, France, ex Enugu R, B.Nuenkirchen, Eintracht Frankfurt, Fenerbahce, on 3/8/2002) PL 59+7/7 FLC 5+1/3 FAC 0+1*

Sean O'Hanlon (left)

OKORONKWO Isaac
Born: Nbene, Nigeria, 1 May 1978
Height: 6'0" **Weight:** 11.9
International Honours: Nigeria
This experienced central defender made just a solitary Carling Cup appearance for Wolves in the first half of last season and in the new year he was called up by Nigeria for the African Nations' Cup finals. It was April before Isaac was considered ready for the Premiership, and he made a good debut at Manchester City. He was very quick, strong in the tackle, but sometimes had lapses of concentration, however, he retained his place for the rest of the campaign.
Wolverhampton W (Free from Shakhtar Donetsk, Ukraine on 30/7/2003) PL 7 FLC 1

OKUONGHAE Magnus
Born: Nigeria, 16 February 1986
Height: 6'3" **Weight:** 13.4
This big centre half made his Football League debut as a substitute for Rushden against Colchester at Nene Park towards the end of their 4-0 home victory last November. Three days later he was leading out the U18 team in the FA Youth Cup against Manchester United in front of a sell-out crowd, with Diamonds going 1-0 up before losing 2-1. Magnus was also involved with the first-team squad near the end of the season and will be looking to gain more senior experience in 2004-05.
Rushden & Diamonds (Trainee) FL 0+1

OLDFIELD David Charles
Born: Perth, Australia, 30 May 1968
Height: 5'11" **Weight:** 13.4
International Honours: E: U21-1
David spent the 2003-04 season as coach and assistant manager at Oxford but managed a handful of first-team appearances, his only start coming early on at Kidderminster. A wily and experienced player, he is capable of taking most positions and not letting anyone down.
Luton T (From apprentice on 16/5/1986) FL 21+8/4 FLC 4+2/2 FAC 0+1 Others 2+1/2
Manchester C (£600,000 on 14/3/1989) FL 18+8/6 FLC 2+1/2 Others 0+1/1
Leicester C (£150,000 on 12/1/1990) F/PL 163+25/26 FLC 10+2/1 FAC 7/3 Others 11+4/2
Millwall (Loaned on 24/2/1995) FL 16+1/6
Luton T (£150,000 on 21/7/1995) FL 99+18/18 FLC 11/2 FAC 2 Others 7+2/4
Stoke C (Free on 2/7/1998) FL 50+15/7 FLC 4+1 FAC 2 Others 1+1

Peterborough U (Free on 23/3/2000) FL 68+10/4 FLC 3 FAC 8+2/1 Others 4+1
Oxford U (Free on 8/8/2002) FL 20+11/2 FLC 2+1 FAC 2/1 Others 0+1

O'LEARY Kristian Denis
Born: Port Talbot, 30 August 1977
Height: 6'0" **Weight:** 13.4
Club Honours: Div 3 '00
International Honours: W: Yth
Despite starting the season in the Swansea defensive line, it was soon evident that Kristian did not figure as an automatic selection under Brian Flynn although he made numerous appearances from the substitutes' bench. When included, he again showed his versatility by performing in a range of defensive positions, and towards the end of the season even played in a midfield role. A local product, Kristian has always given 100 per cent commitment when playing for the Swans.
Swansea C (From trainee on 1/7/1996) FL 170+33/7 FLC 9 FAC 9+2 Others 7+2

O'LEARY Stephen
Born: Barnet, 12 February 1985
Height: 5'10" **Weight:** 11.8
International Honours: RoI: Yth
This promising Luton youngster spent much of last season developing in the club's U19 side, but was called up to the first team for the LDV Vans Trophy match against Rushden in November. He acquitted himself well and featured on a number of occasions in the closing stages of the campaign, scoring a crucial equaliser in the home game against Sheffield Wednesday. A fast and direct midfield player, he was called up to the Republic of Ireland U19 squad during the season.
Luton T (Trainee) FL 3+2/1 Others 1

OLEMBE Salomon
Born: Yaounde, Cameroon, 8 December 1980
Height: 5'7" **Weight:** 10.4
International Honours: Cameroon
One of three players signed by Peter Reid on a season-long loan deal from Marseilles, Salomon had previously spent the whole of his career in France. He featured in midfield and at left back under Reid, but after returning from international duty for Cameroon in the African Nations' Cup finals, he found himself overlooked by new Leeds' boss Eddie Gray.
Leeds U (Loaned from Marseilles, France, ex Nantes, on 31/8/2003) PL 8+4 FLC 2

OLI Dennis Chiedozie
Born: Newham, 28 January 1984
Height: 6'0" **Weight:** 12.4
This tall striker only managed a handful of appearances for Queens Park Rangers last term, his only start coming in the LDV Vans Trophy tie against Kidderminster. He spent large parts of the season out on loan to gain first-team experience, firstly at Gravesend and then at Farnborough.
Queens Park R (From juniors on 24/10/2001) FL 8+15 FLC 0+1 FAC 1+2 Others 2+1

OLIVEIRA Filipe
Born: Braga, Portugal, 27 May 1984
Height: 5'10" **Weight:** 11.2
International Honours: Portugal: Yth
When Jose Mourinho took over as Chelsea boss in June there was at least one familiar face to greet him, ex-Porto starlet Filipe Oliviera. The Portuguese forward joined Chelsea as the previous regime, short of funds and with one eye on the future, scoured Europe to develop the very best of the continent's young talent. The exciting youngster made two substitute appearances during 2003-04: 25 minutes against Scarborough and ten minutes against Everton. A creative right-sided midfielder who is also comfortable in the 'hole' behind the front players, Filipe has a bright future.
Chelsea (£140,000 from FC Porto, Portugal on 11/9/2001) PL 0+4 FLC 0+1 FAC 0+1 Others 0+1

OLIVER Luke John
Born: Hammersmith, 1 May 1984
Height: 6'6" **Weight:** 14.6
Wycombe's giant central defender made a couple of early-season appearances as a substitute last term, but failed to appear again in the first team. Luke joined Conference side Woking in February and went on to make a couple of appearances, signing a new contract in the summer.
Wycombe W (Free from Brook House on 2/7/2002) FL 0+4

OLSEN James Paul
Born: Bootle, 23 October 1981
Height: 5'11" **Weight:** 11.9
James was unable to break into the first-team squad at Tranmere last term and in March his contract was cancelled, allowing him to join Macclesfield on a short-term deal. However, he received few opportunities in the senior side, managing just two appearances from the bench in a wide-left midfield role. James was used as a left-sided player in the reserve side

307

where he showed good pace and scored an excellent goal in the home match against Stockport reserves.
Tranmere Rov *(From trainee at Liverpool on 22/3/2001) FL 1+3 FLC 0+1 Others 0+1*
Macclesfield T *(Free on 25/3/2004) FL 0+2*

OLSEN Kim Plougman
Born: Denmark, 11 February 1979
Height: 6'3" **Weight:** 13.10
This tall, old-fashioned style centre forward joined Sheffield Wednesday after a successful trial period. However, although he featured on a number of occasions he sometimes seemed to struggle to get to grips with Second Division football. After a period of settling in he will be hoping to make his mark at Hillsborough in the 2004-05 campaign.
Sheffield Wed *(Signed from Midtjylland, Denmark on 3/2/2004) FL 6+4 Others 1+1*

OLSZAR Sebastian
Born: Poland, 10 December 1981
Height: 5'11" **Weight:** 11.9
International Honours: Poland: U21
This young striker scored regularly for Pompey reserves last term, but made little impact at first-team level. He featured as a substitute in the FA Cup tie at Liverpool in January, then spent the closing stages of the campaign on loan at Coventry where he failed to impress. He was released by Portsmouth in the summer.
Portsmouth *(£100,000 from Admira Modling, Austria, ex Gornik Zabrze, on 30/1/2004) FAC 0+1*
Coventry C *(Loaned on 17/3/2004) FL 1+4*

OLUGBODI Jide Michael
Born: Lagos, Nigeria, 20 November 1977
Height: 5'11" **Weight:** 11.9
This well-travelled striker spent a couple of months at Brentford in the autumn of 2003. However, he managed just one start, in the LDV Vans Trophy tie against Barnet and failed to impress in his first-team appearances. He was subsequently released before the end of the year.
Brentford *(Free from SC Austria Lustenaua, Austria, ex Mohammedan SC, Bangladesh, Schaffhausen, Rot-Weiss Oberhausen, on 3/10/2003) FL 0+2 FAC 0+1 Others 1+1*

OMOYINMI Emmanuel (Manny)
Born: Nigeria, 28 December 1977
Height: 5'6" **Weight:** 10.7
International Honours: E: Sch
Manny had another frustrating season at Oxford last term and spent much of the campaign out on loan, with two spells at Margate and one at Gravesend. His one

start for the U's came late on against Cambridge as new manager Graham Rix looked to assess his squad. A small tricky winger, he was released in the summer.
West Ham U *(From trainee on 17/5/1995) PL 1+8/2 FLC 0+2 FAC 1+1*
Bournemouth *(Loaned on 30/9/1996) FL 5+2*
Dundee U *(Loaned on 20/2/1998) SL 1+3 SC 0+1*
Leyton Orient *(Loaned on 19/3/1999) FL 3+1/1*
Gillingham *(Loaned on 3/9/1999) FL 7+2/3 FLC 2*
Scunthorpe U *(Loaned on 21/12/1999) FL 6/1 Others 1*
Barnet *(Loaned on 25/2/2000) FL 1+5*
Oxford U *(Free on 10/7/2000) FL 32+35/9 FLC 2+2 FAC 1+2 Others 2+1*

ONE Armand
Born: Paris, France, 15 March 1983
Height: 6'4" **Weight:** 14.0
This talented striker spent time at Wrexham on a short-term deal at the start of last season, showing an impressive level of skill. However, his contract was cancelled due to a breach of club discipline and he later had a brief spell with Conference side Tamworth.
Cambridge U *(£30,000 from Nantes, France on 7/9/2001) FL 18+14/4 FAC 0+2 Others 4+3/5 (Freed on 23/11/2002)*
Northampton T *(Loaned on 10/9/2002) FL 6/1 FLC 0+1*
Wrexham *(Free, following a break from football, on 12/9/2003) FL 2+1*

O'NEIL Brian
Born: Paisley, 6 September 1972
Height: 6'1" **Weight:** 12.4
International Honours: S: 6; U21-7; Yth; Sch
Brian's role at the heart of Preston's midfield ended when he sustained an injury in February which put him out of action for the rest of the campaign. Before that his experience and composure on the ball were of great assistance to the younger players around him, and his distribution created many opportunities for attacks. He demonstrated his versatility by playing at centre half during January's injury crisis and his influence was missed for the rest of the season. His first goal for the club was a flying volley versus Rotherham, and his only other strike came in the FA Cup tie against Reading.
Glasgow Celtic *(Free from Porirua Viard U on 10/7/1991) SL 92+27/8 SLC 6+4/1 SC 10/9 Others 8+3/1*
Nottingham F *(Loaned on 18/3/1997) PL 4+1*

Aberdeen *(Free on 3/7/1997) SL 24+4/1 SLC 4 SC 1 (Transferred to Wolfsburg, Germany on 23/7/1998)*
Derby Co *(Signed on 16/11/2000) P/FL 14+3 FLC 1+1 FAC 2*
Preston NE *(Free on 3/1/2003) FL 39+5/1 FAC 3/1*

O'NEIL Gary Paul
Born: Bromley, 18 May 1983
Height: 5'10" **Weight:** 11.0
Club Honours: Div 1 '03
International Honours: E: Yth
Gary had a frustrating season waiting in the wings for Pompey last term. He featured in the Carling Cup tie against Northampton before joining Walsall on loan at the end of September, showing plenty of energy and commitment in midfield. Soon after his return to Fratton Park he scored twice in the 6-1 win against Leeds, but managed just two more Premiership starts during the campaign.
Portsmouth *(From trainee on 5/6/2000) F/PL 48+30/7 FLC 4+3 FAC 1+1*
Walsall *(Loaned on 26/9/2003) FL 7*

O'NEILL Joseph (Joe)
Born: Blackburn, 28 October 1982
Height: 6'0" **Weight:** 10.12
Joe joined Bury on a season-long loan from Preston North End but he will be disappointed that he managed to start only ten games during that time. He scored his first goal with a diving header against York in September, also netting a last-minute winner at Bristol Rovers the only goal of the game against Northampton. The promising young striker was sidelined by an ankle injury during March and he seldom featured during the second half of the campaign.
Preston NE *(From trainee on 2/7/2002)*
Bury *(Loaned on 8/7/2003) FL 10+13/3 FLC 0+1 FAC 0+1 Others 1+1*

O'NEILL Keith Padre Gerard
Born: Dublin, 16 February 1976
Height: 6'1" **Weight:** 12.7
International Honours: RoI: 13; U21-1; Yth; Sch
Keith appeared as a substitute for Coventry early on last term against Nottingham Forest and suffered a hamstring injury only minutes after coming on. His disconsolate walk to the tunnel would be the last City fans would see of the midfielder and he eventually announced his retirement from the game.
Norwich C *(From trainee on 1/7/1994) P/FL 54+19/9 FLC 8+3/1 FAC 3*

Middlesbrough (£700,000 + on 19/3/1999)
PL 32+5 FLC 3+1 FAC 1
Coventry C (£1,000,000 on 9/8/2001) FL
7+5

O'NEILL Matthew (Matt) Paul
Born: Accrington, 25 June 1984
Height: 5'11" **Weight:** 10.9
It was a disappointing season for the
youngster after his first-team
breakthrough at the end of 2002-03. A
regular on the Burnley bench early on, he
was called into action only rarely and
missed most of the second half of the
season through injury. Matt's pace and
crossing ability, not to mention his long
throw, were skills that the Clarets would
surely have had some use for during a
difficult campaign.
Burnley (From trainee on 2/7/2003) FL 2+9

ONIBUJE Folawiyo (Fola)
Born: Lagos, Nigeria, 25 September 1984
Height: 6'5" **Weight:** 14.9
This giant striker spent the early part of
the 2003-04 campaign developing with
Preston's reserve team before joining
Huddersfield Town on loan. A pacy player
with fine skills in the air, he returned early
to Deepdale with a groin injury. Fola was
later released by North End and had trials
with a number of clubs towards the end
of the season.
Preston NE (From Charlton Ath juniors on
13/11/2002)
Huddersfield T (Loaned on 21/11/2003) FL
0+2

ONUORA Ifem (Iffy)
Born: Glasgow, 28 July 1967
Height: 6'1" **Weight:** 13.10
After spending much of the previous
campaign out injured, this big striker
began the 2003-04 campaign on loan at
Wycombe, where he looked a little rusty.
Next stop was Grimsby where his loan
move was soon converted to a permanent
transfer. Iffy featured regularly for the
Mariners but was then released and
finished the season with spells at
Tranmere and Huddersfield. Despite
suffering a freak knee injury in the warm-
down following his debut appearance for
the Terriers, he recovered to feature in the
end-of-season play-offs.
Huddersfield T (From Bradford University on
28/7/1989) FL 115+50/30 FLC 10+6/4 FAC
12+3/3 Others 13+3/3
Mansfield T (£30,000 on 20/7/1994) FL
17+11/8 FAC 0+1 Others 1
Gillingham (£25,000 on 16/8/1996) FL
53+9/23 FLC 6/1 FAC 4/2 Others 1

Swindon T (£120,000 on 13/3/1998) FL
64+9/25 FLC 4 FAC 2+1
Gillingham (£125,000 on 3/1/2000) FL
69+17/26 FLC 3/1 FAC 4+1/1 Others 3/1
Sheffield U (Free on 4/7/2002) FL 7/1 FLC 1
Wycombe W (Loaned on 20/8/2003) FL 6
Grimsby T (Free on 19/9/2003) FL 18+1/3
FAC 2 Others 1
Tranmere Rov (Free on 27/2/2004) FL 1+2
Huddersfield T (Free on 25/3/2004) FL 0+3
Others 2/1

OPARA Junior Lloyd
Born: Enfield, 6 January 1984
Height: 6'1" **Weight:** 13.0
This young striker made a good
impression when coming off the bench
for Cambridge at Rochdale last August,
and soon afterwards he netted his first
goal for the U's at Cheltenham, finding
the net with a well-taken shot from just
inside the area. However, Lloyd was
released at the end of October and later
played for Braintree, Hornchurch and
Grays Athletic. He was reported to have
signed for Swindon Town in the summer.
Colchester U (Trainee) FL 0+6 FLC 0+1 FAC
0+1 Others 0+1
Cambridge U (Free from trainee on
28/4/2003) FL 1+9/1 Others 1

ORMEROD Brett Ryan
Born: Blackburn, 18 October 1976
Height: 5'11" **Weight:** 11.4
Club Honours: AMC '02
Following Kevin Phillips' arrival at St
Mary's Brett's chances of regular first-team
football were limited, but he was brought
in, to good effect, when both Phillips and
James Beattie were rested, scoring a
double in the home win against Charlton
in December, and a week later, stunning
Liverpool, in a 2–1 victory at Anfield, with
a goal after 76 seconds. An unashamed
grafter rather than a classic striker, he is
nerveless in front of goal, selfless in
providing chances for others, and an
undoubted asset to the Saints' first-team
squad.
Blackpool (£50,000 from Accrington Stanley
on 21/3/1997) FL 105+23/45 FLC 8/4 FAC
5+1/5 Others 7+2/8
Southampton (£1,750,000 on 7/12/2001) PL
44+27/11 FLC 4/4 FAC 5+3/1

ORR Bradley James
Born: Liverpool, 1 November 1982
Height: 6'0" **Weight:** 11.12
Bradley came to Burnley on loan from
Newcastle last January. A strong and
tenacious midfielder, he saw little of the
first-team action hoped for, starting only
one game, the away match at Millwall.

He performed well enough to suggest
that better things lay ahead but was
recalled to St James's Park before his
three-month loan spell had expired. He
was released in the summer.
Newcastle U (From trainee on 12/7/2001)
Burnley (Loaned on 29/1/2004) FL 1+3

OSBORN Simon Edward
Born: Croydon, 19 January 1972
Height: 5'9" **Weight:** 11.4
Simon joined Walsall in the summer of
2003 and missed only three games all
season, playing on for a spell with a
broken toe. His keen tackling made an
immediate impact in midfield and he
scored his first goal for the Saddlers with
a header at Watford in October. In a
traumatic final game he opened the
scoring against Rotherham and was then
sent off as the club slipped to relegation.
Crystal Palace (From trainee on 3/1/1990)
F/PL 47+8/5 FLC 11/1 FAC 2 Others 1+3
Reading (£90,000 on 17/8/1994) FL 31+1/5
FLC 4 Others 3
Queens Park R (£1,100,000 on 7/7/1995) PL
6+3/1 FLC 2
Wolverhampton W (£1,000,000 on
22/12/1995) FL 151+11/11 FLC 7/3 FAC 11+1
Others 2
Tranmere Rov (Free on 22/3/2001) FL 9/1
Port Vale (Free on 7/9/2001) FL 7 FLC 1
Gillingham (Free on 12/10/2001) FL 38+8/5
FAC 2+1
Walsall (Free on 18/7/2003) FL 39+4/3 FLC 2
FAC 1

OSEI-KUFFOUR Jonathan (Jo)
Born: Edmonton, 17 November 1981
Height: 5'7" **Weight:** 10.6
Club Honours: FAYC '00
Jo made excellent progress in his second
season at Torquay, adding better discipline
and awareness to his obvious assets of
speed and trickery. Although occasionally
used out wide, notably when scoring
twice at Bristol Rovers, he established
himself as David Graham's central striking
partner. Jo finished the campaign with ten
goals and a fair number of assists, proof
of a more consistent end product to his
exciting runs at defenders.
Arsenal (From trainee on 18/7/2000)
Swindon T (Loaned on 24/8/2001) FL 4+7/2
FLC 1 Others 1
Torquay U (Free on 18/10/2002) FL
51+20/15 FLC 1 FAC 1+1/1 Others 1+1

O'SHAUGHNESSY Paul Joseph
Born: Bury, 3 October 1981
Height: 6'4" **Weight:** 11.12
Paul missed the opening games of the

2003-04 season for Bury due to a foot injury, but he was quickly back in action and earned an extended run in the team throughout most of the first half of the campaign. A gutsy, spirited midfielder, his fortunes waned following a change in management in December and he was given a free transfer in the summer.
Bury (From trainee on 10/7/2001) FL 27+18/1 FLC 0+1 FAC 2 Others 3

O'SHEA John Francis
Born: Waterford, 30 April 1981
Height: 6'3" **Weight:** 11.12
Club Honours: PL '03; CS '03; FAC '04
International Honours: RoI: 14; U21-13; Yth (UEFA-U16 '98)
A highly talented young central defender who possesses presence, great composure and silky defensive skills, John continued to make his mark in the Manchester United first team with only two Premiership absences from August to December. A leading contender during United's Champions' League campaign, he celebrated his first Premiership goal against Wolves in September, and notched his second against Spurs in December. Though United encountered a tricky spell defensively during the months of January and February, he continued to give some solid performances, and ended the campaign as one of the team's most consistent performers.
Manchester U (Signed from Waterford U on 2/9/1998) PL 62+12/2 FLC 9 FAC 7 Others 18+9
Bournemouth (Loaned on 18/1/2000) FL 10/1 Others 1

OSMAN Leon
Born: Billinge, 17 May 1981
Height: 5'8" **Weight:** 11.0
Club Honours: FAYC '98
International Honours: E: Yth; Sch
One of the few plus points of Everton's disappointing end to the 2003-04 season was the chance given to this goal-scoring midfielder to add to a burgeoning reputation, gained as both a prolific marksman with the Blues' second string and a highly successful loan spell at Derby early in 2004, which saw a string of 'Man of the Match' performances and led to an inquiry from George Burley for a permanent move. Leon lends a nimble and creative presence to the team and he marked his first start for Everton with a typical opportunist goal at Wolves. A slim build hides a committed approach to the game and he will be looking for a regular spot in the Blues' midfield in the future.

Everton (From trainee on 18/8/1998) PL 3+3/1 FLC 0+1
Carlisle U (Loaned on 4/10/2002) FL 10+2/1 Others 3/2
Derby Co (Loaned on 26/1/2004) FL 17/3

OSTER John Morgan
Born: Boston, 8 December 1978
Height: 5'9" **Weight:** 10.8
International Honours: W: 11; B-1; U21-9; Yth
John's career appeared to be going nowhere at Sunderland but last term he established himself as a first-team regular. A diminutive figure who can play on either flank, he contributed five goals for the Black Cats, and his trickery on the ball and crossing ability created numerous opportunities for his colleagues. It was John who came closest to making the Black Cats' fans dreams come true in the FA Cup semi-final at Old Trafford, when his free kick struck the bar in the early stages of the game. He was out of contract in the summer and at the time of writing it was

Leon Osman (left)

uncertain whether he would remain on Wearside.

Grimsby T *(From trainee on 11/7/1996) FL 21+3/3 FAC 0+1/1*
Everton *(£1,500,000 on 21/7/1997) PL 22+18/1 FLC 4+1/1 FAC 2+3/1*
Sunderland *(£1,000,000 on 6/8/1999) P/FL 42+17/5 FLC 7+2/1 FAC 7+3 Others 2*
Barnsley *(Loaned on 19/10/2001) FL 2*
Grimsby T *(Loaned on 1/11/2002) FL 10/5*
Grimsby T *(Loaned on 21/2/2003) FL 7/1*

OTSEMOBOR John

Born: Liverpool, 23 March 1983
Height: 5'10" **Weight:** 12.7
International Honours: E: Yth
This young defender was the only home grown debutant for Liverpool last season. He made an impressive debut in the Carling Cup tie at home to Bolton in December, when he caught the eye with some confident forward runs from right back and held his place for four more games before returning to the reserves. In January he was loaned out to Bolton Wanderers for further experience, but made just one appearance at right back before returning to Anfield in April.
Liverpool *(From trainee on 23/3/2000) PL 4 FLC 2*
Hull C *(Loaned on 13/3/2003) FL 8+1/3*
Bolton W *(Loaned on 2/2/2004) PL 1*

OVENDALE Mark John

Born: Leicester, 22 November 1973
Height: 6'2" **Weight:** 13.2
Mark was first-choice 'keeper for York City for almost all of the 2003-04 campaign. He produced some sound and consistent displays for a team that spent much of the time struggling in the lower reaches of the table prior to their relegation to the Conference. Mark was one of several senior players released by the Minstermen at the end of the season.
Northampton T *(Free from Wisbech on 15/8/1994) FL 6 Others 2 (Free to Barry T during 1995 close season)*
Bournemouth *(£30,000 on 14/5/1998) FL 89 FLC 10 FAC 7 Others 5*
Luton T *(£425,000 on 10/8/2000) FL 44+1 FLC 4 FAC 2 Others 4*
York C *(Free on 4/8/2003) FL 41 FLC 1 FAC 1 Others 1*

OWEN Gareth David

Born: Pontypridd, 21 September 1982
Height: 6'1" **Weight:** 11.6
International Honours: W: Yth
This young Stoke central defender looked to have filled out more and seemed to be a much stronger player last season. He made a couple of appearances from the

bench early on, then joined Oldham Athletic in an extended loan deal in the new year. He impressed at Boundary Park with his rugged, no-nonsense style at the heart of defence. The Wales U20 international signed off with his first-ever senior goal as Latics thrashed champions-elect Plymouth Argyle 4-1.
Stoke C *(From trainee on 5/7/2001) FL 1+2*
Oldham Ath *(Loaned on 16/1/2004) FL 15/1*

OWEN Michael James

Born: Chester, 14 December 1979
Height: 5'9" **Weight:** 11.2
Club Honours: FAYC '96; FLC '01, '03; FAC '01; UEFAC '01; ESC '01; CS '01
International Honours: E: 60; U21-1; Yth; Sch
Liverpool and England's leading striker had something of a mixed season last term, starting out in top form before being laid low by injury, then suffering a goal drought before finishing off on another high. Although the Reds suffered a stuttering start to the season, Michael's own form was good scoring eight goals in the first eight games. However, a series of injury problems including a thigh strain then kept him out of action. Returning to duty in January he took time to find his customary sharpness and went seven games without a goal before finding the net with a trademark effort – a long run followed by an angled dink over the 'keeper – against Manchester City. Having broken his duck he finished the season on a high note with nine more goals, finishing as the Reds' top scorer once more. Michael remained a fixture for his country, featuring in the Euro 2004 finals in the summer.
Liverpool *(From juniors on 18/12/1996) PL 193+23/118 FLC 12+2/9 FAC 14+1/8 Others 48+4/23*

OWUSU Lloyd Magnus

Born: Slough, 12 December 1976
Height: 6'1" **Weight:** 14.0
Club Honours: Div 3 '99
Sheffield Wednesday had high hopes of this experienced striker last term, however although he scored twice on the opening day at Swindon, he only managed to find the net four more times and he eventually joined Reading on loan. Signed to supplement the Royals' attacking options, he became a first-choice striker following the long-term injury to Nicky Forster. The loan period was extended to three months, during which time Lloyd impressed with a string of combative displays in some bruising encounters. He scored two beautifully taken goals in the 2-2 draw at Crystal Palace, and eventually

left Hillsborough permanently on signing a contract with the Royals.
Brentford *(£25,000 from Slough T on 29/7/1998) FL 148+16/64 FLC 3+4/3 FAC 8/2 Others 13+3/4*
Sheffield Wed *(Free on 8/7/2002) FL 24+28/9 FLC 2+1 FAC 3/1 Others 1+1*
Reading *(Signed on 23/12/2003) FL 11+5/4*

OWUSU-ABEYIE Quincy Jamie

Born: Amsterdam, Holland, 15 April 1986
Height: 5'11" **Weight:** 11.10
International Honours: Holland: Yth
Quincy's relaxed style of play belies a steely determination to work hard for the ball and he possesses a whole range of close-control trickery. He started the Carling Cup tie at home to Rotherham in the Second Round and he was back in the team for the first leg of the semi-final with Middlesbrough when he partnered Kanu up front. The talented youngster will be looking for more first-team experience with Arsenal in 2004-05. Quincy also represented Holland at U19 level during the season.
Arsenal *(Trainee) FLC 1+2*

OYEDELE Shola

Born: Kano, Nigeria, 14 September 1984
Height: 5'11" **Weight:** 12.7
A solid and unspectacular right-footed defender, Shola began the 2003-04 season playing in central defence for the Wimbledon reserves and ended it as the club's first choice in the right-back position. He made his debut at Walsall in mid-March and put in a composed performance, not taking too many chances, making all of his tackles when required and rarely venturing over the halfway line. This was a sight to behold for the long-suffering fans who had seen calamity after calamity throughout the campaign, and providing he keeps to the basics he should have a good career ahead of him.
Wimbledon *(Trainee) FL 9*

OYEN Davy

Born: Bilzen, Belgium, 17 July 1975
Height: 6'0" **Weight:** 12.4
International Honours: Belgium: 3
This attacking left back started the first three League games for Nottingham Forest last term before being replaced. He then suffered a knee injury which required an operation and once fit he made his last appearance for the club in a creditable draw against Cardiff in January. Davy was released in March when he returned to Belgium.
Nottingham F *(Free from Anderlecht, Belgium, ex KRC Genk, Paris St Germain, on 29/1/2003) FL 4+4 FLC 1*

Michael Owen

P

PACQUETTE Richard Francis
Born: Paddington, 28 January 1983
Height: 6'0" **Weight:** 12.7
This powerful young forward featured in
the starting line-up for Queens Park
Rangers in the Carling Cup and LDV Vans
Trophy ties, but managed just a couple of
Second Division appearances from the
substitutes' bench. Richard also had spells
on loan at Gravesend and Mansfield,
where he scored with a terrific header at
York before returning to Loftus Road.
Queens Park R (From trainee on 1/2/2000)
FL 13+18/6 FLC 2+1 FAC 0+1 Others 3+3/1
Mansfield T (Loaned on 6/2/2004) FL 3+2/1

PADULA Diego **Gino** Mauro
Born: Buenos Aires, Argentina, 11 July
1976
Height: 5'9" **Weight:** 12.4
This left-sided defender is a great favourite
of the Queens Park Rangers fans. A pacy
player who tackles well and delivers a
useful cross, he was an ever-present in the
side until suffering a broken toe against
Oldham at the beginning of March. Gino
regained fitness and after a successful run
out in the reserves he returned for the last
few games of the season. He was
honoured with a place in the PFA Division
Two team of the season.
Walsall (Free fron Xerez, Spain, ex River
Plate, Argentina, via trial at Bristol Rov, on
11/11/1999) FL 23+2 FAC 2
Wigan Ath (Free on 21/7/2000) FL 2+2 FLC
0+1 FAC 2 Others 2/1
Queens Park R (Free on 8/7/2002) FL 53+4/4
FLC 3 FAC 1+1 Others 5+1/1

PAGE Robert John
Born: Llwynpia, 3 September 1974
Height: 6'0" **Weight:** 12.5
Club Honours: Div 2 '98
International Honours: W: 33; B-1;
U21-6; Yth; Sch
Sheffield United's captain missed three
months of the 2003-04 season following
an ankle injury in September, but
otherwise was more or less a fixture in
the side. Apart from the occasional lapse
he produced a series of reliable
performances at the centre of defence,
showing good anticipation and the
ability to tackle under pressure. Very
good in the air in defence, his first, and
so far only, goal for the Blades was a
long-range shot against Norwich. Robert
remained a regular for Wales, gaining
several more caps, but injury meant he
missed the vital games against Russia.

Watford (From trainee on 19/4/1993) P/FL
209+7/2 FLC 17 FAC 12+1 Others 6/1
Sheffield U (£350,000 on 8/8/2001) FL
106+1/1 FLC 7 FAC 11 Others 3

PAHARS Marian
Born: Latvia, 5 August 1976
Height: 5'9" **Weight:** 10.9
International Honours: Latvia: 62
After an injury and illness ravaged 2002-
03 season it was a slow road back to
fitness for Marian, with recurring ankle
and groin problems making his
rehabilitation in 2003-04 a matter of two
steps forward and one back. His
appearances were thus fleeting and,
because of the presence of Kevin Phillips,
restricted to a midfield role rather than
partnering James Beattie in attack, but
his electric turn of pace, tight ball
control and calmness approaching the
goal, to pass or shoot, remains
undiminished. He was fit enough to
represent Latvia in the Euro 2004 finals
in the summer.
Southampton (£800,000 from Skonto Riga,
Latvia on 25/3/1999) PL 105+24/42 FLC
7+2/1 FAC 8/1

Robert Page

PALMER Jermaine Ashley Clifton
Born: Derby, 28 August 1986
Height: 6'2" **Weight:** 11.3
This highly rated young striker was on the fringes of the Stoke City first-team squad last term and made his senior debut as a substitute against Rotherham in April, adding two more appearances from the bench before the end of the season. Jermaine is the son of former Notts County full back Charlie Palmer.
Stoke C (Trainee) FL 0+3

PALMER Stephen (Steve) Leonard
Born: Brighton, 31 March 1968
Height: 6'1" **Weight:** 12.13
Club Honours: Div 2 '92, '98
International Honours: E: Sch
Steve can play either in central defence or midfield and was the club captain for Queens Park Rangers again last term. He started the season in midfield but moved back into the defence when either Danny Shittu or Clarke Carlisle was unavailable. When he did not start the home game with Bristol City at the end of September, it was his first absence since joining the club and ended a run of 101 successive appearances. Steve is able to make up for his lack of pace by reading the game well and marshalling the players around him. He has never been a prolific goal-scorer and his five goals all came when he was playing in midfield. He was released by the club in the summer.
Ipswich T (Signed from Cambridge University on 1/8/1989) F/PL 87+24/2 FLC 3 FAC 8+3/1 Others 4+2
Watford (£135,000 on 28/9/1995) P/FL 222+13/8 FLC 18+1/1 FAC 9+2 Others 7
Queens Park R (Free on 17/7/2001) FL 116+11/9 FLC 3 FAC 4 Others 7+2/1

PAPADOPULOS Michal
Born: Czechoslovakia, 14 April 1985
Height: 6'0" **Weight:** 12.6
International Honours: Czech Republic: Yth
Michal was a replacement for Jeremie Aliadiere in Arsenal's Carling Cup third round win over Wolves, which proved to be his only first-team performance last season. He also featured on the bench a number of times and made 12 appearances for the club's reserve team. He also appeared for the Czech Republic at U19 level during the season.
Arsenal (Loaned from Banik Ostrava, Czechoslovakia on 1/9/2003) FLC 0+1

PARKER Scott Matthew
Born: Lambeth, 13 October 1980
Height: 5'7" **Weight:** 10.7
Club Honours: Div 1 '00

International Honours: E: 2; U21-12; Yth; Sch
It was a great loss to Charlton Athletic when Scott was sold to Chelsea at the end of the January transfer window. Charlton did not want to part with Scott and the reason was obvious as he was the most influential and skilful player at the club. Unable to replace him due to the closure of the transfer window, the Addicks were to win only four times after his departure, having lost only five Premiership games before his sale. Scott has an excellent touch, reads the game well and is a strong tackler. He is very self-assured with good vision, and distributes the ball well, preferring a central midfield role. Scott opened his goal-scoring account for the Blues in only his second match – a nicely-taken left-foot shot at Portsmouth – and was particularly effective in the two-legged Champions' League victory over Arsenal when his work-rate and all-action style on the right flank were big factors in the Blues' famous triumph. Scott made two England appearances either side of his transfer.
Charlton Ath (From trainee on 22/10/1997) P/FL 104+24/9 FLC 8+2/1 FAC 4+3
Norwich C (Loaned on 31/10/2000) FL 6/1
Chelsea (£10,000,000 on 30/1/2004) PL 7+4/1 FAC 1 Others 4+1

PARKER Sonny
Born: Middlesbrough, 28 February 1983
Height: 6'0" **Weight:** 11.12
International Honours: E; Yth
Sonny found himself out of the Bristol Rovers starting line-up in the opening stages of the 2003-04 campaign but enjoyed a good run in the team at right back in mid-season. He scored a superb first-ever Football League goal with a powerful header to ensure a point against Torquay. Sonny was made available on a free transfer during the summer.
Birmingham C (From trainee on 15/4/1999)
Bristol Rov (Free on 18/12/2002) FL 26+4/1 FLC 0+1 FAC 2

PARKER Wesley (Wes) Jaye
Born: Boston, 7 December 1983
Height: 5'8" **Weight:** 10.5
This promising left-sided defender failed to make a breakthrough into the Grimsby Town first-team squad last term and was restricted to just a handful of appearances from the substitutes' bench. Wes was released by the Mariners at the end of the season.
Grimsby T (Trainee) FL 1+8 FAC 1

PARKIN Jonathan (Jon)
Born: Barnsley, 30 December 1981
Height: 6'4" **Weight:** 15.4
This powerfully built striker struggled to make an impact at York last term as a result of injuries and suspension, netting just two goals for the Minstermen. In February Jon moved on to Macclesfield, where he went straight in the first team. Once he had settled he began to use his huge physical presence to good effect, holding the ball up to allow his colleagues to move forward, and falling back to defend when necessary. Ironically Jon opened his account for Macc against his former club, York.
Barnsley (From trainee on 5/1/1999) FL 8+2 FLC 1+1 FAC 0+1
Hartlepool U (Loaned on 7/12/2001) FL 0+1
York C (Free on 7/2/2002) FL 64+10/14 FAC 2 Others 2/1
Macclesfield T (Free on 20/2/2004) FL 12/1

PARKIN Samuel (Sam)
Born: Roehampton, 14 March 1981
Height: 6'2" **Weight:** 13.0
International Honours: E: Sch
Sam enjoyed another fine season for Swindon in 2003-04, forging an effective strike partnership with Tommy Mooney, which brought a combined tally of 42 goals. A knee injury early in the campaign coincided with Town's bad run of form during October and the side struggled without him. A classy finisher who holds the ball up well, he signed an extended contract as Swindon sought to deter the interest of other clubs.
Chelsea (From juniors on 21/8/1998)
Millwall (Loaned on 12/9/2000) FL 5+2/4
Wycombe W (Loaned on 24/11/2000) FL 5+3/1 FAC 0+3/1 Others 2/1
Oldham Ath (Loaned on 22/3/2001) FL 3+4/3
Northampton T (Loaned on 4/7/2001) FL 31+9/4 FLC 2/1 FAC 0+2 Others 2
Swindon T (Signed on 8/8/2002) FL 79+4/44 FLC 3/3 FAC 3 Others 3+1/2

PARKINSON Andrew (Andy) John
Born: Liverpool, 27 May 1979
Height: 5'8" **Weight:** 10.12
After signing for Sheffield United during the close season Andy had a limited involvement early on last term, making just one start, in the Carling Cup, and several appearances from the bench. After a month's loan at Notts County where he impressed with some more exciting displays, he returned to Bramall Lane, making three starts as a hard-working, attacking midfielder on the right. In mid-March Andy returned to Notts County on

loan to the end of the season.

Tranmere Rov (From trainee at Liverpool on 12/4/1997) FL 102+62/18 FLC 15+9/5 FAC 12+2/2 Others 1
Sheffield U (Free on 18/7/2003) FL 3+4 FLC 1 FAC 1+1
Notts Co (Loaned on 15/1/2004) FL 5/3
Notts Co (Loaned on 19/3/2004) FL 5+4

PARLOUR Raymond (Ray)

Born: Romford, 7 March 1973
Height: 5'10" **Weight:** 11.12
Club Honours: FLC '93; ECWC '94; PL '98, '02, '04; FAC '93, '98, '02, '03; CS '98, '99, '02
International Honours: E: 10; B-1; U21-12

One of the few remaining links to the pre-Arsene Wenger days at Arsenal, Ray suffered an injury-plagued campaign last term. He has been a part of the Arsenal first team since 1992 and remains a vital cog in the team's wheel. Always strong in the tackle, a willing runner and combative player, he found his appearances limited by the competition for places in the centre of midfield, yet he remains very much an Arsenal man who adds passion and courage on the field to complement the flair of his colleagues.

Arsenal (From trainee on 6/3/1991) F/PL 282+57/22 FLC 23+3 FAC 40+4/4 Others 45+12/6

PARNABY Stuart

Born: Durham, 19 July 1982
Height: 5'11" **Weight:** 11.4
Club Honours: FLC '04
International Honours: E: U21-4; Yth; Sch

England U21 star Stuart started last term as Middlesbrough's regular right back but his campaign was interrupted by a torn anterior cruciate ligament in his right knee which took four months out of his season. Fortunately, an operation was not required, but on returning to full fitness he was in a losing battle with on-loan Danny Mills for the right-back berth and he found himself called into the team as a cover player helping out in midfield and

Jon Parkin (centre)

defence for the remainder of the season.
Middlesbrough *(From trainee on 21/7/1999)*
PL 29+5 FLC 2+2 FAC 2
Halifax T *(Loaned on 23/10/2000) FL 6*

PARRISH Sean

Born: Wrexham, 14 March 1972
Height: 5'10" **Weight:** 11.8
Whenever he pulled on his Kidderminster
shirt last term Sean was certain to give
100 per cent effort for the team. He
scored the winning goal in Jan Molby's
first game back in charge, ironically at
Sixfields against one of his former clubs,
Northampton Town. A left-sided
midfielder he also figured at left back on
occasion, but was at his best when
allowed to roam free in support of the
attack. Sean was unlucky to be one of
the players released by Harriers at the end
of the season.
Shrewsbury T *(From trainee on 12/7/1990)*
*FL 1+2 FLC 1 Others 3/1 (Free to Telford
during 1992 close season)*
Doncaster Rov *(£20,000 on 28/5/1994) FL*
64+2/8 FLC 3+1 FAC 2 Others 3
Northampton T *(£35,000 + on 2/8/1996) FL*
103+6/13 FLC 8/1 FAC 2 Others 5/2
Chesterfield *(Free on 19/7/2000) FL*
44+11/11 FLC 4/1 FAC 4 Others 4+1
Kidderminster Hrs *(Free on 8/7/2002) FL*
37+19/8 FLC 1+1 FAC 5 Others 2+2

PARRY Paul Ian

Born: Newport, 19 August 1980
Height: 5'11" **Weight:** 11.12
International Honours: W: 2
This talented left winger made a startling
impact when he stepped up to senior
football with Cardiff City last term.
Snapped up from Conference outfit
Hereford United early in January he was
plunged straight into the first team as the
Bluebirds were in need of a left-sided
player to balance the team following the
departure of Julian Gray. He quickly
settled into First Division football and
completed a meteoric rise when he was
awarded his first full cap for Wales
against Scotland, just a matter of weeks
after entering the full-time game. Paul
capped a fine season when he scored the
winner for Wales in their friendly match
with Canada in May.
Cardiff C *(£75,000 from Hereford U on
9/1/2004) FL 14+3/1*

PARTON Andrew (Andy)

Born: Doncaster, 29 September 1983
Height: 5'10" **Weight:** 11.12
This young striker found senior
opportunities hard to come by at
Scunthorpe in the first half of last season,

and in December he was loaned out to
Harrogate Town. A pacy player who can
also operate on either wing, Andy
returned with quite an impact, coming off
the substitutes' bench to volley his first
senior goal in the FA Cup fourth round tie
at Portsmouth in January. However, he
only managed three further substitute
appearances in the League during the rest
of the campaign.
Scunthorpe U *(From trainee on 2/7/2003) FL
1+11 FLC 0+1 FAC 0+3/1 Others 0+1*

PASANEN Petri Mikael

Born: Lahti, Finland, 24 September 1980
Height: 6'1" **Weight:** 12.11
International Honours: Finland: 20;
U21-6; Yth
This Finnish defender joined Portsmouth
during the January transfer window. He
impressed with some consistent
performances, making the right-back
berth his own in the second half of the
campaign. Petri is a versatile youngster
who can also play in the centre of the
defence.
Portsmouth *(Loaned from Ajax, Holland, ex
Haka, on 5/1/2004) PL 11+1 FAC 4*

PASTON Mark

Born: Hastings, New Zealand, 13
December 1976
Height: 6'5" **Weight:** 14.3
International Honours: New Zealand
Mark can look back on his first season in
English football with some satisfaction. He
began as Bradford's first-choice
goalkeeper and used his height well to
command the penalty area and deal with
crosses. However, Mark suffered a hernia
problem which refused to go away and
he was forced to have an operation early
in the new year. He returned towards the
end of the season to play in a couple
more games.
Bradford C *(Free from Napier C, New
Zealand on 5/8/2003) FL 13 FLC 1*

PATERSON Jamie Ryan

Born: Dumfries, 26 April 1973
Height: 5'5" **Weight:** 10.6
Jamie started last term in residence on the
right-hand side of midfield for Doncaster
Rovers, but lost his place early in
September and failed to win it back. He
was one of several players released by
Rovers in the summer and will be looking
to resurrect his career elsewhere in 2004-
05.
Halifax T *(From trainee on 5/7/1991) FL
34+10/5 FLC 0+2 FAC 1 Others 2*
Falkirk *(Signed on 11/12/1994) SL 1+3*

Scunthorpe U *(£18,000 on 12/10/1995) FL
34+21/2 FAC 4+1/1 Others 3*
Halifax T *(Free on 30/7/1997) FL 56+8/17
FLC 3+1/1 FAC 4/1*
Doncaster Rov *(Free on 26/7/2000) FL 7+1/1
FLC 1+1*

PATTERSON Rory Christopher

Born: Derry, 16 July 1984
Height: 5'10" **Weight:** 10.13
This young Rochdale striker had a couple
of brief spells in the first-team squad
early on last season and then reappeared
in the crucial closing games as Dale
successfully battled to preserve their
Football League status. A regular scorer
for the reserves, he was only denied a
first-ever senior goal by the acrobatics of
the Southend 'keeper in the final home
game of the campaign.
Rochdale *(Trainee) FL 5+10 FAC 0+1 Others
1+1*

PATTERSON Simon George

Born: Harrow, 4 September 1982
Height: 6'4" **Weight:** 14.5
This young Watford striker joined
Wycombe in a three-month loan deal at
the start of the 2003-04 campaign. He
made his debut on the opening day
against Stockport and netted his first goal
at Blackpool, using his considerable
height to score with a well-taken header.
He added another goal, but suffered a
serious knee injury after just five games
and was recalled to Vicarage Road early.
Simon was released in the summer.
Watford *(Signed from Wembley on
23/9/2000)*
Wycombe W *(Loaned on 22/7/2003) FL
3+1/2 FLC 1*

PAYNE Stephen (Steve) John

Born: Pontefract, 1 August 1975
Height: 5'11" **Weight:** 13.3
Club Honours: GMVC '95, '97; FAT '96
International Honours: E: SP-1
A solid and reliable defender with a useful
long throw, Steve was an ever-present for
Chesterfield last term until injury put him
on the sidelines in October. Not long after
he recovered he moved back to
Macclesfield and immediately brought
greater stability to the centre of the
defence, playing in both a back-four
formation and as one of three central
defenders.
Huddersfield T *(From trainee on 12/7/1993)*
Macclesfield T *(Free on 23/12/1994) FL
71+6/2 FLC 6 FAC 6 Others 2*
Chesterfield *(Signed on 8/7/1999) FL
146+5/8 FLC 5+1 FAC 4 Others 9+2/2*
Macclesfield T *(Signed on 5/3/2004) FL 13*

PAYNTER William (Billy) Paul
Born: Liverpool, 13 July 1984
Height: 6'1" **Weight:** 12.0
This promising Port Vale striker began the 2003-04 season in fine style partnering Steve McPhee and hitting the target regularly as Vale raced to the top of the Second Division table. A strong-running player who is also useful in the air, he reverted to a wide role on the right when Steve Brooker returned to full fitness, but still gave his all for the team. Billy finished with a creditable tally of 14 goals and also won the club's 'Young Player of the Year' award for the second time running.
Port Vale *(From trainee on 1/7/2002) FL 60+23/18 FLC 0+1 FAC 2+2/1 Others 3*

PEACOCK Lee Anthony
Born: Paisley, 9 October 1976
Height: 6'0" **Weight:** 12.8
Club Honours: AMC '97, '03
International Honours: S: U21-1; Yth
Lee started the 2003-04 campaign in rich goal-form for Bristol City, netting six times early on including doubles in the opening two games against Notts County and Swansea City. Although the supply of goals dried up to some extent later in the campaign, the well-built striker still finished up as City's leading scorer with 16 in all competitions.
Carlisle U *(From trainee on 10/3/1995) FL 52+24/11 FLC 2+3 FAC 4+1/1 Others 6+4*
Mansfield T *(£90,000 on 17/10/1997) FL 79+10/29 FLC 4/1 FAC 4 Others 4/2*
Manchester C *(£500,000 on 5/11/1999) FL 4+4 FAC 1+1*
Bristol C *(£600,000 on 10/8/2000) FL 131+13/54 FLC 4/3 FAC 11/1 Others 16/5*

PEAD Craig George
Born: Bromsgrove, 15 September 1981
Height: 5'9" **Weight:** 11.6
International Honours: E: Yth
After an excellent season as a full back in 2002-03 Craig was given little opportunity to shine at Coventry last term. He started a handful of games at right back towards the end of the year and scored an excellent long-range winning goal after coming off the bench against Wimbledon. Craig's only other start was in his more familiar central-midfield position against Norwich in February, his other appearances coming as a substitute.
Coventry C *(From trainee on 17/9/1998) FL 24+18/3 FLC 1 FAC 2*

PEARCE Allan David
Born: Wellington, New Zealand, 7 April 1983
Height: 5'10" **Weight:** 11.5
International Honours: New Zealand: U23; Yth
Allan found it difficult to force his way into Lincoln City's first-team squad because of the competition among strikers for places. He spent most of the season in the reserves with his senior chances restricted to just five appearances from the substitutes' bench. During the season Allan gained further international experience with New Zealand but was released at the end of the campaign.
Lincoln C *(From trainee at Barnsley on 25/10/2002) FL 9+10/1 FLC 0+1 Others 0+1*

PEARCE Dennis Anthony
Born: Wolverhampton, 10 September 1974
Height: 5'10" **Weight:** 11.0
Club Honours: Div 3 '98
Dennis had another disappointing time with injuries for Peterborough last term and his only appearance in the starting line-up came against Oldham in October. At the turn of the year his contract was cancelled by mutual consent and he left the club. When fully fit Dennis is a dependable full back who is comfortable on the ball.
Aston Villa *(From trainee on 7/6/1993)*
Wolverhampton W *(Free on 3/7/1995) FL 7+2 FLC 1 FAC 1*
Notts Co *(Free on 21/7/1997) FL 108+10/3 FLC 7+1 FAC 12+1 Others 3*
Peterborough U *(Free on 10/5/2001) FL 11+3 FLC 1 FAC 1*

PEARCE Ian Anthony
Born: Bury St Edmunds, 7 May 1974
Height: 6'3" **Weight:** 14.4
Club Honours: PL '95
International Honours: E: U21-3; Yth
As West Ham fought to regain Premiership status Ian was solid and reliable at the heart of the defence. Used mainly as a central defender he scored the winner against Sunderland in December, but was then surprisingly moved out to Fulham, with the Hammers receiving Andy Melville in return. Ian produced some excellent defensive performances for the West London club, notably at Liverpool and Bolton. His presence was also notable at the other end of the field where he caused havoc amongst opposing defenders at corners.
Chelsea *(From juniors on 1/8/1991) F/PL 0+4 Others 0+1*
Blackburn Rov *(£300,000 on 4/10/1993) PL*

43+19/2 FLC 4+4/1 FAC 1+2 Others 6+1
West Ham U *(£1,600,000 + on 19/9/1997) P/FL 135+7/9 FLC 8 FAC 10+1/1 Others 1+1*
Fulham *(£400,000 + on 23/1/2004) PL 12+1*

PEARSON Gary
Born: Seaham, 7 December 1976
Height: 5'10" **Weight:** 12.5
This strong-tackling central defender enjoyed a run in the Darlington first team in the opening stages of 2003-04, but figured only as a substitute during the remainder of the campaign after struggling with injury problems. His robust tackling and committed play certainly bolstered the defence when it needed it and he contributed a single goal, netting at Rochdale in August.
Sheffield U *(From trainee on 3/7/1995. Free to Stalybridge Celtic on 22/3/1996)*
Darlington *(Signed from Durham C, ex Gateshead, Spennymoor U, Seaham RS, Whitby T, on 8/8/2001) FL 39+9/3 FAC 1+2 Others 1*

PEAT Nathan Neil Martin
Born: Hull, 19 September 1982
Height: 5'9" **Weight:** 10.9
With Hull chasing promotion last term, Nathan found opportunities hard to come by. After outings in City's two LDV Vans Trophy ties, he joined Cambridge on loan, making some favourable impressions early on but never really seeming to settle. Nathan returned to Hull and featured from the bench in the home defeat by Torquay when he came on in place of Andy Holt. A left-sided defender or midfielder, he was rewarded with a further contract for the 2004-05 season.
Hull C *(From trainee on 11/7/2002) FL 0+2 FAC 0+1 Others 2+1*
Cambridge U *(Loaned on 24/12/2003) FL 3+3*

PEDERSEN Henrik
Born: Denmark, 10 June 1975
Height: 6'1" **Weight:** 13.5
International Honours: Denmark: 1
Henrik began the 2003-04 campaign in the Bolton first team, but after just four games found himself confined to the bench for much of the first half of the season. The arrival of Javi Moreno in January seemed to push him further down the pecking order, to such an extent that Henrik hinted that he may have to ply his trade elsewhere. However, a recall to the starting line-up against Charlton at the end of January, and a goal to boot, secured the first-team spot Henrik craved for much of the remainder of the season. A powerful striker, he

317

Henrik Pedersen

contributed massively to Bolton's fine conclusion to the season, scoring four goals in five games and gelling well with Kevin Davies to form an effective strike-partnership.
Bolton W (£650,000 from Silkeborg, Denmark on 11/7/2001) PL 55+22/14 FLC 5+5/3 FAC 4/1

PEETERS Bob
Born: Lier, Belgium, 10 January 1974
Height: 6'5" **Weight:** 13.12
International Honours: Belgium: 2
This giant striker joined Millwall shortly after the start of the 2003-04 season and featured regularly in the line-up before being sidelined by an ankle injury towards the end of the year. His height causes opposition defences all kinds of problems, while he holds the ball up well and has a good shot with either foot. His first goal was a last-gap equaliser against Crystal Palace at home, which was well received by the Millwall faithful.
Millwall (Signed from Vitesse Arnhem, Holland, ex Lierse, Roda JC, on 19/8/2003) FL 16+4/3

PEJIC Shaun Melvyn
Born: Hereford, 16 November 1982
Height: 6'1" **Weight:** 12.3
International Honours: W: U21-6; Yth
Shaun was an ever-present in the Wrexham starting line-up early on last term, but was then rested before returning towards the end of the year. However, he was hampered by injuries in the second half of the campaign which restricted his appearances. A calm, assured defender, he missed the final run-in after suffering a hairline fracture of his fibia. Shaun also featured for Wales at U21 level during the season.
Wrexham (From trainee on 9/8/2002) FL 55+6 FLC 3 FAC 1 Others 3

PEMBERTON Martin Calvin
Born: Bradford, 1 February 1976
Height: 5'11" **Weight:** 12.6
Martin found it hard to break into the Stockport County line-up last term and only managed a handful of starts. The experienced left back went out on loan to Rochdale in January, but lasted just an hour against Yeovil before being forced off by a back injury. Unable to shake it off he returned to Edgeley Park without playing any further part in Dale's campaign.
Oldham Ath (From trainee on 22/7/1994) FL 0+5 FLC 0+1 Others 0+1
Doncaster Rov (Free on 21/3/1997) FL 33+2/2 FLC 0+1

Scunthorpe U (Free on 26/3/1998) FL 3+3
Hartlepool U (Free on 3/7/1998) FL 0+4 FLC 0+1 (Free to Harrogate T on 30/9/1998)
Mansfield T (£10,000 + from Bradford PA on 3/8/2000) FL 49+7/5 FLC 1 FAC 2+1 Others 2
Stockport Co (Free on 30/4/2002) FL 20+6 FLC 2+1 FAC 1 Others 1+1
Rochdale (Loaned on 9/1/2004) FL 1

PEMBRIDGE Mark Anthony
Born: Merthyr Tydfil, 29 November 1970
Height: 5'8" **Weight:** 12.0
International Honours: W: 51; B-2; U21-1; Sch
Mark made a handful of early-season appearances for Everton before moving to Fulham, but the West London club did not see the best of him last term. He quickly established himself in the squad until he was injured against Liverpool in November, causing him to be absent for three months. Upon his return he went straight back into the side and scored his first goal for the club from a free kick at Chelsea. An industrious midfielder with a firm tackle and an explosive shot, he managed just a few appearances before he suffered a recurrence of a calf problem which kept him out for the remainder of the season. Mark continued to feature in the Wales international set-up when fit.
Luton T (From trainee on 1/7/1989) FL 60/6 FLC 2 FAC 4 Others 4
Derby Co (£1,250,000 on 2/6/1992) FL 108+2/28 FLC 9/1 FAC 6/3 Others 15/5
Sheffield Wed (£900,000 on 19/7/1995) PL 88+5/11 FLC 6/1 FAC 7/1 Others 1 (Free to Benfica, Portugal on 1/7/1998)
Everton (£800,000 on 6/8/1999) PL 82+9/4 FLC 1 FAC 8+1
Fulham (£500,000 + on 1/9/2003) PL 9+3/1 FLC 1 FAC 0+2

PENFORD Thomas (Tom) James
Born: Leeds, 5 January 1985
Height: 5'10" **Weight:** 11.3
This promising young central midfielder is not short of confidence despite his lack of big-match experience. Tom started the last three matches of Bradford's season and showed a willingness to look for the ball. He was not frightened to perform a trick or two or set off on a dribble and his attitude bodes well for the future. He was unlucky not to score his first senior goal in the final game at Millwall when a first-time shot from the edge of the penalty area struck the bar.
Bradford C (Trainee) FL 3+4

PENNANT Jermaine
Born: Nottingham, 15 January 1983
Height: 5'6" **Weight:** 10.0
Club Honours: FAYC '00, '01
International Honours: E: U21-19; Yth; Sch
Peter Reid took advantage of the new rule allowing loans between Premiership clubs by recruiting the Arsenal protégé for Leeds on a two-month loan deal last August. Jermaine ended up staying the whole season and was the only one of the many loan signings to remain in the first team following the arrival of new manager Eddie Gray. Highly praised by Gray he showed glimpses of brilliance including a sublime goal in the 1-1 draw against Chelsea in December. In a season of struggle Jermaine showed himself as an intelligent and skilful winger.
Notts Co (Associated Schoolboy) FAC 0+1 Others 0+1
Arsenal (From trainee on 16/3/2000, having been signed for £1,500,000 on 14/1/1999) PL 1+4/3 FLC 5+1 Others 0+3
Watford (Loaned on 10/11/2002) FL 9/2
Watford (Loaned on 15/11/2002) FL 12 FAC 2/1
Leeds U (Loaned on 20/8/2003) PL 34+2/2

PERICARD Vincent
Born: Efok, Cameroon, 3 October 1982
Height: 6'1" **Weight:** 13.8
Club Honours: Div 1 '03
Vincent had a very frustrating season at Portsmouth last term when hampered by a troublesome thigh injury. His only start came in the Carling Cup tie against Northampton and his Premiership outings all came from the substitutes' bench. At his best he is a pacy young striker with a good eye for goal. After a long rehabilitation programme, he hopes to feature more regularly in the 2004-05 campaign.
Portsmouth (£400,000 from Juventus, Italy on 22/7/2002) F/PL 18+20/9 FLC 2+1/1 FAC 0+1

PERPETUINI David Peter
Born: Hitchin, 26 September 1979
Height: 5'8" **Weight:** 10.8
David was a regular for Gillingham last term until being sidelined by a cruciate knee injury, which cut short his season. Prior to that he produced some solid performances for the First Division side. A talented left-sided player, he added balance and width to the side and he scored the club's 'Goal of the Season' in the 1-1 draw at Crewe at the beginning of December.
Watford (From trainee on 3/7/1997) P/FL 17+2/1 FLC 1+1

Gillingham (£100,000 on 9/8/2001) FL
52+31/5 FLC 4+3 FAC 4

PERRETT Russell (Russ)
Born: Barton on Sea, 18 June 1973
Height: 6'3" **Weight:** 13.2
This experienced defender had a rather
frustrating time at Luton last term, and
after returning from injury he managed
just a handful of appearances before
being sidelined once more. The highpoint
of his season came when he scored in
successive games against Tranmere and
Wycombe in October. The classy centre
half was reported to have signed a new
contract in the summer.
Portsmouth (Signed from Lymington on
30/9/1995) FL 66+6/2 FLC 5 FAC 4
Cardiff C (£10,000 on 21/7/1999) FL 28+1/1
FAC 5/1 Others 1
Luton T (Free on 10/8/2001) FL 63+3/7 FLC 3
FAC 1

PERRY Christopher (Chris)
John
Born: Carshalton, 26 April 1973
Height: 5'8" **Weight:** 11.1
Chris initially signed on loan for Charlton
to cover for the injured central defenders
Richard Rufus and Gary Rowett, but the
transfer was made permanent in
December. He put in some steady
performances in the heart of the defence
alongside both Mark Fish and Jon
Fortune, keeping the promising Fortune
out of the side at times. Although not
very tall for a central defender, Chris is
good in the air and is a strong tackler. He
has good ball control and passing ability,
and also reads the game well. He scored
his only goal of the season with a
powerful header against his old club,
Tottenham, at the Valley in February.
Wimbledon (From trainee on 2/7/1991) PL
158+9/2 FLC 21 FAC 24/1
Tottenham H (£4,000,000 on 7/7/1999) PL
111+9/3 FLC 13 FAC 9 Others 4/1
Charlton Ath (£100,000 on 1/9/2003) PL
25+4/1 FLC 1 FAC 1

PESCHISOLIDO Paolo (Paul)
Pasquale
Born: Scarborough, Canada, 25 May
1971
Height: 5'7" **Weight:** 10.12
Club Honours: Div 2 '99
International Honours: Canada: 51;
U23-11; Yth
Paul was a regular member of the
Sheffield United squad last term,
although many of his appearances came
from the bench. He played in his
customary striking role, where he

showed his eye for goal, his anticipation
and running constantly causing
defenders problems. His tally included a
hat-trick at Gillingham, but he was
surprisingly allowed to join Derby
County in March. As usual, Paul arrived
with a bang, scoring the winner against
Rotherham in his first game for the
Rams. Previously, he had scored debut
goals for West Brom, Fulham, QPR and
Sheffield United. He followed up with
two against Nottingham Forest, the first
being his 100th in the League, and gave
an energetic point to Derby's attacks,
quickly blending with Marcus Tudgay.
Birmingham C (£25,000 from Toronto
Blizzards, Canada on 11/11/1992) FL 37+6/16
FLC 2/1 FAC 0+1 Others 1+1
Stoke C (£400,000 on 1/8/1994) FL 59+7/19
FLC 6/3 FAC 3 Others 5+1/2
Birmingham C (£400,000 on 29/3/1996) FL
7+2/1
West Bromwich A (£600,000 on 24/7/1996)
FL 36+9/18 FLC 4+1/3 FAC 1
Fulham (£1,100,000 on 24/10/1997) FL
69+26/24 FLC 7+1/4 FAC 9+1/2 Others 2
Queens Park R (Loaned on 3/11/2000) FL
5/1
Sheffield U (Loaned on 19/1/2001) FL 4+1/2
Norwich C (Loaned on 22/3/2001) FL 3+2
Sheffield U (£150,000 + on 10/7/2001) FL
35+44/17 FLC 3+5/2 FAC 3+5/2 Others 0+2/1
Derby Co (Signed on 12/3/2004) FL 11/4

PETERS Mark
Born: Flint, 6 July 1972
Height: 6'0" **Weight:** 11.8
Club Honours: NC '01; Div 3 '03
Mark joined Leyton Orient shortly after
the start of last season and quickly
became a fixture in the line-up. A
dominant centre half who is effective
both in the air and on the floor, he
possesses a good touch and can bring the
ball out from defence with confidence.
Mark netted twice for the O's including a
far-post header at Yeovil in January.
Manchester C (From trainee on 5/7/1990)
Norwich C (Free on 2/9/1992)
Peterborough U (Free on 10/8/1993) FL
17+2 FLC 2 Others 2
Mansfield T (Free on 30/9/1994) FL 107+1/9
FLC 5/1 FAC 8 Others 7
Rushden & Diamonds (Free on 3/7/1999) FL
65+2/1 FLC 4/1 FAC 5 Others 5
Leyton Orient (Free on 12/9/2003) FL 39/2
FAC 2 Others 1

PETERS Mark William
Born: Frimley, 4 October 1983
Height: 5'8" **Weight:** 10.10
This diminutive striker had rather a
disappointing season for Brentford last

term when he was in and out of the first-
team squad. He had few efforts at goal
and failed to add to his previous tally,
although he led the scoring charts for the
reserves. Mark moved on to join
Farnborough in March.
Southampton (From trainee on 4/10/2000)
Brentford (Free on 18/2/2002) FL 5+15/1
FLC 1 FAC 0+2 Others 1

PETHICK Robert (Robbie)
John
Born: Tavistock, 8 September 1970
Height: 5'10" **Weight:** 11.12
Club Honours: Div 2 '02
Used mainly as defensive cover for
Brighton last term, Robbie also played a
handful of games in midfield. However,
with his contract up at the end of the
season and a clutch of young defenders
emerging, he was released in January and
joined Dr Martens League outfit
Weymouth. Robbie is a solid defender
who makes up for any lack of skill with
versatility, determination and a rocket-like
shot.
Portsmouth (£30,000 from Weymouth on
1/10/1993) FL 157+32/3 FLC 13+3 FAC 9
Others 2+1
Bristol Rov (£15,000 on 19/2/1999) FL
60+3/2 FLC 5 FAC 1 Others 2+1
Brighton & Hove A (Free on 10/7/2001) FL
44+20 FLC 1+2 FAC 3/1 Others 6

PETIT Emmanuel (Manu)
Born: Dieppe, France, 22 September
1970
Height: 6'1" **Weight:** 12.8
Club Honours: PL '98; FAC '98; CS '98,
'99
International Honours: France: 63 (WC
'98, UEFA '00)
One of the first departures from Stamford
Bridge in the summer of 2004 was Manu
Petit whose final season was marred by a
knee and thigh injuries which restricted
him to just four starts. His last match for
the club was at Blackburn when he went
out on a high, putting in a superb
performance where he bossed midfield in
his own inimitable fashion. One incident
in particular was vintage Petit – he won
the ball with a crunching tackle and slid
an inch-perfect left-footed pass to Frank
Lampard who buried his second goal of
the match.
Arsenal (£3,500,000 from AS Monaco,
France, ex ES Argues, on 25/6/1997) PL
82+3/9 FLC 3 FAC 13/2 Others 16+1
(£15,000,000 to Barcelona, Spain on
28/7/2000)
Chelsea (£7,500,000 on 23/7/2001) PL
52+3/2 FLC 3/1 FAC 11+1 Others 5+1

PETTA Robert (Bobby) Alfred Manuel
Born: Rotterdam, Holland, 6 August 1974
Height: 5'7'' **Weight:** 11.3
Club Honours: SPD '01, '02; SLC '01
Bobby found himself out of the first-team picture at Celtic last term, his only appearance coming as a substitute in the Champions' League qualifier against MTK Hungaria. In the January transfer window he joined Fulham on loan and made an immediate impact by setting up the winning goal for Louis Saha in the FA Cup tie against Cheltenham. Used as a squad player thereafter, he appeared mostly as a substitute, his most productive position being as a left-sided midfielder. A player with good pace and an excellent crosser of the ball, Fulham did not pursue a permanent signing.
Ipswich T (Free from Feyenoord, Holland on 12/6/1996) FL 55+15/9 FLC 8+2 FAC 5+1 Others 3
Glasgow Celtic (Free on 10/7/1999) SL 36+16 SLC 3+4/1 SC 3+1/1 Others 14+4/2
Fulham (Loaned on 1/1/2004) PL 3+6 FAC 2+3

PETTEFER Carl James
Born: Burnham, 22 March 1981
Height: 5'7" **Weight:** 10.5
After beginning the 2003-04 season in Portsmouth's reserves, this small but surprisingly combative midfielder joined Southend United on loan early in the new year. Carl added a degree of grit to the centre of the park for the Blues until his season was cruelly ended after suffering a bad ankle injury at Huddersfield's McAlpine Stadium. He was released by Pompey at the end of the campaign and was reported to have signed a permanent deal with the Roots Hall club.
Portsmouth (From trainee on 23/11/1998) FL 1+2
Exeter C (Loaned on 21/10/2002) FL 30+1/1 FAC 4 Others 2
Southend U (Loaned on 10/2/2004) FL 11 Others 1+2

PETTERSON Andrew (Andy) Keith
Born: Fremantle, Australia, 29 September 1969
Height: 6'2" **Weight:** 14.7
This much-travelled goalkeeper began last term on a short-term contract with Rushden, but did not feature in first-team action for the Nene Park club. He then had a brief spell with Southend, keeping goal in the home game with Carlisle, but he was only a stop-gap until Daryl Flahavan returned to the club. In January

he signed for Walsall to cover for Jimmy Walker's suspension, but found himself on the wrong end of a 6-1 home defeat by Coventry on his debut. Then after having a splendid second half in the 3-2 defeat at Stoke Andy bravely played on in the 1-1 draw against Crewe despite badly dislocating a finger. He was released in the summer.
Luton T (Signed from East Freemantle, Australia on 30/12/1988) FL 16+3 FLC 2 Others 2
Ipswich T (Loaned on 26/3/1993) PL 1
Charlton Ath (£85,000 on 15/7/1994) P/FL 68+4 FLC 6 FAC 3 Others 2
Bradford C (Loaned on 8/12/1994) FL 3
Ipswich T (Loaned on 26/9/1995) FL 1
Plymouth Arg (Loaned on 19/1/1996) FL 6
Colchester U (Loaned on 8/3/1996) FL 5
Portsmouth (Loaned on 13/11/1998) FL 13
Portsmouth (Free on 5/7/1999) FL 19 FLC 1+1
Torquay U (Loaned on 15/3/2001) FL 6
West Bromwich A (Free on 26/3/2002)
Brighton & Hove A (Free on 9/8/2002) FL 6+1 FLC 2
Bournemouth (Free on 23/12/2002. Freed in April 2003)
Southend U (Free, via spell with Derry C and trial at Rushden & Diamonds, on 19/9/2003) FL 1 (Free to Derry C on 31/9/2003)
Walsall (Free on 15/1/2004) FL 3

PETTINGER Andrew (Andy) Richard
Born: Scunthorpe, 21 April 1984
Height: 6'0" **Weight:** 12.2
Grimsby Town's reserve 'keeper had the misfortune to suffer a broken finger last term and this kept him out of action for four months. Once he had recovered fitness he was thrust straight back into the first team to replace Aidan Davison who was also sidelined by injury. Although he faced the challenge with confidence, any hopes of establishing permanently in the side were ended after three games by another hand injury. Andy was one of several youngsters released by the club in the summer.
Everton (From trainee on 12/5/2001)
Grimsby T (Signed on 24/12/2002) FL 3

PHILLIPS Kevin Mark
Born: Hitchin, 25 July 1973
Height: 5'7" **Weight:** 11.0
Club Honours: Div 1 '99
International Honours: E: 8; B-1
Kevin hit a 25-yard wonder goal after coming on as a substitute at Leicester on the first day of the season – marking a remarkable return to Southampton where he had been rejected as a trainee full

back 12 years before. For the rest of 2003 goals proved elusive, and he scored just twice more – once in the Premiership, and another in the UEFA Cup – but he worked hard with strike partner James Beattie to overcome the limitations of an erratic Saints' midfield. In the new year he began to hit the back of the net with the characteristic ruthlessness which established his reputation, and has seen him touted for a recall to the England squad.
Watford (£10,000 from Baldock on 19/12/1994) FL 54+5/24 FLC 2/1 FAC 2 Others 0+2
Sunderland (£325,000 + on 17/7/1997) P/FL 207+1/113 FLC 9+1/5 FAC 14/10 Others 3/2
Southampton (£3,250,000 on 14/8/2003) PL 28+6/12 FAC 1 Others 2/1

PHILLIPS Mark Ian
Born: Lambeth, 27 January 1982
Height: 6'2" **Weight:** 13.0
This young central defender managed a solitary appearance for Millwall last season, coming on as a substitute in the Carling Cup tie against Oxford. Mark was otherwise restricted to reserve-team football due to the excellent form of the club's regular central defenders and the strength of the first-team squad.
Millwall (From trainee on 3/5/2000) FL 8 FLC 1+1

PHILLIPS Martin John
Born: Exeter, 13 March 1976
Height: 5'10" **Weight:** 11.10
Club Honours: Div 3 '02
Martin signed a new one-year contract for Plymouth in the summer of 2003, but was again beset by injuries and did not make his first appearance in the starting line-up until the end of December. An out-and-out winger, he has great ability on the ball and many of his crosses led to goal-scoring opportunities for his colleagues. However, he failed to make much of an impact and was released in the summer.
Exeter C (From trainee on 4/7/1994) FL 36+16/5 FLC 1+2 FAC 2+2 Others 1+5
Manchester C (£500,000 on 25/11/1995) P/FL 3+12 FLC 0+1
Scunthorpe U (Loaned on 5/11/1998) FL 2+1 Others 1
Exeter C (Loaned on 19/3/1998) FL 7+1
Portsmouth (£50,000 + on 27/8/1998) FL 4+20/1 FLC 2+2 FAC 0+1
Bristol Rov (Loaned on 24/2/1999) FL 2
Plymouth Arg (£25,000 on 11/8/2000) FL 90+24/10 FLC 4 FAC 7+2/2 Others 4

321

PHILLIPS Steven (Steve) John
Born: Bath, 6 May 1978
Height: 6'1" **Weight:** 11.10
Club Honours: AMC '03
This Bristol City goalkeeper is a brilliant shot-stopper and he enjoyed another fine season in 2003-04, helping the defence become one of the most parsimonious in the Football League, conceding just 37 goals in their 46 games. The play-off semi-final at Hartlepool showed Steve at his best, with a series of brilliant saves throughout the game. Selected by his peers as a member of the PFA Division Two side, he was one of three City players to be so honoured.
Bristol C (Signed from Paulton Rov on 21/11/1996) FL 191+1 FLC 9 FAC 14 Others 19

PHILO Mark
Born: Bracknell, 5 October 1984
Height: 5'11" **Weight:** 11.5

A product of the Wycombe youth set-up, Mark made his senior debut at Barnsley as a substitute last February. He made four starts in total, including the final three of the season, and is highly regarded by manager Tony Adams. As a skilful right-sided midfielder, Mark has the ability to take the game to the opposition and make things happen, and can expect to be a key player in the 2004-05 season.
Wycombe W (From trainee on 1/7/2003) FL 4+8

Thomas Pinault

PIDGELEY Leonard (Lenny) James
Born: Twickenham, 7 February 1984
Height: 6'4" **Weight:** 13.10
International Honours: E: Yth
This young goalkeeper came to Watford on loan in September, initially for a month as cover for the injured Richard Lee. However he was plunged into first-team action after Alec Chamberlain was sent off at Crewe and made the most of the opportunity, becoming a regular thereafter. In January he had the unusual experience of playing against his own club, Chelsea, in the third round of the FA Cup, and acquitted himself well. However, he lost his place following the 4-1 defeat at Ipswich in March. Lenny represented England at U20 level during the season.
Chelsea (From trainee on 11/7/2003)
Watford (Loaned on 16/9/2003) FL 26+1 FAC 2

PIERCY John William
Born: Forest Gate, 18 September 1979
Height: 5'11" **Weight:** 12.4
International Honours: E: Yth
Brighton supporters saw the best of John only in fits and starts last term, as his season was disrupted by persistent injury problems, but he showed briefly why he is considered to be one of the most talented players at the club. Able to play in midfield, as a winger or up front, he scored four excellent goals and proved a useful and versatile substitute towards the end of the season as Albion secured promotion via the play-offs. Although out of contract, John showed enough to earn a three-month deal in 2004-05 to prove his undoubted skills at a higher level.
Tottenham H (From trainee on 2/7/1998) PL 1+7 FLC 1
Brighton & Hove A (Free on 20/9/2002) FL 9+19/4 FLC 1 FAC 0+2 Others 0+3

PILKINGTON George Edward
Born: Rugeley, 7 November 1981
Height: 5'11" **Weight:** 11.6
International Honours: E: Yth
This central defender or full back had an excellent season for Port Vale in 2003-04. After a steady start he got better as the campaign progressed and looked equally adept anywhere in the back four (or five). Not too many opposing forwards got the better of George and the Vale hierarchy were well pleased when he signed a new contract. Towards the end of the season he played on despite carrying an injury as it was all hands to the pump for the play-off push which only failed on the last day.

Everton (From trainee on 18/11/1998)
Exeter C (Loaned on 1/11/2002) FL 7 FAC 4 Others 1
Port Vale (Free on 1/7/2003) FL 44/1 FLC 1 FAC 3 Others 1

PILKINGTON Joel Thomas
Born: Accrington, 1 August 1984
Height: 5'8" **Weight:** 10.4
This diminutive but determined midfielder spent plenty of time on the Burnley bench before finally making his debut as a substitute in the home game against Wimbledon in April. A regular in the Clarets' second string for some time, he will be hoping to make further progress in 2004-05.
Burnley (From trainee on 2/7/2003) FL 0+1

PILKINGTON Kevin William
Born: Hitchin, 8 March 1974
Height: 6'1" **Weight:** 13.0
Club Honours: FAYC '92
International Honours: E: Sch
This ever-reliable 'keeper was once again Mansfield Town's first-choice custodian and club captain last term when he was an ever-present in the side. He produced fine penalty stops against Cambridge United and Darlington in successive matches, although on the second occasion the rebound was put in. Kevin is an excellent shot stopper and a fine servant to the club.
Manchester U (From trainee on 6/7/1992) PL 4+2 FLC 1 FAC 1
Rochdale (Loaned on 2/2/1996) FL 6
Rotherham U (Loaned on 22/1/1997) FL 17
Port Vale (Free on 1/7/1998) FL 23 FLC 1 FAC 1 (Freed during 2000 close season)
Wigan Ath (Free, via a trial at Macclesfield, on 31/8/2000. Freed on 4/9/2000)
Mansfield T (Free from Aberystwyth T on 8/9/2000) FL 125 FLC 3 FAC 9 Others 6

PINAULT Thomas
Born: Grasse, France, 4 December 1981
Height: 5'10" **Weight:** 11.1
Thomas did not make the anticipated progress for Colchester last term, even though his season began well with a goal to knock Plymouth out of the Carling Cup. He partnered Kem Izzet in central midfield, but managed just one more goal, in the LDV Vans Trophy tie against Southend. Thomas eventually lost his place to veteran Bobby Bowry and started only a handful of games from February onwards. He was released in the summer.
Colchester U (Free from AS Cannes, France on 5/7/1999) FL 104+29/5 FLC 4+2/1 FAC 10 Others 8/1

PIPE David Ronald
Born: Caerphilly, 5 November 1983
Height: 5'9" **Weight:** 12.4
International Honours: W: 1; U21-6; Yth
This young right-sided midfielder failed to make progress at Coventry last term and only appeared once, as a substitute in the Carling Cup first round win over Peterborough. He was converted into a right-back with some success in the reserves and went on loan to Notts County before signing for the Magpies in April after his Sky Blues contract was cancelled. David impressed at Meadow Lane with his pace, determination and skill.
Coventry C (From trainee on 8/11/2000) FL 11+10/1 FLC 1+2 FAC 0+1
Notts Co (Free on 15/1/2004) FL 18

PIPER Matthew (Matt) James
Born: Leicester, 29 September 1981
Height: 6'1" **Weight:** 13.5
This flying right winger again had his season ruined by injury, a series of knee operations causing him to miss around six months of the campaign. At his best, Matt is an exciting young player capable of scoring goals himself or providing pinpoint crosses for others. He made an appearance as a substitute in Sunderland's FA Cup semi-final defeat by Millwall and almost saved the game for the Wearsiders when his late shot was brilliantly saved by Andy Marshall.
Leicester C (From trainee on 12/8/1999) PL 14+2/1 FLC 1 FAC 0+1
Mansfield T (Loaned on 20/11/2001) FL 8/1
Sunderland (£3,500,000 on 21/8/2002) P/FL 12+10 FLC 1+1 FAC 0+1

PIRES Robert
Born: Reims, France, 29 October 1973
Height: 6'1" **Weight:** 12.4
Club Honours: PL '02, '04; FAC '03
International Honours: France: 74 (UEFA '00)
Robert enjoyed an outstanding season for Arsenal last term, scoring a total of 19 goals in all competitions including 14 in the Premiership. He contributed crucial strikes against Liverpool, both at Anfield and Highbury, as well as the Gunners' away goal in the Champions' League quarter-final. A player of tremendous flair, balance and skill, Robert pleased the fans by getting on the score sheet both home and away against Tottenham Hotspur, helping to inspire a fight back at Highbury and effectively securing the title. He was named in the France squad for Euro 2004

and in the PFA Premiership team of the season.
Arsenal (£6,000,000 from Olympique Marseilles, France, ex Metz, on 24/7/2000) PL 110+13/41 FLC 1/1 FAC 17+4/6 Others 41+3/8

PISTONE Alessandro (Sandro)
Born: Milan, Italy, 27 July 1975
Height: 5'11" **Weight:** 12.1
International Honours: Italy: U21 (UEFA-U21 '96)
This talented and versatile player continues to have his undoubted abilities hampered by an ongoing battle to

Matt Piper

maintain full fitness. At his best the defender is one of the most skilful players at Goodison Park, adding both pace to the Everton back line and impressive two-footed crossing skills when going forward. After featuring in the first-team at the start of the season he required hernia surgery, and ongoing groin problems prevented a prolonged spell in the side until the new year when he returned with a series of stylish performances. Typically a sprained ankle in the penultimate game of the season ended his campaign.
Newcastle U (£4,300,000 from Inter Milan, Italy, ex Vicenza, Solbiatese, Crevalcore, on

31/7/1997) PL 45+1/1 FLC 1+1 FAC 8 Others 7
Everton (£3,000,000 on 12/7/2000) PL 60+8/1 FLC 4 FAC 3

PITT Courtney Leon
Born: Westminster, 17 December 1981
Height: 5'7" **Weight:** 10.12
This tricky left winger joined Luton on loan at the start of last season and featured regularly in the early fixtures, scoring a classy goal in the Carling Cup tie against Yeovil. An injury saw him return to Portsmouth, but once fit again he was back at Kenilworth Road. After a brief spell on loan at Coventry he was released by Pompey and joined Oxford on a short-term deal on transfer-deadline day, linking up with his former coach Graham Rix. However, he failed to make the expected impact for the U's and his contract was not renewed in the summer.
Chelsea (From trainee on 4/7/2000)
Portsmouth (£200,000 on 5/7/2001) FL 29+10/3 FLC 1 FAC 1
Luton T (Loaned on 8/8/2003) FL 11+1 FLC 1+1/1
Coventry C (Loaned on 28/12/2003) FL 1 FAC 0+1
Oxford U (Free on 25/3/2004) FL 5+3

PLATT Clive Linton
Born: Wolverhampton, 27 October 1977
Height: 6'4" **Weight:** 13.0
This hard-working, powerful target man joined Notts County in the summer of 2003 and was just beginning to settle in at Meadow Lane when he chose to move on to Peterborough in the new year. He impressed for the London Road club with his pace, but will probably be disappointed with his tally of two goals for the Posh.
Walsall (From trainee on 25/7/1996) FL 18+14/4 FLC 1+2/1 FAC 0+1 Others 1+6
Rochdale (£70,000 + on 5/8/1999) FL 151+18/30 FLC 5/1 FAC 13/5 Others 7/1
Notts Co (Free on 7/8/2003) FL 19/3 FLC 3 FAC 3/3
Peterborough U (Free on 7/1/2004) FL 17+1/2

PLUCK Colin Ian
Born: Edmonton, 6 September 1978
Height: 6'0" **Weight:** 13.10
Club Honours: FAT '02; NC '03
This brave, solid and committed defender was a key figure for Yeovil Town last term and was a regular in the line-up despite a series of minor injuries. A big crowd favourite, Colin was always a threat from corners and set pieces and netted six goals during the campaign, mostly with powerful headers.

Watford (From trainee on 13/2/1997) FL 1 Others 1
Morton (Free on 4/2/2000) SL 3+1 (Free to Stevenage Borough on 1/3/2000)
Yeovil T (Free from Dover Ath, ex Hayes, on 30/7/2001) FL 36/4 FAC 3/2 Others 2

POGLIACOMI Leslie (Les)
Amado
Born: Australia, 3 May 1976
Height: 6'4" **Weight:** 14.5
International Honours: Australia: Yth
Les enjoyed another excellent campaign in goal for Oldham Athletic last term, establishing a new club record with 19 clean sheets. He underlined his shot-stopping ability with a series of exceptional saves to deny Stockport County all three points at Edgeley Park on Easter Monday. The giant 'keeper turned down an approach from Crystal Palace in February but was out of contract in the summer, in demand and weighing up his options at the time of writing.
Oldham Ath (Free from Parramatta Power, Australia, ex Marconi Stallions, Wollongong Wolves, Parramatta Power, on 22/7/2002) FL 83 FLC 3 FAC 5 Others 3

POLLITT Michael (Mike)
Francis
Born: Farnworth, 29 February 1972
Height: 6'4" **Weight:** 14.0
This commanding 'keeper played a major role in ensuring that Rotherham United avoided relegation last term. Mike once again proved that he is one of the best goalkeepers in the First Division and earned several points for the Millers with some superb saves. He commands his area well and is a brave shot-stopper.
Manchester U (From trainee on 1/7/1990)
Bury (Free on 10/7/1991)
Lincoln C (Loaned on 24/9/1992) FL 5 FLC 1
Lincoln C (Free on 1/12/1992) FL 52 FLC 4 FAC 2 Others 4
Darlington (Free on 11/8/1994) FL 55 FLC 4 FAC 3 Others 5
Notts Co (£75,000 on 14/11/1995) FL 10 Others 2
Oldham Ath (Loaned on 29/8/1997) FL 16
Gillingham (Loaned on 12/12/1997) FL 6
Brentford (Loaned on 22/1/1998) FL 5
Sunderland (Free on 23/2/1998)
Rotherham U (Free on 14/7/1998) FL 92 FLC 4 FAC 7 Others 5
Chesterfield (Free on 15/6/2000) FL 46 FLC 3 FAC 1 Others 4
Rotherham U (£75,000 on 29/5/2001) FL 130 FLC 9 FAC 5

POOK Michael David
Born: Swindon, 22 October 1985
Height: 5'11" **Weight:** 11.10
This young midfielder was a member of the Swindon Town side that reached the quarter-finals of the FA Youth Cup. He made his senior debut in the LDV Vans Trophy tie at Boston in October when he showed some nice touches and an intelligent use of the ball. Later in the campaign he featured on the bench on a number of occasions although he was never called into the action.
Swindon T (Trainee) Others 1

POOLE Kevin
Born: Bromsgrove, 21 July 1963
Height: 5'10" **Weight:** 12.11
Club Honours: FLC '97
Still competent, despite his advancing years, Kevin featured in cup games only for Bolton last season. The veteran 'keeper, considered by many at the club to be the model professional, performed admirably in these games with performances that belied his age. Kevin is aware that he will never dislodge Jussi Jaaskelainen as the club's primary goalkeeper, but he is a more than capable deputy when required for Sam Allardyce's experimental cup squads.
Aston Villa (From apprentice on 26/6/1981) FL 28 FLC 2 FAC 1 Others 1
Northampton T (Loaned on 8/11/1984) FL 3
Middlesbrough (Signed on 27/8/1987) FL 34 FLC 4 FAC 2 Others 2
Hartlepool U (Loaned on 27/3/1991) FL 12
Leicester C (£40,000 on 30/7/1991) F/PL 163 FLC 10 FAC 8 Others 12
Birmingham C (Free on 4/8/1997) FL 56 FLC 7 FAC 2 Others 2
Bolton W (Free on 25/10/2001) PL 3 FLC 5 FAC 4

POOM Mart
Born: Tallinn, Estonia, 3 February 1972
Height: 6'4" **Weight:** 13.6
International Honours: Estonia: 98
This giant goalkeeper enjoyed an outstanding season at Sunderland, with the undoubted highlight coming away at his former club Derby in September. With the Black Cats seconds away from a 1-0 defeat, Mart strode upfield for a corner and headed a stunning equaliser to etch his name into Wearside folklore forever. Mart's agility and bravery have made him immensely popular with the Sunderland fans and he played a huge part in the club's run to the FA Cup semi-finals and the First Division play-offs. He continued to represent Estonia at international level during the campaign.

Portsmouth (£200,000 from FC Wil,
Switzerland, ex Flora, on 4/8/1994) FL 4 FLC 3 (Signed by Tallinn SC, Estonia on 9/5/1996)
Derby Co (£500,000 on 26/3/1997) P/FL 143+3 FLC 12 FAC 8
Sunderland (£2,500,000 on 23/11/2002) P/FL 47/1 FLC 1 FAC 6 Others 2

POPOVIC Anthony (Tony)
Born: Australia, 4 July 1973
Height: 6'4" **Weight:** 13.11
International Honours: Australia: 43; U23; Yth
This steady central defender had a fine season for Crystal Palace last term and was a regular in the line-up for most of the campaign. He forged an excellent partnership at the back with Mark Hudson in the second half of the season which was instrumental in leading the club from the relegation zone to the play-offs. His only goal came in the 3-0 win at Sheffield United in February.
Crystal Palace (£600,000 from Sanfrecce Hiroshima, Japan on 24/8/2001) FL 90/6 FLC 8/1 FAC 5 Others 3

PORTER Christopher (Chris)
Born: Wigan, 12 December 1983
Height: 6'1" **Weight:** 13.2
Chris started last season in the Bury line-up and grabbed six goals in only seven starts as he made a strong claim for a regular place. He scored his first-ever Football League goal at home to Scunthorpe in August and eventually finished up as the Shakers' second-highest scorer with ten goals. The talented young striker was rewarded with the offer of an extended contact, but found himself included on the substitutes' bench for the closing fixtures.
Bury (Free from Queen Elizabeth Grammar School OB, Blackburn on 3/3/2003) FL 19+20/9 FLC 1 FAC 0+1/1 Others 1

PORTER Christopher (Chris)
Ian
Born: Sunderland, 10 November 1979
Height: 6'2" **Weight:** 13.2
Chris made his senior debut in goal for York City last March when he impressed with some sound handling in a goalless draw at home to promotion candidates Torquay United. He went on to play another five games, keeping a clean sheet in the club's final Football League match at Swansea on the last day of the season.
Sunderland (From trainee on 1/8/1998. Free on 8/3/2000)
Darlington (Free from Leiftur, Iceland on 21/3/2002) FL 9+1 FAC 2
York C (Free on 31/7/2003) FL 5

Mart Poom

PORTER Joel William
Born: Adelaide, Australia, 25 December 1978
Height: 5'9" **Weight:** 11.13
International Honours: Australia: 4
This experienced striker had a rather mixed time at Hartlepool last term. After an unsuccessful trial at Bolton Wanderers, Joel was a mid-season signing for Pool manager Neale Cooper. A strong player, and a hard-working forward, he did not get the goal-scoring rewards his performances deserved. He struggled to find the net regularly, but his fine opportunist goal in the play-off semi-final at home to Bristol City gave Hartlepool a hope that they could still reach the final at Cardiff.
Hartlepool U (Free from Olympic Sharks, Australia on 27/11/2003) FL 18+9/3 FAC 1+1/1 Others 2/1

POSTIGA Manuel **Helder** Marques
Born: Povoa de Varzim, Portugal, 2 August 1982
Height: 5'11" **Weight:** 11.0
International Honours: Portugal: 9; U21; Yth
This talented striker arrived at Tottenham with plenty of promise, but injury, fitness problems and then competition from other strikers restricted his appearances at White Hart Lane. Following the departure of Glenn Hoddle he fell behind Robbie Keane and Fredi Kanoute in the pecking order and when Jermain Defoe arrived he slipped even further back. As a result he never really seemed to become acclimatised to the rigours of Premiership football and made only nine starts, not featuring at all after the beginning of March.
Tottenham H (£6,250,000 + from Porto, Portugal on 18/7/2003) PL 9+10/1 FLC 1+2/1 FAC 2

POSTMA Stefan
Born: Utrecht, Holland, 10 June 1976
Height: 6'6" **Weight:** 14.12
After spending virtually the whole of the previous season as an understudy to Peter Enckelman, Stefan remained as the second-choice goalkeeper for Aston Villa last term following the arrival of Thomas Sorensen. He managed just two first-team appearances from the substitutes' bench, replacing the injured Sorensen in the second half of the home game against Bolton in early October and then again in the home game against Wolves in December. Stefan has proved that he is a reliable understudy, but will unfortunately

have to continue to wait patiently for his chance to prove that he he is worthy of the number one shirt.
Aston Villa (£1,500,000 from De Graafschap, Holland, ex Utrecht, on 28/5/2002) PL 5+3 FLC 1 FAC 1 Others 1

POTTER Graham Stephen
Born: Solihull, 20 May 1975
Height: 6'1" **Weight:** 11.7
International Honours: E: U21-1; Yth
This experienced player was used at both left back and on the left side of midfield after signing for Boston United in the summer. However, he was unable to win a regular first-team place despite some solid performances and was loaned out to Shrewsbury before moving onto Macclesfield. He made a positive impact at Moss Rose, featuring at left back or as a left wing back. It was in the latter role that he scored his first goal for Macc in the home match against Carlisle. Graham performed consistently, showing himself to be a good distributor of the ball.
Birmingham C (From trainee on 1/7/1992) FL 23+2/2 FAC 1 Others 6
Wycombe W (Loaned on 17/9/1993) FL 2+1 FLC 1 Others 1
Stoke C (£75,000 on 20/12/1993) FL 41+4/1 FLC 3+1 FAC 4 Others 5
Southampton (£250,000 + on 23/7/1996) FL 2+6 FLC 1+1
West Bromwich A (£300,000 + on 14/2/1997) FL 31+12 FLC 0+3 FAC 1
Northampton T (Loaned on 24/10/1997) FL 4 Others 1
Reading (Loaned on 2/12/1999) FL 4 Others 1
York C (Free on 7/7/2000) FL 108+6/5 FLC 4 FAC 12/3 Others 1
Boston U (Free on 9/7/2003) FL 11+1 FLC 1 FAC 1 Others 0+1
Macclesfield T (Free on 13/2/2004) FL 16/2

POULTER Robert John
Born: Sheffield, 2 February 1986
Height: 6'1" **Weight:** 12.7
A product of the Sheffield Wednesday youth scheme, this young goalkeeper joined the first-team squad last term following injuries to other 'keepers on the club's books. His only appearance came when he replaced the injured Ola Tidman in the LDV Vans Trophy tie against Blackpool and he kept a clean sheet during his brief spell on the pitch. Robert will be looking to gain more senior experience in the 2004-05 campaign.
Sheffield Wed (Trainee) Others 0+1

POUTON Alan
Born: Newcastle, 1 February 1977
Height: 6'0" **Weight:** 12.8

This battling midfielder missed most of the first half of the 2003-04 season as he fought to regain fitness following close-season knee surgery, and his absence was felt as Grimsby struggled at the wrong end of the table. It was not until December that he returned to the squad and proved that he had lost none of his power and tenacity. However, hopes that his return would contribute to an upturn in the club's fortunes were dashed when he was transferred to Gillingham in the new year. Solid, rather than spectacular, he showed the Priestfield fans that he wasn't afraid to put his foot in and was never found wanting in terms of effort.
Oxford U (From trainee at Newcastle U on 7/11/1995)
York C (Free on 8/12/1995) FL 79+11/7 FLC 5+1 FAC 5/1 Others 2
Grimsby T (£150,000 on 5/8/1999) FL 100+21/10 FLC 11+2 FAC 1+1
Gillingham (£35,000 on 17/1/2004) FL 14+5 FAC 1

POWELL Christopher (Chris) George Robin
Born: Lambeth, 8 September 1969
Height: 5'10" **Weight:** 11.7
Club Honours: Div 1 '00
International Honours: E: 5
Chris is a skilful and unflappable left-sided defender, who can play as an orthodox left back or as a left wing back. He lost his place to Hermann Hreidarsson at the start of the season, and apart from a handful of games when the Iceland international was injured in September, didn't return to Charlton's side until April, when an injury to Mark Fish necessitated Hreidarsson playing in central defence. Chris is very consistent and rarely has a bad game. He loves to push forward down the left wing and get in crosses from the by-line, or cut inside. Although his England international days are over, Chris still looks capable of playing at the highest level for at least another season.
Crystal Palace (From trainee on 24/12/1987) FL 2+1 FLC 0+1 Others 0+1
Aldershot (Loaned on 11/1/1990) FL 11
Southend U (Free on 30/8/1990) FL 246+2/3 FLC 13 FAC 8 Others 21
Derby Co (£750,000 on 31/1/1996) F/PL 89+2/1 FLC 5 FAC 5/1
Charlton Ath (£825,000 on 1/7/1998) P/FL 190+10/1 FLC 8+1 FAC 8/1

POWELL Darren David
Born: Hammersmith, 10 March 1976
Height: 6'3" **Weight:** 13.2
Club Honours: Div 3 '99
Darren was a regular in the Crystal Palace

line-up early on last season, but was then sidelined by a torn thigh muscle. The powerful defender spent a lengthy period out of action, but returned to the squad at the end of the campaign and featured as a substitute in the play-offs. Darren scored the vital late goal in the play-off semi-final second leg against Sunderland which took the match into extra-time and ultimately a penalty shoot-out as the Eagles battled their way back to the Premiership.
Brentford (£15,000 from Hampton on 27/7/1998) FL 128/6 FLC 7 FAC 4 Others 10+1/2

Crystal Palace (£400,000 on 8/8/2002) FL 49/1 FLC 7/1 FAC 2 Others 0+3/1

POYET Gustavo (Gus) Augusto
Born: Montevideo, Uruguay, 15 November 1967
Height: 6'2" **Weight:** 13.0
Club Honours: ECWC '98; ESC '98; FAC '00; CS '00
International Honours: Uruguay: 31; Yth
This lion-hearted central striker or attacking midfielder, struggled against injury in what turned out to be his final season at Spurs last term. An undoubted favourite at White Hart Lane, Gus provided creativity in attack and carved a niche position supporting the front two in attack. His 12 starts brought three Premiership goals, but he was released by the club in the summer.
Chelsea (Free from Real Zaragoza, Spain, ex River Plate, Grenoble, Bella Vista, on 15/7/1997) PL 79+26/36 FLC 3+1/2 FAC 8+1/7 Others 20+7/4
Tottenham H (£2,250,000 on 10/7/2001) PL 66+16/18 FLC 8+1/2 FAC 6+1/3

PRATLEY Darren Antony
Born: Barking, 22 April 1985
Height: 6'0" **Weight:** 10.13
A regular in the Fulham reserve side, which he captained for part of the season, midfielder Darren was given two first-team outings as a substitute including a Premiership appearance at Charlton. A tough-tackling midfielder who demonstrates a will to win and is highly rated within the club, he will be looking to gain a more regular place in 2004-05.
Fulham (From trainee on 29/4/2002) PL 0+1 FLC 0+1

PREECE Andrew (Andy) Paul
Born: Evesham, 27 March 1967
Height: 6'1" **Weight:** 12.0
Andy began last term as player-manager at Bury and featured regularly in the starting line-up in the early months of the season before reverting to a place on the substitutes' bench. However, within days of celebrating four years in the post he was on his way out of Gigg Lane and shortly afterwards he joined Carlisle United on a playing contract. He made an outstanding debut against Torquay, scoring early on and inspiring United's first Third Division win in over three months. Andy combined well with his fellow strikers, some of whom were only half his age, but the improvement in performances was not enough to keep the club in the Football League.
Northampton T (Free from Evesham on 31/8/1988) FL 0+1 FLC 0+1 Others 0+1 (Free to Worcester C during 1989 close season)
Wrexham (Free on 22/3/1990) FL 44+7/7 FLC 5+1/1 FAC 1/2 Others 5/1
Stockport Co (£10,000 on 18/12/1991) FL 89+8/42 FLC 2+1 FAC 7/3 Others 14+2/9
Crystal Palace (£350,000 on 23/6/1994) PL 17+3/4 FLC 4+2/1 FAC 2+3
Blackpool (£200,000 on 5/7/1995) FL 114+12/35 FLC 8+2/1 FAC 2+3/2 Others 12/2

Chris Powell

Bury (Free on 6/7/1998) FL 87+81/27 FLC 7+7 FAC 3+3 Others 4+3/2
Carlisle U (Free on 19/12/2003) FL 23+2/3

PRESSMAN Kevin Paul
Born: Fareham, 6 November 1967
Height: 6'1" **Weight:** 15.5
International Honours: E: B-3; U21-1; Yth; Sch
Kevin was again the number one goalkeeper for Sheffield Wednesday last term and is now the third-highest post-war appearance maker for the Owls. He had something of an up-and-down season in 2003-04, disputing the 'keeper's jersey with Ola Tidman and then having a loan spell at West Bromwich Albion, although he made no appearances during his spell at the Hawthorns. Injuries brought his recall to Hillsborough and he then retained his place until the end of the campaign. Kevin was one of 13 players released by the Owls during the summer.
Sheffield Wed (From apprentice on 7/11/1985) F/PL 400+4 FLC 46 FAC 21 Others 7
Stoke C (Loaned on 10/3/1992) FL 4 Others 2

PRICE Jamie Benjamin
Born: Normanton, 27 October 1981
Height: 5'9" **Weight:** 11.0
Club Honours: Div 3 '04
This versatile Doncaster Rovers defender had two short runs in the first team last season, producing some capable performances. Although most of his appearances came at right back, he can take any defensive position and can also play in the centre of midfield if required.
Doncaster Rov (From trainee on 6/8/1999) FL 17+2 FLC 1 Others 1

PRICE Jason Jeffrey
Born: Pontypridd, 12 April 1977
Height: 6'2" **Weight:** 11.5
Club Honours: Div 3 '00
International Honours: W: U21-7
Jason's last-day goal for Hull City against Bristol Rovers not only ignited remarkable promotion celebrations, it also took his goals tally to ten for the term and meant that four Tigers' players had reached double figures in the same season for the first time since the 1965-66 campaign. Although the right winger added defensive stability to the flank it was his supply of goals that took the eye, most notably when he netted a hat-trick in the top-of-the-table clash against Doncaster last December.

Swansea C (Free from Aberaman on 17/7/1995) FL 133+11/17 FLC 10/1 FAC 4/1 Others 4+1/1
Brentford (Free on 6/8/2001) FL 15/1 FLC 2 Others 1
Tranmere Rov (Free on 8/11/2001) FL 34+15/11 FAC 5/4
Hull C (Free on 1/7/2003) FL 29+4/9 FLC 1 FAC 1/1 Others 1

PRICE Lewis Peter
Born: Bournemouth, 19 July 1984
Height: 6'3" **Weight:** 13.6
International Honours: W: Yth
After being an unused substitute for Ipswich for much of last season Lewis finally made his debut at Gillingham in April when Kelvin Davis had a stomach upset. The promising young 'keeper acquitted himself well and Joe Royle now knows that he would not let him down if he needs to call on him again.
Ipswich T (From Southampton juniors on 9/8/2002) FL 1

PRICE Michael
Born: Ashington, 3 April 1983
Height: 6'0" **Weight:** 13.10
This young 'keeper arrived at Darlington in the summer of 2003 as cover for Andy Collett, but injuries saw him thrust into the first team at the end of September and he retained his place until the end of the season. Michael is a good shot-stopper who possesses a powerful kick and his confidence grew as the campaign wore on.
Leicester C (From trainee on 17/2/2001)
Darlington (Free on 6/8/2003) FL 36 FLC 1 FAC 1 Others 1

PRIEST Christopher (Chris)
Born: Leigh, 18 October 1973
Height: 5'10" **Weight:** 12.0
Chris was not used at the start of last season, but became a regular in the Macclesfield starting line-up when John Askey took up the managerial reins. His introduction into central midfield immediately provided more pace and his hallmark of working from box to box enabled him to move forward and score the occasional goal. When David Flitcroft departed in January Chris was appointed team captain.
Everton (From trainee on 1/6/1992)
Chester C (Loaned on 9/9/1994) FL 11/1 Others 2
Chester C (Free on 11/1/1995) FL 151+5/25 FLC 6 FAC 6/1 Others 6
Macclesfield T (Free on 5/7/1999) FL 140+10/13 FLC 4/1 FAC 12 Others 2+1

PRIET Nicolas
Born: Lyon, France, 31 January 1983
Height: 6'4" **Weight:** 12.10
This tall central defender joined Leicester in the summer of 2003 and captained the club's re s e rves last term, popping up with some crucial goals. Nicolas made his first-team debut in the Carling Cup tie against Crewe, when he gave an a s s u red perfo rmance after appearing as a second-half substitute. Surprisingly, his contract was not renewed as the season ended.
Leicester C (Free from Lyon, France on 29/7/2003) FLC 0+1

PRIMUS Linvoy Stephen
Born: Forest Gate, 14 September 1973
Height: 6'0" **Weight:** 14.0
Club Honours: Div 1 '03
This hard-working Portsmouth defender surprised many critics last term and one several 'Man of the Match' awards for some fine performances. He certainly did not disappoint in any of his Premiership appearances remaining a great favourite of the Pompey fans with his reliable approach.
Charlton Ath (From trainee on 14/8/1992) FL 4 FLC 0+1 Others 0+1
Barnet (Free on 18/7/1994) FL 127/7 FLC 9+1 FAC 8/1 Others 4
Reading (£400,000 on 29/7/1997) FL 94+1/1 FLC 9 FAC 6 Others 4
Portsmouth (Free on 4/8/2000) P/FL 102+4/2 FLC 6/1 FAC 6

PRIOR Spencer Justin
Born: Southend, 22 April 1971
Height: 6'3" **Weight:** 13.4
Club Honours: FLC '97
Spencer was only ever on the fringes of the Cardiff City squad last term and managed just a handful of appearances. A strong central defender who is powerful in the air and effective when he keeps it simple, he was out of contract in the summer and was released by the Bluebirds.
Southend U (From trainee on 22/5/1989) FL 135/3 FLC 9 FAC 5 Others 7/1
Norwich C (£200,000 on 24/6/1993) P/FL 67+7/1 FLC 10+1/1 FAC 0+2 Others 2
Leicester C (£600,000 on 17/8/1996) 61+3 FLC 7 FAC 5 Others 2
Derby Co (£700,000 on 22/8/1998) PL 48+6/1 FLC 5 FAC 4
Manchester C (£500,000 + on 23/3/2000) P/FL 27+3/4 FLC 4 FAC 2+1
Cardiff C (£650,000 on 3/7/2001) FL 72+9/2 FLC 2 FAC 8 Others 5

PRITCHARD Mark Owen
Born: Tredegar, 23 November 1985
Height: 5'9" **Weight:** 11.0
A promising second-year scholar at Swansea, Mark was added to the senior squad for the visit to Scunthorpe United last September after injuries restricted the options available to manager Brian Flynn. A consistent goal-scorer at youth-team level, he had already made his mark in the reserves last term before being given his Football League debut against Cambridge United at the Vetch Field. Mark added a handful of appearances from the substitutes' bench as the campaign progressed.
Swansea C (Trainee) FL 1+3

PROCTOR Michael Anthony
Born: Sunderland, 3 October 1980
Height: 5'11" **Weight:** 12.7
This young striker began the season as a first choice at Sunderland, but ultimately found his path to the first team blocked and was allowed to join Rotherham United in February in a deal which saw Darren Byfield move to the Stadium of Light. Michael scored two goals on his debut for the Millers in the 5-1 home win against Reading and quickly established a good understanding with fellow striker Martin Butler. He was involved in all the goals in the 3-0 home win against Burnley which ensured that United avoided relegation, rounding off the scoring with a cheeky chip shot from the penalty spot to make it three out of three from 12 yards.
Sunderland (From trainee on 29/10/1997)

Michael Price

P/FL 15+23/3 FLC 3+1 FAC 4+2/2
Halifax T (Loaned on 14/3/2001) FL 11+1/4
York C (Loaned on 9/8/2001) FL 40+1/14 FLC
1 FAC 6 Others 1
Bradford C (Loaned on 23/8/2002) FL
10+2/4
Rotherham U (Signed on 6/2/2004) FL
16+1/6

PROUDLOCK Adam David
Born: Telford, 9 May 1981
Height: 6'0" **Weight:** 13.0
International Honours: E: Yth
After a successful time on loan at
Hillsborough during the previous season,
Adam signed permanently for Sheffield
Wednesday shortly after the start of the
2003-04 campaign. Although he suffered
from a lack of service, the young striker
worked hard and the high point of his
season came when he netted a hat-trick
in the FA Cup first round victory over
Salisbury City.
Wolverhampton W (From trainee on
15/7/1999) FL 42+29/13 FLC 4+2/2 FAC
2+3/2 Others 0+2
Clyde (Loaned on 1/8/2000) SL 4/4 SLC 2/1
Nottingham F (Loaned on 19/3/2002) FL 3
Tranmere Rov (Loaned on 25/10/2002) FL 5
Others 1
Sheffield Wed (Loaned on 13/12/2002) FL
3+2/2
Sheffield Wed (Signed on 6/9/2003) FL
26+4/3 FAC 3/3 Others 4+1/3

PROVETT Robert James (Jim)
Born: Stockton, 22 December 1982
Height: 6'0" **Weight:** 13.4
This young Hartlepool goalkeeper was
rewarded for his patience when he was
brought into the side for the second
game of the 2003-04 season, and
immediately earned rave reports for his
performance. One of the real success
stories of the campaign, he was the
recipient of the 'Player of the Year' and
the 'Player's Player of the Year' awards.
Although not the tallest of goalkeepers,
Jim has quickly earned a reputation for his
bravery and agility.
Hartlepool U (From trainee on 3/4/2002) FL
45 FLC 2 FAC 3 Others 3

PRUTTON David Thomas
Born: Hull, 12 September 1981
Height: 6'1" **Weight:** 11.10
International Honours: E: U21-25; Yth
In a season when the Saints' midfield
seriously under performed, David excelled:
hard-running, tenacious and quick witted,
his chief shortcomings being a tendency
to make ill-considered tackles and – until
the last game of the season, in a 2–1

defeat at Charlton – a failure to get on
the score sheet. His versatility saw him
play right across the middle four, but
towards the end of the season, as the
injury list lengthened, he was settled in
the centre alongside the precocious
Yoann Folly, a partnership that promises a
bright future. Another promising
partnership was forged with James
Beattie, with whom he hosts a popular
record programme on the club's own FM
radio station 'The Saint'.
Nottingham F (From trainee on 1/10/1998)
FL 141+2/7 FLC 7 FAC 5
Southampton (£2,500,000 on 31/1/2003) PL
31+8/1 FLC 1+1 FAC 1

PUGH Daniel (Danny) Adam
Born: Manchester, 19 October 1982
Height: 6'0" **Weight:** 12.10
This young Manchester United attacking
midfielder made only one appearance for
the Reds last term against West Bromwich
Albion in the Carling Cup. He will be
hoping to gain further senior experience
in 2003-04.
Manchester U (From trainee on 18/7/2000)
PL 0+1 FLC 2 FAC 0+1 Others 1+2

PULLEN James Daniel
Born: Chelmsford, 18 March 1982
Height: 6'2" **Weight:** 14.2
This young goalkeeper began the 2003-
04 season on loan at Dagenham &
Redbridge. However, in November he was
transferred to Peterborough where he
was required as cover for Mark Tyler.
Although James only started three games
he never let the team down and finished
the season on loan to Heybridge Swifts.
Ipswich T (Free from Heybridge Swifts on
1/10/1999) FL 1 FLC 1
Blackpool (Loaned on 10/8/2001) FL 16 FLC
1 FAC 1 Others 1
Peterborough U (Free on 28/11/2003) FL 3

PUNCHEON Jason David Ian
Born: Croydon, 26 June 1986
Height: 5'8" **Weight:** 12.2
A very left-footed midfielder who can
also play at left back when required,
Jason was given his chance for
Wimbledon at Walsall in mid-March and
immediately impressed with his skill on
the ball and long-range shooting ability.
Given several more opportunities before
the season's end, he became more
involved at set pieces, delivering the
corner that led to his skipper's winning
goal at Wigan, and for one so young
showed amazing maturity in most
situations.
Wimbledon (Trainee) FL 6+2

PURCHES Stephen (Steve) Robert
Born: Ilford, 14 January 1980
Height: 5'11" **Weight:** 12.0
Now a firmly established part of the
Bournemouth side, Stephen again
showed his versatility last term, operating
in both wing-back roles as well as in
midfield. He also maintained his personal
record of finishing on the winning side
every time he scored a goal, including the
match when he netted an own goal
against Luton, only for the Cherries to go
on and win 6-3!
West Ham U (From trainee on 6/7/1998)
Bournemouth (Free on 4/7/2000) FL
151+10/8 FLC 5 FAC 13 Others 8/2

PURSE Darren John
Born: Stepney, 14 February 1977
Height: 6'2" **Weight:** 12.8
International Honours: E: U21-2
Darren struggled to break the central
defensive pairing of Matthew Upson and
Kenny Cunningham at Birmingham last
term. However, when Upson injured his
ankle, Darren got back in and produced
a series of commanding performances,
using his power and presence to make
some good tackles and important
headers. Martin Taylor's signing in
January and Upson recovery put him on
the sidelines again and he required
ankle surgery in April. Darren was
reported to have signed for Premiership
newcomers West Bromwich Albion in
the summer.
Leyton Orient (From trainee on 22/2/1994)
FL 48+7/3 FLC 2 FAC 1 Others 7+1/2
Oxford U (£100,000 on 23/7/1996) FL
52+7/5 FLC 10+1/2 FAC 2
Birmingham C (£800,000 on 17/2/1998)
P/FL 143+25/9 FLC 17+2/2 FAC 6 Others 6+1

PURSER Wayne Montague
Born: Basildon, 13 April 1980
Height: 5'9" **Weight:** 11.13
Wayne was a regular in the Leyton Orient
first-team squad last term, featuring both
as a right winger and at centre forward,
and finished the campaign as the O's
second-top scorer. A tricky winger who
despite his lack of inches is effective in
the air, Wayne will be looking to establish
himself firmly in the starting line-up in
2004-05.
Queens Park R (From trainee on 21/4/1997)
Barnet (Free on 18/8/2000) FL 4+14/3 FLC
1+1 FAC 0+2 Others 1+1/1
Leyton Orient (£9,000 on 27/3/2003) FL
36+12/8 FLC 1 FAC 2/1 Others 1

David Prutton (left)

Q

QUASHIE Nigel Francis
Born: Peckham, 20 July 1978
Height: 6'0" **Weight:** 12.4
Club Honours: Div 1 '03
International Honours: S: 2; E: B-1;
U21-4; Yth
A troublesome knee injury interrupted
Nigel's 2003-04 season for Pompey, but
his 100 per cent commitment to the
cause could not be faulted as he tried his
best among the elite of the Premiership.
A gifted playmaker with an educated left
foot, he scored his only goal at Leicester
with a typical hard-struck shot into the
net from 25 yards. Nigel was called up to
represent Scotland in the summer.
Queens Park R (From trainee on 1/8/1995)
P/FL 50+7/3 FLC 0+1 FAC 4/2
Nottingham F (£2,500,000 on 24/8/1998)
P/FL 37+7/2 FLC 7/1 FAC 1+1
Portsmouth (£200,000 + on 7/8/2000) P/FL
121+8/13 FLC 7/1 FAC 6

QUEUDRUE Franck
Born: Paris, France, 27 August 1978
Height: 6'0" **Weight:** 12.4
Club Honours: FLC '04
Franck missed the first five games of the
2003-04 season because of suspension
carried over from the previous campaign,
but from then on he had a tremendous
season culminating in a Carling Cup
winner's medal and 6 bottles of
champagne (it turned out to be cider,
after all!) from coach Steve Harrison – for
not receiving a red card all season, a bet
the Boro' coach struck with Franck in an
attempt to improve his level of discipline.
He was as cool as a cucumber when he
scored Boro's penalty shoot-out winner
against Tottenham in the Carling Cup
quarter-final in December.
Middlesbrough (£2,500,000 from RC Lens,
France, ex Meaux, on 12/10/2001) PL 88+2/3
FLC 8/1 FAC 9

QUIGLEY Mark
Born: Dublin, 27 October 1985
Height: 5'10" **Weight:** 11.7
International Honours: RoI: Yth
This strong, hard-working forward
produced some excellent performances
for Millwall's U19 and reserve teams last
season and made his senior debut as a
substitute against Ipswich in December.
Mark also represented the Republic of
Ireland at U19 level during the campaign.
Millwall (From trainee on 1/11/2002) FL 0+1

QUINN Alan
Born: Dublin, 13 June 1979
Height: 5'9" **Weight:** 11.7
International Honours: RoI: 4; U21-8;
Yth (UEFA-U18 '98)
This skilful and hard-working midfielder
was a regular for Sheffield Wednesday
early on last term before joining
Sunderland on loan in October. He spent
three months on Wearside, producing
some neat displays on the left-hand side
of the field. Alan duly returned to
Hillsborough, celebrating his return with
the winner at Wrexham in his first game
back. Always popular with the fans for his
wholehearted approach, he was out of
contract at the end of the season and his

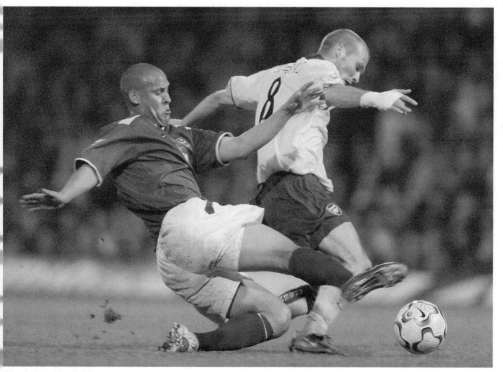

Nigel Quashie (left)

future was unclear at the time of writing.
Sheffield Wed *(Signed from Cherry Orchard on 6/12/1997) P/FL 147+10/16 FLC 14/1 FAC 6+1 Others 2*
Sunderland *(Loaned on 3/10/2003) FL 5+1*

QUINN Barry Scott
Born: Dublin, 9 May 1979
Height: 6'0" **Weight:** 12.2
International Honours: RoI: 4; U21-17; Yth (UEFA-U18 '98)
Barry found himself completely out of the first-team picture at Coventry last term. And in January he joined Rushden on loan. He featured at centre half and left back for the Diamonds but soon returned to Highfield Road, before going out on loan again, this time to Oxford. He impressed in a midfield role for the U's, showing plenty of vision, but was sidelined by an injury for several weeks. Barry was reported to have signed a permanent deal for Oxford in the summer.
Coventry C *(From trainee on 28/11/1996) P/FL 67+16 FLC 5 FAC 2+1*
Rushden & Diamonds *(Loaned on 9/1/2004) FL 4*
Oxford U *(Loaned on 3/3/2004) FL 5+1*

QUINN Robert (Rob) John
Born: Sidcup, 8 November 1976
Height: 5'11" **Weight:** 11.2
Club Honours: Div 3 '99
International Honours: RoI: U21-5; B-1
This hard-working central midfielder featured regularly for Bristol Rovers in the opening stages of last season, scoring against Macclesfield. Thereafter he was often used from the substitutes' bench, although he managed a few games as a central defender and one at right back. Rob was reported to have signed for Stevenage during the summer.
Crystal Palace *(From trainee on 11/3/1995) F/PL 18+5/1 FLC 2+1/1 Others 2+1*
Brentford *(£40,000 on 9/7/1998) FL 98+11/2 FLC 9+1 FAC 6/2 Others 7/1*
Oxford U *(£75,000 on 12/1/2001) FL 23+6/2*
Bristol Rov *(Free on 15/7/2002) FL 67+12/3 FLC 2 FAC 5 Others 2*

QUINN Wayne Richard
Born: Hayle, 19 November 1976
Height: 5'10" **Weight:** 11.12
International Honours: E: B-1; U21-2; Yth
Wayne joined West Ham on an extended loan last September. A left back who can also play in midfield, he stepped straight into the side as a replacement for the injured Rufus Brevett. Wayne gets forward to good effect and puts over some excellent crosses. He was a regular in the side until the arrival of Jon Harley in January after which he did not play for the first team again.
Sheffield U *(From trainee on 6/12/1994) FL 131+8/6 FLC 14+1 FAC 12+1 Others 2*
Newcastle U *(£750,000 + on 1/1/2001) PL 14+1 FLC 1 FAC 0+1 Others 6+1/1*
Sheffield U *(Loaned on 7/1/2003) FL 6 FLC 2 FAC 2*
West Ham U *(Free on 11/9/2003) FL 22 FLC 2 FAC 2+1*

QUINTON Darren Jason
Born: Romford, 28 April 1986
Height: 5'8" **Weight:** 9.11
A member of Cambridge United's successful youth-team squad, Darren was one of several youngsters introduced to senior football by the U's last term. A promising midfield player he made his Football League debut when coming on as a substitute in the closing stages of the match at Leyton Orient on the final day of the season.
Cambridge U *(Trainee) FL 0+1*

Franck Queudrue (right)

R

RACHUBKA Paul Stephen

Born: San Luis Obispo, California, USA, 21 May 1981
Height: 6'1" **Weight:** 13.5
International Honours: E: Yth

After recovering from a bout of glandular fever, Charlton's reserve 'keeper joined Burnley on loan last January as he sought to gain match fitness. He did not appear for the Clarets' first team, but later joined Huddersfield Town, for whom he proved to be a huge success. Paul showed good command of his area and made many top-class saves, being particularly outstanding in the goalless draw at Hull. Paul also did well in the play-off semi-final second leg against Lincoln, and saved the opening Mansfield Town penalty in the shoot-out that clinched promotion from the Third Division.
Manchester U (From trainee on 7/7/1999) PL 1 FLC 0+1 Others 0+1
Oldham Ath (Loaned on 23/11/2001) FL 16 Others 1
Charlton Ath (Signed on 20/5/2002)
Huddersfield T (Loaned on 2/3/2004) FL 13 Others 3

RADEBE Lucas

Born: Johannesburg, South Africa, 12 April 1969
Height: 6'1" **Weight:** 11.8
International Honours: South Africa: 70 (ANC '96)

When your team is struggling, one person you can call on above all others is Lucas Radebe. Unfortunately 'The Chief' suffered another season decimated by injury and his longest run in the Leeds United side was only five games, how sorely he was missed. One of the best defenders to have graced the Premiership he has deservedly been awarded a testimonial at Elland Road, but his contract was up at the end of the season and at the time of writing it seemed likely that he would be moving elsewhere.
Leeds U (£250,000 from Kaizer Chiefs, South Africa on 5/9/1994) PL 179+18 FLC 9+5 FAC 19+2/1 Others 27/2

RADZINSKI Tomasz

Born: Poznan, Poland, 14 December 1973
Height: 5'9" **Weight:** 11.7
International Honours: Canada: 22; U23-3

Tomasz continued to be a regular in the Everton starting line-up without grabbing the headlines generated during a successful 2002-03 campaign. After a goal on the opening day against Arsenal and a run of four goals in eight matches from November onwards, an overall return of eight goals in the campaign bore no relation to the chances presented to him, and he continued to be dogged by inconsistency in his finishing at times. His greatest assets were his blistering pace and high work rate during a season when he was most effective when employed in wide positions.
Everton (£4,500,000 from Anderlecht, Belgium, ex Germinal Ekeren, on 20/8/2001) PL 78+13/25 FLC 2+3 FAC 5/1

RAE Alexander (Alex) Scott

Born: Glasgow, 30 September 1969
Height: 5'9" **Weight:** 11.12
Club Honours: Div 1 '99
International Honours: S: B-4; U21-8

This tough-tackling midfielder was out of the first team for the first few games last term, but soon became a regular again. He scored with one of the most powerful shots of the season at Bolton, which rightly won the 'Goal of the Month' competition, and was instrumental in the dramatic win over Leicester, scoring with a header to equalise as Wolves came back from 3-0 down. Alex then scored in three successive away games in December and eventually finished the campaign as the club's leading scorer with eight goals in all competitions. He was runner-up for the Wolves' 'Player of the Season' award.
Falkirk (Free from Bishopbriggs on 15/6/1987) SL 71+12/20 SLC 5/1 SC 2+1
Millwall (£100,000 on 20/8/1990) FL 205+13/63 FLC 13+2/1 FAC 13/6 Others 10/1
Sunderland (£750,000 on 14/6/1996) F/PL 90+24/12 FLC 12+1/3 FAC 7 Others 0+2
Wolverhampton W (£1,200,000 on 21/9/2001) F/PL 88+19/15 FLC 4+1/4 FAC 2+2/1 Others 2+1/1

RAMMELL Andrew (Andy) Victor

Born: Nuneaton, 10 February 1967
Height: 6'1" **Weight:** 13.12

This veteran marksman spent the pre-season out of action due to a knee operation, but returned to the Bristol Rovers squad in October in spectacular fashion, scoring twice after coming on as substitute in the remarkable 4-0 victory at Darlington. Unfortunately a second knee operation then resulted in Andy having to retire after some 15 years in the professional game.
Manchester U (£40,000 from Atherstone U on 26/9/1989)

Barnsley (£100,000 on 14/9/1990) FL 149+36/44 FLC 11+3/1 FAC 12+1/4 Others 8/1
Southend U (Signed on 22/2/1996) FL 50+19/13 FLC 3+3/1 FAC 2+1 Others 1
Walsall (Free on 15/7/1998) FL 60+9/23 FLC 3/1 FAC 3+1 Others 5/1
Wycombe W (£75,000 on 7/9/2000) FL 69+5/25 FLC 3/1 FAC 12/5 Others 3
Bristol Rov (Free on 27/3/2003) FL 8+4/6 FAC 1 Others 0+1

RAMSDEN Simon Paul

Born: Bishop Auckland, 17 December 1981
Height: 6'0" **Weight:** 12.4

This young right back featured regularly for the reserves last term, but made only one first-team appearance, coming on as a substitute in the dying seconds of the FA Cup tie against Ipswich. Simon was out of contract in the summer and was reported to have signed for Grimsby Town.
Sunderland (From trainee on 7/8/2000) FAC 0+1
Notts Co (Loaned on 16/8/2002) FL 21+11 FLC 1 FAC 1

RANKIN Isaiah (Izzy)

Born: Edmonton, 22 May 1978
Height: 5'10" **Weight:** 11.6

Izzy came into the Barnsley side last October and enjoyed his best spell at the club to date, proving to be sharp in and around the penalty area and scoring six times. However, he then lost his place and after finding it hard to get back in the team, he joined Grimsby Town on loan, the transfer subsequently becoming permanent. Izzy made an immediate impact for the Mariners, scoring after only five minutes of his debut in the home win over Brighton and appeared to have struck up a promising partnership with fellow loanee Lee Thorpe until sidelined by injury. By the time he returned Thorpe had departed and for the remainder of the season injury restricted his appearances.
Arsenal (From trainee on 12/9/1995) PL 0+1
Colchester U (Loaned on 25/9/1997) FL 10+1/5 Others 1
Bradford C (£1,300,000 on 14/8/1998) P/FL 15+22/4 FLC 2/1 FAC 0+2 Others 1+1/1
Birmingham C (Loaned on 19/1/2000) FL 11+2/4
Bolton W (Loaned on 11/8/2000) FL 9+7/2 FLC 2
Barnsley (£350,000 on 19/1/2001) FL 18+29/8 FLC 1+2/1 FAC 2+1/1 Others 1+1
Grimsby T (Signed on 12/2/2004) FL 12/4

Tomasz Radzinski (left)

RANKINE Simon Mark
Born: Doncaster, 30 September 1969
Height: 5'9" **Weight:** 12.11
Club Honours: Div 2 '00
After being on loan at Sheffield United towards the end of the 2002-03 campaign, Mark signed a one-year deal in the close season. He was a regular member of the squad but, due to the form of Stuart McCall and Nick Montgomery, he spent much of the campaign unused on the bench. When called on he filled the role of defensive midfielder with energy and determination, closing down opponents and picking up the loose ball. He was reported to have signed for Tranmere during the summer.
Doncaster Rov (From trainee on 4/7/1988) FL 160+4/20 FLC 8+1/1 FAC 8/2 Others 14/2
Wolverhampton W (£70,000 on 31/1/1992) FL 112+20/1 FLC 9+1 FAC 14+2 Others 7+1
Preston NE (£100,000 on 17/9/1996) FL 217+16/12 FLC 16+4/1 FAC 13/1 Others 6/1
Sheffield U (Free on 27/3/2003) FL 11+8 FLC 1 FAC 0+2 Others 3

RAVEN Paul Duncan
Born: Salisbury, 28 July 1970
Height: 6'1" **Weight:** 12.12
International Honours: E: Sch
Paul headed his only goal of the season for Carlisle against York after just four minutes of the opening fixture. Significantly it was already an equaliser and thereafter it was a season of rather mixed fortunes for this experienced defender. A succession of injuries restricted his contribution to the club, with his final game coming against Darlington towards the end of December.
Doncaster Rov (From juniors on 6/6/1988) FL 52/4 FLC 2 FAC 5 Others 2
West Bromwich A (£100,000 on 23/3/1989) FL 249+10/15 FLC 20/2 FAC 10/3 Others 15/1
Doncaster Rov (Loaned on 27/11/1991) FL 7
Rotherham U (Loaned on 29/10/1998) FL 11/2
Grimsby T (Free on 13/7/2000) FL 21+10 FLC 2 FAC 0+1
Carlisle U (Free on 13/2/2003) FL 24/1 Others 4

RAVENHILL Richard (Ricky) John
Born: Doncaster, 16 January 1981
Height: 5'10" **Weight:** 11.3
Club Honours: Div 3 '04
This central midfield player was a regular in the Doncaster Rovers first-team squad last term, but was often on the substitutes' bench. A tenacious tackler and a hard worker in the centre of the field he had a lengthy run in the first

team in the closing stages of the season when he finally added the one missing dimension to his game: goal-scoring. He netted the winner at Yeovil in March and set Rovers on the way to victory at Bristol Rovers with a fine strike the following month.
Barnsley (From trainee on 29/6/1999)
Doncaster Rov (Free on 18/1/2002) FL 14+22/3 FLC 1+1 FAC 0+1 Others 2

RAWLE Mark Anthony
Born: Leicester, 27 April 1979
Height: 5'11" **Weight:** 12.0
Mark joined Oxford in the summer of 2003 and although not starting the season as a regular became a 'super-sub', coming off the bench on a number of occasions to find the net, with some of his strikes being special efforts. He finished as the club's second-top scorer with eight goals, including an overhead cracker at Kidderminster, a vital header at Huddersfield and the winner on his return to his old club, Southend. Mark played most of his games up front or out wide on the left.
Southend U (£60,000 + from Boston U on 23/2/2001) FL 69+9/15 FLC 2/1 FAC 6+1/3 Others 2/1
Oxford U (Free on 17/7/2003) FL 10+21/8 FLC 1 FAC 0+1

REA Simon
Born: Kenilworth, 20 September 1976
Height: 6'1" **Weight:** 13.2
This talented central defender is a great favourite of the Peterborough United fans. A competitive player who is good in the air, he receives plenty of knocks as a result of his bravery. A regular in the first half of the campaign, he was in and out of the side after Christmas.
Birmingham C (From trainee on 27/1/1995) FL 0+1 Others 1+1
Peterborough U (Free on 24/8/1999) FL 133+12/8 FLC 5+1 FAC 11 Others 6+1

REDDY Michael
Born: Kilkenny City, Ireland, 24 March 1980
Height: 6'1" **Weight:** 11.7
International Honours: RoI: U21-8; Yth
Michael was again unable to force himself into the Sunderland line-up last term and in October he re-joined Sheffield Wednesday in a three-month loan deal. The pacy striker scored a late winner in the LDV Vans Trophy tie against Barnsley, but never seemed to recapture the form he had shown in his previous spell at Hillsborough. He was released by Sunderland in the summer.

Sunderland (£50,000 from Kilkenny C on 30/8/1999) PL 0+10/1 FLC 2+1/1 FAC 0+1
Swindon T (Loaned on 27/1/2001) FL 17+1/4 Others 1+1/1
Hull C (Loaned on 21/9/2001) FL 1+4/4
York C (Loaned on 1/11/2002) FL 10+1/2
Sheffield Wed (Loaned on 30/1/2003) FL 13+2/3
Sheffield Wed (Loaned on 3/10/2003) FL 9+3/1 FAC 2 Others 3/1

REDFEARN Neil David
Born: Dewsbury, 20 June 1965
Height: 5'9" **Weight:** 13.0
Club Honours: Div 2 '91
Neil gave Boston United experience and skill in midfield last term. He appeared on both flanks and in the centre of the park as well as providing some spectacular goals. He combined playing with coaching until the change of management. Shortly after the return of Steve Evans he moved on to Rochdale on a short-term deal. Given squad number 38, to match his age, and continuing to display his skill with crosses and free kicks, his experience of over 900 senior games helped Dale preserve their Football League status.
Bolton W (From Nottingham F juniors on 23/6/1982) FL 35/1 FLC 2 FAC 4
Lincoln C (£8,250 on 23/3/1984) FL 96+4/13 FLC 4 FAC 3/1 Others 7
Doncaster Rov (£17,500 on 22/8/1986) FL 46/14 FLC 2 FAC 3/1 Others 2
Crystal Palace (£100,000 on 31/7/1987) FL 57/10 FLC 6 FAC 1 Others 1
Watford (£150,000 on 21/11/1988) FL 22+2/3 FLC 1 FAC 6/3 Others 5/1
Oldham Ath (£150,000 on 12/1/1990) FL 56+6/16 FLC 3/1 FAC 7+1/3 Others 1
Barnsley (£150,000 on 5/9/1991) F/PL 289+3/71 FLC 21/6 FAC 20/6 Others 5
Charlton Ath (£1,000,000 on 1/7/1998) PL 29+1/3 FLC 2/1 FAC 1
Bradford C (£250,000 on 3/8/1999) PL 14+3/1 FLC 1+1 FAC 2
Wigan Ath (£112,500 on 17/3/2000) FL 18+4/7 FAC 1 Others 5
Halifax T (Free on 16/3/2001) FL 39+3/6 FLC 1 FAC 3 Others 1
Boston U (Free on 3/8/2002) FL 46+8/12 FLC 1+1/1 FAC 1 Others 1
Rochdale (Free on 19/3/2004) FL 9

REDKNAPP Jamie Frank
Born: Barton on Sea, 25 June 1973
Height: 6'0" **Weight:** 12.10
Club Honours: FLC '95; ESC '01
International Honours: E: 17; B-1; U21-19; Yth; Sch
Another season blighted by injury deprived Tottenham of their most talented midfielder and club captain. Jamie is

Jamie Redknapp

undoubtedly a great talent but has become injury prone with recurrences of calf, hamstring and ligament problems. At his best, shown during the relegation battle at the end of the season, Jamie is a playmaker, a striker and a leader and loves to get forward and take on opponents. Spurs suffered as a result of his lack of availability and after signing an extension to his current deal, Jamie will be keen to repay the club's faith in 2004-05.

Bournemouth *(From trainee on 27/6/1990)* FL 6+7 FLC 3 FAC 3 Others 2
Liverpool *(£350,000 on 15/1/1991)* F/PL 207+30/30 FLC 26+1/5 FAC 17+1/2 Others 21+6/4
Tottenham H *(Free on 18/4/2002)* PL 28+6/4

REED Steven
Born: Barnstaple, 18 June 1985
Height: 5'8" **Weight:** 12.2
This promising Yeovil Town defender made his senior debut in the Carling Cup tie against Luton at the start of the 2003-04 season. Steven added a handful more appearances during the campaign producing some competent performances. He is always looking to push forward for goals and was a regular scorer in the club's reserve team last term.
Yeovil T *(From juniors on 26/9/2002)* FL 3+2 FLC 0+1 Others 0+1

REES Matthew (Matt) Richard
Born: Swansea, 2 September 1982
Height: 6'3" **Weight:** 13.2
International Honours: W: U21-4
This young Millwall central defender spent most of the 2003-04 season out on loan, firstly with Conference outfits Aldershot and Dagenham & Redbridge, then joining his hometown club on transfer deadline day. Despite his lack of first-team experience, Matthew impressed with his aerial ability and overall play, scoring on his League debut at Lincoln City. He continued to represent Wales at U21 level, but was released by the Lions during the summer.
Millwall *(From trainee on 19/4/2000)*
Swansea C *(Loaned on 25/3/2004)* FL 3/1

REEVES Alan
Born: Birkenhead, 19 November 1967
Height: 6'0" **Weight:** 12.0
Despite taking control of the reserves for his first season in a coaching role, this evergreen defender remained an important member of the Swindon Town squad last term. If not playing he was a regular on the bench and remained involved in the first team throughout the

campaign, giving his usual wholehearted and committed performances whenever called upon. The visit to Loftus Road in May saw Alan make his 500th senior appearance and there are no signs that he is ready to hang up his boots just yet.
Norwich C *(Free from Heswall on 20/9/1988)*
Gillingham *(Loaned on 9/2/1989)* FL 18
Chester C *(£10,000 on 18/8/1989)* FL 31+9/2 FLC 1+1 FAC 3 Others 3
Rochdale *(Free on 2/7/1991)* FL 119+2/9 FLC 12/1 FAC 6 Others 5
Wimbledon *(£300,000 on 6/9/1994)* PL 52+5/4 FLC 2+2 FAC 8
Swindon T *(Free on 23/6/1998)* FL 184+15/11 FLC 10+2/2 FAC 7 Others 4+1

REEVES David Edward
Born: Birkenhead, 19 November 1967
Height: 6'0" **Weight:** 12.6
Club Honours: Div 3 '95
This veteran striker and hero of the Chesterfield faithful made his 600th Football League appearance in the Spireites' 4-2 win over Queens Park Rangers last January. His experience and enthusiasm were important to the club and its younger players as they fought relegation: his hat-trick in a 4-4 draw with Grimsby turned out to be vital. Age caught up with him at the season's end, though, and his release was met with general sadness.
Sheffield Wed *(Free from Heswall on 6/8/1986)* FL 8+9/2 FLC 1+1/1 FAC 1+1 Others 0+1
Scunthorpe U *(Loaned on 17/12/1986)* FL 3+1/2
Scunthorpe U *(Loaned on 1/10/1987)* FL 6/4
Burnley *(Loaned on 20/11/1987)* FL 16/8 Others 2/1
Bolton W *(£80,000 on 17/8/1989)* FL 111+23/29 FLC 14+1/1 FAC 8+5/5 Others 9+1/7
Notts Co *(£80,000 on 25/3/1993)* FL 9+4/2 FLC 1+1
Carlisle U *(£121,000 on 1/10/1993)* FL 127/48 FLC 9/5 FAC 9/4 Others 23/6
Preston NE *(Signed on 9/10/1996)* FL 45+2/12 FLC 3+1/3 FAC 2/3 Others 1
Chesterfield *(Signed on 6/11/1997)* FL 160+8/46 FLC 10+1/4 FAC 6+1/1 Others 10/5
Oldham Ath *(Free on 19/12/2001)* FL 11+2/3
Chesterfield *(Free on 14/8/2002)* FL 54+17/12 FLC 3 FAC 0+1 Others 1+1

REEVES Martin Lee
Born: Birmingham, 7 September 1981
Height: 6'0" **Weight:** 11.12
This all-action midfield player had a rather miserable time in his first season at Northampton and spent much of the campaign out injured. His best run in the team came in November, but although he

always offered 100 per cent effort he failed to find the net in first-team games.
Leicester C *(From trainee on 1/11/2000)* P/FL 1+7 FLC 1+1
Hull C *(Loaned on 7/3/2003)* FL 5+3/1
Northampton T *(Free on 16/6/2003)* FL 9+5 FLC 1 FAC 2+1 Others 1+2

REGAN Carl Anthony
Born: Liverpool, 14 January 1980
Height: 6'0" **Weight:** 11.5
Club Honours: FAYC '98
International Honours: E: Yth
Carl fell further down the pecking order of right backs at Hull last season following the summer signings of Alton Thelwell and Richard Hinds. His only outing came in the LDV Vans Trophy win at Darlington before going out on loan to Conference club Chester City in December. Carl's contract was cancelled in March and he finished the campaign with Unibond League outfit Droylsden.
Everton *(From trainee on 19/1/1998)*
Barnsley *(£20,000 on 15/6/2000)* FL 31+6 FLC 5
Hull C *(Free on 15/8/2002)* FL 33+5 FLC 1 FAC 1 Others 1

REHMAN Zeshan (Zesh)
Born: Birmingham, 14 October 1983
Height: 6'2" **Weight:** 12.12
International Honours: E: Yth
An impressive defender who is calm in his approach to the game and an excellent distributor of the ball, Zesh featured for Fulham as a substitute in the Carling Cup tie at Wigan, and he was given a further chance in the final minutes of the Premiership game at Anfield in April. He gained useful experience early on in the campaign when he was loaned to Brighton. He was an instant hit for Albion, scoring a cracking goal at Rushden, but unfortunately that was the peak of his success in his spell on the South Coast and his form dipped.
Fulham *(From trainee on 7/6/2001)* PL 0+1 FLC 0+1
Brighton & Hove A *(Loaned on 29/9/2003)* FL 6/2 Others 1
Brighton & Hove A *(Loaned on 14/11/2003)* FL 3+2 Others 1

REICH Marco
Born: Meisenheim, Germany, 30 December 1977
Height: 6'0" **Weight:** 11.13
International Honours: Germany: 1
Marco has a good pedigree: a German cap and a Bundesliga title with Kaiserslautern. He was out of the picture with Werder Bremen when Derby signed

him in the January window. Marco began brilliantly, displaying a classy touch and an ability to go past defenders on his debut, an important victory over Gillingham. Lack of match fitness told and a hamstring injury in March, just as he looked ready to open up Crewe, set him back. Marco was absent for a month and Derby's relegation battle meant he was recalled earlier than was ideal, but he scored against Millwall with a great free kick.
Derby Co *(Free from Werder Bremen, Germany, ex Kaiserslautern, on 16/1/2004) FL 9+4/1*

REID Andrew (Andy) Matthew
Born: Dublin, 29 July 1982
Height: 5'7" **Weight:** 11.12
International Honours: RoI: 7; U21-15; Yth (UEFA-U16 '98)
Andy had an excellent season for Nottingham Forest last term when he was the side's only ever-present and finished as top scorer with 13 goals despite playing mostly on the left-hand side of midfield. He was named as the Nationwide Division One 'Player of the Month' for October and his outstanding form saw him being rewarded with his international debut for the Republic of Ireland against Canada the following month. Andy was named in the PFA Division One team for the season.
Nottingham F *(From trainee on 16/8/1999) FL 96+23/16 FLC 5+2 FAC 4/1 Others 2/1*

REID Levi Stanley Junior
Born: Stafford, 19 January 1983
Height: 5'5" **Weight:** 11.1
Levi made a handful of appearances in the unaccustomed role of full back for Port Vale last term and was then left out of the side. However, he was given his opportunity in a central-midfield role by new manager Martin Foyle and did well, particularly in the final four games of the season. Nothing seems to upset Levi and he will always give everything for the cause.
Port Vale *(From trainee on 1/7/2003) FL 7+5 FAC 3*

REID Paul James
Born: Sydney, Australia, 6 July 1979
Height: 5'10" **Weight:** 10.10
Paul was restricted to reserve-team football for Bradford City last term and on transfer-deadline day he signed for Brighton. The midfielder performed well enough to force his way into the Albion line-up for the final run-in and the play-offs. He was, however, relegated to the substitutes' bench for the promotion

clincher against Bristol City at the Millennium Stadium. A good passer of the ball, Paul looks to have a few goals in him as an attacking midfielder.
Bradford C *(Free from Wollongong Wolves, Australia on 7/9/2002) FL 7+1/2*
Brighton & Hove A *(Free on 25/3/2004) FL 4+1 Others 2+1*

REID Paul Mark
Born: Carlisle, 18 February 1982
Height: 6'2" **Weight:** 12.4
International Honours: E: Yth
Paul had an excellent season at Northampton last term when he captained the side, despite his tender years. A tall, commanding centre back he is effective in the air and sound in the tackle. Paul also enjoyed his trips upfield for set pieces and scored with a text-book header in the home win over Rochdale in February.
Carlisle U *(From trainee on 19/2/1999) FL 17+2 Others 3*
Glasgow R *(£200,000 on 1/7/2000)*
Preston NE *(Loaned on 29/1/2002) FL 0+1/1*
Northampton T *(Loaned on 31/12/2002) FL 19*
Northampton T *(£100,000 on 19/6/2003) FL 33/2 FLC 2 FAC 3 Others 2+2*

REID Steven John
Born: Kingston, 10 March 1981
Height: 6'1" **Weight:** 12.4
Club Honours: Div 2 '01
International Honours: RoI: 13; U21-2; E: Yth
Steven arrived at Blackburn with a hamstring injury and this proved to be the prelude for something of an unfortunate time at Ewood Park, for he then missed four months football with a recurrence of the problem. He never managed to settle in one position, being unable to dislodge Brett Emerton from his role on the right flank, although he looked most comfortable in a brief session at right back. He will be hoping for better things in 2004-05.
Millwall *(From trainee on 18/5/1998) FL 115+24/18 FLC 5+2 FAC 10/1 Others 10+1*
Blackburn Rov *(£1,800,000 + on 30/7/2003) PL 9+7 FLC 1 Others 1+1*

REILLY Andrew (Andy)
Born: Luton, 26 October 1985
Height: 5'10" **Weight:** 12.8
International Honours: S: U21-1; Yth
This fierce-tackling left back made a surprise senior debut for Wycombe at home to Colchester in the LDV Vans Trophy tie last December, covering for the injured Chris Vinnicombe. He produced a

most impressive performance and went on to add several further appearances. Andy was a regular for Scotland U19s during the campaign and also featured for the U21 team. He was rewarded for his progress by receiving the Supporters' Association 'Young Player of the Season' award.
Wycombe W *(From trainee on 2/4/2004) FL 5 Others 1*

REMY Ellis Nathan
Born: City of London, 13 February 1984
Height: 6'2" **Weight:** 13.0
This enthusiastic teenaged striker signed for Lincoln City on a six-month contract and was given his debut when he came on as a late substitute in the opening-day home game with Oxford United. He made only one more appearance as a substitute before being loaned out to Kettering Town in September. The following month he moved on a permanent basis to Grays Athletic.
Wimbledon *(From juniors on 29/6/2001. Free to Hastings T during 2002 close season)*
Lincoln C *(Free on 8/8/2003) FL 0+1 FLC 0+1*

REO-COKER Nigel Shola Andre
Born: Thornton Heath, 14 May 1984
Height: 5'8" **Weight:** 10.5
International Honours: E: U21-3; Yth
Nigel was given the captain's armband by Wimbledon at the start of last season and straightaway showed it was business as usual for the young central midfielder. Always encouraging his team mates even when things were going from bad to worse, it was only a matter of time before the club's administrators cashed in on their number one asset, and that they did early in the new year when he was sold to West Ham. On his debut for the Hammers against Rotherham he sparkled with energy and showed an eagerness to get stuck in. He soon began to stamp his authority on the side and scored his first goal for the club in March against his former colleagues. Nigel also played for England U21s during the campaign.
Wimbledon *(From trainee on 15/7/2002) FL 57+1/6 FLC 2+1 FAC 2+1*
West Ham U *(£575,000 on 23/1/2004) FL 13+2/2 Others 0+3*

REPKA Tomas
Born: Zlin, Czechoslovakia, 2 January 1974
Height: 6'0" **Weight:** 12.7
International Honours: Czech Republic: 46
Tomas played the majority of his games at right back for West Ham last season and

Nigel Reo-Coker

his defensive capabilities improved under new manager Alan Pardew. He has a fierce tackle and gave many solid performances, however, he received a number of unnecessary yellow cards and needs to show an improvement in this area.
West Ham U *(£5,500,000 from Fiorentina, Italy, ex Banik Ostrava, Sparta Prague, on 14/9/2001) FI/PL 103 FLC 3 FAC 5+1 Others 3*

REUSER Martijn Franciscus
Born: Amsterdam, Holland, 1 February 1975
Height: 5'9" **Weight:** 11.7
International Honours: Holland: 1; U21-12
The 2003-4 season proved to be a repeat of the previous campaign for Martijn at Ipswich. His appearances were restricted once again by injury and when he was fit he was often only on the bench. When the midfielder did get some action as a substitute it often changed the course of a game. At Gillingham, for instance, he came on and equalised with a free kick before laying on the winner for Darren Bent with a superb cross.
Ipswich T *(£1,000,000 + from Vitesse Arnhem, Holland, ex Ajax, on 23/3/2000) PI/FL 42+49/14 FLC 5+4/2 FAC 4+2/1 Others 2+6/2*

REVELL Alexander (Alex) David
Born: Cambridge, 7 July 1983
Height: 6'3" **Weight:** 12.0
This young forward had something of a roller-coaster season for Cambridge United last term. He scored two goals early on in the campaign then suffered a groin injury that kept him out until January. Alex returned to action against Bristol Rovers in February, when he scored and was then carried off on a stretcher with a head injury. He was released in the summer.
Cambridge U *(From trainee on 21/4/2001) FL 19+38/5 FLC 0+1 FAC 0+2 Others 1+5*

REWBURY Jamie
Born: Porth, 15 February 1986
Height: 6'0" **Weight:** 12.1
International Honours: W: Yth
This second-year scholar made his first start for Swansea in central defence against promotion-chasing Hull City at the Vetch Field last April, after making an appearance from the subs' bench at Lincoln in the previous match. Also capable of playing as a central striker, Jamie settled into a central defensive position for the Swans U19 side last term, and gaining international recognition for

Wales at U20 level. A youngster who possesses excellent ball skills, both in attack and in defence, he will be looking to gain further senior experience in 2004-05.
Swansea C *(Trainee) FL 1+1*

REYES Jose Antonio
Born: Utrera, Spain, 1 September 1983
Height: 5'9" **Weight:** 11.2
Club Honours: PL '04
International Honours: Spain: 3
Arsenal pulled off a major transfer coup when Jose Reyes arrived during the January transfer window. A pacy and skilful player who is an enthusiastic runner, he made his debut as a substitute in the 2-1 win over Manchester City in February. Later that month he announced his arrival in stunning style as he turned a 1-0 FA Cup deficit to Chelsea into a 2-1 victory, scoring both of the Gunners goals in the fifth round tie. His first goal was a sumptuous long-range strike and he continued to impress throughout the remainder of the campaign adding three more goals.
Arsenal *(£10,500,000 + from Seville, Spain on 30/1/2004) PL 7+6/2 FLC 1 FAC 2+1/2 Others 2+2/1*

REYNA Claudio
Born: Livingston, New Jersey, USA, 20 July 1973
Height: 5'8" **Weight:** 11.3
Club Honours: SPD '00; SC '99
International Honours: USA: 102
Claudio joined Manchester City during the 2003 close season, but he was hampered by injuries in the first half of the campaign and it was not until December that he became a regular in the line-up. An extremely gifted midfield player who commands respect on and off the field, he is a powerful figure who can boss a game when he is in top form.
Glasgow R *(£2,000,000 from VFL Wolfsburg, Germany, ex Virginia University, Beyer Leverkusen, on 31/3/1999) SL 57+6/9 SLC 2/1 SC 6+1 Others 25/1*
Sunderland *(£4,500,000 on 7/12/2001) PL 28/3 FLC 1/1*
Manchester C *(£2,500,000 on 29/8/2003) PL 19+4/1 FLC 1 FAC 3 Others 2+2*

RHODES Alexander (Alex) Graham
Born: Cambridge, 23 January 1982
Height: 5'9" **Weight:** 10.4
This left-footed striker was a prolific goal-scorer for Newmarket Town last term, netting hat-tricks in three consecutive games. His talent brought trials at a

number of clubs before he signed for Brentford in November. However, apart from an appearance from the bench in December Alex did not feature in the side until the last two games of the campaign. Nevertheless, he ended the campaign as the club's hero when he scored the vital goal that guaranteed survival in Division Two by flicking the ball past a defender with his heel and then side-footing home with his left foot.
Brentford *(Signed from Newmarket T on 13/11/2003) FL 0+3/1*

RHODES Christopher (Chris) Kyle
Born: Mansfield, 9 January 1987
Height: 5'9" **Weight:** 10.12
Chris is one of several talented youngsters to develop through the Notts County youth system and experience senior football last term. One of the stars of the team that won the Midland Youth Cup, the promising midfield player came on from the bench in the fixture at Peterborough at the turn of the year.
Notts Co *(Trainee) FL 0+1*

RICHARDS Dean Ivor
Born: Bradford, 9 June 1974
Height: 6'2" **Weight:** 13.5
International Honours: E: U21-4
This talented Spurs defender was plagued by injury last term, restricting his first-team appearances in the second half of the campaign. The team missed his presence and experience and the back four struggled for stability and cohesion. Regaining full fitness will be Dean's priority and Tottenham will be keen for him to feature on a regular basis in 2004-05, adding strength and experience to a relatively young back four.
Bradford C *(From trainee on 10/7/1992) FL 82+4/4 FLC 7/1 FAC 4/1 Others 3+2*
Wolverhampton W *(£1,850,000 on 25/3/1995) FL 118+4/7 FLC 11 FAC 10/1 Others 2*
Southampton *(Free on 28/7/1999) PL 67/3 FLC 7/2 FAC 4+1/2*
Tottenham H *(£8,100,000 on 24/9/2001) PL 73/4 FLC 3 FAC 5*

RICHARDS Marc John
Born: Wolverhampton, 8 July 1982
Height: 6'0" **Weight:** 12.7
International Honours: E: Yth
This talented young striker had a barren time in the early part of last season for Northampton and it was not until early December that he notched his first goals. However, he still finished the campaign in double figures and netted all four goals in

the victory at Macclesfield in March. He thus became the first Cobblers player to net four on an away ground since 1946. Fast, tricky and with a lethal right foot, Marc was a key figure in leading the club into the play-offs.
Blackburn Rov (From trainee on 12/7/1999) FLC 1+1
Crewe Alex (Loaned on 10/8/2001) FLC 1+3 FLC 0+1/1
Oldham Ath (Loaned on 12/10/2001) FL 3+2 Others 1/1
Halifax T (Loaned on 12/2/2002) FL 5
Swansea C (Loaned on 22/11/2002) FL 14+3/7
Northampton T (Free on 7/7/2003) FL 27+14/8 FLC 2 FAC 0+4/2 Others 4+1/1

RICHARDS Matthew (Matt)
Lee
Born: Harlow, 26 December 1984
Height: 5'8" **Weight:** 11.0
Matt established himself as the regular left back for Ipswich Town last term, improving his defensive skills and developing a fine understanding with Ian Westlake on the left-hand side of the pitch. He joined the attack frequently and was not afraid to have a shot on goal. His first and so far only goal for the club came in the home game with Stoke when he hooked home a loose ball following a corner.
Ipswich T (From trainee on 31/1/2002) FL 51+6/1 FLC 2+1 FAC 3 Others 3+1

RICHARDSON Barry
Born: Wallsend, 5 August 1969
Height: 6'1" **Weight:** 12.8
This veteran 'keeper took over as the youth coach at Doncaster Rovers during the 2002-03 campaign, but with the youth team moth-balled last term he was signed up as cover for Andy Warrington. Barry was called upon just twice, playing in the LDV Vans Trophy ties. He left the club at the end of March for pastures new.
Sunderland (From trainee on 20/5/1988)
Scunthorpe U (Free on 21/3/1989)
Scarborough (Free on 3/8/1989) FL 30 FLC 1 Others 1
Northampton T (Free, via trial at Stockport Co, on 10/9/1991) FL 96 FLC 4 FAC 5 Others 8
Preston NE (£20,000 on 25/7/1994) FL 20 FLC 2 FAC 3 Others 2
Lincoln C (£20,000 on 20/10/1995) FL 131 FLC 5 FAC 11 Others 3 (Free to Doncaster Rov on 8/8/2000)
Mansfield T (Loaned on 5/8/1999) FL 6 FLC 2
Halifax T (Free on 21/12/2001) FL 24 (Free to Gainsborough Trinity on 30/6/2002)

Doncaster Rov (Free on 28/7/2003) Others 2

RICHARDSON Frazer
Born: Rotherham, 29 October 1982
Height: 5'11" **Weight:** 12.1
International Honours: E: Yth
This promising young right back featured as a substitute for Leeds in the Premiership game against Southampton last August and in November he joined Stoke City on loan. Despite his defensive pedigree he was used on the right side of midfield and produced some useful performances. He scored his first senior goal at West Ham before being unexpectedly recalled to Elland Road, and went on to feature on a handful of occasions for Leeds during the remainder of the campaign.
Leeds U (From trainee on 2/11/1999) PL 2+2 FAC 1 Others 0+1
Stoke C (Loaned on 10/1/2003) FL 6+1
Stoke C (Loaned on 8/11/2003) FL 6/1

RICHARDSON Ian George
Born: Barking, 22 October 1970
Height: 5'10" **Weight:** 11.1
Club Honours: Div 3 '98
International Honours: E: SP-1
This wholehearted, courageous player was a near ever-present for Notts County last term, but despite some committed displays he was unable to save the team from relegation. Always popular with the club's fans, he featured in both defence and midfield, and contributed four goals for the Magpies during the campaign.
Birmingham C (£60,000 from Dagenham & Redbridge on 23/8/1995) FL 3+4 FLC 3+1 FAC 2 Others 1+2
Notts Co (£200,000 on 19/1/1996) FL 227+16/21 FLC 16 FAC 20/2 Others 8/1

RICHARDSON Kieran Edward
Born: Greenwich, 21 October 1984
Height: 5'9" **Weight:** 10.11
Club Honours: FAYC '03
An excellent all round midfielder with good skills, Kieran was used during Manchester United's short-lived Carling Cup run, playing in both matches against Leeds and West Bromwich Albion. Despite his limited appearances, big things are still expected of him at Old Trafford.
Manchester U (Trainee) PL 0+2 FLC 2+1/1 FAC 1+1 Others 2+3

RICHARDSON Leam Nathan
Born: Leeds, 19 November 1979
Height: 5'7" **Weight:** 11.4
Club Honours: AMC '04
Leam was in and out of the Blackpool

line-up last term when a series of niggling injuries restricted his appearances. He was used to good effect at both full back and in midfield. His season will be remembered for a superb goal in the FA Cup tie at Oldham and also for his appearance from the bench in the LDV Vans Trophy final at Cardiff's Millennium Stadium.
Blackburn Rov (From trainee on 31/12/1997) FLC 1
Bolton W (£50,000 on 13/7/2000) P/FL 5+8 FLC 3+1 FAC 1
Notts Co (Loaned on 9/11/2001) FL 20+1 FAC 1
Blackpool (Loaned on 20/12/2002) FL 20 FAC 1
Blackpool (Free on 15/7/2003) FL 24+4 FLC 1 FAC 1/1 Others 5+1

RICHARDSON Marcus Glenroy
Born: Reading, 31 August 1977
Height: 6'2" **Weight:** 13.2
This powerful target man was a key player for Lincoln City after initially signing on loan from Hartlepool United in August. He spent two months at Sincil Bank scoring four goals in 10 starts before returning to Hartlepool. His improved form saw him restored to the first team, but in three games he had only limited success. Marcus was back on loan at Lincoln in December before signing permanently the following month. He finished with a double-figure goal tally for the Imps with his strength and pace giving problems for opposing defences. He agreed a new contract in the summer.
Cambridge U (Free from Harrow Borough on 16/3/2001) FL 7+9/2 FLC 1
Torquay U (£5,000 on 18/9/2001) FL 21+18/8 FLC 0+1 FAC 1 Others 0+1
Hartlepool U (Free on 1/10/2002) FL 23+4/5 FAC 2/1
Lincoln C (Loaned on 22/8/2003) FL 9+3/4 Others 1/1
Lincoln C (Free on 8/12/2003) FL 25+1/6 Others 2

RICHMOND Andrew (Andy)
John
Born: Nottingham, 9 January 1983
Height: 6'3" **Weight:** 12.10
This young goalkeeper made only one appearance for Chesterfield in 2003-04, thanks to Carl Muggleton's fine form. Tall and agile, Andy has the right attitude to make progress, and the battle for the Spireites' number-one jersey should become interesting as the 2004-05 campaign progresses.
Chesterfield (From trainee on 9/7/2002) FL 6+1 Others 1

343

Liam Ridgewell (left)

RICKARDS Scott
Born: Sutton Coldfield, 3 November 1981
Height: 5'9" **Weight:** 12.6
After seeing regular action with Conference club Tamworth in the first half of last season, Scott was signed up by Kidderminster Harriers as a prospect for the future. A speedy forward, his appearances were mainly from the substitutes' bench and his moment of glory came in the otherwise forgettable home defeat by Macclesfield when he scored Harriers' only goal in a 4-1 defeat.
Kidderminster Hrs (£5,000 from Tamworth, ex Derby Co trainee, on 12/12/2003) FL 5+8/1 FAC 0+1

RICKERS Paul Steven
Born: Pontefract, 9 May 1975
Height: 5'10" **Weight:** 11.0
This busy midfielder had another disappointing season at Northampton last term, when he spent a lengthy period on the injury list. His only first-team action came from the substitutes' bench in the Carling Cup tie against Portsmouth and in December he was loaned to Conference outfit Leigh RMI. In February his contract was cancelled by mutual consent and after trials with Macclesfield and Dundalk he signed for Bury on non-contract terms, but failed to make a senior appearance for the Shakers.
Oldham Ath (From trainee on 16/7/1993) FL 242+19/20 FLC 13/2 FAC 17+2 Others 5+3
Northampton T (Free on 8/7/2002) FL 8+3 FLC 0+2 FAC 1 Others 2/1

RICKETTS Michael Barrington
Born: Birmingham, 4 December 1978
Height: 6'2" **Weight:** 11.12
Club Honours: FLC '04
International Honours: E: 1
Michael scored only three goals for Middlesbrough last season, but still retained the support of his manager Steve McClaren. However, one of those three goals could not have been more significant as it earned Boro' a 1-1 draw at White Hart Lane in the quarter-final of the Carling Cup. Boro' won the game 5-4 on shoot-out penalties and went on to win the trophy at the Millennium Stadium when Michael came on as a substitute (for Joseph-Desire Job) in the club's 2-1 victory over his former club Bolton Wanderers.
Walsall (From trainee on 13/9/1996) FL 31+45/14 FLC 2+4 FAC 2+2 Others 3+1/1
Bolton W (£500,000 on 17/7/2000) P/FL 63+35/37 FLC 0+4/3 FAC 4+3/4 Others 1+2/2
Middlesbrough (£2,200,000 on 31/1/2003) PL 12+20/3 FLC 3+2/1 FAC 2

RICKETTS Rohan Anthony
Born: Clapham, 22 December 1982
Height: 5'9" **Weight:** 11.0
Club Honours: FAYC '01
International Honours: E: Yth
This promising Tottenham youngster enjoyed a good run in the side in the early part of the 2003-04 season as a result of injuries to his colleagues. Rohan produced some impressive performances and contributed goals in the Carling Cup tie against Coventry and in the Premiership victory over Aston Villa in November. The highly rated midfielder will be looking to receive more first-team opportunities in 2004-05.
Arsenal (From trainee on 8/9/2001) FLC 0+1
Tottenham H (Free on 11/7/2002) PL 12+12/1 FLC 3+1/1

RIDGEWELL Liam Matthew
Born: Bexley, 21 July 1984
Height: 5'10" **Weight:** 11.0
Club Honours: FAYC '02
International Honours: E: U21-2; Yth
This young Aston Villa central defender made a number of appearances towards the end of the 2003-04 season and coped well with the step-up to Premiership football. Liam represented England at U19 level during the campaign before moving up to the U21 squad.
Aston Villa (From trainee on 26/7/2001) PL 5+6 FLC 0+2 FAC 0+1
Bournemouth (Loaned on 11/10/2002) FL 2+3

RIDLEY Lee
Born: Scunthorpe, 5 December 1981
Height: 5'9" **Weight:** 11.2
Lee enjoyed his best run in the first-team in his three years as a professional at Scunthorpe during the second half of last term. He came off the bench to score his first League goal, a winner against Northampton in February and started ten of the next 11 league matches. A determined left back who is tidy in defence, he also filled in during the season at right back and as one of three centre halves.
Scunthorpe U (From trainee on 3/7/2001) FL 27+8/1 FAC 3+1 Others 0+2

RIGGOTT Christopher (Chris)
Born: Derby, 1 September 1980
Height: 6'3" **Weight:** 12.2
Club Honours: FLC '04
International Honours: E: U21-8; Yth
Although it was another year of progress and steady consolidation for Chris at Middlesbrough, his season was interrupted by injury, restricting him to 17 Premiership games for the club. He was in

the side for the two Carling Cup semi-final games against Arsenal and was unlucky not to play in the final at the Millennium Stadium, but at least had the consolation of a seat on the substitutes' bench. Considered a player with great potential who has already proven himself in the Premiership, he is expected to challenge both Gareth Southgate and Ugo Ehiogu for one of the centre-back positions and has time on his side providing he can steer clear of injury.
Derby Co (From trainee on 5/10/1998) P/FL 87+4/5 FLC 7/1 FAC 2/1
Middlesbrough (£1,500,000 + on 31/1/2003) PL 18+4/2 FLC 4+1 FAC 1+1

RIGOGLIOSO Adriano
Born: Liverpool, 28 May 1979
Height: 5'11" **Weight:** 11.12
Club Honours: Div 3 '04
International Honours: E: SP-1
Doncaster Rovers manager Dave Penney had been tracking Adriano for some time and he eventually secured his man from Morecambe last November. A midfield player who likes to play in the 'hole' just behind the forwards, he has yet to make a real impact at Belle Vue. He was a regular in the Rovers reserve team, demonstrating plenty of skill and a capacity for hard work.
Doncaster Rov (£30,000 from Morecambe, ex Liverpool trainee, Marine, on 6/11/2003) FL 5+12

RIIHILAHTI Aki
Born: Helsinki, Finland, 9 September 1976
Height: 6'1" **Weight:** 12.6
International Honours: Finland: 51; U21-2; Yth
Aki was mostly a substitute for Crystal Palace early on last season before breaking into the starting line-up in the second half of the campaign. The talented midfielder seemed to blossom following the arrival of new manager Iain Dowie but was out of contract in the summer and his future was unclear at the time of writing. Aki also continued to represent Finland at international level during the season.
Crystal Palace (£200,000 from Valerenga, Norway, ex HJK Helsinki, on 22/3/2001) FL 93+17/7 FLC 7+3/1 FAC 3 Others 3

RIISE Jon Arne
Born: Molde, Norway, 24 September 1980
Height: 6'1" **Weight:** 12.6
Club Honours: ESC '01; CS '01; FLC '03
International Honours: Norway: 35; U21-17; Yth
Jon Arne had a somewhat quiet and subdued season for Liverpool last term,

when he failed to register a single goal. This was mainly due to the fact that he was restricted to the left-back slot following the arrival of Harry Kewell, rather than the more advanced role he has previously featured in. Although untroubled by injury, he started only 28 games last season and lost his place on a number of occasions.
Liverpool (£3,770,000 from AS Monaco, France, ex Aalesund, on 26/7/2001) PL 87+16/13 FLC 5+1 FAC 5+1 Others 30+2/1

RILEY Paul Anthony
Born: Nottingham, 29 September 1982
Height: 5'9" **Weight:** 10.7
Paul featured regularly in the Notts County first-team set-up last term, although he was often used from the bench. However, he fell out of favour following a change in management and was released in the summer. Paul is a promising left back or left-sided midfielder who loves to push down the flank to help out the attack.
Notts Co (From trainee on 4/12/2001) FL 18+10/3 FLC 1+1 FAC 2 Others 1

RITCHIE Paul Simon
Born: Kirkcaldy, 21 August 1975
Height: 5'11" **Weight:** 12.0
Club Honours: SC '98; Div 1 '03
International Honours: S: 7; B-2; U21-7; Sch
Though Walsall picked up only one point in Paul's first six games for them, he became a key figure in the defence last term. He impressed with his inch-perfect tackles and brave blocks, and contributed an injury-time goal to win the final game against Rotherham, but sadly it was not enough to enable the club to avoid relegation. Paul added a further cap for Scotland against Wales in February and was voted as 'Player of the Season' by the Saddlers' supporters.
Heart of Midlothian (Signed from Links U on 31/7/1992) SL 132+1/5 SLC 10+1 SC 11/3 Others 6
Bolton W (Free on 22/12/1999) FL 13+1 FLC 1 FAC 3+1 Others 2
Glasgow R (Free on 26/2/2000)
Manchester C (£500,000 on 22/8/2000) P/FL 11+9 FLC 3+1 FAC 3
Portsmouth (Loaned on 20/9/2002) FL 8+4 FLC 1
Derby Co (Loaned on 27/3/2003) FL 7
Walsall (Free on 22/8/2003) FL 33/1 FLC 1 FAC 1

RIVERS Mark Alan
Born: Crewe, 26 November 1975
Height: 5'11" **Weight:** 11.2

Club Honours: Div 1 '04
Mark scored four goals in Norwich City's first four League matches of the 2003-04 season before sustaining a nasty ankle injury in the match at Nottingham Forest at the end of August. By the time he had recovered fitness several loan signings had been brought in and Nigel Worthington's side had a settled look to it. A winger with a direct style who likes to take his opponent on at pace, he has a good career goal-scoring record and can also operate as an out-and-out striker. After failing to re-establish himself in the side in the latter half of the campaign, he will be hoping for better luck in 2004-05.
Crewe Alex (From trainee on 6/5/1994) FL 177+26/43 FLC 14+1/8 FAC 12/5 Others 5+3/3
Norwich C (£600,000 on 28/6/2001) FL 54+20/10 FLC 1 FAC 2+2 Others 3/1

RIX Benjamin (Ben)
Born: Wolverhampton, 11 December 1982
Height: 5'10" **Weight:** 11.11
This talented left-sided midfield player found it difficult to establish himself as a regular in the Crewe Alexandra first team last season. Ben was in and out of the line-up before dropping out of contention altogether in March. He scored two goals, netting in the 3-0 home win over Derby and the defeat at Bradford City.
Crewe Alex (From trainee on 6/2/2001) FL 41+29/2 FLC 2 FAC 4+4/2 Others 1+1

ROBERT Laurent
Born: Saint-Benoit, Reunion, 21 May 1975
Height: 5'9" **Weight:** 11.2
International Honours: France: 9; B-4
Laurent was a regular on the left wing for Newcastle, from where he delivered whipped in crosses with pace which were extremely difficult to deal with. He is an exciting player when running with the ball, and has a vicious shot with his left foot used to good effect from both open play and set pieces. Laurent can be frustratingly inconsistent, but on his day he is an undoubted match winner; thus for example he scored two stunning thunderbolt goals at home to Tottenham in December and another in the FA Cup tie at Liverpool. He also contributed a remarkable goal at home to Fulham in January with a jumping mid-air back heel, all of which helped him become the club's second-top scorer for the season.
Newcastle U (£10,500,000 from Paris St Germain, France, ex Montpellier, Nancy, on 10/8/2001) PL 90+8/19 FLC 4+1/2 FAC 6/3 Others 21+4/3

ROBERTS Andrew (Andy) James
Born: Dartford, 20 March 1974
Height: 5'10" **Weight:** 13.0
Club Honours: FAYC '91
International Honours: E: U21-5
This experienced midfielder again showed that he has plenty to offer for Millwall last season. A versatile player who can also slot into the back four or operate as a sweeper, he has scored many a wonder goal with his tremendous right foot. He would have been ever present last term if it were not for injury but nevertheless he was once again a hit with the club's supporters.
Millwall (From trainee on 29/10/1991) FL 132+6/5 FLC 12/2 FAC 7 Others 4/1
Crystal Palace (£2,520,000 on 29/7/1995) F/PL 106+2/2 FLC 7+1 FAC 8 Others 6/1
Wimbledon (£1,200,000 + on 10/3/1998) P/FL 92+9/6 FLC 12+1/1 FAC 3+2
Norwich C (Loaned on 28/1/2002) FL 4+1
Millwall (Free on 16/8/2002) FL 60+6/3 FLC 2 FAC 2+1

ROBERTS Benjamin (Ben) James
Born: Bishop Auckland, 22 June 1975
Height: 6'1" **Weight:** 13.0
International Honours: E: U21-1
Ben became first-choice goalkeeper for Brighton last term, despite suffering a number of injuries during the campaign. At the business end of the season he kept a clean sheet for 632 minutes, a crucial factor in Albion's promotion triumph via the play-offs. Indeed, his save from Swindon Town's Tommy Mooney in the penalty shoot-out at Withdean was immense in the context of the whole season, putting Albion well on the way to Cardiff. A great shot-stopper, he still needs to work on his kicking game and to judge situations with a cooler head on occasion.
Middlesbrough (From trainee on 24/3/1993) F/PL 15+1 FLC 2+1 FAC 6 Others 1
Hartlepool U (Loaned on 19/10/1995) FL 4 Others 1
Wycombe W (Loaned on 8/12/1995) FL 15
Bradford C (Loaned on 27/8/1996) FL 2
Millwall (Loaned on 12/2/1999) FL 11 Others 4
Luton T (Loaned on 24/2/2000) FL 14
Charlton Ath (Free on 19/7/2000) PL 0+1
Reading (Loaned on 17/11/2002) FL 6
Luton T (Loaned on 24/8/2002) FL 3
Brighton & Hove A (Loaned on 17/1/2003) FL 3
Brighton & Hove A (Free on 25/7/2003) FL 32 FLC 1 Others 5

ROBERTS Christian John
Born: Cardiff, 22 October 1979
Height: 5'10" **Weight:** 12.8
Club Honours: AMC '03
International Honours: W: U21-1; Yth
With the team struggling for goals towards the end of last season this experienced striker came good for Bristol City just when it mattered, though his late goal that took the team through to the promotion play-off final cost him the chance of a Welsh cap. A regular in the squad throughout the campaign, although often used from the substitutes' bench, he scored eight times.
Cardiff C (From trainee on 8/10/1997) FL 6+17/3 FLC 2 FAC 2+3 Others 0+2
Exeter C (Free on 24/7/2000) FL 67+12/18 FLC 2+1 FAC 2+1 Others 2
Bristol C (Signed on 26/3/2002) FL 59+27/19 FLC 3+1 FAC 4+2/4 Others 10+2/2

ROBERTS Gareth Wyn
Born: Wrexham, 6 February 1978
Height: 5'7" **Weight:** 12.6
Club Honours: FAYC '96
International Honours: W: 6; B-1; U21-10
Gareth was Tranmere's most consistent and reliable player in 2003-04, once again producing a string of impressively solid and steady performances. He can play equally well either in the left-back or left-wing-back positions and is a tenacious tackler who rarely loses his cool. Gareth was recalled to the Wales international squad in March after an absence of three years and picked up a further cap as a substitute in the win over Hungary. Out of contract in the summer, he has since signed a new deal that will keep him at Prenton Park for the foreseeable future.
Liverpool (From trainee on 22/5/1996. £50,000 to Panionios, Greece on 15/1/1999)
Tranmere Rov (Free on 5/8/1999) FL 192+5/8 FLC 19 FAC 19+1 Others 4/1

ROBERTS Gary Steven
Born: Chester, 4 February 1987
Height: 5'8" **Weight:** 10.5
International Honours: E: Yth
Gary made his senior debut for Crewe when coming on as a substitute against Burnley on Boxing Day and added another appearance against Wimbledon soon afterwards. A combative midfield player who was a first-year scholar at Gresty Road last term, Gary also represented England at U17 level.
Crewe Alex (Trainee) FL 0+2

ROBERTS Iwan Wyn
Born: Bangor, 26 June 1968
Height: 6'3" **Weight:** 14.2
Club Honours: Div 1 '04
International Honours: W: 15; B-1; Yth; Sch
Iwan's contract for Norwich City was not extended beyond June 2004 and his emotional farewell from the club he served so fantastically well for seven seasons, coincided with the Canaries' championship celebrations. A tremendous team player he provides an excellent focal point for his side's attack, using his great strength and ability to retain possession and bring his colleagues into play. Powerful in the air and with his goal-scoring instincts intact, he netted eight times in 2003-04, including two in the final game of the season. An outstanding ambassador for Norwich he will surely continue his playing career for a season or two before turning his undoubted talents to coaching.
Watford (From trainee on 4/7/1988) FL 40+23/9 FLC 6+2/3 FAC 1+6 Others 5
Huddersfield T (£275,000 on 2/8/1990) FL 141+1/50 FLC 13+1/6 FAC 12/4 Others 14+1/8
Leicester C (£100,000 on 25/11/1993) P/FL 92+8/41 FLC 5/1 FAC 5/2 Others 1
Wolverhampton W (£1,300,000 + on 15/7/1996) FL 24+9/12 FLC 2 FAC 0+1 Others 2
Norwich C (£900,000 on 9/7/1997) FL 232+46/84 FLC 15+3/10 FAC 6+1/2 Others 0+3/1

ROBERTS Jason Andre Davies
Born: Park Royal, 25 January 1978
Height: 5'11" **Weight:** 12.7
International Honours: Grenada
Jason began last season on loan at Portsmouth, where he did well scoring four times from six starts, including a Premiership goal against Everton. In January he became Wigan Athletic's record signing and got off to a great start, scoring after 33 seconds of his debut against Lancashire rivals Preston North End. A hard working and purposeful striker, he has a great eye for goal and quickly redeveloped a fine understanding with his former Bristol Rovers colleague Nathan Ellington. Their partnership proved to be a handful, Jason netting eight goals including doubles in the home wins over Coventry City and Cardiff City.
Wolverhampton W (£250,000 from Hayes on 12/9/1997)
Torquay U (Loaned on 19/12/1997) FL 13+1/6 Others 1
Bristol C (Loaned on 26/3/1998) FL 1+2/1
Bristol Rov (£250,000 on 7/8/1998) FL 73+5/38 FLC 6/3 FAC 6/7 Others 3
West Bromwich A (£2,000,000 on 27/7/2000) P/FL 75+14/24 FLC 3+1/2 FAC 6 Others 2/1
Portsmouth (Loaned on 1/9/2003) PL 4+6/1 FLC 2/3
Wigan Ath (£2,000,000 on 13/1/2004) FL 14/8

ROBERTS Neil Wyn
Born: Wrexham, 7 April 1978
Height: 5'10" **Weight:** 11.0
Club Honours: Div 2 '03
International Honours: W: 3; B-1; U21-1; Yth
Always a willing worker, Neil found himself limited to a bit-part role for Wigan last term, unable to split the striking partnership of Nathan Ellington and Jason Roberts. Although not a prolific scorer, he impressed with his bravery and a willingness to work hard for the side. At his best he holds the ball up and probes for openings for other players. Only a late West Ham equaliser in the final game of the season prevented him becoming a hero following his goal as the Latics missed out on a play-off place.
Wrexham (From trainee on 3/7/1996) FL 58+17/17 FLC 1/1 FAC 11+1/4 Others 2+2/2
Wigan Ath (£450,000 on 18/2/2000) FL 64+61/19 FLC 6+3/2 FAC 6/1 Others 3+1
Hull C (Loaned on 25/1/2002) FL 3+3

ROBERTS Stephen (Steve) Wyn
Born: Wrexham, 24 February 1980
Height: 6'0" **Weight:** 12.7
International Honours: W: U21-4; Yth
Steve missed the first two months of last season while recovering from surgery to his foot. However, the cultured centre back returned to the side and played a prominent role after Christmas, putting in some fine performances at the heart of the defence. A controlled type of defender who can find colleagues with long pinpoint passes, he notched his team's second goal in the quarter final of the FAW Premier Cup against Total Network Solutions and also the match-winning effort in the penalty shoot-out against Cardiff City in the semi-final of the same competition.
Wrexham (From trainee on 16/1/1998) FL 109+7/3 FLC 2 FAC 6/1 Others 6+1/1

ROBERTS Stuart Ian
Born: Carmarthen, 22 July 1980
Height: 5'7" **Weight:** 9.8
International Honours: W: U21-13

This extremely quick-footed midfielder or striker was a firm favourite with the Wycombe fans, but found it very difficult to establish himself in the line-up last term. He mostly featured from the substitutes' bench before returning to his former club Swansea City in the new year. He scored on his first start for the Swans against Doncaster and generally impressed with his electrifying pace.

Swansea C *(From trainee on 9/7/1998) FL 58+34/14 FLC 4+3 FAC 4 Others 7+2*
Wycombe W *(£102,500 on 19/10/2001) FL 37+33/4 FLC 2+1 FAC 4+2 Others 2+2*
Swansea C *(Free on 24/2/2004) FL 8+4/1*

ROBERTSON Gregor Aedan
Born: Edinburgh, 19 January 1984
Height: 6'0" **Weight:** 12.4
International Honours: S: U21-1
This young Nottingham Forest midfielder made his debut in the Carling Cup tie against Tranmere last September and quickly found himself a regular in the side. He cemented his place in the troublesome left-back role, but after the arrival of Alan Rogers found himself out of favour. Gregor was called up for the first time for Scotland U21s against the Republic of Ireland in May.
Nottingham F *(From Heart of Midlothian juniors on 8/2/2001) FL 12+4 FLC 1+1 FAC 2*

ROBERTSON Hugh Scott
Born: Aberdeen, 19 March 1975
Height: 5'9" **Weight:** 12.7
A left back with an extremely powerful shot, Hugh was a regular with Scottish First Division outfit Ross County during the first half of the 2003-04 season. He moved on to Hartlepool in the new year and very soon became a favourite with the supporters who were quick to call for him to go for goal from free kicks. He scored four first-team goals, the best of the bunch being his long-range effort which clinched victory over Luton Town and was chosen as Pool's 'Goal of the Season'
Aberdeen *(Signed from Lewis U on 24/8/1993) SL 13+9/2 SLC 0+1 SC 1*
Dundee *(Signed on 18/1/1997) SL 41+11/3 SLC 1+1 SC 1*
Brechin C *(Loaned on 20/3/1998) SL 5+2*
Inverness Caledonian Thistle *(Loaned on 3/10/1998) SL 12*
Ayr U *(Loaned on 3/11/2000) SL 8/2*
Ross Co *(Signed on 1/2/2001) SL 100+3/12 SLC 8 SC 4 Others 5*
Hartlepool U *(Free on 31/1/2004) FL 18/4 Others 2*

ROBERTSON Mark William
Born: Sydney, Australia, 6 April 1977
Height: 5'9" **Weight:** 11.4
International Honours: Australia: U23-5; Yth
This combative midfielder spent the first half of last season out on loan with St Johnstone, but after being recalled to his parent club he made a permanent move to Stockport in the new year. He impressed the Edgeley Park faithful with some battling performances in the centre of the park and was a regular until sidelined by a thigh injury at the beginning of March. Mark opened his account for the Hatters with a 'Goal of the Season' contender, a well-struck 25-yarder in the home defeat by Swindon.
Burnley *(Free from Marconi Stallions, Australia on 3/10/1997) FL 27+9/1 FLC 1+2 Others 3+2*
Swindon T *(Loaned on 22/8/2000) FL 4+6/1 FLC 2+1*
Dundee *(Free on 8/3/2001) SL 9+16 SLC 3 SC 1+1 Others 1+1*
St Johnstone *(Loaned on 31/1/2003) SL 10/1*
St Johnstone *(Loaned on 29/8/2003) SL 8+1/1 SLC 3+1*
Stockport Co *(Free on 9/1/2004) FL 9+3/1*

ROBINS Mark Gordon
Born: Ashton under Lyne, 22 December 1969
Height: 5'8" **Weight:** 11.11
Club Honours: FAC '90; ECWC '91; ESC '91; FLC '97
International Honours: E: U21-6
A prolific scorer throughout his career, Mark started in two of the first three games for Rotherham last season without finding the net and from that point he could only manage a handful of substitute appearances. He moved to Sheffield Wednesday in search of regular action and netted twice on his debut at Carlisle in the LDV Vans Trophy tie. There followed a steady if not spectacular integration to the team and a few goals as well. Mark's all-round effort and experience were a terrific help to the Owls, but he then suffered a leg injury which kept him out at a crucial late stage of the season.
Manchester U *(From apprentice on 23/12/1986) FL 19+29/11 FLC 0+7/2 FAC 4+4/3 Others 4+3/1*
Norwich C *(£800,000 on 14/8/1992) PL 57+10/20 FLC 6+3/1 Others 1+1*
Leicester C *(£1,000,000 on 16/1/1995) P/FL 40+16/12 FLC 5+4/5 FAC 4+2 Others 1+1*
Reading *(Loaned on 29/8/1997) FL 5*
(Signed by Deportivo Orense, Spain on 15/11/1998)

Manchester C *(Free from Panionios, Greece on 25/3/1999) FL 0+2*
Walsall *(Free on 5/8/1999) FL 30+10/6 FLC 4/1 FAC 2/1*
Rotherham U *(Free on 5/7/2000) FL 84+24/44 FLC 6+2/4 FAC 3+1 Others 1/1*
Bristol C *(Loaned on 18/2/2003) FL 6/4 Others 1+1/1*
Sheffield Wed *(Signed on 8/12/2003) FL 14+1/3 Others 3/4*

ROBINSON Andrew (Andy) Mark
Born: Birkenhead, 3 November 1979
Height: 5'8" **Weight:** 11.4
Andy initially joined Swansea on a short-term contract, but following some gutsy displays in midfield this was extended until the end of the season. He made his debut for the Swans against Boston United at the Vetch Field, capping a fine display by scoring his side's third goal, and by the end of the campaign he had reached a double-figure goal tally. Andy commanded a regular place in the midfield engine room, where he impressed with his tackling ability and some spectacular long-range goals.
Tranmere Rov *(Free from Cammell Laird on 11/11/2002) Others 0+1*
Swansea C *(Free on 14/8/2003) FL 34+3/8 FAC 5/2*

ROBINSON Carl Phillip
Born: Llandrindod Wells, 13 October 1976
Height: 5'10" **Weight:** 12.10
Club Honours: Div 1 '03
International Honours: W: 17; B-2; U21-6; Yth
This experienced Portsmouth midfielder spent most of last term out on loan and his only appearances for Pompey came as a substitute at the turn of the year. His first stop was Rotherham where he spent three months in the autumn, playing a major role in the club's revival with some cultured performances. In January he spent a month at Sheffield United, where he showed some neat touches in midfield, before finishing the season at Sunderland. He turned in some impressive displays, for the Wearsiders particularly against champions Norwich in May when his header won a vital three points for the team.
Wolverhampton W *(From trainee on 3/7/1995) FL 129+35/19 FLC 12+1/1 FAC 14/3*
Shrewsbury T *(Loaned on 28/3/1996) FL 2+2 Others 1*
Portsmouth *(Free on 31/7/2002) P/FL 11+5 FLC 1+1 FAC 0+2*

Sheffield Wed (Loaned on 17/1/2003) FL 4/1
Walsall (Loaned on 20/2/2003) FL 10+1/1
Rotherham U (Loaned on 18/9/2003) FL 14 FLC 2
Sheffield U (Loaned on 30/1/2004) FL 4+1
Sunderland (Loaned on 25/3/2004) FL 6+1/1
Others 1+1

ROBINSON Jake David
Born: Brighton, 23 October 1986
Height: 5'9" **Weight:** 10.4
In October, Jake became the first 16-year-old to score for Brighton in a peacetime fixture, when he notched a late goal against Forest Green Rovers in the LDV Vans Trophy after coming on as a substitute. By the end of the season the highly promising striker had one start and ten appearances from the bench to his name, plus a long-term professional contract.
Brighton & Hove A (From trainee on 22/12/2003) FL 1+8 FLC 0+1 Others 0+1/1

ROBINSON James Gilbert
Born: Whiston, 18 September 1982
Height: 5'10" **Weight:** 11.6
James was given his first start by Crewe in the opening game of the 2003-04 season against Wimbledon and thereafter featured from the substitutes' bench on several occasions. A promising midfielder who is comfortable on the ball, he netted his first goal for the club in the amazing 6-4 defeat by Ipswich in January.
Crewe Alex (From trainee on 28/11/2001) FL 1+9/1 FAC 0+1

ROBINSON John Robert Campbell
Born: Bulawayo, Rhodesia, 29 August 1971
Height: 5'10" **Weight:** 11.7
Club Honours: Div 1 '00
International Honours: W: 29; U21-5
John was a major signing for Cardiff City as they contemplated their first season at Division One level for 18 years. He was a massive success, inspiring all those around him with his enthusiasm and commitment. A clever right-footed winger with a tremendous work rate, he was a regular for most of the campaign and contributed two goals.
Brighton & Hove A (From trainee on 21/4/1989) FL 57+5/6 FLC 5/1 FAC 2+1 Others 1+2/2
Charlton Ath (£75,000 on 15/9/1992) P/FL 296+36/35 FLC 20+4/5 FAC 17+3/3 Others 5+1
Cardiff C (Free on 10/7/2003) FL 31+3/2

ROBINSON Mark
Born: Guisborough, 24 July 1981
Height: 5'9" **Weight:** 11.0
After being Hartlepool's first-choice left back for the previous three seasons, Mark found himself out in the cold in 2003-04 following a change in management. He gave some good performances for the reserves and was rewarded with a first-team place, but after a handful of games a disastrous 4-0 defeat at Blackpool ended his run. Mark failed to get another chance, was loaned out to Spennymoor United, and was releaseed at the end of the season.
Hartlepool U (From trainee on 2/7/1999) FL 80+5 FLC 2 Others 3

ROBINSON Marvin Leon St Clair
Born: Crewe, 11 April 1980
Height: 6'0" **Weight:** 12.9
International Honours: E: Sch
Marvin joined Chesterfield last September after a successful trial period and used his power and pace to secure important goals as the club sought to climb off the bottom of the Second Division table. He signed for the season after protracted negotiations, but thereafter was used mainly from the bench to pep up a tiring forward line, and the goals dried up. He was released in the summer.
Derby Co (From trainee on 8/7/1998) P/FL 3+9/1
Stoke C (Loaned on 13/9/2000) FL 3/1
Tranmere Rov (Loaned on 29/11/2002) FL 1+5/1 Others 0+1
Chesterfield (Free on 19/9/2003) FL 17+15/6 FAC 1 Others 2/1

ROBINSON Matthew Adam
Born: Ipswich, 22 March 1984
Height: 5'10" **Weight:** 11.6
After being released by Ipswich Town, Matthew had a lengthy spell as a non-contract player at Bournemouth, where he featured as an unused substitute before joining Cambridge United on a similar basis in the new year. A midfielder who can also play up front, he needs a full pre-season behind him to develop his full potential.
Bournemouth (From trainee at Ipswich T on 31/10/2003)
Cambridge U (Free on 9/2/2004) FL 1+2

ROBINSON Matthew (Matt) Richard
Born: Exeter, 23 December 1974
Height: 5'11" **Weight:** 11.8
Matt was an ever-present for Oxford United last term until an achilles strain forced him out of the closing games. He

was one of the U's most impressive players throughout the campaign, featuring in the left-wing-back role from where he put in some telling crosses. Matt netted his annual goal with a fine strike in the home win against Carlisle.
Southampton (From trainee on 1/7/1993) PL 3+11 FAC 1+2
Portsmouth (£50,000 on 20/2/1998) FL 65+4/1 FLC 3+2 FAC 3
Reading (£150,000 on 28/1/2000) FL 62+3 FLC 3+1 FAC 2 Others 4
Oxford U (Free on 12/7/2002) FL 82/2 FLC 5 FAC 3 Others 1+1

ROBINSON Neil David
Born: Liverpool, 18 November 1979
Height: 5'10" **Weight:** 12.12
This young Macclesfield striker found it difficult to break into the first team last season and managed just one appearance from the substitutes' bench, in the home match against Cheltenham in February. Early on in the campaign he had a loan spell at Conference club Leigh RMI and later enjoyed two loan periods at Southport where, during his second spell, he scored seven goals in four matches, earning Neil a permanent move to the Unibond League side in March.
Macclesfield T (£12,000 from Prescot Cables on 29/7/2002) FL 2+9 FLC 0+1

ROBINSON Paul Derrick
Born: Sunderland, 20 November 1978
Height: 5'11" **Weight:** 11.12
A regular goal-scorer in the early part of the 2003-04 season, Paul's best performance for Hartlepool was in the 8-1 victory over Grimsby Town when he netted a hat-trick. He was unlucky with niggling injuries in mid-season, then his scoring touch deserted him. A hamstring injury kept him out for a spell, and he was slightly out of the picture as the season ended, being restricted to substitute appearances. However he began scoring regularly for the reserves, helping them clinch the Pontins League Division One East championship.
Darlington (From trainee on 14/7/1997) FL 7+19/3 FLC 0+1 FAC 2+4/1 Others 0+1
Newcastle U (£250,000 + on 27/3/1998) PL 2+9 FLC 0+1 Others 0+4/1
Wimbledon (£1,500,000 on 9/8/2000) FL 0+4 FLC 1+1
Burnley (Loaned on 10/10/2000) FL 0+4
Dundee U (Loaned on 21/2/2001) SL 2+9
Grimsby T (Loaned on 28/3/2002) FL 1+4
Grimsby T (Loaned on 9/8/2002) FL 5+7/1 FLC 1
Carlisle U (Loaned on 22/11/2002) FL 1+4/1 FAC 2 Others 0+1/1

*Blackpool (Free on 21/3/2003) FL 5+2/1
Hartlepool U (Free on 31/7/2003) FL
19+12/7 FLC 2/2 FAC 2+1 Others 0+3*

ROBINSON Paul Mark James
Born: Barnet, 7 January 1982
Height: 6'1" **Weight:** 12.1
This tall, ball-playing central defender broke into the Millwall first-team squad last September and produced some accomplished performances. However, after a brief run in the line-up Paul was sidelined by an injury and did not feature again during the remainder of the campaign.
*Millwall (From trainee on 25/10/2000) FL
19+4 FAC 3+1/1*

ROBINSON Paul Peter
Born: Watford, 14 December 1978
Height: 5'9'' **Weight:** 11.12
Club Honours: Div 2 '98
International Honours: E: U21-3
Paul's departure to West Bromwich Albion last October came as a bombshell to the Watford faithful. A local lad with more than 250 appearances in eight seasons with the club and much admired for his passion and total commitment, Paul was regarded as the embodiment of Watford FC and a fixture at left back. Signed by manager Gary Megson to add some grit and determination to the team, he made his Albion debut against Norwich City at home, four days after arriving from Vicarage Road. An all-action player, strong and committed in defensive play, he loves to push forward.
*Watford (From trainee on 13/2/1997) P/FL
201+18/8 FLC 15+1/1 FAC 10+2 Others 5
West Bromwich A (£250,000 on
14/10/2003) FL 30+1 FAC 1*

ROBINSON Paul William
Born: Beverley, 15 October 1979
Height: 6'2" **Weight:** 13.4
Club Honours: FAYC '97
International Honours: E: 5; U21-11
Paul reported back for pre-season training at Leeds following the collapse of a reported move to Aston Villa, and his performances were as committed as ever, not least when he joined the exclusive club of goal-scoring keepers. United looked to be heading for a Carling Cup defeat at the hands of Swindon Town, when he raced upfield for a stoppage-time corner, and as the ball looped across his header sailed over the goalie to equalise. An excellent young goalkeeper and regular in the England squad, Paul was seen as a highly saleable asset in troubled times at Elland Road and at the

time of writing it remained to be seen where his immediate future lay.
*Leeds U (From trainee on 13/5/1997) PL
93+2 FLC 5/1 FAC 7 Others 12*

ROBINSON Ryan
Born: Kendal, 13 October 1982
Height: 6'2" **Weight:** 13.2
This young goalkeeper joined Southend as cover for Carl Emberson and found himself thrust into first-team action early on last term. Ryan made his debut at Hull and retained his place for the next game at home to Lincoln, before manager Steve Wignall opted for experience by re-signing former 'keeper Darryl Flahavan. Ryan had a spell on loan at Ryman League club Wivenhoe Town but he was released at the end of the season.
*Blackburn Rov (From trainee on 14/1/2002)
Southend U (Free on 31/7/2003) FL 2*

ROBINSON Stephen (Steve)
Born: Lisburn, 10 December 1974
Height: 5'9" **Weight:** 11.3
International Honours: NI: 5; B-4; U21-1; Yth; Sch
After recovering from a pre-season operation, Steve took his place in the Luton Town line-up at the beginning of October and quickly re-established himself in the side, keeping his place until the end of the campaign. The clever right-sided midfielder enjoyed one of his best-ever seasons for the Hatters and netted the team's 'Goal of the Season' with a fine effort at Blackpool in December. Steve became one of the club's first out-of-contract players to re-sign in the summer.
*Tottenham H (From trainee on 27/1/1993)
PL 1+1
Bournemouth (Free on 20/10/1994) FL
227+13/51 FLC 14/1 FAC 15+1/5 Others 16/3
Preston NE (£375,000 on 26/5/2000) FL
6+18/1 FLC 3+1 FAC 0+1
Bristol C (Loaned on 18/3/2002) FL 6/1
Luton T (£50,000 on 20/6/2002) FL 55+8/3
FLC 1+1 FAC 6/1 Others 3*

ROBINSON Steven (Steve) Eli
Born: Nottingham, 17 January 1975
Height: 5'9" **Weight:** 11.3
This hard-running Swindon midfielder was a regular in the line-up last term until his season ended prematurely after he suffered a broken bone in his leg at Blackpool in January. Tough tackling and always willing to work for the team he has been offered a further contract and will be looking to make a come back in the 2004-05 campaign.

*Birmingham C (From trainee on 9/6/1993) FL
53+28 FLC 6+2/1 FAC 2+2/1 Others 2+1
Peterborough U (Loaned on 15/3/1996) FL 5
Swindon T (£50,000 on 12/2/2001) FL
117+7/5 FLC 3 FAC 5 Others 3/1*

ROBINSON Trevor Kymar
Born: Jamaica, 20 September 1984
Height: 5'9" **Weight:** 12.11
Trevor produced some excellent performances for Millwall's U19 and reserve teams last season and was called up to make his first-team debut against Cardiff in December. A promising and very tricky winger he is another product of the club's successful youth set-up.
Millwall (From trainee on 23/1/2004) FL 0+1

ROBSON Glenn Alan
Born: Sunderland, 25 September 1977
Height: 5'11" **Weight:** 11.7
This young striker was given a number of early-season outings by Darlington last term, but the only time that he found the net was in the penalty shoot-out that put Bradford City out of the first round of the Carling Cup at Valley Parade. Glen's quick, darting runs often surprised defenders but nevertheless he was released in November and linked up with Northern League club Durham City.
*Rochdale (Signed from Murton on
13/11/1996) FL 0+10 (Freed on 12/8/1998)
Darlington (Free from Durham C on
6/8/2003) FL 3+3 FLC 1*

ROBSON Matthew (Matty) James
Born: Durham, 23 January 1985
Height: 5'10" **Weight:** 11.2
A third-year scholar with Hartlepool, Matty is a left-sided utility player who is equally proficient as a defender or when going forward. He was surprisingly included in the first team for the opening game of the 2003-04 season at Peterborough and scored a goal in the great 4-3 win. Matty held his place in the early games, and in mid-season he had another first-team run before returning to the reserves.
*Hartlepool U (From trainee on 16/3/2004) FL
17+6/1 FLC 1 FAC 2 Others 1*

ROCA Carlos Jose
Born: Manchester, 4 September 1984
Height: 5'4" **Weight:** 10.7
A third-year scholar at Boundary Park, Carlos was thrust into the first team earlier than anticipated last term. A diminutive and quick-footed player who usually operates on the right-hand side of midfield, he made several early-season

appearances as a substitute and started two games in the cup competitions. New manager Brian Talbot decided to release him in May and Carlisle United swooped to secure his services.
Oldham Ath *(Trainee) FL 0+7 FLC 1 FAC 1 Others 0+2*

ROCASTLE Craig Aaron
Born: Lewisham, 17 August 1981
Height: 6'1" **Weight:** 12.13
This central midfield player spent much of last season developing in the club's reserves, and made the odd appearance as an unused substitute for the first team. In February Craig had a loan spell at Barnsley where he impressed with his passing skills, but returned following a change in manager at Oakwell. The following month he joined Lincoln City, also on loan. He was give his debut as a second-half substitute in the home game with Kidderminster and started the move that led to the Imps' late equaliser. Craig found it hard to impose his skill in the hustle and bustle of a Third Division promotion campaign and made just one more appearance as a substitute before returning to Stamford Bridge. Craig is the cousin of the late Arsenal and England player David Rocastle.
Chelsea *(Free from Slough T, ex Croydon, Gravesend & Northfleet, Ashford T, Kingstonian, on 1/9/2003)*
Barnsley *(Loaned on 13/2/2004) FL 4+1*
Lincoln C *(Loaned on 25/3/2004) FL 0+2*

ROCHE Barry Christopher
Born: Dublin, 6 April 1982
Height: 6'4" **Weight:** 12.6
International Honours: Rol: Yth
This young goalkeeper finally got his chance to play for Nottingham Forest at the City Ground when he replaced the injured Darren Ward against Gillingham last February. He then had a brief run in the side before being dropped following the visit to Derby, but added a couple more appearances before the season's end.
Nottingham F *(From trainee on 29/6/1999) FL 8+3*

ROCHE Lee Paul
Born: Bolton, 28 October 1980
Height: 5'10" **Weight:** 10.12
International Honours: E: U21-1; Yth
Unable to threaten Gary Neville's place at Old Trafford, this young right back moved to Burnley in the close season of 2003 and made a scoring debut in the opening game against Crystal Palace. It looked set fair for him, but injury allowed Dean West

back into the side and Lee had to be content with a substitute's role behind the steady West. He emerged as the regular first choice after Christmas and was generally reliable and more difficult to shake off the ball than his slight frame would suggest.
Manchester U *(From trainee on 11/2/1999) PL 0+1 FLC 1 Others 1*
Wrexham *(Loaned on 24/7/2000) FL 41 FLC 2 FAC 1 Others 1*
Burnley *(Free on 18/7/2003) FL 21+4/1 FLC 1+1 FAC 3*

RODGER Simon Lee
Born: Shoreham, 3 October 1971
Height: 5'9" **Weight:** 11.9
Club Honours: Div 1 '94
Brighton's main midfield playmaker had his season cut short last term after he suffered a twisted knee in the Carling Cup tie at Middlesbrough. While his absence didn't prevent his colleagues from securing promotion via the play-offs, Simon was sorely missed at times and his vision would surely have led to a more attacking performance on occasion. Out of contract in the summer, his future was unclear at the time of writing.
Crystal Palace *(£1,000 from Bognor Regis T on 2/7/1990) F/PL 242+34/11 FLC 30+1/2 FAC 9+4 Others 5+3 (Free to Woking during 2002 close season)*
Manchester C *(Loaned on 28/10/1996) FL 8/1*
Stoke C *(Loaned on 14/2/1997) FL 5*
Brighton & Hove A *(Free on 23/10/2002) FL 34+2/2 FLC 2*

RODRIGUES Hugo Miguel
Born: Santa Maria do Feira, Portugal, 22 November 1979
Height: 6'8" **Weight:** 15.6
This giant defender joined Yeovil shortly before the start of last term and provided new options for manager Gary Johnson in the back line. A regular in the squad throughout the campaign, Hugo became something of a cult hero for the fans at Huish Park and scored his first goal for the club when he netted against Hull City in the final home game of the season.
Yeovil T *(Free from Pedras Rubras, Portugal on 6/8/2003) FL 23+11/1 FLC 1 FAC 2 Others 1*

ROGERS Alan
Born: Liverpool, 3 January 1977
Height: 5'9" **Weight:** 12.6
Club Honours: Div 1 '98
International Honours: E: U21-3
This pacy left-sided midfielder found his

opportunities for Leicester limited following the arrival of Ben Thatcher and he was allowed out on loan to maintain his match-fitness levels. A spell at Wigan, where he featured at left back, was ended by injury but in the new year he went out on loan to Nottingham Forest. He was used as a left-sided defender at the City Ground and linked up well with Andy Reid down the flank. Alan's contract expired at the end of the season, at which time he was released by Micky Adams.
Tranmere Rov *(From trainee on 1/7/1995) FL 53+4/2 FLC 1 FAC 1*
Nottingham F *(£2,000,000 on 10/7/1997) P/FL 135+2/17 FLC 15/2 FAC 2+1/1*
Leicester C *(£300,000 on 16/11/2001) P/FL 57+5 FLC 3/2 FAC 4*
Wigan Ath *(Loaned on 1/12/2003) FL 5*
Nottingham F *(Loaned on 13/2/2004) FL 12*

ROGERS Kristian Raleigh John
Born: Chester, 2 October 1980
Height: 6'3" **Weight:** 12.6
International Honours: E: Sch
Out of contract at Wrexham, Kristian signed for Sheffield United as understudy for goalkeeper Paddy Kenny. However, following Kenny's injury United signed a more experienced 'keeper and Kristian's appearances were limited to the reserves apart from one Carling Cup appearance against Queens Park Rangers when he performed competently. On transfer-deadline day he moved to Macclesfield on loan but added no further appearances during his stay.
Wrexham *(From Chester C juniors on 14/8/1998) FL 39+1 FLC 2 FAC 1 Others 1*
Sheffield U *(Free on 11/7/2003) FLC 1*

ROGERS Mark Alvin
Born: Guelph, Ontario, Canada, 3 November 1975
Height: 6'1" **Weight:** 12.12
International Honours: Canada: 7
This dependable central defender started last season as an automatic choice at Wycombe. However, with the team struggling, he lost his place, and although he later returned to the line-up he joined Conference club Stevenage Borough in the new year, the transfer later becoming permanent. Mark is a brave and committed team player who continued to turn out for Canada, winning further caps against the Republic of Ireland and the Czech Republic.
Wycombe W *(Free from Burnaby Canadians, Canada on 23/12/1998) FL 123+16/4 FLC 8/1 FAC 14+1/1 Others 7+1/1*

Ronaldo (right)

ROGET Leo Thomas Earl
Born: Ilford, 1 August 1977
Height: 6'1" **Weight:** 12.2
This experienced central defender had a
frustrating time at Brentford last term,
spending a lengthy time out with an
ankle injury and also suffering problems
with suspension. He moved on to
Rushden in the new year, but although he
was a regular in the line-up, he proved
unable to save the Diamonds from
relegation and was one of several players
released in the summer.
*Southend U (From trainee on 5/7/1995) FL
105+15/7 FLC 8 FAC 6/1 Others 3/1*
*Stockport Co (Free on 1/3/2001) FL 28+3/1
FLC 2*
Reading (Loaned on 14/2/2002) FL 1
*Brentford (Free on 9/8/2002) FL 29 FLC 1
FAC 1 Others 4*
*Rushden & Diamonds (Free on 30/1/2004)
FL 16+1*

[RONALDO] AVEIRO DOS
SANTOS Cristiano Ronaldo
Born: Madeira, Portugal, 5 February 1985
Height: 6'0" **Weight:** 12.4
Club Honours: FAC '04
International Honours: Portugal: 13;
U21-15; Yth
Ronaldo started the season with a
massive task in hand. Not only was he
hailed as Britain's most expensive
teenager, he also became heir apparent to
the No 7 shirt, last worn by a certain D
Beckham. Having impressed with a
sublime performance in Manchester
United's opening Premiership game
against Bolton, he found that defences
where quick to tighten up to nullify his
'step over' style. After opening his goal
account with a strike against Portsmouth,
there were also notable efforts against
Tottenham and Birmingham City as the
season progressed. With Sir Alex Ferguson
carefully monitoring his progress, Ronaldo
showed real class as the season reached
its climax. His exciting wing play was
allied with pinpoint crosses, which
became welcome fodder for the likes of
Ruud Van Nistelrooy and Louis Saha.
Ronaldo also established himself at
international level and was a member of
Portugal's squad that reached the final of
Euro 2004 only to be defeated by Greece.
*Manchester U (£7,700,000 + from Sporting
Lisbon, Portugal on 14/8/2003) PL 15+14/4
FLC 1 FAC 5/2 Others 3+2*

ROONEY Wayne Mark
Born: Liverpool, 24 October 1985
Height: 5'10" **Weight:** 12.4
International Honours: E: 17; Yth

Although the 2003-04 campaign was very
much a learning period for Wayne, he
confirmed his reputation as the most
outstanding young talent in the English
game. Abundantly gifted, he has a
footballing brain way beyond his teenage
years and his physical presence belies a
dexterous touch and perceptive passing
ability. Apart from a sparkling goal at
Charlton, some of his best performances
early in the season came for his country
and he became England's youngest-ever
scorer against Macedonia in September.
After three consecutive scoring
appearances as a substitute over
Christmas he produced the most
consistent form of his Everton career in
February and March, contributing a string
of outstanding displays. He scored nine
goals for the Blues in the season, the
majority being from powerful shots from
in and around the edge of the penalty
area. Wayne was outstanding for England
in the Euro 2004 finals in the summer, his
goals ensuring the team enjoyed a
comfortable passage through the group
stage, before he suffered a foot injury
that at the time of writing seemed likely
to keep him out of action for the start of
the 2004-05 campaign.
*Everton (From trainee on 20/2/2003) PL
40+27/15 FLC 4+2/2 FAC 4*

ROPER Ian Robert
Born: Nuneaton, 20 June 1977
Height: 6'3" **Weight:** 13.4
In his ninth season as a Walsall
professional, Ian was his usual brave
committed self at the heart of the
defence. Although suffering a number of
injuries he quickly recovered and one of
his finest displays was in the goalless
draw at West Ham in March when he
came back into the side after a three-
week absence and only one day's training.
Ian passed the 250-appearance mark for
the Saddlers in the course of the season.
*Walsall (From trainee on 15/5/1995) FL
203+25/2 FLC 8+6 FAC 10+3/1 Others 11+3*

ROQUE JUNIOR Jose Vitor
Born: Santa Rita do Spaucai, Brazil, 31
August 1976
Height: 6'1" **Weight:** 12.11
International Honours: Brazil: 33
This experienced defender was one of
several players to join Leeds United in
long-term loan deals at the start of last
season. Unfortunately his arrival coincided
with some heavy defeats and although he
scored two goals in the 3-2 Carling Cup
defeat by Manchester United he struggled
to come to terms with the pace of the

Premiership. Jose was eventually released
and subsequently joined Siena in another
loan deal.
*Leeds U (Loaned from AC Milan, Italy, ex
Palmeiras, on 1/9/2003) PL 5 FLC 2/2*

ROSE Matthew David
Born: Dartford, 24 September 1975
Height: 5'11" **Weight:** 11.1
Club Honours: FAYC '94
International Honours: E: U21-2
This central midfield or left-sided defensive
player missed the first half of the 2003-04
season for Queens Park Rangers with a
back injury sustained during the previous
campaign. His first competitive appearance
was in the reserves in December and he
returned to the first team for the final ten
minutes of the LDV Vans Trophy match
against Brighton, when he received a
warm welcome from the fans. For the rest
of the season Matthew was either on the
bench or in the line-up as cover for
injuries, mostly featuring at left back or in
the centre of the defence.
Arsenal (From trainee on 19/7/1994) PL 2+3
*Queens Park R (£500,000 on 20/5/1997) FL
171+17/6 FLC 7 FAC 4 Others 4+1*

ROSE Richard Alan
Born: Pembury, 8 September 1982
Height: 6'0" **Weight:** 11.9
This promising youngster took advantage
of the club's injury problems to break into
Gillingham side last term and produced a
number of gutsy performances that
earned him a new contract. The versatile
defender enjoyed an extended run in the
side in the second half of the campaign
and will be looking to establish himself in
the line-up in 2004-05.
*Gillingham (From trainee on 10/4/2001) FL
15+11 FLC 0+1*
Bristol Rov (Loaned on 13/12/2002) FL 9

ROSENIOR Liam James
Born: Wandsworth, 9 July 1984
Height: 5'9" **Weight:** 11.8
Club Honours: AMC '03
Following a trial spell at Fulham, Liam
made a permanent move last November
and featured regularly in the club's reserve
team at right back. In the new year he
joined Torquay on loan to gain further
experience of senior football and stayed
until the end of the season. After an
impressive debut for the Gulls in centre
midfield, he was used in a wide-right role
where he proved quick and to have good
technique. Liam is the son of the Torquay
United manager Leroy Rosenior.
*Bristol C (From trainee on 15/8/2001) FL
2+20/2 FAC 0+1 Others 2+3/1*

Wayne Rooney

Fulham (Free on 7/11/2003)
Torquay U (Loaned on 19/3/2004) FL 9+1

ROSS Neil James
Born: Birmingham, 10 August 1982
Height: 6'1" **Weight:** 14.2
Neil found himself well down the pecking order for a place in the Macclesfield team as a striker last term and mostly had to be content with his role in the reserves, for whom he completed the season as joint-top scorer. However, he made a few appearances for the senior side usually coming on from the substitutes' bench late in the match, giving him only limited opportunities to make an impression. Neil had a loan spell at Conference side Northwich Victoria early on in the campaign, but had to return early due to injury.
Leeds U (From trainee on 12/8/1999)
Stockport Co (Free on 28/1/2000) FL 3+6/2 FLC 1+1 FAC 1 Others 1+1
Bristol Rov (Loaned on 23/10/2001) FL 2+3 Others 1
Macclesfield T (£30,000 on 10/1/2003) FL 7+7

ROUGIER Anthony (Tony) Leo
Born: Tobago, 17 July 1971
Height: 6'0" **Weight:** 14.1
International Honours: Trinidad & Tobago
Tony signed for Brentford in the first week of the 2003-04 season and was mostly employed on the right wing, although he sometimes featured as a striker. His laid-back style and deceptive pace made him a great favourite of the Bees' fans and he scored some terrific goals. However, a change in management resulted in a move to Bristol City on transfer-deadline day and he proved to be a useful addition to the squad as the Ashton Gate club fought their way to the play-offs. He was released by City in the summer. Tony continued to represent Trinidad at international level during the campaign.
Raith Rov (Free from Trinity Prospect, Trinidad on 9/3/1995) SL 47+10/2 SLC 3/3 SC 4+1/1 Others 4+1/1
Hibernian (Signed on 10/7/1997) SL 34+11/4 SLC 4
Port Vale (£175,000 on 4/1/1999) FL 41+10/8 FLC 2/1 FAC 1
Reading (£325,000 on 11/8/2000) FL 47+37/6 FLC 2+3 FAC 2+1 Others 3+4
Brighton & Hove A (Loaned on 20/2/2003) FL 5+1/2
Brentford (Free on 15/8/2003) FL 29+2/4 FAC 2/1 Others 1
Bristol C (Free on 25/3/2004) FL 5+1/1 Others 3/1

ROUTLEDGE Wayne Neville
Born: Sidcup, 7 January 1985
Height: 5'6" **Weight:** 10.7
International Honours: E: Yth
This small, tricky right winger was a near ever-present in the Crystal Palace squad last term, featuring in the starting line-up throughout the second half of the campaign. Wayne has become a firm favourite with the Palace faithful and was voted as the club's 'Young Player of the Year' for the second season in a row. Already an established youth international, he represented England at U19 level during the season.
Crystal Palace (From trainee on 9/7/2002) FL 45+27/10 FLC 4+2 FAC 1+1 Others 3

ROWAN Jonathan (Jonny) Robert
Born: Grimsby, 29 November 1981
Height: 5'10" **Weight:** 11.4
Jonny featured on a number of occasions for Grimsby Town in the early stages of the 2003-04 campaign, scoring in the otherwise disastrous defeat at Hartlepool. However, he then dropped out of the reckoning and it was not until a change in management that he featured regularly in the side again. The young striker

Tony Rougier (centre)

contributed another goal in the home draw with Bournemouth in March.
Grimsby T (From trainee on 12/7/2000) FL 32+20/6 FLC 2+4/2 FAC 0+1

ROWETT Gary
Born: Bromsgrove, 6 March 1974
Height: 6'0" **Weight:** 12.10
After his 2002-03 season was decimated by injury, Gary was hoping for better luck when he played in Charlton's opening game against Manchester City at the Valley last term. It was not to be, however, and he made no further appearances for the club. Gary is a strong, hard-tackling and skilful defender who can play at right back or in central defence, but failed to shake off the persistent knee injury that plagued him all season and has now left the club.
Cambridge U (From trainee on 10/9/1991) FL 51+12/9 FLC 7/1 FAC 5+2 Others 5/3
Everton (£200,000 on 21/5/1994) PL 2+2
Blackpool (Loaned on 23/1/1995) FL 17
Derby Co (£300,000 on 20/7/1995) P/FL 101+4/2 FLC 8/2 FAC 5+2
Birmingham C (£1,000,000 on 17/8/1998) FL 87/6 FLC 9/3 FAC 3/1 Others 4/1
Leicester C (£3,000,000 + on 7/7/2000) PL 47+2/2 FLC 2 FAC 4/1 Others 2
Charlton Ath (£2,500,000 + on 14/5/2002) PL 13/1

ROWLAND Stephen (Steve) John
Born: Wrexham, 2 November 1981
Height: 5'10" **Weight:** 12.4
Steve eventually became Port Vale's regular right back last term, although in the early part of the season he was shunted here, there and everywhere after breaking into the line-up. He became settled in the right-back berth after Christmas and looked particularly sharp and effective in the tackle.
Port Vale (From trainee on 2/7/2001) FL 73+6/1 FAC 2 Others 5

ROWLANDS Martin Charles
Born: Hammersmith, 8 February 1979
Height: 5'9" **Weight:** 10.10
Club Honours: Div 3 '99
International Honours: RoI: 3; U21-8
Martin started out at right wing back for Queens Park Rangers last term, covering for the injured Terrell Forbes. When a regular full back became available he moved forward to a conventional right-wing position and he soon made the role his own only missing games through injury or suspension. Although not a prolific scorer he netted some important

goals and finished the season with a total of 12 goals. Martin was voted as the Supporters' Club and players' 'Player of the Season'. He was called up by the Republic of Ireland in the summer, winning his first full caps.
Brentford (£45,000 from Farnborough T on 6/8/1998) FL 128+21/20 FLC 8+3/1 FAC 7+2 Others 17/2
Queens Park R (Free on 6/8/2003) FL 41+1/10 FLC 2/2 FAC 1 Others 3

ROYCE Simon Ernest
Born: Forest Gate, 9 September 1971
Height: 6'2" **Weight:** 12.8
Simon returned to Charlton Athletic for his second spell at the club, and deputised for the suspended Dean Kiely in the opening game of the season against Manchester City at the Valley. It was his only appearance, for although Simon made some very good saves and played well in the 3-0 defeat, Kiely was recalled for the following game and kept his place for the remainder of the season. Simon is a good shot-stopper, comfortable with crosses and commands his area well.
Southend U (£35,000 from Heybridge Swifts on 15/10/1991) FL 147+2 FLC 9 FAC 5 Others 6
Charlton Ath (Free on 2/7/1998) PL 8
Leicester C (Free on 17/7/2000) PL 16+3 FLC 1 FAC 4
Brighton & Hove A (Loaned on 24/12/2001) FL 6
Queens Park R (Loaned on 24/8/2002) FL 16 Others 1
Charlton Ath (Free on 4/7/2003) PL 1

RUDDY John Thomas Gordon
Born: St Ives, 24 October 1986
Height: 6'4" **Weight:** 15.4
John was a regular with Cambridge United's successful youth team last term and was promoted to a position on the substitutes' bench in the closing stages of the campaign. He went on to make his senior debut in the final game of the season at Leyton Orient. In an eventful game, he gave a confident performance, saving a twice-taken penalty and keeping a clean sheet.
Cambridge U (Trainee) FL 1

RUNDLE Adam
Born: Durham, 8 July 1984
Height: 5'10" **Weight:** 11.2
Though he featured in half of Carlisle United's Third Division matches last term, most of Adam's appearances were off the bench and it was often difficult for him to make a telling contribution. A talented

winger with the ability to take on and beat defenders, his only goal for the club came in the LDV Vans Trophy win over Rochdale.
Darlington (Trainee) FL 8+9
Carlisle U (Free on 31/12/2002) FL 25+19/1 FLC 1 Others 4+1/2

RUSHBURY Andrew (Andy) James
Born: Carlisle, 7 March 1983
Height: 5'10" **Weight:** 11.7
Never more than a fringe player for Chesterfield last term, Andy managed just five appearances from the bench. Used mainly down the left wing, he scored his maiden League goal to provide a late equaliser at Wycombe in August. He went on loan to Alfreton Town in December but joined Conference club Telford in March, as the Spireites made room for new signings.
Chesterfield (From trainee on 25/7/2002) FL 23+17/1 FLC 2+2 FAC 1+1 Others 0+1

RUSK Simon Edward
Born: Peterborough, 17 December 1981
Height: 5'11" **Weight:** 12.8
Club Honours: NC '02
Simon picked up a hamstring injury early in the campaign which restricted his appearances for Boston United. He was used on the right side of midfield, but when he returned to action he was switched to right back in the final games. He accepted the offer of a three-month contract with the Pilgrims at the end of the season.
Boston U (Free from Cambridge C on 6/4/2001) FL 28+9/2 FLC 2 FAC 1 Others 1

RUSSELL Alexander (Alex) John
Born: Crosby, 17 March 1973
Height: 5'9" **Weight:** 11.7
It is impossible to overstate the importance of this central midfielder to the smooth running of Torquay's passing game last term. Always looking to receive the ball, Alex was the hub of the team, controlling games with his vision and his fast and accurate distribution. He was deservedly named in the PFA Division Three team for the second year in succession.
Rochdale (£4,000 from Burscough on 11/7/1994) FL 83+19/14 FLC 5/1 FAC 1+1 Others 2+3
Cambridge U (Free on 4/8/1998) FL 72+9/8 FLC 7+1 FAC 6 Others 3
Torquay U (Free on 9/8/2001) FL 114+1/18 FLC 4 FAC 3/1 Others 2

Alex Russell

RUSSELL Craig Stewart
Born: Jarrow, 4 February 1974
Height: 5'10" **Weight:** 12.6
Club Honours: Div 1 '96
Craig began the 2003-04 season on a short-term contract at Carlisle, but although he scored with a clever lob in the Carling Cup tie at Walsall he managed only a handful of appearances before leaving in mid-season. In January he returned to Darlington where his experience in holding the ball and bringing others into play was evident as well as his eye for goal. Craig netted a spectacular winner for the Quakers in the crucial game at Macclesfield in March.
Sunderland (From trainee on 1/7/1992) P/FL 103+47/31 FLC 7+6/1 FAC 6+3/2 Others 2
Manchester C (£1,000,000 on 14/11/1997) FL 22+9/2 FAC 5+1/2
Tranmere Rov (Loaned on 7/8/1998) FL 3+1
Port Vale (Loaned on 29/1/1999) FL 8/1
Darlington (Loaned on 3/9/1999) FL 11+1/2
Oxford U (Loaned on 11/2/2000) FL 5+1
St Johnstone (Loaned on 29/3/2000) SL 1/1
St Johnstone (Free on 12/7/2000) SL 16+19/2 SLC 1+1 SC 1+1/1 Others 2
Carlisle U (Free on 16/1/2003) FL 10+9/1 FLC 1/1 FAC 1 Others 4+1
Darlington (Free on 16/1/2004) FL 6+6/1

RUSSELL Darel Francis Roy
Born: Stepney, 22 October 1980
Height: 5'11" **Weight:** 11.9
International Honours: E: Yth
Despite playing in the thick of the action this competitive midfielder was an ever-present for Stoke City last season. His pacy runs from the centre of the park often gave opposing defences problems and he was also capable of turning up unnoticed in the penalty area to put the finishing touches to attacking moves. A useful player with a good 'engine', he was voted as City's 'Young Player of the Year' by the fans, a fine tribute to his first season with the club.
Norwich C (From trainee on 29/11/1997) FL 99+33/7 FLC 8/2 FAC 6+1
Stoke C (£125,000 on 8/8/2003) FL 46/4 FLC 2 FAC 2

RUSSELL Samuel (Sam) Ian
Born: Middlesbrough, 4 October 1982
Height: 6'0" **Weight:** 10.13
Sam joined Third Division Scunthorpe United on loan last August as reserve goalkeeper but within three weeks, he had forced his way into the first team. He kept the club's first clean sheet of the campaign at Kidderminster on his debut, and then saved a penalty in each of the next two away matches. Sam showed

himself to be a confident goalkeeper during his three months with the Iron before returning to the Riverside Stadium and a place in the reserve team. He was released by Middlesbrough during the summer.
Middlesbrough (From trainee on 7/7/2000)
Darlington (Loaned on 28/12/2002) FL 1
Scunthorpe U (Loaned on 22/8/2003) FL 10 FLC 1 Others 1

RUSTER Sebastien
Born: Marseilles, France, 6 September 1982
Height: 5'10" **Weight:** 12.3
Sebastien was signed up by Swindon after impressing during trials. A wide midfielder with blistering pace, skill and the ability to take players on, he looked a promising player on the few occasions he appeared for the Robins. However, his previous club Cannes subsequently demanded a fee for his transfer and he was there fore released by the Second Division club in January.
Swindon T (Free from Cannes, France on 3/10/2003) FL 0+2 FAC 0+1 Others 1

RYAN Keith James
Born: Northampton, 25 June 1970
Height: 5'11" **Weight:** 12.8
Club Honours: FAT '91, '93; GMVC '93
Club captain at Wycombe Wanderers, Keith had an injury-blighted time in 2003-04, missing the start of the campaign following a hernia operation, with problems to knee and ankle to follow. The latter required an operation in March, and at the time of writing he appeared likely to miss the start of the 2004-05 season. In spite of this he managed a dozen starts, playing either as a forceful midfielder or striker. His only goal, against Bournemouth in December, set up a rare win for the team.
Wycombe W (Signed from Berkhamstead T during 1990 close season) FL 264+49/27 FLC 13+2/3 FAC 20+4/4 Others 17+2/1

RYAN Robert (Robbie) Paul
Born: Dublin, 16 May 1977
Height: 5'10" **Weight:** 12.0
Club Honours: Div 2 '01
International Honours: RoI: U21-12; Yth; Sch
After a slow start at Millwall last term, Robbie firmly established himself in the line-up during the second half of the campaign. The consistent left back rarely had a bad day at the office and was once again a key figure in defence for the club.
Huddersfield T (Free from Belvedere YC on 26/7/1994) FL 12+3 FLC 2

Millwall (£10,000 on 30/1/1998) FL 209+17/2 FLC 9 FAC 16 Others 5

RYAN Timothy (Tim) James
Born: Stockport, 10 December 1974
Height: 5'10" **Weight:** 11.6
Club Honours: Div 3 '04
International Honours: E: SP-14
Tim started the 2003-04 campaign playing in the centre of defence for Doncaster Rovers, but was soon pushed out to the left-back position. This gave him licence to push forward more and in his first match in his new role he blasted in a goal from 30 yards. He repeated the feat a month later and the Belle Vue fans have since urged him to shoot every time he goes forward. Tim enjoyed an excellent season with Rovers and is a popular man around the club and with the fans.
Scunthorpe U (From trainee on 8/4/1993) FL 1+1 (Free to Buxton on 28/11/1994)
Doncaster Rov (Free on 8/8/1996) FL 22+6 FLC 0+1 FAC 1 Others 1 (Free to Southport on 5/8/1997)
Doncaster Rov (Free on 24/5/2000) FL 41+1/2 FLC 2 FAC 1 Others 1

Robbie Ryan

S

SAAH Brian Ebo

Born: Hornchurch, 16 December 1986
Height: 6'1" **Weight:** 11.0
Brian became one of Leyton Orient's youngest-ever players when he made his senior debut at Huddersfield last September. The promising midfielder showed maturity beyond his years and seemed calm on the ball and not afraid to tackle. Brian will be looking to gain further senior experience for the O's in 2004-05.
Leyton Orient (Trainee) FL 4+2

SABIN Eric

Born: Paris, France, 22 January 1975
Height: 6'1" **Weight:** 12.4
This tall striker scored his first goal for Queens Park Rangers in injury-time in the game at Grimsby, giving the club their first-ever victory at Blundell Park. Although he only made three starts, Eric was a regular on the bench, but only came on in a handful of games. He was a regular in the reserve side, for whom he scored some fine individual goals. With his opportunities limited at Loftus Road, he went out on loan to Boston United in March, but signed a permanent transfer for Northampton Town before the transfer deadline at the end off the month. Eric opened his account for the Cobblers with two goals against Hull at the KC stadium.
Swindon T (Free from Wasquehal, France on 13/7/2001) FL 60+13/9 FLC 2 FAC 5 Others 0+1
Queens Park R (Free on 17/7/2003) FL 3+7/1 FLC 0+2 FAC 1 Others 2+1
Boston U (Loaned on 3/3/2004) FL 2
Northampton T (Signed on 12/3/2004) FL 9+2/5 Others 1

SADLER Matthew (Mat) John

Born: Birmingham, 26 February 1985
Height: 5'11" **Weight:** 11.6
International Honours: E: Yth
This young Birmingham City defender joined Northampton Town on loan last November as cover for injuries and international call-ups. Mat produced a series of creditable performances at left back for the Cobblers before returning to continue his development in the Blues' reserve team.
Birmingham C (From trainee on 12/4/2002) PL 2 FLC 2
Northampton T (Loaned on 21/11/2003) FL 7 Others 1

SADLIER Richard Thomas

Born: Dublin, 14 January 1979
Height: 6'2" **Weight:** 12.10
Club Honours: Div 2 '01
International Honours: Rol: U21-2; Yth
This tall, rangy front man managed just a couple of first-team appearances for Millwall last term, coming on as a substitute in the early-season games against Crewe and Stoke. However, he then suffered from a recurrence of the hip injury that had previously threatened his career and in the new year he announced his retirement from the game. He will be a great loss to the club.
Millwall (Signed from Belvedere YC on 14/8/1996) FL 103+42/34 FLC 6/2 FAC 4+1/2 Others 7+2/3

SAFRI Youssef

Born: Morocco, 1 March 1977
Height: 5'10" **Weight:** 11.8
International Honours: Morocco:
Youssef produced some excellent performances as a midfield anchor man for Coventry, impressing with his excellent ball control and distribution. Playing mainly in the deeper 'holding' role he had limited scoring chances and failed to register a goal. However, he suffered hernia problems towards the end of the season and required corrective surgery that kept him out of action for several games.
Coventry C (Free from Raja Casablanca, Morocco on 25/8/2001) FL 87+4/1 FLC 6 FAC 1

SAHA Louis

Born: Paris, France, 8 August 1978
Height: 5'11" **Weight:** 11.10
Club Honours: Div 1 '01
International Honours: France: 5; U21; Yth (UEFA-U18 '97)
This livewire forward displayed exceptional form during the first half of the season with Fulham before a much-publicised move to Old Trafford. A change in system saw Louis often play as a lone striker and he revelled in the responsibility banging in 15 goals, some spectacular but many just simply the clinical finishes from a confident striker. At the time of his move he was enjoying a fine scoring run which included four doubles in an eight game spell. Bought as a long-term spearhead with Ruud Van Nistelrooy in mind, Louis certainly got his United career off with a bang. Having celebrated his debut with a trademark goal against Southampton, he followed it up with a double strike against Everton in his next Premiership game. Showing a positive

understanding with Van Nistelrooy from the off, further strikes against Fulham and Arsenal in the Premiership gave an instant return on his transfer fee. Though injury confined him to the sidelines for most of February, and disappointment came in his first European tie against Porto, the successes outweighed the failings on what seems to be another of Sir Alex's most astute buys.
Newcastle U (Loaned from Metz, France on 8/1/1999) PL 5+6/1 FAC 1/1
Fulham (£2,100,000 from Metz, France on 29/6/2000) P/FL 100+17/53 FLC 3+3/6 FAC 10+1/3 Others 5+4/1
Manchester U (£12,825,000 on 23/1/2004) PL 9+3/7 Others 1+1

SAKHO Lamine

Born: Louga, Senegal, 28 September 1977
Height: 5'10" **Weight:** 11.2
International Honours: Senegal; France: U21
One of several players to join Leeds United in long-term loan deals last season, Lamine impressed during a pre-season tournament in Dublin. The experienced striker began the 2003-04 campaign in the first team and scored in the victory at Middlesbrough in August. However, he was out of the picture under Eddie Gray and only featured once after January. Lamine represented Senegal in the African Nations' Cup finals at the beginning of the year.
Leeds U (Loaned from Marseilles, France, ex Nimes, RC Lens, on 14/8/2003) PL 9+8/1 FLC 1 FAC 0+1

SAKIRI Artim

Born: Struga, Macedonia, 23 September 1973
Height: 5'11" **Weight:** 12.0
International Honours: Macedonia: 61
Following three months of negotiations, Albion manager Gary Megson finally signed this attacking midfielder. After having had the pleasure of scoring for his country in a Euro 2004 qualifying game against England in October 2002, Artim gained his 55th full cap in the return in September 2003. A strong, purposeful player with a great engine, he celebrated his debut for Albion with a wonderful equalising goal in the 4-1 win over Burnley.
West Bromwich A (Signed from CSKA Sofia, Bulgaria, ex Vardar Skopje, Halmstads, TennisBorussia, HIT Gorica, Malatyaspar, on 4/8/2003) FL 6+19/1 FLC 2+2 FAC 1

SALAKO John Akin

Born: Nigeria, 11 February 1969
Height: 5'10" **Weight:** 12.8

Lloyd Sam

Club Honours: FMC '91; Div 1 '94, '00
International Honours: E: 5
Although John made a total of 43 first-team appearances for Reading in 2003-04, he only played the full 90 minutes in 19 of those games, and his future with the club was always in doubt from the time when he was asked to agree to an alteration in his contract. He had filled the left-wing berth with some success and his crossing of the ball was as accurate as ever, but he may now feel the time has come to concentrate on his media career after being released in the summer.
Crystal Palace (From apprentice on 3/11/1986) F/PL 172+43/22 FLC 19+5/5 FAC 20/4 Others 11+3/2
Swansea C (Loaned on 14/8/1989) FL 13/3 Others 2/1
Coventry C (£1,500,000 on 7/8/1995) PL 68+4/4 FLC 9/3 FAC 4/1
Bolton W (Free on 26/3/1998) PL 0+7
Fulham (Free on 22/7/1998) FL 7+3/1 FLC 2/1 FAC 2+2 Others 1
Charlton Ath (£150,000 + on 20/8/1999) P/FL 10+37/2 FLC 1+2 FAC 3+4/1
Reading (£75,000 + on 2/11/2001) FL 96+15/13 FLC 4+1/1 FAC 0+4 Others 1

SALL Abdou Hamed
Born: Senegal, 1 November 1980
Height: 6'3" **Weight:** 14.2
On a trip back from France Abdou asked Jan Molby if he could train with Kidderminster while he was in the area. He was then called into action for his second spell with Harriers to cover in defence for the suspended Wayne Hatswell at Southend. Clearly not ready for Third Division football he spent a few games on the bench before being loaned to Cinderford Town. Abdou was recalled for the final few games of the season and did enough to earn himself a new contract at Aggbrough.
Kidderminster Hrs (Free from Toulouse, France on 10/8/2001) FL 31/2 FAC 1 Others 2/1 (Free to Nuneaton Borough on 14/2/2003)
Oxford U (Loaned on 29/11/2002) FL 0+1 FAC 0+1
Kidderminster Hrs (Free from Revel, France on 12/2/2004) FL 6+1

SAM Hector McLeod
Born: Mount Hope, Trinidad, 25 February 1978
Height: 5'9" **Weight:** 11.5
International Honours: Trinidad & Tobago: 15
Still something of an enigma at Wrexham, Hector only found himself in the starting line up for roughly half the first-team

fixtures last term, but still topped the Racecourse scoring charts in a season when goals were hard to come by. His strength was his unpredictability, and he enjoyed a consistent spell during October and November, netting one of the goals to secure a win at Rushden and also a brace in the 4-2 home win over Blackpool just after Christmas.
Wrexham (£125,000 from CL Financial San Juan Jabloteh, Trinidad on 8/8/2000) FL 58+54/26 FLC 4+1 FAC 3+1 Others 5+3/2

SAM Lloyd Ekow
Born: Leeds, 27 September 1984
Height: 5'8" **Weight:** 10.7
International Honours: E: Yth
This talented youngster made his first-team debut for Charlton in a pre-season friendly and after developing in the reserves he joined Leyton Orient on loan to gain some valuable experience of senior football. He proved to be an exciting winger with the ability to beat a man and deliver his cross. Lloyd signed a further contract with the Addicks in the new year and will be looking to gain more first-team experience in 2004-05.
Charlton Ath (From trainee on 5/7/2002)
Leyton Orient (Loaned on 15/1/2004) FL 5+5

SAMBROOK Andrew (Andy) John
Born: Chatham, 13 July 1979
Height: 5'10" **Weight:** 12.4
Club Honours: Div 3 '03
International Honours: E: Sch
After spending most of the first half of last season on the bench, Andy stepped into the Rushden line-up as a replacement for the injured Paul Underwood just before Christmas. A player who is capable of slotting into several positions – including both full-back roles and as a defensive midfielder – he was a valuable member of the squad in case of injuries or suspensions. Andy had a few more opportunities towards the end of the season but was unable to prevent the Diamonds from slipping to relegation.
Gillingham (Associated Schoolboy) FL 0+1
Rushden & Diamonds (Free from Hartwick College, USA on 9/8/2001) FL 45+16 FAC 2 Others 1+1

SAMPSON Ian
Born: Wakefield, 14 November 1968
Height: 6'2" **Weight:** 13.3
This reliable central defender had another fine season at Northampton last term. He is particularly effective in the air and also likes to push upfield for set pieces, which led to his scoring twice during the campaign. Ian, who is now second in the

list of all-time appearances for the Cobblers, was awarded a benefit match against local rivals Rushden & Diamonds at the end of the season.
Sunderland (Signed from Goole T on 13/11/1990) FL 13+4/1 FLC 1 FAC 0+2 Others 0+1
Northampton T (Loaned on 8/12/1993) FL 8
Northampton T (Free on 5/8/1994) FL 372+10/26 FLC 16+1/1 FAC 19/1 Others 23/2
Tottenham H (Loaned on 22/6/1995) Others 3/1

SAMUEL JLloyd
Born: Trinidad, 29 March 1981
Height: 5'11" **Weight:** 11.4
International Honours: E: U21-7; Yth
This versatile Aston Villa player is comfortable as a right back, left back or in a wing-back role, although he is best used on the left-hand side. Jlloyd was a revelation last term, when he was an ever-present in the side, and was undoubtedly the club's most-improved player. He scored his first Premiership goal with an uncharacteristic right-foot wonder strike against Charlton and then doubled his tally in the Carling Cup semi-final against Bolton. Jlloyd was named in the senior England squad for the friendly against Sweden but has yet to win his first full cap.
Aston Villa (From trainee on 2/2/1999) PL 94+17/2 FLC 10+1/1 FAC 4 Others 5+2
Gillingham (Loaned on 26/10/2001) FL 7+1

SAMWAYS Vincent (Vinny)
Born: Bethnal Green, 27 October 1968
Height: 5'8" **Weight:** 11.0
Club Honours: FAC '91; CS '91, '95
International Honours: E: U21-5; Yth
Walsall fans were delighted when this experienced midfielder rejoined the club in the summer of 2003 after initially announcing that he was staying in Spain. Vinny's crisp passing was a delight and he bagged the match winner at Reading in October with a quickly taken free kick. Unfortunately he seemed to tire of the weekly journeying from Spain and he did not complete the season, playing his last game in the goalless draw at West Ham in March.
Tottenham H (From apprentice on 9/11/1985) F/PL 165+28/11 FLC 27+4/4 FAC 15+1/2 Others 7+1
Everton (£2,200,000 on 2/8/1994) PL 17+6/2 FLC 3/1 Others 2/1 (£600,000 to Las Palmas, Spain on 13/12/1996)
Wolverhampton W (Loaned on 21/12/1995) FL 3
Birmingham C (Loaned on 9/2/1996) FL 12
Walsall (Free from Sevilla, Spain on 26/2/2003) FL 42/2 FLC 2 FAC 1

SANASY Kevin Roy
Born: Leeds, 2 November 1984
Height: 5'8" **Weight:** 10.5
An aggressive forward usually employed on the right, Kevin has come up through the ranks at Bradford and showed his potential in the closing weeks of the season. He scored within four minutes of coming on as a substitute against Wimbledon, starting a passing move which swept from one end of the pitch to the other, which he then finished with an impudent flick from the outside of his right foot. Kevin made his full debut against Stoke in the final home game and kept his place the following week at Millwall.
Bradford C (Trainee) FL 2+4/1

SANDWITH Kevin
Born: Workington, 30 April 1978
Height: 5'11" **Weight:** 12.5
This skilful left back was signed by Lincoln City from Halifax Town following the departure of Paul Mayo to Watford. Kevin made only one start in the final weeks of the season but was a regular on the substitutes' bench. He showed potential as a naturally left-sided player with good tackling and passing skills.
Carlisle U (From trainee on 16/7/1996) FL 2+1 (Free to Barrow on 27/9/1998)
Lincoln C (Free from Halifax T, ex Telford U, Doncaster Rov, on 12/3/2004) FL 1+2

SANTOS Georges
Born: Marseille, France, 15 August 1970
Height: 6'3" **Weight:** 14.0
Georges started last season playing as a defensive midfield player for Ipswich, a role to which he is not particularly suited, and he struggled to produce his best form. His confidence and form improved once he was moved to central defence and his defensive partnership with Richard Naylor blossomed. However, he found himself a casualty after a poor team performance against Crystal Palace at the end of the year and he was unable to re-establish himself in the side.
Tranmere Rov (Free from Toulon, France on 29/7/1998) FL 46+1/2 FLC 6 FAC 1
West Bromwich A (£25,000 on 23/3/2000) FL 8
Sheffield U (Free on 5/7/2000) FL 37+24/6 FLC 2+3 FAC 1+1
Grimsby T (Free on 27/9/2002) FL 24+2/1 FAC 1
Ipswich T (Free on 1/8/2003) FL 28+6/1 FLC 2

SAUNDERS Mark Philip
Born: Reading, 23 July 1971
Height: 5'11" **Weight:** 11.12

Once a stalwart of the Gillingham side, Mark was very much a bit-part player during the 2003-04 campaign. Injuries hampered his season but he was often overlooked when fit. The experienced midfielder or right back netted once during the season, hitting the winner in the 4-3 thriller at Ipswich in November.
Plymouth Arg (Signed from Tiverton T on 22/8/1995) FL 60+12/11 FLC 1+1 FAC 2+3 Others 2
Gillingham (Free on 1/6/1998) FL 114+55/15 FLC 8+2/1 FAC 9+1/1 Others 3+4

SAVA Facundo
Born: Ituzaingo, Argentina, 3 July 1974
Height: 5'11" **Weight:** 12.8
It was a frustrating campaign for the Argentine striker who rarely got much of a look in at first-team level for Fulham, although he did finish as top scorer for the reserve team. His only start of the season came in the Carling Cup tie at Wigan, but he featured regularly on the bench in the first half of the campaign, but his only senior goal of the campaign came in the 2-1 home win over Bolton. Facundo's style as a more orthodox centre forward did not fit in with the system and he struggled to benefit from the lone-striker role.
Fulham (£2,000,000 from Gimnasia y Esgrima la Plata, Argentina, ex Ferrocarril Oeste, Boca Juniors, on 25/6/2002) PL 13+13/6 FLC 2+1 FAC 3+3/1 Others 6

SAVAGE Basir (Bas) Mohammed
Born: Wandsworth, 7 January 1982
Height: 6'3" **Weight:** 13.8
Bas spent most of the 2003-04 campaign in Reading's reserves and despite his total of 17 first-team appearances – mostly as a substitute – he has still to score a goal in the Football League. However, he made a spirited comeback after missing a complete season through injury, and showed sufficient pace and enterprise as an attacker to persuade the manager to give him an extension to his contract. Bas had the satisfaction of captaining the reserve team which won the Pontins Combination by defeating Cardiff City reserves 3-1 in the play-off final at the Madejski Stadium.
Reading (£20,000 from Walton & Hersham on 7/2/2002) FL 6+10 FLC 1 FAC 1

SAVAGE David (Dave) Thomas Patrick
Born: Dublin, 30 July 1973
Height: 6'1" **Weight:** 12.7
International Honours: RoI: 5; U21-5

Dave was a regular in the Bristol Rovers line-up last term until picking up a niggling hamstring injury which ruled him out of the closing fixtures. A hard-working central midfielder, he scored two goals during the campaign, one of which proved to be the winner at Southend shortly before Christmas.
Brighton & Hove A (Signed from Kilkenny on 5/3/1991. Free to Longford T in May 1992)
Millwall (£15,000 on 27/5/1994) FL 104+28/6 FLC 11/2 FAC 6+2/2 Others 2/1
Northampton T (£100,000 on 7/10/1998) FL 98+15/18 FLC 3 FAC 5 Others 2+1
Oxford U (Free on 18/8/2001) FL 85/5 FLC 4 FAC 4 Others 2
Bristol Rov (Free on 1/7/2003) FL 37+1/2 FLC 1 FAC 1 Others 1

SAVAGE Robert (Robbie) William
Born: Wrexham, 18 October 1974
Height: 6'1" **Weight:** 11.11
Club Honours: FAYC '92; FLC '00
International Honours: W: 35; U21-5; Yth; Sch
Robbie provided the heartbeat to the Birmingham City side last term with his dynamic style and determination to chase lost causes. He inspired those around to copy him and his passing was both economical and accurate. Goalkeepers learned to respect him from free kicks as he whipped in vicious shots. Robbie wore his heart on his sleeve, he was booked on a number of occasions, but the Blues fans loved him.
Manchester U (From trainee on 5/7/1993)
Crewe Alex (Free on 22/7/1994) FL 74+3/10 FLC 5 FAC 5 Others 8/1
Leicester C (£400,000 on 23/7/1997) PL 160+12/8 FLC 15+2 FAC 12/1 Others 2+1
Birmingham C (£2,500,000 on 30/5/2002) PL 64/7 FAC 5

SCHEMMEL Sebastien
Born: Nancy, France, 2 June 1975
Height: 5'10" **Weight:** 11.12
International Honours: France: U21
This former West Ham defender was in and out of Pompey's Premiership team last season after a promising start to the campaign. He contributed a goal in the FA Cup tie against Blackpool, but Portsmouth supporters feel they have yet to see the best from this experienced player.
West Ham U (£465,000 from Metz, France, ex Nancy, on 19/1/2001) PL 60+3/1 FLC 2+1 FAC 7
Portsmouth (Free on 14/8/2003) PL 12+2 FLC 2 FAC 1+1/1

Robbie Savage

Paul Scholes

SCHOFIELD Daniel (Danny) James
Born: Doncaster, 10 April 1980
Height: 5'10" **Weight:** 11.3
This skilful winger or striker enjoyed a fruitful season in the Huddersfield Town first-team ranks last term. The youngster served up several fine displays and contributed some great goals, none more so than the double strikes against Yeovil and Swansea at the McAlpine Stadium. Danny made a significant contribution to the Terriers' play-off success, scoring from the penalty spot in the second leg of the semi-final and again in the shoot-out that decided the final after another 'Man of the Match' performance.
Huddersfield T (£2,000 from Brodsworth on 8/2/1999) FL 103+11/18 FLC 5+1 FAC 4+1 Others 10+1/5

SCHOLES Paul
Born: Salford, 16 November 1974
Height: 5'7" **Weight:** 11.10
Club Honours: PL '96, '97, '99, '00, '01, '03; FAC '96, '99, '04; CS '96, '97, '03
International Honours: E: 66; Yth (UEFA-U18 '93)
A central midfielder whose imaginative distribution makes him the fulcrum of the team, Paul once again showed that even amongst United's new elite he was very much the main deal. Scoring in successive Premiership outings against Bolton and Newcastle, his season was then hampered by injury. Despite that, he returned to net against Birmingham, and Manchester City (2) in the Premiership, and by the turn of the year he enjoyed an extended spell of first-team action celebrating with goals against Aston Villa and Manchester City in the Premiership and further contributions against City and Arsenal in the FA Cup. In Europe too his influence propelled United into the knock out stages of the Champions League. Indeed, his strike in the match against Porto at Old Trafford in March seemed likely to propel United to the quarter-finals. A second goal that night was ruled offside, costing United a place in the last eight.
Manchester U (From trainee on 29/1/1993) PL 230+58/78 FLC 10+4/8 FAC 18+8/9 Others 76+11/20

SCHUMACHER Steven (Steve) Thomas
Born: Liverpool, 30 April 1984
Height: 5'10" **Weight:** 11.0
International Honours: E: Yth
This young Everton midfield player joined Third Division Carlisle United on loan last November to gain some valuable

experience of senior football. He featured regularly during his stay at Brunton Park and scored with a neat header in the LDV Vans Trophy clash with Huddersfield. Steve later had a spell on loan at Oldham where he did not feature in the first team and was released by Everton at the end of the season.
Everton (From trainee on 12/5/2001)
Carlisle U (Loaned on 31/10/2003) FL 4 FAC 1 Others 1/1

SCHWARZER Mark
Born: Sydney, Australia, 6 October 1972
Height: 6'5" **Weight:** 13.6
Club Honours: FLC '04
International Honours: Australia: 25; Yth
Mark missed only three Premiership games in Middlesbrough's long, historic season and he must now be considered one of the best goalkeepers in the competition. However, with only a year of his contract left Boro' manager Steve McClaren wanted to tie his number one 'keeper to a long-term contract, but talks were put on hold and the outcome was uncertain at the time of writing.
Bradford C (£350,000 from Kaiserslautern, Germany, ex Blacktown, Marconi, Dynamo Dresden, on 22/11/1996) FL 13 FAC 3
Middlesbrough (£1,500,000 on 26/2/1997) F/PL 239 FLC 23 FAC 13

SCIMECA Riccardo (Riccy)
Born: Leamington Spa, 13 June 1975
Height: 6'1" **Weight:** 12.9
Club Honours: FLC '96
International Honours: E: B-1; U21-9
Equally adept in the centre of defence or in a 'holding' midfield role, Riccy joined Leicester in the summer of 2003. An accomplished and valuable member of the team, his adaptability was stretched further by a spell at right back later in the season. A promising central defensive partnership with Steve Howey was broken up when the latter was allowed to join Bolton in January. Riccy was sidelined with injury for the final few games and was quickly sought after by promoted Norwich City as the season ended.
Aston Villa (From trainee on 7/7/1993) PL 50+23/2 FLC 4+3 FAC 9+1 Others 5+2
Nottingham F (£3,000,000 on 23/7/1999) FL 147+4/7 FLC 8/1 FAC 5 Others 2
Leicester C (Free on 5/7/2003) PL 28+1/1 FLC 1 FAC 1

SCOFFHAM Stephen (Steve)
Born: Germany, 12 July 1983
Height: 5'11" **Weight:** 11.4
At the beginning of the 2003-04 season

Steve was employed in the building trade and playing for Northern Counties East League club Gedling Town. However, in a real-life 'Roy of the Rovers' tale the young striker was snapped up by Notts County and went on to feature regularly at first-team level, albeit mainly from the substitutes' bench. Steve scored his first-ever Football League goal against Grimsby in March, but unfortunately he broke a bone in his leg on the final day of a quite remarkable season.
Notts Co (Signed from Gedling T on 14/2/2004) FL 4+11/2

SCOTT Andrew (Andy)
Born: Epsom, 2 August 1972
Height: 6'1" **Weight:** 11.5
Club Honours: Div 3 '99
Andy suffered a serious leg injury playing for Oxford against Boston United early on last season and this kept him out of action for several months. Once he returned to fitness he was unable to win back his place in the line-up and he eventually moved on to Leyton Orient. An experienced left winger or striker, Andy featured regularly for the O's in the closing fixtures and will be looking to establish himself in the side in 2004-05.
Sheffield U (£50,000 from Sutton U on 1/12/1992) P/FL 39+36/6 FLC 5/2 FAC 2+1 Others 3+1/3
Chesterfield (Loaned on 18/10/1996) FL 4+1/3
Bury (Loaned on 21/3/1997) FL 2+6
Brentford (£75,000 on 21/11/1997) FL 109+9/28 FLC 8+1/4 FAC 3 Others 6/3
Oxford U (£75,000 on 12/11/2001) FL 77+18/24 FLC 3+1/1 FAC 0+1
Leyton Orient (Free on 24/3/2004) FL 8/1

SCOTT Paul
Born: Wakefield, 5 November 1979
Height: 5'11" **Weight:** 12.8
This industrious defender slotted comfortably into the Huddersfield Town back line when called upon last term and never failed to impress. He even managed to score his first senior goal in the defeat at Bury. A good reader of the game, he tackles strongly and has a quick turn of pace. Paul will be looking to establish himself in the side long term once he has recovered from an ankle injury.
Huddersfield T (From trainee on 3/7/1998) FL 18+14/2 FLC 1+1 FAC 1 Others 1+1

SCOTT Paul David
Born: Burnley, 29 January 1985
Height: 5'10" **Weight:** 11.10
When Paul made his Burnley debut as a substitute in the away game at Coventry

Mark Schwarzer

in March, he became the fifth member of his family to represent the Clarets at first-team level, following grandfather Brian Miller, uncle David Miller, father Derek and brother Chris. Primarily a left back, he had shown promise in the reserves and will be looking to gain further senior experience next term.
Burnley (Trainee) FL 0+2

SCOTT Richard Paul
Born: Dudley, 29 September 1974
Height: 5'9" **Weight:** 12.8
Richard struggled to break into the first-team set-up at Peterborough last term and his only appearance came as a substitute in the FA Cup tie against Hereford. A versatile player who can feature at full back or in midfield, he was subsequently released and later joined Stevenage.
Birmingham C (From trainee on 17/5/1993) FL 11+1 FLC 3+1 Others 3
Shrewsbury T (Signed on 22/3/1995) FL 91+14/18 FLC 6 FAC 8+1/3 Others 8+1/1
Peterborough U (Signed on 20/7/1998) FL 65+16/7 FLC 1+3 FAC 1 Others 6+1 (Free to Telford U during 2001 close season)
Peterborough U (Free from Stevenage Borough on 23/12/2002) FL 13+3/1 FAC 0+1

SCOTT Robert (Rob)
Born: Epsom, 15 August 1973
Height: 6'1" **Weight:** 11.10
There can be few players who have been more unfortunate with injuries than Rob over the last couple of seasons. Last term he fought back well from a dislocated shoulder to win back his place in the side and he was showing some of his best-ever form for Rotherham on the right of the back four when he suffered a cruciate knee ligament injury at Sunderland in October, and this kept him out for the rest of the campaign. However, he is now back to full fitness again and will be pushing for a first-team place again in 2004-05.
Sheffield U (£20,000 from Sutton U on 1/8/1993) FL 2+4/1 FLC 0+1 Others 2+1
Scarborough (Loaned on 22/3/1995) FL 8/3
Northampton T (Loaned on 24/11/1995) FL 5 Others 1
Fulham (£30,000 on 10/1/1996) FL 65+19/17 FLC 3+5 FAC 3/1 Others 2+2/1
Carlisle U (Loaned on 18/8/1998) FL 7/3
Rotherham U (£50,000 on 17/11/1998) FL 143+7/7 FLC 9+1 FAC 8/1 Others 6

SCOWCROFT James (Jamie) Benjamin
Born: Bury St Edmunds, 15 November 1975
Height: 6'1" **Weight:** 12.2
International Honours: E: U21-5

James can operate either as a striker or in a withdrawn midfield role, but last season he was again used mostly on the right of midfield for Leicester. A regular in the side throughout the campaign, his form seemed to dip during the latter stages of the season. James scored five goals including a late strike as the Foxes completed a double over Portsmouth in the final home fixture.
Ipswich T (From trainee on 1/7/1994) P/FL 163+39/47 FLC 21+4/7 FAC 9+1 Others 7+3/1
Leicester C (£3,000,000 on 31/7/2001) P/FL 97+5/20 FLC 5+1/1 FAC 4/1

SCULLY Anthony (Tony) Derek Thomas
Born: Dublin, 12 June 1976
Height: 5'7" **Weight:** 11.12
International Honours: RoI: B-1; U21-10; Yth; Sch
Although Tony began last season at Peterborough, he failed to make a first-team appearance for the Posh and drifted off to play in the Conference with Dagenham & Redbridge, Barnet and then Tamworth. New Notts County boss Gary Mills then gave him the chance to resurrect his career at Meadow Lane and he grabbed at the chance. The skilful winger impressed the Magpies fans with three goals from six starts and earned himself a permanent contract with the club.
Crystal Palace (From trainee on 2/12/1993) FL 0+3
Bournemouth (Loaned on 14/10/1994) FL 6+4 Others 2
Cardiff C (Loaned on 5/1/1996) FL 13+1
Manchester C (£80,000 on 12/8/1997) FL 1+8
Stoke C (Loaned on 27/11/1998) FL 7
Queens Park R (£155,000 on 17/3/1998) FL 20+20/2 FLC 4+1 FAC 0+1
Cambridge U (Free on 9/7/2001) FL 20+11/2 FLC 0+1 FAC 2 Others 3
Southend U (Loaned on 1/11/2002) FL 8 FAC 4
Peterborough U (Free to Dagenham & Redbridge on 5/9/2003)
Notts Co (Free from Tamworth, via Barnet, on 12/2/2004) FL 6+4/3

SEAMAN David Andrew
Born: Rotherham, 19 September 1963
Height: 6'4" **Weight:** 14.10
Club Honours: Div 1 '91; PL '98, '02; FAC '93, '98, '02, '03; FLC '93; ECWC '94; CS '98, '02
International Honours: E: 75; B-6; U21-10
David joined Manchester City in the summer of 2003 hoping to enjoy a

swansong season having spent 13 successful years at Arsenal. Things, however, did not quite go according to plan and after damaging a shoulder during the 4-2 defeat at Portsmouth he made the decision to hang up his gloves. He will be remembered as an international-class 'keeper, an excellent shot-stopper with good command over his area.
Leeds U (From apprentice on 22/9/1981)
Peterborough U (£4,000 on 13/8/1982) FL 91 FLC 10 FAC 5 Others 3
Birmingham C (£100,000 on 5/10/1984) FL 75 FLC 4 FAC 5
Queens Park R (£225,000 on 7/8/1986) FL 141 FLC 13 FAC 17 Others 4
Arsenal (£1,300,000 on 18/5/1990) F/PL 405 FLC 38 FAC 48 Others 73
Manchester C (Free on 4/7/2003) PL 19 FLC 1 FAC 1 Others 5

SEARLE Damon Peter
Born: Cardiff, 26 October 1971
Height: 5'11" **Weight:** 10.4
Club Honours: WC '92, '93; Div 3 '93
International Honours: W: B-1; U21-6; Yth; Sch
Damon joined Chesterfield on a monthly contract last August after trials at Colchester and York, and slotted in with some effect as an attacking left back, displaying stamina, a good tackle and crossing ability. With the defence settling, however, he was allowed to leave and he moved on to Conference outfit Forest Green Rovers.
Cardiff C (From trainee on 20/8/1990) FL 232+2/3 FLC 9/1 FAC 13 Others 22
Stockport Co (Free on 28/5/1996) FL 34+7 FLC 2+1 FAC 2 Others 1
Carlisle U (Free on 6/7/1998) FL 57+9/3 FLC 4 FAC 1 Others 4+1/1
Rochdale (Loaned on 17/9/1999) FL 13+1
Southend U (Free on 10/7/2000) FL 126+7/3 FLC 4 FAC 12 Others 9/1
Chesterfield (Free on 15/8/2003) FL 4+1

SEDDON Gareth Jonathan
Born: Burnley, 23 May 1980
Height: 5'11" **Weight:** 11.2
This promising striker made a slow start at Bury last term, but his season gathered momentum as it progressed. Initially at Gigg Lane on a short-term monthly rolling contract, Gareth was a substitute in the early-season games and his first start did not come until mid-September. In February he was awarded a contract until the end of the season and he responded by scoring regularly, finishing the campaign as the Shakers' leading scorer with 11 goals.

Bury (Signed from RAF Codsall, via trail at Everton, ex Accrington Stanley, Atherstone U, on 9/8/2001) FL 53+26/17 FLC 1+1 FAC 1/1

SEDGEMORE Benjamin (Ben) Redwood
Born: Wolverhampton, 5 August 1975
Height: 5'11" **Weight:** 12.10
International Honours: E: Sch
Ben began the 2003-04 season in a central-midfield position for Lincoln City but a hernia operation in late August put him out of action for five weeks. He found himself on the bench when fit again, only getting back in the starting line-up when Richard Butcher was injured. Ben was released at the end of the season.
Birmingham C (From trainee on 17/5/1993)
Northampton T (Loaned on 22/12/1994) FL 1
Mansfield T (Loaned on 25/8/1995) FL 4+5 Others 1
Peterborough U (Free on 10/1/1996) FL 13+4 FAC 1
Mansfield T (Free on 6/9/1996) FL 58+9/6 FLC 1 FAC 2+1 Others 3
Macclesfield T (£25,000 on 19/3/1998) FL 84+18/6 FLC 8/2 FAC 7/1 Others 2
Lincoln C (Signed on 16/2/2001) FL 83+25/5 FLC 3 FAC 4 Others 3+3

SEDGWICK Christopher (Chris) Edward
Born: Sheffield, 28 April 1980
Height: 5'11" **Weight:** 10.10
Chris made further progress for Rotherham last term and passed the landmark figure of 200 appearances although he is still only in his early twenties. He again demonstrated his ability to deliver telling crosses from wide on the right, but he was not very prolific in finding the net himself, although one of his goals brought an unexpected victory at promoted West Bromwich Albion. The young winger was able to maintain a prodigious work rate while his defensive work proved crucial to the club's cause.
Rotherham U (From trainee on 16/8/1997) FL 176+47/15 FLC 8+2/2 FAC 8+5 Others 2+2/1

SEMPLE Ryan David
Born: Belfast, 4 July 1985
Height: 5'11" **Weight:** 10.11
This pacy, wide-attacking player had a lengthy spell on loan at Farnborough last term. His only first-team appearance for Peterborough came in the final game of the season against Wycombe. Ryan will be hoping to make a breakthrough into the first-team squad in 2004-05.
Peterborough U (From trainee on 12/8/2002) FL 2+3

SENDA Daniel (Danny) Luke
Born: Harrow, 17 April 1981
Height: 5'10" **Weight:** 10.0
International Honours: E: Yth
Danny had another good season at right back for Wycombe last term. He was an automatic choice apart from a five-match run in December when a dip in form saw him lose his place under new manager Tony Adams. His pace is his big attribute, along with his work rate and a willingness to bring the ball forward. As a result he was switched to his old wide-right-midfield role in March, responding with some splendid performances. Danny signed a new contract for the Chairboys in the summer.
Wycombe W (From Southampton juniors on 26/1/1999) FL 131+57/5 FLC 3+3 FAC 7+3 Others 6+4

SENIOR Philip (Phil) Anthony
Born: Huddersfield, 30 October 1982
Height: 5'11" **Weight:** 11.1
Phil started the 2003-04 season as understudy to new arrival Ian Gray in goal for Huddersfield Town. However, when injury ruled out Gray, Phil stepped in and enjoyed an extended run in the side until the arrival of Paul Rachubka on loan from Charlton. A great shot-stopper, he commands his area well for a small 'keeper.
Huddersfield T (From trainee on 6/11/1999) FL 32+2 FAC 0+1

SESTANOVICH Ashley Shane
Born: Lambeth, 18 September 1981
Height: 6'3" **Weight:** 13.0
Ashley joined Sheffield United in the summer of 2003 and began the season in the reserves. He enjoyed an impressive loan spell with Scarborough where he was named 'FA Cup Player of Round Two'. Returning to Bramall Lane he made his debut in April as a substitute, playing down the right flank.
Sheffield U (Signed from Hampton & Richmond on 27/2/2003) FL 0+2

SHACKELL Jason Philip
Born: Stevenage, 27 August 1983
Height: 5'11" **Weight:** 11.9
This young Norwich central defender added six more senior appearances last term when he again displayed a maturity beyond his tender years to impress the Canary fans. Solidly built, he is particularly strong in the air with a good range of passing, especially on his favoured left foot. A natural defender, he reads and assesses dangerous situations well, allowing him to avoid last-ditch tackles

and clearances. The highlight of his season was an impressive outing against Cardiff's prolific Robbie Earnshaw at Carrow Road, which will have given him great confidence as he strives to force his way into regular senior duty.
Norwich C (From trainee on 28/1/2003) FL 6+2

SHAKES Ricky Ulric
Born: Brixton, 26 January 1985
Height: 5'10" **Weight:** 12.0
A product of the Bolton youth system, Ricky is a pacy forward with an eye for goal. He figured in only one game for the first team last season, coming off the bench in the FA Cup defeat by Tranmere. Ricky had only been on the pitch for five minutes when he notched his first goal for the club and will be hoping to make inroads into the squad more often during the coming season.
Bolton W (Trainee) FAC 0+1/1

SHARP Kevin Phillip
Born: Ontario, Canada, 19 September 1974
Height: 5'9" **Weight:** 11.11
Club Honours: FAYC '93; Div 3 '97; AMC '99
International Honours: E: Yth (UEFA-U18 '93); Sch
After joining Scunthorpe United during the summer of 2003, Kevin became the Iron's first-choice left back, occasionally moving up in to midfield as he showed himself to be a player who loves to get forward and is comfortable on the ball. He opened his goal account with a penalty against Boston in September and notched a cracking long-range strike at Carlisle the following month. He kept his place throughout the season apart from the occasional period of suspension.
Leeds U (£60,000 from Auxerre, France on 20/10/1992) PL 11+6 Others 0+1
Wigan Ath (£100,000 on 30/11/1995) FL 156+22/10 FLC 7+2/1 FAC 7+3 Others 18+1/1
Wrexham (Free on 2/11/2001) FL 12+3
Huddersfield T (Free on 8/8/2002) FL 38+1 FLC 2 FAC 1 Others 1
Scunthorpe U (Free on 2/7/2003) FL 37+3/2 FLC 2 FAC 5 Others 4

SHARPS Ian William
Born: Warrington, 23 October 1980
Height: 6'4" **Weight:** 13.8
A product of Tranmere's successful youth scheme, this effective central defender possesses the twin advantages of being both outstanding in the air and difficult to

shake off the ball. Ian also has impressive vision as well as accurate distribution skills. Although he was absent from the side for two lengthy spells during the 2003-04 season, he always impressed with his work rate and was given a new contract by Rovers boss Brian Little in the summer.

Tranmere Rov (From trainee on 5/7/1999) FL 80+7/4 FLC 4 FAC 5 Others 2

SHAW Jonathan (Jon) Steven
Born: Sheffield, 10 November 1983
Height: 6'1" **Weight:** 12.9
This young Sheffield Wednesday striker had a few outings as a substitute early on last term, before joining York City on loan in the middle of the season. He impressed for the Minstermen with his strength and control and was given an extended run for the Owls in the closing stages of the campaign. Jon scored his first goal in the penultimate game of the season against Luton and added another in the final game against Queens Park Rangers. He will be looking to win regular first-team football at Hillsborough in 2004-05.

Sheffield Wed (From trainee on 2/7/2003) FL 7+8/2 FAC 0+2 Others 1+2
York C (Loaned on 14/11/2003) FL 5+3

SHAW Paul
Born: Burnham, 4 September 1973
Height: 5'11" **Weight:** 12.4
International Honours: E: Yth
Paul was a regular in the Gillingham line-up last term, producing some intelligent performances. However, with his contract due to expire in the summer he was allowed to move on to Sheffield United in the new year. He made a memorable start for the Blades, coming on as a substitute and scoring with a long-range effort in the 3-3 draw with West Ham. However, after a handful of starts on the left side of midfield, he spent the rest of the season on the bench, generally coming on as a late substitute.

Arsenal (From trainee on 18/9/1991) PL 1+11/2 FAC 0+1
Burnley (Loaned on 23/3/1995) FL 8+1/4
Cardiff C (Loaned on 11/8/1995) FL 6
Peterborough U (Loaned on 20/10/1995) FL 12/5 Others 2
Millwall (£250,000 on 15/9/1997) FL 88+21/26 FLC 6/2 FAC 2 Others 5+2/4
Gillingham (£450,000 on 11/7/2000) FL 118+17/26 FLC 5+3 FAC 8/3
Sheffield U (£75,000 on 12/1/2004) FL 4+9/1

SHAW Richard Edward
Born: Brentford, 11 September 1968
Height: 5'9" **Weight:** 12.8
Club Honours: FMC '91; Div 1 '94
After recovering from a broken foot Richard appeared in a run of consecutive games for Coventry between September and November, featuring either in the heart of defence or at right back. He was always a solid performer using his many years of experience to good effect whilst compensating for a slight slowing down with good positional play. However, he spent most of the second half of the campaign on the bench, rarely being used. At Gillingham in the penultimate game of the season he finally scored his first goal for the Sky Blues after 297 appearances with a thunderous drive which won the club's 'Goal of the Season' award.

Kevin Sharp

Crystal Palace *(From apprentice on 4/9/1986) F/PL 193+14/3 FLC 28+2 FAC 18 Others 12+1*
Hull C *(Loaned on 14/12/1989) FL 4*
Coventry C *(£1,000,000 on 17/11/1995) P/FL 242+17/1 FLC 18+2 FAC 18+1*

SHEARER Alan
Born: Newcastle, 13 August 1970
Height: 6'0" **Weight:** 12.6
Club Honours: PL '95
International Honours: E: 63; B-1; U21-11; Yth
Captain of his hometown club, Alan remains one of the top strikers in the country, contributing not only with an impressive tally of goals for Newcastle, but also through the way he leads the attack, holding up the ball before laying it off or flicking on high balls to bring his colleagues into the game. His shooting remains as powerful and accurate as ever as he proved with his goal against Chelsea in late April, while his commitment and appetite for the game is undiminished. Alan is second only to colleague Gary Speed in the number of Premiership games he has played, and he continues to rack up an impressive tally of landmarks. Thus already the top scorer in Premiership history, he registered his 250th League goal at home to Southampton in October, and netted twice at Fulham in October to become the second-highest scorer in major competitions in Newcastle's history. In December he was voted 'North East Player of the Year' by the local Football Writers' Association.
Southampton *(From trainee on 14/4/1988) FL 105+13/23 FLC 16+2/11 FAC 11+3/4 Others 8/5*
Blackburn Rov *(£3,600,000 on 24/7/1992) PL 132+6/112 FLC 16/14 FAC 8/2 Others 9/2*
Newcastle U *(£15,000,000 on 30/7/1996) PL 238+5/131 FLC 12+1/6 FAC 29/19 Others 37/17*

SHEARER Scott
Born: Glasgow, 15 February 1981
Height: 6'3" **Weight:** 14.8
International Honours: S: B-1
The promising young goalkeeper was never intended to be first choice for Coventry last term, but injuries forced him into the team at the start of the season. He was unconvincing in his early matches and then dropped out of the team until February when he was recalled after the FA Cup defeat at Colchester. Scott kept his place for the rest of the campaign and put in some much more assured performances. His good form earned him

Scotland Future cap and a call-up as a replacement for the full squad in April when he sat on the bench.
Albion Rov *(Signed from Tower Hearts on 6/7/2000) SL 47+2/1 SLC 1 SC 2 Others 1*
Coventry C *(Signed on 7/7/2003) FL 29+1 FLC 2*

SHEERAN Mark John
Born: Newcastle, 9 September 1982
Height: 6'0" **Weight:** 11.10
Mark had a somewhat disappointing campaign for Darlington last term, only managing five substitute appearances and finding the net just once in the LDV Vans Trophy tie against Hull City. He showed he possesses an eye for goal with his quick darting runs and ability to lose defenders, but he was released in February and joined Whitby Town soon afterwards.
Darlington *(From trainee on 9/7/2002) FL 1+31/6 Others 0+3/1*

SHELLEY Brian
Born: Dublin, 15 November 1981
Height: 6'0" **Weight:** 11.12
International Honours: RoI: U21-4
The 2003-04 campaign proved to be something of a season of two halves for Brian at Carlisle. A pacy defender who likes to overlap down the wing, he featured at right back until early December. When he returned to the side in the spring he initially found himself on the more unfamiliar left flank for a while. He adjusted well and his consistent performances in both roles earned more than one 'Man of the Match' citation in the closing weeks of the term.
Carlisle U *(Free from Bohemians on 9/8/2002) FL 60+6/1 FLC 1 FAC 4 Others 8*

SHERIDAN Darren Stephen
Born: Manchester, 8 December 1967
Height: 5'5" **Weight:** 11.5
A combative midfielder, Darren endured a frustrating season for Oldham last term. He struggled to get back into the side following a period of suspension before spending a large chunk of the campaign sidelined after fracturing a leg in the FA Cup victory over Carlisle United. He finally returned to action in March and showed new boss Brian Talbot his worth with an outstanding display as Latics beat promotion-chasing Bristol City at Ashton Gate. However, Darren became out of contract in the summer and the club decided not to offer him a new deal.
Barnsley *(£10,000 from Winsford U on 12/8/1993) F/PL 149+22/5 FLC 9+4/1 FAC 9+2/1 Others 1+1*

Wigan Ath *(Free on 2/7/1999) FL 50+8/3 FLC 5 FAC 1+2 Others 5/1*
Oldham Ath *(Free on 24/7/2001) FL 72+16/3 FLC 4+1 FAC 8 Others 8*

SHERIDAN John Joseph
Born: Stretford, 1 October 1964
Height: 5'10" **Weight:** 12.0
Club Honours: FLC '91; Div 1 '97
International Honours: RoI: 34; B-1; U23-2; U21-2; Yth
John was a central figure on and off the field in Oldham Athletic's battle for survival in 2003-04. After previously retiring from the game in April 2003, he was forced to pull on his boots again as the club's financial problems left manager Iain Dowie with a threadbare squad. John made his comeback in the 2-2 draw with Sheffield Wednesday in August, scoring a penalty and displaying the vision that has marked him out as one of the most gifted players of his generation. John then took over as caretaker manager in December and he remained in charge until early March. It was, however, no surprise when he announced his retirement for a second time to allow him to concentrate on his new role as assistant manager to Brian Talbot.
Leeds U *(From Manchester C juniors on 2/3/1982) FL 225+5/47 FLC 14/3 FAC 11+1/1 Others 11/1*
Nottingham F *(£650,000 on 3/8/1989) FLC 1*
Sheffield Wed *(£500,000 on 3/11/1989) F/PL 187+10/25 FLC 24/3 FAC 17+1/3 Others 5/2*
Birmingham C *(Loaned on 9/2/1996) FL 1+1 FLC 2*
Bolton W *(£180,000 on 13/11/1996) F/PL 24+8/2 FLC 2 FAC 2 (Free to Doncaster Rov in 1998 close season)*
Oldham Ath *(Free on 20/10/1998) FL 132+13/14 FLC 2+2 FAC 14+1/2 Others 1*

SHERINGHAM Edward (Teddy) Paul
Born: Highams Park, 2 April 1966
Height: 5'11" **Weight:** 12.5
Club Honours: Div 2 '88; FMC '92; CS '97; PL '99, '00, '01; FAC '99; EC '99
International Honours: E: 51; U21-1; Yth
Regarded as one of the best players of the modern era with his intelligent and hard-working style of play, Teddy was an immediate inspiration to the Pompey side last season scoring five goals in the first five matches. Despite his advancing years, he played in most of the club's Premiership games, steadying the squad to safety after a rocky mid-winter spell.

He finished with nine goals and will be missed next term as he seeks his final footballing days elsewhere.
Millwall *(From apprentice on 19/1/1984) FL 205+15/93 FLC 16+1/8 FAC 12/5 Others 12+1/5*
Aldershot *(Loaned on 1/2/1985) FL 4+1 Others 1*
Nottingham F *(£2,000,000 on 23/7/1991) FL 42/14 FLC 10/5 FAC 4/2 Others 6/2*
Tottenham H *(£2,100,000 on 28/8/1992) PL 163+3/76 FLC 14/10 FAC 17/13*
Manchester U *(£3,500,000 on 1/7/1997) PL 73+31/31 FLC 1/1 FAC 4+5/5 Others 23+16/9*
Tottenham H *(Free on 16/7/2001) PL 67+3/22 FLC 6+1/3 FAC 3/1*
Portsmouth *(Free on 2/7/2003) PL 25+7/9 FLC 3 FAC 2+1/1*

SHERON Michael (Mike)
Nigel
Born: St Helens, 11 January 1972
Height: 5'10" **Weight:** 11.13
Club Honours: AMC '04
International Honours: E: U21-16
Mike was a regular in the Blackpool line-up throughout the 2003-04 campaign, although a number of his appearances came from the substitutes' bench. The hard-working striker did not find the net until November, but in the new year he hit the target regularly and finished the season with a double-figure goals tally.
Manchester C *(From trainee on 5/7/1990) F/PL 82+18/24 FLC 9+1/1 FAC 5+3/3 Others 1*
Bury *(Loaned on 28/3/1991) FL 1+4/1 Others 2*
Norwich C *(£1,000,000 on 26/8/1994) P/FL 19+9/2 FLC 6/3 FAC 4/2*
Stoke C *(£450,000 on 13/11/1995) FL 64+5/34 FLC 4/5 FAC 1 Others 2*
Queens Park R *(£2,750,000 on 2/7/1997) FL 57+6/19 FLC 2+2/1 FAC 2*
Barnsley *(£1,000,000 on 27/1/1999) FL 114+38/33 FLC 10+2/7 FAC 4+3 Others 1*
Blackpool *(Free on 21/7/2003) FL 28+10/8 FLC 1 FAC 1+1 Others 7/3*

SHERWOOD Timothy (Tim)
Alan
Born: St Albans, 6 February 1969
Height: 6'0" **Weight:** 12.9
Club Honours: PL '95; Div 1 '03
International Honours: E: 3; B-1; U21-4
Tim featured regularly for Portsmouth in the opening stages of the 2003-04 campaign, although he was often on the bench. A cool and composed midfielder, he had the misfortune to suffer a broken leg playing against his former club Tottenham in December and this effectively ended his season.
Watford *(From trainee on 7/2/1987) FL*

23+9/2 FLC 4+1 FAC 9 Others 4+1
Norwich C *(£175,000 on 18/7/1989) FL 66+5/10 FLC 7/1 FAC 4 Others 5+1/2*
Blackburn Rov *(£500,000 on 12/2/1992) F/PL 239+7/25 FLC 24+1/2 FAC 15+2/4 Others 12*
Tottenham H *(£3,800,000 on 5/2/1999) PL 81+12/12 FLC 6+3/2 FAC 13/1 Others 3/1*
Portsmouth *(Free on 29/1/2003) P/FL 24+6/1 FLC 2+1/2*

SHIELDS Anthony (Tony)
Gerald
Born: Londonderry, 4 June 1980
Height: 5'7" **Weight:** 10.10
This tough-tackling midfielder was a regular starter for Peterborough in the early part of the 2003-04 campaign, but then became unsettled. Tony was eventually released by Posh and moved on to join Conference club Aldershot Town before returning to Ireland, signing for Waterford United.
Peterborough U *(From trainee on 6/7/1998) FL 93+31/3 FLC 5+1/1 FAC 4+3/1 Others 1+2*

SHILTON Samuel (Sam) Roger
Born: Nottingham, 21 July 1978
Height: 5'10" **Weight:** 11.6
After experiencing a rebirth of his Kidderminster career under Ian Britton, Sam found himself on the sidelines again following a change in management in October. The left wing back was eventually released early in the new year and moved on to join Burton Albion.
Plymouth Arg *(Trainee) FL 1+2 FAC 0+1*
Coventry C *(£12,500 on 31/10/1995) PL 3+4 FLC 1+1 FAC 0+1*
Hartlepool U *(Free on 9/7/1999) FL 45+9/7 FLC 1+1 FAC 3 Others 3+1*
Kidderminster Hrs *(Free on 11/7/2001) FL 60+19/5 FLC 2+1 FAC 3+2 Others 5/1*

SHIPPERLEY Neil Jason
Born: Chatham, 30 October 1974
Height: 6'1" **Weight:** 13.12
International Honours: E: U21-7
Neil made a successful return to Crystal Palace last term and was appointed as club captain following the departure of Hayden Mullins to West Ham. The big powerful striker was a key figure in the Eagles rise to the play-offs and contributed eight goals in the regular season. However, he will best be remembered for scoring the winner in the play-off final against West Ham which earned the club a return to Premiership status after a six-year absence.
Chelsea *(From trainee on 24/9/1992) PL 26+11/7 FLC 4+2/1 FAC 3/1 Others 2*
Watford *(Loaned on 7/12/1994) FL 5+1/1*

Southampton *(£1,250,000 on 6/1/1995) PL 65+1/12 FLC 5+1/2 FAC 10/5*
Crystal Palace *(£1,000,000 on 25/10/1996) F/PL 49+12/20 FLC 3 FAC 2 Others 5/1*
Nottingham F *(£1,500,000 on 22/9/1998) PL 12+8/1 FAC 1*
Barnsley *(£700,000 on 7/7/1999) FL 70+8/27 FLC 4+1/3 FAC 2 Others 3/1*
Wimbledon *(£750,000 on 25/7/2001) FL 82+5/32 FLC 4/3 FAC 4/1*
Crystal Palace *(Signed on 24/7/2003) FL 40/9 FLC 4 FAC 1 Others 3/2*

SHITTU Daniel (Danny)
Olusola
Born: Lagos, Nigeria, 2 September 1980
Height: 6'3" **Weight:** 16.0
International Honours: Nigeria: 1
This tall and solid central defender produced a series of fine performances for Queens Park Rangers last term when he remained a firm favourite with the fans. However, he was badly affected by injuries, firstly he suffered a minor tear to his cruciate ligament which kept him out for nearly two months, then his campaign ended in January when he was diagnosed as having ruptured his anterior cruciate ligament.
Charlton Ath *(Free from Carshalton Ath on 15/9/1999)*
Blackpool *(Loaned on 16/2/2001) FL 15+2/2 Others 2*
Queens Park R *(£250,000 on 23/10/2002) FL 88+2/9 FLC 3 FAC 1 Others 5*

SHOREY Nicholas (Nicky)
Born: Romford, 19 February 1981
Height: 5'9" **Weight:** 10.10
Generally considered to be one of the best full backs in the Football League, Nicky enjoyed another successful season for Reading last term. It was only spoiled by a foot injury which kept him out of the last ten games of the fixture list and which may threaten to disrupt his pre-season training. Up to that point he had been a classy defender, quick in the tackle and a vital addition to the attack when speeding upfield. His second goal of the campaign, a crashing left-footed strike from a free-kick outside the box in the 2-1 home win over Sheffield United, was a classic.
Leyton Orient *(From trainee on 5/7/1999) FL 12+3 FAC 1*
Reading *(£25,000 on 9/2/2001) FL 110/4 FLC 7 FAC 6 Others 4*

SHORT Craig Jonathan
Born: Bridlington, 25 June 1968
Height: 6'1" **Weight:** 13.8
Club Honours: FLC '02

Craig was one of the few players at Blackburn who could hold his head high last term, his only problem being that his advancing years have impacted on his body. He missed the first half of the season, but his return at Old Trafford brought immediate advances to the club's defending. He figured in all but one of the games in which the defence kept a clean sheet and right to the end he fought with pride. Unfortunately his hamstring problems remain although he was given a contract extension by Rovers.
Scarborough (Free from Pickering T on 15/10/1987) FL 61+2/7 FLC 6 FAC 2 Others 7/1
Notts Co (£100,000 on 27/7/1989) FL 128/6 FLC 6/1 FAC 8/1 Others 16/2
Derby Co (£2,500,000 on 18/9/1992) FL 118/9 FLC 11 FAC 7/4 Others 7
Everton (£2,700,000 on 18/7/1995) PL 90+9/4 FLC 7 FAC 4 Others 3
Blackburn Rov (£1,700,000 + on 3/8/1999) P/FL 118+2/3 FLC 4/1 FAC 6 Others 2

SHOWUNMI Enoch
Born: London, 21 April 1982
Height: 6'3" **Weight:** 14.10
A product of the Willesden Constantine junior club, Enoch had a tremendous season with Luton Town in 2003-04. He made an impressive debut at Plymouth in September and went on to become a regular in the line-up in the second half of the campaign. A tall, but pacy striker, he proved a handful for opposition defenders and scored with a brilliant free kick against Colchester. However, the highlight of his career to date was an excellent hat-trick in the 4-1 home win over Brentford in February.
Luton T (Signed from Willesden Constantine on 5/9/2003) FL 18+8/7 FAC 2 Others 2+1/1

SHUKER Christopher (Chris) Alan
Born: Liverpool, 9 May 1982
Height: 5'5" **Weight:** 10.1
This young Manchester City striker was out of the first-team picture at the start of last term and he began the season on loan at Rochdale. Chris initially played as an out-and-out striker, but looked more comfortable when switched to a wide position. He later spent three months at Hartlepool, also on loan, and had some early successes but after returning to the City of Manchester Stadium he was released and signed for Barnsley. Chris did well as an attacking midfield player at Oakwell, impressing with some all-action displays.

Manchester C (From trainee on 21/9/1999) P/FL 1+4 FLC 0+1/1
Macclesfield T (Loaned on 27/3/2001) FL 6+3/1
Walsall (Loaned on 26/2/2003) FL 3+2
Rochdale (Loaned on 7/8/2003) FL 14/1 FLC 1
Hartlepool U (Loaned on 13/12/2003) FL 14/1 FAC 1
Barnsley (Signed on 17/3/2004) FL 9

SIBIERSKI Antoine
Born: Lille, France, 5 August 1974
Height: 6'2" **Weight:** 12.8
International Honours: France: Yth

A gifted player with the ball at his feet, Antoine is a talented attacking midfield player with an eye for goal. He scored on his debut for Manchester City at Charlton and continued to contribute with some valuable goals in his side's successful fight against relegation from the Premiership.
Manchester C (£700,000 from Lens, France, ex Lille OSC, Auxerre, Nantes, on 7/8/2003) PL 18+15/5 FLC 0+1 FAC 3+2/1 Others 1/1

SIDIBE Mamady
Born: Mali, 18 December 1979
Height: 6'4" **Weight:** 12.4
International Honours: Mali: 7

Mamady Sidibe

This big Gillingham striker impressed everyone with his work rate and a willingness to put himself about and upset opposing defences last term. However, he managed just six goals during the campaign, although this was a slight improvement on the previous campaign. Mamady represented Mali in the African Nations' Cup finals at the beginning of the year, featuring from the bench in the third-place play-off match against Nigeria.
Swansea C *(Free from CA Paris, France, ex Racing Club Paris, on 27/7/2001) FL 26+5/7 FLC 0+1 FAC 2/1 Others 1*
Gillingham *(Free on 9/8/2002) FL 58+13/8 FLC 3+1 FAC 3+1/2*

SIDWELL Steven (Steve)
James
Born: Wandsworth, 14 December 1982
Height: 5'10" **Weight:** 11.2
Club Honours: FAYC '00, '01
International Honours: E: U21-5; Yth
This hugely talented young midfielder was a vital component in Reading's midfield last term. Steve is the archetypal creative maestro, who can spray passes to all parts of the field, yet he also has the resilience to make tackles in his own penalty area. He scores his share of goals too, none better than the long run and shot which brought his team an injury-time goal and a 1-0 home win over West Bromwich Albion. Steve fully deserved the accolades he received during the season, including the *Evening Post* 'Player of the Year' award and further selection for the England U21 team.
Arsenal *(From trainee on 2/7/2001)*
Brentford *(Loaned on 23/10/2001) FL 29+1/4 FAC 2 Others 3*
Brighton & Hove A *(Loaned on 9/11/2002) FL 11+1/5*
Reading *(£250,000 on 21/11/2003) FL 56/10 FLC 3/1 FAC 1+1 Others 2*

SIGURDSSON Larus Orri
Born: Akureyri, Iceland, 4 June 1973
Height: 6'0" **Weight:** 13.11
International Honours: Iceland: 42; U21-16; Yth
Unfortunately for Larus, the 2003-04 season will be one he wants to forget quickly! Owing to injury (a damaged knee that required an operation) he appeared in only five First Division games and spent weeks on end lying on the treatment table at the Hawthorns. He did, however, add to his collection of international caps when he played for Iceland against Germany. Larus is a versatile player who can feature in defence or midfield.

Stoke C *(£150,000 from Thor, Iceland on 21/10/1994) FL 199+1/7 FLC 15 FAC 6+1 Others 6*
West Bromwich A *(£325,000 on 17/9/1999) P/FL 104+12/1 FLC 4 FAC 6+1 Others 0+1*

[SILAS] REBELO FERNANDES Jorge Manuel
Born: Lisbon, Portugal, 1 September 1976
Height: 5'9" **Weight:** 11.3
International Honours: Portugal: 3
This winger looked impressive in training and pre-season friendlies with Wolves, and was the most exciting prospect of the summer signings. However, he made little impact when starting the first two Premiership games and never really had a decent run in the team. The only other starts he made were in cup matches and he did not feature again after February.
Wolverhampton W *(£1,000,000 from Uniao Leiria, Portugal on 21/7/2003) PL 2+7 FLC 2 FAC 1+2*

SILVA Gilberto
Born: Lagoa da Prata, Brazil, 7 October 1976
Height: 6'2" **Weight:** 12.4
Club Honours: CS '02; FAC '03; PL '04
International Honours: Brazil: 27
Gilberto started the 2003-04 season in quiet fashion for Arsenal, playing a defensive role in the centre of midfield although he registered his first Premiership goal against Middlesborough and added three more during the campaign. However, the emergence of Edu midway through the campaign saw him tussle for the 'holding' berth alongside Patrick Vieira during the closing stages. The added competition for places clearly had the required effect as Gilberto returned to figure strongly in the last weeks of Arsenal's historic campaign. He is known for his ability to break up attacks and form the defensive shield in front of the back four.
Arsenal *(£4,500,000 from Atletico Mineiro, Brazil, ex America-MG, on 9/8/2002) PL 61+6/4 FLC 1 FAC 4+2 Others 17+5/3*

SILVESTRE Mikael Samy
Born: Tours, France, 9 August 1977
Height: 6'0" **Weight:** 13.1
Club Honours: PL '00, '01, '03; CS '03; FAC '04
International Honours: France: 34; U21; Yth (UEFA-U18 '96)
A stylish, pacy defender who keeps a cool head under pressure, and combines as an

attacking outlet down the flank, Mikael started the season in outstanding fashion with United's opener in the Community Shield showdown against Arsenal at the Millennium Stadium. Though that was about as good as it got in the goal-scoring stakes, he continued to show his quality as one of the Reds most consistent and adaptable performers from August to December with only three Premiership absences. Indeed his influence was greatly missed in the European showdown with Porto both home and away, when Mikael was an absentee through injury. By the end of the campaign, however, he was near the top of the club's charts for appearances.
Manchester U *(£4,000,000 from Inter Milan, Italy on 10/9/1999) PL 153+11/2 FLC 5 FAC 11/1 Others 50+6/3*

SIMEK Franklin (Frankie)
Michael
Born: St Louis, Missouri, USA, 13 October 1984
Height: 6'0" **Weight:** 11.6
International Honours: USA: Yth
Central defender Frankie made his sole appearance of the campaign for Arsenal in the Carling Cup third round victory over Wolves 5-1 when he produced a highly impressive display. Frankie was paired with Stathis Tavlaridis in the heart of the defence as the club's young guns shone. He was an unused substitute for the quarter-final tie at the Hawthorns and was a mainstay of the club's reserve team, making 19 appearances in all.
Arsenal *(From trainee on 1/7/2002) FLC 1*

SIMONSEN Steven (Steve)
Preben
Born: South Shields, 3 April 1979
Height: 6'3" **Weight:** 13.2
International Honours: E: U21-4; Yth
This talented goalkeeper had a difficult campaign at Goodison, making just one senior appearance in August following an injury to Richard Wright, and then the superb form of Nigel Martyn kept him out of first-team contention for the rest of the season. As a consequence Steve rejected a one-year extension to his contract at the end of the campaign and was released by the club. The former England U21 international is an efficient shot-stopper and is particular adept at handling crosses.
Tranmere Rov *(From trainee on 9/10/1996) FL 35 FLC 4 FAC 3*
Everton *(£3,300,000 on 23/9/1998) PL 28+2 FLC 2 FAC 5*

SIMPEMBA Ian Frederick
Born: Dublin, 28 March 1983
Height: 6'2" **Weight:** 12.8
International Honours: RoI: Yth
This enthusiastic right-sided midfielder
was out of favour at Wycombe early on
last season. All this changed when Tony
Adams took over and he made his full
debut at Wrexham in November. Ian
managed to hold down his place and
eventually made the right-back position
his own. The bravery he displayed scoring
his first goal for the club, a diving header
at Sheffield Wednesday, which saw him
hospitalised after a collision with the
goalkeeper, sums up his tremendous spirit.
*Wycombe W (From trainee on 10/7/2001) FL
17+3/2 FAC 2 Others 1*

SIMPKINS Michael (Mike)
James
Born: Sheffield, 28 November 1978
Height: 6'1" **Weight:** 12.0
Signed by Rochdale manager Alan
Buckley to fill the vacancy for an out-and-
out left back, Michael was a virtual ever-
present for the first half of last season
apart from the odd period of suspension.
However, he failed to win over the Dale
supporters and after Steve Parkin took
over, Michael lost his place firstly to Matt
Doughty and then to new signing Shaun
Smith.
Sheffield Wed (From trainee on 4/7/1997)
*Chesterfield (Free on 26/3/1998) FL 22+4
FLC 2+1 FAC 1 Others 2*
*Cardiff C (Free on 29/5/2001) FL 13+4 FLC 1
Others 2*
Exeter C (Loaned on 20/9/2002) FL 4+1
*Cheltenham T (Loaned on 23/12/2002) FL 2
FAC 0+1*
*Rochdale (Free on 6/8/2003) FL 25+2 FLC 1
FAC 1 Others 1*

SIMPSON Michael
Born: Nottingham, 28 February 1974
Height: 5'9" **Weight:** 10.8
Club Honours: AIC '95
This workaholic, hard-tackling Wycombe
central midfielder missed a handful of
games last term, but found it hard to
consistently reproduce the brilliant form
of the previous campaign. Michael has
been an enormously influential player
over the years for the Chairboys and it
came as a major shock when his contract
was not renewed at the end of the
season, even allowing for the team's
relegation.
*Notts Co (From trainee on 1/7/1992) FL
39+10/3 FLC 4+1 FAC 2+1 Others 7+3*
*Plymouth Arg (Loaned on 4/10/1996) FL
10+2*

*Wycombe W (£50,000 on 5/12/1996) FL
267+18/16 FLC 14+1 FAC 24+2/5 Others 14*

SIMPSON Paul David
Born: Carlisle, 26 July 1966
Height: 5'6" **Weight:** 11.10
Club Honours: AMC '02
International Honours: E: U21-5; Yth
After starting the 2003-04 season on a
playing contract for Carlisle, Paul found
himself in the role of player-manager for
almost the entire campaign. Although a
series of injuries restricted his appearances
on the park, he retained sufficient skill
and craft to enable him to make a series
of telling contributions. His long-range
shooting power brought several goals, the
pick of which came from a curling free
kick against Bury. Paul earned widespread
respect as a manager for almost
preserving United's Football League status
from an almost hopeless mid-term
position.
*Manchester C (From apprentice on
4/8/1983) FL 99+22/18 FLC 10+1/2 FAC
10+2/4 Others 8+3*
*Oxford U (£200,000 on 31/10/1988) FL
138+6/43 FLC 10/3 FAC 9/2 Others 5/2*
*Derby Co (£500,000 on 20/2/1992) P/FL
134+52/48 FLC 12+3/6 FAC 4+4/1 Others
14+2/2*
Sheffield U (Loaned on 6/12/1996) FL 2+4
*Wolverhampton W (£75,000 on
10/10/1997) FL 32+20/6 FLC 2+1 FAC 2+5*
Walsall (Loaned on 17/9/1998) FL 4/1
Walsall (Loaned on 11/12/1998) FL 6
*Blackpool (Free on 11/8/2000) FL 69+7/13
FLC 5+1 FAC 6/1 Others 4+2/1*
*Rochdale (Free on 25/3/2002) FL 37+5/15
FLC 1 FAC 3+1/1 Others 3/1*
*Carlisle U (Free on 7/8/2003) FL 25/6 Others
0+1*

SINAMA-PONGOLLE Florent
Born: Saint Pierre, Reunion, 20 October
1984
Height: 5'9" **Weight:** 10.10
International Honours: France: U21;
Yth
This young striker arrived at Anfield in the
summer of 2003, along with Anthony Le
Tallec from French club Le Havre. He was
introduced to first-team action early in the
season making his debut as a substitute
against Olimpija Ljubljana in the UEFA
Cup and receiving his first start in the
Carling Cup tie at Blackburn shortly
afterwards. Florent remained in the first-
team squad until January, mostly as a
substitute, and scored his first goals for
the Reds in the 3-1 victories over Leeds
and Bolton in December. In the second
half of the season he was troubled by

knee and ankle injuries and made only
occasional entries from the dug-out. A
lively striker who takes up good positions,
he has excellent potential and will be
looking for more first- team opportunities
in 2004-05.
*Liverpool (Signed from Le Havre, France on
18/7/2003) PL 3+12/2 FLC 1+1 FAC 1+2
Others 1+2*

SINCLAIR Frank Mohammed
Born: Lambeth, 3 December 1971
Height: 5'9" **Weight:** 12.9
Club Honours: FAC '97; FLC '98, '00
International Honours: Jamaica: 24
This right-footed wing back or central
defender suffered a thigh injury in an
early-season reserve fixture for Leicester
and this hampered his challenge for a
regular first-team place. Frank then found
plenty of competition for defensive places
throughout the season, although he did
manage to fill in on occasions at both full
back and in the centre of the back four.
The highlight of his year was representing
Jamaica against Brazil on his home
ground of the Walkers Stadium. The low
point came in the aftermath of a well
publicised off-the-field event in the
spring. His final contribution for the
Foxes, at Highbury, was to lay on the goal
that threatened to upset Arsenal's
wonderful run, then present the Gunners
with the opportunity to get back on terms
by felling Andy Cole in the box. Frank's
contract expired at the end of the season
and he was released by the club.
*Chelsea (From trainee on 17/5/1990) F/PL
163+6/7 FLC 17+1/2 FAC 18/1 Others 13/3*
*West Bromwich A (Loaned on 12/12/1991)
FL 6/1*
*Leicester C (£2,000,000 on 14/8/1998) P/FL
153+11/3 FLC 20 FAC 10/1*

SINCLAIR Trevor Lloyd
Born: Dulwich, 2 March 1973
Height: 5'10" **Weight:** 12.10
International Honours: E: 12; B-1; U21-
14; Yth
With his pace and ability to beat
defenders down the left-hand side, Trevor
was a valuable presence in lending width
for Manchester City last term. He was
regularly selected by Kevin Keegan, but
his form went through a series of peaks
and troughs. Trevor scored his first
Premiership goal of the season when
coming on as a substitute in the
Manchester 'derby'.
*Blackpool (From trainee on 21/8/1990) FL
84+28/15 FLC 8 FAC 6+1 Others 8+5/1*
*Queens Park R (£750,000 on 12/8/1993)
P/FL 162+5/16 FLC 13/3 FAC 10/1*

West Ham U *(£2,300,000 + on 30/1/1998)
PL 175+2/37 FLC 10+1 FAC 8 Others 10/1*
Manchester C *(£2,500,000 on 22/7/2003) PL
20+9/1 FLC 2 FAC 3+1 Others 3/1*

SINGH Harpal

Born: Bradford, 15 September 1981
Height: 5'7" **Weight:** 10.9
This talented striker arrived at Bury on a
three-month loan shortly before the start
of the 2003-04 campaign and was a
regular in the line-up, providing some
much-needed width on the left-hand side.
His loan was extended until the end of
the season in November, but almost
immediately afterwards he dislocated his
shoulder – an injury that required an
operation. Harpal was sidelined until
February, but fought his way back into
the first team and began to show
glimpses of his best form before returning
to Elland Road in the summer.
Leeds U *(From trainee on 26/9/1998)*
Bury *(Loaned on 11/9/2001) FL 11+1/2 FAC
2/1 Others 1*
Bristol C *(Loaned on 8/3/2002) FL 3*
Bradford C *(Loaned on 8/11/2002) FL 3*
Bury *(Loaned on 8/8/2003) FL 20+8/2 FLC 1
FAC 1*

SKIVERTON Terence (Terry)
John

Born: Mile End, 26 June 1975
Height: 6'1" **Weight:** 13.6
Club Honours: FAT '02; NC '03
International Honours: E: SP-4
Terry was out of action with an ankle
injury at the start of last term and it was
not until October that he made his first
appearance for Yeovil. Further knocks
interrupted his progress but when fit he
proved to be a captain who led the team
by example. A big powerful defender,
Terry contributed two goals during the
season.
Chelsea *(From trainee on 19/5/1993)*
Wycombe W *(Loaned on 17/2/1995) FL 8+2*
Wycombe W *(Free on 26/3/1996) FL 5+5/1
FAC 0+1 (Free to Welling U on 13/8/1997)*
Yeovil T *(Signed on 3/6/1999) FL 25+1/2 FAC
3 Others 2*

SKORA Eric

Born: Metz, France, 20 August 1981
Height: 6'1" **Weight:** 11.10
This youngster signed a new contract for
Preston in the summer of 2003, but only
appeared in the first two matches before
joining Kilmarnock on loan in January.
Somewhat perversely, he scored against
Celtic in only his second match after
failing to score a League goal for North
End in 42 appearances. A mobile

midfielder, Eric possesses good ball skills
and a surprisingly robust tackle, and
despite his lack of scoring success for
Preston he often pops up in the box for
strikes on goal. He was a regular for the
SPL club in the second half of the
campaign before returning to Deepdale.
Preston NE *(Free from Nancy, France on
22/10/2001) FL 32+10 FLC 3/1 FAC 3/1*
Kilmarnock *(Loaned on 23/1/2004) SL
16+1/3 SC 1*

SKOUBO Morten

Born: Struer, Denmark, 30 June 1980
Height: 6'3" **Weight:** 13.8
International Honours: Denmark: 1;
U21-8
This tall, well-built striker joined West
Bromwich Albion to boost the first-team
squad. He made his debut for the
Baggies in the 3-0 defeat at Preston
North End in early February but was
given very little first-team action after
that. He managed just one more
appearance from the bench and was
released in the summer.
West Bromwich A *(Loaned from Borussia
Monchengladbach, Germany on 2/2/2004) FL
0+2*

SKULASON Olafur-Ingi

Born: Reykjavik, Iceland, 1 April 1983
Height: 6'0" **Weight:** 11.10
International Honours: Iceland: 1, U21-
4; Yth
The Icelandic midfielder made just one
outing for the Arsenal first team in the
2003-04 campaign. He replaced Justin
Hoyte in the Carling Cup third round win
over Wolves. However, he also made the
bench as an unused substitute in the
second round tie at home to Rotherham
United and the two legs of the semi-final
against Middlesborough. Olafur-Ingi made
21 appearances for the reserves in total,
19 of which came as starts.
Arsenal *(Signed from Fylkir, Iceland on
11/7/2001) FLC 0+1*

SMALL Wade Kristopher

Born: Croydon, 23 February 1984
Height: 5'7" **Weight:** 11.6
But for injuries Wade would probably
have been given a chance for Wimbledon
much earlier, but he finally made his
debut as a substitute in mid-October at
Coventry. A busy right-footed attacker, he
initially figured on the left side of
midfield, but as the club's forward
options became thinner and thinner as
the season progressed he ended the
campaign as one of the two central
strikers. A constant threat to defenders

when running with the ball, he looks to
have all the attributes to do well in the
game.
Wimbledon *(From trainee on 17/7/2003) FL
23+4/1 FAC 3*

SMART Allan Andrew Colin

Born: Perth, 8 July 1974
Height: 6'2" **Weight:** 12.10
Club Honours: AMC '97
This well-travelled striker arrived at Crewe
on trial early on last term, but his only
appearances in the side were as a
substitute. He was granted a contract for
the remainder of the season but failed to
appear in the senior squad from
December onwards due to injury
problems. Allan was released in the
summer.
St Johnstone *(From juniors on 24/1/1991)*
Brechin C *(Free on 30/12/1991)*
Inverness Caledonian Thistle *(Free on
28/7/1993) SL 2+2 SLC 1+1*
Preston NE *(£15,000 on 22/11/1994) FL
17+4/6 FAC 2/1 Others 1+1*
Carlisle U *(Loaned on 24/11/1995) FL 3+1*
Northampton T *(Loaned on 13/9/1996) FL 1*
Carlisle U *(Signed on 9/10/1996) FL 41+3/16
FLC 1/1 FAC 4 Others 4+1*
Watford *(£75,000 + on 2/7/1998) P/FL
48+9/12 FLC 1+2 FAC 1 Others 0+3/1*
Hibernian *(Loaned on 14/8/2001) SL 2+3/1*
Stoke C *(Loaned on 6/11/2001) FL 0+2*
Oldham Ath *(£225,000 on 30/11/2001) FL
14+7/6 FAC 1 Others 2/1*
Dundee U *(Free on 19/6/2002) SL 2+15 SLC
0+1*
Crewe Alex *(Free on 15/8/2003) FL 0+6*

SMERTIN Alexei

Born: Barnaul, Russia, 1 May 1975
Height: 5'9" **Weight:** 10.8
International Honours: Russia: 42
Alexei joined Chelsea in the summer of
2003 but was immediately shipped out to
Portsmouth on a season-long loan. He
proved of immense help to Pompey in
their first Premiership season. Cool and
pacy, he set up numerous good moves
with his unselfish style of play, creating
several goals for his colleagues. He
excited the Fratton Park regulars
throughout the campaign, although he
did not get on the score sheet himself,
despite coming close on several occasions.
Chelsea *(£3,450,000 from Bordeaux, France,
ex Uralan, Lokomotiv Moscow, on 26/8/2003)*
Portsmouth *(Loaned on 27/8/2003) PL 23+3
FLC 2 FAC 5*

SMICER Vladimir (Vlad)

Born: Czechoslovakia, 24 May 1973
Height: 5'11" **Weight:** 11.3

Club Honours: FLC '01, '03; FAC '01; UEFAC '01
International Honours: Czech Republic: 72; U21-7. Czechoslovakia: 1
The Czech international midfielder or striker was again unable to win an automatic berth in the Liverpool team last season, when he was essentially a squad player filling in on the wing, in the centre of the park or up front as required. In the early part of the campaign he found a regular place in midfield in the absence of Didi Hamann, and remained in contention until January when he was sidelined with an achilles injury. After a long absence he returned to action for another run of four games.
Liverpool (£3,750,000 from RC Lens, France, ex SK Slavia Praha, on 14/7/1999) PL 67+44/10 FLC 13+2/5 FAC 9+1/1 Others 19+13/2

SMITH Nathan **Adam**
Born: Huddersfield, 20 February 1985
Height: 6'0" **Weight:** 12.5
Adam came up through the ranks at Chesterfield to earn a professional contract and made three appearances from the substitutes' bench last term. With fearsome pace and a keen eye for goal, he has the courage to finish moves: when his talent is blended into a team framework he will become a valuable asset for the Spireites.
Chesterfield (Trainee) FL 0+3 Others 0+1

SMITH Adrian (Adie)
Jonathan
Born: Birmingham, 11 August 1973
Height: 5'10" **Weight:** 12.0
Club Honours: NC '00
International Honours: E: SP-3
Adie once again found himself performing a variety of roles for Kidderminster last term, playing mostly at right back but also in the centre of the defence and in midfield. A fans' favourite, he was sorely missed when he decided to leave the club in January and soon afterwards he joined Conference outfit Tamworth.
Kidderminster Hrs (£19,000 from Bromsgrove Rov on 17/6/1997) FL 112+10/8 FLC 1+2 FAC 8 Others 3/1

SMITH Alan
Born: Rothwell, 28 October 1980
Height: 5'9" **Weight:** 11.10
International Honours: E: 8; U21-10; Yth
A local lad made good, a factor which when combined with his natural talent and commitment made Alan the jewel in

the Leeds' crown last term. In a turbulent season he was again used in various positions as a striker and in a more withdrawn role. This enabled him to become a more complete player and he forced his way back into the England set-up. Every supporter breathed a sigh of relief when the club resisted his sale in the January transfer window, but it was inevitable that he would depart in the summer following the club's relegation.
Leeds U (From trainee on 26/3/1998) PL 148+24/38 FLC 4+2 FAC 11+4/4 Others 28+7/14

SMITH Christopher (Chris)
Alan
Born: Derby, 30 June 1981
Height: 5'11" **Weight:** 11.6
This young central defender had a rather mixed season for York City last term. At his best he showed composure and steadiness at the back, but he sometimes lacked consistency and was unable to maintain a regular slot in the Minstermen's defence. Chris was one of several players released by the club in the summer.
Reading (From trainee on 22/6/1999)
York C (Free on 2/7/2001) FL 71+8 FLC 1 FAC 5 Others 3

SMITH David (Dave)
Christopher
Born: Liverpool, 26 December 1970
Height: 5'10" **Weight:** 13.0
Dave battled with a hamstring injury at Macclesfield throughout last season, when he was limited to just a handful of appearances in the early part of the campaign. He is an experienced central midfield player who is an excellent passer of the ball.
Norwich C (From trainee on 4/7/1989) F/PL 13+5 FAC 2+1 Others 1+1
Oxford U (£100,000 on 5/7/1994) FL 193+5/2 FLC 23+1/1 FAC 9+1 Others 7
Stockport Co (Free on 4/2/1999) FL 64+7/3 FLC 3+1 FAC 2 (Freed during 2000 close season)
Macclesfield T (Loaned on 1/2/2002) FL 8
Macclesfield T (Free from Drogheda U on 31/1/2003) FL 10+3 FLC 1

SMITH Dean
Born: West Bromwich, 19 March 1971
Height: 6'1" **Weight:** 12.10
Dean captained Sheffield Wednesday last season, when he was a near ever-present in the side. Solid as a rock, he looked more comfortable in the centre of a traditional back four than when playing in a three-man defence. An inspiration to his

colleagues at times, he scored his first goal for Wednesday in the home game with Brentford. Dean was one of a number of out-of-contract players released by the club in the summer.
Walsall (From trainee on 1/7/1989) FL 137+5/2 FLC 10 FAC 4 Others 10
Hereford U (£75,000 on 17/6/1994) FL 116+1/19 FLC 10/3 FAC 7 Others 11+1/4
Leyton Orient (£42,500 on 16/6/1997) FL 239/32 FLC 18 FAC 19/4 Others 12/1
Sheffield Wed (Signed on 21/2/2003) FL 55/1 FLC 1 FAC 1+1 Others 4

SMITH Gary Stephen
Born: Middlesbrough, 30 January 1984
Height: 5'8" **Weight:** 10.8
Gary's arrival at Wimbledon on loan from Middlesbrough coincided with an improvement in the club's fortunes in which he undoubtedly played a significant part. A busy central midfielder always keen to run with the ball, by the season's end he had become the focal point of the team's midfield operations. After scoring the club's first goal at the visiting end of their Milton Keynes home against Ipswich at the end of March he immediately became a crowd favourite. However, despite an impressive loan spell with the Dons he was released soon after returning to the Riverside Stadium.
Middlesbrough (From trainee on 6/7/2002)
Wimbledon (Loaned on 22/3/2004) FL 10+1/3

SMITH Grant Gordon
Born: Irvine, 5 May 1980
Height: 6'1" **Weight:** 12.7
A left-footed player with the ability to play in a wide range of positions from midfield to wing back or as a forward, Grant was a regular on the bench for Swindon throughout the 2003-04 season. He will have been disappointed not to have made more appearances, but will take heart from giving a good account of himself during both play-off games against Brighton.
Reading (From trainee at Wycombe W on 7/8/1998)
Heart of Midlothian (Free on 19/3/1999)
Clydebank (Free on 2/12/2000) SL 16+1/2
Sheffield U (Free on 13/7/2001) FL 2+8 FAC 0+1
Halifax T (Loaned on 7/9/2001) FL 11 Others 1
Livingston (Free on 4/7/2000) SL 0+2 SLC 1 Others 1
Plymouth Arg (Loaned on 10/3/2003) FL 4+1/1
Swindon T (Free on 25/7/2003) FL 0+7 FLC 2 FAC 0+1 Others 2+1

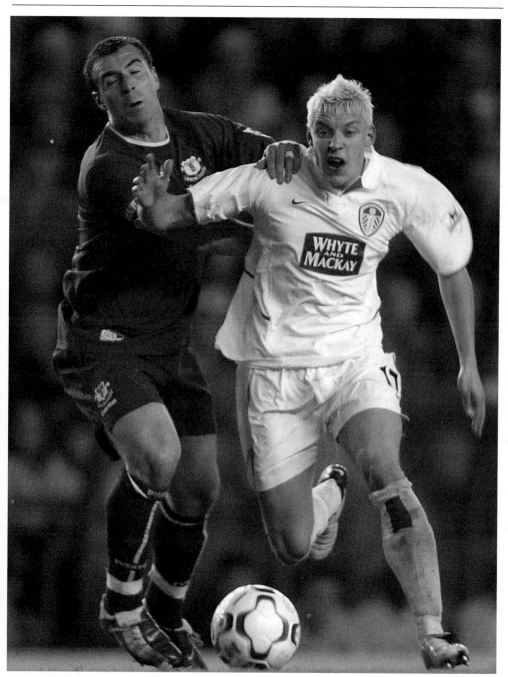

Alan Smith (right)

SMITH Jack David
Born: Hemel Hempstead, 14 October
1983
Height: 5'11" **Weight:** 11.5
Previously best known as the younger
brother of Tommy Smith, Jack began to
carve out a reputation on his own
account for Watford last season. He made
his full debut against Bradford in October
replacing the departed Paul Robinson at
left back, and made his mark immediately
as a sound defender with good vision and
passing skills. He also played at right
back, where he looked even more
comfortable, and got on the score sheet
twice during his sorties upfield. In
February he lined up against brother
Tommy, now of Sunderland: the result
was an honourable draw. Unfortunately, a
badly gashed leg in March brought his
season to an early close, but not before
he had been offered a new contract.
*Watford (From trainee on 5/4/2002) FL
16+2/2 FAC 2*

SMITH James (Jamie) Jade
Anthony
Born: Birmingham, 17 September 1974
Height: 5'7" **Weight:** 11.4
This long-serving right back was again
hampered by injuries at Crystal Palace last
term. Most of his appearances came early
on in the campaign, but he only added a
couple of outings in the new year. Out of
contract in the summer, he was released
by the club.
*Wolverhampton W (From trainee on
7/6/1993) FL 81+6 FLC 10+1 FAC 2 Others
4/1*
*Crystal Palace (Signed on 22/10/1997) P/FL
136+13/4 FLC 16+1/2 FAC 6+2 Others 1+1*
Fulham (Loaned on 25/3/1999) FL 9/1

SMITH Jay Alexander
Born: Lambeth, 24 September 1981
Height: 5'7" **Weight:** 10.6
This hugely popular and influential
Southend player had a somewhat injury-
hit season last term. An attacking
midfielder who, despite a slight frame,
never shirks a tackle, Jay also has a useful
goal-scoring record. Unfortunately his
campaign finished in February after
suffering a bad ankle injury in the home
game with Cambridge United.
Aston Villa (From trainee on 7/7/2000)
*Southend U (Free on 19/8/2002) FL 46+3/6
FLC 1 FAC 8+1/3 Others 4*

SMITH Jay Mark
Born: Hammersmith, 29 December 1981
Height: 5'11" **Weight:** 11.7
Jay started the 2003-04 campaign in the

Brentford first team, but by the end of
September dropped down to the
substitutes' bench. He was then in and
out of the side until January after which
he was left out of the squad for the rest
of the season. A midfielder with good
passing skills, he will be hoping to get
back into contention in 2004-05.
*Brentford (From trainee on 5/7/2000) FL
37+9 FLC 1 FAC 4 Others 3+3*

SMITH Jeffrey (Jeff)
Born: Middlesbrough, 28 June 1980
Height: 5'10" **Weight:** 11.8
A promising left winger, Jeff found it
difficult to make his mark in the Bolton
first team last season, figuring only in the
two FA Cup games against Tranmere. He
spent loan spells with Scunthorpe and
Rochdale before signing for Preston in
March. However, he had a frustrating
time at Deepdale. Signed to cover the
absence of Eddie Lewis, Jeff missed the
chance to start at Derby when he too was
injured, having made five previous
appearances from the bench. Speedy and
nimble in possession, he impressed the
North End fans during his cameo
appearances.
*Hartlepool U (From trainee on 3/7/1998) FL
2+1 Others 1 (Free to Barrow in October
1999)*
*Bolton W (Free from Bishop Auckland on
21/3/2001) P/FL 1+1 FLC 2 FAC 4*
*Macclesfield T (Loaned on 23/11/2001) FL
7+1/2*
Scunthorpe U (Loaned on 16/1/2004) FL 1
Rochdale (Loaned on 20/2/2004) FL 1
Preston NE (Signed on 4/3/2004) FL 0+5

SMITH Martin Geoffrey
Born: Sunderland, 13 November 1974
Height: 5'11" **Weight:** 12.6
Club Honours: Div 1 '96
International Honours: E: U21-1; Yth;
Sch
Wherever Martin played for Northampton
last term he seemed to fit the role
perfectly: out-and-out striker, wide man
and central midfield were all positions in
which he excelled. A skilful player who
was the club's leading scorer during the
campaign, no Cobblers fan will forget his
goal in the FA Cup replay against
Rotherham that earned a money-spinning
fourth round tie against Manchester
United.
*Sunderland (From trainee on 9/9/1992) P/FL
90+29/25 FLC 10+6/2 FAC 7+3/1*
*Sheffield U (Free on 6/8/1999) FL 24+2/10
FLC 3+1/4 FAC 3/1*
*Huddersfield T (£300,000 on 3/2/2000) FL
72+8/29 FLC 2+1 FAC 1 Others 1*

*Northampton T (Free on 7/8/2003) FL
43+1/11 FLC 1 FAC 5/3 Others 4+1/1*

SMITH Ian Paul
Born: Easington, 22 January 1976
Height: 6'0" **Weight:** 13.3
A left-sided midfielder or winger, Paul
followed his old manager Chris Turner to
Sheffield Wednesday last term. He made
a very favourable impression when he got
into the side, and scored a couple of
goals when the team were flying, but
then a bad ligament injury kept him out
of the picture for a lengthy spell and the
Owls' fortunes dipped. When he regained
his fitness he had another run in the line-
up until injury again took its toll and kept
him out until the end of the season.
*Burnley (From trainee on 10/7/1994) FL
79+33/5 FLC 3+1 FAC 6+1 Others 5*
*Oldham Ath (Loaned on 22/9/2000) FL 3+1
FLC 1*
*Hartlepool U (Free, via trial at Torquay U,
on 1/11/2001) FL 45+10/4 FAC 3 Others 2*
*Sheffield Wed (Free on 2/7/2003) FL 12+7/2
Others 2*

SMITH Paul Daniel
Born: Epsom, 17 December 1979
Height: 6'4" **Weight:** 14.0
This quiet and unassuming goalkeeper
again performed miracles as Brentford's
last line of defence during the 2003-04
campaign. Penalty saves against Oldham
and at Stockport earned vital points,
while he also saved two in the shoot-out
that decided the LDV Vans Trophy tie at
Barnet. Eventually the Bees decided to
cash-in on one of the best goalkeepers in
the Nationwide League and Paul was sold
to Southampton, although he has yet to
make his debut for the Saints in
Premiership action.
*Charlton Ath (Free from Walton & Hersham
on 2/7/1998. Free to Walton & Hersham
during 1999 close season)*
*Brentford (Free from Carshalton Ath on
27/7/2000) FL 86+1 FLC 3 FAC 6 Others 8+1*
Southampton (250,000 + on 28/11/2004)

SMITH Paul William
Born: East Ham, 18 September 1971
Height: 5'11" **Weight:** 13.0
This experienced midfielder was in the
same rich vein of form as of old last term,
and Gillingham always looked worse
when he wasn't in the centre of midfield.
His experience and ball-winning
capabilities more than compensated for
his lack of pace, although he scored just
one goal, netting in the FA Cup third
round tie against Charlton.
*Southend U (From trainee on 16/3/1990) FL
18+2/1 Others 0+1*

Brentford (Free on 6/8/1993) FL 159/11 FLC 12/1 FAC 12/3 Others 15/2
Gillingham (Signed on 25/7/1997) FL 298+3/18 FLC 17/1 FAC 19/1 Others 9+2/2

SMITH Ryan Craig Matthew
Born: Islington, 10 November 1986
Height: 5'10" **Weight:** 10.10
International Honours: E: Yth
Ryan is a versatile Arsenal youngster who is comfortable on the left side of midfield or as a centre forward. He made his debut as a substitute in the Carling Cup win over Rotherham United, successfully converting a penalty in the shoot-out, and also featured in the victory against Wolves in the third round. He later replaced David Bentley in the semi-final first leg defeat by Middlesborough. Ryan made 13 appearances for the reserves, starting in seven of those games, before a knee injury brought his season to an abrupt halt in February.
Arsenal (Trainee) FLC 0+3

SMITH Gareth Shaun
Born: Leeds, 9 April 1971
Height: 5'10" **Weight:** 11.0
Shaun was out of contention for a first-team place at Hull last term and his only senior appearance came in the LDV Vans Trophy tie against Darlington. The experienced left back had loan spells at Stockport and Carlisle in the autumn, before eventually joining Rochdale on a short-term contract in March. He was just the sort of player Dale boss Steve Parkin was seeking and some steady defending helped the club avoid dropping into the relegation zone.
Halifax T (From trainee on 1/7/1989) FL 6+1 Others 1 (Free to Emley in May 1991)
Crewe Alex (Free on 31/12/1991) FL 380+22/41 FLC 24+1/4 FAC 19+2/4 Others 19+2/3
Hull C (Free on 12/7/2002) FL 17+5/1 FLC 1 FAC 0+1 Others 1
Stockport Co (Loaned on 5/9/2003) FL 3+3 FLC 1
Carlisle U (Loaned on 21/10/2003) FL 4 FAC 1
Rochdale (Free on 5/3/2004) FL 13

SMITH Stephen Martin
Born: Harlow, 19 September 1986
Height: 5'8" **Weight:** 11.7
This hard-working central midfielder impressed for Cambridge United's youngsters when they knocked Leicester City out of the FA Youth Cup, scoring the winner to take the U's into the fifth round of the competition for the first time. Stephen was handed a surprise first-team

debut at Doncaster in April when he performed well in the intimidating atmosphere of a large crowd.
Cambridge U (Trainee) FL 1+1

SMITH Thomas (Tommy) William
Born: Hemel Hempstead, 22 May 1980
Height: 5'8" **Weight:** 11.4
International Honours: E: U21-1; Yth
This talented striker joined Sunderland shortly after the start of the 2003-04 campaign and proved to be an astute purchase for the Wearsiders. An ability to play through the middle or wide on either flank made him an extremely useful member of the squad and he shone in the club's FA Cup run, scoring four goals, most notably a double at St. Andrews against Birmingham in the fifth round replay and then the only goal in the quarter-final against Sheffield United. Tommy possesses an excellent first touch, is comfortable using either foot, and has a deceptive turn of pace.
Watford (From trainee on 21/10/1997) P/FL 114+35/33 FLC 7+3/1 FAC 5+3/2
Sunderland (Signed on 25/9/2003) FL 22+13/4 FAC 3+1/4 Others 0+2

SOAMES David Michael
Born: Grimsby, 10 December 1984
Height: 5'5" **Weight:** 10.8
This young striker was a regular on the substitutes' bench for Grimsby Town last term, but although he featured in several games he failed to make the starting line-up. The youngster signed a new contract in the summer and will be hoping to establish himself in the side in 2004-05.
Grimsby T (Trainee) FL 0+20/1 FAC 2

SOARES Thomas (Tom) James
Born: Reading, 10 July 1986
Height: 6'0" **Weight:** 11.4
This talented Crystal Palace youngster was called up for his senior debut as a substitute against Gillingham last February and added two further appearances from the bench towards the end of the season. A skilful player, he can feature in midfield or in a role just behind the front strikers.
Crystal Palace (Trainee) FL 0+3

SODJE Efetobore (Efe)
Born: Greenwich, 5 October 1972
Height: 6'1" **Weight:** 12.0
Club Honours: GMVC '96
International Honours: Nigeria
Efe provided a major contribution to Huddersfield Town's promotion success last term. He produced some battling displays in the centre of the defence and

was rewarded by being handed the captain's armband. He was outstanding in the play-offs before an unfortunate neck injury in extra time of the final against Mansfield prevented him from lifting the trophy. Efe continued to represent Nigeria during the campaign and was also selected for the PFA Division Three team of the year.
Macclesfield T (£30,000 from Stevenage Borough on 11/7/1997) FL 83/6 FLC 6 FAC 6/1 Others 1
Luton T (Free on 12/8/1999) FL 5+4 FLC 1 FAC 2+1 Others 1
Colchester U (Free on 23/3/2000) FL 3
Crewe Alex (Free on 21/7/2000) FL 86+12/3 FLC 6+2 FAC 6+3/1 Others 2
Huddersfield T (Free on 7/8/2003) FL 37+2/4 FLC 2 FAC 1 Others 3+1

SOFIANE Youssef
Born: Lyon, France, 8 July 1984
Height: 5'8" **Weight:** 11.0
International Honours: France: Yth
The young French striker made his first-team debut for West Ham in the pre-season friendly against PSV Eindhoven. Normally a striker, he played on the right wing with some effect. Youssef came on as a substitute on the opening day of season at Preston and played very well as the Hammers beat Rushden in the Carling Cup. However, he never played for the first team again and in December he returned to France to join Lille on loan.
West Ham U (Free from Auxerre, France on 26/6/2002) FL 0+1 FLC 1

SOLANO Nolberto (Nobby) Albino
Born: Lima, Peru, 12 December 1974
Height: 5'8" **Weight:** 10.8
International Honours: Peru: 65; Yth
Nobby began the 2003-04 season on the right side of Newcastle's midfield and scored the winner in the away Champions' League qualifier at Partizan Belgrade. A hard-working, skilful player he is always available as an outlet to his defenders and able to take players on and deliver telling crosses. He struggled to hold down a place during the first half of the season, however, around the turn of the year he was playing regularly, so it was a surprise when he was transferred to Aston Villa in the January transfer window and much to the disappointment of the Toon Army. Nobby made an impressive debut in Villa's 5-0 win at Leicester and became an instant hit amongst the fans. He unfortunately pulled up with a hamstring strain just before half time against Blackburn and

Ole Gunnar Solskjaer (right)

subsequently missed the next four games, but was soon back in the line-up. He featured for Peru in the Copa America tournament in the summer.
Newcastle U (£2,763,958 from Boca Juniors, Argentina, ex Cristal Alianza Lima, Sporting, Deportivo Municipal, on 17/8/1998) PL 158+14/29 FLC 10+2 FAC 19/2 Others 27+4/7 Aston Villa (£1,500,000 on 29/1/2004) PL 10

SOLSKJAER Ole Gunnar
Born: Kristiansund, Norway, 26 February 1973
Height: 5'10" **Weight:** 11.10
Club Honours: PL '97, '99, '00, '01, '03; FAC '99, '04; EC '99; CS '03
International Honours: Norway: 62; U21-19
A supremely dedicated striker, who is arguably the most clinical of finishers at Manchester United, Ole played in the club's opening three Premiership games, and scored in the Champions' League opener against Panathinaikos, before disappearing from first-team action for vital knee surgery in September. During that time United sorely missed his goal scoring contribution, and his return in the FA Cup tie against Fulham was greatly welcomed. Although Sir Alex Ferguson used him as a last-minute gamble against Porto in the vital European decider in March, there was to be no 'Viva Barcelona' for Ole on the night.
Manchester U (£1,500,000 from Molde, Norway on 29/7/1996) PL 142+71/84 FLC 7+3/6 FAC 10+12/6 Others 40+44/19

SOMMEIL David
Born: Point-a-Pitre, Guadeloupe, 10 August 1974
Height: 5'11" **Weight:** 11.6
International Honours: France: B-1
A determined ball-winner, David started the 2003-04 season at right back for Manchester City before switching to central defence. He made history by becoming the first Blues' player to score a Premiership goal at the City of Manchester Stadium when he netted a late equaliser against Portsmouth. A strong and powerful defender, he completed the season on loan at Marseilles.
Manchester C (£3,500,000 from Bordeaux, France, ex Caen, Rennes, on 27/11/2003) PL 32/2 FLC 1 FAC 2 Others 4/1

SOMNER Matthew (Matt)
James
Born: Isleworth, 8 December 1982
Height: 6'0" **Weight:** 13.2
International Honours: W: U21-2
Matt started last season in the left-back

position for Brentford, retaining his place until the arrival of Ronnie Bull when he switched to the centre of the defence. However, Matt lost out to Scott Fitzgerald in March and thereafter he was a regular on the substitutes' bench, coming on in a number of different positions. He also represented Wales at U21 level during the campaign.
Brentford (From trainee on 4/7/2001) FL 71+11/1 FLC 1+1 FAC 3+2/1 Others 2

SONKO Ibrahima (Ibu)
Born: Bignona, Senegal, 22 January 1981
Height: 6'3" **Weight:** 13.7
International Honours: Senegal: U21
This cool, composed Brentford centre back was a regular in the side throughout the 2003-04 campaign. While his play didn't quite hit the heights of the previous season he learnt to clear the ball more quickly rather than trying to play his way out of trouble. He scored three goals, two

Matt Somner

of them late in the campaign at Sheffield Wednesday and against Colchester to help secure vital points.

Brentford *(Free from Grenoble, France, ex St Etienne, on 9/8/2002) FL 79+1/8 FLC 3/1 FAC 6 Others 2*

SONNER Daniel (Danny) James

Born: Wigan, 9 January 1972
Height: 5'11" **Weight:** 12.8
International Honours: NI: 11; B-4
This right-side midfielder joined Nottingham Forest after a short trial period and started the 2003-04 season in the line-up. However, he found it hard to sustain his form in the middle part of the campaign, and was mostly used as a substitute in the final run-in. Danny returned to international football for Northern Ireland in March, winning his first caps for three years. He was out of contract at the end of the season and his future was unclear at the time of writing.

Burnley *(From trainee at Wigan Ath on 6/8/1990) FL 1+5 FLC 0+1/1 Others 0+2 (Free to Preussen Koln, Germany during 1993 close season)*
Bury *(Loaned on 21/11/1992) FL 5/3 FAC 3 Others 1/1*
Ipswich T *(Free from FC Erzgebirge Aue, Germany on 12/6/1996) FL 28+28/3 FLC 6+4/1 FAC 1+1 Others 0+1*
Sheffield Wed *(£75,000 on 15/10/1998) PL 42+11/3 FLC 3+1/1 FAC 4+2*
Birmingham C *(Free on 4/8/2000) FL 32+9/2 FLC 12/1 FAC 1 Others 2*
Walsall *(Free on 5/8/2002) FL 20+4/4 FLC 2 FAC 2*
Nottingham F *(Free on 6/8/2003) FL 19+9 FLC 3 FAC 1*

SORENSEN Thomas

Born: Denmark, 12 June 1976
Height: 6'4" **Weight:** 13.10
Club Honours: Div 1 '99
International Honours: Denmark: 40; B-1; U21-6
This talented goalkeeper joined Aston Villa during the 2003 close season and went straight into the side as the first-choice 'keeper. A great all-round goalkeeper, he commands his box well and is developing into a first-class shot-stopper. He produced numerous outstanding saves throughout the campaign, but perhaps his most inspirational performance was against Middlesborough late on in the campaign. Thomas was one of two ever-presents for Villa last term and also represented Denmark on the international scene.

Sunderland *(£500,000 + from Odense BK,*

Denmark on 6/8/1998) P/FL 171 FLC 13 FAC 13*
Aston Villa *(£2,250,000 on 8/8/2003) PL 38 FLC 6 FAC 1*

SORVEL Neil Simon

Born: Whiston, 2 March 1973
Height: 6'0" **Weight:** 12.9
Club Honours: GMVC '95, '97; FAT '96
This hard-working, reliable midfield player was hampered by injuries at Crewe last season and did not feature as often as he had in the previous campaign. However, Neil eventually made a full recovery and played an important part in the run-in to the end of the campaign.

Crewe Alex *(From trainee on 31/7/1991) FL 5+4 FAC 1+1 Others 4*
Macclesfield T *(Free on 21/8/1992) FL 79+7/7 FLC 4+1 FAC 5 Others 0+1*
Crewe Alex *(Free on 9/6/1999) FL 184+20/10 FLC 14 FAC 10+1 Others 4*

SOUTHALL Leslie Nicholas (Nicky)

Born: Stockton, 28 January 1972
Height: 5'10" **Weight:** 12.12
Nicky struggled to find his confidence in a midfield role for Gillingham in the first half of last season, but was then switched to right back where he excelled in the closing stages of the club's successful battle against relegation. A vastly experience player, he failed to add to his tally of goals for the Gills during the campaign.

Hartlepool U *(From Darlington juniors on 21/2/1991) FL 118+20/24 FLC 6+1/3 FAC 4+4 Others 6+2*
Grimsby T *(£40,000 on 12/7/1995) FL 55+17/6 FLC 3+3/1 FAC 4/3/2*
Gillingham *(Free on 9/12/1997) FL 141+13/17 FLC 6+1/1 FAC 10/3 Others 12*
Bolton W *(Free on 2/7/2001) PL 10+8/1 FLC 4 FAC 2*
Norwich C *(Loaned on 27/9/2002) FL 4+5*
Gillingham *(Free on 6/12/2002) FL 56+3/1 FLC 2 FAC 4*

SOUTHERN Keith William

Born: Gateshead, 24 April 1981
Height: 5'10" **Weight:** 12.6
Club Honours: AMC '04
Keith missed the start of the 2003-04 season through injury, and then when he did return to match fitness, he suffered a further injury in the LDV Vans Trophy tie against Stockport and was out of action for another two months. Thereafter the young midfielder returned to the first-team squad, but spent most of the remainder of the campaign on the bench.

Everton *(From trainee on 21/5/1999)*

Blackpool *(Free on 8/8/2002) FL 53+13/3 FLC 2+1/1 FAC 4/1 Others 4+1/1*

SOUTHGATE Gareth

Born: Watford, 3 September 1970
Height: 6'0" **Weight:** 12.8
Club Honours: Div 1 '94; FLC '96, '04
International Honours: E: 57
Gareth is now considered one of the Premiership's elder statesmen but despite this he had yet another memorable season at the Riverside Stadium, proudly leading Middlesbrough to the first major trophy, the Carling Cup, of the club's history. A reliable, experienced defender who can launch attacks from the back he is proving to be an inspirational captain for Boro' and is still an England regular even though he missed the closing games of the domestic season with a knee injury. This injury led to his exclusion from Sven-Göran Eriksson's Euro 2004 squad.

Crystal Palace *(From trainee on 17/1/1989) F/PL 148+4/15 FLC 23+1/7 FAC 9 Others 6*
Aston Villa *(£2,500,000 on 1/7/1995) PL 191/7 FLC 17/1 FAC 20/1 Others 15*
Middlesbrough *(£6,500,000 on 14/7/2001) PL 100/4 FLC 7 FAC 8*

SPARROW Matthew (Matt) Ronald

Born: Wembley, 3 October 1981
Height: 5'11" **Weight:** 10.6
Always a first choice for Scunthorpe United last term, Matt finally found his best form when switched from his normal right-sided position to the centre of midfield. When on form he is an energetic player who loves running at opposition players and he contributed four valuable goals during the campaign.

Scunthorpe U *(From trainee on 30/7/2001) FL 110+16/17 FLC 3+3 FAC 10 Others 7+1/1*

SPEED Gary Andrew

Born: Deeside, 8 September 1969
Height: 5'10" **Weight:** 12.10
Club Honours: Div 2 '90, Div 1 '92; CS '92
International Honours: W: 80; U21-3; Yth
Evergreen Gary is the organiser in Newcastle's midfield, where his consistency, high work rate, and intelligent use of the ball make him a key player. His experience enables him to always be in the thick of the action, and his fine heading ability coupled with an ability to time his runs makes him a regular threat in any opponent's box. Gary's durability is an asset and once again he was a near-ever present for his club, indeed he holds the all-time record

for the most appearances in the Premiership, while he has also passed 600 appearances in all competitions during the campaign. Captain of Wales he became his country's second-most capped player last term, often appearing at left back.

Leeds U *(From trainee on 13/6/1988) F/PL 231+17/39 FLC 25+1/11 FAC 21/5 Others 14+3/2*

Everton *(£3,500,000 on 1/7/1996) PL 58/16 FLC 5/1 FAC 2/1*

Newcastle U *(£5,500,000 on 6/2/1998) PL 206+7/29 FLC 9+2/1 FAC 22/5 Others 39/5*

SPENCER Damian Michael
Born: Ascot, 19 September 1981
Height: 6'1" **Weight:** 14.5
A tall, powerful forward who leads the line with great enthusiasm, Damian made more starting appearances than any other Cheltenham striker last season. He played alongside five different partners in attack as well as featuring as a lone striker and occasionally operating on the left of a five-man midfield. He scored a stunning 12-minute hat-trick in the 3-3 draw at Hull City and finished with a total of ten goals in all competitions.

Bristol C *(From trainee on 14/6/2000) FL 8+5/1 FLC 0+1 Others 1+3/1*

Exeter C *(Loaned on 22/3/2001) FL 2+4*

Cheltenham T *(Free on 7/8/2002) FL 39+27/15 FLC 1 FAC 4+1/1 Others 1+2*

SPENCER James Matthew
Born: Stockport, 11 April 1985
Height: 6'5" **Weight:** 15.2
Stockport's youngest-ever 'keeper found it difficult to make a permanent breakthrough into the first team last season, as a series of loan players kept him out of the side for long periods. When called upon he regularly produced solid displays that belied his young age, one of the best coming at Swindon when he made some superb saves including a great penalty stop.

Stockport Co *(From trainee on 19/4/2002) FL 17+1 FAC 1 Others 3*

SPENDER Simon
Born: Mold, 15 November 1985
Height: 5'8" **Weight:** 11.0
International Honours: W: Yth
A second-year scholar with Wrexham, Simon made his first-team debut when coming on as a substitute at Home Park against eventual champions Plymouth Argyle last March. He came through with flying colours, producing a solid

performance. He featured on several more occasions in the closing stages of the campaign and will be looking to gain further senior experience in 2004-05.

Wrexham *(Trainee) FL 3+3*

SPICER John William
Born: Romford, 13 September 1983
Height: 5'11" **Weight:** 11.7

International Honours: E: Yth
This promising right back made his only first-team appearance in the second round Carling Cup tie when Arsenal faced Rotherham United. His progress can be monitored though the reserves, for whom he featured more times than any other player, making 20 starts and two more appearances as a substitute.

Arsenal *(From trainee on 2/7/2001) FLC 0+1*

Damian Spencer

SPILLER Daniel (Danny)
Born: Maidstone, 10 October 1981
Height: 5'9" **Weight:** 12.3
The 2003-04 season proved to be a real breakthrough for Danny and he was a mainstay in midfield for Gillingham. A regular in the starting line-up, he became a fans' favourite with his tough tackling and non-stop running. A player who rises to the occasion for big games, he scored some vital goals and was named 'Player of the Year' by both the players and the club's supporters.
Gillingham (From trainee on 10/7/2000) FL 37+13/6 FLC 3+1 FAC 2+1

SPRING Matthew John
Born: Harlow, 17 November 1979
Height: 5'11" **Weight:** 11.5
Matthew had a somewhat frustrating time at Luton last term after struggling with a groin problem which eventually required surgery and brought his campaign to a premature close in February. Prior to that the talented midfielder had featured regularly in the side, but sometimes seemed to be struggling to find his best form. Matthew was out of contract in the summer and his future was unclear at the time of writing.
Luton T (From trainee on 2/7/1997) FL 243+7/25 FLC 16/1 FAC 18+1/3 Others 4

SRNICEK Pavel
Born: Ostrava, Czechoslovakia, 10 March 1968
Height: 6'2" **Weight:** 14.9
Club Honours: Div 1 '94
International Honours: Czech Republic: 49
Pavel was third-choice goalkeeper at Fratton Park last term and made just four appearances, keeping a clean sheet in the Premiership clash at Middlesbrough. He moved on to West Ham in the new year, initially on loan, making his debut in difficult circumstances when he came on as a substitute against Millwall to face a penalty after Stephen Bywater had been sent off. He added a couple more first-team appearances but provided plenty of experienced back-up at Upton Park.
Newcastle U (£350,000 from Banik Ostrava, Czechoslovakia on 5/2/1991) F/PL 148+1 FLC 10+1 FAC 11 Others 17 (Free to Banik Ostrava, Czechoslovakia during 1998 close season)
Sheffield Wed (Free on 12/11/1998) PL 44 FLC 2 FAC 6 (Free to Brescia, Italy on 30/6/2000)
Portsmouth (Free on 1/9/2003) PL 3 FLC 1
West Ham U (Loaned on 20/2/2004) FL 2+1

STACK Graham Christopher
Born: Hampstead, 26 September 1981
Height: 6'2" **Weight:** 12.6
Club Honours: FAYC '00
International Honours: RoI: U21-7; Yth
The Republic of Ireland U21 'keeper enjoyed a memorable campaign for Arsenal and figured in all of the club's Carling Cup matches. Against Rotherham he both scored a penalty and saved one, as the Gunners eventually triumphed 9-8 in the shoot-out. His performances earned him rave reviews as the club went all the way to the semi-finals, and he played brilliantly in both legs of the tie against Middlesborough. Injury to Stuart Taylor allowed him the chance to sit on the bench for virtually the whole campaign and he took his full part in the title celebrations at both White Hart Lane and the presentation of the Premiership trophy three weeks later at Highbury. Graham also made the bench for his country when they faced Brazil in a prestige friendly.
Arsenal (From trainee on 18/7/2000) FLC 5

STALLARD Mark
Born: Derby, 24 October 1974
Height: 6'0" **Weight:** 13.6
A great favourite with the Notts County fans, Mark again produced some fine performances as a striker last term. It was therefore something of a shock when he was released early in the new year and he moved on to join Second Division rivals Barnsley. He scored on his debut for the Reds at Brighton and worked hard to link up play between midfield and attack before an injury brought his campaign to a premature close.
Derby Co (From trainee on 6/11/1991) FL 19+8/2 FLC 2+1/2 FAC 2+2 Others 3/2
Fulham (Loaned on 23/9/1994) FL 4/3
Bradford C (£110,000 on 12/11/1996) FL 33+10/10 FLC 2/1 FAC 4/1
Preston NE (Loaned on 14/2/1997) FL 4/1
Wycombe W (£100,000 on 7/3/1997) FL 67+3/23 FLC 5+1/1 Others 2/1
Notts Co (£10,000 on 3/3/1999) FL 168+17/67 FLC 13+1/8 FAC 10/3 Others 2
Barnsley (Free on 21/1/2004) FL 10/1

STAMPS Scott
Born: Birmingham, 20 March 1975
Height: 5'10" **Weight:** 11.10
Club Honours: NC '00
A stalwart of the Kidderminster defence last term, Scott proved to be one of the best left backs in the Third Division. He missed only a handful of games throughout the campaign, but lost out to new signing Steve Burton towards the

end of the season and was one of several players released by Harriers in the summer.
Torquay U (From trainee on 6/7/1993) FL 80+6/5 FLC 5 FAC 2 Others 2+1/1
Colchester U (£10,000 on 26/3/1997) FL 52+4/1 FLC 4 FAC 3+1 Others 1+1
Kidderminster Hrs (Free on 17/9/1999) FL 123+6 FLC 4 FLC 3 FAC 7 Others 4

STANDING Michael John
Born: Shoreham, 20 March 1981
Height: 5'10" **Weight:** 10.12
International Honours: E: Yth; Sch
Michael will be hoping for better luck after a disappointing season for Bradford City when he started only two matches. He added more strength to his obvious ball skills but found first-team opportunities strictly limited. His longest run in the team came just before Christmas when he made substitute appearances against Wigan and Sunderland and started in the 2-0 home defeat to Rotherham, lasting 70 minutes.
Aston Villa (From trainee on 26/3/1998)
Bradford C (Free on 19/3/2002) FL 16+14/2 FLC 1 FAC 1

STANIC Mario
Born: Sarajevo, Yugoslavia, 10 April 1972
Height: 6'2" **Weight:** 12.12
Club Honours: CS '00
International Honours: Croatia: 49
The influx of so many midfielders into Chelsea 'post-Abramovich' has certainly marginalised Mario Stanic. The popular Croatian international made only five substitute appearances during the season – Premiership at Southampton and the final match of the season at home to Leeds United, Carling Cup against Notts County and Reading and Champions' League against MSK Zilinia – for a sum total of just over two hours' playing time! His four years at Stamford Bridge have been blighted by injury but he has always given 100 per cent in whichever role he has been asked to perform and endeared himself to Blues' fans with his wholehearted attitude.
Chelsea (£5,600,000 from Parma, Italy, ex Zeljeznicar Sarajevo, Croatio Zagreb, Sporting Gijon, Benfica, Brugge, on 12/7/2000) PL 39+20/7 FLC 3+3/1 FAC 7+2/2 Others 5+1

STANSFIELD Adam
Born: Plymouth, 10 September 1978
Height: 5'11" **Weight:** 11.6
Club Honours: FAT '02
International Honours: E: SP-3
This effective striker spent much of last season on the substitutes' bench for

Yeovil. Nevertheless he netted six times during the campaign, including strikes in both fixtures against Lincoln City. Adam's pace is his main strength and he will be looking to feature more regularly in the starting line-up in 2004-05.
Yeovil T (Signed from Elmore on 8/11/2001) FL 7+25/6 FAC 0+2 Others 0+2

STANTON Nathan
Born: Nottingham, 6 May 1981
Height: 5'9" **Weight:** 11.3
International Honours: E: Yth
Nathan remained one of the first choices on the Scunthorpe United team sheet last term, playing either at right back, where he mainly operated, or centre half, which remains his favourite position. A very quick, determined defender who is developing his attacking game, he missed two months of the season because of a knee cartilage injury, but returned after Christmas to become an ever-present during the closing three months of the campaign. His performances were rewarded when he was selected in the PFA Division Three team of the year.
Scunthorpe U (From trainee on 19/3/1999) FL 176+18 FLC 6 FAC 15+2 Others 10+1/1

STAUNTON Stephen (Steve)
Born: Drogheda, Ireland, 19 January 1969
Height: 6'1" **Weight:** 12.12
Club Honours: FAC '89; Div 1 '90; FLC '94, '96
International Honours: RoI: 102; U21-4; Yth
Signed on the eve of last season, Steve made an instant impression at Coventry with his vast defensive experience helping a wobbly back line. His positional sense and confidence were obvious, whether he played at left back or in the centre of defence, although his lack of pace was occasionally exposed on a couple of occasions. He suffered several niggling injuries and required a minor operation near the end of the season, missing the last two games.
Liverpool (£20,000 from Dundalk on 2/9/1986) FL 55+10 FLC 6+2/4 FAC 14+2/1 Others 1/1
Bradford C (Loaned on 13/11/1987) FL 7+1 FLC 2 Others 1
Aston Villa (£1,100,000 on 7/8/1991) F/PL 205+3/16 FLC 17+2/1 FAC 19+1/1 Others 15+1
Liverpool (Free on 3/7/1998) PL 38+6 FLC 5/1 FAC 2 Others 5+2
Crystal Palace (Loaned on 20/10/2000) FL 6/1
Aston Villa (Free on 7/12/2000) PL 65+8 FLC 5 FAC 4 Others 5/1

Coventry C (Free on 15/8/2003) FL 34+1/3 FLC 1 FAC 2

STEAD Jonathan (Jon) Graeme
Born: Huddersfield, 7 April 1983
Height: 6'3" **Weight:** 11.7
International Honours: E: U21-2
Jon started the season as a regular striker for Huddersfield and scored at will, producing some classy displays of close control and quick footwork. Fast and skilful, the local hero attracted much attention after leading the goal-scoring charts in Division Three, and he moved up to the Premiership with Blackburn Rovers during the January transfer window. Jon was a revelation at Ewood Park, providing an immediate winner at Middlesbrough, another at Fulham and a late equaliser against Newcastle. Not overawed by the step-up in grade, he scored because he was never afraid to get in an attempt at goal, and with a low back-lift he struck the ball early. His work rate was phenomenal and showed that he could hold and lay the ball off well.
Huddersfield T (From trainee on 30/11/2001) FL 54+14/22 FLC 5/2 FAC 2 Others 2
Blackburn Rov (£1,200,000 on 2/2/2004) PL 13/6

STEELE Lee Anthony James
Born: Liverpool, 2 December 1973
Height: 5'8" **Weight:** 12.7
Club Honours: Div 3 '01; Div 2 '02
Lee missed the start of the 2003-04 season whilst still recovering from a knee injury, but he then endured a frustrating time with further injuries disrupting his campaign and restricting his appearances. He managed just three starts and netted his only goal with a last-minute strike against Scunthorpe to earn a valuable three points for the U's. Lee was reported to have signed for Leyton Orient during the summer break.
Shrewsbury T (£30,000 + from Northwich Vic on 21/7/1997) FL 104+9/37 FLC 5/3 FAC 4+1 Others 3
Brighton & Hove A (Free on 19/7/2000) FL 24+36/11 FLC 1+1 FAC 1+4 Others 4/1
Oxford U (Free on 12/7/2002) FL 6+20/4 FAC 0+1

STEFANOVIC Dejan
Born: Yugoslavia, 28 October 1974
Height: 6'2" **Weight:** 12.10
International Honours: Serbia: 23
Pompey's most expensive player, this experienced left back featured in the majority of Premiership games last season,

scoring important goals against Leeds, Manchester City and Birmingham. A proven, consistent professional, he steadied the back line, pairing up well with Arjan De Zeeuw in the heart of the defence.
Sheffield Wed (£2,000,000 from Red Star Belgrade, Yugoslavia on 22/12/1995) PL 59+7/4 FLC 2 FAC 4/1 (Free to Vitesse Arnhem, Holland on 1/7/1999)
Portsmouth (£1,850,000 on 30/7/2003) PL 32/3 FLC 2 FAC 4

STEPHENS Kevin Alexander
Born: Enfield, 28 July 1984
Height: 5'10" **Weight:** 12.5
This young central defender managed just one appearance from the substitutes' bench for Leyton Orient last term, and spent much of the campaign out on loan with Ryman League clubs Billericay and Hornchurch. He was released by the O's shortly before the end of the season.
Leyton Orient (From trainee on 22/8/2003) FL 2+2

STEVENSON Jonathan (Jon) Ashlee
Born: Leicester, 13 October 1982
Height: 5'6" **Weight:** 11.11
Jon never really got going for Swindon Town last term and failed to establish himself as a regular in the first-team squad. Always behind Tommy Mooney and Sam Parkin in contention for a place in the side, the arrival of Rory Fallon saw his opportunities further reduced, although he was often included on the bench. A small, lively striker, he was leading scorer for the club's reserve team, but nevertheless he was released in the summer.
Leicester C (From trainee on 26/3/2001) P/FL 0+12/2 FLC 0+2
Swindon T (Free on 7/7/2003) FL 1+4 FLC 2 Others 1

STEWART Bryan William
Born: Stockton, 13 September 1985
Height: 5'11" **Weight:** 11.0
One of several youngsters who came up through the ranks at York last term, Bryan produced a number of lively displays up front in the early weeks of the campaign when coming on as a substitute. He returned to first-team action near the end of the season and in his first League start at home to Leyton Orient he gave a fine performance down the left wing showing pace, control and an ability to cross the ball.
York C (Trainee) FL 2+8 FLC 0+1

Jordan Stewart (foreground)

STEWART Gareth John
Born: Preston, 3 February 1980
Height: 6'0" **Weight:** 12.8
International Honours: E: Yth; Sch
Last term proved to be another season of misfortune for this Bournemouth goalkeeper. After losing his number one jersey to Neil Moss, he made just one first-team appearance, at Yeovil in the LDV Vans Trophy, and then in December he damaged his knee in a reserve game at Cardiff. This required surgery and ruled him out for the rest of the campaign.
Blackburn Rov (From trainee on 11/2/1997)
Bournemouth (Free on 2/7/1999) FL 83+1 FLC 1 FAC 6+1 Others 1

STEWART Jordan Barrington
Born: Birmingham, 3 March 1982
Height: 5'11" **Weight:** 11.12
International Honours: E: U21-1
This left-footed midfielder or full back can be tricky and deceptive when going forward, and has the knack of contributing spectacular goals, as witnessed by his scorching effort for Leicester City at Maine Road. Usually employed on the left side of midfield during the season, only occasionally at full back, he suffered from a few injury problems and, because of that, was not always an automatic choice.
Leicester C (From trainee on 22/3/2000) P/FL 53+25/5 FLC 3+2 FAC 4+3
Bristol Rov (Loaned on 23/3/2000) FL 1+3

STEWART William Marcus Paul
Born: Bristol, 7 November 1972
Height: 5'10" **Weight:** 11.0
International Honours: E: Sch
A left-sided striker whose close control and ability to turn sharply are his most notable assets, Marcus finished the 2003-04 season as Sunderland's joint-top goal-scorer with 16. His first strike of the season was a crucial one, as it sealed a 2-0 win at Preston in August, and Marcus proceeded to score in the next three matches as the Wearsiders climbed the First Division table. Although he had to be content at stages with a place on the substitutes' bench, he continued to score vital goals including a last-minute penalty winner against Crystal Palace in September and further strikes against the same opposition in both legs of the play-off semi-finals.
Bristol Rov (From trainee on 18/7/1991) FL 137+34/57 FLC 11/5 FAC 7+1/4 Others 16+1/14
Huddersfield T (£1,200,000 + on 2/7/1996) FL 129+4/58 FLC 18/7 FAC 9/3
Ipswich T (£2,500,000 on 1/2/2000) P/FL

65+10/27 FLC 4+2/11 FAC 4/2 Others 8/7
Sunderland (£3,250,000 on 30/8/2002) P/FL 37+22/15 FLC 4+1/4 FAC 5+2/1 Others 2/2

STEWART Michael James
Born: Edinburgh, 26 February 1981
Height: 5'11" **Weight:** 11.11
International Honours: S: 3; U21-17; Sch
This young Manchester United midfielder was loaned out to Nottingham Forest to gain valuable first-team experience last term. After starting the season in the line-up he struggled to get back in the side after a period of suspension and was then affected by a number of niggling injuries. Michael's final appearance for Forest was in the home defeat by West Ham in December and he returned to Old Trafford in April.
Manchester U (From trainee on 19/3/1998) PL 5+2 FLC 2+2 FAC 0+1 Others 0+2
Nottingham F (Loaned on 29/7/2003) FL 11+2 FLC 1+1

ST LEDGER-HALL Sean Patrick
Born: Birmingham, 28 December 1984
Height: 6'0" **Weight:** 12.0
This promising young defender started just two games for Peterborough last term, the LDV Vans Trophy tie against Torquay and the final match of the season against Wycombe. In between he spent time on loan at Stevenage. Sean plays with a calm assuredness that belies his youth and will be looking to break into the side in 2004-05.
Peterborough U (From trainee on 18/7/2003) FL 1+2 Others 1

STOCK Brian Benjamin
Born: Winchester, 24 December 1981
Height: 5'11" **Weight:** 11.2
International Honours: W: U21-4
This Bournemouth midfielder endured a frustrating season in 2003-04, for despite his obvious talent he could not command a regular place in the line-up. Brian still proved that he has a good eye for goal and on his day was as good as any player on the pitch, but he lacked the consistency required for an extended run in the team.
Bournemouth (From trainee on 25/11/2000) FL 48+30/7 FAC 6 Others 5+3

STOCKDALE Robert (Robbie) Keith
Born: Redcar, 30 November 1979
Height: 5'11" **Weight:** 11.3
International Honours: S: 4; B-2; E: U21-1

Out-of-favour right back Robbie started the campaign by playing in three of Middlesbrough's pre-season friendlies. but he must have known his chances would be as rare as snow in the Sahara desert following the arrival of on-loan Danny Mills from Leeds United. In October he joined West Ham in an extended loan deal and made a creditable start before a hamstring injury forced him out of action. He returned to the Riverside at the end of January and soon afterwards went out on loan again, this time to Rotherham, where his cultured performances proved invaluable in the battle to avoid relegation and he marked the last home game with a tremendous goal in the 3-0 win against Burnley to secure safety. A good tackler and clever ball player, Robbie always seemed to have enough time on the ball to use it properly.
Middlesbrough (From trainee on 2/7/1998) P/FL 62+13/2 FLC 8+1 FAC 7
Sheffield Wed (Loaned on 13/9/2000) FL 6
West Ham U (Loaned on 23/10/2003) FL 5+2 FLC 1 FAC 1
Rotherham U (Loaned on 20/2/2004) FL 16/1

STOCKLEY Samuel (Sam) Joshua
Born: Tiverton, 5 September 1977
Height: 6'0" **Weight:** 12.0
Sam enjoyed his best season to date for Colchester United in 2003-04. A near ever-present in the line-up, he was mostly used as a right back, although he switched to left back during the run-in following injuries to Andy Myers and Karl Duguid. Sam always gave 100 per cent, and finished runner-up to Alan White in the club's 'Player of the Year' standings. He was out of contract in the summer and his future was uncertain at the time of writing.
Southampton (From trainee on 1/7/1996)
Barnet (Free on 31/12/1996) FL 177+5/2 FLC 10 FAC 4 Others 11
Oxford U (£150,000 on 13/7/2001) FL 39+2 FLC 1 FAC 1 Others 1
Colchester U (Free on 30/8/2002) FL 75+2/1 FLC 2 FAC 7 Others 6+1

STOLCERS Andrejs
Born: Latvia, 8 July 1974
Height: 5'10" **Weight:** 11.4
Club Honours: Div 1 '01
International Honours: Latvia: 78
Andrejs did not enjoy the best of seasons at Fulham last term and failed to make a single Premiership appearance. His only first-team outing came in the Carling Cup tie at Wigan and he was unlucky not to

get on the score sheet in that game. Used on the left side of midfield in reserve games, his appearances were limited by injury. His lack of match practise also saw him left out of the Latvia side in which he had been a feature, however, he was a member of the squad for Euro 2004.

Fulham *(£2,000,000 + from Shakhtjor Donetsk, Ukraine, ex Olympija Riga, Skonto Riga, on 7/12/2000) P/FL 8+17/2 FLC 3+1/2 FAC 0+2 Others 0+1*

STONE Steven (Steve) Brian
Born: Gateshead, 20 August 1971
Height: 5'8" **Weight:** 12.7
Club Honours: Div 1 '98, '03
International Honours: E: 9
This experienced midfield campaigner was often a pivotal figure for Pompey last term, and on many occasions he was the diff erence between winning and losing matches. Steve scored on two occasions, net ting in the 4-0 win over Bolton and providing the winner against Manchester United at Fratton Park in April. His intelligence and composure calmed play down in the centre of the park and he was a tremendous influence on the team.

Nottingham F *(From trainee on 20/5/1989) F/PL 189+4/23 FLC 14+1/2 FAC 11 Others 10/2*
Aston Villa *(£5,500,000 on 12/3/1999) PL 66+24/4 FLC 5+3/1 FAC 5+5/2 Others 10+4*
Portsmouth *(Loaned on 24/10/2002) FL 5/1*
Portsmouth *(Free on 20/12/2002) P/FL 42+3/5 FLC 2+1 FAC 1+1/1*

STONEBRIDGE Ian Robert
Born: Lewisham, 30 August 1981
Height: 6'0" **Weight:** 11.4
Club Honours: Div 3 '02; Div 2 '04
International Honours: E: Yth
Ian had another solid season with Plymouth Argyle, when he was generally used as a left-sided midfield player rather than up front. He has excellent touch on the ball and also has good movement. Sometimes used from the bench, Ian scored two crucial goals in successive games in February, which gained Argyle six points at a vital stage of the season.
Plymouth Arg *(From trainee at Tottenham H on 13/7/1999) FL 124+47/38 FLC 2+3/1 FAC 16+2/5 Others 5+2/1*

STORY Owen Grant
Born: Burton, 3 August 1984
Height: 5'11" **Weight:** 10.10
Owen made his senior debut for Rushden as a substitute during the 2-1 defeat at Bournemouth last September. The quick front-runner made a few more

appearances from the bench during the season and was often with the first-team squad for experience, which should prove valuable in his future career. However, following the club's relegation he was one of several out-of-contract players who were released.
Rushden & Diamonds *(Trainee) FL 0+5 Others 0+1*

STOWELL Michael (Mike)
Born: Preston, 19 April 1965
Height: 6'2" **Weight:** 14.2
Mike provided good back-up in the goalkeeping department for Bristol City last term, but such was the form of Steve Phillips that he hardly got a look in. His only appearance came in the LDV Vans Trophy tie at Plymouth when City lost 4-0.
Preston NE *(Free from Leyland Motors on 14/2/1985)*
Everton *(Free on 12/12/1985) Others 1*
Chester C *(Loaned on 3/9/1987) FL 14 Others 2*
York C *(Loaned on 24/12/1987) FL 6*
Manchester C *(Loaned on 2/2/1988) FL 14 FAC 1*
Port Vale *(Loaned on 21/10/1988) FL 7 Others 1*
Wolverhampton W *(Loaned on 17/3/1989) FL 7*
Preston NE *(Loaned on 8/2/1990) FL 2*
Wolverhampton W *(£250,000 on 28/6/1990) FL 377+1 FLC 30 FAC 22 Others 11*
Bristol C *(Free on 27/7/2001) FL 25 FLC 2 FAC 1 Others 1*

STRACHAN Craig Scott
Born: Aberdeen, 19 May 1982
Height: 5'8" **Weight:** 10.6
After missing virtually the whole of the 2002-03 campaign due to injury problems, this young midfielder joined Rochdale shortly before the start of last season. However, Craig managed just one brief taste of first-team action when he came on as a late substitute against Macclesfield last September. A shin splints problem then led to his leaving senior football, although he spent the closing stages of the campaign with Dr Martens League club Halesowen Town.
Coventry C *(From trainee on 20/12/1999)*
Rochdale *(Free on 5/8/2003) FL 0+1*

STRACHAN Gavin David
Born: Aberdeen, 23 December 1978
Height: 5'11" **Weight:** 11.7
International Honours: S: U21-8; Yth
One of Hartlepool manager Neale Cooper's close season signings, Gavin had

been a trialist at Sheffield Wednesday during the summer before arriving at the Victoria Ground. Gavin got off to a good start, scoring from a free kick on his debut against Peterborough United, and in the early months of the season he found the net on two more occasions. However, after establishing himself in a central-midfield role he was sidelined for a lengthy period with a knee injury.
Coventry C *(From trainee on 28/11/1996) P/FL 5+11 FLC 1+3/1 FAC 2+2*
Dundee *(Loaned on 27/1/1999) SL 4+2*
Peterborough U *(Free on 14/3/2003) FL 1+1*
Southend U *(Free on 27/3/2003) FL 6+1*
Hartlepool U *(Free on 8/8/2003) FL 34+2/5 FLC 2 FAC 3 Others 1*

STREET Kevin
Born: Crewe, 25 November 1977
Height: 5'10" **Weight:** 10.8
This central midfielder started the 2003-04 campaign in Bristol Rovers first team, but after scoring what proved to be a consolation goal at Torquay in September he was allowed to move on. Kevin subsequently joined Conference club Shrewsbury Town and was a regular in the line-up as the Shrews fought their way back into the Third Division after a season's absence.
Crewe Alex *(From trainee on 4/7/1996) FL 57+58/9 FLC 4+3 FAC 1+1 (Free to Northwich Vic during 2002 close season)*
Luton T *(Loaned on 20/11/2001) FL 1+1*
Bristol Rov *(Free on 29/11/2002) FL 21+12/2 FLC 1 Others 0+1*

STRONG Gregory (Greg)
Born: Bolton, 5 September 1975
Height: 6'2" **Weight:** 12.12
International Honours: E: Yth; Sch
This powerful left-footed central defender joined Bury on loan shortly before the start of the 2003-04 campaign as a direct replacement for Michael Nelson, who had signed for Hartlepool. Greg was a regular in a flat back four during two months at Gigg Lane, but failed to make much of an impression. Back at Hull, he was restricted to just a couple of outings in the LDV Vans Trophy games, but showed his professionalism by turning out for the reserves as a striker and bagging a hat-trick against Rotherham. Greg's move to Boston in March was immediately followed by a training ground injury that prevented him appearing for the Pilgrims.
Wigan Ath *(From trainee on 1/10/1992) FL 28+7/3 FLC 5 FAC 1 Others 3+1*
Bolton W *(Signed on 10/9/1995) P/FL 10+2/1 FLC 8+2*

Blackpool (Loaned on 21/11/1997) FL 11/1 Others 1
Stoke C (Loaned on 24/3/1999) FL 5/1
Motherwell (Loaned on 17/3/2000) SL 11
Motherwell (£150,000 on 14/7/2000) SL 62+2/3 SLC 1/1 SC 2
Hull C (Free on 17/6/2002) FL 3 Others 2
Cheltenham T (Loaned on 4/2/2003) FL 3+1
Scunthorpe U (Loaned on 25/3/2003) FL 7 Others 2
Bury (Loaned on 1/8/2003) FL 10 FLC 1
Boston U (Signed on 12/3/2004)

STUART Graham Charles
Born: Tooting, 24 October 1970
Height: 5'9" **Weight:** 11.10
Club Honours: FAC '95; Div 1 '00
International Honours: E: U21-5; Yth
Graham was a regular in Charlton's midfield for most of the season, building up useful partnerships with new signings Matt Holland and Claus Jensen. He suffered a back injury in March, which forced him to miss six games, but fully recovered to regain his place before the end of the campaign. Graham is a hard-working attacking midfielder who is a good distributor of the ball as well as being a strong tackler. He is often involved in build-up play and likes to get a shot on goal where possible, in addition to setting up others. He found the net on three occasions including the winning goal at Goodison Park against Everton, one of his former clubs.
Chelsea (From trainee on 15/6/1989) F/PL 70+17/14 FLC 11/2 FAC 5+2/1 Others 3+2/1
Everton (£850,000 on 19/8/1993) PL 116+20/22 FLC 9/3 FAC 10+3/5 Others 2+1/1
Sheffield U (£850,000 on 28/11/1997) FL 52+1/11 FLC 4 FAC 10+1/1 Others 0+1
Charlton Ath (£1,100,000 on 25/3/1999) P/FL 132+12/22 FLC 6 FAC 8/2

STUART Jamie Christopher
Born: Southwark, 15 October 1976
Height: 5'10" **Weight:** 11.0
International Honours: E: U21-4; Yth
This experienced left back never really managed to hold down a regular place in the Southend United defence last term. Jamie also featured in the left-sided centre-back berth and always displayed total commitment. His rugged and combative style made him popular with the Roots Hall crowd but he finished the season as a regular on the substitutes' bench. Jamie was released by the Blues at the end of the campaign.
Charlton Ath (From trainee on 18/1/1995) FL 49+1/3 FLC 8+1 FAC 3 Others 0+1
Millwall (Free on 25/9/1998) FL 42+3 FLC 2 FAC 1 Others 6

Bury (Free, via trial at Cambridge U, on 8/10/2001) FL 56+5/1 FLC 2+1/1 FAC 2+1 Others 4
Southend U (Free on 6/6/2003) FL 23+3 FAC 3 Others 4

STUBBS Alan
Born: Liverpool, 6 October 1971
Height: 6'2" **Weight:** 13.10
Club Honours: SPD '98, '00; SLC '97, '99
International Honours: E: B-1
There are few players more committed to the Everton cause than this locally born centre half who captained the side for long periods during the season, setting a fine professional example in a struggling team. Alan was absent on two occasions, for a total of eight weeks, as a result of a troublesome groin injury, but in the remainder of the campaign he was the bedrock of the Blues' defence. He is a dominating presence in the air and has better distribution skills than most central defenders. For the second consecutive season he failed to find the target, which, considering his dead-ball skills, remained a mystery.
Bolton W (From trainee on 24/7/1990) P/FL 181+21/9 FLC 23/4 FAC 16+2/2 Others 12+1
Glasgow Celtic (£3,500,000 on 10/7/1996) SL 101+5/3 SLC 8+1 SC 11 Others 16+1/2
Everton (Free on 13/7/2001) PL 88+5/2 FLC 3+2 FAC 8/1

STURRIDGE Dean Constantine
Born: Birmingham, 27 July 1973
Height: 5'8" **Weight:** 12.5
Dean was in the line-up for Wolves in their first-ever Premiership game at Blackburn, but found there was plenty of competition for strikers at the club and injury put him out of contention. In December he was given a run and was involved in four successive games, but he did not make the required impact and in January he joined Sheffield United on loan. However, although he showed glimpses of his striking ability he did not play a full game, being hampered by his lack of match fitness and a knee problem. A hamstring injury against Crystal Palace meant an early return to Molineux and he later had surgery on his knee.
Derby Co (From trainee on 1/7/1991) P/FL 142+48/53 FLC 9+4/4 FAC 8/2 Others 2
Torquay U (Loaned on 16/12/1994) FL 10/5
Leicester C (£350,000 on 19/11/2001) PL 20+2/6 FLC 1 FAC 2
Wolverhampton W (£375,000 on 23/11/2001) P/FL 46+25/30 FLC 1+2 FAC 1+1 Others 2+3/1
Sheffield U (Loaned on 2/1/2004) FL 2+2 FAC 1

STURROCK Blair David
Born: Dundee, 25 August 1981
Height: 6'0" **Weight:** 11.1
Club Honours: Div 3 '02; Div 2 '04
Although Blair did not achieve a starting role in Plymouth's first team last season, he came off the substitutes' bench on 25 occasions. A pacy right-sided midfield player, he is very quick, able to turn defenders and has good movement off the ball. Blair is the son of Southampton manager Paul Sturrock.
Dundee U (From juniors on 5/9/1999)
Brechin C (Loaned on 8/8/2000) SL 20+7/6 SC 1+2 Others 3+1/3
Plymouth Arg (Free on 26/10/2001) FL 9+54/2 FLC 1/1 FAC 0+5 Others 1+1

SUFFO Herve Patrick
Born: Ebolowa, Cameroon, 17 January 1978
Height: 5'9" **Weight:** 12.12
International Honours: Cameroon (ANC '02)
Patrick's early-season form for Coventry was good and he notched fine goals against Sheffield United and Stoke. His best performances came at Derby, when he scored two goals, and at Burnley. He returned to first-team action in February and scored the winner at Forest before suffering a broken foot that kept him out for the last two months of the season. A skilful striker who looked more comfortable playing in a slightly withdrawn role, he used his body strength well and was awkward to dislodge from the ball.
Sheffield U (£150,000 from Nantes, France, ex Tonerre Yaounde, Barcelona, on 20/11/2000) FL 16+20/5 FLC 0+1/1 FAC 0+1 (Freed on 3/4/2002)
Coventry C (Free from Numancia, Spain on 30/7/2003) FL 20+7/7 FLC 2

SULLIVAN Neil
Born: Sutton, 24 February 1970
Height: 6'0" **Weight:** 12.1
International Honours: S: 27
A cruciate ligament injury sustained by Chelsea's new number two 'keeper Jurgen Macho gave Neil Sullivan an unexpected chance to emerge from football's wilderness. The experienced Scottish international made his debut in the Carling Cup fourth round tie at Reading 21 months after his previous first-team match at Spurs! Neil filled in competently for Carlo Cudicini when the Blues' first choice was sidelined with a groin strain but Cudicini's broken finger in March coincided with Neil developing a thigh strain in training which curtailed his

season and allowed Marco Ambrosio to undertake his surprise 11-match run in the first team.

Wimbledon *(From trainee on 26/7/1988)*
F/PL 180+1 FLC 18 FAC 25
Crystal Palace *(Loaned on 1/5/1992) FL 1*
Tottenham H *(Free on 5/6/2000) PL 64 FLC 8 FAC 9*
Chelsea *(Free on 29/8/2003) PL 4 FLC 2 FAC 1+1*

SUMMERBEE Nicholas (Nicky) John
Born: Altrincham, 26 August 1971
Height: 5'11" **Weight:** 12.8
Club Honours: Div 1 '99
International Honours: E: B-1; U21-3
Nicky proved to be Nicky Law's final signing for Bradford when he joined the Bantams a month into the season. The much-travelled right winger made his debut at home to Preston and celebrated by scoring the winning goal from close range. Nicky likes to get the ball in early and he remains one of the best crossers of the ball in the Football League. However, he is no longer an out-and-out winger who hugs the touchline, tending to operate more centrally on the right of a midfield three. Nicky often found himself back in his own penalty area and has improved his defensive skills, so much so that he played one game at right back.

Swindon T *(From trainee on 20/7/1989) F/PL 89+23/6 FLC 9+1/3 FAC 2+3 Others 7/1*
Manchester C *(£1,500,000 on 24/6/1994) P/FL 119+12/6 FLC 11+2/2 FAC 12/2*
Sunderland *(£1,000,000 on 14/11/1997) P/FL 87+6/7 FLC 6+1 FAC 4+1 Others 3/1*
Bolton W *(Free on 4/1/2001) FL 9+3/1 FAC 3*
Nottingham F *(Free on 9/11/2001) FL 17/2 FAC 1*
Leicester C *(Free on 9/8/2002) FL 7+22 FLC 1+1 FAC 2*
Bradford C *(Free on 12/9/2003) FL 33+2/1*

SUMMERBELL Mark
Born: Durham, 30 October 1976
Height: 5'9" **Weight:** 11.9
Mark saw relatively little first-team action for Carlisle United in 2003-04, featuring in just half-a-dozen early-season games. A ball-winning midfielder, he will be hoping for better things in the 2004-05 campaign.

Middlesbrough *(From trainee on 1/7/1995) F/PL 35+16/1 FLC 4+3/3*
Bristol C *(Loaned on 28/9/2001) FL 5*
Portsmouth *(Loaned on 28/3/2002) FL 5*
Carlisle U *(Free on 23/8/2002) FL 43+2/1 FLC 1 FAC 2 Others 5*

SUTCH Daryl
Born: Lowestoft, 11 September 1971
Height: 6'0" **Weight:** 12.0
International Honours: E: U21-4; Yth
Daryl began the season at right back for Boston United but lost his place and found it difficult to break into the first-team line-up again. He was released early in the new year and later underwent an operation to solve a problem with his achilles tendon.

Norwich C *(From trainee on 6/7/1990) F/PL 255+50/9 FLC 24+3 FAC 10+3 Others 2+5*
Southend U *(Free on 3/1/2003) FL 16/1*
Boston U *(Free on 9/7/2003) FL 6 FLC 1 FAC 0+1 Others 0+1*

SUTTON John William Michael
Born: Norwich, 26 December 1983
Height: 6'0" **Weight:** 14.2
International Honours: E: Yth
This exciting young striker was in prolific form for Raith Rovers last season, bagging 16 goals from 24 appearances, including a hat-trick against Brechin City. Chris was snapped up by Millwall during the January transfer window and made his debut just 24 hours later, coming on as a substitute in the away win at Crewe. A player with good pace and a cracking shot, he featured on a number of occasions later on in the campaign. John is the brother of Celtic striker Chris Sutton.

Tottenham H *(From trainee on 12/7/2001)*
Carlisle U *(Loaned on 4/10/2002) FL 7/1 FAC 1 Others 2*
Swindon T *(Free on 20/12/2002) FL 0+1 (Freed on 20/1/2003)*
Raith Rov *(Free on 19/7/2003) SL 20/13 SC 1 Others 3/3*
Millwall *(£60,000 on 30/1/2004) FL 2+2 FAC 0+1*

SVARD Sebastian
Born: Hividovre, Denmark, 15 January 1983
Height: 6'1" **Weight:** 12.11
Club Honours: FAYC '01
International Honours: Denmark: U21-7; Yth
This talented Arsenal youngster spent the whole of last season out on loan. Sebastian was back in Denmark with FC Copenhagen until the new year when he returned, only to go out almost immediately to Stoke City. A versatile player who is comfortable in a number of positions including midfield, central defence and full back, he produced some fine performances for the Potters and netted a superb goal at Sunderland. He

represented Denmark at U20 level during the campaign.

Arsenal *(Signed from FC Copenhagen, Denmark on 1/11/2000) FLC 1+1 FAC 1*
Stoke C *(Loaned on 1/1/2004) FL 9+4/1 FAC 1*

SVENSSON Anders
Born: Sweden, 17 July 1976
Height: 5'10" **Weight:** 12.11
International Honours: Sweden: 50
Three seasons at St Mary's have verified that, in Anders Svensson, the Saints have an enigma on their hands. Sublimely skilful and capable of inspired passing (Kevin Phillips has credited him with having 'eyes in the back of his head,') he manifests flashes of genius amidst performances that can, at best, be termed mediocre. In a perversely erratic midfield it is hard to know whether this inconsistency has influenced, or been a result of, Anders' exasperating unpredictability and he spent the season alternating between the starting line-up and the bench. Ironically, towards the end of the campaign, with injuries piling up, Anders' form, on the left of an *ad hoc* middle four, was nothing short of breathtaking.

Southampton *(£750,000 from IF Elfsborg, Sweden, ex Hestrafors, on 16/7/2001) PL 76+21/6 FLC 5/2 FAC 8+1/2 Others 2*

SVENSSON Mathias
Born: Boras, Sweden, 24 September 1974
Height: 6'0" **Weight:** 12.4
Club Honours: Div 1 '00, '04
International Honours: Sweden: 3
Unable to force his way into Charlton's starting line-up, Mathias was loaned to Derby County, where he created an excellent impression and scored three goals in ten appearances before returning to the Valley in November. He is a strong, aggressive striker who is excellent in the air, works very hard and is unselfish. He made his first appearance of the season for Charlton as a substitute in the 2-1 win at Birmingham City, and after a further substitute appearance at Leicester, he started the next game, a 1-0 home defeat by Leeds. It was to be his final appearance for the Addicks as he completed a permanent move to Norwich City in December. He scored some great goals for the Canaries, including a cracker against Wigan at Carrow Road on Good Friday. His all-action style made him popular with the fans who will be hoping that his previous Premiership experience will be an advantage as City embark on

their first top-flight season since 1994-95.
Portsmouth *(£200,000 from Elfsborg,*
Sweden on 6/12/1996) FL 34+11/10 FLC 1/1
FAC 3+2/1 (£100,000 to Tirol Innsbruck,
Austria on 15/7/1998)
Crystal Palace *(£100,000 on 29/9/1998) FL*
26+6/10 FLC 2 FAC 1
Charlton Ath *(£600,000 on 28/1/2000) P/FL*

Mathias Svensson

42+28/7 FLC 0+2 FAC 2+4/1
Derby Co *(Loaned on 22/8/2003) FL 9+1/3*
Norwich C *(£50,000 on 19/12/2003) FL*
16+4/7

SVENSSON Michael
Born: Sweden, 25 November 1975
Height: 6'2" **Weight:** 13.8

International Honours: Sweden: 25
In combination with Claus Lundekvam,
Michael makes for a splendid obstacle in
the heart of the Saints' defence. His lanky,
almost gawky, physique and boyish
physiognomy are deceptive: he is a quick,
strong, natural athlete, adept in the air
and on the grass with a tenacious
approach to the game, which, in the
opinion of some opponents and referees,
can be a tad over-enthusiastic – he isn't
known in his native Sweden as 'Killer' for
nothing! He was having a magnificent
season until a bizarre calf injury, sustained
while warming up before the game at
Portsmouth in March, saw him sidelined
for the rest of the campaign.
Southampton *(£2,000,000 from Troyes,*
France, ex Halmstads BK, on 12/7/2002) PL
59+1/4 FLC 5/1 FAC 8/1 Others 2

SWAILES Christopher (Chris)
William
Born: Gateshead, 19 October 1970
Height: 6'2" **Weight:** 12.11
If there is one player who epitomises
Rotherham United's never-say-die attitude
then Chris is the one. His battling qualities
at the centre of the defence just cannot
be bettered and he is always willing to
thrust himself into situations with little
fear, hence the number of cuts he
sustained to his forehead. Always willing
to join the attack from corners and free
kicks, Chris can cause havoc in opposing
penalty areas and he weighed in with
three vital goals. He took over the
skipper's reins from the injured Martin
McIntosh and proved to be an inspired
leader.
Ipswich T *(From trainee on 23/5/1989)*
Peterborough U *(£10,000 on 28/3/1991.*
Free to Boston U in August 1991)
Doncaster Rov *(Free from Bridlington T on*
27/10/1993) FL 49 FLC 2/1 FAC 1 Others 2
Ipswich T *(£225,000 on 23/3/1995) P/FL*
34+3/1 FLC 3 Others 2
Bury *(£200,000 on 14/11/1997) FL 125+1/10*
FLC 9 FAC 8 Others 3/1
Rotherham U *(Free on 1/7/2001) FL 130/12*
FLC 9/2 FAC 5

SWAILES Daniel (Danny)
Born: Bolton, 1 April 1979
Height: 6'3" **Weight:** 13.0
Danny enjoyed another successful season
for Bury last term when he was a near
ever-present. Despite playing alongside a
succession of diff erent central defensive
partners, he remained consistent,
although he seemed to step up a gear
once the experienced Dave Challinor

arrived on loan from Stockport in January. Danny missed the last few games of the campaign after suffering a medial ligament injury at Yeovil, but nevertheless he was voted runner-up in the 'Player of the Season' poll by the fans.
Bury (From trainee on 9/7/1997) FL 134+10/12 FLC 4+3 FAC 7+1 Others 10+2/1

SWEENEY Antony Thomas
Born: Stockton, 5 September 1983
Height: 6'0" **Weight:** 11.9
For much of the 2003-04 season Antony was out of the first-team picture and it looked as if his career at Hartlepool could be over. However, he was brought into the team in the last month of the campaign, and can be satisfied with his contribution as the club went for a play-off place. He grew in maturity and his headed goal in the play-off semi-final at Bristol City almost earned a place in the Millennium Stadium final.
Hartlepool U (From trainee on 10/1/2002) FL 10+7/1 Others 3/1

SWEENEY Peter Henry
Born: Glasgow, 25 September 1984
Height: 6'0" **Weight:** 12.0
International Honours: S: U21-3; Yth
Peter broke into the Millwall first-team squad last October and from then on featured regularly, although he was often used from the substitutes' bench. The pacy, tricky winger produced some impressive displays and was a thorn in the side of many an opposition defender.
Millwall (From juniors on 13/12/2000) FL 22+13/3 FAC 2+4

SYMES Michael
Born: Great Yarmouth, 31 October 1983
Height: 6'3" **Weight:** 12.4
This big strong target man had featured for Everton reserves last term before joing Crewe Alexandra on loan in April. He made a handful of appearances in the closing stages of the campaign, scoring his only start, which came in the 3-1 win over Coventry. He was released by Everton in the summer.
Everton (From trainee on 13/2/2002)
Crewe Alex (Loaned on 24/3/2004) FL 1+3/1

SYMONS Christopher (Kit) Jeremiah
Born: Basingstoke, 8 March 1971
Height: 6'2" **Weight:** 13.7
Club Honours: Div 2 '99; Div 1 '01
International Honours: W: 37; B-1; U21-2; Yth
This experienced central defender was in and out of the Crystal Palace line-up last term, and made his last appearance in the FA Cup tie against Tottenham in January. However, Kit was a key figure off the field for the Eagles. He took over as acting manager following the departure of Steve Kember, helping turn the club's season around, and then when Iain Dowie came to Selhurst Park he was appointed as assistant-manager.
Portsmouth (From trainee on 30/12/1988) FL 161/10 FLC 19 FAC 10 Others 14+1/1
Manchester C (£1,600,000 on 17/8/1995) P/FL 124/4 FLC 6 FAC 9
Fulham (Free on 30/7/1998) P/FL 96+6/13 FLC 15+1/1 FAC 12
Crystal Palace (£400,000 on 7/12/2001) FL 42+7 FLC 5 FAC 6

Chris Swailes

T

TABB Jay Anthony
Born: Tooting, 21 February 1984
Height: 5'5" **Weight:** 9.7
International Honours: RoI: U21-1
Although Jay was mostly used as a substitute by Brentford in the early stages of last season, he made a real breakthrough during a magical week in October. Moved up front at half time in the LDV Vans Trophy tie at Barnet he scored twice to register his first goals for the Bees. The following Saturday he came off the bench to coolly side-foot home two more against Luton, then he swept in a cross against Brighton. A change in management saw him used in a wide-attacking role and he clearly benefited, finding the net regularly to finish with a double-figure goals tally. Jay also featured for the Republic of Ireland at U21 level during the season.
Brentford (From trainee on 23/7/2001) FL 24+22/9 FLC 1 FAC 2+1 Others 2+1/2

TAGGART Gerald (Gerry) Paul
Born: Belfast, 18 October 1970
Height: 6'1" **Weight:** 13.12
Club Honours: Div 1 '97; FLC '00
International Honours: NI: 51; U23-2; Yth; Sch
This left-footed central defender found it tough going trying to steady a rocky Leicester back line single-handedly during the early weeks, and found himself out of favour. A subsequent loan move to Stoke coincided with an upturn in the Potters' fortunes as he brought some much-needed stability to a young looking defence. After a brief recall to the Walkers Stadium, when Stoke conceded nine goals in three games, his transfer was made permanent.
Manchester C (From trainee on 1/7/1989) FL 10+2/1 Others 1
Barnsley (£75,000 on 10/1/1990) FL 209+3/16 FLC 15/1 FAC 14/2 Others 6/1
Bolton W (£1,500,000 on 1/8/1995) F/PL 68+1/4 FLC 8/1 FAC 4
Leicester C (Free on 23/7/1998) P/FL 105+12/9 FLC 12+2/2 FAC 8+1 Others 2/1
Stoke C (Loaned on 9/12/2003) FL 8/2
Stoke C (Free on 27/2/2004) FL 13

TAIT Paul
Born: Newcastle, 24 October 1974
Height: 6'1" **Weight:** 11.10
This experienced striker started the 2003-04 season in goal-scoring mood for Bristol Rovers, netting six in the early matches. However, Paul then underwent a knee operation in December, although he was back within four weeks. He finished the season as Rovers' leading scorer with 12 goals, the best of which was a delightful chip over the Southend goalkeeper at the Memorial Stadium, considered by many fans as the club's 'Goal of the Season'.
Everton (From trainee on 8/7/1993)
Wigan Ath (Free on 22/7/1994) FL 1+4 (Free to Runcorn on 16/2/1996)
Crewe Alex (Signed from Northwich Vic on 9/6/1999) FL 31+32/6 FLC 0+1 FAC 1+1
Hull C (Loaned on 5/11/2001) FL 0+2
Bristol Rov (Free on 12/7/2002) FL 61+13/19 FLC 2 FAC 4/1 Others 1

TALBOT Daniel Brian
Born: Enfield, 30 January 1984
Height: 5'9" **Weight:** 10.9
Club Honours: Div 3 '03
Daniel again struggled to make much of an impact at Rushden last term and started just three games, although he claimed an early goal at home to Bristol City in December. A young left-sided player who can feature in defence or midfield, he later had a spell on loan at Conference club Stevenage Borough but did not make a single appearance before returning to Nene Park. Daniel is the son of Oldham Athletic manager Brian Talbot.
Rushden & Diamonds (From juniors on 10/2/2001) FL 10+13/1 FLC 1 Others 2+1

TALBOT Stewart Dean
Born: Birmingham, 14 June 1973
Height: 5'11" **Weight:** 13.7
This all-action midfield player was in the Rotherham line-up at the beginning of the 2003-04 season, but from the end of September he became more of a squad player than an automatic choice. Nevertheless he could always be relied upon to give his best with his strong tackling and powerful running. Stewart moved to Brentford in search of more regular first-team football in the new year and initially found it tough going in a struggling team. As time went on, however, he built up an understanding with Eddie Hutchinson and began to show the fans his ability. He scored two goals for the Bees with long-range right-foot efforts against Rushden and Barnsley.
Port Vale (Signed from Moor Green on 10/8/1994) FL 112+25/10 FLC 4+3 FAC 4+1 Others 2+3/1
Rotherham U (Free on 13/7/2000) FL 100+14/8 FLC 6 FAC 6+1

Shrewsbury T (Loaned on 11/2/2003) FL 5 Others 2
Brentford (Free on 17/2/2004) FL 15/2

TALBOTT Nathan Anthony
Born: Wolverhampton, 21 October 1984
Height: 6'1" **Weight:** 13.0
A full back signed by Yeovil from Wolves on a short-term contract on deadline day, Nathan made a two-minute substitute appearance against Bury before moving on.
Yeovil T (From trainee at Wolverhampton W on 25/3/2004) FL 0+1

TALIA Francesco (Frank)
Born: Melbourne, Australia, 20 July 1972
Height: 6'1" **Weight:** 13.6
Club Honours: Div 2 '96
International Honours: Australia: Sch
Wycombe's first-choice 'keeper missed the opening games of the 2003-04 campaign after recovering from a cartilage operation in the summer. Although he returned to the team at the end of August, he lost his place to reserve 'keeper Steve Williams in December. After one more appearance, a hamstring injury picked up in training at the end of February ended his season. Frank is a great shot-stopper and a firm favourite with the supporters. He will be hoping to reclaim his number one spot in 2004-05.
Blackburn Rov (Free from Sunshine George Cross, Australia on 28/8/1992)
Hartlepool U (Loaned on 29/12/1992) FL 14 Others 1
Swindon T (£150,000 on 8/9/1995) FL 107 FLC 9 FAC 2
Sheffield U (Free, via trial at Wolverhampton W on 26/9/2000) FL 6 (Freed during 2001 close season)
Reading (Free from Royal Antwerp, Belgium on 15/3/2002)
Wycombe W (Free on 9/8/2002) FL 52 FLC 1 FAC 3 Others 3

TANN Adam John
Born: Fakenham, 12 May 1982
Height: 6'0" **Weight:** 11.5
International Honours: E: Yth
An accomplished defender who can play either at centre half or right back, Adam was switched to a defensive-midfield role by Cambridge mid-way through last season and adapted well. A regular in the line-up for most of the campaign, he also contributed three valuable goals.
Cambridge U (From trainee on 7/9/1999) FL 77+8/3 FLC 1 FAC 8+1/3 Others 13/1

393

TAPP Alexander (Alex) Nicholas
Born: Redhill, 7 June 1982
Height: 5'8" **Weight:** 11.10
A fiercely competitive left-footed midfielder, Alex's season for Wimbledon ended in mid-January when he damaged knee ligaments in the home game against Stoke. Until then he had displayed his usual commitment and willingness to make tackles others would shy clear of, and it is to be hoped he will make a full recovery in time for the new season.
Wimbledon (From trainee on 10/1/2000) FL 35+3/3 FLC 3/1 FAC 2

TARICCO Mauricio Ricardo
Born: Buenos Aires, Argentine, 10 March 1973
Height: 5'9" **Weight:** 11.7
A pacy defender who likes to play wide and get forward in attack, Mauricio has great distribution skills and likes to take on opponents in midfield. His temperament has calmed over the last season and he has shrugged off his reputation for getting involved with opponents, thus enabling him to focus on producing some gritty performances. A regular throughout the campaign, Mauricio scored his only Premiership goal in the 2-1 win over Leeds in August.
Ipswich T (£175,000 from Argentinos Juniors, Argentina on 9/9/1994) FL 134+3/4 FLC 18/3 FAC 8 Others 7
Tottenham H (£1,800,000 on 4/12/1998) PL 125+5/2 FLC 12 FAC 9+2 Others 3

TARNAT Michael
Born: Dusseldorf, Germany, 27 October 1969
Height: 6'2" **Weight:** 12.10
International Honours: Germany: 19
Michael did not take long to win over the Manchester City supporters last term, producing a series of highly polished performances in his opening games for the club following his move from Bayern Munich. He quickly became something of a cult figure amongst the fans following two incredible strikes within the space of a few weeks against Blackburn Rovers and Aston Villa, courtesy of an excellent striking technique. Despite a brief injury lay-off in the lead up to Christmas, he remained the side's first-choice left back. However, City decided not to renew his contract and he left after the final game of the season.
Manchester C (Free from Bayern Munich, Germany, ex MSV Duisburg, Karlsruher SC, on 9/7/2003) PL 32/3 FLC 2 FAC 4/1 Others 3

TATE Alan
Born: Easington, 2 September 1982
Height: 6'1" **Weight:** 13.9
Alan came back for a second loan spell at Swansea last October, and after spending a successful two months with the Third Division club he returned to Old Trafford. However, he was made available on a free transfer soon afterwards and promptly returned to the Vetch Field, signing a long-term deal. A composed defender, who is a good striker of the ball, he suffered a foot injury late in the season which saw him miss a few games.
Manchester U (From trainee on 18/7/2000)

Swansea C (Loaned on 22/11/2002) FL 27
Swansea C (Loaned on 24/10/2003) FL 9 Others 1
Swansea C(Free on 6/2/2004) FL 16+1/1 FAC 1

TATE Christopher (Chris) Douglas
Born: York, 27 December 1977
Height: 6'0" **Weight:** 11.10
This experienced striker remained a crowd favourite at Leyton Orient last term, even though most of his first-team appearances came from the substitutes' bench. He managed just a single goal, but always gave his best to the cause when

Michael Tarnat

called upon. Chris was released by the O's during the summer.
Sunderland *(From trainee at York C on 17/7/1996)*
Scarborough *(Free on 5/8/1997) FL 21+28/13 FLC 0+1 FAC 0+1 Others 2+1*
Halifax T *(£150,000 on 5/7/1999) FL 18/4 FLC 2 FAC 2/1 (£80,000 to Scarborough on 16/12/1999)*
Leyton Orient *(£25,000 on 3/11/2000) FL 34+41/10 FLC 0+1 FAC 1+2/1 Others 2+2/1*

TAVLARIDIS Efstathios (Stathis)
Born: Greece, 25 January 1980
Height: 6'2" **Weight:** 12.11
International Honours: Greece: U21
This Arsenal youngster played his part in the early rounds of the club's quest for Carling Cup glory. He featured in the second round win over Rotherham, the 5-1 victory over Wolves in the fourth round and the impressive quarter-final success at the Hawthorns against West Bromwich Albion. Stathis is a solid central defender who is as equally comfortable winning possession in the air as he is with the ball at his feet. He moved to French club Lille on loan during the January transfer window and has since agreed a permanent move to Paris Saint Germain.
Arsenal *(£600,000 from Iraklis, Greece on 21/9/2001) PL 0+1 FLC 7*
Portsmouth *(Loaned on 2/1/2003) FL 3+1 FAC 1*

TAYLOR Cleveland Ken Wayne
Born: Leicester, 9 September 1983
Height: 5'8" **Weight:** 11.5
An exciting right-sided midfielder, Cleveland found it difficult to make his mark in the Bolton first team last season. He made just one appearance, as a substitute in the FA Cup replay against Tranmere, and, seemingly frustrated by his lack of chances at the Reebok, joined Scunthorpe on a free transfer in March, having previously been on loan at Glanford Park. He quickly settled into a role on the right wing for the Iron and his fantastic attitude, great pace and skill made him a huge crowd favourite.
Bolton W *(From trainee on 5/8/2002) FAC 0+2*
Exeter C *(Loaned on 9/8/2002) FL 1+2*
Scunthorpe U *(Signed on 16/1/2004) FL 18+2/3 Others 1*

TAYLOR Craig
Born: Plymouth, 24 January 1974
Height: 6'1" **Weight:** 13.2
After an impressive loan spell the previous

season, Craig was snapped up by Torquay in the summer of 2003 and was immediately appointed club captain. Organised and disciplined, dominant in the air and sound on the ground, he formed an outstanding centre-back partnership with Steve Woods. Craig was rarely absent all season and was a key figure in helping the team win promotion from the Third Division.
Exeter C *(From trainee on 13/6/1992) FL 2+3 FLC 1 Others 2+2 (Free to Bath C on 18/3/1994)*
Swindon T *(£25,000 from Dorchester T on 15/4/1997) FL 47+8/2 FLC 0+1 FAC 3*
Plymouth Arg *(Loaned on 16/10/1998) FL 6/1*
Plymouth Arg *(£30,000 on 20/8/1999) FL 80+2/6 FLC 2 FAC 7 Others 1/1*
Torquay U *(Loaned on 24/2/2003) FL 5*
Torquay U *(Free on 2/7/2003) FL 43/4 FLC 1 FAC 1 Others 1*

TAYLOR Gareth Keith
Born: Weston super Mare, 25 February 1973
Height: 6'2" **Weight:** 13.8
International Honours: W: 14; U21-7
This powerful striker started the 2003-04 campaign on the treatment table after suffering an eye injury in a pre-season friendly for Burnley against Leeds. He was allowed to join Nottingham Forest in September and although not completely match fit he was forced to play immediately as a replacement for the injured David Johnson. Gareth found goals difficult to come by early on, but rediscovered his touch following a change in management and netted vital goals against Walsall and Bradford to gain valuable points for Forest. His season finished early after he was forced to have a knee operation in April. Gareth also scored his first goal for Wales against Scotland in February.
Bristol Rov *(From trainee at Southampton on 29/7/1991) FL 31+16/16 FLC 3 FAC 1+1 Others 5*
Crystal Palace *(£750,000 on 27/9/1995) FL 18+2/1 FAC 2/1*
Sheffield U *(Signed on 8/3/1996) FL 56+28/25 FLC 8+3/2 FAC 5+2 Others 1+2*
Manchester C *(£400,000 on 26/11/1998) FL 28+15/9 FLC 2+1/1 FAC 3 Others 1+3*
Port Vale *(Loaned on 21/1/2000) FL 4*
Queens Park R *(Loaned on 14/3/2000) FL 2+4/1*
Burnley *(Free on 20/2/2001) FL 88+7/36 FLC 4+1 FAC 6/1*
Nottingham F *(£500,000 on 27/8/2003) FL 28+6/8 FLC 2 FAC 2*

TAYLOR Ian Kenneth
Born: Birmingham, 4 June 1968
Height: 6'1" **Weight:** 12.4
Club Honours: AMC '93; FLC '96
After two injury-hit seasons with Aston Villa, Ian proved remarkably resilient at Derby. Only suspensions - and he collected too many cards - kept the captain out. He was Derby's leading scorer, helped by a previously untested accuracy from the penalty spot. Even when asked to play wide in midfield, hardly his best position, he continued to set a fine example, maintaining a high energy level. Ian exceeded even George Burley's hopes by his consistency and was unlucky not to be named 'Player of the Year'.
Port Vale *(£15,000 from Moor Green on 13/7/1992) FL 83/28 FLC 4/2 FAC 6/1 Others 13/4*
Sheffield Wed *(£1,000,000 on 12/7/1994) PL 9+5/1 FLC 2+2/1*
Aston Villa *(£1,000,000 on 21/12/1994) PL 202+31/28 FLC 20+2/8 FAC 14+3/2 Others 18+1/5*
Derby Co *(Free on 4/7/2003) FL 42/11 FLC 1/1 FAC 1*

TAYLOR John Patrick
Born: Norwich, 24 October 1964
Height: 6'2" **Weight:** 13.12
Club Honours: Div 3 '91
In his testimonial season, Cambridge United's manager was forced to pull on his boots again as an injury crisis left the club short of strikers. In spite of his advancing years, he performed valiantly and came close to scoring on a number of occasions. Replaced as manager in March, he joined Northampton Town on non-contract terms. John became the oldest outfield player to play in the Football League for the Cobblers, using his experience to assist the younger players around him and showing that he was not afraid to put himself about.
Colchester U *(From juniors on 17/12/1982) FLC 0+1 (Freed during 1984 close season)*
Cambridge U *(Signed from Sudbury T on 24/8/1988) FL 139+21/46 FLC 9+2/2 FAC 21/10 Others 12+2/2*
Bristol Rov *(Signed on 28/3/1992) FL 91+4/44 FLC 4 FAC 3 Others 5*
Bradford C *(£300,000 on 5/7/1994) FL 35+1/11 FLC 4/2 FAC 2 Others 3*
Luton T *(£200,000 on 23/3/1995) FL 27+10/3 FLC 2 Others 1/1*
Lincoln C *(Loaned on 27/9/1996) FL 5/2*
Colchester U *(Loaned on 8/11/1996) FL 8/5 Others 1*

395

Cambridge U *(Free on 10/1/1997) FL*
103+72/40 FLC 3+6/1 FAC 9+6/1 Others
2+2/1
Northampton T *(Free on 24/3/2004) FL*
3+5/1 Others 0+2

TAYLOR Kris
Born: Stafford, 12 January 1984
Height: 5'9" **Weight:** 13.5
Kris was the first player to move to
Walsall under a new agreement with
Manchester United. He played regularly in
the reserve team, mainly in midfield,
before netting on his first-team debut at
Stoke in January. He consistently
demonstrated a zest for the game and
seemed to cover every inch of the pitch in
the goalless draw at West Ham in March.
Kris also showed his versatility by playing
at wing back in the penultimate home
game against Sheffield United.
Manchester U *(From trainee on 2/2/2001)*
Walsall *(Free on 19/2/2003) FL 5+6/1*

TAYLOR Maik Stefan
Born: Hildeshein, Germany, 4 September
1971
Height: 6'4" **Weight:** 14.2
Club Honours: Div 2 '99; Div 1 '01
International Honours: NI: 38; B-1;
U21-1
Maik began the season on loan with
Birmingham City, and the move was such
a success that a permanent transfer was
eventually arranged. He had an
outstanding campaign, pushing Mikael
Forssell close for the club's 'Player of the
Year' award. Tall and imposing, he
consistently relieved pressure by coming
out to take free kicks and corners. His
reflexes were of the highest order and his
double save at Manchester City in
February, when he seemingly clawed the
ball out when it was behind him, was
world class.
Barnet *(Free from Farnborough on 7/6/1995)*
FL 70 FLC 6 FAC 6 Others 2
Southampton *(£500,000 on 1/1/1997) PL 18*
Fulham *(£800,000 + on 17/11/1997) P/FL*
183+1 FLC 22 FAC 20 Others 6
Birmingham C *(Signed on 8/8/2003) PL 34*
FLC 1 FAC 4

TAYLOR Martin
Born: Ashington, 9 November 1979
Height: 6'4" **Weight:** 15.0
Club Honours: FLC '02
International Honours: E: U21-1; Yth
When Craig Short missed the first half of
the season for Blackburn, Martin was
viewed as an ideal replacement. However,
he never really seemed to fit in and would
have seen very little first-team action but

for injuries and suspension to other
defenders on the club's books. He was
allowed to leave during the January
transfer window when he signed for
Birmingham City. Martin made an
immediate impression at St Andrews,
showing a calmness in the heat of battle
and an ability to use the ball coming out
of defence. He coped adequately at right
back, but looked even better in the centre
of the defence.
Blackburn Rov *(From trainee on 13/8/1997)*
P/FL 68+20/5 FLC 17 FAC 13+2/1 Others 3+2
Darlington *(Loaned on 18/1/2000) FL 4*
Stockport Co *(Loaned on 23/3/2000) FL 7*
Birmingham C *(£1,250,000 on 2/2/2004) PL*
11+1/1

TAYLOR Matthew Simon
Born: Oxford, 27 November 1981
Height: 5'10" **Weight:** 11.10
Club Honours: Div 1 '03
International Honours: E: U21-3
This talented midfielder was lucky to
survive unscathed in a serious car
accident last October, but matured as a
player throughout the campaign. A
troublesome heel injury kept him out of
the Pompey line-up for a while but he
came back with some good
performances. Matthew can play on the
left-hand side whether at wing back or
in midfield. He scored four cup goals,
including a dramatic equaliser in the FA
Cup fifth round tie at Anfield.
Luton T *(From trainee on 9/2/1999) FL*
127+2/16 FLC 6 FAC 10/1 Others 1
Portsmouth *(£400,000 + on 3/7/2002) F/PL*
53+12/7 FLC 5/1 FAC 5+1/3

TAYLOR Robert (Bob)
Born: Horden, 3 February 1967
Height: 5'10" **Weight:** 12.12
This vastly experienced striker joined
Cheltenham Town shortly after the start
of the 2003-04 season. His link-up play
and calmness in front of goal proved to
be a class above Division Three level in the
opening weeks of the campaign, but as
the team began to struggle the service
and support for him dried up. Bob scored
twice in the 4-1 win at Leyton Orient and
grabbed both goals in a 2-1 defeat of
Carlisle but his season was truncated by
injury. First a cracked rib, then an achilles
problem restricted his appearances in the
second half of the season and he was
released at the end of the campaign.
Leeds U *(Free from Horden Colliery on*
27/3/1986) FL 33+9/9 FLC 5+1/3 FAC 1
Others 4+1/1
Bristol C *(£175,000 on 23/3/1989) FL*
96+10/50 FLC 6+1/2 FAC 9+1/5 Others 3/1

West Bromwich A *(£300,000 on 31/1/1992)*
FL 211+27/96 FLC 16/6 FAC 6+2/3 Others
16+3/8
Bolton W *(Free on 8/11/1998) P/FL 57+20/21*
FLC 6+5/2 FAC 4+1/2 Others 3/2
West Bromwich A *(£90,000 on 23/3/2000)*
P/FL 45+41/17 FLC 5+1 FAC 0+2/1 Others
0+2
Cheltenham T *(Free on 19/8/2003) FL*
19+9/7 FAC 2/1 Others 1

TAYLOR Ryan Anthony
Born: Liverpool, 19 August 1984
Height: 5'8" **Weight:** 10.4
International Honours: E: Yth
This promising youngster established
himself in the Tranmere Rovers line-up last
term, playing either at right wing back or
on the right-hand side of midfield. A
regular in the side apart from a brief spell
towards the end of the season, he looks
comfortable on the ball and is developing
as a specialist with free kicks and
penalties.
Tranmere Rov *(From trainee on 3/4/2002) FL*
39+16/6 FLC 3+1/1 FAC 8+1/1 Others 3/1

TAYLOR Scott James
Born: Chertsey, 5 May 1976
Height: 5'10" **Weight:** 11.4
Club Honours: AMC '02, '04
Scott was in tremendous form for
Blackpool in 2003-04 when he finished
the season, with a total of 27 goals
despite his campaign finishing early due
to an injury. His tally included hat-tricks
against Hartlepool and in the FA Cup tie
at Oldham, and several doubles. The
talented striker was selected for the PFA's
Division Two team of the season.
Millwall *(£15,000 from Staines on 8/2/1995)*
FL 13+15 FLC 0+2/2 FAC 1+1
Bolton W *(£150,000 on 29/3/1996) P/FL*
2+10/1 FLC 0+4/1 FAC 1/1
Rotherham U *(Loaned on 12/12/1997) FL*
10/3 Others 1
Blackpool *(Loaned on 26/3/1998) FL 3+2/1*
Tranmere Rov *(£50,000 on 9/10/1998) FL*
78+30/17 FLC 16/5 FAC 2+5
Stockport Co *(Free on 10/8/2001) FL 19+9/4*
FLC 2/3 FAC 0+1
Blackpool *(Free on 25/1/2002) FL 73+19/31*
FLC 4/3 FAC 4+1/8 Others 7+2/5

TAYLOR Steven Vincent
Born: Greenwich, 23 January 1986
Height: 6'1" **Weight:** 13.0
International Honours: E: U21-2; Yth
A product of Newcastle's Academy, this
young centre back is on the verge of
becoming a regular in the first-team
squad despite his age. Tall and well built,
but composed on the ball he has played

for England at all levels from U16 to U21, making his debut for the latter age group prior to appearing in his club's first team. Loaned out for a month to Wycombe, he proved to be possibly the most impressive loan signing the Chairboys have ever made. His anticipation, positioning and distribution were exceptional for a teenager and his performances were priceless. Steven made his Newcastle debut as a late substitute in the UEFA Cup tie at Real Mallorca in March and this was followed by his first Premiership start at Bolton three days later, both in the unaccustomed position of right back.
Newcastle U (From trainee on 30/1/2003) PL 1 Others 0+1
Wycombe W (Loaned on 12/12/2003) FL 6

TEALE Gary
Born: Glasgow, 21 July 1978
Height: 6'0" **Weight:** 11.6
Club Honours: Div 2 '03
International Honours: S: U21-6
After being used mainly as a substitute in the first three months of the season Gary became one of the stars in the Wigan Athletic side after the new year, making the right-wing berth his own with a sustained run in the side. One of the quickest players in the First Division, his blistering pace and direct running troubled most defences. He was particularly effective late in the game, when his searing speed was used as a springboard for telling counter attacks. Gary scored several spectacular goals, including stunning efforts in the away wins at Ipswich and Preston. An expected recall to the Scotland squad was halted after he broke his collarbone in February and he wasn't quite able to discover his true form on his return.
Clydebank (From juniors on 19/6/1996) SL 52+16/14 SLC 3+1 SC 1 Others 4
Ayr U (£70,000 on 2/10/1998) SL 94+7/13 SLC 5+1/1 SC 10/3 Others 4/1
Wigan Ath (£200,000 on 14/12/2001) FL 65+24/5 FLC 2+3 FAC 2+1 Others 2/2

TEBILY Olivier
Born: Ivory Coast, 19 December 1975
Height: 6'1" **Weight:** 13.4
Club Honours: SLC '99
International Honours: Ivory Coast; France: U21
A muscular and powerful player, Olivier put in some fine performances at right back for Birmingham City last term, not allowing many opponents to get the better of him. Sometimes it was hard to tell what he was going to do next, especially when attacking, but he was

never found wanting when it came to the battle. He made an incredible athletic goal-line clearance at Chelsea in January's 0-0 draw.
Sheffield U (£175,000 from Chateauroux on 24/3/1999) FL 7+1
Glasgow Celtic (£1,250,000 on 8/7/1999) SL 29+9 SLC 4+1/1 SC 2+1 Others 5/1
Birmingham C (£700,000 on 22/3/2002) P/FL 36+10 FLC 1 FAC 2 Others 3

TEGGART Neil
Born: Downpatrick, NI, 16 September 1984
Height: 6'2" **Weight:** 12.4

International Honours: NI: Yth
This young striker arrived at Darlington on loan from Sunderland for the final three months of the season and soon impressed with his strong running and good link-up play with the other forwards. Although he contributed to a number of goals for others he failed to score for the Quakers.
Sunderland (From trainee on 17/4/2002)
Darlington (Loaned on 6/2/2004) FL 9+6

TELFER Paul Norman
Born: Edinburgh, 21 October 1971
Height: 5'9" **Weight:** 11.6
International Honours: S: 1; B-2; U21-3

Gary Teale

Paul has what football pundits refer to as a great 'engine'. And none of the three managers that graced Southampton last season felt that the team could manage without it – or indeed him! Undoubtedly, in a midfield that failed to sparkle last season, his industry and doggedness made-up for a lot of failings; and when skipper Jason Dodd was sidelined with injury in March, Paul resumed the right-back position he'd filled with aplomb for much of the 2002-03 campaign.

Luton T (From trainee on 7/11/1988) FL 136+8/19 FLC 5 FAC 14/2 Others 2/1
Coventry C (£1,500,000 on 11/7/1995) PL 178+13/6 FLC 15/2 FAC 15+4/4
Southampton (Free on 2/11/2001) PL 86+12/1 FLC 4+1 FAC 8 Others 1+1

TEN HEUVEL Laurens
Born: Duivendrecht, Holland, 6 June 1976
Height: 6'0" **Weight:** 12.3
This well-travelled striker impressed during the pre-season for Grimsby and joined the Mariners on loan. However, when the serious football started he failed to live up to expectations and after only a handful of appearances he returned to Bramall Lane. Soon afterwards Laurens moved back to Holland where he joined De Graafschap.

Barnsley (£75,000 from FC Den Bosch, Holland on 12/3/1996) F/PL 1+7 FLC 0+1 (Freed to First Vienna, Austria during 1998 close season)
Sheffield U (Signed from Telstar U, Holland on 31/7/2002) FL 0+5 FLC 0+3 FAC 0+1
Bradford C (Loaned on 27/3/2003) FL 4+1
Grimsby T (Loaned on 8/8/2003) FL 3+1 FLC 1

TERRY John George
Born: Barking, 7 December 1980
Height: 6'0" **Weight:** 12.4
Club Honours: FAC '00
International Honours: E: 11; U21-9
From the Sukru Saracoglu Stadium to Scarborough and all points in between, both geographically and in footballing terms, John Terry played his football with the same lion-hearted determination that has marked him as one of the outstanding modern defenders. Due to Rio Ferdinand's indisposition, John was thrown into the deep end for the difficult Euro 2004 qualifier against Turkey and, in only his fifth international, played heroically to ease England's path to the finals. At the other end of the spectrum, Chelsea were facing a bumpy ride in the FA Cup fourth round tie at Scarborough

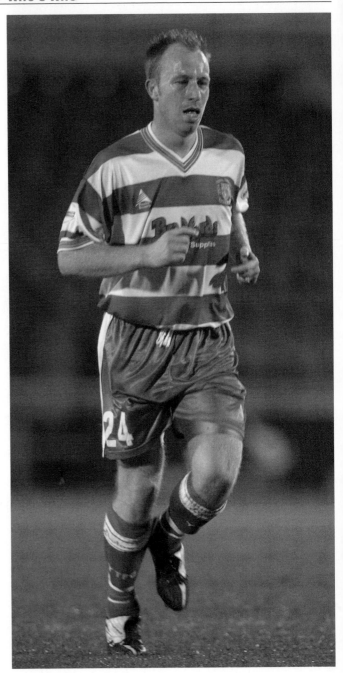

Paul Terry

when John bravely threw himself into a melee to head the only goal of the match and spare the team's blushes. The Blues were also under the cosh at Bolton when he strode forward purposefully, played a one-two and calmly slotted the ball home to set up another away Premiership victories. 'JT' formed a tremendous central defensive partnership with William Gallas and the pairing was a major factor in the Blues' 32 clean sheets, second-place Premiership finish and magnificent Champions' League run. John was selected for the PFA Premiership team of the season and for the England squad for the Euro 2004 finals.

Chelsea (From trainee on 18/3/1998) PL 102+12/7 FLC 12+1 FAC 18+5/6 Others 19/2 Nottingham F (Loaned on 23/3/2000) FL 5+1

TERRY Paul Edward
Born: Dagenham, 3 April 1979
Height: 5'10" **Weight:** 12.6
International Honours: E: SP-3
Paul was one of several new signings for Yeovil Town during the 2003 close season. A defensive midfielder, he added some much-needed stability for the Glovers in the centre of the park. A tough-tackling player who can also play at full back, he scored his only goal in the 2-1 win at York in April. Paul is the older brother of Chelsea's John Terry.

Yeovil T (Signed from Dagenham & Redbridge, ex Charlton Ath trainee, on 20/8/2003) FL 22+12/1 FAC 3 Others 1+1

TESSEM Jo
Born: Orlandet, Norway, 28 February 1972
Height: 6'3" **Weight:** 12.10
International Honours: Norway: 9; B-1
A utility player, Jo has, over the last five years, played his best football for the Saints and Norway on the right of midfield. Most effective on the offensive he, nonetheless, works well chasing back and as a man-marker. Unfortunately Gordon Strachan never fancied him in midfield, preferring him as an occasional striker. Nor did caretaker Steve Wigley see Jo as the solution to the Saints' midfield malaise and, having made just one start in 2003–04, he was loaned to his old club Lyn Oslo in March, less than a month after Paul Sturrock arrived to manage at St Mary's. At the time of writing it remained to be seen if he would return to Southampton in July, to see out the last year of his contract.

Southampton (£600,000 from Molde, Norway, ex Lyn, on 19/11/1999) PL 67+43/12 FLC 4+2/1 FAC 7+6/3 Others 0+1

THATCHER Benjamin (Ben) David
Born: Swindon, 30 November 1975
Height: 5'10" **Weight:** 12.7
International Honours: W: 3; E: U21-4; Yth
This hard-working and inspirational full back or central defender was an instant hit with the Leicester fans with his wholehearted and committed approach and was very much the star man of the difficult early weeks of the campaign. The team clearly suffered when Ben had a spell out of action in October, when suffering from pneumonia, but he came back to net his first goal for some time with a header against his old club, Tottenham, in the eight-goal thriller at White Hart Lane. A Welsh grandparent meant that a switch of international allegiance was possible and he duly made his debut for Wales in March. He missed the last few fixtures after having an operation on a broken nose.

Millwall (From trainee on 8/6/1992) FL 87+3/1 FLC 6 FAC 7 Others 1
Wimbledon (£1,840,00 on 5/7/1996) PL 82+4 FLC 12 FAC 5
Tottenham H (£5,000,000 on 12/7/2000) PL 29+7 FLC 6+1 FAC 3
Leicester C (£300,000 + on 17/7/2003) PL 28+1/1

THELWELL Alton Anthony
Born: Islington, 5 September 1980
Height: 6'0" **Weight:** 12.7
International Honours: E: U21-1
Alton took something of a gamble in dropping down from the Premiership to the Third Division when he signed for Hull City, but the move paid immediate dividends as he enjoyed promotion success. He got off to a flying start in the right-back berth with a goal-scoring debut in the 4-1 defeat of Darlington and soon established a promising partnership down the right flank with Jason Price. However, a series of injuries including a broke a bone in the base of his foot and a groin problem then restricted his appearances.

Tottenham H (From trainee on 27/1/1999) PL 13+5 FAC 0+3
Hull C (Free on 1/7/2003) FL 22+4/1 FLC 1

THIRLWELL Paul
Born: Washington, 13 February 1979
Height: 5'11" **Weight:** 11.4
International Honours: E: U21-1
This central midfielder will remember the 2003-04 season as one of incredible highs and lows. Paul had the honour of being made captain of Sunderland, the club he

supported as a boy, and he impressed in the role of the 'holding' player in the middle of the park where his powerful tackling provided extra defensive cover. However, a succession of injuries including two calf strains, a broken nose and a fractured skull severely disrupted his campaign. Paul was out of contract in the summer and his future was unclear at time of writing.

Sunderland (From trainee on 14/4/1997) P/FL 55+22 FLC 6+2/1 FAC 5+2
Swindon T (Loaned on 8/9/1999) FL 12

THOMAS Daniel (Danny) Justin
Born: Leamington, 1 May 1981
Height: 5'7" **Weight:** 11.2
This lightning quick winger started the season in the Bournemouth first team, but lost his place after three games, and eventually left to join Boston United. Danny was brought in as a deadline transfer and proceeded give some superb displays on the left side of the Pilgrims' midfield. His skill and ability to beat defenders set up plenty of chances and he also got on the score sheet himself.

Leicester C (From trainee at Nottingham F on 13/5/1998) PL 0+3
Bournemouth (Signed on 8/2/2002) FL 35+24/2 FLC 2/1 FAC 6/1 Others 5+2
Boston U (Signed on 19/3/2004) FL 8/3

THOMAS James Alan
Born: Swansea, 16 January 1979
Height: 6'0" **Weight:** 13.0
International Honours: W: U21-21
Although James signed a new contract for Swansea during the 2003 close season, he had a rather disappointing time last term. He struggled to win a place in the starting line-up, initially being unable to break up the Kevin Nugent/ Lee Trundle partnership, and then being sidelined by a foot injury. The pacy striker then suffered a thigh injury, which further complicated matters for him during the second half of the campaign.

Blackburn Rov (From trainee on 2/7/1996) FL 1+3/1 FAC 1/2
West Bromwich A (Loaned on 29/8/1997) FL 1+2
Blackpool (Loaned on 21/3/2000) FL 9/2
Sheffield U (Loaned on 24/11/2000) FL 3+7/1 FAC 0+1
Bristol Rov (Loaned on 22/3/2002) FL 7/1
Swansea C (Free on 9/7/2002) FL 42+13/16 FLC 1+1/1 FAC 2+3 Others 2/1

THOMAS Jerome William
Born: Wembley, 23 March 1983
Height: 5'10" **Weight:** 11.10

Jerome Thomas

Club Honours: FAYC '00, '01
International Honours: E: Yth
Jerome featured for Arsenal on three occasions in Carling Cup ties last term before moving on to Charlton in the new year. Unfortunately he picked up an ankle injury in his first outing for the Addicks' reserves which kept him sidelined for several weeks, but he returned to earn a first-team debut as a half-time substitute against Leicester City in the penultimate home game of the season. Jerome is an attacking left-sided wingman who likes to run at defenders and get a strike on goal when the opportunity arises, as well as creating chances for others. He had a promising debut, and will be hoping to break into the first team on a regular basis in 2004-05.
Arsenal (From trainee on 3/7/2001) FLC 1+2
Queens Park R (Loaned on 27/3/2002) FL 4/1
Queens Park R (Loaned on 29/8/2002) FL 5+1/2
Charlton Ath (£100,000 on 2/2/2004) PL 0+1

THOMAS Stephen
Born: Hartlepool, 23 June 1979
Height: 5'10" **Weight:** 12.0
International Honours: W: U21-5; Yth
Stephen's career at Wrexham was re-ignited last season and he was a regular in the side for most of the campaign. He was the most attacking of the club's midfield line and showed a willingness to strike from distance, scoring with a cracking long-range effort against Swindon Town at the Racecourse in March. Although mainly a midfield player, manager Denis Smith also introduced him to the wing-back position last term.
Wrexham (From trainee on 4/7/1997) FL 85+31/7 FLC 2+2 FAC 1+1 Others 5+1/2

THOMAS Wayne Junior Robert
Born: Gloucester, 17 May 1979
Height: 5'11" **Weight:** 11.12
After spending the previous two seasons playing as an emergency right back, Wayne moved back to his preferred position of centre half for Stoke City last season. He managed to cut out the defensive errors that he once made and became a firm favourite of the club's fans. Voted as the 'Player's Player of the Year' he even created time to move forward and find the net three times before Christmas. Strong and effective in the air, it is hoped that he will be a fixture in the side for some time to come.
Torquay U (From trainee on 4/7/1997) FL 89+34/5 FLC 2+1/1 FAC 7/1 Others 6+4

Stoke C *(£200,000 + on 5/6/2000) FL*
153+1/5 FLC 6+1 FAC 9 Others 10

THOME Emerson Augusto
Born: Porto Alegre, Brazil, 30 March 1972
Height: 6'1" **Weight:** 13.4
Emerson is a physical, domineering centre back who certainly takes no prisoners. He was pitched into action for Bolton early on due to Florent Laville's injury, and he formed an effective central-defensive partnership with Bruno N'Gotty until a hamstring injury in late October sidelined him for a month. He then returned to the starting line-up, where he remained until the end of the season, proving to be a vital part of the club's success.
Sheffield Wed (Free from Benfica, Portugal on 23/3/1998) PL 60+1/1 FLC 5+1 FAC 4/1
Chelsea (£2,700,000 on 23/12/1999) PL 19+2 Others 1
Sunderland (£4,500,000 on 1/9/2000) PL 43+1/2 FLC 4 FAC 5
Bolton W (Free on 28/8/2003) PL 25+1 FLC 5 FAC 1

THOMPSON David Anthony
Born: Birkenhead, 12 September 1977
Height: 5'7" **Weight:** 10.0
Club Honours: FAYC '96
International Honours: E: U21-7; Yth
After spending the end of the previous season recuperating from a knee operation, it was disappointing that David had to undergo further surgery to save his Blackburn career last term and was only able to play in a handful of games. Used in both flank position and the middle he was his usual aggressive self, although his frustration with the efforts of those around him was clearly visible.
Liverpool (From trainee on 8/11/1994) PL 24+24/5 FLC 5 FAC 0+1 Others 2
Swindon T (Loaned on 21/11/1997) FL 10
Coventry C (£3,000,000 on 8/8/2000) P/FL 61+5/15 FLC 3+1/1 FAC 2
Blackburn Rov (£1,500,000 on 28/8/2002) PL 33+1/5 FLC 5/1 FAC 2 Others 5/1

THOMPSON Glyn William
Born: Telford, 24 February 1981
Height: 6'1" **Weight:** 12.4
Glyn started last term as first-choice 'keeper for Northampton Town, but lost his place following the 4-3 defeat at Cheltenham in September and from then on had to play second fiddle to Lee Harper. His next appearance came when Harper received a red card against Hull and Glyn stepped off the bench to save the resultant penalty. Cool under pressure

and excellent with crosses, he will be looking for more senior experience in 2004-05.
Shrewsbury T (From trainee on 14/12/1998) FL 1 FLC 1
Fulham (£50,000 on 20/11/1999)
Mansfield T (Loaned on 21/1/2000) FL 16
Northampton T (Free on 29/11/2002) FL 18+1 FLC 1 FAC 1

THOMPSON John
Born: Dublin, 12 October 1981
Height: 6'1" **Weight:** 11.11
International Honours: RoI: 1; U21-11; Yth
John can play in a variety of roles and started the 2003-04 season in his favoured central-defensive position for Nottingham Forest, retaining his place until October. Thereafter he was in and out of the side, featuring in both full-back roles before injury finished his campaign early. John made his full international debut for the Republic of Ireland against Canada during the season.
Nottingham F (Signed from Home Farm, ex River Valley Rgrs, on 6/7/1999) FL 52+8/4 FLC 4+1 FAC 2 Others 1+1

THOMPSON Justin
Born: Prince Rupert, Canada, 9 January 1981
Height: 6'2" **Weight:** 13.10
International Honours: Canada: U23-7
This central defender signed non-contract forms for Bury last November after a trial period at Gigg Lane and made his debut for the Shakers in the LDV Vans Trophy tie against Oldham when he scored the winning goal. Almost immediately he was called away to represent Canada at U23 level but returned to make a couple more appearances for the Shakers. Justin released in December and after a short trial with Leyton Orient he signed for Hornchurch.
Bury (Free from Fairfield Univ, Canada, via trials at Kaiserslautern, Barnsley, ex Union, on 31/10/2003) FL 1 Others 2/1

THOMPSON Lee Jonathan
Born: Sheffield, 25 March 1983
Height: 5'7" **Weight:** 11.2
International Honours: E: Sch
Lee showed plenty of energy and determination in his second season at Boston United. He proved popular with the fans and was voted 'Player of the Year' by the junior supporters. He was equally at home on the right side of midfield or up front as an emergency striker.
Sheffield U (From juniors on 7/7/2000)

Boston U (Free on 4/10/2002) FL 32+18/9 FAC 2 Others 4/2

THOMPSON Tyrone I'Yungo
Born: Sheffield, 8 May 1982
Height: 5'9" **Weight:** 11.2
After being released by Sheffield United, this skilful midfielder joined Huddersfield Town during the 2003 close season. Tyrone made his debut for the Terriers in the opening game at home to Cambridge United and showed he had a good turn of pace and could use the ball well. However, he subsequently only featured from the substitutes' bench and was released before the end of the campaign.
Sheffield U (From trainee on 10/7/2000) FLC 1+1 FAC 1
Lincoln C (Loaned on 18/10/2002) FL 0+1 Others 2
Huddersfield T (Free on 7/8/2003) FL 1+1

THOMSON Andrew (Andy) John
Born: Swindon, 28 March 1974
Height: 6'3" **Weight:** 14.12
This strong and reliable Wycombe central defender could not break into the line-up until September last term. Andy then enjoyed a run of starts, scoring three goals, before losing his place in December to loan players, firstly Steve Taylor and then Stuart Nethercott. He missed the remainder of the campaign after suffering knee ligament damage in January and was released in the summer in the big post-relegation clear out at Adams Park.
Swindon T (From trainee on 1/5/1993) P/FL 21+1 FLC 5/1 Others 3
Portsmouth (£75,000 on 29/12/1995) FL 85+8/3 FLC 4 FAC 6+1
Bristol Rov (£60,000 on 15/11/1999) FL 124+3/6 FLC 8 FAC 6 Others 5
Wycombe W (Free on 28/3/2002) FL 48+2/2 FLC 3 FAC 3/1 Others 5+1/1

THOMSON Steven (Steve)
Born: Glasgow, 23 January 1978
Height: 5'8" **Weight:** 10.4
International Honours: S: Yth
Steve joined Peterborough shortly after the start of the 2003-04 season and soon established himself in the line-up. A hard-working, combative midfield player, he forged a good partnership with Curtis Woodhouse in the centre of the park. The highlight of his season was undoubtedly his amazing goal against Swindon which was struck home from all of 50 yards.
Crystal Palace (From trainee on 9/12/1995) FL 68+37/1 FLC 8+4/2 FAC 3+1/1 Others 1+1
Peterborough U (Free on 5/9/2003) FL 28+7/1 FAC 3/1 Others 3

THORNE Peter Lee
Born: Manchester, 21 June 1973
Height: 6'0" **Weight:** 13.6
Club Honours: Div 2 '96; AMC '00
Although Peter remained a crucial player for Cardiff City last term his season was badly disrupted by injuries. A major contributor to Robert Earnshaw's goal-scoring success, he continued to produce some intelligent play and scored a total of 13 goals during the campaign. However, his season finished early after he suffered a fracture in a bone at the bottom of his foot.
Blackburn Rov (From trainee on 20/6/1991) Others 0+1
Wigan Ath (Loaned on 11/3/1994) FL 10+1

Swindon T (£225,000 on 18/1/1995) FL 66+11/27 FLC 5+1/4 FAC 4+2 Others 1+1/1
Stoke C (£350,000 + on 25/7/1997) FL 147+11/65 FLC 12+1/6 FAC 5+1 Others 9+3/9
Cardiff C (£1,700,000 on 13/9/2001) FL 88+7/34 FLC 2/1 FAC 5/1 Others 6/1

THORNLEY Benjamin (Ben) Lindsay
Born: Bury, 21 April 1975
Height: 5'9" **Weight:** 11.12
Club Honours: FAYC '92
International Honours: E: U21-3; Sch
This experienced midfielder signed non-contract forms for Bury in September and the following day played a major part in helping to defeat his former club Huddersfield Town at Gigg Lane, having a hand in both goals. Ben gave Bury some vital width on the right-hand side but was troubled by injuries during his time at the club, with a groin strain being particularly troublesome. As a result he was released in November and after a trial at Partick Thistle he signed for Halifax Town.
Manchester U (From trainee on 29/1/1993) PL 1+8 FLC 3 FAC 2
Stockport Co (Loaned on 6/11/1995) FL 8+2/1 Others 1
Huddersfield T (Loaned on 22/2/1996) FL 12/2
Huddersfield T (£175,000 + on 3/7/1998) FL 77+22/5 FLC 10 FAC 5/1
Aberdeen (Signed on 1/8/2001) SL 17+13/3 SLC 2+1/1 SC 0+2/1
Blackpool (Free on 31/12/2002) FL 7+5 FAC 1
Bury (Free on 5/9/2003) FL 5

THORNTON Sean
Born: Drogheda, Ireland, 18 May 1983
Height: 5'10" **Weight:** 11.0
International Honours: RoI: U21-8; Yth
Sean is considered to be the most creative midfielder on the books at Sunderland, but found it surprisingly difficult to win a regular first-team berth at the Stadium of Light last term. Although most effective in a central role, where his passing ability can be best used, he was often asked to fill in wide on the right where his pinpoint crossing skills were put to good effect. His delivery from set pieces was exceptional and he scored with stunning free kicks against Gillingham and Preston in March.
Tranmere Rov (Trainee) FL 9+2/1 FAC 0+1 Others 0+1
Sunderland (Signed on 4/7/2002) P/FL 25+8/5 FLC 2 FAC 3+4 Others 1+1
Blackpool (Loaned on 7/11/2002) FL 1+2 Others 1

THORPE Anthony (Tony) Lee
Born: Leicester, 10 April 1974
Height: 5'9" **Weight:** 12.6
This experienced striker got off to a good start for Luton last term, netting twice in the opening game against Rushden, but soon afterwards he was sold to Queens Park Rangers. Tony was not a regular starter until Paul Furlong was out injured, but once in the side struck up a good understanding with Kevin Gallen. He was soon scoring goals, including a run of five in seven matches. However, once Furlong had regained fitness Tony was back on the bench but he did make a number of appearances as a substitute before being sidelined by injury.

Lee Thompson

Luton T (From trainee at Leicester C on 18/8/1992) FL 93+27/50 FLC 5+4/5 FAC 5+3/2 Others 4+3/3
Fulham (£800,000 on 26/2/1998) FL 5+8/3 Others 1+1
Bristol C (£1,000,000 on 23/6/1998) FL 102+26/50 FLC 5+2/4 FAC 6+1/3 Others 9/4
Reading (Loaned on 5/2/1999) FL 6/1
Luton T (Loaned on 25/3/1999) FL 7+1/4
Luton T (Loaned on 26/11/1999) FL 3+1/1
Luton T (Free on 1/7/2002) FL 30+2/15 FLC 1/1 FAC 1/1 Others 2/2
Queens Park R (£50,000 on 22/8/2003) FL 22+9/10 FAC 1 Others 1+2/1

THORPE Lee Anthony
Born: Wolverhampton, 14 December 1975
Height: 6'1" **Weight:** 12.4
Lee made a promising start to the 2003-04 season, netting two early goals for Leyton Orient, but then a combination of injuries, loss of form and suspensions led to his being out of the team for long periods. In January he was allowed to join Grimsby Town on loan, where he struck up a fine partnership with Izzy Rankin, seen to best effect in the 6-1 demolition of Barnsley. However, Lee returned to the O's and eventually moved out permanently, signing for Bristol Rovers shortly before the transfer deadline. He worked tirelessly for the Pirates' cause and opened his goal-scoring account in the last home match of the season against one of his former clubs, Lincoln City.
Blackpool (From trainee on 18/7/1994) FL 2+10 FLC 0+1 FAC 1 Others 1
Lincoln C (Free on 4/8/1997) FL 183+9/58 FLC 5+1/1 FAC 14/1 Others 9+1/7
Leyton Orient (Free on 3/5/2002) FL 42+13/12 FLC 2/1 FAC 1 Others 1+1
Grimsby T (Loaned on 6/2/2004) FL 5+1
Bristol Rov (Free on 12/3/2004) FL 8+2/1

THORRINGTON John Gerard
Born: Johannesburg, South Africa, 17 October 1979
Height: 5'8" **Weight:** 10.12
International Honours: USA: 1
The lively winger started the 2003-04 campaign as a regular in the Huddersfield Town line-up. He was always a threat to the opposing defences with his close control and quick turn of pace and scored a close-range winner in the Carling Cup tie against Derby County, before a knee injury blighted his season. Once recovered John left for pastures new at Grimsby, but he failed to establish himself in the side and departed shortly before the end of the campaign.

Manchester U (Signed from Mission Viejos Pateadores, California, USA, on 7/10/1997. Free to Bayer Leverkusen, Germany during 1999 close season)
Huddersfield T (Free on 16/3/2001) FL 48+19/7 FLC 1+2/1 FAC 0+1 Others 4
Grimsby T (Free on 12/3/2004) FL 2+1

TIATTO Daniele (Danny)
Amadio
Born: Melbourne, Australia, 22 May 1973
Height: 5'7" **Weight:** 12.0
Club Honours: Div 1 '02
International Honours: Australia: 21; U23
Danny proved to be a hugely important, committed and versatile team member for Manchester City when available last term. He can play as an orthodox left winger, left back or wing back, but spent much of the campaign on the sidelines through injury. He was released by City following the last game of the season.
Stoke C (Loaned from FC Baden, Switzerland on 25/11/1997) FL 11+4/1
Manchester C (£300,000 from FC Baden, Switzerland on 15/7/1998) P/FL 112+28/3 FLC 10/1 FAC 3+1 Others 3+2

TIDMAN Ola
Born: Sweden, 11 May 1979
Height: 6'2" **Weight:** 11.13
International Honours: Sweden: U21-2; Yth
This young goalkeeper started last season as first choice for Sheffield Wednesday, but then a leg injury put paid to him for several months and when he eventually regained fitness, his place in the side, he struggled to find his confidence. He was rested for a while, but will be hoping to become first choice again in 2004-05.
Stockport Co (Free from La Louviere, Belgium, ex BK Kick, Malmo FF, KAA Gent, on 24/1/2003) FL 18
Sheffield Wed (Free on 8/7/2003) FL 9 FLC 1 Others 2

TIE Li
Born: Liaoning, China, 18 September 1977
Height: 6'0" **Weight:** 11.10
International Honours: China
After an excellent first season with Everton, this feisty, experienced Chinese international midfielder had a difficult campaign, which followed the signing of a new contract and a fine goal at Ibrox in a pre-season friendly. He was sidelined early on with a foot injury and then he sustained a broken leg in February, following a freak training ground accident whilst on international duty, that ended

his season. He has excellent two-footed passing ability which he combines with great stamina.
Everton (£1,000,000 from Liaoning Bodao, China on 8/8/2002) PL 32+2 FLC 4+1 FAC 0+1

TIERNEY Francis (Fran)
Born: Liverpool, 10 September 1975
Height: 5'10" **Weight:** 11.0
Club Honours: Div 3 '04
International Honours: E: Yth
Fran started last term in exceptionally good form for Doncaster Rovers but was put out of action with an ankle injury that took rather a long time to mend. Before the season closed he managed a few games in the reserves and returned to the first team in the last match against Carlisle United. Fran is a left- or right-sided midfield player who is exceedingly skilful on the ball.
Crewe Alex (From trainee on 22/3/1993) FL 57+30/10 FLC 6 FAC 1+4 Others 5+6/3
Notts Co (Free on 2/7/1998) FL 19+14/4 FLC 0+1 FAC 1+4/1 Others 2 (Freed on 30/6/2000)
Exeter C (Free from Witton A on 10/11/2000) FL 4+3/1 FAC 0+1 (Free to Witton A on 1/2/2001)
Doncaster Rov (Free on 20/3/2001) FL 10+3/3 FLC 0+1 Others 1/1

TIERNEY Marc
Born: Prestwich, 23 August 1985
Height: 5'11" **Weight:** 11.2
This promising left-sided defender caught the eye during Oldham Athletic's pre-season tour of Northern Ireland and went on to become a regular member of the first-team squad last term. He made two starts for the Latics in the Carling Cup and LDV Vans Trophy competitions and was rewarded with the offer of a new contract in May by manager Brian Talbot. Marc is the younger brother of Manchester United defender Paul Tierney.
Oldham Ath (From juniors on 8/8/2003) FL 0+2 FLC 1 Others 1

TIERNEY Paul Thomas
Born: Salford, 15 September 1982
Height: 5'10" **Weight:** 12.10
International Honours: RoI: U21-7
This promising young defender made his bow for Manchester United in the Carling Cup match against West Bromwich Albion in December. He later had a spell on loan at Colchester but never really seemed to settle and returned to Old Trafford early.
Manchester U (From trainee on 18/7/2000) FLC 1

Ola Tidman

Crewe Alex (Loaned on 8/11/2002) FL 14+3/1 FAC 2 Others 3
Colchester U (Loaned on 30/1/2004) FL 2 FAC 1 Others 1

TILSON Stephen (Steve) Brian

Born: Wickford, 27 July 1966
Height: 5'11" **Weight:** 12.6
Club Honours: FAT '01

Steve was asked to take over as caretaker-manager at Southend following the departures of both Steve Wignall and Dave Webb. The veteran midfielder steered the Blues out of the murky waters of the relegation zone and was rewarded with a two-year deal as manager. Despite his advancing years, Steve managed a brief appearance from the substitutes' bench in the home game with Oxford United when he demonstrated that his left foot was still in fine fettle.

Southend U (Free from Witham T on 7/2/1989) FL 199+40/26 FLC 9+1 FAC 5 Others 12+2/5 (Free to Canvey Island on 18/7/1997)
Brentford (Loaned on 16/9/1993) FL 2
Southend U (Free on 7/10/2002) FL 2+2 FAC 0+2 Others 1

TINDALL Jason

Born: Mile End, 15 November 1977
Height: 6'1" **Weight:** 11.10

Jason is a player who can be relied upon whether appearing at the back, in the middle of the park or, occasionally, as a forward. Injuries prevented him from making many starts for Bournemouth last term, but he was a regular on the bench. He went under the surgeon's knife at the end of the season to resolve a troublesome knee problem in readiness for the 2004-05 season.

Charlton Ath (From trainee on 18/7/1996)
Bournemouth (Free on 3/7/1998) FL 124+36/6 FLC 4+3 FAC 8+3 Others 4+2

TINKLER Mark Roland

Born: Bishop Auckland, 24 October 1974
Height: 5'11" **Weight:** 13.3
Club Honours: FAYC '93
International Honours: E: Yth (UEFA-U18 '93); Sch

Mark had another good season for Hartlepool in 2003-04, having few problems in adjusting to Second Division football after being an important member of Hartlepool's promotion side of the previous campaign. A tireless worker and ball winner, the midfield playmaker was a near ever-present and added a new string

to his bow by successfully playing a lengthy spell as a central defender.

Leeds U (From trainee on 29/11/1991) PL 14+11 FLC 1 Others 0+1
York C (£85,000 on 25/3/1997) FL 88+2/8 FLC 6 FAC 5 Others 2
Southend U (£40,000 on 13/8/1999) FL 55+1/1 FLC 2+1 FAC 1 Others 1
Hartlepool U (Free on 2/11/2000) FL 155+2/31 FLC 4 FAC 6 Others 9/1

TINNION Brian

Born: Stanley, 23 February 1968
Height: 6'0" **Weight:** 13.0
Club Honours: AMC '03

Last season saw the launch of Brian's testimonial year, which will see a meeting with Portsmouth at the start of the 2004-05 campaign, a deserved reward for this fine servant who has now played over 500 games for Bristol City. A fine long-distance goal in the League game at Hartlepool was one of the highlights of the 2003-04 season, which brought his inclusion in the PFA divisional side for the second successive season. Although at the veteran stage of his career, Brian is still a talented midfield player with wonderful passing skills.

Newcastle U (From apprentice on 26/2/1986) FL 30+2/2 FLC 5 Others 1+1
Bradford C (£150,000 on 9/3/1989) FL 137+8/22 FLC 12/1 FAC 9/4 Others 7+1/2
Bristol C (£180,000 on 23/3/1993) FL 400+36/35 FLC 26+1 FAC 27+2/6 Others 21+6

TIPTON Matthew John

Born: Conwy, Wales, 29 June 1980
Height: 5'10" **Weight:** 13.8
International Honours: W: U21-6; Yth

Matthew was mostly used from the bench by Macclesfield in the early part of last term and missed several matches as a result of routine treatment to slow down his heart rate. After his return to action in October he became a regular in the starting line-up and hit a rich vein of form, but then suffered a goal drought coinciding with a dip in form of the team. However, he regained his goal-scoring form and completed the season as the team's top scorer equalling the Macclesfield record for the most League goals scored in a season. A pacy striker who can cause all sorts of problems for the opposition, Matthew was voted 'Player of the Year' by both players and supporters.

Oldham Ath (From trainee on 1/7/1997) FL 51+61/15 FLC 3+4 FAC 4+7/1 Others 3+3/1
Macclesfield T (Free on 13/2/2002) FL 74+13/29 FLC 2+1/1 FAC 7/5 Others 2/1

TODD Andrew (Andy) John James

Born: Derby, 21 September 1974
Height: 5'10" **Weight:** 11.10
Club Honours: Div 1 '97, '00

Andy received few first-team opportunities early on last season for Blackburn and in September he joined Burnley on loan. The Clarets' often-suspect defence looked much more solid during his spell at Turf Moor, his partnership in the centre with the equally experienced David May reminding Burnley's supporters of the value of a safe pair of centre backs. It was therefore a blow when he returned to Ewood Park, but he looked a much better player for the experience, reading the game cleverly and using his physical strength to advantage. He settled into the side with some useful performances and at one point even looked a candidate for 'Player of the Season' before a dip in form.

Middlesbrough (From trainee on 6/3/1992) FL 7+1 FLC 1+1 Others 5
Swindon T (Loaned on 27/2/1995) FL 13
Bolton W (£250,000 on 1/8/1995) P/FL 66+18/2 FLC 14+5/1 FAC 1 Others 3
Charlton Ath (£750,000 on 18/11/1999) P/FL 27+13/1 FLC 4 FAC 6+1
Grimsby T (Loaned on 21/2/2002) FL 12/3
Blackburn Rov (£750,000 on 31/5/2002) PL 26+5/1 FLC 4 FAC 3 Others 2
Burnley (Loaned on 4/9/2003) FL 7 FLC 1

TODOROV Svetoslav

Born: Bulgaria, 30 August 1978
Height: 6'0" **Weight:** 11.11
Club Honours: Div 1 '03
International Honours: Bulgaria: 31; Yth

After leading the scoring chart for Pompey in 2002-03, Svetoslav was extremely unlucky in damaging his knee in training the day before the Premiership campaign started. The knee became troublesome and required a major operation in USA in the autumn. He eventually made a comeback in the reserves, scoring three goals, and started one first-team game at Anfield, but this proved too much. After missing out on Euro 2004 action he will be hoping to make a full recovery in 2004-05.

West Ham U (£500,000 + from Liteks Lovech, Bulgaria on 30/1/2001) PL 4+10/1 FLC 1 FAC 0+2/1
Portsmouth (£750,000 on 20/3/2002) P/FL 47+2/27 FLC 2 FAC 1

TOMLINSON Stuart Charles

Born: Chester, 10 May 1985
Height: 6'0" **Weight:** 11.0

Kolo Toure (foreground)

This promising young 'keeper signed his first professional contract for Crewe in the summer of 2003, but managed just one appearance as a substitute last term. Stuart replaced the injured Clayton Ince in the game at West Ham in March.
Crewe Alex (From trainee on 16/7/2003) FL 0+2

TONER Ciaran
Born: Craigavon, 30 June 1981
Height: 6'1" **Weight:** 12.4
International Honours: NI: 2; U21-17; Yth; Sch
Ciaran was hampered by injuries in the first half of last season, and only featured regularly for Leyton Orient after Christmas. He is a midfield playmaker who on his day is an excellent passer of the ball. Ciaran was called up by Lawrie Sanchez for the full Northern Ireland squad and was an unused substitute against Estonia. Ciaran was released by the O's during the summer.
Tottenham H (From trainee on 14/7/1999)
Peterborough U (Loaned on 21/12/2001) FL 6 FAC 1
Bristol Rov (Free on 28/3/2002) FL 6
Leyton Orient (Free on 7/5/2002) FL 41+11/2 FLC 2 FAC 1 Others 2

TONGE Dale
Born: Doncaster, 7 May 1985
Height: 5'10" **Weight:** 10.6
A promising defender or midfield player, Dale progressed from the Academy via the reserves to the Barnsley first team last term. He made his debut as a substitute against Brentford in April and will be hoping to gain further senior experience in 2004-05.
Barnsley (Trainee) FL 0+1

TONGE Michael William
Born: Manchester, 7 April 1983
Height: 6'0" **Weight:** 11.10
International Honours: E: U21-2; Yth
Last term proved to be a period of consolidation for Michael at Sheffield United and he found himself more closely marked than before. Playing as an attacking midfielder, he was always keen to be involved and worked hard to win the ball. He is good in the tackle and distributes the ball well, but is perhaps most dangerous when attacking down the left flank, from where he has the ability to beat an opponent and produce searching crosses. He was ever-present in First Division fixtures and won more England U21 caps during the campaign.

Sheffield U (From trainee on 16/3/2001) FL 114+8/13 FLC 9/2 FAC 9 Others 3

TONKIN Anthony Richard
Born: Newlyn, 17 January 1980
Height: 5'11" **Weight:** 12.2
Club Honours: FAT '02
Recruited from Stockport County soon after the start of the 2003-04 campaign, Anthony made his debut for Crewe against Rotherham soon afterwards, but it was not until November that he established himself as a regular in the line-up at left back. He retained his place in the side until injury ruled him out towards the end of the campaign.
Stockport Co (£50,000 from Yeovil T on 26/9/2002) FL 23+1 FLC 1 FAC 2
Crewe Alex (£150,000 on 26/8/2003) FL 20+6 FLC 0+1 FAC 1

TORPEY Stephen (Steve) David James
Born: Islington, 8 December 1970
Height: 6'3" **Weight:** 14.6
Club Honours: AMC '94
Scunthorpe's target man continued to provide a threat to opposition defences with his strength in the air and ability to hold the ball up in the 2003-04 season. A virtual ever-present, he ended the campaign with 15 goals, including the strike against Macclesfield in April which guaranteed Scunthorpe's Football League status and two in the FA Cup tie against Sheffield Wednesday in December.
Millwall (From trainee on 14/2/1989) FL 3+4 FLC 0+1
Bradford C (£70,000 on 21/11/1990) FL 86+10/22 FLC 6 FAC 2+1 Others 8/6
Swansea C (£80,000 on 3/8/1993) FL 151+11/44 FLC 9+2/2 FAC 10/5 Others 15+3/5
Bristol C (£400,000 on 8/8/1997) FL 53+17/13 FLC 4+1/1 FAC 3 Others 3+1
Notts Co (Loaned on 7/8/1998) FL 4+2/1 FLC 1+1/1
Scunthorpe U (£175,000 on 3/2/2000) FL 160+5/45 FLC 5/2 FAC 16/7 Others 8+2/4

TOURE Kolo Abib
Born: Ivory Coast, 19 March 1981
Height: 5'10" **Weight:** 11.13
Club Honours: CS '02; FAC '03; PL '04
International Honours: Ivory Coast
Without question the most improved player at Highbury, Kolo was paired with Sol Campbell in central defence as Arsenal negotiated a series of pre-season friendlies. Written off as title contenders by many at the start of the campaign, the Gunners produced wonderful football allied with resolute defending and no one

typified this more than Kolo. He became the model of consistency throughout a tremendously impressive campaign and contributed three goals, becoming a fans favourite along the way.
Arsenal (Signed from ASEC Mimosa, Ivory Coast on 18/2/2002) PL 45+18/3 FLC 3 FAC 7+3/2 Others 14+5

TOWNSEND Ryan Matthew George
Born: Tameside, 2 September 1985
Height: 6'0" **Weight:** 12.5
Defender Ryan made his debut from the bench along with fellow Burnley graduate Paul Scott towards the end of a 4-0 hammering at Coventry in March. He appeared much too late to rescue the situation but did little wrong and will hope for further chances in 2004-05.
Burnley (Trainee) FL 0+1

TOWNSLEY Derek Johnstone
Born: Carlisle, 21 March 1973
Height: 6'5" **Weight:** 13.1
This tall midfielder joined Oxford United in the summer of 2003 and netted a hat-trick in a pre-season game which promised much for the campaign. However, he took time to adjust to the different requirements of the English game and in February he returned to Scotland where he joined Gretna. Derek ended the campaign in fine goal-scoring form, netting nine times in 15 games including a hat-trick against East Stirling.
Queen of the South (Signed from Gretna, ex Carlisle U trainee, on 27/8/1996) SL 77+10/19 SLC 2/1 SC 3+1/1 Others 5
Motherwell (Signed on 10/6/1999) SL 38+16/6 SLC 5/1 SC 4+1
Hibernian (Signed on 8/7/2001) SL 22+21/9 SLC 3 SC 5+1
Oxford U (Free on 10/7/2003) FL 9+2 FLC 2 Others 1

TOWNSON Kevin
Born: Liverpool, 19 April 1983
Height: 5'8" **Weight:** 10.3
International Honours: E: Yth
Rochdale fans' favourite Kevin bounced back from a disappointing time in 2002-03, scoring regularly in the early part of last term. However, the diminutive goal poacher was unable to convince successive managers that he deserved a regular place in the side, never starting more than two games in a row and netting nearly half his goals after coming off the bench. Even so, he finished as the side's top scorer for the second time in three seasons.

Kevin Townson

Rochdale *(From Everton juniors on 6/7/2000) FL 40+61/25 FLC 0+3/3 FAC 2+4/1 Others 5+1/1*

TRAORE Djimi
Born: Paris, France, 1 March 1980
Height: 6'3" **Weight:** 13.10
Club Honours: FLC '03
International Honours: France: U21; Yth
Djimi began last term in Liverpool's re s e rves, b ut was recalled to the first team in October as a replacement at left back for Jon Arne Riise. Djimi enjoyed a run of eight games during which he scored his first and only goal for Liverpool, in the tricky UEFA Cup tie away to Steaua Bucharest. It was a spectacular eff o rt from wide on the left, which eluded defenders and goalkeeper alike to sail into the far corner of the net. After Riise's recall in December, Djimi played only three more first-team games, two in January and one in April, all at left back.
Liverpool *(£550,000 from Laval, France on 18/2/1999) PL 45+2 FLC 7+1 FAC 2 Others 16+2/1*

TREMARCO Carl
Born: Liverpool, 11 October 1985
Height: 5'11" **Weight:** 12.3
Carl signed his first professional contract with Tranmere during the 2003-04 season and was a regular with the club's reserve team last term. A calm and classy defender whose maturity belies his age, he stepped up to the senior side during an injury crisis, making his debut in the potentially tricky FA Cup tie at Hornchurch when he performed with great composure. Carl will be looking to gain further experience of first-team football in the 2004-05 campaign.
Tranmere Rov *(From trainee on 2/4/2004) FAC 1*

TROLLOPE Paul Jonathan
Born: Swindon, 3 June 1972
Height: 6'0" **Weight:** 12.6
Club Honours: Div 2 '99
International Honours: W: 9; B-1
This experienced central midfielder enjoyed his best season since joining Northampton in 2003-04. Sometimes helping out in defence and occasionally moving upfield to snap up the odd goal, Paul was effective wherever he played. A near ever-present, he was the Cobblers' club captain and led the team by example.
Swindon T *(From trainee on 23/12/1989)*

Torquay U *(Free on 26/3/1992) FL 103+3/16 FLC 9+1/1 FAC 7 Others 8+1*
Derby Co *(£100,000 on 16/12/1994) F/PL 47+18/5 FLC 3+2/1 FAC 3+1*
Grimsby T *(Loaned on 30/8/1996) FL 6+1/1*
Crystal Palace *(Loaned on 11/10/1996) FL 0+9*
Fulham *(£600,000 on 28/11/1997) FL 54+22/5 FLC 9+2 FAC 3+5 Others 4/1*
Coventry C *(Free on 22/3/2002) FL 5+1*
Northampton T *(Free on 31/7/2002) FL 84/8 FLC 3 FAC 7 Others 5+1*

TRUNDLE Lee Christopher
Born: Liverpool, 10 October 1976
Height: 6'0" **Weight:** 13.3
Lee followed his former boss Brian Flynn to Swansea during the 2003 close season and the move paid off for both player and club. He netted a total of 22 goals in all competitions, including a hat-trick in the away game at Cheltenham, and was included in the PFA Third Division team of the season. An exciting left-sided front runner with the ability to take on the

Lee Trundle

opposition, Lee, also possesses a good strike rate, and the ability to play his team mates into goal-scoring positions.
Wrexham *(£60,000 from Rhyl, ex Burscough, Chorley, Stalybridge Celtic, Southport, on 16/2/2001) FL 73+21/27 FLC 0+2 FAC 1 Others 4+1/3*
Swansea C *(Free on 14/7/2003) FL 29+2/16 FLC 1 FAC 5/5 Others 0+1*

TUDGAY Marcus
Born: Shoreham, 3 February 1983
Height: 6'3" **Weight:** 13.2
Initially on a monthly contract while he recovered from knee surgery, Marcus had every reason to be pleased with his progress at Derby last term. His intelligent forward play earned him a deal for the remainder of the season once he was fit, followed by a longer contract. Never a prolific scorer, Marcus showed more of an eye for goal and has much to offer in his all-round game, able to accept the ball, hold it and use it well. He was impressively quick to tune in to Paul Peschisolido's runs and advanced his career significantly.
Derby Co *(From trainee on 16/7/2002) FL 20+17/6 FAC 2*

TUDOR Shane Anthony
Born: Wolverhampton, 10 February 1982
Height: 5'8" **Weight:** 11.2
Shane is a hard-working Cambridge United midfielder who usually features on the wing, but can also play in a more central role. Dangerous when running at defenders, a series of injuries seemed to take an edge of his explosive pace and limited him to just three goals during the season.
Wolverhampton W *(From trainee on 9/8/1999) FL 0+1*
Cambridge U *(Free on 22/11/2001) FL 87+8/15 FLC 3/1 FAC 10/1 Others 11/2*

[TUGAY] KERIMOGLU Tugay
Born: Istanbul, Turkey, 24 August 1970
Height: 5'9" **Weight:** 11.6
Club Honours: SPD '00; SC '00; FLC '02
International Honours: Turkey: 92
With the departure of Damien Duff and David Dunn, Tugay was left as the only truly creative player at Blackburn last term and the responsibility weighed heavily on his aging legs. At times his passing was supreme, but when the midfield became congested and the tackles were flying he was seldom comfortable. He scored with a stunning strike against Birmingham (voted the club's 'Goal of the Season') and there was never a doubt that he cared about results. Late in the season he

played as front man in the diamond formation and recovered much of his old zest. Out of contract there was some doubt at the time of writing as to whether he would accept the deal that was on the table.
Glasgow R *(Signed from Galatasaray, Turkey on 15/1/2000) SL 26+16/4 SLC 2+1 SC 3+4 Others 6*
Blackburn Rov *(£1,300,000 on 20/7/2001) PL 94+12/5 FLC 10+1 FAC 6+2 Others 6*

TURLEY William (Billy) Lee
Born: Wolverhampton, 15 July 1973
Height: 6'4" **Weight:** 15.0
Club Honours: NC '01; Div 3 '03
Billy had a somewhat difficult start to the 2003-04 campaign with Rushden and was sidelined by a knee ligament problem in October. He did not return to action until February and then only won his place back when Jamie Ashdown was recalled by Reading. An influential 'keeper who commands his box effectively, he will be hoping to have a better time in 2004-05.
Northampton T *(Free from Evesham on 10/7/1995) FL 28 FAC 2 Others 4*
Leyton Orient *(Loaned on 5/2/1998) FL 14*
Rushden & Diamonds *(£135,000 on 15/6/1999) FL 111+1 FLC 5 FAC 4 Others 4*

TURNBULL Ross
Born: Bishop Auckland, 4 January 1985
Height: 6'4" **Weight:** 13.5
International Honours: E: Yth
This young Middlesbrough 'keeper spent time on loan with both Darlington and Barnsley last term. Signed by the Quakers in the wake of the disastrous FA Cup defeat by Hornchurch, he played just once, keeping a clean sheet against Lincoln City. Later on he was given special permission by the Football League to join Barnsley after the transfer deadline to cover for an injury crisis at Oakwell and acquitted himself well after a rather nervous start. Ross also featured on the substitutes' bench for Boro' on a handful of occasions during the season.
Middlesbrough *(From trainee on 6/7/2002)*
Darlington *(Loaned on 14/11/2003) FL 1*
Barnsley *(Loaned on 22/4/2004) FL 3*

TURNER John Andrew James
Born: Harrow, 12 February 1986
Height: 6'2" **Weight:** 11.0
After bursting onto the scene at Cambridge United towards the end of the previous season, this promising young striker developed at a more steady pace last term. John featured in three-quarters of the first-team games, although often

used from the bench, and added his name to the U's history books when he scored the club's 2000th Football League goal.
Cambridge U *(From trainee on 3/12/2003) FL 17+20/4 FAC 2/2 Others 0+1*

TWIGG Gary
Born: Glasgow, 19 March 1984
Height: 6'0" **Weight:** 11.12
This young left-sided striker spent much of last season in Derby's reserve team. His only senior action came during loan spells at Burton Albion and Bristol Rovers. He made his debut for Rovers at left back, and impressed during his spell at the Memorial Stadium, creating several goals with his accurate crosses.
Derby Co *(From trainee on 20/3/2001) P/FL 1+8*
Bristol Rov *(Loaned on 16/3/2004) FL 7+1*

TYLER Mark Richard
Born: Norwich, 2 April 1977
Height: 6'0" **Weight:** 12.9
International Honours: E: Yth
Mark was once again a near ever-present for Peterborough last term and has now made over 300 senior appearances for Posh. Still one of the best shot-stoppers in the lower divisions, he commands his penalty area well and has a confident approach to the game.
Peterborough U *(From trainee on 7/12/1994) FL 268+1 FLC 12 FAC 21 Others 19*

TYSON Nathan
Born: Reading, 4 May 1982
Height: 5'10" **Weight:** 11.12
International Honours: E: Yth
Nathan played in nine first-team games for Reading during the season, always as a second-half substitute in an attempt to liven up the attack with his undoubted pace. However, incoming manager Steve Coppell allowed him to move to nearby Wycombe Wanderers, originally on a two-month loan deal, then permanently. He made a huge impression as a striker at Adams Park, setting up two goals on his debut against Grimsby, and it was not long before he was scoring himself. The best was one of two goals at Oldham when he picked the ball up in his own half and weaved down the wing before floating it into the net.
Reading *(From trainee on 18/3/2000) FL 9+24/1 FLC 0+2 FAC 2+1 Others 0+2*
Swansea C *(Loaned on 30/8/2001) FL 7+4/1*
Cheltenham T *(Loaned on 22/3/2002) FL 1+7/1*
Wycombe W *(Signed on 2/1/2004) FL 21/9*

UV

U'DDIN Anwar
Born: Tower Hamlets, 1 November 1981
Height: 6'2" **Weight:** 13.0
Anwar struggled to regain full fitness last term and subsequently spent part of the season out on loan with Hereford United and Telford where he gained valuable experience. The young central defender returned to the Memorial Stadium to make one full start and one appearance as a substitute for Bristol Rovers before being released in the summer.
West Ham U (From trainee on 9/7/2001)
Sheffield Wed (Free on 28/2/2002)
Bristol Rov (Free on 2/7/2002) FL 18+1/1 FLC 1 Others 1+1

UHLENBEEK Gustav (Gus)
Reinier
Born: Paramaribo, Surinam, 20 August 1970
Height: 5'10" **Weight:** 12.6
Club Honours: Div 2 '99
Gus joined Chesterfield last August after a short trial and showed fine form early on as an attacking right back. Disciplinary problems appeared to affect this form, though, and he was dropped after the team lost at home to Stockport. Gus left the club by mutual consent in April.
Ipswich T (£100,000 from Tops SV, Holland, ex Ajax, Cambuur, on 11/8/1995) FL 77+12/4 FLC 5+3 FAC 4+3 Others 7+1
Fulham (£250,000 on 22/7/1998) FL 22+17/1 FLC 4+1 FAC 3+2 Others 1
Sheffield U (Free on 10/8/2000) FL 47+4 FLC 5 FAC 3
Walsall (Loaned on 28/3/2002) FL 5
Bradford C (Free on 9/8/2002) FL 42/1 FLC 1 FAC 1
Chesterfield (Free on 5/8/2003) FL 36+4 Others 1

ULLATHORNE Robert (Rob)
Born: Wakefield, 11 October 1971
Height: 5'8" **Weight:** 11.3
International Honours: E: Yth
After being released by Sheffield United during the close season, Rob had trials with a number of clubs including Walsall and Derby County before joining Northampton Town on a short-term contract in February. The experienced defender settled into the left-back spot at Sixfields and made it his own, looking effective when pushing forward down the flank and also when tracking back.
Norwich C (From trainee on 6/7/1990) F/PL 86+8/7 FLC 10+2/1 FAC 7+1 Others 1 (Free

to Osasuna, Spain during 1996 close season)
Leicester C (£600,000 on 18/2/1997) PL 28+3/1 FLC 8+1 FAC 2/1
Sheffield U (Free, following an injury and trials at Huddersfield T, Real Zaragoza, Tenerife, Newcastle, on 1/12/2000) FL 39+1 FLC 2 FAC 2 (Freed on 8/5/2003)
Northampton T (Free, via trials at Stoke C, Walsall, Derby Co, on 20/2/2004) FL 13/1 Others 2

UNDERWOOD Paul Victor
Born: Wimbledon, 16 August 1973
Height: 5'11" **Weight:** 12.8
Club Honours: NC '01; Div 3 '03
International Honours: E: SP-4
This cultured left back was an ever-present for Rushden until Christmas when he was forced to have a knee operation which kept him out of action for several weeks. Soon after he recovered he was transferred to Luton, but had the misfortune to suffer a hamstring injury just 17 minutes into his debut for the Hatters and spent the rest of the season on the sidelines.
Rushden & Diamonds (£50,000 from Enfield, ex Kingstonian, Molesey, Sutton U, Carshalton Ath, on 6/6/1997) FL 110/1 FLC 4 FAC 6 Others 6
Luton T (Free on 25/3/2004) FL 1

UNSWORTH David Gerald
Born: Chorley, 16 October 1973
Height: 6'1" **Weight:** 14.2
Club Honours: FAC '95; CS '95
International Honours: E: 1; U21-6; Yth
This lion-hearted and versatile defender had yet another committed season in the Blue jersey of Everton. After beginning the campaign on the left-hand side of the team, David found a new lease of life when he was moved to the centre of defence in November, using his great experience and reading of the game to produce a series of impressively robust displays. Although the return of Joseph Yobo in February hastened a switch to the bench, he still managed to reach a personal milestone when making his 300th Premiership appearance for the club against Middlesbrough.
Everton (From trainee on 25/6/1992) F/PL 108+8/11 FLC 5+2 FAC 7 Others 4/1
West Ham U (£1,000,000 + on 18/8/1997) PL 32/2 FLC 5 FAC 4
Aston Villa (£3,000,000 on 28/7/1998)
Everton (£3,000,000 on 22/8/1998) PL 164+24/23 FLC 10+1/1 FAC 16+1/4

UNSWORTH Lee Peter
Born: Eccles, 25 February 1973
Height: 5'11" **Weight:** 11.8

Lee enjoyed a satisfying season for Bury in 2003-04, despite suffering various injury problems. He played in the right-back position for the first half of the campaign, but soon after losing his place to Matt Barrass he suffered a groin injury, which required surgery. Lee returned to the Shakers' line-up in February but then tore medial ligaments in his left knee and did not return until the closing games of the season when he featured as a central defender.
Crewe Alex (Signed from Ashton U on 20/2/1995) FL 93+33 FLC 10+1/1 FAC 5+1/1 Others 8+2
Bury (Free on 4/8/2000) FL 107+5/5 FLC 6 FAC 5 Others 9

UPSON Matthew James
Born: Stowmarket, 18 April 1979
Height: 6'1" **Weight:** 11.4
Club Honours: PL '02
International Honours: E: 6; U21-11; Yth
Matthew was an imposing figure alongside Kenny Cunningham in the centre of defence for Birmingham City last term. He used his pace and physique to dominate strikers more instead of relying solely upon his anticipation and reading of play. When he was at his peak, Matthew fell awkwardly and damaged ankle ligaments in January. It cost him his England place, and on his return Matthew was asked to fill-in at left back, which he did very well.
Luton T (From trainee on 24/4/1996) FL 0+1 Others 1
Arsenal (£1,000,000 on 14/5/1997) PL 20+14 FLC 8 FAC 3+1 Others 8+2
Nottingham F (Loaned on 8/12/2000) FL 1
Crystal Palace (Loaned on 2/3/2001) FL 7
Reading (Loaned on 6/9/2002) FL 13+1 FLC 1/1
Birmingham C (£2,000,000 + on 23/1/2003) PL 44 FLC 1 FAC 2

VAESEN Nico Jos-Theodor
Born: Ghent, Belgium, 28 September 1969
Height: 6'3" **Weight:** 12.8
After recovering from a serious knee injury suffered towards the end of the previous campaign, Nico found it impossible to win his place back at Birmingham last term and he spent most of the second half of the campaign out on loan, His first port of call was Gillingham, where he kept two clean sheets in five appearances, producing some superb displays. In February he joined Bradford City, where his spell coincided with the club's best spell of the

David Unsworth (left)

season. Finally, he concluded his travels by
helping Crystal Palace into the play-offs
and kept a clean sheet in the decider
against West Ham which ensured a return
to the Premiership for the Eagles.
Huddersfield T *(£80,000 from SC Eendracht
Aalst, Belgium on 10/7/1998) FL 134 FLC 12
FAC 7*
Birmingham C *(£800,000 on 19/6/2001)
P/FL 49+1 FLC 2 FAC 1 Others 3*
Gillingham *(Loaned on 24/12/2003) FL 5*
Bradford C *(Loaned on 13/2/2004) FL 6*
Crystal Palace *(Loaned on 18/3/2004) FL 10
Others 3*

VALAKARI Simo Johannes
Born: Helsinki, Finland, 28 April 1973
Height: 5'10" **Weight:** 11.10
International Honours: Finland: 32;
U21-2
After four injury-hit seasons, Simo
Valakari's contract with Derby County was
ended in March, allowing him to move to
the USA and MLS club Dallas Burn. Derby
followers were sorry to see him go
because his tidy passing, coupled with a
highly professional attitude, should have
earned more success. Simo added two
more Finland caps in the first half of the
season, when he was a regular member
of the Rams' squad.
Motherwell *(Signed from FinnPa, Finland on
6/2/1997) SL 98+6 SLC 3+1 SC 7+2*
Derby Co *(Free on 6/7/2000) P/FL 34+12/3
FLC 5*

VALENTINE Ryan David
Born: Wrexham, 19 August 1982
Height: 5'10" **Weight:** 11.11
International Honours: W: U21-8; Yth
Ryan was once again a regular for
Darlington last term, and surprised
everyone by netting in consecutive games
in April after previously registering just
one goal in over 80 appearances for the
Quakers. A versatile player who can
perform on either side of the defence, he
is quick into the tackle and enjoys
overlapping down the left flank to link up
with the midfield.
Everton *(From trainee on 1/9/1999)*
Darlington *(Free on 8/8/2002) FL 76+7/3 FLC
3 FAC 3 Others 2*

VAN BRONCKHORST
Giovanni (Gio) Christiaan
Born: Rotterdam, Holland, 5 February
1975
Height: 5'10" **Weight:** 11.10
Club Honours: SPD '99, '00; SC '99, '00;
SLC '98; PL '02; FAC '03
International Honours: Holland: 41
Arsenal fans would be the first to admit

Matthew Upson

413

Simo Valakari

that they have not seen the best of Giovanni. The former Rangers man has had an injury-plagued career so far at Highbury and the only opportunity for him in a Gunners shirt last season came as a substitute in the FA Community Shield. He replaced Freddie Ljungberg in the traditional curtain raiser and was then sent out on loan to Barcelona for the rest of the season. He enjoyed fine form at the Nou Camp and was instrumental in the club's La Liga championship challenge.
Glasgow R (£5,000,000 from Feyenoord, Holland on 15/7/1998) SL 72+1/13 SLC 6/1 SC 10+1/3 Others 28/5
Arsenal (£8,500,000 on 22/6/2001) PL 22+19/2 FLC 4 FAC 5+2 Others 8+4

VAN BUYTEN Daniel
Born: Chimay, Belgium, 7 February 1978
Height: 6'5" **Weight:** 13.10
International Honours: Belgium: 21
Daniel arrived at Manchester City during the January transfer window in the deal which saw David Sommeil move in the opposite direction. Signed on loan until the end of the season, he proved to be a quick, imposing defender with a silky smooth touch. He slotted comfortably into the defence but then an innocuous slip in training saw him tear muscles in his groin and he returned to Marseilles to recuperate.
Manchester C (Loaned from Marseilles, France, ex Charleroi, Standard Liege, on 31/1/2004) PL 5 FAC 1

VAN DER SAR Edwin
Born: Leiden, Holland, 29 October 1970
Height: 6'5" **Weight:** 13.6
International Honours: Holland: 89
After making a full recovery from the injury which saw him miss the second half of the previous campaign, Edwin once again made the first-team goalkeeping slot his own at Fulham, missing only one Premiership game all season. He produced some magnificent performances particularly away from home and was outstanding at Arsenal. Edwin is almost unbeatable in one-on-one situations and is an effective shot-stopper. He was a fixture in the Holland international squad.
Fulham (£7,000,000 from Juventus, Italy, ex Noordwijk, Ajax, on 10/8/2001) PL 93 FAC 10 Others 11

VAN HEUSDEN Arjan
Born: Alphen, Holland, 11 December 1972
Height: 6'3" **Weight:** 14.7
Arjan started the 2003-04 season as first-

Arjan Van Heusden

choice 'keeper for Torquay, but lost his place twice through injury and had a longish spell on the bench after the second layoff due to Kevin Dearden's impressive form. Arjan is an excellent shot stopper, but sometimes needs to show greater command of his area.
Port Vale *(£4,500 from VV Noordwijk, Holland on 15/8/1994) FL 27 FLC 4 Others 2*
Oxford U *(Loaned on 26/9/1997) FL 11 FLC 2*
Cambridge U *(Free on 4/8/1998) FL 41+1 FLC 6 FAC 1 Others 4*
Exeter C *(Free on 31/7/2000) FL 74 FLC 2 FAC 4 Others 1*
Mansfield T *(Free on 27/9/2002) FL 5*
Torquay U *(Free on 1/11/2002) FL 40 FLC 1 FAC 2*

VAN NISTELROOY Rutgerus (Ruud) Johannes Martinus
Born: Oss, Holland, 1 July 1976
Height: 6'2" **Weight:** 12.13
Club Honours: PL '03; CS '03; FAC '04
International Honours: Holland: 38
An archetypal centre forward who is blessed with all-round technique, powerful in the air, and packing a fearsome shot in either foot, Ruud continued to show just why he is lauded as one of the best strikers in world football today. His goal scoring prowess continued at a phenomenal rate when he set two new records for the Reds right from the off. A nicely executed goal against Bolton in the opening Premiership game of the season was his ninth in nine games (a Premiership record) and 11 out of 11 (a new United record). Having then gone through a somewhat barren spell, he equalled Denis Law's old European goal-scoring record of 28 goals with a strike against Stuttgart. He then sailed to the forefront of the Premiership sharp shooters with more notable efforts adding a hat-trick in Holland's Euro 2004 play-off match against Scotland. Though his goal tally dipped ever so slightly from January to May, he started the new year in great form, showing an immediate understanding with his new partner Louis Saha up front. Ruud was selected for the PFA Premiership team of the season and also featured for his country in the Euro 2004 finals in the summer.
Manchester U *(£19,000,000 from PSV Eindhoven, Holland, ex Den Bosch, Heerenveen, on 5/7/2001) PL 93+5/68 FLC 4/1 FAC 6+3/12 Others 33+1/29*

VARNEY Luke
Born: Leicester, 28 September 1982
Height: 5'11" **Weight:** 11.7
Luke made his debut in senior football for

Crewe on the opening day of the 2003-04 campaign when he came on as a substitute at Wimbledon. The promising young striker enjoyed a brief run in the line-up at the turn of the year, scoring on his first start against Crystal Palace. Luke was injured in the FA Cup tie against Telford and did not play for the first team again during the season.
Crewe Alex (Signed from Quorn on 25/3/2003) FL 5+3/1 FLC 0+1 FAC 1

VASSELL Darius
Born: Birmingham, 13 June 1980
Height: 5'7" **Weight:** 12.0
International Honours: E: 22; U21-11; Yth

Luke Varney

Darius is a quick and skilful striker who loves to take defences on. He struggled with niggling injuries during the early part of the season, but returned to hit the target twice in Aston Villa's 3-0 victory over Fulham at the end of December – just what he needed after going so long without a goal. He eventually reached a double-figure goals tally, but never really found a consistent vein of form. He was a regular for England during the season and featured in the squad for the Euro 2004 finals in the summer.
Aston Villa (From trainee on 14/4/1998) PL 90+51/33 FLC 9+8/4 FAC 4+4/1 Others 3+11/4

VAUGHAN Anthony (Tony) John
Born: Manchester, 11 October 1975
Height: 6'1" **Weight:** 11.2
International Honours: E: Yth; Sch
This central or left-sided defender joined Mansfield Town on a one-year contract in the summer of 2003. Although he missed the opening games with an ankle injury, and belatedly starting his season at Southend at the end of August, he soon settled into Town's defence. He was the first choice left back until the closing stages of the campaign when Adam Eaton returned to fitness. Tony was one of several payers released by the Stags in the summer.
Ipswich T (From trainee on 1/7/1994) P/FL 56+11/3 FLC 4+2 FAC 2 Others 4
Manchester C (£1,350,000 on 9/7/1997) FL 54+4/2 FLC 6+1 FAC 3 Others 3+1
Cardiff C (Loaned on 15/9/1999) FL 14 Others 1
Nottingham F (£350,000 on 8/2/2000) FL 38+5/1 FLC 2 FAC 1
Scunthorpe U (Loaned on 26/3/2002) FL 5
Mansfield T (Loaned on 25/10/2002) FL 4
Motherwell (Loaned on 31/1/2003) SL 12/1 SC 3
Mansfield T (Free on 4/8/2003) FL 32/2 FAC 3

VAUGHAN David Owen
Born: Rhuddlan, 18 February 1983
Height: 5'7" **Weight:** 10.10
International Honours: W: 2; U21-3; Yth
This versatile left-sided player was a regular in the Crewe line-up at the beginning of the 2003-04 campaign, but was then sidelined by a knee injury which required surgery. He eventually recovered to take his place in the team again in March. He added a further cap for Wales against Hungary towards the end of the season.
Crewe Alex (From trainee on 6/2/2001) FL 69+8/3 FLC 3 FAC 7/1 Others 2/1

VAZ TE Ricardo Jorge
Born: Lisbon, Portugal, 1 October 1986
Height: 6'2" **Weight:** 12.7
International Honours: Portugal: Yth
A very exciting centre forward, Ricardo joined Bolton in the summer of 2003. He scored eight goals in his first three Academy games and was quickly promoted to the reserve team. His only taste of first-team football came in the two FA Cup games against Tranmere, including a start in the replay, when he gave a very good account of himself.
Bolton W (Trainee) PL 0+1 FAC 1+1

VENUS Mark
Born: Hartlepool, 6 April 1967
Height: 6'0" **Weight:** 13.11
Club Honours: Div 3 '89
This experienced central defender signed for Cambridge United in the 2003 close season to bolster the defence and support the younger players in the squad. He fitted in well, occasionally featuring on the left-hand side of midfield as cover for the injury-ravaged squad. However, in March he was allowed to move on loan to Dagenham & Redbridge and at the end of the campaign he joined Hornchurch as assistant manager.
Hartlepool U (From juniors on 22/3/1985) FL 4 Others 0+1
Leicester C (Free on 6/9/1985) FL 58+3/1 FLC 3 FAC 2 Others 2+1
Wolverhampton W (£40,000 on 23/3/1988) FL 271+16/7 FLC 17+1/1 FAC 15+1 Others 17/2
Ipswich T (£150,000 on 29/7/1997) P/FL 144+4/16 FLC 18/3 FAC 4 Others 14
Cambridge U (Free on 4/8/2003) FL 21 FLC 1 FAC 0+1

VERNAZZA Paolo Andrea Pietro
Born: Islington, 1 November 1979
Height: 6'0" **Weight:** 11.10
International Honours: E: U21-2; Yth
Paolo, a cultured midfield player, suffered an unfulfilling season at Watford last term. He made a slow start, but discovered a rich vein of form after his return from a period of suspension and seemed set for a productive run. However, he lost momentum around Christmas and had to be content with substitute appearances thereafter. His failure to score was another source of disappointment, and he was released at the end of the season.
Arsenal (From trainee on 18/11/1997) PL 2+3/1 FLC 4 Others 1+2
Ipswich T (Loaned on 2/10/1998) FL 2
Portsmouth (Loaned on 14/1/2000) FL 7
Watford (£350,000 + on 15/12/2000) FL 71+25/2 FLC 3/1 FAC 8

VERNON Scott Malcolm
Born: Manchester, 13 December 1983
Height: 6'1" **Weight:** 11.6
This young striker exploded into Oldham Athletic's first team last term with a tally of 14 goals in his first full season in professional football. Scott embarked on a run of seven goals in eight games in January and enjoyed the highlight of his career the following month when he notched a memorable first-half hat-trick against Grimsby Town. Difficult to

dispossess, he uses his tall frame to good effect and is a threat both aerially and when allowed to run at defenders. Scott is the son of former Stockport striker John Vernon.
Oldham Ath (From trainee on 3/7/2002) FL 30+23/13 FLC 1 FAC 1+1 Others 3/4

VERON Juan Sebastian
Born: Buenos Aires, Argentina, 9 March 1975
Height: 6'1" **Weight:** 12.7
Club Honours: PL '03
International Honours: Argentina: 56
Many eyebrows were raised when one of the modern-day enigmas Juan Sebastian Veron joined the 'Roman Revolution' on the eve of the season. Claudio Ranieri seemed to have no doubts describing the Argentine as "the best midfielder in the world" and to rubber stamp that endorsement Juan Sebastian scored the Blues' first Premiership goal of the season at Liverpool with a sweetly struck shot to set up Chelsea's second League victory since 1935 on their bogey ground. Although used sparingly in the Premiership, Juan Sebastian was a crucial figure in Chelsea's Champions' League odyssey – where his pinpoint passing and subtle changes of pace and direction orchestrated the Blues' attempts to unlock the obdurate European defences. He produced a memorable performance at one of his former clubs, Lazio, where he inspired Chelsea to a crushing four-goal victory and received tumultuous applause from the Lazio *tifosi*. Juan Sebastian's season was unfortunately virtually ended in November after masterminding Chelsea's 5-0 victory over Newcastle. He travelled to Colombia for an international and ruptured a disc in his back during the match; this serious injury required an operation and a lengthy period of recuperation in his homeland. He eventually returned to three late substitute appearances after Easter.
Manchester U (£28,100,000 from Lazio, Italy, ex Estudiantes, Boca Juniors, Sampdoria, Parma, on 13/7/2001) PL 45+6/7 FLC 4+1 FAC 2 Others 24/4
Chelsea (£15,000,000 on 7/8/2003) PL 5+2/1 FLC 1 Others 5+1

VIANA Hugo Miguel
Born: Barcelos, Portugal, 15 January 1983
Height: 5'9" **Weight:** 11.8
International Honours: Portugal: 12; B-1; U21-9; Yth
Hugo had a frustrating time last term when he struggled to establish himself as

a first choice in Newcastle's midfield, for despite being in the squad throughout the season he was limited to a handful of starts plus a few more substitute appearances, insufficient experience to enable him to adapt his game to the particular tempo, pace, and aggression demands of the Premiership. He is a talented player with a cultured left foot and his outings were mainly on the left side of midfield rather than in his preferred central role. Despite his infrequent appearances for his club he continued to be capped by Portugal although he missed out on Euro 2004.
Newcastle U (£8,500,000 from Sporting Lisbon, Portugal on 19/7/2002) PL 16+23/2 FLC 2 FAC 0+1 Others 10+9/2

VICTORY Jamie Charles
Born: Hackney, 14 November 1975
Height: 5'10" **Weight:** 12.0
Club Honours: FAT '98; NC '99
International Honours: E: SP-1
Jamie was again a near ever-present for Cheltenham Town last term. He operated mostly at left back in a four-man defence but also played in the centre or on the left of a five-man set-up. He contributed goals in the vital wins over Kidderminster Harriers and Darlington, and was among the leading contenders for the 'Player of the Season' awards.
West Ham U (From trainee on 1/7/1994)
Bournemouth (Loaned on 1/7/1995) FL 5+11/1 FLC 1+1 Others 1+1
Cheltenham T (Free on 1/7/1996) FL 183+1/16 FLC 7/1 FAC 12 Others 9/1

VIDMAR Anthony (Tony)
Born: Adelaide, Australia, 15 April 1969
Height: 6'1" **Weight:** 12.10
Club Honours: SPD '99, '00; SLC '99, '02; SC '99, '00, '02
International Honours: Australia: 63; Yth
Tony won just about every award going at the Cardiff City 'Player of the Year' dinner last season. He was voted top man by sponsors Redrow Homes, Cardiff City Supporters Club and Cardiff Valley RAMS. A very skilful and versatile defender who operated at left back and in the centre of the defence, Tony was a major success for the Bluebirds last term.
Glasgow R (Free from NAC Breda, Holland, ex Ekeren, Adelaide C, on 30/6/1997) SL 89+18/7 SLC 6+2 SC 15/2 Others 23+6/2
Middlesbrough (Free on 5/9/2002) PL 9+3 FLC 2 FAC 1
Cardiff C (Free on 22/7/2003) FL 45/1 FLC 2 FAC 1

Hugo Viana

VIDUKA Mark Anthony

Born: Australia, 9 October 1975
Height: 6'2" **Weight:** 13.9
Club Honours: SLC '00
International Honours: Australia: 23; U23; Yth

Mark started the 2003-04 season with a goal in the opening game for Leeds against Newcastle. He then suffered a barren spell and was dropped after falling out of favour, only to be given a reprieve by new boss Eddie Gray. He featured as the sole striker in a 4-5-1 formation and then in a two-man attack alongside Alan Smith. Mark looked to have regained his form and began scoring regularly, showing sublime skills for a big man, but nevertheless he was unable to save the club from relegation.

Glasgow Celtic (Signed from NK Croatia Zagreb, Croatia, ex Melbourne Knights, on 2/12/1998) SL 36+1/30 SLC 4/1 SC 3/3 Others 4/1
Leeds U (£6,000,000 on 25/7/2000) PL 126+4/59 FLC 3/1 FAC 8/5 Others 25/7

VIEIRA Magno Silva

Born: Brazil, 13 February 1985
Height: 5'9" **Weight:** 11.0
This young Wigan Athletic striker joined Northampton Town on loan early in the new year to gain experience of senior football. Although he looked a little lightweight for Third Division football, he showed good ball control and clever skills. He scored two opportunist goals for the Cobblers before returning to the JJB Stadium to continue his development.

Wigan Ath (From juniors on 15/8/2003)
Northampton T (Loaned on 16/1/2004) FL 7+3/2

VIEIRA Patrick

Born: Dakar, Senegal, 23 June 1976
Height: 6'4" **Weight:** 13.0
Club Honours: PL '98, '02, '04; FAC '98, 02; CS '98, '99, '02
International Honours: France: 72 (WC '98, UEFA '00)
An inspirational captain who leads by example, Patrick was injured for almost two months early on last season, yet Arsenal recorded some fine results without him, beating Newcastle, Liverpool and Chelsea among others. He contributed vital goals, at Chelsea, Spurs and, fittingly, in Arsenal's last game of their record-breaking campaign against Leicester. Patrick has blossomed under the managerial reins of Arsene Wenger and having held aloft consecutive FA Cups as vice-captain, he lifted the Premiership

Trophy proudly on his own on 15 May. Patrick was a member of the France Euro 2004 squad and was named in the Premiership team of the season for the sixth season running, a feat no other player has previously achieved.

Arsenal (£3,500,000 from AC Milan, Italy, ex Cannes, on 14/8/1996) PL 240+7/22 FLC 7 FAC 40+2/2 Others 65+1/2

VINCENT Jamie Roy

Born: Wimbledon, 18 June 1975
Height: 5'10" **Weight:** 11.8
Out of the first-team picture at Portsmouth, Jamie made an immediate impact when loaned to Walsall in October. Only one goal was conceded in his first three games, as he proved himself defensively strong on the left flank and he always looked comfortable in possession. His readiness to join in attacks was popular with fans, who were sorry when his loan spell ended in December. He later joined Derby on a permanent basis and made an ideal start 13 minutes into his debut against Gillingham by curving in a precise free kick. Naturally suited to the left and able to use the ball well from the back, Jamie settled quickly until a hamstring injury at Wigan put him out for nine matches, although he returned before the end of the season.

Crystal Palace (From trainee on 13/7/1993) FL 19+6 FLC 2+1/1 FAC 1
Bournemouth (Loaned on 18/11/1994) FL 8
Bournemouth (£25,000 + on 30/8/1996) FL 102+3/5 FLC 7+1 FAC 8 Others 9/1
Huddersfield T (£440,000 + on 25/3/1999) FL 54+5/2 FLC 3+2 FAC 2
Portsmouth (£800,000 on 23/2/2001) FL 43+5/1 FLC 1
Walsall (Loaned on 17/10/2003) FL 12 FAC 0+1
Derby Co (Free on 16/1/2004) FL 7/1

VINE Rowan Lewis

Born: Basingstoke, 21 September 1982
Height: 6'1" **Weight:** 12.2
This promising young Portsmouth striker once again spent the whole of the season out on loan in 2003-04. Rowan ensured that his name will be recorded in Colchester United history books after plundering a breathtaking hat-trick to dump Coventry City out of the FA Cup. He was transformed into a left winger by U's manager Phil Parkinson and scored several vital goals while showing some powerful running and the ability to cut in from the left. Rowan returned to Fratton Park in the summer.

Portsmouth (From trainee on 27/4/2001) FL 3+10

Brentford (Loaned on 7/8/2002) FL 37+5/10 FLC 1+1/1 FAC 3/2 Others 3
Colchester U (Loaned on 7/8/2003) FL 30+5/6 FLC 1 FAC 5+2/4 Others 4+2/2

VINNICOMBE Christopher (Chris)

Born: Exeter, 20 October 1970
Height: 5'9" **Weight:** 10.12
Club Honours: SPD '91
International Honours: E: U21-12
Wycombe's left back continued to be a first choice throughout the 2003-04 season, apart from the occasional period of suspension or injury. A tough tackler who likes to get forward whenever possible, by his own high standards Chris was probably not as consistent as in previous seasons. He was one of many seasoned professionals released by the club at the end of the campaign following relegation.

Exeter C (From trainee on 1/7/1989) FL 35+4/1 FLC 5/1 Others 2
Glasgow R (£150,000 on 3/11/1989) SL 14+9/1 SLC 1+2 Others 1
Burnley (£200,000 on 30/6/1994) FL 90+5/3 FLC 9 FAC 2 Others 7+1/1
Wycombe W (Free on 6/8/1998) FL 217+4/2 FLC 14 FAC 20 Others 8

VIRGO Adam John

Born: Brighton, 25 January 1983
Height: 6'2" **Weight:** 13.7
Although he prefers playing as a central defender, Adam took his chance of a first-team place at Brighton and claimed the right-back berth under new manager Mark McGhee. A good tackler, he is also renowned for the length of his passing, and is capable of hitting 50-yard balls diagonally across the pitch. He scored his first senior goal at Stockport in February to secure a vital point, but the highlight of his season was the flying header at the end of extra time against Swindon to force the play-off semi-final to a penalty shoot-out. Adam then bravely took the fourth Albion spot kick and scored, putting the Seagulls well on the way to the Millennium Stadium.

Brighton & Hove A (From juniors on 4/7/2000) FL 29+8/1 FLC 1 Others 4+2/1
Exeter C (Loaned on 29/11/2002) FL 8+1

VIVEASH Adrian Lee

Born: Swindon, 30 September 1969
Height: 6'2" **Weight:** 12.13
This experienced left-footed defender began the 2003-04 season as a regular in the Swindon Town line-up as a member of a three-man back line. However, he lost his place in October and was then

Adrian Viveash

sidelined by a knee injury. On returning to fitness he had a successful loan period at Kidderminster where he formed a fine central defensive partnership with Wayne Hatswell. On his return to the County Ground he made the odd appearance on the substitutes' bench, but failed to win his place back in the team.

Swindon T *(From trainee on 14/7/1988) FL 51+3/2 FLC 6+1 FAC 0+1 Others 2*
Reading *(Loaned on 4/1/1993) FL 5 Others 1/1*
Reading *(Loaned on 20/1/1995) FL 6*
Barnsley *(Loaned on 10/8/1995) FL 2/1*
Walsall *(Free on 16/10/1995) FL 200+2/13 FLC 12 FAC 15/2 Others 13/1*
Reading *(Free on 6/7/2000) FL 62+1/3 FLC 3+1 FAC 5 Others 7*
Oxford U *(Loaned on 6/9/2002) FL 11 FLC 3 Others 1*
Swindon T *(Free on 14/7/2003) FL 14+1 FLC 1 Others 1*
Kidderminster Hrs *(Loaned on 2/3/2004) FL 7*

VOLMER Joost Gerard Bernard
Born: Enschede, Holland, 7 March 1974
Height: 6'2" **Weight:** 13.5
After being recommended to the club by former Baggies' player Romeo Zondervan, Joost made his debut for West Bromwich Albion on the opening day of the season in the 4-1 defeat at Walsall. A solid performer, strong in the air and on the ground, he deputised initially for Darren Moore and also for Phil Gilchrist.
West Bromwich A *(Free from AZ Alkmaar, Holland, ex Twente Enschede, V V Venlo, Maastricht V V, Fortuna Sittard, on 7/8/2003) FL 10+5 FLC 2+1*

VOLZ Moritz
Born: Siegen, Germany, 21 January 1983
Height: 5'11" **Weight:** 12.10
Club Honours: FAYC '00, '01
International Honours: Germany: U21-4; Yth
One of the success stories of Fulham's season, Moritz initially arrived on loan from Arsenal before signing permanently in January. He went on to make the right-back spot his own. An effective defender he is crisp in the tackle, and an excellent passer of the ball. A player who likes to join the attack and who often makes surging runs into the opposing box, he was unlucky not to get on the score sheet on several occasions.
Arsenal *(Free from Schalke 04, Germany on 25/1/2000) FLC 1+1*
Wimbledon *(Loaned on 3/2/2003) FL 10/1*
Fulham *(£2,200,000 on 8/8/2003) PL 32+1 FAC 5*

W

WAINWRIGHT Neil
Born: Warrington, 4 November 1977
Height: 6'0" **Weight:** 11.5
Neil began last term playing in a much deeper role for Darlington, but following a change in management he reverted to his more familiar position on the right wing. A player who is at his best when running at defenders with the ball, he has the ability to cut in effectively towards goal. Neil finished the campaign as the Quakers' second-top scorer with seven goals to his credit.
Wrexham (From trainee on 3/7/1996) FL 7+4/3 FAC 1 Others 1
Sunderland (£100,000 + on 9/7/1998) FL 0+2 FLC 5+1
Darlington (Loaned on 4/2/2000) FL 16+1/4
Halifax T (Loaned on 13/10/2000) FL 13 FAC 1 Others 2
Darlington (£50,000 on 17/8/2001) FL 83+20/12 FLC 0+1 FAC 6+2/2 Others 2

WAKE Brian Christopher
Born: Stockton, 13 August 1982
Height: 6'0" **Weight:** 11.2
This young striker was mostly restricted to appearances from the substitutes' bench for Carlisle last term and his only goals came in the LDV Vans Trophy ties. He subsequently moved on to join Scottish Third Division side Gretna for whom he ended the season in goal-scoring form, netting four times in the closing stages of the campaign including a double in the 4-1 win at Montrose.
Carlisle U (Signed from Tow Law T on 10/5/2002) FL 12+31/9 FLC 2 FAC 1+1 Others 1+4/2

WALES Gary
Born: East Calder, 4 January 1979
Height: 5'10" **Weight:** 11.2
International Honours: S: U21-1
This pacy young striker found it difficult to break into the Hearts first team last season and his only senior action came as a late substitute against Dunfermline in December. In January he joined Walsall on loan where he impressed with his readiness to run at defenders and powerful shooting. Although he scored in the 3-3 draw at Nottingham Forest, he later chose to sign for Gillingham. Although he picked up an injury during his time at Priestfield, he was in good form against Coventry, when he bagged his first goal for the Gills.
Hamilton Academical (Signed from Links U

on 17/10/1997) SL 28+5/11 SLC 2 SC 2/1
Heart of Midlothian (£50,000 on 28/7/1999) SL 52+37/17 SLC 4+2 SC 5+2/2
Walsall (Loaned on 30/1/2004) FL 5+2/1
Gillingham (Free on 25/3/2004) FL 3+3/1

WALKER Desmond (Des) Sinclair
Born: Hackney, 26 November 1965
Height: 5'11" **Weight:** 11.13
Club Honours: FLC '89, '90; FMC '89, '92
International Honours: E: 59; U21-7
This veteran defender was no longer a regular in the Nottingham Forest line-up last season, but when chosen he never let the side down. He suffered a couple of niggling hamstring injuries but continued to show great determination to regain his place and when selected he always led the side as captain. Des was out of contract in the summer and was offered a coaching job with Forest's youngsters.
Nottingham F (From apprentice on 2/12/1983) FL 259+5/1 FLC 40 FAC 28 Others 14 (£1,500,000 to Sampodoria on 1/8/92)
Sheffield Wed (£2,700,000 on 22/7/1993) P/FL 307 FLC 28 FAC 24 Others 3 (Freed during 2001 close season)
Nottingham F (Free, via a spell at Burton A, on 9/7/2002) FL 52+4 FLC 1 FAC 2 Others 2

WALKER Ian Michael
Born: Watford, 31 October 1971
Height: 6'2" **Weight:** 13.1
Club Honours: FAYC '90; FLC '99
International Honours: E: 4; B-1; U21-9; Yth
This experienced goalkeeper had something of an up-and-down season with Leicester City last term. Ian started in fine fettle and later ended the campaign in the same manner, but in between he sometimes struggled to find his best form. He was a regular choice in the England squad for most of the season and won a place in the Euro 2004 squad during the summer.
Tottenham H (From trainee on 4/12/1989) F/PL 257+2 FLC 22+1 FAC 25 Others 6
Oxford U (Loaned on 31/8/1990) FL 2 FLC 1
Leicester C (£2,500,000 on 26/7/2001) P/FL 118 FLC 6 FAC 6

WALKER James Barry
Born: Sutton in Ashfield, 9 July 1973
Height: 5'11" **Weight:** 13.5
James kicked off the 2003-04 season with a pre-season testimonial game against Birmingham City. He went on to enjoy another great campaign for Walsall when he was a near ever-present and produced many outstanding displays. However, in

the close season it was reported that he had been transferred to West Ham.
Notts Co (From trainee on 9/7/1991)
Walsall (Free on 4/8/1993) FL 401+2 FLC 24+1 FAC 30 Others 19

WALKER Justin Matthew
Born: Nottingham, 6 September 1975
Height: 5'11" **Weight:** 12.12
International Honours: E: Yth; Sch
This hard-working midfield player made an immediate impact for Cambridge in the early part of the 2003-04 season. However, he fell out of favour in November and spent two months on loan at York, where he battled hard but was unable to help the team out of relegation trouble. Justin returned to the Abbey Stadium following a change in management and helped set up a goal against Cheltenham in his first match back.
Nottingham F (From juniors on 10/9/1992)
Scunthorpe U (Signed on 26/3/1997) FL 126+6/2 FLC 8 FAC 6 Others 7/1
Lincoln C (Free on 12/7/2000) FL 68+8/4 FLC 1+2 FAC 3+1 Others 6/1
Exeter C (Free on 6/8/2002) FL 35+4/5 FLC 1 FAC 3+1/1 Others 1
Cambridge U (Free on 9/6/2003) FL 23/1 FLC 1/1 Others 1
York C (Loaned on 6/1/2004) FL 7+2

WALKER Richard Martin
Born: Birmingham, 8 November 1977
Height: 6'0" **Weight:** 12.0
Club Honours: AMC '02
This pacy striker struggled to make an impact at Blackpool last term and spent time on loan at Northampton in the autumn, impressing with some strong running. Later in the season he had a loan spell at Oxford, but a change in management during his stay meant that he featured less often than he would have liked before returning to Bloomfield Road.
Aston Villa (From trainee on 13/12/1995) PL 2+4/2 FLC 1+1 FAC 0+1 Others 1
Cambridge U (Loaned on 31/12/1998) FL 7+14/3 Others 1+2/1
Blackpool (Loaned on 9/2/2001) FL 6+12/3
Wycombe W (Loaned on 13/9/2001) FL 10+2/3 FAC 1/1
Blackpool (£50,000 + on 21/12/2001) FL 38+24/12 FLC 0+1 FAC 1+2 Others 3+1/3
Northampton T (Loaned on 21/10/2003) FL 11+1/4 FAC 4/2 Others 3/2
Oxford U (Free on 17/3/2004) FL 3+1

WALKER Richard Stuart
Born: Stafford, 17 September 1980
Height: 6'2" **Weight:** 13.0

This solid central defender made a number of appearances for Crewe last season, although he has yet to establish himself as a regular in the side. Richard is a hard-working youngster and contributed one goal during the campaign, netting in the 2-0 win at Rotherham in September.

Crewe Alex *(From trainee on 6/7/1999) FL 50+9/3 FLC 3 FAC 1+1 Others 4*

Justin Walker

WALKER Robert (Rob) Stephen

Born: Bolton, 20 September 1985
Height: 5'9" **Weight:** 11.0
Rob burst onto the first-team scene at Oldham with some outstanding displays in the club's 2003 pre-season tour of Northern Ireland. The teenaged left back made his senior debut on the opening day of the new campaign against Brighton at Boundary Park and performed admirably. A solid defender, Rob likes to push forward down the flank and possesses a useful left foot. A member of the Latics' side that won the Lancashire FA Youth Cup final at Burnley in May, he will be looking for more first-team involvement again in 2004-05.
Oldham Ath *(Trainee) FL 1*

WALKER Scott Edward

Born: Glasgow, 5 March 1975
Height: 6'1" **Weight:** 13.9
Club Honours: S Div 1 '00
This experienced left-sided central defender had spells with St Mirren and Alloa in the early part of the 2003-04 campaign before joining Hartlepool on a short-term contract. He received a few chances as cover for injuries, but struggled to adjust to Second Division football, and could not force his way into the side. He was released in the summer.
East Stirling *(Signed from Kilwinning Rgrs on 19/12/1997) SL 47/6 SLC 1 SC 2/2*
St Mirren *(Signed on 19/5/1999) SL 97/9 SLC 6/2 SC 4 Others 1*
Dunfermline *(Signed on 17/6/2002) SL 12+8/2 SLC 0+2 SC 0+2*
St Mirren *(Free on 13/9/2003) SL 1*
Alloa Ath *(Free on 19/9/2003) SL 10 SC 2/1*
Hartlepool U *(Free on 16/1/2004) FL 5+1*

WALLACE Rodney (Rod) Seymour

Born: Greenwich, 2 October 1969
Height: 5'7" **Weight:** 11.6
Club Honours: Div 1 '92; CS '92; SPD '99, '00; SC '99, '00; SLC '98
International Honours: E: B-2; U21-11
This vastly experienced striker struggled to make an impact at Gillingham last term and his only goal came in the 4-3 win at Ipswich in November. Rod battled against injuries and loss of form, rarely featuring in the second half of the campaign. He was released by the club in the summer.
Southampton *(From trainee on 19/4/1988) FL 111+17/45 FLC 18+1/6 FAC 10/3 Others 3+1/2*
Leeds U *(£1,600,000 on 7/6/1991) F/PL 187+25/53 FLC 18+1/8 FAC 16+5/4 Others 1+4/1*
Glasgow R *(Free on 17/7/1998) SL 73+4/39 SLC 6/4 SC 10+1/4 Others 24+2/7*
Bolton W *(Free on 17/9/2001) PL 14+5/3 FLC 1+2/1 FAC 1*
Gillingham *(Free on 8/8/2002) FL 27+9/12 FLC 2 FAC 1+1*

WALLWORK Ronald (Ronnie)

Born: Manchester, 10 September 1977
Height: 5'10" **Weight:** 12.9

Club Honours: FAYC '95; PL '01
International Honours: E: Yth
A versatile performer, who prefers a midfield role, Ronnie failed to gain a regular place in Albion's first team and after just seven outings (two as a substitute) he was loaned out to Bradford City where he made an immediate impact on the right-hand side of midfield. He scored on his debut against Crystal Palace and this began something of a goals spree for the former Manchester United trainee who netted three more in the next six games, including two in a 2-1 win at Rotherham after renewing his loan into a second month. Unfortunately he broke a bone in his foot towards the end of that game and had to return to the Hawthorns six weeks ahead of schedule.
Manchester U *(From trainee on 17/3/1995)* PL 4+15 FLC 4+1 FAC 1+1 Others 1+1
Carlisle U *(Loaned on 22/12/1997)* FL 10/1 Others 2
Stockport Co *(Loaned on 18/3/1998)* FL 7
West Bromwich A *(Free on 2/7/2002)* P/FL 27+5 FLC 2+1 FAC 2
Bradford C *(Loaned on 22/1/2004)* FL 7/4

WALSH Gary

Born: Wigan, 21 March 1968
Height: 6'3" **Weight:** 15.10
Club Honours: ECWC '91; ESC '91; FAC '94
International Honours: E: U21-2
Paul Jewell's only close-season signing saw this experienced goalkeeper join his hometown club. A tall and commanding figure, Gary would be content to sit on the bench for Wigan for most of the campaign with regular 'keeper John Filan in such fine form. His only League start came at home to Wimbledon although he managed appearances in the Carling Cup ties against Hull and Middlesbrough. Out of contract in the summer, his future had yet to be decided at the time of writing.
Manchester U *(From juniors on 25/4/1985)* F/PL 49+1 FLC 7 Others 6
Airdrie *(Loaned on 11/8/1988)* SL 3 SLC 1
Oldham Ath *(Loaned on 19/11/1993)* PL 6
Middlesbrough *(£500,000 on 11/8/1995)* PL 44 FLC 9 FAC 4
Bradford C *(£500,000 + on 26/9/1997)* P/FL 131+1 FLC 7 FAC 4 Others 1
Middlesbrough *(Loaned on 15/9/2000)* PL 3
Wigan Ath *(Free on 14/7/2003)* FL 1+2 FLC 2

WALSH Michael Shane

Born: Rotherham, 5 August 1977
Height: 6'0" **Weight:** 13.2
Club Honours: AMC '01

This talented Port Vale defender was once again affected by injury last term. Michael began the season in the line-up, but lasted only five games before renewing acquaintances with the treatment room. When fit he is the club's best defender and this was demonstrated when he returned at Bristol City to help Vale to a 1-0 victory, soon after to be followed by a 2-0 win over fellow promotion-chasers Queens Park Rangers. Unfortunately a long-standing back problem reared its head again and Michael was forced to spend another four months on the sidelines, then when he returned a further injury brought his campaign to a close.
Scunthorpe U *(From trainee on 3/7/1995)* FL 94+9/1 FLC 4 FAC 9 Others 5
Port Vale *(£100,000 on 30/7/1998)* FL 122+6/4 FLC 6+1 FAC 2 Others 7

WALTERS Jonathan (Jon) Ronald

Born: Birkenhead, 20 September 1983
Height: 6'1" **Weight:** 12.0
International Honours: RoI: U21-1; Yth
Jon began last season on loan at Crewe, but did not feature at first-team level and in November he went out on loan again to Barnsley where he led the forward line well, but sustained a knee injury that led to his return to the Reebok Stadium. Once he had recovered fitness Jon made a permanent move to Hull, scoring in his first game and generally being used as a substitute, coming off the bench to partner his former Blackburn colleague Ben Burgess.
Blackburn Rov *(From trainee on 3/8/2001)*
Bolton W *(Signed on 30/4/2002)* PL 0+4 FLC 1 FAC 0+1
Hull C *(Loaned on 24/2/2003)* FL 11/5
Barnsley *(Loaned on 12/11/2003)* FL 7+1 FAC 3 Others 0+1
Hull C *(£50,000 on 5/2/2004)* FL 5+11/1

WALTON David (Dave) Lee

Born: Bedlington, 10 April 1973
Height: 6'2" **Weight:** 14.8
Club Honours: Div 3 '94
What seemed a good move for Dave turned into an injury nightmare. George Burley saw him as the pillar of Derby's defence but, after playing through the pre-season games, Dave needed a cartilage operation. Once recovered from that, a series of strains hampered his progress and he became a background figure. Only during a loan with Stockport did Dave play regularly, forming an impressive partnership with Danny Griffin in the heart of the County defence.

However, after being recalled, he suffered another thigh strain playing for Derby's reserves.
Sheffield U *(Free from Ashington on 13/3/1992)*
Shrewsbury T *(Signed on 5/11/1993)* FL 127+1/10 FLC 7 FAC 10/1 Others 11/1
Crewe Alex *(£500,000 + on 20/10/1997)* FL 146+9/3 FLC 8+1/1 FAC 7
Derby Co *(Free on 3/7/2003)* FL 3+2
Stockport Co *(Loaned on 6/2/2004)* FL 7

WANCHOPE Watson **Pablo (Paulo)** Cesar

Born: Costa Rica, 31 July 1976
Height: 6'4" **Weight:** 12.6
Club Honours: Div 1 '02
International Honours: Costa Rica
An awkward gangling striker, Paulo is one of the most unpredictable strikers in the Premiership, providing Manchester City with a welcome alternative in their attacking options. The experienced Costa Rican international has had his injury problems but they seemed to be behind him last term and he featured prominently in the Blues' battle against relegation, scoring four vital goals in the last three games of the season.
Derby Co *(£600,000 from CS Heridiano, Costa Rica on 27/3/1997)* PL 65+7/23 FLC 6+1/5 FAC 4
West Ham U *(£3,250,000 on 28/7/1999)* PL 33+2/12 FLC 3 FAC 4/1
Manchester C *(£3,650,000 on 16/8/2000)* P/FL 51+13/27 FLC 4/1 FAC 3/1 Others 1+3

WANLESS Paul Steven

Born: Banbury, 14 December 1973
Height: 6'1" **Weight:** 13.12
Paul returned to his former club Oxford United in the summer of 2003 and was seen by many fans as providing the final piece in the jigsaw to build a promotion-winning squad. A hard-working, driving force in the U's midfield he weighed in with five goals, most of them towering headers. Paul was rarely absent during the campaign, but proved unable to lead the club to the promotion they sought.
Oxford U *(From trainee on 3/12/1991)* FL 12+20 FLC 0+3/1 Others 2+2
Lincoln C *(Free on 7/7/1995)* FL 7+1 Others 2
Cambridge U *(Free on 8/3/1996)* FL 264+20/44 FLC 13 FAC 19+2/2 Others 16/3
Oxford U *(Free on 7/8/2003)* FL 38/5 FLC 1 FAC 1

WAPENAAR Harald Paul

Born: Vlaardingen, Holland, 10 April 1970
Height: 6'1" **Weight:** 13.7

Paulo Wanchope

This experienced goalkeeper was understudy to Shaka Hislop at Portsmouth last term and made a handful of first-team appearances when his rival was sidelined by injury. Harald showed himself to be a capable 'keeper, and made a number of excellent point-blank saves.

Portsmouth (Free from FC Utrecht, Holland, ex Roosendal BC, Helmond Sport, on 11/7/2003) PL 5 FLC 2 FAC 1

WARD Ashley Stuart
Born: Manchester, 24 November 1970
Height: 6'2" **Weight:** 13.10
Ashley joined Sheffield United during the 2003 close season and was employed up front as a target man where he used his height, experience and strength to win, hold and distribute the ball. Even when played as a lone striker he caused problems for defenders. He missed several games through injuries and his season was brought to an early end with a medial ligament problem suffered in the FA Cup tie at Sunderland.

Manchester C (From trainee on 5/8/1989) FL 0+1 FAC 0+2
Wrexham (Loaned on 10/1/1991) FL 4/2 Others 1
Leicester C (£80,000 on 30/7/1991) FL 2+8 FLC 2+1 FAC 0+1 Others 0+1
Blackpool (Loaned on 21/11/1992) FL 2/1
Crewe Alex (£80,000 on 1/12/1992) FL 58+3/25 FLC 4/2 FAC 2/4 Others 7/6
Norwich C (£500,000 on 8/12/1994) P/FL 53/18 FLC 6/3 FAC 1
Derby Co (£1,000,000 on 19/3/1996) F/PL 32+8/9 FLC 1/4 FAC 2/1
Barnsley (£1,300,000 + on 5/9/1997) P/FL 45+1/20 FLC 9/4 FAC 6/1
Blackburn Rov (£4,250,000 + on 31/12/1998) P/FL 52+2/13 FLC 2 FAC 4+1
Bradford C (£1,500,000 on 18/8/2000) P/FL 75+9/17 FLC 4+1/3 FAC 1
Sheffield U (Free on 7/8/2003) FL 20+3/4 FLC 1 FAC 2

WARD Darren
Born: Worksop, 11 May 1974
Height: 6'2" **Weight:** 14.2
Club Honours: Div 3 '98
International Honours: W: 5; B-1; U21-2
Darren was an ever-present for Nottingham Forest last term until suffering a back injury against Gillingham in March, this required surgery and ruled him out for the rest of the season. A great shot-stopper, he was capped by Wales as a substitute against Scotland during the campaign.

Mansfield T (From trainee on 27/7/1992) FL 81 FLC 5 FAC 5 Others 6

Notts Co (£160,000 on 11/7/1995) FL 251 FLC 18 FAC 23 Others 10
Nottingham F (Free on 21/5/2001) FL 123 FLC 8 FAC 4 Others 2

WARD Darren Philip
Born: Harrow, 13 September 1978
Height: 6'0" **Weight:** 12.6
Darren had an excellent season for Millwall last term when he was the club's only ever-present. A consistent central defender, he was in outstanding form and established a great understanding with Matt Lawrence in the heart of the defence. Tall and strong, he has a commanding presence and reads the game well.

Watford (From trainee on 13/2/1997) P/FL 56+3/2 FLC 6/1 FAC 2 Others 0+1
Queens Park R (Loaned on 17/12/1999) FL 14 FAC 1
Millwall (£500,000 on 3/10/2001) FL 92+7/4 FLC 2 FAC 12 Others 2

WARD Gavin John
Born: Sutton Coldfield, 30 June 1970
Height: 6'3" **Weight:** 14.12
Club Honours: Div 3 '93; WC '93; AMC '00
Gavin joined Coventry last summer, but suffered a slipped disc in his back a week before the 2003-04 season started. He finally got his first-team chance at the end of November and enjoyed a decent run of consecutive games. His handling and shot-stopping were excellent and he was one of the best kickers the club have had for some time. Gavin conceded only 18 goals in 15 games, but was dropped following the FA Cup defeat by Colchester and failed to win his place back. He later had a brief spell on loan at Barnsley to cover for an injury-crisis and was released by Coventry in the summer.

Shrewsbury T (From trainee at Aston Villa on 26/9/1988)
West Bromwich A (Free on 18/9/1989) FLC 1
Cardiff C (Free on 5/10/1989) FL 58+1 FAC 1 Others 7
Leicester C (£175,000 on 16/7/1993) F/PL 38 FLC 3 FAC 0+1 Others 4
Bradford C (£175,000 on 13/7/1995) FL 36 FLC 6 FAC 3 Others 2
Bolton W (£300,000 on 29/3/1996) F/PL 19+3 FLC 2 FAC 4
Burnley (Loaned on 14/8/1998) FL 17
Stoke C (Free on 25/2/1999) FL 79 FLC 7 FAC 2 Others 12
Walsall (Free on 9/8/2002) FL 5+2
Coventry C (Free on 4/8/2003) FL 12 FAC 3
Barnsley (Loaned on 29/4/2004) FL 1

WARD Graham William
Born: Dublin, 25 February 1983
Height: 5'8" **Weight:** 11.12
International Honours: RoI: U21-3; Yth
When called upon by Kidderminster last term Graham showed himself to be a talented midfielder with good passing skills and surprisingly effective in the air, despite being relatively small in height. Graham became the first Kidderminster player to appear for his country at a senior level when he was called up to represent the Republic of Ireland at U21 level last August. He also featured in the World Youth Championships held in Dubai in December. However, he was one of several players released by Harriers in the summer.

Wolverhampton W (From trainee on 17/7/2000)
Kidderminster Hrs (Free on 8/8/2003) FL 17+4 FLC 1 FAC 2 Others 1

WARD Mitchum (Mitch) David
Born: Sheffield, 19 June 1971
Height: 5'8" **Weight:** 11.7
This experienced midfielder was an influential figure for York City in the first half of the 2003-04 campaign with his control and passing ability. Unfortunately he sustained an injury playing against his former club Barnsley in the FA Cup and upon his return never really recovered his form. Mitch was one of a number of senior players released by the Minstermen in the summer.

Sheffield U (From trainee on 1/7/1989) F/PL 135+19/11 FLC 8+3/2 FAC 7+2/2 Others 5+1/1
Crewe Alex (Loaned on 1/11/1990) FL 4/1 FAC 1/1 Others 2
Everton (£850,000 on 25/11/1997) PL 18+6 FLC 2+1 FAC 2
Barnsley (£20,000 on 14/7/2000) FL 68+9 FLC 5+1 FAC 2
York C (Free on 1/8/2003) FL 27+4 FLC 1 FAC 1

WARHURST Paul
Born: Stockport,, 26 September 1969
Height: 6'1" **Weight:** 13.6
Club Honours: PL '95
International Honours: E: U21-8
After being released by Bolton at the end of the previous season, Paul was unable to find a new club and re-joined Wanderers on a short-term contract in September. He made no first-team appearances and then had a brief spell at Chesterfield, scoring a fine goal in the LDV Vans Trophy tie against Lincoln. Paul was subsequently attached to a number

of clubs on trial or on short-term contracts and featured in turn for Barnsley, Carlisle and Grimsby during the campaign. A versatile player, most of his appearances came in defence or midfield, although he also featured as an emergency striker for the Mariners.

Manchester C *(From trainee on 1/7/1988)*
Oldham Ath *(£10,000 on 27/10/1988) FL 60+7/2 FLC 8 FAC 5+4 Others 2*
Sheffield Wed *(£750,000 on 17/7/1991) F/PL 60+6/6 FLC 9/4 FAC 7+1/5 Others 5/3*
Blackburn Rov *(£2,700,000 on 17/8/1993) PL 30+27/4 FLC 6+2 FAC 2+1 Others 4+2*
Crystal Palace *(£1,250,000 on 31/7/1997) P/FL 27/4 FLC 2 FAC 1*
Bolton W *(£800,000 on 25/11/1998) P/FL 81+10 FLC 3+3 FAC 3+2 Others 2+2*
Stoke C *(Loaned on 27/3/2003) FL 4+1/1*
Chesterfield *(Free on 16/10/2003) FL 3+1 FAC 1 Others 1/1*
Barnsley *(Free on 12/12/2003) FL 3+1*
Carlisle U *(Free on 20/2/2004) FL 0+1*
Grimsby T *(Free on 12/3/2004) FL 5+2*

WARNE Paul

Born: Norwich, 8 May 1973
Height: 5'9" **Weight:** 11.2
Despite the fact that Paul was originally signed by Rotherham as a striker, he rarely got the opportunity to play in that position last term and had to be content with appearances in wide positions both on the right and left. However, he tackled those demands with great enthusiasm and always gave his best with some willing running. If there was one aspect of his play with which he would be disappointed it was the fact that he failed to get on the score sheet but he made up for that with his hard work on behalf of the team.

Wigan Ath *(£25,000 from Wroxham on 30/7/1997) FL 11+25/3 FLC 0+1 FAC 1 Others 1+2/1*
Rotherham U *(Free on 15/1/1999) FL 160+46/27 FLC 5+6/1 FAC 10/1 Others 5*

WARNER Anthony (Tony) Randolph

Born: Liverpool, 11 May 1974
Height: 6'4" **Weight:** 13.9
Club Honours: Div 2 '01
Tony was once again in outstanding form for Millwall last term being an ever-present in the team until he was sidelined by a neck injury in January and this kept him out of action until the end of the season. Tall and commanding, he confirmed his reputation as one of the best goalkeepers outside of the Premiership.

Liverpool *(From juniors on 1/1/1994)*

Swindon T *(Loaned on 5/11/1997) FL 2*
Glasgow Celtic *(Loaned on 13/11/1998) SL 3*
Aberdeen *(Loaned on 31/3/1999) SL 6*
Millwall *(Free on 16/7/1999) FL 200 FLC 10 FAC 10 Others 5*

WARNER Scott John

Born: Rochdale, 3 December 1983
Height: 5'11" **Weight:** 11.11
Scott found himself out of favour at Rochdale in the early part of last term, but was reinstated to the side for Steve Parkin's second game back in charge. The Dale youngster then made the most of the situation and showed good progress during the remainder of the season. Scott's hard work and non-stop covering in the centre of the park were particularly effective when Dale played with a midfield five, and his first-ever senior goal earned a vital point in the relegation battle against Scunthorpe.

Rochdale *(From trainee on 29/7/2003) FL 16+5/1 FAC 2*

WARNOCK Stephen

Born: Ormskirk, 12 December 1981
Height: 5'7" **Weight:** 12.1
International Honours: E: Yth; Sch
On a season-long loan from Liverpool, Stephen had an outstanding season for Coventry last term. He started out at left back and rarely let the side down, then impressed even more as a left-sided or central-midfield player with some gutsy tackling, good ball control and shrewd passing. His tireless running pleased City's fans and he was often a goal threat with his accurate shooting. Stephen's overall consistency deservedly won him several 'Player of the Year' awards.

Liverpool *(From trainee on 27/4/1999)*
Bradford C *(Loaned on 13/9/2002) FL 12/1*
Coventry C *(Loaned on 31/7/2003) FL 42+2/3 FLC 2 FAC 2+1*

WARREN Mark Wayne

Born: Clapton, 12 November 1974
Height: 6'0" **Weight:** 12.2
International Honours: E: Yth
This veteran campaigner added some much-needed experience to a youthful Southend squad last term. He was often a colossus in the defence and forged a great partnership with Leon Cort. Mark's wholehearted style was often at the expense of self-preservation and he sustained a collection of niggling injuries throughout the campaign. Also something of a free-kick specialist, few

present at Aggborough will forget his 30-yard thunderbolt against Kidderminster Harriers.

Leyton Orient *(From trainee on 6/7/1992) FL 134+18/5 FLC 8+1/2 FAC 5+1 Others 10+4/1*
Oxford U *(Loaned on 24/12/1998) FL 4*
Notts Co *(Signed on 28/1/1999) FL 76+8/1 FLC 9 FAC 1 Others 4*
Colchester U *(Free on 9/8/2002) FL 20 FAC 1*
Southend U *(Free on 11/6/2003) FL 27+5/2 FLC 1 FAC 2 Others 4*

WARRINGTON Andrew (Andy) Clifford

Born: Sheffield, 10 June 1976
Height: 6'3" **Weight:** 12.13
Club Honours: Div 3 '04
Andy enjoyed another consistent season in goal for Doncaster Rovers in 2003-04 and he equalled a club record by keeping 19 clean sheets in Third Division games. A very reliable last line of defence, he produced some fine saves when called upon and was one of the best 'keepers in the division.

York C *(From trainee on 11/6/1994) FL 61 FLC 7 FAC 4 Others 4*
Doncaster Rov *(Free on 8/6/1999) FL 46 FLC 2 FAC 1*

WATERMAN David (Dave) Graham

Born: Guernsey, 16 May 1977
Height: 5'10" **Weight:** 13.2
International Honours: NI: U21-14
Dave benefited from the appointment of his former Pompey club manager Graham Rix as manager of Oxford towards the end of last season and from then on featured regularly in the line-up. He let no one down when selected, appearing mainly at right back and right wing back and producing some committed displays.

Portsmouth *(From trainee on 4/7/1995) FL 60+20 FLC 4+1 FAC 3*
Oxford U *(Free on 28/3/2002) FL 37+10/1 FAC 4 Others 2/1*

WATSON Benjamin (Ben)

Born: Lambeth, 9 July 1985
Height: 5'10" **Weight:** 10.11
A talented young midfielder with great passing skills, Ben was hampered by injuries last term and had to undergo a hernia operation. Most of his appearances came in the early part of the season and he scored his first goal in senior football when he netted in the 1-1 draw at Millwall at the end of August.

Crystal Palace *(Trainee) FL 11+10/1 FLC 1+3 FAC 1*

WATSON Kevin Edward
Born: Hackney, 3 January 1974
Height: 6'0" **Weight:** 12.6
Used mainly as a substitute during the season, Kevin only completed the full 90 minutes in eight of his 25 first-team appearances. It was predictable, therefore, that he would be given a free transfer during the summer. His style of play is steady and orthodox, and despite his careful passing, he lost out to more creative midfielders such as Jamie Harper and Steve Sidwell. He captained Reading in one first-team game, the 3-0 home defeat by Crystal Palace just before Christmas.
Tottenham H *(From trainee on 15/5/1992)* PL 4+1 FLC 1+1/1 FAC 0+1 Others 4
Brentford *(Loaned on 24/3/1994)* FL 2+1
Bristol C *(Loaned on 2/12/1994)* FL 1+1
Barnet *(Loaned on 16/2/1995)* FL 13
Swindon T *(Free on 15/7/1996)* FL 39+24/1 FLC 2+2 FAC 1+2
Rotherham U *(Free on 31/7/1999)* FL 109/7 FLC 6/1 FAC 7 Others 3
Reading *(Loaned on 2/11/2001)* FL 6
Reading *(£150,000 + on 14/3/2002)* FL 40+20/2 FLC 2 FAC 0+1 Others 0+1

WATSON Paul Douglas
Born: Hastings, 4 January 1975
Height: 5'8" **Weight:** 10.10
Club Honours: Div 3 '99, '01; Div 2 '02
Paul will be happy to see the back of the 2003-04 campaign. Plagued by foot, hamstring, groin and pelvis problems, he enjoyed his best run for Brighton in the middle of the season, stringing together a run of games at both right back and on the left side of midfield. With a clutch of good youngsters coming through the ranks, Paul may find it difficult to regain a place in the Albion side in 2004-05.
Gillingham *(From trainee on 8/12/1992)* FL 57+5/2 FLC 4 FAC 6 Others 5+3
Fulham *(£13,000 on 30/7/1996)* FL 48+2/4 FLC 3/1 FAC 2 Others 2
Brentford *(£50,000 on 12/12/1997)* FL 37 FLC 2 FAC 2 Others 0+1
Brighton & Hove A *(£20,000 on 9/7/1999)* FL 190+3/14 FLC 8/1 FAC 10/3 Others 6

WATSON Stephen (Steve) Craig
Born: North Shields, 1 April 1974
Height: 6'0" **Weight:** 12.7
International Honours: E: B-1; U21-12; Yth
Steve began the season in great style for Everton, showing his keen eye for goal by scoring twice from the right side of midfield in the opening three matches and then hitting a superb hat-trick in 25

minutes against Leeds. However he was then sidelined for four months by a double-hernia operation in October. When he returned to the team he understandably was unable to reproduce the peak form of the early part of the campaign and was clearly lacking in match fitness. Steve is a popular member of the Everton team and he adds a versatile and diligent presence to the squad, being at home in both defence and midfield.
Newcastle U *(From trainee on 6/4/1991)* F/PL 179+29/12 FLC 10+6/1 FAC 13+4 Others 18+4/1
Aston Villa *(£4,000,000 on 15/10/1998)* PL 39+2 FLC 8+1/1 FAC 4
Everton *(£2,500,000 on 12/7/2000)* PL 94+7/14 FLC 4+1/1 FAC 2+1/1

WATTLEY David Anthony
Born: Enfield, 5 September 1983
Height: 5'11" **Weight:** 11.10
This young defender found it difficult to break into the Lincoln City squad after signing on a 12-month contract in the summer of 2003. He spent most of the season in the reserves where he was used at both centre back and wing back. David's only first-team start was as a replacement for the injured Mark Bailey at Cheltenham in March. He was released at the end of the campaign.
Queens Park R *(From trainee on 8/9/2000)*
Lincoln C *(Free on 4/7/2003)* FL 1+2 Others 0+1

WAY Darren
Born: Plymouth, 21 November 1979
Height: 5'7" **Weight:** 11.0
Club Honours: FAT '02; NC '03
International Honours: E: SP-3
Darren was one of the mainstays in central midfield for Yeovil Town for most of the 2003-04 season. A terrier of a player who always gives 100 per cent commitment, he scored five goals during the campaign. Darren stood in as captain when Terry Skiverton was absent and was one of the stars of the FA Cup tie against Liverpool.
Norwich C *(From trainee on 11/9/1998)*
Yeovil T *(Free on 19/8/2000)* FL 38+1/5 FLC 1 FAC 2 Others 2

WEALE Christopher (Chris)
Born: Chard, 9 February 1982
Height: 6'2" **Weight:** 13.3
Club Honours: FAT '02; NC '03
International Honours: E: SP-4
Chris was an ever-present in Third Division matches for Yeovil last season until the beginning of March when a training accident left him with a broken bone in

his hand. The talented goalkeeper produced a series of consistent displays for the Glovers, earning him a place in the PFA Division Three team of the season and also a spell training with West Ham, although no transfer materialised.
Yeovil T *(From juniors on 5/6/2000)* FL 35 FLC 1 FAC 3 Others 1

WEATHERSTONE Simon
Born: Reading, 26 January 1980
Height: 5'10" **Weight:** 12.0
Club Honours: NC '02
International Honours: E: SP-3
Simon had another good season at Boston, showing skill and persistence both as a striker and in different midfield roles. In January he moved on to Yeovil for personal reasons, but failed to make much of an impact at Huish Park. The highlight of his spell came when he scored a stunning goal against his old club in April.
Oxford U *(From trainee on 27/3/1997)* FL 25+27/3 FLC 1+3/1 Others 1
Boston U *(Free on 16/2/2001)* FL 57+5/10 FLC 2/1 Others 4/1
Yeovil T *(£15,000 on 23/1/2004)* FL 11+4/1

WEAVER Nicholas (Nick) James
Born: Sheffield, 2 March 1979
Height: 6'3" **Weight:** 13.6
Club Honours: Div 1 '02
International Honours: E: U21-10
Nick's appearances for Manchester City have been restricted over the past few seasons due to problems with his right knee. Last term he played just once for the first team, that outing coming in the UEFA Cup tie against TNS. Following a visit to the orthopaedic surgery department of sports medicine at the Cleveland Clinic in the USA where he under went pioneering surgery Nick is now on the long road back to recovery and will be hoping to resume his career, fully fit, in 2004-05.
Mansfield T *(Trainee)* FL 1
Manchester C *(£200,000 on 2/5/1997)* P/FL 145+1 FLC 14 FAC 11 Others 4

WEAVER Simon Daniel
Born: Doncaster, 20 December 1977
Height: 6'1" **Weight:** 10.7
This hard-working defender was used by Lincoln City on the right side of a three-man centre-back system. He was a first-team regular for most of the season missing just one game until being rested in mid-March. He then found it difficult to get back in the starting line-up but was offered a new deal at the end of the campaign.

Sheffield Wed (From trainee on 24/5/1996. Freed during 1998 close season)
Doncaster Rov (Loaned on 14/2/1997) FL 2
Lincoln C (Free from Nuneaton Borough, ex Ilkeston T, on 7/8/2002) FL 83/3 FLC 1 FAC 3 Others 8/1

WEBB Daniel (Danny) John
Born: Poole, 2 July 1983
Height: 6'1" **Weight:** 11.8

Club Honours: Div 2 '02
Danny was only on the fringes of the first-team squad at Hull last term, and scored his only goal in the LDV Vans Trophy tie against Scunthorpe. This turned out to be the enthusiastic striker's penultimate appearance in the Tigers' colours as he joined Cambridge on loan in December before securing a permanent move to the Abbey Stadium in February.

A replacement for the departed Dave Kitson, he seized his chance to gain regular first-team football and scored three times for the U's. Danny is the son of former Chelsea star David Webb.
Southend U (From trainee at Southampton on 4/12/2000) FL 16+15/3 FLC 1 FAC 1+1 Others 3+2/1
Brighton & Hove A (Loaned on 12/12/2001) FL 7+5/1 FAC 1

Danny Webber (left)

Brighton & Hove A *(Loaned on 8/11/2002)*
FL 0+3
Hull C *(Free on 13/12/2002) FL 4+12 Others*
2/1
Lincoln C *(Loaned on 14/3/2003) FL 4+1/1*
Cambridge U *(Free on 18/12/2003) FL*
19+2/3

WEBBER Daniel (Danny)
Vaughn
Born: Manchester, 28 December 1981
Height: 5'9" **Weight:** 10.8
International Honours: E: Yth
Danny joined Watford in the summer
from Manchester United after two
successful loan spells, during which he
had impressed with his speed, close
control and hard-working attitude. Great
things were expected of him, but he
suffered a series of setbacks which made
his season one to forget. Foremost among
these was the death of his close friend
and former United colleague Jimmy Davis,
which understandably had a profound
effect and suddenly rendered his football
an irrelevance. His partnership with Bruce
Dyer failed to flourish, and he found goals
hard to come by. In December he
sustained an ankle injury and in January
he dislocated his shoulder in training – a
recurrence of an old injury – and this
effectively ended his season.
Manchester U *(From trainee on 7/1/1999)*
FLC 1+1 Others 0+1
Port Vale *(Loaned on 23/11/2001) FL 2+2*
Others 0+1
Watford *(Loaned on 28/3/2002) FL 4+1/2*
Watford *(Loaned on 13/8/2002) FL 11+1/2*
Watford *(Signed on 7/7/2003) FL 24+3/5 FLC*
2 FAC 0+2

WEIR David (Davie) Gillespie
Born: Falkirk, 10 May 1970
Height: 6'2" **Weight:** 13.7
Club Honours: S Div 1 '94; B&Q '94; SC
'98
International Honours: S: 37
After being a fixture in the Everton
defence since he joined the club, this
classy and composed centre half endured
an exasperating season in 2003-04. He
started the campaign on the bench and,
after regaining his place in the starting
line-up in October, was then sidelined for
four months with a ligament injury. He
returned to the side in time to produce an
excellent performance at Chelsea in April,
but his lack of match practice was
apparent in the final few games. Davie
has been an excellent servant to the
Blues, remaining a solid presence in the
back-line, as well as scoring some vital
goals, and he has been the most

consistent performer during his time at
the club. It is hoped that a good pre-
season will see him return to his best
form.
Falkirk *(From Glasgow Celtic juniors on*
1/8/1992) SL 133/8 SLC 5 SC 6 Others 5
Heart of Midlothian *(Signed on 29/7/1996)*
SL 92/8 SLC 10/2 SC 9/2 Others 6
Everton *(£250,000 on 17/2/1999) PL*
155+8/7 FLC 8 FAC 13

WELCH Michael Francis
Born: Crewe, 11 January 1982
Height: 6'3" **Weight:** 13.3
International Honours: RoI: Yth
This tall Macclesfield central defender
mostly played in a back-four formation
last term, although there were times
when he operated in a three-man central
defence. Michael is known for his long
clearances and he is not afraid to make
timely tackles. He initially partnered Karl
Munroe, but ended the season in good
form playing alongside the more
experienced Steve Payne.
Macclesfield T *(From trainee at Barnsley on*
9/8/2001) FL 77+6/3 FLC 3 FAC 4 Others 2

WELLENS Richard Paul
Born: Manchester, 26 March 1980
Height: 5'9" **Weight:** 11.6
Club Honours: AMC '02, '04
International Honours: E: Yth
Blackpool's outstanding midfield player
enjoyed another fine season during 2003-
04. A regular in the line-up throughout
the campaign, he was a member of the
side that won the LDV Vans Trophy at
Cardiff's Millennium Stadium and also
gained a place in the PFA Division Two
team of the year. To cap a great campaign
he won the Seasiders' 'Player of the Year'
title, while his brilliant long-range effort
against Port Vale was voted as the club's
'Goal of the Season'.
Manchester U *(From trainee on 19/5/1997)*
FLC 0+1
Blackpool *(Signed on 23/3/2000) FL*
146+14/13 FLC 8+1 FAC 8 Others 12+3/1

WELLER Paul Anthony
Born: Brighton, 6 March 1975
Height: 5'8" **Weight:** 11.2
Burnley's longest-serving player had
another steady season last term.
Something of a utility man in the past,
Paul's appearances in 2003-04 were
almost exclusively as a 'holding' player in
midfield, probably the role to which he is
best suited. Rarely conceding possession
willingly, he is a player who seldom goes
for glory but can hardly ever be accused
of not pulling his weight for the side, and

despite his lack of height his opponents
always know they have been in a game.
Although failing to find the net, he is
never afraid to try his luck in front of
goal.
Burnley *(From trainee on 30/11/1993) FL*
199+53/11 FLC 12+2 FAC 8+6/2 Others 7

WELLS Dean Thomas
Born: Hammersmith, 25 March 1985
Height: 6'1" **Weight:** 13.2
This promising young Brentford central
defender made his senior debut against
Sheffield Wednesday in October after
coming off the bench to replace Leo
Roget. Dean subsequently returned to the
club's reserve and junior teams to
continue his football education.
Brentford *(Trainee) FL 0+1*

WELSH Andrew (Andy)
Born: Manchester, 24 November 1983
Height: 5'8" **Weight:** 9.8
International Honours: S: Yth
This talented young Stockport winger was
restricted to substitute appearances
during the early stages of last season and
had to wait until mid-September to make
his first start. He then became a regular
name on the team sheet as his traditional
wing play often terrorised opponents
down the flanks, although he was
sometimes let down by a poor final ball.
He scored his only goal of the campaign
with a fine left-foot strike in the 3-3 draw
at Barnsley in November.
Stockport Co *(From trainee on 11/7/2001) FL*
40+22/3 FLC 1+1 FAC 2 Others 2+2
Macclesfield T *(Loaned on 30/8/2002) FL*
4+2/2

WELSH John Joseph
Born: Liverpool, 10 January 1984
Height: 5'7" **Weight:** 11.6
International Honours: E: U21-1; Yth
This young Liverpool midfielder added
two more substitute appearances last
term. These came early in the season in
the away leg of the UEFA Cup tie in
Ljubljana in September and, perhaps more
surprisingly, in the last ten minutes of the
crucial home game with Arsenal in
October.
Liverpool *(From trainee on 29/1/2001) PL*
0+1 FLC 0+1 Others 0+1

WEST Dean
Born: Morley, 5 December 1972
Height: 5'10" **Weight:** 12.2
Club Honours: Div 2 '97
Things looked bleak for Dean, one of
Burnley's most consistent players of the
previous two seasons, when his number

two shirt was given to new signing Lee Roche, and it was Roche who began the season at right back. However, an early injury to the newcomer let Dean back in and he retained his place up to Christmas with his usual composure and sure-footedness at the back, also finding the net in an away win at Gillingham. After the new year, though, he was relegated to the bench, returning when Roche was injured but missing the end of the season with an injury of his own.
Lincoln C (From trainee on 17/8/1991) FL 93+26/20 FLC 11/1 FAC 6/1 Others 5+2/1
Bury (Signed on 29/9/1995) FL 100+10/8 FLC 6 FAC 3 Others 2+1
Burnley (Free on 26/7/1999) FL 145+13/5 FLC 6+2/1 FAC 11 Others 1

WESTCARR Craig Naptali
Born: Nottingham, 29 January 1985
Height: 5'11" **Weight:** 11.8
International Honours: E: Yth
This talented young Nottingham Forest forward found himself out of the picture early on last season. However, after regaining his form in the reserves he worked his way back into the side and made a handful more appearances, all from the substitutes' bench.
Nottingham F (From trainee on 31/1/2002) FL 2+20/1 FLC 1+1 FAC 0+1

WESTLAKE Ian John
Born: Clacton, 10 July 1983
Height: 5'10" **Weight:** 11.6
Who would have thought that after making his first full appearance against West Ham last August that Ian would have gone on to enjoy such a remarkable season in 2003-04? He quickly established himself in the Ipswich line-up and his industrious style of play made it difficult to leave him out. Used mainly on the left-hand side of midfield, he proved that he could also man-mark effectively when he completely dominated Jason McAteer when Sunderland visited Portman Road. Ian opened his goal-scoring account with a cracking volley against Gillingham and at the season's end he was voted as the club's 'Player of the Year'.
Ipswich T (From trainee on 9/8/2002) FL 30+13/6 FLC 1+1 FAC 1 Others 2

WESTON Curtis James
Born: Greenwich, 24 January 1987
Height: 5'11" **Weight:** 11.9
This very talented attacking midfielder is another product of the Millwall youth system. Skilful with both feet and possessing a terrific 'engine' Curtis produced some excellent performances

for the U19s last term and went on to make his senior debut as a substitute against Bradford City on the last day of the season, acquitting himself well.
Millwall (From trainee on 17/3/2004) FL 0+1 FAC 0+1

WESTON Rhys David
Born: Kingston, 27 October 1980
Height: 6'1" **Weight:** 12.3
International Honours: W: 6; U21-4; E: Yth; Sch
Full back Rhys started in half of Cardiff City's First Division games last term but ended the campaign on a low note when, having fought back to fitness, he limped off during the first half of a testimonial match with an ankle problem. The Welsh international defender missed several spells through injury and will be hoping to come back stronger in the 2004-05 campaign.
Arsenal (From trainee on 8/7/1999) PL 1 FLC 1+1
Cardiff C (£300,000 on 21/11/2000) FL 121+6/2 FLC 4 FAC 11+1 Others 7

WESTWOOD Ashley Michael
Born: Bridgnorth, 31 August 1976
Height: 6'0" **Weight:** 12.8
Club Honours: FAYC '95
International Honours: E: Yth
After signing for Northampton Town during the 2003 close season, Ashley missed the opening matches of the new term due to injury. Then, when he finally made his debut for the club against Cheltenham, he lasted just 60 minutes before being taken off with a dislocated shoulder! Sadly this was Ashley's fate for much of the campaign, although he finished off with a short run in the line-up and the experienced defender will be hoping for a better time in the 2004-05 season.
Manchester U (From trainee on 1/7/1994)
Crewe Alex (£40,000 on 26/7/1995) FL 93+5/9 FLC 8 FAC 9/2 Others 10
Bradford C (£150,000 on 20/7/1998) P/FL 18+6/2 FLC 1 FAC 2+1 Others 1+1
Sheffield Wed (£150,000 + on 10/8/2000) FL 79+3/5 FLC 10+2/4 FAC 2
Northampton T (Free on 15/7/2003) FL 8+1 FAC 1 Others 1

WESTWOOD Christopher (Chris) John
Born: Dudley, 13 February 1977
Height: 6'0" **Weight:** 12.2
This consistent central defender enjoyed another fine season for Hartlepool in 2003-04 when he formed a highly effective partnership at the back with

Michael Nelson. Occasionally switched to right back, Chris is a model professional who does the job required and is rarely in trouble with referees. He was chosen by the supporters as the club's 'Away Player of the Year' for the second season running and passed the landmark figure of 200 Football League appearances for Hartlepool during the campaign.
Wolverhampton W (From trainee on 3/7/1995) FL 3+1/1 FLC 1+1 (Released during 1998 close season)
Hartlepool U (Signed from Telford U on 24/3/1999) FL 208+5/3 FLC 6 FAC 9 Others 15

WETHERALL David
Born: Sheffield, 14 March 1971
Height: 6'3" **Weight:** 13.12
International Honours: E: Sch
Bradford City's captain ended a two-year wait for a goal when he headed home the first in the 2-1 win over Reading on Easter Saturday. The influential centre half was a calming influence throughout another difficult season both on-and-off the field, and remained a huge favourite with the supporters. David was carried off with a knee injury against Watford in October which ruled him out for ten weeks, during which time City managed to win only once. He returned for the much-needed 1-0 home victory over Coventry straight after Christmas and missed only one more game from that point. As Bradford's PFA representative, David also made an important contribution in the dressing room when the club went back into administration.
Sheffield Wed (From trainee on 1/7/1989)
Leeds U (£125,000 on 15/7/1991) F/PL 188+14/12 FLC 19+1/2 FAC 21+3/4 Others 4
Bradford C (£1,400,000 on 7/7/1999) P/FL 123+3/6 FLC 7/2 FAC 2 Others 3

WHALEY Simon
Born: Bolton, 7 June 1985
Height: 5'11" **Weight:** 11.7
This young Bury midfielder was given occasional substitute appearances during the first half of last season but then picked up a knee injury in training and was out of action until January. Simon battled back to earn another appearance on the bench for the home game against Cambridge but soon afterwards suffered medial ligament damage – and yet another lay off. A player who catches the eye with his electric pace and confident, skilful approach, he gamely returned in April and was rewarded with a starting place in midfield for the closing fixtures, claiming his first-ever Football League

goal with a great volley in the final game at home to Macclesfield.
Bury (From trainee on 30/10/2002) FL 3+9/1 Others 0+4

WHALLEY Gareth
Born: Manchester, 19 December 1973
Height: 5'10" **Weight:** 11.12
This skilful midfield player found it difficult to win a regular place in the line-up for Cardiff last term, although by the end of the season there were signs that he was beginning to establish himself in the side once more. Gareth is a talented player with the ability to unlock the tightest of defences and will be hoping to become firmly established in the side in 2004-05.
Crewe Alex (From trainee on 29/7/1992) FL 174+6/9 FLC 11+1/1 FAC 15+1/3 Others 24/3
Bradford C (£600,000 on 24/7/1998) P/FL 99+4/3 FLC 10+2/2 FAC 2 Others 5+1
Crewe Alex (Loaned on 28/3/2002) FL 7
Cardiff C (Free on 9/7/2002) FL 33+8/2 FLC 2 FAC 1 Others 3

WHELAN Glenn David
Born: Dublin, 13 January 1984
Height: 6'0" **Weight:** 12.5
International Honours: RoI: U21-6; Yth
A player who is comfortable anywhere in defence or midfield, Glenn made his senior debut for Manchester City in the UEFA Cup qualifying victory over TNS. Unable to nail down a regular spot in the first-team squad he spent some time on loan at Bury where he slotted effortlessly into a central midfield role. He eventually spent three months at Gigg Lane showing great stamina and passing ability. Glenn represented the Republic of Ireland in the World Youth Championships in December and later stepped up to appear for the U21s.
Manchester C (From trainee on 25/1/2001) Others 0+1
Bury (Loaned on 29/9/2003) FL 13 FAC 1 Others 1

WHELAN Noel David
Born: Leeds, 30 December 1974
Height: 6'2" **Weight:** 12.3
Club Honours: FAYC '93
International Honours: E: U21-2; Yth (UEFA-U18 '93)
Noel signed for Millwall in the summer of 2003 and formed an impressive partnership up front with Neil Harris in the early stages of the campaign. All was going well until Noel sustained a bad hamstring pull and was out for eight weeks in which time he returned to his home in Middlesbrough and he was then

released by Millwall. His first contact with Derby County was to ask for treatment and training facilities. George Burley was impressed by his progress and, with Derby short of goals, offered him a contract for a month. Although lending physical presence to the attack, Noel was unable to score and was released after a second month.
Leeds U (From trainee on 5/3/1993) PL 28+20/7 FLC 3+2/1 FAC 2 Others 3
Coventry C (£2,000,000 on 16/12/1995) PL 127+7/31 FLC 6/1 FAC 15+1/7
Middlesbrough (£2,200,000 on 4/8/2000) PL 33+28/6 FLC 4/2 FAC 5+3/3
Crystal Palace (Loaned on 7/3/2003) FL 7+1/3
Millwall (Free on 5/8/2003) FL 8+7/4 FLC 1
Derby Co (Free on 29/1/2004) FL 3+5

WHING Andrew (Andy) John
Born: Birmingham, 20 September 1984
Height: 6'0" **Weight:** 12.0
Andy followed up his promising first season with some excellent performances at right back for Coventry in the early part of the 2003-04 season and he netted his first-ever senior goal in the home defeat by Nottingham Forest. Although occasionally exposed for pace, his never-say-die attitude more than made up for his limitations. Andy was given a break in November but soon regained his place and enjoyed another short run in the line-up.
Coventry C (From trainee on 7/4/2003) FL 39+3/1 FLC 1 FAC 2

WHITAKER Daniel (Danny) Phillip
Born: Wilmslow, 14 November 1980
Height: 5'10" **Weight:** 10.12
Danny generally featured as a wide-right midfielder for Macclesfield last term, having mostly operated in a central-midfield role before. He is a pacy, attacking player capable of scoring goals and netted six times during the season. Danny is a young player who always tries hard and wants to make a good impression.
Macclesfield T (Signed from Wilmslow Sports on 5/7/2000) FL 89+4/17 FLC 3/4 FAC 7/1 Others 2

WHITE Alan
Born: Darlington, 22 March 1976
Height: 6'1" **Weight:** 13.2
Alan got off to a low-key start for Colchester last term and it was not until December that he began to establish himself as a regular in the line-up. However, once in the side he never

looked back. He produced some towering performances alongside Wayne Brown in the centre of the defence and scooped no fewer than three awards at the end-of-the season ceremony including the club's 'Player of the Year' trophy.
Middlesbrough (From trainee on 8/7/1994) Others 1
Luton T (£40,000 on 22/9/1997) FL 60+20/3 FLC 3+3 FAC 2 Others 4
Colchester U (Loaned on 12/11/1999) FL 4 Others 1
Colchester U (Free on 19/7/2000) FL 128+11/4 FLC 7+1 FAC 6+2 Others 6

WHITE Andrew (Andy)
Born: Swanwick, 6 November 1981
Height: 6'4" **Weight:** 13.4
This tall central striker signed a new one-year contract for Mansfield during the summer of 2003, but most of his appearances came for the Stags from the bench and he failed to find the net. He spent much of the campaign out on loan, firstly at Boston, where he showed plenty of skill, then at Conference club Burton Albion, and finally at Kidderminster. He caused plenty of problems for opposition defenders during his spell at Aggborough and scored against Boston, one of his former clubs. Andy was reported to have signed for Crewe Alexandra during the summer.
Mansfield T (Signed from Hucknall T on 13/7/2000) FL 37+31/10 FLC 1+2/1 FAC 0+3 Others 0+2
Crewe Alex (Loaned on 24/10/2002) FL 0+2
Boston U (Loaned on 11/9/2003) FL 3+3
Kidderminster Hrs (Loaned on 31/10/2003) FL 6+1/1 FAC 2

WHITEHEAD Dean
Born: Oxford, 12 January 1982
Height: 5'11" **Weight:** 12.1
After sitting out the first few games on the bench Dean came into his own for Oxford United last term, dominating the midfield and also weighing in with seven goals. A specialist with free kicks and corners, he netted the club's final goal of the season with his ear (counted as a rare bullet header)! A local boy who is highly rated at the Kassam Stadium, Dean deservedly won the 'Player of the Year' trophy, just reward for an excellent campaign.
Oxford U (From trainee on 20/4/2000) FL 92+30/9 FLC 5+1 FAC 3+2 Others 1+2

WHITFIELD Paul Michael
Born: St Asaph, 6 May 1982
Height: 6'0" **Weight:** 12.8
International Honours: W: U21-1; Yth

Paul received few opportunities at Wrexham last term due to the excellent form shown by first-choice 'keeper Andy Dibble. Even when Dibble was sidelined through injury Paul lost out to on-loan signing Michael Ingham and he was among those released by the club in May.

Wrexham *(From trainee on 16/7/2001) FL 7+3 FLC 1 FAC 1 Others 4+1*

WHITLEY James (Jim)
Born: Zambia, 14 April 1975
Height: 5'9" **Weight:** 11.0
International Honours: NI: 3; B-1
This industrious Wrexham midfielder was again a key figure for Wrexham last term and on the occasions when he was absent he was sorely missed. A perfect example came in the home match against Hartlepool on Easter Monday. After dominating the proceedings and with the team looking in charge, Jim had to leave the field with a pulled hamstring (which put him out for the rest of season) and his absence changed the complexion of the game, with the visitors returning home 2-1 winners.

Manchester C *(From juniors on 1/8/1994) FL 27+11 FLC 3+1/1 FAC 2+1 Others 0+1*
Blackpool *(Loaned on 20/8/1999) FL 7+1 FLC 1*
Norwich C *(Loaned on 24/8/2000) FL 7+1/1*
Swindon T *(Loaned on 15/12/2000) FL 2 FAC 1*
Northampton T *(Loaned on 27/2/2001) FL 13*
Wrexham *(Free on 11/10/2001) FL 112+2/1 FLC 3 FAC 3 Others 5*

WHITLEY Jeffrey (Jeff)
Born: Zambia, 28 January 1979
Height: 5'8" **Weight:** 11.2
International Honours: NI: 12; B-2; U21-17
A tenacious midfield anchorman Jeff joined Sunderland in the summer of 2003 following a short trial period, making his debut in the Carling Cup win at Mansfield. He took advantage of an injury to Paul Thirlwell to establish himself in the side in September, enjoying an uninterrupted run until the closing stages of the campaign when suspension led to an enforced rest.

Manchester C *(From trainee on 19/2/1996) P/FL 96+27/8 FLC 9+1 FAC 2+2 Others 4*
Wrexham *(Loaned on 14/1/1999) FL 9/2*
Notts Co *(Loaned on 21/3/2002) FL 6*
Notts Co *(Loaned on 18/10/2002) FL 12 FAC 1 Others 1*
Sunderland *(Free on 7/8/2003) FL 33/2 FLC 2 FAC 5 Others 2*

WHITLOW Michael (Mike) William
Born: Northwich, 13 January 1968
Height: 6'0" **Weight:** 12.12
Club Honours: Div 2 '90, Div 1 '92; FLC '97
Out of contract, Mike signed a one-year deal with Sheffield United in the summer, spending the 2003-04 campaign as defensive cover at Bramall Lane. In the autumn he had a run of nine games, playing both on the left side of the defence and as a central defender. He performed reliably, using his experience and positional sense to compensate for his lack of pace. Other opportunities arose, but he spent most of the latter part of the season on the bench.

Leeds U *(£10,000 from Witton A on 11/11/1988) FL 62+15/4 FLC 4+1 FAC 1+4 Others 9*
Leicester C *(£250,000 on 27/3/1992) F/PL 141+6/8 FLC 12/1 FAC 6 Others 14*
Bolton W *(£500,000 + on 19/9/1997) P/FL 124+8/2 FLC 13+2 FAC 10+1 Others 2+3*
Sheffield U *(Free on 22/7/2003) FL 13+4/1 FLC 1 FAC 1+1*

Mike Whitlow

WHITTINGHAM Peter Michael
Born: Nuneaton, 8 September 1984
Height: 5'10" **Weight:** 10.5
Club Honours: FAYC '02
International Honours: E: U21-1; Yth
This lively young midfielder proved to be
the find of the season for Aston Villa,
firmly establishing himself as a member of
the senior squad. A calm player both on
and off the pitch, his classy performances
in the centre of the park belied his tender
years. Peter scored his first senior goal in
the Carling Cup tie against Wycombe and
was a member of the England U19 and
U21 squads during the campaign.
*Aston Villa (From trainee on 2/11/2002) PL
21+15 FLC 4+2/1 FAC 1*

WHITTLE Justin Phillip
Born: Derby, 18 March 1971
Height: 6'1" **Weight:** 12.12
Although Justin lost his regular place in
the Hull City line-up last autumn when
Marc Joseph and Damien Delaney forged
a formidable partnership at the heart of
the defence, he remained a hugely
popular figure at the KC Stadium. He has
publicly declared that he wishes to end
his career with the Tigers and will be
hoping to add more valuable
contributions to the club's cause in the
2004-05 campaign.
*Glasgow Celtic (Signed from Army during
1994 close season)*
*Stoke C (Free on 20/10/1994) FL 66+13/1
FLC 3+4 FAC 2 Others 2*
*Hull C (£65,000 on 27/11/1998) FL 184+9/2
FLC 9 FAC 8+2 Others 7/1*

**WIDDRINGTON Thomas
(Tommy)**
Born: Newcastle, 1 October 1971
Height: 5'10" **Weight:** 12.2
Club Honours: AMC '01
Tommy joined Macclesfield at the start of
last season and was a regular in the side
apart from a brief spell in March when he
suffered a problem with a disc in his back.
His vast experience proved useful to the
side and he showed considerable ability in
the centre of the midfield, often holding
up the ball to allow others to move into
more forward positions. Tommy's style of
play quickly gained many admirers
amongst the supporters at Moss Rose.
*Southampton (From trainee on 10/5/1990)
F/PL 67+8/3 FLC 3+1 FAC 11*
*Wigan Ath (Loaned on 12/9/1991) FL 5+1
FLC 2*
*Grimsby T (£300,000 on 11/7/1996) FL
72+17/8 FLC 10+3 FAC 3+1 Others 1*
*Port Vale (Free on 24/3/1999) FL 77+5/8 FLC
2 FAC 2 Others 3*

*Hartlepool U (Free on 30/7/2001) FL 50+6/5
FLC 1 FAC 1+1 Others 2*
*Macclesfield T (Free on 19/8/2003) FL 34+1
FAC 3 Others 1*

WIEKENS Gerard
Born: Tolhuiswyk, Holland, 25 February
1973
Height: 6'0" **Weight:** 13.4
Club Honours: Div 1 '02
This intelligent, versatile player was a
reliable member of the Manchester City
squad last term. Gerard accepted that his
first-team opportunities would be limited
and despite being the longest-serving
player at the club he managed just a
solitary appearance. With no sign of his
contract being extended he moved on
following the last game of the season.
*Manchester C (£500,000 from SC Veendam,
Holland on 28/7/1997) P/FL 167+15/10 FLC
13+2 FAC 11+1 Others 4*

WILBRAHAM Aaron Thomas
Born: Knutsford, 21 October 1979
Height: 6'3" **Weight:** 12.4
Stockport's longest-serving player had
another good season at Edgeley Park last
term, scoring eight goals from 32 League
starts. He netted twice in the 2-2 draw at
Sheffield Wednesday in September and
also contributed important winners at
Swindon and Brighton and a late
equaliser at Blackpool. Towards the end of
the season he formed a strong
partnership with Jon Daly as the Hatters
went 11 games unbeaten to ensure
relegation was avoided.
*Stockport Co (From trainee on 29/8/1997) FL
118+54/35 FLC 5+2/1 FAC 3+1 Others 2*

WILCOX Jason Malcolm
Born: Farnworth, 15 July 1971
Height: 5'11" **Weight:** 11.10
Club Honours: PL '95
International Honours: E: 3; B-2
Jason made only a limited number of
appearances for Leeds United last term,
featuring early on and again in the very
last few matches. In between he lost out
to on-loan signing Jermaine Pennant for a
place on the right-hand side of midfield.
Jason was out of contract in the summer
and his future was unclear at the time of
writing.
*Blackburn Rov (From trainee on 13/6/1989)
F/PL 242+27/31 FLC 16+1/1 FAC 18+2/2
Others 7*
*Leeds U (£3,000,000 on 17/12/1999) PL
52+29/4 FLC 3 FAC 6+1 Others 9+6/2*

WILES Simon
Born: Preston, 22 April 1985
Height: 5'11" **Weight:** 11.4

One of several promising youngsters on
the books at Blackpool, Simon made his
senior debut as a substitute in the LDV
Vans Trophy game against Tranmere last
October when he came close to scoring.
The speedy winger added a handful more
appearances from the bench and will be
looking to receive further senior action in
2004-05.
*Blackpool (From trainee on 10/5/2004) FL
0+4 Others 0+1*

WILFORD Aron Leslie
Born: Scarborough, 14 January 1982
Height: 6'2" **Weight:** 14.2
This young striker impressed at times in
the York City attack in the early part of
the 2003-04 season, scoring when
coming off the bench against Rochdale
and in the home win over Bristol Rovers.
However, he struggled to establish himself
in the side, and after spells on loan with
Harrogate Town and Worksop he was
released. Aron signed for Lincoln City in
March and was used as back-up for the
Imps' strike force in the closing weeks of
the season. He never made the starting
line-up but was regularly on the
substitutes' bench, with his only goal
being from his first touch against Yeovil
Town in the final game of the regular
season. Aron was released at the end of
the campaign.
*Middlesbrough (From Harrogate College on
14/7/1999. Free to Whitby T on 23/11/2001)*
*York C (Free on 29/7/2003) FL 4+2/2 FAC
0+1 Others 1*
*Lincoln C (Free on 25/3/2004) FL 0+5/1
Others 0+1*

WILKINSON Andrew (Andy)
Gordon
Born: Stone, 6 August 1984
Height: 5'11" **Weight:** 11.0
This pacy young central defender had
been developing patiently in Stoke City's
reserve team for some time and in
November he joined Conference outfit
Telford United to gain experience of
senior football. On his return Andy made
his first-team debut as a substitute at
home to Walsall and then received his
first start in the penultimate game of the
season against West Bromwich Albion
when he put on a superb performance.
*Stoke C (From trainee on 8/7/2002) FL 1+2
FLC 1 Others 0+1*

WILKINSON Jack Lloyd
Born: Beverley, 12 September 1985
Height: 5'8" **Weight:** 10.8
This promising striker looked good at U19
and reserve-team levels for Hartlepool in

the first half of the 2003-04 season. A second-year scholar, Jack was given an early chance to prove himself as Neale Cooper added youth to his first-team squad. He got off to a great start, scoring twice in his first three appearances, before resuming his football education with the juniors.

Hartlepool U *(Trainee) FL 2+2/2 FAC 0+2*

WILKINSON Shaun Frederick

Born: Portsmouth, 12 September 1981
Height: 5'8" **Weight:** 11.2
Shaun managed just three appearances from the substitutes' bench for Brighton last term and in November he moved on to Dr Martens League club Havant & Waterlooville, where he had spent a successful loan period earlier in the campaign. A versatile player, Shaun was used as a defender, in midfield and as a forward during his spell with the Seagulls.

Brighton & Hove A *(From trainee on 7/8/2001) FL 4+13 FLC 1/1 FAC 0+1*
Chesterfield *(Loaned on 27/11/2002) FL 0+1*

WILKINSON Wesley (Wes)

Born: Wythenshawe, 1 May 1984
Height: 5'10" **Weight:** 11.1
This pacy young striker scored regularly for Nantwich Town last term and in March he signed for Oldham Athletic following a successful trial period. Wes made an immediate impact, and although he only started two games, he was outstanding after coming on as a first-half substitute in the club's shock 2-0 win at promotion-chasing Bristol City. A recurring knee problem then restricted his involvement, but the promising youngster was rewarded with a 12-month contract by manager Brian Talbot in May.

Oldham Ath *(Signed from Nantwich T on 4/3/2004) FL 2+3*

WILKSHIRE Luke

Born: Wollongong, Australia, 2 October 1981
Height: 5'9" **Weight:** 11.5
International Honours: Australia: U23-9; Yth
This skilful midfielder joined Bristol City as a replacement for the departed Scott Murray. Luke had a difficult task to replace one of the stars of the Ashton Gate team, but persevered and produced some fine performances. He also featured for Australia in their qualifying ties for the Olympic Games.

Middlesbrough *(Signed from AIS, Australia on 12/5/1999) PL 13+8 FLC 2 FAC 1*
Bristol C *(£250,000 on 6/8/2003) FL 35+2/2 FLC 3 FAC 3/1 Others 0+2*

WILLIAMS Adrian

Born: Reading, 16 August 1971
Height: 6'2" **Weight:** 13.2
Club Honours: Div 2 '94
International Honours: W: 13
Despite approaching the veteran stage of his career, Adrian completed another fine season as Reading's captain, proving to be an excellent example to younger players both on the field and off it. He is as fit as ever, jumps just as high to head away incoming crosses, and frequently uses his body to block goal-bound shots. His long passing out of defence is tidy too, and he showed a striker's awareness with his only goal of the campaign, a well-timed bullet header in the 2-1 win at Sheffield United.

Reading *(From trainee on 4/3/1989) FL 191+5/14 FLC 17/1 FAC 16/2 Others 14/2*
Wolverhampton W *(£750,000 on 3/7/1996) FL 26+1 FLC 3 FAC 2+2 Others 2/1*
Reading *(Loaned on 15/2/2000) FL 5/1 Others 1*
Reading *(Free on 26/3/2000) FL 119+2/3 FLC 6+1 FAC 3 Others 5*

WILLIAMS Anthony Simon

Born: Bridgend, 20 September 1977
Height: 6'1" **Weight:** 13.5
International Honours: W: U21-16; Yth
Anthony started the 2003-04 campaign as Hartlepool's first-choice goalkeeper, but was quickly replaced by Jim Provett and found it difficult to get back in the side. He was loaned out firstly to Swansea City, where he only featured on the substitutes' bench, and then to Stockport in the new year. He became a regular for County in the closing stages of the campaign and played a big part in ensuring the club avoided relegation. Anthony was released by Hartlepool in the summer.

Blackburn Rov *(From trainee on 4/7/1996)*
Macclesfield T *(Loaned on 16/10/1998) FL 4*
Bristol Rov *(Loaned on 24/3/1999) FL 9*
Gillingham *(Loaned on 5/8/1999) FL 2 FLC 2*
Macclesfield T *(Loaned on 28/11/2000) FL 11*
Hartlepool U *(Free on 7/7/2000) FL 131 FLC 2 FAC 4 Others 9*
Stockport Co *(Loaned on 23/1/2004) FL 15*

WILLIAMS Ashley Errol

Born: Wolverhampton, 23 March 1984
Height: 6'0" **Weight:** 11.2
The former Hednesford Town defender was a revelation at Stockport last term and played a key role in ensuring County avoided relegation. After sitting on the bench on a number of occasions he finally made his debut in the 2-2 draw at Hartlepool United in mid-March and then

kept his place in the side. Ashley received the club's 'Young Player of the Year' award for some solid performances.

Stockport Co *(Free from Hednesford T on 31/12/2003) FL 10*

WILLIAMS Benjamin (Ben) Philip

Born: Manchester, 27 August 1982
Height: 6'0" **Weight:** 13.4
International Honours: E: Sch
This young Manchester United goalkeeper joined Crewe on loan in March as a replacement for the injured Clayton Ince. Ben was an ever-present in the closing stages of the campaign and proved to be a very capable custodian. He was reported to have signed permanently for the Alex in the summer.

Manchester U *(From juniors on 3/7/2001)*
Chesterfield *(Loaned on 30/12/2002) FL 14*
Crewe Alex *(Loaned on 19/3/2004) FL 10*

WILLIAMS Christopher (Chris) Jonathan

Born: Manchester, 2 February 1985
Height: 5'8" **Weight:** 9.6
This young striker was in and out of the Stockport line-up last term. Chris scored his first goal when he came off the bench in the 2-1 home defeat by Queens Park Rangers at the start of November and then four days later he was on the mark again in the incredible 5-4 LDV Vans Trophy win against Wrexham. He had to make do with substitute appearances for the majority of the campaign but still managed to score the club's 'Goal of the Season' with a fine effort in the 2-0 win at Brentford.

Stockport Co *(From trainee on 5/3/2002) FL 5+17/3 FLC 1 FAC 0+2 Others 2/1*

WILLIAMS Daniel (Danny) Ivor Llewellyn

Born: Wrexham, 12 July 1979
Height: 6'1" **Weight:** 13.0
International Honours: W: U21-9
Danny started the 2003-04 season in good form for Kidderminster, scoring directly from free kicks in the games at Darlington and Cheltenham. However, the goals became less frequent as the season wore on and his form began to suffer. Danny had a spell on loan with Conference club Chester City then on transfer-deadline day he moved on to join Bristol Rovers. He produced a fine performance on his debut for Rovers, scoring a super goal against York and soon became a popular figure with the club's supporters.

Liverpool *(From trainee on 14/5/1997)*
Wrexham *(Free on 22/3/1999)* FL 38+1/3
FLC 4 FAC 4/1 Others 1
Kidderminster Hrs *(Free on 11/7/2001)* FL
108+3/8 FLC 2 FAC 7 Others 5+1
Bristol Rov *(Free on 25/3/2004)* FL 6/1

WILLIAMS Darren
Born: Middlesbrough, 28 April 1977
Height: 5'10" **Weight:** 11.12
Club Honours: Div 1 '99
International Honours: E: B-1; U21-2
The longest-serving player at Sunderland,
utility man Darren is now the last
surviving link on the playing staff from the
Roker Park days. A tough tackler with a
fair turn of pace and the ability to get
forward from defence, he featured mainly
at right back last term, filling in when
Stephen Wright was out injured. Darren
also had the honour of captaining the
side for the last game of the regular
season at Burnley.
York C *(From trainee on 21/6/1995)* FL 16+4
FLC 4+1 FAC 1 Others 3/1
Sunderland *(£50,000 on 18/10/1996)* F/PL
154+44/4 FLC 19+2/2 FAC 11+2 Others 4+1

WILLIAMS Eifion Wyn
Born: Anglesey, 15 November 1975
Height: 5'11" **Weight:** 11.12
International Honours: W: B-1
A tireless front runner for Hartlepool,
Eifion had spells when he struggled to
find the net last term, but he can be
content with the knowledge that for the
second season running he was an
automatic choice and the team's leading
goal-scorer. His efforts were recognised
when he was called up for the Wales
international squad for their two games in
the summer, but unfortunately an injury
received in the play-offs forced him to pull
out.
Torquay U *(£70,000 from Barry T on
25/3/1999)* FL 84+27/24 FLC 4+1 FAC 3
Others 3
Hartlepool U *(£30,000 on 6/3/2002)* FL
88+6/32 FLC 3/1 FAC 5 Others 5/2

WILLIAMS Gareth Ashley
Born: Cardiff, 10 September 1982
Height: 5'10" **Weight:** 11.13
International Honours: W: U21-5; Yth
Gareth was on the substitutes' bench on
a number of occasions for Crystal Palace
last term, but his only appearance was in
the Carling Cup game against Doncaster.
He spent much of the season out on loan
to gain experience of senior football.
Gareth scored a great goal on his debut

for Cambridge at Kidderminster and then
had a brief spell at Bournemouth where
he played just 20 minutes of first-team
football before suffering a training ground
injury. Finally, the talented midfielder
spent the closing stages of the campaign
at Colchester, where he once again
showed himself to be a lethal finisher. He
added further caps for Wales at U21 level
during the campaign.
Crystal Palace *(From trainee on 9/7/2002)* FL
0+5 FLC 2+1
Colchester U *(Loaned on 24/1/2003)* FL
6+2/6
Cambridge U *(Loaned on 30/10/2003)* FL 4/1
Bournemouth *(Loaned on 20/2/2004)* FL
0+1
Colchester U *(Loaned on 22/3/2004)* FL
5+2/2

WILLIAMS Gareth John
Born: Glasgow, 16 December 1981
Height: 5'11" **Weight:** 11.10
International Honours: S: 4; B-1; U21-9;
Yth
This talented Scotland international
started the 2003-04 season in his
customary position in front of the back
four for Nottingham Forest, but after a
change of management he was
encouraged to play a more attacking role
in midfield. The Forest fans saw a new
side to his game emerge, and he scored
five goals in the closing stages, including
a double against Crystal Palace. Gareth
also captained the side during the season
but was out of contract in the summer
and his future was unclear at the time of
writing.
Nottingham F *(From trainee on 23/12/1998)*
FL 132+10/9 FLC 4+1 FAC 5 Others 2

WILLIAMS Gavin John
Born: Pontypridd, 20 June 1980
Height: 5'10" **Weight:** 11.5
Club Honours: NC '03
This talented midfielder was the star
performer for Yeovil Town last term and
deservedly swept the board in voting for
the club's 'Player of the Year', winning
five awards. A near ever-present, he
finished as the club's leading scorer with
13 goals in all competitions. His probing
runs and defence-splitting passes are the
main features of his game and after
narrowly missing out on the play-offs he
will be hoping to lead the Glovers to
promotion in 2004-05.
Hereford U *(From trainee on 13/8/1998)*
Yeovil T *(£20,000 on 16/5/2002)* FL 42/9 FLC
1 FAC 3/3 Others 2/1

WILLIAMS John Nelson
Born: Birmingham, 11 May 1968
Height: 6'1" **Weight:** 13.12
If the veteran striker John Williams is only
remembered for one thing from his time
at Kidderminster last term, it will be the
goal he scored in the FA Cup tie against
Wolves. For 12 minutes his name was in
the headlines until a last-minute equaliser
broke Harriers' hearts. Although not as
speedy as he once was, John still gave his
all for the cause despite playing most of
the season on a week-to-week contract
with no job security. He was one of
several players released in the summer.
Swansea C *(£5,000 from Cradley T on
19/8/1991)* FL 36+3/11 FLC 2+1 FAC 3 Others
1
Coventry C *(£250,000 on 1/7/1992)* PL
66+14/11 FLC 4 FAC 2
Notts Co *(Loaned on 7/10/1994)* FL 3+2/2
Stoke C *(Loaned on 23/12/1994)* FL 1+3
Swansea C *(Loaned on 3/2/1995)* FL 6+1/2
Wycombe W *(£150,000 on 15/9/1995)* FL
34+1/9 FLC 4+1/2 FAC 5/4 Others 2
Hereford U *(Free on 14/2/1997)* FL 8+3/3
Walsall *(Free on 21/7/1997)* FL 0+1
Exeter C *(Free on 29/8/1997)* FL 16+20/4
Cardiff C *(Free on 3/8/1998)* FL 25+18/12
FLC 2/1 FAC 5/3 Others 1
York C *(£20,000 on 12/8/1999)* FL 29+13/3
FLC 2 FAC 0+1 Others 1
Darlington *(Free on 21/12/2000)* FL 23+1/5
Others 1
Swansea C *(Free on 17/7/2001)* FL 37+31/5
FLC 1+1 FAC 2+1/1 Others 1
Kidderminster Hrs *(Free on 8/8/2003)* FL
28+16/4 FLC 1 FAC 2+2/1 Others 1

WILLIAMS Marcus Vincent
Born: Doncaster, 8 April 1986
Height: 5'8" **Weight:** 10.9
A left winger in his second season as a
scholar at Scunthorpe United, Marcus
made a surprise first-team debut as a
substitute in the 3-0 home win against
Yeovil last March. He was mainly used as
a left wing back for the reserves, for
whom he proved to be a pacy, skilful
player.
Scunthorpe U *(Trainee)* FL 0+1

WILLIAMS Mark Stuart
Born: Stalybridge, 28 September 1970
Height: 6'0" **Weight:** 13.0
Club Honours: Div 3 '94
International Honours: NI: 30; B-1
Mark returned to Wimbledon after a spell
playing in the USA, and after a couple of
settling-in games quickly showed that he
had lost none of the central defensive
power and determination that had served
him so well during his previous spell.

Never the quickest of players, he had plenty of speedy legs around him to help out in that department, and the joy with which he celebrated his late headed equaliser in the draw at Cardiff spoke volumes as to the affection he clearly holds for the club. Mark was offered a new deal at the end of the season, which his performances undoubtedly deserved.

Shrewsbury T *(Free from Newtown on 27/3/1992) FL 96+6/3 FLC 7+1 FAC 6 Others 6/1*
Chesterfield *(£50,000 on 7/8/1995) FL 168/12 FLC 10 FAC 13/1 Others 7/1*
Watford *(Free on 13/7/1999) P/FL 20+2/1 FLC 2*
Wimbledon *(Signed on 26/7/2000) FL 69+1/7 FLC 5/1 FAC 8/1*
Stoke C *(Free on 11/3/2003) FL 5+1 (Freed during 2003 close season)*
Wimbledon *(Signed from Columbus Crew, USA on 6/2/2004) FL 11/1*

WILLIAMS Matthew
Born: Flint, 5 November 1982
Height: 5'8" **Weight:** 9.11
International Honours: W: U21-10; Yth
This skilful striker failed to make a breakthrough with Manchester United, despite featuring regularly for Wales at U21 level and shortly before the transfer deadline he signed for Notts County. Matthew showed plenty of promise in his outings for the Magpies and will be looking to establish himself in the line-up in 2004-05.

Manchester U *(From trainee on 1/2/2000)*
Notts Co *(Free on 18/3/2004) FL 5+2*

WILLIAMS Paul Darren
Born: Burton, 26 March 1971
Height: 6'0" **Weight:** 13.0
International Honours: E: U21-6
This uncompromising left-sided central defender arrived at Stoke during the 2003 close season and brought some much-needed experience to a young defence last term. He went straight into the side, despite not having played a full match for some time, and put on a good display. Injury and illness however laid him low for much of the campaign and he subsequently found it difficult to regain a position in the starting line-up.

Derby Co *(From trainee on 13/7/1989) FL 153+7/26 FLC 10+2/2 FAC 8/3 Others 14+1/2*
Lincoln C *(Loaned on 9/11/1989) FL 3 FAC 2 Others 1*
Coventry C *(£975,000 on 6/8/1995) P/FL 153+16/5 FLC 16+1/1 FAC 13*
Southampton *(Free on 26/10/2001) PL 37+2 FLC 1 FAC 2*
Stoke C *(Free on 20/8/2003) FL 16+3 FLC 1*

WILLIAMS Robert (Robbie) Ian
Born: Pontefract, 2 October 1984
Height: 5'10" **Weight:** 11.13
Robbie suffered a broken bone in his foot during pre-season training and was out of action until late in the campaign. He returned at left back for Barnsley and again showed immense promise, also taking on the responsibility of penalty taker. He will be looking for an injury-free season in 2004-05 to allow him to develop at first-team level.

Barnsley *(Trainee) FL 10+2/1 FAC 1 Others 0+1*

WILLIAMS Ryan Neil
Born: Sutton in Ashfield, 31 August 1978
Height: 5'5" **Weight:** 11.4
International Honours: E: Yth
Ryan was forced to sit out the first six weeks of the season due to a viral complaint, but after recovering he managed just one appearance for Hull City, playing (and scoring) in the LDV Vans Trophy win over Darlington. Soon afterwards he joined Bristol Rovers on loan, scoring a spectacular winner against the Tigers during his spell at Memorial Stadium. The tricky winger signed permanent forms for Rovers and settled in on the left hand-side of midfield, but only kept his place briefly and was made available for transfer in the summer.

Mansfield T *(Trainee) FL 9+17/3 FLC 2 FAC 0+1*
Tranmere Rov *(£70,000 + on 8/8/1997) FL 2+3*
Chesterfield *(£80,000 on 10/11/1999) FL 69+6/13 FLC 3 FAC 1 Others 5+1/1*
Hull C *(£150,000 on 9/7/2001) FL 40+12/2 FLC 1 FAC 2+1 Others 4+1/1*
Bristol Rov *(Free on 30/10/2003) FL 15+4/1 FAC 1*

WILLIAMS Steven (Steve)
Born: Oxford, 21 April 1983
Height: 6'4" **Weight:** 12.8
An injury to first-choice goalkeeper Frank Talia gave Steve the opportunity to make his debut for Wycombe at the start of last season and although he lost his place after four games he had three more spells in the team during the campaign. After a shaky start Steve visibly grew in confidence, particularly in the air, and is now a more than worthy first-team 'keeper. His season ended prematurely after he dislocated a finger during a training session.

Wycombe W *(From trainee on 12/4/2002) FL 19 FLC 2 FAC 1 Others 1*

WILLIAMS Thomas (Tommy) Andrew
Born: Carshalton, 8 July 1980
Height: 6'0" **Weight:** 11.8
Out of the first-team picture at Birmingham, Tommy joined Queens Park Rangers on loan at the start of last season where he operated on the left-hand side of defence and midfield. After returning to St Andrews Tommy went out on loan again, this time to Peterborough where he impressed with some confident, skilful displays and he was eventually signed on a contract until the end of the season.

West Ham U *(£60,000 from Walton & Hersham on 3/4/2000)*
Peterborough U *(Free on 22/3/2001) FL 32+4/2 FLC 1+1 FAC 4+1 Others 1*
Birmingham C *(£1,000,000 on 12/3/2002) FL 4*
Queens Park R *(Loaned on 8/8/2002) FL 22+4/1 FLC 1 FAC 2 Others 2+2*
Queens Park R *(Loaned on 4/8/2003) FL 4+1*
Peterborough U *(Free on 1/2/2004) FL 20+1/1 FAC 1*

WILLIAMSON Lee Trevor
Born: Derby, 7 June 1982
Height: 5'10" **Weight:** 10.4
This Mansfield Town youngster looked in impressive form in a central-midfield role at the start of the 2003-04 season, but then suspension and a cartilage injury kept him out of action. Lee made the starting line-up for over half the Stags fixtures, but was in and out of the side in the second half of the campaign.

Mansfield T *(From trainee on 3/7/2000) FL 111+29/3 FLC 3+3 FAC 8+1 Others 7*

WILLIAMSON Michael (Mike) James
Born: Stoke, 8 November 1983
Height: 6'4" **Weight:** 13.3
This young Southampton defender returned to his former club on loan and initially covered for the suspended Craig Taylor at centre back, before switching to the right-back position. Mike produced some effective performances, looking very comfortable with the ball at his feet. Later in the campaign he had a loan spell at Doncaster, signing as cover for injury and suspension, but was restricted to appearances as an unused substitute during his spell with the Yorkshire club.

Torquay U *(Trainee) FL 3 Others 1*
Southampton *(£100,000 on 21/11/2001)*
Torquay U *(Loaned on 15/9/2003) FL 9+2 Others 1*

WILLIS Adam Peter
Born: Nuneaton, 21 September 1976
Height: 6'1" **Weight:** 12.2

Adam proved to be one of Ian Britton's best signings for Kidderminster after arriving during the 2003 close season. He quickly settled into the centre of the defence, reading the game well and looking strong in the air. However, when manager Jan Molby returned to the club he sent Adam out on loan to Burton. He was then involved in a car crash suffering whiplash injuries, and he played no further games for Harriers before being released at the end of the campaign.
Coventry C *(From trainee on 1/7/1995)*
Swindon T *(Free on 21/4/1998) FL 76+16/1 FLC 2+1/1 FAC 3+1/1 Others 3*
Mansfield T *(Loaned on 25/3/1999) FL 10*
Kidderminster Hrs *(Free on 8/8/2003) FL 12/1 FLC 1*

WILLIS Scott Leon
Born: Liverpool, 20 February 1982
Height: 5'10" **Weight:** 11.5
This battling midfield man was given few opportunities to shine by Lincoln City last term, with his only appearances being from the substitutes' bench. Scott was loaned to Northwich Victoria but on his return failed to win a place in the Imps' squad. He was then loaned to Hereford United in February staying at Edgar Street until the end of the season when he was released by Lincoln.
Mansfield T *(From trainee at Wigan Ath on 23/3/2000. Freed on 23/2/2001)*
Carlisle U *(Free from Doncaster Rov on 10/8/2001) FL 0+1 (Free to Bamber Bridge on 17/10/2001)*
Lincoln C *(Free from Droylesden on 7/8/2002) FL 23+10/3 FLC 1 FAC 1 Others 1+4*

WILLMOTT Christopher (Chris) Alan
Born: Bedford, 30 September 1977
Height: 6'2" **Weight:** 11.12
Chris was a regular in the Northampton Town line-up last term, helping his side reach the Third Division play-offs. He bottled up the centre of defence with some strong tackling and the ability to push opposition forwards out to the flanks. He is also effective in the air and has been known to pop upfield and score the odd goal.
Luton T *(From trainee on 1/5/1996) FL 13+1*
Wimbledon *(£350,000 on 14/7/1999) P/FL 50+3/2 FLC 3+1 FAC 2*
Luton T *(Loaned on 1/2/2003) FL 7+1*
Luton T *(Loaned on 8/4/2003) FL 5*
Northampton T *(Free on 7/7/2003) FL 35+1/1 FLC 2 FAC 4 Others 5*

WILLOCK Calum Daniel
Born: London, 29 October 1981
Height: 5'11" **Weight:** 12.7
International Honours: St Kitts; E: Sch
Calum began last season on loan at Bristol Rovers, but although he tried hard he only featured from the bench and failed to find the net. Later he made a permanent move to Peterborough and established himself as a regular in the line-up. The pacy young striker discovered his goal touch to find the net on several occasions towards the end of the campaign and looked an exciting prospect. Calum ended a fine season when he was called up for international duty by St Kitts for their World Cup qualifying ties.
Fulham *(From ADT College, Putney on 18/7/2000) P/FL 0+5*
Queens Park R *(Loaned on 7/11/2002) FL 3*
Bristol Rov *(Loaned on 8/8/2003) FL 0+5*
Peterborough U *(£25,000 on 13/10/2003) FL 22+7/8 FAC 1+1/1 Others 2*

WILLS Kevin Michael
Born: Torquay, 15 October 1980
Height: 5'8" **Weight:** 10.7
Club Honours: Div 3 '02
Kevin was regularly involved at first-team level for Torquay in the opening half of the 2003-04 campaign, often featuring as a substitute but with a number of starts, most successfully as a slightly withdrawn second striker in away matches. His equaliser at Macclesfield and a neatly taken brace in a 2-1 win at Kidderminster earned vital points for the Gulls' promotion campaign. However, he received limited opportunities in the new year and was a little unfortunate to be released at the end of the season.
Plymouth Arg *(From trainee on 16/7/1999) FL 17+15/1 FLC 1 FAC 1+3 Others 2+1*
Torquay U *(Free on 29/11/2002) FL 12+31/4 FLC 0+1 FAC 0+2 Others 1/1*

WILNIS Fabian
Born: Surinam, 23 August 1970
Height: 5'8" **Weight:** 12.6
Fabian enjoyed a successful season in the right-back berth for Ipswich Town last term and produced some excellent attacking performances down the flank. He used his experience to good effect when faced with marauding wingers and there were not many that got past him. The best indication of his season was that he was most certainly missed when he was unable to play.
Ipswich T *(£200,000 from De Graafschap, Holland, ex NAC Breda, on 6/1/1999) P/FL 154+18/5 FLC 10+3 FAC 9 Others 11+1*

WILSON Brian Jason
Born: Manchester, 9 May 1983
Height: 5'10" **Weight:** 11.0
This promising young right back did well with Stoke's reserve team last season, but managed only three first-team appearances, all from the substitutes' bench. Brian made a big impression at Cheltenham Town during a one-month loan spell at the turn of the year and eventually made a permanent move to Whaddon Road on transfer-deadline day. A composed defender with good positional sense and comfortable on the ball, he loves to get forward and support the attack. He is not afraid to shoot from distance and almost scored with an audacious 40-yard effort against Hull City. Brian can also play on the right-hand side of midfield.
Stoke C *(From trainee on 5/7/2001) FL 1+5 FLC 0+1 Others 1*
Cheltenham T *(Loaned on 12/12/2003) FL 7 FAC 1*
Cheltenham T *(Signed on 25/3/2004) FL 7*

WILSON Che Christian Aaron Clay
Born: Ely, 17 January 1979
Height: 5'9" **Weight:** 11.3
Che proved to be a useful squad player for Southend United last term after signing from Dr Martens League club Cambridge City. Although primarily employed at left back, he also produced some sterling performances in a central-midfield role. His overall contribution to the squad was sufficient to earn a new contract at Roots Hall.
Norwich C *(From trainee on 3/7/1997) FL 16+6 FLC 3*
Bristol Rov *(Free on 13/7/2000) FL 74+1 FLC 7 FAC 6 Others 3+1 (Free to Cambridge C during 2002 close season)*
Southend U *(Free on 30/7/2003) FL 11+3 FAC 2 Others 3+4*

WILSON Kelvin
Born: Nottingham, 3 September 1985
Height: 6'2" **Weight:** 12.3
A versatile defender who can play either at right back or in the centre of defence, Kelvin was a member of the Notts County youth team that won the Midland Youth Cup last term. An excellent prospect, he made his Football League debut as a substitute at Hartlepool in April and went on to feature in the starting line-up in the final two games of the season.
Notts Co *(Trainee) FL 2+1*

WILSON Laurie James
Born: Brighton, 5 December 1984
Height: 5'10" **Weight:** 11.4

Steve Wilson

International Honours: NI: Yth
This promising young midfield player did well in the reserves for Sheffield Wednesday last term, but received few first-team opportunities and was released by the Owls when his contract expired in the summer. Laurie is the son of the former Bristol City manager Danny Wilson.
Sheffield Wed (Trainee) FAC 0+2 Others 1

WILSON Mark Antony
Born: Scunthorpe, 9 February 1979
Height: 5'11" **Weight:** 13.0
Club Honours: E: Yth; Sch
International Honours: E: U21-2; Yth; Sch
This young Middlesbrough midfield player was unable to break into the first-team squad last term and in September he joined Swansea City on loan. He had a successful time at the Vetch Field, showing plenty of skills and vision in the centre of the park and scoring twice. However, he returned to the Riverside with a hamstring injury. Once fit again he went out on loan to Sheffield Wednesday, but after a couple of promising performances he suffered a cruciate ligament injury in the match at Port Vale and returned to the North-East to recuperate.
Manchester U (From trainee on 16/2/1996) PL 1+2 FLC 2 Others 3+2
Wrexham (Loaned on 23/2/1998) FL 12+1/4
Middlesbrough (£1,500,000 on 9/8/2001) PL 6+10 FLC 4/2 FAC 2+1
Stoke C (Loaned on 14/3/2003) FL 4
Swansea C (Loaned on 12/9/2003) FL 12/2 Others 1
Sheffield Wed (Loaned on 22/1/2004) FL 3

WILSON Stephen (Steve) Lee
Born: Hull, 24 April 1974
Height: 5'10" **Weight:** 11.2
Steve found himself on the substitutes' bench for Macclesfield at the start of last season when Boaz Myhill was preferred, but resumed his place as goalkeeper at the end of October when Myhill was injured. Steve soon proved his worth and whilst he commands his area well and has improved his handling of high crosses, his greatest attribute is undoubtedly as a shot-stopper. This was best illustrated in the FA Cup tie at home to Cambridge United when he saved two penalties to earn Macclesfield a replay and then went on to play his part in the penalty shoot-out which followed the replay, and which saw Macc progress to the next round.

Hull C *(From trainee on 13/7/1992) FL 180+1 FLC 13 FAC 13 Others 11+1*
Macclesfield T *(Free on 22/3/2001) FL 114+1 FLC 2 FAC 11 Others 3*

WILTORD Sylvain
Born: Paris, France, 10 May 1974
Height: 5'9" **Weight:** 12.2
Club Honours: FAC '02, '03; PL '02, '04; CS '02
International Honours: France: 65 (UEFA '00)
Sylvain started the season as first choice and in his preferred role of centre forward for Arsenal, but after three early goals he suffered an injury-hit campaign and one that was also blighted by poor form. He missed the vast majority of the run-in, only returning against Leeds in April when his impact was minimal. A member of the France squad for Euro 2004, it was announced he would leave the club during the summer.
Arsenal *(£13,000,000 from Bordeaux, France, ex Rennes, Girondins, on 31/8/2000) PL 78+28/31 FLC 7/5 FAC 14+6/10 Others 25+17/3*

WINDASS Dean
Born: Hull, 1 April 1969
Height: 5'10" **Weight:** 12.6
Dean began his second spell at Bradford as a central midfielder or playing just behind the strikers. However, he was soon moved back to centre forward where he scored his first goal against former club Sheffield United. The wholehearted player did not want to miss any games and put off a double hernia operation for a month. He finally went under the knife after breaking his hand in an FA Cup defeat against Luton. When Dean returned fully fit, the difference was immediate and he scored in four of the next five games.
Hull C *(Free from North Ferriby on 24/10/1991) FL 173+3/57 FLC 11/4 FAC 6 Others 12/3*
Aberdeen *(£700,000 on 1/12/1995) SL 60+13/21 SLC 5+2/6 SC 7/3 Others 6/1*
Oxford U *(£475,000 on 6/8/1998) FL 33/15 FLC 2 FAC 3/3*
Bradford C *(£950,000 + on 5/3/1999) P/FL 64+10/16 FLC 6/2 FAC 2 Others 6/3*
Middlesbrough *(£600,000 + on 15/3/2001) PL 16+21/3 FLC 2 FAC 4+3*
Sheffield Wed *(Loaned on 6/12/2001) FL 2*
Sheffield U *(Loaned on 11/11/2002) FL 4/3*
Sheffield U *(Signed on 16/1/2003) FL 16/3 Others 2*
Bradford C *(Free on 14/7/2003) FL 34+2/6 FLC 1 FAC 1*

WINTERS Thomas (Tom) Richard
Born: Banbury, 11 December 1985
Height: 5'9" **Weight:** 10.10
A second-year scholar with Oxford United, Tom enjoyed an impressive season with the club's reserves in 2003-04 and was rewarded when he was given his senior debut when coming off the bench in the final game of the season against Rochdale. A wide-left midfield player, he made a good impression with some probing runs and came close to finding the net with a long-range drive.
Oxford U *(Trainee) FL 0+1*

WISE Dennis Frank
Born: Kensington, 15 December 1966
Height: 5'6" **Weight:** 10.10
Club Honours: FAC '88, '97, '00; FLC '98; ECWC '98; ESC '98; CS '00
International Honours: E: 21; B-3; U21-1
Dennis proved the doubters wrong last season by making his mark as a player-manager with Millwall. After succeeding Mark McGhee early on in the campaign, his hard-work ethic producing the very best out of a squad that had previously stumbled along. He was a huge inspiration to all around him and was one of the main reasons why the club reached the FA Cup final for the first time in their history. A thorn to opponents, he has great energy and motivation and formed an excellent managerial partnership with Ray Wilkins.
Wimbledon *(From trainee at Southampton on 28/3/1985) FL 127+8/27 FLC 14 FAC 11/3 Others 5*
Chelsea *(£1,600,000 on 3/7/1990) F/PL 322+10/53 FLC 30/6 FAC 38/8 Others 44+1/8*
Leicester C *(£1,600,000 + on 23/6/2001) PL 15+2/1 FLC 1 FAC 1*
Millwall *(Free on 24/9/2002) FL 54+6/4 FAC 9/1*

WISE Stuart
Born: Middlesbrough, 4 April 1984
Height: 6'1" **Weight:** 13.2
The powerfully built central defender missed a large part of York City's 2003-04 campaign due to injury. Stuart eventually recovered and regained his place in the closing weeks. He impressed with his strength, heading ability and commitment in the Minstermen defence and scored his first senior goal in City's last home game of the season against Leyton Orient.
York C *(From trainee on 8/7/2003) FL 24+9/1 FLC 1 Others 1*

WISEMAN Scott Nigel Kenneth
Born: Hull, 9 October 1985
Height: 6'0" **Weight:** 11.6
This promising young right back's rise through the Hull ranks was duly rewarded last April when he was given his first professional contract and then made his senior debut from the substitutes' bench at Kidderminster. Scott came on to give an impressive and confident display as the promotion-chasing Tigers earned a point in a bruising 1-1 draw. His undoubted potential was recognised when he won Hull's 'Young Player of the Year' award.
Hull C *(From trainee on 8/4/2004) FL 0+2*

WOLFENDEN Matthew (Matty)
Born: Oldham, 23 July 1987
Height: 5'9" **Weight:** 11.1
Matthew became one of the youngest-ever players in the history of Oldham Athletic when he made his first-team debut against Swindon last November aged 16 years and 115 days. A hard-working and gifted talent, Matthew is primarily a striker but can also switch to a wide position when required. A local lad, he played no further part in the first team thereafter but will be hoping to benefit from new manager Brian Talbot's expressed belief in giving the club's youngsters their chance in 2004-05.
Oldham Ath *(Trainee) FL 0+1*

WOLLEASTON Robert Ainsley
Born: Perivale, 21 December 1979
Height: 5'11" **Weight:** 12.2
A skilful attacking midfielder, Robert joined Bradford shortly before the start of the season after finding himself well down the pecking order at Stamford Bridge. He was used extensively as a substitute, coming off the bench in four of the first six matches, but was unable to break through into the starting line-up. Robert finally made his full debut against Reading on Easter Saturday and scored his first senior goal two days later at Derby.
Chelsea *(From trainee on 3/6/1998) PL 0+1 FLC 0+1*
Bristol Rov *(Loaned on 23/3/2000) FL 0+4*
Portsmouth *(Loaned on 8/3/2001) FL 5+1*
Northampton T *(Loaned on 4/7/2001) FL 2+5 FLC 0+1*
Bradford C *(Free on 14/7/2003) FL 6+8/1 FLC 0+1*

WOOD Leigh James
Born: Selby, 21 May 1983
Height: 6'1" **Weight:** 11.2
Leigh had a mixed campaign for York City in 2003-04 when he was troubled by a

Jonathan Woodgate (left)

shoulder injury mid-term. He figured for the Minstermen in central defence and at full back, but was at his best and most comfortable in a central-midfield role where he impressed with his ball control and passing skills. Leigh was one of several senior players released by City in the summer.
York C (From trainee on 7/3/2002) FL 44+20 FLC 1 Others 1

WOOD Neil Anthony
Born: Manchester, 4 January 1983
Height: 5'10" **Weight:** 13.2
This Manchester United youngster had a spell on loan with Peterborough early on last term when he scored once. In the new year he was out on loan again, this time to Burnley. His three months at Turf Moor saw much promise, with Neil usually lying just behind the forwards, but always keen to both instigate and finish off attacking moves. His only goal came in one of his best performances, in the home game against Norwich, and he is a player that the Clarets' fans would be delighted to see more of in the future.
Manchester U (From trainee on 7/11/2000)
Peterborough U (Loaned on 12/9/2003) FL 2+1/1
Burnley (Loaned on 30/1/2004) FL 8+2/1 FAC 1

WOOD Richard Mark
Born: Wakefield, 5 July 1985
Height: 6'3" **Weight:** 11.11
This young Sheffield Wednesday defender had something of an up-and-down season last term. An excellent covering player, who is good at tackling and more than useful in the air at both ends of the pitch, he failed to establish himself in the side. However, Richard was in the line-up for the closing fixtures and will be hoping to retain his place in the 2004-05 campaign.
Sheffield Wed (From trainee on 7/4/2003) FL 12+3/1 FLC 1/1 FAC 0+1 Others 2+1

WOODGATE Jonathan Simon
Born: Middlesbrough, 22 January 1980
Height: 6'2" **Weight:** 13.0
Club Honours: FAYC '97
International Honours: E: 5; U21-1; Yth
Injuries proved disruptive for Jonathan in his first full season in the heart of Newcastle's back four. Stomach problems led to him missing early-season matches, he then underwent a double hernia operation in October, suffered a torn hamstring in December, and his campaign was brought to a premature close when

he tore a thigh muscle in the home game with Chelsea in April. When fit he brought a touch of class to Newcastle's defence through both his own performances and his motivation and organisation of his colleagues. His straight-backed gait hides a surprising turn of speed, while his timing and reading of the game enable him to snuff out attacks before they become too dangerous, rarely having to go to ground. After missing several England calls up because of his injuries he played against Sweden in March, but another injury kept him out of the squad for Euro 2004 in the summer.
Leeds U (From trainee on 13/5/1997) PL 100+4/4 FLC 7 FAC 11 Others 20
Newcastle U (£9,000,000 on 31/1/2003) PL 28 FAC 2 Others 7

WOODHOUSE Curtis
Born: Beverley, 17 April 1980
Height: 5'8" **Weight:** 11.0
International Honours: E: U21-4; Yth
Curtis was once again out of the first-team picture at Birmingham last term and in October he moved on to sign for Peterborough. A powerful and skilful midfielder, he produced some spirited performances and was a key figure in turning the club's fortunes around. A hard-working box-to-box player, he was voted as 'Player of the Year' by the Posh supporters.
Sheffield U (From trainee on 31/12/1997) FL 92+12/6 FLC 5+3 FAC 10
Birmingham C (£1,000,000 on 2/2/2001) P/FL 35+13/2 FLC 3+1 FAC 1 Others 2
Rotherham U (Loaned on 1/2/2003) FL 11
Peterborough U (Free on 13/10/2003) FL 26+1/7 FAC 3 Others 3

WOODMAN Andrew (Andy) John
Born: Camberwell, 11 August 1971
Height: 6'3" **Weight:** 13.7
Club Honours: Div 3 '99
Andy was an ever-present in goal for Oxford United under Ian Atkins, but by a twist of fate in Graham Rix's first game as manager an injury let in young Simon Cox and the popular 'keeper ended the season sharing the gloves with the youngster. A very experienced professional, Andy kept 16 clean sheets during the campaign, mostly early on when the U's defence was at its meanest. Andy was out of contract in the summer and it was reported he had signed for Stevenage.
Crystal Palace (From trainee on 1/7/1989)

Exeter C (Free on 4/7/1994) FL 6 FLC 1 FAC 1 Others 2
Northampton T (Free on 10/3/1995) FL 163 FLC 13 FAC 8 Others 13
Brentford (Signed on 22/1/1999) FL 61 FLC 1 FAC 2 Others 3
Southend U (Loaned on 8/8/2000) FL 17 FLC 2
Colchester U (Free on 10/11/2000) FL 54 FLC 2 FAC 2 Others 1
Oxford U (Free on 18/1/2002) FL 101 FLC 5 FAC 4 Others 2

WOODMAN Craig Alan
Born: Tiverton, 22 December 1982
Height: 5'9" **Weight:** 9.11
This left wing back featured regularly for Bristol City in the middle of last term and was then brought back for the end-of-season play-offs. The promising youngster will have learnt from his experiences, despite the disappointment at the failure to win promotion, and will be looking to establish himself in the line-up in the 2004-05 campaign.
Bristol C (From trainee on 17/2/2000) FL 27+12 FLC 2 FAC 3 Others 10

WOODS Stephen (Steve) John
Born: Northwich, 15 December 1976
Height: 5'11" **Weight:** 12.3
After spending much of the previous campaign on the injury list, Steve came back last term to establish a useful centre-back partnership with Craig Taylor – their solid combination forming the bedrock of Torquay's promotion campaign. An excellent organiser, strong in the air and solid on the ground with good distribution skills, he chipped in with six goals including two penalties and a crucial volley in the decisive last-day win at Southend. Steve was United's only ever-present and runner-up in the poll for 'Player of the Year'.
Stoke C (From trainee on 3/8/1995) FL 33+1 FLC 2 FAC 2 Others 2
Plymouth Arg (Loaned on 26/3/1998) FL 4+1
Chesterfield (Free on 7/7/1999) FL 22+3 FLC 4 Others 0+1
Torquay U (Free on 17/8/2001) FL 89+4/8 FLC 2 FAC 3 Others 1

WOODTHORPE Colin John
Born: Ellesmere Port, 13 January 1969
Height: 5'11" **Weight:** 11.8
Bury's utility man started 39 Third Division fixtures for last season, and would have played more games had he not been forced out by suspensions. Nevertheless, Colin continued to give the Shakers great service, whether at left back – where he

Andy Woodman

appeared throughout the first half of the season – or in the centre of a back five where he featured latterly.
Chester C *(From trainee on 23/8/1986) FL 154+1/6 FLC 10 FAC 8+1 Others 18/1*
Norwich C *(£175,000 on 17/7/1990) P/FL 36+7/1 FLC 0+2 FAC 6 Others 1+1*
Aberdeen *(£400,000 on 20/7/1994) SL 43+5/1 SLC 5+1/1 SC 4 Others 5+2*
Stockport Co *(£200,000 on 29/7/1997) FL 114+39/4 FLC 12+1/2 FAC 4+1/1*
Bury *(Free on 23/8/2002) FL 69+2 FLC 3+1 FAC 2 Others 8/1*

WOOZLEY David James
Born: Ascot, 6 December 1979
Height: 6'0" **Weight:** 12.10
After being a regular at centre back for Torquay during the previous season, David had a somewhat different campaign at Plainmoor last term. He played two games as an emergency centre forward and one as a left back before a knee injury led to a four-month lay-off. On his return he had another two games at left back before a marathon spell on the bench, as Steve Woods and Craig Taylor firmly established themselves at centre back.
Crystal Palace *(From trainee on 17/11/1997) FL 21+9 FLC 3+1 FAC 0+1*
Bournemouth *(Loaned on 15/9/2000) FL 6*
Torquay U *(Loaned on 28/8/2001) FL 12 FLC 1*
Torquay U *(Free on 27/3/2002) FL 52+8/3 FLC 2 FAC 2 Others 1*

WORGAN Lee John
Born: Eastbourne, 1 December 1983
Height: 6'1" **Weight:** 13.10
International Honours: W: Yth
Lee made his debut for Wimbledon as a substitute 'keeper against Bradford City in November, but it was his next match, away at Rotherham, that proved to be the turning point in his Wimbledon career. Once again used from the bench, he was judged at fault for a headed goal from a corner, and later received a red card. He was subsequently loaned out to Wycombe who required special dispensation to sign him as the transfer deadline had passed. However, he only had two games to show what a superb shot-stopper he is before being recalled by the Dons, ironically to cover for the injured Scott Bevan, Wycombe's previous loan 'keeper last season.
Wimbledon *(From trainee on 9/4/2003) FL 0+3*
Wycombe W *(Loaned on 12/4/2004) FL 2*

WORRELL David
Born: Dublin, 12 January 1978
Height: 5'11" **Weight:** 12.4
Club Honours: Div 3 '02; Div 2 '04
International Honours: RoI: U21-17
David was a regular in the starting line-up for Plymouth last term in his familiar position at right back before losing his place to Paul Connolly in November. He was then restricted to the reserves and managed just one more first-team appearance, but nevertheless remained an important member of Argyle's Second Division championship-winning squad.
Blackburn Rov (Signed from Shelbourne on 12/1/1995)
Dundee U (Free on 30/3/1999) SL 13+4 SLC 2
Plymouth Arg (Signed on 23/11/2000) FL 117 FLC 2 FAC 9 Others 6

WORTHINGTON Jonathan (Jon) Alan
Born: Dewsbury, 16 April 1983
Height: 5'9" **Weight:** 11.0
This energetic midfielder was given an opportunity by Huddersfield Town last term and grabbed it with both hands. He impressed with some displays of strong running and tenacious tackling and contributed three goals. Jon finished the season by winning the Terriers' 'Player of the Year' award.
Huddersfield T (From trainee on 10/9/2001) FL 46+15/3 FLC 2 FAC 2 Others 4

WOTTON Paul Anthony
Born: Plymouth, 17 August 1977
Height: 5'11" **Weight:** 12.0
Club Honours: Div 3 '02; Div 2 '04
Paul once again had a solid season for Plymouth Argyle in 2003-04. He served the team as captain and initially formed a powerful central-defensive partnership with Graham Coughlan. Then, after losing his place, he fought his way back into the side as a central midfield player. He notched a total of nine goals during the campaign including Argyle's 5000th goal in the Football League, a 45-yard wind-assisted effort against Bournemouth on Boxing Day.
Plymouth Arg (From trainee on 10/7/1995) FL 250+29/29 FLC 7+1 FAC 21/5 Others 9+1/2

WRACK Darren
Born: Cleethorpes, 5 May 1976
Height: 5'9" **Weight:** 12.10
Darren featured intermittently for Walsall early on last season and it was not until October that he won a regular place in the team. The experienced wing back netted five times in a run of four games in the autumn, including doubles against Wigan and Nottingham Forest in the space of a week. He willingly played out of position when it was in the interests of the team, and although injured against Sunderland early in March he was back for the last two games, running and tackling as tirelessly as ever as his tally of games for the Saddlers approached the 300 mark.
Derby Co (From trainee on 12/7/1994) FL 4+22/1 FLC 0+3 FAC 0+2
Grimsby T (£100,000 + on 19/7/1996) FL 5+8/1 Others 0+1
Shrewsbury T (Loaned on 17/2/1997) FL 3+1 Others 1
Walsall (Free on 6/8/1998) FL 197+34/37 FLC 12+1/1 FAC 13+1/2 Others 7+1/1

WRIGHT Alan Geoffrey
Born: Ashton under Lyne, 28 September 1971
Height: 5'4" **Weight:** 9.9
Club Honours: FLC '96
International Honours: E: U21-2; Yth; Sch
In the summer of 2003 Middlesbrough boss Steve McClaren brought defender Alan Wright in as full-back cover, and with his Villa career in decline Alan accepted the opportunity to try his luck on Teesside. However, Alan's chances of first-team football were restricted to just two games – he made his Boro' debut against Fulham on the opening day of the

Lee Worgan

season – and his final game was in the 4-0 defeat at the Riverside by Arsenal. Alan went to Sheffield United on loan, before making the move a permanent one in January. He initially played as a left wing back for the Blades, followed by a brief spell in midfield, but after a few games on the bench he returned to his defensive role. He is quick and decisive in the tackle and positive coming forward.

Blackpool *(From trainee on 13/4/1989) FL 91+7 FLC 10+2 FAC 8 Others 11+2*
Blackburn Rov *(£400,000 on 25/10/1991) F/PL 67+7/1 FLC 8 FAC 5+1 Others 3*
Aston Villa *(£1,000,000 on 10/3/1995) PL 255+5/5 FLC 19 FAC 25 Others 26*
Middlesbrough *(Free on 12/8/2003) PL 2*
Sheffield U *(Free on 31/10/2003) FL 21/1 FAC 2+1*

WRIGHT David
Born: Warrington, 1 May 1980
Height: 5'11" **Weight:** 10.8
International Honours: E: Yth
This consistent right back was a near ever-present for Crewe last season, contributing a rare goal in the 2-2 draw at West Bromwich Albion in December. David is a versatile player who can take any position in the back line and captained the side last term in the absence of Dave Brammer.
Crewe Alex *(From trainee on 18/6/1997) FL 206+5/3 FLC 10+1 FAC 12 Others 3+1*

WRIGHT Jermaine Malaki
Born: Greenwich, 21 October 1975
Height: 5'9" **Weight:** 11.9
International Honours: E: Yth
This underrated Ipswich player quietly goes about his midfield work, delivering a telling pass or a weighted through ball to set up goal attempts for his colleagues. Jermaine has an excellent shot with either foot and is not afraid to have a try at goal. It was his spectacular equaliser from some way out that provided the springboard at Rotherham for Town to go on and win the game after trailing at the interval. He is also very versatile and is capable of filling in at full back if required.
Millwall *(From trainee on 27/11/1992)*
Wolverhampton W *(£60,000 on 29/12/1994) FL 4+16 FLC 1+3/1 Others 0+1*
Doncaster Rov *(Loaned on 1/3/1996) FL 13*
Crewe Alex *(£25,000 on 19/2/1998) FL 47+2/5 FLC 5 FAC 1*
Ipswich T *(£500,000 on 23/7/1999) P/FL 147+37/10 FLC 15+2 FAC 8+1/1 Others 10+1*

WRIGHT Mark Anthony
Born: Wolverhampton, 24 February 1982
Height: 5'11" **Weight:** 11.4

This promising young midfielder featured regularly for Walsall in the closing stages of the 2003-04 campaign, although most of his appearances were from the substitutes' bench. He consistently livened games up with his running and accurate crossing from the right flank, opening his first-team scoring account with the match winner at Preston in March and finding the net again in the final game against Rotherham.
Walsall *(From trainee on 26/1/2001) FL 5+15/2 FLC 0+1 Others 2*

WRIGHT Richard Ian
Born: Ipswich, 5 November 1977
Height: 6'2" **Weight:** 13.0
Club Honours: FAC '02; PL '02
International Honours: E: 2; U21-15; Yth; Sch
Richard was another Everton player to suffer an injury-plagued campaign last term. After suffering a domestic accident that upset his pre-season arrangements, he started the first three games only for a troublesome knee injury to keep him out for six months. The brilliant form of Nigel Martyn kept the England international on the bench for the remainder of the campaign. Richard is a fine 'keeper, excelling in shot-stopping as well as being good at dealing with high balls.
Ipswich T *(From trainee on 2/1/1995) P/FL 240 FLC 27 FAC 13 Others 11*
Arsenal *(£6,000,000 on 13/7/2001) PL 12 FLC 1 FAC 5 Others 4*
Everton *(£3,500,000 + on 26/7/2002) PL 37 FLC 3 FAC 1*

WRIGHT Stephen John
Born: Liverpool, 8 February 1980
Height: 6'2" **Weight:** 12.0
Club Honours: UEFAC '01
International Honours: E: U21-6; Yth
Sunderland's first choice right back had his 2003-04 season interrupted by a succession of injuries. A committed, powerful competitor, Stephen has become a popular figure at the Stadium of Light and his first-ever goal in a red-and-white shirt against Watford in August was arguably the Black Cats' 'Goal of the Season', scored after he made a 70-yard run upfield to fire home a Marcus Stewart pass. Stephen returned to the side to feature in the FA Cup semi-final against Millwall but aggravated a thigh injury, which meant another spell on the sidelines.
Liverpool *(From trainee on 13/10/1997) PL 10+4 FLC 1+1 FAC 2 Others 2+1/1*
Crewe Alex *(Loaned on 6/8/1999) FL 17+6 FLC 1*

Sunderland *(£3,000,000 on 15/8/2002) P/FL 45+3/1 FLC 0+1 FAC 8*

WRIGHT Thomas (Tommy) Andrew
Born: Kirby Muxloe, 28 September 1984
Height: 6'0" **Weight:** 11.12
International Honours: E: Yth
This young Leicester City striker signed a long-term contract in the summer of 2003 and in September he joined Brentford on loan. He made a great early impression for the Bees, netting on his first two starts against Hartlepool and Chesterfield, but then injuries and international call-ups disrupted his season and he eventually returned to the Walker Stadium when he was injured again in April. Tommy represented England at U20 level during the World Youth Championships in Dubai during the campaign.
Leicester C *(From trainee on 10/6/2003) P/FL 2+12 FAC 0+1*
Brentford *(Loaned on 12/9/2003) FL 18+7/3*

WRIGHT-PHILLIPS Shaun Cameron
Born: Greenwich, 25 October 1981
Height: 5'6" **Weight:** 10.1
Club Honours: Div 1 '02
International Honours: E: U21-6
Shaun is a player of real pace and skill with the ability to lift spectators from their seats. He can operate in a variety of roles but his preferred territory is on the right wing. Shaun has skill, speed, determination and courage and he can score goals as well as make them. One of the stars of the Manchester City side last term, he thoroughly deserved his call-up to the full England squad for the friendly against Sweden in Gothenburg. Shaun deservedly won the Blues' supporters' 'Player of the Year' award.
Manchester C *(From trainee on 28/10/1998) P/FL 97+22/16 FLC 7+4/2 FAC 7+1/1 Others 4+2/1*

WROE Nicholas (Nicky)
Born: Sheffield, 28 September 1985
Height: 5'11" **Weight:** 10.7
Nicky was on the fringe of the Barnsley first team for nearly all of the 2003-04 season, but had to wait until near the end of the campaign to get his chance. A young midfielder of immense promise, he scored his first-ever Football League goal at Stockport on the final day of the campaign.
Barnsley *(Trainee) FL 2+1/1*

XYZ

YAKUBU Ayegbeni
Born: Benin City, Nigeria, 22 November 1982
Height: 6'0" **Weight:** 13.1
Club Honours: Div 1 '03
International Honours: Nigeria
Pompey's top scorer in 2003-04 with 16 Premiership goals and three in cup competitions, this powerful striker was in electric form at the end of the season with 11 goals in 10 games; 4 of which were struck in the last game against Middlesbrough. Strong in the challenge, fast and able to take on players, he remains an exciting prospect for the future.
Portsmouth *(Loaned from Maccabi Haifa, Israel, ex Okomo Oil, Julius Berger, Hapoel Kfar-Saba, on 13/1/2003) P/FL 47+4/23 FLC 1+1/2 FAC 4/1*

YALCIN Levent (Lev)
Born: Middlesbrough, 25 March 1985
Height: 6'0" **Weight:** 12.2
International Honours: Turkey: Yth
After missing the first half of the 2003-04 season through injury Lev was a regular member of York City's first-team squad in the closing months. Although still to score at senior level, the young striker showed plenty of promise with his pace, control and skill.
York C *(Trainee) FL 5+15 FLC 0+1*

YATES Mark Jason
Born: Birmingham, 24 January 1970
Height: 5'11" **Weight:** 13.2
Club Honours: NC '99
International Honours: E: SP-2
Mark began last term as captain of Cheltenham Town, but following a change in management he lost his place in the side in December. In February he returned to his former club Kidderminster to provide leadership and a ball-winning

Ayegbeni Yakubu

Mark Yates

presence in the centre of the park. He scored twice for the Harriers, including a late penalty to save a point in the game at Leyton Orient, but despite some useful performances he was released at the end of the season.

Birmingham C *(From trainee on 8/7/1988) FL 38+16/6 FLC 5/1 FAC 0+2 Others 5*
Burnley *(£40,000 on 30/8/1991) FL 9+9/1 FLC 1 FAC 0+2 Others 2+1*
Lincoln C *(Loaned on 19/2/1993) FL 10+4*
Doncaster Rov *(Signed on 30/7/1993) FL 33+1/4 FLC 2 FAC 1 Others 1 (Transferred to Kidderminster Hrs on 13/8/1994)*
Cheltenham T *(Signed on 28/1/1999) FL 190+4/19 FLC 8 FAC 13+1/2 Others 8+2*
Kidderminster Hrs *(Free on 26/2/2004) FL 14/2*

YATES Steven (Steve)
Born: Bristol, 29 January 1970
Height: 5'11" **Weight:** 12.2
Club Honours: Div 3 '90
This veteran defender slotted perfectly into the back line for Huddersfield Town last term. Strong and uncompromising in the tackle, he provided experience and leadership to the younger players around him and after recovering from a groin injury he became a real rock in the team. Steve was voted 'Players' Player of the Year' for the Terriers.
Bristol Rov *(From trainee on 1/7/1988) FL 196+1 FLC 9 FAC 11 Others 21*
Queens Park R *(£650,000 on 16/8/1993) P/FL 122+12/2 FLC 8 FAC 7*
Tranmere Rov *(Free on 5/8/1999) FL 109+4/7 FLC 13+1/2 FAC 10/5*
Sheffield U *(Free on 4/7/2002) FL 11+1 FLC 1*
Huddersfield T *(Free on 7/8/2003) FL 35/1 FLC 3 Others 3*

YEATES Mark Stephen
Born: Dublin, 11 January 1985
Height: 5'9" **Weight:** 10.7
International Honours: RoI: U21-2; Yth
This promising Tottenham teenager spent two months on loan at Brighton last term. Introduced as a winger, he blossomed when switched to a central-midfield role, impressing with his vision and shooting ability. By the time he left the youngster had become an important cog in the Albion midfield. Mark later stepped up to make his bow in the Premiership when he featured in the starting line-up against Wolves on the final day of the season.
Tottenham H *(From trainee on 25/7/2002) PL 1*
Brighton & Hove A *(Loaned on 14/11/2003) FL 9 Others 1*

Mark Yeates

YEO Simon John
Born: Stockport, 20 October 1973
Height: 5'10" **Weight:** 11.8
Simon reached a double-figure goal tally for Lincoln City last term, despite having few opportunities in the starting line-up. He proved most effective as a substitute capable of changing the game with his pace when used on the left side of a three-man attack. Eight of his goals came from the bench including a number of important strikes in the run-in to the end of the campaign. Simon was offered a new deal by Lincoln in the summer.
Lincoln C (Free from Hyde U on 7/8/2002) FL 35+43/16 FLC 0+1 FAC 3/1 Others 5+5/6

YETTON Stewart David
Born: Plymouth, 27 July 1985
Height: 5'8" **Weight:** 10.3
This promising Plymouth Argyle youngster added a further appearance as a substitute last term, coming off the bench at Hartlepool in May. A pacy striker who never stops running, he is always quick to close down opposing defenders. Stewart will be looking to gain further experience of senior football in 2004-05.
Plymouth Arg (Trainee) FL 0+2

YOBO Joseph
Born: Kano, Nigeria, 6 September 1980
Height: 6'2" **Weight:** 11.6
International Honours: Nigeria
After signing a long-term contract in pre-season, Joseph's season at Everton was split into two separate periods. Prior to his departure for the African Nations' Cup he remained a competent presence in the Blues defence, without looking the top-class centre half he had seemed in 2002-03. However, when he returned to the club in February his confidence was restored and he produced a series of superb displays, showing the class and form that makes him one of the best young defenders in the top-flight. At his best he shows awesome pace and presence, which is combined with good skill on the ball and fine, crisp tackling. During the season he also became a greater threat in the opposition box, scoring his first two goals for the club.
Everton (£4,500,000 from Marseilles, France, ex Mechelen, Standard Liege, on 6/8/2002) PL 49+3/2 FLC 4 FAC 0+1

YORKE Dwight
Born: Canaan, Tobago, 3 November 1971
Height: 5'10" **Weight:** 12.4
Club Honours: FLC '96; FAC '99; PL '99, '00, '01; EC '99

Joseph Yobo

International Honours: Trinidad & Tobago

Although he started the season keeping out Andy Cole, Dwight was generally a peripheral figure at Blackburn last term. He featured in over half the Premiership games, but was often on the bench and scored just six goals. His best moment was a headed equaliser against Wolves and his meagre goal tally was unusual in that most were scored with his head rather than his feet. Dwight made a surprise return to international duty during the summer, featuring as a substitute for Trinidad in their friendly against Northern Ireland in June.

Aston Villa (£120,000 from Signal Hill, Tobago on 19/12/1989) F/PL 195+36/73 FLC 20+2/8 FAC 22+2/14 Others 10/3
Manchester U (£12,600,000 on 22/8/1998) PL 80+16/48 FLC 3/2 FAC 6+5/3 Others 31+11/12
Blackburn Rov (£2,000,000 on 26/7/2002) PL 40+16/12 FLC 5/4 FAC 3+1/3 Others 4+1

YOUNG Ashley Simon
Born: Stevenage, 9 July 1985
Height: 5'9" **Weight:** 9.13
Ashley, a pacy and direct winger who can operate on either side, made a handful of appearances for Watford early on last season after impressing in the reserves. He scored in his first two matches, making him briefly top scorer, and his final return of three League goals from five substitute appearances was very creditable. Ashley, who is slightly built, also demonstrated a good work rate and excellent vision, suggesting that he might be effective in central midfield in the future.

Watford (From juniors on 12/7/2002) FL 0+5/3 FLC 1

YOUNG Gregory (Greg) James
Born: Doncaster, 25 April 1983
Height: 6'1" **Weight:** 12.3
Greg was the only one of Grimsby's promising young players to establish himself firmly in the senior squad last season. Able to operate anywhere in defence he was unfortunate to have his campaign curtailed by a shoulder injury received in the 4-4 draw against fellow strugglers Chesterfield in March. However, he will be looking forward to regular senior football in 2004-05 as the Mariners adjust to life in the Third Division.

Grimsby T (From trainee at Sheffield Wed on 26/7/2002) FL 11+7 FAC 0+1 Others 0+1

YOUNG Jamie Iain
Born: Brisbane, Australia, 25 August 1985
Height: 5'11" **Weight:** 12.9
International Honours: E: Yth
A promising young 'keeper, Jamie finally made his first-team debut for Reading in the home game against Stoke City, after having warmed the bench for the previous 21 matches. He came on to replace the injured Marcus Hahnemann, and immediately confirmed his potential by making a breathtaking tip-over save from a close-range header. After that experience it was back to the bench and reserve-team football, where he gained a winner's tankard when he was on duty in the Pontins Combination play-off final against Cardiff City. He continued to be an important member of the England U19 squad.

Reading (From trainee on 20/10/2003) FL 0+1

YOUNG Luke Paul
Born: Harlow, 19 July 1979
Height: 6'0" **Weight:** 12.4
Club Honours: FLC '99
International Honours: E: U21-12; Yth
Luke played some of the best football of his career for Charlton Athletic during the season. He started as first-choice right back until he suffered an ankle injury in the 1-0 win at Blackburn Rovers in October. He was to miss the next three months before returning to the squad in January. After a couple of games as a substitute he regained his right-back spot, which he kept for the remainder of the season. Luke is a good tackler and distributes the ball well. He can play as an orthodox right back or right wing back, and is also able to play in central defence. He possesses a very long throw, which is put to good use on occasions.

Tottenham H (From trainee on 3/7/1997) PL 44+14 FLC 1+3 FAC 9+2 Others 2+1
Charlton Ath (£3,000,000 + on 27/7/2001) PL 84+6 FLC 4 FAC 3

YOUNG Neil Anthony
Born: Harlow, 31 August 1973
Height: 5'9" **Weight:** 12.0
The 2003-04 season proved to be another frustrating campaign for this Bournemouth right back. An ankle injury flared up in October, requiring surgery, and he did not return to the first team until April. A substitute appearance at Peterborough that month was Neil's 300th Football League outing for the club

and excellent performances after that showed what the Cherries had missed.

Tottenham H (From trainee on 17/8/1991)
Bournemouth (Free on 11/10/1994) FL 291+11/4 FLC 19+1 FAC 20 Others 19

YOUNGS Thomas (Tom) Anthony John
Born: Bury St Edmunds, 31 August 1979
Height: 5'9" **Weight:** 10.4
Last term proved to be a rather frustrating season for this Northampton Town striker. Tom was in and out of the side without being able to put a decent run of appearances together before being sidelined by an injury. He will be hoping to establish himself in the line-up in the 2004-05 campaign.

Cambridge U (From juniors on 3/7/1997) FL 118+32/43 FLC 3+3 FAC 10/3 Others 12+3/2
Northampton T (£50,000 on 27/3/2003) FL 7+10 FLC 1 Others 0+1

ZAKUANI Gabriel (Gaby)
Born: Congo, 31 May 1986
Height: 6'0" **Weight:** 10.10
Gaby started the 2003-04 season in the Leyton Orient U19 team, but due to injuries to others and his own superb form he was given a brief run in the first team towards the end of the year. Gaby is a confident central defender who shows an experience beyond his years and managed to contribute goals at Kidderminster and in the home game with Bury.

Leyton Orient (Trainee) FL 9+2/2 FAC 1

ZAMORA Robert (Bobby) Lester
Born: Barking, 16 January 1981
Height: 6'0" **Weight:** 11.0
Club Honours: Div 3 '01; Div 2 '02
International Honours: E: U21-6
This prolific striker combines all the natural predatory qualities: pace, accuracy and instinct for goal, so it was disappointing that Tottenham manager Glenn Hoddle should give Bobby so few chances to impress last term. The arrival of Freddie Kanoute and Helder Postiga at the same time only further pushed him down the pecking order and he eventually moved on to West Ham in part-exchange for Jermain Defoe. Bobby was soon on the score sheet for the Hammers, netting with a header at Bradford on his debut and adding another goal in the home game with Cardiff. Perhaps his best strike came against Wimbledon when he cut inside one player and unleashed an 18-yarder into the corner of the net.

449

Bristol Rov (From trainee on 1/7/1999) FL 0+4 FLC 0+1 FAC 0+1
Brighton & Hove A (Loaned on 11/2/2000) FL 6/6
Brighton & Hove A (£100,000 on 10/8/2000) FL 117+2/70 FLC 4/2 FAC 6/4 Others 1/1
Tottenham H (£1,500,000 on 22/7/2003) PL 6+10 FLC 1/1 FAC 0+1
West Ham U (Signed on 3/2/2004) FL 15+2/5 Others 3

ZAVAGNO Luciano
Born: Rosario, Argentina, 6 August 1977
Height: 6'0" **Weight:** 12.0
Luciano was on his way to Spartak Moscow early on last season but, to Derby's surprise, failed his medical. He returned to compete with Paul Boertien for the left-back position, always showing

a willingness to attack, and was credited with the goal that earned a point off Crystal Palace at Selhurst Park. Luciano gave way to loan signing Peter Kennedy for five games and stepped down again when Jamie Vincent was signed. In January, he moved to Italy's Serie A when Ancona took over his contract.

Derby Co (Signed from ES Troyes, France, ex Santa Fe, Strasbourg, on 19/10/2001) P/FL 48+4/3 FAC 2+1

ZENDEN Boudewijn (Bolo)
Born: Maastricht, Holland, 15 August 1976
Height: 5'9" **Weight:** 11.5
Club Honours: FLC '04
International Honours: Holland: 53
Bolo Zenden arrived at Middlesbrough on a year-long loan from Premiership big-spenders Chelsea and, thanks to the long

arm of coincidence, made his Boro' debut in the 2-0 defeat at Bolton Wanderers. He was a little rusty at the start but grew in stature with each passing game as he adjusted to his new surroundings. In the Carling Cup final, also against Bolton, he provided the inch-perfect cross for Joseph-Desire Job to tap-in Boro's early goal; then he added a controversial second from the penalty spot minutes later to create an unforgettable moment in the club's history.

Chelsea (£7,500,000 from Barcelona, Spain, ex PSV Eindhoven, on 10/8/2001) PL 24+19/4 FLC 2+3 FAC 1+6 Others 3+1
Middlesbrough (Loaned on 30/8/2003) PL 31/4 FLC 5+1/2 FAC 2/1

ZIEGE Christian
Born: Germany, 1 February 1972
Height: 6'1" **Weight:** 12.12
Club Honours: FLC '01
International Honours: Germany: 72 (UEFA '96)
This hugely talented left back was again badly affected by injuries last term restricting his availability for Tottenham. Pacy, strong in the tackle and a consummate professional on and off the pitch, Spurs fans have been cruelly robbed of the phenomenal talent that saw Christian achieve so much at club and international level. In his rare appearances he looked to be enjoying his football and showed a great level of fitness, awareness and determination. Sadly, with the prospect of rebuilding after a dismal season for the club, Christian was released by the club at the end of the season but earned a surprising call-up to the Germany squad for Euro 2004.

Middlesbrough (£4,000,000 from AC Milan, Italy, ex Bayern Munich, on 6/8/1999) PL 29/6 FLC 3+1/1 FAC 1
Liverpool (£5,500,000 on 29/8/2000) PL 11+5/1 FLC 1+3/1 FAC 2+1 Others 6+3
Tottenham H (£4,000,000 on 1/8/2001) PL 44+3/7 FLC 5/1 FAC 3/2

ZIVKOVIC Boris
Born: Zivinice, Croatia, 15 November 1975
Height: 6'0" **Weight:** 12.8
International Honours: Croatia: 38
A tall Croatian international who can operate on either flank as a full back, Boris played in 18 Premiership games for Pompey last season before losing his place following the defeat at Villa Park. He was released soon afterwards and returned to Germany, signing for VfB Stuttgart. Boris was a member of the Croatia squad for Euro 2004.

Tom Youngs

Bolo Zenden

Portsmouth *(Free from Beyer Leverkusen, Germany, ex Sarajevo, Marsonia, Hrvatski Zagreb, on 17/7/2003) PL 17+1 FLC 1 FAC 1*

ZOLA-MAKONGO Calvin
Born: Kinshasha, DR Congo, 31 December 1984
Height: 6'1" **Weight:** 12.0

Calvin joined Oldham Athletic on a season-long loan from Newcastle United last September and was handed the number nine shirt by then manager Iain Dowie. A tall striker who is comfortable on the ball, he is a real handful for defenders and found the net seven times for the Latics. However, he fell out of

favour when Brian Talbot became manager and after returning to St James's Park he was reported to have signed for Tranmere Rovers during the summer.
Newcastle U *(From trainee on 17/1/2002)*
Oldham Ath *(Loaned on 30/8/2003) FL 21+4/5 FAC 1/1 Others 2/1*

Christian Ziege (right)

FA Barclaycard Premiership and Nationwide League Clubs
Summary of Appearances and Goals for 2003-2004

KEY TO TABLES: P/FL = Premier/Football League. FLC = Football League Cup. FAC = FA Cup. Others = Other first team appearances.
Left hand figures in each column list number of full appearances + appearances as substitute. Right hand figures list number of goals scored.

	P/FL App	P/FL Goals	FLC App	FLC Goals	FAC App	FAC Goals	Others App	Others Goals
ARSENAL (PREM: 1st)								
ALIADIERE Jeremie	3 + 7		3	4	1		0 + 1	
BENTLEY David	1		4		0 + 2	1	0 + 1	
BERGKAMP Dennis	21 + 7	4			3	1	5 + 2	
CAMPBELL Sol	35	1			5		10	
CLICHY Gael	7 + 5		5		1 + 3		1	
COLE Ashley	32		1		4		10	1
CYGAN Pascal	10 + 8		3				2 + 1	
EDU	13 +17	2	4	1	4 + 1	1	7 + 2	3
FABREGAS Cesc			2 + 1	1				
HENRY Thierry	37	30			2 + 1	3	11	6
HOYTE Justin	0 + 1		2					
JEFFERS Francis							0 + 1	
KANU Nwankwo	3 + 7	1	4	2	1 + 2		1 + 6	
KEOWN Martin	3 + 7		3		1		1	
LAUREN	30 + 2		1		5		9	
LEHMANN Jens	38				5		11	
LJUNGBERG Freddie	27 + 3	4			4	4	9 + 1	2
OWUSU-ABEYIE Quincy			1 + 2					
PAPADOPULOS Michal			0 + 1					
PARLOUR Ray	16 + 9		3		2 + 1		5 + 1	
PIRES Robert	33 + 3	14			3 + 1	1	10 + 1	4
REYES Jose Antonio	7 + 6	2	1		2 + 1	2	2 + 2	1
SILVA Gilberto	29 + 3	4	1		3		6 + 3	
SIMEK Frankie			1					
SKULASON Olafur-Ingi			0 + 1					
SMITH Ryan			0 + 3					
SPICER John			0 + 1					
STACK Graham			5					
TAVLARIDIS Stathis			3					
THOMAS Jerome			1 + 2					
TOURE Kolo	36 + 1	1	2		4 + 1	2	11	
VAN BRONCKHORST Giovanni							0 + 1	
VIEIRA Patrick	29	3	2		5		7 + 1	
WILTORD Sylvain	8 + 4	3	3	1			3 + 2	
ASTON VILLA (PREM: 6th)								
ALLBACK Marcus	7 + 8	1	1 + 3					
ALPAY	4 + 2	1						
ANGEL Juan Pablo	33	16	5	7	1			
BARRY Gareth	36	3	6		1	1		
CROUCH Peter	6 +10	4	1 + 1					
DE LA CRUZ Ulises	20 + 8		3		1			
DELANEY Mark	23 + 2		5					
DUBLIN Dion	12 +11	3	4 + 1					
HADJI Moustapha	0 + 1							
HENDRIE Lee	32	2	4		1			
HITZLSPERGER Thomas	22 +10	3	2 + 3	2	0 + 1			
JOHNSEN Ronny	21 + 2	1	2 + 1		1			
KINSELLA Mark	2							
McCANN Gavin	28		6	2	1			
MELLBERG Olof	33	1	5		1			
MOORE Luke	0 + 7							
MOORE Stefan	2 + 6	1	1 + 2		0 + 1			
POSTMA Stefan	0 + 2							
RIDGEWELL Liam	5 + 6		0 + 2					
SAMUEL Jlloyd	38	2	6	1	1			
SOLANO Nobby	10							
SORENSEN Thomas	38		6		1			
VASSELL Darius	26 + 6	9	5 + 1	1	1			
WHITTINGHAM Pete	20 +12		4 + 2	1	1			
BARNSLEY (DIV 2: 12th)								
ALCOCK Danny	0 + 1							
ATKINSON Rob	0 + 1							
AUSTIN Neil	32 + 5		0 + 1		4 + 1		0 + 1	
BAKER Tom	0 + 1							
BERESFORD Marlon	14							
BETSY Kevin	42 + 3	10	1		5	1	2	
BIRCH Gary	8	2						
BOULDING Mick	5 + 1							
BURNS Jacob	16 + 6	1			4		1	
CAIG Tony	3							
CARSON Stephen	9 + 2	1			3 + 1		1 + 1	
CROOKS Lee	20 + 3				1		2	
DAVIES Arron	1 + 3							

	P/FL App	P/FL Goals	FLC App	FLC Goals	FAC App	FAC Goals	Others App	Others Goals
FALLON Rory	12 + 4	4	1				1	
GALLIMORE Tony	20		1		2		2	
GIBBS Paul	0 + 3		1				1	
GORRE Dean	16 + 3	7	1	1			1	
HANDYSIDE Peter	28		1		2		1	
HAYWARD Steve	24 + 8	1	1		4		1	
ILIC Sasa	25		1		5		2	
IRELAND Craig	43	3	1		5		2	
JACK Darren					0 + 1			
KAY Antony	39 + 4	3	1		5		1	2
LUMSDON Chris	17 +11	3	0 + 1		1 + 3		1 + 1	
MONK Garry	14 + 3				4		1	
MULLIGAN David	2 + 2							
MURPHY David	10	2						
NARDIELLO Danny	14 + 2	7						
NEIL Alex	17 +14	2			1 + 2			
O'CALLAGHAN Brian	25 + 4		1		4 + 1		2	
RANKIN Izzy	9 +11	5	0 + 1		2 + 1	1	1 + 1	
ROCASTLE Craig	4 + 1							
SHUKER Chris	9							
STALLARD Mark	10	1						
TONGE Dale	0 + 1							
TURNBULL Ross	3							
WALTERS Jon	7 + 1				3		0 + 1	
WARD Gavin	1							
WARHURST Paul	3 + 1							
WILLIAMS Robbie	3 + 1	1						
WROE Nicky	1 + 1	1						
BIRMINGHAM CITY (PREM: 10th)								
BARROWMAN Andrew	0 + 1							
BENNETT Ian	4 + 2						0 + 3	
CARTER Darren	1 + 4		1				0 + 1	
CISSE Aliou	5 +10		1				0 + 1	
CLAPHAM Jamie	22 + 3		1				1 + 1	1
CLEMENCE Stephen	32 + 3	2	1		1		1 + 1	
CUNNINGHAM Kenny	36		1		4			
DEVLIN Paul	0 + 2							
DUGARRY Christophe	12 + 2	1			0 + 1			
DUNN David	20 + 1	2	1		3			
FIGUEROA Lucho	0 + 1		0 + 1					
FORSSELL Mikael	32	17	0 + 1		3 + 1	2		
GRAINGER Martin	3 + 1	1						
HORSFIELD Geoff	2 + 1							
HUGHES Bryan	17 + 9	3			3 + 1	2		
JOHN Stern	7 +22	4	1		1 + 1			
JOHNSON Damien	35		1	1	4			
KENNA Jeff	14 + 3	2			4			
KIROVSKI Jovan	0 + 6		0 + 1		0 + 1			
LAZARIDIS Stan	25 + 5	2	1		4			
MORRISON Clinton	19 +13	4	1		4	1		
PURSE Darren	9				3			
SAVAGE Robbie	31	3			4			
TAYLOR Maik	34		1		4			
TAYLOR Martin	11 + 1	1			2			
TEBILY Olivier	17 +10				2			
UPSON Matthew	30		1		2			
BLACKBURN ROVERS (PREM: 15th)								
AMORUSO Lorenzo	11 + 1	3					2	
ANDRESEN Martin	11							
BABBEL Markus	23 + 2	3	1		1		1	
BAGGIO Dino	0 + 9	1			0 + 1		1 + 1	
COLE Andy	27 + 7	11	1		1		0 + 1	
DANNS Neil	0 + 1							
DOUGLAS Jonathan	14	1						
EMERTON Brett	31 + 6	2	0 + 1				2	1
ENCKELMAN Peter	2							
FERGUSON Barry	14 + 1	1	1	1				
FLITCROFT Garry	29 + 2	3	1		1			
FRIEDEL Brad	36	1	1		1			
GALLAGHER Paul	12 +14	3	0 + 1		1			
GRABBI Ciccio	0 + 5						1 + 1	
GRAY Michael	14							
GRESKO Vratislav	22 + 2	1	1				2	
JANSEN Matt	9 +10	2					2	1
JOHANSSON Nils-Eric	7 + 7		0 + 1					

	P/FL App	Goals	FLC App	Goals	FAC App	Goals	Others App	Goals
MAHON Alan	1 + 2				1			
NEILL Lucas	30 + 2	2	1		1		1	
REID Steven	9 + 7		1				1 + 1	
SHORT Craig	19				1			
STEAD Jon	13	6						
TAYLOR Martin	10 + 1				0 + 1		0 + 1	
THOMPSON David	10 + 1	1	1		1		2	
TODD Andy	19				1		1	
TUGAY	30 + 6	1	1		1		2	
YORKE Dwight	15 + 8	4	1		2		0 + 1	1 + 1

BLACKPOOL (DIV 2: 14th)

	P/FL App	Goals	FLC App	Goals	FAC App	Goals	Others App	Goals
BARNES Phil	19		1		1		1	
BLINKHORN Matthew	4 + 8	1					0 + 4	1
BULLOCK Martin	33 +11		2 + 1		3		6 + 1	
CLANCY Sean	1 + 1							
CLARKE Chris	11 + 7	1	2 + 1		1 + 2		2	
COID Danny	30 + 5	3	1 + 1		2	1	4	2
DANNS Neil	12		2				1	
DAVIS Steve	22 + 7	1	3		3		1 + 1	
DINNING Tony	10	3					3	
DOHERTY Sean	0 + 1							
DONNELLY Ciaran	8 + 1							
DOUGLAS Jonathan	15 + 1	3	3				1	
EDGE Lewis	1							
ELLIOTT Steve	28						5	
EVANS Gareth	21 + 2		2		2		4 + 1	
FLYNN Mike	29 + 1	1	1		2 + 1		6 + 1	
GRAYSON Simon	28 + 5	1	2 + 1		2		4 + 1	
HESSEY Sean	4 + 2						0 + 1	
HILTON Kirk	12 + 2	1	1		1		2	
JASZCZUN Tommy	5 + 2				1		1	
JOHNSON Simon	3 + 1	1			0 + 1			
JONES Bradley	5						2	
JONES Lee	21		2		2		4	
McMAHON Stephen	7 + 5				0 + 2		2 + 3	
MANGAN Andrew	0 + 2							
MATIAS Pedro	7				1			
MURPHY John	27 + 3	9	1 + 1		3		3	4
RICHARDSON Leam	24 + 4		1		1	1	5 + 1	
SHERON Mike	28 +10	8	2 + 1		1 + 1		7	3
SOUTHERN Keith	15 +13	2	1 + 1	1	2	1	3 + 1	1
TAYLOR Scott	30 + 1	16	3	3	3	6	4	2
WALKER Richard	3 + 6							
WELLENS Richard	40 + 1	3	3		2		4	
WILES Simon	0 + 4						0 + 1	

BOLTON WANDERERS (PREM: 8th)

	P/FL App	Goals	FLC App	Goals	FAC App	Goals	Others App	Goals
BA Ibrahim	0 + 9		5 + 1		1			
BARNESS Anthony	11 + 4		4 + 2		2			
CAMPO Ivan	37 + 1	4	6					
CHARLTON Simon	28 + 3		5 + 2					
COMYN-PLATT Charlie	0 + 1							
DAVIES Kevin	38	9	4 + 1	1				
DJORKAEFF Youri	24 + 3	8	4 + 1	1				
FACEY Delroy	0 + 1				2			
FRANDSEN Per	22 +11	1	3		1 + 1			
GARDNER Ricardo	20 + 2		2 + 2					
GIANNAKOPOULOS Stelios	17 +14	2	4 + 2	2	2			
HOWEY Steve	2 + 1							
HUNT Nicky	28 + 3	1	6		1			
JAASKELAINEN Jussi	38		3					
JARDEL	0 + 7		3 + 1	3	1			
LAVILLE Florent	5							
LITTLE Glen	0 + 4				2			
LIVESEY Danny								
MORENO Javi	1 + 7		0 + 2					
N'GOTTY Bruno	32 + 1	2	6		1			
NOLAN Kevin	37	9	4 + 1	2	0 + 2	1		
OKOCHA Jay Jay	33 + 2		5 + 1	3				
OTSEMOBOR John	1							
PEDERSEN Henrik	19 +14	7	4 + 3	2	2			
POOLE Kevin			4		2			
SHAKES Ricky					0 + 1	1		
SMITH Jeff					2			
TAYLOR Cleveland					0 + 1			
THOME Emerson	25 + 1		5					
VAZ TE Ricardo	0 + 1				1 + 1			

BOSTON UNITED (DIV 3: 11th)

	P/FL App	Goals	FLC App	Goals	FAC App	Goals	Others App	Goals
AKINFENWA Adebayo	2 + 1				1		1	
ANGEL Mark	12 +11	1			1			
BALMER Stuart	25 + 1	3			1			

	P/FL App	Goals	FLC App	Goals	FAC App	Goals	Others App	Goals
BASTOCK Paul	46		1		1		2	
BEEVERS Lee	40	2			1		2	1
BENNETT Tom	35	1	1	1	1		1	
BOYD Adam	14	4						
BROUGH Scott							0 + 1	
BROWN Jermaine	3 + 2							
CHAPMAN Ben	33 + 4	1					0 + 1	
CLARKE Ryan	1 + 3						2	
CROPPER Dene	4 + 1	1						
DOUGLAS Stuart	14 +15	1	1		0 + 1			
DUFFIELD Peter	12 +17	5	1		1		1 + 1	1
ELLENDER Paul	42	4	1		1		1	
GREAVES Mark	34 + 3		1		1		1	
HOCKING Matt	16 + 6		1		0 + 1		2	
HOGG Chris	10				1		2	
HOLLAND Chris	3 + 2							
HURST Kevan	3 + 4	1						
JONES Graeme	31 + 2	6	0 + 1					
LOGAN Richard	4 + 4		0 + 1					
MELTON Steve	9	1						
MORROW Sam	0 + 2							
NOBLE David	14	2						
POTTER Graham	11 + 1	1	1		1		0 + 1	
REDFEARN Neil	19 + 4	6	0 + 1	1	1		1	
RUSK Simon	16 + 3		1					
SABIN Eric	2							
SUTCH Daryl	6		1		0 + 1		0 + 1	
THOMAS Danny	8	3						
THOMPSON Lee	20 +15	5			1		2	
WEATHERSTONE Simon	14 + 3	4					2	
WHITE Andy	3 + 3							

BOURNEMOUTH (DIV 2: 9th)

	P/FL App	Goals	FLC App	Goals	FAC App	Goals	Others App	Goals
BROADHURST Karl	36 + 3	1	1		3		0 + 1	
BROWNING Marcus	41 + 1	1	1		3	1	1	
BUXTON Lewis	24 + 2				1 + 1			
CONNELL Alan	1 + 6							
COOKE Stephen	3							
CUMMINGS Warren	42	2	1		3			
ELLIOTT Wade	23 +16	3	1		3	1	1	
FEENEY Warren	34 + 6	12	0 + 1		3		1	
FLETCHER Carl	40	2	1		3			
FLETCHER Steve	40 + 1	9	1		3		0 + 1	
HAYTER James	37 + 7	14	1		1 0 + 2		0 + 1	
HOLMES Derek	10 +16	2	0 + 1		1			
JORGENSEN Claus	16 + 1							
MAHER Shaun	23 + 6	1			0 + 1			
MOSS Neil	46				3			
O'CONNOR Gareth	28 + 9	2	1		3		1	
PURCHES Steve	42	3	1		3		1	
STEWART Gareth							1	
STOCK Brian	11 + 8	3			2			
THOMAS Danny	2 + 8						1	
TINDALL Jason	2 +17		0 + 1		0 + 2		1	
WILLIAMS Gareth	0 + 1							
YOUNG Neil							1	

BRADFORD CITY (DIV 1: 23rd)

	P/FL App	Goals	FLC App	Goals	FAC App	Goals	Others App	Goals
ARMSTRONG Alun	6	1			1			
ATHERTON Peter	27	2						
BERESFORD Marlon	5							
BOWER Mark	11 + 3				1			
BRANCH Michael	29 + 4	6	1		0 + 1			
CADAMARTERI Danny	14 + 4	3						
COMBE Alan	21				1			
CORNWALL Luke	2 + 1		0 + 1					
DAVIES Clint	1 + 1							
EDDS Gareth	19 + 4				1			
EMANUEL Lewis	18 +10	2	1					
EVANS Paul	20 + 3	3	1		1			
FARRELLY Gareth	14				1			
FORREST Danny	2 +11							
FRANCIS Simon	25 + 5				1			
GAVIN Jason	37 + 1				0 + 1			
GRAY Andy	33	5	1		1	1		
HECKINGBOTTOM Paul	43		1		1			
JACOBS Wayne	11 + 2							
KEARNEY Tom	13 + 4				1			
McHUGH Frazer	3							
MUIRHEAD Ben	12 +16	2	0 + 1		0 + 1			
PASTON Mark	13		1					
PENFORD Tom	3 + 1							
SANASY Kevin	2 + 3	1						
STANDING Michael	2 + 4							

Kevin Nolan (Bolton Wanderers)

	P/FL App	P/FL Goals	FLC App	FLC Goals	FAC App	FAC Goals	Others App	Others Goals
SUMMERBEE Nicky	33 + 2	1						
VAESEN Nico	6							
WALLWORK Ronnie	7	4						
WETHERALL David	34	1	1		1			
WINDASS Dean	34 + 2	6	1					
WOLLEASTON Robert	6 + 8	1	0 + 1					

BRENTFORD (DIV 2: 17th)

	P/FL App	P/FL Goals	FLC App	FLC Goals	FAC App	FAC Goals	Others App	Others Goals
ALLEN-PAGE Danny							0 + 1	
BEADLE Peter	1							
BLACKMAN Lloyd	0 + 3		0 + 1					
BULL Ronnie	20							
DOBSON Michael	42	1	1		1		2	
EVANS Steve	14 +11	2			0 + 2		2	
FIELDWICK Lee	4 + 1							
FITZGERALD Scott	9							
FRAMPTON Andy	10 + 6		1		1	1	2	
HARROLD Matt	5 + 8	2			1	3	1	
HUGHES Steve	1 + 8		0 + 1		0 + 2		0 + 1	
HUNT Steve	38 + 2	11	1		2		2	2
HUTCHINSON Eddie	36	5	1		1		0 + 1	
JULIAN Alan	13		0 + 1					
KITAMIRIKE Joel	21 + 1				1			
MAY Ben	38 + 3	7	1		1			
NELSON Stuart	9							
O'CONNOR Kevin	36 + 7	1	1		2	1	1 + 1	
OLUGBODI Jide	0 + 2				0 + 1		1 + 1	
PETERS Mark	2 + 7				0 + 1		1	
RHODES Alex	0 + 3	1						
ROGET Leo	15						1	
ROUGIER Tony	29 + 2	4			2	1	2	
SMITH Jay	12 + 5		1		2		1 + 1	
SMITH Paul	24		1		2		2	
SOMNER Matt	30 + 9		1		2		1	
SONKO Ibu	42 + 1	1	1		2			
TABB Jay	22 +14	9	1		2		1	2
TALBOT Stewart	15	2						
WELLS Dean	0 + 1							
WRIGHT Tommy	18 + 7	3						

BRIGHTON & HOVE ALBION (DIV 2: 4th)

	P/FL App	P/FL Goals	FLC App	FLC Goals	FAC App	FAC Goals	Others App	Others Goals
BECK Dan	0 + 1							
BENJAMIN Trevor	10	5						
BUTTERS Guy	43	3	1		6			
CARPENTER Richard	40 + 2	4	1 + 1		1		6	2
CULLIP Danny	40		1		1		2	
EL-ABD Adam	6 + 5						2	
FLITNEY Ross	3							
HARDING Dan	17 + 6		0 + 2				4 + 1	
HART Gary	35 + 7	3	2		1		3 + 3	
HENDERSON Darius	10	2						
HINSHELWOOD Adam	16 + 1		2		1		1 + 1	
IWELUMO Chris	10	4					3	
JONES Nathan	34 + 2		2		1		5 + 1	
JONES Stuart	2 + 1							
KNIGHT Leon	43 + 1	25	2		1		6	2
KUIPERS Michel	9 + 1		1		1		1	
LEE David	1 + 3						1	
McPHEE Chris	17 +12	4	2	1	1	1	2 + 1	3
MARNEY Danny	0 + 3						0 + 1	
MAYO Kerry	31 + 2		2				3	
OATWAY Charlie	29 + 2	1	1				3	
PETHICK Robbie	6 + 8		0 + 1		1		3	
PIERCY John	8 +16	4			0 + 1		0 + 3	
REHMAN Zesh	9 + 2	2					2	
REID Paul	4 + 1						2 + 1	
ROBERTS Ben	32						5	
ROBINSON Jake	1 + 8		0 + 1				0 + 1	1
RODGER Simon	7		2					
VIRGO Adam	20 + 2	1	1				3	1
WATSON Paul	14 + 1		1				1	
WILKINSON Shaun	0 + 2				0 + 1			
YEATES Mark	9						1	

BRISTOL CITY (DIV 2: 3rd)

	P/FL App	P/FL Goals	FLC App	FLC Goals	FAC App	FAC Goals	Others App	Others Goals
AMANKWAAH Kevin	4 + 1		1		1	2		
BELL Mickey	20 + 7		2	1	0 + 1			
BROWN Aaron	29 + 1	5	1		3			
BROWN Marvin	1 + 1							
BURNELL Joe	14 + 3	1	2		1		1 + 1	
BUTLER Tony	37 + 1	1	3		1		4	
CAREY Louis	41	1			2		4	
CLIST Simon	1		2 + 1					
COLES Danny	45	2	3		3		4	
DOHERTY Tommy	28 + 5	2	2				4	
FORTUNE Clayton	1 + 5		0 + 1					
GOODFELLOW Marc	7 + 8	4					0 + 2	1
HILL Matt	40 + 2	2	2		3		3 + 1	
HULBERT Robin			0 + 2				0 + 1	
LITA Leroy	2 +24	5	0 + 1		0 + 2		1 + 1	
MATTHEWS Lee	1 + 7	2	0 + 2		0 + 2	1	0 + 1	
MILLER Lee	32 +10	8	2 + 1	1	2		1	
MURRAY Scott	4 + 2						0 + 3	
PEACOCK Lee	39 + 2	14	2	2	3		3	
PHILLIPS Steve	46		3		3		3	
ROBERTS Christian	24 +14	6	2 + 1		1 + 2	1	4	1
ROUGIER Tony	5 + 1	1					3	1
STOWELL Mike							1	
TINNION Brian	36 + 9	2	2 + 1		2		3	
WILKSHIRE Luke	35 + 2	2	3		3	1	0 + 2	
WOODMAN Craig	14 + 7		1		3		4	

BRISTOL ROVERS (DIV 3: 15th)

	P/FL App	P/FL Goals	FLC App	FLC Goals	FAC App	FAC Goals	Others App	Others Goals
AGOGO Junior	28 +10	6	1					
ANDERSON Ijah	37 + 2		1				1	
ANDERSON John	8							
ARNDALE Neil	1 + 2							
AUSTIN Kevin	21 + 2				1			
BARRETT Adam	45	4	1		1		1	
BOXALL Danny	23 + 1		1				1	
BRYANT Simon	7 + 5		0 + 1					
CARLISLE Wayne	22 + 3	7	1		0 + 1		1	
CLARKE Ryan	2							
EDWARDS Christian	40 + 2		1		1		1	
GIBB Ally	8	1						
GILROY David	1 + 3				0 + 1			
HALDANE Lewis	16 +11	5			1		1	1
HENRIKSEN Bo	1 + 3							
HOBBS Shane	0 + 2							
HODGES Lee	5 + 8	2	0 + 1					
HYDE Graham	33 + 4	2			1		1	
LESCOTT Aaron	8							
MATTHEWS Lee	9							
MILLER Kevin	44		1		1		1	
PARKER Sonny	13 + 2	1	0 + 1		1		1	
QUINN Rob	23 +12	1	1		1		1	
RAMMELL Andy	1 + 4	2			1		0 + 1	
SAVAGE Dave	37 + 1	2	1		1		1	
STREET Kevin	8 + 5		1				0 + 1	
TAIT Paul	28 + 5	12	1		1		1	
THORPE Lee	8 + 2	1						
TWIGG Gary	7 + 1							
UDDIN Anwar	1						0 + 1	
WILLIAMS Danny	6		1					
WILLIAMS Ryan	15 + 4	1			1			
WILLOCK Calum	0 + 5							

BURNLEY (DIV 1: 19th)

	P/FL App	P/FL Goals	FLC App	FLC Goals	FAC App	FAC Goals	Others App	Others Goals
ADEBOLA Dele	0 + 3	1						
BLAKE Robbie	44 + 1	19	3	1	3	2		
BRANCH Graham	30 + 8	3	2		0 + 1			
CAMARA Mo	45		3		2 + 1			
CHADWICK Luke	23 +13	5	2	1	1 + 1			
CHAPLOW Richard	30 + 9	5	1 + 1		3			
FACEY Delroy	12 + 2	5	2					
FARRELLY Gareth	9 + 3		1 + 1					
GNOHERE Arthur	12 + 2	1	2					
GRANT Tony	34 + 3				3			
JENSEN Brian	46		3		3			
JOHNROSE Lenny	4 + 3							
LITTLE Glen	33 + 1	3	2		2			
McEVELEY Jay	0 + 4				1			
McGREGOR Mark	20 + 3	1	1		3			
MAY David	34 + 1	4	1		3			
MOORE Alan	5 + 8		1		1 + 2			
MOORE Ian	38 + 2	9	2	1	3	3		
O'NEILL Matt	0 + 4							
ORR Bradley	1 + 3							
PILKINGTON Joel	0 + 1							
ROCHE Lee	21 + 4	1	1 + 1		3			
SCOTT Paul	0 + 2							
TODD Andy	7		1					
TOWNSEND Ryan	0 + 1							
WELLER Paul	25 + 8		2		1 + 1			
WEST Dean	25 + 7	1	2 + 1					
WOOD Neil	8 + 2	1			1			

BURY (DIV 3: 12th)

	P/FL App	P/FL Goals	FLC App	FLC Goals	FAC App	FAC Goals	Others App	Others Goals
BARRASS Matt	19 + 3	1					1	
CARTLEDGE Jon	7 + 4	1						
CHALLINOR Dave	15							
CHARNOCK Phil	3							
CLEGG George	4 + 2		1				1	
CONNELL Lee	23 + 5	6	1		1		2	
DALY Jon	7	1						
DUNFIELD Terry	28 + 2	2					2	
DUXBURY Lee	36 + 1		1		1			
FLITCROFT Dave	17							
GARNER Glyn	46		1		1		2	
GULLIVER Phil	10				1			
GUNBY Steve	1 + 4						0 + 1	
KENNEDY Tom	22 + 5						1	
NUGENT David	20 + 6	3	1		1		0 + 1	
O'NEILL Joe	10 +13	3	0 + 1		0 + 1		1 + 1	
O'SHAUGHNESSY Paul	21 + 6	1			1			
PORTER Chris	19 +18	9	1		0 + 1	1	1	
PREECE Andy	10 + 4	5	0 + 1		1		2	1
SEDDON Gareth	28 +12	11	0 + 1		1			
SINGH Harpal	20 + 8	2	1		1			
STRONG Greg	10		1					
SWAILES Danny	42	5			2			
THOMPSON Justin	1				2		1	
THORNLEY Ben	5							
UNSWORTH Lee	27	2	1		2			
WHALEY Simon	3 + 7	1					0 + 1	
WHELAN Glenn	13				1		1	
WOODTHORPE Colin	39		1		1		2	

CAMBRIDGE UNITED (DIV 3: 13th)

	P/FL App	P/FL Goals	FLC App	FLC Goals	FAC App	FAC Goals	Others App	Others Goals
ANGUS Stev	39 + 1	1	1		3		1	
BIMSON Stuart	21 + 3		1		1			
BRIDGES David	11 +10	2			0 + 1		1	
CHILLINGWORTH Dan	10 + 3	7	1					
CLARKE Chris	0 + 1							
DANIELS Dave	0 + 1							
DUNCAN Andy	37	2			3		1	
DUTTON Brian	0 + 3				0 + 2			
EASTER Jermaine	10 + 5	2						
FLEMING Terry	17 + 1	1			1			
FULLER Ashley	0 + 1							
GLEESON Dan	3 + 4							
GOODHIND Warren	25 + 1				3			
GUTTRIDGE Luke	46	11	1		3	1	1	
KITSON Dave	17	10	1		1	1		
LOCKETT Ryan	1 + 1							
McCAFFERTY Neil	5 + 1							
MARSHALL Shaun	45		1		3		1	
MURRAY Fred	34 + 4		1		2 + 1		1	
NACCA Franco	2 + 7				3		0 + 1	
NICHOLLS Ashley	15 + 1	1						
OPARA Lloyd	1 + 7	1					1	
PEAT Nathan	3 + 3							
QUINTON Darren	0 + 1							
REVELL Alex	10 +10	3	0 + 1					
ROBINSON Matthew	1 + 2							
RUDDY John	1							
SMITH Stephen	1 + 1							
TANN Adam	31 + 3	2	1		2 + 1	1	1	
TAYLOR John	6 + 3				3		1	
TUDOR Shane	30 + 6	3	1		3		1	
TURNER John	17 +19	3			2	2	0 + 1	
VENUS Mark	21		1		0 + 1		1	
WALKER Justin	23		1	1			1	
WEBB Danny	19 + 2	3						
WILLIAMS Gareth	4	1						

CARDIFF CITY (DIV 1: 13th)

	P/FL App	P/FL Goals	FLC App	FLC Goals	FAC App	FAC Goals	Others App	Others Goals
ALEXANDER Neil	24 + 1							
BARKER Chris	33 + 6		2					
BOLAND Willie	33 + 4		1 + 1		1			
BONNER Mark	14 + 6		2					
BOWEN Jason	0 + 2		2					
BULLOCK Lee	4 + 7	3						
CAMPBELL Andy	6 +19	2	1 + 1	1	0 + 1			
COLLINS James	15 + 5	1	1					
CROFT Gary	23 + 4	1			0 + 1			
EARNSHAW Robert	44 + 2	21	2		2	5	1	
FLEETWOOD Stuart	0 + 2		0 + 1					
GABBIDON Danny	41		3		2			
GORDON Gavin	7 + 8	1	0 + 1					
GRAY Julian	5 + 4							
KAVANAGH Graham	27	7	1		1			
LANGLEY Richard	39 + 5	6			1			
LEE Alan	17 + 6	3			0 + 1			
MARGETSON Martyn	22		2		1			
MAXWELL Layton	0 + 1		1					
PARRY Paul	14 + 3	1						
PRIOR Spencer	4 + 3				1			
ROBINSON John	31 + 3	2						
THORNE Peter	19 + 4	13	1		1			
VIDMAR Tony	45	1	2		1			
WESTON Rhys	23 + 1		1		1			
WHALLEY Gareth	16 + 6	2	1		1			

CARLISLE UNITED (DIV 3: 23rd)

	P/FL App	P/FL Goals	FLC App	FLC Goals	FAC App	FAC Goals	Others App	Others Goals
ANDREWS Lee	33 + 4		1		1		3	
ARNISON Paul	20 + 6	1					1	
BALDACCHINO Ryan	0 + 1							
BILLY Chris	39	1	0 + 1				3	
BIRCH Mark	2							
BOYD Mark	9		1					
BYRNE Des	9 + 2						1	
COWAN Tom	20	1						
DUFFIELD Peter	10	3						
FARRELL Craig	21 + 9	7			1		1 + 1	
FORAN Richie	20 + 3	4	1				2	
FRYATT Matty	9 + 1	1						
GLENNON Matty	44		1		1		3	
GRAY Kevin	25	3						
HENDERSON Kevin	10 + 9	2			0 + 1		2	
JACK Michael	0 + 3				1		0 + 1	
KEEN Peter	2 + 1				0 + 1			
KELLY Darren	9 + 1	1	0 + 1				1	
LANGMEAD Kelvin	3 + 8	1						
LIVINGSTONE Steve	6		0 + 1				2	
McDONAGH Will	23 + 4	1	1		1		3	
McGILL Brendan	42 + 2	7			1		3	
MADDISON Lee	2		1					
MOLLOY David	3 + 4				0 + 1		0 + 1	
MURPHY Peter	33 + 2	1	1		1			
PREECE Andy	23 + 2	3						
RAVEN Paul	13	1						
RUNDLE Adam	6 +17		1				1	1
RUSSELL Craig	3 + 3		1	1	1		1 + 1	1
SCHUMACHER Steve	4				1		1	
SHELLEY Brian	28 + 3		1		1		3	
SIMPSON Paul	25	6			1		0 + 1	
SMITH Shaun	4				1			
SUMMERBELL Mark	4 + 2							
WAKE Brian	2 +13		1		1		1 + 1	2
WARHURST Paul	0 + 1							

CHARLTON ATHLETIC (PREM: 7th)

	P/FL App	P/FL Goals	FLC App	FLC Goals	FAC App	FAC Goals	Others App	Others Goals
BARTLETT Shaun	13 + 6	5						
CAMPBELL-RYCE Jamal	0 + 2		0 + 2					
COLE Carlton	8 +13	4			1	1		
DI CANIO Paolo	23 + 8	4	1	1	0 + 1			
EUELL Jason	24 + 7	10	1 + 1		0 + 1			
FISH Mark	23		2					
FORTUNE Jon	21 + 7	2	1 + 1		1			
HOLLAND Matt	38	6	2		1			
HREIDARSSON Hermann	33	2	1		1			
JENSEN Claus	27 + 4	4	2	1	1			
JOHANSSON JJ	16 +10	4	1 + 1		1			
KIELY Dean	37		2		1			
KISHISHEV Radostin	30 + 3		1		1			
KONCHESKY Paul	17 + 4		1					
LISBIE Kevin	5 + 4	4			1			
PARKER Scott	20	2	2		1			
PERRY Chris	25 + 4	1	1		1			
POWELL Chris	11 + 5		1					
ROWETT Gary	1							
ROYCE Simon	1							
STUART Graham	23 + 5	3	2		1			
SVENSSON Mathias	1 + 2		0 + 1					
THOMAS Jerome	0 + 1							
YOUNG Luke	21 + 3		1		1			

CHELSEA (PREM: 2nd)

	P/FL App	P/FL Goals	FLC App	FLC Goals	FAC App	FAC Goals	Others App	Others Goals
AMBROSIO Marco	8		1				3	
BABAYARO Celestine	5 + 1	1	3		2		3	
BRIDGE Wayne	33	1			2		11 + 2	2
COLE Joe	18 +17	1	2 + 1	2	2 + 1		3 + 6	
CRESPO Hernan	13 + 6	10	1 + 1				7 + 3	2

APPEARANCES/GOALS — PFA FOOTBALLERS' WHO'S WHO

(continued)

Name	P/FL App	Goals	FLC App	Goals	FAC App	Goals	Others App	Goals
CUDICINI Carlo	26				3		11	
DESAILLY Marcel	15		1		1		7 + 1	
DUFF Damien	17 + 6	5	2		0 + 1		7 + 4	1
FORSSELL Mikael							1	
GALLAS William	23 + 6		1		4		11	1
GEREMI	19 + 6	1	3		1		7 + 3	
GRONKJAER Jesper	19 +12	2	2 + 1	1	4		6 + 4	1
GUDJOHNSEN Eidur	17 + 9	6	1	2	2 + 2	2	8 + 2	3
HASSELBAINK Jimmy Floyd	22 + 8	12	3	2	3	1	4 + 4	2
HUTH Robert	8 + 8		1		0 + 1		0 + 2	1
JOHNSON Glen	17 + 2	3	3		1		8 + 1	1
LAMPARD Frank	38	10	1 + 1	1	4	1	13 + 1	4
MAKELELE Claude	26 + 4		1 + 1	1	3		11	
MELCHIOT Mario	20 + 3	2			2		4 + 1	
MUTU Adrian	21 + 4	6	0 + 1	1	3	3	6 + 1	1
NICOLAS Alexis	1 + 1				1			
OLIVEIRA Filipe	0 + 1				0 + 1			
PARKER Scott	7 + 4	1			1		4 + 1	
PETIT Manu	3 + 1				0 + 1		1 + 1	
STANIC Mario	0 + 2		0 + 2				0 + 1	
SULLIVAN Neil	4				1 + 1			
TERRY John	33	2	2		3	1	13	
VERON Juan Sebastian	5 + 2	1	1				5 + 1	

CHELTENHAM TOWN (DIV 3: 14th)

Name	P/FL App	Goals	FLC App	Goals	FAC App	Goals	Others App	Goals
AMANKWAAH Kevin	11 + 1							
BIRD David	18 + 6		1		2		1	
BOOK Steve	4 + 1		1					
BRAYSON Paul	20 +11	7	0 + 1		1		1	1
BROUGH John	23 + 3	2	1		3			
CLEVERLEY Ben	2 + 6				1		1	
CORBETT Luke	0 + 1							
COZIC Bertrand	7	1	0 + 1					
DEVANEY Martin	32 + 8	5	0 + 1		2		1	1
DOBSON Craig	0 + 2						0 + 1	
DUFF Michael	42				3			
DUFF Shane	13 + 2	1			0 + 1		1	
FINNIGAN John	32 + 1	1	1		3		1	
FORSYTH Richard	16 +11	2			1 + 1		1	
FYFE Graham	15 + 5		1				1	
GILL Jerry	5 + 2							
GRIFFIN Antony	10 + 5		1					
HENRY Karl	8 + 1	1						
HIGGS Shane	42				3		1	
HOWELLS Lee	7 + 2				1			
HYNES Peter	2 + 2							
JONES Darren	14	1						
McCANN Grant	43	8	1	1	3	3	1	
ODEJAYI Kay	14 +16	5	1		0 + 2		0 + 1	
SPENCER Damian	29 + 7	9	1		3	1	0 + 1	
TAYLOR Bob	19 + 9	7			2	1	1	
VICTORY Jamie	44	2	1		2		1	
WILSON Brian	14				1			
YATES Mark	20 + 1	2	1		2		1	

CHESTERFIELD (DIV 2: 20th)

Name	P/FL App	Goals	FLC App	Goals	FAC App	Goals	Others App	Goals
ALLOTT Mark	35 + 5	2	1		1		0 + 2	
BLATHERWICK Steve	36	2	1		0 + 1		2	
BRANDON Chris	39 + 4	4	1		1		2	2
BURT Jamie	0 + 1							
CADE Jamie	9 + 1	2			1		1 + 1	1
DAVIES Gareth	18 +10		0 + 1		1	1	1	
DAWSON Kevin	22 + 2		1					
DE BOLLA Mark	3 + 5	1			1			
EVATT Ian	43	5	1		1	1	1 + 1	
FOLAN Caleb	4 + 3							
FULLARTON Jamie	0 + 1							
HOWSON Stuart	6 + 3						1	
HUDSON Mark	32 + 3	2	1				2	
HURST Glynn	28 + 1	13	1					
INNES Mark	17 + 5						0 + 1	
McMASTER Jamie	4 + 2	2						
MUGGLETON Carl	46		1		1		1	
NIVEN Derek	22	1						
N'TOYA-ZOA Tcham	3 + 3							
O'HALLORAN Matt	1 + 2							
O'HARE Alan	40		1		1		1	
PAYNE Steve	20	1	1		1		2	
REEVES David	18 +13	4	1		0 + 1		1 + 1	
RICHMOND Andy							1	
ROBINSON Marvin	17 +15	6	1		1		2	1
RUSHBURY Andy	0 + 5	1	0 + 1					
SEARLE Damon	4 + 1							
SMITH Adam	0 + 3							

(continued)

Name	P/FL App	Goals	FLC App	Goals	FAC App	Goals	Others App	Goals
UHLENBEEK Gus	36 + 1						1	
WARHURST Paul	3 + 1				1		1	1

COLCHESTER UNITED (DIV 2: 11th)

Name	P/FL App	Goals	FLC App	Goals	FAC App	Goals	Others App	Goals
ANDREWS Wayne	32 + 9	12			4 + 1		3 + 1	2
BALDWIN Pat	1 + 3		1				0 + 2	
BOWRY Bobby	18 + 6		1		1 + 1		2 + 1	
BROWN Jermaine							0 + 1	1
BROWN Simon	40		2		6		5	
BROWN Wayne	16						0 + 1	
CADE Jamie	6 + 9							
CHILVERS Liam	29 + 3				7		5	
COOTE Adrian			0 + 1					
DUGUID Karl	30	2	2		6		4	
FAGAN Craig	30 + 7	9	2	1	5		4	
FITZGERALD Scott	22 + 1		1		2		2	
GERKEN Dean	1							
HADLAND Phil	0 + 1		0 + 1					
HALFORD Greg	15 + 3	4			2		4	
IZZET Kem	43 + 1	3	2		6		4	1
JOHNSON Gavin	14 + 4	1			1		1 + 1	
JOHNSON Richard							0 + 1	
KEITH Joe	16 +12	2	2		4 + 1	2	5 + 1	1
McGLEISH Scott	25 + 9	10	1		6 + 1	1	4 + 2	6
McKINNEY Richard	5				1		1	
MYERS Andy	21		1		2		2	
PINAULT Thomas	31 + 9		1 + 1	1	7		5	
STOCKLEY Sam	44		2		6		5 + 1	
TIERNEY Paul	2				1		1	
VINE Rowan	30 + 5	6	1		5 + 2	4	4 + 2	2
WHITE Alan	30 + 3	1	2		5 + 1		5	
WILLIAMS Gareth	5 + 2	2	2					

COVENTRY CITY (DIV 1: 12th)

Name	P/FL App	Goals	FLC App	Goals	FAC App	Goals	Others App	Goals
ADEBOLA Dele	15 +13	2	2	1			2 + 1	
ARPHEXAD Pegguy	5							
BARRETT Graham	20 +11	2	1 + 1		1			
CLARKE Peter	5							
DAVENPORT Calum	31 + 2				3			
DELOUMEAUX Eric	19	1			2			
DOYLE Michael	38 + 2	5	2		3			
GIDDINGS Stuart	0 + 1							
GORDON Dean	3 + 2				1 + 1			
GRAINGER Martin	7							
GUDJONSSON Bjarni	17 + 1	3			1 + 1			
JACKSON Johnnie	2 + 3	2						
JEPHCOTT Avun			0 + 1					
JOACHIM Julian	27 + 2	8			3	3		
JORGENSEN Claus	4 + 4		1 + 1					
KERR Brian	5 + 4							
KONJIC Mo	36 + 6	2	2		3			
LOWE Onandi	1 + 1	1						
McALLISTER Gary	14	3						
McSHEFFREY Gary	16 + 3	11			2 + 1	1		
MANSOURI Yazid	9 + 5		1					
MORRELL Andy	19 +11	9	1 + 1		2			
OLSZAR Sebastian	1 + 4							
O'NEILL Keith	0 + 1							
PEAD Craig	6 +11	1	1					
PIPE David			0 + 1					
PITT Courtney	1						0 + 1	
SAFRI Youssef	31		2		1			
SHAW Richard	11 + 8	1	1		1			
SHEARER Scott	29 + 1		2					
STAUNTON Steve	34 + 1	3	1		1			
SUFFO Patrick	20 + 7	7	2					
WARD Gavin	12				3			
WARNOCK Stephen	42 + 2	3	2		2 + 1			
WHING Andy	26 + 2	1	1		2			

CREWE ALEXANDRA (DIV 1: 18th)

Name	P/FL App	Goals	FLC App	Goals	FAC App	Goals	Others App	Goals
ASHTON Dean	43 + 1	19	2	1	1			
BARROWMAN Andrew	3 + 1	1	1					
BELL Lee	0 + 3							
BRAMMER Dave	16	1	2					
COCHRANE Justin	37 + 1	2	2					
EDWARDS Paul	2 + 8		2					
FOSTER Steve	45	2	2		1			
HIGDON Michael	7 + 3	1			1			
HIGNETT Craig	11 + 4							
INCE Clayton	36				1			
JEFFS Ian					0 + 1			
JONES Billy	23 + 4	1			1			
JONES Steve	43 + 2	15	1	1	1			

	P/FL App	P/FL Goals	FLC App	FLC Goals	FAC App	FAC Goals	Others App	Others Goals
LUNT Kenny	43 + 2	7	2		1			
McCREADY Chris	15 + 7		0 + 1					
MOSES Adie	15 + 6		1					
RIX Ben	18 + 8	2	2		1			
ROBERTS Gary	0 + 2							
ROBINSON James	1 + 8	1			0 + 1			
SMART Allan	0 + 6							
SORVEL Neil	26 + 5							
SYMES Michael	1 + 3	1						
TOMLINSON Stuart	0 + 1							
TONKIN Anthony	20 + 6		0 + 1		1			
VARNEY Luke	5 + 3	1	0 + 1		1			
VAUGHAN David	29 + 2		2					
WALKER Richard	17 + 3	1	1					
WILLIAMS Ben	10							
WRIGHT David	40	1	2		1			

CRYSTAL PALACE (DIV 1: 6th)

	P/FL App	P/FL Goals	FLC App	FLC Goals	FAC App	FAC Goals	Others App	Others Goals
BERTHELIN Cedric	17		3		1			
BLACK Tommy	12 +13		1 + 1		1			
BORROWDALE Gary	14 + 9		2 + 1		1			
BUTTERFIELD Danny	45	4	4		1		3	1
CLARKE Matt	4							
DERRY Shaun	25 +12	2	4				1 + 2	
EDWARDS Rob	6 + 1	1						
FLEMING Curtis	15 + 2		1 + 1					
FREEDMAN Dougie	20 +15	13	3	2	0 + 1		0 + 1	
GRANVILLE Danny	21	3			0 + 1		3	
GRAY Julian	24	2			1		2	
HEEROO Gavin	0 + 1							
HUDSON Mark	14							
HUGHES Michael	34	3	3		1		3	
JOHNSON Andy	40 + 2	27	3	4	1		3	1
LEIGERTWOOD Mikele	7 + 5						3	
MULLINS Hayden	10		1					
MYHRE Thomas	15		1					
POPOVIC Tony	34	1	2		1		3	
POWELL Darren	10		2				0 + 3	1
RIIHILAHTI Aki	24 + 7		2 + 2				3	
ROUTLEDGE Wayne	32 +12	6	2 + 2		1		3	
SHIPPERLEY Neil	40	9	4		1		3	2
SMITH Jamie	13 + 2		1 + 1		0 + 1			
SOARES Tom	0 + 3							
SYMONS Kit	12 + 3		3		1			
VAESEN Nico	10						3	
WATSON Ben	8 + 8	1	1 + 3		1			
WILLIAMS Gareth			1					

DARLINGTON (DIV 3: 18th)

	P/FL App	P/FL Goals	FLC App	FLC Goals	FAC App	FAC Goals	Others App	Others Goals
ALEXANDER John	0 + 3							
BOSSY Fabien	4 + 2		1					
CLARK Ian	20 +14	4	1 + 1		1		1	
CLARKE Matthew	44 + 1	4	2		1		1	
CLOSE Brian	8 + 4							
COGHLAN Michael	0 + 3				0 + 1			
COLLETT Andy	9		1					
CONLON Barry	38 + 1	14	2		1			
CONVERY Mark	17 + 8	2			0 + 1			
GRAHAM Danny	7 + 2	2						
HUGHES Chris	24 + 6	2	1 + 1		1		1	
HUTCHINSON Joey	38 + 1		1		0 + 1		1	
JAMES Craig	10							
KELTIE Clark	23 + 8	1	2		1		1	
LIDDLE Craig	43		2				1	
McGURK David	22 + 5	4	2		1		1	
MADDISON Neil	30 + 2	1	1		1		1	
MASON Christopher	0 + 1							
MATTHEWS Lee	6	1						
MELLANBY Danny	5 + 2							
MORGAN Alan	4 + 1	1			1		1	
NICHOLLS Ashley	25 + 1		2		1		1	
PEARSON Gary	11 + 7	1			1			
PRICE Michael	36		1		1			
ROBSON Glenn	3 + 3		1					
RUSSELL Craig	6 + 6	1						
SHEERAN Mark	0 + 6						0 + 1	1
TEGGART Neil	9 + 6							
TURNBULL Ross	1							
VALENTINE Ryan	33 + 7	2	2		1			
WAINWRIGHT Neil	30 + 5	7			0 + 1			

DERBY COUNTY (DIV 1: 20th)

	P/FL App	P/FL Goals	FLC App	FLC Goals	FAC App	FAC Goals	Others App	Others Goals
BOERTIEN Paul	10 + 8		1					
BOLDER Adam	11 +13	1			1			

	P/FL App	P/FL Goals	FLC App	FLC Goals	FAC App	FAC Goals	Others App	Others Goals
BRADBURY Lee	7							
CALDWELL Gary	6 + 3		1					
COSTA Candido	23 +11	1	1					
DICHIO Danny	6	1						
DOYLE Nathan	1 + 1							
EDWARDS Rob	10 + 1	1						
ELLIOTT Steve	2 + 2		1					
GRANT Lee	36		1		1			
HOLMES Lee	17 + 6	2			0 + 1			
HUDDLESTONE Tom	42 + 1		1		1			
HUNT Lewis	1							
JACKSON Richard	34 + 2		1					
JOHNSON Michael	39	1			1			
JUNIOR	6 + 6	4						
KENNA Jeff	9							
KENNEDY Peter	5	1						
LABARTHE TOME Gianfranco	0 + 3		1					
McLEOD Izzy	4 + 6	1	0 + 1					
MANEL	12 + 4	3			1			
MAWENE Youl	30				1			
MILLS Pablo	13 + 6		1		1			
MORRIS Lee	21 + 2	5	0 + 1		1			
OAKES Andy	10							
OSMAN Leon	17		3					
PESCHISOLIDO Paul	11	4						
REICH Marco	9 + 4	1						
SVENSSON Mathias	9 + 1	3						
TAYLOR Ian	42	11	1	1	1			
TUDGAY Marcus	20 + 9	6			1			
VALAKARI Simo	14 + 6		1					
VINCENT Jamie	7		1					
WALTON Dave	3 + 2							
WHELAN Noel	3 + 5							
ZAVAGNO Luciano	16 + 1	1			1			

DONCASTER ROVERS (DIV 3: 1st)

	P/FL App	P/FL Goals	FLC App	FLC Goals	FAC App	FAC Goals	Others App	Others Goals
AKINFENWA Adebayo	4 + 5	4					1	
ALBRIGHTON Mark	27 + 1	3			1		1	
BARNES Paul	2 + 5		0 + 2	1	0 + 1		2	
BEECH Chris	11		1				1	
BLACK Chris	1							
BLUNDELL Gregg	41 + 3	18	2		2	1	1	
BROWN Chris	17 + 5	10					0 + 1	
BURTON Steve	1 + 5						0 + 1	
DOOLAN John	36 + 3		2		1		1	
FORTUNE-WEST Leo	28 +11	11	2	1	1		0 + 1	
FOSTER Steve	44	1	2				2	
GILL Robert	0 + 1						2	
GREEN Paul	38 + 5	8	1		1		1	
HYNES Peter	0 + 5	1						
McGRATH John	4 + 7		1		1		1	
McINDOE Michael	45	10	2		1		2	
MALONEY Jon	0 + 1						0 + 1	
MARPLES Simon	16		1		1		1	
MELLIGAN JJ	21	2						
MORLEY Dave	15 + 6	1	1		1		2	
MULLIGAN David	14		1					
O'BRIEN Rob	1							
PATERSON Jamie	7 + 1	1	1 + 1				1	
PRICE Jamie	17 + 2		1				1	
RAVENHILL Ricky	14 +22	3	1 + 1		0 + 1		1	
RICHARDSON Barry							2	
RIGOGLIOSO Adriano	5 +12							
RYAN Tim	41 + 1	2	2		1		1	
TIERNEY Fran	10 + 3	3	0 + 1				1	1
WARRINGTON Andy	46		2		1			

EVERTON (PREM: 17th)

	P/FL App	P/FL Goals	FLC App	FLC Goals	FAC App	FAC Goals	Others App	Others Goals
CAMPBELL Kevin	8 + 9	1			0 + 1			
CARSLEY Lee	15 + 6	2	2		2			
CHADWICK Nicky	1 + 2		1	1				
CLARKE Peter	1				0 + 1			
FERGUSON Duncan	13 + 7	5	2	2	2	2		
GRAVESEN Thomas	29 + 1	2	3		3			
HIBBERT Tony	24 + 1		3		3			
JEFFERS Francis	5 +13	1			0 + 3	2		
KILBANE Kevin	26 + 4	3			3	1		
LINDEROTH Tobias	23 + 4		1 + 1	1	1			
McFADDEN James	11 +12		3		1			
MARTYN Nigel	33 + 1		3		3			
NAYSMITH Gary	27 + 2	2	2		2 + 1			
NYARKO Alex	7 + 4		1		2			
OSMAN Leon	3 + 1	1	0 + 1					
PEMBRIDGE Mark	4							

	P/FL		FLC		FAC		Others	
	App	Goals	App	Goals	App	Goals	App	Goals
PISTONE Sandro	20 + 1		1		2			
RADZINSKI Tomasz	28 + 6	8	0 + 2		2			
ROONEY Wayne	26 + 8	9	2 + 1		3			
SIMONSEN Steve	1							
STUBBS Alan	25 + 2		1 + 1		2			
TIE Li	4 + 1		1 + 1					
UNSWORTH David	22 + 4	3	1 + 1		3			
WATSON Steve	22 + 2	5	1		0 + 1			
WEIR Davie	9 + 1		2					
WRIGHT Richard	4							
YOBO Joseph	27 + 1	2	2		0 + 1			

FULHAM (PREM: 9th)

	P/FL		FLC		FAC		Others	
BOA MORTE Luis	32 + 1	9	0 + 1		5	1		
BOCANEGRA Carlos	15				4			
BONNISSEL Jerome	16							
BUARI Malik	1 + 2		1					
CLARK Lee	25	2			2			
CROSSLEY Mark	1		1					
DAVIS Sean	22 + 2	5			6	1		
DJETOU Martin	19 + 7		1		4			
GOMA Alain	23				6			
GREEN Adam	4		1		2			
HARLEY Jon	3 + 1							
HAYLES Barry	10 +16	4			3 + 3	1		
INAMOTO Junichi	15 + 7	2	1		2	1		
JOHN Collins	3 + 5	4						
KNIGHT Zat	30 + 1				5 + 1			
LEACOCK Dean	3 + 1		1					
LEGWINSKI Sylvain	30 + 2		1		4			
McBRIDE Brian	5 +11	4			3	1		
MALBRANQUE Steed	38	6			6	2		
MARLET Steve	1	1						
MELVILLE Andy	9		1		0 + 1			
PEARCE Ian	12 + 1							
PEMBRIDGE Mark	9 + 3	1	1		0 + 2			
PETTA Bobby	3 + 6				2 + 3			
PRATLEY Darren	0 + 1		0 + 1					
REHMAN Zesh	0 + 1		0 + 1					
SAHA Louis	20 + 1	13			1	2		
SAVA Facundo	0 + 6	1	1		0 + 2			
STOLCERS Andrejs			1					
VAN DER SAR Edwin	37				6			
VOLZ Moritz	32 + 1				5			

GILLINGHAM (DIV 1: 21st)

	P/FL		FLC		FAC		Others	
AGYEMANG Patrick	20		6					
ASHBY Barry	22 + 1	1	2		1			
BANKS Steve	13							
BARTRAM Vince	1							
BENJAMIN Trevor	1 + 3	1						
BOSSU Bert	3 + 1				2			
BROWN Jason	22		3					
BROWN Wayne	4	1						
COX Ian	32 + 1		3		1			
CROFTS Andrew	1 + 7		0 + 1					
HENDERSON Darius	4				1 + 1	1		
HESSENTHALER Andy	27 + 9	2	1 + 1		1			
HILLS John	27 + 2	2	3	1	2			
HIRSCHFELD Lars	2							
HOPE Chris	37	3	3		2			
JAMES Kevin	12 + 5	1	0 + 1		0 + 1			
JARVIS Matt	2 + 8				0 + 1			
JOHNSON Leon	18 + 2				0 + 1			
JOHNSON Tommy	6 + 9	3	0 + 2		2	1		
KING Marlon	9 + 2	4	1 + 1	1	1			
NOSWORTHY Nyron	26 + 1	2	3	1	2			
PERPETUINI David	14 + 6	2	1 + 1					
POUTON Alan	14 + 5				1			
ROSE Richard	12 + 5							
SAUNDERS Mark	8 +13	1	2	1				
SHAW Paul	20 + 1	6	2		1			
SIDIBE Mamady	34 + 7	5	2 + 1		1	1		
SMITH Paul	31 + 2		2		2	1		
SOUTHALL Nicky	34 + 1		2		1			
SPILLER Danny	32 + 7	6	2		2			
VAESEN Nico	5							
WALES Gary	3 + 3	1						
WALLACE Rod	10 + 4	1	1					

GRIMSBY TOWN (DIV 2: 21st)

	P/FL		FLC		FAC		Others	
ANDERSON Iain	24 + 5	5	1	1	2		1	
ANTOINE-CURIER Mickael	3 + 2							
ARMSTRONG Craig	9							

	P/FL		FLC		FAC		Others	
	App	Goals	App	Goals	App	Goals	App	Goals
BARNARD Darren	34	2	1		2		1	
BOLDER Chris	6 + 1							
BOULDING Mick	27	12	1		1	1	0 + 1	
CAMPBELL Stuart	39	1	1	1	2		0 + 1	
CAS Marcel	13 + 7	2	1		0 + 2	1	1	
COLDICOTT Stacy	13 + 1							
CRANE Tony	37	3	1		2			
CROWE Jason	27 + 5		1		2		1	
DAVISON Aidan	32		1		2		1	
DAWS Nicky	17						1	
EDWARDS Mike	32 + 1	1			2		1	
FETTIS Alan	11							
FORD Simon	21 + 5	1	1				1	
GROVES Paul	7 + 4		0 + 1		1			
HAMILTON Des	20 + 7		1		2		1	
HOCKLESS Graham	4 + 9	2						
JEVONS Phil	21 + 8	12	1		1	1		
LAWRENCE Jamie	5	1						
McDERMOTT John	21							
MANSARAM Darren	11 +20	3	0 + 1		0 + 1		1	1
NIMMO Liam	0 + 2							
ONUORA Iffy	18 + 1	3			2		1	
PARKER Wes	0 + 4							
PETTINGER Andy	3							
POUTON Alan	5							
RANKIN Izzy	12	4						
ROWAN Jonny	9 + 5	2						
SOAMES David	0 +10							
TEN HEUVEL Laurens	3 + 1		1					
THORPE Lee	5 + 1							
THORRINGTON John	2 + 1							
WARHURST Paul	5 + 2							
YOUNG Greg	10 + 7				0 + 1		0 + 1	

HARTLEPOOL UNITED (DIV 2: 6th)

	P/FL		FLC		FAC		Others	
ARNISON Paul	2 + 2							
BARRON Micky	32	1	1 + 1		3		3	
BOYD Adam	10 + 8	12					2 + 1	
BRACKSTONE John	5 + 1				1	1		
BYRNE Danny	2				1			
CARSON Stephen	1 + 2							
CLARKE Darrell	23 +10	5	1		0 + 2		1 + 2	2
CRADDOCK Darren	9 + 1				0 + 1			
DANNS Neil	8 + 1	1					0 + 2	
EASTER Jermaine	0 + 3							
FOLEY David	0 + 1							
GABBIADINI Marco	9 + 6	5	1		1	2	1	
HENDERSON Kevin	1 + 2		0 + 1					
HUMPHREYS Richie	46		3	2	3	1	3	
ISTEAD Steven	1 +30	1	0 + 2	1	0 + 1			
JORDAN Andy	4 + 1		1					
McCANN Ryan	0 + 4		0 + 1					
NELSON Michael	38 + 2	3	2		3		3	
PORTER Joel	18 + 9	3			1 + 1	1	2	1
PROVETT Jim	45		2		3		2	
RICHARDSON Marcus	3							
ROBERTSON Hugh	18	4					2	
ROBINSON Mark	4						1	
ROBINSON Paul	19 +12	7	2	2	2 + 1		0 + 3	
ROBSON Matty	17 + 6	1	1		2			
SHUKER Chris	14	1			1			
STRACHAN Gavin	34 + 2	5	2		3		1	
SWEENEY Antony	8 + 3	1					2	1
TINKLER Mark	43 + 1	6	2		3		3	
WALKER Scott	5 + 1							
WESTWOOD Chris	45		2		3		3	
WILKINSON Jack	2 + 2				0 + 2			
WILLIAMS Anthony	1							
WILLIAMS Eifion	39 + 2	13	2		3		3	1

HUDDERSFIELD TOWN (DIV 3: 4th)

	P/FL		FLC		FAC		Others	
ABBOTT Pawel	12 + 1	5					1 + 1	
AHMED Adnan	0 + 1							
BOOTH Andy	36 + 1	13	2	1	1		4	
BOOTY Martyn	3 + 1							
BROWN Nat	13 + 8		0 + 2		0 + 1		0 + 1	
CARSS Tony	35 + 1	2	3	1	1		1	
CLARKE Nathan	25 + 1	1	1		1			
EDWARDS Robbie	11 + 6	1	1				2 + 1	1
FOWLER Lee	27 + 2		3				0 + 1	
GRAY Ian	17		3		1		1	
HARKINS Gary	1 + 2							
HOLDSWORTH Andy	31 + 5		2	1	1		4	
HOLLAND Chris	0 + 3				1		1	

Junichi Inamoto (Fulham) on right of picture

	P/FL		FLC		FAC		Others	
	App	Goals	App	Goals	App	Goals	App	Goals
HUGHES Ian	12 + 1	1	1				1	
LLOYD Anthony	30 + 1	3			1		4	
McALISKEY John	5 + 3	4					0 + 2	
MATTIS Dwayne	2 + 3				0 + 1			
MIRFIN David	15 + 6	2	1				4	1
NEWBY Jon	10 + 4		1					
ONIBUJE Fola	0 + 2							
ONUORA Iffy	0 + 3						2	1
RACHUBKA Paul	13						3	
SCHOFIELD Danny	38 + 2	8	3		1		4	1
SCOTT Paul	16 + 3	2	1		1		1 + 1	
SENIOR Phil	16				0 + 1			
SODJE Efe	37 + 2	4	2		1		3 + 1	
STEAD Jon	26	16	3	2	1		1	
THOMPSON Tyrone	1 + 1							
THORRINGTON John	3 + 2		1	1				
WORTHINGTON Jon	36 + 3	3	2		1		4	
YATES Steve	35	1	3				3	

HULL CITY (DIV 3: 2nd)

	App	Goals	App	Goals	App	Goals	App	Goals
ALLSOPP Danny	31 + 5	15	1					
ASHBEE Ian	39	2	1		1			
BURGESS Ben	44	18	1		1			
BURTON Steve					1			
DAWSON Andy	32 + 1	3			1			
DELANEY Damien	46	2	1		1			
DONALDSON Clayton							0 + 2	
ELLIOTT Stuart	42	14	1		0 + 1			
FETTIS Alan	3		1				2	
FORRESTER Jamie	6 +15	4	1		0 + 1		1	1
FRANCE Ryan	7 +21	2					2	1
FRY Russell							0 + 1	
GREEN Stuart	38 + 4	6	1		1			
HINDS Richard	34 + 5	1	1		1		0 + 1	
HOLT Andy	6 +19	1			1		1	
JOSEPH Marc	32				1		1	
KEATES Dean	9 + 5		0 + 1				2	
KUIPERS Michel	3							
LEWIS Junior	13	1						
MARSHALL Lee	10 + 1							
MELTON Steve	0 + 5		0 + 1				2	
MUSSELWHITE Paul	17 + 1							
MYHILL Boaz	23							
PEAT Nathan	0 + 1						1 + 1	
PRICE Jason	29 + 4	9	1		1	1	1	
REGAN Carl							1	
SMITH Shaun							1	
STRONG Greg							2	
THELWELL Alton	22 + 4	1	1					
WALTERS Jon	5 +11	1						
WEBB Danny	0 + 4						2	1
WHITTLE Justin	15 + 3		1		1		1	
WILLIAMS Ryan							1	1
WISEMAN Scott	0 + 2							

IPSWICH TOWN (DIV 1: 5th)

	App	Goals	App	Goals	App	Goals	App	Goals
ARMSTRONG Alun	5 + 2	2	0 + 1				0 + 1	
BART-WILLIAMS Chris	23 + 3	2			1		0 + 1	
BENT Darren	32 + 5	16	1		1		2	1
BENT Marcus	4	1	0 + 1					
BLOOMFIELD Matt			0 + 1					
BOWDITCH Dean	7 + 9	4	1 + 1	1	0 + 1		0 + 1	
COUNAGO Pablo	18 +11	11	2	1	2		2	
DAVIS Kelvin	45		2		2			
DIALLO Drissa	16 + 3		1					
ELLIOTT Matt	10						2	
KUQI Shefki	29 + 7	11			1 + 1		1 + 1	
McGREAL John	18	1			2		1	
MAGILTON Jim	46	1	2		1 + 1		2	
MAHON Alan	7 + 4	1	1					
MAKIN Chris	5		1					
MILLER Tommy	27 + 7	11	1		2	1	2	
MITCHELL Scott	0 + 2							
MORROW Sam			0 + 1					
NASH Gerard	0 + 1							
NAYLOR Richard	28 +11	5	1 + 1		2	1	2	
PRICE Lewis	1							
REUSER Martijn	3 +14	3	1		1 + 1	1	0 + 1	
RICHARDS Matt	41 + 3	1	2		2		2	
SANTOS Georges	28 + 6	1	2					
WESTLAKE Ian	30 + 9	6	1		1		2	
WILNIS Fabian	41		1		2		2	
WRIGHT Jermaine	42 + 3	5	2		2		2	

KIDDERMINSTER HARRIERS (DIV 3: 16th)

	P/FL		FLC		FAC		Others	
	App	Goals	App	Goals	App	Goals	App	Goals
ANTOINE-CURIER Mickael	0 + 1							
BENNETT Dean	34 + 4	3	1		4	4	0 + 1	
BETTS Robert	8 + 1				0 + 1			
BISHOP Andy	8 + 3	2						
BROCK Stuart	37		1		4		1	
BROWN Simon	8	2						
BURTON Steve	10 + 2				1	1		
CHRISTIANSEN Jesper	11 +10	1			2			
CLARKE Leon	3 + 1							
COLEMAN Kenny	10		1		0 + 1		1	
DANBY John	9							
DYER Lloyd	5 + 2	1						
FLYNN Sean	4 + 2		1					
FOSTER Ian	10 + 1	3						
GADSBY Matt	23 + 9	2			2 + 1		1	
HATSWELL Wayne	32		2		4			
HENRIKSEN Bo	14 + 8	2			2 + 2			
HINTON Craig	41 + 1	1	1		4		1	
JENKINS Lee	5 + 2							
KEATES Dean	8	2						
LEWIS Matt	1 + 3		0 + 1		0 + 1		0 + 1	
McHALE Chris	0 + 1							
MELLIGAN JJ	5	1					1	
MURRAY Adam	19 + 3	3						
PARRISH Sean	16 +11	3	0 + 1		3		0 + 1	
RICKARDS Scott	5 + 8	1			0 + 1			
SALL Abdou	6 + 1							
SHILTON Sam	9 + 5		1		1 + 1		1	
SMITH Adie	19 + 3		0 + 1		4		1	
STAMPS Scott	34 + 1		1		3		1	
VIVEASH Adrian	7							
WARD Graham	17 + 4		1		2		1	
WHITE Andy	6 + 1	1			2			
WILLIAMS Danny	28	5	1		4		1	
WILLIAMS John	28 +16	4	1		2 + 2	1	1	
WILLIS Adam	12	1	1					
YATES Mark	14	2						

LEEDS UNITED (PREM: 19th)

	App	Goals	App	Goals	App	Goals	App	Goals
BAKKE Eirik	8 + 2	1			1			
BARMBY Nicky	1 + 5							
BATTY David	10 + 2		1		1			
BRIDGES Michael	1 + 9		1 + 1					
CALDWELL Steve	13	1						
CAMARA Zoumana	13	1	2					
CARSON Scott	2 + 1							
CHAPUIS Cyril	0 + 1		1 + 1					
DOMI Didier	9 + 3		0 + 2					
DUBERRY Michael	19	3	1		1			
HARTE Ian	21 + 2	1	2		1	1	1	
JOHNSON Seth	24 + 1	2	1					
JOHNSON Simon	1 + 4							
KELLY Garry	37		2					
KILGALLON Matthew	7 + 1		2		1			
LENNON Aaron	0 +11		1 + 1		0 + 1			
McPHAIL Stephen	8 + 4	1	1					
MATTEO Dominic	33		2		1			
MILNER James	27 + 3	3	1		1			
MORRIS Jody	11 + 1							
OLEMBE Salomon	8 + 4		2					
PENNANT Jermaine	34 + 2	2						
RADEBE Lucas	11 + 3		0 + 1					
RICHARDSON Frazer	2 + 2				1			
ROBINSON Paul	36		2		1			
ROQUE JUNIOR Jose Victor	5		2		2	2		
SAKHO Lamine	9 + 8	1	1		0 + 1			
SMITH Alan	35	9	2		1			
VIDUKA Mark	30	11	1		1		1	
WILCOX Jason	3 + 3		1					

LEICESTER CITY (PREM: 18th)

	App	Goals	App	Goals	App	Goals	App	Goals
BENJAMIN Trevor	2 + 2							
BENT Marcus	28 + 5	9			2	1		
BROOKER Paul	0 + 3		2		0 + 1			
CANERO Peter	2 + 5							
COYNE Danny	1 + 3		1					
CURTIS John	14 + 1		1					
DABIZAS Nikos	18							
DAVIDSON Callum	8 + 5				2			
DEANE Brian	0 + 5		2					
DICKOV Paul	28 + 7	11	2	1	2	1		
ELLIOTT Matt	3 + 4				0 + 1			

	P/FL App	P/FL Goals	FLC App	FLC Goals	FAC App	FAC Goals	Others App	Others Goals
FERDINAND Les	20 + 9	12			1 + 1	1		
FREUND Steffen	13 + 1							
GILLESPIE Keith	7 + 5		0 + 1					
GUPPY Steve	9 + 6							
HEATH Matt	13				2			
HIGNETT Craig	3 +10	1	1		1			
HOWEY Steve	13	1	2					
IMPEY Andy	11 + 2		2		1			
IZZET Muzzy	30	2	0 + 2	1	1			
McKINLAY Billy	15 + 1		1		2			
NALIS Lilian	11 + 9	1	2					
PRIET Nicolas			0 + 1					
ROGERS Alan	7 + 1							
SCIMECA Riccy	28 + 1	1	1		1			
SCOWCROFT Jamie	33 + 2	5	1 + 1		2			
SINCLAIR Frank	11 + 3	1	2		1			
STEWART Jordan	16 + 9	1	1 + 1		1 + 1			
TAGGART Gerry	9							
THATCHER Ben	28 + 1	1						
WALKER Ian	37		1		2			

LEYTON ORIENT (DIV 3: 19th)

	P/FL App	P/FL Goals	FLC App	FLC Goals	FAC App	FAC Goals	Others App	Others Goals
AKINFENWA Adebayo	0 + 1				0 + 1			
ALEXANDER Gary	44	15	1		2	1	0 + 1	
BARNARD Donny	17 + 6							
BRAZIER Matthew	5	1	1					
COOPER Shaun	9							
DOWNER Simon	1 + 2							
DUNCAN Derek	0 + 1							
EBDON Marcus	10 + 4		1				1	
FORBES Boniek	0 +10				0 + 1		1	
HAMMOND Dean	6 + 2				1			
HARNWELL Jamie	1 + 2							
HARRISON Lee	19 + 1		1		1 + 1		1	
HEALD Greg	4							
HUNT David	35 + 3	1	1		2		1	
HUNT Warren	6							
IBEHRE Jabo	17 +18	4	0 + 1	1	1 + 1		1	
JONES Billy	29 + 2		1				0 + 1	
JOSEPH Matthew	23 + 1				2			
LOCKWOOD Matthew	24 + 1	2	1		2	1	1	1
McCORMACK Alan	8 + 2				1			
McGHEE Dave	10		1		1			
MACKIE John	20	1						
MILLER Justin	27 + 7	2	1		1 + 1			
MORRIS Glenn	27		0 + 1		1			
NEWEY Tom	31 + 3	2	1		2			
PETERS Mark	39				2		1	
PURSER Wayne	29 +12	5	1		2	1	1	1
SAAH Brian	4 + 2							
SAM Lloyd	5 + 5							
SCOTT Andy	8	1						
STEPHENS Kevin	0 + 1							
TATE Chris	5 +18		0 + 1	1			1	
THORPE Lee	15 + 2	4			1		0 + 1	
TONER Ciaran	19 + 8	1	1		1			
ZAKUANI Gaby	9 + 1	2			1			

LINCOLN CITY (DIV 3: 7th)

	P/FL App	P/FL Goals	FLC App	FLC Goals	FAC App	FAC Goals	Others App	Others Goals
BAILEY Mark	34 + 1	1			0 + 1		4	2
BLOOMER Matt	14 +13		1		2	1	4 + 1	
BUTCHER Richard	26 + 6	6	1		2		5	1
CARBON Matt	1							
CROPPER Dene	5 +16				1			
ELLISON Kevin	11				2			
FLETCHER Gary	42	16			2		4	3
FRECKLINGTON Lee							1 + 1	
FUTCHER Ben	43	2	1		2		5	
GAIN Peter	42	7			2		3	
GREEN Francis	28 + 7	7			1		2 + 2	1
LIBURD Richard	19 + 5		1				2 + 1	
McCOMBE Jamie	8						1 + 1	
McNAMARA Niall	2 + 8		1		1 + 1		1	
MARRIOTT Alan	46		1		2		5	
MAY Rory	1 + 4				0 + 2		0 + 1	
MAYO Paul	31	6	1		2	1	3	1
MORGAN Paul	41		1		2		1	
PEARCE Allan	0 + 3		0 + 1				0 + 1	
REMY Ellis	0 + 1		0 + 1					
RICHARDSON Marcus	34 + 4	10			3		1	
ROCASTLE Craig	0 + 2							
SANDWITH Kevin	1 + 2							
SEDGEMORE Ben	24 + 3		1				1 + 2	
WATTLEY David	1 + 2						0 + 1	

	P/FL App	P/FL Goals	FLC App	FLC Goals	FAC App	FAC Goals	Others App	Others Goals
WEAVER Simon	39		1		2		3	
WILFORD Aron	0 + 5	1					0 + 1	
WILLIS Scott	0 + 3						0 + 1	
YEO Simon	13 +28	11	0 + 1		2	1	4 + 1	1

LIVERPOOL (PREM: 4th)

	P/FL App	P/FL Goals	FLC App	FLC Goals	FAC App	FAC Goals	Others App	Others Goals
BAROS Milan	6 + 7	1			0 + 1		2 + 2	1
BISCAN Igor	27 + 2		2		1		5 + 2	
CARRAGHER Jamie	22				3		4	
CHEYROU Bruno	9 + 3	2			3 + 1	2	1 + 2	
DIAO Salif	2 + 1		1				2 + 1	
DIOUF El Hadji	20 + 6		2		1		3 + 1	
DUDEK Jerzy	30		1		3		4	
FINNAN Steve	19 + 3				3		5 + 1	
GERRARD Steven	34	4	1 + 1		3		7 + 1	2
HAMANN Dietmar	25		0 + 1		4		5	1
HENCHOZ Stephane	15 + 3		1		4		3 + 1	
HESKEY Emile	25 +10	7	1		2		3 + 1	1	4 + 2	2
HYYPIA Sami	38	4	1		4		8	1
JONES Paul	2							
KEWELL Harry	36	7	0 + 2	1	3		8	3
KIRKLAND Chris	6		1		1		4	
LE TALLEC Anthony	3 +10		2		1 + 3		2 + 2	1
LUZI-BERNARDI Patrice	0 + 1							
MURPHY Danny	19 +12	5	2		2		1 + 1	1	6 + 1	
OTSEMOBOR John	4		1					
OWEN Michael	29	16			3	1	6	2
RIISE Jon Arne	22 + 6		1		1		4	
SINAMA-PONGOLLE Florent	3 +12	2	1 + 1		1 + 2		1 + 2	
SMICER Vladimir	15 + 5	3	1		1	1	2 + 1	
TRAORE Djimi	7		2				2	1
WELSH John	0 + 1						0 + 1	

LUTON TOWN (DIV 2: 10th)

	P/FL App	P/FL Goals	FLC App	FLC Goals	FAC App	FAC Goals	Others App	Others Goals
BARNETT Leon					1		2	
BAYLISS Dave	6		1	1				
BECKWITH Robert	13		2					
BERESFORD Marlon	11				5			
BOYCE Emmerson	42	4	2		5	1		
BRILL Dean	4 + 1						2	
BRKOVIC Ahmet	24 + 8	1	1		5		2	
COYNE Chris	44	2	2	1	5		2	
CROWE Dean	0 + 8		0 + 1		0 + 3		2	
DAVIES Curtis	4 + 2						0 + 1	
DAVIS Sol	34 + 2		1 + 1		4		3	
DEENEY David							1 + 1	
FOLEY Kevin	32 + 1	1	2	2	3			
FORBES Adrian	21 + 6	9			4	5	0 + 1	
HILLIER Ian	8 + 3		0 + 1		2 + 1		3	
HOLMES Peter	11 + 5	3			2 + 1		1	
HOWARD Steve	34	14	2	1	3		1	
HUGHES Paul	20 + 2	1	2					
HYLDGAARD Morten	18							
JUDGE Matthew	0 + 1						0 + 1	1
KEANE Keith	14 + 1	1			0 + 1		1	
LEARY Michael	8 + 6	2	0 + 1		1 + 1		2 + 1	1
McSHEFFREY Gary	18	9	1	1				
MANSELL Lee	12 + 4	2			5	1	3	
NEILSON Alan	11 + 3	1	1		1			
NICHOLLS Kevin	21	2	1		1			
OKAI Parys			0 + 1		0 + 1		1	
O'LEARY Stephen	3 + 2	1					1	
PERRETT Russ	5 + 1	2						
PITT Courtney	11 + 1		1 + 1	1				
ROBINSON Steve	32 + 2	2			4	1	2	
SHOWUNMI Enoch	18 + 8	7			2		2 + 1	1
SPRING Matthew	24	1	2		3		1	
THORPE Tony	2	2	1					
UNDERWOOD Paul	1							

MACCLESFIELD TOWN (DIV 3: 20th)

	P/FL App	P/FL Goals	FLC App	FLC Goals	FAC App	FAC Goals	Others App	Others Goals
ABBEY George	23 + 2		1		3		1	
ADAMS Danny	27		1		4		1	1
BERESFORD David	5						0 + 1	
BESWETHERICK Jon	3 + 1							
BRACKENRIDGE Steve	2 + 5	2			1 + 1			
CARR Michael	7				1			
CARRAGHER Matthew	18							
CARRUTHERS Martin	30 + 9	8	1		3 + 1	2	1	
CLARK Steve	1 + 3							
FLITCROFT Dave	14 + 1						1	
HADDRELL Matt	4 + 6	1	1		2 + 1			
HARSLEY Paul	16	2						
HITCHEN Steve	8 + 1		0 + 1		0 + 1			

Player	P/FL App	Goals	FLC App	Goals	FAC App	Goals	Others App	Goals
JONES Rob	1							
LITTLE Colin	18 + 6	5	1		4	1		
MACAULEY Steve	16				1		1	
MILES John	23 + 6	6	1		1 + 1	1	0 + 1	
MUNROE Karl	35 + 1		1		3		1	
MYHILL Boaz	15		1					
OLSEN James	0 + 2							
PARKIN Jon	12		1					
PAYNE Steve	13							
POTTER Graham	16		2					
PRIEST Chris	26 + 3	2			4		0 + 1	
ROBINSON Neil	0 + 1							
ROSS Neil	1 + 5							
SMITH Dave	7 + 3		1					
TIPTON Matthew	34 + 4	16	0 + 1		4	3	1	
WELCH Michael	33 + 5		1		2		1	
WHITAKER Danny	33 + 3	5	1	1	4		1	
WIDDRINGTON Tommy	34 + 1				3		1	
WILSON Steve	31 + 1				4		1	

MANCHESTER CITY (PREM: 16th)

Player	P/FL App	Goals	FLC App	Goals	FAC App	Goals	Others App	Goals
ANELKA Nicolas	31 + 1	16	2		4	4	5	4
ARASON Arni					2			
BARTON Joey	24 + 4	1	2		3 + 1		2 + 3	
BERKOVIC Eyal	1 + 3		0 + 1				2	
BISCHOFF Mikkel							1	
BOSVELT Paul	22 + 3		1		4	1	4 + 1	
DISTIN Sylvain	38		2		5	1	5	
DUNNE Richard	28 + 1		2		5		3 + 1	
ELLEGAARD Kevin	2 + 2		1					
ELLIOTT Stephen	0 + 2							
FLOOD Willo							1	
FOWLER Robbie	23 + 8	7	2	1	4		4	1
HUCKERBY Darren							1	1
JAMES David	17							
JIHAI Sun	29 + 4	1	1		3		5	1
JORDAN Steve	0 + 2							
MACKEN Jon	7 + 8	1	0 + 1	1	1 + 2	2	1 + 1	
McMANAMAN Steve	20 + 2		0 + 1		2 + 1		4	
NEGOUAI Christian							1	1
REYNA Claudio	19 + 4	1	1		3		2 + 2	
SEAMAN David	19		1		1		5	
SIBIERSKI Antoine	18 +15	5	0 + 1	1	3 + 2	1	1	1
SINCLAIR Trevor	20 + 9	1	2		3 + 1		3	1
SOMMEIL David	18		1		2		4	1
TARNAT Michael	32		3		2		4	1	3
TIATTO Danny	1 + 4						2 + 2	
VAN BUYTEN Daniel	5				1			
WANCHOPE Paulo	12 +10	6					1 + 3	
WEAVER Nick							1	
WHELAN Glenn							0 + 1	
WIEKENS Gerard							1	
WRIGHT-PHILLIPS Shaun	32 + 2	7	2	2	3 + 1	1	4 + 2	1

MANCHESTER UNITED (PREM: 3rd)

Player	P/FL App	Goals	FLC App	Goals	FAC App	Goals	Others App	Goals
BARDSLEY Phil			1		0 + 1			
BELLION David	4 +10	2	2	1	1 + 1		0 + 4	
BROWN Wes	15 + 2		2		5 + 1		2	
BUTT Nicky	12 + 9	1	2		3 + 2		5 + 1	1
CARROLL Roy	6		2		2 + 1		1	
DJEMBA DJEMBA Eric	10 + 5		1		0 + 1		1 + 4	1
EAGLES Chris			0 + 2					
FERDINAND Rio	20						7	
FLETCHER Darren	17 + 5		2		4 + 1		3 + 3	
FORLAN Diego	10 +14	4	1		2	1	2 + 3	2
FORTUNE Quinton	18 + 5		1		3		7 + 1	2
GIGGS Ryan	29 + 4	7			5		9	1
HOWARD Tim	32				4		8	
JOHNSON Eddie			0 + 1					
KEANE Roy	25 + 3	3			4 + 1		6	
KLEBERSON	10 + 2	2	1		1		1 + 1	
NARDIELLO Danny			0 + 1					
NEVILLE Gary	30		2		4		7	
NEVILLE Phil	29 + 2				2 + 1		8	1
O'SHEA John	32 + 1	2	2		6		6 + 2	
PUGH Danny			1		0 + 1			
RICHARDSON Kieran			2		0 + 1			
RONALDO	15 +14	4	1		5	2	3 + 2	
SAHA Louis	9 + 3	7					1 + 1	
SCHOLES Paul	24 + 4	9			6	4	6	1
SILVESTRE Mickael	33 + 1				5	1	7	2
SOLSKJAER Ole Gunnar	7 + 6				1 + 2		2 + 1	1
TIERNEY Paul			1					
VAN NISTELROOY Ruud	31 + 1	20			3 + 1	6	8	4

MANSFIELD TOWN (DIV 3: 5th)

Player	P/FL App	Goals	FLC App	Goals	FAC App	Goals	Others App	Goals
ARTELL Dave	24 + 2	3	1		3 + 1		0 + 1	
BEARDSLEY Chris	2 +13	1			0 + 1		1	
BUXTON Jake	9		1		0 + 1		1	
CHRISTIE Iyseden	24 + 3	8	1		2 + 1	1		
CLARKE Jamie	11 + 1		1		1 + 1		1	
CORDEN Wayne	40 + 4	8	1		2 + 1		4	
CURLE Tom	0 + 1							
CURTIS Tom	34 + 4		1		3		3	1
D'JAFFO Laurent	4 + 4	1					0 + 3	
DAY Rhys	40 + 1	6	0 + 1		4		4	2
DIMECH Luke	17 + 3	1	1		1 + 1			
DISLEY Craig	18 +16	5			3 + 1		4	
EATON Adam	3						3	
HASSELL Bobby	33 + 1		1		4		3	
JOHN-BAPTISTE Alex	14 + 3						4	
LARKIN Colin	19 +18	7			1 + 1	1	1 + 3	
LAWRENCE Liam	41	18	1		4	3	3	
MacKENZIE Neil	25 + 7	2	0 + 1		2	3	1 + 1	
MENDES Junior	36 + 3	11	1		4	1	3	1
MITCHELL Craig	0 + 1							
MULLIGAN Lance	0 + 1							
PACQUETTE Richard	3 + 2	1			3			
PILKINGTON Kevin	46		1		4		4	
VAUGHAN Tony	32		2		3			
WHITE Andy	2 +12		0 + 1				0 + 1	
WILLIAMSON Lee	29 + 6	5	1		3		4	

MIDDLESBROUGH (PREM: 11th)

Player	P/FL App	Goals	FLC App	Goals	FAC App	Goals	Others App	Goals
BOATENG George	35		6		2			
CHRISTIE Malcolm	7 + 3	1	0 + 1	1				
COOPER Colin	17 + 2		2					
DAVIES Andrew	8 + 2							
DORIVA	19 + 2		4 + 1					
DOWNING Stewart	7 +13		1 + 1		2			
EHIOGU Ugo	16		2		1			
GREENING Jonathan	17 + 8	1	4					
JOB Joseph-Desire	19 + 5	5	1 + 2	1	2	1		
JONES Brad	1				1			
JUNINHO	26 + 5	8	5 + 1	1	0 + 1			
MACCARONE Massimo	13 +10	6	5		0 + 2			
MARINELLI Carlos	1		1					
MENDIETA Gaizka	30 + 1	2	6	1	1			
MILLS Danny	28		7		2			
MORRISON James	0 + 1				0 + 1			
NASH Carlo	1							
NEMETH Szilard	17 +15	9	2 + 2		1 + 1			
PARNABY Stuart	8 + 5		0 + 2		1			
QUEUDRUE Franck	31		7		2			
RICKETTS Michael	7 +16	2	3 + 2	1	2			
RIGGOTT Chris	14 + 3		4 + 1		1 + 1			
SCHWARZER Mark	36		7		1			
SOUTHGATE Gareth	27		6		1			
STOCKDALE Robbie	0 + 2							
WRIGHT Alan	2							
ZENDEN Bolo	31	4	5 + 1	2	2	1		

MILLWALL (DIV 1: 10th)

Player	P/FL App	Goals	FLC App	Goals	FAC App	Goals	Others App	Goals
BRANIFF Kevin	6 +10		0 + 1		1 + 3	1		
CAHILL Tim	40	9	1		7	3		
CHADWICK Nicky	11 + 4	4						
COGAN Barry	0 + 3				0 + 1			
CRAIG Tony	8 + 1		1					
DICHIO Danny	15	7			5	1		
DOLAN Joe	0 + 1							
DUNNE Alan	4 + 4		0 + 1					
ELLIOTT Marvin	14 + 7				1 + 3			
FOFANA Aboubaka	9 + 7				0 + 1			
GUERET Willy	2				2			
HARRIS Neil	26 +12	9	1		7	1		
HEARN Charley	3 + 4		1					
IFILL Paul	29 + 4	8			6	1		
JUAN	2 + 1		1					
LAWRENCE Matt	34 + 2		1		7			
LIVERMORE David	35 + 1	1			7			
McCAMMON Mark	3 + 4				0 + 1			
MARSHALL Andy	16				4			
MUSCAT Kevin	27				4			
NETHERCOTT Stuart	11 + 3	1	1					
PEETERS Bob	16 + 4	3			7			
PHILLIPS Mark			0 + 1					
QUIGLEY Mark	0 + 1							
ROBERTS Andy	29 + 4	1			2 + 1			

	P/FL		FLC		FAC		Others	
	App	Goals	App	Goals	App	Goals	App	Goals
ROBINSON Paul	7 + 2							
ROBINSON Trevor	0 + 1							
RYAN Robbie	28 + 2				6			
SADLIER Richard	0 + 2							
SUTTON John	2 + 2				0 + 1			
SWEENEY Peter	21 + 8	2			2 + 3			
WARD Darren	46	3	1		7			
WARNER Tony	28		1		1			
WESTON Curtis	0 + 1				0 + 1			
WHELAN Noel	8 + 7	4	1					
WISE Dennis	26 + 5	1			6	1		

NEWCASTLE UNITED (PREM: 5th)

	P/FL		FLC		FAC		Others	
	App	Goals	App	Goals	App	Goals	App	Goals
AMBROSE Darren	10 +14	2	0 + 1		0 + 1		6 + 5	1
AMEOBI Shola	18 + 8	7	1		0 + 1		8 + 5	3
BELLAMY Craig	13 + 3	4					7 + 1	5
BERNARD Olivier	35	1	1		2		13	
BOWYER Lee	17 + 7	2					0 + 1	
BRAMBLE Titus	27 + 2		1		1		11	3
BRIDGES Michael	0 + 6						1 + 2	
BRITTAIN Martin	0 + 1						0 + 1	
CALDWELL Steve	3 + 2		1				0 + 1	
CHOPRA Michael	1 + 5							
DYER Kieron	25	1			2	2	6 + 1	
GIVEN Shay	38				2		13	
GRIFFIN Andy	5		1				2	
HARPER Steve			1				1	
HUGHES Aaron	34				2		11	
JENAS Jermaine	26 + 5	2	1		2		10 + 2	1
LUA LUA Lomano	2 + 5		1		0 + 1		0 + 2	
O'BRIEN Andy	27 + 1	1			1		12 + 1	
ROBERT Laurent	31 + 4	6	1		1	2	12 + 2	3
SHEARER Alan	37	22	0 + 1		2		12	6
SOLANO Nobby	8 + 4		1		2		4 + 1	1
SPEED Gary	37 + 1	3	0 + 1		2		13	1
TAYLOR Steven	1						0 + 1	
VIANA Hugo	5 +11				0 + 1		5 + 4	
WOODGATE Jonathan	18				2		7	

NORTHAMPTON TOWN (DIV 3: 6th)

	P/FL		FLC		FAC		Others	
	App	Goals	App	Goals	App	Goals	App	Goals
ABIDALLAH Nabil	0 + 1						0 + 1	
AMOO Ryan	0 + 1							
ASAMOAH Derek	4 +27	3			4 + 1	1	3 + 1	
BURGESS Oliver	3 + 6		1 + 1					
CARRUTHERS Chris	19 + 5		1		4		2	
CHAMBERS Luke	19 + 5		2		0 + 2		1	
CLARK Peter	6		1					
DOIG Chris	9							
DUDFIELD Lawrie	12 + 7	3	1 + 1	1	0 + 1		0 + 2	2
HARGREAVES Chris	41 + 1	3	1 + 1	1	5	1	4	1
HARPER Lee	39		1		5		5	
HARSLEY Paul	5 + 9		1		0 + 2		1 + 1	
LINCOLN Greg	4 + 3	1			2		1	
LOW Josh	28 + 5	3	1		1	1	2	1	4	
LYTTLE Des	23 + 4				5		3	
MORISON Steve	2 + 3	1						
REEVES Martin	9 + 5		1		1 + 2		1 + 2	
REID Paul	33		2		3		2 + 2	
RICHARDS Marc	27 +14	8	2		0 + 4	2	4 + 1	1
RICKERS Paul	0 + 1							
SABIN Eric	9 + 2	5			1			
SADLER Mat	7							
SAMPSON Ian	35 + 2	2	0 + 1		5		4	
SMITH Martin	43 + 1	11	1		5	3	4 + 1	1
TAYLOR John	3 + 5	1					0 + 2	
THOMPSON Glyn	7 + 1		1					
TROLLOPE Paul	43	6	1				3 + 1	
ULLATHORNE Rob	13		1				2	
VIEIRA Magno	7 + 3	2						
WALKER Richard	11 + 1	4			4	2	3	2
WESTWOOD Ashley	8 + 1				1		1	
WILLMOTT Chris	35 + 1	1	2		4		1	
YOUNGS Tom	2 +10		1				0 + 1	

NORWICH CITY (DIV 1: 1st)

	P/FL		FLC		FAC		Others	
	App	Goals	App	Goals	App	Goals	App	Goals
ABBEY Zema	1 + 2							
BRENNAN Jim	7 + 8	1			1	1		
BRIGGS Keith	1 + 2							
COOPER Kevin	6 + 4							
CROUCH Peter	14 + 1	4			1			
DRURY Adam	42		1		1			
EASTON Clint	8 + 2	2	1		1			
EDWORTHY Marc	42 + 1		1		1			
FLEMING Craig	46	3			1			
FRANCIS Damien	39 + 2	7	1		1			
GREEN Robert	46		1		1			
HAMMOND Elvis	0 + 4							
HARPER Kevin	9							
HENDERSON Ian	14 + 5	4	1		0 + 1			
HOLT Gary	46	1	1		1			
HUCKERBY Darren	36	14	1		1			
JARVIS Ryan	0 +12	1	1		0 + 1			
MACKAY Malky	45	4	1		1			
McKENZIE Leon	12 + 6	9						
McVEIGH Paul	36 + 8	5	0 + 1		1			
MULRYNE Phil	14 +20	3	0 + 1		0 + 1			
NIELSEN David	2		0 + 1					
NOTMAN Alex	0 + 1							
RIVERS Mark	7 + 5	4	1					
ROBERTS Iwan	13 +28	8						
SHACKELL Jason	4 + 2							
SVENSSON Mathias	16 + 4	7						

NOTTINGHAM FOREST (DIV 1: 14th)

	P/FL		FLC		FAC		Others	
	App	Goals	App	Goals	App	Goals	App	Goals
BARMBY Nick	6	1						
BIGGINS James			1					
BOPP Eugene	9 + 6	1	1 + 1	2	1			
CASH Brian	0 + 1							
CHOPRA Michael	3 + 2							
DAWSON Michael	30	1	1					
DOIG Chris	7 + 3		0 + 1		1			
EVANS Paul	8							
GARDNER Ross	1 + 1							
GERRARD Paul	8							
GUNNARSSON Brynjar	9 + 4				1			
HAREWOOD Marlon	19	12	3					
IMPEY Andy	15 + 1	1						
JESS Eoin	21 +13	2	0 + 2					
JOHNSON David	10 + 7	7	1					
KING Marlon	23 + 1	5			2	1		
LOUIS-JEAN Mathieu	37 + 1	1	2		2			
McPHAIL Stephen	13 + 1		2					
MORGAN Wes	30 + 2	2	3					
OYEN Davy	4		1					
REID Andy	46	13	3		2			
ROBERTSON Gregor	12 + 4		1 + 1		2			
ROCHE Barry	6 + 2							
ROGERS Alan	12							
SONNER Danny	19 + 9		3		1			
STEWART Michael	11 + 2		1 + 1					
TAYLOR Gareth	28 + 6	8	2		2			
THOMPSON John	26 + 6	1	3		1			
WALKER Des	23 + 2		1		2			
WARD Darren	32		3		2			
WESTCARR Craig	0 + 3				0 + 1			
WILLIAMS Gareth	38 + 1	6	1 + 1		2			

NOTTS COUNTY (DIV 2: 23rd)

	P/FL		FLC		FAC		Others	
	App	Goals	App	Goals	App	Goals	App	Goals
ANTOINE-CURIER Mickael	4	1						
ARPHEXAD Pegguy	3							
BALDRY Simon	32 + 3	1	2	1	3		1	
BARACLOUGH Ian	30 + 4		3		3		0 + 1	
BARRAS Tony	38 + 2	2	3	1	2	1	0 + 1	
BEWERS Jonathan	0 + 3							
BOERTIEN Paul	5							
BOLLAND Paul	35 + 4	1	0 + 2		1		1	
BROUGH Michael	5 + 5		1		0 + 2		1	
CASKEY Darren	29 + 4	2	2		3		0 + 1	
DEENEY Saul	3							
FENTON Nicky	42 + 1	1	3		3	2	1	
FRANCIS Willis	0 + 3							
GARDEN Stuart	12 + 1							
HACKWORTH Tony	4 + 8		0 + 1				1	
HARRAD Shaun	0 + 8				0 + 1			
HEFFERNAN Paul	31 + 7	20	2 + 1		1 + 1	1	1	
JENKINS Steve	17		3		2		1	
LIVESEY Danny	9 + 2						1	
McFAUL Shane	2 + 4						1	
McGOLDRICK David	2 + 2							
McHUGH Frazer	9 + 4							
MILDENHALL Steve	28		3		3		1	
MURRAY Adam	1 + 2				0 + 1		1	
NICHOLSON Kevin	16 + 7		2 + 1		2 + 1	1	1	
OAKES Stefan	14							
PARKINSON Andy	10 + 4	3						
PIPE David	18							
PLATT Clive	19	3	3		3	3		
RHODES Chris	0 + 1							

	P/FL App	P/FL Goals	FLC App	FLC Goals	FAC App	FAC Goals	Others App	Others Goals
RICHARDSON Ian	40	3	3		3	1		
RILEY Paul	13 + 6	3	1 + 1		2			
SCOFFHAM Steve	4 +11	2						
SCULLY Tony	6 + 4	3						
STALLARD Mark	18 + 4	4	2 + 1	2	2			
WILLIAMS Matthew	5 + 2							
WILSON Kelvin	2 + 1							

OLDHAM ATHLETIC (DIV 2: 15th)

	P/FL App	P/FL Goals	FLC App	FLC Goals	FAC App	FAC Goals	Others App	Others Goals
ANTOINE-CURIER Mickael	5 + 3	2	1		1			
BARLOW Matty	0 + 1							
BEHARALL Dave	7	2			2		2	
BONNER Mark	6 + 1							
BOSHELL Danny	16 + 6		1		1 + 1		2	1
CARNEY Dave			0 + 1					
CLEGG Michael	28 + 4				2		2	
COOKSEY Ernie	22 +14	4			2	2	1 + 1	
CROWE Dean	2 + 3	1						
EYRE John	42 + 1	6	1		1	1	1	
EYRES David	22 + 7	3			0 + 1			
FLEMING Craig	0 + 1							
GRIFFIN Adam	25 + 1	1			0 + 1			
HAINING Will	30 + 1	2	1		1			
HALL Chris	0 + 1				0 + 1			
HALL Danny	28 + 3	1	1		1 + 1		1	
HOLDEN Dean	37 + 2	4			2		1 + 1	
HUDSON Mark	15						1	
JOHNSON Jermaine	18 + 2	5						
KILLEN Chris	7 + 6	2						
LOMAX Kelvin	0 + 1							
MURRAY Paul	41	9	1		1		1 + 1	
NDIWA-LORD Kangana	3 + 1							
O'HALLORAN Matt	2 +11		0 + 1		0 + 1		1 + 1	
OWEN Gareth	15	1						
POGLIACOMI Les	46		1		2		2	
ROCA Carlos	0 + 7		1		1		0 + 2	
SHERIDAN Darren	18 + 9		1		1		2	
SHERIDAN John	19 + 3	5	0 + 1		2			
TIERNEY Marc	0 + 2		1				1	
VERNON Scott	28 +17	12	1		1		2	2
WALKER Rob	1							
WILKINSON Wes	2 + 3							
WOLFENDEN Matty	0 + 1							
ZOLA-MAKONGO Calvin	21 + 4	5			1	1	2	1

OXFORD UNITED (DIV 3: 9th)

	P/FL App	P/FL Goals	FLC App	FLC Goals	FAC App	FAC Goals	Others App	Others Goals
ALSOP Julian	26 + 3	5	1		1			
ASHTON Jon	30 + 4		2		1		1	
BASHAM Steve	38	14	1	1	1		1	
BOUND Matt	33 + 4	1	2		1		1	
BROWN Danny	12		1				1	
COX Simon	5							
CROSBY Andy	41 + 1	5	2		1		1	
FORAN Richie	3 + 1							
HACKETT Chris	6 +16	1	0 + 1		0 + 1		1	
HUNT James	36 + 5	2	1		1			
LOUIS Jefferson	6 +14	2	0 + 1	1	0 + 1		1	
McCARTHY Paul	28 + 1	2						
McNIVEN Scott	41		2		1		1	
OLDFIELD David	1 + 2		0 + 1					
OMOYINMI Manny	1 + 2						0 + 1	
PITT Courtney	5 + 3							
QUINN Barry	5 + 1							
RAWLE Mark	10 +21	8	1		0 + 1		1	
ROBINSON Matt	40		1		2		1	
SCOTT Andy	2 + 4		0 + 1					
STEELE Lee	3 +13	1						
TOWNSLEY Derek	9 + 2		2				1	
WALKER Richard	3 + 1							
WANLESS Paul	38	5	1		1		1	
WATERMAN Dave	6 + 7				1			
WHITEHEAD Dean	37 + 7	7	2		1			
WINTERS Tom	0 + 1							
WOODMAN Andy	41		2		1		1	

PETERBOROUGH UNITED (DIV 2: 18th)

	P/FL App	P/FL Goals	FLC App	FLC Goals	FAC App	FAC Goals	Others App	Others Goals
ARBER Mark	43 + 1	3	1		3		2	
BOUCAUD Andre	7 + 1		1		1			
BRANSTON Guy	14							
BURTON-GODWIN Sagi	27 + 3	1	1		1		2	1
CLARKE James	28 +17	9	1		1 + 1	2	2	1
FARRELL David	30 +14	5	0 + 1		3		3	1
FOTIADIS Andy	0 + 8						0 + 2	
GILL Matthew	27 + 6		1		1 + 1		1 + 1	

	P/FL App	P/FL Goals	FLC App	FLC Goals	FAC App	FAC Goals	Others App	Others Goals
GREEN Francis	0 + 3		0 + 1					
JELLEYMAN Gareth	13 + 4				2		3	
JENKINS Steve	6 + 2							
KANU Christopher	16 + 5		1		2		2 + 1	
LEGG Andy	38 + 4		1		1 + 1		0 + 2	
LOGAN Richard	12 +17	7			2 + 1	1	1 + 1	1
McKENZIE Leon	19	9	1		1		2	3
NEWTON Adam	28 + 9	2	0 + 1		2 + 1	1	2 + 1	
NOLAN Matt	0 + 1							
PEARCE Dennis	1 + 2							
PLATT Clive	17 + 1	2						
PULLEN James	3							
REA Simon	25 + 3	1	1		3		1	
SCOTT Richard					0 + 1			
SEMPLE Ryan	1 + 1							
SHIELDS Tony	9		1					
ST LEDGER-HALL Sean	1 + 1						1	
THOMSON Steve	28 + 7	1			3	1	3	
TYLER Mark	43		1		3		3	
WILLIAMS Tommy	20 + 1	1	1		1			
WILLOCK Calum	22 + 7	8			1 + 1	1	2	
WOOD Neil	2 + 1	1						
WOODHOUSE Curtis	26 + 1	7			3			

PLYMOUTH ARGYLE (DIV 2: 1st)

	P/FL App	P/FL Goals	FLC App	FLC Goals	FAC App	FAC Goals	Others App	Others Goals
ADAMS Steve	25 +11	2	1		1		1	
ALJOFREE Hasney	20 + 4		1				1	
BENT Jason	13 + 5	1	1		1		2	
BERESFORD David	0 + 1							
CAPALDI Tony	29 + 4	7	1				0 + 2	
CONNOLLY Paul	28 + 1							
COUGHLAN Graham	46	7	1		1		1	1
EVANS Micky	35 + 9	11	1	1	1		1	1
FRIIO David	35 + 1	14	0 + 1		1	1	2	
GILBERT Peter	40	1	1		1		2	1
HODGES Lee	28 + 9	3			0 + 1		1 + 1	
KEITH Marino	28 +12	9	1		1		2	1
LARRIEU Romain	6		1					
LOWNDES Nathan	18 +15	8			0 + 1		1 + 1	2
McCORMICK Luke	40				1		2	
NORRIS David	42 + 3	5	1		1		0 + 1	
PHILLIPS Martin	3 + 6	1			0 + 1			
STONEBRIDGE Ian	21 + 9	5	0 + 1		1	1	2	
STURROCK Blair	0 +24						0 + 1	
WORRELL David	18		1		1		2	
WOTTON Paul	31 + 7	9	0 + 1		1		2	
YETTON Stewart	0 + 1							

PORTSMOUTH (PREM: 13th)

	P/FL App	P/FL Goals	FLC App	FLC Goals	FAC App	FAC Goals	Others App	Others Goals
BERGER Patrik	20	5	1 + 1	1	1			
BERKOVIC Eyal	10 + 1	1			4			
BURTON Deon	0 + 1				1			
CURTIS John	5 + 1							
DE ZEEUW Arjan	36	1	2		4			
DUFFY Richard	0 + 1							
FAYE Amdy	27		1		2 + 1			
FOXE Hayden	8 + 2	1	2 + 1		2			
HARPER Kevin	0 + 7				2			
HISLOP Shaka	30				4			
HUGHES Richard	8 + 3				2 + 2	1		
LUA LUA Lomano	10 + 5	4			1			
MORNAR Ivica	3 + 5	1			2			
O'NEIL Gary	3	2	1 + 1					
OLSZAR Sebastian					0 + 1			
PASANEN Petri	11 + 1				4			
PERICARD Vincent	0 + 2		1					
PRIMUS Linvoy	19 + 2		1		4			
QUASHIE Nigel	17 + 4	1	1		3			
ROBERTS Jason	4 + 6	1	2	3				
ROBINSON Carl	0 + 1				0 + 2			
SCHEMMEL Sebastien	12 + 2		2		1 + 1	1		
SHERINGHAM Teddy	25 + 7	9	3		2 + 1	1		
SHERWOOD Tim	7 + 6		2 + 1	2				
SMERTIN Alexei	23 + 3		2		5			
SRNICEK Pavel	3							
STEFANOVIC Dejan	32	3	2		4			
STONE Steve	29 + 3	2	2 + 1		0 + 1			
TAYLOR Matthew	18 +12		3		4 + 1	3		
TODOROV Svetoslav	1							
WAPENAAR Harald	5		2		1			
YAKUBU Ayegbeni	35 + 2	16	1 + 1	2	4		1	
ZIVKOVIC Boris	17 + 1		1		1			

	P/FL App	P/FL Goals	FLC App	FLC Goals	FAC App	FAC Goals	Others App	Others Goals
PORT VALE (DIV 2: 7th)								
ARMSTRONG Ian	4 +16	1			0 + 1		1	
BIRCHALL Chris	1 + 9				1 + 2			
BOYD Marc	20 + 2				3		0 + 1	
BRAIN Jonny	32				3		1	
BRIDGE-WILKINSON Marc	27 + 5	7	1		0 + 2		1	
BRIGHTWELL Ian	2						1	
BRISCO Neil	20 + 7				1 + 1		1	
BROOKER Steve	29 + 3	8	1		1			
BROWN Ryan	17		1					
BURNS Liam	19 + 8				3	1		
COLLINS Sam	43	4	1		3			
CUMMINS Micky	42	4	1		2		1	
DELANY Dean	14							
JAMES Craig	8							
LIPA Andreas	27 + 3	2	1		2			
LITTLEJOHN Adrian	24 +12	7	1		3		1	
McPHEE Steve	46	25	1		3	1	1	1
PAYNTER Billy	42 + 2	13	0 + 1		2	1	1	
PILKINGTON George	44	1	1		3		1	
REID Levi	7 + 4				3			
ROWLAND Steve	26 + 3						1	
WALSH Michael	12 + 1		1					
PRESTON NORTH END (DIV 1: 15th)								
ABBOTT Pawel	2 + 7	2	0 + 1		0 + 3			
ALEXANDER Graham	45	9	1		3			
BRISCOE Lee	2							
BROOMES Marlon	30				1			
BURLEY Craig	1 + 3							
CARTWRIGHT Lee	2 +10		1		1			
CRESSWELL Richard	41 + 4	2	1		1	1		
DAVIS Claude	16 + 6	1			2			
EDWARDS Rob	16 + 8		1		1			
ETUHU Dickson	23 + 8	3	1		2	1		
FULLER Ricardo	37 + 1	17	1		2	2		
GEMMILL Scot	7	1						
GOULD Jonathan	37				3			
HEALY David	27 +11	15	0 + 1		3			
JACKSON Mark	0 + 1							
JACKSON Michael	41 + 2		1		1			
KEANE Michael	21 + 9	1	1		2			
KOUMANTARAKIS George	1 + 6	1			2	1		
LEWIS Eddie	26 + 7	6			2			
LONERGAN Andy	8							
LUCAS David	1 + 1							
LUCKETTI Chris	37		1	1	1			
LYNCH Simon	6 +13	1						
McCORMACK Alan	2 + 3							
McKENNA Paul	39	6			3			
MEARS Tyrone	11 + 1	1	0 + 1		1			
O'NEIL Brian	27 + 2	1			3	1		
SKORA Eric	0 + 2		1					
SMITH Jeff	0 + 5							
QUEEN'S PARK RANGERS (DIV 2: 2nd)								
AINSWORTH Gareth	21 + 8	6	2 + 1	1	1		2	
BARTON Warren	2 + 1						2	
BEAN Marcus	23 + 8	1	1		1		3	
BIGNOT Marcus	6							
BIRCHAM Marc	36 + 2	2	3				2	
CAMP Lee	12							
CARLISLE Clarke	32 + 1	1	2		1		3	
CULKIN Nick	5						3	
CURETON Jamie	2 +11	2						
DALY Wes	0 + 2				0 + 1			
DAY Chris	29		3		1		1	
EDGHILL Richard	15 + 5		2				1 + 1	
FORBES Terrell	30		3				4	
FURLONG Paul	31 + 5	16	2				1 + 1	
GALLEN Kevin	44 + 1	17	3		1		2 + 2	
GNOHERE Arthur	17 + 1				1		1	
JOHNSON Richard	10 + 1							
LANGLEY Richard	1	1	1	1				
McLEOD Kevin	26 + 9	3	2		1		1	
MARNEY Dean	1 + 1						1	
OLI Dennis	0 + 3				0 + 1		1 + 1	
PACQUETTE Richard	0 + 2		1				2	
PADULA Gino	36	3	3				3	
PALMER Steve	24 +11	4	1		1		2 + 2	1
ROSE Matthew	15 + 5						1 + 1	
ROWLANDS Martin	41 + 1	10	2	2	1		3	
SABIN Eric	3 + 7	1	0 + 2		1		2 + 1	
SHITTU Danny	18 + 2		2				2	
THORPE Tony	22 + 9	10			1		1 + 2	1
WILLIAMS Tommy	4 + 1							
READING (DIV 1: 9th)								
ASHDOWN Jamie	10							
BROOKER Paul	5 + 6							
BROWN Steve	19		2		1			
BUTLER Martin	0 + 3							
DALEY Omar	0 + 6		0 + 1					
FORSTER Nicky	28 + 2	7	4	4				
GOATER Shaun	30 + 4	12	1 + 1		2		2	
GORDON Dean	0 + 3							
HAHNEMANN Marcus	36		4		2			
HARPER Jamie	35 + 4	1	2		1		2	
HENDERSON Darius	0 + 1							
HUGHES Andy	42 + 1	3	4		1			
INGIMARSSON Ivar	24 + 1	1	2		1			
KITSON Dave	10 + 7	5						
MACKIE John	7 + 2	1	1		1 + 1			
MORGAN Dean	3 +10	1			1 + 1			
MURRAY Scott	25 + 9	5	3 + 1		2			
MURTY Graeme	37 + 1		2		2			
NEWMAN Ricky	25 + 5		3		2			
OWUSU Lloyd	11 + 5	4						
SALAKO John	32 + 5	3	3 + 1	1	0 + 2			
SAVAGE Bas	6 + 9		1		1			
SHOREY Nicky	35		2	4	2			
SIDWELL Steve	43	8	3	1	1 + 1			
TYSON Nathan	0 + 8		0 + 1		1			
WATSON Kevin	10 +12		2		0 + 1			
WILLIAMS Adrian	33	1	3		2			
YOUNG Jamie	0 + 1							
ROCHDALE (DIV 3: 21st)								
ANTOINE-CURIER Mickael	5 + 3	1			0 + 1		0 + 1	
BEECH Chris	9 + 5		1		1			
BERTOS Leo	40	9	1		1	1	1	
BETTS Robert	4 + 1	2	0 + 1		1			
BISHOP Andy	8 + 2	1			1		1	
BRANNAN Ged	11				1			
BURGESS Daryl	33 + 2		1		2			
CONNOR Paul	21 + 3	5	1		1			
DONOVAN Kevin	4 + 3							
DOUGHTY Matt	25 + 6		1		1 + 1		1	
EDWARDS Neil	34		1		2		1	
EVANS Wayne	45		1		2		1	
FLOOD Willo	6							
GILKS Matt	12		1		0 + 1		1	
GRAND Simon	11 + 6		1		2		1	
GRIFFITHS Gareth	29 + 4	1			1		1	
HEALD Greg	10	1						
HILL Stephen	1							
HOLT Grant	14	4						
JONES Gary	26	4			1			
LIVESEY Danny	11 + 2							
McCLARE Sean	33 + 5		1		1		1	
McCOURT Paddy	6 +18	2	0 + 1		2		0 + 1	
McEVILLY Lee	15 +15	6			1 + 1			
NDIWA-LORD Kangana	0 + 1							
PATTERSON Rory	3 + 4				0 + 1		1	
PEMBERTON Martin	1							
REDFEARN Neil	9							
SHUKER Chris	14	1	1					
SIMPKINS Mike	25 + 2		1		1		1	
SMITH Jeff	1							
SMITH Shaun	13							
STRACHAN Craig	0 + 1							
TOWNSON Kevin	17 +16	10	0 + 1	1	1 + 1	1	1	
WARNER Scott	10 + 4	1			1			
ROTHERHAM UNITED (DIV 1: 17th)								
BARKER Richie	12 +20	1	1 + 1		2	1		
BARKER Shaun	36	2	3		2			
BAUDET Julien	8 + 3		0 + 1		3			
BRANSTON Guy	7 + 1		1		1			
BUTLER Martin	36 + 1	15	1		0 + 1			
BYFIELD Darren	26 + 2	7	3		1		2	
DAWS Nick	3 + 1		1		1			
GARNER Darren	10 + 3				0 + 1			
GILCHRIST Phil	10							
HOSKINS Will	0 + 4	2			0 + 1			
HURST Paul	23 + 5	1	1 + 1		2	1		
LEE Alan	23		1		1			

Player	P/FL App	Goals	FLC App	Goals	FAC App	Goals	Others App	Goals
McINTOSH Martin	18	2	2					
MINTO Scott	28 + 4		2		1			
MONKHOUSE Andy	17 +10	3	2				0 + 1	
MONTGOMERY Gary	3 + 1		0 + 1					
MORRIS Jody	9 + 1	1						
MULLIN John	35 + 3	4	1 + 1		1			
POLLITT Mike	43		3					
PROCTOR Michael	16 + 1	6						
ROBINS Mark	2 + 7		0 + 1					
ROBINSON Carl	14		2					
SCOTT Rob	8 + 2							
SEDGWICK Chris	40	2	3	2	2			
STOCKDALE Robbie	16	1						
SWAILES Chris	43		3		3	1	2	
TALBOT Stewart	19 + 4	1	3		2			
WARNE Paul	23 +12	1	1 + 2		2			

RUSHDEN & DIAMONDS (DIV 2: 22nd)

Player	P/FL App	Goals	FLC App	Goals	FAC App	Goals	Others App	Goals
ASHDOWN Jamie	19							
BELL David	31 + 6	1	1		1		1	
BENJAMIN Trevor	5 + 1	1	1					
BIGNOT Marcus	35		2		1		2	
BURGESS Andy	32 + 5	4	1		1		1 + 1	
DARBY Duane	9 + 3	2	0 + 1		1			
DEMPSTER John	11 + 8		0 + 1		0 + 1		2	
DUFFY Robert	4 + 4							
EDWARDS Andy	29	3	1		1		2	
EVANS Paul	2		1		1		2	
GRAY Stuart	33 + 2	5	0 + 1		1		2	
HALL Paul	28 + 5	2	1		0 + 1		0 + 1	
HANLON Richie	18 + 9	1			0 + 1		2	
HUNTER Barry	43		4		1			
JACK Rodney	44 + 1	12	1		1		2	1
KELLY Marcus	4 + 4							
KITSON Paul	18 +10	5					2	
LOWE Onandi	24 + 2	15	1	1	1			
MANANGU Eric	0 + 1							
MILLS Garry	25 + 5	1	1		1		2	
OKUONGHAE Magnus	0 + 1							
QUINN Barry	4							
ROGET Leo	16 + 1							
SAMBROOK Andy	14 + 6						0 + 1	
STORY Owen	0 + 5						0 + 1	
TALBOT Daniel	3 + 4	1					0 + 1	
TURLEY Billy	25		1					
UNDERWOOD Paul	30		1				2	

SCUNTHORPE UNITED (DIV 3: 22nd)

Player	P/FL App	Goals	FLC App	Goals	FAC App	Goals	Others App	Goals
BARWICK Terry	27 + 3	1			6		3 + 1	
BEAGRIE Peter	28 + 4	11	1 + 1	1	5		3	
BUTLER Andy	34 + 1	2	1		4		3	
BYRNE Cliff	39	1	2		6		4	
CALVO-GARCIA Alex	8 + 4	2	0 + 1		1			
EVANS Tommy	36		1		6		3	
FEATHERSTONE Lee	7 + 4		1		0 + 3		0 + 2	
GRAVES Wayne	12 + 9		0 + 1		3		1 + 1	
GROVES Paul	13	3			1			
GULLIVER Phil	2							
HAYES Paul	12 +23	2	1 + 1	2	3 + 2	2	1 + 2	1
HOLLOWAY Darren	5	1						
HUNT Jonathan	0 + 1				0 + 1			
JACKSON Mark	15 + 2		1		1		1 + 1	1
KEEGAN Paul	0 + 2							
KELL Richard	21 + 3	2	2		4 + 1		2 + 2	1
KILFORD Ian	11 + 7		1		2 + 1		2	
McCOMBE Jamie	8 + 7		1		0 + 1	1	1	
MacLEAN Steve	37 + 5	23	1 + 1	1	5	3		1
PARTON Andy	0 + 3				0 + 1	1	1	
RIDLEY Lee	15 + 3	1			2 + 1		0 + 1	
RUSSELL Sam	10		1		1			
SHARP Kevin	37 + 3	2	2		5		4	
SMITH Jeff	1							
SPARROW Matt	37 + 1	3	2		6		4	1
STANTON Nathan	31 + 2		1		3 + 1		2	
TAYLOR Cleveland	18 + 2	3			1			
TORPEY Steve	42 + 1	11	2		5	3	3 + 1	1
WILLIAMS Marcus	0 + 1							

SHEFFIELD UNITED (DIV 1: 8th)

Player	P/FL App	Goals	FLC App	Goals	FAC App	Goals	Others App	Goals
ALLISON Wayne	14 +25	1	1 + 1		2 + 2	2		
ARMSTRONG Chris	4 + 8	1	1					
BAXTER Lee	1							
BOUSSATTA Dries	3 + 3				1			
BROWN Michael	14 + 1	2	1					
CRYAN Colin	0 + 1		0 + 1					
FETTIS Alan	2 + 1							
FORTE Jonathan	1 + 6						0 + 1	
FRANCIS Simon	4 + 1							
GERRARD Paul	16							
GRAY Andy	14	9						
HARLEY Jon	5							
HURST Kevan			0 + 1					
JAGIELKA Phil	43	3	2		3			
KABBA Steve	0 + 1							
KENNY Paddy	27		1		4			
KOZLUK Rob	42	1	2		3			
LESTER Jack	25 + 7	12	2	2	2	1		
McCALL Stuart	37	2	1		4			
McLEOD Izzy	1 + 6							
MONTGOMERY Nick	32 + 4	3	1		4			
MORGAN Chris	32		1		3	1		
NDLOVU Peter	28 + 8	9	1		2			
PAGE Robert	30		1		4			
PARKINSON Andy	3 + 4		1		1 + 1			
PESCHISOLIDO Paul	12 +15	8	0 + 1		2 + 2	1		
RANKINE Mark	6 + 7		1		0 + 2			
ROBINSON Carl	4 + 1							
ROGERS Kristian			1					
SESTANOVICH Ashley	0 + 2							
SHAW Paul	4 + 9	1						
STURRIDGE Dean	2 + 2							
TONGE Michael	46	4	2		3			
WARD Ashley	20 + 3	4	1		2			
WHITLOW Mike	13 + 4	1	1		1 + 1			
WRIGHT Alan	21		1		2 + 1			

SHEFFIELD WEDNESDAY (DIV 2: 16th)

Player	P/FL App	Goals	FLC App	Goals	FAC App	Goals	Others App	Goals
ANTOINE-CURIER Mickael	0 + 1							
ARMSTRONG Craig	5 + 5		1				2	
BARRY-MURPHY Brian	38 + 3		1		2		6	
BESWETHERICK Jon	4 + 1				1 + 1		1 + 1	
BROMBY Leigh	29		1		3		5	
BRUNT Chris	8 + 1	2						
BURCHILL Mark	4 + 1							
CARR Chris	0 + 2							
CHAMBERS Adam	8 + 3				1			
COOKE Terry	19 + 4	2	0 + 1		0 + 1		0 + 1	
EVANS Richard	5 + 1		1					
GEARY Derek	41		1		3		5	
HASLAM Steve	16 + 9				2 + 1		1 + 1	
HOLT Grant	9 + 8	2	0 + 1		2	1	1 + 2	
KUQI Shefki	7	5	1					
LEE Graeme	30	3	1	1	3		3	1
LUCAS David	17				1			
McLAREN Paul	23 + 2	2	1		1			
McMAHON Lewis	9 + 1						0 + 1	
MUSTOE Robbie	22 + 3	1			3		1	
NDUMBU-NSUNGU Guylain	20 + 4	9			1 + 1		5 + 1	
NIXON Eric	0 + 1							
OLSEN Kim	6 + 4						1 + 1	
OWUSU Lloyd	12 + 8	5	1		3	1	1 + 1	
POULTER Robert							0 + 1	
PRESSMAN Kevin	20 + 1				3		3	
PROUDLOCK Adam	26 + 4	3			3	3	4 + 1	3
QUINN Alan	23 + 1	4	1		3		1	
REDDY Michael	9 + 3	1			2		3	1
ROBINS Mark	14 + 1	3			3		4	
SHAW Jon	7 + 7	2			0 + 1		1 + 2	
SMITH Jon	41		1		1 + 1		4	
SMITH Paul	12 + 7	2					2	
TIDMAN Ola	9		1				2	
WILSON Laurie					0 + 2		1	
WILSON Mark	3							
WOOD Richard	10 + 2		1	1	0 + 1		2 + 1	

SOUTHAMPTON (PREM: 12th)

Player	P/FL App	Goals	FLC App	Goals	FAC App	Goals	Others App	Goals
BAIRD Chris	1 + 3							
BEATTIE James	32 + 5	14	2		3	1	2	
BLAYNEY Alan	2							
CRAINEY Stephen	5							
CRAINIE Martin	1							
DELAP Rory	26 + 1	1	3				1 + 1	
DELGADO Agustin	0 + 4		1 + 1					
DODD Jason	27 + 1		3		1		2	
FERNANDES Fabrice	21 + 6	1	2				2	
FOLLY Yoann	9							
GRIFFIT Leandre	2 + 3	2						
HALL Fitz	7 + 4		1					

	P/FL		FLC		FAC		Others	
	App	Goals	App	Goals	App	Goals	App	Goals
HIGGINBOTHAM Danny	24 + 3		2		1		1	
JONES Paul	8		0 + 1				1	
KENTON Darren	3 + 4						1	
LE SAUX Graeme	19		1	1			1	
LUNDEKVAM Claus	31	1	2		1		2	
McCANN Neil	9 + 9		0 + 2				0 + 1	
MARSDEN Chris	9 + 4		2 + 1				1	
NIEMI Antti	28		3		1		1	
OAKLEY Matt	7						1	
ORMEROD Brett	14 + 8	5	3	1	0 + 1		1	
PAHARS Marian	6 + 8	2	1				1	
PHILLIPS Kevin	28 + 6	12	1		1		2	1
PRUTTON David	22 + 5	1	1 + 1		1		1	
SVENSSON Anders	17 +13		1		1		2	
SVENSSON Michael	26	2	3		1		2	
TELFER Paul	33 + 4		2 + 1		1		1 + 1	
TESSEM Jo	1 + 2						0 + 1	

SOUTHEND UNITED (DIV 3: 17th)

	P/FL		FLC		FAC		Others	
BENTLEY Mark	15 + 6	2						
BRAMBLE Tes	16 +18	4	0 + 1		5	2	5 + 1	2
BROUGHTON Drewe	27 + 8	2	1	1	0 + 2		4 + 3	5
CLARK Steve	2 + 4				0 + 1		1 + 2	1
CONSTANTINE Leon	40 + 3	21			2 + 1		6 + 1	4
CORBETT Jim	13 + 4	1	1		3 + 1	1	1	1
CORT Leon	46		1		5		6	
DUDFIELD Lawrie	13	5						
EMBERSON Carl	6	1						
FLAHAVAN Darryl	37				5		7	
FULLARTON Jamie	7							
GOWER Mark	40	6	1		5	2	7	1
HUNT Lewis	23 + 3				3		5	
HUSBANDS Michael	3 + 6				0 + 2		0 + 2	
JENKINS Neil	7 + 9	1			4		2 + 2	
JUPP Duncan	39 + 1		1		2		5	
KIGHTLY Michael	2 + 9				1 + 2		2 + 1	1
McSWEENEY Dave	16 + 5	1	1		3		3	
MAHER Kevin	42	1	1	1	5		7	
NICOLAU Nicky	9							
NIGHTINGALE Luke	0 + 4							
ODUNSI Leke	12	1	1					
PETTEFER Carl	11						1 + 2	
PETTERSON Andy	1							
ROBINSON Ryan	2							
SMITH Jay	16 + 2	1			5	3	3	
STUART Jamie	23 + 3				3		4	
TILSON Steve	0 + 1							
WARREN Mark	27 + 5	2	1		2		4	
WILSON Che	11 + 3				2		3 + 2	

STOCKPORT COUNTY (DIV 2: 19th)

	P/FL		FLC		FAC		Others	
ADAMS Danny	12							
BARLOW Stuart	15 +15	8	1 + 1	1	1		2 + 1	3
BECKETT Luke	6 + 2	4	1					
BYRNE Michael	1		1					
CARTWRIGHT Lee	14 + 1							
CHALLINOR Dave	14 + 3		1		1		2 + 1	
CLARE Rob	36	3	2		1		2	
COLGAN Nicky	14 + 1							
COLLINS Wayne	0 + 2							
DALY Jon	19 + 6	3	0 + 1		1			
ELLISON Kevin	10 + 4	1	1				1	
GIBB Ally	23 + 3				1		2	
GOODWIN Jim	29 + 5	4	1		1	1	3	
GRIFFIN Danny	15	1						
HARDIKER John	38 + 1		1 + 1		1		3	
HEATH Matt	8						2	
JACKMAN Danny	27	2					2	
JONES Rob	14 + 2	2	2				1	
LAMBERT Rickie	39 + 1	12	2		1		2	1
LESCOTT Aaron	12 + 2		1				1 + 1	
LYNCH Simon	9	3						
McLACHLAN Fraser	14 + 6	3	1				0 + 1	
MORRISON Owen	11 +11	1	1		0 + 1		0 + 2	1
MYHILL Boaz	2						1	
PEMBERTON Martin	5 + 1		1		1		1 + 1	
ROBERTSON Mark	9 + 3	1						
SMITH Shaun	3 + 3		1					
SPENCER James	15						2	
WALTON Dave	7							
WELSH Andy	24 +10	1	1 + 1		1		2 + 1	
WILBRAHAM Aaron	32 + 9	8	1		0 + 1		2	
WILLIAMS Anthony	15							
WILLIAMS Ashley	10							

	P/FL		FLC		FAC		Others	
	App	Goals	App	Goals	App	Goals	App	Goals
WILLIAMS Chris	4 +12	3	1		0 + 1		2	1

STOKE CITY (DIV 1: 11th)

	P/FL		FLC		FAC		Others	
AKINBIYI Ade	23 + 7	10	0 + 1		1			
ANDREWS Keith	16							
ASABA Carl	26 +11	8	1		2			
CLARKE Clive	41 + 1	3	2		2			
COMMONS Kris	14 +19	4	0 + 2		0 + 1			
CUTLER Neil	9 + 4		1		2			
DE GOEY Ed	37		1					
EUSTACE John	26	5	2		1			
GOODFELLOW Marc	0 + 4		2	1	1			
GREENACRE Chris	8 + 5	2	1		1 + 1			
GUNNARSSON Brynjar	1 + 2							
HALL Marcus	34 + 1		2		1			
HALLS John	34							
HENRY Karl	14 + 6		1					
HILL Clint	9 + 3							
HOEKSTRA Peter	20 + 4	4	1		1 + 1			
IWELUMO Chris	3 + 6		1 + 1	1	0 + 1			
JOHNSON Richard	3 + 4				1 + 1			
MARTEINSSON Petur	3							
NEAL Lewis	6 +13	1	1 + 1		1			
NOEL-WILLIAMS Gifton	40 + 2	10	1		1			
OWEN Gareth	1 + 2							
PALMER Jermaine	0 + 3							
RICHARDSON Frazer	6	1						
RUSSELL Darel	46	4	2		2			
SVARD Sebastian	9 + 4	1	1		1			
TAGGART Gerry	21	2						
THOMAS Wayne	39	3	1		2			
WILKINSON Andy	1 + 2		1					
WILLIAMS Paul	16 + 3		1					
WILSON Brian	0 + 2		0 + 1					

SUNDERLAND (DIV 1: 3rd)

	P/FL		FLC		FAC		Others	
ARCA Julio	31	4			6	2		
BABB Phil	22		1		5		2	
BJORKLUND Joachim	19 + 6		1		3		1 + 1	
BLACK Chris	0 + 1							
BREEN Gary	32	4			4		2	
BUTLER Thomas	7 + 5		1		0 + 1			
BYFIELD Darren	8 + 9	5						
CLARK Ben	2 + 3		2		1			
COOPER Colin	0 + 3							
COOPER Kevin	0 + 1							
DOWNING Stewart	7	3						
FLO Tore Andre	1							
GRAY Michael	0 + 1		1					
HEALY Colin	16 + 4							
INGHAM Michael	1		1					
JAMES Craig	1							
KILBANE Kevin	5		1					
KYLE Kevin	36 + 8	10	1 + 1	3	5	1	2	2
LEADBITTER Grant			0 + 1					
McATEER Jason	18	2	1		4		2	
McCARTNEY George	40 + 1		1		6		2	
MYHRE Thomas	3 + 1							
OSTER John	35 + 3	5	1 + 1		5 + 1		2	
PIPER Matt	4 + 5				0 + 1			
POOM Mart	43	1	1		6		2	
PROCTOR Michael	4 +13	1	1		1			
QUINN Alan	5 + 1							
RAMSDEN Simon					0 + 1			
ROBINSON Carl	6 + 1	1	1		1		1 + 1	
SMITH Tommy	22 +13	4			3 + 1	4	0 + 2	
STEWART Marcus	28 +12	14	1 + 1		3 + 2		2	2
THIRLWELL Paul	21 + 8				3 + 1			
THORNTON Sean	14 + 8	4			0 + 4		1 + 1	
WHITLEY Jeff	33	2			5		2	
WILLIAMS Darren	24 + 5		1 + 1		1 + 1		1 + 1	
WRIGHT Stephen	20 + 2	1	0 + 1		5			

SWANSEA CITY (DIV 3: 10th)

	P/FL		FLC		FAC		Others	
BRITTON Leon	42	3	1		5			
BYRNE Shaun	9				1			
COATES Jonathan	14 +13		0 + 1		1 + 3		1	
CONNOLLY Karl	4 + 6	1	1	1	1			
CONNOR Paul	12	5			1			
CORBISIERO Antonio	1 + 4							
DUFFY Richard	16 + 2	1			3		1	
DURKAN Kieron	11 + 4	1	1		2	1	1	
FIELDWICK Lee	4 + 1							
FREESTONE Roger	35 + 2				5			

469

	P/FL App	P/FL Goals	FLC App	FLC Goals	FAC App	FAC Goals	Others App	Others Goals
HOWARD Michael	25				5		1	
HYLTON Leon	10 + 1		1		0 + 1			
IRIEKPEN Izzy	33 + 1	1			5			
JENKINS Lee	8 + 3						0 + 1	
JOHNROSE Lenny	21 + 4		1		3			
JONES Richard							1	
JONES Stuart	16 + 8		1		1		1	
MARTINEZ Roberto	24 + 3		1		2			
MAXWELL Layton	1 + 2							
MAYLETT Brad	26 + 7	5	1		3			
MURPHY Brian	11		1					
NARDIELLO Danny	3 + 1						1	1
NUGENT Kevin	31 + 8	8	0 + 1		2 + 2	2		
O'LEARY Kristian	28 + 6		1		4 + 1			
PRITCHARD Mark	1 + 3							
REES Matt	3	1						
REWBURY Jamie	1 + 1							
ROBERTS Stuart	8 + 4	1						
ROBINSON Andy	34 + 3	8			5	2		
TATE Alan	25 + 1	1			1		1	
THOMAS James	8 + 8	3	0 + 1		1 + 3		1	
TRUNDLE Lee	29 + 2	16	1		5	5	0 + 1	
WILSON Mark	12	2					1	
SWINDON TOWN (DIV 2: 5th)								
BURTON Deon	4	1						
DUKE David	35 + 7	1	1 + 1		1		1 + 1	
EVANS Rhys	41		1 + 1		2			
FALLON Rory	6 +13	6					0 + 2	1
GARRARD Luke	0 + 1						0 + 1	
GRIEMINK Bart	5 + 1		1				1	
GURNEY Andy	42	6	1	1	1	1	2	
HERRING Ian	1		0 + 1				1	
HEWLETT Matt	43		2				2	
HEYWOOD Matty	39 + 1	1	2		1		2	
HOWARD Brian	21 +14	4	1 + 1		1		3	
IFIL Jerel	16							
IGOE Sammy	33 + 3	5	2				2	
LEWIS Junior	4							
MARTIN Ben							0 + 1	
MIGLIORANZI Stefani	34 + 1	4	1 + 1		1		1	
MILNER James	6		2					
MOONEY Tommy	41 + 4	19	0 + 1	1	1		2	
NICHOLAS Andrew	28 + 3	1			1		2 + 1	
O'HANLON Sean	17 + 2	2					1	
PARKIN Sam	38 + 2	19	2	3	1		2	1
POOK Michael								
REEVES Alan	17 +10		2		1		1 + 1	
ROBINSON Steve	20 + 2	1	1		1		1	
RUSTER Sebastien	0 + 2				0 + 1			
SMITH Grant	0 + 7		2		0 + 1		2 + 1	
STEVENSON Jon	1 + 4		2					
VIVEASH Adrian	14 + 1		1				1	
TORQUAY UNITED (DIV 3: 3rd)								
BEDEAU Tony	13 +11	1			1		1	
BENEFIELD Jimmy	3 +12		0 + 1		1	1	1	
BERNARD Narada	0 + 1							
BOND Kain	0 + 1							
BROAD Joe	4 +10						1	
CANOVILLE Lee	32 + 1	1	1		1			
DEARDEN Kevin	21 + 1						1	
FOWLER Jason	24 + 7	2	1		1		1	
GRAHAM David	41 + 4	22	0 + 1	1	1		0 + 1	
GRITTON Martin	17 +14	4						
HANKIN Sean	1		1					
HAZELL Reuben	12 + 7	1			1			
HILL Kevin	42 + 3	5	1		0 + 1			
HOCKLEY Matt	44 + 1	5	1		1		1	
KILLOUGHERY Graham	0 + 3						0 + 1	
McGLINCHEY Brian	34							
McMAHON Daryl	0 + 1							
OSEI-KUFFOUR Jo	33 + 8	10					0 + 1	
ROSENIOR Liam	9 + 1							
RUSSELL Alex	42 + 1	2	1		1		1	
TAYLOR Craig	43	4	1		1		1	
VAN HEUSDEN Arjan	25		1					
WILLIAMSON Mike	9 + 2						1	
WILLS Kevin	7 +16	1	0 + 1		0 + 1		1	1
WOODS Steve	46	6	1		1		1	
WOOZLEY David	4 + 6		1					
TOTTENHAM HOTSPUR (PREM: 14th)								
ANDERTON Darren	16 + 4	1	3		2	1		

	P/FL App	P/FL Goals	FLC App	FLC Goals	FAC App	FAC Goals	Others App	Others Goals
BLONDEL Jonathan	0 + 1		1 + 1					
BROWN Michael	17	1			2			
BUNJEVCEVIC Goran	3 + 4							
CARR Steve	32	1	4		3			
DALMAT Stephane	12 +10	3	1 + 2		2 + 1			
DAVIES Simon	17	2			2 + 1			
DEFOE Jermain	14 + 1	7						
DOHERTY Gary	16 + 1		2 + 1		2	1		
GARDNER Anthony	33		4		3			
JACKSON Johnnie	9 + 2	1			1 + 2			
KANOUTE Fredi	19 + 8	7	2 + 1	2	1	3		
KEANE Robbie	31 + 3	14	4	1	3	1		
KELLER Kasey	38		4		3			
KELLY Stephen	7 + 4							
KING Ledley	28 + 1	1	3		3			
KONCHESKY Paul	10 + 2		2 + 1					
MABIZELA Mbulelo	0 + 6		0 + 1					
MARNEY Dean	1 + 2							
POSTIGA Helder	9 +10	1	1 + 2	1	2			
POYET Gus	12 + 8	3	2 + 1		1 + 1			
REDKNAPP Jamie	14 + 3	1						
RICHARDS Dean	23		2		1			
RICKETTS Rohan	12 +12	1	3 + 1	1				
TARICCO Mauricio	31 + 1	1	3		2			
YEATES Mark	1							
ZAMORA Bobby	6 +10	1	1	1	0 + 1			
ZIEGE Christian	7 + 1		1		1		1	
TRANMERE ROVERS (DIV 2: 8th)								
ACHTERBERG John	45		2		8		1	
ALLEN Graham	40 + 1	1	2		7		1	
ASHTON Neil	0 + 1							
BERESFORD David	13 +12	1			6			
CONNELLY Sean	33 + 4		2		5		1	
DADI Eugene	29 + 9	16	1 + 1	1	6 + 2	2	1	
DAGNALL Chris	5 + 5	1	0 + 1					
GOODISON Ian	12				2			
GRAY Kevin	2						1	
HALL Paul	9	2						
HARRISON Danny	32	2	2		7			
HAWORTH Simon	21 + 1	6	2		2	1	1	
HAY Alex	3 +16				0 + 4			
HOWARTH Russell	1							
HUME Iain	32 + 8	10	2		7	3	0 + 1	1
JENNINGS Steve	1 + 3				1			
JONES Gary	36 + 6	9	2		7 + 1	2	1	
LINWOOD Paul	18 + 2				3 + 1		1	
LORAN Tyrone	26 + 2		1		2		1	
MELLON Micky	39 + 4		2		7	2	1	
NAVARRO Alan	9 +10				1 + 2		0 + 1	
NICHOLSON Shane	9 + 7	2	1		0 + 3		0 + 1	1
ONUORA Iffy	1 + 2							
ROBERTS Gareth	44	1	2		7		1	
SHARPS Ian	25 + 2	1	2		3			
TAYLOR Ryan	21 + 9	5	1 + 1		6 + 1	1		
TREMARCO Carl					1			
WALSALL (DIV 1: 22nd)								
ANDREWS Keith	10	2						
ARANALDE Zigor	29 + 7		2		1			
BAIRD Chris	10							
BAZELEY Darren	35 + 4		2		1			
BENNETT Julian	0 + 1							
BIRCH Gary	25 +10	4	0 + 1		1			
BRADBURY Lee	7 + 1	1						
BURLEY Craig	5							
BURTON Deon	2 + 1		1					
CARBON Matt	7 + 1							
CORICA Steve	17 + 2	2	2					
DINNING Tony	2 + 3							
EMBLEN Neil	27 +12	5	2		1			
FRYATT Matt	4 + 7	1	0 + 1					
HAWLEY Karl					0 + 1			
HAY Danny	14 + 2							
LAWRENCE Jamie	8 + 9	1	1		0 + 1			
LEITAO Jorge	29 +10	7	1	1	1	1		
McSPORRAN Jermaine	2 + 4							
MATIAS Pedro	6 + 9	1	0 + 1					
MERSON Paul	31 + 3	4	2	2				
OAKES Stefan	1 + 4							
O'NEIL Gary	7							
OSBORN Simon	39 + 4	3	2		1			
PETTERSON Andy	3							
RITCHIE Paul	33		1		1			

Andrew Nicholas (Swindon Town) on right of picture

	P/FL App	Goals	FLC App	Goals	FAC App	Goals	Others App	Goals
ROPER Ian	33		1		1			
SAMWAYS Vinny	29		2	2	1			
TAYLOR Kris	5 + 6	1						
VINCENT Jamie	12				0 + 1			
WALES Gary	5 + 2	1						
WALKER James	43		2		1			
WRACK Darren	23 + 4	6	1		1			
WRIGHT Mark	3 + 8	2	2					

WATFORD (DIV 1: 16th)

	P/FL App	Goals	FLC App	Goals	FAC App	Goals	Others App	Goals
ARDLEY Neal	35 + 3	1	1		2			
BAIRD Chris	8							
BLIZZARD Dominic	1 + 1	1						
BOUAZZA Hameur	6 + 3	1						
BROWN Wayne	12							
CHAMBERLAIN Alec	20 + 1		2					
COOK Lee	20 +21	7	0 + 2		2			
COX Neil	35	4	2		1			
DEVLIN Paul	39	3	1		2			
DOYLEY Lloyd	7 + 2		2		0 + 1			
DYCHE Sean	22 + 3		1		1			
DYER Bruce	18 +14	3	2		1			
FISKEN Gary	0 + 1		1					
FITZGERALD Scott	28 +16	10	0 + 1	1	0 + 1			
GAYLE Marcus	32	1	1		2			
HAND Jamie	16 + 6		0 + 2		1			
HELGUSON Heidar	20 + 2	8	1		1	1		
HYDE Micah	28 + 5	1	1 + 1		2			
IFIL Jerel	9 + 1							
JOHNSON Richard			1					
KELLY Stephen	13							
McNAMEE Anthony	0 + 2							
MAHON Gavin	32		2		2	1		
MAYO Paul	12							
PIDGELEY Lenny	26 + 1				2			
ROBINSON Paul	10		1					
SMITH Jack	16 + 1	2			2			
VERNAZZA Paolo	17 +12				1			
WEBBER Danny	24 + 3	5	2		0 + 2			
YOUNG Ashley	0 + 5	3	1					

WEST BROMWICH ALBION (DIV 1: 2nd)

	P/FL App	Goals	FLC App	Goals	FAC App	Goals	Others App	Goals
BERTHE Sekou	2 + 1		1					
CHAMBERS Adam			0 + 1					
CHAMBERS James	14 + 3							
CLEMENT Neil	25 +10	2	4 + 1	1	1			
DICHIO Danny	5 + 6		2 + 1					
DOBIE Scott	14 +17	5	2 + 3	2	0 + 1			
DYER Lloyd	2 +15	2			0 + 1			
FACEY Delroy	2 + 7							
GAARDSOE Thomas	45	4	5		1			
GILCHRIST Phil	16 + 1		3 + 1					
GREGAN Sean	40 + 3	1	4					
HAAS Bernt	36	1	5		2		1	
HORSFIELD Geoff	20	7			1			
HOULT Russell	44		5		1			
HUGHES Lee	21 +11	11	1 + 3	1	1			
HULSE Rob	29 + 4	10	5	3	1			
JOHNSON Andy	33 + 5	2	4 + 1					
KINSELLA Mark	15 + 3	1						
KOUMAS Jason	37 + 5	10	3					
MOORE Darren	20 + 2	2			1			
MURPHY Joe	2 + 1							
N'DOUR Alassane	2		1					
O'CONNOR James	27 + 3		5		1			
ROBINSON Paul	30 + 1				1			
SAKIRI Artim	6 +19	1	2 + 2		1			
SIGURDSSON Larus	5							
SKOUBO Morten	0 + 2							
VOLMER Joost	10 + 5		2 + 1					
WALLWORK Ronnie	4 + 1		1 + 1					

WEST HAM UNITED (DIV 1: 4th)

	P/FL App	Goals	FLC App	Goals	FAC App	Goals	Others App	Goals
ALEXANDERSSON Niclas	5 + 3							
BREVETT Rufus	2		1					
BYRNE Shaun			0 + 1					
BYWATER Steve	17				3		3	
CAROLE Sebastien	0 + 1							
CARRICK Michael	34 + 1	1	1		4		3	
COHEN Chris	1 + 6							
CONNOLLY David	37 + 2	10	2	2	4	2	3	
DAILLY Christian	43		2	3	3 + 1		3	1
DEANE Brian	9 +17	6			3		0 + 3	
DEFOE Jermain	19	11	3		4		3	

	P/FL App	Goals	FLC App	Goals	FAC App	Goals	Others App	Goals
ETHERINGTON Matthew	34 + 1	5	3		4		3	1
FERDINAND Anton	9 +11		2 + 1		3			
GARCIA Richard	2 + 5		0 + 3					
HAREWOOD Marlon	28	13			4	1	3	
HARLEY Jon	15	1			1			
HORLOCK Kevin	23 + 4	1	2		4			
HUTCHISON Don	10 +14	4	1		0 + 1		0 + 1	
JAMES David	27		3		1			
KILGALLON Matthew	1 + 2		1					
LEE Rob	12 + 4		2		0 + 1			
LOMAS Steve	5				0 + 2		3	
McANUFF Jobi	4 + 8	1					0 + 1	
MELLOR Neil	8 + 8	2	1 + 1		0 + 3			
MELVILLE Andy	11 + 3						3	
MULLINS Hayden	27				4	1	3	
NOBLE David	0 + 3		1					
NOWLAND Adam	2 + 9							
PEARCE Ian	24	1	1		1			
QUINN Wayne	22		2		2 + 1			
REO-COCKER Nigel	13 + 2	2					0 + 3	
REPKA Tomas	40		2		2		3	
SOFIANE Youssef	0 + 1		1					
SRNICEK Pavel	2 + 1							
STOCKDALE Robbie	5 + 2		1		1			
ZAMORA Bobby	15 + 2	5					3	

WIGAN ATHLETIC (DIV 1: 7th)

	P/FL App	Goals	FLC App	Goals	FAC App	Goals	Others App	Goals
BAINES Leighton	23 + 3		1		1			
BRECKIN Ian	43 + 2		3		1			
BULLARD Jimmy	46	2	3	1	1			
BURCHILL Mark	1 + 3							
DE VOS Jason	25 + 2	2			1			
DINNING Tony	11 + 2		1					
EADEN Nicky	46		3		1			
ELLINGTON Nathan	43 + 1	18	1 + 1	1	1			
FARRELLY Gareth	3 + 4							
FILAN John	45		1		1			
FLYNN Michael	1 + 7		0 + 1					
HORSFIELD Geoff	16	7	1					
JACKSON Matt	23 + 1	1	3		0 + 1			
JARRETT Jason	33 + 8	1	2	1				
KENNEDY Peter	10 + 2	1	3					
LAWRENCE Jamie	0 + 4							
LIDDELL Andy	35 + 5	9	3		1			
McCULLOCH Lee	31 +10	6	3	1	1			
McMILLAN Steve	13 + 2		1					
MAHON Alan	13 + 1	1						
MITCHELL Paul	1 +11		0 + 1		1			
ROBERTS Jason	14	8						
ROBERTS Neil	9 +19	2	2 + 1		1			
ROGERS Alan	5							
TEALE Gary	15 +13	2	0 + 1		1			
WALSH Gary	1 + 2		2					

WIMBLEDON (DIV 1: 24th)

	P/FL App	Goals	FLC App	Goals	FAC App	Goals	Others App	Goals
AGYEMANG Patrick	23 + 3	7	1		1			
BANKS Steve	24		1		3			
BARTON Warren	5							
BEVAN Scott	10							
CAMPBELL-RYCE Jamal	3 + 1							
CHORLEY Ben	33 + 2	2	1		1 + 1			
DARLINGTON Jermaine	40 + 1	1	1		3			
GIER Rob	24 + 1		0 + 1		3			
GORDON Michael	8 +10		1		0 + 1			
GRAY Wayne	20 +13	4			1 + 2			
HARDING Ben	10 + 5				1			
HAWKINS Peter	16 + 2		1		0 + 1			
HEALD Paul	10							
HERZIG Nico	18 + 1							
HOLDSWORTH Dean	14 +14	3	0 + 1		2			
HOLLOWAY Darren	8 + 5		1					
JARRETT Albert	3 + 6		0 + 1					
KAMARA Malvin	15 +12	2						
LEIGERTWOOD Mikele	27	2	1		3			
LEWINGTON Dean	28	1			3			
McANUFF Jobi	25 + 2	5			3			
McDONALD Scott	0 + 2							
MACKIE Jamie	8 + 5				2 + 1			
McKOY Nick	1 + 2							
MARTIN David	2							
MORGAN Lionel	2 + 1							
NOWLAND Adam	24 + 1	3	1		2		2	2
NTIMBAN-ZEH Harry	9 + 1							
OYEDELE Shola	9							

	P/FL App	P/FL Goals	FLC App	FLC Goals	FAC App	FAC Goals	Others App	Others Goals
PUNCHEON Jason	6 + 2							
REO-COKER Nigel	25	4	1		1			
SMALL Wade	23 + 4	1			3			
SMITH Gary	10 + 1	3						
TAPP Alex	12 + 2	1	1		1			

	P/FL App	P/FL Goals	FLC App	FLC Goals	FAC App	FAC Goals	Others App	Others Goals
WILLIAMS Mark	11	1						
WORGAN Lee	0 + 3							
WOLVERHAMPTON WANDERERS (PREM: 20th)								
ANDREWS Keith	1		1		1			

Denis Irwin (Wolverhampton Wanderers) on right of picture

	P/FL App	Goals	FLC App	Goals	FAC App	Goals	Others App	Goals
BLAKE Nathan	10 + 3	1	1					
BUTLER Paul	37		2		2			
CAMARA Henri	29 + 1	7	2					
CAMERON Colin	25 + 5	4	1		2			
CLARKE Leon			0 + 2		0 + 1			
CLYDE Mark	6 + 3				3			
COOPER Kevin	0 + 1							
CORT Carl	13 + 3	5						
CRADDOCK Jody	31 + 1	1	3	1	2 + 1			
GANEA Ivo	6 +10	3			2 + 1	1		
GUDJONSSON Joey	5 + 6		3	1	1 + 1			
INCE Paul	32		2		1			
IRWIN Denis	30 + 2				1			
IVERSEN Steffen	11 + 5	4	2		1 + 1			
JONES Paul	16							
KACHLOUL Hassan	0 + 4							
KENNEDY Mark	28 + 3	2	1 + 1		3			
LUZHNY Oleg	4 + 2		2		2			
MARSHALL Andy			1					
MILLER Kenny	17 + 8	2	2	1	3	2		
MURRAY Matt	1		1					
NAYLOR Lee	37 + 1		3					
NEWTON Shaun	20 + 8		0 + 2		2			
OAKES Michael	21		1 + 1		3			
OKORONKWO Isaac	7		1					
RAE Alex	27 + 6	5	2 + 1	2	1	1		
SILAS	2 + 7		2		1 + 2			
STURRIDGE Dean	2 + 3		0 + 1					

WREXHAM (DIV 2: 13th)

	P/FL App	Goals	FLC App	Goals	FAC App	Goals	Others App	Goals
ARMSTRONG Chris	19 + 7	5			0 + 1	1	1	1
BARRETT Paul	19 + 8	2					1	
CAREY Brian	32 + 2	2	1		1			
CROWELL Matty	9 + 6	1	0 + 1				1 + 1	
DIBBLE Andy	35		1		1		1	
EDWARDS Carlos	42	5	1		1		1	
EDWARDS Paul	40 + 1		1		1		1	
FERGUSON Darren	39	1	1		1		1	
HOLMES Shaun	3 +10	2			1		1	1
INGHAM Michael	11							
JONES Lee	13 + 9	5	1		1		1	3
JONES Mark	0 +13	1			1 + 1	1	1	1
LAWRENCE Denis	45	5	1		1		1	
LLEWELLYN Chris	46	8	1		1		1 + 1	
MACKIN Levi	1							
McNULTY Jimmy							0 + 1	
MORGAN Craig	14 + 4				0 + 1		2	
ONE Armand	2 + 1							
PEJIC Shaun	20 + 1	1					1	
ROBERTS Steve	24 + 3				1		2	
SAM Hector	24 +13	10	0 + 1		1		2	2
SPENDER Simon	3 + 3							
THOMAS Stephen	31 + 9	2	1		0 + 1		1 + 1	
WHITFIELD Paul	0 + 2						2	
WHITLEY Jim	34 + 2		1		1		1	

WYCOMBE WANDERERS (DIV 2: 24th)

	P/FL App	Goals	FLC App	Goals	FAC App	Goals	Others App	Goals
BELL Andy	3 + 8	3	1		1			
BEVAN Scott	5							
BLOOMFIELD Matt	10 + 2	1						
BRANSTON Guy	9						2	1
BROWN Steve	18 + 7	1	1		0 + 1		0 + 2	
BULMAN Dannie	30 + 8		0 + 1		2		2	
COOK Lewis	1 + 4		0 + 1				0 + 1	
CURRIE Darren	42	7	2		2	2	3	
DELL Steve	3 + 1							
DIXON Jonny	2 + 6				1			
FAULCONBRIDGE Craig	11 + 5	2			2		0 + 1	
HARDING Billy	0 + 2							
HARRIS Richard	6 + 4		1 + 1	2				
HENDERSON Wayne	3							
HOLE Stuart	0 + 1							
HOLLIGAN Gavin	8 + 5	2	1		1	1	1	
JOHNSON Roger	28		2		3		3	1
McSPORRAN Jermaine	29 + 4	7	1		3	3	2	2
MAPES Charlie	10 + 5	3	1		0 + 1		1	
MARSHALL Scott	8				1			
MOORE Luke	6	4						
NETHERCOTT Stuart	22	1						
OLIVER Luke	0 + 2							
ONUORA Iffy	6							
PATTERSON Simon	3 + 1	2	1					
PHILO Mark	4 + 8							
REILLY Andy	5				1			

	P/FL App	Goals	FLC App	Goals	FAC App	Goals	Others App	Goals
ROBERTS Stuart	5 +11		0 + 1		2 + 1		2	
ROGERS Mark	15		2		1		1	
RYAN Keith	10 + 7	1			1 + 1		1 + 1	
SENDA Danny	37 + 3		2		2		2	
SIMPEMBA Ian	17 + 2	2			2		1	
SIMPSON Michael	38	2			2		3	
TALIA Frank	17				2		2	
TAYLOR Steven	6							
THOMSON Andy	11	1	1		2	1	2 + 1	1
TYSON Nathan	21	9						
VINNICOMBE Chris	36		2		3		2	
WILLIAMS Steve	19	2	2		1		1	
WORGAN Lee	2							

YEOVIL TOWN (DIV 3: 8th)

	P/FL App	Goals	FLC App	Goals	FAC App	Goals	Others App	Goals
BISHOP Andy	4 + 1	2						
BULL Ronnie	7							
COLLIS Steve	11						1	
CRITTENDEN Nick	20 + 9	2	1		3	1	1	
DANI	3 + 1	4						
EDWARDS Jake	17 +10	6			1 + 1	2	2	2
EL KHOLTI Abdou	19 + 4	1	0 + 1		0 + 1		1	
ELAM Lee	6 + 6	1						
GALL Kevin	39 + 4	8	1		3	1	2	1
GILES Chris	0 + 1							
GOSLING Jamie	4 + 8	1	1		0 + 2		0 + 2	
JACKSON Kirk	19 +11	5	1		1 + 2			
JOHNSON Lee	45	5	1		3		2	
LINDEGAARD Andy	12 +11	2	2 + 1		0 + 1			
LOCKWOOD Adam	43	4	1		3		2	
MATTHEWS Lee	2 + 2							
O'BRIEN Roy	13		1					
PLUCK Colin	36	4			3	2	2	
REED Steven	3 + 2		0 + 1				0 + 1	
RODRIGUES Hugo	23 +11	1	1		2		1	
SKIVERTON Terry	25 + 1	2			3		2	
STANSFIELD Adam	7 +25	6			0 + 2		0 + 2	
TALBOTT Nathan	0 + 1							
TERRY Paul	22 +12	1			3		1 + 1	
WAY Darren	38 + 1	5	1		2		2	
WEALE Chris	35				3		1	
WEATHERSTONE Simon	11 + 4	1						
WILLIAMS Gavin	42	9	1		3	3	2	1

YORK CITY (DIV 3: 24th)

	P/FL App	Goals	FLC App	Goals	FAC App	Goals	Others App	Goals
ARTHUR Adam	2 + 1							
ASHCROFT Kane	1 + 1							
BELL Andy	3 + 7	1						
BRACKSTONE Steve	4 + 5	2			0 + 1		1	
BRASS Chris	39	1	1		1			
BROWNE Gary	2 + 4							
BULLOCK Lee	34 + 1	7	1		1			
COAD Matthew	0 + 3							
COOPER Richard	26 +11	2			1		1	
CROWE Dean	2 + 3							
DAVIES Sean	6 + 2							
DICKMAN Jonjo	2							
DOVE Craig	1						1	
DOWNES Stephen	4 + 2						1	
DUNNING Darren	42	3	1		1		1	1
EDMONDSON Darren	26 + 1	1	1		1			
FOX Christian	2 + 3							
GEORGE Liam	14 + 8	3			0 + 1		0 + 1	
HAW Robbie	0 + 1							
HOPE Richard	36	2	1		1		1	
LAW Graeme	2 + 2							
MERRIS David	42 + 2	1	1	1	1		0 + 1	
NEWBY Jon	6 + 1							
NOGAN Lee	38 + 1	8	1		1	1	0 + 1	
OFFIONG Richard	2 + 2							
OVENDALE Mark	41		1		1		1	
PARKIN Jon	9 + 6	2					1	
PORTER Chris	5							
SHAW Jon	5 + 3							
SMITH Chris	26 + 2				1		1	
STEWART Bryan	2 + 8		0 + 1					
WALKER Justin	7 + 2							
WARD Mitch	27 + 4		1		1			
WILFORD Aron	4 + 2	2			0 + 1		1	
WISE Stuart	18 + 1	1	1				1	
WOOD Leigh	21 + 5		1					
YALCIN Lev	5 +10							

Where Did They Go?

Below is a list of all players who were recorded in the previous edition as making a first-team appearance in 2002-2003, but failed to make the current book. They are listed alphabetically and show their last League club, their approximate leaving dates, as well as their next club, for which a minimum stay of three months is the requisite. Of course, they may well have moved on by now, but space does not allow further reference.

* Shows that the player in question is still with his named club but failed to make an appearance in 2003-2004, the most common reason being injury.

+ Players retained by Exeter City and Shrewsbury Town, who were relegated to the Conference.

Player	Last club	Date	Next club
ABBEY Nathan	Northampton T	06.03	Burnley
ACIMOVIC Milenko	Tottenham H	01.04	Lille OSC (France) loan
ACUNA Clarence	Newcastle U	10.03	Rosario Central (Argentina)
AISTON Sam	Shrewsbury T	+	
AKIN Bulent	Bolton W	03.03	Genclerbiru (Turkey)
ALCIDE Colin	Exeter C	12.02	Retired
ALDRIDGE Paul	Macclesfield T	06.03	Derry C (Ireland)
ALLEN Bradley	Bristol Rov	06.03	Hornchurch
AMPADU Kwame	Exeter C	+	
ANDERSEN Trond	Wimbledon	08.03	Aalborg (Denmark)
ANDRE Pierre-Yves	Bolton W	05.03	Guingamp (France)
ANGELL Brett	Queens Park R	07.03	Retired
ANTWI Will	Crystal Palace	06.03	Aldershot T
APPLEBY Matty	Oldham Ath	*	
APPLEBY Richie	Hull C	12.03	Retired
ARMSTRONG Gordon	Burnley	06.03	Accrington Stanley
ASHCROFT Lee	Wigan Ath	02.03	Southport
ASHIKODI Moses	Millwall		
ASHINGTON Ryan	Torquay U	11.02	Newport Co
ASKEY John	Macclesfield T	06.03	Retired
ASTAFJEVS Vitas	Bristol Rov	06.03	Admira Wacker (Austria)
ATANGANA Simon	Colchester U	03.03	Halstead T
ATKINS Mark	Shrewsbury T	06.03	Harrogate T
ATTWELL Jamie	Torquay U	12.02	
AUSTIN Dean	Crystal Palace	11.02	Woking
AWUAH Jones	Gillingham	*	
AYRES Lee	Kidderminster Hrs	11.03	Tamworth
BAARDSEN Espen	Everton	02.03	Retired
BACON Danny	Mansfield T	07.03	Hucknall T
BAILEY John	Preston NE	01.04	
BAKER Phil	Exeter C	05.03	Aberystwyth T
BALIS Igor	West Bromwich A	06.03	Retired
BALTACHA Sergei	Millwall	03.03	Queens Park
BAMPTON Dave	Swindon T	*	
BANKOLE Ade	Crewe Alex	*	
BARNARD Lee	Tottenham H	*	
BARRETT Scott	Leyton Orient	06.03	Grays Ath
BARROWCLOUGH Carl	Barnsley	10/03	Leigh RMI
BARTHEZ Fabien	Manchester U	01.04	O.Marseille (France) loan
BASS Jon	Hartlepool U	02.04	Retired
BATES Tom	Coventry C	*	
BATTERSBY Tony	Rushden & Diamonds	03.03	Stevenage Borough
BEARD Mark	Southend U	06.03	Kingstonian
BEASANT Dave	Brighton & Hove A	06.03	Retired
BECKHAM David	Manchester U	07.03	Real Madrid (Spain)
BELGRAVE Barrington	Southend U	06.03	Farnborough T
BELMADI Djemel	Manchester C	05.03	O. Marseilles (France)

Player	Last club	Date	Next club
BENALI Francis	Southampton	06.03	Retired
BENARBIA Ali	Manchester C	07.03	United Arab Emirates
BENNETT Dan	Wrexham	06.03	
BENNETT Neil	Rochdale	05.03	
BERG Henning	Blackburn Rov	06.03	Glasgow Rangers
BERGSSON Gudni	Bolton W	05.03	Retired
BERNARD Paul	Plymouth Arg	05.03	St Johnstone
BETTS Simon	Darlington	06.03	Whitby T
BISHOP Ian	Rochdale	01.03	Burscough
BJORNEBYE Stig Inge	Blackburn Rov	04.03	Retired
BLACK Kingsley	Lincoln C	10.02	Retired
BLACKWELL Dean	Brighton & Hove A	*	
BLANC Laurent	Manchester U	05.03	Retired
BLOMQVIST Jesper	Charlton Ath	06.03	Retired
BOGARDE Winston	Chelsea	*	
BOKSIC Alen	Middlesbrough	02.03	Retired
BOTHROYD Jay	Coventry C	07.03	
BRADLEY Shayne	Chesterfield	06.03	
BRADSHAW Gary	Hull C	03.03	North Ferriby U
BRAVO Raul	Leeds U	05.03	Real Madrid (Spain)
BRENNAN Martin	Cambridge U	*	
BRESLAN Geoff	Exeter C	06.03	Taunton T
BROAD Steve	Southend U	06.03	Kingstonian
BRYAN Marvin	Rotherham U	06.03	
BUCKLEY Adam	Lincoln C	06.03	Harrowby U
BURNS John	Carlisle U	11.02	Hucknall T
BURROWS David	Sheffield Wed	06.03	Retired
BYRNE Chris	Macclesfield T	04.03	Retired
BYRNE Paul	Port Vale	06.03	Southport
CAMARA Titi	West Ham U	01.03	Al Ittihad (Saudi Arabia)
CAMARA Ben	Torquay U	01.04	Stevenage Borough
CAME Shaun	Macclesfield T	10.02	Northwich Victoria
CAMM Mark	Lincoln C	10.03	Kings Lynn
CAMPBELL Darren	Reading	*	
CAMPBELL Paul	Darlington	06.03	Whitby T
CANHAM Marc	Colchester U	06.03	Team Bath
CANHAM Scott	Leyton Orient	03.03	Woking
CANSDELL-SHERIFF Shane	Leeds U	06.03	Aarhus GF (Denmark)
CARBONARI Horacio	Derby Co	01.03	Rosario Central (Argentina)
CARTWRIGHT Mark	Shrewsbury T	09.03	Halifax T
CARVALHO Rogerio	York C	01.03	
CASTLE Peter	Reading	*	
CHALLIS Trevor	Bristol Rov	06.03	Telford U
CHAPMAN Liam	Hull C	06.03	Wakefield & Emley
CHETTLE Steve	Grimsby T	06.03	Burton A
CHIPPO Youssef	Coventry C	08.03	Al Sadd (Qatar)
CISSE Edouard	West Ham U	07.03	AS Monaco (France)
CLARE Daryl	Boston U	10.02	Chester C
CLARIDGE Steve	Millwall	06.03	Weymouth

Name	Club	Date	Destination
CLARKE Lee	Peterborough U	01.04	St Albans C
CLIFFORD Mark	Boston U	03.03	Nuneaton Borough
COLLINS Aidan	Ipswich T	*	
COLLINS John	Fulham	06.03	Retired
COLLINS Lee	Blackpool	06.03	Morecambe
COLY Ferdinand	Birmingham C	05.03	RC Lens (France)
CONNOR Dan	Peterborough U	04.03	Waterford U (Ireland)
COOK Jamie	Boston U	02.03	Stevenage Borough
COOK Paul	Burnley	06.03	Accrington Stanley
COOKE Andy	Stoke C	07.03	Busan Icons (Korea)
COONEY Sean	Coventry C	*	
COPPINGER James	Exeter C	+	
CORAZZIN Carlo	Oldham Ath	06.03	
CORNELLY Chris	Lincoln C	*	
CORREIA Albano	Bristol C	03.03	Hereford U
COSTELLO Peter	Boston U	06.03	Stevenage Borough
COTTERILL James	Scunthorpe U	06.03	Barrow
CRAMB Colin	Bury	06.03	Shrewsbury T
CRONIN Glenn	Exeter C	+	
CULLEN Jon	Darlington	10.02	Spennymoor U
CURLE Keith	Mansfield T	06.03	Retired
CURRAN Chris	Exeter C	06.03	
CUSACK Nick	Swansea C	09.02	Retired
DACOURT Olivier	Leeds U	01.03	AS Roma (Italy)
DALGLISH Paul	Blackpool	06.03	Linfield (N. Ireland)
DANIELSSON Helgi	Peterborough U	05.03	Fylkir (Iceland)
DANKS Mark	Bradford C	06.03	Hednesford T
DARBY Brett	Southend U	05.03	Tamworth
DAVIS Jimmy	Manchester U	08.03	Deceased
DE LUCAS Enrique	Chelsea	10.03	Deportivo Alaves (Spain)
DE VOGT Wilko	Sheffield U	01.03	Roosendal BC (Holland)
DE-VULGT Leigh	Swansea C	12.02	Carmarthen T
DEBEC Fabien	Coventry C	06.03	
DEENEY Joe	Luton T	03.03	Enfield
DELORGE Laurent	Coventry C	10.02	Lierse SK (Belgium)
DEVINE Sean	Exeter C	+	
DI PIEDI Michele	Sheffield Wed	05.03	
DIABATE Lassina	Portsmouth	06.03	
DIGBY Fraser	Kidderminster Hrs	04.03	Retired
DILLON Dan	Carlisle U	*	
DOANE Ben	Sheffield U	05.03	
DONNELLY Simon	Sheffield Wed	06.03	St Johnstone
DOUDOU	Queens Park R	06.03	Farnborough T
DOUGHTY Phil	Blackpool	*	
DOUGLIN Troy	Torquay U	01.03	
DOYLE Daire	Kidderminster Hrs	01.03	Nuneaton Borough
DRYSDALE Leon	Shrewsbury T	10.03	Nuneaton Borough
DUCROS Andy	Kidderminster Hrs	02.03	Burton A
DUFFY Lee	Rochdale	02.04	Radcliffe Borough
DUNBAVIN Ian	Shrewsbury T	+	
DURNIN John	Port Vale	06.03	Accrington Stanley
DYKES Daren	Swindon T	05.03	
DYSON Jon	Huddersfield T	01.03	Nuneaton Borough
EATON David	Macclesfield T	06.03	Witton A
EDGE Roland	Gillingham	06.03	Hibernian
EDUSEI Akwasi	Gillingham	*	
EDWARDS David	Shrewsbury T	+	
EDWARDS Nathan	Swindon T	06.03	Chippenham T
EL KARKOURI Talal	Sunderland	05.03	Paris Saint Germain (France)
EL KHALEJ Tahar	Charlton Ath	06.03	
ELDERSHAW Simon	Port Vale	*	
ELDING Anthony	Boston U	02.03	Stevenage Borough
ELLIOTT Robbie	Newcastle U	*	

Name	Club	Date	Destination
ENGONGA Vicente	Coventry C	05.03	Real Oviedo (Spain)
ERIBENNE Chukki	Bournemouth	06.03	Havant & Waterlooville
EVANS Mark	Wrexham	01.03	Colwyn Bay
EVANS Terry	Swansea C	6.03	Newport Co
FARR Craig	Swindon T	09.03	Chippenham T
FENG Li Wei	Everton	01.03	Shenzhen (China)
FENN Neale	Peterborough U	06.03	
FENTON Graham	Blackpool	06.03	Blyth Spartans
FERRER Albert	Chelsea	06.03	Retired
FESTA Gianluca	Portsmouth	06.03	Cagliari (Italy)
FEUER Ian	Wolverhampton W	12.02	
FLACK Steve	Exeter C	+	
FLOWERS Tim	Leicester C	06.03	Retired
FOE Marc-Vivien	Manchester C	06.03	Deceased
FOLEY Dominic	Watford	06.03	SC Braga (Portugal)
FORD Mark	Darlington	06.03	Harrogate T
FORD Bobby	Oxford U	06.03	Bath C
FORINTON Howard	Torquay U	09.02	Yeovil T
FORREST Martyn	Bury	10.03	Droylsden
FOYEWA Amos	Bournemouth	03.03	Woking
FRADIN Karim	Stockport Co	04.03	Chateauraux (France)
FRAIN John	Northampton T	06.03	Moor Green
FRASER Stuart	Exeter C	06.03	Tiverton T
FREEMAN David	Carlisle U	10.02	St Patricks Ath (Ireland)
GAIA Santos	Exeter C	+	
GALLACHER Kevin	Huddersfield T	10.02	Retired
GALLOWAY Mick	Carlisle U	12.02	Gretna
GARRY Ryan	Arsenal	*	
GAY Daniel	Southend U	06.03	Hornchurch
GEORGE Finidi	Ipswich T	07.03	RCD Mallorca (Spain)
GHENT Matthew	Barnsley	06.03	
GLASS Stephen	Watford	06.03	Hibernian
GLOVER Lee	Mansfield T	10.02	Corby T
GODFREY Elliott	Watford	*	
GOLDBAEK Bjarni	Fulham	06.03	Retired
GOODLAD Mark	Port Vale	*	
GOODMAN Don	Exeter C	06.03	Stafford R
GOULD James	Boston U	06.03	Stevenage Borough
GRAYDON Keith	Sunderland	05.03	Scarborough
GRAZIOLI Giuliano	Bristol Rov	07.03	Barnet
GREEN Ryan	Sheffield Wed	05.03	Hereford U
GREEN Scott	Wrexham	06.03	Telford U
GREER Gordon	Blackburn Rov	08.03	Kilmarnock
GRENET Francois	Derby Co	02.03	Stade Rennais (France)
GRIFFITHS Carl	Luton T	06.03	Harlow T
GRIFFITHS Leroy	Queens Park R	06.03	Grays Ath
HAMSHAW Matt	Sheffield Wed	*	
HANKEY Dean	Mansfield T	*	
HARDY Lee	Macclesfield T	06.03	Burscough
HARRIES Paul	Exeter C	10.02	
HARRIS Andy	Leyton Orient	06.03	Chester C
HATCHER Danny	Leyton Orient	12.02	Newport (IoW)
HEARD Jamie	Hull C	06.03	Chester C
HEARY Thomas	Huddersfield T	05.03	
HEATH Nick	Kidderminster Hrs	02.04	Stratford T
HEATHCOTE Jonathan	Cambridge U	11.03	Mildenhall T
HEATHCOTE Mick	Shrewsbury T	01.03	Colwyn Bay
HEIKKINEN Markus	Portsmouth	04.03	HJK Helsinki (Finland)
HENDON Ian	Peterborough U	05.03	Barnet
HENDRY Colin	Bolton W	06.03	Retired
HENRY Ronnie	Tottenham H	11.03	Fisher Ath
HERIVELTO Moriera	Walsall	01.03	Ionikos (Greece)
HERRERA Martin	Fulham	07.03	Estudiantes (Argentina)
HEVICON Ryan	Carlisle U	09.02	Mossley
HIGGINS Alex	Boston U	*	

Name	Old club	Date	New club
HILEY Scott	Exeter C	+	
HILL Nicky	Bury	06.03	Hyde U
HJELDE Jon Olav	Nottingham F	06.03	Busan Icons (Korea)
HOBSON Gary	York C	05.03	North Ferriby U
HOCKENHULL Darren	Blackburn Rov	06.03	Halifax T
HODGSON Richard	Darlington	06.03	Farnborough T
HOGG Lewis	Bristol Rov	06.03	Weston super Mare
HOLDSWORTH David	Bolton W	11.02	Scarborough
HOLMES Paul	Torquay U	06.03	Retired
HOLMES Richard	Notts Co	06.03	Harrowby U
HOLYOAK Danny	Mansfield T	01.03	Kings Lynn
HOWARD Jon	Chesterfield	03.03	Burton A
HOWARTH Neil	Cheltenham T	06.03	Telford U
HOWE Eddie	Portsmouth	*	
HOWIE Scott	Bristol Rov	06.03	Shrewsbury T
HUNTER Roy	Oxford U	06.03	Hucknall T
HURST Mark	Mansfield T	*	
HUTCHINGS Carl	Leyton Orient	06.03	Farnborough T
INGRAM Rae	Port Vale	06.03	Bangor C
INVINCIBILE Danny	Swindon T	06.03	Kilmarnock
IPOUA Guy	Gillingham	06.03	Livingston
IRONS Kenny	Huddersfield T	06.03	Retired
JACKSON Michael	Swansea C	11.02	Cirencester T
JAGIELKA Steve	Shrewsbury T	11.03	Sheffield U
JAVARY Jean-Phillipe	Sheffield U	09.03	
JEMSON Nigel	Shrewsbury T	06.03	Retired
JENSEN Niclas	Manchester C	07.03	Borussia Moenchen. Gladbach (Germany)
JERVIS Dave	Mansfield T	01.03	Gainsborough Trinity
JOBSON Richard	Rochdale	05.03	Retired
JOHNSON Marvin	Luton T	06.02	Retired
JOHNSTON Allan	Middlesbrough	*	
JONES Andy	Mansfield T	*	
JONES Griff	Barnsley	*	
JONES Matt	Leicester C	*	
JONES Scott	York C	09.03	Alfreton T
JONES Steve	Cheltenham T	06.03	Bath C
JORDAN Tom	Southend U	06.03	Tamworth
JORDAO	West Bromwich A	*	
JOY Ian	Kidderminster Hrs	01.03	Columbus Crew (USA)
JUANJO	Bradford C	06.03	
JUDGE Alan	Oxford U	05.03	Retired
KANCHELSKIS Andrei	Southampton	02.03	Al Hilal (Saudi Arabia)
KARLSSON Par	Wimbledon	08.02	Elfsborg (Sweden)
KAWAGUCHI Yoshi	Portsmouth	09.03	Nordjylland (Denmark)
KEAVENY Jonathan	Swansea C	11.02	Carmarthen T
KEEBLE Chris	Colchester U	06.03	Heybridge Swifts
KEENAN Joe	Chelsea	*	
KELLY Alan	Blackburn Rov	*	
KELLY Gary	Sheffield U	05.03	Leigh RMI
KERR Scott	Hull C	03.03	Scarborough
KHELA Inderpaul	Kidderminster Hrs	06.03	Evesham U
KILHEENEY Ciaran	Exeter C	05.03	Droylsden
KIMBLE Alan	Luton T	06.03	Dagenham & Redbridge
KINET Christophe	Millwall	04.03	FC Bruxelles (Belgium)
KINKLADZE Giorgiou	Derby Co	06.03	
KOLINKO Alex	Crystal Palace	06.03	Rostov (Russia)
LABANT Vladimir	West Ham U	01.03	Sparta Prague (Czechosolvakia)
LACEY Damian	Swansea C	01.03	Retired
LAWSON Ian	Bury	07.03	
LE PEN Ulrich	Ipswich T	06.03	Strasbourg (France)
LEE Andy	Bradford C	06.03	Aberystwyth T
LEE Jason	Peterborough U	06.03	Falkirk
LEE Martyn	Wycombe W	06.03	Maidenhead U
LEE Richard	Watford	*	
LEONHARDSEN Oyvind	Aston Villa	07.03	
LESCOTT Joleon	Wolverhampton W	*	
LEVER Mark	Mansfield T	01.03	Ilkeston T
LIGHTBOURNE Kyle	Macclesfield T	06.03	Retired
LOCK Matthew	Exeter C	06.03	Team Bath
LODGE Andy	Boston U	11.02	Ilkeston T
LOGAN Richard	Lincoln C	07.03	Retired
LOPES Osvaldo	Plymouth Arg	05.03	
LOURENCO	Oldham Ath	12.02	Sporting Lisbon (Portugal)
LOVETT Jay	Brentford	06.03	Lewes
LOWE Ryan	Shrewsbury T	+	
LOWER Scott	Kidderminster Hrs	06.03	Bedworth U
LUCIC Teddy	Leeds U	06.03	Bayer Leverkusen (Germany)
LYNCH Mark	Manchester U	*	
McANESPIE Kieran	Plymouth Arg	06.03	Falkirk
McAULEY Hugh	Kidderminster Hrs	06.03	Forest Green Rov
McCARTHY Jon	Carlisle U	06.03	Hucknall T
McCARTHY Paddy	Manchester C	*	
McCLEN Jamie	Newcastle U	*	
McCOMBE John	Huddersfield T	*	
McCONNELL Barry	Exeter C	+	
MacDONALD Gary	Peterborough U	10.02	Stevenage Borough
McGIBBON Pat	Tranmere Rov	09.02	Portadown (N.Ireland)
McGOVERN Brian	Peterborough U	01.03	St Patricks Ath (Ireland)
McGOVERN Jon-Paul	Sheffield U	06.03	Livingston
McGREGOR Paul	Northampton T	06.03	
McINNES Derek	West Bromwich A	06.03	Dundee U
McKEEVER Mark	Bristol Rov	06.03	Weston super Mare
McKENZIE Colin	Hartlepool U	06.03	Bedlington Terriers
McLEAN Aaron	Leyton Orient	03.03	Aldershot T
MACARI Paul	Huddersfield T	10.03	Leek T
MACHO Jurgen	Sunderland	07.03	Chelsea
MACKEY Ben	Coventry C	*	
MADDIX Danny	Sheffield Wed	05.03	Barnet
MAGENNIS Mark	Carlisle U	11.02	Ards (N.Ireland)
MALCOLM Stuart	Plymouth Arg	05.03	Ross Co
MARRIOTT Andy	Birmingham C	06.03	Beira Mar (Portugal)
MARSH Chris	Northampton T	06.03	Retired
MARTIN John	Leyton Orient	06.03	Hornchurch
MARTIN Lee	Macclesfield T	06.03	Retired
MATHIE Alex	York C	03.03	Pickering T
MAYE Danny	Southend U	10.02	Corby T
MAZZINA Nicolas	York C	11.02	
MEDINA Nicolas	Sunderland	08.03	CD Leganes (Spain) (on loan)
MELAUGH Gavin	Rochdale	05.03	
MENDY Bernard	Bolton W	05.03	Paris Saint Germain (France)
METTOMO Lucien	Manchester C	08.03	Kaiserslautern (Germany)
MICHOPOULOS Nik	Burnley	06.03	Retired
MIKE Adie	Lincoln C	01.03	Mossley
MILLEN Keith	Bristol C	05.03	Retired
MILLIGAN Jamie	Blackpool	05.03	Droylsden
MILLS Lee	Stoke C	06.03	Telford U
MILOSEVIC Danny	Leeds U	10.03	Glasgow Celtic
MILTON Russell	Cheltenham T	06.03	Bath C
MISKELLY David	Oldham Ath	06.03	Portadown (N.Ireland)
MOILANEN Tepi	Preston NE	01.03	Heart of Midlothian
MOLENAAR Robert	Bradford C	06.03	Roosendal BC (Holland)
MOLLOY Trevor	Carlisle U	10.02	Shamrock Rov (Ireland)
MONCUR John	West Ham U	06.03	Retired
MONINGTON Mark	Boston U	12.02	Halifax T
MOOR Reinier	Exeter C	+	

Name	Club	Date	Destination
MOORE Neil	Mansfield T	12.02	Southport
MORLEY Ben	Boston U	09.02	Telford U
MORTIMER Alex	Kidderminster Hrs	01.03	Southport
MOSS Darren	Shrewsbury T	+	
MOSS David	Swansea C	01.03	Carmarthen T
MUMFORD Andrew	Swansea C	03.04	Newport Co
MURDOCK Colin	Preston NE	06.03	Hibernian
MURPHY Chris	Shrewsbury T	06.03	Telford U
MURPHY Danny	Queens Park R	06.03	Margate
MURPHY Matt	Swansea C	06.03	Ford Sports Daventry
MURPHY Shaun	Sheffield U	08.03	Perth Glory (Australia)
MURRAY Antonio	Ipswich T	*	
MURRAY Karl	Shrewsbury T	12.03	Woking
MUSTAFA Tarkan	Rushden & Diamonds	02.03	Dagenham & Redbridge
NAISBITT Danny	Carlisle U	09.02	Barnet
NASH Martin	Macclesfield T	05.03	
NAYLOR Tony	Cheltenham T	06.03	Telford U
NAYLOR Glenn	Darlington	06.03	Harrogate T
NDAH George	Wolverhampton W	*	
NEDERGAARD Steen	Norwich C	05.03	Odense BK (Denmark)
NIELSEN Allan	Watford	06.03	Herfolge (Denmark)
NIXON Marc	Carlisle U	06.03	
NOON Mark	Coventry C	03.04	Tamworth
NORMANN Runar	Coventry C	10.02	Brann Bergen (Norway)
NORVILLE Jason	Watford	*	
O'CONNOR Aaron	Scunthorpe U	02.03	Ilkeston T
O'CONNOR Martin	Walsall	06.03	Shrewsbury T
O'GRADY Chris	Leicester C	*	
O'KANE John	Blackpool	06.03	Hyde U
OKOLI James	York C	03.03	
OKON Paul	Leeds U	08.03	
OLIVER Michael	Rochdale	06.03	Barrow
O'NEILL Paul	Macclesfield T	06.03	Gretna
OSBORN James	Luton T	03.03	Harrow Borough
OSBOURNE Isaac	Coventry C	*	
OSTENSTAAD Egil	Blackburn Rov	08.03	Glasgow Rangers
OUADDOU Abdeslam	Fulham	07.03	Stade Rennais (France)
PACKHAM Will	Brighton & Hove A	06.03	Worthing
PALMER Carlton	Stockport Co	02.03	Retired
PAPADOPOULOS Demi	Burnley	07.03	Panathanaikos (Greece)
PARKINSON Phil	Reading	02.03	Retired
PARTRIDGE Richie	Liverpool	*	
PARTRIDGE Scott	Shrewsbury T	06.03	Weymouth
PATTERSON Mark	Gillingham	12.02	Dover Ath
PAYNTER Owen	Cambridge U	02.03	Mildenhall T
PAYTON Andy	Burnley	06.03	Retired
PELZER Marc Sebastian	Blackburn Rov	01.04	Eintracht Trier (Germany)
PENNOCK Adrian	Gillingham	01.03	Gravesend & Northfleet
PETRESCU Tomi	Leicester C	*	
PETTINGER Paul	Lincoln C	02.03	Kettering T
PETTY Ben	Hull C	12.02	Moor Green
PHILLIPS Gareth	Swansea C	06.03	Newport Co
PHILLIPS Waynne	Wrexham	06.03	Caernarfon T
PHILPOTT Lee	Hull C	06.03	Weymouth
PLUMMER Chris	Queens Park R	06.03	Barnet
POLLET Ludo	Wolverhampton W	06.03	
POWELL Darryl	Sheffield Wed	06.03	Colorado Rapids (USA)
POWELL Paul	Oxford U	05.03	Didcot T
POWER Graeme	Exeter C	06.03	Tiverton T
PRICE Michael	Hull C	12.02	Scarborough
PRINCE Neil	Torquay U	11.02	Lancaster C
QUINN Niall	Sunderland	11.02	Retired
RAHIM Brent	Northampton T	05.03	Falkirk
RAPLEY Kevin	Colchester U	06.03	Chester C
RASMUSSEN Mark	Burnley	06.03	Gateshead
RAVANELLI Fabrizio	Derby Co	09.03	Dundee
REDDINGTON Stuart	Mansfield T	11.02	Burton A
REDMILE Matt	Shrewsbury T	06.03	Scarborough
REDMOND Steve	Bury	06.03	Leigh RMI
REED Adam	Darlington	06.03	Whitby T
REID Brian	Blackpool	12.02	Falkirk
REID Paul	Swansea C	03.03	Carmarthen T
RICARDO	Manchester U	08.03	Racing Santander (Spain) on loan
RICHARDS Justin	Bristol Rov	12.02	Stevenage Borough
RICHARDSON Lee	Chesterfield	01.07	Retired
RICKETTS Sam	Oxford U	06.03	Telford U
RIDLER Dave	Macclesfield T	03.03	Shrewsbury T
RIZA Omer	Cambridge U	06.03	Denizlispor (Turkey)
RODGERS Luke	Shrewsbury T	+	
RODRIGO	Everton	05.03	Botafogo (Brazil)
RODWELL Jim	Boston U	08.02	Farnborough T
ROGERS Paul	Brighton & Hove A	06.03	Worthing
ROSCOE Andy	Exeter C	06.03	Leigh RMI
ROSSITER Mark	Sunderland	*	
ROWLAND Keith	Chesterfield	12.02	Hornchurch
RUBINS Andrejs	Crystal Palace	02.03	Shinnik Yaroslavi (Russia)
RUFUS Richard	Charlton Ath	*	
RUSSELL Kevin	Wrexham	06.03	Retired
RUSSELL Simon	Hull C	*	
RYAN Leon	Scunthorpe U	10.02	Whitley Bay
RYAN Richie	Sunderland	*	
SAGARE Jake	Grimsby T	05.03	Halifax T
SALTER Mark	Southend U	06.03	Bath C
SALVA	Bolton W	05.03	Malaga (Spain)
SANKOFA Osei	Charlton Ath	*	
SARA Juan	Coventry C	05.03	Dundee
SCHMEICHEL Peter	Manchester C	05.03	Retired
SCHWARZ Stefan	Sunderland	06.03	Retired
SCOTT Dion	Kidderminster Hrs	06.03	Nuneaton Borough
SELLARS Scott	Mansfield T	05.03	Retired
SELLEY Ian	Wimbledon	06.03	Woking
SETCHELL Gary	Rushden & Diamonds	06.03	Tamworth
SHAABAN Rami	Arsenal	*	
SHANDRAN Anthony	Burnley	06.03	Spennymoor U
SHARP James	Hartlepool U	06.03	Falkirk
SHARP Neil	Swansea C	06.03	Woking
SHARPE Lee	Exeter C	09.02	Retired
SHELDON Gareth	Exeter C	+	
SHTANIUK Sergei	Stoke C	07.03	Shinnik Yaroslavi (Russia)
SIBON Gerald	Sheffield Wed	01.03	Heerenveen (Holland)
SIMMS Gordon	Hartlepool U	06.03	
SIMPSON Fitzroy	Walsall	06.03	Telford U
SINCLAIR Dean	Norwich C	*	
SKELTON Aaron	Luton T	06.03	Havant & Waterlooville
SLABBER Jamie	Tottenham H	02.04	
SLAVEN John	Carlisle U	08.03	Cowdenbeath
SMITH Alex	Reading	06.03	Chester C
SMITH David	Swansea C	01.03	Retired
SMITH Jason	Swansea C	01.04	Retired
SMITH Paul	Lincoln C	02.04	Retired
SOLKHON Brett	Rushden & Diamonds	01.03	Kettering T
SOLLITT Adam	Rushden & Diamonds	06.03	Scarborough
SOLTVEDT Trond Egil	Sheffield Wed	06.03	Retired
SPEDDING Duncan	Northampton T	06.03	
STAMP Darryn	Northampton T	08.03	Chester C
STANFORD Eddie	Coventry C	*	
STEELE Danny	Colchester U	11.02	Fisher Ath
STEPANOVS Igors	Arsenal	08.03	Beveren (Belgium) loan
STEPHENS Ross	Shrewsbury T	+	

PFA FOOTBALLERS' WHO'S WHO — WHERE DID THEY GO?

Name	Club	Date	Destination
STEVENS Dean	Torquay U	*	
STEVENS Ian	Shrewsbury T	06.03	Gretna
STIENS Craig	Leeds U	01.04	Merthyr Tydfil
STOCKDALE David	York C	*	
STOCKWELL Mick	Colchester U	06.03	Maldon T
STONE Danny	Notts Co	06.03	Southport
STRINGER Chris	Sheffield Wed	*	
STRUPAR Branko	Derby Co	06.03	
SUKUR Hakan	Blackburn Rov	05.03	Galatasaray (Turkey)
SWIERCZEWSKI Piotr	Birmingham C	05.03	O.Marseille (France)
SWONNELL Sam	Watford	*	
TARDIF Chris	Portsmouth	*	
TAYLOR Chris	Swindon T	*	
TAYLOR Martin	Wycombe W	06.03	Telford U
TAYLOR Michael	Blackburn Rov	*	
TAYLOR Robert	Scunthorpe U	04.03	Retired
TAYLOR Stuart	Arsenal	*	
THEOBALD David	Cambridge U	05.03	Canvey Island
THEOKLITOS Michael	Blackpool	06.03	
THOMAS Andrew	Stockport Co	06.03	Kidsgrove Ath
THOMAS Martin	Exeter C	+	
THOMPSON Andy	Shrewsbury T	06.03	Retired
THOMPSON Chris	Grimsby T	06.03	Northwich Vic
THOMPSON Neil	Boston U	09.02	Retired
THOMSON Andy	Queens Park R	06.03	Partick Thistle
THURGOOD Stuart	Southend U	06.03	Grays Ath
TILER Carl	Portsmouth	06.03	Retired
TILLSON Andy	Rushden & Diamonds	12.02	Team Bath
TIMM Mads	Manchester U	*	
TINSON Darren	Macclesfield T	07.03	Shrewsbury T
TOD Andy	Bradford C	08.03	Dunfermline Ath
TODA Kazuyuki	Tottenham H	01.04	Shimizu (Japan)
TODD Chris	Exeter C	+	
TOFTING Stig	Bolton W	04.03	Retired
TOGWELL Sam	Crystal Palace	*	
TOLLEY Glenn	Shrewsbury T	+	
TOLLEY Jamie	Shrewsbury T	+	
TOWN David	Boston U	06.03	Havant & Waterlooville
TOWNSEND Ben	Wycombe W	01.03	Woking
TRAYNOR Rob	Brentford	04.04	Crawley T
TURNER Andy	Northampton T	03.03	Moor Green
TURNER Michael	Charlton Ath	*	
TUTTLE David	Millwall	01.03	Retired
UDEZE Iffy	West Bromwich A	05.03	PAOK Salonika (Greece)
VAN BLERK Jason	Shrewsbury T	06.03	Colwyn Bay
VAN DEURZEN Jurgen	Stoke C	01.03	KFC Dessel (Belgium)
VARGA Stanislav	Sunderland	01.03	Glasgow Celtic
VICKERS Steve	Birmingham C	06.03	Retired
VIGNAL Gregory	Liverpool	08.03	Stade Rennais (France) on loan
WAINE Andrew	Burnley	06.03	Accrington Stanley
WALKER Richard	Cheltenham T	09.03	Retired
WALSH Steve	Coventry C	09.02	Tamworth
WALSHE Ben	Queens Park R	11.03	Gravesend & Northfleet
WARBURTON Ray	Boston U	01.03	Aldershot T
WARD Chris	Lincoln C	06.03	Northwich Victoria
WARD Iain	Grimsby T	*	
WARDLEY Stuart	Rushden & Diamonds	*	
WARNE Steve	Chesterfield	*	
WARNER Phil	Cambridge U	01.03	Eastleigh
WARREN Christer	Bristol Rov	12.02	Eastleigh
WATKIN Steve	Swansea C	06.03	Caernarfon T
WATSON Alex	Exeter C	06.03	Taunton T
WATSON Gordon	Hartlepool U	06.03	Retired
WATTS Steve	Shrewsbury T	10.03	Dagenham & Redbridge
WEATHERSTONE Ross	Boston U	03.03	Farnborough T
WELCH Keith	Mansfield T	06.03	Retired
WHEATCROFT Paul	Scunthorpe U	01.03	Southport
WHELAN Phil	Southend U	06.03	Retired
WHITBREAD Adrian	Reading	05.03	Retired
WHITE Jason	Mansfield T	*	
WHITEHEAD Phil	Reading	05.03	Tamworth
WHITEHEAD Stuart	Darlington	06.03	Telford U
WHITWORTH Neil	Exeter C	06.03	Southport
WIJNHARD Clyde	Oldham Ath	06.03	Vitoria Guimaraes (Portugal)
WILD Peter	Stockport Co	06.03	Kidsgrove Ath
WILDING Craig	York C	06.03	Stafford R
WILDING Peter	Shrewsbury T	06.03	Welshpool T
WILLIAMS Lee	Cheltenham T	06.03	Telford U
WILLIAMS Mark	Brentford	06.03	Barnet
WILLIS Roger	Peterborough U	10.02	Cambridge C
WINTERBURN Nigel	West Ham U	06.03	Retired
WINTERS Robbie	Luton T	08.02	Brann Bergen (Norway)
WOAN Ian	Shrewsbury T	05.03	Retired
WOME Pierre	Fulham	06.03	RCD Espanyol (Spain)
WOOD Jamie	Swansea C	06.03	Total Network Solutions
WRIGHT Stephen	Scunthorpe U	12.02	Retired
XAVIER Abel	Liverpool	01.03	Galatasaray (Turkey)
YOUDS Eddie	Huddersfield T	06.03	Grays Ath
YOUNG Alan	Swindon T	12.03	Swindon Supermarine
YOUNG Scott	Cardiff C	*	
YULU Christian	Coventry C	06.03	
ZDRILIC David	Walsall	08.03	Aberdeen
ZHIYI Fan	Cardiff C	06.03	
ZOLA Franco	Chelsea	06.03	Cagliari (Italy)

IN MEMORIAM

Jimmy Davis

Jimmy was killed in a car accident on 9th August 2003, the opening day of the season. A highly-promising wide-right midfield player who had played for England at under-20 level, Jimmy was on a year's loan from Manchester United and had earlier completed a successful loan period with Swindon Town. Having played for Watford in pre-season tour matches, he had already made himself an integral part of the squad, so his loss was keenly felt by Watford's players, staff and supporters alike, as well as by his many friends in Manchester and Swindon. As a tribute, Jimmy's name remained on the Watford squad list all season and the players took the field for home matches after an extract from Coolio's 'Gangsta's Paradise' – Jimmy's favourite song. This tribute was written by Audrey Adams.

Marc-Vivien Foe

Having recently returned to play for Olympique Lyonnais in France, after spending 2002-03 on loan at Manchester City, Marc-Vivien tragically collapsed and died during the second half of a Confederations Cup match between Cameroon and Colombia in Paris on 26 June 2003. It was a huge blow to all who knew the tigerish 6'3" defensive midfielder, who had first come to notice internationally for Cameroon at the age of 17 while playing for Canon de Yaounde. From there, he moved to the French club, Racing Lens, where he became an integral part of the team that won the French title in 1997-98, before spending 18 months with West Ham and moving back to France with Olympique Lyonnais. A motivational figure for Cameroon, he was a member of the side that won the African Nations' Cup in 2000 and 2002 and will be sorely missed.

PFA AWARDS 2004

Player of the Year
THIERRY HENRY
(ARSENAL)

Young Player of the Year
SCOTT PARKER
(CHELSEA)

Special Merit Award
DARIO GRADI
(CREWE ALEXANDRA)

DIVISIONAL AWARDS

FA Barclaycard Premiership

Tim Howard	Manchester United
Lauren	Arsenal
Sol Campbell	Arsenal
John Terry	Chelsea
Ashley Cole	Arsenal
Steven Gerrard	Liverpool
Frank Lampard	Chelsea
Patrick Vieira	Arsenal
Robert Pires	Arsenal
Thierry Henry	Arsenal
Ruud van Nistelrooy	Manchester United

Nationwide League Division One

Robert Green	Norwich City
Phil Jagielka	Sheffield United
Danny Gabbidon	Cardiff City
Malky Mackay	Norwich City
Julio Arca	Sunderland
Tim Cahill	Millwall
Michael Carrick	West Ham United
Jason Koumas	West Bromwich Albion
Andy Reid	Nottingham Forest
Robert Earnshaw	Cardiff City
Andy Johnson	Crystal Palace

Nationwide League Division Two

Steve Phillips	Bristol City
Louis Carey	Bristol City
Graham Coughlan	Plymouth Argyle
Danny Cullip	Brighton & Hove Albion
Gino Padula	Queens Park Rangers
Carlos Edwards	Wrexham
David Friio	Plymouth Argyle
Brian Tinnion	Bristol City
Richard Wellens	Blackpool
Leon Knight	Brighton & Hove Albion
Scott Taylor	Blackpool

Nationwide League Division Three

Chris Weale	Yeovil Town
Nathan Stanton	Scunthorpe United
Andy Crosby	Oxford United
Efe Sodje	Huddersfield Town
Andy Dawson	Hull City
Peter Beagrie	Scunthorpe United
Liam Lawrence	Mansfield Town
Michael McIndoe	Doncaster Rovers
Alex Russell	Torquay United
David Graham	Torquay United
Lee Trundle	Swansea City

PFA Fans Divisional Player of the Year Awards —Premiership: Thierry Henry (Arsenal). Division One: Darren Huckerby (Norwich City). Division Two: Neil Moss (Bournemouth). Division Three: Lee Harper (Northampton Town).

For information on how to vote during the season, go to the Official PFA website: www.givemefootball.com